فضائلِ اعمال

FAZAIL
-E-
AMAAL

FULL VERSION OF ORIGINAL BOOK
FAZAIL E AMAAL

PUBLISHED BY:
ISLAMIC BOOK STORE

SHAIKHUL HADITH HADHRAT MOULANA
MUHAMMAD ZAKARIYYA SAAHIB
(RAHMATULLAHI ALAYH)

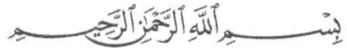

Compiled by: Shaikhul Hadith, Hadhrat Moulana Muhammad Zakariyya Saahib (RA)

Jamiatul Ulama (KZN)
Ta'limi Board
4 Third Avenue
P.O.Box 26024
Isipingo Beach
4115
South Africa

Tel: (+27) 31 912 2172
E-mail: info@talimiboardkzn.org
Website: talimiboardkzn.org

Revised Translation
First Edition: Jumaadal Ula 1443 / January 2022

Permission is granted for reprinting this book without any alterations. A humble appeal is made to the readers to offer suggestions, corrections, etc. to improve the quality of future publications. May Allah Ta'ala reward you.

The publishers, translators, editors and typesetters humbly request your duas for them, their parents, families, Asaatizah and Mashaaikh.

Published by: Islamic Book Store, Gujarat, India 394601

SECTIONS

	PAGE NO.
Stories of the Sahaabah رَضِىَٱللَّهُعَنْهُمْ	4
Virtues of Qur-aan	255
Virtues of the Salaah	365
Virtues of Zikr	487
Virtues of Tabligh	727
Virtues of Ramadhaan	773
The Downfall of the Muslims & it's Only Remedy	865
6 Points	903

حكايات صحابة
رَضِيَ ٱللَّهُ عَنْهُمْ

STORIES OF THE SAHAABAH
رَضِيَ ٱللَّهُ عَنْهُمْ

Contents

Author's Foreword 11

CHAPTER 1 TO TOLERATE HARDSHIPS & NOT TO GIVE UP DEEN WHEN FACED WITH DIFFICULTY 14
   1. Nabi ﷺ goes to Taa'if 14
   2. Martyrdom of Hadhrat Anas bin Nadhr ؓ 17
   3. The truce of Hudeybiah and the incident of Hadhrat Abu Jandal ؓ and Hadhrat Abu Baseer ؓ 18
   4. Hadhrat Bilal ؓ and his sufferings 20
   5. Hadhrat Abu Zarr Ghiffaari ؓ accepts Islam 21
   6. The difficulties faced by Hadhrat Khabbaab ibnul Arat ؓ 24
   7. Hadhrat Ammaar ؓ and his Parents 25
   8. Hadhrat Suhaib ؓ accepts Islam 25
   9. Hadhrat 'Umar ؓ accepts Islam 27
   10. Escaping to Abyssinia and being boycotted in the valley of Abu Taalib 29

CHAPTER 2 THE FEAR OF ALLAH TA'ALA 34
   1. Nabi's ﷺ worry at the time of a storm 34
   2. What Hadhrat Anas ؓ used to do at the time of a storm 36
   3. What Nabi ﷺ did at the time of a solar eclipse (sun being blocked by the moon) 36
   4. Nabi ﷺ crying the whole night 37
   5. Hadhrat Abu Bakr ؓ and the fear of Allah Ta'ala 37
   6. Hadhrat Umar ؓ and the fear of Allah Ta'ala 39
   7. A warning by Hadhrat Abdullah bin Abbaas ؓ 41
   8. Nabi's ﷺ passing near the ruins (Broken buildings) of Samood during the Tabuk Journey 42
   9. Hadhrat Ka'ab ؓ does not join the Battle of Tabuk 43
   10. Nabi's ﷺ warning on the Sahaabah's ؓ Laughing 49
   11. Hadhrat Hanzalah's ؓ fear of Nifaaq (hypocrisy) 50
   12. A few stories about the fear of Allah Ta'ala 51

CHAPTER 3 STAYING AWAY FROM LUXURIES 56
   1. Nabi ﷺ does not like gold 56
   2. Nabi's ﷺ life of simplicity (staying away from luxuries) 56

3. Hadhrat Abu Hurayrah's ﷺ hunger 58
4. Hadhrat Abu Bakr's ﷺ daily allowance from the Bait-ul-Maal (public treasury).. 59
5. Hadhrat 'Umar's ﷺ daily allowance from the Bait-ul-Maal (public treasury) 60
6. Hadhrat Bilal's ﷺ story about Nabi ﷺ 63
7. Another story of Hadhrat Abu Hurayrah's ﷺ hunger 65
8. Nabi's ﷺ opinion about two people 66
9. Poverty is for those who love Nabi ﷺ 67
10. The story of the Al-Ambar fish 67

CHAPTER 4 PIETY AND BEING CAUTIOUS DUE TO THE FEAR OF ALLAH TA'ALA
.... 69
1. Nabi ﷺ accepts a woman's invitation 69
2. Nabi ﷺ does not sleep for the whole night................................ 70
3. Hadhrat Abu Bakr ﷺ and a fortune-teller's food 70
4. Hadhrat Umar ﷺ vomits the milk of Sadaqah............................ 71
5. Hadhrat Abu Bakr ﷺ gives his garden to Bait-ul-Maal............. 72
6. The story of Ali bin Ma'bad (rahmatullahi alayh) 72
7. Hadhrat Ali ﷺ passes by a grave.. 73
8. Nabi ﷺ speaks about haraam food... 74
9. Hadhrat 'Umar ﷺ does not like his wife to weigh musk.......... 75
10. Hadhrat 'Umar-bin-Abdul Aziz (rahmatullahi alayh) removes a governor 76

CHAPTER 5 BEING CAREFUL ABOUT SALAAH 77
1. Rewards of Nafl (optional) Salaah 77
2. Nabi ﷺ spends the whole night in Salaah 78
3. Nabi's ﷺ reading of the Qur-aan in Salaah................................ 79
4. Salaah of a few well-known Sahaabah ﷺ..................................... 79
5. Salaah of two Sahaabah (A muhaajir and an ansaari) ﷺ who were standing guard at night 81
6. Hadhrat Abu Talha ﷺ and his Salaah 82
7. Hadhrat Ibn Abbaas ﷺ and his Salaah 83
8. Sahaabah ﷺ stopping business at the time of Salaah............. 83
9. Shahaadat of Hadhrat Khubaib, Hadhrat Zaid and Hadhrat 'Aasim ﷺ 85
10. Nabi's ﷺ friends in Jannah... 88

CHAPTER 6 SACRIFICING FOR OTHERS 90
   1. Feeding the guest in darkness... 90
   2. Feeding a fasting Sahaabi ﷺ... 91
   3. Overpaying of Zakaat... 91
   4. Hadhrat 'Umar ﷺ trying to copy Hadhrat Abu Bakr ﷺ 93
   5. Sahaabah ﷺ dying thirsty for others 94
   6. Hadhrat Hamzah's ﷺ kafan (burial cloth)... 94
   7. The story of the goat's head 96
   8. The wife of Hadhrat 'Umar ﷺ acts as a midwife (a lady who helps during childbirth) 96
   9. Hadhrat Abu Talha ﷺ gives his garden to Allah Ta'ala..................... 98
   10. Hadhrat Abu Zarr ﷺ scolds his servant... 99
   11. The story of Hadhrat Abdullah bin Ja'far ﷺ and Hadhrat Abdullah bin Zubair ﷺ 101

CHAPTER 7 BRAVERY AND HEROISM 104
   1. Ibn Jahsh ﷺ and Sa'ad ﷺ make dua for each other 104
   2. Hadhrat Ali's ﷺ bravery in the Battle of Uhud................................. 105
   3. Hadhrat Hanzalah ﷺ becomes a shaheed... 106
   4. Hadhrat Amr bin Jamooh's ﷺ wish for shahaadat (dying in the path of Allah Ta'ala) 107
   5. Hadhrat Mus'ab bin 'Umair ﷺ gets martyred 109
   6. Hadhrat Sa'ad's ﷺ message to Rustam 110
   7. Hadhrat Wahb bin Qabus ﷺ gets martyred...................................... 111
   8. The incident of Bi'r Ma'oona 112
   9. Hadhrat 'Umair ﷺ stops eating dates.. 114
   10. Hadhrat 'Umar's ﷺ emigration to Madinah 115
   11. An army is sent to Moota 115
   12. The Story of Sa'eed bin Jubair (rahmatullahi alayh) and Hajjaaj bin Yusuf 118

CHAPTER 8 THIRST FOR KNOWLEDGE 124
   1. Sahaabah's ﷺ group of Muftis 126
   2. Hadhrat Abu Bakr ﷺ burns his collection... 126
   3. Hadhrat Mus'ab bin Umair ﷺ does tabligh....................................... 127
   4. Hadhrat 'Ubayy bin Ka'ab ﷺ teaches Hadith.................................... 129
   5. Hadhrat Huzayfah's ﷺ worry about evil... 130
   6. Hadhrat Abu Hurayrah's ﷺ memory for Hadith 132
   7. The killing of Musaylamah and the compilation of the Qur-aan........... 133

Fazaail-e-A'maal - Stories of the Sahaabah

8. Hadhrat Abdullah bin Mas'ood's ﷺ carefulness about Hadith............ 135
9. A person travels from Madinah Munawwarah to Hadhrat Abu Darda ﷺ in Damascus to learn one Hadith 136
10. Hadhrat Ibn Abbaas's ﷺ thirst for knowledge 138
11. Miscellaneous stories about knowledge.................................... 139

CHAPTER 9 PLEASING NABI ﷺ 148

1. Hadhrat Abdullah bin Amr ﷺ burns his sheet............................. 148
2. An Ansaari Sahaabi ﷺ demolishes his building........................... 149
3. Sahaabah's ﷺ throwing away red sheets of saddle cloth 150
4. Hadhrat Waail ﷺ has his hair cut 151
5. Hadhrat Suhail ﷺ and Hadhrat Khuraym ﷺ give up what is not liked by Nabi ﷺ 151
6. Hadhrat Ibn-Umar ﷺ stops speaking to his son 152
7. Hadhrat Ibn 'Umar ﷺ answers a question.................................... 153
8. Hadhrat Ibn Mughaffal ﷺ stops speaking to his nephew 154
9. Hadhrat Hakeem bin Hizaam ﷺ gives up begging 154
10. Hadhrat Huzayfah ﷺ is sent to spy on the enemy 155

CHAPTER 10 WOMEN'S COURAGE & LOVE FOR ISLAM................ 158

1. Hadhrat Faatimah's ﷺ tasbeeh... 158
2. Hadhrat Aa'ishah's ﷺ spending in the path of Allah Ta'ala.............. 160
3. Hadhrat Aa'ishah ﷺ gets angry with Hadhrat Ibn Zubair ﷺ 161
4. Hadhrat Aa'ishah ﷺ and the fear of Allah Ta'ala........................... 162
5. The Story of Hadhrat Umm-e-Salamah ﷺ 163
6. Women in the Battle of Khaibar 164
7. Hadhrat Ummu Haraam ﷺ in the Battle of Cyprus 165
8. Story of Hadhrat Ummu Sulaim ﷺ 166
9. Hadhrat Ummu Habibah's ﷺ behavior towards her father 167
10. The story of Hadhrat Zainab ﷺ 169
11. Hadhrat Khansa ﷺ encourages her sons to be brave.................. 171
12. Hadhrat Safiyyah ﷺ kills a Jew on her own............................... 173
13. Hadhrat Asma's ﷺ discussion with Nabi ﷺ regarding the rewards for women 174
14. The Story of Hadhrat Ummu Ammaarah ﷺ 175
15. Story of Hadhrat Ummu Hakeem ﷺ 177
16. Martyrdom of Hadhrat Sumayya ﷺ.. 178
17. The story of Hadhrat Asma bint Abu Bakr ﷺ............................. 179
18. Hadhrat Asma ﷺ comforts her grandfather............................... 180

19. Hadhrat Asma's ﷺ spending in charity.. 181
20. The story of migration and demise of Nabi's ﷺ daughter,
Hadhrat Zainab ﷺ.. 182
21. Hadhrat Rubayyi's ﷺ honour.. 184
The lives of the Ummahaat-ul-Mu'mineen (Mothers of the believers
who were The pure wives of Nabi ﷺ).. 185
  (1) Hadhrat Khadijah ﷺ.. 185
  (2) Hadhrat Sauda ﷺ.. 186
  (3) Hadhrat Aa'ishah ﷺ.. 186
  (4) Hadhrat Hafsah ﷺ.. 188
  (5) Hadhrat Zainab bint Khuzaimah ﷺ.. 189
  (6) Hadhrat Ummu Salamah ﷺ... 190
  (7) Hadhrat Zainab bint Jahsh ﷺ... 192
  (8) Hadhrat Juwairiyyah bintul-Haaris ﷺ.. 193
  (9) Hadhrat Ummu Habibah ﷺ... 194
  (10) Hadhrat Safiyyah ﷺ.. 195
  (11) Hadhrat Maimoonah ﷺ... 196
The sons of Nabi ﷺ.. 196
The Daughters of Nabi ﷺ.. 198
  (1) Hadhrat Zainab ﷺ.. 198
  (2) Hadhrat Ruqayyah ﷺ.. 198
  (3) Hadhrat Umme Kulsum ﷺ.. 199
  (4) Hadhrat Faatimah ﷺ.. 200

CHAPTER 11 CHILDREN AND THEIR LOVE FOR ISLAM 203
1. Children keep Fast... 203
2. Hadhrat Aa'ishah's ﷺ thirst for knowledge.. 204
3. Hadhrat 'Umair ﷺ desire to go for Jihaad... 205
4. Hadhrat 'Umair bin Abi Waqqaas ﷺ hides himself to go to badr....... 205
5. Two youngsters of the Ansaar kill Abu Jahl.. 206
6. A contest between Raafi' ﷺ and Samurah ﷺ..................................... 207
7. Hadhrat Zaid ﷺ gets chosen for his knowledge of Qur-aan.............. 209
8. The father of Hadhrat Abu Sa'eed Khudri ﷺ passes away 209
9. Hadhrat Salamah bin Akwah ﷺ challengers a group of robbers
single handedly 210
10. Hadhrat Baraa ﷺ wanting to join in the Battle of Badr 212
11. Hadhrat Abdullah bin Abdullah bin Ubayy ﷺ disgraces his
munaafiq father 213
12. Hadhrat Jaabir's ﷺ eagerness to fight... 215
13. Hadhrat Ibn Zubair's ﷺ bravery against the Romans....................... 216

14. Hadhrat Amr bin Salamah رضي الله عنه learns the Qur-aan in the state of kufr 217
15. Hadhrat Abdullah Ibn Abbaas رضي الله عنه ties his slave with chains 218
16. Hadhrat Abdullah Ibn Abbaas رضي الله عنه memorizes the Qur-aan in his childhood 218
17. Abdullah bin Amr bin Aas رضي الله عنه memorises Hadith 219
18. Hadhrat Zaid bin Saabit رضي الله عنه memorizes the Qur-aan 220
19. Hadhrat Hasan's رضي الله عنه knowledge of Islam 221
20. Hadhrat Husain's رضي الله عنه thirst for learning 223

CHAPTER 12 LOVE FOR NABI ﷺ 226

1. Hadhrat Abu Bakr رضي الله عنه undergoes difficulty for the sake of Islam 226
2. The sadness of Hadhrat 'Umar رضي الله عنه at the passing away of Nabi ﷺ 229
3. An Ansaari Woman's concern about Nabi ﷺ 231
4. The behaviour of the Sahaabah رضي الله عنهم at Hudaybiyyah 232
5. Hadhrat Ibn Zubair رضي الله عنه drinks the blood of Nabi ﷺ 235
6. Hadhrat Abu 'Ubaidah رضي الله عنه loses his teeth 236
7. Hadhrat Zaid رضي الله عنه refuses to go with his father 236
8. Anas bin Nadhr's رضي الله عنه martyrdom in Uhud 238
9. .... Sa'ad's
10. A woman dies after seeing Nabi's ﷺ grave 240
11. miscellaneous stories of The love of Sahaabah رضي الله عنهم for Nabi ﷺ 240

   Story 1 - The love of Hadhrat 'Umar رضي الله عنه for Nabi ﷺ 242
   Story 2 - On the Day of Qiyaamah you will be with whom you love 242
   Story 3 - Hadhrat Haarisah رضي الله عنه offers his house to Nabi ﷺ for Faatimah رضي الله عنها 243
   Story 4 - Company of Nabi ﷺ after death 244
   Story 5 - Followers coming after Nabi ﷺ wish to see him 245
   Story 6 - Abu Bakr رضي الله عنه wishes for the uncle of Nabi ﷺ to accept Islam 246
   Story 7 - An old lady singing poems in love of Nabi ﷺ 246
   Story 8 - Hadhrat Bilal رضي الله عنه wishes to meet Nabi ﷺ after death 247
   Story 9 - Zaid's رضي الله عنه love for Nabi ﷺ 247
   Conclusion – Our conduct with the Sahaabah رضي الله عنهم and their virtues 248

AUTHOR'S FOREWORD

We glorify Allah Ta'ala and send blessings and salutations of peace on our noble Nabi ﷺ and his Sahaabah ﭬ and those who follow him in upholding the cause of Deen.

It was in the year 1353 A.H. (1934) that an eminent Sheikh, who is my mentor and for whom I have every respect, asked me to compile a book containing stories of the Sahaabah ﭬ of Nabi ﷺ, with special mention of the belief and Practices of the women and children of his time. The main idea of this request was that Muslim mothers, while going to bed at night, instead of telling stories and fables to their children, may narrate to them the real and true incidents of the golden age of Islam that would create an Islamic spirit of love and esteem in them for the Sahaabah ﭬ and thereby strengthen their 'Imaan'. The proposed book will be a useful substitute for the current story books.

It became essential for me to fulfil the desire of my Sheikh, for, besides being under moral debt and obligation to him for his immense beneficence, I consider the good will of such pious people to be the source of success in this world and the Hereafter.

I knew my shortcomings and difficulties and, therefore, had been postponing the carrying out of this work for four years, when in Safar 1357 A.H., it so happened that I was advised by the doctors to suspend my regular responsibility of teaching for some time. I decided to utilize this period of rest for complying with the long-standing desire of the Sheikh, with the belief that even if my attempt did not meet up to his expectation, it would anyhow be a pleasant engagement for me and in addition bring me spiritual blessings.

It is an admitted fact that the stories of the pious people deserve to be studied rather deeply, in order to derive proper benefit from them. This is more important in case of the Sahaabah ﭬ, who were chosen by Allah Ta'ala for the company of His beloved and our dear Nabi ﷺ. Their stories not only help to strengthen our Imaan and make us practice on Deen but also cause Allah Ta'ala's blessings and mercy to descend on the readers.

Junaid Baghdaadi *(rahmatullahi alayh)*, a head of the Soofis, once said: "Stories of the pious and saintly people are Allah Ta'ala's special ways, which strengthen the hearts of those who strive in His Path."

Somebody inquired of Junaid *(rahmatullahi alayh)* if he could mention something in support of his statement. He replied: "Yes; Allah Ta'ala has said in His Book:

وَ كُلًّا نَقُصُّ عَلَيْكَ مِنْ اَنْبَآءِ الرُّسُلِ مَا نُثَبِّتُ بِهٖ فُؤَادَكَ ۚ وَجَآءَكَ فِىْ هٰذِهِ الْحَقُّ وَمَوْعِظَةٌ وَّذِكْرٰى لِلْمُؤْمِنِيْنَ

"And we narrate to you (O Muhammad ﷺ) all the stories of the Rasools so that your heart may be strengthened (consoled) by them. In these (stories) the truth has come to you as well as advice and a reminder for the Mu'mineen." (Surah Hood - Aayah 120)

One cannot lay too much stress on the point that whether these be the sayings of Nabi ﷺ or the stories of other pious people, or the books on Islamic practices, or the advices and written discourses (majlis) of the Auliyaa. It is not enough to go through them once only, but they have to be studied over and over again in order to derive proper benefit from them.

Abu Sulaymaan Daaraani *(rahmatullahi alayh)*, a famous saint, writes: "I attended a discourse (majlis) by a Sheikh at his residence. It had some effect on me, but only till the time that I rose from the meeting. I went to his audience for the second time to listen to his advices, and this time the effect remained with me till I reached my home. When I visited him for the third time, the effect of his advices stayed with me even after reaching home. Then I broke the shackles that had kept me away from Allah Ta'ala, and set out on His path to seek His pleasure."

The case with Deeni books is similar; a quick reading hardly produces the desired effect; rather a frequent and thorough study of these books is therefore necessary.

For the convenience of the readers, and to create more interest in them, I have divided this book into the following twelve chapters together with an important note in conclusion.

- Chapter 1 - To tolerate hardships and not to give up Deen when faced with difficulty.
- Chapter 2 - The fear of Allah Ta'ala.
- Chapter 3 - Staying away from luxuries.
- Chapter 4 - Piety and being cautious due to the fear of Allah Ta'ala.
- Chapter 5 - Being careful about Salaah.
- Chapter 6 - Sacrificing for others.
- Chapter 7 - Bravery and Heroism.
- Chapter 8 - Thirst for knowledge.
- Chapter 9 - Pleasing Nabi ﷺ.
- Chapter 10 - Women's courage and love for Islam.
- Chapter 11 - Children and their love for Islam.
- Chapter 12 - Love for Nabi ﷺ.
- Important note in conclusion – The Virtues and Privileges of the Sahaabah رضي الله عنهم.

CHAPTER 1

TO TOLERATE HARDSHIPS & NOT TO GIVE UP DEEN WHEN FACED WITH DIFFICULTY

It is really very hard for the Muslims of today to imagine and much less to bear or even attempt to bear the hardships that were experienced by Nabi ﷺ and his Sahaabah رضى الله عنهم in the path of Allah Ta'ala. Books of history are full of stories of their sufferings. It is a pity that our attitude is so indifferent and our knowledge so poor with regard to those events. I open this chapter with a story about Nabi ﷺ himself whose name is sure to attract the blessings of Allah Ta'ala.

1. NABI ﷺ GOES TO TAA'IF

For nine years, since Allah Ta'ala selected him for His mission, Nabi ﷺ had been preaching the message of Allah Ta'ala in Makkah and making all out efforts to guide and reform his people. Besides a few people, who had accepted Islam, or who helped him though not accepting Islam, all the rest in Makkah opposed him and went all out to persecute and ridicule him and his followers.

His uncle Abu Taalib was one of those good-hearted people who helped him although he did not accept Islam. The following year on the death of Abu Taalib, the kuffaar increased their oppression (causing problems) without anyone to support and protect Nabi ﷺ.

Ch.1 - Tolerating Hardships

At Taa'if, the second biggest town of Arabia, there lived a clan called Banu Saqeef which was strong in number. Nabi ﷺ went to Taa'if hoping to win them over to Islam. Taa'if would then be a safe place for the Muslims where the Quraish would not be able to harm them and also be a base for the propagation of Islam. When he reached Taa'if, Nabi ﷺ visited the three chiefs of the clan separately, and gave them the message of Allah Ta'ala, and asked each of them to help him in his mission.

Instead of accepting his message, they refused to even listen to him. Inspite of the famous hospitality of the Arabs, each of them treated him very badly and rudely. They told him that they did not like him to be in their town. Nabi ﷺ had expected a friendly treatment and kind words from them as they were the leaders of their clans.

But one of them mockingly said: "Hey, Allah Ta'ala has made you a Nabi!"

The other teased him: "Could Allah not find anyone else besides you to make him His Nabi?"

The third one mockingly said: "I do not want to talk to you, because if you are really a Nabi, then to oppose you is to invite trouble, and if you only pretend to be one, then why should I talk with a person pretending to be a Nabi?"

Nabi ﷺ, who was very patient, did not give up after meeting the chiefs and tried to speak to the common people in the town, but nobody would listen to him and they instead asked him to leave their town and go wherever he liked. When he realised that his efforts were in vain, he decided to leave the town.

But they did not allow him to leave in peace and sent the street hooligans after him to tease him and throw stones at him. He was hit with stones so much that his whole body was covered with blood and his shoes were stuck to his feet. He left the town in this terrible condition. When he was far out of the town and safe from the people, he made dua to Allah Ta'ala, asking for forgiveness.

اَللّٰهُمَّ اِلَيْكَ اَشْكُوْا ضَعْفَ قُوَّتِيْ وَقِلَّةَ حِيْلَتِيْ وَهَوَانِيْ عَلَى النَّاسِ يَا اَرْحَمَ الرَّاحِمِيْنَ اَنْتَ رَبُّ الْمُسْتَضْعَفِيْنَ وَاَنْتَ رَبِّيْ اِلٰى مَنْ تَكِلُنِيْ اِلٰى بَعِيْدٍ يَتَجَهَّمُنِيْ اَمْ اِلٰى عَدُوٍّ مَلَّكْتَهُ

اَمْرِیْ اِنْ لَّمْ یَکُنْ بِكَ عَلَىَّ غَضَبٌ فَلَا اُبَالِیْ وَلٰكِنْ عَافِیَتُكَ هِیَ اَوْسَعُ لِیْ اَعُوْذُ بِنُوْرِ وَجْهِكَ الَّذِیْ اَشْرَقَتْ لَهُ الظُّلُمَاتُ وَصَلَحَ عَلَیْهِ اَمْرُ الدُّنْیَا وَالْاٰخِرَةِ مِنْ اَنْ تُنْزِلَ بِیْ غَضَبَكَ اَوْ یَحِلَّ عَلَیَّ سَخَطَكَ لَكَ الْعُتْبٰی حَتّٰی تَرْضٰی وَلَا حَوْلَ وَلَا قُوَّةَ اِلَّا بِكَ

"O Allah, I complain to You alone that I am weak, that I do not have any resources and that I do not hold any significance in the eyes of the people. O, Most Merciful of all those who show mercy, You are the Rabb (master) of the weak, and You are my own Rabb (master). To whom are You going to entrust me? To a stranger who would look at me harshly or to an enemy, to whom You have given control over my affairs? If You are not angry with me, then I do not care for anything except that I should enjoy Your protection. I seek shelter in Your light (noor), which removes all sorts of darkness's and controls the affairs of this world and the hereafter. May it never be that You become angry with me or You are displeased with me. I must please You until You are happy with me. There is neither strength (to refrain from evil) nor any power (to do any good) except with You."

The heavens were moved by His dua and Jibraa-eel عَلَيْهِ السَّلَام came before Nabi صَلَّى اللَّهُ عَلَيْهِ وَسَلَّم, greeted him with *Assalamu Alaykum* and said: "Allah Ta'ala knows all that has happened between you and these people. He has sent the angel in charge of the mountains to do whatever you decide."

Saying this, Jibraa-eel عَلَيْهِ السَّلَام brought the angel before Nabi صَلَّى اللَّهُ عَلَيْهِ وَسَلَّم. The angel greeted Nabi صَلَّى اللَّهُ عَلَيْهِ وَسَلَّم with *Assalamu Alaykum* and said: "O, Nabi of Allah, I am at your service. If you wish, I can cause the mountains on both sides of this town to collide with each other, so that all the people would be crushed to death, or you may suggest any other type of punishment for them."

The merciful Nabi صَلَّى اللَّهُ عَلَيْهِ وَسَلَّم said: "Even if these people do not accept Islam, I do hope from Allah Ta'ala that there will be people from among their children who would worship Allah Ta'ala and serve His Deen."

Look at the behaviour of our noble Nabi ﷺ, whom we say we follow. We get so irritated over a little trouble or some bad words from somebody that we keep on harming him and taking revenge throughout our lives in every possible way. Is this good behaviour for one who claims to follow Nabi ﷺ? Look, even after so much suffering at Taa'if, he does not curse the people of Taa'if nor take any revenge, even when he had the opportunity to do so.

2. MARTYRDOM OF HADHRAT ANAS BIN NADHR ﷺ

Hadhrat Anas bin Nadhr ﷺ was one of the Sahaabah ﷺ who could not take part in the Battle of Badr. He regretted to have missed the honour of participating in the first battle of Islam. He waited for a chance so that he could compensate for Badr. He did not have to wait long as the battle of Uhud took place the next year. He joined the army with much eagerness.

Although they were less in number and the Muslims were gaining the upper hand, some people made a mistake and the Muslims had to suffer a temporary loss. Nabi ﷺ had sent a group of fifty archers (men with bows and arrows) to guard a road behind the mountain against the enemy troops who were mounted on animals. They had firm instructions not to move from their places until they received further orders from Nabi ﷺ. When they saw the Muslims winning and the enemy escaping, they left their places thinking that the battle was over and it was time to join in the chase and share the booty. The leader tried his best to stop them from leaving by reminding them of Nabi's ﷺ command and begged them to stay on, but only ten people listened to him, arguing that the order given by Nabi ﷺ was only while they were actually fighting.

The mounted troops of the enemy then noticed the unguarded road in the back, and attacked the Muslims from behind who were busy with sharing the booty. It was at this time that Hadhrat Anas ﷺ saw Hadhrat Sa'ad bin Mu'aaz ﷺ passing in front of him. He shouted to him: "O, Sa'ad! Where are you going? By Allah! I smell the sweet smell of Jannah coming from Mount Uhud." Saying this, he ran into the middle of the enemy and fought fiercely till he attained martyrdom.

After the battle, it was found that his body had been wounded so much that only his sister could identify him and that too only from his fingertips. More than eighty wounds which were inflicted by arrows and swords were counted on his body.

Those who strive in the path of Allah Ta'ala with sincerity and love, taste the pleasures of Jannah even in this world and so did Anas رضي الله عنه smell the sweet smell of Jannah.

3. THE TRUCE OF HUDEYBIAH AND THE INCIDENT OF HADHRAT ABU JANDAL رضي الله عنه AND HADHRAT ABU BASEER رضي الله عنه

In the sixth year of the Hijrah, Nabi صلى الله عليه وسلم and 1400 of his Sahaabah رضي الله عنهم left for Makkah to perform Umrah. The Quraish heard of the news and decided to stop him coming into Makkah even for Umrah, so he had to camp at Hudaybiyyah. However, the Sahaabah رضي الله عنهم were determined to enter even if it involved an open fight. Despite the eagerness of Sahaabah رضي الله عنهم to fight, Nabi صلى الله عليه وسلم did not agree and, he entered into an agreement with the Quraish, accepting all their conditions.

This one-sided and seemingly unfair agreement was very difficult on the Sahaabah رضي الله عنهم, but their love for Nabi صلى الله عليه وسلم made them accept his decision and even the most brave man like Umar رضي الله عنه had no choice but to accept the decision. According to one of the points of the agreement, converts to Islam must be returned to the Quraish, but those who left the Muslims to join the Quraish will not be returned to the Muslims.

Hadhrat Abu Jandal رضي الله عنه, a Muslim in Makkah, was suffering great persecution at the hands of the Quraish. They always kept him in chains. On hearing about the arrival of Nabi صلى الله عليه وسلم in Hudaybiyyah, he somehow escaped and managed to reach the Muslim camp at a time when the agreement was about to be signed. His father Suhail (at that time a non-Muslim), was the messenger of the Quraish in the discussions for the agreement. He slapped Hadhrat Abu Jandal رضي الله عنه on his face and insisted on taking him back to Makkah. Nabi صلى الله عليه وسلم said that, since

Ch.1 - Tolerating Hardships

the agreement had not yet been signed, Abu Jandal رضي الله عنه should not be returned. However, Suhail would not listen to anyone and was not prepared to leave his son with the Muslims even at the request of Nabi ﷺ and would have even cancelled the agreement. Abu Jandal رضي الله عنه, describing his hardships, complained at the top of his voice but much to the shock of the Sahaabah رضي الله عنهم, Nabi ﷺ agreed to his return. However he asked him to be patient saying: "Oh! Abu Jandal رضي الله عنه, do not be distressed, Allah Ta'ala will soon open a way for you."

After the agreement was signed and Nabi ﷺ had returned to Madinah, another Makkan Muslim Hadhrat Abu Baseer رضي الله عنه escaped to Madinah and asked Nabi's ﷺ for protection. Nabi ﷺ refused to listen to him and according to the agreement, handed him over to the two persons who had been sent by the Quraish to fetch him. However, he advised him as he had advised Hadhrat Abu Jandal رضي الله عنه to be patient and to hope for the help of Allah Ta'ala.

When Hadhrat Abu Baseer رضي الله عنه and his two guards were on their way back to Makkah, Hadhrat Abu Baseer رضي الله عنه said to one of them: "Friend, your sword is extremely fine."

The man was flattered and took it out from its sheath and said: "Yes it is really very fine, and I have tried it on so many people. You can have a look at it."

He quite foolishly gave the sword to Abu Baseer رضي الله عنه, who immediately used it on its owner and killed him. The other man ran off and reached Madinah to report to Nabi ﷺ. In the meantime Abu Baseer رضي الله عنه also arrived. He said to Nabi ﷺ: "Oh, Nabi of Allah, you returned me once as you had to abide by the agreement. I was not obliged to the agreement and I managed to escape from them with this trick, as I was afraid they would force me to leave Islam."

Nabi ﷺ said: "You are a trouble-maker. I wish you could be helped."

Hadhrat Abu Baseer رضي الله عنه understood from this that he would be returned to the Quraish again when they asked for him. Therefore, he left Madinah and escaped to a place in the desert on the sea shore. Abu Jandal رضي الله عنه also managed to escape and joined him there. More Muslims of Makkah followed and in a few days quite a large group of

Muslims gathered in the desert. They had to suffer in the desert, where there were no people or vegetation. However, because they had not signed any agreement, they troubled the Quraish by attacking their caravans passing that way. This forced the Quraish to come to Nabi ﷺ and request him to call the Muslims in the desert to Madinah. Then they will also follow the agreement like the other Muslims and the caravans could pass in safety.

It is said that Hadhrat Abu Baseer رضي الله عنه was on his deathbed when the letter sent by Nabi ﷺ asking him to return to Madinah reached him. He died while holding Nabi's ﷺ letter in his hand.

No power on earth can make a person give up his Imaan, as long as it is true Imaan. Allah Ta'ala has promised to help those who are genuine Muslims.

4. HADHRAT BILAL رضي الله عنه AND HIS SUFFERINGS

Hadhrat Bilal رضي الله عنه, who was the muazzin of Nabi's ﷺ Masjid, is one of the most famous of the Sahaabah رضي الله عنهم. He was an Abyssinian slave belonging to a kaafir in Makkah. His master, Umayyah bin Khalaf, who was the worst enemy of Islam, did not like him accepting Islam and, therefore, punished him severely. He would make him lie down on the burning sand at midday and place a heavy stone on his chest, so that he could not even move.

He would then say to him: "Leave Islam or burn and die."

Even then, Bilal رضي الله عنه would shout out: "**Ahad**" - The One (Allah), "**Ahad**" - The One (Allah).

He was whipped at night causing many cuts on his body. He was then forced to lie on the burning ground during the day to make him either leave Islam or to die a slow death from the wounds. Abu Jahl, Umayyah and others, would take turns in punishing Hadhrat Bilal رضي الله عنه and would get tired competing with one another in causing more and more painful punishment, but Hadhrat Bilal رضي الله عنه never gave up. At last Hadhrat Abu Bakr رضي الله عنه bought him and he became a free Muslim.

While Islam taught the oneness of our creator Allah Ta'ala, the idol worshipers of Makkah believed in many gods, therefore Hadhrat Bilal رضى الله عنه repeated: **"Ahad (The One), Ahad (The One)."**

This shows his love for Allah Ta'ala, Who was so dear to him, that no amount of punishment could stop him from repeating His pure name. It is said that the street children of Makkah would drag him in the streets, while he would continue saying: **"Ahad! Ahad!"**

Look how Allah Ta'ala rewarded his steadfastness. He had the honour to become the muazzin of Nabi صلى الله عليه وسلم. He was always to remain with him to call out the Azaan for his Salaah at home and also while travelling. After the death of Nabi صلى الله عليه وسلم, it became very hard for him to stay in Madinah as he would miss Nabi صلى الله عليه وسلم at every step and in every corner. He, therefore, left Madinah, and decided to pass the rest of his life in the path of Allah Ta'ala. Once he saw Nabi صلى الله عليه وسلم in his dream saying to him: "O, Bilal! How is it that you never visit me?"

As soon as he got up, he left for Madinah. On reaching Madinah, Hadhrat Hasan رضى الله عنه and Hadhrat Husain رضى الله عنه, the grandsons of Nabi صلى الله عليه وسلم, asked him to call out the Azaan. He could not refuse them, for they were very dear to him. As soon as the Azaan was called out, the people of Madinah cried openly remembering the happy old days of Nabi صلى الله عليه وسلم. Even the women came out of their houses weeping. After a few days Hadhrat Bilal رضى الله عنه left Madinah and passed away in Damascus in the year 20 A.H.

5. HADHRAT ABU ZARR GHIFAARI رضى الله عنه ACCEPTS ISLAM

Hadhrat Abu Zarr Ghiffaari رضى الله عنه is very famous among the Sahaabah رضى الله عنهم for his piety and knowledge. Hadhrat Ali رضى الله عنه used to say: "Abu Zarr رضى الله عنه has such knowledge that other people cannot cope to learn."

When he first heard about Nabi صلى الله عليه وسلم, he sent his brother to go to Makkah and find out whether he was really a Nabi. After making enquiries his brother returned and told him that he found Muhammad ﷺ to be a man of good habits and excellent behaviour and that his wonderful message was neither poetry nor magic. This report did not satisfy him. He, therefore, decided to go to Makkah and find out the truth for himself. When he reached Makkah, he went straight to the Haram He did not know Nabi ﷺ, and he did not know who to ask about him considering the fearful conditions prevailing at that time in Makkah.

When it became dark, Hadhrat Ali رضي الله عنه noticed him and could not ignore him as he was a stranger. Looking after and caring for the travellers, the poor and the strangers was a habit of Sahaabah رضي الله عنهم. He therefore took him to his house without asking him why he had come to Makkah and Abu Zarr رضي الله عنه also did not tell Ali رضي الله عنه the purpose of his visit. The next day, he again went to the Haram and stayed there till the night without being able to learn who Nabi ﷺ was. In fact, everybody knew that Nabi ﷺ and his Sahaabah رضي الله عنهم were being punished in Makkah and Abu Zarr رضي الله عنه knew it was dangerous to ask about Nabi ﷺ. Hadhrat Ali رضي الله عنه again took him home for the night and once again did not ask him why he had come to Makkah. However, on the third night, after Hadhrat Ali رضي الله عنه had entertained him, he asked him: "Brother, what brings you to this town?"

Before replying, Hadhrat Abu Zarr رضي الله عنه asked Hadhrat Ali رضي الله عنه to promise that he would speak the truth. He then asked him about Nabi Muhammad ﷺ. Hadhrat Ali رضي الله عنه replied: "He is certainly the Nabi of Allah Ta'ala. You come with me tomorrow and I shall take you to him, but you have to be very careful, in case the people come to know that you are with me, and you could get into trouble. If I see some trouble on the way, I shall move to the side pretending to adjust my shoes, and you may carry on without stopping so that the people may not think that we are together."

The next day, he followed Hadhrat Ali رضي الله عنه, who took him to Nabi ﷺ. In the very first meeting he accepted Islam. Fearing that the Quraish might harm him, Nabi ﷺ asked him to keep his conversion to Islam a secret. He also asked him to go back home to his clan and return when the Muslims had become much stronger.

Hadhrat Abu Zarr ﵁ replied: "O, Nabi of Allah! I take an oath in the name of Allah, I must go and recite the Kalimah in the middle of these kuffaar."

True to his word, he went straight to the Haram Shareef and right in the centre of the crowd, at the top of his voice, he recited the Shahaadah:

$$\text{اَشْهَدُ اَن لَّا اِلٰهَ اِلَّا اللهُ وَاَشْهَدُ اَنَّ مُحَمَّدًا رَسُوْلُ اللهِ}$$

"I bear witness that there is no deity except Allah, and I bear witness that Muhammad (ﷺ) is the Nabi of Allah."

People attacked him from all sides and would have beaten him to death if Abbaas ﵁, (the uncle of Nabi ﷺ, who had not yet accepted Islam), had not protected him and saved him from death.

Abbaas ﵁ said to the mob: "Do you know who he is? He belongs to the Ghiffaar clan, who live on the way of our caravans to Syria. If he is killed, they will attack us and we shall not be able to do business with that country." This stopped them and they left him alone.

Hadhrat Abu Zarr ﵁ repeated the Shahaadah the next day and would have surely been beaten to death by the crowd had not Abbaas ﵁ once again saved him for the second time.

The action of Hadhrat Abu Zarr ﵁ was due to his extreme love for shouting out the Kalimah among the kuffaar. The advice of Nabi ﷺ of stopping him was due to the love in his heart for Hadhrat Abu Zarr ﵁. Nabi ﷺ did not want him to be put to hardships by the Kuffaar which may be too much for him.

There is absolutely no disobedience in this story. Since Nabi ﷺ himself was going through all sorts of hardships in spreading the message of Islam. Abu Zarr ﵁ also thought it better to follow his example rather than to avoid danger. It was this quality of Sahaabah ﵃ that took them very far in their Dunya and in their Deen. When a person had recited the Kalimah and entered the Deen of Islam, no power on earth could turn him back and no oppression or cruelty could stop him from Tabligh.

6. THE DIFFICULTIES FACED BY HADHRAT KHABBAAB IBNUL ARAT ﷺ

Hadhrat Khabbaab ﷺ is also one of those blessed persons who offered themselves for sacrifice and suffering for the sake of Allah Ta'ala. He was the sixth or seventh person to accept Islam and therefore suffered long. He was made to put on steel armour and lie in the sun to sweat and suffer. Very often he was made to lie flat on the burning sand, which caused the flesh on his back to melt.

He was the slave of a woman. When she came to know that he was visiting Nabi ﷺ, she used to burn his head with a hot iron rod. Hadhrat 'Umar ﷺ, once asked Hadhrat Khabbaab ﷺ about his sufferings after accepting Islam. He showed him his back. Hadhrat 'Umar ﷺ said, "I have never seen such a back before." He said, "My body was dragged over heaps of burning charcoal and the blood and fat coming out of my back put out the fire."

It is said that, when Islam spread and the Muslims conquered all the surrounding lands, he used to weep and say: "Allah Ta'ala seems to be rewarding us in this world for all our sufferings and perhaps no reward would be left for us in the Hereafter."

Hadhrat Khabbaab ﷺ says: "Nabi ﷺ once read a very long rakaat while performing Salaah. When the Sahaabah ﷺ mentioned it to him, he said, 'This was a Salaah of desiring from Allah Ta'ala and humility. I asked three favours from Allah Ta'ala. I begged Him: O Allah! Do not let my Ummat die by famine; do not let my Ummat be destroyed by an enemy overpowering them; and do not let my Ummat fight amongst themselves.' Allah Ta'ala accepted the first two duas, but not the third one."

Hadhrat Khabbaab ﷺ passed away in 37 A.H. He was the first of the Sahaabah ﷺ to be buried at Koofah.

Hadhrat Ali ﷺ, once passing his grave, said: "May Allah Ta'ala bless and show mercy on Hadhrat Khabbaab ﷺ. He accepted Islam happily. He made hijrat with great pleasure in the path of Allah Ta'ala, and spent his whole life in struggling and suffering for Islam. Blessed is the person who remembers the day of Qiyaamah, prepares for his questioning, remains satisfied with very little of this world and is able to please Allah Ta'ala."

To be able to please Allah Ta'ala, was really the Sahaabah رضي الله عنهم greatest achievement, for this was the only purpose of their life.

7. Hadhrat Ammaar رضي الله عنه and his Parents

Hadhrat Ammaar رضي الله عنه and his parents were also severely punished. They were tortured on the burning hot sands of Makkah. While passing by them, Nabi صلى الله عليه وسلم would ask them to be patient, giving them good news about Jannah. Ammaar's رضي الله عنه father, Yaasir رضي الله عنه, died after suffering at the hands of the kuffaar. His mother Sumayya رضي الله عنها was killed by Abu Jahl, who put his spear through the most private part of her body, causing her death. She had refused to leave Islam in spite of suffering terrible torture in her old age. The blessed lady was the first person to become a shaheed (to die in the path of Allah Ta'ala).

The first Masjid in Islam was built by Ammaar رضي الله عنه. When Nabi صلى الله عليه وسلم moved to Madinah, Ammaar رضي الله عنه built a room for him where he could sit, take a rest in the afternoon and read his Salaah under its roof. He first collected the stones and then built the Masjid in Quba. He fought against the enemies of Islam very bravely.

Once when he was fighting in a battle he happily said: "I am going to meet my friends very soon. I am going to meet Muhammad صلى الله عليه وسلم and his Sahaabah رضي الله عنهم." He then asked for water. He was given some milk. He took it and said: "I heard Nabi صلى الله عليه وسلم saying to me, 'Milk shall be the last drink of your life'." He then fought till he was made shaheed. He was about ninety-four years old at that time.

8. Hadhrat Suhaib رضي الله عنه accepts Islam

Hadhrat Suhaib رضي الله عنه and Hadhrat Ammaar رضي الله عنه became Muslims at the same time. Nabi صلى الله عليه وسلم was staying at Arqam's رضي الله عنه place, when they both came separately with the same intention of accepting Islam and met each other at the door of the house. Like other poor

Muslims of that time, Suhaib ﷺ also suffered a lot at the hands of the Kuffaar.

At last he decided to emigrate to Madinah. The Quraish would not tolerate this, and soon after he left, a group went after him to bring him back to Makkah. As they came near, he shouted to them: "You know that I am better with the bow and arrow than all of you. As long as I have a single arrow left with me, you will not be able to catch me, and when I finish all my arrows, I shall fight you with my sword, as long as it is in my hand. If you like, you can take my money and my two women slaves which I have left in Makkah, instead of me."

When they agreed, he told them where to find his money, and they allowed him to go to Madinah. At this, Allah Ta'ala sent down the following Aayat of the Qur-aan to Nabi ﷺ:

$$\text{وَمِنَ النَّاسِ مَن يَشْرِىْ نَفْسَهُ ابْتِغَآءَ مَرْضَاتِ اللهِ ۗ وَاللهُ رَءُوْفٌ بِالْعِبَادِ}$$

"And from the people is he who would sell himself, seeking the pleasure of Allah Ta'ala, and Allah Ta'ala is most Compassionate (Kind) towards His bondsmen." (Surah Baqarah - Aayah 207)

Nabi ﷺ was at that time at Quba. When he saw Hadhrat Suhaib ﷺ coming, he remarked: "A good bargain, Suhaib!"

Suhaib ﷺ says: "Nabi ﷺ was eating dates at that time. I also joined him in eating. One of my eyes was sore. He said, 'Suhaib! You are eating dates when your eye is sore'. 'But I am taking them by the side of the other eye, which is not sore, O, Nabi of Allah,' I replied. Nabi ﷺ was amused with my reply."

Hadhrat Suhaib ﷺ was very generous and freely spent his money on others. 'Umar ﷺ once told him that he was over-generous. He replied: "But I spend only where it is right."

When Hadhrat 'Umar ﷺ was about to die, he wanted Suhaib ﷺ to perform his janaazah salaah.

Ch.1 - Tolerating Hardships

9. Hadhrat 'Umar ﺭﺿﻲ ﺍﻟﻠﻪ ﻋﻨﻪ Accepts Islam

Hadhrat 'Umar ﺭﺿﻲ ﺍﻟﻠﻪ ﻋﻨﻪ, of whom all the Muslims are proud and the disbelievers still fear, was very strong in opposing Nabi ﺻﻠﻰ ﺍﻟﻠﻪ ﻋﻠﻴﻪ ﻭﺳﻠﻢ and famous for persecuting the Muslims before he accepted Islam. One day, in a meeting, the Quraish asked for someone to volunteer to kill Nabi ﺻﻠﻰ ﺍﻟﻠﻪ ﻋﻠﻴﻪ ﻭﺳﻠﻢ. 'Umar ﺭﺿﻲ ﺍﻟﻠﻪ ﻋﻨﻪ offered himself for this job, at which everybody said: "Surely you can do it, 'Umar!"

With a sword hanging from his neck, he left immediately to carry out this evil deed. On his way he met Sa'ad bin Abi Waqqaas ﺭﺿﻲ ﺍﻟﻠﻪ ﻋﻨﻪ of the Zuhrah clan.

"Where are you going, 'Umar?" asked Sa'ad ﺭﺿﻲ ﺍﻟﻠﻪ ﻋﻨﻪ.

Umar ﺭﺿﻲ ﺍﻟﻠﻪ ﻋﻨﻪ replied: "I am going to kill Muhammad."

Sa'ad ﺭﺿﻲ ﺍﻟﻠﻪ ﻋﻨﻪ warned 'Umar ﺭﺿﻲ ﺍﻟﻠﻪ ﻋﻨﻪ: "But don't you see that Banu Haashim, Banu Zuhrah and Banu Abdi Munaaf will kill you in revenge?"

'Umar ﺭﺿﻲ ﺍﻟﻠﻪ ﻋﻨﻪ gets upset with the warning and replies: "It seems that you have also accepted Islam. Let me kill you first."

'Umar ﺭﺿﻲ ﺍﻟﻠﻪ ﻋﻨﻪ pulled out his sword. Sa'ad ﺭﺿﻲ ﺍﻟﻠﻪ ﻋﻨﻪ, declaring his conversion to Islam, also took out his sword. They were about to start a fight when Sa'ad ﺭﺿﻲ ﺍﻟﻠﻪ ﻋﻨﻪ said to him: "You better first put your own house in order. Your sister and your brother-in-law have accepted Islam."

Hearing this, 'Umar ﺭﺿﻲ ﺍﻟﻠﻪ ﻋﻨﻪ became very angry and immediately went to his sister's house. The door was locked from inside and both husband and wife were learning the Qur-aan from Hadhrat Khabbaab ﺭﺿﻲ ﺍﻟﻠﻪ ﻋﻨﻪ. 'Umar ﺭﺿﻲ ﺍﻟﻠﻪ ﻋﻨﻪ knocked at the door and shouted for his sister to open it. When Hadhrat Khabbaab ﺭﺿﻲ ﺍﻟﻠﻪ ﻋﻨﻪ heard the voice of 'Umar ﺭﺿﻲ ﺍﻟﻠﻪ ﻋﻨﻪ, he hid himself in a room, forgetting to take the pages of the Noble Qur-aan with him. When his sister opened the door, 'Umar ﺭﺿﻲ ﺍﻟﻠﻪ ﻋﻨﻪ hit her on the head, saying: "O, enemy of yourself, have you also left your religion?"

Her head began to bleed. 'Umar ﺭﺿﻲ ﺍﻟﻠﻪ ﻋﻨﻪ then went inside and asked, "What were you doing and who was the stranger I heard from outside?" His brother-in-law replied, "We were talking to each other." 'Umar ﺭﺿﻲ ﺍﻟﻠﻪ ﻋﻨﻪ asked him, "Have you also left the religion of your forefathers and become a Muslim?" His brother-in-law replied, "But what if the new religion is the better and the true one?" 'Umar ﷺ became furious and jumped on him, pulling his beard and beating him up terribly. When his sister tried to stop him, he smacked her face so violently, that it bled profusely.

She was, after all, 'Umar's sister. She burst out: "'Umar! You are hitting us only because we have become Muslims. Listen! We are ready to die as Muslims. You can do whatever you like."

When 'Umar ﷺ had cooled down and felt ashamed over his sister's bleeding, he saw the pages of the Qur-aan left behind by Hadhrat Khabbaab ﷺ. He said, "Alright show me, what these are?" "No," said his sister, "you are dirty and no dirty person can touch the Qur-aan." He asked again, but his sister was not prepared to allow him to touch the Qur-aan unless he washed his body. 'Umar ﷺ at last agreed. He washed his body and then began to read the Qur-aan. It was Surah "Taaha". He started from the beginning of the Surah, and he was a completely changed man when he came to the aayat:

اِنَّنِىْ اَنَا اللّٰهُ لَآ اِلٰهَ اِلَّآ اَنَا فَاعْبُدْنِىْ ۙ وَ اَقِمِ الصَّلٰوةَ لِذِكْرِىْ

"Verily I am Allah. There is none worthy of worship besides Me, so worship me and establish Salaah for My remembrance."
(Surah Taahaa - Aayah 14)

He said: "Alright, take me to Muhammad ﷺ."

On hearing this, Hadhrat Khabbaab ﷺ came out from inside and said: "O, 'Umar! Good news for you. Yesterday (on Thursday night) Nabi ﷺ made dua to Allah Ta'ala, 'O Allah, strengthen Islam with either 'Umar or Abu Jahl, whomsoever You like.' It seems that his dua has been answered in your favour."

'Umar ﷺ then went to Nabi ﷺ and accepted Islam on Friday morning. Although 'Umar's ﷺ conversion to Islam was terrible news for the Quraish, the Muslims were still few in number and the whole country was against them. The kuffaar increased their efforts to completely wipe out the Muslims and Islam. With Umar ﷺ now on their side, the Muslims started to perform their Salaah openly in the Haram.

Hadhrat Abdullah bin Mas'ood ؓ says: "'Umar's ؓ Islam was a big victory, his hijrat to Madinah a very great help, and his becoming the Khalifah, a great blessing for the Muslims."

10. Escaping to Abyssinia and being boycotted in the valley of Abu Taalib

The problems and sufferings of the Muslims were increasing all the time. Nabi ﷺ at last allowed them to emigrate to some other place. Abyssinia at that time was ruled by a Christian King (who later on accepted Islam), who was very merciful and just. In Rajab, in the fifth year of Nubuwwat, the first group of Muslims emigrated to Abyssinia. This group had about twelve men and five women. The Quraish chased after them to catch them, but their boats had already left the shore. When they reached Abyssinia, they heard the false news that the whole tribe of the Quraish had accepted Islam. They were very happy to hear this news and returned to their country. When they reached Makkah, they learnt that the news was false and the problems were going on as before. Some of them decided to return to Abyssinia but the rest entered Makkah, under the protection of a few noble people. This is known as the first migration (Hijrat) to Abyssinia.

Later on, a bigger group of eighty-three men and eighteen women emigrated to Abyssinia. This is called the second migration to Abyssinia. Some Sahaabah ؓ took part in both the migrations. The Quraish did not like the migrations, and the thought of peace enjoyed by the Muhaajireen gave them no rest. They sent a group to Abyssinia with beautiful presents for the king, his chiefs and the priests. The group first met the chiefs and the priests, and by giving them the presents, they won their hearts.

They then came to the king's palace and bowed down in front of him. After presenting the gifts, they said: "O, king! A few lads of our people have left their religion, and have joined an absolutely new religion, which is opposed to our as well as your religion. They have come to settle in your country. The people of Makkah, their parents and families have sent us to take them back to their country. We request you to hand them over to us."

The king replied: "Without proper investigation, we cannot hand them over to you. Let us call them and hear what they have to say. If what you are saying is true, that they have forsaken their religion, then we will happily hand them over to you."

Thereafter, the king called the Muslims to his court. At first, they were very worried and did not know what to do, but Allah Ta'ala gave them courage, and they decided to go and speak the truth before the king. When they came before him, they greeted him with 'Salaam'. Someone objected that according to the rules of the land, they had not bowed down before the king.

They explained: "Our Nabi ﷺ has forbidden us from prostrating before anyone except Allah Ta'ala." The king then asked them to explain the charges brought against them.

Hadhrat Ja'far رضى الله عنه stood up and said: "O, king! We were an ignorant nation. We neither knew Allah Ta'ala nor His Ambiyaa عليهم السلام. We worshipped stones. We used to eat dead meat and did all sorts of terrible and disgraceful things. We did not fulfil the rights of our relatives. The strong among us would oppress the weak. At last, Allah Ta'ala sent a Nabi ﷺ to guide and reform us. His noble lineage, beautiful character, sincerity of his mission and pure life is well known to us. He invited us to worship Allah Ta'ala, and encouraged us to give up idol and stone worship. He commanded us with good behaviour, and stopped us from shameless things. He taught us to tell the truth, to return the trust (amaanah), to take care of our families and to do good to our neighbours. He taught us to read Salaah, to Fast, to pay Zakaat, to have good behaviour; and to avoid all evil, bad behaviour and killing.

He stopped us from adultery, rude behaviour, telling of lies, stealing the wealth of an orphan, falsely accusing anyone, and all other evil things. He taught us the Qur-aan, the wonderful book of Allah Ta'ala. We believed in him, followed him and practised on his teachings. Then, our people began to harm and torture us, thinking that we might give up our Islam and go back to idol-worship. However, when their cruelties became too much, we escaped to your country with the permission of our Nabi ﷺ."

The king said: "Let us hear something of the Qur-aan that your Nabi ﷺ has taught you."

Hadhrat Ja'far ؓ recited a few Aayaat from the beginning of 'Surah Maryam', which touched the hearts of the king and the priests so much so that tears flowed down their cheeks and wet their beards.

The king remarked: "By Allah, these words and the words revealed to Moosa ؑ are the rays of one and the same light."

He then told the Quraish delegation that he would not hand over the Muslims to them. The Kuffaar, disappointed and disgraced, had a meeting. One of them said: "I have a plan that is sure to make the king angry with the Muslims."

Although the others did not agree, yet he would not listen to them. The next day, they told the king that the Muslims do not believe in Hadhrat 'Isa ؑ and in his religion. The Muslims were again called to the court. They were much more worried this time.

When the king asked about their belief in Hadhrat 'Isa ؑ, they said: "We believe in what Allah Ta'ala has sent down about him to our Nabi ﷺ, that is he is a servant and Nabi of Allah Ta'ala and is the word of Allah Ta'ala, which He gave to the virgin and pure Maryam ؓ."

Negus (the king) said: "Hadhrat 'Isa ؑ himself does not say anything more than that."

The priests then began to protest, but the king would not listen to them. He returned the presents to the Kuffaar and told the Muslims: "Go and live in peace. If anybody ill-treats you, he will have to answer to me."

The king's decision was announced all over. This gave the Muslims some respect in the country, and the Quraish delegation had to return in failure.

This failure of the Quraish in Abyssinia, and the victory of the Muslims over them, caused an increase in the frustration of the Kuffaar. Hadhrat 'Umar's ؓ accepting Islam made them even more furious. They became more and more angry, until their anger reached such a point that a large number of the Quraish chiefs planned to kill Muhammad ﷺ. But this was not so easy because Banu Haashim, the family of Nabi ﷺ, were strong in number and still stronger in position. Although all of them were not Muslims, yet even the non-

Muslims among them would not agree to, nor tolerate the murder of Nabi ﷺ.

Therefore, the Quraish decided to completely boycott the Banu Haashim family. Their chiefs wrote a document saying that none of them or their families would mix with or buy from or sell to those who sided with the Banu Haashim, unless and until they hand over Muhammad ﷺ for the death penalty. All of them signed this document on the 1st Muharram in the seventh year of Nubuwwat and the document was hung up in the Ka'bah in order to give it full importance.

For three long years, Nabi ﷺ and all his family were shut up in the valley, which was a small section in one of the valleys that ran down to Makkah. For three long years nobody could see them nor have any contact with them. They could not buy anything in Makkah or from anyone else coming from outside.

Any person found outside this valley, was beaten mercilessly and if he asked for anything it was refused. Soon their food stock was reduced to a bare minimum and they were rationed. Their women, and more especially their children and babies would cry with hunger. This was harder on them than their own starvation. During the last part of this period, their only food was the little food that the husbands of the Banu Haashim women married into other families managed to smuggle into the valley in the darkness of night.

At last after three years, by the Grace of Allah Ta'ala, the document was eaten up by white ants and the boycott ended. We cannot even imagine the sufferings that they had to go through. During this period, the Sahaabah ﷺ not only remained firm on their Imaan, but also kept busy in spreading the light of Islam amongst themselves.

Look! How much the Sahaabah ﷺ have suffered in the path of Allah Ta'ala for the cause of Islam. We claim to follow their footsteps and dream of being like them, but how much have we suffered for Islam? What sacrifice have we made for the sake of Allah Ta'ala? Success is always according to the sacrifice. We wish to live in luxury and comfort, and are racing with the non-Muslims in enjoying the good things of this world, forgetting the Aakhirat, and then at the same time we expect to receive the same help from Allah Ta'ala which the Sahaabah ﷺ

received. We cannot bluff anybody but ourselves by behaving like this. A poet has said,

> *"O Traveller, I am afraid that you will not reach the Ka'bah because the road that you are following leads (in the opposite direction) to Turkey."*

CHAPTER 2
THE FEAR OF ALLAH TA'ALA

Together with the amazing level of sacrifice, the Sahaabah رضى الله عنهم also had a genuine and deep fear of Allah Ta'ala in their hearts.

I wish that the Muslims of today could have a speck of that fear of Allah Ta'ala. Here are a few stories about the fear of Allah Ta'ala in the lives of Sahaabah رضى الله عنهم.

1. NABI'S ﷺ WORRY AT THE TIME OF A STORM

Hadhrat Aa'ishah رضى الله عنها says that whenever a strong wind started to blow, bringing with it thick clouds, then Nabi's ﷺ face would change colour with the fear of Allah Ta'ala. He would become restless and would go in and out with worry, and would recite the following dua:

اَللّٰهُمَّ اِنِّيْ اَسْئَلُكَ خَيْرَهَا وَخَيْرَ مَا فِيْهَا وَخَيْرَ مَا اُرْسِلَتْ بِهِ وَاَعُوْذُ بِكَ مِنْ شَرِّهَا وَشَرِّ مَا فِيْهَا وَشَرِّ مَا اُرْسِلَتْ بِهِ

"O my Allah! I ask of You the good out of this wind, the good out of that which is in this wind, and the good out of that which is the outcome of this wind. I seek protection in You from the evil of this wind, from the evil out of that which is in this wind, and from the evil out of that which is the outcome of this wind."

She says: "And then when it began to rain, signs of happiness appeared on his face. I said to him once, 'O Nabi of Allah, when clouds appear everybody is happy because it will rain, but why is it that I see you so worried at that time?' He replied, 'O, 'Aa'ishah! How can I feel safe that this wind does not warn of the anger of Allah Ta'ala? The people of A'ad were punished with the wind. They were happy when they saw the thick clouds (gathering), believing that they had brought rain; but actually those clouds brought no rain but total destruction to the people of 'Aad.'"

Nabi ﷺ was obviously talking about the following Aayaat of the Qur-aan:

فَلَمَّا رَأَوْهُ عَارِضًا مُّسْتَقْبِلَ أَوْدِيَتِهِمْ قَالُوا هَذَا عَارِضٌ مُّمْطِرُنَا ۚ بَلْ هُوَ مَا اسْتَعْجَلْتُم بِهِ ۖ رِيحٌ فِيهَا عَذَابٌ أَلِيمٌ ۝ تُدَمِّرُ كُلَّ شَيْءٍ بِأَمْرِ رَبِّهَا فَأَصْبَحُوا لَا يُرَىٰ إِلَّا مَسَاكِنُهُمْ ۚ كَذَٰلِكَ نَجْزِي الْقَوْمَ الْمُجْرِمِينَ

"Then, when they saw it (the punishment) as a cloud coming toward their valleys, they said: 'This is a cloud that will bringing us rain.' Rather, it was that very thing (punishment) which you sought to hasten, a fierce wind bearing a painful punishment, it demolished everything (in its path) by the command of its Rabb and it transpired that only their homes could be seen. Thus did We punish the sinful nation." (Surah A'hqaaf - Aayah 24-25)

Look at the fear of Allah Ta'ala in the heart of a person who is the best of all creation. In spite of a clear Aayat in the Qur-aan[1] that Allah Ta'ala would not punish the people so long as Nabi ﷺ was with them he has so much fear of Allah Ta'ala in him, that a strong wind reminds him of the punishment given to the people in the past. Now let us look into our own hearts for a moment. Although we are full of sins, yet earthquakes, lightning, etc., do not cause any fear of Allah Ta'ala in our hearts and, instead of making Istighfaar or Salaah at such times, we only get busy in silly inquiries.

---

[1] *Surah Anfaal – Aayah 33*

2. WHAT HADHRAT ANAS ﷺ USED TO DO AT THE TIME OF A STORM

Hadhrat Nadhr-bin-Abdullah ﷺ says: "One day while Hadhrat Anas ﷺ was alive, it became very dark during the day time. I went to him and asked, 'Did you ever see such a thing in the time of Nabi ﷺ?' He replied, 'I seek refuge in Allah Ta'ala! In those days, if the breeze grew a little stronger than normal, we would rush towards the Masjid, fearing the coming of the Last Day.'"

Hadhrat Abu Darda ﷺ says: "Whenever there was a storm, Nabi ﷺ would get worried and go to the Masjid."

Nowadays, even at the time of the worst of problems, who thinks of going to the Masjid? Leave aside the common people, even those who regard themselves as good and practicing Muslims, do not practice this Sunnat.

3. WHAT NABI ﷺ DID AT THE TIME OF A SOLAR ECLIPSE (SUN BEING BLOCKED BY THE MOON)

The sun was once in eclipse in Nabi's ﷺ time. The Sahaabah ﷺ left their jobs. Even the young boys practicing with their bow and arrows rushed towards the Masjid to know what Nabi ﷺ would do at that time. Nabi ﷺ started Salaah of two rakaat, which were so long that some people fainted and fell down.

He wept in his Salaah and said: "O Allah! You have said that You will not punish them as long as I am with them and so long as they seek Your forgiveness."

This refers to an Aayat in the Qur-aan wherein Allah Ta'ala says:

وَمَا كَانَ اللّٰهُ لِيُعَذِّبَهُمْ وَاَنْتَ فِيْهِمْ ۚ وَمَا كَانَ اللّٰهُ مُعَذِّبَهُمْ وَهُمْ يَسْتَغْفِرُوْنَ

"But Allah Ta'ala would not punish them while You are with them, nor will He punish them while they seek forgiveness."
(Surah Anfaal - Aayah 33)

Ch.2 – The Fear of Allah Ta'ala

He then addressed the people saying: "You should rush for Salaah whenever you find the Sun or the Moon in eclipse. If you know the signs of the Last Day as I do, then surely you would weep more and laugh less. In all such occasions, read Salaah; make dua to Allah Ta'ala and give sadaqah (charity) to the poor."

4. NABI ﷺ CRYING THE WHOLE NIGHT

Once Nabi ﷺ kept crying the whole night, again and again repeating the following aayat:

اِنْ تُعَذِّبْهُمْ فَاِنَّهُمْ عِبَادُكَ ۖ وَ اِنْ تَغْفِرْ لَهُمْ فَاِنَّكَ اَنْتَ الْعَزِيْزُ الْحَكِيْمُ

"If You punish them, they are Your slaves; and if You forgive them, You only are the Mighty, the Wise." (Surah Maai'dah - Aayah 118)

It is said about Imaam Abu Haneefah *(rahmatullahi alayh)* that he also once wept the whole night, reciting the following aayat of the Qur-aan in Tahajjud:

وَامْتَازُوا الْيَوْمَ اَيُّهَا الْمُجْرِمُوْنَ

"Separate yourselves on this day, O sinful people."
(Surah Yaaseen - Aayah 59)

This aayat means that on the Day of Qiyaamah, the sinful people will be asked to separate themselves from the good people, and will not be allowed to mix with them as they were doing in the world. Why should the people, with fear of Allah Ta'ala in their hearts, not weep in anxiety regarding to which class they will belong to on that Day?

5. HADHRAT ABU BAKR ﷺ AND THE FEAR OF ALLAH TA'ALA

According to our belief, Hadhrat Abu Bakr ﷺ is the highest person after the Ambiyaa ﷺ. Nabi ﷺ himself gave him the good news of his being the head of a group of people in Jannah.

Nabi ﷺ once said: "Abu Bakr's رضي الله عنه name shall be called out from all the gates of Jannah, and he will be the first of my followers to enter it."

With all these virtues, Hadhrat Abu Bakr رضي الله عنه used to say: "I wish I was a tree that would be cut and finished off."

Sometimes he would say: "I wish I was a blade of grass, whose life ended with the grazing of an animal."

He also said: "I wish I was a strand of hair on the body of a Mu'min."

Once he went to a garden, where he saw a bird singing. He sighed deeply and said: "O, Bird! How lucky you are! You eat, you drink and fly under the shade of the trees, and you fear no questioning on the Day of Qiyaamah. I wish I was just like you."

Hadhrat Rabi'ah Aslami رضي الله عنه says: "I once had an argument with Hadhrat Abu Bakr رضي الله عنه and he said a word that I did not like. He realised it immediately and said to me; 'Brother, please say that word back to me.' I refused to do so. He insisted, and even spoke of telling Nabi ﷺ about it, but I did not agree to say that word. He got up and left me. A few people of my family said, 'Look! How strange! The person does wrong to you and on top of that, he wants to complain to Nabi ﷺ.' I said, 'Do you know who he is. He is Hadhrat Abu Bakr رضي الله عنه. To displease him is to displease Nabi ﷺ and to displease Nabi ﷺ is to displease Allah Ta'ala, and if Allah Ta'ala is displeased then who can save Rabi'ah from destruction?' I went to Nabi ﷺ and mentioned the whole story to him. He said, 'You were quite right in refusing to say that word. But you could have said this much in reply: O, Abu Bakr, may Allah Ta'ala forgive you!'"

Look at the fear of Allah Ta'ala in Hadhrat Abu Bakr رضي الله عنه. He wants to clear his books in this world. As soon as he spoke something slightly wrong to a person, he regrets it and asks that person to say that word back to him. He even threatens to have the problem solved by taking it to Nabi ﷺ. We are in the habit of saying bad words to others, but we do not fear the consequences or the reckoning in the Aakhirat.

6. HADHRAT UMAR ﷺ AND THE FEAR OF ALLAH TA'ALA

Hadhrat Umar ﷺ would often hold a straw (piece of dry grass) in his hand and say: "I wish I were a straw like this."
Sometimes he would say: "I wish my mother had not given birth to me."

Once he was busy with some important work when a person came to him and complained about a small problem and requested him to solve it. Hadhrat 'Umar ﷺ lashed him across his shoulders, saying: "When I sit for that job, you do not come to me, but when I am busy in other important work you come with your complaints and disturb me."

The person walked away. Hadhrat 'Umar ﷺ sent for him and handing his whip over to him, said: "You lash me now to even things up." The person said: "I forgive you for the sake of Allah Ta'ala."

Hadhrat 'Umar ﷺ went home, read two rakaats Salaah in repentance and scolded himself, saying: "O, Umar! You were low but Allah Ta'ala raised you. You were lost but Allah Ta'ala guided you. You were an ordinary person but Allah Ta'ala honoured you and made you rule over the people. Now one of them comes and asks you for help in the wrong done to him, and you beat him. What answer will you give before Allah Ta'ala?" He kept on scolding himself for a very long time.

Once, when Hadhrat Umar ﷺ was going towards Harrah (a suburb of Madinah) with his slave Aslam, he saw a fire in the desert. He said: "There seems to be a camp. Perhaps, it is a caravan that could not enter the town because it was too dark. Let's go and look after them and arrange for their protection during the night."

When he reached there, he found a woman and some children. The children were crying. The woman had a pot of water over the fire. Hadhrat 'Umar ﷺ greeted her with salaam and with her permission, went near her.

'Umar ﷺ asked: "Why are these children crying?"

The woman replied: "Because they are hungry."

'Umar ﷺ again asked: "What is in the pot?"

The woman replied: "Only water, to calm the children, so that they may go to sleep thinking that food is being prepared for them. Ah! On the Day of Qiyaamah, Allah Ta'ala will judge between Umar ﷺ and me, for not taking care of me when I am in difficulty."

'Umar ﷺ, (weeping), said: "May Allah Ta'ala have mercy on you! How can 'Umar know of your problem?"

The Woman replied: "When he is our Amir, he must keep himself informed about us."

Hadhrat 'Umar ﷺ returned to the town and immediately went to Baitul-Maal to fill a sack with flour, dates, fat and clothes, and also took some money. When the sack was ready, he said to his slave Aslam: "Put this sack on my back, Aslam."

Aslam said: "No please, Amirul-Mu'mineen! I shall carry this sack."

Hadhrat 'Umar ﷺ refused to listen to Aslam, even when he tried to force him, and said: "What! Will you carry my load on the Day of Qiyaamah? I must carry this bag, because I will be questioned about this woman in the Aakhirat."

Aslam unhappily placed the bag on Hadhrat Umar's ﷺ back and he carried it quickly right to the woman's tent. Aslam followed him. He put a little flour and some dates and fat in the pot and began to stir. He blew (with his mouth) into the fire to light it.

Aslam says: "I saw the smoke passing through his thick beard."

After some time, the food was ready. He himself served it to the family. After they had eaten to their full, he gave them the little that was left for their next meal. The children were very happy after their meal and began to play about happily. The woman felt very grateful and said: "May Allah Ta'ala reward you for your kindness! In fact you deserve to take the place of the Khalifah instead of 'Umar."

'Umar ﷺ said: "When you come to see the Khalifah, you will find me there."

He sat for a while at a place close by and kept on watching the children. He then returned to Madinah. On his way back, he said to Aslam: "Aslam, Do you know why I sat there? I had seen them crying out of hunger; I liked to see them laughing and happy for some time."

It is said that Hadhrat 'Umar ﷺ used to recite Surah Kahf, Surah Thaahaa and other such Surahs when leading the Fajr Salaah and would weep so much, that his crying could be heard a few rows back. Once he was reading Surah Yusuf in Fajr, when he came to the Aayat:

$$\text{اِنَّمَآ اَشْكُوْا بَثِّیْ وَحُزْنِیْٓ اِلَی اللّٰہِ}$$

"*I only complain of my problems and grief to Allah Ta'ala,*"
(Surah Yoosuf - Aayah 86)

He wept so much, that he could not recite any further. In Tahajjud Salaah, he would sometimes fall to the ground because of his excessive weeping.

Such was the fear of Allah Ta'ala in Hadhrat 'Umar رضى الله عنه, whose name struck terror in the hearts of the strongest kings of his time. Even today, the people are filled with awe (fear) when they read about him. Is there any person in power today who is prepared to show such kindness to the people he is in charge of?

7. A WARNING BY HADHRAT ABDULLAH BIN ABBAAS رضى الله عنهما

Wahab bin Munabbah *(rahmatullahi alayh)* says: "Abdullah bin Abbaas رضى الله عنه became blind in his old age. I once led him to the Haram Shareef in Makkah, where he heard a group of people arguing. He asked me to lead him to them. He greeted them with '*Assalaamu Alaikum.*' They asked him to sit down, but he refused and said: 'May I tell you about people who hold a high position in the sight of Allah Ta'ala? They are those whom His fear has caused them to be silent, even though they are able to speak. In fact they are able to speak very well and have a good understanding. The zikr of Allah Ta'ala has over-powered them and they do not speak much. They only do good actions. Why are you not like these people?' After this scolding, I never even saw a group of two people in the Haram."

It is said that Hadhrat Ibn Abbaas رضى الله عنه used to weep so much with Allah Ta'ala's fear that the tears flowing down his cheeks had left marks on them.

In this story, Hadhrat Abdullah bin Abbaas رضى الله عنه has shown a very easy way to do good actions. This is, to think about the greatness of Allah Ta'ala. If this is done, it becomes very easy to do all other good actions with full sincerity. Is it so difficult to spend a few minutes, out of the twenty four hours of a day, to think about the greatness of Allah Ta'ala?

8. NABI'S ﷺ PASSING NEAR THE RUINS (BROKEN BUILDINGS) OF SAMOOD DURING THE TABUK JOURNEY

The Tabuk journey is one of the major battles of Nabi ﷺ and the last one in which he took part in. When he heard that the Caesar (king of Rome) had gathered a large army to wipe out Islam and was on his way (through Syria) to Madinah, he decided to lead the Sahaabah رضي الله عنهم to stop him on his way. On Thursday, the 5th Rajab, 9 A.H., the Muslims marched out of Madinah.

As the weather was hot and the fighting was expected to be very tough, Nabi ﷺ made a clear announcement that the Muslims should gather in strength and prepare fully to face the Roman army. He also encouraged them to spend towards the equipment of the army. It was at this time that Hadhrat Abu Bakr رضي الله عنه gave all his wealth and belongings. When he was asked by Nabi ﷺ as to what he had left for his family, he replied: "I have left Allah Ta'ala and His Nabi ﷺ for them."

Hadhrat 'Umar رضي الله عنه gave half of his belongings and Hadhrat 'Usmaan رضي الله عنه gave enough for the equipment of one-third of the army. Although everyone gave more than what he could afford, the equipment was still short. Ten people had to share a camel which they rode in turns. This is why this battle is known as, "The campaign of hardship."

The journey was long and the weather hot and dry. The orchards were full of ripe dates (the main food of Madinah) and it was just the time for harvesting, when all of a sudden the Sahaabah رضي الله عنهم were asked to go for this battle. It was really a severe test of their Imaan. They imagined the long and difficult journey ahead, the boiling heat, the strong enemy, and to top it all, losing the entire year's crop of dates, but they could not even dream of missing this battle because of the deep fear of Allah Ta'ala in their hearts.

Except for the women, children (who were excused), those who were excused to stay behind by Nabi ﷺ himself and the munaafiqeen, nearly everybody else joined the army. Also amongst those who were left behind were people who did not have any animal to ride on, nor could

Nabi ﷺ provide them with any. It is about them that Allah Ta'ala says in his Qur-aan:

$$\text{تَوَلَّوْا وَاَعْيُنُهُمْ تَفِيْضُ مِنَ الدَّمْعِ حَزَنًا اَلَّا يَجِدُوْا مَا يُنْفِقُوْنَ}$$

"They turned back with eyes flowing with tears in sorrow that they could not find something to spend." (Surah Taubah - Aayah 92)

From the true believers, there were three who had stayed behind without any excuse. Their story will be presented later.

On their way to Syria, when the Muslims reached the area of the nation of Samood, Nabi ﷺ covered his face with his upper garment and quickened the speed of his camel. He also instructed the Sahaabah ﷺ to do the same, since that was the place of destruction of the nation of Samood. They were told to pass there weeping and fearing that Allah Ta'ala punishes them as he had punished the people of Samood.

The dearest and the most beloved Nabi of Allah ﷺ and his Sahaabah ﷺ pass by the area of the punished people in fear and tears, before they are also punished. On the other hand today, if any place is struck with an earthquake, it becomes a place of sightseeing for us and, if we see any ruins, our eyes remain dry and our hearts unaffected. What a change of attitude!

9. HADHRAT KA'AB ﷺ DOES NOT JOIN THE BATTLE OF TABUK

Amongst the Munaafiqeen (hypocrites who pretend to be Muslims) who did not join in The Battle of Tabuk, there were more than eighty people from the Ansaar and another eighty from the desert Arabs and a large number from the outskirts. They themselves did not go and they encouraged others not to go as well. They said,

$$\text{لَا تَنْفِرُوْا فِى الْحَرِّ}$$

"Don't go out in the heat." (Surah Taubah - Aayah 81)

Allah Ta'ala's reply to this was:

$$\text{قُلْ نَارُ جَهَنَّمَ أَشَدُّ حَرًّا}$$

"Say, the fire of Jahannam is much hotter." (Surah Taubah - Aayah 81)

From amongst the Sahaabah رضي الله عنهم, there were only three people who failed to join Nabi صلى الله عليه وسلم. They were Muraarah bin Rabi, Hilaal bin Umayyah and Ka'ab bin Maalik رضي الله عنهم. Muraarah رضي الله عنه had orchards full of dates. He decided to stay behind saying: "I have taken part in all the battles so far. What can happen if I miss this one?" He feared losing his crop of dates and this stopped him from going out. Later when he realised his mistake, he gave away the whole crop with the garden in charity.

Hadhrat Hilaal's رضي الله عنه case was different. Some of his family who had been away for a long time, had just returned to Madinah. It was for the sake of their company that he did not join the Battle. He had also taken part in all the battles before and thought (like Muraarah رضي الله عنه) that it would not matter if he missed just this one battle. When he came to know of the seriousness of his mistake, he made up his mind not to speak to all those relatives who had been the cause of this mistake.

Hadhrat Ka'ab رضي الله عنه himself explains his story as follows: He says, "I had never been as rich as I was at the time of Tabuk. I had two camels of my own which I never owned before. It was a habit of Nabi صلى الله عليه وسلم that he never disclosed the destination of his expeditions, but he would keep enquiring about the conditions of other places. But this time because Tabuk was very far, the weather extremely hot and the very strong enemy, he had announced his destination, so that thorough and complete preparations could be made.

The number of Muslims was so large that it was difficult to write down their names, so much so, that those who were absent would not even be noticed in the large crowd.

The gardens of Madinah were full of fruit. I intended every morning to prepare for the journey, but somehow or the other, the days passed by and I had not even started. I knew that I had all that I needed and that I could be ready whenever I wanted.

Ch.2 – The Fear of Allah Ta'ala

I had still not yet decided when I learnt that Nabi ﷺ had already left with the Sahaabah ﷺ. I still knew in my mind that I could take a day or two to get ready and catch up with them. This delay continued till the time of Nabi's ﷺ arrival in Tabuk. I then tried to get ready but again, somehow or the other, I did not do so. Now, when I came to look at the people left behind, I realised that there was no one in Madinah except those who were known to be Munaafiqeen or had been specially allowed to stay behind for certain valid reasons.

On reaching Tabuk, Nabi ﷺ asked: 'How is it that I do not see Ka'ab?' Somebody said, 'O, Nabi of Allah: His wealth has caused him to stay behind.' Hadhrat Muaaz ﷺ quickly said, 'No, this is wrong. As far as our knowledge goes, he is a true Muslim.' However, Nabi ﷺ kept quiet."

Hadhrat Ka'ab ﷺ says: "After a few days I heard the news of Nabi's ﷺ return. I was full of grief and sadness. Good excuses, one after the other, entered my mind and I was sure that I could escape Nabi's ﷺ anger with one of them for the time being, and later on ask for Allah Ta'ala's forgiveness. I also asked the wise men of my family for advice. However, when I came to know that Nabi ﷺ had returned, I was certain that nothing but the truth would save me. So I decided to speak the truth.

It was the noble habit of Nabi ﷺ that whenever he returned from a journey, he would first go to the Masjid and perform two rakaat 'Tahiyyatul Masjid' and then stay there for a while to meet visitors. As he sat in the Masjid, the Munaafiqeen came and gave their excuses taking oaths as to why they did not join him in the battle. He accepted their excuses leaving the matter to Allah Ta'ala.

Just then I came and greeted him with salaam. He turned his face away with a sarcastic smile. I begged him with the words: 'O, Nabi of Allah! You turn your face away from me. By Allah! Neither am I a Munaafiq, nor do I have the least doubt on my Imaan.' He asked me to come near and I did so.

He then asked me: 'What stopped you from coming with me? Did you not purchase the two camels?' I replied: 'O, Nabi of Allah, if I was talking to a worldly man, then I am sure that I would escape his anger by making good excuses, because Allah Ta'ala has gifted me with the ability

45

to speak very well. But in your case, I am sure that if I speak lies, Allah Ta'ala would be angry with me. I also know that if I displease you by speaking the truth, then Allah Ta'ala would very soon remove your displeasure. I will therefore speak the truth. By Allah, I had no excuse at all. I had never been as rich as I was at that time.'

Nabi ﷺ said: 'He is speaking the truth.' He then told me: 'You go away; Allah Ta'ala will decide your matter.' When I left the Masjid, many people from my family scolded me saying, 'Never before had you done any wrong. If, after making some good excuse, you had asked Nabi ﷺ to make dua for you, then surely his dua would have been enough for you.' I asked them if there were any more people like me. They told me that there were two other people: Hilaal bin Umayyah ؓ and Muraarah bin Rabi ؓ, who also had spoken the truth like me and received the same reply from Nabi ﷺ.

I knew that both of them were very good Muslims and had taken part in the Battle of Badr. Nabi ﷺ instructed that no one should speak to the three of us."

Hadhrat Ka'ab ؓ continues: "Because of the instructions of Nabi ﷺ, the Sahaabah ؓ completely ignored us. Nobody was prepared to mix with or even speak to us. It seemed as if I was living in a strange land. My own birth-place looked like a strange land and my best friends behaved like strangers towards me.

حَتَّى إِذَا ضَاقَتْ عَلَيْهِمُ الْأَرْضُ بِمَا رَحُبَتْ

'Until the earth narrowed for them despite its vastness'
(Surah Taubah - Aayah 118)

The thing that worried me most was that, if I died in this condition, Nabi ﷺ would not lead my Janaazah Salaah and if Nabi ﷺ passed away in the meantime, I would be doomed forever, with no one to talk to and with no one to make dua at my funeral. The other two friends of mine stayed in their houses. I was the most daring of the three. I would go to the market and join the Jamaat for Salaah, but nobody would talk to me. I would come to Nabi ﷺ and say, '*Assalaamu Alaikum*' and would watch eagerly to see if his lips moved in reply. After

Fardh, I used to complete the Salaah standing close to him, and I would look at him from the corner of my eye to see if he ever looked at me. I noticed that when I was busy in Salaah he did look at me, but when I had finished, he would turn his face away from me."

Hadhrat Ka'ab رضي الله عنه continues: "When this social boycott became too difficult for me to bear, I one day climbed up the wall of my dear cousin, Qataadah رضي الله عنه, and greeted him with '*Assalaamu Alaikum*'. He did not return my salaam. I told him, 'For the sake of Allah Ta'ala, do answer my question. Don't you know that I love Allah Ta'ala and His Nabi صلى الله عليه وسلم?' He kept quiet. I repeated my question, but again he would not speak. When I asked for the third time, he simply said, Allah Ta'ala and His Nabi صلى الله عليه وسلم know best.' At this, tears flowed out of my eyes and he left me alone.

Once, whilst passing through a street of Madinah, I noticed a Coptic Christian, who had come from Syria to sell grain, asking about Ka'ab bin Maalik. When the people pointed me out to him, he gave me a letter from the Christian King of Ghassaan. It read: 'We have come to know that your master has ill-treated you. Allah Ta'ala will not keep you in disgrace. You should come to us. We shall help you.' When I read this letter, I said: '*Inna-lillahi-wa-Inna-ilaihi-raaji-oon*' (To Allah we belong and to Him is our return and said); 'So my situation is so bad that even the Kuffaar are trying to make me leave Islam.' I could not imagine anything worse than that. I threw the letter into the fire and then went to Nabi صلى الله عليه وسلم and said: 'O, Nabi of Allah! Your treatment towards me has lowered me so much that even the Kuffaar are trying to convert me.'

When forty days had passed in this condition, a messenger of Nabi صلى الله عليه وسلم brought me this command: 'Be separated from your wife,' I asked him, 'Must I divorce her?' He replied: 'No, only be separated.' A similar message was delivered to my other two friends as well. I therefore told my wife: 'Go to your parents and wait till Allah Ta'ala decides my case.'

Hadhrat Hilaal's رضي الله عنه wife went to Nabi صلى الله عليه وسلم and said; 'O, Nabi of Allah! Hilaal رضي الله عنه is an old man and there is nobody else to look after him. If I go away from him, he will die. If it is not very serious, kindly allow me to look after him.' Nabi صلى الله عليه وسلم replied; 'You may do so provided that you do not fulfil his conjugal rights.' She remarked! 'O,

Nabi of Allah: He has no urge for such a thing; since the day his ordeal has started, he has been spending his entire time weeping.'"

Hadhrat Ka'ab رضي الله عنه says: "It was suggested to me that I should also ask Nabi ﷺ for permission to keep my wife with me, but I said; 'Hilaal is old, while I am young. I do not know what reply I will get and besides, I have no courage to ask him.'

Another ten days had passed and now our test had lasted a full fifty days. On the morning of the fiftieth day, I had performed my Fajr Salaah and was sitting on the roof of my house full of grief. The earth had closed upon me and life had become miserable for me. I heard an announcer from over the top of mount Sala, 'Good news to you, O, Ka'ab.' The moment I heard this, I fell on the ground in sajdah and tears of joy rolled down my cheeks, as I understood that our test was now over.

In fact, after the Salaah that morning, Nabi ﷺ had announced Allah Ta'ala's forgiveness for all three of us. A person ran up to the top of the mountain and announced the forgiveness in a loud voice and this was the announcement that had reached me. Thereafter, a rider came galloping to deliver the same happy news to me.

I gave away the clothes that I was wearing as a gift to the person who brought the good news to me. I swear by Allah Ta'ala, that I had no other clothes at that time. I dressed up by borrowing clothes from some friend and went to Nabi ﷺ. As I entered the Masjid, the people around Nabi ﷺ ran to congratulate me. Hadhrat Abu Talha رضي الله عنه was the first to reach me. He shook my hand with such warmth that I shall never forget.

Thereafter I made salaam to Nabi ﷺ. I found his face shining like the full moon. This was normal whenever he was very happy. I told him, 'O, Nabi of Allah! I wish to give away in charity all that I own as thanks for the acceptance of my Taubah.' He said: 'This will be too much for you. Keep some with you.' I agreed and kept some behind with me. I agreed to keep my share of the booty that fell in our hands in the Khaiber campaign."

Hadhrat Ka'ab رضي الله عنه says: "It is the truth that had saved me. I am determined to speak nothing but the truth in future."
This story explains the following beautiful qualities of the Muslims of that time:

1. The importance of going out in the path of Allah Ta'ala. Even those who had taken part in every battle had to face the anger of Nabi ﷺ when they failed to listen to Allah Ta'ala's call, even though it was for the first time in their lives.

2. Their love and obedience to Nabi ﷺ. For full fifty days all the Muslims, including their nearest and dearest ones, would not speak to these three people because of the order Nabi ﷺ. The three persons were themselves most steadfast through the entire ordeal imposed on them.

3. Their strong faith (Imaan). Hadhrat Ka'ab ؓ was very worried when he received the letter from the Christian King, asking him to defy Nabi ﷺ. His words and his action at that time are a proof of the strong Imaan in his heart.

Let us search our hearts and see how devoted we are to our deen of Islam. Leave alone Zakaat and Hajj, which involve sacrifice and money, how many of us are particular about Salaah which is the most important pillar of Islam after Imaan?

10. NABI'S ﷺ WARNING ON THE SAHAABAH'S ؓ LAUGHING

Once, when Nabi ﷺ came to the Masjid for Salaah, he noticed some people laughing and giggling.

He said: "If you remembered your death, I would not see you like this. Think of your death often. Not a single day passes when the Qabr (grave) does not call out: 'I am a place of loneliness; I am a place of dust; I am a place of worms.' When a Muslim is placed in the Qabr (grave), it says; 'Welcome to you. It is good of you to have come into me. Of all the people walking on the earth, I liked you the best. Now that you have come into me, you will see how I treat you.' The grave then expands as far as the eye can see. A door from Jannah is then opened for him in the Qabr (grave), and through this door he gets the fresh and sweet air of Jannah.

But when an evil man is placed in the Qabr (grave) it says; 'No welcome for you. Your coming into me is very bad for you. Of all the people walking on the earth, I hated you the most. Now that you have come to me, you will see how I treat you!' The Qabr (grave) then closes upon him so much that his ribs of one side go into the ribs of the other side. As many as seventy snakes are then set upon him to keep biting him till the Day of Qiyaamah. These snakes are so poisonous that if one of them spits its poison upon the earth, not a single blade of grass would ever grow again."

After this, Nabi ﷺ said: "The grave is either a garden of Jannah or a pit of Jahannam."

'The fear of Allah Ta'ala' is a very basic and important aspect of a Muslim's life. Nabi ﷺ asked us to remember death often and to always keep the fear of Allah Ta'ala in our hearts.

11. HADHRAT HANZALAH'S رضى الله عنه FEAR OF NIFAAQ (HYPOCRISY)

Hadhrat Hanzalah رضى الله عنه says: "We were once with Nabi ﷺ when he delivered a khutbah. Our hearts became soft, our eyes were flowing with tears, and we realised where we stood. Thereafter, I left Nabi ﷺ and returned home. I sat with my wife and children and joked with them, and suddenly realised that the effect of Nabi's ﷺ advices had completely vanished from my heart.

I thought to myself that I was not what I had been, and I told myself; 'O, Hanzalah! You are a Munaafiq (hypocrite - one who claims to be a Muslim but hides disbelief in his heart)'. I was extremely worried and I left my house repeating these words in sorrow, 'Hanzalah has become a Munaafiq'.

I saw Hadhrat Abu Bakr رضى الله عنه coming towards me and I told him; 'Hanzalah has become a Munaafiq.' He said; *Subhaanallah!* What are you saying? Hanzalah can never be a Munaafiq!'"

I explained to him: "When we are with Nabi ﷺ and listen to his talks about Jannah and Jahannam, we feel as if both are in front of us, but when we return home and are busy at home, we forget all about the Aakhirah. Hadhrat Abu Bakr رضي الله عنه said: "My case is exactly the same."

We both went to Nabi ﷺ and I said; "I have turned Munaafiq, O Nabi of Allah!" He asked what I meant, and I repeated what I had said to Hadhrat Abu Bakr رضي الله عنه.

Thereupon Nabi ﷺ said: "By him who controls my life, If you could stay at home like how you are when you are with me, then the Malaa'ikah would greet you whilst you are walking and in your beds. But, O, Hanzlah! This is almost impossible. This is almost impossible."

We have to look after our homes and jobs, and therefore we cannot be thinking about the Aakhirah twenty-four hours of the day. According to what has been said by Nabi ﷺ, to always think about the Aakhirah is almost impossible and it should not be expected by all. Only the Malaa'ikah remain like that at all times. In the case of men, the state of their mind changes with conditions and environments. But we can see from this story how concerned the Sahaabah رضي الله عنهم were about the condition of their Imaan. Hanzalah رضي الله عنه suspects Nifaq in himself when he feels that the condition of his mind at home is not the same as it is when he is with Nabi ﷺ.

12. A FEW STORIES ABOUT THE FEAR OF ALLAH TA'ALA

It is very difficult to write all that is said in the Qur-aan and the Hadith about the importance of the fear of Allah Ta'ala. However, remember that the fear of Allah Ta'ala is very important for progressing in our Deen.

Nabi ﷺ has said: "The fear of Allah Ta'ala is the root of all wisdom."

Hadhrat Ibn 'Umar رضي الله عنه used to weep so much with the fear of Allah Ta'ala that he lost his eyesight. He told somebody: "You wonder at my weeping. Even the sun weeps with the fear of Allah Ta'ala."

On another occasion, he said: "Even the moon weeps with His fear."

Nabi ﷺ once passed by a Sahaabi رضي الله عنه who was reading the Qur-aan, when he came to the Aayat:

$$\text{فَإِذَا انشَقَّتِ السَّمَاءُ فَكَانَتْ وَرْدَةً كَالدِّهَانِ}$$

"And when the skies will split and become rosy (red) like hide (leather)," (Surah Rahmaan - Aayah 37)

The hair of his body stood on end, and he was nearly choked, because of crying so much. He would cry and say: "Alas, what will happen to me on the day when even the Heavens will split? Woe to me!"

Nabi ﷺ told him: "Your crying has made even the Malaa'ikah weep."

Once an Ansaari Sahaabi ﷺ sat and wept after Tahajjud, saying: "I cry to Allah Ta'ala for protection from the fire of Jahannam."

Nabi ﷺ told him: "You have made the Malaa'ikah weep today."

Hadhrat Abdullah bin Rawahah ﷺ was once weeping. His wife also began to weep on seeing him crying. He asked her: "Why are you weeping?" She replied: "Whatever makes you weep makes me weep too." He said: "The idea that I have to cross the bridge of Siraat across Jahannam makes me weep. I don't know whether I shall be able to cross over or fall into Jahannam."

Zurarah bin Aufa ﷺ was leading the Salaah in a Masjid when he read the Aayat:

$$\text{فَإِذَا نُقِرَ فِي النَّاقُورِ ۞ فَذَٰلِكَ يَوْمَئِذٍ يَوْمٌ عَسِيرٌ}$$

"When the trumpet is blown, surely that day will be a day of difficulty!" (Surah Muddatthir Aayah 8-9)

He fell down and passed away. Thereafter, people carried his body to his house.

Khulaid was reading his Salaah. During his Qiraat, he reached the Aayat:

$$\text{كُلُّ نَفْسٍ ذَائِقَةُ الْمَوْتِ}$$

"Every person will taste of death" (Surah Aale I'mraan - Aayah 185)

He began to repeat it again and again. He heard a voice from a corner of the room saying: "How often are you going to repeat this Aayat? Your recitation has already caused the death of four Jinns."

It is said about another Shaikh that (while reading the Qur-aan) when he reached the Aayat:

$$ثُمَّ رُدُّوْۤا اِلَى اللّٰهِ مَوْلٰىهُمُ الْحَقِّ ۚ اَلَا لَهُ الْحُكْمُ$$

"Then they will be returned to Allah, their true Master, Lo! Judgement is (exclusively) His?" *(Surah An'aam - Aayah 62)*

He gave out a cry, shivered and breathed his last.

There are many stories of this type. Fudhail *(rahmatullahi alayh)*, a famous Shaikh, says: "The fear of Allah Ta'ala leads to everything that is good."

Shibli *(rahmatullahi alayh)*, another Shaikh of high position, says: "Whenever I have felt Allah's fear in me, I have found a fresh door of knowledge and wisdom opened for me."

In a Hadith, it is said: "Allah Ta'ala says; 'I do not give two fears to my slave. If he does not fear me in this world, I shall give him fear in the next, and if he fears me in this world I shall save him from all fears in the Hereafter.'"

Nabi ﷺ said: "All things fear a person who fears Allah Ta'ala, while everything is a source of fear to him who fears somebody besides Allah Ta'ala."

Yahya bin Ma'az *(rahmatullahi alayh)* says: "If a man fears Jahannam as much as he is afraid of poverty then he may enter into Jannah."

Abu Sulaymaan Daaraani *(rahmatullahi alayh)* says: "There is nothing but destruction for a heart that is empty of the fear of Allah Ta'ala."

Nabi ﷺ says: "The face that gets wet with the smallest drop of tear because of the fear of Allah Ta'ala is safe from entering into the fire of Jahannam."

He also said: "When a Muslim shivers with the fear of Allah Ta'ala, his sins fall away from him like leaves falling off a tree."

Nabi ﷺ has said: "A person weeping with the fear of Allah Ta'ala cannot go to Jahannam until milk goes back into the udders, (which is impossible)."

Hadhrat Uqbah bin Aamir ؓ once asked Nabi ﷺ, "What is the way for salvation (i.e. being saved from the fire of Jahannam)?" He replied: "Guard your tongue, stay indoors and cry over your sins."

Hadhrat Aa'ishah ؓ once asked Nabi ﷺ: "Is there anybody from your followers who will go to Jannah without reckoning?" "Yes," replied Nabi ﷺ, "The person who often cries over his sins."

There is another Hadith, in which my dear Master, Hadhrat Muhammad ﷺ has said: "No drop is more dear to Allah Ta'ala than two drops; a drop of tear shed in the fear of Allah Ta'ala, and a drop of blood shed in the path of Allah Ta'ala."

It is said in a Hadith that seven people would be under the shade of the Arsh on the day of Qiyaamah. One of them would be the person who remembered Allah Ta'ala when he was all alone, and tears flowed from his eyes with the fear of Allah Ta'ala and in repentance for his sins.

Hadhrat Abu Bakr ؓ says: "One who can weep should do so, and one who cannot should make the face of a weeping person."

It is said that when Muhammad bin Munkadir *(rahmatullahi alayh)* wept, he wiped his tears over his face and beard saying: "I have heard that the fire of Jahannam does not touch the place touched by these tears."

Saabit Bunaani *(rahmatullahi alayh)* was suffering from a disease of the eyes. His doctor said told him: "Your eyes would be all right, if you do not weep in future." He replied: "What is the good of an eye if it cannot shed tears."

Yazid bin Maisarah *(rahmatullahi alayh)* says: "There can be seven reasons for weeping viz., extreme joy, madness, extreme pain, horror, pretending, being drunk and the fear of Allah Ta'ala. A single tear shed in the fear of Allah Ta'ala (is enough to put out oceans of fire (of Jahannam)."

Hadhrat Ka'ab Ahbaar ؓ says: "By Him who holds my life in His (hands), I love to weep for the fear of Allah Ta'ala, with tears flowing down my cheeks, rather than spending a mountain of gold in charity."

Ch.2 – The Fear of Allah Ta'ala

There are many other sayings of the Auliyaa and other pious people which prove that weeping, because of the fear of Allah Ta'ala and also over one's sins, is very effective and beneficial in attaining piety. However, we should not lose hope in Allah Ta'ala. His Mercy is unlimited.

Hadhrat 'Umar رَضِيَ اللّٰهُ عَنْهُ says: "If it were to be announced on the Day of Qiyaamah that all shall go to Jahannam except one person, my belief in the Mercy of Allah Ta'ala would make me hope that I may be that chosen one. Again, if it were to be announced on that day that all shall go to Jannah except one person, then my sins would make me fear that I may be that one."

It is, therefore, necessary that we should have both fear and hope together in our hearts, especially when the time of death is close, we should have more hope than fear.

Nabi صَلَّى اللّٰهُ عَلَيْهِ وَسَلَّمَ says: "None of you should die, except with a strong hope in the Mercy of Allah Ta'ala."

When Imaam Ahmad bin Hambal *(rahmatullahi alayh)* was about to pass away, he sent for his son and asked him to read to him the Ahaadith that shows hope in Allah Ta'ala and His Mercy.

CHAPTER 3

STAYING AWAY FROM LUXURIES

There is such a wealth of Ahaadith about this aspect of the life of Nabi ﷺ that, it is really difficult to choose a few examples. He said: "Abstinence (staying away from luxuries) is an asset of a believer."

1. NABI ﷺ DOES NOT LIKE GOLD

Rasulullah ﷺ has said: "My Allah wanted to turn the mountains of Makkah into gold for me, but my dua to Him was; 'O, Allah! I like to eat one day and feel hungry the next, so that I will make dua to You and remember You when I am hungry and be grateful and thankful to You and praise You when my hunger is gone!'"

We claim to follow Nabi ﷺ and are proud of being his followers. Isn't it very important for us to follow him in practice also?

2. NABI'S ﷺ LIFE OF SIMPLICITY
(STAYING AWAY FROM LUXURIES)

Once, Nabi ﷺ decided to stay away from his wives for one month as he was unhappy with them about something. For that one month he lived in a separate room upstairs in his house. A rumour began spreading among the Sahaabah ﷺ that Nabi ﷺ had divorced

Ch.3 - *Staying Away from Luxuries*

his wives. When Hadhrat 'Umar ؓ heard of this, he came running to the Masjid and found the Sahaabah ؓ sitting in groups, very worried of Nabi's ﷺ suffering. He went to his daughter Hafsah ؓ, who was a wife of Nabi ﷺ, and found her weeping in her room. He told her: "Why are you weeping now? Have I not warned you not to do anything that will make Nabi ﷺ angry?"

He returned to the Masjid and found some of the Sahaabah ؓ sitting near the mimbar (pulpit) and weeping. He sat there for some time, but could not sit for long because of his concern. He went towards the room where Nabi ﷺ was staying.

He found Rabah ؓ, a slave, sitting on the steps. He asked him to go and ask Nabi ﷺ if he would allow Hadhrat 'Umar ؓ to see him. Rabah went inside and came back to tell him that Nabi ﷺ remained silent and said nothing. Hadhrat 'Umar ؓ returned to the Masjid and sat near the mimbar.

The worry in his heart would not allow him any rest, and he asked Rabah ؓ to ask Nabi ﷺ for a second time. Nabi ﷺ did not give any answer this time too. After sitting near the mimbar again, Hadhrat 'Umar ؓ asked for the third time for permission to see Nabi ﷺ.

This time, permission was given. When he was taken inside, he saw Nabi ﷺ lying on a date leaf mat. The pattern of the mat could easily be seen on his handsome body. His pillow was a leather bag filled with the bark of the date tree.

Hadhrat 'Umar ؓ says: "I greeted him with *Assalaamu Alaykum* and asked: 'Have you divorced your wives, O, Nabi of Allah?' He answered that he had not done so. Hearing this, I began to say a joke or two; 'O, Nabi of Allah! We the Quraish have always controlled our women, but the Ansaar of Madinah are controlled by their women. Our women have also got influenced by the women over here.'

I said a few more things which made him smile. I noticed that his room had only three pieces of skin and a handful of barley lying in a corner. I looked about, but I failed to find anything else. I began to weep.

He asked; 'Why are you weeping?' I replied: 'O Nabi of Allah! Why should I not weep? I can see the marks of the mat on your body, and I have also noticed all your belongings that you have in this room. O, Nabi of Allah! Make dua that Allah Ta'ala grants us more provisions also. The Persians and the Romans who have no Imaan and do not worship Allah Ta'ala but worship their kings, Caesar and Chosroes, live in gardens with streams but you as the Nabi and accepted slave of Allah Ta'ala live in such poverty!' Nabi ﷺ was resting against his pillow, but when he heard me talk like this, he sat up and said; 'O, 'Umar! Are you still in doubt? Ease and comfort in the Aakhirah is much better than ease and comfort in this world. The kuffaar are enjoying their share of the good things in this world, but we have all wonderful things waiting for us in the next.' I begged him: 'O Nabi of Allah! Ask forgiveness for me. I was really in the wrong.'"

Look at the few possessions of the beloved Nabi of Allah Ta'ala. See how he scolds Hadhrat 'Umar ﷺ when he asks him to make dua for some things of comfort in this world.

Somebody asked Aa'ishah ﷺ about the bedding of Nabi ﷺ in her house. She said: "It was just a skin filled with the bark of a date tree."

Hafsah ﷺ was asked the same question. She said: "His bedding was a piece of thick cloth, which I double folded under him. Once I folded it four times to make it softer. The next morning he asked me: 'What did you spread under me last night?' I replied: 'The same cloth, but I folded it four times instead of two.' He said: 'Keep it as it was before. The extra softness makes it difficult to get up for Tahajjud.'"

Now let us look around and see the furniture of our bedrooms. We, who live in so much comfort, instead of being thankful and more obedient to Allah Ta'ala for His gifts, always complain of hard times.

3. HADHRAT ABU HURAYRAH'S ﷺ HUNGER

Once, Hadhrat Abu Hurayrah ﷺ, after wiping his nose with a beautiful expensive cloth, told himself: "Look at me! I am cleaning my nose with an expensive cloth today. I remember the time when I used to lie down between the mimbar (pulpit) and the house of Nabi ﷺ. People thought that I was suffering from fits and put their feet on my neck (to try and make me better). But it was no sickness, instead it was pangs of hunger."

Hadhrat Abu Hurayrah ﷺ had to remain hungry for days at a time. Sometimes he used to get so hungry that he would faint and people would think that he was having fits. It seems that in those days they treated fits by placing their foot on the neck of the patient.

Hadhrat Abu Hurayrah ﷺ is one of those people who suffered from extreme poverty in the early days of Islam. However, he saw better days in his later years. He was very pious and loved performing Nafl Salaah.

He had a bag full of date seeds with him. He used these seeds for his Zikr. When the bag was empty, his maid filled it again with date seeds. Somebody was always busy in Salaah in his house during the night. His wife and his servant would take turns with him in performing Salaah.

4. HADHRAT ABU BAKR'S ﷺ DAILY ALLOWANCE FROM THE BAIT-UL-MAAL (PUBLIC TREASURY)

Hadhrat Abu Bakr ﷺ used to buy and sell cloth (material). After the death of Nabi ﷺ, people selected him as the Khalifah (leader). The next day, with some cloth in his arms, he was going to the market as usual when Hadhrat 'Umar ﷺ met him on the way.

'Umar ﷺ asked: "Where are you going to, Abu Bakr?"

Abu Bakr ﷺ replied: "To the market."

'Umar ﷺ asked: "If you get busy with your business, who will do the job of the Khalifah?"

Abu Bakr ﷺ asked: "How am I supposed to feed my family?"

'Umar ﷺ suggested: "Let us go to Hadhrat Abu 'Ubaidah ﷺ (who was in charge of the Baitul Maal) to fix a wage for you from the Baitul Maal."

They both went to Hadhrat Abu 'Ubaidah ﷺ who fixed a small amount as wages for Abu Bakr ﷺ. He fixed for Abu Bakr an allowance equal to what was usually paid to an average Muhaajir.

Once, Hadhrat Abu Bakr's ﷺ wife told him: "I would like to eat a sweet dish."

Hadhrat Abu Bakr ﷺ replied: "I have no money to arrange for the dish."

His wife said: "If you allow me, I shall try to save something daily from our spending, which will one day be enough to buy the ingredients for the sweet dish."

He agreed and a little money was saved in many days. When his wife brought him the money to buy the sweet dish, he said: "It seems that we have received so much more than what we need."

He returned the savings to the Baitul Maal and from then on got his wages cut down by the amount saved by his wife.

Hadhrat Aa'ishah ﷺ says: "When Hadhrat Abu Bakr ﷺ was chosen as the Khalifah, he told the people: 'You know that I am a businessman. Now that I have to spend all my time looking after the country, my wages shall, therefore, be paid from the 'Baitul Maal'."

Hadhrat Aa'ishah ﷺ says: "At the time of his death, Hadhrat Abu Bakr ﷺ instructed me to hand over, to the next Khalifah, all that was given to him from the Baitul Maal for his household needs."

It is said that Hadhrat Abu Bakr ﷺ left no cash after him. Hadhrat Anas ﷺ says: "Hadhrat Abu Bakr ﷺ left behind a she camel used for providing milk, a bowl and a servant."

Some say that he also left a bedding. When all these were given to Hadhrat 'Umar ﷺ, he remarked: "May Allah Ta'ala show mercy to Hadhrat Abu Bakr ﷺ! He has set an example for us which is very hard to follow."

5. HADHRAT 'UMAR'S ﷺ DAILY ALLOWANCE FROM THE BAIT-UL-MAAL (PUBLIC TREASURY)

Hadhrat 'Umar ﷺ also used to do business. When he was made the Khalifah after Hadhrat Abu Bakr ﷺ, he gathered the people and told them: "I earned my money doing business. As you people have now made me the Khalifah, I cannot continue with my business. How will I live?"

Different amounts of money from the Baitul-Maal were suggested by different people. Hadhrat Ali رَضِيَ اللَّهُ عَنْهُ did not speak. 'Umar رَضِيَ اللَّهُ عَنْهُ asked him: "O Ali, what is your suggestion?"

He replied: "I suggest that you should take an average amount that may be enough for your family."

Hadhrat Umar رَضِيَ اللَّهُ عَنْهُ accepted his suggestion and a moderate amount was fixed as his daily wage.

Later on, some people including Hadhrat Ali رَضِيَ اللَّهُ عَنْهُ, Hadhrat Usmaan رَضِيَ اللَّهُ عَنْهُ, Hadhrat Zubair رَضِيَ اللَّهُ عَنْهُ and Hadhrat Talhah رَضِيَ اللَّهُ عَنْهُ once felt that Hadhrat 'Umar's رَضِيَ اللَّهُ عَنْهُ wages should be increased, as it was not enough for him, but nobody dared to suggest that to Hadhrat 'Umar رَضِيَ اللَّهُ عَنْهُ.

Some people came to his daughter, Ummul-Mu'mineen Hadhrat Hafsah رَضِيَ اللَّهُ عَنْهَا, and asked her to find out Hadhrat 'Umar's رَضِيَ اللَّهُ عَنْهُ reaction to the suggestion without mentioning their names to him. When Hadhrat Hafsah رَضِيَ اللَّهُ عَنْهَا talked about it to Hadhrat 'Umar رَضِيَ اللَّهُ عَنْهُ, he became angry and said: "Who are the people making this suggestion?"

Hadhrat Hafsah رَضِيَ اللَّهُ عَنْهَا said: "First let me know your opinion."

Hadhrat 'Umar رَضِيَ اللَّهُ عَنْهُ replied: "If I knew them, I would slap them on their faces. Hafsah! Just tell me what was Nabi's صَلَّى اللَّهُ عَلَيْهِ وَسَلَّمَ best clothing in your house?"

Hadhrat Hafsah رَضِيَ اللَّهُ عَنْهَا replied: "It was a pair of reddish brown clothes, which Nabi صَلَّى اللَّهُ عَلَيْهِ وَسَلَّمَ wore on Friday or while receiving some prominent people."

Hadhrat 'Umar رَضِيَ اللَّهُ عَنْهُ asked: "What was the best food that Nabi صَلَّى اللَّهُ عَلَيْهِ وَسَلَّمَ ate at your house?"

Hadhrat Hafsah رَضِيَ اللَّهُ عَنْهَا replied: "The only food we used to eat was simple barley bread. One day I spread the remains of an empty butter tin on a piece of bread which he ate with enjoyment and offered it to others as well."

Hadhrat 'Umar رَضِيَ اللَّهُ عَنْهُ asked: "What was the best bedding that Nabi صَلَّى اللَّهُ عَلَيْهِ وَسَلَّمَ ever used in your house?"

Hadhrat Hafsah ؓ replied: "It was a piece of thick cloth. In summer it was spread in four layers, and the winter in two layers, half of which he spread underneath and with the other half he covered himself."

Hadhrat 'Umar ؓ advising Hadhrat Hafsah ؓ said: "Hafsah! Go and tell these people that Nabi ﷺ has set an example for us which I must follow. My example and that of my other two friends viz., Nabi ﷺ and Hadhrat Abu Bakr ؓ is like that of three men travelling on the same road. The first man started with a provision and reached the goal. The second followed the first and joined him. Now the third is on his way. If he follows their way, he will also join them; otherwise he can never reach them."

Such is the life of the person who was feared by the kings of the world. What a simple life he lived! Once, while reading the Khutbah, it was noticed that his lower clothing had as many as twelve patches, including one of leather.

Once he came late for his Jumu'ah salaah and told the people: "Excuse me, people! I got late because I was washing my clothes and had no other clothes to put on."

Once he was having his meal when 'Utbah bin Abi Farqad ؓ asked permission to see him. He allowed him in and invited him to share the food with him. 'Utbah ؓ started eating, but the bread was so rough that he could not swallow it. 'Utbah bin Abi Farqad ؓ asked: "Why don't you use fine flour for your bread, 'Umar?"

Hadhrat 'Umar ؓ asked: "Can every Muslim afford fine flour for his bread?"

'Utbah ؓ replied, "No. Everybody cannot afford it."

Hadhrat 'Umar ؓ said, "Alas! You wish to fulfil all my pleasures while I am in this world."

There are thousands of such stories about the noble Sahaabah ؓ. Everybody should not try to copy them, for we are not as strong as they were and that is why the Sufi Sheikhs of our time do not ask us to do those things which tire the body too much, as the people are already weak.

We should however keep the life of the Sahaabah ؓ as an example before us, so that we may at least give up some of our luxuries

Ch.3 - Staying Away from Luxuries

and lead a simpler life. With the Sahaabah's ﷢ lives as an example, we can at least feel ashamed when competing with one another in running after the luxuries of this world.

6. HADHRAT BILAL'S ﷠ STORY ABOUT NABI ﷺ

Someone asked Hadhrat Bilal ﷠ how Nabi ﷺ met his expenses.

Hadhrat Bilal ﷠ replied: "He never kept back anything for later. Whenever a poor person, whether hungry or naked came to him, he would send him over to me and I would then arrange for his needs by borrowing money from somebody. This is what usually happened.

Once a Mushrik came to me and said: 'Look here! I have a lot of extra money. Don't borrow money from anybody else. Whenever you need it, come straight to me.' I said: 'This is really fine.' I began to borrow money from him to meet the needs of Nabi ﷺ.

One day, after I had made wudhu and was about to call the Azaan, the same Mushrik came with some people and shouted, 'O, Negro!' When I went to him, he began to abuse me, using filthy language and said: 'How many days are left of this month?' I said: 'It is about to finish.' He said most rudely: 'Look here! There are only four days left of this month. If you fail to clear up your debts by the end of the month, I shall take you as my slave for my money and then you will be grazing sheep as you had been doing before.'

After saying this he went away. I remained very sad and full of grief throughout the day. After Isha Salaah, when Nabi ﷺ was alone, I went and told him the story, saying: 'O, Nabi of Allah! You have nothing with you, nor can I arrange any money from somewhere so quickly. I am afraid the Mushrik will disgrace me. I therefore intend to keep away until such time that you get enough money to clear the debts.'

I went home, took my sword, shield and shoes and waited for the morning to leave for some other place. Just before dawn, somebody came to me and said. 'Hurry up! Nabi ﷺ wants to see you.' I hurried to the Masjid and found four loaded camels sitting near Nabi ﷺ. He said: 'Good news, Bilal. Allah Ta'ala has made arrangements for clearing your debts. Take these camels with their load. The Chief of Fidak has sent them as a gift to me.'

I thanked Allah Ta'ala and took the camels and cleared up all the debts. In the meantime, Nabi ﷺ kept sitting in the Masjid. When I returned, I said: *'Alhamdulillah!* All the debts are now clear, O, Nabi of Allah.' He asked: 'Is there anything left from the gift?' I said, 'Yes, something is still left.' He said, 'Go and spend that as well. I shall not go home until the whole lot is spent.' Nabi ﷺ kept sitting in the Masjid all day long.

After Isha Salaah he asked again if everything had been spent. I said: 'Something is still left unspent. A few of the poor have not come as yet.' He slept in the Masjid that night. The next day after Isha Salaah he again called me and asked: 'Bilal! Is everything finished now?' I said: 'Yes, Allah Ta'ala has blessed you with peace. Everything is now spent and gone.'

Nabi ﷺ began to praise Allah Ta'ala over this news, for he did not like death to come to him while any of the riches were with him. He then went home and met his family."

Pious people do not like to keep any wealth with them. How could Nabi ﷺ, being the leader of the pious, like to keep anything with him?

It is said of Maulana Abdur Rahim (May Allah have mercy on him), who was a Saint of our time, immediately spent all that he received as gifts from the people and he did not keep anything for himself. A few days before his death, he gave all his clothes to one of his attendants and said: "If I need to wear any clothes in my life, I shall borrow them from you."

I also know about my late father; whenever he had any money left after Maghrib, would give it to one of his creditors,(someone that he was owing money to) as he was several thousand rupees in debt and would say: "I would not like to keep this trouble with me for the night."

Ch.3 - *Staying Away from Luxuries*

7. ANOTHER STORY OF HADHRAT ABU HURAYRAH'S رَضِىَٱللَّهُعَنْهُ HUNGER

Hadhrat Abu Hurayrah رَضِىَٱللَّهُعَنْهُ says: "I wish you had seen some of us living on a starvation diet for many days, so much so that we could not even stand straight. Because of hunger, I would lie on my stomach and press my stomach against the ground or keep a stone tied to my stomach.

Once, I intentionally sat waiting for some known person to pass that way. As Hadhrat Abu Bakr رَضِىَٱللَّهُعَنْهُ came along, I began to talk to him, intending to continue the talk until we reach his home, where I expected him to invite me to share his meals, as was his habit. But his answer was short, and my plan did not work.

The same thing happened with Hadhrat Umar رَضِىَٱللَّهُعَنْهُ, when he passed that way. Next to pass that way was Nabi صَلَّىٱللَّهُعَلَيْهِوَسَلَّمَ himself. A smile spread over his face when he saw me, for he at once knew why I was sitting there. 'Come with me, Abu Hurayrah,' he said, and I went with him to his house.

He took me in and a bowl of milk was brought before him. He asked, 'Who brought this milk?' and was told that somebody had sent it as a present. He asked me to go and invite all the Suffah friends. The Suffah people were treated as everyone's guests by all the Muslims. They were such people who had neither family nor home of their own and no means of livelihood. Their number changed all the time, but at that particular time, they were seventy in total. Nabi صَلَّىٱللَّهُعَلَيْهِوَسَلَّمَ would send them in groups of two or four to the well-to-do Sahaabah رَضِىَٱللَّهُعَنْهُمْ as guests. He himself would give them all that came to him as 'Sadaqah', and would also share the gifts with them."

Hadhrat Abu Hurayrah رَضِىَٱللَّهُعَنْهُ says: "When Nabi صَلَّىٱللَّهُعَلَيْهِوَسَلَّمَ asked me to invite all these people, I became disappointed because the milk was so little that it was not even enough for one person. I knew that Nabi صَلَّىٱللَّهُعَلَيْهِوَسَلَّمَ would ask me to serve the milk to the others first and a server is always the last, and usually gets the least. Anyway, out I went, and fetched all of them.

Nabi صَلَّىٱللَّهُعَلَيْهِوَسَلَّمَ told me: 'Abu Hurayrah, serve the milk to them.' I took the bowl to each person until he drank to his fill and returned the bowl to me, till all of them were served. Nabi ﷺ then held the bowl in his own hand, smiled at me, and said; 'Only the two of us are left now!' 'Yes,' I replied. 'He then requested me to drink.' I took it and drank. He encouraged me to have more, and I drank to my fill, till I said that I had no space for any more. He then took the bowl, and drank the remaining milk."

8. NABI'S ﷺ OPINION ABOUT TWO PEOPLE

Some people were sitting with Nabi ﷺ when a person passed by. Nabi ﷺ asked the people: "What do you think of this person?"

They replied: "O Nabi of Allah! He comes from a good family. By Allah, he is such that if he wants to marry a woman of the most well-known family, she will agree to marry him. If he advises someone, they will listen to him."

Nabi ﷺ remained silent. A little later, another person happened to pass that way and Nabi ﷺ asked the same question to his Sahaabah ؓ about that person also.

They replied: "O, Nabi of Allah! He is a very poor Muslim. If he wants to marry someone, nobody will marry him. If he makes a suggestion, it will not be accepted. If he talks, few people would listen to him."

Nabi ﷺ then said: "This second person is better than a whole lot of such persons as the first."

Belonging to a good family means nothing to Allah Ta'ala. A poor Muslim, who is not thought of highly and who is not respected much in this world, is much nearer to Allah Ta'ala than hundreds of the so-called important people who, though respected by the worldly people, are far from the path of Allah Ta'ala.

It is said in a Hadith: "It will be the end of this world when there will not be a single person remaining to recite the name of Allah Ta'ala. It is by the pure name of Allah Ta'ala that this universe is running."

9. POVERTY IS FOR THOSE WHO LOVE NABI ﷺ

A person came to Nabi ﷺ and said: "O Nabi of Allah! I love you very much."

Nabi ﷺ replied: "Think properly before you say this."

The person said: "I have already thought about it. I love you very much, O, Nabi of Allah."

Nabi ﷺ again replied: "Think once again before you say such a thing."

The person again said: "I still love you very much, O Nabi of Allah."

Nabi ﷺ then said: "Well, if you are true in what you say, then be prepared for difficulties and hard times coming to you from all sides, because it follows all those who love me as quickly as water flows downstream."

That is why we find the Sahaabah رضي الله عنهم mostly living a life of poverty. Similarly, the famous Muhaddithin, Sufis and Ulama lived in poverty throughout their lives.

10. THE STORY OF THE AL-AMBAR FISH

Nabi ﷺ sent an army of three hundred men towards the seashore in 8 A.H. The leader was Hadhrat Abu Ubaidah رضي الله عنه. He gave them a bag full of dates as their food. They had been out for fifteen days when they ran short of food.

In order to provide the men with food, Hadhrat Qais رضي الله عنه began buying three camels daily from his own men to feed them, promising to pay them after returning to Madinah. The Amir (leader) stopped him from doing that because they needed the camels for riding.

He collected the dates that had been left with each person and stored them in a bag. He would give one date to each man as his daily share. When Hadhrat Jaabir رضي الله عنه later on mentioned this story to the people, someone asked him: "How did you manage to live on one date only for the whole day?"

He replied: "When all the dates were finished, we wished even for that one date. We were facing starvation. We soaked dry tree-leaves with water and ate them."

When they reached this stage, Allah Ta'ala had mercy on them, for He always brings ease after every hardship, provided it is borne patiently.

A big fish known as 'Ambar' was thrown out of the sea for them. The fish was so big that they ate from it for eighteen days. They also filled their bags with the leftover, which lasted them right up to Madinah. When this story was told to Nabi ﷺ, he said: "The fish was arranged for you by Allah Ta'ala."

Difficulties and hardships in this world will come to the people of Allah Ta'ala.

Nabi ﷺ says: "The hardest tests in this world are for the Ambiyaa عَلَيْهِمُ السَّلَام, then for those who are next to them, and then for those who are the best from the rest."

The test of a person depends on his nearness to Allah Ta'ala. He always makes things easy through His kindness after each test. Look at how much the Sahaabah رَضِيَ اللهُ عَنْهُم have suffered in the path of Allah Ta'ala. They had to live on leaves of trees, starve and even lose their lives because of our true Deen, which now we fail to preserve.

CHAPTER 4

PIETY AND FEAR OF ALLAH TA'ALA

The habits and character of the Sahaabah رضى الله عنهم are worth following because they were the people specially chosen by Allah Ta'ala to be the friends of His beloved Nabi صلى الله عليه وسلم.

Nabi صلى الله عليه وسلم says: "I have been sent in the best period of human history."

The time of Nabi صلى الله عليه وسلم was itself a blessed period and his companions were really the best of all people.

1. NABI صلى الله عليه وسلم ACCEPTS A WOMAN'S INVITATION

Nabi صلى الله عليه وسلم was once returning from a funeral, when a woman invited him to have some food at her house. He went in with some of his Sahaabah رضى الله عنهم. When the food was served, it was noticed that Nabi صلى الله عليه وسلم was trying to chew a morsel, but it would simply not go down his throat. He said: "It seems that the animal has been slaughtered without the permission of its owner."

The woman said: "O, Nabi of Allah! I had asked a man to buy a goat for me from the market, but he could not get one. My neighbour had recently also bought a goat, so I sent the man there with some money to buy the goat from him. My neighbour was out and his wife sold the goat to my man."

Nabi صلى الله عليه وسلم asked her to go and serve the meat to the prisoners.

It has been seen in the lives of many pious Muslims that doubtful food would simply not go down their throats, so this is not such a surprising thing in the case of Nabi ﷺ, who is the most pious of all people.

2. NABI ﷺ DOES NOT SLEEP FOR THE WHOLE NIGHT

Once, Nabi ﷺ could not sleep at night. He was turning from side to side. His wife asked him: "O Nabi of Allah! Why can't you get sleep?"

He answered: "A date was lying about. I picked it up and ate it so that it does not go to waste. Now I am worried that it might be from Sadaqah (charity)."

Most probably the date belonged to Nabi ﷺ himself, but because people sent him their Sadaqah as well (for distribution), he could not sleep with the worry that it might be from Sadaqah. This shows the perfect honesty of Nabi ﷺ that he could not sleep because of a doubt in his mind. How is it that those who claim themselves to be the slaves of that very master ﷺ, but indulge in usury, corruption, theft, plunder and every other type of 'haraam' business without the least conscience?

3. HADHRAT ABU BAKR ؓ AND A FORTUNE-TELLER'S FOOD

Hadhrat Abu Bakr ؓ had a slave who used to give him some of his daily wages as the master's share. Once he brought him some food and Hadhrat Abu Bakr ؓ took a morsel from it.

Then the slave said: "You always ask about the things that I bring to you, but today you have not done so."

He replied: "I was feeling so hungry that I did not do that. Tell me how did you get this food?"

The slave said: "Before I accepted Islam, I practiced fortune-telling. During those days I met some people for whom I practiced some of my magic. They promised to pay me for that later on. I saw those people today, while they were busy in a wedding, and they gave me this food."

Hadhrat Abu Bakr رَضِيَ اللّٰهُ عَنْهُ said: "Ah! You would have surely killed me?"

He then tried to vomit the morsel he had swallowed, but could not do so, as his stomach had been quite empty. Somebody suggested to him to drink water to his fill and then try to vomit the morsel. He sent for a cup of water and kept on drinking water and forcing it out, until the morsel was vomited out.

Somebody said: "May Allah Ta'ala have mercy on you! You put yourself to so much trouble for one single morsel."

To this he replied: "I would have forced it out even if I had to lose my life. I have heard Nabi صَلَّى اللّٰهُ عَلَيْهِ وَسَلَّمَ saying, 'The flesh that is fed by haraam food, will end up in the fire of Jahannam.' I therefore hurried to vomit this morsel, in case any part of my body should receive nourishment from it."

Many stories like this have been reported about Hadhrat Abu Bakr رَضِيَ اللّٰهُ عَنْهُ. He was very particular and would not taste anything unless he was perfectly sure about it. Even the slightest doubt about it being halaal would make him vomit what he had eaten.

4. HADHRAT UMAR رَضِيَ اللّٰهُ عَنْهُ VOMITS THE MILK OF SADAQAH

A person once brought some milk for Hadhrat Umar رَضِيَ اللّٰهُ عَنْهُ. When he drank it, he saw that it tasted funny and asked the person where he got the milk from.

The person replied: "The camels given in Sadaqah were grazing in the desert, and the person looking after them gave me this milk from those camels."

Hadhrat Umar رَضِيَ اللّٰهُ عَنْهُ put his hand in his throat and vomited all the milk that he had drank.

These Allah-fearing people not only totally stayed away from haraam food, but would also avoid eating any doubtful food. They would not dare eat anything that was haraam, which is so common these days.

5. HADHRAT ABU BAKR ﷺ GIVES HIS GARDEN TO BAIT-UL-MAAL

Ibn-Seereen writes: "When Hadhrat Abu Bakr ﷺ was about to pass away, he told his daughter Hadhrat Aa'ishah ﷺ, 'I did not like to take anything from the Bait-ul-Maal, but Hadhrat 'Umar ﷺ insisted on it, to relieve me of my business and to allow me to spend all my time on the duties of the Khilaafat and I was left no choice. Now give that garden of mine to the next Khalifah, in exchange of what I have received from the Bait-ul-maal.'"

When Hadhrat Abu Bakr ﷺ passed away, Aa'ishah ﷺ asked Hadhrat 'Umar ﷺ to take that garden, as instructed by her late father.

Hadhrat 'Umar ﷺ said: "May Allah Ta'ala bless your father! He has left no chance for anybody to open his lips against him."

Hadhrat Abu Bakr ﷺ received his allowance (wages) from the Bait-ul-Maal in the interest of all the Muslims, and that too at the request of the most important Sahaabi ﷺ. The amount taken was almost the minimum possible, and hardly enough for him, as we have already seen in the story (in the last chapter) about his wife's not able to cook one sweet dish during the whole month.

In spite of all this, he was so particular that he gave his garden to the Bait-ul-Maal in exchange for what he had received from the public funds.

6. THE STORY OF ALI BIN MA'BAD
(RAHMATULLAHI ALAYH)

Ali bin Ma'bad *(rahmatullahi alayh)* was a Muhaddith. He says: "I was living in a rented house. Once I wrote something which I wanted to dry up quickly. The house walls were made of mud and I wanted to scrape a little mud from there to dry up the ink, but I thought: 'This house is not mine, and I cannot scrape the walls without the owner's permission.'

After a moment I thought: 'After all what difference does it make? It is only a very little mud that I am using.' So, I scraped a little mud from a wall and used it. That night, while asleep, I saw a person in my dream, scolding me: 'Maybe tomorrow, on the Day of Qiyaamah, you may regret that saying of yours; It is only a very little mud that I am using.'"

Piety in different people is of different levels. The high rank of the Muhaddith demanded that he should have been particular even about a small amount of mud; though for a common man it was something within permissible limits.

7. HADHRAT ALI ﷺ PASSES BY A GRAVE

Hadhrat Kumail ﷺ says: "Once, I was with Hadhrat Ali ﷺ on a journey. When we reached a lonely place; he came to a grave and said: 'O you people of the graves! O you who live amongst ruins! O you who live alone in the wilderness! How is it with you in the other world? How has it gone with you there?'

He continued: 'The news from our side is that all the wealth and riches you left behind, has long been distributed. Your children are orphans and your widows have long since remarried. Now let us hear about you.'

He then turned to me and said: 'O Kumail! If they could speak, they would have told us that the best provision for the Hereafter is Taqwa.' Tears flowed out of his eyes, as he added: 'O Kumail! The grave is a container of the deeds; but one realises it only after death.'"

Our good or bad actions are stored in our graves. It is said in a Hadith that every person meets his good deeds in the grave in the form of a good friend who befriends and consoles him there. But his bad deeds come to him in ugly shapes and with bad smells, which add to his suffering.

In another Hadith it is said: "Three things go with a person to his grave, namely: His wealth (as was the habit of the early Arabs of the time), his relatives and his deeds. His wealth and his relatives turn back after his burial, but his actions go in and stay with him in the grave."

Once, Nabi ﷺ asked the Sahaabah ﷺ: "Do you know how your relatives, your wealth, and your deeds are related to you?"

The Sahaabah ﷺ wanted to know about it. He replied: "It is like a person who has three brothers. When he is about to die, he calls one of his brothers and asks him: 'Brother! You know my problem? How can you help me?' The brother replies: 'I shall call the doctor, nurse you and

73

look after you. When you pass away, I shall bathe you, enshroud you in kaffan and carry you to the grave. Then I shall make Dua for you after you are buried.' This brother is his closest family."

He puts the same question to the second brother, who replies like this: "I shall remain with you as long as you are alive. As soon as you are dead then I shall go to someone else." This brother is his worldly wealth.

He then asks the third brother in the same way, who replies: "I shall not leave you even in your grave and I shall come with you into that place of total loneliness. When your deeds are weighed on the scale, I shall immediately put my weight to the scale of your good deeds and weigh it down." This brother represents his good deeds.

"Now, tell me which of the brothers was most useful to the person?" The Sahaabah رَضِىَ اللّٰهُ عَنْهُ replied: "O, Nabi of Allah! The last brother is really the most useful to him. There is no doubt about it. The other two brothers were of no use."

8. NABI ﷺ SPEAKS ABOUT HARAAM FOOD

Nabi ﷺ once said; "Because Allah Ta'ala Himself has no faults, He, therefore, blesses only pure things. He instructed the Muslims, as He had instructed His Ambiyaa عَلَيْهِمُ السَّلَام. He says in the Noble Qur-aan:

$$\text{يَٰٓأَيُّهَا الرُّسُلُ كُلُوا۟ مِنَ ٱلطَّيِّبَٰتِ وَٱعْمَلُوا۟ صَٰلِحًا ۖ إِنِّى بِمَا تَعْمَلُونَ عَلِيمٌ}$$

"O Ambiyaa! Eat of the pure things and do good actions. I am definitely aware of what you do." (Surah Mu'minoon - Aayah 51)

$$\text{يَٰٓأَيُّهَا ٱلَّذِينَ ءَامَنُوا۟ كُلُوا۟ مِن طَيِّبَٰتِ مَا رَزَقْنَٰكُمْ}$$

"O You who believe! Eat of the pure things which we have given you."
(Surah Baqarah - Aayah 172)

Then Nabi ﷺ spoke about a person who is a traveller with untidy hair and dusty clothes. He raises his hands towards the skies and calls out: "O, Allah! O, Allah!" but his food, drink and clothing are all haraam. So, Allah Ta'ala would never listen to him and would not answer his duas, even though outwardly he seems to be worthy of help.

People wonder why the duas of the Muslims are not always answered by Allah Ta'ala. The reason is easy to understand from the above Hadith.

Allah Ta'ala does sometimes accept the dua of even a Kaafir (and also the dua of a sinful Muslim). It is the dua of a pious person that is always answered. That is the reason why people ask the pious people to make dua for them.

Therefore, those who wish to have their duas accepted must stay away from haraam. No wise person would take a chance of his duas being rejected.

9. HADHRAT 'UMAR ﷺ DOES NOT LIKE HIS WIFE TO WEIGH MUSK

Hadhrat 'Umar ﷺ once received some musk from Bahrain. He said: "I want someone to weigh it, so that it may be equally distributed among the Muslims."

His wife said: "I shall weigh it."

Hadhrat 'Umar ﷺ kept quiet. A little later he again asked for someone to weigh the musk and again his wife offered to do so. He kept quiet this time too. When she repeated her offer for the third time, he said: "I do not like you touching the musk with your hands (while weighing it) and rubbing those hands on your body afterwards, as that little extra would be more than my rightful share."

Any other person weighing the musk would, have had the same advantage, but Hadhrat 'Umar ﷺ did not like this little extra for any member of his own family. Look at how particular he was so that no one could point a finger at him.

A similar story is related about Hadhrat 'Umar bin Abdul Aziz *(rahmatullahi alayh)* (who is known as the second 'Umar). While he was Khalifah, musk belonging to the Baitul-Maal was being weighed. He closed his own nostrils, saying: "The use of musk is to smell it."

This was how particular the Sahaabah رَضِيَ اللهُ عَنْهُم, their followers and our elders in Islam were.

10. Hadhrat 'Umar-bin-Abdul Aziz
(Rahmatullahi Alayh) Removes a Governor

Hadhrat 'Umar-bin-Abdul Aziz *(rahmatullahi alayh)* appointed a person as the governor of a province. Somebody said that this person had been the governor of Hajjaaj-bin-Yusuf (a very big oppressor) also. Hadhrat 'Umar bin Abdul Aziz *(rahmatullahi alayh)* immediately removed that person.

The man said: "I had been with Hajjaaj only for a very short time." The Khalifah said: "His company for a day or even less is enough to regard a man unfit for public service."

"A man is known by the company he keeps." The company of pious people leaves a mark of piety on the character of a person and, likewise, evil company has its evil effect. That is why keeping company of bad people is always discouraged. Even the company of animals is not without its own effect.

Nabi ﷺ said: "Pride and arrogance are to be found in those who own camels and horses, while softness and humility are found in those who look after sheep and goats."

Nabi ﷺ said, "A person who joins a pious man is like one who sits with a musk-seller. Although he does not receive any musk, the lovely smell would still be enjoyed by him. But bad company is like a fire; a man sitting near it cannot escape the smoke and the fumes, even though a spark does not fall on him."

CHAPTER 5

BEING CAREFUL ABOUT SALAAH

Salaah is the most important type of all ibaadaat. In fact, it is the first thing we will be questioned about on the Day of Qiyaamah.

Nabi ﷺ said: "Salaah is the only line separating the difference between Kufr and Islam." There are many other Ahaadith about Salaah, which I have collected in another book.

1. REWARDS OF NAFL (OPTIONAL) SALAAH

Nabi ﷺ said that Allah Ta'ala told him: "My anger comes on a person who dislikes My friends, and only those are blessed with My love who always perform their Fardh actions. A person keeps on coming closer to Me through nafl, till I choose him as 'My beloved'. I then become his ear with which he listens, his eye with which he looks, his hands with which he holds, and his feet with which he walks (i.e. his listening, looking, holding and walking are according to My wishes and commands, and he would never even dream of using any part of his body in any action against My commands). If such a person asks for anything, I give it to him and if he asks for My protection, I will protect him."

Those people are really blessed who, after reading their Fardh, are in the habit of reading Nafl also. May Allah Ta'ala give me and all my friends the strength to earn this blessing.

2. NABI ﷺ SPENDS THE WHOLE NIGHT IN SALAAH

Someone asked Aa'ishah رضي الله عنها: "Tell me something special about Nabi ﷺ."

She answered: "There was nothing which was not special about him. Everything he did was wonderful. One night he came and lay down next to me. After sometime, he got up saying, 'Now let me pray to my Allah.'

He then stood up in Salaah with such humility and sincerity that tears rolled down his cheeks, onto his beard and on his chest. He then went into Ruku and Sajdah, and his tears flowed down as fast as before and after lifting his head from Sajdah, he continued weeping in this way till Hadhrat Bilal رضي الله عنه called out the azaan of Fajr Salaah."

I begged him: "O, Nabi of Allah! You are sinless, because Allah Ta'ala has forgiven each and every sin of yours committed in the past and which may happen in the future and still you cry so much."

Nabi ﷺ replied: "Why should I not be a grateful slave of Allah Ta'ala?" He then said, "Why should I not pray like this when Allah Ta'ala has today revealed to me these Aayaat?"

اِنَّ فِيْ خَلْقِ السَّمٰوٰتِ وَالْاَرْضِ وَاخْتِلَافِ الَّيْلِ وَالنَّهَارِ لَاٰيٰتٍ لِّاُولِى الْاَلْبَابِ ۙ الَّذِيْنَ يَذْكُرُوْنَ اللّٰهَ قِيَامًا وَّقُعُوْدًا وَّعَلٰى جُنُوْبِهِمْ

"Certainly in the creation of the Heavens and the Earth, and in the changing of the night and the day, are signs (of His Power) for the people of understanding. They are those who remember Allah, standing, sitting and lying down." (Surah Aale I'mraan - Aayah 190-191)

It has been mentioned in many Ahaadith that Nabi's ﷺ feet would get swollen because of his very long rakaats in Salaah. People told him: "O, Nabi of Allah! You are sinless and you still exert yourself so much!"

He would reply: "Should I not be a grateful slave of my Allah Ta'ala, then?"

3. NABI'S ﷺ READING OF THE QUR-AAN IN SALAAH

Hadhrat 'Auf رضي الله عنه says: "I was once with Nabi ﷺ. He brushed his teeth with a Miswaak, performed his Wudhu and stood up for Salaah. I also joined him. He read surah 'Baqarah' in his first rakaat; he would ask for mercy when he read any ayat praising the grace of Allah Ta'ala, and would make dua for forgiveness when reading any aayah about His anger. He took as much time in Ruku and Sajdah each as he had taken in Qiyaam. In Ruku he read:

سُبْحَانَ ذِى الْجَبَرُوْتِ وَالْمَلَكُوْتِ وَالْعَظْمَةِ

'Glory to Allah! The possessor of majesty, sovereignty and magnificence.'

He read the next three Surahs in the remaining three rakaats and each rakaat was about as long as the first one."

Hadhrat Huzayfah رضي الله عنه has also narrated a similar story about his Salaah with Nabi ﷺ.

The Qiraat (reading) of the Qur-aan by Nabi ﷺ in four rakaats comes to more than one-fifth of the Qur-aan and Nabi ﷺ read the Qur-aan with proper Tajweed. He would also make dua and ask forgiveness after some of the Aayaat. His Ruku and Sajdah would also last as long as his Qiyaam (standing).

We can therefore have an idea of how much time he must have taken to read his Salaah. This can only be possible when Salaah brings inner satisfaction and spiritual enjoyment. That is why Nabi ﷺ had often been heard saying: "The comfort of my eyes is in Salaah."

4. SALAAH OF A FEW WELL-KNOWN SAHAABAH رضي الله عنهم

Hadhrat Mujahid رضي الله عنه, describing the Salaat of Hadhrat Abu Bakr رضي الله عنه and Hadhrat Abdullah bin Zubair رضي الله عنه says: "They used to stand in salaah without moving at all as though they were pieces of wood stuck in the ground."

Ulama agree that Hadhrat Abdullah bin Zubair ﷺ learnt to read his Salaah from Hadhrat Abu Bakr ﷺ, who learnt it direct from Nabi ﷺ.

Hadhrat Abdullah bin Zubair ﷺ remained in Sajdah for so long and stood so still that birds would come and sit on his back. He would sometimes remain in Sajdah or Ruku all night long. Once, someone attacked him. An object came and hit the wall of the Masjid where he was reading his Salaah. A piece of stone flew from the wall and passed in between his beard and throat. He neither shortened his Salaah nor did it worry him in the least bit.

Once, he read his Salaah while his son Haashim slept near him. A snake fell from the ceiling and coiled around the child. The child woke up screaming. All the people of the house gathered around him. They killed the snake after a lot of struggle. In the meanwhile Abdullah Ibn Zubair ﷺ, calmly and quietly, remained busy in his Salaah. When he had completed his Salaah, he asked his wife: "What was the noise that I heard during my Salaah?"

His wife said: "May Allah Ta'ala have mercy on you! The child's life was in danger and you did not even notice it."

He replied: "If I turned my attention to anything else, what would have happened to my Salaah?"

Towards the end of his Khilaafat, Hadhrat 'Umar ﷺ was stabbed and the same wound caused his death. He bled quite a bit and remained unconscious for long periods, but when he was told of the time of Salaah, he would immediately read it in that very condition and say: "There is no place in Islam for the person who leaves out his Salaah."

Hadhrat Usmaan ﷺ would remain in Salaah all night long, finishing the whole Qur-aan in one rakaat.

It is reported that Hadhrat Ali ﷺ would turn pale and tremble at the time of Salaat. Somebody asked him the reason, and he said: "It is the time to discharge that trust which Allah Ta'ala offered to the Heavens and the Earth and the hills, but they shrank from bearing it, and I have taken responsibility for it."

Somebody asked Khalaf bin Ayyub ﷺ: "Don't the flies annoy you in your Salaah?"

He replied: "Even the thieves patiently tolerate the hiding given by the police and afterwards boast about it. Why should I be disturbed by mere flies when standing in the presence of my Allah?"

When Muslim bin Yasaar رَحْمَةُٱللَّه stood up for Salaah, he told his family members: "You may keep on talking; I will not hear what you say."

Once he was reading his Salaah in the Jaami' Masjid of Basrah. A part of the Masjid wall fell down with a crash and everybody ran for safety, but he did not even hear the noise.

Somebody asked Haatim Asam رَحْمَةُٱللَّه as to how he performed his Salaah. He replied: "When the time for Salaah comes, I perform Wudhu and go to the place where I have to read my Salaah. I sit down for some time till all the parts of my body are relaxed. I then stand up for Salaah, imagining the Ka'bah in front of me, my feet on the Bridge of Siraat, with Jannah to my right and Jahannam to my left and Izraa-eel عَلَيْهِٱلسَّلَام (angel of death) close behind me thinking that it may be my last Salaah. I then read my Salaah with full sincerity and love. I then finish my Salaah between fear and hope of it being accepted.

5. SALAAH OF TWO SAHAABAH (A MUHAAJIR AND AN ANSAARI) رَضِىَٱللَّهُعَنْهُمَا WHO WERE STANDING GUARD AT NIGHT

While returning from a battle, Nabi صَلَّىٱللَّهُعَلَيْهِوَسَلَّم stopped for the night at a place. He asked: "Who would keep watch over the camp tonight?"

Hadhrat Ammaar bin Yaasir رَضِىَٱللَّهُعَنْهُ and Hadhrat Abbaad bin Bishr رَضِىَٱللَّهُعَنْهُ offered to guard. Both of them were instructed to watch from a hill-top for any night attack by the enemy.

Abbaad رَضِىَٱللَّهُعَنْهُ told Ammaar رَضِىَٱللَّهُعَنْهُ: "Let us keep watch and sleep by taking turns. In the first half of the night I shall keep watch, while you go to sleep. In the next half, you may keep watch while I go to sleep."

Hadhrat Ammaar رَضِىَٱللَّهُعَنْهُ agreed and went to sleep and Hadhrat Abbaad رَضِىَٱللَّهُعَنْهُ started his Salaah. An enemy saw him in the dark from a distance and shot an arrow at him. Seeing that he did not move, he shot another and still another arrow at him. Hadhrat Abbaad رَضِىَٱللَّهُعَنْهُ pulled out and threw away each arrow as it hit him and at last awakened his friend. The enemy ran away when he saw them both together, fearing that there may be many more of them. Hadhrat Ammaar رضي الله عنه noticed Hadhrat Abbaad رضي الله عنه bleeding from three places. He said: "*Subhaanallah!* Why did you not wake me up earlier?"

Hadhrat Abbaad رضي الله عنه replied: "I had started reciting Surah Kahf in my Salaah. I did not like to shorten it, but when I was shot by the third arrow, I was very worried that if I die, there may be danger to Nabi صلى الله عليه وسلم. I therefore finished the Salaah and awakened you. If Nabi صلى الله عليه وسلم was not in danger, I would have definitely finished the Surah, even if I had been killed."

Look at the love of the Sahaabah رضي الله عنهم for Salaah. One arrow after another pierces the body of Hadhrat Abbaad رضي الله عنه and he is bleeding heavily, but is not prepared to stop reading the Qur-aan in his Salaah. On the other hand, the bite of a wasp or even of a mosquito is enough to distract us from our Salaah.

According to the Hanafiyyah school of jurisprudence, wudhu breaks with bleeding, while according to the Shafi'iyyah it does not. It is just possible that Abbaad رضي الله عنه might be having the view of the Shafi'iyyah or that this mas'alah might not have been discussed till then.

6. HADHRAT ABU TALHA رضي الله عنه AND HIS SALAAH

Hadhrat Abu Talha رضي الله عنه was once reading his Salaah in his garden. His attention went towards a bird that flew about, but could not find a way out of the thick branches and leaves. For a short moment, he followed the bird with his eyes and forgot the number of rakaats. Upon this mistake, he became very sad. He immediately went to Nabi صلى الله عليه وسلم and said: "O Nabi of Allah, this garden of mine has disturbed me in my Salaah. I give it away for the sake of Allah Ta'ala. Kindly use it as you wish."

Once in the time of Hadhrat Usmaan رضي الله عنه, one of the Ansaar was reading his Salaah in his garden. The branches of the trees which were full and heavy with ripe juicy dates caught his eyes and he felt pleased with it. This made him forget the number of rakaats in his Salaah. He was so much saddened that he decided to give away the garden that had distracted him from his Salaah.

He came to Hadhrat Usmaan رضي الله عنه and gave the garden to him for using in the path of Allah Ta'ala. Hadhrat Usmaan رضي الله عنه had the garden sold for fifty thousand dirhams and spent the money on the poor. This shows the value the Sahaabah رضي الله عنهم had for their Imaan. Hadhrat Abu Talha رضي الله عنه was prepared to give away his orchard worth fifty thousand dirhams because it had interfered with his Salaah. According to Shah Waliullah, the Sufis choose obedience to Allah Ta'ala over anything that distracts from it.

7. HADHRAT IBN ABBAAS رضي الله عنه AND HIS SALAAH

Hadhrat Abdullah bin Abbaas رضي الله عنه suffered from cataract (a type of disease) of the eye. A doctor told him: "Treatment is possible, but you have to be careful. You cannot make sajda on the ground for five days. However, you can use a wooden desk for performing Sajdah."

He said: "This cannot be so. I would not say a single rakaat like that. I have heard Nabi صلى الله عليه وسلم saying, 'A person who intentionally leaves out a single Salaah, shall have to face Allah Ta'ala's anger on the Day of Qiyaamah.'"

It is actually permissible to perform Salaah in the way advised by the doctors. Yet, due to his love for Salaah and complete fear for Nabi's صلى الله عليه وسلم warning, Hadhrat Abdullah bin Abbaas رضي الله عنه was ready to lose his eyesight rather than allow the slightest change in the Salaah as performed by Nabi صلى الله عليه وسلم himself. In fact, the Sahaabah رضي الله عنهم would sacrifice the whole world for their Salaah. We may call them fanatics, but the decision in the Hereafter would prove that they were those persons who really feared and loved their Creator above everything else in this world.

8. SAHAABAH رضي الله عنهم STOPPING BUSINESS AT THE TIME OF SALAAH

Hadhrat Abdullah bin 'Umar رضي الله عنه once visited the market place. He noticed that at the time of Salaah, everybody closed his shop and went to the Masjid.

He said: "These are people about whom Allah Ta'ala has written:

$$رِجَالٌ لَّا تُلْهِيهِمْ تِجَارَةٌ وَّلَا بَيْعٌ عَنْ ذِكْرِ اللّٰهِ وَإِقَامِ الصَّلٰوةِ وَإِيتَآءِ الزَّكٰوةِ ۙ يَخَافُوْنَ يَوْمًا تَتَقَلَّبُ فِيْهِ الْقُلُوْبُ وَالْاَبْصَارُ$$

"Men, whom business and selling does not distract them from the zikr of Allah Ta'ala, establishing Salaah and paying of Zakaat. They fear a day when hearts and eyeballs will be overturned. (i.e. The Day of Qiyaamah)" (Surah Noor - Aayah 37)

Hadhrat Ibn Abbaas ؓ says: "These people were very busy in their business, but when they heard the Azaan, they left everything and rushed towards the Masjid."

He once said: "By Allah, they were such businessmen whose business did not stop them from the remembrance of Allah Ta'ala."

Hadhrat Abdullah bin Masood ؓ was once in the marketplace when Azaan was called out. He noticed everybody leaving his shop as it was, and proceeding to the masjid. He remarked: "These are surely the persons of whom Allah says:

$$رِجَالٌ لَّا تُلْهِيهِمْ تِجَارَةٌ وَّلَا بَيْعٌ عَنْ ذِكْرِ اللّٰهِ وَإِقَامِ الصَّلٰوةِ وَإِيتَآءِ الزَّكٰوةِ ۙ$$

Men, whom business and selling does not distract them from the zikr of Allah Ta'ala, establishing Salaah and paying of Zakaat.
(Surah Noor - Aayah 37)

Another Hadith says: "When all the people shall be gathered on the Day of Qiyaamah, it will be asked, 'Who are those who praised Allah Ta'ala in good and difficult times?' A group will get up and enter Jannah without any questions. Again it will be asked, 'Who are those who kept away from their beds and spent their nights in worshipping Allah Ta'ala.' Another group will get up and enter Jannah without any questions. The Malaaikah will ask yet again, 'Where are those whom business did not stop from remembering Allah Ta'ala,' and yet another group will get up and enter Jannah without any questions. After these three groups have gone, questioning would start for the rest of the people."

9. Shahaadat of Hadhrat Khubaib, Hadhrat Zaid and Hadhrat 'Aasim رَضِيَ اللّٰهُ عَنْهُمْ

The Quraish were very angry at the loss of some of their greatest men in the battle of Uhud. Sulaifah, whose two sons had been killed, had taken a vow that she would drink wine in the skull of Hadhrat 'Aasim رَضِيَ اللّٰهُ عَنْهُ, if she could get hold of his head. Hadhrat 'Aasim رَضِيَ اللّٰهُ عَنْهُ had killed both her sons.

She had announced a prize of one hundred camels for the person who brought Hadhrat 'Aasim's رَضِيَ اللّٰهُ عَنْهُ head to her. One hundred camels was a huge reward at that time. Sufyan bin Khalid worked out a plan to get this prize. He sent a few men to Madinah, who pretended to accept Islam. They asked Nabi صَلَّى اللّٰهُ عَلَيْهِ وَسَلَّمَ to send some Sahaabah رَضِيَ اللّٰهُ عَنْهُمْ to their locality to preach Islam to the people.

They made a special request for Hadhrat 'Aasim رَضِيَ اللّٰهُ عَنْهُ saying: "Our people are very happy with his method of teaching."

Nabi صَلَّى اللّٰهُ عَلَيْهِ وَسَلَّمَ sent ten (or six according to another report) of his Sahaabah رَضِيَ اللّٰهُ عَنْهُمْ to go with them and Hadhrat 'Asim رَضِيَ اللّٰهُ عَنْهُ was also included. They started very pleasantly from Madinah Munawwarah not knowing that treachery awaited them on the way. They were attacked by more than two hundred of the enemy including one hundred crack selected archers (masters of the bow and arrow). The Sahaabah رَضِيَ اللّٰهُ عَنْهُمْ climbed up a hill called Fadfad.

The enemy called out to them: "We do not want to kill you. We shall only take you to Makkah and sell you to the Quraish."

The Sahaabah رَضِيَ اللّٰهُ عَنْهُمْ refused this offer and chose to fight to the end. When they ran short of arrows, they attacked the enemy with their spears.

Hadhrat 'Aasim رَضِيَ اللّٰهُ عَنْهُ called out to his companions: "No doubt you have been betrayed by these terrible people, but you should not lose heart because martyrdom is itself what you are hoping for. Allah Ta'ala, the most beloved, is with you and your hoorein (women of Jannah) are waiting for you. With these words, he rushed into the very thick of the enemy and when his spear broke, he fought on with his sword until he fell fighting to the last.

His last dua was: "O Allah! Inform Nabi ﷺ about our fate." Allah Ta'ala, in his compassion, answered his dua by revealing the news to Nabi ﷺ.

Hadhrat 'Aasim رضي الله عنه knew about Sulaifah's vow to drink wine in his skull, so he also asked Allah Ta'ala: "O, Allah! I have given my life for you, O Allah, save my head from the hands of these kuffaar."

This dua was also accepted. After his death, a swarm of bees or wasps covered his body and stopped the enemy from cutting off his head. They left the body alone intending to do their dirty job during the night when the bees would have gone, but during the night, there was a very heavy rain, which washed away the body.

Returning to the fight, when seven out of the ten Sahaabah رضي الله عنهم were made shaheed and the remaining three, Hadhrat Khubaib رضي الله عنه, Hadhrat Zaid bin Wathnah رضي الله عنه and Hadhrat Abdullah bin Taariq رضي الله عنه were still sticking to their position on the hill-top, the enemy again called out to them: "You three should come down from the hill, of course we would not cause any harm to you."

The three trusted them and came down the hill, but the enemy immediately pounced upon them and held them down with the strings of their bows. Upon this, Hadhrat Abdullah bin Taariq رضي الله عنه complained: "So this is the very first breach of your promise. I would rather join my martyred brothers than go alive with you."

He then refused to follow them as a prisoner. They tried their best to make him walk, but would not and realising that he would not move an inch from the spot, killed him there and then. The two remaining prisoners were taken by them to Makkah and sold to the Quraish.

Safwaan bin Umayyah paid fifty camels for Hadhrat Zaid bin Wathna رضي الله عنه to kill him in revenge for the death of his father Umayyah in the battle of 'Uhud and Hujair bin Abi Ahaab bought Hadhrat Khubaib رضي الله عنه for one hundred camels to avenge the death of his father in the same battle.

Safwaan gave Hadhrat Zaid رضي الله عنه to his slave to be killed outside the boundary of the Haram. A crowd followed them to watch Hadhrat Zaid رضي الله عنه meet his end and Abu Sufyan also happened to be one of the spectators. When Zaid رضي الله عنه stood ready to meet his death, Abu Sufyaan asked him: "Don't you wish that Muhammad (ﷺ) to be in your place today and you be freed to enjoy life with your family?"

Hadhrat Zaid's رضي الله عنه reply amazed them all: "By Allah!" he said, "The very thought of enjoying life with my family is unbearable to me, even if Nabi ﷺ was to suffer a thorn-prick in his foot."

The Quraish simply could not understand this reply, and Abu Sufyan said: "There is absolutely no example, anywhere in the world, for the love that the Sahaabah رضي الله عنهم of Muhammad (ﷺ) have for him." Hadhrat Zaid رضي الله عنه was then martyred.

Hadhrat Khubaib رضي الله عنه remained as a prisoner of Hujair for a long time. A woman slave of Hujair (who later on accepted Islam) says: "When Hadhrat Khubaib رضي الله عنه was a prisoner with us, I noticed one day that he was eating grapes from a bunch as big as a human head, although it was not the season of grapes in Makkah at that time.

When the day for his killing came close, he asked for a razor, which was given to him. Meanwhile a child of the house, while playing, went close to Hadhrat Khubaib رضي الله عنه. All the people of the house got worried. They thought that there was nothing to stop Hadhrat Khubaib رضي الله عنه from killing the child with the razor as he himself was soon to be killed. On seeing their worry, Hadhrat Khubaib رضي الله عنه removed their fears by saying: 'Do you think that I would stoop so low and kill an innocent child? This horrible crime is simply not possible for me.'"

When he was brought out to be killed and asked to make his last wish, if any, he requested: "Allow me to read two rakaat of Salaah, for it is time for me to leave the world and meet my Allah."

They let him read his Salaah. After finishing the two rakaat most calmly, he said: "But if you people were thinking that I was afraid of death, I would have read another two rakaats."

He was then tied up. At that time he said: "O, Allah! There is nobody to convey my last Salaam to Nabi ﷺ."

Allah Ta'ala sent his Salaam to Nabi ﷺ through an angel. Nabi ﷺ answered: "Waalaykumus salaam! O Khubaib," and informed the Sahaabah رضي الله عنهم: "Khubaib has been martyred by the Quraish."

Forty of the Quraysh speared him at one and the same time. One of those teased him: "Say by Allah, if you now wish Muhammad (ﷺ) to be in your place and you be freed."

He replied: "By Allah! the Most Magnificent, I will not tolerate a thorn pricking Nabi ﷺ in exchange for my life."

Every word of this story is a lesson for all of us. The devotion and love of the Sahaabah رضي الله عنهم mentioned here is really something to admire and desire. They would lay down their own lives but would not tolerate even a thorn pricking Nabi ﷺ. Again, look at Hadhrat Khubaib's رضي الله عنه last wish. He neither remembers his family members nor wishes to see any of them. What he wishes is to send his last Salaam to Nabi ﷺ and to say two last rakaats of Salaah.

10. NABI'S ﷺ FRIENDS IN JANNAH

Rabee'ah رضي الله عنه says: "I used to do the khidmat (service) of Nabi ﷺ at night. I would keep water, miswaak, musallah (praying mat), etc., ready for his Tahajjud Salaah. Once he was very pleased with me and asked me, 'What would you wish for the most?' I replied, 'O, Nabi of Allah, I wish to be with you in Jannah.' He asked me if there was anything else I wished for, but I replied, 'This is the only thing I wish for.' He then said, 'All right, you should help me by prostrating (i.e. joining me in performing abundant Salaah).'"

Here is a lesson for us. We should not depend on duas only, but should also make an effort. The best of all efforts is Salaah. It would also be wrong to depend only on the duas of the Auliyaa and the pious people. This is a world of cause and effect; and, no doubt, Allah Ta'ala sometimes, in His Wisdom and Might, brings into effect things which are out of the norm, but this happens only on very rare occasions. In this world we make all possible efforts, and do not depend on duas alone nor be satisfied with what we have. So with regards to the Hereafter, we should also try our best to make the required effort, and do not depend on dua only, nor like an irresponsible person leave all to taqdeer (destiny). No doubt, the duas of pious people and lovers of Allah Ta'ala have their effect, but they only go as far as to boost our own sincere efforts, and even Nabi ﷺ asked Rabee'ah ﷺ to 'help' him by prostrating frequently (i.e., saying Salaah in his leisure hours also).

CHAPTER 6

SACRIFICING FOR OTHERS

The Sahaabah رضي الله عنهم were an example of goodness. They set a standard that sometimes will be hard to follow in our times. We would be lucky if we can get even a part of their character. One of their beautiful qualities was sacrificing for others. Allah Ta'ala mentions this in the Noble Quraan.

يُؤْثِرُونَ عَلَىٰ أَنفُسِهِمْ وَلَوْ كَانَ بِهِمْ خَصَاصَةٌ

"They choose others over themselves, even though they themselves are poor." (Surah Hashr - Aayah 9)

1. FEEDING THE GUEST IN DARKNESS

A Sahaabi رضي الله عنه came to Nabi ﷺ and complained of hunger and suffering. At that time Nabi ﷺ had nothing on himself or at his home to feed him.

He asked the Sahaabah رضي الله عنهم: "Who will take him home as a guest for me tonight?"

One Ansaari Sahaabi رضي الله عنه said: "O, Nabi of Allah! I will do that."
The Ansaari Sahaabi رضي الله عنه took the person to his house and instructed his wife: "Look, this man is a guest of Nabi ﷺ. We will feed him as best as we can."

The wife replied: "By Allah! I have no food in the house, except very little which is just enough for the children."

The Sahaabi رَضِىَ اللهُ عَنْهُ said: "You put the children to sleep without feeding them, while I sit with the guest for the small meal. When we start eating put out the lamp by pretending to set it right, so that the guest will not know that I did not eat."

The plan worked out nicely and the whole family, including the children, stayed hungry so that the guest could eat properly. It was over this incident that Allah Ta'ala sent down the aayah:

يُؤْثِرُونَ عَلَىٰ أَنْفُسِهِمْ وَلَوْ كَانَ بِهِمْ خَصَاصَةٌ

"They choose others over themselves, even though they themselves are poor." *(Surah Hashr - Aayah 9)*

There are quite a number of similar stories about the Sahaabah رَضِىَ اللهُ عَنْهُمْ. The next story is one of them.

2. FEEDING A FASTING SAHAABI رَضِىَ اللهُ عَنْهُ

One of the Sahaabah رَضِىَ اللهُ عَنْهُمْ was keeping fast after fast, as he could not get anything to eat. Hadhrat Saabit رَضِىَ اللهُ عَنْهُ came to know of this. He told his wife: "I shall bring a guest tonight. When we sit for the meal, put out the lamp, pretending to set it right and you must not eat anything until the guest has finished eating to his fill."

The plan worked out as in the last story. The husband and wife sat with the guest and he never suspected in the least that neither of them had eaten, though their hands and jaws seemed to be moving.

When Hadhrat Saabit رَضِىَ اللهُ عَنْهُ went to Nabi صَلَّى اللهُ عَلَيْهِ وَسَلَّم the next morning, he was greeted with the happy news; "O, Saabit! Allah Ta'ala has tremendously liked your action of looking after the guest last night."

3. OVERPAYING OF ZAKAAT

Hadhrat Ubay bin Ka'ab رَضِىَ اللهُ عَنْهُ says: "Nabi صَلَّى اللهُ عَلَيْهِ وَسَلَّم once sent me to collect Zakaat from a locality. I went to a person there and asked about the details of his belongings. A baby camel, one year old, was due from him in Zakaat. When he heard this, he said, 'Of what use is a one year old baby camel? You can neither milk it, nor ride it. Here is a fine grown up she camel. You had better take this instead.'

I replied, 'My job does not allow me to take more than what is actually due from you. Therefore, I cannot accept what you offer. Nabi ﷺ is visiting this locality and he will be camping tonight at a place not very far from here. It is better that you go and place your offer before him. If he does not object, I would gladly accept your offer, otherwise you shall have to give me exactly what is due from you.'

The man then took the she-camel to Nabi ﷺ and pleaded with him: 'O Nabi of Allah! Your collector came to receive Zakaat from me. By Allah! I have never had the honour of paying anything to Nabi ﷺ or his collector before. I therefore placed before him everything that I owned. He decided that a one year old baby camel was due from me. O Nabi of Allah! This baby camel is of no use. It can neither give milk nor carry a load. I therefore asked him to accept a fine grown up she-camel. Instead, he refused to accept without your permission. I have now come to you with the she-camel.'

Nabi ﷺ replied, 'No doubt only that much is due from you which he has worked out, but if you are willing to give more than that from your own side, it would be accepted.' I then presented the she-camel to Nabi ﷺ, which he accepted and made dua of barkat for the man."

Look with what generosity of heart the Sahaabah رضي الله عنهم gave away their best things for the sake of Allah Ta'ala. On the other hand, we also claim to be the true followers of Islam and those who love Nabi ﷺ, but leave alone the giving of charity in general to the poor and the needy, we find it hard to pay the actual fardh amount.

Zakaat, as a pillar of Islam, is not even known to our rich people. Of the middle classes, those who think themselves to be the pious people of our community, pay their Zakaat in such a way that even what they spend on their own relatives and friends and all other donations which they are forced to give out of necessity, are given with the intention of zakaat.

Ch. 6 – *Sacrificing for Others*

4. HADHRAT 'UMAR رَضِيَ اللَّهُ عَنْهُ TRYING TO COPY HADHRAT ABU BAKR رَضِيَ اللَّهُ عَنْهُ

Hadhrat 'Umar رَضِيَ اللَّهُ عَنْهُ says: "Once Nabi صَلَّى اللَّهُ عَلَيْهِ وَسَلَّمَ asked us to spend in the path of Allah Ta'ala. At that time I had some money. I thought to myself that, every time Hadhrat Abu Bakr رَضِيَ اللَّهُ عَنْهُ beats me in spending for the sake of Allah Ta'ala. By the grace of Allah Ta'ala I shall beat him today because I have some money. I went home happy with the idea. I divided all my wealth into exactly two equal parts. I left one half for my family and I presented the other half to Nabi صَلَّى اللَّهُ عَلَيْهِ وَسَلَّمَ.

Nabi صَلَّى اللَّهُ عَلَيْهِ وَسَلَّمَ asked me: 'Did you leave anything for your family, 'Umar?' 'Yes, O Nabi of Allah,' I replied. 'How much 'Umar?' asked Nabi صَلَّى اللَّهُ عَلَيْهِ وَسَلَّمَ. 'Exactly one-half,' I replied.

In the meantime, Hadhrat Abu Bakr رَضِيَ اللَّهُ عَنْهُ came along with his contribution. He had brought everything that he owned. Nabi صَلَّى اللَّهُ عَلَيْهِ وَسَلَّمَ asked Hadhrat Abu Bakr رَضِيَ اللَّهُ عَنْهُ: 'What did you leave for your family, Abu Bakr?' Hadhrat Abu Bakr رَضِيَ اللَّهُ عَنْهُ replied: 'I have left Allah and His Nabi صَلَّى اللَّهُ عَلَيْهِ وَسَلَّمَ for them.'"

Hadhrat 'Umar رَضِيَ اللَّهُ عَنْهُ says that on that day he told himself that he could never compete with Hadhrat Abu Bakr رَضِيَ اللَّهُ عَنْهُ.

Allah Ta'ala says in the Noble Qur-aan,

$$\text{فَاسْتَبِقُوا الْخَيْرَاتِ}$$

"Compete with one another in good works." (Surah Maa'idah - Aayah 48)

Such healthy competition in sacrifice is, therefore, quite desirable and welcome. This incident happened at the time of Tabuk, when the Sahaabah رَضِيَ اللَّهُ عَنْهُمْ, in response to Nabi's صَلَّى اللَّهُ عَلَيْهِ وَسَلَّمَ appeal for help, contributed beyond their means. This has already been mentioned in Chapter two.

$$\text{جَزَاهُمُ اللهُ عَنَّا وَعَنْ سَائِرِ الْمُسْلِمِينَ أَحْسَنَ الْجَزَاءِ}$$

May Allah Ta'ala reward them with the best reward on our behalf and on behalf of all the Muslims. Aameen

5. SAHAABAH ﷺ DYING THIRSTY FOR OTHERS

Hadhrat Abu Jahm bin Huzayfah ﷺ says: "During the battle of Yarmuk, I went out to look for my cousin, who was right in the front of the battlefield. I also took some water with me for him. I found him in the middle of the battle, about to pass away. I went forward to help him with the little water I had but, as I reached him, another badly wounded soldier next to him gave a groan. My cousin turned his face and directed me to take the water to that person first.

I went to the other person with the water. He was Hishaam bin Abil Aas ﷺ, but I had just reached him, when I heard the groan of yet another person lying not very far away. Hishaam ﷺ pointed me in his direction. Unfortunately, before I could reach him, he had breathed his last. I hurried back to Hishaam ﷺ and found him dead as well. I hurried as fast as I could to my cousin and, in the meantime, he had also passed away.

إِنَّا لِلّٰهِ وَ إِنَّآ اِلَيْهِ رَاجِعُوْنَ

"Surely we belong to Allah Ta'ala and to Him is our return"

Many an incident of such self-denial and heroic sacrifice is recorded in the books of Hadith. This is the last word in self-sacrifice, that each dying person would forego quenching his own thirst in favour of his needy brother. May Allah Ta'ala bless their souls with His choicest favours for their sacrifice for others even at the time of death, when a person has seldom the sense to make a choice.

6. HADHRAT HAMZAH'S ﷺ KAFAN (BURIAL CLOTH)

Hadhrat Hamzah ﷺ, who was the dear uncle of Nabi ﷺ and one of his earliest supporters, became shaheed in Uhud. The cruel enemy cut off his nose, ears and organs. He was ripped open and his heart, lungs and liver were torn out and the whole body was thoroughly disfigured. While Nabi ﷺ was making arrangements for the burial of the dead, he saw the body of Hadhrat Hamzah ﷺ and was shocked to find it in that condition. He covered the body with a sheet of cloth.

Hadhrat Hamzah's ﷺ sister Safiyyah ﷺ also came to see her martyred brother for the last time. Nabi ﷺ, fearing that the sight might be too much for her to bear, asked her son Hadhrat Zubair ﷺ to stop her from seeing the body.

She however, said: "Yes, I have heard that they have disfigured my dear brother's body. It is not too much in the path of Allah Ta'ala and we should accept it. I will bear all this patiently and may Allah Ta'ala in His Grace have mercy on us all."

Hadhrat Zubair ﷺ informed Nabi ﷺ of his mother's words. Nabi ﷺ gave her permission to see the body. When she saw what they had done to it, she simply said, 'Inna lillahi wa inna ilaihi raaji-oon' and made dua for him.

In another Hadith, Hadhrat Zubair ﷺ himself narrates what happened. He says: "We saw a woman coming to the place where the Shuhadaa of Uhud had been gathered. As she came near to us, I recognised her to be my own mother. I tried to stop her, but she was too strong for me. She pushed me aside, saying, 'Leave me alone,' When I told her that Nabi ﷺ had stopped her from seeing the body, she immediately stopped and explained, 'On hearing the news of my brother's death, I have brought a couple of sheets for his kaffan. Take these sheets and use them.' When we took the sheets and began covering the body, we noticed the corpse of an Ansaari named Suhail ﷺ lying close by in the same condition. We felt ashamed to cover the body of Hadhrat Hamzah ﷺ in two sheets, while the body of another Muslim brother lay bare. We, therefore, decided to use one sheet for each of the two bodies. We discovered that one sheet was bigger than the other, so we drew lots and the bigger sheet came to Hadhrat Suhail ﷺ and the smaller one to Hadhrat Hamzah ﷺ. We found that the sheet meant for Hadhrat Hamzah ﷺ was too small and would not cover his body. When we covered the head, the feet were exposed and when we pulled it down to cover the feet, the head was exposed. Nabi ﷺ said, 'Cover the head with the sheet and the feet with leaves from the tree.'"

This is how Hadhrat Hamzah ﷺ, the dear uncle of Nabi ﷺ, was buried. Look at the spirit of the Sahaabah ﷺ, who could not tolerate Hadhrat Hamzah ﷺ being covered in two sheets and another Muslim brother remaining without a sheet. Although Hadhrat Hamzah ﷺ deserved the bigger sheet because of his position, his body was covered with a smaller sheet that had come to him. Can there be a better example of equality and self-sacrifice? Is it not shameful on our part, that we, who call ourselves the followers of these noble people, do not have any of their qualities?

7. THE STORY OF THE GOAT'S HEAD

Hadhrat Ibn 'Umar ﷺ says: "One of the Sahaabah ﷺ received a goat's head as a present. He thought of a neighbour who had a bigger family and was more in need of it than himself and presented it to him. This brother, after receiving the present, remembered yet another person who he thought was more deserving than himself and sent the head to him. In this way the goat's head changed hands seven times and finally came back to the first person.

From this story we learn that although the Sahaabah ﷺ were poor and needy, they chose others over themselves.

8. THE WIFE OF HADHRAT 'UMAR ﷺ ACTS AS A MIDWIFE
(A LADY WHO HELPS DURING CHILDBIRTH)

During the time of his Khilaafat, Ameer-ul-Mu'mineen Hadhrat 'Umar ﷺ, used to walk around the streets of Madinah during the night to keep watch. One night he noticed a camel-hair tent pitched in an open space. He had never seen this particular tent before. When he came close to the tent, he found a person sitting outside and heard a sort of groan coming from inside the tent. Hadhrat 'Umar ﷺ greeted the stranger with "Assalaam-u-Alaikum" and sat down beside him.

Hadhrat 'Umar ﷺ asked him: "From where are you brother?"

The person replied: "I am from the desert and a stranger to this place. I have come to request Ameer-ul-Mu'mineen for some help in my need."

Hadhrat 'Umar ؓ asked: "Who is groaning like this inside the tent?"

The person angrily replied: "Please mind your own business."

Hadhrat 'Umar ؓ said: "Do tell me please. Maybe I can help you."

The person replied: "If you must know, then inside the tent is my wife groaning with the pains of childbirth."

Hadhrat 'Umar ؓ asked: "Is there anybody else to help her?"

"No one," replied the person.

Hadhrat 'Umar ؓ got up and hurried to his house. He told his wife Hadhrat Ummu-Kulsum ؓ: "Allah Ta'ala has given you a chance to earn a lot of thawaab."

"What is it, O, Ameer-ul-Mu'mineen?" asked his wife.

Hadhrat 'Umar ؓ replied: "Out there, is a poor woman of the desert in child birth, with nobody to help her."

His wife offered herself saying: "I am ready to help her, if it pleases you."

Hadhrat Ummu-Kulsum ؓ was, after all the daughter of Hadhrat Faatimah ؓ and the grand-daughter of Nabi ﷺ. How could she hesitate to help a desperate sister at the time of need?

Hadhrat 'Umar ؓ told her: "Then you should hurry up. Also take a pan, some butter, food and other things needed during the child birth."

Hadhrat Ummu-Kulsum ؓ did so and left for the place where the tent was pitched. Hadhrat 'Umar ؓ followed her closely. She entered the tent while Hadhrat 'Umar ؓ made a fire and began cooking something which those people could eat.

After some time, Hadhrat Ummu-Kulsum ؓ called out from inside the tent, "O, Ameer-ul-Mu'mineen, congratulate your friend on the birth of a son."

The person was embarrassed when he heard her saying Ameerul-Mu'mineen' and realised the high position of the person who had been serving him, but Hadhrat 'Umar ؓ put him at ease, saying: "That is all right, there is nothing to worry about."

He then placed the pan near the tent and asked his wife to take it and feed the woman. She fed her and returned the pan. Then Hadhrat 'Umar رضي الله عنه asked the Bedouin to have some food, as he had been awake the whole night.

Hadhrat 'Umar رضي الله عنه then returned home with his wife, telling the person, "Come to me tomorrow and I shall see what I can do for you."

Is there any king, or even a small chief, or even an ordinary middle class person of our time, who will take his wife out in the middle of the night, to help a poor strange woman while he himself makes a fire and cooks food? Leave alone the worldly rich people, how many of the pious people would do that? We should realize that unless we really follow in the footsteps of those Allah fearing people, whom we claim to be our role models, we cannot wish for the special blessings that Allah Ta'ala gave them.

9. HADHRAT ABU TALHA رضي الله عنه GIVES HIS GARDEN TO ALLAH TA'ALA

Hadhrat Anas رضي الله عنه says, "Abu Talhah رضي الله عنه owned the best gardens in Madinah and they were more in number than those of any other Ansaari. One of his favourite gardens was known by the name of *'Bi'r Haa'*. It was close to Nabi's ﷺ Masjid and the water of its well was sweet and plentiful. Nabi ﷺ often visited that garden and drank its water. When Allah Ta'ala sent down the verse,

$$لَنْ تَنَالُوا الْبِرَّ حَتَّىٰ تُنْفِقُوا مِمَّا تُحِبُّونَ$$

"You shall never reach righteousness/ piety until you spend of that which you love." (Surah Aale I'mraan - Aayah 92)

Hadhrat Abu Talhah رضي الله عنه came to Nabi ﷺ and spoke out from his heart, "O, Nabi of Allah! I love Bi'r Haa very much. As Allah Ta'ala wants us to spend that which we love, I give that garden to be spent in the path of Allah Ta'ala as you please."

Nabi ﷺ was very pleased and said: "What a fine present (to Allah)! I think it would be best if you share it among your own heirs (close family)."Hadhrat Abu Talhah رَضِىَ اللهُ عَنْهُ did as Nabi ﷺ suggested.

After reading an Aayat of the Qur-aan or listening to a good bayaan, are we prepared to give away any of our belongings so quickly for the sake of Allah Ta'ala?

Even when we wish to give something in charity, we usually do it from our death-beds only, or else when we are so displeased with some of our relatives that we decide to disinherit them. But, at the time of weddings, we are ready to show off and spend thousands even if we have to take a loan on interest.

10. HADHRAT ABU ZARR رَضِىَ اللهُ عَنْهُ SCOLDS HIS SERVANT

Hadhrat Abu Zarr رَضِىَ اللهُ عَنْهُ was well known for his piety and simplicity. He kept no money with him and did not like others to hoard it. He was always scolding the rich. Therefore, Hadhrat Usmaan رَضِىَ اللهُ عَنْهُ, during his caliphate, advised him to shift to Rabzah (a small village in the desert). He had a few camels to live on and an old servant to look after them.

A tribesman from Banu Sulaim once came to him and said: "I wish to stay with you to benefit from your knowledge of Allah Ta'ala's commandments and Nabi's ﷺ sunnats. I shall also help your servant in looking after the camels."

Hadhrat Abu Zarr رَضِىَ اللهُ عَنْهُ replied: "I cannot keep a person with me who does not listen to me, but if you will always do as I tell you, then you can stay with me, otherwise I wish you good-bye."

The person asked: "In what way would you like me to obey you?"

Hadhrat Abu Zarr رَضِىَ اللهُ عَنْهُ replied: "When I ask you to spend from my belongings, you must spend the best of them."

The person says, "I accepted Hadhrat Abu Zarr's رَضِىَ اللهُ عَنْهُ condition and stayed with him.

One day, somebody told him that there were some poor people camping near the spring close-by and were in need of food. He asked me to fetch a camel. I went and intended to choose the best of the lot, as I had promised to do. It was a very kind and obedient animal which was good for riding, so I decided to leave it and chose the second best. After all, it was only going to be slaughtered and eaten and for this it was just as good as the other. The other one was very good for riding and much more useful to Hadhrat Abu Zarr رضي الله عنه and his family, while the poor would find this one just as tasty as the other. I, therefore, led the other camel to Hadhrat Abu Zarr رضي الله عنه.

He shouted: 'So, after all you have broken your promise.' Knowing well what he meant, I went back and fetched the best camel instead.

He requested the people around him, 'I want two persons to do a job for Allah Ta'ala.' Two people came forward. He asked them to go and slaughter the camel and distribute the meat equally among the families camping near the water, including his own, saying, 'My family will also share equally with the rest.' Those two people carried out his instructions.

He then sent for me and asked: 'Did you intentionally ignore my instructions about spending the best out of my belongings, or did you just happen to forget about it?'

I replied: 'I did not forget your instructions, but thought it better to keep the good camel for riding, while the other was just as good for eating.'

Abu Zarr رضي الله عنه asked: 'Did you leave it for my personal needs?' 'Yes,' I replied.

Then Hadhrat Abu Zarr رضي الله عنه advised me: 'Come; let me tell you about my needs. That is the day when I shall be left alone in the darkness of the grave. Remember, there are three partners in your wealth-: firstly your fate (taqdeer), which does not wait to take away its share, good or bad. It will take away all that it has to take. Secondly, your heirs who are waiting for the day of your death, so that they may take over their share, and thirdly yourself. If you can manage, don't be the most helpless of the three partners. Take your full share, while you can. Allah Ta'ala says:

$$\text{لَنْ تَنَالُوا الْبِرَّ حَتَّىٰ تُنْفِقُوا مِمَّا تُحِبُّونَ}$$

"You shall never reach righteousness/ piety until you spend of that which you love." (Surah Aale I'mraan - Aayah 92)

I, therefore, think it best to send things which I love in advance (to the Aakhirat), so that they may be kept safely for me over there.'"

The worst loser of the three partners is that man who does not spend his wealth in the path of Allah Ta'ala, and keeps delaying till at last fate (taqdeer) takes it away from him, or he dies and his heirs distribute amongst themselves. Very seldom do heirs give away the wealth, inherited from another person, in the path of Allah Ta'ala so that his soul may benefit by it.

Nabi ﷺ once said: "Man loves his worldly belongings, hugging them to his soul, and boasting, 'My wealth, my wealth,' but in reality only that much of his wealth belongs to him, which he either enjoys in the form of food and clothes or that which he spends in the path of Allah Ta'ala, which will be stored up for him in the hereafter. The remainder of his wealth belongs to others; he is acting only as a guardian."

Once Nabi ﷺ asked the Sahaabah ؓ, "Which of you would like to see his wealth in the hands of his heirs rather than keeping it himself?"

They replied, "Who would like to be such a person, O Nabi of Allah Ta'ala?"

Nabi ﷺ explained: "Whatever you send in advance by spending it in the path of Allah Ta'ala is yours, and whatever is left behind belongs to your heirs."

11. THE STORY OF HADHRAT ABDULLAH BIN JA'FAR ؓ AND HADHRAT ABDULLAH BIN ZUBAIR ؓ

Hadhrat Ja'far Tayyaar ؓ is a cousin of Nabi ﷺ and a brother of Hadhrat Ali ؓ. His whole family is famous for justice, generosity, bravery and heroism, but Hadhrat Ja'far ؓ had a special love for the poor and often mixed with them. When the Quraish were persecuting the Muslims, he emigrated to Abyssinia with the other Muslims, and was the spokesman who so successfully defended the Muslims in the court of the Negus. This story has already been given in Chapter one.

After returning from Abyssinia, he emigrated to Madinah and was martyred in Mootah. When Nabi ﷺ heard about his death, he went to his house to comfort the family. He called his sons Abdullah ﷺ, Aun ﷺ and Muhammad ﷺ, comforted them and blessed them with his duas. All his sons were exactly like their father, but Hadhrat Abdullah ﷺ was so generous and big-hearted that people called him "Qutbus Sakhaa" (the chief of the generous). He accepted Islam at the hands of Nabi ﷺ when he was just seven years old.

Once he asked his uncle Hadhrat Ali ﷺ to help someone in his need. The person sent four thousand Dirhams as a present to Hadhrat Abdullah ﷺ, but he returned the whole lot saying: "We people don't sell our good deeds." On another occasion, somebody sent him two thousand Dirhams as a present, all of which he spent in charity immediately.

A businessman once brought a large amount of sugar for sale in the market, but unfortunately, there was no demand for sugar just then and this grieved him very much. Hadhrat Abdullah ﷺ bought the whole lot and gave it free of charge to the people. He always looked after all the strangers who were stranded in the city during the night.

In one battle, Hadrat Zubair ﷺ called his son Abdullah ﷺ and told him that he had a strong feeling that this was going to be his last battle and that he would pass away in battle. If he did really pass away, then Abdullah ﷺ must pay off all his debts. He then told him that if he had any problem in paying the debts, he should ask his 'Master' for help. Abdullah ﷺ was confused and asked who his 'Master' was? Allah Ta'ala, replied Hadrat Zubair ﷺ. That very same day Hadrat Zubair ﷺ passed away. When Abdullah ﷺ checked his father's books, he saw that the debts amounted to over Two million dirhams.

Having the reputation of being an honest and trustworthy person, people came to him for the safe keeping of their money. He always addressed them like this: "Dear brothers, I have no vaults for the safe keeping of your monies. I will treat them as loans to me, and you may take them back when you please." He would then spend the money on the poor and the needy. However, Abdullah ﷺ cleared all his father's debts.

He says: "Whenever I had any difficulty, I would make dua (to Allah Ta'ala) 'O, Master of Zubair, help me,' and the difficulty would be removed."

Once he went to Hadhrat Abdullah bin Ja'far رضي الله عنه and the following conversation took place.

Abdullah bin Zubair رضي الله عنه: "I find from my father's accounts that you owe him one million Dirhams."

Abdullah bin Ja'far رضي الله عنه: "All right. You can have the money whenever you please."

However, after checking the accounts again, he found that it was his mistake, and in fact this amount of money was owed to Hadhrat Abdullah bin Ja'far رضي الله عنه by his father. He, therefore, went to him and said: "Forgive me. It was my mistake. In fact my father owed you that amount of money."

Abdullah bin Ja'far رضي الله عنه: "If that is the case, then I free you of the debt."

Abdullah bin Zubair رضي الله عنه: "No, I must pay it."

Abdullah bin Ja'far رضي الله عنه: "All right. You may pay it whenever you can."

Abdullah bin Zubair رضي الله عنه: "Will you accept a piece of land for the debt?"

Abdullah bin Ja'far رضي الله عنه: "Yes, if that is easier for you."

Abdullah bin Zubair رضي الله عنه says, "I gave him a piece of waterless land. He asked his slave to spread his musallah on that land. He then went and read two rakaats of Salaah, spending a long time in sajdah. After finishing the Salaah, he pointed out a certain spot to his slave and ordered him to dig at that spot. After a little digging, water gushed out from there."

The qualities of the Sahaabah رضي الله عنهم mentioned here was part of their everyday life. In fact, these things were not considered to be anything strange.

Chapter 7

Bravery and Heroism

The Sahaabah رضى الله عنهم were not afraid of death at all. Therefore, they were fearless and brave. A person who is not afraid of death is ready for anything. They neither had love for wealth nor any fear for the enemy. I wish I could also acquire this quality from the Sahaabah رضى الله عنهم.

1. Ibn Jahsh رضى الله عنه and Sa'ad رضى الله عنه make Dua for each other

One day before the Battle Uhud, Abdullah bin Jahsh رضى الله عنه told Sa'ad bin Abi Waqqaas رضى الله عنه: "O, Sa'ad! Come, let us make dua together. Let each one ask Allah Ta'ala to accept his only wish, whilst the other would say 'Aameen' to it. In this way, the duas are more likely to be answered by Allah Ta'ala."

Sa'ad رضى الله عنه agreed, and they both went to a corner to make dua. Sa'ad رضى الله عنه was first to ask Allah Ta'ala, saying: "O Allah! When the battle starts tomorrow, let me face a very strong and fierce enemy. Let him attack me with all his might and power, and let me fight him with all my strength. Then, O Allah! let me be successful by killing him for your sake, and allow me to have his belongings as booty."

Abdullah رضى الله عنه said: "Aameen."

Ch.7 – Bravery & Heroism

Then Abdullah رَضِىَ اللّٰهُ عَنْهُ started his dua, saying: "O Allah! let me face one of the toughest fighters from the enemy tomorrow. Let him attack me with full force and let me attack him with my full strength. Then let him overpower and kill me. He may cut my nose and ears from my body. When I appear before you on the Day of Qiyaamah, You may ask me, 'How did you lose your nose and ears, O, Abdullah!' and I will say, 'These were lost in the way of Allah Ta'ala and His Nabi صَلَّى اللّٰهُ عَلَيْهِ وَسَلَّمَ.' Then You will say, 'Yes! Surely these were lost in My way.'"

Hadhrat Sa'ad رَضِىَ اللّٰهُ عَنْهُ said: "Aameen."

In the battlefield the next day, both of the Sahaabah رَضِىَ اللّٰهُ عَنْهُمْ saw their duas answered exactly as they had asked.

Sa'ad رَضِىَ اللّٰهُ عَنْهُ says: "Abdullah's رَضِىَ اللّٰهُ عَنْهُ dua was better than mine. In the evening I noticed his ears and nose tied with string."

This story shows the great courage and bravery of Sahaabah رَضِىَ اللّٰهُ عَنْهُمْ, who were anxious to face the brave and the strong from amongst the enemy, and on the other hand it shows their devotion and their love for Allah Ta'ala. Abdullah رَضِىَ اللّٰهُ عَنْهُ wishes Allah Ta'ala to prove on the Day of Qiyaamah that his sacrifice was really for His sake.

رہے گا کوئی تو تیغ ستم کے یادگاروں میں

مرے لاشے کہ ٹکڑے دفن کرنا سو مزاروں میں

2. Hadhrat Ali's رَضِىَ اللّٰهُ عَنْهُ Bravery in the Battle of Uhud

Not understanding Nabi's صَلَّى اللّٰهُ عَلَيْهِ وَسَلَّمَ orders properly changed the victory at Uhud into a loss for a short while, the details of which we have already seen in Chapter one. This was a very hard time for the Muslims. They were caught between two groups of the enemy and many of them were killed. Nabi صَلَّى اللّٰهُ عَلَيْهِ وَسَلَّمَ himself was surrounded by the enemy, who spread the rumour that he had been killed. Most of the Sahaabah رَضِىَ اللّٰهُ عَنْهُمْ could not think properly when they heard this rumour and this was the main cause of their confusion.

Hadhrat Ali ؓ says: "We were surrounded by the enemy and I could not see Nabi ﷺ. I first looked for him among the living and then among the dead, but I could not find him anywhere. I told myself that, 'It is impossible for him to run away from the battlefield. It seems that Allah Ta'ala is angry with us because of our sins and he has lifted Nabi ﷺ to the heavens. There is no way left for me except to jump into the enemy and fight till I am killed.' I therefore attacked the enemy, clearing them with my sword, till I saw Nabi ﷺ. I was very happy and was sure that Allah Ta'ala had been protecting him through His Malaa'ikah. I came to him and stood by his side.

Meanwhile a group of the enemy tried to attack Nabi ﷺ. He told me, 'Ali go and stop them.' I fought and chased them away by myself, killing quite a few of them. After this, yet another group came to attack him. He again called out, 'Ali go and stop them.' I fought with that group also myself till they ran away."

Hadhrat Jibraa-eel عليه السلام came and praised Hadhrat Ali ؓ for his bravery and his love for Nabi ﷺ. Nabi ﷺ said:

اِنَّهُ مِنِّيْ وَاَنَا مِنْهُ

"Ali belongs to me and I belong to him."

Then, Hadhrat Jibraa-eel عليه السلام said:

وَاَنَا مِنْكُمَا

"I belong to you both."

Look at the bravery of Hadhrat Ali ؓ. When he cannot find Nabi ﷺ, he jumps into the enemy all alone. This shows his genuine love for Nabi ﷺ.

3. HADHRAT HANZALAH ؓ BECOMES A SHAHEED

When the Battle of Uhud started, Hadhrat Hanzalah ؓ had just been married and therefore did not join the battle from the beginning. It is said that he had just left the bed of his wife and had hardly started taking his bath, when he heard somebody announcing about the defeat. He delayed the bath and with sword in hand, rushed towards the battle-field. He jumped into the enemy lines, fighting and going forward into the enemy, until he was killed.

The body of the person killed in the path of Allah Ta'ala is not washed, unless a bath has been compulsory on him before his death. The Sahaabah رضي الله عنهم did not know that he had needed a bath and, therefore, buried him without a bath.

Just before his burial, Nabi ﷺ said: "I see the Malaaikah washing Hanzalah's رضي الله عنه body."

Hadhrat Abu Sa'eed Sa'adi رضي الله عنه says: "After hearing this from Nabi ﷺ, I went to have a look at Hanzalah's رضي الله عنه face and I noticed drops of water flowing down from his hair."

When Nabi ﷺ returned to Madinah, he made enquiries and found out that Hadhrat Hanzalah رضي الله عنه had delayed his bath. This again shows the courage of those people. A brave person cannot accept any delay and jumps into the jaws of death. Hadhrat Hanzalah رضي الله عنه also could not wait to finish the bath which was compulsory on him.

4. HADHRAT AMR BIN JAMOOH'S رضي الله عنه WISH FOR SHAHAADAT (DYING IN THE PATH OF ALLAH TA'ALA)

'Amr bin Jamooh رضي الله عنه would limp and walk because he was lame. He had four sons, who often spent time with Nabi ﷺ and took part in many battles. On the occasion of Uhud, Amr رضي الله عنه also wished to join the battle.

People told him: "You have an excuse because you are lame. You don't have to join the battle."

He replied: "How sad that my sons go to Jannah and I stay behind."

His wife also wanted him to fight and get martyred. To encourage him, she told him: "I do not believe that people have stopped you from going. It seems that you are yourself afraid to go to the battlefield."

Hearing this, Hadhrat 'Amr رضي الله عنه took his weapons and facing the Qiblah, made dua to Allah Ta'ala:

$$\text{اَللّٰهُمَّ لَا تَرُدَّنِىْ اِلٰٓى اَهْلِىْ}$$

"O, Allah! Do return me to my family."

He then went to Nabi ﷺ and said: "I had always wished for shahadat (martyrdom), but my people have always stopped me from going to the battlefield. O, Nabi of Allah! I cannot wait any more. Please allow me to join the battle. I hope to walk in Jannah with my lame foot."

Nabi ﷺ told him: "You have an excuse. There is no harm if you stay behind."

However he still insisted, and at last Nabi ﷺ allowed him to fight. Hadhrat Abu Talha رضي الله عنه says: "I saw 'Amr رضي الله عنه fighting. He walked proudly and said, 'By Allah! I am fond of Jannah.' One of his sons was following him from behind. Both the father and the son fought till they were killed."

After hearing about the death of her husband and son, his wife came with a camel to fetch their bodies. When the bodies were loaded on the camel, it refused to stand up. When it was forced to stand up after a big struggle, it would not go to Madinah and would turn towards Uhud, again and again. When Nabi ﷺ was told about this, he said: "The camel has been commanded to do that. Did 'Amr رضي الله عنه say anything at the time of leaving his home?"

His wife told Nabi ﷺ that whilst facing Qiblah he had made dua to Allah Ta'ala,:

$$\text{اَللّٰهُمَّ لَا تَرُدَّنِىْ اِلٰٓى اَهْلِىْ}$$

"O Allah! Do not return me to my family"

Nabi ﷺ said: "This is why the camel refuses to go towards his home."

Look at Hadhrat 'Amr's رضي الله عنه wish to die in the path of Allah Ta'ala. It was their love for Allah Ta'ala and his Nabi ﷺ that made the Sahaabah رضي الله عنهم attain such heights. Even after his death, 'Amr رضي الله عنه wanted to remain in the battlefield and therefore the camel refused to take his body back to Madinah.

5. HADHRAT MUS'AB BIN 'UMAIR رضي الله عنه GETS MARTYRED

Hadhrat Mus'ab bin 'Umair رضي الله عنه had been brought up with great love and affection by his wealthy parents. Before accepting Islam, he lived in luxury and comfort. It is said that he was the best dressed youth of Makkah. His parents would buy clothes worth two hundred dirhams for him. He accepted Islam in its early days, without informing his parents. When they came to know of it, they tied him up with a rope and forced him to stay at home. He got a chance to escape and emigrated to Abyssinia. After returning from Abyssinia, he again emigrated to Madinah.

Thus, a person like him who was brought up in luxury and comfort, was now living a life of poverty and difficulty. Once, Nabi ﷺ was sitting with the Sahaabah رضي الله عنهم when Mus'ab رضي الله عنه passed in front of them. He had only one sheet of cloth to cover his body. This sheet had many patches, including one of leather. Nabi ﷺ with tears in his eyes mentioned Mus'ab's رضي الله عنه life of luxury before Islam.

In the Battle of Uhud, Mus'ab رضي الله عنه held the flag of Islam. When the Muslims were temporarily scattered in confusion, he held the flag and stood at his post like a rock. An enemy came and cut his hand with a sword, so that the flag might fall resulting in the defeat of the Muslims. He at once took the flag in the other hand. The enemy then cut the other hand also. He held the flag to his chest with the help of his bleeding arms. The enemy at last stabbed his body with an arrow. He fell down dead and with him fell the flag that he had not allowed to fall while he was alive. Another Muslim ran and took over the flag.

At the time of his burial, he had only one sheet of cloth to cover his body. This sheet was too short for his size. When it was pulled to cover the head, the feet would be left open, and when it was pulled to cover the feet, the head would become uncovered. Nabi ﷺ said: "Cover his head with the sheet and his feet with 'Azkhar' leaves."

Such was the end of the youth who was brought up in luxury and comfort. The person who used to wear clothes worth two hundred dirhams does not have enough clothing to cover his dead body.

Look with what bravery he tried to keep up the flag and did not allow it to fall till he was dead. This is the miracle of Imaan. Once Imaan gets into a person, it makes him forget everything else, whether wealth, luxury or life itself.

6. HADHRAT SA'AD'S ﷺ MESSAGE TO RUSTAM

In the Iraq expedition, Hadhrat 'Umar ﷺ wanted to lead the army himself. There were discussions (mashwara), over several days, separately among the common people and among the leaders, whether Ameer-ul-Muminin should lead the expedition or stay in Madinah so that he could direct the operations and arrange for reinforcements from the headquarters. The common people were in favour of Hadhrat 'Umar ﷺ leading the expedition, and the leaders in favour of him staying in Madinah. Somebody mentioned the name of Hadhrat Sa'd bin Abi Waqqaas ﷺ as a substitute for Umar ﷺ to command the expedition. Both the groups agreed, and it was decided that Hadhrat Sa'd ﷺ should lead the expedition and Hadhrat 'Umar ﷺ should stay behind in Madinah. Hadhrat Sa'ad ﷺ was very brave and was one of the heroes of Arabia.

Iraq was part of the Persian Empire, and Yazdjard was the emperor at that time. He called one of his best generals named Rustam and ordered him to stop the Muslim army. Rustam did not want to go to battle because of his fear of the Muslims. He asked the emperor again and again to keep him back, saying: "I shall make all the arrangements from here and I shall be of use to you when you will need any advice." The Emperor did not agree and he had to go to the battlefield.

When Hadhrat Sa'ad ﷺ was about to leave Madinah, Hadhrat Umar ﷺ gave him the following advices: "O, Sa'd! Let not this fact deceive you that you are a Sahaabi of Nabi ﷺ and that people call you his uncle. Allah Ta'ala does not stop evil with evil, but He stops evil with good. Allah Ta'ala has no relationship with His creation. All men, high and low, are equal before Him, because all are His creation and He is their only Rabb. One can win His favours only if he devotes himself to His service. Remember that the Sunnah of Nabi ﷺ is the only correct way of doing things. You are going on a very heavy mission. You can only complete it by following the truth. Inculcate good habits in yourself and your companions. Choose the fear of Allah Ta'ala because this will lead you to His obedience and stop you from His disobedience. Obedience to the commandments of Allah Ta'ala is for those who hate this world and love the Hereafter."

Sa'ad رضي الله عنه faced the huge army with full hope in Allah Ta'ala. When both armies were ready to fight, he sent a message to Rustam, which read:

$$\text{فَاِنَّ مَعِیَ قَوْمًا یُّحِبُّوْنَ الْمَوْتَ کَمَا یُحِبُّوْنَ الْاَعَاجِمُ الْخَمْرَ}$$

"Rustam! There are people with me to whom death (in the path of Allah Ta'ala) is more enjoyable than is wine to the people in your army."

Ask the people who are addicted to liquor, how much they love to taste it. The Sahaabah رضي الله عنهم loved to meet death in the Path of Allah Ta'ala even more. This was the main cause of their success.

7. HADHRAT WAHB BIN QABUS رضي الله عنه GETS MARTYRED

Wahb bin Qabus رضي الله عنه was a shepherd and had been a Muslim for some time. He lived in his village in the desert. When he came to Madinah to see Nabi ﷺ, he brought with him his nephew and his herd of goats, which he had tied with a rope. He learnt that Nabi ﷺ was in Uhud. He left his goats and went to Uhud to fight by the side of Nabi ﷺ. A group of the enemy was at that time about to attack Nabi ﷺ.

Nabi ﷺ announced: "The person who gets rid of these people will be my friend in Jannah."

Hadhrat Wahb رضي الله عنه attacked them fiercely and forced all of them back. A second and third group of the enemy tried to come forward and each time it was Hadhrat Wahb رضي الله عنه who fought them and chased them away by himself. Nabi ﷺ gave him the good news of Jannah. As soon as he heard this he jumped into the enemy and fought till he was killed.

Hadhrat Sa'ad bin Abi Waqqaas ﷺ says: "I have never seen a person fighting so bravely as Wahb ﷺ. I saw Nabi ﷺ standing beside his body, saying, 'O Wahb! You have pleased me. May Allah Ta'ala be pleased with you.'"

Although Nabi ﷺ himself was wounded in this battle, yet he buried Wahb's ﷺ body with his own hands. Hadhrat 'Umar ﷺ used to say: "I never envied anybody more than Wahb ﷺ. I wish I could appear before Allah Ta'ala with a record as good as his."

What was there in life of Hadhrat Wahb ﷺ that makes a famous person like Hadhrat 'Umar ﷺ envy him? It is the same quality of sacrifice for the sake of Allah Ta'ala and His Nabi ﷺ even though Hadhrat Umar ﷺ and other Sahaabah ﷺ have better deeds.

8. THE INCIDENT OF BI'R MA'OONA

At Bi'r Ma'oona, seventy Sahaabah ﷺ were made shaheed. All of them were Hafiz of the Qur-aan. They were called the Jamaat (group) of Quraa and were mainly from the Ansaar. Nabi ﷺ loved them very much because they busied themselves in Zikr and reading the Qur-aan during the night. During the day they remained in the service of Nabi ﷺ and his family.

A person by the name of Aamir bin Maalik who was known as Abu Bara, from the Bani Aamir tribe of Najd, came to Nabi ﷺ and took this Jama'at with him for the Tabligh (preaching) and the Ta'leem (teaching) of his people. Nabi ﷺ was worried saying: "I fear that some harm may come to my Sahaabah ﷺ." However, the person guaranteed him that he will himself see to their safety. After much thought, Nabi ﷺ agreed to send the group of seventy Sahaabah ﷺ with him. He also gave them a message for 'Aamir bin Tufail (the head of the tribe), inviting him to Islam.

The group of Sahaabah ﷺ camped at Bi'r Ma'oona. Hadhrat 'Umar bin Umayyah ﷺ and Hadhrat Munzir bin 'Umar ﷺ took the camels for grazing and Hadhrat Haraam ﷺ with two Sahaaba went to deliver Nabi's ﷺ message to 'Aamir bin Tufail.

Ch.7 – Bravery & Heroism

When they reached near his place, Hadhrat Haraam رَضِىَاللّٰهُعَنْهُ told his friends: "You both stay here while I shall go to him alone. If I am safe, you may also come after me, but if I am killed then you should escape from here, as the loss of one person is better than the loss of three."

'Aamir bin Tufail was the nephew of 'Aamir bin Maalik, who had brought the group. He was a bitter enemy of Islam and bitterly hated the Muslims. When Hadhrat Haraam رَضِىَاللّٰهُعَنْهُ delivered Nabi's صَلَّىاللّٰهُعَلَيْهِوَسَلَّمَ message to him, he did not even read it and attacked Hadhrat Haraam رَضِىَاللّٰهُعَنْهُ with his spear which pierced his body. Hadhrat Haraam رَضِىَاللّٰهُعَنْهُ shouted out, *"By the Rabb of the Ka'bah, I am successful,"* and passed away. The cruel person did not worry about the guarantee given by his uncle, or for the accepted rule all over the world, that nobody will kill the envoy (messenger).

He then called the people of his tribe and encouraged them to kill all the Sahaabah رَضِىَاللّٰهُعَنْهُمْ camping at Bi'r Ma'oona. The people were hesitant because of the guarantee given by 'Aamir bin Maalik. He then gathered a large number of people from the neighbouring tribes and attacked the Muslims. They murdered each one of them except Hadhrat Ka'b bin Zaid رَضِىَاللّٰهُعَنْهُ, who still had some life left in him, but the enemy thought that he was dead.

While grazing the camels, Hadhrat Munzir رَضِىَاللّٰهُعَنْهُ and Hadhrat 'Umar رَضِىَاللّٰهُعَنْهُ noticed vultures flying in the air. They said, "Something terrible has happened," and returned to the camp. They saw from a distance that their friends were dead and the murderers were standing around their bodies with bloody swords in their hands. They stopped a while to think of what they should do.

Hadhrat 'Umar رَضِىَاللّٰهُعَنْهُ said: "Let us go back to Madinah and tell Nabi صَلَّىاللّٰهُعَلَيْهِوَسَلَّمَ."

Hadhrat Munzir رَضِىَاللّٰهُعَنْهُ did not agree. He said: "Nabi صَلَّىاللّٰهُعَلَيْهِوَسَلَّمَ will get the news sooner or later. I do not like to miss martyrdom and run away from the place where our friends are lying in their peaceful sleep. Let us go forward and meet them."

They both went and jumped into the thick of battle. Hadhrat Munzir رَضِىَاللّٰهُعَنْهُ was killed and Hadhrat 'Umar رَضِىَاللّٰهُعَنْهُ was captured. Since

'Aamir's mother had to set free a slave because of an oath that she had made, 'Aamir set Hadhrat 'Umar رضي الله عنه free and let him go.

'Aamir bin Fuhairah رضي الله عنه, a slave of Abu Bakr رضي الله عنه, was also among those who were killed at Bi'r Ma'oona. Jabbaar bin Sulami, who killed him, says: "When I stabbed my spear through him, he said 'By Allah, I have been successful' and to my surprise I saw his body moving up towards the sky. I asked later on as to what was the success that 'Aamir bin Fuhairah رضي الله عنه meant when he said, *'By Allah, I have been successful.'* I was told that it was that of entering into Jannah. This made me accept Islam."

These are the wonderful people, of whom Islam is proud. Death was more enjoyable for them than wine for their enemies. They felt most successful at the time of their death as they had done those deeds which had made Allah Ta'ala happy with them.

9. HADHRAT 'UMAIR رضي الله عنه STOPS EATING DATES

In the Battle of Badr, Nabi ﷺ was sitting in a tent. He encouraged the Sahaabah رضي الله عنهم to fight, saying: "Rise up and race with one another for a Jannah as wide as the Heavens and the Earth, prepared for the Muttaqeen (pious)."

Hadhrat 'Umair ibnul Humaam رضي الله عنه was also listening to this. He said: "Bakh! Bakh! How wonderful."

Nabi ﷺ asked Hadhrat 'Umair رضي الله عنه what he meant by saying that. He said: "I wish to be one of those for whom this Jannah has been prepared."

Nabi ﷺ said: "Certainly, you are one of them."

Hadhrat 'Umair رضي الله عنه then took out a few dates from his bag and began to eat. While he was eating, he suddenly said: "To wait till the dates finish will be a very long time. I cannot do that."

Saying this, he threw away the dates, and with sword in hand jumped into the battlefield and fought till he was killed.

The fact is that these people appreciated the value of Jannah because their Yaqeen (faith) was firm. If we too get that Yaqeen in our hearts, nothing will be too difficult or too much for us.

10. HADHRAT 'UMAR'S ﷺ EMIGRATION TO MADINAH

Hadhrat 'Umar ﷺ is well known for his bravery by one and all. In the beginning, when the Muslims were very weak, Nabi ﷺ made dua to Allah Ta'ala to strengthen the Muslims with Hadhrat 'Umar ﷺ accepting Islam. This dua was answered by Allah Ta'ala in no time, (as we have seen in Chapter one)

Hadhrat Abdullah bin Mas'ood ﷺ says: "We could not read our Salaah in the Haram till Hadhrat 'Umar ﷺ had accepted Islam."

Hadhrat Ali ﷺ says: "People emigrating to Madinah Munawwarah left Makkah Mukarramah quietly and secretly, because they feared the Quraish. However, when Hadhrat 'Umar ﷺ decided to go, he hung his sword from his neck, held his bow in his hand and took a large number of arrows with him.

He first went to the Haram Shareef, performed Tawaaf comfortably, performed his Salaah most calmly and then went to the different groups of the Quraish, saying to each of them, 'Whoever does not mind his mother crying for him, his wife becoming a widow and his children becoming orphans, may come out of Makkah Mukarramah and face me.' No one was prepared to accept his challenge."

11. AN ARMY IS SENT TO MOOTA

Of the letters that Nabi ﷺ sent to various kings, inviting them to Islam, one was sent to the King of Busra with Hadhrat Haaris bin Umair Azdi ﷺ. When Hadhrat Haaris ﷺ reached Moota, he was killed by Shurahbeel Ghassani, one of the governors of the emperor Caesar. The murder of the envoy (messenger) was against all laws.

Nabi ﷺ was very upset when the news reached him. He collected an army of 3 000 Sahaabah ﷺ, to fight against the enemy. Nabi ﷺ said, "Hadhrat Zaid bin Haarisah ﷺ will be the Amir of the army, If Zaid ﷺ is killed, then Ja'far bin Abi Taalib ﷺ will be your Amir and if he also passes away, then Abdullah bin Rawaahah ﷺ will be your Amir. If he also dies, then you can choose an Amir from amongst yourselves."

A Jew who was listening to this, said: "All three must die. This is exactly how the earlier Ambiyaa عَلَيْهِمُ ٱلسَّلَام used to foretell about future events."

Nabi صَلَّى ٱللَّهُ عَلَيْهِ وَسَلَّم gave Hadhrat Zaid رَضِىَ ٱللَّهُ عَنْهُ a white flag which he personally made. He then walked with the army for some distance out of Madinah and made dua for them saying: "May Allah Ta'ala bring you back safely and successfully. May He guard you against all evils."

At that moment Hadhrat Abdullah bin Rawaahah رَضِىَ ٱللَّهُ عَنْهُ, who was a poet, recited the following three couplets:

"I only wish forgiveness of my sins and a sword to cause my blood to gush out like water from a fountain,

Or a spear to stab me through my liver and stomach, And when people pass my grave they should say:

'May you, who have died for Allah's Ta'ala cause, be successful and do well. You are really successful.'"

Shurahbeel received the news about this army. He prepared himself to meet them with an army of 100 000 men. When the Muslim army proceeded further, they heard the news that the emperor Caesar himself was coming with another army of 100 000 men to help Shurahbeel. The Sahaabah رَضِىَ ٱللَّهُ عَنْهُم, who were only 3 000, began to doubt whether they should fight this army or ask Nabi صَلَّى ٱللَّهُ عَلَيْهِ وَسَلَّم what to do.

At this Hadhrat Abdullah bin Rawaahah رَضِىَ ٱللَّهُ عَنْهُ called aloud: "Friends! What are you worried about? What are you here for? You are here to attain shahaadat. We have never fought because of our strength in weapons and numbers. We have always fought on the strength of Islam, through which Allah Ta'ala has honoured us. You are sure of one of two successes, either victory or Martyrdom (shahaadat)."

After being encouraged by Hadhrat Abdullah bin Rawaahah رَضِىَ ٱللَّهُ عَنْهُ, the Sahaabah رَضِىَ ٱللَّهُ عَنْهُم decided to go on till they faced the Christian army in the battlefield of Moota. Hadhrat Zaid رَضِىَ ٱللَّهُ عَنْهُ, with the flag in his hand, gave out instructions on the battlefield. A fierce battle started and Shurahbeel's brother was killed in action. Shurahbeel himself escaped and hid in a fort. He sent a message to the emperor Caesar, who immediately sent an army, of 200 000 men. The Muslims were fighting against a very huge army.

Hadhrat Zaid رضي الله عنه was killed and the flag was taken over by Hadhrat Ja'far رضي الله عنه. He intentionally disabled his horse to remove any thought he had about returning home. He then read a few couplets, which meant:

> "O, people! What a beautiful place Jannah is. How fine and how cool is its water. The Roman army's doom is near. I must finish them all."

With the flag in one hand and his sword in the other, he jumped into the enemy. The enemy cut his right hand, which held the flag with. He at once carried it with his left hand. When that too was cut off, he held the flag with his teeth and supported it with his bleeding arms. His body was cut into two by somebody from behind and he fell dead. He was thirty-three years old at that time.

Hadhrat Abdullah bin Umar رضي الله عنه says: "When we removed him from the battlefield, we counted as many as ninety wounds on his body which were all on the front."

When Hadhrat Ja'far رضي الله عنه was killed, Hadhrat Abdullah bin Rawaahah رضي الله عنه was eating a piece of meat in a corner of the battle-field. He had been hungry for three days. On hearing about the death of Hadhrat Ja'far رضي الله عنه, he threw away the piece of meat, telling himself: "Abdullah! You are busy eating, while Ja'far has reached Jannah."

He took the flag and began to fight. His finger was severely injured and hung loose. He placed the hanging finger under his foot and tore it off from the hand, and then rushed forward. Knowing that the Muslims were fighting a very large army, he paused for a moment in despair. He at once recovered from his despair and told himself: "O, heart! What makes you wait now? Is it for the love of the wife? If so, then I divorce her this very moment. Is it for the slaves? Then I set them all free. Is it for the garden? I then give it over in Sadaqah."

He then read a few couplets, which meant:

> "O, Abdullah! You have to die one day whether you like it or not. You have had enough good times. Oh you! Who are a drop of dirty fluid, See how the kuffaar are attacking the Muslims. Why does Jannah not

attract you? Even if you are not killed in this battle, remember you have to die one day."

He then got down from his horse. Meanwhile his cousin brought him a piece of meat, saying, "You have not eaten or slept for many days. Eat this and take a little rest before you fight." He held the slice and was about to eat it when he heard the enemy attack from one side. He at once threw away the slice and jumped into the crowd, striking with his sword till he was killed.

The history of Sahaabah رضى الله عنهم is full of stories which show that the pleasures of this world were nothing in their eyes, and their only concern was to be successful in the Hereafter.

12. THE STORY OF SA'EED BIN JUBAIR (RAHMATULLAHI ALAYH) AND HAJJAAJ BIN YUSUF

We see the same qualities even in the Tabi'een (those people who saw the Sahaabah رضى الله عنهم). I close this chapter with the story of Sa'eed bin Jubair *(rahmatullahi alayh)*, who is a famous Tabi'ee.

Nabi صلى الله عليه وسلم has said:

اَفْضَلُ الْجِهَادِ كَلِمَةُ حَقٍّ عِنْدَ سُلْطَانٍ جَآئِرٍ (سنن ابن ماجه # 4011)

"To speak the truth in the face of a cruel ruler is the best Jihaad."

This is a story of Jihaad of that type. At that time, Hajjaaj bin Yusuf, the well-known murderer was the governor of an area. Hajjaaj's cruelty and oppression is well known to all. The rulers in those days, in spite of their shortcomings, never lagged behind in propagating Deen, yet we treat them as the worst among rulers because of comparing them to the just and Allah-fearing rulers. It was for this reason that people disliked such rulers.

He was the governor of King Abdul Malik bin Marwaan over Hejaz and Iraq. The King lived in Damascus and Hajjaaj had his base at Koofah. Sa'eed bin Jubair *(rahmatullahi alayh)* had fought against Hajjaaj. After the defeat, Sa'eed *(rahmatullahi alayh)* ran away and hid in Makkah Mukarramah. The Government sent a very strict person as the Governor of Makkah, with instructions to arrest Sa'eed *(rahmatullahi alayh)*. The Governor gathered all the people of Makkah Shareef and read to them the order of Abdul Malik, which said: "Any person who gives shelter to Hadhrat Sa'eed *(rahmatullahi alayh)* shall be killed with Hadhrat Sa'eed *(rahmatullahi alayh)*."

He then announced to the people: "By Allah, I must kill the person who gives shelter to Hadhrat Sa'eed *(rahmatullahi alayh)*.His and his neighbour's houses would be demolished."

Hadhrat Sa'eed *(rahmatullahi alayh)* was arrested with great difficulty and sent to Koofah. When he was brought before Hajjaaj, the following conversation took place:

Hajjaaj asked: "What is your name?"

Hadhrat Sa'eed *(rahmatullahi alayh)* replied: "My name is Sa'eed (which means fortunate)."

Hajjaaj asked: "What is your father's name?"

Hadhrat Sa'eed *(rahmatullahi alayh)* replied: "Jubair (which means trimmed)."

Hajjaaj remarked: "No, you are in fact Shaqi (which means terrible), son of Kusair (which means a broken thing)."

Hadhrat Sa'eed *(rahmatullahi alayh)* said: "My mother knew my name better than you do."

Hajjaaj remarked: "You are despicable and your mother is also despicable."

Hadhrat Sa'eed *(rahmatullahi alayh)* said: "The Knower of the hidden things is someone else."

Hajjaaj said: "Look! I am going to kill you."

Hadhrat Sa'eed *(rahmatullahi alayh)* said: "Then my mother was right in giving me this name."

Hajjaaj said: "I shall send you to Jahannam."

Hadhrat Sa'eed *(rahmatullahi alayh)* said: "If I knew that you had that power, I would have taken you as my god."

Hajjaaj asked: "What is your belief about Nabi ﷺ?"

Hadhrat Sa'eed *(rahmatullahi alayh)* replied: "He was a messenger of Mercy and a Nabi of Allah Ta'ala, sent with the best guidance for the whole creation."

Hajjaaj asked: "What do you say about the Khulafaa?"

Hadhrat Sa'eed *(rahmatullahi alayh)* replied: "I am not a guardian over them. Everybody is responsible for his own actions."

Hajjaaj asked: "Who is the highest of the four Khulafaa?"

Hadhrat Sa'eed *(rahmatullahi alayh)* replied: "The one who had been able to please Allah Ta'ala the most."

Hajjaaj asked: "Which of them had been able to please Allah Ta'ala the most?"

Hadhrat Sa'eed *(rahmatullahi alayh)* replied: "This is known only to Him, Who knows what is hidden in the hearts."

Hajjaaj asked: "Is Ali in Jannah or in Jahannam?"

Hadhrat Sa'eed *(rahmatullahi alayh)* replied: "I can only answer that after I visit the two places and meet their people."

Hajjaaj asked: "What will happen to me on the Day of Qiyaamah?"

Hadhrat Sa'eed *(rahmatullahi alayh)* replied: "I have no knowledge of the unseen?"

Hajjaaj said: "You do not wish to tell me the truth."

Hadhrat Sa'eed *(rahmatullahi alayh)* replied: "But I did not tell a lie either."

Hajjaaj asked: "Why do you never laugh?"

Hadhrat Sa'eed *(rahmatullahi alayh)* replied: "I do not see anything to laugh at. Why should one laugh when he is created from dust and has to appear on the Day of Qiyaamah and is always surrounded by problems?"

Hajjaaj said: "But I laugh."

Hadhrat Sa'eed *(rahmatullahi alayh)* replied: "Allah Ta'ala has created us differently."

Hajjaaj said: "I am going to kill you now."

Hadhrat Sa'eed *(rahmatullahi alayh)* replied: "The time and manner of my death has already been decided."

Hajjaaj said: "Allah Ta'ala has favoured me over you."

Hadhrat Saeed *(rahmatullahi alayh)* replied: "Nobody can be proud of his closeness to Allah Ta'ala, unless he knows his position; and Allah Ta'ala is the only knower of the unseen."

Hajjaaj asked: "Why should I not be proud of my relationship with Allah Ta'ala, when I am with the Ameer-ul-Mu'mineen and you are with the rebels?"

Hadhrat Sa'eed *(rahmatullahi alayh)* replied: "I am with the other Muslims. I myself avoid mischief, but nobody can change the decision of Allah Ta'ala."

Hajjaaj asked: "What do you say about what we collect for the Ameer-ul-Mu'mineen?"

Hadhrat Sa'eed *(rahmatullahi alayh)* replied: "I do not know what you collect for him."

Hajjaj sent for gold, silver and dresses from the treasury and showed these to Sa'eed *(rahmatullahi alayh)*.

Hadhrat Saeed *(rahmatullahi alayh)* said: "These are useful, provided you are able to obtain with them the things that may provide you peace on the Day of Qiyaamah, when every nursing mother will forget her child and every pregnant one will be delivered of her burden, and when nothing but good deeds will be of any benefit."

Hajjaaj asked: "Are our collections not good?"

Hadhrat Sa'eed *(rahmatullahi alayh)* replied: "You have collected them, and you are the best judge."

Hajjaaj asked: "Do you like any of these things for yourself?"

Hadhrat Sa'eed *(rahmatullahi alayh)* replied: "I only like the things which Allah Ta'ala likes."

Hajjaaj said: "Curse to you!"

Hadhrat Sa'eed *(rahmatullahi alayh)* replied: "Curse is for the person who cannot go to Jannah and is made to enter Jahannam."

Hajjaaj angrily asked: "Tell me how I should kill you?"

Hadhrat Sa'eed *(rahmatullahi alayh)* replied: "As you would like to be killed yourself."

Hajjaaj asked: "Should I forgive you?"

Hadhrat Sa'eed *(rahmatullahi alayh)* replied: "Allah's forgiveness is real. Your forgiveness is of no value."

Hajjaaj ordering the executioner: "Kill this man!"

Hadhrat Sa'eed *(rahmatullahi alayh)* laughed while he was being taken to be killed. Hajjaaj was told of this. He called him back.

Hajjaaj asked: "What made you laugh?"

Hadhrat Sa'eed *(rahmatullahi alayh)* replied: "Your courage with Allah Ta'ala and His mercy to you."

Hajjaaj said: "I am killing a person who has caused disunity amongst the Muslims." Hajjaaj ordering the executioner: "Kill him in front of me."

Hadhrat Sa'eed *(rahmatullahi alayh)* requested: "Let me perform two rakaats salaah."

After finishing Salaah, he faced the Qiblah and read:

$$إِنِّي وَجَّهْتُ وَجْهِيَ لِلَّذِيْ فَطَرَ السَّمٰوٰتِ وَالْأَرْضَ حَنِيْفًا وَّمَآ اَنَا مِنَ الْمُشْرِكِيْنَ$$

"Verily I have turned my face (my devotion and worship) to that being Who created the heavens and earth, as a Haneef (one who worships Allah Ta'ala alone and is not inclined to any deviation) and I am not from those who ascribe partners to Allah Ta'ala"
(Surah An'aam – Aayah 79)

Hajjaaj: "Turn him away from our Qiblah and let him face the Qiblah of the Christians who also caused problems amongst their people." His face was immediately turned towards the other direction.

Hadhrat Sa'eed *(rahmatullahi alayh)* replied:

$$اَيْنَمَا تُوَلُّوْا فَثَمَّ وَجْهُ اللهِ$$

"And whichever direction you turn, there is Allah Ta'ala's presence",
(Surah Baqarah - Aayah 115)

Hadhrat Sa'eed (rahmatullahi alayh) said: "Allah Ta'ala knows about the Imaan that is concealed within me"

Hajjaaj said: "Make him face towards the ground. We are only responsible to act on what is apparent to us." (Hadhrat Sa'eed (rahmatullahi alayh) was made to lie on his face.)

Hadhrat Sa'eed *(rahmatullahi alayh)*:

$$مِنْهَا خَلَقْنٰكُمْ وَفِيْهَا نُعِيْدُكُمْ وَمِنْهَا نُخْرِجُكُمْ تَارَةً اُخْرٰى$$

"From it (the earth) did we create you, and into it shall we return you, and from it shall we bring you out once again."
(Surah Thaahaa - Aayah 55)

Hajjaaj said: "Kill him"

Hadhrat Sa'eed *(rahmatullahi alayh)* said: "I call you to witness what I say;

أَشْهَدُ اَنْ لَّا اِلٰهَ اِلَّا اللّٰهُ وَحْدَهُ لَا شَرِيْكَ لَهُ وَاَشْهَدُ اَنَّ مُحَمَّدًا عَبْدُهُ وَرَسُوْلُهُ

I bear witness that there is no deity except Allah, who is all alone and who has no partner and I bear witness that Muhammad (ﷺ) is His slave and His Nabi."

He was then beheaded (his head was cut off).

اِنَّا لِلّٰهِ وَاِنَّا اِلَيْهِ رَاجِعُوْنَ

"Indeed to Allah we belong and to him shall we return"

After his killing, a great amount of blood flowed from Hadhrat Sa'eed's *(rahmatullahi alayh)* body. Hajjaaj himself wondered at this. When he asked the doctors the reason for this, they said: "His calmness at the time of death had kept his blood normal. Usually, people who are going to be killed are scared and so afraid of death that their blood becomes thick and does not flow easily."

There are many such stories about the Taabi'een. Hadhrat Imaam Abu Hanifah *(rahmatullahi alayh)*, Hadhrat Imaam Maalik *(rahmatullahi alayh)*, Hadhrat Imaam Ahmad bin Hambal *(rahmatullahi alayh)* and other pious people had to suffer alot because of their truthfulness; but they remained firm on the right path.

CHAPTER 8
THIRST FOR KNOWLEDGE

Since the Kalimah is the foundation of Islam and the basis for all achievements, no good action is, therefore, acceptable without belief in the Kalimah. Therefore, the Sahaabah رضي الله عنهم devoted most of their energy, especially in the early days of Islam, in the propagation of the Kalimah and by fighting against the kuffaar. Although their activities left them very little time to devote themselves in the pursuit of knowledge, yet their zeal even in this direction has preserved for us 14 centuries later a legacy in the form of knowledge about the Qur-aan and Hadith, which is a shining example for us. Later, when the Sahaabah رضي الله عنهم we're not as preoccupied in the field of da'wat and jihaad, and the number of people in Islam also grew considerably, Allah Ta'ala revealed the following verse in the Qur-aan:

وَمَا كَانَ الْمُؤْمِنُونَ لِيَنْفِرُوا كَآفَّةً ۚ فَلَوْلَا نَفَرَ مِنْ كُلِّ فِرْقَةٍ مِنْهُمْ طَآئِفَةٌ لِيَتَفَقَّهُوا فِي الدِّينِ وَلِيُنْذِرُوا قَوْمَهُمْ إِذَا رَجَعُوا إِلَيْهِمْ لَعَلَّهُمْ يَحْذَرُونَ

"And it is not (correct) for the believers to go out (in the path of Allah) all together. Why does a small group from every large party not proceed to attain deep understanding of Deen, so that they may warn their people (who had been engaged in the part of Allah Ta'ala) when they return to them so that they may beware (of sin)?" (Surah Taubah - Aayah 122)

Hadhrat Abdullah bin Abbas (Radhiyallaho anho) says: "The verses of the Qur-aan which were revealed in the beginning of Islam, demanding every Muslim to move out in the path of Allah Ta'ala; for example:

$$\text{اِلَّا تَنْفِرُوْا يُعَذِّبْكُمْ عَذَابًا اَلِيْمًا}$$

"If you do not go forth, He (Allah Ta'ala) shall punish you severely;"
(Surah Taubah - Aayah 39)

$$\text{اِنْفِرُوْا خِفَافًا وَّثِقَالًا وَّجَاهِدُوْا بِاَمْوَالِكُمْ وَاَنْفُسِكُمْ فِيْ سَبِيْلِ اللهِ}$$

"Proceed (in the path of Allah Ta'ala) when light or heavy (in good conditions and adverse conditions), and exert yourselves (for the welfare of deen) with your wealth and your lives in the way of Allah Ta'ala;" (Surah Taubah - Aayah 41)

These verses were later on superseded by the foregoing verse, which advised only a party from each group to leave their places.

$$\text{وَمَا كَانَ الْمُؤْمِنُوْنَ لِيَنْفِرُوْا كَآفَّةً فَلَوْلَا نَفَرَ مِنْ كُلِّ فِرْقَةٍ مِّنْهُمْ طَآئِفَةٌ}$$
$$\text{لِّيَتَفَقَّهُوْا فِي الدِّيْنِ وَلِيُنْذِرُوْا قَوْمَهُمْ اِذَا رَجَعُوْٓا اِلَيْهِمْ لَعَلَّهُمْ يَحْذَرُوْنَ}$$

"And it is not (correct) for the believers to go out (in the path of Allah) all together. Why does a small group from every large party not proceed to attain deep understanding of Deen, so that they may warn their people (who had been engaged in the part of Allah Ta'ala) when they return to them so that they may beware (of sin)?" (Surah Taubah - Aayah 122)

The Sahaabah (Radhiyallaho anhum) were very few in number and they had to assume the responsibilities of Islam in all fields. Therefore, Allah Ta'ala gifted them with the talent in all fields of Deen. In the time of the Tabieen, Islam spread far and wide and the Muslims grew in number. Since the later people lacked the talent in all fields of Deen like that of the Sahaabah (Radhiyallaho anhum), Allah Ta'ala used different people to specialize in different branches of Islamic learning.

Muhadditheen devoted themselves to the collection and propagation of Hadith. Similarly, the Fuqaha (jurists), Soofia (Experts in Zikr), Qurraa (Experts in recitation of Qur-aan), Mujahidin (Fighters in the path of Allah Ta'ala), etc; each group specialised in its own field. This was very necessary at that time because the different branches of Islamic learning would not have developed to the level of perfection, as it is difficult for one man to specialise in all the branches. The Ambiyaa عَلَيْهِمُ ٱلسَّلَام, and especially Muhammad ﷺ, who was the leader amongst them, were specially gifted with such a capability. This will explain why the stories of other eminent personalities, besides the Sahaabah رَضِىَ ٱللَّهُ عَنْهُم have also been narrated in this chapter.

1. SAHAABAH'S رَضِىَ ٱللَّهُ عَنْهُم GROUP OF MUFTIS

Most of the Sahaabah رَضِىَ ٱللَّهُ عَنْهُم, were involved in Jihaad, daawat, learning and teaching. However, there was a group of Sahaabah رَضِىَ ٱللَّهُ عَنْهُم who were totally responsible for issuing Fatwa, even during the lifetime of Nabi ﷺ.

They were the following Sahaabah رَضِىَ ٱللَّهُ عَنْهُم: Hadhrat Abu Bakr رَضِىَ ٱللَّهُ عَنْهُ, Hadhrat 'Umar رَضِىَ ٱللَّهُ عَنْهُ, Hadhrat Usmaan رَضِىَ ٱللَّهُ عَنْهُ, Hadhrat Ali رَضِىَ ٱللَّهُ عَنْهُ, Hadhrat Abdur Rahmaan bin 'Auf رَضِىَ ٱللَّهُ عَنْهُ, Hadhrat Ubayy bin Ka'ab رَضِىَ ٱللَّهُ عَنْهُ, Hadhrat Abdullah bin Mas'ood رَضِىَ ٱللَّهُ عَنْهُ, Hadhrat Mu'aaz bin Jabal رَضِىَ ٱللَّهُ عَنْهُ, Hadhrat Ammaar bin Yaasir رَضِىَ ٱللَّهُ عَنْهُ, Hadhrat Huzayfah رَضِىَ ٱللَّهُ عَنْهُ, Hadhrat Salmaan Farsi رَضِىَ ٱللَّهُ عَنْهُ, Hadhrat Zaid bin Saabit رَضِىَ ٱللَّهُ عَنْهُ, Hadhrat Abu Musa رَضِىَ ٱللَّهُ عَنْهُ and Hadhrat Abu Darda رَضِىَ ٱللَّهُ عَنْهُ. To give Fatwa during the lifetime of Nabi ﷺ was a great honour for these Sahaabah رَضِىَ ٱللَّهُ عَنْهُم, and it gives us an idea of their deep and great knowledge.

2. HADHRAT ABU BAKR رَضِىَ ٱللَّهُ عَنْهُ BURNS HIS COLLECTION

Hadhrat Aa'ishah رَضِىَ ٱللَّهُ عَنْهَا says: "My father, Hadhrat Abu Bakr رَضِىَ ٱللَّهُ عَنْهُ, had a book of 500 Ahaadith. One night I noticed that he was very restless. He was tossing about in bed and could not sleep. I got worried and asked him, 'Are you suffering from any illness or worried about something?' However he did not speak and remained restless throughout the night. The next morning he called me and said, 'Bring the book of Hadith that I gave you to keep.' I brought the book and he set fire to it, till it was burnt. He said, 'The book had many Ahaadith that I had heard from other people. I thought that if I passed away and left behind a Hadith accepted as true by me, but really not authentic, then I should have to answer for that.'"

It was Hadhrat Abu Bakr's رضى الله عنه thirst for knowledge that caused him to write a book of 500 Ahaadith. But it was due to his extreme carefulness that he burnt the collection.

The Sahaabah رضى الله عنهم were very careful and cautious about Hadith. That is why we find very few Ahaadith narrated by the famous Sahaabah رضى الله عنهم. People who nowadays quote Hadith (without first checking) in their lectures from the mimbar should take a lesson from this story. Hadhrat Abu Bakr رضى الله عنه remained in the company of Nabi صلى الله عليه وسلم most of his time, in Madinah and on journeys, and was his companion during Hijrah.

Many of the Sahaabah رضى الله عنهم used to say: "Hadhrat Abu Bakr رضى الله عنه was the most learned amongst us."

Hadhrat Umar رضى الله عنه has mentioned that, "After the death of Nabi صلى الله عليه وسلم, when discussion regarding the selection of the Khalifah was taking place, Hadhrat Abu Bakr رضى الله عنه advised the people mentioning all the Aayaat of the Qur-aan and all those Ahaadith of Nabi صلى الله عليه وسلم which spoke about the virtues and qualities of the Ansaar. This shows how much knowledge of the Qur-aan he had and how many Ahaadith he remembered. Despite all this, there are very few Ahaadith which have been narrated by Hadhrat Abu Bakr رضى الله عنه. This is the underlying reason because of which Imaam Abu Hanifah *(rahmatullahi alayh)* too was not so free in reporting Hadith.

3. HADHRAT MUS'AB BIN UMAIR رضى الله عنه DOES TABLIGH

A story about Hadhrat Mus'ab bin Umair رضى الله عنه has already been given in Chapter seven. When the first group of people from Madinah

Munawwarah accepted Islam in Mina, Nabi ﷺ chose Hadhrat Mus'ab bin Umair رضي الله عنه to go with them to Madinah to teach Islam and also preach to others. He was busy all the time teaching the Qur-aan and other Islamic practices to the people. He stayed with Hadhrat As'ad bin Zurarah رضي الله عنه and was known as 'Muqree' (the teacher).

Sa'd bin Mu'aaz and Usaid bin Hudhair, who were from the chiefs of Madinah Munawwarah, did not like what Hadhrat Mus'ab رضي الله عنه was doing.

Sa'd told Usaid: "You go to As'ad and tell him that we do not like him bringing a stranger to Madinah, who will mislead the poor and simple people of the town."

Usaid went to Hadhrat As'ad رضي الله عنه and talked to him very rudely.

Hadhrat As'ad رضي الله عنه told him: "You listen to him first and if you like his teachings, you may accept them. If not, then you can stop him." Usaid said, "This is a fair proposal".

Hadhrat Mus'ab رضي الله عنه then explained the beauty of Islam and read a few Aayaat of the Noble Qur-aan to him.

Usaid said: "These teachings are excellent and these Aayaat are really beautiful. How does a person accept Islam?"

Hadhrat Mus'ab رضي الله عنه said: "You take a bath, put on clean clothes and read the Kalimah."

Usaid immediately followed these instructions and accepted Islam. He then went to Sa'd and brought him to Hadhrat Mus'ab رضي الله عنه to listen to his dawat to Islam. Sa'd also accepted Islam. As soon as Sa'd accepted Islam, he went to the people of his tribe (Banu Ash-hal) and told them: "What type of a person do you think I am?"

They replied: "You are the best and the noblest of the tribe."

He then said: "I have taken a qasm (oath) not to talk to you until you all accept Islam and believe in Muhammad ﷺ."

All the men and women of the Banu Ash-hal tribe immediately accepted Islam. Hadhrat Mus'ab رضي الله عنه began to teach and train them in Islam.

Note: It was a common practise of the Sahaabah رضي الله عنهم that when any of them accepted Islam, then he immediately began to preach it. Every one of them considered it compulsory upon himself to preach and teach to others what he knew about Islam. His business, farm, job or studies did not stop him from inviting others to Islam.

4. Hadhrat 'Ubayy bin Ka'ab رضي الله عنه teaches Hadith

Hadhrat Ubayy bin Ka'ab رضي الله عنه is one of the most famous Sahaabah رضي الله عنه and was an expert Qaari of the Qur-aan. Very few Arabs knew how to read and write before Islam, and he was one of them. Nabi ﷺ used to read out the revealed verses of the Qur-aan to him. He memorised the Qur-aan during the lifetime of Nabi ﷺ and had a very good understanding of it.

Nabi ﷺ said: "Ubayy bin Ka'ab رضي الله عنه is the greatest Qaari of my Ummat."

He used to finish reciting the entire Qur-aan in eight nights in Tahajjud Salaah.

Nabi ﷺ once told him: "I have been commanded by Allah Ta'ala to read the Qur-aan to you."

He said: "O, Nabi of Allah! Did Allah Ta'ala mention me by my name?"

Nabi ﷺ replied: "Yes, He mentioned you by your name." Tears began to roll down his cheeks with extreme joy.

ذکر میرا مجھ سے بہتر ہے کہ اس محفل میں ہے

My name being taken is better than me being in the gathering

Hadhrat Jundub bin Abdullah رضي الله عنه says: "When I went to Madinah Munawwarah to study, I found that the people were sitting in groups and each group had a teacher. In one of the groups I saw a person dressed in two sheets of cloth, teaching Hadith and looking like a traveller. I asked the people, 'Who is this person?' They said, 'He is our respected Imaam, Hadhrat Ubayy bin Ka'ab رضي الله عنه.' When he finished teaching, I followed him to his house. He lived in a very old and simple building, with little or no furniture. I noticed Hadhrat Ubayy رضي الله عنه living a very simple and poor life."

Hadhrat Ubayy رضي الله عنه says: "Once Nabi ﷺ tested me in my knowledge of the Qur-aan. He asked me, 'Ubayy, which is the best Aayat of the Qur-aan?' I said, 'Allah and His Nabi ﷺ know best.' He again asked me the same question and I gave the same humble and respectful reply. When he asked me once again, I replied, 'The best Aayah in the Qur-aan is Aayatul Kursi.' My reply made him very happy. He said, 'May Allah Ta'ala bless you through your knowledge.'

Once, when Nabi ﷺ was leading the Salaah, he missed one Aayah. Hadhrat Ubayy رضي الله عنه corrected the mistake from behind. After finishing the Salaah, Nabi ﷺ asked, 'Who corrected me?' He was told that it was Hadhrat Ubayy bin Ka'ab رضي الله عنه. He said, 'I also thought that it was him.'"

Note: Together with his love for knowledge and his special job of writing the Qur-aan, he took part in all the battles by the side of Nabi ﷺ. He did not miss a single battle with Nabi ﷺ.

5. HADHRAT HUZAYFAH'S رضي الله عنه WORRY ABOUT EVIL

Hadhrat Huzayfah رضي الله عنه is one of the well-known Sahaabah رضي الله عنهم. He is known as the 'Keeper of Secrets'. Nabi ﷺ had told him the names of the Munaafiqeen (hypocrites) and had informed him of the order of all the evils which the Muslims were to face till the last day. He gave him full details (namely, the name of the mischief maker, his parent's names, his community, etc.) about the incidents that were going to affect 300 or more people.

Hadhrat Huzayfah رضي الله عنه says: "Other people used to ask Nabi ﷺ about good things, while I always asked him about the evil things, so that I may save myself from them."

He then mentioned the following conversation with Nabi ﷺ:-

Huzayfah رضي الله عنه asked: "O Nabi of Allah, shall we slip back to evil, after the good that you have brought to us?"

Nabi ﷺ replied: "Yes. The evil is coming."

Huzayfah رضي الله عنه asked: "Shall we have good again after that evil?"

Nabi ﷺ replied: "Huzayfah! Go and read the Qur-aan, think about its meaning and follow its orders."

However Huzayfah's رضي الله عنه worry grew even more and he continued his questions about evils that were to come to the Muslims.

Huzayfah رضي الله عنه asked again: "O Nabi of Allah, tell me if good will come after the evil?"

Nabi ﷺ replied: "Yes, good will come again, but the hearts of the people will not be as clean as before."

Huzayfah رضي الله عنه asked: "And will there be any evil coming after this good?"

Nabi ﷺ replied: "Yes, There will be such persons who will mislead the people and take them to Jahannam."

Huzayfah رضي الله عنه asked: "What should I do if I see that time?"

Nabi ﷺ replied: "If the Muslims are united under one ruler, then join them; otherwise separate yourself from all such groups and be hidden in a corner, or take safety under a tree (i.e. in a forest) and remain there till you pass away."

As Nabi ﷺ had told him the names of the Munaafiqeen of that time, Hadhrat 'Umar رضي الله عنه used to ask him: "Is there any Munaafiq among my governors?"

He once replied: "Yes. There is one, but I shall not tell you his name." Hadhrat 'Umar رضي الله عنه sent the man home, probably by his own judgment.

Whenever somebody passed away, Hadhrat 'Umar رضي الله عنه would ask if Hadhrat Huzayfah رضي الله عنه was taking part in the Janaazah Salaah. If Huzayfah رضي الله عنه was not present, then Hadhrat 'Umar رضي الله عنه would also not attend that funeral. When Hadhrat Huzayfah رضي الله عنه was about to pass away, he cried in worry and discomfort.

People asked him: "Are you weeping because you are leaving this world?"

He replied: "No, I am not weeping over that. I love to die. I am weeping because I don't know, whether Allah Ta'ala is pleased with me or not."

He then made dua: "O, Allah! These are the last moments of my life. You know that I have always loved You. Bless my meeting with You."

6. HADHRAT ABU HURAYRAH'S ﷺ MEMORY FOR HADITH

Hadhrat Abu Hurayrah ﷺ is another famous Sahaabi. No other person has narrated as many Ahaadith as him. He had been with Nabi ﷺ for only four years, as he accepted Islam in 7 A.H. and Nabi ﷺ passed away in 11 A.H. People used to wonder as to how he could remember so many Ahaadith in such a short period.

He explains this himself, saying: "People wonder how I remember so many Ahaadith. The fact is that while my Muhaajir brothers were busy in business and my Ansaar brothers did their farming, I was always with Nabi ﷺ. I was from the people of Suffah. I never cared to earn my living. I was happy with the little food that Nabi ﷺ gave me. I would be with Nabi ﷺ at times when no one else was there. I once complained to Nabi ﷺ about my poor memory. He said, 'Spread your shawl!' I did so. He made some signs on the shawl with his own hands and said, 'Now wrap this shawl around yourself.' I wrapped it around my chest. Since then, I have never forgotten anything that I had wished to remember."

Note: The people of Suffah were living in Nabi's ﷺ Masjid. They had no means of income. They were the guests of Nabi ﷺ, who gave them Sadaqah and shared with them the gifts that he received. Abu Hurayrah ﷺ was one of them. He would sometimes go without food for days together and would sometimes behave like a mad person because of hunger, as we have already seen in Chapter three. Despite these difficulties, he was always busy in memorising the sayings of Nabi ﷺ.This enabled him to narrate such a large number of Ahaadith. Imaam Ibn Jauzi *(rahmatullahi alayh)* has attributed as many as 5374 Ahaadith to him.

Once he mentioned the following Hadith: "A person taking part in a funeral gets one Qeeraat of reward if he returns after the Janaazah salaah, but gets two Qeeraats of reward if he remains there till the burial is over, and one Qeeraat is heavier than mount Uhud."

Hadhrat Abdullah bin 'Umar ﷺ heard this and had some doubt. He said: "O, Abu Hurayrah! Think before you speak."

Hadhrat Abu Hurayrah ﷺ got upset and took Hadhrat Abdullah bin 'Umar ﷺ to Hadhrat Aa'ishah ﷺ and told her: "O, Ummul-Mu'mineen, I request you to say by Allah if you have heard from Nabi ﷺ the Hadith regarding Qeeraats of reward?" She replied: "Yes. I have heard this Hadith."

Hadhrat Abu Hurayrah ﷺ then said to Hadhrat Abdullah bin 'Umar ﷺ: "During the time of Nabi ﷺ, I had no tree to plant in the orchard and no goods to sell in the market. I was always with Nabi ﷺ. My only job was to memorise what Nabi ﷺ had said, and to eat only what he gave me."

Hadhrat Abdullah bin 'Umar ﷺ said: "No doubt, of us all, you were always with him and therefore you know the most about Nabi ﷺ."

With all this achievements, Hadhrat Abu Hurayrah ﷺ says: "I read *Istighfaar* 12 000 times daily."

He had a piece of string with 1000 knots. He would not go to sleep until he had read **'Subhaanallah'** on all of these knots.

7. THE KILLING OF MUSAYLAMAH AND THE COMPILATION OF THE QUR-AAN

Musaylamah, who was a liar, called himself a prophet even during the lifetime of Nabi ﷺ. After the death of Nabi ﷺ, people of weak Imaan began to leave Islam. Musaylamah took advantage of the situation and caused many people to follow him. Hadhrat Abu Bakr ﷺ took up arms against him. A fierce battle was fought with Musaylamah, in which the Muslims won with the help of Allah Ta'ala and Musaylamah was killed. However, many Sahaabah ﷺ, including many Huffaaz, lost their lives.

After this battle, Hadhrat 'Umar ﷺ went to Hadhrat Abu Bakr ﷺ and said: "Many Huffaaz have been killed in this battle. I am afraid that we will lose a good part of the Qur-aan if we have to fight a few more battles and lose more Huffaaz. I, therefore, suggest that the Qur-aan may be compiled and protected in the form of one complete book."

Hadhrat Abu Bakr رضي الله عنه said: "How can I do something that was not done in the lifetime of Nabi صلى الله عليه وسلم?"

However, Hadhrat 'Umar رضي الله عنه insisted so much that Hadhrat Abu Bakr رضي الله عنه agreed to it. He sent for Hadhrat Zaid bin Saabit رضي الله عنه and told him what had been discussed between him and Hadhrat 'Umar رضي الله عنه and then said: "You are young and intelligent. Everybody considers you to be trustworthy. You were also chosen by Nabi صلى الله عليه وسلم to write the Qur-aan during his lifetime. I therefore request you to go to the people and collect the Qur-aan from them and put it into a book form."

Hadhrat Zaid رضي الله عنه says: "By Allah, if Hadhrat Abu Bakr رضي الله عنه had asked me to shift the rocks of a mountain from one place to another, it would not have been so hard for me as compared to the collecting of the Qur-aan. I said, 'How do you both dare to do something which was not done by Nabi صلى الله عليه وسلم?'. In one Hadith it is mentioned that Hadhrat Abu Bakr رضي الله عنه told Hadhrat Zaid رضي الله عنه, "If you are in agreement with Hadhrat Umar's رضي الله عنه proposal, I will give the instruction to proceed, otherwise I shall also hold back". Hadhrat Zaid رضي الله عنه says, "After a lengthy discussion Allah Ta'ala opened my heart to the merit of this task. I then started going to the people and collecting the Qur-aan from those who had written it and from those who had learnt it by heart, till the final compilation was ready."

Note: From this incident gauge at how strictly the Sahaabah رضي الله عنهم followed Nabi صلى الله عليه وسلم. Shifting of a mountain from its place was not as difficult for them as doing a thing that they had not seen Nabi صلى الله عليه وسلم doing. Allah Ta'ala gave them the honour of providing the greatest service to Islam by compiling the Qur-aan into one book. Hadhrat Zaid رضي الله عنه was so careful that he would only accept the Aayaat when these were proved to be written during the lifetime of Nabi صلى الله عليه وسلم and only after they were confirmed by those who had memorised the Qur-aan.

Many thanks to the efforts of Hadhrat Zaid رضي الله عنه. No doubt, he had to go from door to door and person to person, before Allah Ta'ala made it possible for every word to be compiled and written down. Hadhrat Zaid

رَضِيَ اللّٰهُ عَنْهُ was helped by Hadhrat Ubayy bin Ka'ab رَضِيَ اللّٰهُ عَنْهُ, whom Nabi صَلَّى اللّٰهُ عَلَيْهِ وَسَلَّمَ had called a great expert in Qur-aanic knowledge. It was with this effort that these Sahaabah رَضِيَ اللّٰهُ عَنْهُمْ were the first people to compile the Qur-aan Shareef.

8. HADHRAT ABDULLAH BIN MAS'OOD'S رَضِيَ اللّٰهُ عَنْهُ CAREFULNESS ABOUT HADITH

Hadhrat Abdullah bin Mas'ood رَضِيَ اللّٰهُ عَنْهُ is one of those famous Sahaabah رَضِيَ اللّٰهُ عَنْهُمْ who was given the task of issuing Fatwa, even during the lifetime of Nabi صَلَّى اللّٰهُ عَلَيْهِ وَسَلَّمَ. He was one of the very early Muslims who emigrated to Abyssinia. He joined Nabi صَلَّى اللّٰهُ عَلَيْهِ وَسَلَّمَ in all his battles and worked as his attendant. He carried the shoes of Nabi صَلَّى اللّٰهُ عَلَيْهِ وَسَلَّمَ, gave him a pillow when he needed one, and brought him water for his wudhu. He was therefore called, "The keeper of the shoes," "The keeper of the pillow" and "The manager of wudhu."

Nabi صَلَّى اللّٰهُ عَلَيْهِ وَسَلَّمَ once said: "Abdullah bin Mas'ood رَضِيَ اللّٰهُ عَنْهُ is the only person whom I can choose as an Ameer (leader) without asking anybody."

On one occasion Nabi صَلَّى اللّٰهُ عَلَيْهِ وَسَلَّمَ said to him, "You have permission to visit me at all times."

Nabi صَلَّى اللّٰهُ عَلَيْهِ وَسَلَّمَ said:

"If you want to read the Qur-aan as it was revealed to me, then copy the reading of Abdullah bin Mas'ood."

"Believe in what Abdullah bin Mas'ood says about me."

Hadhrat Abu Musa Ash'ari رَضِيَ اللّٰهُ عَنْهُ says: "Abdullah bin Mas'ood رَضِيَ اللّٰهُ عَنْهُ and his mother visited Nabi's صَلَّى اللّٰهُ عَلَيْهِ وَسَلَّمَ house so often and were so comfortable there that the people of Yemen, who had come to see Nabi صَلَّى اللّٰهُ عَلَيْهِ وَسَلَّمَ, thought that they were part of the Ahl-e-Bayt (family members of Nabi صَلَّى اللّٰهُ عَلَيْهِ وَسَلَّمَ)." Although he was so close to Nabi صَلَّى اللّٰهُ عَلَيْهِ وَسَلَّمَ, yet he was very careful about narrating the words of Nabi صَلَّى اللّٰهُ عَلَيْهِ وَسَلَّمَ.

Hadhrat Abu Aamir Shaybaani *(rahmatullahi alayh)* says: "I stayed with Hadhrat Abdullah bin Mas'ood رضي الله عنه for one year. I never heard him quoting any words directly to Nabi ﷺ. Whenever he intended doing so, he would shiver with fear."

Hadhrat 'Amr bin Maimoon *(rahmatullahi alayh)* says: "I visited Abdullah bin Mas'ood رضي الله عنه every Thursday for one year. I never heard him saying; 'Nabi ﷺ said this.' Once, when narrating a Hadith, he said the words; 'Nabi ﷺ said so,' suddenly his body began to shiver, his eyes became full of tears, his forehead sweated, his veins became swollen and he said, '*InshaAllah* Nabi ﷺ said so,' or he may have said something similar or a bit less or a bit more."

Note: Look at the Sahaabah's رضي الله عنهم caution and care about Hadith. This is because Nabi ﷺ said: "A person who says that I have said something, which I did not say, is making his home in Jahannam."

Because of this warning, the Sahaabah رضي الله عنهم explained everything that Nabi ﷺ said or did, but, they were afraid of saying; "Nabi ﷺ said this," in case they should differ from what Nabi ﷺ had actually said. On the other hand, we go on quoting Ahaadith without being sure of their authenticity and do not fear the serious consequences of attributing anything wrongly to Nabi ﷺ. It may be mentioned that the Fiqah Hanifiyah is based mostly on the Ahaadith narrated by Hadhrat Abdullah bin Mas'ood رضي الله عنه.

9. A PERSON TRAVELS FROM MADINAH MUNAWWARAH TO HADHRAT ABU DARDA رضي الله عنه IN DAMASCUS TO LEARN ONE HADITH

Kaseer bin Qais *(rahmatullahi alayh)* says: "I was sitting with Hadhrat Abu Darda رضي الله عنه in a Masjid in Damascus, when someone came to him and said, 'O, Abu Darda رضي الله عنه, I have come all the way from Madinah to learn one Hadith from you, because you have heard it directly from Nabi ﷺ.'"

Hadhrat Abu Darda ﺭﺿﻲﺍﻟﻠﻪﻋﻨﻪ asked: "Do you have any other work in Damascus?"

The person replied: "No."

Hadhrat Abu Darda ﺭﺿﻲﺍﻟﻠﻪﻋﻨﻪ again asked: "Are you sure that you have no other work in Damascus?"

The person replied: "I have come to this place only to learn this Hadith."

Hadhrat Abu Darda ﺭﺿﻲﺍﻟﻠﻪﻋﻨﻪ then said: "I have heard Nabi ﺻﻠﻰﺍﻟﻠﻪﻋﻠﻴﻪﻭﺳﻠﻢ saying, 'Allah Ta'ala makes the way to Jannah easy for the one who travels some distance to seek knowledge. The Malaa'ikah (Angels) spread their wings under his feet in his honour and all things in the heavens and earth, even the fish in the water, make dua for his forgiveness. The greatness of a person who has knowledge over a person doing ibaadat is like the greatness of the moon over the stars. The Ulama are the inheritors of the Ambiyaa ﻋﻠﻴﻬﻢﺍﻟﺴﻼﻡ. The inheritance of the Ambiyaa ﻋﻠﻴﻬﻢﺍﻟﺴﻼﻡ is not gold or silver. Their inheritance is knowledge. A person who obtains knowledge receives a great wealth.'"

Note: Hadhrat Abu Darda ﺭﺿﻲﺍﻟﻠﻪﻋﻨﻪ was a leader amongst the Sahaabah ﺭﺿﻲﺍﻟﻠﻪﻋﻨﻬﻢ and had a very good knowledge of Deen. He is called 'Hakeemul Ummah' (The wise person of this Ummah).

He once said: "Before accepting Islam, I did business. After accepting Islam, I tried to serve Allah Ta'ala together with my business, but I could not do so. I, therefore, gave up the business for the service of Allah Ta'ala. Now, if I have a shop at the gate of a Masjid and therefore have no fear of losing a single Salaah, and even if the shop gives me a daily profit of forty Dinars (gold coins) to spend the whole lot in the path of Allah Ta'ala, even then I am not going to go back to business."

Somebody asked the reason, "Why are you not happy to do such business which will not lead you to the missing of salaah and you will also earn much profit which you can also spend in the path of Allah. Then too you do not prefer this. He replied: "Because of the fear of answering on the day of Qiyaamah."

He used to say: "I love death, so that I may meet Allah Ta'ala. I love poverty, so that I may be humble. I love sickness, so that I may be forgiven of my sins by Allah Ta'ala."

In this story, we find a person travelling all the way from Madinah Shareef to Damascus for the sake of one Hadith. This was not at all difficult for those people.

Hadhrat Sha'abi *(rahmatullahi alayh)* is a famous Muhaddith of Koofah. He once narrated a Hadith to one of his students and said: "You are listening to this Hadith while sitting in your home town. People had to travel all the way to Madinah for even less important things, because Madinah was the only seat of learning in those days."

Sa'eed ibnul Musayyab *(rahmatullahi alayh)* is a famous Tabi'ee. He says: "For each Hadith that I have learnt, I had to travel on foot for days and nights together."

Imaam Bukhaari *(rahmatullahi alayh)* was born in Shawwal 194 A.H. He started learning Hadith in 205 A.H. That is when he was only eleven years old. He had memorised all the books written by Abdullah bin Mubarak *(rahmatullahi alayh)* while he was in his early teens. After collecting Ahaadith from all the learned men of his own locality, he set out in 216 A.H. in search of further knowledge. His father died and he could not leave his widowed mother alone. He therefore took her with him on his long and strenuous journey to Balkh, Baghdad, Mecca, Basra, Koofah, Asqalan, Hims and Damascus. He collected all the available Ahaadith from these seats of learning. He was accepted as an expert in Hadith, while he did not have a single hair on his chin.

He writes: "I was eighteen when I compiled the Fatwah of the Sahaabah and Tabi'ees."

Haashid *(rahmatullahi alayh)* and one of his companions say: "Bukhaari and the two of us used to go together to the same teacher. We noted down all the Ahaadith that we learnt, but he wrote nothing. After many days we told him, 'Bukhaari, you are wasting your time.' He kept quiet. When we warned him again and again, he said, 'You are now annoying me too much. Bring your notes.' We brought our notes, which covered about 15,000 Ahaadith. To our utter amazement, he recited all those Ahaadith by heart."

10. HADHRAT IBN ABBAAS'S رَضِىَ اللّٰهُ عَنْهُ THIRST FOR KNOWLEDGE

Hadhrat Abdullah bin Abbaas رَضِىَ اللّٰهُ عَنْهُ says: "After Nabi صَلَّى اللّٰهُ عَلَيْهِ وَسَلَّمَ had passed away, I told an Ansaari friend of mine, 'Nabi صَلَّى اللّٰهُ عَلَيْهِ وَسَلَّمَ is no more with us, but many Sahaabah ﷺ are still with us. Let us go to them and learn the knowledge of Islam.' He said, 'Who is going to come to you for learning in the presence of these famous Sahaabah ﷺ?' I was not discouraged. I continued learning and went to every person who was thought to have heard something from Nabi ﷺ. I managed to learn a lot from the Ansaar. If, on my visit to one of the Sahaabah ﷺ, I found him asleep, I spread my shawl at the gate and sat waiting. Sometimes my face and body would get covered with dust, but I kept sitting till they woke up. I then asked what I needed to. Some of them said: 'Abdullah! You are the cousin of Nabi ﷺ, you could have sent for us. Why did you take all the trouble of coming to our homes?' I told them: 'I must come to you, for I am a student and you are my teachers.' Some people for whom I had waited said: 'How long have you been waiting for us?' I informed them that I had been sitting there for a pretty long time. They said: 'What a pity, you could have awakened us from our sleep.' I said: 'I did not like to disturb you for my own sake.' I continued learning till there came a time when people began to flock to me for learning. My Ansaari friend realised this at that time and said with regret, 'This boy has surely proven himself more intelligent than us.'"

11. MISCELLANEOUS STORIES ABOUT KNOWLEDGE

Note: It was this love, pursuit and sacrifice for knowledge, which caused Hadhrat Abdullah bin Abbaas ﷺ to be known as Hibr-ul-Ummat (the most learned man of Islam) and Bahrul Uloom (ocean of knowledge) in his time.

At the time of his death, he was in Taa'if. Hadhrat Muhammad bin Ali ﷺ performed the janazah salaah and said: "Today we have lost our saintly leader."

Hadhrat Abdullah bin 'Umar ﷺ says: "Abdullah bin Abbaas ﷺ is known for his knowledge regarding the occasions when the different Aayaat of the Qur-aan were revealed."

Hadhrat 'Umar ﷺ used to seat Hadhrat Ibn Abbaas ﷺ with honour amongst the most knowledgeable Ulama of his time. This is all due to his hard work in acquiring knowledge. He could not have reached this position if he had thought himself to be part of Nabi's ﷺ family and demanded respect from the people instead of going to them for knowledge.

Nabi ﷺ has said: "Be most humble and respectful to those from whom you receive knowledge."

Mujaahid *(rahmatullahi alayh)* says: "A proud or shy student cannot gain much."

Hadhrat Ali رضى الله عنه says: "I am a slave to the person who has taught me even a single word. He may sell me or set me free."

Hadhrat Yahya bin Kaseer *(rahmatullahi alayh)* says: "Knowledge and easy living cannot go together."

Hadhrat Imaam Shaafi *(rahmatullahi alayh)* says: "A student who learns half-heartedly and ungratefully can never succeed. A student who is humble and hard-living often reaches his goal."

Mughirah *(rahmatullahi alayh)* says: "We feared our teacher Hadhrat Ibrahim *(rahmatullahi alayh)* more than even the kings of our times."

Hadhrat Imaam Bukhaari *(rahmatullahi alayh)* writes about Yahya bin Ma'een *(rahamatullahi alaih)*, the famous Muhaddith: "I have never seen a person more respectful to the Muhadditheen than Yahya."

Imaam Abu Yusuf *(rahmatullahi alayh)* says: "I have heard from famous people that a student who does not respect his teacher is never successful."

This story shows that Hadhrat Abdullah bin Abbaas رضى الله عنه was very humble and respectful to those from whom he learnt Islam. It also shows his thirst for knowledge. He did not mind any amount of effort or difficulty in going to those who had some knowledge of Hadith. In fact, nothing can be achieved without hardship.

As the Arabic saying goes:

$$\text{مَنْ طَلَبَ الْعُلٰى سَهِرَ اللَّيَالِيْ}$$

"A person who wishes for high positions must burn the midnight oil."
(Study till late at night)

It is said about Hadhrat Haaris bin Yazid, Hadhrat Ibn Shubrumah, Hadhrat Qa'qaa, and Hadhrat Mughirah *(rahmatullahi alaihim)* that they discussed Deeni matters amongst themselves after Isha and would continue till the Azaan of Fajr.

Hadhrat Lais bin Sa'eed *(rahmatullahi alayh)* says: "Imaam Zuhri *(rahmatullahi alayh)* sat after Isha Salaah with wudhu and continued his discussion on Hadith until it was time for Fajr Salaah."

Daraawardi *(rahamatullahi alaih)* says: "I saw Imaam Abu Hanifah *(rahmatullahi alayh)* and Imaam Maalik *(rahmatullahi alayh)* in Nabi's ﷺ Masjid after Isha, discussing a mas'ala very calmly without offending each other. They returned only after performing Fajr Salaah."

Ibn Furat Baghdadi *(rahmatullahi alayh)*, a Muhaddith, left eighteen boxes full of books when he passed away. Most of these books were written with his own hand. His book is famously known to be a source of reference among the Muhaddithin for its authenticity and systematic record.

Ibn Jauzi *(rahmatullahi alayh)* was another famous Muhaddith. He was brought up as an orphan, as he lost his father when he was only three. He was so studious that he would not leave his village except for Jumuah Salaah. He once mentioned from the mimbar, pointing to his fingers: "With these fingers I have written or copied 2000 books."

He himself was the author of more than 250 books. It is said that he never remained idle. He used to write four parts of a book daily. His lessons were so famous that as many as 100 000 students at a time listened to him. The kings, their ministers and chiefs would also sit for his lectures.

He himself says: "As many as 100 000 followers have taken bay'at to me and 20 000 kuffaar have accepted Islam at my hands."

He also suffered a lot at the hands of Shiahs, who were in power those days. He saved the shavings when sharpening his pen and at the time of his death, instructed that those shavings be used for warming the water for washing his dead body. It is said that the shavings were more than enough for warming the water and a part was still left unused.

Yahya bin Ma'een *(rahmatullahi alayh)* is a famous Shaikh of Hadith. He says: "I have written one million Ahaadith with my own hand."

Ibn Jarir Tabari *(rahmatullahi alayh)* is a famous historian. He is an expert on the history of the Sahaabah and Tabi'een. For forty years, he wrote forty pages daily. After his death, his output in written work (since his maturity) was calculated to come to fourteen pages daily. The book on history written by him is very famous. When he planned to write this book, he told the people around him: "You will be pleased to know that I intend writing a book on world history."

They asked: "How big will that book be?"

He replied: "About 30 000 pages."

They said: "Who will live to finish this book?"

He said: "*Innaa lillahi wa innaa ilaihi raaji-oon.* People do not have any hope."

He then decided to keep it short, which still came to 6000 pages. The same thing happened when he wrote a book on the meaning of the Qur-aan. This is also a very famous book.

Daaraqutni *(rahmatullahi alayh)* is a famous writer on Hadith. He travelled to Baghdad, Basra, Koofah, Waasit, Egypt and Syria for learning Hadith. Once, while sitting in the class of his teacher, he was seen copying from a certain book.

One of the other students scolded him saying: "How can you listen to the Shaikh while doing that work?"

He replied: "There is a difference in my listening and yours. Tell me how many Ahaadith has the Shaikh recited so far?"

The student began to think.

Daaraqutni *(rahmatullahi alayh)* said: "Now let me tell you. The Shaikh has so far recited eighteen Ahaadith and they are ......"

He then repeated all the eighteen Ahaadith that the Shaikh had recited in the same order, quoting the chain of narration in each case.

Haafiz Athram *(rahmatullahi alayh)* is a Muhaddith. He had an excellent memory for Ahaadith. Once, when he was in Makkah for Hajj, two famous Shaikhs from Khuraasaan were giving lectures on Hadith in the Haram separately and a large number of people were listening to each Shaikh. He sat between the two groups and wrote down the lectures of both the Shaikhs at one and the same time.

Abdullah bin Mubaarak *(rahmatullahi alayh)* is a famous Muhaddith. His efforts in collecting Ahaadith are well known to everybody. He says: "I have learnt Hadith from four thousand teachers."

Ali bin Hasan *(rahmatullahi alayh)* says: "It was a very cold night when Ibn Mubaarak and I stepped out from the Masjid after Isha Salaah.

Ch. 8 - Thirst for Knowledge

As we stepped out of the Masjid a discussion on a certain Hadith began. We remained standing there in discussion till the Fajr Azaan was heard."

Humaydi *(rahmatullahi alayh)* is a Muhaddith who has combined Bukhaari and Muslim Shareef in one book. He used to write throughout the night. When it was very hot, he would write while sitting in a tub of water. He also wrote poetry. The following lines have been written by him:

$$ لِقَآءُ النَّاسِ لَيْسَ يُفِيْدُ شَيْئًا \qquad سِوَى الْهَذَيَانِ مِنْ قِيْلٍ وَّقَالِ $$

$$ فَاَقْلِلْ مِنْ لِقَاءِ النَّاسِ اِلَّا \qquad لِاَخْذِ الْعِلْمِ اَوْ اِصْلَاحِ حَالٍ $$

Mixing with people does not benefit, except wasting time in gossip.

Don't go to the people, except for learning knowledge and piety.

Imaam Tabraani *(rahmatullahi alayh)* is a famous Muhaddith and writer of many books. Somebody asked: "How could you write so many books, Shaikh?" He replied: "I have been on my mat for thirty years."

Abul Abbaas Shirazi *(rahmatullahi alayh)* says: "I have learnt 300 000 Ahaadith from Tabraani."

Imaam Abu Hanifah *(rahmatullahi alayh)* worked very hard in explaining those Ahaadith which contradict one another. Koofah was the centre of Islamic learning in those days. He had collected Hadith from all the Muhadditheen of that place. Whenever a Muhaddith from outside came to Koofah, he sent his students to him to find out if he knew any Hadith that he had not yet learnt. The Imaam gathered a group of famous Ulama who were experts in Hadith, Fiqh and Philology (study of languages). They had discussions on masaail regarding Islamic practices. Sometimes the discussions continued for one month before a point was agreed upon, and written in the book of Fiqh for the people of his mazhab (school of thought).

Imaam Tirmizi *(rahmatullahi alayh)* is known to one and all. He was known for memorising Ahaadith. His memory was excellent. Some Muhadditheen once tested his memory. They read before him forty one Ahaadith. Imaam Tirmizi *(rahmatullahi alayh)* immediately repeated all of them.

He himself writes: "On my way to Makkah, I copied two parts from the collections of Hadith by a Shaikh. I happened to come across that Shaikh personally. I told him, 'I have copied two parts of your collections. I wish to compare those Ahaadith by listening to them directly from you.' The Shaikh agreed. While going to his place, I took a blank book by mistake instead of the notebook in which I had copied the Ahaadith. The Shaikh started reciting the Ahaadith, while I held the blank book in my hand. When he noticed it, he was very angry with me and said, "Don't you have any shame?!". I explained to him how that had happened, and said, 'Shaikh, your time is not wasted. I remember everything that you have said.' He did not believe me and asked me to repeat all that he had recited. I repeated all the Ahaadith. He thought that I had memorised them before I came to him. I said, 'You may recite some other Ahaadith.' He recited forty new Ahaadith. I repeated all of them without any error."

It is very difficult to work hard as much as these Muhadditheen did in collecting, memorising and teaching Hadith. It is difficult even to mention all their stories. Qartamah *(rahmatullahi alayh)* is a Muhaddith who is not very famous. One of his students, Dawood, says: "People speak about the memory of Abu Haatim *(rahmatullahi alayh)*. I have never seen a person with a better memory than Qartamah. Once he told me, 'Pick any of the books from my library. I shall recite it from my memory.' I picked up 'Kitabul-Ashribah.' He recited the whole book in the reverse order i.e. reading from the end to the beginning of each chapter."

Abu Zur'ah *(rahmatullahi alayh)* says: "Imaam Ahmad bin Hambal *(rahmatullahi alayh)* remembered one million Ahaadith by heart. Ishaaq bin Raahwaih *(rahmatullahi alayh)* says: I have collected 100 000 Ahaadith and I know 30 000 of them by heart."

Khaffaaf *(rahmatullahi alayh)* says: "Ishaaq *(rahmatullahi alayh)* once read out to us 11 000 Ahaadith from his memory. He then repeated all of them in the same order, without any mistake."

Abu Sa'd Isbahaani, *(rahmatullahi alayh)* was only sixteen when he left from Baghdad to learn Hadith from Abu Nasr *(rahmatullahi alayh)*. He heard about Abu Nasr's *(rahmatullahi alayh)* death on the way. He cried bitterly like a child and would say: "Were will I get his sanad (chain of narration) from?" Such crying is not possible without love and devotion. He knew the kitaab "Muslim Shareef" by heart and taught the book to his pupils from memory. He performed Haj eleven times. When he sat for meals, his eyes used to fill up with tears.

Abu Umar Dharir *(rahmatullahi alayh)*, who was blind from birth, is from the Huffaaz of Hadith. He was an expert in History, Fiqh, Law of inheritance and Mathematics.

Abul Husain Isfahaani *(rahmatullahi alayh)* remembered both the Bukhaari and Muslim Shareef kitaabs by heart. Bukhaari Shareef was so deeply fixed in his memory that he would give the chain of narrators for any text or vice versa.

Shaikh Taqiud-Deen Ba'albakki *(rahmatullahi alayh)* memorised the 'Muslim Shareef' in four months. He was also a Haafiz of Ahaadith which were common in Muslim and Bukhaari's kitaabs. He was a saint and many miracles were performed by him. He had also memorised the Qur-aan Shareef. It is said that Surah Al-An'aam was memorised by him in one day.

Ibnus-Sunni *(rahmatullahi alayh)* is a famous student of Imaam Nasaai *(rahmatullahi alayh)*. He wrote Ahaadith even up to the last moments of his life. His son says: "While my father was writing Hadith, he put aside the pen, lifted his hands in dua and breathed his last."

Allamah Saaji *(rahmatullahi alayh)* mastered Fiqh (Islamic laws) in his teens. Then he began to learn Hadith. He stayed in Herat for ten years and wrote by hand the whole of Tirmizi Shareef six times during that stay. His teacher Ibn Mandah *(rahmatullahi alayh)* passed away while teaching him 'Gharaib Shu'bah' after Isha. It was the yearning of students and teachers to remain engaged in learning and teaching till their death.

Abu-Umar Khaffaaf *(rahmatullahi alayh)* remembered 100 000 Ahaadith by heart. More than 100 000 people sat for the lectures of Aasim bin Ali *(rahmatullahi alayh)*, the teacher of Imaam Bukhaari *(rahmatullahi alayh)*, when he was in Baghdad. One day, during his lecture, the audience was estimated to be 120 000. The words spoken by him were relayed (repeated) many times, before these could be heard by all the people. Once he said something which had to be relayed fourteen times.

After reaching Baghdad, Abu Muslim Basri *(rahmatullahi alayh)* took his class to a big ground. Seven men were relaying (repeating) his lecture and 40 000 ink-pots, for taking down his lecture, were counted.

There were many more people who only listened without writing. In the lectures by Faryabi *(rahmatullahi alayh)*, there used to be 316 people who would repeat his words to allow all the people to write these down. It was this sacrifice and love which has protected the knowledge of Hadith till today.

Imaam Bukhaari *(rahmatullahi alayh)* says: "I wrote down 7 275 Ahaadith after choosing from 600 000 Ahaadith. I have been reading a Salaah of two rakaats before writing each Hadith."

When Imaam Bukhaari *(rahmatullahi alayh)* came to Baghdad, the Muhadditheen tested his knowledge. Ten people were chosen for the test. Each of these people chose ten Ahaadith of his choice and after making some changes in the wording, read each Hadith before Imaam Bukhaari *(rahmatullahi alayh)*. After each Hadith, he would say: "I do not know this Hadith."

When all had finished, he spoke to each man saying: "Brother, the first Hadith you read was this (repeating the Hadith word for word), but actually it is like this (saying the correct Hadith) and so on." He repeated all 100 Ahaadith first in the wrong way in which those men had read, and again in the correct way in that very order.

Imaam Muslim *(rahmatullahi alayh)* started learning Hadith when he was fourteen, and remained busy in its pursuit till his death. He says: "I have gathered my book of 12 000 Ahaadith after choosing from 300 000 Ahaadith."

Abu Dawood *(rahmatullahi alayh)* says: "I had collected 500 000 Ahaadith, but I chose only 4 800 for my book."

Yusuf Muzi *(rahmatullahi alayh)* is a famous Muhaddith. He is an Imaam in Asmaa-ur-Rijaal (information about the chain of narrators of Hadith). After learning Fiqh and Hadith from the teachers in his own town, he went to Makkah, Madinah, Halab, Hamat, Ba'albak,etc, for more knowledge. He is the writer of many books. 'Tahzib-ul-Kamal' is in 200 volumes and 'Kitaab-ul-Atraaf' has more than 80 volumes. He often kept quiet and spoke very little and most of the time he was busy in reading or writing. He suffered at the hands of his enemies, who were jealous of him, but he never took revenge.

It is really very difficult to cover all the stories of other famous people about all their efforts in attaining knowledge. The details of their hard work cannot be covered even in several volumes. The very few examples mentioned above is only meant to give a small idea of the pains that our elders in Islam have taken for the preservation and development of the knowledge of Hadith, thus leaving it for us in such a complete form.

Let those people who claim to seek knowledge see for themselves what sacrifices they are really making. It is useless to hope that the knowledge about Nabi ﷺ, which has reached us, will be spread and brought into practice while we remain busy in our luxuries, comforts, pleasures and other worldly activities.

CHAPTER 9

PLEASING NABI ﷺ

As we have already seen from the stories in previous chapters, that obedience to Allah Ta'ala and His Nabi ﷺ was the guiding factor in the lives of Sahaabah رضي الله عنهم. Stories given exclusively in this chapter are to enable us to examine our way of living and see how far we are prepared to please Allah Ta'ala and His Nabi ﷺ. We often desire the help and blessings of Allah Ta'ala which the Sahaabah رضي الله عنهم received. If we desire similar results, then we shall have to live the way they had lived.

1. HADHRAT ABDULLAH BIN AMR رضي الله عنه BURNS HIS SHEET

Hadhrat Abdullah bin Amr ibnul Aas رضي الله عنه says: "Once we were with Nabi ﷺ on a journey. When I went to see him, I was wearing a light red sheet. He asked me, 'What is this that you are wearing?' I felt that he did not like my red clothes. When I reached home, I found a fire burning in the fireplace. I threw my sheet into the fire. The next day when I went to Nabi ﷺ, he asked, 'Where is that sheet?' I told him what I had done to it. He said, 'You could have given it to one of the ladies in your house. Women are allowed to wear clothes of that colour.'"

Note: In fact, Hadhrat Abdullah رضي الله عنه was so worried when Nabi ﷺ became unhappy, that he did not waste any time and

Ch. 9 - Pleasing Nabi ﷺ

destroyed the sheet. He did not even think of using it in another way. If we had been in his place, we would have thought of many excuses for keeping it, or at least we would have found some other use for it.

2. AN ANSAARI SAHAABI ؓ DEMOLISHES HIS BUILDING

Nabi ﷺ once passed through a street of Madinah Munawwarah and saw a high building with a dome. He asked the Sahaabah ؓ, "What is this?" They told him that it was a new building built by one of the Ansaari Sahaabah ؓ. Nabi ﷺ remained silent.

Once, the Sahaabi ؓ who had built that house had come to Nabi ﷺ and greeted him with *'Assalamu Alaikum.'* Nabi ﷺ turned his face away from him and did not give a reply. Thinking that Nabi ﷺ may not have heard, he repeated the salaam, but Nabi ﷺ again turned his face away. He was very shocked to notice Nabi ﷺ angry with him. How could he withstand this displeasure?. He asked the Sahaabah ؓ who were there, what the reason was. He was told that Nabi ﷺ had asked about his new building. He immediately went and demolished the new building and did not even tell Nabi ﷺ what he had done.

When Nabi ﷺ passed that way again, He asked: "Where is that building with a dome that I saw at this spot before?" The Sahaabah ؓ told him that the Sahaabi ؓ broke it down because Nabi ﷺ was not happy with it.

Nabi ﷺ said: "Every new building is a sinful burden, except that which is necessary."

Note: These are lessons of intense love and devotion. The Sahaabah ؓ could not see Nabi ﷺ being unhappy. As soon as they saw that he was unhappy with something, then at all costs, they immediately removed that which caused his displeasure.

That Sahaabi ؓ did not even tell Nabi ﷺ that he had demolished the building, as perhaps it may be seen as boasting. Nabi ﷺ himself noticed it later on. Nabi ﷺ did not like people wasting their money on buildings. His own house was built with date trees, with mats being used as walls for privacy.

Once, when he was not in Madinah Munawwarah, his wife Ummu Salamah رَضِيَ اللَّهُ عَنْهَا, who received some money, built walls of unbaked bricks for her house. When Nabi صَلَّى اللَّهُ عَلَيْهِ وَسَلَّمَ returned from his journey, he asked her: "Why did you do this?" She replied: "O, Nabi of Allah. This is only to have better privacy." Nabi صَلَّى اللَّهُ عَلَيْهِ وَسَلَّمَ said, "The worst use of money is to spend it on buildings."

Hadhrat Abdullah bin Amr رَضِيَ اللَّهُ عَنْهُ says: "My mother and I were once repairing a wall of our house. Nabi صَلَّى اللَّهُ عَلَيْهِ وَسَلَّمَ saw us working and said, 'Your own death is nearer than the falling of this wall.'"

3. SAHAABAH'S رَضِيَ اللَّهُ عَنْهُمْ THROWING AWAY RED SHEETS OF SADDLE CLOTH

Raafi' رَضِيَ اللَّهُ عَنْهُ says: "We were once with Nabi صَلَّى اللَّهُ عَلَيْهِ وَسَلَّمَ on a journey. The sheets that we had spread on our camels were decorated with red cotton. Nabi صَلَّى اللَّهُ عَلَيْهِ وَسَلَّمَ said, 'I notice that the colour red is beginning to attract you.' We stood up and ran around in confusion because of this scolding so much so that our camels also began to run about. We immediately removed the sheets from their backs."

Note: We are surprised on hearing such stories about Sahaabah رَضِيَ اللَّهُ عَنْهُمْ, as we live in a different time with quite a different way of thinking. When the treaty of Hudaybiyyah was being discussed, Urwah bin Mas'ood رَضِيَ اللَّهُ عَنْهُ, who was a messenger of the Quraish, had a chance of carefully studying the behaviour of the Sahaabah رَضِيَ اللَّهُ عَنْهُمْ.

When he returned to his people, he told them: "I have met many great kings and rulers. I have met the Emperors of Persia, Rome and Abyssinia. Nowhere have I seen people showing respect to their ruler as the Sahaabah رَضِيَ اللَّهُ عَنْهُمْ showed respect to Nabi Muhammad صَلَّى اللَّهُ عَلَيْهِ وَسَلَّمَ. When he spits, his saliva is not allowed to fall on the ground. It is taken by somebody in his hands to wipe his face and body with it. When he gives an order, every person rushes to carry it out. When he makes wudhu, the Sahaabah رَضِيَ اللَّهُ عَنْهُمْ compete with one another to grab the water falling down from his limbs so much so that someone will think that they are going to fight over that water. When he speaks, everybody is silent. Nobody lifts his eyes to look at him, out of respect for him."

4. HADHRAT WAAIL رَضِىَ اللّٰهُ عَنْهُ HAS HIS HAIR CUT

Waail ibn Hujar رَضِىَ اللّٰهُ عَنْهُ says: "I once visited Nabi ﷺ when the hair on my head was long. While I was sitting with him, he said, 'Zubaab, Zubaab' (Meaning something evil or bad). I thought that he was unhappy with my hair. I returned home and had my hair cut. The next day when I again went to him, he said, 'I was not talking about your hair yesterday. However, it is good that you had your hair cut.'"

Note: This shows the obedience of those people. They did not delay in acting upon the wishes of Nabi ﷺ. They acted on the slightest remark or indication of Nabi ﷺ, irrespective of whether their conclusion proved to be correct or not. They never thought it necessary to further enquire or clarify.

In the early years, talking in Salaah was allowed. Once, Hadhrat Abdullah bin Mas'ood رَضِىَ اللّٰهُ عَنْهُ visited Nabi ﷺ while he was performing his Salaah. As per his normal practise, he greeted him with "*Assalaamu Alaykum*" but received no reply, because to talk in Salaah had now been forbidden. He says, "After receiving no reply, all sorts of thoughts began to trouble my mind. I thought perhaps he is displeased with me, or he is angry with me, for something that I may have done. At last when Nabi ﷺ finished his Salaah and told me that Allah Ta'ala had forbidden talking in Salaah, I knew that he was not upset with me and I heaved a sigh of relief."

5. HADHRAT SUHAIL رَضِىَ اللّٰهُ عَنْهُ AND HADHRAT KHURAYM رَضِىَ اللّٰهُ عَنْهُ GIVE UP WHAT IS NOT LIKED BY NABI ﷺ

One Sahaabi Suhail bin Hanzalah رَضِىَ اللّٰهُ عَنْهُ, lived a reserved life in Damascus. He did not mix much with people, or go anywhere. He was either busy in Salaah or in zikr throughout the day. While going to the Masjid, he would pass by Hadhrat Abu Darda رَضِىَ اللّٰهُ عَنْهُ, who was one of the famous Sahaabah رَضِىَ اللّٰهُ عَنْهُمْ.

Hadhrat Abu Darda ؓ would tell him: "O, Suhail! Let us hear some good words from you. We shall learn a lot and you will lose nothing." Suhail ؓ would then say something that he had heard from Nabi ﷺ, or that he had seen in his lifetime.

One day as he was passing, Hadhrat Abu Darda ؓ made his usual request. Hadhrat Suhail ؓ said: "Once Nabi ﷺ spoke about Hadhrat Khuraym Asadi ؓ and said, 'He is a good man except for two habits, he keeps the hair of his head too long and he allows his 'Izaar' (trouser) to flow below his ankles.' When Khuraym ؓ learnt about this, he immediately cut his hair up to his ears and began to keep his 'Izaar' up to the middle of the calf of his leg."

Note: It is mentioned in some narrations that Rasulullah ﷺ had mentioned both these aspects to him and he took a qasam that he will not do this in the future. There is no contradiction between these two narrations. It could be that Rasulullah ﷺ said it to him directly and in his absence and thereafter someone else mentioned it to him.

6. HADHRAT IBN-UMAR ؓ STOPS SPEAKING TO HIS SON

Abdullah-bin-'Umar ؓ said: "I have heard Nabi ﷺ saying, 'Allow your women to go to the Masjid.'"

One of his sons said: "We cannot allow our women to go to the Masjid, as this can cause problems later on."

Ibn 'Umar ؓ became very angry and scolded his son, saying: "When I tell you that Nabi ﷺ has allowed our women to go to the Masjid, how dare you say that you cannot allow them?" He then refused to speak to him throughout his life.

Note: Ibn-Umar's ؓ son clearly had no intention of disobeying Nabi ﷺ. He feared many problems in allowing the women of that time to go to the Masjid and this was according to the social conditions of his era.

For the same reason, Hadhrat Aa'ishah ؓ said: "If Nabi ﷺ had seen the women of our time, he would have stopped them from going to the Masjid."

Hadhrat Aa'ishah ﷺ said this not very long after the death of Nabi ﷺ. Still, Ibn-Umar ﷺ could not allow his son to refuse something which Nabi ﷺ had allowed and he stopped talking to him for the rest of his life. Other Sahaabah ﷺ also faced the problem regarding women visiting the Masjid. On the one hand, there was the wish of Nabi ﷺ allowing them to go to the Masjid, and on the other hand there was the possibility of looseness in society (the signs of which were beginning) that demanded stopping them from going to the Masjid.

A'atikah ﷺ, the wife of Hadhrat 'Umar ﷺ, went to the Masjid regularly but Hadhrat 'Umar ﷺ did not like it. Somebody told her that Hadhrat 'Umar ﷺ did not like her going to the Masjid. She said: "Why does he not stop me from going to Masjid?"

After the death of Hadhrat 'Umar ﷺ, A'atikah ﷺ was married to Hadhrat Zubair ﷺ. He also did not like her going to the Masjid, but could not stop her for the above reason. Once he sat in her way to the Masjid and, as she passed by him, he teased her. In the dark, she could not make out who it was. After this incident, she stopped going to the Masjid. On a later occasion, Hadhrat Zubair ﷺ asked her: "Why don't you go to the Masjid now?" She replied: "Times have changed."

7. HADHRAT IBN 'UMAR ﷺ ANSWERS A QUESTION

Somebody told Ibn 'Umar ﷺ: "Allah Ta'ala has said something in the Qur-aan about Salaah in peace and Salaah in fear, but He has not said anything about Salaah during a journey."

He replied: "O, my nephew! When we knew nothing, Allah Ta'ala sent Nabi Muhammad ﷺ as his Nabi to us. We must do what we have seen him doing."

Note: This shows that it is not necessary that each and every rule should be clearly mentioned in the Qur-aan. The actions of Nabi ﷺ are sufficient for us to practice on.

Nabi ﷺ says: "I have been given the Qur-aan and also other commands. Beware of the time which is coming shortly, when carefree people sitting on their couches will say, 'Stick to the Qur-aan only. Carry out only the commands contained in it.'"

This carefree attitude often afflicts those people who are intoxicated by their wealth.

8. HADHRAT IBN MUGHAFFAL رضي الله عنه STOPS SPEAKING TO HIS NEPHEW

A young nephew of Abdullah-bin-Mughaffal رضي الله عنه was playing 'Khazaf' (A game played with stones). He told him: "O, Nephew! Stop doing that. Nabi ﷺ has said that it has no benefit. It cannot shoot a bird nor harm an enemy. But somebody's eye or tooth can be injured accidently."

The boy stopped playing. As he was still small, after some time when he thought that his uncle was not watching him, he started again.

Ibn Mughaffal رضي الله عنه saw him playing. He got very angry and said: "How dare you do a thing after knowing what Nabi ﷺ has said? By Allah! I will never speak to you again." In another narration it is mentioned that he said further, "I will never visit you when you are sick, nor join your funeral if you die during my lifetime."

Note: 'Khazaf' is a game in which a pebble is placed on the thumb and then thrown with the force of the other fingers. Children are fond of playing such games. This game is such that one cannot hunt with it but somebody's eye can be injured accidently. Ibn Mughaffal رضي الله عنه could not allow his nephew ignoring the words of Nabi ﷺ. Don't we know the instructions of Nabi ﷺ about many things which we are in a habit of doing from morning till evening? How worried are we about his commands? Let everybody think about it himself and answer.

9. HADHRAT HAKEEM BIN HIZAAM رضي الله عنه GIVES UP BEGGING

Hadhrat Hakeem bin Hizaam رضي الله عنه came to Nabi ﷺ and asked for something. Nabi ﷺ gave him something. He again came for the second time and asked for something. Nabi ﷺ gave him something this time also. When he came to ask for the third time, after giving him something, Nabi ﷺ said: "Hakeem! Money will mislead you. It appears to be very sweet (but it is really not so). It is a blessing when earned with satisfaction of the heart (by working), but there is no barakah in it when it is acquired with greed." It is like a sickness where one eats but does not get filled.

Hakeem said: "O, Nabi of Allah, I will not bother anybody after this." Hadhrat Abu Bakr رضى الله عنه, in the time of his Khilaafat, wanted to help Hakeem رضى الله عنه from the Baitul Maal, but he refused. Again Hadhrat 'Umar رضى الله عنه as Ameer-ul-Mu'mineen asked Hakeem many times to accept something from him, but he did not agree.

Note: It is because of our greed that we find no barakah in what we earn.

10. HADHRAT HUZAYFAH رضى الله عنه IS SENT TO SPY ON THE ENEMY

Hadhrat Huzayfah رضى الله عنه says: "In the Battle of Khandaq, we faced a very big army of the enemy, including the kuffaar from Makkah Mukarramah and other groups. At the same time, the Jews of Banu Quraizah in Madinah Munawwarah were about to break their promise, and we feared that they will destroy our houses and families, because we were outside defending Madinah Munawwarah against the enemies. The Munaafiqeen started asking permission from Nabi ﷺ to go back to Madinah Munawwarah, giving the excuse of their homes not being guarded. He allowed every one of them.

One night, during those difficult days, such a storm came the like of which wasn't seen before or since then. It was so dark that one could not see one's own hand, and the wind was blowing wildly. The Munaafiqeen were returning to their homes. 300 of us stuck to our positions. Nabi ﷺ approached everyone and asked about him. I had neither weapons to defend myself, nor any clothes to keep me warm. I had only one small sheet, which I had borrowed from my wife. I wrapped it around my waist and sat with my knees on the ground. When Nabi ﷺ passed by me, he said, 'Who are you?' I said, 'Huzayfah!' I could not stand up because of the severe cold and I held onto the ground more tightly with shame.

He said, 'Huzayfah, stand up and go to the enemy camp and bring us some news about them.' Of all the Sahaabah رَضِيَ اللهُ عَنْهُم, I was the most ill equipped, both against the enemy and against the cold that night, but as soon as I got the order, I stood up and left for the enemy camp. As I left, Nabi ﷺ made dua for me saying,

اَللّٰهُمَّ احْفَظْهُ مِنْ بَيْنِ يَدَيْهِ وَمِنْ خَلْفِهِ وَعَنْ يَمِيْنِهِ وَعَنْ شِمَالِهِ وَمِنْ فَوْقِهِ وَمِنْ تَحْتِهِ

'O Allah! Protect him from the front, from the back, from the right, from the left, from above and from below.'

Immediately after his dua, I was completely relieved of my fear and cold. I felt as if I was walking in a warm and peaceful place. Nabi ﷺ warned me, 'Return immediately after seeing what they are doing. Do not do anything else.'

When I reached the enemy camp, I found a fire burning with people sitting around it. Each person warmed his hands before the fire and then rubbed them over his body. The shouts of "Go Back" were heard from all directions. Everyone was shouting to the people of his tribe to pack up and return. The wind was causing the stones to fly and strike against their tents. The ropes of the tents were breaking and the animals were dying.

I found Abu Sufyaan, the leader of the enemy forces, sitting near the fire warming himself. I thought of killing him. I had actually taken out an arrow from my quiver and placed it in my bow, when I remembered the order of Nabi ﷺ. I put the arrow back into the quiver. Whilst I was amongst them, they seemed to become aware of my presence. They shouted, 'There is a spy amongst us. Each one of us should catch the hand of the person next to him.' I immediately caught the hand of a person and shouted, 'Who are you?' He said, '*Subhaanallah!* You don't know me. I am so and so.'

I then returned to my camp. While I was on my way back, I met twenty horsemen with turbans on their heads (these were angels). They said to me, 'Tell your master that Allah Ta'ala has taken care of his enemy and that he has nothing to worry about now.' When I reached my camp, I found Nabi ﷺ performing Salaah with a small shawl around him.

Ch. 9 - Pleasing Nabi ﷺ

Whenever he was in any problem, he immediately began reading Salaah. When he had finished, I told him what I had seen in the enemy camp. When I told him how I escaped their 'search for the spy', I could see his beautiful teeth shining. He then asked me to lie down near his feet and put a corner of his shawl over my body. I lay down and pressed my chest against the soles of his feet."

Note: Look at their desire to carry out the orders of Nabi ﷺ in all conditions. May Allah Ta'ala favour us with the same type of obedience, even though we do not deserve it. *Aameen*!

CHAPTER 10
WOMEN'S COURAGE & LOVE FOR ISLAM

The lap of the mother is known to be the best madrasah. The reality is that if women have the love for Deen and good actions then its effect will also naturally be found in their children. In these times, our children are brought up in an un-Islamic environment that either pulls them away from Islam or at the least they are not bothered about their duties towards Allah Ta'ala. When the early years are spent in this way, the consequences that follow are obvious.

1. HADHRAT FAATIMAH'S رضى الله عنها TASBEEH

Hadhrat Ali رضى الله عنه once told one of his pupils: "Shall I tell you the story of Hadhrat Faatimah رضى الله عنها, the dearest and the most beloved daughter of Nabi صلى الله عليه وسلم?"

When the pupil replied "Yes", he said: "Hadhrat Faatimah رضى الله عنها used to grind the grain herself, which caused sores on her hands. She carried water for the house in a leather bag, which left a mark on her chest. She cleaned the house herself, which made her clothes dirty. Once, when some prisoners of war were brought to Madinah Munawwarah, I told her, 'Go to Nabi صلى الله عليه وسلم and ask him for a servant to help you in your house-work.' She went to him but found many people around him. As she was very shy, she did not have the courage to ask Nabi صلى الله عليه وسلم in front of other people.

The next day Nabi ﷺ came to our house and said, 'Faatimah! What made you come to me yesterday?' She felt shy and kept quiet. I said, 'O, Nabi of Allah! Faatimah has sores on both her hands and marks on her chest because of grinding grain and carrying water. She is always busy in cleaning the house causing her clothes to remain dirty. I told her about the prisoners of war and told her to go and ask you for a servant.'"

It has also been reported that Hadhrat Faatimah رضى الله عنها herself made a request; "'Ali and I own only one bedding, which is a goatskin. We use it at night to sleep on and during the day to put the feed of the camel.' Nabi ﷺ said, 'Faatimah! Be patient. Nabi Musa عليه السلام and his wife owned only one bedding for ten years, which was also the cloak of Musa عليه السلام. Acquire the fear Allah Ta'ala and keep on fulfilling the commands of Allah Ta'ala and do all your own housework. Before going to bed read:-

1. **Subhanallah 33 times,**
2. **Al-hamdulillah 33 times,**
3. **And Allahu Akbar 34 times.**

You will find this better than a servant.' Hadhrat Faatimah رضى الله عنها replied, 'I am happy with what Allah Ta'ala and His Nabi ﷺ would be pleased with.'"

Note: Look! This is the life of the dear daughter of the King of both the worlds. Nowadays, even when a little wealth enters a family, the ladies think that it is below their dignity to do the housework. Let alone the housework, they even want help with their own work - even in their bathrooms!

In this Hadith, the above zikr should be read before sleeping. In other Ahaadith, Nabi ﷺ advised Hadhrat Faatimah رضى الله عنها to read after every Salaah,

1. **Subhanallah 33 times,**
2. **Al-hamdulillah 33 times,**
3. **Akbar 33 times**
4. **and one time, the following:-**

لَااِلٰهَ اِلَّا اللّٰهُ وَحْدَهُ لَا شَرِيْكَ لَهُ لَهُ الْمُلْكُ وَلَهُ الْحَمْدُ وَهُوَ عَلٰى كُلِّ شَيْءٍ قَدِيْرٌ

Lailaha illallaho wahdahu lasharikalahu lahulmulku walahulhamdu wahuwa ala kulli shayin Qadir

2. HADHRAT AA'ISHAH'S ﷺ SPENDING IN THE PATH OF ALLAH TA'ALA

Once, Hadhrat Aa'ishah ﷺ received a gift of more than one hundred thousand (100000) Dirhams. She started distributing it to the poor, till not a single Dirham was left with her by the evening. She was fasting that day. Her maid servant brought her a loaf of bread and a little olive oil for Iftaar, and said "I wish we had kept one Dirham for ourselves to get some meat for Iftaar."

Hadhrat Aa'ishah ﷺ said; "What's the use of complaining now. If you had told me at that time, I would have bought some meat."

Note: Gifts were often received by Hadhrat Aa'ishah ﷺ from Hadhrat Mu'aawiyah ﷺ, Hadhrat Abdullah bin Zubair ﷺ and others, as that was the time of ease and wealth for the Muslims as country after country came into their control. In spite of all this wealth, Hadhrat Aa'ishah ﷺ led a life of poverty. Look! She gives 100 000 Dirhams to the poor, but she does not remember to get some meat for her own Iftaar.

Today, such stories seem to be impossible but to the people who had understood the Sahaabah ﷺ, hundreds of such stories are quite possible. There are many stories like this about Hadhrat Aa'ishah ﷺ.

Once she was fasting and had nothing for her Iftaar except one piece of bread. A poor man came and begged for some food. She asked her maid to give him that piece of bread. The maid said: "If I give him the piece of bread, there will be nothing left for your Iftaar." She said: "Never mind. Let him have the piece."

Once she killed a snake. She saw someone in her dream, saying: "Aa'ishah ﷺ, you killed a Muslim." She replied: "How could a Muslim come into the house of Nabi's ﷺ widow?" The person replied: "But he had come in purdah (disguise)." She immediately got up

Ch. 10 – Women's Courage & Love for Islam

from her sleep and at once spent twelve thousand (12 000) Dirhams in Sadaqah, which was the blood-money (compensation) fixed for a Muslim killed by mistake.

Hadhrat Urwah رضي الله عنه says: "I once saw Hadhrat Aa'ishah رضي الله عنها spending seventy thousand (70 000) Dirhams in charity, while she herself, was wearing a dress with patches."

3. HADHRAT AA'ISHAH رضي الله عنها GETS ANGRY WITH HADHRAT IBN ZUBAIR رضي الله عنه

Hadhrat Abdullah bin Zubair رضي الله عنه was Hadhrat Aa'ishah's رضي الله عنها sister's son (nephew). He was very dear to her, as she had brought him up. He did not like her spending so much in charity, while she herself lived in difficulty and poverty. He mentioned this to somebody and said: "My aunt must be stop from doing that."

She heard about this and was so unhappy that she took an oath not speak to Hadhrat Abdullah رضي الله عنه for the rest of her life. Hadhrat Abdullah bin Zubair رضي الله عنه was very upset by her oath. He sent many people to speak to her for him, but she told them, "I have taken an oath and I am not ready to break it."

When Hadhrat Abdullah bin Zubair رضي الله عنه was extremely worried, he at last, took two people from the family of Nabi's ﷺ mother to her house to plead for him. Hadhrat Aa'ishah رضي الله عنها allowed them to enter the house and to speak to her from behind a curtain. Ibn Zubair رضي الله عنه also quietly got in with them. When they started talking, he crossed the curtain and hugged his aunt, crying and begging her for forgiveness. The two people also begged and reminded her of Nabi's ﷺ stopping a Muslim from refusing to speak with another Muslim. When she heard this Hadith, she could not control herself and began to cry very bitterly. She forgave Hadhrat Abdullah bin Zubair رضي الله عنه and began to speak with him. She then began freeing slave after slave because of her breaking her oath, until forty slaves had been set free by her. Even later on, whenever she thought of the breaking of her oath, she cried so much that her shawl would become wet with her tears.

Note: How much do we worry about the oaths we take from morning till evening? It is for everyone to check his own self and answer. Come and see the people who had real respect for Allah Ta'ala and understood the importance of fulfilling vows. How deeply did they feel when they were unable to fulfil an oath? That is why we see Hadhrat Aa'ishah رضى الله عنها crying so much whenever she remembered that incident about the breaking of her oath.

4. HADHRAT AA'ISHAH رضى الله عنها AND THE FEAR OF ALLAH TA'ALA

Who does not know about the love that Nabi ﷺ had for his dear wife Hadhrat Aa'ishah رضى الله عنها? It is said that when he was asked whom he loved the most, he replied, "Aa'ishah." She was so learned in Fiqh (Islamic laws) that many famous Sahaabah رضى الله عنهم would go to her to find out Islamic laws. Hadhrat Jibraa-eel عليه السلام used to greet her with 'Assalamu Alaikum.' Nabi ﷺ told her that she would be his wife in Jannah.

When she was falsely accused by the Munaafiqeen (Hypocrites), Allah Ta'ala cleared her name and declared her innocence in the Qur-aan. Hadhrat Aa'ishah رضى الله عنها once counted ten special qualities that Allah Ta'ala had given her over the other wives of Nabi ﷺ. They have been mentioned in detail by Hadhrat Ibn Sa'd رحمه الله, Her spending in the path of Allah Ta'ala has already been narrated in the earlier stories.

In spite of all these virtues, she feared Allah Ta'ala so much that she was often heard saying;

"I wish I was a tree, so that I could be always busy with Allah's tasbih and be saved from answering on the Day of Qiyaamah."

"I wish I had been a stone or a piece of earth."

"I wish I had been a leaf on a tree or a blade of grass."

"I wish I had not been born at all."

Note: The stories about the fear of Allah Ta'ala which the Sahaabah رضى الله عنهم had in their hearts, has already been given in Chapter two. This was the guiding factor of their lives.

5. THE STORY OF HADHRAT UMM-E-SALAMAH ﺭﺿﻲ ﺍﻟﻠﻪ ﻋﻨﻬﺎ

Ummul-Mu'mineen, Hadhrat Ummu Salamah ﺭﺿﻲ ﺍﻟﻠﻪ ﻋﻨﻬﺎ was first married to Abu Salamah ﺭﺿﻲ ﺍﻟﻠﻪ ﻋﻨﻪ. The husband and wife were very close to each other. Once Ummu Salamah ﺭﺿﻲ ﺍﻟﻠﻪ ﻋﻨﻬﺎ told her husband: "I have heard that if a husband does not marry another woman during the life or after the death of his wife, and also if the wife does not remarry after the death of her husband, when entered into Jannah, the couple is allowed to live there as husband and wife. Give me your word that you will not marry after my death, and I too promise that I will not marry again if you pass away before me."

Hadhrat Abu Salamah ﺭﺿﻲ ﺍﻟﻠﻪ ﻋﻨﻪ said: "Will you do as I say?"

She replied: "That is why I am asking you so that I can obey you."

He said: "I want you to take a husband after my death." He then made dua, saying, "O, Allah! After my death let Ummu Salamah be married to a husband better than me. May he not give her any trouble at all."

In the beginning, the couple emigrated to Abyssinia. After their return, they then again emigrated to Madinah Munawwarah.

Hadhrat Ummu Salamah ﺭﺿﻲ ﺍﻟﻠﻪ ﻋﻨﻬﺎ says: "When my husband made up his mind to emigrate to Madinah Munawwarah, he loaded the camel with the luggage. He then made sure that I should ride the camel with our son Salamah. He led the camel out of the town, holding the string in his hand. The people of my father's family (Banu Mughirah) saw us leaving. They came and grabbed the string from Hadhrat Abu Salamah's ﺭﺿﻲ ﺍﻟﻠﻪ ﻋﻨﻪ hand saying, 'You can go wherever you like but we cannot allow our girl to go and travel from place to place.' Then by force they took my son and me back to their family. When the people of my husband's family, Banu Abdul As'ad, learnt this, they came to Banu Mughirah and began to fight with them saying, 'You can keep your girl if you like, but you have no right over the child who belongs to our family. Why should we allow him to stay in your family, when you have not allowed your girl to go with her husband?' They forcefully took the boy away. Hadhrat Abu Salamah ﺭﺿﻲ ﺍﻟﻠﻪ ﻋﻨﻪ had already gone to Madinah Munawwarah.

All the members of my family were now separated from one another. I would go out to the desert daily and cry there from morning till night. I lived in this condition for one full year, separated from my husband and my son. One day, one of my cousins, taking pity on me, told the people of the family, 'You have separated this poor woman from her husband and son. Why don't you have mercy on her and let her go?' Due to the caring efforts of this cousin of mine, the people of Banu Mughirah agreed to let me go and join my husband. Banu Abdul As'ad also gave me back my son. I got a camel ready and with my son in my lap, I sat on its back and left for Madinah Munawwarah all alone.

I had only gone four miles, when Hadhrat Usmaan bin Talhah رضي الله عنه met me at Tan'eem. He asked me, 'Where are you going?' I replied, 'To my husband in Madinah Munawwarah.' He said, 'Are you going alone?' I said, 'Yes, nobody besides Allah Ta'ala is with me.' He took the rope of my camel and began to lead. By Allah, I had never come across a person more righteous than Hadhrat Usmaan رضي الله عنه. When I had to get down, he would make the camel sit and himself go behind a tree and when I had to climb up he would bring the camel and make it sit close to me. He would then hold the rope and lead the animal. In this way we reached Quba (a village on the outskirts of Madinah Munawwarah). He told me that Hadhrat Abu Salamah رضي الله عنه was staying there. He then took us to my husband and then returned all the way back to Makkah Mukarramah. By Allah, I have never seen anybody more honourable and kind than Hadhrat Usmaan bin Talhah رضي الله عنه and by Allah, no one else could bear the hardships that I suffered during that year."

Note: Look at Hadhrat Ummu Salamah's رضي الله عنها Imaan and trust in Allah Ta'ala. She set out on a long and dangerous journey all alone. See how Allah Ta'ala sent his help to her. No doubt Allah Ta'ala can send anybody to offer help to those who place their trust in Him, because the hearts of all the people are in His control. As a rule, a female is not allowed to travel alone on a long journey, except for the fardh hijrat for the sake of Allah Ta'ala. There is thus no objection on her traveling alone in this incident.

6. WOMEN IN THE BATTLE OF KHAIBAR

During the time of Nabi ﷺ, just as the men loved to go out in the path of Allah Ta'ala, the women also wanted to sacrifice in the path of Allah Ta'ala whenever they had a chance.

Hadhrat Ummu Ziyaad رَضِيَ اللَّهُ عَنْهَا says: "In the Battle of Khaibar, six of us (women) reached the battlefield. When Nabi صَلَّى اللَّهُ عَلَيْهِ وَسَلَّمَ came to know of it, he called us and said with anger, 'Who allowed you to come over here? Who brought you to this place?' We said, 'O Nabi of Allah! We know knitting and we have some medicines with us. We shall help the men by passing arrows to them, by helping them when they are sick and by preparing food for them.' Nabi صَلَّى اللَّهُ عَلَيْهِ وَسَلَّمَ allowed us to stay."

Note: The women of that time were braver than even the men of our times. Look at the courage of these women who reached the battlefield on their own and offered to do different jobs in the battlefield.

Hadhrat Ummu Sulaim رَضِيَ اللَّهُ عَنْهَا joined the battle of Hunayn whilst she was pregnant, carrying Abdullah bin Abi Talhah رَضِيَ اللَّهُ عَنْهُ. She kept a dagger with her. Nabi صَلَّى اللَّهُ عَلَيْهِ وَسَلَّمَ asked, "What is this dagger for, O, Ummu Sulaim?" She replied: "I shall stab the stomach of any Kaafir who comes close to me." She had also taken part in the battle of Uhud, where she took care and treated the injured.

Hadhrat Anas رَضِيَ اللَّهُ عَنْهُ says: "I saw Hadhrat Aa'ishah رَضِيَ اللَّهُ عَنْهَا and Hadhrat Ummu Sulaim رَضِيَ اللَّهُ عَنْهَا in the battlefield, bringing water for the injured very diligently."

7. HADHRAT UMMU HARAAM رَضِيَ اللَّهُ عَنْهَا IN THE BATTLE OF CYPRUS

Ummu Haraam رَضِيَ اللَّهُ عَنْهَا was the maternal aunt of Hadhrat Anas رَضِيَ اللَّهُ عَنْهُ. Nabi صَلَّى اللَّهُ عَلَيْهِ وَسَلَّمَ often visited her and sometimes had his afternoon nap at her place. Once he was sleeping in her house, when he woke up smiling.

Hadhrat Ummu Haraam رَضِيَ اللَّهُ عَنْهَا said: "O, Nabi صَلَّى اللَّهُ عَلَيْهِ وَسَلَّمَ may my parents be sacrificed for you, tell me what made you smile."

He replied: "I saw in my dream a few of my followers going for Jihaad across the sea. They looked like kings sitting on their thrones in their ships."

Hadhrat Ummu Haraam رَضِيَ اللَّهُ عَنْهَا said: "O, Nabi of Allah! Make dua that I may also be from those people."

"You will be one of them!" He replied and went to sleep again, and got up smiling for the second time.

Hadhrat Ummu Haraam ﷺ again asked him why he was smiling, Nabi ﷺ gave a similar reply.

Hadhrat Ummu Haraam ﷺ asked him to make dua for her to join them also, but he said: "You are with the first group only."

During the Khilaafat (rule) of Hadhrat Usmaan ﷺ, Ameer Muaawiyyah ﷺ, the Governor of Syria, wanted permission to attack the Island of Cyprus. This permission was given by Hadhrat Usmaan ﷺ. Hadhrat Ummu Haraam ﷺ, with her husband Hadhrat Ubaadah ﷺ, was in that army. While returning from the island, she fell from her mule, broke her neck and passed away. She was buried in Cyprus.

Note: Look at the spirit of Hadhrat Ummu Haraam ﷺ. She wanted to join both the armies. As she was meant to pass away during the first journey, Nabi ﷺ did not make dua for her taking part in the second one.

8. Story of Hadhrat Ummu Sulaim ﷺ

Hadhrat Ummu Sulaim ﷺ was the mother of Hadhrat Anas ﷺ. After her husband passed away, she did not marry again for some time so that she could bring up her son properly. She then married Hadhrat Abu Talhah ﷺ and had a son named Abu Umair from him. Nabi ﷺ used to go to her house and play with the child.

One day, Abu Umair was ill and Hadhrat Abu Talha ﷺ was fasting. While Hadhrat Abu Talhah ﷺ was out on his job, the child passed away. Hadhrat Ummu Sulaim ﷺ washed and enshrouded the body and laid it in the cot. She then took a bath, changed her clothes and beautified herself.

When Abu Talhah ﷺ returned home and had his Iftaar, he asked her: "How is the child?"

She replied: "He is now in peace."

The husband was satisfied with the reply. The couple then shared the bed for the night. When they got up in the morning, they had the following conversation.

Hadhrat Ummu Sulaim رضى الله عنها said: "I have a question to ask you." Hadhrat Abu Talhah رضى الله عنه asked: "What is it?"

Hadhrat Ummu Sulaim رضى الله عنها asked: "If a person borrowed something, should he give it back or not if he is asked for it?"

Hadhrat Abu Talhah رضى الله عنه replied: "He must give it back. He has no right to keep it."

Hadhrat Ummu Sulaim رضى الله عنها then said: "Abu Umair was given to us by Allah Ta'ala. He has taken him back."

Hadhrat Abu Talhah رضى الله عنه was filled with grief. He simply said: "But why did you not tell me before?"

He went to Nabi صلى الله عليه وسلم and told the story to him. Nabi صلى الله عليه وسلم made dua for him and said: "Allah Ta'ala will bless your sharing the bed with your wife last night."

An Ansaari Sahaabi رضى الله عنه says: "I lived to see the effect of Nabi's صلى الله عليه وسلم dua. As a result of his union with his wife on that night, Hadhrat Abu Talhah رضى الله عنه got a son named Abdullah. This Abdullah had nine sons, all of whom were Qurraa."

It is an act of great courage and patience to do what Hadhrat Ummu Sulaim رضى الله عنها did when her son had passed away. She did not like her husband to know about the death of the child while he was fasting and needed food and rest.

9. HADHRAT UMMU HABIBAH'S رضى الله عنها BEHAVIOR TOWARDS HER FATHER

Ummul Mu'mineen Hadhrat Ummu Habibah رضى الله عنها was first married to Ubaidullah bin Jahsh. Both together accepted Islam and migrated to Abyssinia. Her husband became a Christian and died there as a Christian. While she was still passing her days in Abyssinia as a widow, Nabi صلى الله عليه وسلم sent his offer through King Negus to marry her. She accepted the offer and came to Madinah Munawwarah to live with Nabi صلى الله عليه وسلم.

During the period of the truce between the Muslims and the kuffaar of Mecca, her father Abu Sufyaan رضى الله عنه (who was not yet a Muslim) once came to Madinah Munawwarah for negotiations in connection with reinforcing the truce. He went to visit Ummu Habibah ﺭﺿﻲﺍﻟﻠﻪﻋﻨﻬﺎ. As he was about to sit on the bedding in her room, she pulled it from under him. He was surprised that instead of spreading a bedding for him, she removed the bedding that was there. He asked: "Was the bedding unfit for me or I unfit for the bedding?"

She replied: "This bedding is for the pure and dear Nabi ﺻﻠﻰﺍﻟﻠﻪﻋﻠﻴﻪﻭﺳﻠﻢ, while you are a kaafir (disbeliever) and, therefore, unclean. How can I allow you to sit on this bedding?"

This hurt Abu Sufyaan and he remarked, "Since you left me, you have learnt bad manners."

The great respect that she had for Nabi ﺻﻠﻰﺍﻟﻠﻪﻋﻠﻴﻪﻭﺳﻠﻢ, would not allow her to let an unclean mushrik, even though he was her own father, to sit on Nabi's ﺻﻠﻰﺍﻟﻠﻪﻋﻠﻴﻪﻭﺳﻠﻢ bedding.

Once she came to know from Nabi ﺻﻠﻰﺍﻟﻠﻪﻋﻠﻴﻪﻭﺳﻠﻢ about the rewards of twelve rakaats of Chaasht (nafl salaat read in the late morning). Since that time, she always read this Salaah regularly.

Her father Hadhrat Abu Sufyaan ﺭﺿﻲﺍﻟﻠﻪﻋﻨﻪ later accepted Islam. On the third day after his death, she sent for some perfume and used it saying: "I don't desire or even need perfume. I have heard Nabi ﺻﻠﻰﺍﻟﻠﻪﻋﻠﻴﻪﻭﺳﻠﻢ saying, 'A woman is not allowed to mourn over the death of any person *(except her husband's)* for more than three days. *(The mourning period in the case of a husband's death is four months and ten days).* I am using the perfume only to show that I am not mourning."

When she was about to die, she sent for Hadhrat Aa'ishah ﺭﺿﻲﺍﻟﻠﻪﻋﻨﻬﺎ and said: "We were co-wives, sharing the love of Nabi ﺻﻠﻰﺍﻟﻠﻪﻋﻠﻴﻪﻭﺳﻠﻢ, and co-wives generally do cause hurt to one another. I forgive you. Please forgive me too."

Hadhrat Aa'ishah ﺭﺿﻲﺍﻟﻠﻪﻋﻨﻬﺎ said: "I forgive you by all means. May Allah Ta'ala also forgive you."

She replied: "O, Aa'ishah, you have made me very happy. May Allah Ta'ala also keep you happy."

She also sent for Hadhrat Ummu Salamah ﺭﺿﻲﺍﻟﻠﻪﻋﻨﻬﺎ and asked her for forgiveness.

Ch. 10 – Women's Courage & Love for Islam

Note: The jealousy between co-wives is natural and often intense. Hadhrat Ummu Habibah ﷺ wanted to be forgiven by the people before she appeared before Allah Ta'ala. Her respect and love for Nabi ﷺ can be understood from her behaviour towards her own father.

10. THE STORY OF HADHRAT ZAINAB ﷺ

Ummul Mu'mineen Hadhrat Zainab ﷺ was a cousin of Nabi ﷺ. She accepted Islam in the early days. At first, she was married to Hadhrat Zaid ﷺ, who was a freed slave and the adopted son of Nabi ﷺ. He was therefore known as Hadhrat Zaid bin Muhammad. Hadhrat Zaid ﷺ could not get on well with Hadhrat Zainab ﷺ and eventually divorced her.

Now, according to the Arab customs before Islam, an adopted son was treated as a real son, so much so that his widow or divorced wife could not be married to his adopted father. Nabi ﷺ wanted to break this custom, so he asked Hadhrat Zainab ﷺ to marry him. When Hadhrat Zainab ﷺ received the offer, she said: "Let me ask Allah Ta'ala!" She then made wudhu and stood up in Salaah. Her action was liked by Allah Ta'ala and the following aayat was revealed to Nabi ﷺ.

$$\text{فَلَمَّا قَضَىٰ زَيْدٌ مِّنْهَا وَطَرًا زَوَّجْنَاكَهَا لِكَيْلَا يَكُونَ عَلَى الْمُؤْمِنِينَ حَرَجٌ فِي أَزْوَاجِ أَدْعِيَائِهِمْ إِذَا قَضَوْا مِنْهُنَّ وَطَرًا ۚ وَكَانَ أَمْرُ اللَّهِ مَفْعُولًا}$$

"So when Zaid had divorced her, we gave her to you in marriage, so that there may be no sin for believers in marrying the wives of their adopted sons, when they have divorced them. The command of Allah must be fulfilled." (Surah A'hzaab - Aayah 37)

When Hadhrat Zainab ﷺ was told of the good news that Allah Ta'ala had married her to Nabi ﷺ and had revealed an aayah about her, then in happiness, she gave away all her jewellery that she was wearing at that time to the person who had brought the news to her. Then she went down in Sajdah and promised to fast for two months. She was very proud of the fact that, while every other wife of Nabi ﷺ was given in marriage to him by their relatives, she was given over in marriage by Allah Ta'ala, as stated in the Qur-aan.

Hadhrat Aa'ishah رضي الله عنها was also proud of being the most beloved wife of Nabi ﷺ and there was always some competition between the two wives. In spite of all this, when Nabi ﷺ asked Hadhrat Zainab رضي الله عنها amongst others, of her opinion about Hadhrat Aa'ishah رضي الله عنها in the matter of the slander against Hadhrat Aa'ishah رضي الله عنها, she said: "I find everything good in Aa'ishah"

Look at her honesty and strong character. This was an occasion where, she could have harmed the reputation of her rival and lowered her, in the eyes of their common husband, who loved Hadhrat Aaishah رضي الله عنها very much. On the other hand, she praised her in very strong words.

Hadhrat Zainab رضي الله عنها was a very pious lady. She fasted very often and would read Nafl Salaah regularly. She earned by working with her hands, and spent all that she earned in the path of Allah Ta'ala.

At the time of the death of Nabi ﷺ, his wives asked him: "Which one of us will join you first?"

He said: "The one with the longest arms."

They began to measure their arms with a stick. They however, came to know later that long hands meant generous spending in charity. Hadhrat Zainab رضي الله عنها was the first to pass away after Nabi ﷺ.

Hadhrat Barazah رضي الله عنه says: "Hadhrat 'Umar رضي الله عنه decided to pay a yearly allowance to the Ummahaat-ul-Mu'mineen (wives of Nabi ﷺ) from the Baitul Maal. He sent me with 12 000 dirhams to Hadhrat Zainab رضي الله عنها as her share. She thought that the 12 000 was to be shared by all the wives, and told me, 'Umar رضي الله عنه should have asked somebody else to distribute this money.' I said, 'It is the yearly share for you alone.' She asked me to throw it in the corner of the room and cover it with a piece of cloth. Then she mentioned the names of some poor people, widows and her relatives, and asked me to give one handful to each of them. After I had distributed the money according to her wishes, some money was still left under the cloth. I asked her if I could have something for myself. She said, 'You may take the rest.' I counted the money. It was eighty-four Dirhams. She then lifted her hands in dua and said, 'O, Allah! Keep this money away from me, because it brings temptation.' She passed away before the allowance for the next year could be paid to her. When Hadhrat 'Umar ﺭﺿﻰ came to know of what she had done with the money, he sent her another 1000 dirhams for her own needs, but even those she distributed very quickly.

During the last part of her life, the Muslims were taking over country after country, and wealth was pouring into Madinah Munawwarah. Yet she left no money or other wealth after her death, except the house where she lived. She was called Ma'wal Masaakeen (shelter of the poor), due to her generous spending in charity."

A woman says: "Once Hadhrat Zainab ﺭﺿﻰ and I were colouring our clothes with red dye. Nabi ﷺ came in, but went out again when he saw us colouring our clothes. Hadhrat Zainab ﺭﺿﻰ felt that Nabi ﷺ had perhaps not liked our clothes being dyed in that colour. She immediately washed all the dyed clothes till their colour was gone." Later when Nabi ﷺ came and saw that there was no dying of clothes, he went inside.

Note: Everybody knows the love women have for money and colourful clothes. But look at these ladies, who gave away the money received by them in charity and got rid of any colour which caused Nabi ﷺ to be unhappy.

11. HADHRAT KHANSA ﺭﺿﻰ ENCOURAGES HER SONS TO BE BRAVE

Hadhrat Khansa ﺭﺿﻰ was a famous poetess. She and some others of her clan embraced Islam in Madinah. Ibn Athir writes: "All masters of literature were unanimous in declaring that the best woman poet in Arabic was Hadhrat Khansa ﺭﺿﻰ. No woman in history has ever written such Arabic poetry as Hadhrat Khansa ﺭﺿﻰ.

During the time of Hadhrat 'Umar ﺭﺿﻰ, in the year 16 A.H., the famous battle of Qadisiyyah was fought between the Muslims and the

Persians. Hadhrat Khansa ﵂ and her four sons took part in this battle.

Before the battle, she encouraged her four sons, saying: "O, my sons! You accepted Islam and made Hijrat of your own free will. By Allah Ta'ala, besides whom there is no deity, you all are the sons of the same father, just as you are the sons of the same mother. I was never unfaithful to your father, nor did I disgrace your uncle (my brother). I neither allowed a bad name to come on your high birth, nor spoiled your noble family pedigree. You know what rewards Allah Ta'ala has promised for those who fight against the kuffaar in His path. You must remember that the everlasting life of the Aakhirat is far better than the short life of this world. Allah Ta'ala has said in the Qur-aan-e-Kareem:

يَٰٓأَيُّهَا ٱلَّذِينَ ءَامَنُوا۟ ٱصْبِرُوا۟ وَصَابِرُوا۟ وَرَابِطُوا۟ وَٱتَّقُوا۟ ٱللَّهَ لَعَلَّكُمْ تُفْلِحُونَ

'O you, who have Imaan! Be patient, compete in having patience, continue doing good deeds and fear Allah Ta'ala so that you may be successful.' (Surah Aale I'mraan - Aayah 200)'

When you get up tomorrow morning, be prepared to give off your best in the battle. Go ahead into the enemy lines, asking for help from Allah Ta'ala. When you see the fighting becoming severe, go right into the centre and face the enemy chiefs. *Insha-Allah*! You will get your home in Jannah with honour and success."

The next day, when the battle was in full swing, all four sons went towards the enemy lines. One by one, while saying their mother's poem they attacked the enemy and fought till all of them were martyred.

When the mother got the news, she said: "*Alhamdulillah*! All praise be to Allah Ta'ala, who has honoured me with their martyrdom. I hope that Allah Ta'ala will join me with them under the shade of His Mercy."

Note: Look at a mother of that time. She encouraged her sons to jump into the thick of battle and when all her sons are killed one after the other, she praises Allah Ta'ala and thanks Him.

12. HADHRAT SAFIYYAH ﷺ KILLS A JEW ON HER OWN

Hadhrat Safiyyah ﷺ was the aunt of Nabi ﷺ and a real sister of Hadhrat Hamzah ﷺ. She took part in the battle of Uhud. When the Muslims were losing and some of them began to escape from the battle, she would hit their faces with her spear and send them back.

In the battle of Khandaq (Trench), Nabi ﷺ had collected all the Muslim women in a fortress and had ordered Hadhrat Hassaan bin Saabit ﷺ to look after them. The Jews, who were hostile to the muslims, were always looking for such opportunities for doing mischief. A group of them approached the place and sent one of their men to spy. Hadhrat Safiyyah ﷺ saw the Jew coming to the fort. She told Hadhrat Hassaan ﷺ: "There is a Jew coming to spy on us. You go out and kill him."

Hadhrat Hassaan ﷺ was a weak person. He did not have the courage to do such a job. Safiyyah ﷺ took a tent peg and went outside the fortress and gave a blow on the head of the Jew and killed him on the spot.

She came back and said to Hassaan ﷺ: "The man is dead. I did not remove the clothes and weapons from his body because of shame and modesty. Now you go and remove everything from his body. Also bring his head after cutting it off from the body."

Hadhrat Hassaan ﷺ was too weak-hearted to do that even. She herself went again and brought his head, and threw it over the wall amongst the Jews. When they saw this, they said: "We were wondering how Muhammad (ﷺ) could keep the women alone in this fort. Surely, there are men inside to guard the ladies."

Note: Hadhrat Safiyyah ﷺ passed away in 20 A.H. at the age of seventy-three. The war of the Trench was fought in 5 A.H. Therefore, in the war of the Trench, she was 58 years old. These days, a lady of that age is hardly able to do her household work. But look how Hadhrat Safiyyah ﷺ goes and kills a Jew all alone.

13. Hadhrat Asma's رضى الله عنها Discussion with Nabi صلى الله عليه وسلم Regarding the Rewards for Women

Hadhrat Asma bint Yazid Ansaari رضى الله عنها came to Nabi صلى الله عليه وسلم and said: "O, Nabi of Allah! I love you more than my parents. The Muslim women have sent me to ask you on their behalf, because you are the Nabi of Allah Ta'ala for men and women. So we, women, have brought Imaan on you and on Allah Ta'ala. We remain in purdah (concealed), confined to our homes. We fulfil the marital rights of our husbands, bearing children for them and looking after their homes. Despite all this, the men get more rewards than us for actions which we are unable to do. They read their daily Salaah and weekly Jumu'ah in the Masjid, visit the sick, go to the funerals, perform Hajj after Hajj and, above all, fight in the path of Allah Ta'ala. When they go for Hajj or Jihaad, we look after their belongings, bring up their children and weave cloth for them. Do we also have a share in their rewards?"

Nabi صلى الله عليه وسلم said to the Sahaabah رضى الله عنهم sitting around him: "Did you ever hear a woman asking a better question?"

The Sahaabah رضى الله عنهم replied: "O, Nabi of Allah! We never thought that a woman could ever ask such a question."

Then Nabi صلى الله عليه وسلم said to Asma رضى الله عنها, "Listen carefully and then go and tell the ladies that sent you, that when a woman looks after her husband, seeks his pleasure and fulfils her responsibilities, then she also gets the same reward as the men for all their ibaadat to Allah Ta'ala." Hadhrat Asma رضى الله عنها returned very happily after getting this reply to her question.

Note: Obedience and good behaviour towards the husband is a great thing for women. But generally they are negligent in this matter.

The Sahaabah رضى الله عنهم once told Nabi صلى الله عليه وسلم: "In other countries, people bow down before their kings and chiefs. You deserve much more respect so allow us to make sajdah to you."

Nabi صلى الله عليه وسلم said, "No. If it were allowed to bow down (make sajdah) before anybody besides Allah Ta'ala, then I would ask the women to make sajdah to their husbands."

He then said, "By Him (by Allah) who has my life in His hand, a woman cannot fulfil her rights to Allah Ta'ala until she fulfils the rights of her husband."

It is reported in a Hadith that once a camel made sajdah before Nabi ﷺ. The Sahaabah رضى الله عنهم said: "When this animal makes sajdah before you, why should we also not make sajdah to you?"

He replied: "Never! If I could ask somebody to make sajdah to anybody besides Allah Ta'ala, I would ask the wives to make sajdah to their husbands."

Regarding this Nabi ﷺ said:

"A woman whose husband is pleased with her at the time of her death goes straight into Jannah."

"A woman who is angry with her husband and she stays away from him in anger for the night, is cursed by the Malaai'kah."

"The Salaah of two people hardly rises above their heads in its journey to the skies. These two people are a run-away slave and a disobedient wife."

14. THE STORY OF HADHRAT UMMU AMMAARAH رضى الله عنها

Hadhrat Ummu Ammarah رضى الله عنها is one of those Ansaar women who accepted Islam in the very beginning. She was from the group that took bay'at to Nabi ﷺ at Al-Aqabah. Al-Aqabah in Arabic means a narrow mountain road. In the early days of Islam, the new Muslims were ill-treated very badly by the Quraish. They would put all sorts of difficulties in the way of Tabligh. Therefore, Nabi ﷺ carried on his work quietly and secretly. People from Madinah Munawwarah who used to come to Makkah Mukarramah for Hajj usually accepted Islam secretly in a mountain pass near Mina, so that the Quraish might not see them. Hadhrat Ummu Ammarah رضى الله عنها was in the third such group from Madinah Munawwarah. She joined most of the battles that were fought after Hijrah (migration). She took an important part in Uhud, Hudaibiyyah, Khaibar, Umratul Qadhaa, Hunayn and Yamaamah.

At time of the battle of Uhud, She was forty-three years old. Her husband and two sons were also fighting in this battle. She herself narrates, "I took a leather bottle full of water and went to Uhud to help the wounded and the thirsty. In the beginning, the Muslims were winning, but things changed in a moment and the enemies were in a winning position. I had reached Nabi ﷺ, when many of the enemy troops rushed to attack and kill him. I protected Nabi ﷺ whenever anybody came close to him." Initially she did not even have a shield. After receiving one, she would stop the attacks of the kuffaar on Nabi ﷺ by using it.

She had a cloth-belt round her waist, full of pieces of cloth, with which she cared for the wounded. She herself got about twelve to thirteen wounds, one of which was very serious."

Hadhrat Ummu Sa'eed رضي الله عنها says: "I once saw a very deep cut on the shoulder of Hadhrat Ummu Ammarah رضي الله عنها. I asked her how she had got that. She said, 'I got it in the Battle of Uhud. When people were running about in confusion, I saw Ibn Qumayyah coming towards us and shouting, Where is Muhammad ﷺ. Let somebody tell me where he is. If he is saved today, I am no more.' Mus'ab bin Umair رضي الله عنه and some others stopped him. And I was amongst them. He gave me this deep cut on my shoulder. I also attacked him, but he escaped because of the double coat of armour that he was wearing."

After treating it for one year, the wound would not heal. In the meantime, Nabi ﷺ decided to go to Hamraaul-Asad. Hadhrat Ummu Ammarah رضي الله عنها also got ready but she could not join as her wound had still not healed. When Nabi ﷺ returned from this battle, he first went to visit Hadhrat Ummu Ammarah رضي الله عنها. He was very happy to find her better. Besides this wound, she suffered many other injuries in the battle of Uhud.

She says: "We were quite weak in Uhud. The enemies were on horseback, while we fought on foot. There would have been a fair fight if they too had been on foot. When somebody on horseback would attack me, I stopped his sword with my shield and when he turned around, I attacked his horse from the back and cut its leg. This caused the horse as well as the rider to fall on the ground. As soon as this happened, Nabi

ﷺ would shout to my son, who would run to help me and then we both finished the man."

Her son Hadhrat Abdullah bin Zaid رضى الله عنه says: "I had a wound on my left arm, which would not stop bleeding. Nabi ﷺ told my mother, 'Put a bandage over it.' My mother took out a bandage from her belt and after bandaging my wound, said, 'Now, son! Go and fight again with the kuffaar.' Nabi ﷺ was watching us. He said, 'O, Ummu Ammarah, who can have courage like yours?'"

At that time, Nabi ﷺ made dua again and again for Hadhrat Ummu Ammarah رضى الله عنها and her family and He mentioned some words of praise as well. Hadhrat Ummu Ammarah رضى الله عنها said, "I was standing with Nabi ﷺ when one of the enemies passed by in front of me. Nabi ﷺ told me, 'Ummu Ammarah! He is the man who wounded your son.' I jumped at him and hit his leg. This caused him to fall down. We then went forward and finished him. Nabi ﷺ smiled and said, 'Ummu Ammarah has taken revenge for her son,' When Nabi ﷺ was making dua for us, I told him, 'O, Nabi of Allah! Make dua so that I may join you in Jannah.' He made this dua too. After this I did not worry over anything that came to me in this life."

As has already been said, she also joined many other battles with the same courage. After the death of Nabi ﷺ, she took part in the fierce battle of Yamaamah, which was fought with the rebels. She lost one of her arms and received eleven other wounds in this battle. She returned to Madinah in this injured condition.

Note: These are the achievements of one woman, who was forty-three in Uhud and fifty-two in Yamaamah. Her great courage in these battles at that age was really amazing.

15. STORY OF HADHRAT UMMU HAKEEM رضى الله عنها

Hadhrat Ummu Hakeem رضى الله عنها was the wife of Ikramah bin Abi Jahl. She took part in Uhud on the enemy side. She accepted Islam when Makkah Mukarramah was conquered. She loved her husband very much. He would not become Muslim because of his father. After the conquest of Makkah Mukarramah, her husband escaped to Yemen. She got pardon for him from Nabi ﷺ and went to Yemen and after great difficulty, she managed to convinced her husband to return home.

She told him: "You can be safe from the sword of Muhammad ﷺ only when you put yourself in his lap."(i.e. if you accept Islam).

She returned with him to Madinah Munawwarah, where Ikramah accepted Islam and the couple began to live together happily. They both took part in the battle against the romans during the rule of Hadhrat Abu Bakr ؓ. Ikramah ؓ was killed in this battle. She then married another Mujaahid, Hadhrat Khaalid bin Sa'eed ؓ who wanted to meet her at a place called Marjus-Suffar.

She said: "We have the enemy on all sides. We shall meet after they are conquered."

He said: "I am sure I shall not survive this battle."

They then shared the bed for the first time in a tent at that place. The next day, Hadhrat Khaalid bin Sa'eed ؓ was arranging for the waleemah when the enemy attacked with full force and he was martyred in the battle. Hadhrat Ummu Hakeem ؓ packed up her tent and other luggage and thereafter fought the enemy with a tent-peg in her hand, till she had killed seven of them.

Note: In times of war, not to speak of a woman, no man would like to get married under such conditions. Look at her marriage in the battle-field and her fight with the enemy. Instead of crying about the loss of her husband, on the day of his death she rushes onto the battlefield and kills seven of the enemy soldiers single-handed. Is this not enough to show the wonderful strength of Imaan in the women of that time?

16. MARTYRDOM OF HADHRAT SUMAYYA ؓ

Hadhrat Sumayya ؓ is the mother of Hadhrat Ammaar ؓ whose story we already read in chapter 5. Just like her son Hadhrat Ammaar ؓ and her husband Yaasir ؓ, she experienced many hardships for the cause of Islam. She was made to lie on hot stones in the hot sun. She was also made to wear steel armour and stand in the hot sun which heated the armour, causing her intense difficulty. When Nabi

Ch. 10 – Women's Courage & Love for Islam

ﷺ passed by, he would encourage her to be patient and promised her Jannah.

One day, Hadhrat Sumayya رضي الله عنها was standing when Abu Jahl passed that way. He spoke rudely and insulted her most severely and then stabbed her through her private part with his spear. She died because of the wound. She was the first to be martyred (give her life) for the sake of Islam.

Note: The patience, perseverance and sacrifice of these ladies are really enviable. For a person blessed with true Islam, no hardship is too difficult to bear. We hear about hundreds of people dying for one cause or the other. It is only dying for the cause of Allah Ta'ala that brings everlasting happiness and comfort in the life hereafter. People losing their lives for the things of the world really lose twice, i.e. in this world, as well as in the hereafter.

17. THE STORY OF HADHRAT ASMA BINT ABU BAKR رضي الله عنها

Hadhrat Asma bint Abu Bakr رضي الله عنها is the daughter of Hadhrat Abu Bakr رضي الله عنه, mother of Abdulla bin Zubair رضي الله عنه and the step-sister of Hadhrat Aa'ishah رضي الله عنها. She is one of the famous women of her time. She was the eighteenth person to accept Islam. She was twenty-seven years old at the time of Hijrat.

After emigrating from Makkah Mukarramah, when Nabi ﷺ and Hadhrat Abu Bakr رضي الله عنه reached Madinah Munawwarah safely, they sent Hadhrat Zaid رضي الله عنه and some other Sahaabah رضي الله عنهم to bring their families from Makkah Mukarramah. Hadhrat Asma رضي الله عنها came to Madinah Munawwarah with Hadhrat Abu Bakr's رضي الله عنه family. When she reached Quba, she gave birth to Hadhrat Abdullah bin Zubair رضي الله عنه, the first Muslim baby born since Hijrat. In those days poverty and constraints were common but at the same time courage, valour and bravery were also unmatched. In Bukhaari Shareef Hadhrat Asma رضي الله عنها narrates herself the manner in which she lived.

She says, "When I was married to Hadhrat Zubair رضي الله عنه, he had no money, property or any servant. He had only one camel for carrying water and one horse. I would bring fodder (food) for the animals and date seeds to feed them instead of grass. I also brought water from the well, fixed the bucket myself and did all my housework myself. Looking after the horse was the most difficult of all the jobs. Because I was not good at baking, after kneading (preparing) the flour, I would take it to the Ansaar women in my neighbourhood, who would bake bread for me. They were sincere and kind.

When we arrived in Madinah Munawwarah, Nabi ﷺ chose a piece of land for Hadhrat Zubair ؓ two miles away from the town. I would bring date seeds from there on my head. One day when I was coming along that way with a bundle on my head, I met Nabi ﷺ with a group of Ansaar on the road. He stopped his camel, made it sit and showed me a sign that he wished to give me a lift. I felt shy of going with men and I also remembered that Hadhrat Zubair ؓ (my husband) was very sensitive in this matter. Nabi ﷺ understood my hesitation and left me alone. When I reached home, I told the story to Hadhrat Zubair ؓ and told him that, because of my own shyness and his feelings, I did not accept the offer of Nabi ﷺ. He said, 'By Allah I am more worried about your carrying the load over such a long distance, but I cannot help it.'

When Sahaabah ؓ went out in the path of Allah Ta'ala, all other jobs had to be done mostly by their women. Sometime later, Hadhrat Abu Bakr ؓ sent us a servant that Nabi ﷺ had given him. So I did not have to look after the horse, which had been really very hard for me."

Note: It was, and still is, the custom in Arabia to grind the date pit, soak it in water and feed it to the animals.

18. HADHRAT ASMA ؓ COMFORTS HER GRANDFATHER

When Hadhrat Abu Bakr ؓ made hijrat to Madinah Munawwarah with Nabi ﷺ, he took all his money with him, thinking that Nabi ﷺ might need it. It was about 6000 Dirhams. After he had left, his father Abu Quhaafah ؓ, who was blind and who had not yet accepted Islam, came to comfort his granddaughters.

Hadhrat Asma رَضِىَاللهُعَنْها says: "Our grandfather came to us and said with grief, 'Your father has caused distress to you with his Hijrat to Madinah Munawwarah, and has put you through a lot of hardship by taking all his money with him.' I said, 'No grandfather, do not worry. He has left a lot of money for us.' I collected some small stones and put them in the place where my father used to keep his money; I covered it with a cloth. I then took my grandfather to that place and placed his hand over the cloth. He thought that it was really full of Dirhams. He said: 'It is good that he has left something for you to live on.' By Allah, my father had not left a single Dirham for us. I played this trick just to put my grandfather at ease."

Note: Look at this brave Muslim girl. Actually speaking, the girls needed more comfort than their grandfather. Normally, they should have complained of their condition to their grandfather because he was their only support. Their father had left, they had no money and the people of Makkah were unfriendly towards them, and they did not have any other relatives in Makkah Mukarramah to help them. Allah Ta'ala had given such understanding to the Muslim men and women of those days that everything they did was really wonderful and worthy of admiration.

Hadhrat Abu Bakr رَضِىَاللهُعَنْهُ was a rich businessman in the beginning, but he always spent generously in the path of Allah Ta'ala. At the time of Tabuk, he gave all that he owned (this we have already seen in chapter six).

Nabi صَلَّىاللهُعَلَيْهِوَسَلَّم once said: "Nobody's wealth has benefited me so much as that of Hadhrat Abu Bakr رَضِىَاللهُعَنْهُ. I have paid back everybody for the good done to me, except Hadhrat Abu Bakr رَضِىَاللهُعَنْهُ. He shall be rewarded by Allah Ta'ala Himself."

19. HADHRAT ASMA'S رَضِىَاللهُعَنْها SPENDING IN CHARITY

Hadhrat Asma رَضِىَاللهُعَنْها loved to spend in the path of Allah Ta'ala. In the beginning, she used to spend calculating by measuring and weighing.

Once Nabi صَلَّىاللهُعَلَيْهِوَسَلَّم told her, "O Asma, don't hoard and don't give in the path of Allah Ta'ala by calculating, but rather spend freely." After this, she started spending most generously.

Asma رضى الله عنها would advise her daughters and house-maids: "Don't wait for any extra requirements before spending in the path of Allah Ta'ala. Our needs go on increasing and the chances of having something extra will become more and more difficult and the time for spending in the path of Allah Ta'ala will never come (as one's needs naturally keep on increasing). Remember that you will not lose by spending in charity."

Note: Although these people were poor and lived a simple life, yet they were free in spending and generous at heart. The Muslims today complain of their poverty, but there will be hardly any group of people among them who are so poor and needy as the Sahaabah رضى الله عنهم used to be. We have already read how they had to go without food for a few days at a time and how some of them had to keep stones tied to their stomach to ease their hunger.

20. THE STORY OF MIGRATION AND DEMISE OF NABI'S صلى الله عليه وسلم DAUGHTER, HADHRAT ZAINAB رضى الله عنها

Hadhrat Zainab رضى الله عنها was born five years after Nabi's صلى الله عليه وسلم marriage to Hadhrat Khadija رضى الله عنها, ten years before nubuwwat. At that time Nabi صلى الله عليه وسلم was thirty years old. She grew up and thereafter accepted Islam. She was married to her cousin Abul Aas bin Rabi. She could not join Nabi صلى الله عليه وسلم during the Hijrat (migration). Her husband fought in Badr for the Quraish and was taken prisoner by the Muslims.

When the Quraish were paying ransom (fines) for their prisoners, Hadhrat Zainab رضى الله عنها also gave what she had for the ransom of her husband. Included in this was the necklace she had received as a gift from her mother Hadhrat Khadijah رضى الله عنها. When Nabi صلى الله عليه وسلم saw the necklace, the memories of Hadhrat Khadijah رضى الله عنها overcame him and tears filled his eyes. After consulting with the Sahaabah رضى الله عنهم, it was decided that the necklace be returned to Hadhrat Zainab رضى الله عنها and her husband will be freed without ransom on the condition that he would send Hadhrat Zainab رضى الله عنها to Madinah Munawwarah when he returned to Makkah Mukarramah.

182

Two men were sent to wait outside Makkah Mukarramah and bring Hadhrat Zainab رَضِيَ اللهُ عَنْهَا safely to Madinah Munawwarah. Her husband asked his brother Kinaanah to take Hadhrat Zainab رَضِيَ اللهُ عَنْهَا outside Makkah Mukarramah and hand her over to the Muslims. As Hadhrat Zainab رَضِيَ اللهُ عَنْهَا and Kinaanah were moving out of the town on camel-back, the Quraish became infuriated. They sent a group to stop them in which was Her cousin Habbaar bin Aswad. He flung a spear at her, which wounded her and caused her to fall from the camel. At that time she was expecting and suffered a miscarriage. Kinaanah started shooting arrows towards the trouble-makers.

Abu Sufyaan told Kinaanah: "We cannot allow the daughter of Muhammad صَلَّى اللهُ عَلَيْهِ وَسَلَّمَ leaving Makkah Mukarramah so openly. Let her go back and we will send her secretly after a few days." Kinaanah agreed. Hadhrat Zainab رَضِيَ اللهُ عَنْهَا was sent off after a few days. She suffered from this wound for a long time, till she passed away because of the wound in 8 A.H.

At the time of her death Nabi صَلَّى اللهُ عَلَيْهِ وَسَلَّمَ said: "She was my best daughter, for she has suffered because of me."

Nabi صَلَّى اللهُ عَلَيْهِ وَسَلَّمَ buried her with his own hands. As he went into the grave to lay her down, he looked very sad but when he came out of the grave, he was quite calm. After being asked by the Sahaabah رَضِيَ اللهُ عَنْهُمْ, he said: "Because of the weakness of Zainab رَضِيَ اللهُ عَنْهَا, I made dua to Allah Ta'ala to save her from the punishment of the grave, and this dua has been answered by Allah Ta'ala."

Note: Just imagine, even the daughter of Nabi صَلَّى اللهُ عَلَيْهِ وَسَلَّمَ who sacrificed her life for Islam needed the dua of Nabi صَلَّى اللهُ عَلَيْهِ وَسَلَّمَ for being saved from the problems in the grave. What about us who are drowned in sins? It is necessary that we should always make dua to be saved from the punishment of the grave. Nabi صَلَّى اللهُ عَلَيْهِ وَسَلَّمَ would often seek protection in Allah Ta'ala from the horrors of the grave. This was to teach his followers.

اَللّٰهُمَّ احْفَظْنَا مِنْهُ بِمَنِّكَ وَكَرَمِكَ وَفَضْلِكَ

(O, Allah! protect us from the horrors of the grave by your special Favour, Grace and Bounty). Aameen

21. HADHRAT RUBAYYI'S ﷺ HONOUR

Rubayyi-bint-Mu'awwiz ﷺ was a women from the Ansaar, who had taken part in many battles by the side of Nabi ﷺ. She nursed the wounded and carried the dead bodies during the battle. She had accepted Islam before Nabi ﷺ had come to Madinah Munawwarah. She was married after Nabi ﷺ made Hijrat. He visited her on the day of her marriage. He heard some girls singing a heroic poem about the Battle of Badr at her place. One of them sang a verse, which meant:

$$\text{وَفِينَا نَبِيٌّ يَعْلَمُ مَا فِيْ غَدٍ}$$

"We have amongst us a Nabi, who knows what is going to happen tomorrow." (ie. In the future)

He stopped her from saying such things, because nobody except Allah Ta'ala knows what is going to happen in the future.

It was Hadhrat Rubayyi's ﷺ father, Hadhrat Mu'awwiz ﷺ, who was one of those who killed Abu Jahl in Badr. Abu Jahl, as we know, was one of the big chiefs of the Quraish and the worst enemy of Islam.

There was a woman named Asma who used to sell perfumes to the ladies. She once came to Hadhrat Rubayyi ﷺ to sell perfume. In the discussion Hadhrat Rubayyi ﷺ said that she was the daughter of Hadhrat Mu'awwiz ﷺ, Asma remarked: "So you are the daughter of the one who killed his chief."

Hadhrat Rubayyi ﷺ could not bear a terrible person like Abu Jahl to be mentioned as the chief of her father. She therefore, replied angrily, "No. I am the daughter of the one who killed his slave."

Asma did not like Abu Jahl being called a slave and said with anger: "It is haraam for me to sell perfume to you."

Hadhrat Rubayyi ﷺ replied in a similar way, "It is haraam for me to buy perfume from you. I have never found a stench in any perfume except yours."

Hadhrat Rubayyi ﷺ says: "I said the last words just to annoy her."

Note: Look at her feelings for Islam. She could not bear an enemy of Islam being mentioned as a chief. We hear from the lips of Muslims very flowery and wonderful descriptions being used for the open enemies of Islam. When they are corrected, they call it narrow mindedness.

Nabi ﷺ says: "Don't call a Munaafiq a chief. You displease Allah Ta'ala when you take him as a chief."

THE LIVES OF THE UMMAHAAT-UL-MU'MINEEN (MOTHERS OF THE BELIEVERS WHO WERE THE PURE WIVES OF NABI ﷺ)

Every Muslim likes to know about the family of Nabi ﷺ. Therefore, a short history of their lives is given in the following pages. The Muhadditheen and historians all agree that eleven ladies had the honour of being the wives of Nabi ﷺ.

(1) HADHRAT KHADIJAH رَضِيَ اللَّهُ عَنْهَا

Hadhrat Khadijah رَضِيَ اللَّهُ عَنْهَا was the first wife of Nabi ﷺ. At the time of her marriage, she was forty years old and Nabi ﷺ was twenty-five. She gave birth to all his children, except his son Ibrahim.

She was first supposed to be married to Waraqah bin Naufal, but this marriage could not take place. Her first husband was Ateeq bin Aa'iz. She had a daughter from him, whose name was Hind. Hind grew up, accepted Islam and had many children. When Ateeq passed away Hadhrat Khadijah رَضِيَ اللَّهُ عَنْهَا married Abu Haalah and had two children from him, by the names of Hind and Haalah. Hind lived right up to the time of Hadhrat Ali's رَضِيَ اللَّهُ عَنْهُ Khilaafat.

When Abu Haalah passed away, Nabi ﷺ married Hadhrat Khadijah رَضِيَ اللَّهُ عَنْهَا as his first wife. She passed away in Ramadhaan in the 10th year of Islam at the age of sixty-five. He loved her very much and did not marry any other woman during her lifetime. Even before Islam, she was popularly known as Taahirah (clean and pure). Her children from her other husbands are, therefore, known as Banu Taahirah. Her goodness and high position have been mentioned in many Ahaadith.

Nabi ﷺ placed her in the grave with his own hands. Till then, there was no Janaazah Salaah.

(2) Hadhrat Sauda رضي الله عنها

Hadhrat Sauda bint Zam'ah bin Qais رضي الله عنها was first married to her cousin Hadhrat Sukraan bin 'Amr رضي الله عنه. The couple accepted Islam and emigrated to Abyssinia. Hadhrat Sukraan رضي الله عنه passed away in Abyssinia. Hadhrat Sauda رضي الله عنها, now a widow, returned to Makkah Mukarramah. Nabi ﷺ, after the death of Hadhrat Khadijah رضي الله عنها (in Shawwal of the same year), married Hadhrat Sauda رضي الله عنها.

We know the devotion of Nabi ﷺ in his salaah. Hadhrat Sauda رضي الله عنها once stood behind him in Tahajjud. The next day she told him: "O, Nabi of Allah! Last night you took so long in your Ruku that I feared bleeding from my nose." (As she was heavy, the strain might have been too much for her).

Nabi ﷺ once intended to divorce her. Meanwhile Hadhrat Aa'ishah رضي الله عنها had also been married to Nabi ﷺ. Hadhrat Sauda رضي الله عنها said: "O, Nabi of Allah! I am ready to give up my turn (with you) in favour of Hadhrat Aa'ishah رضي الله عنها, but I do not like to be divorced by you. I wish to be one of your wives in Jannah." Nabi ﷺ agreed to this suggestion.

She passed away in about 55 A.H. towards the end of the Khilaafat of Hadhrat 'Umar رضي الله عنه. There was another Quraishi woman of the same name. She was also a widow who had about six children. Nabi ﷺ offered to marry her, but she said: "O, Nabi of Allah! You are dearer to me than any other person in this world. I do not like my children to be of any trouble to you." He appreciated this and decided not to marry her.

(3) Hadhrat Aa'ishah رضي الله عنها

Hadhrat Aa'ishah رضي الله عنها was married to Nabi ﷺ in Shawwaal in the tenth year of Nubuwwat. She was born in the fourth year of

Nubuwwat and was married when she was six, but was actually sent by her parents to live with Nabi ﷺ, after his hijrat to Madinah Munawwarah, when she was nine. She was eighteen at the time of the death of Nabi ﷺ. She passed away on the night of Tuesday, the 17th Ramadhaan, 57 A.H., at the age of sixty-six. She wished at the time of her death that she might be buried along with the other Ummahaatul-Mu'mineen, in the public graveyard, though she could be buried by the side of Nabi's ﷺ grave, which was in her house.

She was the only wife of Nabi ﷺ who had not been married before. All the other wives had either been widowed or divorced, some quite a few times, before they became Ummahaatul-Mu'mineen. To be married in Shawwaal was considered evil among the Arab women.

Hadhrat Aa'ishah رضي الله عنها says: "I was married and sent to live with Nabi ﷺ in Shawwaal. Which of Nabi's ﷺ wives has been more blessed with his love and Allah Ta'ala's and other favours than me?"

When Hadhrat Khadijah رضي الله عنها passed away, Hadhrat Khaulah bint Hakeem رضي الله عنها came to Nabi ﷺ and said: "O, Nabi of Allah! Don't you like to marry again?"

Nabi ﷺ asked: "Whom can I marry?"

Khaulah replied: "I know a virgin (a woman who was not married before) and a widow."

Nabi ﷺ said: "Name them."

Khaulah replied: "The virgin is Aa'ishah, the daughter of your best friend Abu Bakr رضي الله عنه and the widow is Sauda bint Zam'ah."

Nabi ﷺ said: "All right! You may make the proposal."

Hadhrat Khaulah رضي الله عنها then went to Hadhrat Aa'ishah's رضي الله عنها mother Ummu-Rooman رضي الله عنها and told her: "I have come with something of goodness and barakah for your family."

Ummu Rooman رضي الله عنها asked: "What is that?"

Hadhrat Khaulah رضي الله عنها replied: "Nabi ﷺ has sent me to seek Hadhrat Aa'ishah's رضي الله عنها hand in marriage for him."

Ummu Rooman رضي الله عنها said: "But Aa'ishah is like his niece. How can she be married to him? Let me talk to her father."

Hadhrat Abu Bakr رضي الله عنه was not at home at that time. When he came, the proposal was mentioned to him, and he gave the same reply. Hadhrat Khaulah رضي الله عنها returned to Nabi ﷺ and told him of their difficulty.

Nabi ﷺ said: "Abu Bakr is my best friend and brother-in-Islam, but this does not stop me from marrying his daughter."

Hadhrat Khaulah رضي الله عنها went back and informed Hadhrat Abu Bakr رضي الله عنه of what Nabi ﷺ had said. Abu Bakr رضي الله عنه was extremely happy. He called Nabi ﷺ to his home and performed Hadhrat Aa'ishah's رضي الله عنها nikaah with him. A few months later, when Nabi ﷺ had emigrated to Madinah Munawwarah, Hadhrat Abu Bakr رضي الله عنه told Nabi ﷺ: "Why don't you have your wife Hadhrat Aa'ishah رضي الله عنها living with you?"

He replied: "I have to make some preparations, etc., before I do that."

Hadhrat Abu Bakr رضي الله عنه gave him some money, with which the necessary things were arranged. Hadhrat Aa'ishah رضي الله عنها then started living with Nabi ﷺ from Shawwaal of 1 or 2 A.H. She shared the bed with Nabi ﷺ for the first time in Hadhrat Abu Bakr's رضي الله عنه house.

These are the three marriages of Nabi ﷺ before Hijrah. All the remaining wives were married to him in Madinah Munawwarah.

(4) HADHRAT HAFSAH رضي الله عنها

Hadhrat Hafsah رضي الله عنها, the daughter of Hadhrat 'Umar رضي الله عنه, was born in Makkah Mukarramah five years before Nubuwwat. She was first married to Hadhrat Khunais bin Huzayfah رضي الله عنه, who was one of the very early Muslims. He first emigrated to Abyssinia and then to Madinah Munawwarah. He took part in the Battle of Badr, and was seriously wounded in Badr (or in Uhud) and passed away because of the wound in the year 1 or 2 A.H. Hadhrat Hafsah رضي الله عنها had also moved to Madinah Munawwarah with her husband.

When her husband passed away, Hadhrat 'Umar رضي الله عنه went to Hadhrat Abu Bakr رضي الله عنه and said: "I want to give Hafsah in marriage to you." Hadhrat Abu Bakr رضي الله عنه kept quiet and said nothing. Meanwhile Ruqayyah رضي الله عنها, the daughter of Nabi صلى الله عليه وسلم and the wife of Hadhrat Usmaan رضي الله عنه passed away. Hadhrat 'Umar رضي الله عنه went to Hadhrat Usmaan رضي الله عنه and offered Hadhrat Hafsah's رضي الله عنها hand to him. He refused by saying, "I don't have any intention to marry at the moment."

Hadhrat 'Umar رضي الله عنه complained of this to Nabi صلى الله عليه وسلم. Nabi صلى الله عليه وسلم said: "Can I tell you of a husband for Hafsah better than 'Usmaan, and of a wife for 'Usmaan better than Hafsah."

He then took Hadhrat Hafsah رضي الله عنها as his next wife, and gave his own daughter Hadhrat Ummu Kulsum رضي الله عنها in marriage to Hadhrat Usmaan رضي الله عنه. Hadhrat Abu Bakr رضي الله عنه later told Hadhrat 'Umar رضي الله عنه: "When you offered Hafsah's hand to me and I kept quiet, this may have displeased you. However as Nabi صلى الله عليه وسلم had told me that he wanted to marry her. I could not accept your offer or tell Nabi's صلى الله عليه وسلم secret to you. I, therefore, kept quiet. If Nabi صلى الله عليه وسلم had changed his mind, I would have gladly married her."

Hadhrat 'Umar رضي الله عنه says: "Abu Bakr's silence over the offer was in fact more painful to me than Usmaan's refusal."

Hadhrat Hafsah رضي الله عنها was a very pious woman who busied herself in Salaah. She would often fast during the day and spend the night in Ibaadat. Once Nabi صلى الله عليه وسلم was unhappy with Hafsah رضي الله عنها for some reason and said the first divorce to her. Hadhrat 'Umar رضي الله عنه was very distressed over this, as he naturally would have been.

Jibraeel عليه السلام came to Nabi صلى الله عليه وسلم and said: "Allah Ta'ala wants you to take Hafsah back, as she is often fasting and spending her nights in Salaah, and also Allah wants it for Hadhrat Umar's رضي الله عنه sake." Nabi صلى الله عليه وسلم therefore took her back. She passed away in Jumadil Oola, 45 A.H., at the age of sixty-three.

(5) HADHRAT ZAINAB BINT KHUZAIMAH رضي الله عنها

Hadhrat Zainab رضي الله عنها was the next lady to be married to Nabi صلى الله عليه وسلم. There are different reports about her earlier husbands.

According to one report, she was first married to Hadhrat Abdullah bin Jahsh ﷺ who was killed in Uhud (as we have already seen in chapter seven). According to another report, she was first married to Tufail ibnul Haaris and when he divorced her she married his brother Ubaidah ibnul Haaris, who was killed in Badr.

Nabi ﷺ married her in Ramadhaan, 3 A.H. She lived with Nabi ﷺ for eight months only, as she passed away in Rabiul-Aakhir, 4 A.H. Hadhrat Zainab and Hadhrat Khadijah ﷺ are the only two wives of Nabi ﷺ who passed away during his lifetime. All the other wives lived after him and passed away later.

Hadhrat Zainab ﷺ spent very generously on the poor, and was known as 'Ummul Masaakeen' (mother of the poor) even before Islam. After her death, Nabi ﷺ married Hadhrat Ummu Salamah ﷺ.

(6) HADHRAT UMMU SALAMAH ﷺ

Hadhrat Ummu Salamah ﷺ was the daughter of Hadhrat Abu Umayyah ﷺ. She was first married to her cousin Abdullah bin Abdul As'ad known as Abu Salamah ﷺ. The couple accepted Islam in the beginning and because of being troubled by the Quraish, they emigrated to Abyssinia. A son, who was born to them in Abyssinia, was named Salamah. After returning from Abyssinia, the family emigrated to Madinah Munawwarah.

Hadhrat Ummu Salamah's ﷺ story about her migration to Madinah Munawwarah has already been given in the early part of this chapter. After reaching Madinah Munawwarah, Hadhrat Ummu Salamah ﷺ had another son 'Umar and two daughters, Durrah ﷺ and Zainab ﷺ. Hadhrat Abu Salamah ﷺ was the eleventh man to accept Islam. He took path in both the battles of Badr as well as in Uhud. He got a very bad wound in Uhud, which did not heal for a long time. He was sent by Nabi ﷺ on an experdition in Safar, 4 A.H. When he returned, the old wound started giving trouble and he passed away because of it on 8th Jumadil-Aakhir, 4 A.H. Hadhrat Ummu Salamah

Ch. 10 – Women's Courage & Love for Islam

رَضِيَ اللَّهُ عَنْهَا was expecting a child at that time. Zainab was born to her after the death of her husband.

After she had completed her Iddat (the waiting period), Hadhrat Abu Bakr رَضِيَ اللَّهُ عَنْهُ proposed to marry her, but she refused. Later, Nabi صَلَّى اللَّهُ عَلَيْهِ وَسَلَّمَ offered to marry her. She said: "O, Nabi of Allah! I have quite a few children with me and I am very sensitive by nature. For getting remarried, I don't have any guardian here in Madinah Munawwarah."

Nabi صَلَّى اللَّهُ عَلَيْهِ وَسَلَّمَ said: "Allah Ta'ala will look after your children and your sensitiveness will disappear shortly. None of your family will dislike the marriage."

She then asked her eldest son Hadhrat Salamah رَضِيَ اللَّهُ عَنْهُ to be her guardian and give her in marriage to Nabi صَلَّى اللَّهُ عَلَيْهِ وَسَلَّمَ. She was married in the end of Shawwal, 4 A.H.

She says: "I had heard from Nabi صَلَّى اللَّهُ عَلَيْهِ وَسَلَّمَ that a person who is struck by a calamity should read this dua,

اَللّٰهُمَّ أُجُرْنِيْ فِيْ مُصِيْبَتِيْ وَاَخْلِفْ لِيْ خَيْرًا مِنْهَا

"O Allah! From You do I hope for reward for this difficulty of mine. So reward me in it and give me something better in return."

Then Allah Ta'ala would accept his dua. I used to read this dua after the death of Hadhrat Abu Salamah رَضِيَ اللَّهُ عَنْهُ, but I could not imagine a husband better than him, until Allah Ta'ala fixed my marriage to Nabi صَلَّى اللَّهُ عَلَيْهِ وَسَلَّمَ."

Hadhrat Aa'ishah رَضِيَ اللَّهُ عَنْهَا says: "Ummu Salamah رَضِيَ اللَّهُ عَنْهَا was famous for her beauty. I once made a plan to see her. I found her much more beautiful than I had heard. I mentioned this to Hafsah who said. "In my opinion, she is not as beautiful as people say."

She passed away in 59 A.H. or 62 A.H. and was the last of the wives of Nabi صَلَّى اللَّهُ عَلَيْهِ وَسَلَّمَ to pass away. She was eighty-four at the time of her death. She was, therefore, born nine years before Nubuwwat.

Nabi صَلَّى اللَّهُ عَلَيْهِ وَسَلَّمَ married her after the death of Hadhrat Zainab bint Khuzaimah رَضِيَ اللَّهُ عَنْهَا. She, therefore, lived in Hadhrat Zainab's رَضِيَ اللَّهُ عَنْهَا house. She found a hand-mill, a kettle and some barley in an earthen jar, lying in the house. She ground some barley and, after adding some fat, cooked a meal, which she served to Nabi ﷺ on the very first day of her marriage with him.

(7) Hadhrat Zainab bint Jahsh رضى الله عنها

After her Nabi ﷺ married Hadhrat Zainab bint Jahsh رضى الله عنها. Hadhrat Zainab bint Jahsh رضى الله عنها was the cousin of Nabi ﷺ. She was first given in marriage by Nabi ﷺ to his adopted son Hadhrat Zaid bin Haarisah رضى الله عنه. When Hadhrat Zaid رضى الله عنه divorced her, she was married to Nabi ﷺ by the command of Allah Ta'ala, as mentioned in Surah Al-Ahzaab. This took place in 5 A.H., when she was thirty-five years old. She was, therefore, born seventeen years before Nubuwwat.

She was always proud of the fact that, while all the other wives were given in marriage to Nabi ﷺ by their guardians, it was Allah Ta'ala Himself Who gave her in marriage to Nabi ﷺ. When Hadhrat Zaid رضى الله عنه divorced her and she had completed her Iddat, Nabi ﷺ sent her his proposal.

She said: "I cannot give an answer until I have asked for advice from my Allah Ta'ala." She performed Wudhu, read two rakaat of Salaah and made dua to Allah, "O, Allah! Your Nabi ﷺ offers to marry me. If I am fit for the honour, then give me in his marriage."

Allah answered her dua by revealing the following verse to Nabi ﷺ:

فَلَمَّا قَضَىٰ زَيْدٌ مِّنْهَا وَطَرًا زَوَّجْنَٰكَهَا لِكَيْ لَا يَكُونَ عَلَى الْمُؤْمِنِينَ حَرَجٌ فِي أَزْوَاجِ أَدْعِيَآئِهِمْ إِذَا قَضَوْا مِنْهُنَّ وَطَرًا ۚ وَكَانَ أَمْرُ اللَّهِ مَفْعُولًا

"So when Zaid رضى الله عنه performed the necessary formality (of divorce) from her, we gave her to you in marriage, so that there may be no sin for the believers in respect of the wives of their adopted sons, when they have divorced them. The order of Allah must be fulfilled." (Surah A'hzaab – Aayah 37)

When she received the good news about this Aayah, she made sajdah before Allah Ta'ala thanking Him. Nabi ﷺ made the walimah in a grand style for this marriage. A goat was slaughtered. Mutton with bread was served to the guests. People came in groups, and were served till all of them were fed.

Hadhrat Zainab رضى الله عنها was very generous in spending in the path of Allah Ta'ala. She earned by working with her hands and spent all her wealth in charity. It was about her that Nabi ﷺ had foretold: "My wife who has long hands will be the first to meet me after my death." The wives understood this to mean the actual length of their arms and began to measure their arms with a stick. When measured, the arm of Hadhrat Sauda رضى الله عنها was the longest. But when Hadhrat Zainab رضى الله عنها passed away first, they understood the true meaning of "long arms" (meaning the most generous). She fasted very often. She passed away in 20 A.H. Hadhrat 'Umar رضى الله عنه performed the Janaazah Salaah. She was fifty at the time of her death.

(8) Hadhrat Juwairiyyah Bintul-Haaris رضى الله عنها

After her Nabi ﷺ married Hadhrat Juwairiyyah رضى الله عنها. Hadhrat Juwairiyyah رضى الله عنها was the daughter of Haaris, the chief of Banu Mustaliq and was married to Musafi bin Safwaan. She was one of the many prisoners who were captured by the Muslims after the Battle of Muraisee'. She was given to Hadhrat Saabit bin Qais رضى الله عنه. He offered to free her for 9 Awqiyyah of gold.

She came to Nabi ﷺ and said: "O, Nabi of Allah! I am the daughter of Haaris, who is the chief of the tribe. You know what difficulty has come to me. The ransom asked by Hadhrat Saabit رضى الله عنه is too much for me. I have come to ask your help."
Nabi ﷺ said, "I will show you something better". Nabi ﷺ offered to pay her ransom, set her free, and offered to take her as his wife. She was very glad to accept this offer. She was married to Nabi ﷺ in 5 A.H. and as a result of this marriage, the prisoners of Banu Mustaliq (Juwairiyyah's رضى الله عنها tribe) numbering about a hundred families, were all set free by the Muslims. They said, "The tribe which

was honoured by Nabi's ﷺ marriage should not remain as slaves."

All the marriages of the Nabi ﷺ were not because of self-interest but rather keeping the interest of Deen in front of him. Hadhrat Juwairiyyah رضى الله عنها was very beautiful and attractive. Three days before she became a prisoner in the battle, she had seen in a dream that the moon came out from Madinah Munawwarah and fell into her lap. She says: "When I was captured, I began to hope that my dream would come true."

She was twenty years old at the time of her marriage to Nabi ﷺ. She passed away in Rabi-ul-Awwal, 50 A.H., in Madinah Munawwarah at the age of sixty-five.

(9) HADHRAT UMMU HABIBAH رضى الله عنها

She was the daughter of Abu Sufyaan, and was first married to Ubaidullah bin Jahsh in Makkah Mukarramah. The couple accepted Islam, and then moved to Abyssinia because of the harassment of the Quraish. One night she saw her husband in a dream in the most ugly and horrible form. The next day she came to know that he had become a Christian. She, however, remained a Muslim and was, therefore, separated from him.

She was now all alone in Abyssinia. Allah Ta'ala soon rewarded her for her loss. Nabi ﷺ sent her an offer of marriage through the King Negus, who sent a woman named Abrahah to her with the message. She was so happy with the good news that she gave the bracelets and other jewellery that she was wearing to the woman in delight. King Negus represented Nabi ﷺ in the Nikaah and gave her 400 Dinaars and many other gifts as dowry. He also gave a feast and Dinaars as gifts to all those who were present in the ceremony. Negus then sent her to Madinah Munawwarah with her dowry and other gifts such as perfume, etc. This marriage took place in 7 A.H. Her father was not a Muslim then. She most probably passed away in 44 A.H.

(10) HADHRAT SAFIYYAH رَضِيَ اللّٰهُ عَنْهَا

She was the daughter of Huyay, who was from the family of Hadhrat Haroon عَلَيْهِ السَّلَام, the brother of Hadhrat Moosa عَلَيْهِ السَّلَام. She was first married to Salam bin Mishkam. She was then in the marriage of Kinaanah bin Abil Huqaiq at the time of the battle of Khaibar. Kinaanah was killed in the battle and she was captured by the Muslims.

Hadhrat Dihyaa Kalbi رَضِيَ اللّٰهُ عَنْهُ asked for a maid, and Nabi ﷺ gave her to him. The other Sahaabah رَضِيَ اللّٰهُ عَنْهُم came to Nabi ﷺ and said: "O, Nabi of Allah! Banu Nazir and Banu Quraizah (the Jewish tribes of Madinah Munawwarah) will feel very offended to see the daughter of a Jewish chief working as a maid. We, therefore, suggest that she may be taken as your wife."

Nabi ﷺ paid a fair amount of money to Hadhrat Dihya رَضِيَ اللّٰهُ عَنْهُ as ransom, and told Safiyyah رَضِيَ اللّٰهُ عَنْهَا: "You are now free; if you like, you can go back to your tribe or if you wish you can be my wife."

She said: "I wanted to be married to you while I was a Jew. How can I leave you now, when I am a Muslim?"

This is because she once saw in her dream a piece of the moon falling into her lap. When she mentioned her dream to her husband Kinaanah, he slapped her face so hard that he left a mark on her eye. He said: "You wish to become the wife of the King of Madinah Munawwarah!"

Her father also beat her when she told him her dream. Then she saw, in her dream, the sun lying on her chest. When she mentioned this to her husband, He said: "You seem to be wishing to become the Queen of Madinah."

She says: "I was seventeen years old when I was married to Nabi ﷺ."

She came to live with Nabi ﷺ when he was returning from Khaibar and camping at the first stage of the return journey. The next morning he told the Sahaabah رَضِيَ اللّٰهُ عَنْهُم: "Let everybody bring whatever he has to eat." They brought their own dates, cheese, butter, etc. A long leather cloth was spread and all of them sat around it to share the food amongst them. This was the walimah for the marriage. She passed away in Ramadhaan, 50 A.H., when she was about sixty years old.

(11) HADHRAT MAIMOONAH ﷺ

Hadhrat Maimoonah ﷺ was the daughter of Haarish bin Hazan. Her original name was Barrah, but she was later renamed Maimoonah by Nabi ﷺ. She was first married to Abu Rahm bin Abdul Uzza. According to some reports, she was married twice before she became Ummul Mu'mineen.

She had been widowed when Nabi ﷺ married her at Sarif, a place on his way to Makkah Mukarramah for 'Umrah in Zul Qa'dah 7 A.H. He had intended to start living with her in Makkah Mukarramah after performing 'Umrah, but because the Quraish did not allow him to enter Makkah Mukarramah, he called her over to him in the same place on his return journey.

Many years later in 51 A.H. she passed away and was buried exactly at the same place when she was eighty-one years old. This is a strange coincidence that at a certain place during one journey she is married, at the same place on the return journey she starts living with Nabi ﷺ, and at the very same place during another journey she passes away and is buried.

Hadhrat Aa'ishah ﷺ says: "Amongst Nabi's ﷺ wives, Maimoonah was the most pious and the most mindful of her family relatives."

Hadhrat Yazeed bin A'sam ﷺ says: "She was seen either busy in Salaah or in her housework. When she was free, she was often seen making Miswaak."

She was the last woman married by Nabi ﷺ. However, Some Muhaditheen have also mentioned one or two other marriages of Nabi ﷺ. But since there isn't consensus on this, it hasn't been mentioned. Of the eleven wives, two passed away in the lifetime of Nabi ﷺ (ie. Hadhrat Khadijah ﷺ and Hadhrat Zainub ﷺ). The remaining nine were alive at the demise of Nabi ﷺ.

THE SONS OF NABI ﷺ

Nabi ﷺ had three sons and four daughters. All the children were born from Hadhrat Khadija ﷺ, except his son Ibrahim. Qaasim was his first son, born to him before Nubuwwat. He passed away when he was two. Abdullah, the second son, was born after Nubuwwat. He was also called Tayyab and Taahir. He also passed away in his childhood.

At the time of his death, the Quraish were overjoyed and said: "Muhammad has no son, and will, therefore, have no one to continue with his family name after him. His name will also die with his death."

It was on this occasion that Surah Al-Kausar was revealed by Allah Ta'ala. It said:

إِنَّآ أَعْطَيْنٰكَ الْكَوْثَرَ ۞ فَصَلِّ لِرَبِّكَ وَانْحَرْ ۞ إِنَّ شَانِئَكَ هُوَ الْأَبْتَرُ ۞

*"Verily We have granted you (O Rasulullah ﷺ) abundant good. So **(as a token of gratitude)** perform Salaah for your Rabb and sacrifice **(animals in His name)**. Certainly, it is your enemy who shall be unknown (without posterity)."*

(Surah Kauthar - Aayaat 1-3)

Even after more than 1400 years, today there are millions who are proud to be connected to Nabi ﷺ in love and devotion.

Ibrahim, the third son and last child, was born in Madinah Munawwarah in 8 A.H. Nabi's ﷺ slave woman Maariyah Qibtiyyah gave birth to him. Nabi ﷺ performed the Aqeeqah ceremony on the seventh day of his birth. Two lambs were slaughtered, the child's head was shaved by Hadhrat Abu Hind Bayazi رضی اللہ عنہ, silver in weight equal to his hair was spent in charity and the hair was buried.

Nabi ﷺ said: "I am naming my child after the name of my forefather Ibrahim عليه السلام."

This son also passed away, on the 10th Rabi-ul-Awwal, 10 A.H., when he was only eighteen months old. Nabi ﷺ then said: "Allah Ta'ala has arranged a heavenly nurse to look after Ibrahim in the gardens of Jannah."

THE DAUGHTERS OF NABI ﷺ

(1) HADHRAT ZAINAB رَضِيَ اللَّهُ عَنْهَا

She was the eldest daughter of Nabi ﷺ and was born in the fifth year of his first marriage, when he was thirty years old. She accepted Islam and was married to her cousin Abul Aas bin Rabi. The story of her emigrating to Madinah Munawwarah and her getting wounded by the Quraish has already been given in the early part of this chapter. She suffered for a long time from that wound and passed away because of it in the beginning of 8 A.H.

Her husband later accepted Islam and joined her in Madinah Munawwarah. She had a son Ali رَضِيَ اللَّهُ عَنْهُ, and a daughter Umaamah. Ali رَضِيَ اللَّهُ عَنْهُ passed away during the lifetime of Nabi ﷺ. This same Ali رَضِيَ اللَّهُ عَنْهُ was the person who sat with Nabi ﷺ on the camel's back at the time of his victorious entry into Makkah Mukarramah. We often read in the Hadith about a little girl riding on the back of Nabi ﷺ as he went down into sajda in his Salaah. This was Umaamah, Zainab's رَضِيَ اللَّهُ عَنْهَا daughter. She lived for a long time after the death of Nabi ﷺ. Hadhrat Ali رَضِيَ اللَّهُ عَنْهُ married her on the death of Hadhrat Faatimah رَضِيَ اللَّهُ عَنْهَا his first wife. It is said that Hadhrat Faatimah رَضِيَ اللَّهُ عَنْهَا, at the time of her death had, said that Hadhrat Ali رَضِيَ اللَّهُ عَنْهُ should marry her. She had no children from Hadhrat Ali رَضِيَ اللَّهُ عَنْهُ. After Hadhrat Ali's رَضِيَ اللَّهُ عَنْهُ death she was married to Hadhrat Mughirah bin Naufal رَضِيَ اللَّهُ عَنْهُ, from whom she had one son named Yahya. She passed away in 50 A.H.

(2) HADHRAT RUQAYYAH رَضِيَ اللَّهُ عَنْهَا

She was born three years after the birth of Hadhrat Zainab رَضِيَ اللَّهُ عَنْهَا, when Nabi ﷺ was thirty-three years old. In her childhood, she was married to Utbah, the son of Abu Lahab, Nabi's ﷺ uncle, and had not yet started living with him when Surah Al-Lahab was revealed.

Abu Lahab called his sons Utbah and Utaibah (to whom Ummu Kulsum, another daughter of Nabi ﷺ was married), and told them: "Unless both of you divorce the daughters of Muhammad, I am not going to see your faces." They divorced their wives.

Later, when Makkah Mukarramah was conquered by the Muslims, Utbah accepted Islam. After this divorce, Hadhrat Ruqayyah رَضِيَ اللهُ عَنْها was married to Hadhrat 'Usmaan رَضِيَ اللهُ عَنْهُ. The couple made hijrat to Abyssinia twice, as we have already seen in chapter one. Nabi ﷺ had announced to the Sahaabah رَضِيَ اللهُ عَنْهُم that he was waiting to receive Allah ta'ala's command for making hijrat to Madinah Munawwarah. The Sahaabah رَضِيَ اللهُ عَنْهُم started making hijrat to Madinah Munawwarah even before Nabi's ﷺ Hijrat. Hadhrat Usmaan رَضِيَ اللهُ عَنْهُ and Hadhrat Ruqayyah رَضِيَ اللهُ عَنْها had also made hijrat to Madinah Munawwarah before Nabi ﷺ.

At the time of Badr, Hadhrat Ruqayyah رَضِيَ اللهُ عَنْها was ill and she later passed away of this illness. Hadhrat 'Usmaan رَضِيَ اللهُ عَنْهُ was, therefore, asked by Nabi ﷺ to stay in Madinah Munawwarah and look after her. The news about the victory in Badr was received in Madinah Munawwarah when the people were returning from Hadhrat Ruqayyah's رَضِيَ اللهُ عَنْها funeral. Thus, Nabi ﷺ was not able to be present at her burial.

A son was born to Hadhrat Ruqayyah رَضِيَ اللهُ عَنْها in Abyssinia. He was named Abdullah and lived longer than his mother but passed away in 4 A.H. when he was six years old. Some reports indicate that he passed away one year before his mother.

(3) Hadhrat Umme Kulsum رَضِيَ اللهُ عَنْها

She is the third daughter of Nabi ﷺ. She was married to Utaibah, the son of Abu Lahab, but had not yet started living with him when Utaibah divorced her after the revelation of Surah Al-Lahab, as has already been mentioned. After divorcing her, Utaibah came to Nabi ﷺ and said the rudest words to him.

Nabi ﷺ cursed him by making this dua: "O, Allah! Order one of your dogs to punish him."

Abu Taalib, who had also not accepted Islam, was terrified and told Utaibah; "You have no way out from this curse."

Once, Utaibah and Abu Lahab went with a group of people to Syria. Abu Lahab, in spite of his kufr and hatred, told the people: "I am afraid of Muhammad's (ﷺ) curse. Everybody should take care of my son."

They happened to camp at a place where there were many lions. The people had piled up all their luggage and Utaibah was made to sleep on top of the pile, while the rest of the people slept around the pile. A lion came at night and smelt all the people sleeping around the pile. The lion then jumped over the people and reached Utaibah. He screamed, but the lion had bitten off his head from his body.

It is extremely necessary that we avoid offending people who are dear to Allah Ta'ala. Nabi ﷺ has reported Allah Ta'ala as saying:

مَنْ عَادٰى لِيْ وَلِيًّا فَقَدْ اٰذَنْتُهُ بِالْحَرْبِ (صحيح البخارى # 6502)

"He who insults my friends I announce war with him."

After the death of Hadhrat Ruqayyah رضى الله عنها, Hadhrat Ummu Kulsum رضى الله عنها was married to Hadhrat Usmaan رضى الله عنه in Rabi-ul-Awwal, 3 A.H. Nabi ﷺ said: "I have given Ummu Kulsum in marriage to Usmaan by Allah's command."

She passed away in Sha'ban, 9 A.H. without having any children. After her death, Nabi ﷺ is reported to have said: "Even if I had one hundred daughters, I would have given all of them in marriage to 'Usmaan رضى الله عنه one after the other, if each one had passed away."

(4) Hadhrat Faatimah رضى الله عنها

Hadhrat Faatimah رضى الله عنها, the fourth and the youngest daughter of Nabi ﷺ will be the leader of the women in Jannah. She was born in the first year of Nubuwwat, when he was forty-one years old. It is said that the name Faatimah (meaning safe from fire) was revealed by Allah Ta'ala. She was married to Hadhrat Ali رضى الله عنه in 2 A.H. She began to live with him seven and a half months later. She was about fifteen and Hadhrat Ali رضى الله عنه was twenty-one at the time of their marriage.

Of all the daughters, she was the most beloved of Nabi ﷺ. Whenever he went out on a journey, she was the last one to meet him and when he returned home, she was the first one to meet him. When Hadhrat Ali ﷺ was thinking of marrying Abu Jahal's daughter, she was very upset and mentioned her grief to Nabi ﷺ.

Nabi ﷺ told Hadhrat Ali ﷺ: "Faatimah is a part of my body. Whoever upsets her upsets me."

Hadhrat Ali ﷺ gave up the idea of the second marriage during her lifetime. After her death, he married her niece Umaamah ﷺ, as we have already read in the previous pages. It was about six months after the death of Nabi ﷺ that Hadhrat Faatimah ﷺ fell ill.

One day, she told her maid: "I want to take a bath. Arrange some water for me." She took a bath and changed her clothes. She then asked for her bed to be placed in the middle of the room. She laid herself down on the bedding, with her face towards the Qiblah, with her right hand under her right cheek, she said: "I am now going to pass away." The next moment she had passed away.

Nabi's ﷺ family continued and shall, Insha Allah, continue through her children. She had three sons and three daughters. Hadhrat Hasan ﷺ and Hadhrat Husain ﷺ were born in the second and the third year respectively, after marriage. Muhassan ﷺ, the third son, was born in 4 A.H., but passed away in childhood.

Ruqayyah, her first daughter, also passed away in childhood and has not been mentioned much in history. Her second daughter Ummu Kulsum, who was first married to Hadhrat 'Umar ﷺ, had one son, Zaid and one daughter Ruqayyah. After Hadhrat 'Umar's ﷺ death, Hadhrat Ummu Kulsum ﷺ was married to Aun bin Ja'far ﷺ, but had no children from him. After his death, his brother Muhammad bin Ja'far ﷺ married her. A daughter was born to them, who passed away in childhood. Even her husband Muhammad ﷺ passed away in her lifetime and she was then married to the third brother, Abdullah bin Ja'far ﷺ, from whom she had no child. She passed away as Abdullah's ﷺ wife. Her son Zaid also passed away the same day and they both were carried for burial at the same time.

Abdullah, 'Aun and Muhammad ﷺ have already been mentioned as sons of Ja'far ﷺ and nephews of Ali ﷺ in chapter six. Zainab, Hadhrat Fatimah's ﷺ third daughter, was married to Abdullah bin Ja'far ﷺ and had two sons Abdullah and Aun from him. After her death, he married her sister Hadhrat UmmuKulsum ﷺ. Hadhrat Ali ﷺ had many other children from his wives after Faatimah ﷺ. It is stated that he had as many as thirty-two children, sixteen sons and sixteen daughters. Hadhrat Hasan ﷺ had fifteen sons and eight daughters, while Hadhrat Husain ﷺ was the father of six sons and three daughters.

رَضِيَ اللهُ تَعَالٰى عَنْهُمْ وَاَرْضَاهُمْ اَجْمَعِيْنَ وَجَعَلَنَا بِهَدْيِهِمْ مُتَّبِعِيْنَ وَاللهُ اَعْلَمُ وَعِلْمُهُ اَتَمُّ

CHAPTER 11

CHILDREN AND THEIR LOVE FOR ISLAM

The true love of Islam in the children of Sahaabah رضي الله عنهم was because of how they were brought up. Parents nowadays spoil their children by over petting them. If, instead, they teach them the importance of Islamic practices, these will become their habits when they grow up.

When we see a child doing something wrong, we say, 'He is only a child.' Some foolish parents actually feel proud when their beloved child misbehaves. We bluff ourselves when we say that, 'he will be all right when he grows up.'

How can a bad seed grow up into a good plant? If you really wish your child to be a good Muslim when he is grown up, then you have to plant the seed of Imaan and Islam in his heart right from childhood. The Sahaabah رضي الله عنهم were very careful about training their children Islamically and they kept a watchful eye over them.

In Hadhrat 'Umar's رضي الله عنه time, a person was arrested by the police for drinking in Ramadhaan. When he was brought before Hadhrat 'Umar رضي الله عنه, he told him: "Destruction to you! Even our children are fasting in this month." The person was punished with eighty lashes and was chased away from Madinah Munawwarah forever.

1. CHILDREN KEEP FAST

Hadhrat Rubbayi' bint Mu'awwaz رضي الله عنها says: "Once Nabi صلى الله عليه وسلم asked us to fast on the tenth of Muharram. Since then we have always fasted on that day. Even the children were made to fast with us. When they cried out of hunger, we kept them busy with toys till the time of Iftaar."

From the Ahaadith we learn that even the breastfeeding mothers of those days would not feed their babies during the fast. They could manage all this, as their health and strength were far better than ours. But, are we really doing even what we could easily manage? Surely we should not force on our children what they cannot manage, but we must encourage them do what they can easily manage.

2. HADHRAT AA'ISHAH'S رَضِيَ اللهُ عَنْهَا THIRST FOR KNOWLEDGE

Hadhrat Aa'ishah رَضِيَ اللهُ عَنْهَا was given in nikah to Nabi ﷺ when she was six years old. She started living with Nabi ﷺ when she was nine years old. She was only eighteen years old at the time of Nabi's ﷺ passing away. Despite her age, she is responsible for reporting many Ahaadith and Islamic laws.

Masrooq *(rahmatullahi alayh)* says: "I saw many famous Sahaabah رَضِيَ اللهُ عَنْهُمْ coming to Hadhrat Aa'ishah رَضِيَ اللهُ عَنْهَا for seeking knowledge about Islamic laws."

'Ata *(rahmatullahi alayh)* says: "Hadhrat Aa'ishah رَضِيَ اللهُ عَنْهَا was more learned than many of the men of her time."

Hadhrat Abu Moosa رَضِيَ اللهُ عَنْهُ says: "With the help of Hadhrat Aa'ishah رَضِيَ اللهُ عَنْهَا, an answer was found to each and every problem we had regarding Islamic knowledge."

The books of Hadith contain as many as 2210 Ahaadith narrated by Hadhrat Aa'ishah رَضِيَ اللهُ عَنْهَا. She says: "I was a child and playing with my friends in Makkah Mukarramah when the following Aayah, was revealed to Nabi ﷺ."

$$\text{بَلِ السَّاعَةُ مَوْعِدُهُمْ وَالسَّاعَةُ أَدْهَى وَأَمَرُّ}$$

"The fact is that the Hour (Qiyaamah) is their appointment and the Hour (Qiyaamah) shall e most severe and most bitter."
(Surah Qamar – Aayah 46)

We know that she made hijrat to Madinah Munawwarah when she was only eight years old. She would have been much younger when this Aayat was revealed in Makkah Mukarramah. This clearly shows her great thirst and love for Islamic knowledge right from her childhood.

3. HADHRAT 'UMAIR ﷺ DESIRE TO GO FOR JIHAAD

Hadhrat 'Umair ﷺ was a slave of Abul Lahm ﷺ and was very young. Every person in those days, young or old wished to go out in the path of Allah Ta'ala. 'Umair ﷺ asked Nabi ﷺ to allow him to fight in the Battle of Khaibar. His master also recommended him very strongly. Nabi ﷺ allowed him and gave him a sword, which 'Umair ﷺ hung around his neck. Now the sword was so big for him that he had to drag it. He fought in the battle till it ended in victory.

As 'Umair ﷺ was a minor and a slave, he was not allowed a full share in the booty. However, Nabi ﷺ gave him a share as a very special case.

Note: Hadhrat 'Umair ﷺ was so eager to fight in the battle that he asked others to intercede on his behalf, even though he knew that he will not get any share from the booty. What could be his reason other than the reward of the Aakhirat, as promised by Allah Ta'ala and His Nabi ﷺ?

4. HADHRAT 'UMAIR BIN ABI WAQQAAS ﷺ HIDES HIMSELF TO GO TO BADR

Hadhrat 'Umair bin Abi Waqqaas ﷺ was a young Sahaabi who had accepted Islam in its early days. He was a brother of Hadhrat Sa'ad bin Abi Waqqaas ﷺ, the famous Muslim General.

Hadhrat Sa'ad ﷺ says: "At the time when we were preparing to march to Badr, I noticed 'Umair ﷺ trying to hide himself. This surprised me. I told him, 'What has happened to you? What makes you hide like this?' He replied, 'Although I wish to go and get martyred in the path of Allah Ta'ala, I am afraid that Nabi ﷺ may stop me from taking part in the battle because of my young age."

'Umair's رضى الله عنه fear turned out to be true. Nabi ﷺ spotted him and then stopped him from going with the army. Hadhrat 'Umair رضى الله عنه could not bear this and began to cry. When Nabi ﷺ was informed of this eagerness and disappointment, he allowed him to go. He fought in the battle and his other desire was fulfilled, he was martyred in the battle.

Hadhrat Sa'ad رضى الله عنه, Hadhrat Umair's رضى الله عنه brother, says: "The sword of Umair رضى الله عنه was too big for him. I had to put a number of knots in the belt, so that it might not touch the ground."

5. TWO YOUNGSTERS OF THE ANSAAR KILL ABU JAHL

Hadhrat Abdur Rahmaan bin 'Auf رضى الله عنه, who is a famous Sahaabi, says: "In the battle of Badr, I was standing in the fighting line when I noticed two Ansaari youngsters, one on either side of me. I thought that it would have been better if I had been between strong men who could help me in need. Suddenly one of the boys caught my hand and said, 'Uncle, do you know Abu Jahl?' I said, 'Yes, but what do you mean by this?' He said, 'I have come to know that this terrible man speaks bad things about Nabi ﷺ. By Him who holds my life in His hand, if I see him, I will not leave him until I kill him or I am killed.' His words left me amazed. Then the other boy had a similar talk with me. I happened to notice Abu Jahl moving about in the battlefield on horseback. I told the boys, 'There is Abu Jahl.' Both of them immediately rushed towards him and attacked him with their swords, until I saw him fall from his horse."

Note: These boys were Hadhrat Muaaz bin Amr bin Jamooh رضى الله عنه and Muaaz bin 'Afra رضى الله عنه.

Muaaz bin Amr bin Jamooh رضى الله عنه says: "I had heard the people say, 'No one can kill Abu Jahl. He is very well guarded.' At that time, I promised to finish him. Abu Jahl was arranging his lines for attack, when he was spotted by Hadhrat Abdur Rahmaan bin Auf رضى الله عنه. The boys were on foot, while Abu Jahl was on horseback. This made it difficult for them to attack Abu Jahl, thus one of the boys hit a leg of the horse and the other that of Abu Jahl. This caused both to fall down and Abu Jahl was unable to get up. The boys left him in this condition. Mu'awwaz bin

Afra ﷺ, the brother of Hadhrat Muaaz bin Afra ﷺ, then went and wounded him even more with his sword, so that he might not drag himself to his camp. Finally, Hadhrat Abdullah bin Mas'ood ﷺ attacked him and cut-off his head from his body."

Hadhrat Muaaz bin Amr bin Jamooh ﷺ says: "When I hit Abu Jahl with my sword, his son Ikramah was with him. He attacked me on my shoulder and cut off my arm, leaving it hanging by the skin only. I threw the broken arm over my shoulder and kept on fighting with one hand, but when it became too difficult, I separated it from my body by placing it under my foot and pulling myself up and threw it away."

6. A CONTEST BETWEEN RAAFI' ﷺ & SAMURAH ﷺ

Whenever an army of Mujaahideen came out of Madinah Munawwarah for battle, Nabi ﷺ inspected them outside Madinah Munawwarah to see that nothing was short in the men and the equipment. It was here that he usually returned all the young boys to Madinah Munawwarah, who had come out with the army wishing to fight for Islam.

While setting out for Uhud, Nabi ﷺ carried out an inspection just outside Madinah Munawwarah. He ordered the young boys to go back. Among them were Abdullah bin 'Umar, Zaid bin Saabit, Usaamah bin Zaid, Zaid bin Arqam, Baraa bin Aazib, Amr bin Hazam, Usaid bin Zuhair, 'Uraabah bin Aus, Abu Sa'eed Khudri, Samurah bin Jundub and Raafi' bin Khudaij ﷺ. All of them were around the ages of thirteen to fourteen.

Khudaij said to Nabi ﷺ: "O Nabi of Allah! My son Raafi' is a very good archer." Hadhrat Raafi' ﷺ stood on his toes to show himself to be taller than he actually was. Nabi ﷺ allowed him to stay on.

When Samurah bin Jundub ﷺ learnt about this, he complained to his step-father Murrah bin Sanaan ﷺ saying: "Nabi ﷺ has allowed Raafi' and rejected me. I am stronger than him and I am sure to beat him in a wrestling match.

This was mentioned to Nabi ﷺ who allowed Samurah to wrestle with Raafi'. Samurah did actually beat Raafi' in the fight and he too was allowed to join the army. A few more boys tried to stay on and some of them were given permission.

Meanwhile it became dark. Nabi ﷺ made the arrangements for the guarding of the camp during the night, and then asked: "Now, who is going to guard my tent during the night?"

A person (standing at his place) replied: "I, O Nabi of Allah!"

Nabi ﷺ asked: "What is your name?"

The person replied: "Zakwaan."

Nabi ﷺ said: "All right. Sit down."

He again asked: "Who else will guard my tent tonight?"

A voice replied: "I, O Nabi of Allah!"

Nabi ﷺ asked: "Who are you?"

A voice replied: "Abu Saba' (father of Saba')."

Nabi ﷺ said: "All right. Sit down."

He asked for the third time: "Who will be the third man to guard my tent tonight?"

Again a voice came from the crowd: "I, O Nabi of Allah!"

Nabi ﷺ asked: "Your name?"

The voice replied: "Ibn Abdul Qais (son of Abdul Qais)."

Nabi ﷺ said: "All right. You also sit down."

Then Nabi ﷺ asked all three to come to him. Only one person came forward: "Where are your other two friends?"

The person replied: "O Nabi of Allah! It was I who stood up all three times."

Nabi ﷺ blessed him with his duas and allowed him to guard his tent. He kept guarding the tent all night long.

Note: Just look! How eager were the Sahaabah رضي الله عنهم to face death for the sake of Allah Ta'ala and His Nabi ﷺ. The children and adults, young and old, men and women, all had the same burning spirit of sacrifice and love. That is why success greeted them at every step.

Raafi' bin Khudaij رضي الله عنه had offered to fight in Badr too, but he was not allowed. However, he was allowed to fight for the first time in Uhud. Since then, he had been taking part in almost all the battles. In Uhud, the enemy's arrow struck him in his chest. When it was taken out, a small piece remained inside his body. This caused a wound, which finally caused his death in old age.

7. HADHRAT ZAID رضي الله عنه GETS CHOSEN FOR HIS KNOWLEDGE OF QUR-AAN

Hadhrat Zaid bin Saabit رضي الله عنه was six years old when his father passed away. At the time of Hijrah he was eleven years old. He wanted to join in the battle of Badr, but was sent back because of his young age. He again tried to join in the battle of Uhud. He was not allowed this time also. After Uhud, he took part in all the battles. When the Muslims were marching towards Tabuk, the flag of the Banu Maalik family was held by Ammaarah رضي الله عنه. Nabi ﷺ took the flag from him and gave it to Zaid رضي الله عنه. Ammaarah رضي الله عنه thought that perhaps this was because of some fault of his, which had displeased Nabi ﷺ.

He therefore asked: "O, Nabi of Allah! Did somebody complain about me?"

Nabi ﷺ said: "No, but Zaid knows more Qur-aan than you. His Qur-aan has given him preference over you."

Note: It was the noble habit of Rasulullah ﷺ that he chose people according to their good qualities. Although over here it was the occasion of fighting and there was no direct link with regards to having more knowledge of the Qur-aan, yet Rasulullah ﷺ had given preference to him to carry the flag. In most instances Rasulullah ﷺ would give preference to this, so much so that if there was a need to bury many people in one grave the one who was more learned in the Qur-aan was given preference like was done in the Battle of Uhud.

8. THE FATHER OF HADHRAT ABU SA'EED KHUDRI رضي الله عنه PASSES AWAY

Hadhrat Abu Sa'eed Khudri رضي الله عنه says, "When I was thirteen years old, I was brought to Nabi ﷺ by my father for fighting in Uhud. My father recommended me saying: 'O, Nabi of Allah! He has a very good body. His bones are very well formed.' Nabi ﷺ looked at me again and again and finally sent me back due to my young age.

However, my father took part in the battle and was killed. He left me nothing to live on. I went to Nabi ﷺ to ask for help. Before I could even speak, he said: "Abu Sa'eed! Whoever asks for patience from Allah Ta'ala, Allah Ta'ala blesses him with patience, whoever asks for chastity from Him, He protects his chastity, and whoever asks for contentment from Him will surely be blessed with it." After hearing this, I returned home without asking him for anything.

Because of this, Allah Ta'ala blessed him with such a high position that, from the younger Sahaabah رضى الله عنهم, there was nobody gifted with so much knowledge and learning as Hadhrat Abu Sa'eed رضى الله عنه.

Note: Look at the patience of Hadhrat Abu Sa'eed رضى الله عنه at such a young age. As we know, in Uhud, he had lost his father, who had left him nothing to live on and, therefore, he fully deserved all the help yet a few words of Nabi ﷺ stopped him from talking of his suffering and asking for a favour.

Can a person much older than him show such strength of character? In fact, the persons selected by Allah Ta'ala for the company of his dear Nabi ﷺ did really deserve that honour. That is why Nabi ﷺ had said: "Allah has preferred my Sahaabah رضى الله عنهم over all other men."

9. HADHRAT SALAMAH BIN AKWAH رضى الله عنه CHALLENGERS A GROUP OF ROBBERS SINGLE HANDEDLY

Ghaabah was a small village about four or five miles (approximately seven to eight kilometers) from Madinah Munawwarah. The camels of Nabi ﷺ were sent there for grazing. Abdur Rahmaan Fazari and a few kuffaar killed the person looking after the camels and stole them. The robbers were on horseback and all of them were armed. That morning Salamah bin Akwah رضى الله عنه was walking in that direction with his bow and arrows when he saw the robbers. Although he was only a boy, he ran very fast. It is said that he could beat the fastest horse in a race. He was also a very good archer.

As soon as he saw the robbers, he climbed up a hill and shouted towards Madinah Munawwarah to call for help. He then chased the robbers till he got close and started shooting arrows at them one after the other. He did this so quickly that the robbers thought they were being chased by a large number of people. If any of the robbers turned his horse towards him, he hid behind a tree and shot the animal with his arrows. The robbers at once ran off at full speed to save themselves from getting caught.

Salamah رضى الله عنه says: "I kept on chasing the robbers until all the camels stolen by them were left behind me. While escaping they left behind thirty spears and thirty sheets of cloth of their own. Meanwhile, Uyaynah bin Hisn (another robber) and his group arrived to help the robbers. They had meanwhile come to know that I was all alone. They now came towards me in large numbers and I was forced to climb up a hill.

As they were about to come close to me, I shouted, 'Stop. First listen to me. Do you know who am I? I am Ibnul Akwah. By Him who has given honour to Nabi Muhammad ﷺ, if anyone of you wishes to catch me, he will not be able to do so. But if I choose to attack any of you he cannot escape me.' I kept on talking to them in this manner to buy some time till, I thought, help would reach me from Madinah Munawwarah. I looked anxiously through the trees, as I talked to them when at last I noticed a group of riders headed by Akhram Asadi رضى الله عنه coming towards me. As Akhram رضى الله عنه approached the robbers, he attacked Abdur Rahmaan and cut one leg of his horse. As Abdur Rahmaan fell down from his horse, he attacked Akhram and killed him. Abu Qataadah رضى الله عنه had meanwhile arrived. In the fighting that took place, Abdur Rahmaan lost his life and Abu Qatadah رضى الله عنه lost his horse."

Note: It is written in some books of history that, when Akhram was going to attack Abdur Rahmaan, Salamah رضى الله عنه advised him to wait till the rest of his people had joined him but he did not wait, saying: "I wish to die in the path of Allah Ta'ala."

He was the only person killed from the Muslims. The robbers lost many of their men. More help reached the Muslims and the robbers ran away. Salamah رضي الله عنه asked for Nabi's ﷺ permission to go after the robbers saying: "O, Nabi of Allah! Let me have one hundred men, I shall teach them a lesson."

Nabi ﷺ said: "No. They would have reached their homes by now."

Most of the historians say that Salamah رضي الله عنه was about twelve or thirteen years old at that time. Look how a boy of such a young age was able to chase so many robbers by himself. He recovered all the stolen goods and also took a great amount of booty from them. This was the result of Imaan and Ikhlaas, which Allah Ta'ala had filled in the hearts of the Sahaabah رضي الله عنهم.

10. HADHRAT BARAA رضي الله عنه WANTING TO JOIN IN THE BATTLE OF BADR

The battle of Badr was the greatest battle ever fought by the Muslims in virtue and importance. It was a very difficult occasion. The Muslim army were faced with a well-equipped army of the enemy. The Muslim army had 313 men, three horses, seventy camels, six or nine coats of armour and eight swords, while on the other hand the Quraish had about 1000 men, 100 horses, 700 camels and were fully armed. The Quraish were so sure of victory that they had brought with them musical instruments and female singers to celebrate the victory. On the other hand, Nabi ﷺ was very worried because of the extreme weakness of the Muslims.

Nabi ﷺ made dua to Allah Ta'ala saying: "O, Allah! Your faithful slaves are on foot, You and only You can provide them with animals to ride upon. They are naked, You and only You can clothe them. They are hungry, only You can fill their bellies. They are poor, You and only You can look after their needs." Allah Ta'ala accepted his dua and gave the Muslims a most wonderful victory.

Although they knew the strength of the Quraish, Abdullah bin 'Umar رضي الله عنه and Baraa bin Aazib رضي الله عنه, wanted to join the battle and came out with the Mujahidin. However, because of their young age, Nabi

ﷺ did not allow them to go to the battlefield. As we have already seen, both these boys were also sent back for the same reason at the time of Uhud, which took place one year after Badr. Look at the youngsters of that time. They were restless to get permission to take part in every battle.

11. HADHRAT ABDULLAH BIN ABDULLAH BIN UBAYY ؓ DISGRACES HIS MUNAAFIQ FATHER

During the famous battle of Banul Mustaliq in 5 A.H., a Muhaajir and an Ansaari had some misunderstanding. Each of them called his own people for help and there was a serious danger of a fight between the two groups of the Muslims, but this was avoided through the efforts of some sensible people.

Abdullah bin Ubayy, who was the chief of the Munaafiqeen, was a very bitter enemy of Islam. Outwardly he acted like a Muslim, and was treated as one by the other Muslims. And this was the general approach towards all the Munaafiqeen. When he came to know of this incident, he used some rude words for Nabi ﷺ and told his people: "All this is because of what you people have done with your own hands. You provided a home to these strangers (meaning the Muhaajireen) in your town and shared your wealth equally with them. If you take back your help from them, they will be forced to go back."

He also said: "By Allah! After returning to Madinah Munawwarah, we, the respected people, shall chase out these evil people from there."

Hadhrat Zaid bin Arqam ؓ, an Ansaari boy, was listening to him. He could not tolerate these words and at once replied angrily by telling him: "By Allah! You are evil. Even your own people look down upon you, and nobody will support you. Muhammad ﷺ is most honoured. He is given respect by Rahmaan (Allah Ta'ala) and respected by his followers."

Abdullah bin Ubayy said: "All right. Do not mention it to anybody. It was only a joke. I was not serious in what I said."

However, Hadhrat Zaid ؓ went straight to Nabi ﷺ and told him what the Munaafiq had said. Hadhrat 'Umar ؓ asked for

Nabi's ﷺ permission to kill Abdullah bin Ubayy but Nabi ﷺ refused.

When Abdullah bin Ubayy learnt that Nabi ﷺ had received the news about his disrespectful talk, he came to him and swore by Allah saying: "I never said such a thing. Zaid is a liar as he has given you false news."

A few of the Ansaar were also sitting with Nabi ﷺ. They also supported him by saying: "O, Nabi of Allah! He is the chief of his tribe and is a noble man. His words are more reliable than those of a young boy. It is possible that Zaid might have misheard or misunderstood him."

Nabi ﷺ accepted this statement and took no action against him. When Zaid ؓ came to know that the Munaafiq had lied to Nabi ﷺ through false oaths, he would not come out for shame of being called a liar by the people. He would not even go to Nabi ﷺ. At last, Allah Ta'ala revealed Surah Al-Munaafiqoon, in which the words of Zaid ؓ were shown to be true and the Munaafiq was shown to be a liar. After this, all the people began to honour Hadhrat Zaid ؓ and look down upon the Munaafiq.

The Munaafiq (Abdullah bin Ubayy) had a son. His name was also Abdullah and he was a very sincere Muslim. When the Mujaahideen were about to reach Madinah Munawwarah, he pulled out his sword and stood just outside the town and, in a challenging tone, told his Munaafiq father: "I will not allow you to enter Madinah Munawwarah, until you admit with your own tongue that it is you who is mean and Muhammad ﷺ is most honoured."

This surprised him very much, as the son had always been very respectful to him, but now he was prepared to kill him, his own father, for the honour of Nabi ﷺ. The Munaafiq had to say: "By Allah! I am mean, and Muhammad ﷺ is most honoured." He was then allowed to enter the town.

12. HADHRAT JAABIR'S ﺭﺿﻲ ﺍﻟﻠﻪ ﻋﻨﻪ EAGERNESS TO FIGHT

When the Battle of Uhud was over and the Sahaabah ﺭﺿﻲ ﺍﻟﻠﻪ ﻋﻨﻬﻢ had just returned to Madinah Munawwarah, they got the news that Abu Sufyaan was prepairing to attack them. They were very tired and even injured. The Quraish, on their way back to Makkah Mukarramah, camped at a place called Hamraaul Asad. Their chief, Abu Sufyaan, sat in a meeting with his chiefs. They spoke among themselves: "The Muslims were defeated in Uhud so their confidence must be very low. This is the best time to kill Muhammad. We do not know if we will get another opportunity or not."

They, therefore, decided to return and attack Madinah Munawwarah. When Nabi ﺻﻠﻰ ﺍﻟﻠﻪ ﻋﻠﻴﻪ ﻭﺳﻠﻢ heard about this meeting, he ordered all those Sahaabah ﺭﺿﻲ ﺍﻟﻠﻪ ﻋﻨﻬﻢ who had taken part in Uhud, and who had just returned from the battle, to move out of Madinah Munawwarah and meet the enemy on the way. Although the Muslims were very tired, they all got ready to go. Because Nabi ﺻﻠﻰ ﺍﻟﻠﻪ ﻋﻠﻴﻪ ﻭﺳﻠﻢ's instruction was that, only those people who participate in Uhud should go out again.

Hadhrat Jaabir ﺭﺿﻲ ﺍﻟﻠﻪ ﻋﻨﻪ made a request to Nabi ﺻﻠﻰ ﺍﻟﻠﻪ ﻋﻠﻴﻪ ﻭﺳﻠﻢ saying: "O, Nabi of Allah! I was very eager to fight in Uhud, but my father stopped me from going, saying that there was no other male in the house to look after my seven sisters and that only one of us could join the battle. As he had made up his mind to go, he asked me to remain with the family. He was killed in Uhud. Now I am very eager to go with you and fight the Quraish."

Nabi ﺻﻠﻰ ﺍﻟﻠﻪ ﻋﻠﻴﻪ ﻭﺳﻠﻢ allowed him to go. He was the only person in that battle who had not fought in Uhud.

Note: Hadhrat Jaabir's ﺭﺿﻲ ﺍﻟﻠﻪ ﻋﻨﻪ request is worthy of admiration. Since, Hadhrat Jaabir's ﺭﺿﻲ ﺍﻟﻠﻪ ﻋﻨﻪ father had just been martyred in Uhud. He left Jaabir ﺭﺿﻲ ﺍﻟﻠﻪ ﻋﻨﻪ a big family to look after and large debts to pay. The debts were due to one of the Jews, who as we know hardly ever have mercy in their hearts for their debtors. And in this case, they were been put under a lot of pressure. Besides this, his seven sisters, for whose sake he was not allowed to go to Uhud, still had to be cared for. Now look! In spite of all these difficulties, Jaabir ﺭﺿﻲ ﺍﻟﻠﻪ ﻋﻨﻪ requests Nabi ﺻﻠﻰ ﺍﻟﻠﻪ ﻋﻠﻴﻪ ﻭﺳﻠﻢ for permission to go to battle. His enthusiasim for jihaad is really wonderful!

13. HADHRAT IBN ZUBAIR'S رضي الله عنه BRAVERY AGAINST THE ROMANS

In 26 A.H. the Khalifah 'Usmaan رضي الله عنه appointed Abdullah bin Abi Sarah رضي الله عنه as the Governor of Egypt in place of Amr bin Aas رضي الله عنه. Hadhrat Abdullah رضي الله عنه, with 20 000 Mujaahideen, went to meet the Roman Army of 200 000. It was a very fierce battle. The Roman commander Jarjir made an announcement saying: "The person who kills Abdullah, will get my daughter's hand in marriage and also 100 000 Dinars in prize."

Some of the Muslims became worried over this announcement. When Abdullah bin Zubair رضي الله عنه was informed of this, he said: "There is nothing to worry about. We may also announce that the person killing Jarjir will get Jarjir's daughter in marriage, 100 000 Dinars in prize, and also a chance to rule over Jarjirs' land."

The fighting was very fierce and went on for a long time. Ibn Zubair رضي الله عنه saw Jarjir seated behind his army, under an umbrella of peacock feathers held by two maids. Ibn Zubair رضي الله عنه went immediately around the Roman army and approached Jarjir directly, who mistakenly thought that somebody was coming to ask for a truce. He attacked Jarjir with his sword and cut off his head from the body. He then fixed the head onto his spear and returned to his camp, to the utter amazement of both the armies at his fantastic bravery.

Note: When the Sahaabah رضي الله عنهم emigrated to Madinah Munawwarah, no son was born to any of them for one year. The Jews of Madinah Munawwarah said: "We have put a spell on the newcomers. They cannot have any sons born to them."

Abdullah bin Zubair رضي الله عنه was the first male child born to the Muhaajireen. The Muslims were, therefore, very happy over his birth. Nabi صلى الله عليه وسلم would usually not allow the children to take the oath of allegiance to him (i.e. hold his hand and promise to obey him) but Abdullah bin Zubair رضي الله عنه had the honour of pledging allegiance to Nabi صلى الله عليه وسلم when he was only seven years old. During this battle, he was in his early twenties (twenty-four or twenty-five). To go alone and

Ch. 11 - Children & their Love for Islam

kill the commander, after by-passing his army of 200 000 men, at this age is really marvellous.

14. HADHRAT AMR BIN SALAMAH رَضِىَ اللّٰهُ عَنْهُ LEARNS THE QUR-AAN IN THE STATE OF KUFR

Hadhrat Amr bin Salamah رَضِىَ اللّٰهُ عَنْهُ says: "We lived with our father at a place on the caravan road to Madinah Munawwarah. When a caravan from Madinah Munawwarah passed our village, we asked those people about Nabi Muhammad صَلَّى اللّٰهُ عَلَيْهِ وَسَلَّمَ. What's the latest about the person who claimed to be receiving wahi (revelation) from Allah Ta'ala?. They would give us information and would also read a few Aayaat of the Qur-aan to us to give us an idea about his claim. I was still a child, but I would immediately learn those Aayaat. In this way, I remembered a good part of the Qur-aan Shareef even before I accepted Islam.

All the desert tribes were waiting for Makkah Mukarramah to come into the control of Nabi صَلَّى اللّٰهُ عَلَيْهِ وَسَلَّمَ before they accepted Islam. When he conquered Makkah Mukarramah, people from all the tribes began to come to Nabi صَلَّى اللّٰهُ عَلَيْهِ وَسَلَّمَ in order to accept Islam. My father was in charge of the group who went to Nabi صَلَّى اللّٰهُ عَلَيْهِ وَسَلَّمَ to pledge allegiance to him on behalf of our tribe. Nabi صَلَّى اللّٰهُ عَلَيْهِ وَسَلَّمَ taught them the basic rules about Salaah and other Islamic practices. He taught them the method of Salaah with jamaat and said, "it is best that the person who knows more Qur-aan should lead (be the Imaam) in Salaah." Because I used to memorise the Aayaat that had been revealed, it so happened that no one in my tribe knew so much Qur-aan as I did. They looked for an Imaam, but they could not find a person who knew more Qur-aan than me. I was therefore, made the Imaam. At that time, I was only about six or seven. I led the Jamaat Salaah and Janaazah Salaah."

Note: It was his natural liking and attraction towards Islam that made him remember so much of the Qur-aan when he was only a boy and he had not even accepted Islam. There is a diffenerce of opinion (amongst the Fuqaha) as to whether a child can perform the Salaah or not. Those who say that it is permissible then there is no objection and those who say that it is not permissible say that Rasulullah صَلَّى اللّٰهُ عَلَيْهِ وَسَلَّمَ mentioned to these people that the one who knows the most amount of

Qur-aan amongst you should lead the salaah, he did not mean a child in this statement.

15. HADHRAT ABDULLAH IBN ABBAAS رَضِىَ اللّٰهُ عَنْهُ TIES HIS SLAVE WITH CHAINS

Ikramah *(rahmatullahi alayh)* the slave of Hadhrat Abdullah bin Abbaas رَضِىَ اللّٰهُ عَنْهُ is one of the well-known Ulama. He says: "During my days of learning the Qur-aan and Hadith, I was chained up by my master, so that I might not go anywhere."

Note: In fact, real knowledge can only be learnt when one is totally devoted. The students who are in the habit of roaming about, going to shopping centres and enjoying themselves are ruining their lives. It was because of this effort that Ikramah *(rahmatullahi alayh)* was later on called. "The ocean of knowledge" and "The most learned man of the Ummah."

Qatadah *(rahmatullahi alayh)* says: "There are four most learned men among the Tabi'ees and Ikramah is one of them."

16. HADHRAT ABDULLAH IBN ABBAAS رَضِىَ اللّٰهُ عَنْهُ MEMORIZES THE QUR-AAN IN HIS CHILDHOOD

Hadhrat Abdullah bin Abbaas رَضِىَ اللّٰهُ عَنْهُ used to tell the people: "Come to me for understanding the Qur-aan. I memorised it while I was only a child."

Once he said: "I finished reading the Qur-aan when I was only ten years old."

Note: The reading of the Qur-aan by Sahaabah رَضِىَ اللّٰهُ عَنْهُمْ was not done like the reading by the non-Arabs of today. Whatever they read, they read with full meaning and explanation. Anything memorised in childhood is very deep and lasting, so Abdullah bin Abbaas رَضِىَ اللّٰهُ عَنْهُ is accepted as the Imaam in Tafseer. None of the Sahaabah رَضِىَ اللّٰهُ عَنْهُمْ has narrated more Ahaadith explaining the meaning of Qur-aan than was done by Ibn Abbaas رَضِىَ اللّٰهُ عَنْهُ.

Abdullah bin Mas'ood رَضِىَ اللّٰهُ عَنْهُ says: "Abdullah bin Abbaas رَضِىَ اللّٰهُ عَنْهُ is the best commentator (explainer) of the Qur-aan."

Abu Abdur Rahmaan *(rahmatullahi alayh)* says: "The Sahaabah ﷺ from whom we learnt Qur-aan used to say, "We learnt ten Aayaat of the Qur-aan at a time from Nabi ﷺ. We would not take the next lesson until we mastered and began practising those ten Aayaat."

Abdullah bin Abbaas ﷺ was thirteen years old at the time of Nabi's ﷺ death. It is a miracle that he knew so much of the Qur-aan and Hadith at such a young age. Many senior Sahaabah ﷺ used to come to him to solve their difficulties about the meanings of the Qur-aan. However, this was all due to the fruits of the dua of Nabi ﷺ, who, once while coming out from the toilet, had found water kept ready for his use and asked, "Who placed this water here?" Somebody said: "Ibn Abbaas."

Nabi ﷺ was very happy and made dua for Ibn Abbaas ﷺ saying: "O, Allah! Give him the knowledge and understanding of the Qur-aan and the practices of Islam."

On another occasion, Nabi ﷺ was performing his Salaah. Ibn Abbaas ﷺ joined him in Salaah by standing behind him. Nabi ﷺ caught him by the hand and pulled him to his side. (When there is only one follower in Salaah with Jamaat, he stands by the side of Imaam and not behind him). While Nabi ﷺ was busy in Salaah, he moved back a little. When the Salaah was over, Nabi ﷺ asked him: "What made you go back?"

He said: "You are the Nabi of Allah! How could I stand in line with you?"

On this occasion too, Nabi ﷺ made dua for his knowledge and understanding.

17. ABDULLAH BIN AMR BIN AAS ﷺ MEMORISES HADITH

Abdullah bin Amr bin Aas ﷺ was one of the most pious Sahaabah ﷺ. He used to fast daily and finish one Qur-aan during the night. Nabi ﷺ stopped him from this difficult program and said: "You will get weak by fasting daily, and your eyesight will suffer by keeping awake every night. You owe some duty to your body, the members of your family and those who come to visit you."

He says: "Nabi ﷺ then advised me to take a month to finish one Qur-aan. I said, 'O, Nabi of Allah! This is too little. Let me make full use of my strength while I am still young.' He then reduced the period to twenty days. I kept on repeating my words and Nabi ﷺ continued reducing the period, till finally I was permitted to take three days in finishing one reading of the Qur-aan."

He had compiled a collection of Ahaadith compiled by him which he had named "Saadiqah (True)." He says: "I used to write down all that I heard from Nabi ﷺ. People once told me that, Nabi ﷺ is after all a human being and many words said by him in anger or humour are actually not meant by him. You should not write down each and every thing spoken by him. I accepted the advice. When I told this to Nabi ﷺ, he said, 'You keep doing as before. By Him who holds my life in His hand, my lips do not say anything except the truth even in anger or joy.'"

Note: Abdullah bin Amr رضي الله عنه is most well-known for his excessive ibaadat. In spite of this, he had collected many Ahaadith. Hadhrat Abu Hurayrah رضي الله عنه says: "No one has narrated from Nabi ﷺ more than me, except Abdullah bin Amr رضي الله عنه. This is because he used to write down what he heard, while I relied on my memory." From this we understand that his narrations of Ahaadith is much more than that of Hadhrat Abu Hurayrah رضي الله عنه. Although in our times we see that the narrations of Hadhrat Abu Hurayrah رضي الله عنه are much more than that of Abdullah bin Amr رضي الله عنه. There are many reasons for this.

This is really wonderful, especially when we know that most of his time was spent in reading the Qur-aan and other ibaadat.

18. HADHRAT ZAID BIN SAABIT رضي الله عنه MEMORIZES THE QUR-AAN

Hadhrat Zaid bin Saabit رضي الله عنه is one of those famous Sahaabah رضي الله عنهم who were known to be the most learned in his time and whose words in deeni matters was most reliable. He was an expert in regulations regarding inheritance. It is said that he was from the most learned Ulama, Qadhis (judges) and Qurra of this Ummat.

He was only eleven years old when Nabi ﷺ made Hijrat to Madinah Munawwarah. That is why he was not allowed to take part in the early battles like Badr, etc. although he very much wanted to. He had lost his father when he was six years old. When Nabi ﷺ came to Madinah Munawwarah, people brought their children to him for duas.

Zaid ؓ was also brought to him. He says: "When I was brought to Nabi ﷺ, he was told that I was a youngster from the Banu Najjaar and that I had already memorised seventeen surahs of the Qur-aan. In order to test me, he asked me to read some of these. I read Surah Qaaf. He rewarded me with his kind words."

When Nabi ﷺ used to write letters to the Jews outside Madinah Munawwarah, he used the local Jews to write for him. Once he told Zaid ؓ: "I am not at ease with what the Jews write and read for me. I fear mischief from them in writing or reading incorrectly. I want you to learn the Jewish language."

Zaid ؓ says: "I mastered Hebrew (the Jewish language) in fifteen days and after that I started doing all the correspondence for Nabi ﷺ." Zaid ؓ is reported to have also mastered the Syrian language at the command of Nabi ﷺ. He managed this within the short period of only seventeen days.

19. HADHRAT HASAN'S ؓ KNOWLEDGE OF ISLAM

The head of the Sayyids (family of Nabi ﷺ), Hadhrat Hasan ؓ was born in 3 A.H., in the month of Ramadhaan. He was, therefore, a little over seven years old at the time of Nabi's ﷺ death. What could a child of this age accomplish in the field of knowledge. In spite of his young age, quite a few Ahaadith have been narrated by him.

Someone once asked him: "Do you remember any sayings of Nabi ﷺ?"

He said: "Yes. Once I was going with him. On the way I saw a large amount of the dates of Sadaqah kept in one place. I took a date from the pile and put it into my mouth. Nabi ﷺ shouted, 'Kakh! Kakh!' (No! No!) and then took out the date from my mouth with his finger, saying: 'Eating Sadaqah is not allowed for us (i.e. family of the Nabi).' Nabi ﷺ had taught me how to read my five times daily Salaah."

Hasan ؓ says: "Nabi ﷺ advised me to read the following dua in my Witr Salaah;

اَللّٰهُمَّ اهْدِنِيْ فِيْمَنْ هَدَيْتَ وَعَافِنِيْ فِيْمَنْ عَافَيْتَ وَتَوَلَّنِيْ فِيْمَنْ تَوَلَّيْتَ وَبَارِكْ لِيْ فِيْمَا اَعْطَيْتَ وَقِنِيْ شَرَّ مَا قَضَيْتَ فَاِنَّكَ تَقْضِيْ وَلَا يُقْضٰى عَلَيْكَ اِنَّهُ لَا يَذِلُّ مَنْ وَّالَيْتَ تَبَارَكْتَ رَبَّنَا وَتَعَالَيْتَ

"O, Allah! Guide me together with those whom you have guided. Keep me in ease together with those whom you have kept in ease. Be my protecting friend together with those whose protecting friend you have been. Bless me in what you have given me. Give me protection against the bad effects of what may have been ordered for me, for Your decision is final and nobody can decide against your will. He who has You as the protecting friend cannot be disgraced. O, Our Rabb! You are blessed and You are the Highest."

Hadhrat Hasan ؓ narrates that he heard Nabi ﷺ saying: "The person who keeps sitting till sunrise at the place where he read his Fajr Salaah shall be saved from the fire of Jahannam."

Hadhrat Hasan ؓ performed his Haj many times by going from Madinah Munawwarah to Makkah Mukarramah on foot and when asked about his reasons for going through such hardships, he said: "I feel ashamed to face Allah Ta'ala (after my death) without going to His House, Makkah Mukarramah walking for Haj."

Hadhrat Hasan ؓ is famous for his piety and tolerance and is the narrator of many Ahaadith collected by Imaam Ahmad *(rahmatullahi alayh)* in his Musnad. The author of 'Talqih' has included Hasan ؓ among those who have reported as many as thirteen Ahaadith. To have remembered so many Ahaadith at the age of seven shows his love for

Islam and his amazing memory. It is unfortunate that we have not even taught our children the basics of Islam at this age.

20. HADHRAT HUSAIN'S ﷺ THIRST FOR LEARNING

Hadhrat Husain ﷺ was one year younger than Hadhrat Hasan ﷺ, his brother. He was a little over six at the time of Nabi's ﷺ death. Nothing much can be expected from a child of this age, but there are quite a few Ahaadith narrated by Hadhrat Husain ﷺ. Muhadditheen count him from those Sahaabah ﷺ who narrated at least eight Ahaadith. The following Ahaadith are from those narrated by Hadhrat Husain ﷺ:

1. *"Each time any Muslim, male or female, recites 'Inna-lillahi-wa-inna-Ilaihi-raaji-oon' when he remembers a difficulty which he experienced before, he receives a reward from Allah Ta'ala just as he would have had at the time of the actual difficulty."*

2. *"A Muslim gets protection from drowning while crossing a river if, at the time of boarding (the boat) he reads:*

بِسْمِ اللّٰهِ مَجْرٖهَا وَمُرْسٰهَا ۚ اِنَّ رَبِّیْ لَغَفُوْرٌ رَّحِیْمٌ

"In the name of Allah Ta'ala shall it travel and anchor. Certainly! My Rabb is surely, most forgiving, most Merciful."
(Surah Hood – Aayah 41)

3. *"To avoid useless things is from the beauty of Islam."*

Rabee'ah *(rahmatullahi alayh)* says: "I once asked Hadhrat Husain ﷺ if he remembered any incident in the life of Nabi ﷺ. He said, 'Yes. I once found a few dates lying near a window and put one of them into my mouth. Nabi ﷺ made me take it out and throw away the dates, as we (i.e. his family members) were not allowed to eat anything from Sadaqah." Many other Ahadith have also been narrated from him.

Husain ؓ had gone twenty-five times for haj on foot to Makkah Mukarramah. He was very punctual in fasting, reading Nafl Salaah, spending on the poor and particular about all matters of Deen.

Note: We find quite a few Sahaabah ؓ narrating many Ahadith in their childhood.

Mahmood bin Rab-ee' ؓ was only five at the time of Nabi's ﷺ death. He says: "Once Nabi ﷺ came to our house. We had a well inside the house. He filled some water in his mouth from that well and then squirted it on my face. I shall never forget this incident."

We are in the habit of useless talk with our children confusing their minds by telling them made up stories and by frightening them about giants and jinns. If, instead, we ask them to read the lives of the great men of Islam, tell them stories of the pious people and warn them of the punishment of Allah's disobedience, they will benefit in this world and in the Hereafter. Children's memories are very good. Anything that they memorise is not forgotten. If children are made to memorise the Qur-aan, they will be able to do so very easily and quickly. I have heard very often from the elderly ladies of my family and from my respected father himself that he had memorised one quarter (¼) of the 30th para of the Qur-aan even before he was weaned (before the age of two). When he was only seven years old, he had finished memorising the whole Qur-aan and in addition to that, he had studied a few standard books in Persian literature (on his own).

He once told me: "When I had finished memorising the Qur-aan, my father required me to repeat (from memory) the full Qur-aan once daily, and allowed me to play for the rest of the day. In the summer months, I used to sit on the roof of the house and start reading the Qur-aan just after Fajr. I would finish the whole Qur-aan in about seven hours. I then had my lunch. In the evening, I used to have lessons in Persian, though it was not compulsory for me. I did this for six months."

It is not something small for a child of seven to read the Qur-aan once daily for a full six months, together with learning other things. As a result, he would never forget or make a mistake when reading the Qur-aan from memory.

As a livelihood, he used to sell kitaabs. He was found reading the Qur-aan with his lips, even when his hands were busy in his job. Sometimes he would even teach us, boys (who wanted to learn from him out of madrasah), while he himself read the Qur-aan while doing his work. He thus did three things at the same time. However, his way of teaching with us was different from that of the normal madrasah. He simply listened to the student reading, translating and explaining the meaning. If the student was correct, he simply said, 'Go ahead,' but if the student made a mistake or needed some explanation, then only would he correct or explain. Now, this story is not of olden times; this has happened only recently. It is, therefore, wrong to believe that the Muslims of today, with weak bodies cannot try to follow the footsteps of the pious people of the past in Islam.

CHAPTER 12

LOVE FOR NABI ﷺ

What we have read so far about the achievements of the Sahaabah رضي الله عنهم in their time was because of their love for Allah Ta'ala and His Nabi ﷺ. Love was a very important force in the lives of Sahaabah رضي الله عنهم. It was this love that made them sacrifice their comfort, forget their lives, give up all their wishes and wealth, ignore all suffering and have no fear of death.

Love is not a thing that can be expressed by words but rather it is a condition of the heart. Love is such a thing that once a heart is filled with it, it makes the mind unmindful of everything else except that of the beloved. Nothing else is of importance, neither honour nor disgrace. May Allah Ta'ala through His Grace give us His own love and that of his Nabi ﷺ, so that we may be blessed with being devoted to his ibaadat and find comfort in all our difficulties faced in His service.

1. HADHRAT ABU BAKR رضي الله عنه UNDERGOES DIFFICULTY FOR THE SAKE OF ISLAM

Those who accepted Islam in the beginning had to keep their Imaan a secret as far as possible. As the Muslims were always being treated badly by the Quraish, even Nabi ﷺ asked all the new Muslims to practice Islam secretly, so that they might not have to suffer at the hands of the Quraish. However, when the number of Muslims reached thirty-

Ch. 12 - Love for Nabi ﷺ

nine, Hadhrat Abu Bakr رضي الله عنه suggested the open preaching and practicing of Islam. Nabi ﷺ did not agree, but when Hadhrat Abu Bakr رضي الله عنه insisted, he gave him permission and so all of them went to the Haram Shareef to invite the people to Islam.

Hadhat Abu Bakr رضي الله عنه began to speak and the Khutbah (lecture) given by him was the first ever in the history of Islam. Hadhrat Hamzah رضي الله عنه who was Nabi's ﷺ uncle and the leader of the Shuhadaa (martyrs) accepted Islam on that very day, while Hadhrat 'Umar رضي الله عنه came into Islam on the third day after this lecture.

As soon as Hadhrat Abu Bakr رضي الله عنه started speaking, the idol worshippers and disbelievers of the Quraish attacked the Muslims from all sides. Despite the fact that he was considered to be one of the noblest and most respectable of all the people in Makkah Mukarramah, Hadhrat Abu Bakr رضي الله عنه was beaten so much that his nose, ears and his whole face were covered in blood. He was kicked, thrashed with shoes, trampled and handled very roughly and brutally. He fell down unconscious and looked half dead. No one believed that he would ever survive this brutal attack.

Banu Teem, the people of his family, came and carried him to his house. They also announced in the Haram that if Hadhrat Abu Bakr رضي الله عنه passed away because of his injuries, they would kill Utbah bin Rabee'ah in revenge, who had assaulted Hadhrat Abu Bakr رضي الله عنه the most. Hadhrat Abu Bakr رضي الله عنه remained unconscious for the whole day. People around him shouted his name again and again to know if he was in his senses, but he would not speak.

However, late in the evening he opened his eyes and showed signs of consciousness. As soon as he was able to speak, he asked: "How is Nabi ﷺ?" The people were most disappointed with him and they said: "How is it that, despite all this hardship and after remaining close to death all day long because of Nabi ﷺ, he has nothing else to talk about but asking about Nabi ﷺ himself, as soon as he becomes conscious again."

Hadhrat Abu Bakr's رضي الله عنه, love for Nabi ﷺ left them disappointed, but they were satisfied that he was out of danger. They advised his mother Ummu Khair to give him something to eat. However, not worried about his food, Hadhrat Abu Bakr رضي الله عنه would again and again and impatiently ask his mother the same question i.e. "How is Nabi صلى الله عليه وسلم?"

Because she did not know about the condition of Nabi صلى الله عليه وسلم, Hadhrat Abu Bakr رضي الله عنه begged her to go to Ummu Jamil رضي الله عنها (Umar's sister) and find out from her the latest news about Nabi صلى الله عليه وسلم. The mother could not refuse her son in this sorry condition and hurried to Ummu Jamil's house to ask about the condition of Nabi Muhammad صلى الله عليه وسلم.

Like other Muslims of that time, Ummu Jamil رضي الله عنها was also keeping her Imaan a secret. She, therefore, acted as if she did not know about Nabi صلى الله عليه وسلم saying: "Who is Muhammad and who is Abu Bakr? I am sorry to learn about the condition of your son. If you like, I can go with you to see him."

Ummu Khair agreed and they both came to Hadhrat Abu Bakr رضي الله عنه. On seeing Hadhrat Abu Bakr رضي الله عنه in that miserable condition, Ummu Jamil رضي الله عنها could not contain herself and began to cry uncontrollably, saying: "Destruction to the ruffians for what they have done to a man like Abu Bakr رضي الله عنه. May Allah Ta'ala punish them for what they have done!" Regardless of what Ummu Jamil رضي الله عنها said, Hadhrat Abu Bakr رضي الله عنه had the same words on his; lips: "How is Nabi صلى الله عليه وسلم?"

Ummu Jamil رضي الله عنها (pointing towards Ummu Khair) asked: "Is it safe to say anything in front of her?"

Abu Bakr رضي الله عنه replied: "Do not worry about her."

Ummu Jamil رضي الله عنها answered: "He is quite well." And she gave futher reassurance.

Abu Bakr رضي الله عنه asked: "Where is he at this moment?"

Ummu Jamil رضي الله عنها replied: "He is at Arqam's place."

Abu Bakr رضي الله عنه took an oath: "By Allah! I will not eat or drink anything until I see him."

His mother was very eager to feed him. She knew that when he had sworn by Allah, he would not break his oath; therefore, he would not eat under any circumstances. She, therefore, agreed to take him to Arqam's place. She had to wait till the later part of the night, when the streets were quiet and she was able to take him without being seen by the Quraish. When they both reached Arqam's place, Hadhrat Abu Bakr رَضِيَ اللَّهُ عَنْهُ saw Nabi ﷺ and held onto him weeping profusely. Nabi ﷺ also held him close and cried, and all the Muslims who were present there also began to weep over the condition of Hadhrat Abu Bakr رَضِيَ اللَّهُ عَنْهُ.

Hadhrat Abu Bakr رَضِيَ اللَّهُ عَنْهُ then introduced his mother Ummu Khair to Nabi ﷺ, saying: "She is my mother, O, Nabi of Allah! Make dua for her and encourage her to accept Islam." Nabi ﷺ first made dua for her and then invited her towards Islam. She accepted Islam there and then.

Note: Many people can claim to be lovers while they are in ease and comfort, but a true lover is he who is able to prove his love even in difficulty and hardship.

2. THE SADNESS OF HADHRAT 'UMAR رَضِيَ اللَّهُ عَنْهُ AT THE PASSING AWAY OF NABI ﷺ

Everyone knows of the bravery, courage and strength of Hadhrat 'Umar رَضِيَ اللَّهُ عَنْهُ. Even after 1400 years, hearts shiver with fear and respect when his name is mentioned. A person could not announce that he was a Muslim, nor could he preach Islam openly before 'Umar رَضِيَ اللَّهُ عَنْهُ accepted Islam. As soon as he accepted Islam, the Muslims started performing Salaah in the Haram, as no one could dare harm them with 'Umar رَضِيَ اللَّهُ عَنْهُ on their side.

Despite all this, he could not bear the shock of the passing away of Nabi ﷺ. He stood with a sword in his hand, very confused and dazed saying: "I shall cut off the head of the person who says that Nabi ﷺ has passed away. Nabi ﷺ has only gone to visit Allah Ta'ala, just as Hadhrat Musa عَلَيْهِ السَّلَامُ had gone to Mount Toor. He will shortly return and cut off the hands and feet of those who were spreading the false news of his death."

On the other hand, Hadhrat 'Usmaan ؓ was stunned with grief on this occasion. He could not speak a single word, even till the next day and walked about without speaking. Hadhrat Ali ؓ too, was in terrible grief. He sat still and didn't move.

Only Hadhrat Abu Bakr ؓ, with all his love for Nabi ﷺ as we have seen in the last story stood, firm as a rock and did not lose himself in this atmosphere of grief. He calmly entered Nabi's ﷺ house, kissed his forehead and came back to the people. He asked Hadhrat 'Umar ؓ to sit down, and began to speak to the people.

He began his lecture as follows: "Whoever worshipped Muhammad ﷺ, let him know that Muhammad ﷺ is no more and whoever worshipped Allah Ta'ala then he should know that Allah Ta'ala is ever-living and forever." He then read the following Aayat of the Qur-aan:

$$\text{وَمَا مُحَمَّدٌ اِلَّا رَسُوْلٌ قَدْ خَلَتْ مِنْ قَبْلِهِ الرُّسُلُ اَفَاِنْ مَّاتَ اَوْ قُتِلَ انْقَلَبْتُمْ عَلٰى اَعْقَابِكُمْ وَمَنْ يَّنْقَلِبْ عَلٰى عَقِبَيْهِ فَلَنْ يَّضُرَّ اللهَ شَيْئًا وَسَيَجْزِى اللهُ الشّٰكِرِيْنَ}$$

"Muhammad ﷺ is a messenger. Indeed many messengers have passed before him. If He passes away or is martyred, would you (Muslims) then turn on your heels? He who turns back on his heels can never harm Allah Ta'ala in the least. Allah Ta'ala shall soon reward those who are grateful."
(Surah Aale I'mraan – Aayah 144)

Since Hadhrat Abu Bakr ؓ was destined to be the Khalifah after Nabi ﷺ, it was important that, unlike other Sahaabah ؓ, he behaved with the calmness and patience that was needed on an occasion like this. Again, it was Hadhrat Abu Bakr ؓ alone who knew better than anybody else about the laws regarding the burial, inheritance, etc, of Nabi ﷺ. When there was a difference of opinion amongst Sahaabah ؓ whether Nabi ﷺ should be buried in Makkah Mukarramah or Madinah Munawwarah or Jerusalem, it was Hadhrat

Ch. 12 - Love for Nabi ﷺ

Abu Bakr رضي الله عنه who explained that Ambiyaa عليهم السلام are buried where they had passed away.

There were many other Ahaadith known only to Hadhrat Abu Bakr رضي الله عنه that helped solve many of the other problems on the demise of Nabi ﷺ. Some of these Ahaadith were:

1. "Ambiyaa عليهم السلام have no heirs. All that a Nabi leaves behind is Sadaqah."

2. "The curse of Allah Ta'ala is on the Ameer who does not take proper care in choosing his deputies."

3. "The leadership shall remain with the Quraish."

3. AN ANSAARI WOMAN'S CONCERN ABOUT NABI ﷺ

In the battle of Uhud, the Muslims suffered heavy losses and quite a large number of them were killed. When the shocking news of their heavy losses reached Madinah Munawwarah, the women came out of their houses to know who had been killed. On seeing a crowd of people at a place, a woman of the Ansaar asked: "How is Nabi ﷺ?" When she was told that her father was killed in the battle, she said '*Inna Lillahi wainna ilayhi rajioon*' and impatiently asked the same question about Nabi ﷺ, This time she was told that her husband had been killed, her brother was dead and that her son too had passed away. With even more worry, she repeated the same question about Nabi ﷺ. She was told that he was safe and sound, but she could not be at rest and insisted on seeing Nabi ﷺ herself.

When at last she had seen him, she said: "O Nabi of Allah, every difficulty is easy and every worry removed after seeing you." She then held onto Nabi's ﷺ robes and said: "O Nabi of Allah! You are dearer to me than my parents. The death of my family has lost its pain for me when I have seen you living."

Note: There are several incidents of this kind that occurred after the battle of Uhud. It is, perhaps, for the large number of such incidents that different names have been reported by different narrators about these women. In fact, such incidents happened in large numbers with many women of that time.

4. THE BEHAVIOUR OF THE SAHAABAH رَضِيَٱللَّهُعَنْهُم AT HUDAYBIYYAH

The campaign of Hudaybiyyah took place in the year 6 A.H., when Nabi صَلَّىٱللَّهُعَلَيْهِوَسَلَّم with a large number of Sahaabah رَضِيَٱللَّهُعَنْهُم were going to Makkah Mukarramah to perform 'Umrah. The Quraish came to know of this and decided to stop them from entering Makkah Mukarramah. They also decided to invite the neighbouring tribes of Makkah Mukarramah for help and made full preparations for battle.

When Nabi صَلَّىٱللَّهُعَلَيْهِوَسَلَّم reached Zul Hulayfah, he sent a man to find out about the Quraish. When Nabi صَلَّىٱللَّهُعَلَيْهِوَسَلَّم reached Asfaan, the person returned from Makkah Mukarramah with the news that the Quraish were fully armed and ready to stop Nabi صَلَّىٱللَّهُعَلَيْهِوَسَلَّم entering Makkah Mukarramah and that the neighbouring tribes were also with them. At this, Nabi صَلَّىٱللَّهُعَلَيْهِوَسَلَّم made mashwara (consulted) with the Sahaabah رَضِيَٱللَّهُعَنْهُم about the situation. One idea was to attack the houses of the tribes who had sent their men to help the Quraish so that they might leave the Quraish in order to protect their own homes and another idea was to march straight towards Makkah Mukarramah.

Hadhrat Abu Bakr رَضِيَٱللَّهُعَنْهُ said: "O Nabi of Allah! You have come to perform 'Umrah. There is no intention of fighting with the Quraish. Let us go ahead. If they stop us we shall fight, otherwise not."

Nabi صَلَّىٱللَّهُعَلَيْهِوَسَلَّم agreed to the suggestion of Hadhrat Abu Bakr رَضِيَٱللَّهُعَنْهُ and decided to march ahead towards Makkah Mukarramah. When he reached Hudaybiyyah, Budail bin Waraqa Al-Khuzaa'ee met him with a group of people. He said: "Under no circumstances will the Quraish allow you to enter Makkah Mukarramah. They are ready for battle."

Nabi صَلَّىٱللَّهُعَلَيْهِوَسَلَّم replied: "We have come to perform 'Umrah only, and have no intention to fight. Many battles have already caused heavy losses for the Quraish. Therefore, if they agree, I am prepared to talk about a peace agreement with them, that they stop their opposition towards me and I too would not fight them. However, if the Quraish do not accept this suggestion, then by Him who holds my life in His hand, I will fight them till at last either Islam succeeds or I am made shaheed."

Budail returned to the Quraish and explained to them what Nabi ﷺ had told him. They did not agree to the peace agreement of Nabi ﷺ. However, discussions between the two sides continued, and at one time Urwah bin Mas'ood Saqafi was sent by the Quraish for discussions. Urwah had not until then accepted Islam. He accepted Islam later. Nabi ﷺ talked to him in the same way as he had talked to Budail.

'Urwah said: "O Muhammad (ﷺ), If you want to kill all the Arabs you cannot possibly do so, as none before you has ever finished off all the Arabs. On the other hand if the Arabs are victorious over you, then these people around you will disappear in no time, leaving you all alone, for I don't find any people of high birth among them. In fact they are all from a low class, coming from all corners and will desert you in times of trouble."

Hadhrat Abu Bakr رضي الله عنه, who was standing close by, was very angry at this, and angrily told 'Urwah: "Go and please your goddess Laat! We will never run away and leave Nabi ﷺ by himself."

'Urwah asked: "Who is he?"

Nabi ﷺ replied: "He is Abu Bakr."

'Urwah then said: "Abu Bakr! I am thankful to you for a favour you have done to me in the past. If it was not for this, I would have replied to your vulgarity."

'Urwah then continued his discussion with Nabi ﷺ. According to the Arab custom, 'Urwah occasionally touched the beard of Nabi ﷺ as he talked to assist in persuading. The Sahaabah رضي الله عنهم could not bear this. 'Urwah's own nephew, Mughirah bin Shu'bah رضي الله عنه, was standing nearby armed with his face concealed by a helmet. He struck 'Urwah's hand with the handle of his sword and said: "Keep your hand away."

'Urwah asked: "Who is he?"

Nabi ﷺ replied: "He is Mughirah."

'Urwah responded: "Oh! You traitor! How dare you hurt your uncle, who is still suffering because of your crimes?" (Before Islam, Mughirah رضي الله عنه had killed a few people. Urwah paid the blood money for him, and was referring to this).

During his long talk with Nabi ﷺ, 'Urwah had been quietly watching the behaviour of the Sahaabah رضي الله عنهم towards Nabi ﷺ. When he returned to the Quraish he told them: "O, Quraish! I have been sent to many great kings as an envoy. I have seen the courts of Caesar, Chosroes and Negus. By Allah! Nowhere have I seen the people around a king so respectful to him as I found the friends of Muhammad ﷺ.

When Muhammad ﷺ spits, they rush to receive the saliva in their hands before it touches the ground and wipe their faces with it. When he gives a command, all of them run to carry out his wish. When he makes wudhu, they fight with one another to collect some of the used water before it falls to the ground. If anyone fails to get that water, he touches the wet hands of the person who had got it and then rubs his hands on his own face. When they speak in his presence, they speak softly. They do not lift their eyes to look at his face, out of respect for him. A hair falling from his head or beard is kept safely to get blessings from it and is seen as very mubaarak. In short, I have never seen any group of people as loving and devoted to their master as I have seen the Sahaabah رضي الله عنهم of Muhammad ﷺ towards him."

Finally, Hadhrat Usmaan رضي الله عنه was chosen by Nabi ﷺ to go and negotiate with the Quraish, as he was still respected by them in spite of him accepting Islam and there wasn't great fear for his safety in Makkah. When Hadhrat 'Usmaan رضي الله عنه had left for Makkah Mukarramah, some of the Sahaabah رضي الله عنهم envied the opportunity given to Hadhrat 'Usmaan رضي الله عنه, as they thought that he would be able to perform Tawaaf of the Ka'bah. Nabi ﷺ on the other hand said: "I do not think that Hadhrat 'Usmaan رضي الله عنه will ever like to do Tawaaf without me."

However, when Hadhrat 'Usmaan رضي الله عنه entered Makkah Mukarramah, Abaan Bin Sa'eed took the responsibility for his protection and told him: "You can move around freely. Nobody can touch you."

Hadhrat 'Usmaan ﷺ continued the negotiations with Abu Sufyaan and the other chiefs of Makkah Mukarramah on behalf of Nabi ﷺ and when he was about to return, the Quraish themselves told him: "While you are here at Makkah Mukarramah, you can perform Tawaaf before you return."

He replied: "How can it be possible for me when Nabi ﷺ has been stopped by you people from entering Makkah Mukarramah."

This reply was not liked by the Quraish and they decided to detain Hadhrat 'Usmaan ﷺ in Makkah Mukarramah. A rumour reached the Muslims that Hadhrat 'Usmaan ﷺ had been killed. On receiving this news, Nabi ﷺ took an oath from all the Sahaabah ﷺ to fight to the last drop of their blood. When the Quraish learnt of this, they got frightened and immediately freed 'Usmaan ﷺ.

Note: In this story, Hadhrat Abu Bakr's ﷺ scolding 'Urwah, Mughirah's ﷺ striking his uncle, the Sahaabah's ﷺ behaviour towards Nabi ﷺ, as 'Urwah had seen and 'Usmaan's ﷺ refusing to do Tawaaf without Nabi ﷺ, all show clearly the intense love of the Sahaabah ﷺ for Nabi ﷺ. The oath of allegiance mentioned in this story is known as Bay'atush Shajarah (The oath under the tree) and is mentioned in the Qur-aan (Surah Fath - Aayah 18). This ayah will be referred to later.

5. HADHRAT IBN ZUBAIR ﷺ DRINKS THE BLOOD OF NABI ﷺ

Once Nabi ﷺ had some blood removed by cupping and the blood was given to Abdullah bin Zubair ﷺ to be buried somewhere. He returned and informed Nabi ﷺ that the blood had been taken care of. Nabi ﷺ asked him: "What did you do with it?"

Ibn-Zubair ﷺ replied: "I have swallowed it."

Nabi ﷺ said: "The person who has my blood in his body, cannot be touched by the fire of Jahannam. However, you will kill people and people will kill you," (referring to something that will take place later in his life).

Note: Everything coming out of Nabi's ﷺ body is clean. Therefore, no doubt remains in understanding Ibn Zubair's رضي الله عنه action. However, the last words of Nabi ﷺ refer to the battles for power which Ibn Zubair رضي الله عنه had to fight with Yazid and Abdul Maalik. In the latter part of his life, Ibn Zubair رضي الله عنه was killed in one of these battles. Even at the time of Ibn Zubair's رضي الله عنه birth, Nabi ﷺ had mentioned that he was a sheep among the cloaked wolves.

6. HADHRAT ABU 'UBAIDAH رضي الله عنه LOSES HIS TEETH

At one time, during the battle of Uhud, Nabi ﷺ was fiercely attacked by the enemy and two pieces of the helmet worn by him were stuck deep into his head (or face). Hadhrat Abu Bakr رضي الله عنه and Hadhrat Abu 'Ubaidah رضي الله عنه ran to help him. Abu 'Ubaidah رضي الله عنه started pulling out the pieces with his teeth. By the time one piece was out, he had lost one of his teeth. Without caring about his lost tooth, he again used his teeth to pull out the other piece as well. He managed to take out that one too, but lost another tooth in the effort. When all the pieces were pulled out, blood began to flow out from Nabi's ﷺ body. Maalik bin Sinaan رضي الله عنه, the father of Abu Sa'eed Khudri رضي الله عنه, licked the blood with his lips. At this, Nabi ﷺ said: "The fire of Jahannam cannot touch the person who has my blood mixed with his."

7. HADHRAT ZAID رضي الله عنه REFUSES TO GO WITH HIS FATHER

Before Islam, Zaid رضي الله عنه was once travelling in a caravan with his mother who was going to her father's town, when the caravan was attacked by the Qais tribe. They took Zaid رضي الله عنه as a slave and sold him in Makkah Mukarramah. Hakeem bin Hizaam bought him for his aunt Khadijah رضي الله عنها, who offered him as a present to Nabi ﷺ when she married him.

Zaid's ﷺ father was in great grief at the loss of his son as it ought to have been. He roamed about in search of him, crying for Zaid in the following heart-breaking poem:

> "I weep in memory of Zaid, whilst I do not know whether he is alive (to be hoped for) or finished by death. O! Zaid, By Allah, I have no knowledge, whether you are killed on soft soil or on a rock. Ah, I wish I knew whether you would ever come back to me, for that is the only desire I am living for. I remember Zaid when the sun rises in the East. I remember him when the rain falls from the clouds. The blowing wind makes stronger the fire of his memory. Alas, my grief and suffering are very long. I shall run my swift camels in search of him. I shall search for him throughout the world. The camels may get tired, but I shall not rest, till I die, for death is the end of every hope. I shall still command my sons and such and such people, to keep searching for Zaid even after my death."

Some people of his family once met Zaid ﷺ during their journey to Makkah Mukarramah. They told him the story of his father's grief and pain and read to him the couplets which he sang in his memory. Zaid ﷺ sent a letter to his father with these people. The letter had three couplets addressed to his father telling him that he was in Makkah, quite well and that they should not worry because he was with very noble people. When the people went back, they informed his father of his location and delivered Zaid's ﷺ message to him.

After receiving the letter, his father and his uncle left for Makkah Mukarramah with enough money to buy Zaid ﷺ. When they came to Nabi ﷺ they said: "O, son of Haashim and the chief of Quraish. You are living in the Haram and you are the neighbour of Allah Ta'ala. You are known for freeing the prisoners and feeding the hungry. We have come to you asking for our son. Accept the ransom money for Zaid and set him free. We are willing to pay even more than the ransom money. Please, show mercy and be kind to us."

Nabi ﷺ asked: "What do you wish to do with Zaid?"

Zaid's father replied: "We want to take him back home with us."

"Is that all?" asked Nabi ﷺ. "All right, then call Zaid and ask him. If he wishes to go with you, I shall let him go without taking any money, but I shall not send him if he doesn't want to go."

Zaid's father replied: "You have shown us more favour than we deserve. We most gladly agree to what you say."

Zaid رضي الله عنه was sent for. When he came, Nabi ﷺ asked Zaid رضي الله عنه: "Do you know these men?"

Zaid رضي الله عنه replied: "Yes, I know them. This is my father and that is my uncle."

Nabi ﷺ then said: "And you know me too. They have come to take you back to your home. You have my full permission to go with them. If on the other hand, you choose to stay on with me, you may do so."

Zaid رضي الله عنه replied: "How can I prefer anybody else over you? You are everybody for me, including my father and my uncle."

Zaid's father and uncle were surprised and said: "O, Zaid! Do you prefer to be a slave? How can you leave your own father, uncle and other members of your family, and remain a slave?"

Zaid رضي الله عنه replied: "I have seen something in my master that makes me choose him over everybody else in the world."

Nabi ﷺ then took Zaid رضي الله عنه in his lap and said: "From today, I adopt Zaid as my son."

The father and uncle were quite satisfied with the situation and gladly left Zaid رضي الله عنه with Nabi ﷺ and returned without him. Zaid رضي الله عنه was only a child at that time. His choosing to remain a slave and refusing to go with his own father, giving up his home and family, shows his great love for Nabi ﷺ.

8. ANAS BIN NADHR'S رضي الله عنه MARTYRDOM IN UHUD

When the Muslims were losing in Uhud, somebody spread the rumour that Nabi ﷺ had been killed. You can imagine the Sahaabah's رضي الله عنهم grief and sadness over this terrible news. Quite naturally, this caused most of them to lose heart.

Anas bin Nadhr رضى الله عنه saw Hadhrat 'Umar رضى الله عنه and Hadhrat Talhah رضى الله عنه with a group of Muhaajireen and Ansaar in a state of total panic. He told them: "Why am I seeing you all so confused?"

They replied: "Nabi ﷺ is killed!"

Anas رضى الله عنه said: "Then who will like to live after him? Come, let us go forward with our swords and join our dear Nabi ﷺ."

After saying these words, he attacked the enemy and fought till he was killed.

Note: In fact, Hadhrat Anas رضى الله عنه had such an extreme love for Nabi ﷺ that he did not consider this life worth living without seeing and being in the company of Nabi ﷺ.

9. SA'AD'S رضى الله عنه MESSAGE FOR THE MUSLIMS

During the battle of Uhud, Nabi ﷺ asked: "What about Sa'ad bin Rabee'? I don't know how things have gone with him." One of the Sahaabah رضى الله عنهم was sent to search for him. He went to the spot where the bodies of the dead lay in heaps. He shouted Sa'ad's رضى الله عنه name to know if he was alive. At one place, while he was announcing that he was sent by Nabi ﷺ to find out about Sa'ad bin Rabee' رضى الله عنه, he heard a weak voice coming from one side. He turned in that direction and found that Sa'ad رضى الله عنه was lying amongst those who were killed and was about to breathe his last.

Sa'ad رضى الله عنه was heard saying: "Give my Salaams to Nabi ﷺ with my message, 'O Nabi of Allah! May Allah Ta'ala give you on my behalf a reward higher and more handsome than the one Allah Ta'ala has ever given to a Nabi on behalf of any of his followers and tell my Muslim brothers, 'Nothing will save them from blame on the Day of Qiyaamah, if the enemy reaches Nabi ﷺ before all of you have been killed.'"

With these words, Sa'ad رضى الله عنه breathed his last and passed away.

فَجَزَاهُ اللهُ عَنَّا أَفْضَلَ مَا جَزَى صَحَابِيًّا عَنْ أُمَّةِ نَبِيِّهِ

"May Allah Ta'ala give you on my behalf a reward higher and more handsome than the one Allah Ta'ala has ever given a Nabi on behalf of any of his followers,"

As a matter of fact, the Sahaabah ﺭﺿﻲﺍﻟﻠﻪﻋﻨﻬﻢ have clearly shown their love for Nabi ﺻﻠﻰﺍﻟﻠﻪﻋﻠﻴﻪﻭﺳﻠﻢ. While they suffered wound after wound and were on their last breath, they had no complaint, no worry nor any wish on their lips and could not think of anything else except the safety of Nabi ﺻﻠﻰﺍﻟﻠﻪﻋﻠﻴﻪﻭﺳﻠﻢ. How I wish that a sinner like me be blessed with an atom of the love that the Sahaabah ﺭﺿﻲﺍﻟﻠﻪﻋﻨﻬﻢ had for Nabi ﺻﻠﻰﺍﻟﻠﻪﻋﻠﻴﻪﻭﺳﻠﻢ.

10. A WOMAN DIES AFTER SEEING NABI'S ﺻﻠﻰﺍﻟﻠﻪﻋﻠﻴﻪﻭﺳﻠﻢ GRAVE

A woman came to Hadhrat Aa'ishah ﺭﺿﻲﺍﻟﻠﻪﻋﻨﻬﺎ and said: "Take me to the grave of Nabi ﺻﻠﻰﺍﻟﻠﻪﻋﻠﻴﻪﻭﺳﻠﻢ, so that I may be fortunate to look at it."

Hadhrat Aa'ishah ﺭﺿﻲﺍﻟﻠﻪﻋﻨﻬﺎ opened the room in which was the grave of Nabi ﺻﻠﻰﺍﻟﻠﻪﻋﻠﻴﻪﻭﺳﻠﻢ and let her go inside. The woman after seeing the grave started crying in love and memory of Nabi ﺻﻠﻰﺍﻟﻠﻪﻋﻠﻴﻪﻭﺳﻠﻢ. In fact she wept so bitterly and continuously that she fainted and passed away there and then (May Allah bless her). The blessed lady remembered the happy days when Nabi ﺻﻠﻰﺍﻟﻠﻪﻋﻠﻴﻪﻭﺳﻠﻢ was alive, and the pain of separation caused her to pass away.

Note: Can the records of history show another example of such love, that the lover is giving up his life at the grave of the beloved?

11. MISCELLANEOUS STORIES OF THE LOVE OF SAHAABAH ﺭﺿﻲﺍﻟﻠﻪﻋﻨﻬﻢ FOR NABI ﺻﻠﻰﺍﻟﻠﻪﻋﻠﻴﻪﻭﺳﻠﻢ

Somebody asked Hadhrat Ali ﺭﺿﻲﺍﻟﻠﻪﻋﻨﻪ: "How much was the Sahaabah's ﺭﺿﻲﺍﻟﻠﻪﻋﻨﻬﻢ love for Nabi ﺻﻠﻰﺍﻟﻠﻪﻋﻠﻴﻪﻭﺳﻠﻢ."

He replied: "By Allah! To us Nabi ﺻﻠﻰﺍﻟﻠﻪﻋﻠﻴﻪﻭﺳﻠﻢ was dearer than our money, our children and our mothers, and was more valuable than a drink of cold water at the time of severest thirst."

Ch. 12 - Love for Nabi ﷺ

Note: There is no doubt in Hadhrat Ali's ؓ words. As a matter of fact, the Sahaabah ؓ reached this state because of the perfection of their Imaan. It had to be so because Allah Ta'ala has written in the Qur-aan-e-Kareem;

$$\text{قُلْ اِنْ كَانَ اٰبَآؤُكُمْ وَاَبْنَآؤُكُمْ وَاِخْوَانُكُمْ وَاَزْوَاجُكُمْ وَعَشِيْرَتُكُمْ وَاَمْوَالُ اقْتَرَفْتُمُوْهَا وَتِجَارَةٌ تَخْشَوْنَ كَسَادَهَا وَمَسٰكِنُ تَرْضَوْنَهَآ اَحَبَّ اِلَيْكُمْ مِّنَ اللّٰهِ وَرَسُوْلِهٖ وَجِهَادٍ فِيْ سَبِيْلِهٖ فَتَرَبَّصُوْا حَتّٰى يَأْتِيَ اللّٰهُ بِاَمْرِهٖ ۗ وَاللّٰهُ لَا يَهْدِى الْقَوْمَ الْفٰسِقِيْنَ}$$

"Say! If your fathers, your sons, your brothers, your spouses, your families, your wealth that you have earned, your businesses in which you fear a loss, and your houses that you love so dearly are more beloved to you than Allah, His messenger and striving in His path, then wait till Allah brings His command (punishment). Allah Ta'ala does not guide the sinful ones." (Surah Taubah – Aayah 24)

This Aayat warns against anything else becoming more attractive than the love of Allah Ta'ala and His Nabi ﷺ. Hadhrat Anas ؓ and Hadhrat Abu Hurayrah ؓ reported that Nabi ﷺ once said: "None of you can be a believer until his love for me is more than his love for his parents, children and all the people of the world."

Ulama say that the love mentioned in this Hadith refers to the love which is developed in the heart and not the natural love. If, however, it is taken to mean the natural and instinctive love, then the word Mo'min will mean the imaan of the highest degree, for instance that of Sahaabah ؓ.

Hadhrat Anas ؓ says that he heard Nabi ﷺ saying, "There are three things which, when found in a person, will cause him to taste the sweetness of real Imaan. These are:

1. When Allah Ta'ala and His Nabi ﷺ are dearer to him than anything else in this world.

2. When his love for anyone is only for the pleasure of Allah Ta'ala, and

3. When turning to 'Kufr' is as hateful to him as being thrown into the fire."

STORY 1 - THE LOVE OF HADHRAT 'UMAR ﷺ FOR NABI ﷺ

Hadhrat 'Umar ﷺ once told Nabi ﷺ: "O Nabi of Allah, you are dearer to me than anybody else in the world except my own self."

Nabi ﷺ replied: "Nobody can be a perfect believer until I am dearer to him than even his own self."

Hadhrat 'Umar ﷺ then said: "Now you are dearer to me than even my own self."

Nabi ﷺ replied: "Now, O 'Umar."
The 'Ulama have given two meanings to the last words of Nabi ﷺ namely:

1. "Now you have real Imaan."

2. "Why is it that it is only now that I am dearer to you than your own self? This should have been a long time ago."

Sahal Tastari *(rahmatullahi alayh)* says: "No one can have enjoyment of the Sunnah until he takes Nabi ﷺ as his Master and considers himself as Nabi's ﷺ slave."

STORY 2 - ON THE DAY OF QIYAAMAH YOU WILL BE WITH WHOM YOU LOVE

A person once came to Nabi ﷺ and asked: "When shall be the Day of Qiyaamah? O, Nabi of Allah!"

Nabi ﷺ asked him: "What preparations have you made for that Day, that you are awaiting it?"

The person replied: "O, Nabi of Allah! I do not have much Salaah, Fast and Sadaqah, but I do have the love of Allah Ta'ala and His Nabi ﷺ in my heart."

Nabi ﷺ said: "On the Day of Qiyaamah, you will surely be with those whom you love."

Nabi ﷺ has also said: "A person shall be resurrected with those that he loves." This has also been mentioned by other Sahaabah رضي الله عنهم, amongst whom are Abdullah bin Mas'ood, Abu Musa Ash'ari, Safwan, Abu Zar رضي الله عنهم, etc.

Hadhrat Anas رضي الله عنه says: "Nothing made the Sahaabah رضي الله عنهم happier than these words of Nabi ﷺ."

They had every reason to be happy because the love of Nabi ﷺ had gone deep into every part of their body.

STORY 3 - HADHRAT HAARISAH رضي الله عنه OFFERS HIS HOUSE TO NABI ﷺ FOR FAATIMAH رضي الله عنها

In the beginning, Hadhrat Faatimah's رضي الله عنها house was a bit far from Nabi ﷺ. Nabi ﷺ once told her: "I wish that you were living near me." Faatimah رضي الله عنها replied: "Haarisah's رضي الله عنه house is close by. If you ask him to exchange his house with mine, he will very gladly do it."

Nabi ﷺ said: "He has already exchanged once when I asked him, I feel shy to ask him again."

However Haarisah رضي الله عنه somehow came to know that Nabi ﷺ wanted Faatimah رضي الله عنها to live near him. He at once came to Nabi ﷺ and said: "O, Nabi of Allah! I have come to know that you wish Faatimah رضي الله عنها to live near you. Here are my houses for you to choose from. No other house is closer to yours than these. Faatimah رضي الله عنها can have her house exchanged with any of these. O, Nabi of Allah. By the name of Allah, what you accept from me is dearer to me than what you leave for me."

Nabi ﷺ accepted the offer, saying: "I know that you are quite sincere in what you say," and made dua for him.

STORY 4 - COMPANY OF NABI ﷺ AFTER DEATH

A person came to Nabi ﷺ and said: "O Nabi of Allah! You are dearer to me than my life, my wealth and my family. When I am at home and think of you, I become restless till I come and see you. O, Nabi of Allah, death is sure to come to both of us. After death, you will be in the high position of the Ambiyaa عَلَيْهِمُ السَّلَام, while I shall be somewhere else and perhaps I may not be able to see you. I am very worried and troubled when I think of this separation from you."

Nabi ﷺ remained quiet and he did not know what to say; Then Jibraa-eel عَلَيْهِ السَّلَام came with this Aayat:

وَمَن يُطِعِ اللّهَ وَالرَّسُولَ فَأُولَٰئِكَ مَعَ الَّذِينَ أَنْعَمَ اللّهُ عَلَيْهِم مِّنَ النَّبِيِّينَ وَالصِّدِّيقِينَ وَالشُّهَدَاءِ وَالصَّالِحِينَ ۚ وَحَسُنَ أُولَٰئِكَ رَفِيقًا ۞ ذَٰلِكَ الْفَضْلُ مِنَ اللّهِ ۚ وَكَفَىٰ بِاللّهِ عَلِيمًا

"Those who obey Allah Ta'ala and the Rasool, (in the Aakhirah) they will be with those upon whom Allah Ta'ala has shown favours from the Ambiyaa, the Siddeeqeen, the Shuhadaa (martyrs) and the Righteous ones. These are really the best of companions. This is a favour from Allah Ta'ala, and Allah Ta'ala is sufficient as the knower."

(Surah Nisaa' – Aayaat 69-70)

These type of stories happened quite often with the Sahaabah رَضِىَ اللّٰهُ عَنْهُم. Such fear, in the hearts of lovers, is quite normal.

عشق است و هزار بد گمانی

Intense love brings forth thoughts of thousands of suspicions

Nabi ﷺ read these Aayaat to remove their fears.

A person once came to Nabi ﷺ and said: "O Nabi of Allah, my love for you is such that when I think of you, I cannot rest till I run to see you, for I am sure I would die if I did not see you. Now I am very worried when I think that, even if I am able to enter Jannah, it will be very difficult for me to see you, for you will be in a position which will

Ch. 12 - Love for Nabi ﷺ

be far above me. I will have great difficulty not being able to see you." Nabi ﷺ comforted him by reading the above Aayaat.

In another Hadith, it is mentioned that a person from the Ansaar came to Nabi ﷺ looking very worried. He asked: "What makes you look so sad?"

The person replied: "O, Nabi of Allah! I am concerned about something."

Nabi ﷺ asked: "What is it?"

The person replied: "O, Nabi of Allah! We come to you every morning and evening. We are blessed with seeing you and are delighted to be in your presence. But one day, we will be separated from you, as you will be in the Jannah of the Ambiyaa عليهم السلام which we cannot reach."

Nabi ﷺ kept silent, but when the above Aayaat were revealed, he sent for that person and gave him the good news contained in these Aayaat.

According to another Hadith, many Sahaabah رضى الله عنهم had these fears until Nabi ﷺ read these Aayaat to them, and they were satisfied.

The Sahaabah رضى الله عنهم once asked Nabi ﷺ: "Ambiyaa عليهم السلام will surely be in a much higher position than their followers. How will their followers be able to see them?"

Nabi ﷺ replied: "Those in higher positions will come down to their friends in lower positions to sit with them and talk to them."

STORY 5 - FOLLOWERS COMING AFTER NABI ﷺ WISH TO SEE HIM

Nabi ﷺ once said: "Some of my followers coming after me will love me very much. They will wish that they could see me, even if they had to spend their wealth, leave their families and give away all their possessions for it."

Khaalid's رضى الله عنه daughter, Abdah رضى الله عنها says: "My father, while in bed, would talk about and remember Nabi ﷺ with love and eagerness. He would also remember each and every Muhaajir and Ansaari (by name) and would say, 'Some of them are my elders and others are my juniors. My heart is eager to meet them all. O, Allah! Call me back soon, so that I may be able to meet all of them.' He would keep on doing this until he would fall asleep."

Story 6 - Abu Bakr رَضِيَ اللَّهُ عَنْهُ WISHES FOR THE UNCLE OF NABI ﷺ TO ACCEPT ISLAM

Hadhrat Abu Bakr رَضِيَ اللَّهُ عَنْهُ once told Nabi ﷺ: "My desire is greater for your uncle Abu Taalib to accept Islam than for my own father, as I know that it would please you more."

Similarly, Hadhrat 'Umar رَضِيَ اللَّهُ عَنْهُ once told 'Abbaas رَضِيَ اللَّهُ عَنْهُ, the uncle of Nabi ﷺ: "I was more pleased at your accepting Islam than that of my father, because your Islam made Nabi ﷺ happier."

Story 7 - An old lady singing poems in love of Nabi ﷺ

One night, while Hadhrat 'Umar رَضِيَ اللَّهُ عَنْهُ was on his security patrol, he saw a light and heard a sound coming from a house. He heard the voice of an old lady who was spinning wool and singing a few couplets with the following meaning:

> "May Allah Ta'ala accept the duas of the pious and the chosen ones who are seeking blessings for Muhammad ﷺ."

> "O, Allah's Nabi! You worshipped each night and you wept before dawn each day."

> "I wish to know if I could be together with my beloved [Nabi ﷺ]."

> "For death comes in different ways and I do not know how I shall die."

> "And whether I'll have the opportunity of meeting You or not."

Hadhrat 'Umar رَضِيَ اللَّهُ عَنْهُ on hearing these couplets also sat down weeping in love and memory of Nabi ﷺ.

Ch. 12 - Love for Nabi ﷺ

Story 8 - Hadhrat Bilal رضي الله عنه wishes to meet Nabi ﷺ after death

The story of Hadhrat Bilal رضي الله عنه is known to all. At the time of his death, his wife sat by his side crying in grief: "O, dear! Alas!"

He replied angrily; "*Subhaanallah!* What a lovely thing it is to die and be able to meet Nabi Muhammad ﷺ and his Sahaabah رضي الله عنهم."

Story 9 - Zaid's رضي الله عنه love for Nabi ﷺ

We have already read the story of Hadhrat Zaid رضي الله عنه in Chapter five. When he was about to be killed, Abu Sufyaan told him: "How would you like it if Muhammad ﷺ is killed in your place, and you be set free to enjoy life with your family."

Zaid رضي الله عنه replied: "By Allah, I cannot sit happily with my family while even a thorn is pricking Nabi ﷺ."

Abu Sufyaan then said: "There is no example anywhere in the world for the love which the friends of Muhammad ﷺ have for him."

Important Note: The Ulama have given different signs of what is true love. Qaadhi Iyaadh writes: "A lover prefers his beloved above all other things and persons. If this is not the case, then it is merely a claim of love, but not true love. Therefore, it is necessary for those who claim to love Nabi ﷺ that they follow him in his words and actions, carry out his orders, give up everything that he has disliked and follow his way of life, the Sunnah, in good and bad times."

Allah Ta'ala has said in the Qur-aan-e-kareem:

قُلْ اِنْ كُنْتُمْ تُحِبُّوْنَ اللهَ فَاتَّبِعُوْنِىْ يُحْبِبْكُمُ اللهُ وَ يَغْفِرْ لَكُمْ ذُنُوْبَكُمْ ۚ وَاللهُ غَفُوْرٌ رَّحِيْمٌ

"*Say (O, Muhammad ﷺ), If you love Allah then follow me (Muhammad ﷺ), Allah Ta'ala will then love you and forgive you your sins. Allah Ta'ala is most Forgiving, most Merciful.*" (Surah Aale I'mraan - Aayah 31)

CONCLUSION – OUR CONDUCT WITH THE SAHAABAH ﷺ AND THEIR VIRTUES

The stories given in the previous pages are examples for us. In fact a detailed account of the lives Sahaabah ﷺ cannot be covered even in big volumes. It is now quite a few months since I started writing this small book. My engagements in Madrasah and other matters needing immediate attention have already delayed this work. I, therefore, propose to finish the book at this stage, so that people may at least benefit from these pages.

However, I have to write an important warning before I conclude. In this era of freedom, just as we are falling short in our duties we owe to Islam, so are we very seriously neglectful in our respect and admiration that we ought to show the Sahaabah ﷺ. Some neglectful people even say bad words against them. We must remember that the Sahaabah ﷺ are those people who laid the foundations of Islam. They are the ones who propagated Islam to the rest of the world. We can never be grateful enough to them. May Allah Ta'ala shower His choicest blessings on them for their efforts in learning Islam from Nabi ﷺ and teaching it to those after them.

In this regard, as a conclusion to this kitaab (book), I am reproducing below the translation of a chapter from "Shifa" by Qaadhi Iyaadh: "If we claim to admire and honour Nabi ﷺ, we must also respect his Sahaabah ﷺ. As Muslims, it is necessary for us to understand their rights over us, to follow them, to praise them and to ask forgiveness of Allah Ta'ala for them. No doubt they had their differences, but we have no right to talk bad about them. We must beware and distance ourselves from the stories made up by the Shiah's, innovators and even some biased historians, whose ulterior motive is to slander and cause harm to some of the Sahaabah ﷺ and insult others.

We must never doubt the sincerity and honesty of Sahaabah ﷺ. When we read or hear about something which appears to lower their position in our eyes, we must give a positive explanation on their behalf and attribute it to sincere motives, for they really deserve this. We should always speak of their good habits and stop our tongues from saying anything that would belittle them. Nabi ﷺ himself has said,

'Don't say anything about my Sahaabah ﷺ when they are mentioned with disrespect.'"

There are many virtues of the Sahaabah ﷺ given in the Qur-aan and Hadith. Allah Ta'ala says in the Qur-aan-e-Kareem:

مُحَمَّدٌ رَّسُوۡلُ اللّٰهِ ؕ وَ الَّذِيۡنَ مَعَهٗۤ اَشِدَّآءُ عَلَى الۡكُفَّارِ رُحَمَآءُ بَيۡنَهُمۡ تَرٰىهُمۡ رُكَّعًا سُجَّدًا يَّبۡتَغُوۡنَ فَضۡلًا مِّنَ اللّٰهِ وَ رِضۡوَانًا ۫ سِيۡمَاهُمۡ فِيۡ وُجُوۡهِهِمۡ مِّنۡ اَثَرِ السُّجُوۡدِ ؕ ذٰلِكَ مَثَلُهُمۡ فِي التَّوۡرٰىةِ ۖۛۚ وَ مَثَلُهُمۡ فِي الۡاِنۡجِيۡلِ ۚ۟ۛ كَزَرۡعٍ اَخۡرَجَ شَطۡـَٔهٗ فَاٰزَرَهٗ فَاسۡتَغۡلَظَ فَاسۡتَوٰى عَلٰى سُوۡقِهٖ يُعۡجِبُ الزُّرَّاعَ لِيَغِيۡظَ بِهِمُ الۡكُفَّارَ ؕ وَعَدَ اللّٰهُ الَّذِيۡنَ اٰمَنُوۡا وَ عَمِلُوا الصّٰلِحٰتِ مِنۡهُمۡ مَّغۡفِرَةً وَّاَجۡرًا عَظِيۡمًا

"Muhammad ﷺ is a Rasool of Allah Ta'ala. And those with him (the Sahaabah ﷺ) are stern against the disbelievers, (yet) compassionate among themselves. You (O, Muhammad ﷺ) will see them sometimes making ruku and sometimes falling in sajdah (in Salaah), (always) seeking the bounty of Allah Ta'ala and His pleasure. Their hallmark (sign by which they are recognised) is on their faces because of the effects of making sajdah. This is their description in the Torah. Their description in the Injeel is like that of a plant that sprouts out its shoot and makes it strong, after which it becomes thick and stands on its own stem, pleasing the farmer so that He may make the disbelievers angry with (the sight of) them. Allah Ta'ala has promised forgiveness and a great reward for those of them who have Imaan and do good deeds." (Surah Fath – Aayah 29)

لَقَدۡ رَضِيَ اللّٰهُ عَنِ الۡمُؤۡمِنِيۡنَ اِذۡ يُبَايِعُوۡنَكَ تَحۡتَ الشَّجَرَةِ فَعَلِمَ مَا فِيۡ قُلُوۡبِهِمۡ فَاَنۡزَلَ السَّكِيۡنَةَ عَلَيۡهِمۡ وَ اَثَابَهُمۡ فَتۡحًا قَرِيۡبًا ۙ وَّ مَغَانِمَ كَثِيۡرَةً يَّاۡخُذُوۡنَهَا ؕ وَ كَانَ اللّٰهُ عَزِيۡزًا حَكِيۡمًا

"Allah Ta'ala was very pleased with the believers (the Sahaabah ﷺ) when they pledged their allegiance to you (O Rasulullah ﷺ) under the tree. Allah Ta'ala knew what was in their hearts, so He sent down peace/ tranquillity to them and rewarded them with a close victory, and abundant booty that they will take. Allah Ta'ala is ever Mighty, Wise." (Surah Fath – Aayaat 18-19)

مِنَ الْمُؤْمِنِيْنَ رِجَالٌ صَدَقُوْا مَا عَاهَدُوا اللهَ عَلَيْهِ ۖ فَمِنْهُمْ مَّنْ قَضٰى نَحْبَهٗ وَ مِنْهُمْ مَّنْ يَّنْتَظِرُ ۖ وَمَا بَدَّلُوْا تَبْدِيْلًا

"From the believers there are men who are true to what they promise with Allah Ta'ala. Some of them have fulfilled their vow/ pledge (by being martyred in battle), and some of them are still waiting (to receive their martyrdom), and they have not changed in the least."
(Surah A'hzaab – Aayah 23).

وَالسّٰبِقُوْنَ الْاَوَّلُوْنَ مِنَ الْمُهٰجِرِيْنَ وَالْاَنْصَارِ وَالَّذِيْنَ اتَّبَعُوْهُمْ بِاِحْسَانٍ ۙ رَّضِيَ اللهُ عَنْهُمْ وَرَضُوْا عَنْهُ وَاَعَدَّ لَهُمْ جَنّٰتٍ تَجْرِىْ تَحْتَهَا الْاَنْهٰرُ خٰلِدِيْنَ فِيْهَآ اَبَدًا ۚ ذٰلِكَ الْفَوْزُ الْعَظِيْمُ

"And Allah Ta'ala is pleased with the first to lead the way (in accepting Islam) from the Muhaajireen, the Ansaar, and those who followed them with sincerity and they are very pleased with Him. He has prepared for them such Gardens beneath which rivers flow, where they will live forever. That is the ultimate success."
(Surah Taubah – Aayah 100)

In the above Aayaat of the Qur-aan-e-Kareem, Allah Ta'ala has praised the Sahaabah ﷺ and expressed His pleasure with them. Similarly in the books of Hadith, numerous virtues of the Sahaabah ﷺ are mentioned:

1. *"After Me, follow Abu Bakr and 'Umar."*

2. "My Sahaabah ﷺ are like (guiding) stars. Whoever you follow, you will be guided (on the right path)."

3. Hadhrat Anas ﷺ narrates that Nabi ﷺ said: "The example of my Sahaabah ﷺ (in the people) is as the example of salt in food. There is no taste in the food without the salt."

4. "Beware (of using your tongue) in insulting (saying bad things about) my Sahaabah ﷺ. Do not make them the target of your insults. Who loves them, loves them for his love for me, and who hates them hates them for his hatred for me. Who causes hurt to them, has caused hurt to Me, and who causes hurt to Me, annoys Allah Ta'ala. Allah Ta'ala will very soon catch the person who annoys Him."

5. "Do not insult my Sahaabah ﷺ. If any of you (persons coming after Sahaabah ﷺ) has spent gold (in Sadaqah) equal in weight to Mount Uhud, he cannot get a reward equal to what my Sahaabah ﷺ get while spending one or even half a mudd of grain only." (A mudd is about 1kg.)

6. "On the person who insults my Sahaabah ﷺ is the curse of Allah Ta'ala, the Malaaikah and of all men put together. Neither his Fardh nor his Nafl is accepted by Allah Ta'ala."

7. "After the Ambiyaa ﷺ, Allah Ta'ala has chosen my Sahaabah ﷺ above all His creation. He has again favoured four of my Sahaabah ﷺ over the rest of them. They are Abu Bakr ﷺ, 'Umar ﷺ, 'Usmaan ﷺ and Ali ﷺ."

8. "O, people! I am pleased with Abu Bakr ﷺ. You should realise his high position. I am also pleased with 'Umar, Ali, 'Usmaan, Talhah, Zubair, Sa'ad, Sa'eed, Abdur Rahmaan bin Auf and Abu Ubaidah ﷺ. You should realise their high position. O, people! Allah Ta'ala has announced the forgiveness of all those who took part in Badr and who took part at Hudaybiyyah. O, people! You should think of me when dealing with my Sahaabah ﷺ, especially those who are my family by marriage. Beware of doing

wrong to them, otherwise they may complain against you on the Day of Qiyaamah and you may not be forgiven."

9. "Think of me when dealing with My Sahaabah ﷺ and My sons in law. The person who has regard for Me shall be in the protection of Allah Ta'ala on the Day of Qiyaamah. Allah Ta'ala is free of any responsibility to him who has no regard for Me. He may catch him at any time."

10. "On the Day of Qiyaamah, I shall be the guardian (protector) of those who have regard for me in their dealing with my Sahaabah ﷺ."

11. "The person who has regard for me in his dealing with my Sahaabah ﷺ, shall be able to reach me when I shall be at Kausar, while the person who has no regard for me in his dealing with them shall not be able to come to me. He may have a look at me from far."

Ayyub Sakhtiyaani *(rahmatullahi alayh)* says: "Whoever loves Abu Bakr ﷺ, strengthens his Imaan. Whoever loves 'Umar ﷺ, receives guidance on the right path. Whoever loves Usmaan ﷺ, is brightened with the light of Allah Ta'ala. Whoever loves Ali ﷺ, holds fast to the rope of Allah Ta'ala. Whoever honours the Sahaabah ﷺ, can never be a Munaafiq (hypocrite). Whoever insults them, he is surely an innovator, or a Munaafiq or one who is against the Sunnah. I am afraid that no good action of such a person will be accepted by Allah Ta'ala, until he cleans his heart of their hatred and begins to love all of them."

Sahl bin Abdullah *(rahmatullahi alayh)* says: "He who does not honour the Sahaabah ﷺ, has actually not believed in Nabi ﷺ."

May Allah Ta'ala, in his grace and kindness, save me, my friends, my supporters, my colleagues, my Mashaaikh, my pupils and all the Muslims from His anger and from His beloved Nabi's ﷺ displeasure, and may He fill our hearts with the true love for the Sahaabah ﷺ. *Aameen*.

بِرَحْمَتِكَ يَا اَرْحَمَ الرَّاحِمِيْنَ وَاٰخِرُ دَعْوَانَا اَنِ الْحَمْدُ لِلّٰهِ رَبِّ الْعَالَمِيْنَ وَالصَّلَاةُ وَالسَّلَامُ الْاَتَمَّانِ الْاَكْمَلَانِ عَلٰى سَيِّدِ الْمُرْسَلِيْنَ وَعَلٰى اٰلِهِ وَاَصْحَابِهِ الطَّيِّبِيْنَ الطَّاهِرِيْنَ وَعَلٰى اَتْبَاعِهِمْ حَمَلَةِ الدِّيْنِ الْمَتِيْنِ

تَمَّتْ

by (Hadhrat Moulana) Muhammad Zakariyya Kandhlavi (RA)
12 Shawwaal 1357 (HIJRI)

محمد ﷺ

فضائلِ قرآن

Virtues of the Qur-aan

CONTENTS

Foreword 258
  Respect for the Qur-aan Shareef 262
  Etiquettes of recitation 263
  Rules of External Respect 264
  Rules of Internal Respect 264
  An Important Rule (Mas-alah) 265

CHAPTER 1 - FORTY AHAADITH   267
  Hadith 1 - The Best person is one who learns the Qur-aan and teaches it 267
  Hadith 2 - A Person busy with the Qur-aan and has no time for Dua and Zikr 268
  Hadith 3 - Reading Qur-aan is better than acquiring She-Camels 269
  Hadith 4 - Double reward for a person who learns the Qur-aan Shareef with difficulty 272
  Hadith 5 - A thing to be envious of 273
  Hadith 6 - Reciter of the Qur-aan Shareef is compared to a citron 273
  Hadith 7 - the effect of the Qur-aan in the rising and the falling of nations 275
  Hadith 8 - The intercession of the Qur-aan 277
  Hadith 9 - A Haafiz Climbs as he recites 282
  To recite with Tarteel 283
  Hadith 10 - ten rewards for every letter 286
  Hadith 11 - The virtues of teaching your children the Qur-aan 287
  Hadith 12 - One special virtue of a Haafiz 289
  Hadith 13 - The Haafiz will have the right to intercede for 10 members of his family for whom Jahannam is compulsory 290
  Hadith 14 - Qur-aan is like a bag of musk 292
  Hadith 15 - A heart with no Qur-aan is like an empty house 292
  Hadith 16 - The virtue of reciting Qur-aan over zikr and tasbeeh 293
  Hadith 17 - The best wealth 294
  Hadith 18 - The reward for looking inside and reading Qur-aan 295
  Hadith 19 - Reciting the Qur-aan is a means of cleansing the rust of the heart 296
  Hadith 20 - The Qur-aan is the Pride of this Ummah 298
  Hadith 21 - Reciting the Qur-aan is Noor 299
  Hadith 22 - Reciting Qur-aan in the Masjid 303
  Hadith 23 - The Qur-aan brings a person closer to Allah Ta'ala 305
  Hadith 24 - People of the Qur-aan are the family of Allah Ta'ala 309

Hadith 25 - To recite in a beautiful voice 310
Hadith 26 - Allah Ta'ala listens to people reciting Qur-aan 310
Hadith 27 - Do not use the Qur-aan as a pillow 312
Hadith 28 - The Qur-aan is the substitue of all previous scriptures with additions 315
Hadith 29 - Nabi ﷺ joins a group of Muhaajireen reciting Qur-aan 316
Hadith 30 – Separate Rewards for reading and listening to the Qur-aan Shareef 318
Hadith 31 - Reciting the Qur-aan loudly or silently 319
Hadith 32 - The Qur-aan is an Interceder (i.e. It will speak on your behalf) 320
Hadith 33 - Fasting and Qur-aan intercedes on behalf of a person 321
Hadith 34 - The Qur-aan is the best interceder 325
Hadith 35 - Reciter of the Qur-aan safeguards the knowledge of Nubuwwat (Prophethood) 326
Hadith 36 – 3 fortunate people who will be saved from questioning on the day of Qiyaamah 326
Hadith 37 - Rewards for Learning one Aayah 327
Hadith 38 – The reward of reciting at least 10 Aayaat 328
Hadith 39 – reward for reciting 100 Aayaat at night 328
Hadith 40 - Reciting the Qur-aan Shareef will save a person from Fitnahs 329

CHAPTER 2 - CONCLUDING SECTION 330

Hadith 1 - Virtues of Surah Faatihah (Surah Faatihah is a cure for all sicknesses) 330
Hadith 2 - Virtues of Surah Yaaseen 333
Hadith 3 - Virtues of Surah Waaqi'ah 335
Hadith 4 - Virtues of Surah Mulk and Surah Sajdah 336
Hadith 5 - When one completes a complete recitation of the Qur-aan, he should immediately start with the next recitation 337
Hadith 6 - Guard the Qur-aan, because it escapes more quickly than camels 339
Hadith 7 - Punishment for the person who reads the Qur-aan for worldly benefits 341

CHAPTER 3 - FINAL NOTE - SUMMARY OF THE FORTY AHAADITH MENTIONED IN PART ONE 343

Conclusion 354

CHAPTER 4 - 40 AHAADITH OF HADHRAT SALMAAN ﷺ 361

FOREWORD

بِسْمِ اللَّهِ الرَّحْمَنِ الرَّحِيْمِ

اَلْحَمْدُ لِلَّهِ الَّذِىْ خَلَقَ الْإِنْسَانَ وَعَلَّمَهُ الْبَيَانَ وَاَنْزَلَ لَهُ الْقُرْاٰنَ وَجَعَلَهُ مَوْعِظَةً وَّشِفَاءً وَّهُدًى وَّرَحْمَةً لِّذَوِى الْإِيْمَانِ لَا رَيْبَ فِيْهِ وَلَمْ يَجْعَلْ لَّهُ عِوَجًا وَّاَنْزَلَهُ قَيِّمًا حُجَّةً نُّوْرًا لِّذَوِى الْإِيْقَانِ وَالصَّلَاةُ وَالسَّلَامُ الْاَتَمَّانِ الْاَكْمَلَانِ عَلٰى خَيْرِ الْخَلَائِقِ مِنَ الْإِنْسِ وَالْجَانِّ الَّذِىْ نَوَّرَ الْقَلْبَ وَالْقُبُوْرَ نُوْرُهٗ وَرَحْمَةً لِّلْعَالَمِيْنَ ظُهُوْرُهٗ وَعَلٰى اٰلِهٖ وَصَحْبِهِ الَّذِيْنَ هُمْ نُجُوْمُ الْهِدَايَةِ وَنَاشِرُ الْفُرْقَانِ وَعَلٰى مَنْ تَبِعَهُمْ بِالْإِيْمَانِ وَبَعْدُ: فَيَقُوْلُ الْمُفْتَقِرُ اِلٰى رَحْمَةِ رَبِّهِ الْجَلِيْلِ عَبْدُهُ الْمَدْعُوُّ بِزَكَرِيَّا بْنِ يَحْيٰى بْنِ اِسْمَاعِيْلَ: هٰذِهِ الْعُجَالَةُ اَرْبَعُوْنَةٌ فِىْ فَضَائِلِ الْقُرَاٰنِ اَلَّفْتُهَا مُمْتَثِلًا لِّأَمْرِ مَنْ اِشَارَتُهٗ حُكْمٌ وَّطَاعَتُهٗ غُنْمٌ

All praise be to Allah Ta'ala Who created man, gave him the gift of speech and revealed the Qur-aan Shareef to him, which is a source of advice, healing, guidance and mercy for those who have Imaan. The Qur-aan Shareef contains nothing that is doubtful or crooked. It is absolutely straight, an authority and Noor (enlightenment) for the believers. Abundant Salawaat and salaam be on Rasulullah ﷺ (blessing and peace from Allah Ta'ala be upon him), the person who is the best of all creation, whose Noor illuminated the hearts of the living and their graves after death, whose appearance was a bounty for the whole universe. Peace be upon his descendants and Sahaabah, who are the stars of guidance and propagators of the Qur-aan Shareef, and also upon all the Muslims.

After this praise and salaam, I (the author), Zakariyya, son of Yahya, son of Isma'il, state that these hurriedly written pages contain forty Ahaadith (Plural of Hadith, sayings of Nabi ﷺ), which, I have collected on virtues of the Qur-aan Shareef, in obedience to such

Foreword

people whose words are law for me and following those people is most valuable to me.

One of the special favours of Allah Ta'ala, which He blessed the Madrasah of Mazahir-ul-Ulum, Saharanpur with, has been the annual jalsah (gathering) of this Madrasah for the purpose of briefly mentioning the progress of the Madrasah. For this jalsah at the Madrasah, not much effort is made to invite speakers, preachers and the famous people of India, but more attention is paid to invite men whose hearts are full of love for Allah Ta'ala and the Mashaaikh (saintly people) who prefer to live unknown.

Those glorious days have passed when *'Hujjat-ul-Islam'* (a title meaning a great authority on Islam) Moulana Muhammad Qaasim Nanotwi Saahib *(rahmatullahi alayh)* and *'Qutbul Irshad'* (a title meaning a great servant) Hadhrat Moulana Rashid Ahmad Gangohi Saahib *(nawwarAllahu marqadahu)* used to honour this jalsah with their presence and enlighten the hearts of all who attended. The scene has not yet disappeared from the eyes when the spiritual descendants of those revivalists of Islam, Hadhrat Shaikh-ul-Hind (*rahmatullahi alayh*), Hadhrat Shah Abdur Rahim Raipuri (*rahmatullahi alayh*), Hadhrat Moulana Khalil Ahmad Saahib Sahaaranpuri (*rahmatullahi alayh*), and Hadhrat Moulana Ashraf Ali Thanwi Saahib *(NawwarAllahu marqadahu)* used to assemble at the annual jalsah of the Madrasah. Their presence was a fountain source of life and noor for deadened souls and quenched the thirst of those who sought the love of Allah Ta'ala.

Although the present annual jalsah lacks the noor of such sources of guidance, the pious people who succeeded them still honour these jalsahs with their presence and enrich the audience with bounties and blessings. The people who attended the jalsah this year are witnesses to this. Only those who possess eyes that see, can experience the noor, but people like us who cannot see also feel something unusual.

At the annual jalsah of this Madrasah, if a person comes to listen to polished speeches and forceful lectures, perhaps he will not return so happy as one whose heart seeks spiritual upliftment.

$$\text{فَلِلّٰهِ الْحَمْدُ وَالْمِنَّةُ}$$

"All praise and thanks are for Allah Ta'ala."

This year, on 27th Zul Qadah 1348 Hijri, Hadhrat Shah Haafiz Muhammad Yasin Naginwi *(rahmatullahi alayh)* had visited the Madrasah. His coming was like a shower of affection and kindness and I can not adequately thank him for this. As he is one of the Khulafaa of Hadhrat Moulana Gangohi *(rahmatullahi alayh)*, there is no need of mentioning his fine qualities of devotion and piety and his Anwaaraat (Plural of 'Noor' enlightenment and blessings). When this jalsah was over, he returned home and honoured me with a kind letter asking me to compile forty Ahaadith regarding the virtues of the Qur-aan Shareef and send them to him along with their translations. He also wrote to me that if I did not carry out his wishes, he would ask the successor to my Shaikh, my respected uncle, Hadhrat Moulana Muhammad Ilyaas Saahib *(rahmatullahi alayh)*, to order me to fulfill his request. He made it known to me that he certainly wanted me to do this job. Incidentally, I received that honoured message when I was out on my travels and my uncle was present (at Saharanpur). On my return, my uncle gave me this letter, ordering me to carry out this task. Now, there was no way I could make any excuses nor could I plead that I was unable to carry out this task. Although I had an excuse that I was busy with the commentary of *'Mu'atta'* (a book of Ahaadith) of Imam Maalik *(rahmatullahi alayh)*, I had to postpone that work for a few days and comply with this urgent request. I beg for forgiveness for my shortcomings because I am incapable.

رَجَاءَ الْحَشْرِ فِي سِلْكِ مَنْ قَالَ فِيْهِمُ النَّبِيُّ صَلَّى اللهُ عَلَيْهِ وَسَلَّمَ مَنْ حَفِظَ عَلٰى أُمَّتِيْ أَرْبَعِيْنَ حَدِيْثًا مِنْ أَمْرِ دِيْنِهِ بَعَثَهُ اللهُ فَقِيْهًا وَكُنْتُ لَهُ يَوْمَ الْقِيَامَةِ شَافِعًا وَشَهِيْدًا قَالَ الْعَلْقَمِيُّ رَحِمَهُ اللهُ: اَلْحِفْظُ هُوَ ضَبْطُ الشَّيْءِ وَمَنْعُهُ مِنَ الضِّيَاعِ فَتَارَةً يَكُوْنُ حِفْظُ الْعِلْمِ بِالْقَلْبِ وَإِنْ لَمْ يَكْتُبْ وَتَارَةً فِي الْكِتَابِ وَإِنْ لَمْ يَحْفَظْهُ بِقَلْبِهِ فَلَوْ حَفِظَ فِي كِتَابِهِ ثُمَّ نَقَلَ إِلَى النَّاسِ دَخَلَ فِي وَعْدِ الْحَدِيْثِ قَالَ الْمُنَاوِيْ رَحِمَهُ اللهُ قَوْلُهُ مَنْ حَفِظَ عَلٰى أُمَّتِيْ أَيْ نَقَلَ إِلَيْهِمْ بِطَرِيْقِ التَّخْرِيْجِ وَالْإِسْنَادِ وَقِيْلَ مَعْنٰى حَفِظَهَا أَنْ يَنْقُلَهَا إِلَى الْمُسْلِمِيْنَ وَإِنْ لَمْ يَحْفَظْهَا وَلَا عَرَفَ مَعْنَاهَا وَقَوْلُهُ أَرْبَعِيْنَ حَدِيْثًا صِحَاحًا أَوْ حِسَانًا أَوْ ضِعَافًا يُعْمَلُ بِهَا فِي الْفَضَائِلِ. فَلِلّٰهِ دَرُّ الْإِسْلَامِ مَا أَيْسَرَهُ وَلِلّٰهِ دَرُّ أَهْلِهِ مَا أَجْوَدَ مَا

اسْتَنْبَطُوْا رَزَقَنِيَ اللهُ تَعَالٰى وَاِيَّاكُمْ كَمَالَ الْاِسْلَامِ وَمِمَّا لَا بُدَّ مِنَ التَّنْبِيْهِ عَلَيْهِ اَنِّيْ اعْتَمَدْتُ فِي التَّخْرِيْجِ عَلَى الْمِشْكَاةِ وَتَخْرِيْجِهٖ وَشَرْحِهٖ الْمِرْقَاةِ وَشَرْحِ الْاِحْيَاءِ لِلسَّيِّدِ مُحَمَّدٍ الْمُرْتَضٰى وَالتَّرْغِيْبِ لِلْمُنْذِرِيّ وَمَا عَزَوْتُ اِلَيْهَا لِكَثْرَةِ الْاَخْذِ عَنْهَا وَمَا اَخَذْتُ عَنْ غَيْرِهَا عَزَوْتُهٗ اِلٰى مَأْخَذِهٖ وَيَنْبَغِيْ لِلْقَارِئِ مُرَاعَاةُ اٰدَابِ التِّلَاوَةِ عِنْدَ الْقِرَاءَةِ

I have done it in the hope of being raised together on the day of Qiyaamah with such people who were mentioned by Rasulullah ﷺ when he said: "Whoever will preserve for my Ummah forty Ahaadith concerning important matters of their Deen, Allah Ta'ala will raise him, on the Day of Qiyaamah, as an Aalim and I will intercede on his behalf and stand witness in his favour."

Alqami (rahmatullahi alayh) says that the word 'preserve' in this Hadith is used in the sense of securing something and guarding it against loss by either memorising it without recording it, or by recording it in black and white without memorising it. Therefore, anyone writing them in the form of a book and passing them on to others will also be included in the blessings mentioned in this Hadith.

Munaawi (rahmatullahi alayh) is of the opinion that "preserve for my Ummah" means reporting of a Hadith along with its chain of narrators. According to some, "preserve" includes even those who are reporting it to other Muslims without memorising it or even without knowing its meanings. The expression "forty Ahaadith" has been used in a general sense, i.e., these Ahaadith may be all sahih (authentic), hasan (correct) or even da'if (weak) to the degree that can be acted upon because of their virtues.

Allahu Akbar! (How great Allah Ta'ala is!). Many are the facilities provided in Islam. Commendable indeed has been the role of the Muhadditheen and Ulama who took great pains to explain the finer points or meanings of various expressions. May Allah Ta'ala bless us all with perfection in Islam.

It is important to note that whenever I have quoted a Hadith without mentioning the name of the book, it should be considered to have been taken from one of the five books, viz. Mishkaat, Tanqih-ur-Ruwat, Mirqaat, Sharhul-Ihyaa and At-Targhib of Imaam Munziri, on which I have relied and from which I have drawn extensively. Whenever I have quoted from any other book, the reference has been mentioned. It is necessary for the reader of the Qur-aan Shareef to respect the Qur-aan.

RESPECT FOR THE QUR-AAN SHAREEF

Before proceeding further, it is necessary to mention some of the requirements of respect for reading the Qur-aan Shareef because we admit that;

بے ادب محروم گشت از فضلِ رب

"One who is devoid of respect is deprived of Allah Ta'ala's special favour."

In brief, the essence of all the rules of respect is to consider the Qur-aan Shareef as the words of Allah Ta'ala, Whom we worship, and as the Word of One Whom we love and seek.

Those who have experienced love will know how worthy of respect a letter or the speech of the beloved is. The delight caused by such a communication is beyond all rules and laws of teaching love because, as it is said:

محبت تجھ کو آداب محبت خود سکھا دے گی

"Love itself will teach one the rules of conduct in love."

While reading the Qur-aan Shareef, if we attempt to imagine the real beauty and limitless bounty of our Beloved Allah Ta'ala, our hearts will feel the immense love of Allah Ta'ala. At the same time, the Qur-aan is the Word of the Master of all masters and the commands of the King of all kings. It is the law set out by the most powerful King, Who remains unequalled forever. Those who have served at the courts of kings know by experience, while others can only imagine the extreme awe inspired by the king's orders. The Qur-aan Shareef is the word of our Beloved Rabb, Who is also the Supreme King. We should therefore read the Qur-aan Shareef with the feelings of love and awe.

Whenever Hadhrat Ikrimah رَضِىَ اللهُ عَنْهُ opened the Qur-aan Shareef, he would become unconscious and fall down. He would then say:

هٰذَا كَلَامُ رَبِّي هٰذَا كَلَامُ رَبِّي

"This is the Word of my Allah! This is the Word of my Allah!"

The above-mentioned incident briefly explains the spirit of the requirements of respect as written in great detail by the Ulama. It will further be explained in the following paragraphs. In short, a Muslim should read the book of Allah Ta'ala not just as a servant, but as a slave in the spirit of complete humility towards his Rabb, Master and Benefactor. The Sufia have written that, if a person feels he has shortcomings in showing respect and reverence while reciting the Qur-aan Shareef, then he will continue to progress towards gaining the nearness of Allah Ta'ala. But a person who regards himself to be perfect or with pride, will not progress.

ETIQUETTES OF RECITATION

After cleaning the teeth with a miswaak and making wudhu, one should sit in a quiet place with grace and humility and face towards the Qiblah. Then, with an attentive heart, deep concentration and love, one should recite, all the time being mindful that one is reciting to Allah Ta'ala. If one understands the meaning, one should pause and reflect on the aayaat of promise and mercy and should beg Allah Ta'ala for His forgiveness and compassion. On the aayaat of punishment and warnings, one should seek His protection, as there is no Helper besides Him. On the aayaat relating to His Majesty and Greatness, one should say *"Subhanallah"* (Glory be to Allah Ta'ala). If one does not naturally shed tears while reading the Qur-aan Shareef, one must try to make oneself weep a little.

وَأَلَذُّ حَالَاتِ الْغَرَامِ لِمُغْرِمٍ   شَكْوَى الْهَوٰى بِالْمُدْمَعِ الْمُهْرَاقِ

"For a lover, the moments of greatest pleasure are those when, in the presence of his beloved, he is shedding tears profusely due to his weakness."

One should not read fast unless one desires to memorise it. The Qur-aan Shareef should be placed in a slightly high position on a stand or a pillow. One should not talk to others during recitation. If one is forced by necessity to speak to someone, it should be done after closing the Book, and then recite Ta'awwuz (seeking refuge of Allah Ta'ala against shaytaan), before reading again. If there are people nearby busy in their work, then it is suggested to read in a low voice, otherwise reading loudly is more rewarding.

The Ulama have mentioned six external and six internal rules of respect for reading the Qur-aan Shareef which are given below:

RULES OF EXTERNAL RESPECT

1. After cleaning the teeth with a miswaak, perform wudhu whilst sitting respectfully facing the Qiblah.
2. Do not read fast but rather at a medium speed with correct tajweed (pronunciation).
3. Try to weep (cry) even if you have to force yourself to do so.
4. When reading the Aayaat of mercy or of punishment, do as explained above.
5. Read in a loud voice. However, if you fear showing off or if others will be disturbed by your recitation, then read softly.
6. Read in a sweet voice because there are numerous Ahaadith that emphasise this.

RULES OF INTERNAL RESPECT

1. The heart should be full of the glory (greatness) of the Qur-aan Shareef.
2. The Qur-aan Shareef is the revelation of Allah Ta'ala, so keep in mind His Greatness, Majesty and Magnificence.

3. The heart should be free from distractions and doubts.

4. Ponder over the meaning and enjoy reciting it. Rasulullah ﷺ once spent the whole night repeating the following aayah over and over:

$$\text{اِنْ تُعَذِّبْهُمْ فَاِنَّهُمْ عِبَادُكَ ۖ وَاِنْ تَغْفِرْ لَهُمْ فَاِنَّكَ اَنْتَ الْعَزِيْزُ الْحَكِيْمُ}$$

"If You punish them, they are Your servants, and if You forgive them, You are the Mighty, the Wise." (Surah Maaidah- Aayah 118)

Once, Hadhrat Sa'eed ibn Jubair رضى الله عنه spent the whole night repeating the following aayah;

$$\text{وَامْتَازُوا الْيَوْمَ اَيُّهَا الْمُجْرِمُوْنَ}$$

"And separate yourselves today (from the Mu'mineen), O you criminals!" (Surah Yaaseen – Aayah 59)

5. If you understand the meaning, you should stop and think about the Aayaat of mercy and beg Allah Ta'ala for forgiveness and compassion. On the Aayaat of punishment and warning, you should seek the protection of Allah Ta'ala, as no one can protect us except Him.

6. The ears should be made attentive as if Allah Ta'ala Himself is speaking and the reader is listening to Him.

May Allah Ta'ala, out of His mercy and kindness, grant us all the ability to read the Qur-aan Shareef with respect. *Aameen.*

An Important Rule (Mas-alah)

It is compulsory on every Muslim to memorise that much of the Qur-aan which is needed for performing Salaah. Memorising the entire Qur-aan is Fardh-e-Kifaayah, i.e. such an act, though obligatory, but it can be fulfilled by few individuals. If there was not a single Haafiz (may Allah Ta'ala forbid), all the Muslims would be held responsible for this sin. Mulla Ali Qari *(rahmatullahi alayh)* has reported from Zarkashi *(rahmatullahi alayh)* that, if in a town or a village, there was no Haafiz to read the Qur-aan Shareef, the entire Muslim community of that place would be considered sinful. In this age of darkness and ignorance, when the Muslims have become misguided in respect of many aspects of Islam, it is generally considered useless and foolish to memorise the Qur-aan Shareef and a total waste of time and mental energy to repeat its words without understanding its meaning. If this was the only thing that we disliked about our Deen, then something in detail could be written about it. But today all our acts are full of faults and all our thoughts are leading us astray. For how many people should we cry and about how many should we keep complaining about.

$$فَاِلَى اللهِ الْمُشْتَكٰى وَاللهُ الْمُسْتَعَانُ$$

"So to Allah Ta'ala do we complain and from Him do we seek help."

CHAPTER 1
FORTY AHAADITH

HADITH 1 - THE BEST PERSON IS ONE WHO LEARNS THE QUR-AAN AND TEACHES IT

عَنْ عُثْمَانَ رَضِيَ اللهُ عَنْهُ قَالَ قَالَ النَّبِيُّ صَلَّى اللهُ عَلَيْهِ وَسَلَّمَ خَيْرُكُمْ مَنْ تَعَلَّمَ الْقُرْاٰنَ وَعَلَّمَهُ (صحيح البخارى # 5027)

Hadhrat Usmaan رَضِىَ اللهُ عَنْهُ says that Rasulullah ﷺ said: "The best amongst you is he who learns the Qur-aan and teaches it."

Note: In most books of Hadith it is quoted with the word '**and**' between '**learns and teaches**' as above. Thus, the greatest reward would be for that person who learns the Qur-aan Shareef and thereafter teaches it to others. But in some of the books this Hadith is narrated with the word '**or**', in which case the meaning would be: "The best amongst you is he who learns the Qur-aan or teaches it."

According to this version, the reward is general, i.e. equally great whether one learns himself or teaches it to others. Thus, there would be equal reward for both.

The Qur-aan Shareef is the basis of the Deen of Islam and the existence of this Deen depends on the preservation and propagation of the Qur-aan Shareef. Therefore, the reward of learning and teaching the Qur-aan Shareef is obvious and does not need further explanation.

However, there are different levels of learning. The highest is to learn the Qur-aan Shareef with its meaning and the least is to learn its words only.

The Hadith mentioned above is also supported by another saying of Rasulullah ﷺ as reported by Hadhrat Sa'eed ibn Sulaim رضي الله عنه: *"If a person who has learnt the knowledge of the Qur-aan thinks that another person, who has been gifted with something else, to be more fortunate than himself, has shown disrespect to the blessings of Allah Ta'ala upon him."*

Since the Qur-aan Shareef is the Word of Allah Ta'ala, to recite and teach it is better than everything else.

Mulla Ali Qari *(rahmatullahi alayh)* quotes from another Hadith that whoever learns the knowledge of the Qur-aan Shareef stores the knowledge of Nubuwat in his forehead.

Sahl Tastari *(rahmatullahi alayh)* says that the proof of love that one has for Allah Ta'ala, is the love for the word of Allah Ta'ala in one's heart.

It is written in *'Sharhul Ihyaa'* that, amongst the people who will be given shelter in the shade of the Arsh (Throne) of Allah Ta'ala on the fearful Day of Qiyaamah will be those who teach the Qur-aan Shareef to the children of Muslims and also those who learn the Qur-aan whilst young and read it throughout their lives.

HADITH 2 - A PERSON BUSY WITH THE QUR-AAN AND HAS NO TIME FOR DUA AND ZIKR

عَنْ اَبِيْ سَعِيْدٍ رَضِيَ اللهُ عَنْهُ قَالَ قَالَ رَسُوْلُ اللهِ صَلَّى اللهُ عَلَيْهِ وَسَلَّمَ يَقُوْلُ الرَّبُّ عَزَّ وَجَلَّ مَنْ شَغَلَهُ الْقُرْاٰنُ عَنْ ذِكْرِيْ وَمَسْئَلَتِيْ اَعْطَيْتُهُ اَفْضَلَ مَا اُعْطِى السَّائِلِيْنَ وَفَضْلُ كَلَامِ اللهِ عَلٰى سَائِرِ الْكَلَامِ كَفَضْلِ اللهِ عَلٰى خَلْقِهٖ (سنن الترمذى # 2926)

Hadhrat Abu Sa'eed رضي الله عنه says that Rasulullah ﷺ said: "Allah Ta'ala says, 'If anybody finds no time for My zikr and for making dua to Me, because he is busy with the Qur-aan Shareef, I shall give him more than what I give to those who make dua to Me.

The greatness of the Word of Allah Ta'ala (the Qur-aan) over all other words is like the greatness of Allah Ta'ala over the entire creation.'"

Note: In other words, compared to those who are making dua to Allah Ta'ala, He will surely give a better reward to that person who remains so busy memorising the Qur-aan or learning and understanding it that he barely gets time for dua.

It is commonly known that when a man distributes sweets etc., a share is set aside for him also because of the job of distribution given to him by the distributor himself.

In another Hadith with a similar meaning it is mentioned that Allah Ta'ala would give such a person a better reward than what He would give to His ever-grateful servants.

HADITH 3 - READING QUR-AAN IS BETTER THAN ACQUIRING SHE-CAMELS

عَنْ عُقْبَةَ بْنِ عَامِرٍ رَضِيَ اللهُ عَنْهُ قَالَ خَرَجَ رَسُوْلُ اللهِ صَلَّى اللهُ عَلَيْهِ وَسَلَّمَ وَنَحْنُ فِي الصُّفَّةِ فَقَالَ اَيُّكُمْ يُحِبُّ اَنْ يَغْدُوَ كُلَّ يَوْمٍ اِلٰى بُطْحَانَ اَوْ اِلَى الْعَقِيْقِ فَيَأْتِيَ مِنْهُ بِنَاقَتَيْنِ كَوْمَاوَيْنِ فِيْ غَيْرِ اِثْمٍ وَلَا قَطِيْعَةِ رَحِمٍ فَقُلْنَا يَا رَسُوْلَ اللهِ نُحِبُّ ذٰلِكَ قَالَ اَفَلَا يَغْدُوْ اَحَدُكُمْ اِلَى الْمَسْجِدِ فَيُعَلِّمَ اَوْ يَقْرَأُ اٰيَتَيْنِ مِنْ كِتَابِ اللهِ عَزَّ وَجَلَّ خَيْرٌ لَهُ مِنْ نَاقَتَيْنِ وَثَلَاثٌ خَيْرٌ لَهُ مِنْ ثَلَاثٍ وَاَرْبَعٌ خَيْرٌ لَهُ مِنْ اَرْبَعٍ وَمِنْ اَعْدَادِهِنَّ مِنَ الْاِبِلِ (صحيح مسلم # 803)

Hadhrat 'Uqbah ibn Aamir ﷺ has said, "Rasulullah ﷺ came to us while we were sitting on the 'Suffah' (a certain spot in Masjidun Nabawi ﷺ) and asked if any one of us would like to go to the market of Buthaan or Aqeeq every day and fetch two she camels of the best quality from there without committing any sin or cutting off family relations. We replied that every one of us would love to do so. Rasulullah ﷺ said that going to the Masjid and reading or teaching two aayaat of Qur-aan Shareef is much better than two she camels, and reading or teaching four aayaat is better than four she camels and an equal number of camels. (i.e. and so on)."

Note: 'Suffah' is the name of a raised platform in the Masjid of Nabi ﷺ in Madinah Munawwarah where the poor Muhaajireen used to stay. These Muhaajireen (those who left Makkah Mukarramah and settled down in Madinah Munawwarah) were known as the "Ashaab-us-Suffah" (The people of the Suffah). The number of these men varied from time to time. Allamah Suyuti *(rahmatullahi alayh)* has listed 101 names and also written an independent booklet about their names.

Buthaan and Aqeeq were the two markets for camels near Madinah Munawwarah. The camel, especially a she camel with a fat hump, was a favourite of the Arabs.

The expression "without sin" is significant. A thing can be obtained without working for it, either by blackmail, through illegal inheritance (by forcefully taking over the property of some relative) or by theft. Rasullullah ﷺ thus ruled out obtaining something incorrectly. Obtaining a thing without committing any sin is certainly liked by all, but much more valuable than that is the learning of a few Aayaat of the Qur-aan Shareef.

Leave alone one or two camels, even if someone owns all the seven continents, he will be forced to leave it behind at the time of death. However, the reward of one Aayah will be ever-lasting. We see even in this life that a man feels happier when he is given only one Rupee (without having to return it), rather than if he is given 1000 Rupees for safe keeping for a while only. By safe keeping he is only burdened with a trust without getting any benefit out of it. In fact, this Hadith indirectly warns us not to compare something temporary with something everlasting. Whether he is busy with some work or resting, a man should ponder if his efforts are being wasted on acquiring the temporary gains of this world or are directed towards achieving the everlasting ones. We should grieve over all our wasted efforts for which we earn everlasting misery.

The last part of the Hadith which says "superior to an equal number of camels" has three meanings. The reward for four camels has been mentioned in detail. Thereafter it is mentioned that the more Aayaat a person reads or teaches, the greater will be their superiority over the number of camels. In this case, the word "camels" at the end refers to either he-camels or she-camels and the number implied is more than four, because up to the number four, the reward has been mentioned in detail.

The second meaning is that the numbers mentioned are the same as referred to earlier, the significance is that different people have different choices. Some people like she camels while others prefer he camels. Therefore Rasulullah ﷺ has used this expression to show that every Aayah is superior to a she or he-camel, whichever one a person prefers.

The third meaning is that the numbers mentioned are the same as referred to before and not more than four. According to the second meaning, the explanation that an Aayah is superior to a she-camel or he-camel refers to both he and she camel, i.e., one Aayah is superior to both a he-camel and a she-camel considered together, and likewise every Aayah is superior to the combination of an equal number of he-camels or she-camels. Thus, a single Aayah has been compared to a pair or couple (of camels). My late father (May Allah Ta'ala bless his grave with noor) has preferred the latter interpretation because of its superior virtue.

The Hadith does not mean that the reward of an aayah is equivalent to a camel or two camels; rather this example is given for our understanding. Actually, the Qur-aan Shareef cannot be compared to camels which will one day die. It has been clearly written before that the reward for even a single aayah is everlasting and is superior to being made a king over the seven continents, which will certainly be destroyed.

Mulla Ali Qari *(rahmatullahi alayh)* has written about a pious person who went to Makkah Mukarramah for Haj. When he landed at Jeddah, some of his business friends asked him to stay longer in Jeddah, so that they could earn more money because of his blessed presence. In fact, they also wanted that some of the servants of the Shaikh to benefit from the profits of their business. At first the Shaikh refused to stay longer. When they insisted, he asked them how much they hoped to earn. They explained that they hoped to double their profits. The Shaikh said, "You have taken all this trouble for such a small amount. I cannot miss out one Salaah in the 'Haram Shareef' (the blessed Masjid in Makkah Mukarramah), where the reward of one Salaah is multiplied one hundred thousand times." We should reflect how we sometimes lose great amounts of reward just for little worldly gain.

Hadith 4 - Double Reward for a Person who Learns the Qur-aan Shareef with Difficulty

عَنْ عَائِشَةَ رَضِيَ اللهُ عَنْهَا قَالَتْ قَالَ رَسُوْلُ اللهِ صَلَّى اللهُ عَلَيْهِ وَسَلَّمَ اَلْمَاهِرُ بِالْقُرْاٰنِ مَعَ السَّفَرَةِ الْكِرَامِ الْبَرَرَةِ وَالَّذِىْ يَقْرَأُ الْقُرْاٰنَ وَيَتَتَعْتَعُ فِيْهِ وَهُوَ عَلَيْهِ شَاقٌّ لَهُ اَجْرَانِ

(صحيح مسلم # 798)

Hadhrat Aa'ishah رَضِيَ اللهُ عَنْهَا narrates that Rasulullah ﷺ once said, "A person who reads the Qur-aan Shareef well will be with those noble and pious Malaaikah who are scribes (writers), and the person who has difficulty in reading the Qur-aan and has to exert himself to learn it, gets double the reward."

Note: The person who "reads the Qur-aan well" in the Hadith refers to the one who memorises the Qur-aan Shareef well and reads it fluently. It is highly praiseworthy if one also learns its meaning and significance as well. "To be with the Malaaikah" means that, just like how the Malaaikah brought the Qur-aan Shareef from the Lowhul Mahfooz (The Protected Tablet in the Heavens), he also conveys it to others by reciting it. Therefore, both have the same job, or it means that he will join the company of the Malaaikah on the Day of Qiyaamah. The person who has difficulty in reading the Qur-aan Shareef will get double reward, one for reading and the other for making effort in reading the Qur-aan Shareef, even though he makes many mistakes. It does not mean that his reward will be more than the person who reads it well. The reward that is mentioned for a good reader is far greater, so much so that he will be with the special Malaaikah. The explanation is that the hard work and effort in the reading of the Qur-aan Shareef has a separate reward. Therefore, reading of the Qur-aan Shareef should not be given up, even though you may struggle to read.

Mulla Ali Qari *(rahmatullahi alayh)* has mentioned from the narration of Tabraani and Bayhaqi *(rahmatullahi alayhima)* that if a person cannot memorise the Qur-aan Shareef well and yet tries to memorise it gets double the reward. Similarly, one who has a love for memorising the Qur-aan Shareef, and in spite of not having the ability to do so, does not give up his efforts, he will be counted by Allah Ta'ala amongst the Huffaaz on the Day of Qiyaamah.

HADITH 5 - A THING TO BE ENVIOUS OF

وَعَنْ عَبْدِ اللهِ رَضِيَ اللهُ عَنْهُ قَالَ قَالَ رَسُوْلُ اللهِ صَلَّى اللهُ عَلَيْهِ وَسَلَّمَ لَا حَسَدَ اِلَّا فِي اثْنَتَيْنِ رَجُلٌ اٰتَاهُ اللهُ الْقُرْاٰنَ فَهُوَ يَقُوْمُ بِهِ اٰنَاءَ اللَّيْلِ وَاٰنَاءَ النَّهَارِ وَرَجُلٌ اٰتَاهُ اللهُ مَالًا فَهُوَ يُنْفِقُهُ اٰنَاءَ اللَّيْلِ وَاٰنَاءَ النَّهَارِ (اخرجه المنذرى فى الترغيب # 942)

Hadhrat ibn Umar رَضِيَ اللهُ عَنْهُ says that Rasulullah ﷺ said, "Hasad (Jealousy) is not permissible except for two people: One whom Allah Ta'ala blesses with the Qur-aan Shareef and he remains busy reading it day and night, and the other who is given a lot of wealth by Allah Ta'ala and he spends it day and night."

Note: According to many Aayaat of the Qur-aan and Ahaadith, jealousy is a bad quality and is absolutely haraam. This Hadith, however, allows one to be jealous of two people. The Ulama have explained this Hadith in two ways. Firstly, jealousy here means *ghibtah* (envy). There is a difference between jealousy and envy. Jealousy is when you see someone who has something that you like and you wish that he should lose it whether it comes to you or not, while envy is a feeling within yourself to also own a thing which someone else has and which you like. Since jealousy is haraam, the Ulama have explained the word jealousy here to mean '*ghibtah*' (envy). '*Ghibtah*' is permissible in worldly things (e.g. a car, etc.) and commendable in Deeni matters.

The second meaning is that if jealousy was permissible, it would have been permissible for the two people mentioned above.

HADITH 6 - RECITER OF THE QUR-AAN SHAREEF IS COMPARED TO A CITRON

عَنْ اَبِيْ مُوْسَى الْاَشْعَرِيِّ رَضِيَ اللهُ عَنْهُ قَالَ قَالَ رَسُوْلُ اللهِ صَلَّى اللهُ عَلَيْهِ وَسَلَّمَ مَثَلُ الْمُؤْمِنِ الَّذِيْ يَقْرَاُ الْقُرْاٰنَ كَمَثَلِ الْاُتْرُجَّةِ رِيْحُهَا طَيِّبٌ وَطَعْمُهَا طَيِّبٌ وَمَثَلُ الْمُؤْمِنِ

الَّذِىْ لَا يَقْرَأُ الْقُرْاٰنَ كَمَثَلِ الثَّمَرَةِ لَا رِيْحَ لَهَا وَطَعْمُهَا حُلْوٌ وَمَثَلُ الْمُنَافِقِ الَّذِىْ يَقْرَأُ الْقُرْاٰنَ مَثَلُ الرَّيْحَانَةِ رِيْحُهَا طَيِّبٌ وَطَعْمُهَا مُرٌّ وَمَثَلُ الْمُنَافِقِ الَّذِىْ لَا يَقْرَأُ الْقُرْاٰنَ كَمَثَلِ الْحَنْظَلَةِ لَيْسَ لَهَا رِيْحٌ وَطَعْمُهَا مُرٌّ (صحيح البخارى # 5427)

Hadhrat Abu Musa ﷺ says that Rasulullah ﷺ said, "The example of a Mu'min who reads the Qur-aan Shareef is like that of a citron (type of orange), which has a nice smell and a sweet taste. The example of a Mu'min who does not read the Qur-aan Shareef is like that of a date, which has no smell, but its taste is sweet. And the hypocrite who reads the Qur-aan Shareef is like a rayhaan (sweet-smelling flower), which has a good smell but has a bitter taste. The hypocrite (one who pretends to be a Muslim) who does not read the Qur-aan Shareef is like a wild gourd (a bitter fruit), which has a bitter taste and no smell."

Note: In this Hadith, reading of the Qur-aan Shareef has been compared to worldly objects in order to make us understand the difference between reading and not reading the Qur-aan Shareef. Otherwise it is obvious that material objects of this world like citrons and dates cannot match the sweetness and perfume of the Qur-aan Shareef. However, there are special points in this example, which indicates the deep knowledge of Nubuwwat and proves the vast understanding of Rasulullah ﷺ.

Consider the example of the citron, which gives flavour to the mouth, cleans the stomach and helps digestion. These qualities are specially associated with the recitation of the Qur-aan Shareef which results in fragrance in the mouth, internal purity and spiritual strength. It is also said that if there is citron in the house, no jinn can enter it and if this is true, then this is the speciality of the Qur-aan Shareef also. Some doctors say that citron strengthens the memory. It is reported in *'Ihyaa'* by Hadhrat Ali ﷺ that, three things strengthen the memory i.e., cleaning the teeth with miswaak, fasting and reading the Qur-aan Shareef.

In the kitaab of *'Abu Dawood'*, it is mentioned at the end of the Hadith given above that a good companion is like a person having musk. Even if you do not get the musk, you will at least enjoy its fragrance. An evil companion is like a person with a fire place. If you do not get blackened in his company, you certainly cannot avoid the smoke. It is, therefore, important that one should be very careful in choosing his companions, with whom he has to generally mix.

HADITH 7 - THE EFFECT OF THE QUR-AAN IN THE RISING AND THE FALLING OF NATIONS

عَنْ عُمَرَ بْنِ الْخَطَّابِ رَضِىَ اللهُ عَنْهُ قَالَ قَالَ رَسُوْلُ اللهِ صَلَّى اللهُ عَلَيْهِ وَسَلَّمَ اِنَّ اللهَ يَرْفَعُ بِهٰذَا الْكِتَابِ اَقْوَامًا وَيَضَعُ بِهِ اٰخَرِيْنَ (صحيح مسلم # 817)

Hadhrat Umar رَضِىَاللهُعَنْهُ says that Rasulullah صَلَّىاللهُعَلَيْهِوَسَلَّمَ said, "Allah Ta'ala gives honour to many people because of the Qur-aan Shareef and He also disgraces many people because of the Qur-aan."

Note: People who believe in the Qur-aan Shareef and practice upon it are given honour and respect by Allah Ta'ala, both in this life as well as in the Aakhirah, while those who do not act upon it are disgraced by Allah Ta'ala. Allah Ta'ala says in the Qur-aan;

يُضِلُّ بِهٖ كَثِيْرًا وَّيَهْدِىْ بِهٖ كَثِيْرًا

"Allah misleads many with this Qur-aan and guides many with it."
(Surah Baqarah – Aayah 26)

At another place in the Qur-aan Shareef we come across:

وَنُنَزِّلُ مِنَ الْقُرْاٰنِ مَا هُوَ شِفَآءٌ وَّرَحْمَةٌ لِّلْمُؤْمِنِيْنَ وَلَا يَزِيْدُ الظّٰلِمِيْنَ اِلَّا خَسَارًا

"And We have revealed such a Qur-aan that is a cure and mercy for the believers, and it only increases the loss of the oppressors."
(Surah Bani Israaeel – Aayah 82)

Nabi صَلَّىاللهُعَلَيْهِوَسَلَّمَ is also reported to have said: "Many hypocrites of this Ummah will be the Qurraa, i.e., those who recite the Qur-aan Shareef correctly." In *Ihyaaul-Ulum* it is reported from some Mashaaikh, "As soon as a man starts reciting a surah of the Qur-aan Shareef, the Malaaikah make dua of mercy for him. They continue to do so till he

275

stops. On the other hand, another person begins reciting a surah, and the Malaaikah curse him. They continue to do so till he completes his recitation.

Sometimes, a person invites the curse of Allah Ta'ala on himself whilst reading the Qur-aan Shareef without him even knowing. For example, a person has the habit of oppressing others. He reads the aayah of the Qur-aan:

$$\text{اَلَا لَعْنَةُ اللّٰهِ عَلَى الظّٰلِمِيْنَ}$$

"Beware, the curse of Allah Ta'ala is on the oppressors."
(Surah Hood – Aayah 18)

He exposes himself to this warning because of his wrong doings. In the similar manner, he reads in the Qur-aan Shareef;

$$\text{لَعْنَتُ اللّٰهِ عَلَى الْكٰذِبِيْنَ}$$

"The curse of Allah Ta'ala is upon the liars."
(Surah Aale I'mraan - Aayah 61)

In reality he is cursing himself because he himself speaks lies.

Aamir ibn Waathilah (رضي الله عنه) says that Hadhrat Umar (رضي الله عنه) had appointed Naafi ibn Abdul Haaris as the Governor of Makkah Mukarramah. Once Hadhrat Umar (رضي الله عنه) asked Naafi as to whom he had appointed as the administrator of the forests. "Ibn Abzi" replied Naafi. "Who is Ibn-e-Abzi?" asked Hadhrat Umar (رضي الله عنه). "He is one of our slaves," was the reply. "Why have you appointed a slave as the ameer (leader)?" objected Hadhrat Umar (رضي الله عنه). "Because he recites the kitaab of Allah Ta'ala" said Naafi. At this, Hadhrat Umar (رضي الله عنه) narrated the Hadith where Rasullullah (صلى الله عليه وسلم) said, that because of this Book, Allah Ta'ala honours many people and disgraces many.

HADITH 8 - THE INTERCESSION OF THE QUR-AAN

عَنْ عَبْدِ الرَّحْمٰنِ بْنِ عَوْفٍ رَضِيَ اللهُ عَنْهُ عَنِ النَّبِيِّ صَلَّى اللهُ عَلَيْهِ وَسَلَّمَ قَالَ ثَلَاثَةٌ تَحْتَ الْعَرْشِ يَوْمَ الْقِيَامَةِ الْقُرْاٰنُ يُحَاجُّ الْعِبَادَ لَهُ ظَهْرٌ وَبَطْنٌ وَالْأَمَانَةُ وَالرَّحِمُ تُنَادِىْ اَلَا مَنْ وَصَلَنِىْ وَصَلَهُ اللهُ وَمَنْ قَطَعَنِىْ قَطَعَهُ اللهُ (اخرجه البغوى فى شرح السنة # 3433)

Hadhrat 'Abdur Rahmaan ibn Auf ؓ narrates that Rasulullah ﷺ said, "On the Day of Qiyaamah, three things will be under the shade of Allah's Arsh; Firstly, the Qur-aan Shareef which will argue on behalf of the people. The second will be 'Amaanat' (trust) and the third will be 'Family Relations', which will say, 'O Allah! Have mercy on the person who joined family ties and don't have mercy on him who cut off family ties.'"

Note: "Three things being under the shade of the Arsh" shows their nearness and importance to Allah Ta'ala. The Qur-aan Shareef will "argue" means that it will beg for forgiveness for those who recited it, respected it and acted upon it. It will plead on their behalf and beg for their rank to be raised.

Mulla Ali Qaari *(rahmatullahi alayh)* has narrated from *'Tirmizi Shareef'* that, in the presence of Allah Ta'ala, the Qur-aan Shareef will beg for clothing to be granted to its reader. Allah Ta'ala will give him a crown of honour. The Qur-aan Shareef will again beg for additional favours whereupon Allah Ta'ala will award the reader clothing of honour. The Qur-aan Shareef will again ask Allah Ta'ala to be pleased with him. Allah Ta'ala will then become happy with the reader.

We find in this life that the pleasure of the beloved is considered to be the most desired gift. In the Aakhirah there will be no gift greater than the pleasure of our Beloved Allah Ta'ala. As for those who did not care about the Qur-aan Shareef and ignored it, it will challenge them saying, "Did you care for me? Did you fulfil your duty towards me?"

It has been reported on the authority of Imam Abu Hanifa *(rahmatullahi alayh)* in *'Ihya'* that it is the right of the Qur-aan Shareef that it should be recited completely twice a year. Those of us who never care to recite the Qur-aan Shareef should first consider how they will defend themselves against such a strong accuser. Death is certain and there can be no escape from it.

The meaning of the expression "exterior and interior of the Qur-aan" is obvious. The Qur-aan Shareef has an outward meaning which can be understood by all, but the deeper spiritual meaning is not understood by everybody. It is in this connection that Rasulullah ﷺ has said: "Whoever gives his personal opinion in respect of anything in the Qur-aan Shareef commits a mistake, even if his opinion is correct."

Some Ulama are of the opinion that the word "exterior" refers to its words, which can be recited properly by everybody and the word "interior", refers to its meanings and its underlying ideas, the understanding of which varies with the ability of the readers.

Hadhrat Ibn Mas'ood رضي الله عنه said, "If you seek knowledge, you should meditate on the meanings of the Qur-aan, because it contains the history of past as well as of latter times." However, it is necessary to know the requirements for interpreting the Qur-aan Shareef. In today's time even those who have little or no knowledge of the Arabic vocabulary offer their personal opinions using translations of the Qur-aan in their own language. Mufassireen say that anyone trying to do a commentary of the Qur-aan Shareef should have the knowledge of fifteen subjects. These subjects, which are briefly given below, will show that it is not possible for everybody to understand and comment on the real meanings of the Qur-aan Shareef.

1) **Lughat:** A study of language. It helps in understanding the appropriate meanings of words. Mujaahid *(rahmatullahi alayh)* says, "One who believes in Allah Ta'ala and the Day of Qiyaamah should not open his lips in respect of the Qur-aan Shareef, unless he is thoroughly familiar with the lughat of the Arabic language. Quite often, an Arabic word has several meanings. A person may know only one or two of them, though, in a given context, the actual meaning may be quite different."

2) **Nahwu (syntax)** is a branch of grammar, which helps to understand the relation of one sentence with another and also of the I'raab (vowel sounds/harkats) of the letters of a word. A change in I'raab (vowel sounds/harkats) often leads to a change in the meaning.

3) **Sarf (etymology)** is a branch of grammar, which helps in knowing the root words and conjugations. The meaning of a word changes with the change in the root and with a change in its conjugation.

Ibn Faaris *(rahmatullahi alayh)* says, "One who loses the knowledge of sarf loses a great deal.' Allamah Zamakhshari *(rahmatullahi alayh)* mentions that, when a certain person wanted to translate the Aayah:

يَوْمَ نَدْعُوْا كُلَّ اُنَاسٍ بِاِمَامِهِمْ

"The day when We will call every person with his leader,"
(Surah Bani Israaeel – Aayah 71)

he ignorantly translated it as: "On the day that We shall call each people after their mothers." He assumed that the singular Arabic word "imam" (leader) was the plural of the Arabic word "umm" (mother). If he had been familiar with sarf (etymology), he would have known that the plural of "umm" is not "imam".

4) **Ish-tiqaaq (derivatives):** It is necessary to have the knowledge of ish-tiqaaq (derivatives) and their root words, because if a word has been derived from two different root words, it will have two different meanings, e.g. the word "maseeh" is derived from "masah" which means to touch or to pass wet hands over something, and also from "masaahat" which means measurement.

5) **Ilmul Ma'aani (knowledge of semantics):** because phrase constructions are understood from their meanings.

6) **Ilmul Bayaan (knowledge of figures of speech):** like similes and metaphors, due to which expressions or shades of meaning or similes and metaphors become known.

7) **Ilmul Badee' (knowledge of idioms):** the knowledge which reveals the beauty of language and its implications.

The last three are the branches of Ilmul Balaaghah (knowledge of speaking fluently with the right choice of words) and are considered very important subjects, which a commentator should master, because the Qur-aan Shareef is a perfect miracle and its amazing sentence constructions can only be understood after mastering these subjects.

8) **Ilmul Qiraa'ah (knowledge of the art of pronunciation):** The different methods of recitation of Qur-aan Shareef sometimes convey different meanings, and sometimes one meaning is to be preferred over the other.

9) **Ilmul Aqaaid (The knowledge of the fundamental beliefs of Deen):** This is necessary to explain certain analogies or comparisons. The literal meaning of certain Aayaat referring to Allah Ta'ala is not the correct one. For example, the comparison in the Aayah:

$$يَدُ اللهِ فَوْقَ اَيْدِيْهِمْ$$

"The hand of Allah Ta'ala is over their hands." *(Surah Fath – Aayah 10)*

will have to be explained because Allah Ta'ala has no physical hands.

10) **Usoolul Fiqh (Principles of Islamic jurisprudence):** These are necessary for finding proofs and deriving masaail (Islamic Laws).

11) **Asbaabun Nuzool (Specific situations due to which Allah Ta'ala sent down wahy (revelation):** The meaning of an Aayah will be better understood if we know how and when it had been revealed. Sometimes the true meaning of an Aayah is understood only if we know the situations in which the Aayah had been revealed.

12) **Naasikh wal Mansookh:** This is the knowledge of those commandments that were later on cancelled or changed so that the cancelled commandments may be distinguished from the commandments that were revealed later.

13) **Ilmul Fiqh (knowledge of Islamic Jurisprudence):** It is only through this knowledge that we arrive at a complete understanding of general principles.

14) **Knowledge of Ahaadith:** Those Ahaadith that happen to be a commentary on certain Aayaat of the Qur-aan.

15) The last but most important is the **Wahbi ilm**, or the gifted understanding, bestowed by Allah Ta'ala upon His selected servants, as is referred to in the Hadith;

$$مَنْ عَمِلَ بِمَا عَلِمَ وَرَّثَهُ اللهُ عِلْمَ مَا لَمْ يَعْلَمْ$$

"Whosoever acts upon what he knows, Allah Ta'ala grants him the knowledge of things not known to him." [1]

It is this special understanding that was meant in the reply of Hadhrat Ali رَضِىَ اللّٰهُ عَنْهُ when he was asked by the people if he received from Rasulullah ﷺ any special knowledge or instructions which were not received by others. Hadhrat Ali رَضِىَ اللّٰهُ عَنْهُ said, "I swear by Him Who created Jannah and created life that I possess nothing special, except the clear understanding which Allah Ta'ala grants a person in respect of the Qur-aan."

Ibnu Abid Dunyaa *(rahmatullahi alayh)* says that the knowledge of the Qur-aan Shareef and that which can be derived from it is such an ocean which has no shores.

The branches of knowledge described above are like tools that are an essential requirement for a commentator. A commentary written by a person who is not learned in these branches of knowledge will be based on his personal opinion, which is prohibited. The Sahaabah رَضِىَ اللّٰهُ عَنْهُمْ already had the advantage of the Arabic language as their mother-tongue, and they reached the depth of the rest of the knowledge by means of their personal contact that they had with Rasulullah ﷺ.

Allamah Suyuti *(rahmatullahi alayh)* says that those who think that it is beyond the capacity of a man to acquire Wahbi ilm, or gifted understanding, are not right. To get this knowledge from Allah Ta'ala, one should adopt the means to this end, which are, acting upon the knowledge that one has acquired and creating a dislike towards the world.

It is stated in *'Keemiyaa-e-Sa'aadat'* that three people are not blessed with the complete understanding of the Qur-aan Shareef. Firstly, the one who is not well versed in Arabic. Secondly, one who persists in committing a major sin or indulges in acts of bidat (innovations), because these actions blacken his heart, which in turn prevents him from understanding the Qur-aan Shareef. Thirdly, one who wants proofs and reasoning for everything, even in the matters of Deen, and feels

---

[1] (اخرجه ابو نعيم فى حلية الأولياء 15/10)

embarrassed when he reads an Aayah of the Qur-aan which he is not able to fully understand and comprehend.

اَللّٰهُمَّ احْفَظْنَا مِنْهُمْ

May Allah Ta'ala protect us from all such sins and evils.

HADITH 9 - A HAAFIZ CLIMBS AS HE RECITES

عَنْ عَبْدِ اللهِ بْنِ عَمْرٍو رَضِيَ اللهُ عَنْهُ قَالَ قَالَ رَسُوْلُ اللهِ صَلَّى اللهُ عَلَيْهِ وَسَلَّمَ يُقَالُ لِصَاحِبِ الْقُرْاٰنِ اِقْرَاْ وَارْتَقِ وَرَتِّلْ كَمَا كُنْتَ تُرَتِّلُ فِي الدُّنْيَا فَاِنَّ مَنْزِلَكَ عِنْدَ اٰخِرِ اٰيَةٍ تَقْرَؤُهَا (سنن ابى داود # 1464)

Hadhrat Abdullah ibn Amr ﷺ reports that Rasulullah ﷺ said, "On the Day of Qiyaamah, it will be said to the Haafiz of the Qur-aan, 'Go on reading the Qur-aan and continue climbing the high positions of Jannah and read slowly like how you used to read in the world; your final place in Jannah will be where you reach at the time of the last aayah of your recitation."

Note: "The man of the Qur-aan" apparently means a Haafiz. Mulla Ali Qari *(rahamatullahi alayh)* has explained it fully that this honour is reserved for a haafiz, and that this hadith does not apply to one who reads by looking into the Qur-aan Shareef. Firstly, because the words "Man of Qur-aan" refers to a haafiz and secondly, there is a Hadith in *'Musnad Ahmad'*:

حَتّٰى يَقْرَاَ شَيْئًا مَّعَهُ

Till he reads of whatever Qur-aan is with him

This word more clearly refers to a haafiz, although a reader who remains very often engaged in reciting the Qur-aan may also be included.

It is written in *'Mirqaat'* that this Hadith does not apply to a reader who is cursed by the Qur-aan Shareef. This is with reference to the Hadith that there are many readers of the Qur-aan who read the Qur-aan but the Qur-aan curses them. Therefore, the reading of Qur-aan by a person who does not have the correct Aqaaid (beliefs) does not justify

Him to be acceptable to Allah Ta'ala. Many Ahaadith of this type relate to the Khawaarij (a sect who were opposed to Hadhrat Ali رَضِىَٰاللَّهُعَنْهُ).

TO RECITE WITH TARTEEL

In this commentary, Shah Abdul Aziz *(rahmatullahi alayh)* has written that 'tarteel' literally means reading with good and clear pronunciation, while according to Islamic principles it means reading in accordance with certain rules as follows:

(1) The letters of the alphabet should be correctly pronounced so that ط is not read as ت and ض is not read as ظ and so on.

(2) Stopping correctly at the pauses, so that the joining or finishing of the Aayaat may not be at the wrong places.

(3) The correct pronunciation of the vowel sounds.

(4) Raising the voice slightly so that the sound of the recitation of the Qur-aan may reach the ears and thus influence the heart.

(5) Setting the sound in a way that it may become full of sorrow and may affect the heart quickly, because a sad voice influences the heart at once and moves and strengthens the soul more effectively.

The doctors are of the opinion that if a medicine is required to affect the heart quickly, it should be given a sweet smell by means of a perfume, because the heart is sensitive to sweet smell. If the medicine is required to affect the liver, it should be sweetened with sugar because the liver likes sweet things. Therefore, if a perfume is used at the time of recitation, it will have a better influence on the heart.

(6) Tashdeed ّ - (doubling of letters) and madd ٓ - (pulling of letters) should be fully pronounced because this reveals the beauty of the Quraan Shareef and adds to its effectiveness.

(7) As stated earlier, the reader's heart should respond to the Aayah indicating mercy or punishment of Allah Ta'ala.

The above-mentioned seven rules explain the correct way of reciting the Qur-aan Shareef, which is called tarteel, and the object of all this is to get the correct understanding of the deeper meaning of the Qur-aan Shareef.

Hadhrat Umm-e-Salamah رَضِىَ اللّٰهُ عَنْهَا was once asked by someone as to how Rasulullah صَلَّى اللّٰهُ عَلَيْهِ وَسَلَّمَ used to recite the Qur-aan Shareef. She said, "In a way that all vowel sounds were clear and the pronunciation of each letter was distinct." It is desirable to recite the Qur-aan correctly with tarteel (correctly and properly) even if one may not understand the meaning.

Ibn Abbaas رَضِىَ اللّٰهُ عَنْهُ said that he preferred to recite short surahs like Al-Qaari'ah (اَلْقَارِعَةُ) or Az-Zilzaal (اِذَا زُلْزِلَتْ) with tarteel correctly, rather than to recite long surahs like Surah Baqarah and Surah Aali Imraan (آلِ عِمْرَانَ) without tarteel (incorrectly without tajweed).

The Mufassireen and Ulama explain the above Hadith to mean that, for each Aayah recited, the reciter will be raised up to a higher level in Jannah. From other Ahaadith, it appears that there are as many levels in Jannah equal to the number of Aayaat in the Qur-aan Shareef. Therefore, the status of a person will be raised by as many levels in Jannah as the number of Aayaat which he knows well. Therefore, the one who is the most learned in the whole Qur-aan will reach the highest level in Jannah.

According to Mulla Ali Qari *(rahmatullahi alayh)*, it is mentioned in a Hadith that there is no level in Jannah higher than that given to the reader of the Qur-aan. So the position of the readers will be raised according to the number of Aayaat recited by them in the world.

Allamah Daani *(rahmatullahi alayh)* says that the Ulama agree there are 6000 aayaat in the Qur-aan Shareef. But there is some difference of opinion about the numbers over and above 6000. These are variously reported to be 204, 14, 19, 25, 36.

It is written in *'Sharhul-Ihya'* that each Aayah corresponds to a higher level in Jannah. So a reader will be asked to climb according to his recitation. One who reads the whole Qur-aan Shareef will reach the highest level in Jannah. One who knows only a part of the Qur-aan Shareef will rise up to the corresponding level. In brief, the stage or level reached will be fixed by the number of Aayaat recited.

According to my humble understanding, the above Hadith has a different meaning;

فَاِنْ كَانَ صَوَابًا فَمِنَ اللهِ وَاِنْ كَانَ خَطَأً فَمِنِّيْ وَمِنَ الشَّيْطَانِ وَاللهُ وَرَسُوْلُهُ مِنْهُ بَرِيْئَانِ

If my interpretation is correct, it is from Allah Ta'ala and, if it is wrong, it is from me and from shaytaan, and Allah Ta'ala and His Nabi ﷺ are free from it.

I think that the raising of the level referred to in this Hadith is not that which can be determined by the number of Aayaat to be recited, that is when one Aayah is recited, then the status will be raised by one step, whether it be read correctly or not. But this Hadith indicates to the raising of the inner spiritual level of a person which is related to the recitation either being read correctly or incorrectly. So a person will be able to read in the same way as he read in this worldly life. Mullah Ali Qari *(rahmatullahi alayh)* has quoted from one Hadith which says that if a person reads the Qur-aan Shareef very often in this life, he will remember it in the Aakhirah, otherwise he will forget it. May Allah Ta'ala help us there also. There are many who memorised the Qur-aan Shareef in their childhood through the Deeni enthusiasm of their parents, but through carelessness and negligence, have forgotten it. It is mentioned in other Ahaadith that a person who dies while attempting to memorise the Qur-aan Shareef, will be counted amongst the Huffaaz. Allah Ta'ala's favours have no limits. We should only look for it. As a poet says:

اس کے الطاف تو ہیں عام شہیدیؔ سب پر   تجھ سے کیا ضد تھی اگر تو کسی قابل ہوتا

O Shaheedi! His bounties are common for all, You could not be denied (these bounties), if you were all worthy,

HADITH 10 - TEN REWARDS FOR EVERY LETTER

عَنْ عَبْدِ اللهِ بْنِ مَسْعُوْدٍ رَضِيَ اللهُ عَنْهُ قَالَ قَالَ رَسُوْلُ اللهِ صَلَّى اللهُ عَلَيْهِ وَسَلَّمَ مَنْ قَرَأَ حَرْفًا مِّنْ كِتَابِ اللهِ فَلَهُ بِهِ حَسَنَةٌ وَالْحَسَنَةُ بِعَشْرِ أَمْثَالِهَا لَا أَقُوْلُ الٓمّٓ حَرْفٌ وَلَٰكِنْ اَلِفٌ حَرْفٌ وَلَامٌ حَرْفٌ وَمِيْمٌ حَرْفٌ (سنن الترمذى # 2910)

Hadhrat Abdullah ibn Mas'ood ﷺ narrates that Rasulullah ﷺ said, "Whosoever reads one letter of the Book of Allah Ta'ala is rewarded with one blessing, and one blessing is multiplied ten times in reward. I do not say that alif laam meem is one letter, but alif is one letter, laam is one letter, and meem is one letter."

Note: Usually a reward is given for a whole action, but in the case of the Qur-aan Shareef it is not so. Reading each letter is counted as one good deed, and the reward of each good deed will be increased ten times, as promised by Allah Ta'ala:

مَنْ جَآءَ بِالْحَسَنَةِ فَلَهٗ عَشْرُ اَمْثَالِهَا

"A person who does a good deed, for him will be ten times its reward."
(Surah An'aam - Aayah 60)

Ten times, however, is the least.

وَاللهُ يُضْعِفُ لِمَنْ يَّشَآءُ

"Allah Ta'ala multiplies the reward for whomsoever He wishes as much as He desires." (Surah Baqarah – Aayah 261)

The reading of each letter of the Qur-aan Shareef equals to a good deed. This has been explained to us by Rasulullah ﷺ that, الٓمّٓ (Alif Laam Meem) is not one letter, but ا (alif), ل (laam) and م (meem) are three separate letters, so it will add up to thirty rewards.

There is a difference of opinion amongst the Ulama whether; الٓمّٓ (Alif, Laam, Meem) is the beginning of Surah Baqarah or Surah Feel اَلَمْ تَرَ. If it is the beginning of Surah Baqarah, and they are counted as they are written i.e. مِيْمْ لَامْ اَلِفْ, ا (alif اَلِفْ), ل (laam لَامْ) and م (meem مِيْمْ), it will be nine letters. Therefore, its rewards will be ninety. If it is the beginning of Surah Feel (اَلَمْ تَرَ) and only three letters are counted, the reward will be thirty.

Bayhaqi *(rahmatullahi alayh)* has reported another Hadith similar to the one mentioned above; "I do not say that بِسْمِ اللهِ (bismillah) is one letter, but that ب (ba) س (sin) and م (meem), etc, are separate letters."

HADITH 11 - THE VIRTUES OF TEACHING YOUR CHILDREN THE QUR-AAN

عَنْ مُعَاذِنِ الْجُهَنِيِّ رَضِيَ اللهُ عَنْهُ قَالَ قَالَ رَسُوْلُ اللهِ صَلَّى اللهُ عَلَيْهِ وَسَلَّمَ مَنْ قَرَاَ الْقُرْاٰنَ وَعَمِلَ بِمَا فِيْهِ اُلْبِسَ وَالِدَاهُ تَاجًا يَوْمَ الْقِيَامَةِ ضَوْءُهُ اَحْسَنُ مِنْ ضَوْءِ الشَّمْسِ فِيْ بُيُوْتِ الدُّنْيَا لَوْ كَانَتْ فِيْكُمْ فَمَا ظَنُّكُمْ بِالَّذِيْ عَمِلَ بِهٰذَا (سنن ابى داود # 1453)

Hadhrat Mu'aaz Juhani ﷺ reports that Rasulullah ﷺ said, "Whosoever reads the Qur-aan Shareef and acts upon what is in it, his parents will be made to wear a crown on the Day of Qiyaamah, the brightness of which will be far more than that of the sun, if the sun was inside your worldly houses. So, what do you think about the person who himself acts upon it?"

Note: Thus, it is because of reading the Qur-aan Shareef and acting upon it that the parents of the reader will be honoured with a crown, the brightness of which will be more than the brightness of the sun, as if the sun was inside your house. Even though the sun is very far from us, its light is very bright. Imagine if the sun comes down into our house, how much brighter it will be. The brightness of the crown to be worn by the parents of the Haafiz will be even brighter. When this is the reward for the parents, what will be the reward of the reader himself? Surely if the parents get so much, the reward of the person who is the real cause should be much more. The parents get this reward because they were the cause of the reader coming into this world and were responsible for his education.

In addition to the fact that the light of the sun will be far greater if it were inside one's own house, this example explains another delicate point. A person becomes attached and likes something when it always remains with him. Therefore, the feeling of strangeness for the sun due to being very far away, will be replaced with the feeling of attachment because it is very close to him in his house. Therefore, in addition to describing the brightness of the crown, the Hadith indicates this attachment with the crown and also the great satisfaction that it belongs to him. Everybody benefits from the sun, but if it were to be given entirely to a single person, how proud would he feel.

Haakim *(rahmatullahi alayh)* has reported from Buraidah, رضى الله عنه the saying of Rasulullah صلى الله عليه وسلم; *"A person who reads the Qur-aan Shareef and acts upon it will be made to wear a crown made of noor, and his parents will be made to wear clothing, which will be more valuable than the entire world. They will say, 'O Allah! Why are we being given these clothes?' 'Because your child learnt the Qur-aan,' will be the reply."*

It is mentioned in *'Jam'ul Fawaa'id'* by Tabrani *(rahmatullah alayh)* that Hadhrat Anas رضى الله عنه had reported the saying of Rasulullah صلى الله عليه وسلم, "Whoever teaches his son to read the Qur-aan Shareef (without memorising it), then all his future and past sins will be forgiven and whoever makes his child memorise the Qur-aan Shareef will be raised on the Day of Qiyaamah shining like the full moon and his son will be asked to start reciting. For every Aayah read by the child, the status of the parent will be raised to the next higher stage of Jannah, till the recitation of the entire Qur-aan Shareef is completed."

There are great rewards for teaching the Qur-aan Shareef to your children. But on the other hand, Allah Ta'ala save us, if you deprive your child of the knowledge of Deen for the sake of a few cents, not only shall you be deprived of everlasting reward but you shall also be held responsible before Allah Ta'ala. Is it not a fact that you are depriving your dear child of reading the Qur-aan Shareef for fear that Ulama and Huffaaz, after memorising the Qur-aan Shareef, become dependent on others for their living? Please remember that not only do you expose your children to everlasting misery, but you will also have to answer for this. The Hadith that says;

$$\text{كُلُّكُمْ رَاعٍ وَكُلُّكُمْ مَسْئُوْلٌ عَنْ رَعِيَّتِهِ} \text{ (صحيح البخارى # 5200)}$$

"Each one of you is a guardian, and will be questioned about those under his control"

This means that everyone shall be questioned about those that are under him and his dependents, as to how much Deen he taught them. Surely one should guard himself and his dependents against these shortcomings. But as the saying goes; "Should one get rid of his clothes because of the fear of lice?" Not at all! Rather one should surely try to keep his clothes clean. If you taught Deeni knowledge to your child, then you would have fulfilled your responsibility towards him. Whatever good deeds he does for the rest of his life, i.e. he performs Salaah and he seeks forgiveness from Allah Ta'ala on your behalf, makes dua for you, this will raise your position in Jannah. If, for the sake of this life and for the desire of a few cents, you keep him ignorant of Deen, then you will have to suffer for this wrong and whatever evil and sins he does, will be your responsibility and also be written in your account. For Allah Ta'ala's sake, have pity on yourselves. This life is only a passing phase and death will put an end to all its hardships, but the sufferings of the Aakhirah will be everlasting.

HADITH 12 - ONE SPECIAL VIRTUE OF A HAAFIZ

$$\text{عَنْ عُقْبَةَ بْنِ عَامِرٍ رَضِيَ اللهُ عَنْهُ قَالَ سَمِعْتُ رَسُوْلَ اللهِ صَلَّى اللهُ عَلَيْهِ وَسَلَّمَ يَقُوْلُ}$$
$$\text{لَوْ جُعِلَ الْقُرْاٰنُ فِيْ اِهَابٍ ثُمَّ اُلْقِيَ فِي النَّارِ مَا احْتَرَقَ} \text{ (سنن الدارمى # 3353)}$$

Hadhrat 'Uqbah ibn Aamir ﷺ narrated that Rasulullah ﷺ said, "If the Qur-aan is placed in a skin and then put in the fire, it will not get burnt."

Note: The Ulama have explained this in two ways. Some of them take the words 'skin' and 'fire' to mean the actual skin and a normal fire. In this case the Hadith refers to a miracle which took place in the lifetime of Rasulullah ﷺ and is specific to his time in the same way as the miracles of other Ambiyaa *(alayhimus salam)* were specific to their lifetime. In the second case, the word 'skin' means the human skin and the word 'fire' means the fire of Jahannam. Therefore this Hadith is general and not limited to any particular period. Thus the Hadith means that if any Haafiz of the Qur-aan Shareef is thrown into Jahannam due to any sin, the fire of Jahannam will not burn him. In another Hadith it is said that the fire will not even touch him. The second interpretation of the above Hadith is also supported by another Hadith reported by Abu Umaamah رضي الله عنه and also given in the book *'Sharhus Sunnah'*, by Mulla Ali Qari *(rahmatullahi alayh)*, which says, "**Learn the Qur-aan by heart, because Allah Ta'ala does not punish the heart which contains the Qur-aan Shareef.**" The meaning of this Hadith is clear and confirmed by the Qur-aan Shareef. Those who regard memorising the Qur-aan Shareef as useless and a waste of time should, for Allah Ta'ala's sake, think about these benefits. The last Hadith alone should encourage a person to spend his whole life learning the Qur-aan Shareef by heart, as there is no one who has not done any sins and does not deserve the fire of Jahannam.

In *'Sharhul Ihya'* there is a list of people who will rest in the shade of Allah Ta'ala's mercy (protection) on the dreadful Day of Qiyaamah. It is mentioned therein that, according to a Hadith reported from Hadhrat Ali رضي الله عنه by Daylami *(rahmatullahi alayh)*, those who guard the Qur-aan Shareef, in other words those who learn the Qur-aan Shareef by heart, will be in the shade of Allah Ta'ala, in the company of the Ambiyaa *(alayhimus salaam)* and other pious people.

HADITH 13 - THE HAAFIZ WILL HAVE THE RIGHT TO INTERCEDE FOR 10 MEMBERS OF HIS FAMILY FOR WHOM JAHANNAM IS COMPULSORY

عَنْ عَلِيِّ بْنِ أَبِيْ طَالِبٍ رَضِيَ اللهُ عَنْهُ قَالَ قَالَ رَسُوْلُ اللهِ صَلَّى اللهُ عَلَيْهِ وَسَلَّمَ مَنْ قَرَأَ الْقُرْآنَ وَاسْتَظْهَرَهُ فَأَحَلَّ حَلَالَهُ وَحَرَّمَ حَرَامَهُ أَدْخَلَهُ اللهُ بِهِ الْجَنَّةَ وَشَفَّعَهُ فِيْ عَشَرَةٍ مِنْ أَهْلِ بَيْتِهِ كُلُّهُمْ قَدْ وَجَبَتْ لَهُ النَّارُ (سنن الترمذى # 2905)

Hadhrat Ali رضي الله عنه says that Rasulullah ﷺ said, "Whoever reads the Qur-aan and learns it by heart, and then regards what is halaal as halaal and what is haraam as haraam, will be entered into

Jannah by Allah Ta'ala, Who will also accept his begging forgiveness for ten people of his family who were destined to go to Jahannam."

Note: By the mercy of Allah Ta'ala, entry into Jannah is promised for every Muslim though he may first be punished for his sins. The Haafiz, however, will be allowed to go straight to Jannah. The ten people who will be forgiven through his intercession will be those sinful and disobedient Muslims who are guilty of major sins. There will be no forgiveness, however, for non-Muslims.
Allah Ta'ala has said:

اِنَّهُ مَنْ يُّشْرِكْ بِاللّٰهِ فَقَدْ حَرَّمَ اللّٰهُ عَلَيْهِ الْجَنَّةَ وَمَأْوٰىهُ النَّارُ ۖ وَمَا لِلظّٰلِمِيْنَ مِنْ اَنْصَارٍ

"Allah Ta'ala has definitely forbidden Jannah for the one who attributes a partner to Allah Ta'ala (commits shirk), and his abode shall be the fire (of Jahannam). The evil doers will have no helpers."
(Surah Maaidah – Aayah 72)

It is also mentioned in the Qur-aan Shareef:

مَا كَانَ لِلنَّبِيِّ وَالَّذِيْنَ اٰمَنُوْۤا اَنْ يَّسْتَغْفِرُوْا لِلْمُشْرِكِيْنَ وَلَوْ كَانُوْۤا اُولِيْ قُرْبٰى

"It is not (permissible) for Nabi ﷺ and the believers to seek forgiveness for the mushrikeen (plural of mushrik) the polytheists (those worshiping many Gods and ascribing partners with Allah Ta'ala) even if they be their relatives." (Surah Taubah – Aayah 113)

The Qur-aanic Aayah clearly says that the mushrikeen (polytheists) will never be forgiven. The intercession of the Huffaaz will therefore, be for those Muslims who will be sent to Jahannam for their sins.

Those who are not Huffaaz and cannot memorise the Qur-aan should at least make one of their relatives a Haafiz, so that by His intercession they may be saved from Jahannam because of their sins.
Allah Ta'ala be thanked for this gracious favour on the person whose father, uncles and grandfathers, both maternal and paternal, were all

Huffaaz. (This refers to the author. May Allah Ta'ala bless him with more favours).

HADITH 14 - QUR-AAN IS LIKE A BAG OF MUSK

عَنْ اَبِىْ هُرَيْرَةَ رَضِىَ اللهُ عَنْهُ قَالَ قَالَ رَسُوْلُ اللهِ صَلَّى اللهُ عَلَيْهِ وَسَلَّمَ تَعَلَّمُوا الْقُرْاٰنَ وَاقْرَءُوْهُ وَارْقُدُوْا فَاِنَّ مَثَلَ الْقُرْاٰنِ وَمَنْ تَعَلَّمَهُ فَقَامَ بِهٖ كَمَثَلِ جِرَابٍ مَحْشُوٍّ مِسْكًا يَفُوْحُ رِيْحُهٗ كُلَّ مَكَانٍ وَمَثَلُ مَنْ تَعَلَّمَهُ فَرَقَدَ وَهُوَ فِىْ جَوْفِهٖ كَمَثَلِ جِرَابٍ اُوْكِىَ عَلٰى مِسْكٍ

(سنن ابن ماجه # 217)

Hadhrat Abu Hurayrah ﷺ narrated that Rasulullah ﷺ said, "Learn the Qur-aan and read it and then sleep, because the example of a person who learns the Qur-aan, reads it and recites it in Tahajjud Salaah is like an open bag full of musk whose beautiful fragrance spreads over the whole place. A person who has learnt the Qur-aan but sleeps while the Qur-aan is in his heart, is like a bag full of musk with its lid closed."

Note: The example of a person who learns the Qur-aan Shareef and cares for it and recites it in Tahajjud Salaah is like that of a musk container which, if opened, fills the whole house with its sweet smell. In the same way, the whole house is lit up with noor and *barakah* because of the reading of the Qur-aan Shareef by the Haafiz. Even if the Haafiz remains asleep or does not read because of laziness, the Qur-aan in his heart is, in any case, like musk. This negligence and laziness cause others to be deprived of the barakah of the Qur-aan Shareef. In spite of this laziness, the heart of the Haafiz still contains the musk of Qur-aan Shareef.

HADITH 15 - A HEART WITH NO QUR-AAN IS LIKE AN EMPTY HOUSE

عَنِ ابْنِ عَبَّاسٍ رَضِىَ اللهُ عَنْهُ قَالَ قَالَ رَسُوْلُ اللهِ صَلَّى اللهُ عَلَيْهِ وَسَلَّمَ اِنَّ الَّذِىْ لَيْسَ فِىْ جَوْفِهٖ شَىْءٌ مِّنَ الْقُرْاٰنِ كَالْبَيْتِ الْخَرِبِ (سنن الترمذى # 2913)

Hadhrat Abdullah ibn Abbaas رَضِيَ اللّٰهُ عَنْهُ has narrated that Rasulullah صَلَّى اللّٰهُ عَلَيْهِ وَسَلَّمَ said, "He in whose heart there is no part of the Qur-aan Shareef is like an empty house."

Note: The example of an empty house is explained by the saying that, "An idle mind is the devil's workshop." (In reality, shaytaan gets hold of an empty house). Similarly, a heart without any Qur-aan Shareef is taken over by shaytaan. Great stress is laid in this Hadith for memorising the Qur-aan Shareef, because the heart which has not memorised the Qur-aan Shareef has been compared to an abandoned house.

Hadhrat Abu Hurayrah رَضِيَ اللّٰهُ عَنْهُ says: "The house in which the Qur-aan Shareef is read, the members of the house increase, virtues and barakah multiply, Malaaikah come down upon them and shaytaan runs far away from there. The house in which the Qur-aan Shareef is not read, life there becomes difficult and empty of barakah, Malaaikah leave the house and shaytaan stays in it."

Hadhrat ibn Mas'ood رَضِيَ اللّٰهُ عَنْهُ and some others reported Rasulullah صَلَّى اللّٰهُ عَلَيْهِ وَسَلَّمَ to have said, **"An empty house is one in which the Qur-aan Shareef is not read."**

HADITH 16 - THE VIRTUE OF RECITING QUR-AAN OVER ZIKR AND TASBEEH

عَنْ عَائِشَةَ رَضِيَ اللهُ عَنْهَا اَنَّ النَّبِيَّ صَلَّى اللهُ عَلَيْهِ وَسَلَّمَ قَالَ قِرَاءَةُ الْقُرْاٰنِ فِي الصَّلَاةِ اَفْضَلُ مِنْ قِرَاءَةِ الْقُرْاٰنِ فِي غَيْرِ الصَّلَاةِ وَقِرَاءَةُ الْقُرْاٰنِ فِي غَيْرِ الصَّلَاةِ اَفْضَلُ مِنَ التَّكْبِيْرِ وَالتَّسْبِيْحِ وَالتَّسْبِيْحُ اَفْضَلُ مِنَ الصَّدَقَةِ وَالصَّدَقَةُ اَفْضَلُ مِنَ الصَّوْمِ وَالصَّوْمُ جُنَّةٌ مِنَ النَّارِ (اخرجه البيهقى فى شعب الايمان # 2049)

Hadhrat Aa'ishah رَضِيَ اللّٰهُ عَنْهَا says that Rasulullah صَلَّى اللّٰهُ عَلَيْهِ وَسَلَّمَ said, "Reading the Qur-aan Shareef in Salaah is more rewarding than reading outside Salaah. Reading outside Salaah is better than takbeer and tasbeeh (zikr). Tasbeeh is better than sadaqah (charity), sadaqah *is better than (nafl) fasting and fasting protects you from the fire of Jahannam."*

Note: The superiority of recitation of the Qur-aan Shareef over zikr (remembrance of Allah Ta'ala) is obvious because the Qur-aan Shareef is the Word of Allah Ta'ala. As mentioned earlier, the superiority of the Word of Allah Ta'ala over the speech of others is like His superiority over His creation. The superiority of zikr over sadaqah has been stressed in other Ahaadith as well. But the superiority of sadaqah over fasting as given in this Hadith, seems contrary to that given in some other Ahaadith where fasting is said to be better than sadaqah. This contradiction is due to the differences in the type of people and their conditions of life. According to this Hadith, fasting comes last in the order of merit. When fasting is protection against the Fire of Jahannum, we can imagine the great reward of the recitation of the Qur-aan Shareef.

The author of *'Ihya'* reports a narration of Hadhrat Ali ﷺ which says that, for every letter read, there are 100 rewards for one who reads it while standing in Salaah, fifty rewards for one who reads while sitting in Salaah, twenty-five rewards for one who reads with wudhu outside Salaah, ten rewards for one who reads without wudhu, and one reward for him who does not read himself but listens to the reader.

HADITH 17 - THE BEST WEALTH

عَنْ أَبِي هُرَيْرَةَ رَضِيَ اللهُ عَنْهُ قَالَ قَالَ رَسُولُ اللهِ صَلَّى اللهُ عَلَيْهِ وَسَلَّمَ أَيُحِبُّ أَحَدُكُمْ إِذَا رَجَعَ إِلَى أَهْلِهِ أَنْ يَجِدَ فِيهِ ثَلَاثَ خَلِفَاتٍ عِظَامٍ سِمَانٍ قُلْنَا نَعَمْ قَالَ فَثَلَاثُ آيَاتٍ يَقْرَأُ بِهِنَّ أَحَدُكُمْ فِي صَلَاتِهِ خَيْرٌ لَهُ مِنْ ثَلَاثِ خَلِفَاتٍ عِظَامٍ سِمَانٍ (صحيح مسلم # 802)

Hadhrat Abu Hurayrah ﷺ *says, "Rasulullah* ﷺ *asked us, 'Does anyone of you like that when he returns home, he should find three she-camels, pregnant and fat?' We replied, 'We would love to do so.' Rasulullah* ﷺ *said, 'Three aayaat which one of you reads in Salaah, are better than three big, pregnant and fat she-camels.'"*

Note: A similar subject-matter has been described in Hadith No. 3. In this Hadith we understand that reading Qur-aan in Salaah is better than reading it out of Salaah. That is why a comparison has been made to pregnant she-camels. Because, just as in one case, there is a reference to two virtues, that is Salaah and tilaawat, in the other case there is a reference to two things that is a she-camel and her pregnancy. It has been mentioned under Hadith No. 3 that Ahaadith of this kind are only examples given for our understanding. Otherwise, the everlasting reward of one aayah of the Qur-aan Shareef is more valuable than thousands of she-camels.

HADITH 18 - THE REWARD FOR LOOKING INSIDE AND READING QUR-AAN

عَنْ عُثْمَانَ بْنِ عَبْدِ اللهِ بْنِ أَوْسٍ الثَّقَفِيِّ عَنْ جَدِّهِ رَضِيَ اللهُ عَنْهُمْ قَالَ قَالَ رَسُوْلُ اللهِ صَلَّى اللهُ عَلَيْهِ وَسَلَّمَ قِرَاءَةُ الرَّجُلِ الْقُرْآنَ فِيْ غَيْرِ الْمُصْحَفِ أَلْفُ دَرَجَةٍ وَقِرَاءَتُهُ فِى الْمُصْحَفِ تُضَعَّفُ عَلَى ذٰلِكَ اِلٰى اَلْفَىْ دَرَجَةٍ (اخرجه البيهقى فى شعب الايمان # 2026)

Hadhrat Usman bin Abdullah bin Aus Saqafi ﷺ narrates from his grandfather that Rasulullah ﷺ said, "Reading the Qur-aan Shareef from memory carries 1000 rewards, while reading the Qur-aan looking inside increases it up to 2000 rewards."

Note: Many rewards of being a Haafiz have been mentioned before. In this Hadith however, we see that a person gets more reward for reading whilst looking inside the Qur-aan as compared to reading it from memory. The reason is that reading whilst looking inside the Qur-aan helps in understanding it, pondering over it and also includes many other ibaadaat, such as looking into the Qur-aan and touching it, etc.

The difference in the apparent meanings of the various Ahaadith has led to a difference of opinion among the Muhaditheen as to whether reading whilst looking inside the Qur-aan Shareef is better than reciting it from memory. Some Ulama give preference to reading by looking inside the Qur-aan because this safeguards the reader from making mistakes and includes the virtuous act of looking into the Qur-aan.

However, other Ulama have mentioned that it is better to read the Qur-aan Shareef from memory because reciting from memory helps in greater devotion and is free from *riyaa* (showing off) and also because this was the way of the recitation of Rasulullah ﷺ himself.

Imaam Nawawi *(rahmatullahi alayh)* has mentioned that this depends upon the individual. Some people concentrate better whilst reading by looking inside the Qur-aan Shareef, whereas others have better concentration when reading from memory. Therefore, reading by looking inside the Qur-aan Shareef is better for some whilst reading from memory is better for others. Haafiz Ibn Hajar *(rahmatullahi alayh)* also has favoured this interpretation in his book *'Fathul Baari'*.

It is said that due to excessive reading of the Qur-aan by Hadhrat Usmaan ؓ, two copies of the Qur-aan Shareef tore. Amr ibn Maimun *(rahmatullahi alayh)* has mentioned in *'Sharhul Ihya'* that, a person who opens the Qur-aan Shareef after Fajr Salaah and reads 100 Aayaat gets a reward as huge as the entire world.

Reading the Qur-aan Shareef by looking into it is good for the eyesight.

Hadhrat Abu Ubaydah ؓ has mentioned a long Hadith in which each narrator says that he had some trouble with his eyes and that his teacher asked him to read the Qur-aan Shareef by looking into it. Hadhrat Imaam Shaafi *(rahmatullahi alayh)* often used to open the Qur-aan Shareef after Esha Salaah and close it just before Fajr Salaah (meaning that he would read the Qur-aan Shareef for the entire night).

HADITH 19 - RECITING THE QUR-AAN IS A MEANS OF CLEANSING THE RUST OF THE HEART

عَنِ ابْنِ عُمَرَ رَضِيَ اللهُ عَنْهُمَا قَالَ قَالَ رَسُوْلُ اللهِ صَلَّى اللهُ عَلَيْهِ وَسَلَّمَ اِنَّ هٰذِهِ الْقُلُوْبَ تَصْدَأُ كَمَا يَصْدَأُ الْحَدِيْدُ اِذَا اَصَابَهُ الْمَاءُ قِيْلَ يَا رَسُوْلَ اللهِ وَمَا جِلَاؤُهَا قَالَ كَثْرَةُ ذِكْرِ الْمَوْتِ وَتِلَاوَةُ الْقُرْاٰنِ (اخرجه البيهقى فى شعب الايمان # 1859)

Hadhrat Abdullah ibn Umar ؓ narrated that Rasulullah ﷺ said, "The hearts rust just as iron rusts with water." When someone asked, "What could clean the hearts again?" Rasulullah

ﷺ said, *"Frequent remembrance of death and recitation of the Qur-aan Shareef."*

Note: Committing too much of sins and failing to make the zikr of Allah Ta'ala, causes the hearts to rust just as water causes iron to rust. Reading of the Qur-aan Shareef and the remembrance of death polishes the rusted hearts. The heart is like a mirror. If it is not cleaned, it will not reflect the (ma'rifat) recognition of Allah Ta'ala. The more polished and brighter it is, the better will it reflect the (ma'rifat) recognition of Allah Ta'ala. Therefore, the more we sin, the more we will lose the recognition of Allah Ta'ala. It is with a view of polishing the mirror of the heart that the Mashaaikh encourage their mureeds to devote themselves to self-discipline, to complete their ma'mulaat, zikr and remembrance of Allah Ta'ala.

It is mentioned in some Ahaadith, that when a person commits a sin, a black dot stains his heart. If he makes proper taubah, this dot is removed. If he commits another sin, another black dot appears. In this way, if he goes on committing sin after sin, his heart becomes completely black. When this happens, the heart doesn't feel like doing any good actions and keeps on doing evil.

اَللّٰهُمَّ احْفَظْنَا مِنْهُ

May Allah Ta'ala save us from such a stage

Allah Ta'ala, in the following aayaat, makes mention of this rust;

كَلَّا بَلْ ۜ رَانَ عَلٰى قُلُوْبِهِمْ مَّا كَانُوْا يَكْسِبُوْنَ

"Never! In fact, the rust of their sins has covered (sealed) their hearts."
(Surah Mutaffifeen-Aayah 14)

This refers to this blackening of the heart.

According to another Hadith, Rasulullah ﷺ said, "I leave behind for you two warners. One who speaks and one who remians silent. That which speaks is the Qur-aan Shareef and that which remains silent is the remembrance of death."

Certainly, the words of Rasulullah ﷺ are worthy of the greatest respect. But only those who take heed derive benefit from his advices. On the other hand, if we consider Deen itself to be a useless occupation and an obstacle in the way of our material progress, we will neither feel the need for spiritual advice nor act upon it.

Hadhrat Hasan Basri *(rahmatullahi alayh)* says, "People of the past knew the Qur-aan Shareef to be the Command of Allah Ta'ala, they pondered over it throughout the night and acted upon it during the day. Today we have learnt how to read the Qur-aan Shareef correctly, but do not understand it to be the command of Allah Ta'ala, and we do not ponder over its meanings."

HADITH 20 - THE QUR-AAN IS THE PRIDE OF THIS UMMAH

عَنْ عَائِشَةَ رَضِيَ اللهُ عَنْهَا قَالَتْ قَالَ رَسُوْلُ اللهِ صَلَّى اللهُ عَلَيْهِ وَسَلَّمَ اِنَّ لِكُلِّ شَىْءٍ شَرَفًا يَتَبَاهَوْنَ بِهِ وَاِنَّ بَهَاءَ اُمَّتِىْ وَشَرَفَهَا الْقُرْآنُ (اخرجه ابو نعيم فى حلية الأولياء 175/2)

Hadhrat Aa'ishah رضي الله عنها says that Rasulullah ﷺ said,
"Certainly there is always something in which people take pride. The glory and pride for my Ummah is the Qur-aan Shareef."

Note: People show their nobility and dignity because of their lineage, their family and other similar things. The Qur-aan Shareef is the source of nobility and pride for the Ummah because reading it, memorising it, teaching it, acting upon it and everything else related to it, will grant them honour. Why should it not be so? After all, it is the Word of the Beloved and the Commandment of the Master. Its honour is far greater than all worldly honours. The wonderful achievements of this worldly life are temporary, while the magnificence and dignity of the Qur-aan Shareef is everlasting and limitless.

Even the minor aspects of the Qur-aan Shareef are such that we should be proud of, besides its excellence in other respects, for example, its beautiful composition, wonderful logic, the right choice of words, the proper development of arguments and the narration of past and future events. Its strong remarks concerning other people are such that they cannot be contradicted. For example, the remark about the Jews, that they say that they love Allah Ta'ala, but they do not wish to die. The listener is impressed by its recitation and the reader never gets tired of reading it. No matter how interesting a book may be, or it may even be a letter from someone you love, you will become tired of reading it for the 20th time if not the 10th, or the 40th time, if not the 20th. On the other hand, if we just memorise one section of the Qur-aan Shareef, one may read it 200 times or 400 times or go on doing so for one's entire life, one will never lose interest. If something prevents us from enjoying it, it will be for a short while only. In fact, the more we read the Qur-aan Shareef, the greater will be our enjoyment and satisfaction. Even if a few of the above excellent qualities were to be found in any book, we would all praise it. So, if all these qualities were present in a single book, to a perfect degree, surely it would have to be regarded with the greatest honour and pride.

We should think about our own condition. How many of us feel really proud of having memorised the entire Qur-aan Shareef? Does a Haafiz command real respect in our eyes? Alas! Our honour and pride is in high university degrees, in big titles, in worldly show, and in wealth which we will have to leave behind one day. O Allah! Have mercy on us.

HADITH 21 - RECITING THE QUR-AAN IS NOOR

عَنْ اَبِیْ ذَرٍّ رَضِیَ اللهُ عَنْهُ قَالَ قُلْتُ یَا رَسُوْلَ اللهِ اَوْصِنِیْ قَالَ عَلَیْكَ بِتَقْوَى اللهِ فَاِنَّهُ رَأْسُ الْاَمْرِ كُلِّهِ قُلْتُ یَا رَسُوْلَ اللهِ زِدْنِیْ قَالَ عَلَیْكَ بِتِلَاوَةِ الْقُرْاٰنِ فَاِنَّهُ نُوْرٌ لَّكَ فِی الْاَرْضِ وَذُخْرٌ لَّكَ فِی السَّمَاءِ (اخرجه المنذرى فى الترغيب # 2193)

Hadhrat Abu Zar رَضِيَ اللهُ عَنْهُ says that he asked Rasulullah ﷺ to give him some advice. Rasulullah ﷺ said: "Develop the fear of Allah Ta'ala, as this is the root of all things." I asked, "O Rasulullah! Add something more" and he said, "Hold firmly onto the reading of the Qur-aan, because it is a Noor in this life and a provision for the Aakhirah."

Note: The fear of Allah Ta'ala is the root of all actions. The person whose heart is filled with the fear of Allah Ta'ala does not commit any sin or experiences any difficulty.

وَ مَنْ يَّتَّقِ اللهَ يَجْعَلْ لَّهُ مَخْرَجًا ۞ وَ يَرْزُقْهُ مِنْ حَيْثُ لَا يَحْتَسِبُ

"Whoever fears Allah Ta'ala, Allah Ta'ala will make a way out for him (from every difficulty) and shall provide for him (what he requires) from sources which he never expected."
(Surah Talaaq – Aayah 2-3)

Some of the above-mentioned Ahaadith also say that the Qur-aan Shareef is full of noor. In *'Sharahul Ihyaa'*, Hadhrat Abu Na'eem *(rahmatullahi alayh)* states that Hadhrat Baasit رضى الله عنه has reported from Rasulullah ﷺ that, the houses in which the Qur-aan Shareef is read shine for the Malaaikah in the Heavens just like how the stars shine for the people of the Earth.

This Hadith, which has been quoted from *'At-Targhib'* is part of a long Hadith reported from Ibn Hibban *(rahmatullahi alayh)* by Mulla Ali Qari *(rahmatullahi alayh)* in detail and by Allamah Suyuti *(rahmatullahi alayh)* in brief. Although the above-mentioned part of the Hadith is sufficient for the purpose of this book, yet the whole Hadith includes many essential and useful subjects and therefore, it is discussed in the following paragraphs.

Hadhrat Abu Zar Ghifaari رضى الله عنه says that he asked Rasulullah ﷺ about the number of books revealed by Allah Ta'ala. Rasulullah ﷺ replied, "One hundred booklets and four books. Fifty booklets were revealed to Hadhrat Shees *(alayhis salaam)*, thirty to Hadhrat Idrees *(alayhis salaam)*, ten to Hadhrat Ibraheem *(alayhis salaam)* and ten to Hadhrat Musa *(alayhis salaam)* before the Torah. In addition to this, four books, i.e., the Torah, the Injeel, the Zaboor and the Qur-aan Shareef have been revealed by Allah Ta'ala." Hadhrat Abu Zar رضى الله عنه enquired about the contents of the booklets revealed to Hadhrat Ibrahim *(alayhis salaam)*. Rasulullah ﷺ replied that they consisted of proverbs, e.g., "O, you strong and proud king! I did not appoint you to hoard wealth, but to prevent the complaint of the oppressed from reaching me by resolving it before hand, because I do not reject the complaint of the oppressed person, even though he may be a disbeliever."

The author states that whenever Rasulullah ﷺ deputed any of the Sahaabah رضى الله عنه as an Ameer or governor, in addition to giving other advice, he used to emphasise:

وَاتَّقِ دَعْوَةَ الْمَظْلُوْمِ فَاِنَّهُ لَيْسَ بَيْنَهَا وَبَيْنَ اللهِ حِجَابٌ (صحيح البخارى # 4347)

Beware of the Dua of the oppressed because between him and Allah Ta'ala there is no veil or intermediary.

As a Persian verse says:

بترس از آه مظلوماں کہ ہنگام دعا کردن

اجابت از در حق بہر استقبال می آید

Beware of the sigh of those oppressed, when they make Dua, Divine acceptance readily greets them.

These booklets also mentioned that a wise man should divide his time in three parts; one for the ibaadat of Allah Ta'ala, one for muhaasabah (self-inspection) to see what good or bad acts you did and one for earning his halaal rizq (livelihood). It is also necessary for him to look after and guard his time and make an effort to improve his personal spiritual condition, and also to guard his tongue against unnecessary and useless talk. Whoever keeps a check on his own speech, his tongue will indulge less in useless talk.

A wise man should not travel except for three reasons, viz., for making preparation for the Aakhirah, or in search of livelihood, or for such recreation which is permissible.

Hadhrat Abu Zar رضى الله عنه then asked about what the booklets contained which were revealed to Hadhrat Musa *(alayhis salaam)*. Rasulullah ﷺ said, "They contained warnings such as, "I am surprised by one who finds pleasure in anything in spite of his belief in the certainty of death." (Naturally when a person is sentenced to death, he can never find pleasure in anything). "I am surprised by one who laughs in spite of his belief in certainty of death. I am surprised by one who witnesses accidents, changes and revolutions of the world all the time and still finds satisfaction in it. I am surprised by one who believes in Taqdeer (predestination) and still suffers from grief and hardship. I am surprised by one who believes that he will soon be required to give an account of his deeds and still does no good deed."

Hadhrat Abu Zar رَضِىَ اللهُ عَنْهُ goes on saying that he asked for more advice. Rasulullah صَلَّى اللهُ عَلَيْهِ وَسَلَّمَ advised that he should develop fear of Allah Ta'ala, because it is the root and basis of all actions. Hadhrat Abu Zar رَضِىَ اللهُ عَنْهُ then begged for more advice. Rasulullah صَلَّى اللهُ عَلَيْهِ وَسَلَّمَ said, "Be consistent in the recitation of the Qur-aan Shareef and zikr, remembrance of Allah Ta'ala, because it is a noor in this world and a provision in the Aakhirah,"

Hadhrat Abu Zar رَضِىَ اللهُ عَنْهُ again asked for more advice and was told, "Stay away from too much laughter, because it causes the heart to die and causes the face to lose its noor." (Too much of laughter is harmful both for the outward and inward nature of man.)

Hadhrat Abu Zar رَضِىَ اللهُ عَنْهُ sought further advice, whereupon Rasulullah صَلَّى اللهُ عَلَيْهِ وَسَلَّمَ said, "Stick to jihaad because this is the rahbaaniyyat of my Ummah." (Rahbaan - singular raahib - were those people of previous Ummahs who cut off all their worldly connections and turned towards Allah Ta'ala.)

Hadhrat Abu Zar رَضِىَ اللهُ عَنْهُ asked for more advice and Rasulullah صَلَّى اللهُ عَلَيْهِ وَسَلَّمَ said, "Remain with the poor and the needy. Be friendly with them and sit with them." When Hadhrat Abu Zar رَضِىَ اللهُ عَنْهُ again asked for more advice, Rasulullah صَلَّى اللهُ عَلَيْهِ وَسَلَّمَ said, "Look at those who are poorer than you (so that you may be thankful) and do not look at those who are richer than yourself, in case you do not appreciate the favours of Allah Ta'ala upon you."

When Hadhrat Abu Zar رَضِىَ اللهُ عَنْهُ again asked for more advice, Rasulullah صَلَّى اللهُ عَلَيْهِ وَسَلَّمَ said: "Let your own faults stop you from criticising others and do not try to find fault with others, because you have those faults yourself. It is enough to prove you guilty that you should find in others such faults which you yourself have, though you may not be aware of them, and that you should find in others such sins which you yourself commit."

After this, Rasulullah ﷺ patted the chest of Abu Zar رضى الله عنه with his loving hand and said, "O Abu Zar! There is nothing wiser than preparation, no piety better than staying away from haraam and no honour better than being polite." (In the explanation of this Hadith, the broad meaning has been kept in view, in preference to the literal translation.)

HADITH 22 - RECITING QUR-AAN IN THE MASJID

عَنْ اَبِىْ هُرَيْرَةَ رَضِىَ اللهُ عَنْهُ اَنَّ رَسُوْلَ اللهِ صَلَّى اللهُ عَلَيْهِ وَسَلَّمَ قَالَ مَا اجْتَمَعَ قَوْمٌ فِىْ بَيْتٍ مِنْ بُيُوْتِ اللهِ يَتْلُوْنَ كِتَابَ اللهِ وَيَتَدَارَسُوْنَهُ بَيْنَهُمْ اِلَّا نَزَلَتْ عَلَيْهِمُ السَّكِيْنَةُ وَغَشِيَتْهُمُ الرَّحْمَةُ وَحَفَّتْهُمُ الْمَلَائِكَةُ وَذَكَرَهُمُ اللهُ فِيْمَنْ عِنْدَهُ (صحيح مسلم # 2699)

Hadhrat Abu Hurayrah رضى الله عنه says that Rasulullah ﷺ said, "When people gather in one of the houses (Masjids) of Allah Ta'ala reading the Qur-aan and reading it out to one another, Sakeenah (peace) comes down upon them, Rahmat (mercy) covers them, the Malaaikah sit around them and Allah Ta'ala speaks about them in the gathering of the Malaaikah."

Note: This Hadith describes the special rewards of Madrasahs and Maktabs. To get the rewards mentioned above is such a high achievement that even if one spends his whole life to acquire it, it will be worthwhile. There are so many rewards mentioned, especially the last one. Allah Ta'ala mentioning and remembering us in the company of the Malaaikah is such a bounty that cannot be surpassed.

The coming down of sakeenah has been mentioned in many Ahaadith. The Ulama have interpreted its real meaning in many ways. However, the different interpretations do not contradict each other and can be meaningfully put together.

Hadhrat Ali رضى الله عنه has interpreted sakeenah as a special breeze, which has a face like that of a human being.

Allamah Suddi *(rahmatullahi alayh)* is reported to have said that it is the name of a large golden dish in Jannah used for washing the hearts of the Ambiyaa *(alayhimus salaam)*. Some have said that it is a special form of mercy.

Tabari *(rahmatullahi alayh)* prefers the view that it means peace of heart. Some interpret it as grace, others consider it as dignity and some take it to mean the Malaaikah. There are other views as well. Haafiz ibn Hajar *(rahmatullahi alayh)* has written in *'Fathul Baari'* that sakeenah includes all the above mentioned rewards and blessings. In the opinion of Nawawi *(rahmatullahi alayh),* it is a combination of peace, mercy, etc., and comes down with the Malaaikah. It is mentioned in the Qur-aan as follows:

فَاَنْزَلَ اللهُ سَكِيْنَتَهٗ عَلَيْهِ

"Then Allah Ta'ala caused His sakeenah to descend upon him."
(Surah Taubah – Aayah 40)

هُوَ الَّذِيْۤ اَنْزَلَ السَّكِيْنَةَ فِيْ قُلُوْبِ الْمُؤْمِنِيْنَ

"It is He Who sent down sakeenah into the hearts of the believers."
(Surah Fath – Aayah 4)

فِيْهِ سَكِيْنَةٌ مِّنْ رَّبِّكُمْ

"Wherein is sakeenah from your Lord." *(Surah Baqarah – Aayah 248)*

In short, this blessing is mentioned in several Aayaat of the Qur-aan Shareef and there are many Ahaadith that also mention these glad tidings.

It is narrated in *'Ihyaa'* that once Ibn Saubaan had promised one of his relatives that he would break his fast with him, but reached the house of his relative the next morning. When the host complained about the guest being so late, the guest said, "If it was not for the promise that I owe you, I would have never disclosed what prevented me from coming to you. I got late by chance until it was the time of Esha Salaah. I thought I should complete my Witr Salaah as well, in case I die during the night without offering this Salaah, because one cannot be sure about death. While I was reciting the Qunoot (a Dua in Witr Salaah), I saw a green garden of Jannah, which had all sorts of flowers. I was so absorbed in what I was seeing that it became dawn." There have been hundreds of similar incidents in the lives of our pious ancestors. However, such things are only experienced when there is complete separation from everyone besides Allah Ta'ala and complete attention towards Him.

There are many Ahaadith which mention about being surrounded by the Malaaikah. A story about Usaid bin Hudhair رَضِىَ اللّٰهُ عَنْهُ is given in the books of Hadith. It is said that while he was reading the Qur-aan Shareef, he felt a cloud spread over him. Nabi صَلَّى اللّٰهُ عَلَيْهِ وَسَلَّمَ told him that these were Malaaikah who had gathered to listen to the reading of the Qur-aan Shareef. Due to their large numbers, they appeared like a cloud.

Once a Sahaabi رَضِىَ اللّٰهُ عَنْهُ felt like there was a sort of a cloud over himself. Rasulullah صَلَّى اللّٰهُ عَلَيْهِ وَسَلَّمَ told him that it was sakeenah, which was sent down due to the recitation of the Qur-aan Shareef.

In '*Muslim Shareef*', this Hadith is given in greater detail. The last sentence is;

مَنْ بَطَّأَ بِهِ عَمَلُهُ لَمْ يُسْرِعْ بِهِ نَسَبُهُ (صحيح مسلم # 2699)

One whose evil deeds drive him away from the mercy of Allah Ta'ala, the superiority of his lineage or nobility of his family cannot bring him near it.

Thus, a person who comes from a noble family, but is involved in disobedience and sin, cannot be equal in the presence of Allah Ta'ala to a Muslim who is from a simple family and who is looked down upon by the people, but is Allah-fearing and pious.

اِنَّ اَكْرَمَكُمْ عِنْدَ اللّٰهِ اَتْقٰكُمْ

"Verily the noblest of you in the sight of Allah is the one who is most Allah-fearing." (Surah Hujuraat – Aayah 13)

HADITH 23 - THE QUR-AAN BRINGS A PERSON CLOSER TO ALLAH TA'ALA

عَنْ اَبِىْ ذَرٍّ رَضِىَ اللّٰهُ عَنْهُ قَالَ قَالَ رَسُوْلُ اللّٰهِ صَلَّى اللّٰهُ عَلَيْهِ وَسَلَّمَ اِنَّكُمْ لَا تَرْجِعُوْنَ اِلَى اللّٰهِ بِشَىْءٍ اَفْضَلَ مِمَّا خَرَجَ مِنْهُ يَعْنِى الْقُرْاٰنَ (اخرجه الحاكم فى المستدرك # 2039)

Hadhrat Abu Zar رَضِيَ اللهُ عَنْهُ says that Rasulullah صَلَّى اللهُ عَلَيْهِ وَسَلَّمَ said, "You cannot turn to Allah Ta'ala and get closer to Him with anything better than that which directly came from Him, i.e. the Qur-aan."

Note: It is obvious from many Ahaadith that there is no better way of becoming closer to Allah Ta'ala than reading the Qur-aan Shareef. Imaam Ahmad ibn Hambal *(rahmatullahi alayh)* says, "I saw Allah Ta'ala in a dream and asked Him, 'What was the best way of getting closer to Him?' Allah Ta'ala said, 'O Ahmad! It is My Word (i.e. the Qur-aan).' I asked whether it is only reading while understanding the meaning or reading without understanding. Allah Ta'ala said, 'Whether with understanding the meaning or without understanding, it is a way of coming closer to me.'"

The reading of the Qur-aan Shareef is the best means of getting access to Allah Ta'ala. This is explained in the commentary of Hadhrat Moulana Shah Abdul Aziz Dehlawi *(rahmatullahi alayh)*, who is from our pious ancestors and an authority in Deen for those who came after him. The object of reciting the Qur-aan Shareef is sulook ilallaah (the path of the sufis towards Allah Ta'ala) which is also called the stage of Ihsaan, which can be achieved in three ways:

(1) **Tasawwur**: Which is known as meditation in Shariah and muraqabah in the language of the sufis.

(2) **Zikr-e-Lisaani**: Remembrance of Allah Ta'ala by repeating words of praise for Him.

(3) **Tilaawat**: Reading of the Qur-aan Shareef.

Since the first method is zikre qalbi (remembrance in the heart), so only two ways remain; firstly zikr by heart or by the tongue, and secondly recitation of the Qur-aan Shareef. The essence of zikr is that the word which is used for or refers to Allah Ta'ala should be repeated over and over again. This repetition helps the mudrikah (the faculty of understanding) in concentrating upon that Being who is being remembered. It would give the feeling of that person being present. Always being in this state is called ma'iyyat (togetherness), which is referred to in the Hadith below:

وَمَا يَزَالُ عَبْدِىْ يَتَقَرَّبُ اِلَىَّ بِالنَّوَافِلِ حَتّٰى اَحْبَبْتُهٗ فَكُنْتُ سَمْعَهُ الَّذِىْ يَسْمَعُ بِهٖ وَبَصَرَهُ الَّذِىْ يُبْصِرُ بِهٖ وَيَدَهُ الَّتِىْ يَبْطِشُ بِهَا وَرِجْلَهُ الَّتِىْ يَمْشِىْ بِهَا (صحيح البخارى # 6502)

My servant continues to gain nearness to Me through nafl (optional) deeds, until I make him My favourite, and thus I become his ears with which he hears, his eyes with which he sees, and his hands with which he holds, and his feet with which he walks.

It means that when a person becomes a favourite of Allah Ta'ala through excessive ibaadah, Allah Ta'ala then becomes a guardian of all the limbs of his body so that his eyes, ears, etc., all submit to His will. This blessing is said to be the result of a lot of nafl Salaah and not fardh Salaah because fardh (obligatory) Salaah is fixed and cannot be increased, whereas nearness and close attachment to Allah Ta'ala demands regular excessive ibaadah with concentration as mentioned above.

But this method of seeking nearness is only specially for that pure and beloved being (Allah Ta'ala). It is impossible to seek nearness to anybody else by remembering his name over and over again. This is because the one who we are seeking to be near to must have two qualities. Firstly, he must be Muheet (i.e. all-knowing, all-seeing, wise, etc.) so that he understands the zikr of all the Zaakireen, whether by word of mouth or by heart, irrespective of language, time and place.

Secondly, he should have the ability to put nur (light) in his understanding and fulfill the desire of the person who remembers Him, which is known as 'dunuww' (nearness), 'tadalli' (proximity), 'nuzul' (to come down) and Qurb (nearness). Since these two requirements are possessed only by Allah Ta'ala, the abovementioned method of seeking nearness is effective only in respect of him. The following Hadith-e-Qudsi (a revelation of Allah Ta'ala quoted by Rasulullah ﷺ) explains:

وَمَنْ تَقَرَّبَ اِلَىَّ شِبْرًا تَقَرَّبْتُ اِلَيْهِ ذِرَاعًا وَمَنْ تَقَرَّبَ اِلَىَّ ذِرَاعًا تَقَرَّبْتُ اِلَيْهِ بَاعًا وَاِذَا اَقْبَلَ اِلَىَّ يَمْشِىْ اَقْبَلْتُ اِلَيْهِ اُهَرْوِلُ (صحيح مسلم # 2675)

"Whoever comes near me by one span, I go near him by an arm's length, whoever comes near me by one arm's length, I go near him by

one 'baah' (stretch of both arms): whoever comes to me walking, I go towards him running."

The example given above is only to make us understand. In reality, Allah Ta'ala is above walking and running. It only means that those who remember and search for him are helped and looked after by Allah Ta'ala far in excess of their expectations. This is because it befits His kindness and compassion. So, those who are always in the zikr of Allah Ta'ala will always attract His attention towards themselves which will result in the favours of Allah Ta'ala being showered upon them. The Qur-aan Shareef altogether is the zikr of Allah Ta'ala, in the sense that no Aayah of the Qur-aan Shareef is devoid of the remembrance and attention towards Allah Ta'ala, and as such, it has the quality of zikr as mentioned above. However, there is another quality of the Qur-aan which is the cause of gaining the nearness of Allah Ta'ala. Every book or speech has the qualities and ideas of the speaker which can influence you. It is obvious that recitation of the poetry of sinful and wicked people has its evil effects, whilst the verses of the pious people have a good influence. It is for this reason that excessive study of the knowledge of logic and philosophy produces pride and superiority, while excessive devotion to the study of Hadith leads to humility. Although as languages, both English and Persian are equal, they have varying influences upon the readers due to the differences in the beliefs and attitudes of the various authors. It can be concluded that repeated recitation of the Qur-aan Shareef will result in the reader's being influenced by the qualities of the Originator of the Aayaat and in developing a natural love for them. Moreover, if a person is devoted to the publications of a particular author, he naturally starts liking and favouring that person. In the same way, the reader of the Qur-aan Shareef is sure to attract Allah Ta'ala's constant attention towards himself, which in turn will draw him near to Allah Ta'ala. May Allah Ta'ala bless us all with His favours.

Hadith 24 - People of the Qur-aan are the Family of Allah Ta'ala

عَنْ اَنَسٍ رَضِىَ اللهُ عَنْهُ قَالَ قَالَ رَسُوْلُ اللهِ صَلَّى اللهُ عَلَيْهِ وَسَلَّمَ اِنَّ لِلّٰهِ اَهْلِيْنَ مِنَ النَّاسِ قَالُوْا مَنْ هُمْ يَا رَسُوْلَ اللهِ قَالَ اَهْلُ الْقُرْاٰنِ هُمْ اَهْلُ اللهِ وَخَاصَّتُهُ

(اخرجه الحاكم فى المستدرك # 2046)

Hadhrat Anas ﺭﺿﻰﺍﻟﻠﻪﻋﻨﻪ says that Rasulullah ﺻﻠﻰﺍﻟﻠﻪﻋﻠﻴﻪﻭﺳﻠﻢ said, "For Allah Ta'ala, amongst the people, there are those who are His family." The Sahaabah ﺭﺿﻰﺍﻟﻠﻪﻋﻨﻬﻢ asked, "Who are these people?" He replied "The people of the Qur-aan. They are the family of Allah and His special ones."

Note: The people of the Qur-aan are those who are always busy with the Qur-aan Shareef and have a special love for it. Therefore, it is obvious that such people are of the household of Allah Ta'ala and are His favourites. It is clear, that as long as these people remain busy with the Qur-aan, special favours of Allah Ta'ala continue to be showered upon them. Those who keep on living with somebody become as one of the people of the household. What a great honour it is to belong to the family of Allah Ta'ala, to be counted from the people of Allah Ta'ala and to be His favourite, with just a little effort.

    People make so much of effort to become famous and to be counted as part of the royal family or to be elected as members of the government. They flatter the voters and sacrifice their comforts and money and even go through disgrace, but consider all this as worthwhile. But effort and struggle for the Qur-aan Shareef is considered as a waste of time and energy.

ببیں تفاوتِ راہ از کجاست تابکجا

Look at the difference between the paths; what a great deviation!

Hadith 25 - To Recite in a Beautiful Voice

عَنْ اَبِىْ هُرَيْرَةَ رَضِىَ اللهُ عَنْهُ قَالَ قَالَ رَسُوْلُ اللهِ صَلَّى اللهُ عَلَيْهِ وَسَلَّمَ مَا اَذِنَ اللهُ لِشَىْءٍ مَّا اَذِنَ لِنَبِىٍّ يَتَغَنّٰى بِالْقُرْاٰنِ (صحيح مسلم # 792)

Hadhrat Abu Hurayrah ﷺ says that Rasulullah ﷺ said, "Allah Ta'ala does not pay attention so much to anything as He does to the voice of a Nabi reading the Qur-aan in a sweet voice."

Note: Allah Ta'ala gives special attention to the reading of the Qur-aan, which is His Word. Since the Ambiyaa *(alayhimus salaam)* follow all the rules of respect etc. when reciting the Qur-aan Shareef, it is clear that Allah Ta'ala listens to them with greater attention. The sweetness of the voice adds to the beauty of the Qur-aan Shareef.

As for people besides the Ambiyaa *(alayhimus salaam)*, their recitation attracts the attention of Allah Ta'ala according to its quality.

Hadith 26 - Allah Ta'ala Listens to People Reciting Qur-aan

عَنْ فَضَالَةَ بْنِ عُبَيْدٍ رَضِىَ اللهُ عَنْهُ قَالَ قَالَ رَسُوْلُ اللهِ صَلَّى اللهُ عَلَيْهِ وَسَلَّمَ لَلّٰهُ اَشَدُّ اُذُنَا اِلٰى قَارِىءِ الْقُرْاٰنِ مِنْ صَاحِبِ الْقَيْنَةِ اِلٰى قَيْنَتِهٖ (احياء علوم الدين ص۔ 273)

Hadhrat Fudaalah ibn Ubaid ﷺ says that Rasulullah ﷺ said, "Allah Ta'ala listens to the voice of the reader of the Qur-aan more eagerly than does the master to the song of his singing slave girl."

Note: It is natural that singing should attract attention. But Deeni inclined people do not listen to singing because of the restriction in Islam. However, Islam does not prohibit listening to the song of a slave woman who is in one's lawful possession, even though this may attract the fullest attention.

The Qur-aan Shareef should not be read in a singing tone. Doing so is forbidden according to many Ahaadith. In one Hadith it is said:

اِيَّاكُمْ وَلُحُوْنَ اَهْلِ الْعِشْقِ (مشكاة المصابيح # 2207)

Beware of reciting the Qur-aan in a musical tone, like that of lovers singing their love poems as musical compositions.

The Mashaaikh say that one who reads the Qur-aan Shareef in a tone of a musical song is a faasiq (evil-doer) and even the person who is listening to such a recitation is committing a sin. However, it is better to read the Qur-aan Shareef in a sweet voice but without singing. There are various Ahaadith which encourage the reading of the Qur-aan Shareef in a sweet voice. Nabi ﷺ said in one Hadith, "Beautify the Qur-aan with a good voice." In another Hadith it is said, "A sweet voice makes the beauty of the Qur-aan twice as beautiful."

Hadhrat Shaikh Abdul Qaadir Jilani *(rahmatullahi alayh)* has written in his book *'Ghunyah'* that, once Hadhrat Abdullah ibn Mas'ood ﷺ happened to pass a place in Kufa and saw a gathering of sinners in a house. A singer named Zaa'zaan was singing and playing his guitar. After hearing his voice, Ibn Mas'ood ﷺ said, "What a sweet voice, if only it was used for reading the Qur-aan Shareef." Saying this, he covered his head with a cloth and went away.

Zaa'zaan saw him saying something. After asking the people, he came to know that Ibn Mas'ood ﷺ was a Sahaabi who had passed by saying those words. Zaa'zaan became very worried and broke all his musical instruments, changed his life and became a follower of Ibn Mas'ood ﷺ. Later on, he became a great Aalim of his time.

There are various Ahaadith that encourage reading of the Qur-aan Shareef in a good voice and at the same time prohibit reading it in a voice resembling singing, as has been stated before.

Hadhrat Huzayfah ﷺ says that Rasullullah ﷺ said, "Read the Qur-aan Shareef in the Arabic style. Do not read it like lovers or in the style of the Jews and the Christians. There will soon come some people who will read the Qur-aan Shareef to impress others like singers and mourners. Their reading will be of no benefit to them at all. They themselves as well as those who admire their reading will get into trouble."

Taa'oos *(rahmatullahi alayh)* writes that someone asked Rasulullah ﷺ, "Who is it that reads the Glorious Qur-aan in the best voice?" Rasulullah ﷺ replied, "It is he whom you hear and feel that he is full of the fear of Allah Ta'ala, i.e. his voice shows that he is overcome with fear." However, this is the extreme kindness of Allah Ta'ala that He does not expect from a person anything beyond what he is capable of. There is a Hadith that Allah Ta'ala has deputed an angel on a special duty. If there is somebody who recites the Qur-aan Shareef, but is unable to recite correctly as it should be done, this angel corrects his recitation before he takes it up to the Heavens."

اَللّٰهُمَّ لَا اُحْصِیْ ثَنَاءً عَلَیْكَ

"O Allah! I cannot count the praises due to You."

HADITH 27 - DO NOT USE THE QUR-AAN AS A PILLOW

عَنْ عُبَيْدَةَ الْمُلَيْكِيِّ رَضِيَ اللهُ عَنْهُ قَالَ قَالَ رَسُوْلُ اللهِ صَلَّى اللهُ عَلَيْهِ وَسَلَّمَ يَا اَهْلَ الْقُرْاٰنِ لَا تَتَوَسَّدُوا الْقُرْاٰنَ وَاتْلُوْهُ حَقَّ تِلَاوَتِهٖ مِنْ اٰنَاءِ اللَّيْلِ وَالنَّهَارِ وَاَفْشُوْهُ وَتَغَنَّوْهُ وَتَدَبَّرُوْا مَا فِيْهِ لَعَلَّكُمْ تُفْلِحُوْنَ وَلَا تَعْجَلُوْا ثَوَابَهُ فَاِنَّ لَهُ ثَوَابًا (مشكاة المصابيح # 2210)

Hadhrat Ubaidah Mulaiki ؓ says that Rasulullah ﷺ said, "O people of the Qur-aan! Do not use the Qur-aan Shareef as a pillow, but read it properly day and night as it should be read. Teach the Qur-aan, read it in a good voice and ponder over its meanings, so that you may be successful. Do not look for a reward for it (in this life), because it has a wonderful reward (in the Aakhirah)."

Note: A few points in this Hadith are:

(1) It is said that the Qur-aan Shareef should not be used as a pillow. Doing so is disrespecting it. It has been written by Ibn Hajar *(rahmatullahi alayh)* that using the Qur-aan Shareef as a pillow, stretching your feet towards it, and trampling over it are all haraam acts. Secondly, the expression "using as a pillow" also means showing disregard to the Qur-aan Shareef. It is useless to place it on a pillow, as it is sometimes found placed on a stand by the side of a grave in a shrine for barakah (blessings). This is total disrespect of the Qur-aan Shareef. It is our duty to the Qur-aan Shareef that it should be read.

(2) The expression "Read it as it supposed to be read" means that it should be read with the highest amount of respect. A commandment to this effect is in the Qur-aan Shareef itself;

$$\text{اَلَّذِيْنَ اٰتَيْنٰهُمُ الْكِتٰبَ يَتْلُوْنَهٗ حَقَّ تِلَاوَتِهٖ}$$

"Those whom we have given the Book, read it as it supposed to be read." *(Surah Baqarah – Aayah 121)*

The orders of a king are received with great respect. A letter from the beloved is read with great fondness. Similarly, the Qur-aan Shareef should be read with great respect and fondness.

(3) The expression "Teach the Qur-aan" means that we should teach it by talks, writing, practicing and all other possible ways. Rasulullah ﷺ ordered its teaching and spreading, but some of our so-called 'intelligent' people consider it a useless task, and at the same time they claim that they have great love for Rasulullah ﷺ and for Islam.

According to a Persian verse:

$$\text{ترسم نرسی بکعبه اے اعرابی   کیں رہ کہ تو میروی بترکستان است}$$

"I am afraid, O, Bedouin! you can never reach Ka'bah. Because the path you are following leads to Turkey."

Rasulullah ﷺ has ordered the teaching and spreading of the Qur-aan, but we do not hesitate to put all sorts of obstacles in the way of its propagation. We make laws for compulsory secular education so that children, instead of learning the Qur-aan Shareef, are forced to join primary schools. We are displeased with teachers in madrasahs for spoiling the lives of our children and therefore, do not send our children to them. Even if this fear of ours is correct, it does not free us of our responsibility. On the other hand, our responsibility becomes even greater because we are all responsible, individually and collectively, to teach the Qur-aan Shareef. No doubt, the Ustaad (teacher) is responsible for his own shortcomings, but if because of his shortcomings we prevent children from going to Madrasah and send notices to their parents in the name of compulsory primary education, convincing them to deprive their children of learning the Qur-aan Shareef, then this is like killing a tuberculosis patient by giving him poison. An attempt to justify our unfriendly conduct towards the Ustaaz due to him not teaching properly is a lame excuse. This argument will be of no use in the court of Allah Ta'ala. We may consider it necessary to educate our children in subjects like Maths to train them to run a small grocery shop or for getting employment with the government, but, according to Allah Ta'ala, the learning of the Qur-aan Shareef is the most important.

(4) The recitation should be in a sweet voice which has already been explained under the previous Hadith.

(5) We are required to ponder over the meaning of the Qur-aan Shareef. There is a quotation from the Torah in *'Ihya'* in which Allah Ta'ala says, "My servant! Are you not ashamed of your behaviour towards Me? If you receive a letter from a friend while you are going on a road, then you stop and sit at a suitable place and read it with full attention and try to understand every word of it. But in the case of My Qur-aan, in which I have explained everything and have repeatedly emphasised important matters, so that you may ponder over and understand them, you show an attitude of indifference. Do you consider Me inferior to your friend? O, My servant! Some of your friends sit with you and talk to you and you give them full attention. You listen to them and try to understand them. If anybody tries to interrupt you, you stop him with a sign. I talk to you through My Qur-aan, but you pay no attention. Do you consider Me inferior to your friends?" The rewards of meditation and contemplation on the contents of the Qur-aan Shareef have already been mentioned in the Foreword of this book and again under Hadith eight.

6. "Do not ask for any reward," means that no gifts should be accepted for reading the Qur-aan Shareef, because you are going to get a great reward in the Aakhirah for your reading.

To accept reward for it in this life is just like being content with empty shells instead of money. Rasulullah ﷺ said, "When my Ummah will attach more value to money, it will lose the dignity which Islam has given it, and when it will give up enjoining good and forbidding evil, it will be deprived of the barakaat of Wahi (Divine Revelation), i.e. the understanding of the Qur'aan Shareef."

اَللّٰهُمَّ احْفَظْنَا مِنْهُ

"O, Allah Ta'ala! Guard us against this."

HADITH 28 - THE QUR-AAN IS THE SUBSTITUE OF ALL PREVIOUS SCRIPTURES WITH ADDITIONS

عَنْ وَاثِلَةَ بْنِ الْأَسْقَعِ رَضِيَ اللهُ عَنْهُ رَفَعَهُ أُعْطِيتُ مَكَانَ التَّوْرَاةِ السَّبْعَ وَأُعْطِيتُ مَكَانَ الزَّبُورِ الْمِيْنَ وَأُعْطِيتُ مَكَانَ الْإِنْجِيلِ الْمَثَانِيَ وَفُضِّلْتُ بِالْمُفَصَّلِ (مسند أحمد # 16982)

Hadhrat Waasilah ibnul Asqa'i ﷺ says that Rasulullah ﷺ said, *"I have been given Sab'a Tuwal in place of the Torah, Mi'een in place of the Zabur, Masaani in place of the Injeel, and Mufassal as a special favour to me."*

Note: The first seven Surahs are called *'Sab'a Tuwal'* (the seven longest ones). The next eleven are called *'Mi'een'* (surahs having about 100 Aayaat each). The next twenty Surahs are known as *'Masaani'* (often repeated Surahs), while all the remaining Surahs are called *'Mufassal'* (the clear ones). This division is according to a popular interpretation, but there is some difference of opinion as to whether a certain surah is included in *'Sab'a Tuwal'* or *'Mi'een'*. Similarly, there is a difference of opinion as to whether a Surah falls under *'Masaani'* or *'Mufassal'*. But this difference of opinion does not affect the meaning or purpose of this Hadith. This Hadith shows that the Qur-aan Shareef contains the message of all the important kitaabs of Allah Ta'ala that had been sent down earlier. It contains *'Mufassal'* as a special favour, which was not found in the earlier Kitaabs.

HADITH 29 - NABI ﷺ JOINS A GROUP OF MUHAAJIREEN RECITING QUR-AAN

عَنْ اَبِىْ سَعِيْدٍ الْخُدْرِيِّ رَضِىَ اللهُ عَنْهُ قَالَ جَلَسْتُ فِىْ عِصَابَةٍ مِّنْ ضُعَفَاءِ الْمُهَاجِرِيْنَ وَاِنَّ بَعْضَهُمْ لَيَسْتَتِرُ بِبَعْضٍ مِّنَ الْعُرْىِ وَقَارِئٌ يَّقْرَاُ عَلَيْنَا اِذْ جَاءَ رَسُوْلُ اللهِ صَلَّى اللهُ عَلَيْهِ وَسَلَّمَ فَقَامَ عَلَيْنَا فَلَمَّا قَامَ رَسُوْلُ اللهِ صَلَّى اللهُ عَلَيْهِ وَسَلَّمَ سَكَتَ الْقَارِئُ فَسَلَّمَ ثُمَّ قَالَ مَا كُنْتُمْ تَصْنَعُوْنَ قُلْنَا كُنَّا نَسْتَمِعُ اِلٰى كِتَابِ اللهِ فَقَالَ الْحَمْدُ لِلّٰهِ الَّذِىْ جَعَلَ مِنْ اُمَّتِىْ مَنْ اُمِرْتُ اَنْ اَصْبِرَ نَفْسِىْ مَعَهُمْ قَالَ فَجَلَسَ وَسْطَنَا لِيَعْدِلَ بِنَفْسِهٖ فِيْنَا ثُمَّ قَالَ بِيَدِهٖ هٰكَذَا فَتَحَلَّقُوْا وَبَرَزَتْ وُجُوْهُهُمْ لَهٗ فَقَالَ اَبْشِرُوْا يَا مَعْشَرَ صَعَالِيْكِ الْمُهَاجِرِيْنَ بِالنُّوْرِ التَّامِّ يَوْمَ الْقِيَامَةِ تَدْخُلُوْنَ الْجَنَّةَ قَبْلَ اَغْنِيَاءِ النَّاسِ بِنِصْفِ يَوْمٍ وَّذٰلِكَ خَمْسُ مِائَةِ سَنَةٍ (سنن ابى داود # 3666)

Hadhrat Abu Sa'eed Khudri ﷺ says, "Once I was sitting with a group of poor Muhaajireen, who did not even have enough clothes to cover their bodies, therefore some of them were hiding behind others. One of them was reading the Qur-aan Shareef. Suddenly Rasulullah ﷺ came and stood near us. When he came, the reader stopped reading. He greeted us and asked what we were doing. We replied that we were listening to the Qur-aan Shareef. Rasulullah ﷺ then said, 'All praise is for Allah Ta'ala, Who has created such people in my Ummah that I have been ordered to remain with them.' Rasulullah ﷺ sat with us. He then asked us to come closer to him. All of us sat facing him. Thereafter, Rasulullah ﷺ said, 'O you poor Muhaajireen! I give you good news of a perfect noor on the Day of Qiyaamah, and you shall enter Jannah before the wealthy people by half a day. This half day will be equal to five hundred years."

Note: The Muhaajireen did not have enough clothes to cover their bodies. This means that they only had clothes to cover their satr (private areas) and not more than that. However, in front of other people, we feel shy to open this part of the body as well (e.g. stomach). This is why they were sitting behind one another.

They did not become aware of the arrival of Rasulullah ﷺ because of being busy listening to the Qur-aan Shareef. They only saw him when he had come very near to them and then, out of respect, the reader stopped reading.

Although Rasulullah ﷺ had seen one of them reading the Qur-aan Shareef, he still asked them what they had been doing. This was to show that he was happy with them.

One day in the Aakhirah will be equal to one thousand years of this world, as is given in the Qur-aan Shareef:

$$وَإِنَّ يَوْمًا عِنْدَ رَبِّكَ كَأَلْفِ سَنَةٍ مِّمَّا تَعُدُّوْنَ$$

"Verily a day with your Rabb is like a thousand years of what you count." (Surah Hajj – Aayah 47)

This is the reason why the Arabic word غَدًا - ghadan (tomorrow) is generally used while referring to the Day of Qiyaamah. Even this will be the probable length of a day for the believers in general. As for the disbelievers, the Qur-aan Shareef says that:

$$فِيْ يَوْمٍ كَانَ مِقْدَارُهُ خَمْسِيْنَ أَلْفَ سَنَةٍ$$

"A day will be equal to fifty thousand years." (Surah Ma'aarij – Aayah 4)

For true believers, this day will be shorter according to their status. It is reported that, for some true Muslims, it will be like the time spent in two rakaats of Fajr Salaah.

The rewards of reading the Qur-aan Shareef are given in many Ahaadith. Similarly, the rewards for listening to the Qur-aan Shareef are also found in many Ahaadith. Listening to the Qur-aan Shareef is so rewarding that Rasulullah ﷺ had been ordered to stay amongst those engaged in reading the Qur-aan Shareef, as given in this Hadith. Some Ulama are of the opinion that listening to the Qur-aan Shareef is more rewarding than reading it, because reading the Qur-aan Shareef is nafl and listening is fardh and a fardh act is always better than a nafl one.

From this Hadith there is one more deduction, in respect of which the Ulama differ in their opinion. There is disagreement as to whether a poor but steadfast person, who conceals his poverty from others, is better, or a wealthy person who is grateful to Allah Ta'ala and discharges his obligations. This Hadith provides an argument in favour of the poor person who is steadfast.

HADITH 30 – SEPARATE REWARDS FOR READING AND LISTENING TO THE QUR-AAN SHAREEF

عَنْ اَبِىْ هُرَيْرَةَ رَضِىَ اللّٰهُ عَنْهُ قَالَ قَالَ رَسُوْلُ اللّٰهِ صَلَّى اللّٰهُ عَلَيْهِ وَسَلَّمَ مَنِ اسْتَمَعَ اِلٰى اٰيَةٍ مِّنْ كِتَابِ اللّٰهِ كُتِبَ لَهُ حَسَنَةٌ مُّضَاعَفَةٌ وَمَنْ تَلَاهَا كَانَتْ لَهُ نُوْرًا يَوْمَ الْقِيَامَةِ

(مسند احمد # 8494)

Hadhrat Abu Hurayrah رَضِىَ اللّٰهُ عَنْهُ reports that Rasulullah صَلَّى اللّٰهُ عَلَيْهِ وَسَلَّمَ said, "Whoever listens to one aayah of the Qur-aan Shareef, there is written for him a double reward, and whoever reads one aayah, it shall be a noor for him on the Day of Qiyaamah."

Note: The Muhaditheen have questioned the above Hadith with respect to its authenticity, but its subject matter is also supported by various other Ahaadith to the effect that even listening to the Qur-aan Shareef has a great reward, so much so that according to some Ulama, listening to the Qur-aan Shareef is better than reading it. Ibn Mas'ood رَضِىَ اللّٰهُ عَنْهُ says that once Rasulullah صَلَّى اللّٰهُ عَلَيْهِ وَسَلَّمَ, while sitting on the mimbar, said to him, "Read the Qur-aan for me." Ibn Mas'ood رَضِىَ اللّٰهُ عَنْهُ replied, "It is not appropriate for me to recite the Qur-aan Shareef to you, because it was revealed to you." Rasulullah صَلَّى اللّٰهُ عَلَيْهِ وَسَلَّمَ said, "It is my heart's desire to listen." Ibn Mas'ood رَضِىَ اللّٰهُ عَنْهُ says that when he read the Qur-aan Shareef, tears flowed from the eyes of Rasulullah صَلَّى اللّٰهُ عَلَيْهِ وَسَلَّمَ. Once Saalim رَضِىَ اللّٰهُ عَنْهُ, the freed slave of Huzayfah رَضِىَ اللّٰهُ عَنْهُ, was reading the Qur-aan Shareef. Rasulullah صَلَّى اللّٰهُ عَلَيْهِ وَسَلَّمَ stood by, listening to him for a long time. Once, Rasulullah صَلَّى اللّٰهُ عَلَيْهِ وَسَلَّمَ listened to the reading of the Qur-aan by Abu Musa Ash'ari رَضِىَ اللّٰهُ عَنْهُ and liked his reading.

Hadith 31 - Reciting the Qur-aan loudly or silently

عَنْ عُقْبَةَ بْنِ عَامِرٍ رَضِىَ اللهُ عَنْهُ قَالَ سَمِعْتُ رَسُوْلَ اللهِ صَلَّى اللهُ عَلَيْهِ وَسَلَّمَ يَقُوْلُ
اَلْجَاهِرُ بِالْقُرْاٰنِ كَالْجَاهِرِ بِالصَّدَقَةِ وَالْمُسِرُّ بِالْقُرْاٰنِ كَالْمُسِرِّ بِالصَّدَقَةِ

(سنن الترمذى # 2919)

Hadhrat Uqbah bin Aamir ﷺ reports that Rasulullah ﷺ said, "The one reading the Qur-aan Shareef loudly is like the one who gives charity openly, and the one who reads silently is like the one who gives charity secretly."

Note: It is more rewarding to give charity openly, when there is some good reason and the intention is to encourage others to do the same. At other times, giving charity secretly is more rewarding. For instance, when the intention is to avoid pride and show or to save the poor from disgrace.

In the same way, reading of the Qur-aan Shareef in a loud voice has more reward when the intention is to encourage others. Besides, in this there is reward also for those who listen. At times it would be better to read silently, so that you don't disturb others or to save yourself from pride and show. Thus, reading either way has its own benefits. Sometimes one way is better and sometimes the other.

Many people have argued on the basis of this Hadith that reading in a low voice is more rewarding. Imam Bayhaqi *(rahmatullahi alayh)* in his book, *'Kitabush Shu'ab'*, has written that Hadhrat Aa'ishah ﷺ had reported that the reward of doing a good act secretly is seventy times more than that of doing it openly. But, according to the rules set by the Muhadditheen (scholars of Ahaadith), this Hadith is dha'eef (weak).

Hadhrat Jaabir ﷺ reports that Rasulullah ﷺ said, "Do not read in a loud voice, otherwise the voice of one person will get mixed up with another person." Hadhrat Umar ibn Abdul Aziz *(rahmatullahi alayh)* found a person reading the Qur-aan Shareef in a loud voice in Masjidun Nabawi ﷺ and had stopped him. However, the reader tried to argue, whereupon Hadhrat Umar ibn Abdul Aziz *(rahmatullahi alayh)* said; "If you are reading for the sake of Allah Ta'ala then read in a low voice, and if you are reading for the sake of people, then such reading is of no use."

Similarly, an advice of Rasulullah ﷺ for reading the Qur-aan in a loud voice, has also been reported.

'*Sharhul Ihya*' contains both riwaayaat (narrations) and 'Aathaar' (sayings of the Sahaabah ﵁), which encourages reading the Qur-aan Shareef in both a loud and soft voice.

HADITH 32 - THE QUR-AAN IS AN INTERCEDER (I.E. IT WILL SPEAK ON YOUR BEHALF)

عَنْ جَابِرٍ رَضِيَ اللهُ عَنْهُ عَنِ النَّبِيِّ صَلَّى اللهُ عَلَيْهِ وَسَلَّمَ الْقُرْآنُ شَافِعٌ مُشَفَّعٌ وَمَاحِلٌ مُصَدَّقٌ مَنْ جَعَلَهُ أَمَامَهُ قَادَهُ إِلَى الْجَنَّةِ وَمَنْ جَعَلَهُ خَلْفَ ظَهْرِهِ سَاقَهُ إِلَى النَّارِ

(اخرجه المنذرى فى الترغيب # 2194)

Hadhrat Jaabir ﵁ reports that Rasulullah ﷺ said, "The Qur-aan Shareef is such an interceder (someone who speaks for another) whose speaking/dua is accepted, and a disputant whose dispute is listened to. Whoever keeps it in front of him, it pulls him to Jannah, and whoever puts it behind his back (ignores it), it throws him into Jahannam."

Note: This means that if the Qur-aan Shareef speaks on behalf of anyone, its intercession is accepted by Allah Ta'ala. The meaning of the "pleading of the Qur-aan" has already been explained under Hadith No.8. The Qur-aan Shareef begs Allah Ta'ala on behalf of those who follow it and to punish those who neglect it. If a person keeps it in front of him, i.e. follows it and follows its rules throughout his life, it leads him to Jannah, and if someone turns his back towards it, i.e. does not follow it, he will definitely fall into Jahannam. According to the author, indifference to the Qur-aan Shareef can also amount to putting it behind the back.

In many Ahaadith there are warnings for those who neglect the Word of Allah Ta'ala. Once, Allah Ta'ala showed Nabi ﷺ the different punishments which will be given to the sinful ones. He was shown a person on whose head a stone was being smashed with such force that his head was crushed. After asking, it was said that Allah Ta'ala had taught His Glorious Qur-aan Shareef to that person, but he did not read it during the night and did not follow it during the day, so now this punishment for him will continue till the Day of Qiyaamah.

May Allah Ta'ala, through His kindness, save us from His punishment. *Aameen*. In fact, the Qur-aan Shareef is such a great gift that ignoring it certainly deserves the worst punishment.

HADITH 33 - FASTING AND QUR-AAN INTERCEDES ON BEHALF OF A PERSON

عَنْ عَبْدِ اللهِ بْنِ عَمْرٍو رَضِيَ اللهُ عَنْهُ قَالَ قَالَ رَسُوْلُ اللهِ صَلَّى اللهُ عَلَيْهِ وَسَلَّمَ اَلصِّيَامُ وَالْقُرْاٰنُ يَشْفَعَانِ لِلْعَبْدِ يَقُوْلُ الصِّيَامُ رَبِّ اِنِّيْ مَنَعْتُهُ الطَّعَامَ وَالشَّرَابَ بِالنَّهَارِ فَشَفِّعْنِيْ فِيْهِ وَيَقُوْلُ الْقُرْاٰنُ رَبِّ مَنَعْتُهُ النَّوْمَ بِاللَّيْلِ فَشَفِّعْنِيْ فِيْهِ فَيُشَفَّعَانِ

(اخرجه المنذري فى الترغيب # 2205)

Hadhrat Abdullah ibn Amr ﷺ reports that Rasulullah ﷺ said, "Fasting and the Qur-aan will both speak to Allah Ta'ala for the obedient person. The fast will say, 'O Allah! I stopped him from eating and drinking during the day, so You accept my intercession on his behalf.' The Qur-aan Shareef will say, 'O Allah! I stopped him from sleep at night, so You accept my dua for him.' Thus, the duas of both of them will be accepted."

Note: In the book *'Targhib'*, the Hadith mentions the words. 'ta'aam' and 'sharaab' i.e. food and drink, as translated above, but in the book of Haakim we find the word *'shahawaat'* (passions) in place of *'sharaab'* i.e. fasting prevented a person from eating and indulging in his passions. It is implied here that one should abstain even from such acts of physical pleasure which are permissible e.g. kissing and embracing (one's own wife). It is mentioned in some Ahaadith that the Qur-aan Shareef will appear in the form of a youth and will say, "It is I who kept you awake during the night and thirsty during the day."

This Hadith also tells us that a Haafiz should read the Qur-aan Shareef in Nafl Salaah at night, as explained already in detail under

Hadith twenty-seven. In the Qur-aan Shareef itself in many places, we are encouraged to read the Qur-aan Shareef in Salaah at night. Some aayaat are given below:

$$\text{وَ مِنَ الَّيْلِ فَتَهَجَّدْ بِهِ نَافِلَةً لَكَ}$$

In a portion of the night perform the Tahajjud salaah that is an extra for you." (Surah Bani Israaeel – Aayah 79)

$$\text{وَ مِنَ الَّيْلِ فَاسْجُدْ لَهُ وَ سَبِّحْهُ لَيْلًا طَوِيلًا}$$

"And worship Allah in a part of the night and praise Him during the long night." (Surah Dahr – Aayah 26)

$$\text{يَتْلُوْنَ اٰيٰتِ اللهِ اٰنَآءَ الَّيْلِ وَ هُمْ يَسْجُدُوْنَ}$$

"They read the aayaat (verses) of Allah Ta'ala (which He revealed) during the night and they go into sajdah (before Him)." (Surah Aali I'mraan – Aayah 113)

$$\text{وَ الَّذِيْنَ يَبِيْتُوْنَ لِرَبِّهِمْ سُجَّدًا وَّ قِيَامًا}$$

"And those who spend the night before their Rabb, in sajdah and standing." (Surah Furqaan – Aayah 64)

Thus, Rasulullah ﷺ and his Sahaabah رضى الله عنهم sometimes spent the whole night in reading the Qur-aan Shareef. It is reported about Hadhrat Usmaan رضى الله عنه that sometimes he read the entire Qur-aan Shareef in a single rakaat of his Witr Salaah. Hadhrat Abdullah ibn Zubair رضى الله عنه used to read the entire Qur-aan Shareef in a single night. Sa'eed ibn Jubair رضى الله عنه read the entire Qur-aan Shareef in two rakaats inside the Ka'bah Shareef. Saabit Bunaani and Hadhrat Abu Hurayrah رضى الله عنه used to read the entire Qur-aan Shareef in one day and night. Abu Shaikh Hannaa'i *(rahmatullahi alayh)* said, "I completed the whole Qur-aan twice and another ten paras in addition in a single night. If I wanted, I could have completed the third reading as well." During the journey for Haj, Salih ibn Kaisaan *(rahmatullahi alayh)* used to often complete the

Qur-aan Shareef twice each night. Mansoor ibn Zaazaan *(rahmatullahi alayh)* completed one reading during Nafl Salaah before noon and the second reading in the interval between Zuhr and Asr Salaah and he spent the whole night in offering Nafl Salaah, weeping so much that the end of his turban would become wet. Similar had been the case with many others, as described by Muhammad ibn Nasr *(rahmatullahi alayh)* in his book *'Qiyaamul Layl'*.

It is written in *'Sharhul Ihya'* that the pious people of the past differed from one another in their practices of completing the reading of the whole Qur-aan. Some of them completed one reading of the whole Qur-aan every day, as was the practice of Imam Shaafi'ee *(rahmatullahi alayh)* in months other than Ramadhaan and some completed two readings every day, as was also done by Imaam Shaafi'ee *(rahmatullahi alayh)* during the month of Ramadhaan. Such was also the practice of Aswad, Salih bin Kaisaan, Sa'eed bin Jubair *(rahmatullahi alayhim)* and of many others. Some used to complete three readings every day. This was the practice of Sulaim ibn Atar, who was an eminent Taabi'ee (the follower of a Sahaabi). He had taken part in the conquest of Egypt during the khilaafat of Hadhrat Umar رَضِيَ اللّٰهُ عَنْهُ and was also appointed ruler of Qasas by Hadhrat Mu'aawiyah رَضِيَ اللّٰهُ عَنْهُ. He used to complete three readings of the whole Qur-aan every night.

Imaam Nawawi *(rahmatullahi alayh)* writes in *'Kitabul Azkaar'* that the maximum daily recitation reported is of Ibnul Kaatib *(rahmatullahi alayh)* who used to complete eight readings of the Qur-aan Shareef during each day and night. Ibn Qudaamah *(rahmatullahi alayh)* has reported that, according to Imaam Ahmad *(rahmatullahi alayh)*, there is no limitation in this respect and that it entirely depends on the keenness of the reader. Historians have stated that Imam Abu Hanifah *(rahmatullahi alayh)* used to complete sixty-one readings in the month of Ramadhaan; once every day, once every night, and one reading was completed in the Taraaweeh Salaah.

On the other hand, Rasulullah ﷺ has said that one who completes one reading of the Qur-aan Shareef in less than three days cannot ponder over it. For this reason, Ibn Hazm *(rahmatullahi alayh)* and others are of the opinion that reading the whole Qur-aan in less than three days is forbidden. According to the author, this Hadith refers to the ability of the readers in general, otherwise completion of one reading of the Qur-aan Shareef in less than three days by a group of Sahaabah رَضِيَ اللّٰهُ عَنْهُمْ has been reported. Similarly, according to the opinion of the Jamhur (general body of Ulama), there is no limitation on the maximum period in which one reading should be completed. The reading should be completed within such time as is convenient. But some Ulama say that the maximum period should not exceed forty days. This means that at least three-quarter of a para should be read daily, and if for any reason this much of reading is not done on any day, the missed portion should also be covered the next day, so that the whole reading is completed within forty days. According to the consensus of opinion, this is not obligatory but, in view of the belief of some Ulama, it is better that the daily reading should not be less than this. This view is supported by some Ahaadith. The author of *'Majma'* has reported in one Hadith:

مَنْ قَرَاَ الْقُرْاٰنَ فِيْ اَرْبَعِيْنَ لَيْلَةً فَقَدْ عَزَبَ (مجمع بحر الانوار 583/3)

Whoever completed the reading of the whole Qur-aan in forty nights, had delayed the matter.

Some Ulama say that the Qur-aan Shareef should be completed once every month, though it is better to complete it every week, as was the practice of most of the Sahaabah رَضِيَ اللّٰهُ عَنْهُمْ. One should start on Friday and read one manzil daily, thus to complete on Thursday. It has already been stated that, according to Imam Abu Hanifah *(rahmatullahi alayh)*, we owe it to the Qur-aan Shareef that it must be read at least twice a year. Therefore, under no circumstances should one do less than this.

There is a Hadith according to which, if the reading of the whole Qur-aan is completed in the beginning of the day, the Malaaikah make dua for mercy for the reader throughout the rest of the day and for rest of a night if completed in the beginning of the night. Therefore, some Mashaa'ikh have concluded that the reading of the whole Qur-aan should be completed preferably in the early part of the day during the summer season and in the early part of the night during winter, so that the reader is benefited for a longer period by the dua of the Malaaikah.

HADITH 34 - THE QUR-AAN IS THE BEST INTERCEDER

عَنْ سَعِيْدِ بْنِ سُلَيْمٍ رَحِمَهُ اللهُ مُرْسَلًا قَالَ قَالَ رَسُوْلُ اللهِ صَلَّى اللهُ عَلَيْهِ وَسَلَّمَ مَا مِنْ شَفِيْعٍ اَفْضَلَ مَنْزِلَةً عِنْدَ اللهِ يَوْمَ الْقِيَامَةِ مِنَ الْقُرْاٰنِ لَا نَبِيٍّ وَلَا مَلَكٌ وَلَا غَيْرُهُ

(احياء علوم الدين ص ـ 273)

Hadhrat Sa'eed ibn Sulaim (RA) has reported that Rasulullah ﷺ said, "On the Day of Qiyaamah, before Allah Ta'ala, no other intercessor (someone who will speak for you) will be better than the Qur-aan; neither a Nabi nor an angel or anything else."

Note: It has been mentioned in many other Ahaadith that the Qur-aan Shareef is such an intercessor whose dua and intercession will be accepted. May Allah Ta'ala make the Qur-aan Shareef intercede (speak) for us all, and may He not make it complain about us. *Aameen.*

In *'La'aali Masnoo'ah'* it is reported from the riwaayah of Bazzaar, which is not fabricated, when a man dies and his family is busy with his funeral, an extremely handsome man stands by his head. When the dead body is covered, the man gets in between the cloth and the chest of the dead person. When the people return home after the burial, the two Malaaikah, Munkar and Nakeer, come in the grave and try to separate this handsome man so that they may be able to question the dead person in private about his Imaan. But the handsome man says, "He is my friend, he is my friend. I will never leave him alone. If you have to question him, then do your job. I cannot leave him until I get him admitted into Jannah." Thereafter he turns to his dead friend and says, "I am the Qur-aan Shareef, which you used to read, sometimes in a loud voice and sometimes in a soft voice. Do not worry! After the questions of Munkar and Nakeer, you will have no worries." When the questioning is over, the handsome man arranges for him from *Al-Malail-A'ala* (the Malaaikah in Heaven) silk bedding filled with musk. May Allah Ta'ala grant this favour to all of us. *Aameen.*

This Hadith in its complete form contains a description of many rewards and has not been quoted in full for the sake of keeping it short.

HADITH 35 - RECITER OF THE QUR-AAN SAFEGUARDS THE KNOWLEDGE OF NUBUWWAT (PROPHETHOOD)

عَنْ عَبْدِ اللهِ بْنِ عَمْرٍو رَضِيَ اللهُ عَنْهُمَا أَنَّ رَسُوْلَ اللهِ صَلَّى اللهُ عَلَيْهِ وَسَلَّمَ قَالَ مَنْ قَرَاَ الْقُرْاٰنَ فَقَدِ اسْتَدْرَجَ النُّبُوَّةَ بَيْنَ جَنْبَيْهِ غَيْرَ اَنَّهٗ لَا يُوْحٰى اِلَيْهِ لَا يَنْبَغِيْ لِصَاحِبِ الْقُرْاٰنِ اَنْ يَّجِدَ مَعَ مَنْ وَّجَدَ وَلَا يَجْهَلَ مَعَ مَنْ جَهِلَ وَفِيْ جَوْفِهٖ كَلَامُ اللهِ

(اخرجه المنذري في الترغيب # 2204)

Hadhrat Abdullah ibn Amr ﷺ reports that Rasulullah ﷺ said, "Whoever reads the Qur-aan Shareef, guards the knowledge of Nubuwat within his chest, though Wahi (revelation) is not sent to him. It is not correct for the one blessed with the Qur-aan Shareef that he should get angry when others get angry, nor should he do something of ignorance (something wrong) with those who are ignorant, while the Qur-aan Shareef is in his chest."

Note: Since Wahi (revelation) ended with Rasulullah ﷺ, more Wahi cannot come. Since the Qur-aan Shareef is the word of Allah Ta'ala, it certainly contains the knowledge of Nubuwwat. If anybody is blessed with this knowledge, it is necessary for him to behave respectfully and to stay away from bad manners.

Fudhail bin Ayaaz *(rahmatullahi alayh)* said that a Haafiz of the Qur-aan carries the flag of Islam. Therefore, it is not correct for him to join those who are involved in useless activities or keep company with the neglectful, or mix with those who waste time.

HADITH 36 – 3 FORTUNATE PEOPLE WHO WILL BE SAVED FROM QUESTIONING ON THE DAY OF QIYAAMAH

عَنْ عَبْدِ اللهِ بْنِ عُمَرَ رَضِيَ اللهُ عَنْهُمَا قَالَ قَالَ رَسُوْلُ اللهِ صَلَّى اللهُ عَلَيْهِ وَسَلَّمَ ثَلَاثَةٌ لَا يَهُوْلُهُمُ الْفَزَعُ الْاَكْبَرُ وَلَا يَنَالُهُمُ الْحِسَابُ هُمْ عَلٰى كَثِيْبٍ مِّنْ مِّسْكٍ حَتّٰى يَفْرُغَ مِنْ حِسَابِ الْخَلَائِقِ رَجُلٌ قَرَاَ الْقُرْاٰنَ ابْتِغَاءَ وَجْهِ اللهِ وَاَمَّ بِهٖ قَوْمًا وَهُمْ بِهٖ رَاضُوْنَ وَدَاعٍ

$$يَدْعُوْ اِلَى الصَّلَاةِ اِبْتِغَاءَ وَجْهِ اللهِ وَعَبْدٌ اَحْسَنَ فِيْمَا بَيْنَهُ وَبَيْنَ رَبِّهِ وَفِيْمَا بَيْنَهُ وَبَيْنَ$$

$$مَوَالِيْهِ \text{ (اخرجه المنذرى فى الترغيب # 2901)}$$

Hadhrat ibn Umar رَضِىَاللهُعَنْهُ reports that Rasulullah صَلَّىاللهُعَلَيْهِوَسَلَّمَ said, "Three people are such that they will have no fear of the horrors on the Day of Qiyaamah, nor will they be questioned (for their actions). They will relax happily on hills of musk until all the people are questioned. One is a person who learnt the Qur-aan, seeking Allah's pleasure and then leads people in Salaah in such a way that they are pleased with him. The second person is one who invites people to Salaah for the pleasure of Allah alone. The third person is one who is very fair to his master, as well as to those under him."

Note: The punishment, horror and miseries of the Day of Qiyaamah are so great that a true Muslim does not forget them. To be saved from those worries on the Day of Qiyaamah, is a favour that is much more than thousands of blessings and millions of pleasures. Those who will then be made to relax and enjoy themselves will be the fortunate ones indeed. Complete destruction and loss is for those foolish people who think that reading the Qur-aan Shareef is useless and a waste of time.

In *'Mu'jamul Kabeer'*, it is written about this Hadith that its reporter, Hadhrat Abdullah bin Umar رَضِىَاللهُعَنْهُ, who was a Sahaabi of Rasulullah صَلَّىاللهُعَلَيْهِوَسَلَّمَ said, "If I had not heard this Hadith from Rasulullah صَلَّىاللهُعَلَيْهِوَسَلَّمَ once, once again and once again (he repeated it seven times), I would never have reported it."

HADITH 37 - REWARDS FOR LEARNING ONE AAYAH

$$عَنْ اَبِىْ ذَرٍّ رَضِىَ اللهُ عَنْهُ قَالَ قَالَ رَسُوْلُ اللهِ صَلَّى اللهُ عَلَيْهِ وَسَلَّمَ يَا اَبَا ذَرٍّ لَاَنْ تَغْدُوَ فَتَعَلَّمَ اٰيَةً مِّنْ كِتَابِ اللهِ خَيْرٌ لَّكَ مِنْ اَنْ تُصَلِّىَ مِائَةَ رَكْعَةٍ وَلَاَنْ تَغْدُوَ فَتَعَلَّمَ بَابًا مِّنَ الْعِلْمِ عُمِلَ بِهٖ اَوْ لَمْ يُعْمَلْ خَيْرٌ مِّنْ اَنْ تُصَلِّىَ اَلْفَ رَكْعَةٍ \text{ (سنن ابن ماجة # 219)}$$

Hadhrat Abu Zar رَضِىَاللهُعَنْهُ reports that Rasulullah صَلَّىاللهُعَلَيْهِوَسَلَّمَ said, "O, Abu Zar! If you go in the morning and learn one aayah from the kitaab of Allah, it will be better for you than reading 100 rakaats of nafl Salaah, and if you learn one chapter of knowledge, which may or may not be practiced upon at that time, it will be better for you than reading 1000 rakaats of nafl Salaah."

Note: It is mentioned in many Ahaadith that learning the knowledge of Deen is better than ibaadah. There are so many Ahaadith on the rewards of learning that all cannot be mentioned here. Rasulullah ﷺ said, "The greatness of an Aalim over an Aabid (worshipper) is like my greatness over the lowest amongst you." He also said that a single Faqeeh (jurist) is harder against shaytaan than 1000 worshippers.

HADITH 38 – THE REWARD OF RECITING AT LEAST 10 AAYAAT

عَنْ اَبِيْ هُرَيْرَةَ رَضِيَ اللهُ عَنْهُ قَالَ قَالَ رَسُوْلُ اللهِ صَلَّى اللهُ عَلَيْهِ وَسَلَّمَ مَنْ قَرَاَ عَشْرَ اٰيَاتٍ فِيْ لَيْلَةٍ لَمْ يُكْتَبْ مِنَ الْغَافِلِيْنَ (اخرجه الحاكم فى المستدرك # 2041)

Hadhrat Abu Hurayrah رضي الله عنه reports that Rasulullah ﷺ said, "Whoever reads ten aayaat at night, will not be counted amongst the neglectful."

Note: It takes only a few minutes to read ten Aayaat. Doing so saves a person from being included in the list of the neglectful for that night. Indeed, it is really a great reward.

HADITH 39 – REWARD FOR RECITING 100 AAYAAT AT NIGHT

عَنْ اَبِيْ هُرَيْرَةَ رَضِيَ اللهُ عَنْهُ قَالَ قَالَ رَسُوْلُ اللهِ صَلَّى اللهُ عَلَيْهِ وَسَلَّمَ مَنْ حَافَظَ عَلٰى هٰؤُلَاءِ الصَّلَوَاتِ الْمَكْتُوْبَاتِ لَمْ يُكْتَبْ مِنَ الْغَافِلِيْنَ وَمَنْ قَرَاَ فِيْ لَيْلَةٍ مِائَةَ اٰيَةٍ كُتِبَ مِنَ الْقَانِتِيْنَ (صحيح ابن خزيمة # 1142)

Hadhrat Abu Hurayrah رضي الله عنه says that Rasulullah ﷺ said, "Whoever reads the five Salaah will not be written amongst the *neglectful; and whoever reads 100 Aayaat at night will be written among the Qaniteen (the obedient ones)."*

Note: Hadhrat Hasan Basri *(rahmatullahi alayh)* reports that Rasulullah ﷺ said, "Whoever reads 100 Aayaat in a night will be safe from the rights of the Qur'aan Shareef, and one who reads 200 Aayaat will get a reward for performing Salaah throughout the night, and one who recites 500 to 1000 Aayaat will get one Qintaar. The Sahaabah رضي الله عنهم asked, 'What is meant by a Qintaar?' Rasulullah ﷺ replied, 'It is equal to 12 000 Dirhams or Dinaars."

HADITH 40 - RECITING THE QUR-AAN SHAREEF WILL SAVE A PERSON FROM FITNAHS

عَنِ ابْنِ عَبَّاسٍ رَضِيَ اللهُ عَنْهُ قَالَ نَزَلَ جِبْرَئِيْلُ عَلَيْهِ السَّلَامُ عَلَى رَسُوْلِ اللهِ صَلَّى اللهُ عَلَيْهِ وَسَلَّمَ فَأَخْبَرَهُ أَنَّهُ سَتَكُوْنُ فِتَنٌ قَالَ فَمَا الْمَخْرَجُ مِنْهَا يَا جِبْرَئِيْلُ قَالَ كِتَابُ اللهِ

(اخرجه رزين كذا فى الرحمة المهداة ص- 111)

Hadhrat ibn Abbaas رضي الله عنه has reported, "Hadhrat Jibraa-eel عليه السلام once told Rasulullah ﷺ that many fitnahs (evils) will certainly appear. Rasulullah ﷺ asked, 'What will be the way out, O Jibraa-eel?' He replied, 'The Book of Allah Ta'ala.'"

Note: To practice on the Book of Allah Ta'ala is a protection against evil. Its reading saves a person from these evils. It has already been mentioned in Hadith twenty-two that if the Qur-aan Shareef is read in a house, peace and mercy comes down on it and shaytaan leaves that place. The Ulama interpret fitnahs to mean the coming of Dajjaal, the invasion by the Tatars and similar events. A long narration from Hadhrat Ali رضي الله عنه also includes the subject matter of this Hadith.

Hadhrat Ali رضي الله عنه says that Hadhrat Yahya *(alayhis salaam)* told the Bani Israa-eel, "Allah Ta'ala orders you to read His book. If you do so, you will be like the people protected in a fort. From whichever side the enemy wants to attack you, they will find the Word of Allah Ta'ala there as a guard to keep them away."

CHAPTER 2
CONCLUDING SECTION

فِيْ عِدَّةِ رِوَايَاتٍ زَائِدَةٍ عَلَى الْأَرْبَعِيْنَ لَا بُدَّ مِنْ ذِكْرِهَا لِأَغْرَاضٍ تُنَاسِبُ الْمَقَامَ

There are a few ahaadith over and above the forty already discussed, which certainly need to be mentioned.

In this section, some special virtues of certain Surahs are given. These Surahs are short, but have many virtues and rewards. In addition, there are one or two important matters, regarding which the readers of the Qur-aan Shareef need to be warned.

HADITH 1 - VIRTUES OF SURAH FAATIHAH (SURAH FAATIHAH IS A CURE FOR ALL SICKNESSES)

عَنْ عَبْدِ الْمَلِكِ بْنِ عُمَيْرٍ رَضِيَ اللهُ عَنْهُ قَالَ قَالَ رَسُوْلُ اللهِ صَلَّى اللهُ عَلَيْهِ وَسَلَّمَ فِيْ فَاتِحَةِ الْكِتَابِ شِفَاءٌ مِّنْ كُلِّ دَاءٍ (سنن الدارمى # 3413)

Hadhrat Abdul Malik ibn Umair رَضِيَ اللهُ عَنْهُ reports that Rasulullah صَلَّى اللهُ عَلَيْهِ وَسَلَّمَ said, "In Surah Faatihah, there is a cure for all sicknesses."

Note: The virtues of Surah Faatihah are found in many Ahaadith. It is reported in one Hadith that while a Sahaabi رَضِيَ اللهُ عَنْهُ was reading Nafl Salaah, Rasulullah صَلَّى اللهُ عَلَيْهِ وَسَلَّمَ called him. Since he was reading Salaah he did not answer. After completing the Salaah he went to Rasulullah صَلَّى اللهُ عَلَيْهِ وَسَلَّمَ, who asked him why he did not answer as soon as he was called. He replied that he could not do so because he was reading Salaah. Rasulullah ﷺ asked if he did not read the following Aayah in the Qur-aan Shareef:

يَاَيُّهَا الَّذِيْنَ اٰمَنُوا اسْتَجِيْبُوْا لِلّٰهِ وَلِلرَّسُوْلِ اِذَا دَعَاكُمْ

"O you who believe! Answer the call of Allah Ta'ala and His Messenger whenever they call you." (Surah Anfaal – Aayah 24)

Rasulullah ﷺ then said, "I will tell you of a Surah which is the greatest and the most virtuous in the Qur-aan Shareef. It is Surah Faatihah, which has seven aayaat. These are the Sab'ul Masaani (seven aayaat that are often repeated) and represent the Glorious Qur-aan Shareef." Some pious Ulama have mentioned that whatever was in the earlier Books revealed by Allah Ta'ala is found in the Qur-aan, and the message of the Qur-aan is found in Surah Faatihah, and that which is in Surah Fatihah is found in Bismillaah and that which is in Bismillah is to be found in its first letter ب (ba). It is explained that ب (ba) is a letter used to join and stands for uniting. Surely the final aim is to unite an aabid (worshiper) with Allah Ta'ala. Some Sufia have gone still further and have said that whatever there is in ب (ba) is to be found in its dot, which signifies the Unity of Allah Ta'ala, a thing which is undividable or united as a single dot.

Some Ulama are reported to have said that the following Aayah is a Dua for fulfilling both our worldly and Deeni objects.;

اِيَّاكَ نَعْبُدُ وَ اِيَّاكَ نَسْتَعِيْنُ

"Only You do we worship and only Your help do we seek."
(Surah Faatihah – Aayah 4)

According to another Hadith, Rasulullah ﷺ said, "By Him Who is the owner of my life, a Surah like this has neither been revealed in the Torah nor in the Injeel nor in the Zaboor nor in the rest of the Qur-aan."

The Ulama have stated that the reading of Surah Faatihah with firm Imaan and Yaqeen cures all sicknesses whether spiritual or worldly, external or internal. To use its aayaat as a taaweez (amulet) and also licking its writing is useful in the treatment of diseases. It is mentioned in the Sihaah books of Hadith (the six authentic books of Hadith) that the Sahaabah رَضِيَ اللهُ عَنْهُمْ used to read Surah Faatihah and blow upon those bitten by a snake or a scorpion and even on the person suffering from fits and on the mentally ill. Rasulullah صَلَّى اللهُ عَلَيْهِ وَسَلَّمَ had also allowed this. There is another narration to the effect that Rasulullah صَلَّى اللهُ عَلَيْهِ وَسَلَّمَ recited this surah and blew on Saa'ib bin Yazeed رَضِيَ اللهُ عَنْهُ and applied his saliva on the spot where he had some pain. According to another Hadith it is said that if, at the time of going to sleep, one reads surah Faatihah and Surah Ikhlaas and blows on himself, he will be protected from all dangers except death.

According to one narration, Surah Faatihah is equivalent to two-thirds of the Qur-aan Shareef in reward. It is also reported that Rasulullah صَلَّى اللهُ عَلَيْهِ وَسَلَّمَ has said, "I have been given four things from the special treasure of the Arsh, from which nothing has ever been given to anyone before. These are Surah Faatihah, Aayatul Kursi, the last few aayaat of surah Baqarah and Surah Kausar." Hadhrat Hasan Basri *(rahmatullahi alayh)* reports the saying of Rasulullah صَلَّى اللهُ عَلَيْهِ وَسَلَّمَ that whoever reads Surah Faatihah is like one who reads the Torah, the Zaboor, the Injeel and the Qur-aan Shareef.

It is reported in one Hadith that shaytaan cried, wept and threw dust on his head four times;

(1) When he was cursed.
(2) When he was thrown out of Jannah onto the earth.
(3) When Hadhrat Muhammad صَلَّى اللهُ عَلَيْهِ وَسَلَّمَ was made a Nabi.
(4) When Surah Faatihah was revealed.

Sha'bi *(rahmatullahi alayh)* says that once a man came to him and complained of pain in his kidney. Sha'bi *(rahmatullahi alayh)* asked him to read Asaasul Qur-aan (the foundation of the Qur-aan) and blow on the aching spot. When he asked what was meant by Asaasul Qur-aan, Sha'bi *(rahmatullahi alayh)* replied, Surah Faatihah.

It is written in the established practices of Mashaa'ikh that Surah Faatihah is the Isme A'zam (اِسْمُ أَعْظَمْ), the Most Glorious Name of Allah Ta'ala and it should be read for achieving all our objects. There are two ways of reading it:

One method is to read this surah forty-one times for forty days, in the time between the sunnat and fardh of the Fajr Salaah. The meem of بِسْمِ اللهِ الرَّحْمٰنِ الرَّحِيْمِ (Bismillaahir rahmaanir raheem) should be read jointly with the laam of اَلْحَمْدُ لِلّٰهِ (Alhamdu lillaahi). Whatever it is intended for, it will Insha-Allah (if Allah Ta'ala wills) be fulfilled. In the treatment of a patient or of one who is affected by sihr (black magic), it should be recited and blown on water to be used for drinking.

The second method is to read it seventy times between the sunnat and fardh of the Fajr Salaah on the first Sunday of a new moon, after which the number is reduced by ten every day until the course ends with a reading of ten times on the seventh day. This weekly course should be repeated for four weeks. If the purpose is achieved at the end of the first month, well and good, otherwise this course should be repeated for the second and, if necessary, for the third month.

The surah is also written with rosewater, musk and saffron, on a porcelain plate, then the writing is washed off and the water is given to the patient for drinking for forty days. This is a sure treatment of chronic diseases. To read it seven times and blow on the patient is a good treatment for toothache, headache and pain in the stomach. All these points have been briefly quoted from the kitaab *'Mazaahir-e-Haq'*.

'Muslim Shareef' has a Hadith in which Ibn Abbaas رَضِىَ اللهُ عَنْهُ says that once Rasulullah صَلَّى اللهُ عَلَيْهِ وَسَلَّمَ was sitting amongst us and said; "Today, a door has been opened in Jannah which was never opened before, and out of it came down an angel who had never come down before. The angel said to me, 'Receive the good news of two anwaar (two lights) which have not been given to anyone before you. One is Surah Faatihah and the other is the last few aayaat of Surah Baqarah.'" These two Surahs have been called Noor because on the Day of Qiyaamah they will travel in front of their readers (brightening up their path).

HADITH 2 - VIRTUES OF SURAH YAASEEN

عَنْ عَطَاءِ بْنِ اَبِيْ رَبَاحٍ رَضِىَ اللهُ عَنْهُ قَالَ بَلَغَنِيْ اَنَّ رَسُوْلَ اللهِ صَلَّى اللهُ عَلَيْهِ وَسَلَّمَ قَالَ مَنْ قَرَاَ يٰسٓ فِىْ صَدْرِ النَّهَارِ قُضِيَتْ حَوَائِجُهُ (سنن الدارمى # 3461)

Hadhrat Ata ibn Abi Rabaah ؓ says that Rasulullah ﷺ said, *"Whoever reads Surah Yaaseen in the beginning of the day, all his needs for that day are fulfilled."*

Note: Many rewards of surah Yaaseen are mentioned in the Ahaadith. It is said in one Hadith;

"Everything has a heart, and the heart of the Qur-aan is Surah Yaaseen. Whoever reads Surah Yaaseen, Allah Ta'ala records for him a reward equal to that of reading the entire Qur-aan Shareef ten times."

According to another Hadith, Allah Ta'ala recited Surah Yaaseen and Surah Taaha 1000 years before the creation of the Heavens and the Earth, and after hearing this, the Malaaikah said, "Blessed be that Ummah onto whom the Qur-aan Shareef will be sent down, and blessed be the hearts that will memorise it, and blessed be the tongues that will recite it."

Nabi ﷺ said, **"Whoever reads Surah Yaaseen only for the pleasure of Allah, all his earlier sins are forgiven. Therefore, make it a practice of reading this Surah for your dead."**

According to one Hadith, Surah Yaaseen is named in the Torah as Mun'imah (giver of good things), because it contains benefits for its reader in this life as well as in the Aakhirah, it removes from him the afflictions of this world and the next and takes away the fear of the next life.

This Surah is also known as Raafi'ah and Khaafidah, i.e. that which gives honour and respect to the believers and disgraces the disbelievers. According to a Hadith, Rasulullah ﷺ said, "My heart wishes that Surah Yaaseen be in the heart of every person of my Ummah." According to another Hadith, if anybody reads Surah Yaaseen every night and then dies, he dies as a shaheed (martyr).

It is reported in yet another Hadith, "Whoever reads Surah Yaaseen is forgiven. Whoever reads it in hunger, is satisfied. Whoever reads it having lost his way, finds the way. Whoever reads it on losing an animal, finds it. When one reads it, fearing that the food will run short, that food becomes enough. If one reads it next to a person who is suffering the pain of death, his death is made easy for him. If anyone reads it for a woman experiencing difficulty in child-birth, her delivery becomes easy."

Muqri *(rahmatullahi alaih)* said, "If Surah Yaaseen is read by one who fears the ruler or an enemy, he gets rid of this fear." According to another Hadith, if somebody reads Surah Yaaseen and Surah Was-Saaffaat on Friday and begs of Allah Ta'ala for something, his Dua is granted. (Most of the above has been drawn from '*Mazaahir-e-Haq*', though the Ulama of Hadith have questioned some of the narrations).

HADITH 3 - VIRTUES OF SURAH WAAQI'AH

عَنِ ابْنِ مَسْعُودٍ رَضِيَ اللّٰهُ عَنْهُ قَالَ قَالَ رَسُوْلُ اللّٰهِ صَلَّى اللّٰهُ عَلَيْهِ وَسَلَّمَ مَنْ قَرَاَ سُوْرَةَ الْوَاقِعَةِ فِى كُلِّ لَيْلَةٍ لَمْ تُصِبْهُ فَاقَةٌ اَبَدًا وَكَانَ ابْنُ مَسْعُوْدٍ رَضِيَ اللّٰهُ عنْهُ يَأْمُرُ بَنَاتِهِ يَقْرَأْنَ بِهَا كُلَّ لَيْلَةٍ (اخرجه البيهقى فى شعب الايمان # 2269)

Hadhrat Ibn Mas'ood ؓ reports that Rasulullah ﷺ said, "Whoever reads Surah Al-Waaqi'ah every night will never starve." Hadhrat Ibn Mas'ood ؓ used to instruct his daughters to recite this Surah every night.

Note: The rewards of Surah Waaqi'ah are also reported in many Ahaadith. There is a narration to the effect that whoever reads Surah Hadeed, Waaqi'ah and Ar-Rahmaan, is counted amongst the dwellers of Jannatul-Firdaus (the highest level of Jannah). There is a Hadith in which it is stated that Surah Waaqi'ah is Surah Al-Ghina (wealth, contentment). Read it and teach it to your children. Another narration says: "Teach it to your wives." Hadhrat Aa'ishah ؓ is reported to have emphasised its reading. It is foolish of us to read it only for the sake of worldly wealth. If instead, it is read for the contentment of the heart and for the sake of the next world, then worldly wealth will come to us without asking.

HADITH 4 - VIRTUES OF SURAH MULK AND SURAH SAJDAH

عَنْ اَبِىْ هُرَيْرَةَ رَضِىَ اللهُ عَنْهُ قَالَ قَالَ رَسُوْلُ اللهِ صَلَّى اللهُ عَلَيْهِ وَسَلَّمَ اِنَّ سُوْرَةً فِى الْقُرْاٰنِ ثَلَاثُوْنَ اٰيَةً شَفَعَتْ لِرَجُلٍ حَتّٰى غُفِرَ لَهُ وَهِىَ تبَارَكَ الَّذِىْ بِيَدِهِ الْمُلْكُ

(اخرجه المنذرى فى الترغيب # 2265)

Hadhrat Abu Hurayrah ؓ narrates that Rasulullah ﷺ said, *"In the Qur-aan there is a Surah consisting of thirty aayaat which will intercede for its reader until he is forgiven. This is Surah Tabaarakal-lazi."*

Note: About Surah Mulk, there is also a narration that Rasulullah ﷺ said, **"My heart wishes that this surah be in the heart of every believer."**

According to a Hadith, a person who reads Surah Mulk and Surah Sajdah between Maghrib and Esha Salaah, is like a person who stands in Salaah throughout Laylatul-Qadr.

It is also reported that if someone reads these two Surahs, seventy rewards are added to his account and seventy sins are wiped out.

According to another narration, if one reads these two surahs, a reward equal to that of standing in Salaah throughout Laylatul Qadr is written for him. This is also mentioned in *'Mazaahir'*.

Tirmizi *(rahmatullahi alayh)* reports from Ibn Abbaas ؓ, *"Some Sahaabah ؓ put up a tent at a place without knowing that there was a grave there. Suddenly, they heard someone reading Surah Tabaarakal-lazi. They reported this to Rasulullah ﷺ who explained to them that this Surah guards a person against Allah's punishment and frees him (from Jahannam)."*

Hadhrat Jaabir ؓ reports that Rasulullah ﷺ would not go to sleep until he had recited Surah Alif-Laam-Meem Sajdah and Tabaarakal-Lazi.

Khalid bin Ma'daan ؓ has said that a narration reached him as follows; "There was a man who was a great sinner, but he used to recite Surah Sajdah. He never read anything else besides this. This Surah spread its wings over that man and submitted to Allah Ta'ala, 'O My Rabb! This man used to recite me very frequently. So the intercession of this surah was accepted. It was ordered that each sin in his account should be replaced by a reward." Khalid bin Ma'daan رَضِيَ اللهُ عَنْهُ has also reported; "This Surah pleads for its reader in the grave and says, 'O, Allah Ta'ala! If I am contained in Your Book, then accept my intercession, otherwise write me off from Your Book.' This Surah appears in the form of a bird, spreads its wings over the dead and guards against the punishment in the grave." He has reported all these rewards for Surah Tabarakal-lazi as well. He himself would never go to sleep unless he had read these two surahs.

Taa'oos *(rahmatullahi alayh)* has said, "These two surahs carry sixty virtues more than that of those carried by any other surah."

The punishment in the grave is not an ordinary thing. After death, the first stage that one has to pass through is the grave. Whenever Hadhrat Usmaan رَضِيَ اللهُ عَنْهُ stood by a grave, he used to weep so much that his beard would become wet with tears. Somebody asked him why he wept more at the mention of the grave than he did at the mention of Jannah and Jahannam. He replied, "I have heard from Rasulullah صَلَّى اللهُ عَلَيْهِ وَسَلَّمَ that the grave is the first stage towards the Aakhirah. Whoever is saved from the punishment in the grave, the stages that follow will become easy for him, and whoever is not saved from the punishment in it, the coming stages will be more difficult for him. I have also heard that no scene is more horrible than that of the grave."

اَللّٰهُمَّ احْفَظْنَا مِنْهُ بِفَضْلِكَ وَمَنِّكَ

"O, Allah Ta'ala! save us from this punishment through Your Mercy and Grace."

Hadith 5 - When one completes a complete recitation of the Qur-aan, he should immediately start with the next recitation

عَنِ ابْنِ عَبَّاسٍ رَضِيَ اللهُ عَنْهُمَا أَنَّ رَجُلًا قَالَ يَا رَسُوْلَ اللهِ أَيُّ الْأَعْمَالِ أَفْضَلُ قَالَ اَلْحَالُّ الْمُرْتَحِلُ قَالَ يَا رَسُوْلَ اللهِ وَمَا الْحَالُّ الْمُرْتَحِلُ قَالَ صَاحِبُ الْقُرْاٰنِ يَضْرِبُ مِنْ أَوَّلِهِ

حَتّٰى يَبْلُغَ اٰخِرَهُ وَمِنْ اٰخِرِهٖ حَتّٰى يَبْلُغَ اَوَّلَهُ كُلَّمَا حَلَّ اِرْتَحَلَ

(اخرجه الحاكم فى المستدرك # 2089)

Hadhrat Ibn Abbaas ﷺ says, "Somebody asked Rasulullah ﷺ as to which act is the most rewarding. Rasulullah ﷺ replied, 'Al-haal wal-murtahil.' The man asked, 'O, Rasulullah! What is Al-haal wal-murtahil?' Rasulullah ﷺ replied, 'It is that reader of the Qur-aan who starts reading from the beginning and continues till he reaches its end, and after the end, he starts at the beginning again. Whenever he stops, he starts again.'"

Note: The Arabic word اَلْحَالُ (al-haal) means one who reaches a halting place and the word اَلْمُرْتَحِلُ (al-murtahil) means one who departs. In other words, as soon as the reading of the Qur-aan Shareef is finished, one should begin another recitation. It should not be that when one reading is finished the next may be started later on. The term وَالْمُرْتَحِلُ الْحَالُ al-haal wal murtahil is explained in a narration in *'Kanzul-Ummaal'* to mean (اَلْخَاتِمُ الْمِفْتَاحُ) al-khaatimatul miftaah (one who concludes and opens), i.e. one who completes the whole reading of the Qur-aan Shareef and then immediately starts another. Probably this has led to the practice generally prevalent in our country, according to which, when the reader finishes the entire Qur-aan Shareef, he does not stop after reading the last surah but also reads from the beginning of the Qur-aan up to (مُفْلِحُوْنَ) muflihoon. Doing so has only become a custom and the people do not care to continue further and complete the next reading. This Hadith teaches us that as soon as one reading of the Qur-aan Shareef is completed, a new reading should be started immediately and brought to completion. It is written in *'Sharhul Ihya'* as well as in Allamah Suyuti's (rahmatullahi alayh) *'Al-Itqaan'* that according to Daarami (rahmatullahi alayh) whenever Rasulullah ﷺ read surah Naas (the last surah), he would also read surah Baqarah up to (مُفْلِحُوْنَ) muflihoon after which he would make dua which is read on completion of the entire Qur-aan.

HADITH 6 - GUARD THE QUR-AAN, BECAUSE IT ESCAPES MORE QUICKLY THAN CAMELS

عَنْ اَبِىْ مُوْسَى الْاَشْعَرِيِّ رَضِىَ اللهُ عَنْهُ قَالَ قَالَ رَسُوْلُ اللهِ صَلَّى اللهُ عَلَيْهِ وَسَلَّمَ تَعَاهَدُوا الْقُرْاٰنَ فَوَالَّذِىْ نَفْسِىْ بِيَدِهٖ لَهُوَ اَشَدُّ تَفَصِّيًا مِّنَ الْاِبِلِ فِىْ عُقُلِهَا

(صحيح البخارى # 5033)

Hadhrat Abu Musa Ash'ari ﷺ reports that Rasulullah ﷺ said, *"Guard the Qur-aan well. I swear by Him in Whose hands my life is, the Qur-aan escapes from the hearts more quickly than camels do from their strings."*

Note: If a man becomes careless when looking after an animal and the animal frees itself from the string, it will escape. Similarly, if the Qur-aan Shareef is not looked after and it is neglected, it will not be remembered and will disappear from the heart. The fact that the Qur-aan Shareef is memorised is a miracle of the Qur-aan Shareef itself. Otherwise memorising a book half or even one-third its size is not only difficult but rather impossible. Therefore, the fact that the Qur-aan Shareef is memorised is mentioned by Allah Ta'ala as a favour in Surah Qamar, where it is repeated over and over:

وَلَقَدْ يَسَّرْنَا الْقُرْاٰنَ لِلذِّكْرِ فَهَلْ مِنْ مُّدَّكِرٍ

"We have made the Qur-aan easy for memorising it, so is there anyone who will memorise it?" (Surah Qamar – Aayah 17)

The author of *'Jalalain'* writes that the question in this aayah is in fact a command. Therefore, Allah Ta'ala has stressed over and over again the importance of memorising the Qur-aan Shareef, but if we Muslims are so foolish as to think that this act is useless and a waste of time and energy, then this mistake on our part is sufficient to justify our destruction. It is a matter of surprise indeed that, when Hadhrat Uzair *(alayhis salaam)* recited the Torah from memory, he was raised to such a level that he was called the "Son of God". Indeed we are ungrateful to Allah Ta'ala for His blessing and favour on us, where He has made the memorising of the

Qur-aan Shareef so easy for all of us (and not only for an individual as in the case of Taurah). It is for such people that the Qur-aan Shareef says;

$$وَسَيَعْلَمُ الَّذِيْنَ ظَلَمُوْٓا اَىَّ مُنْقَلَبٍ يَّنْقَلِبُوْنَ$$

"And those who do wrong will come to know to which place they will return." (Surah Shua'raa – Aayah 227)

It is only through the grace and blessing of Allah Ta'ala that the Qur-aan Shareef gets memorised. Afterwards, if a person neglects it, he is made to forget it. There are severe warnings for those who forget the Qur-aan Shareef after having memorised it. Rasulullah ﷺ is reported to have said, **"The sins of my Ummah were shown to me. I did not find any sin as great as that of forgetting the Qur-aan after having learnt it."** In another Hadith it is mentioned, **"The one who forgets the Qur-aan after having learnt it, will appear in the Court of Allah Ta'ala as a leper (a person with a very bad skin disease)."** According to a narration of Razeen *(rahmatullahi alayh)* in *'Jam'ul-Fawaa'id'*, the following Aayah refers to it:

$$وَمَنْ اَعْرَضَ عَنْ ذِكْرِيْ فَاِنَّ لَهٗ مَعِيْشَةً ضَنْكًا وَّنَحْشُرُهٗ يَوْمَ الْقِيٰمَةِ اَعْمٰى ۝ قَالَ رَبِّ لِمَ حَشَرْتَنِيْٓ اَعْمٰى وَقَدْ كُنْتُ بَصِيْرًا ۝ قَالَ كَذٰلِكَ اَتَتْكَ اٰيٰتُنَا فَنَسِيْتَهَا وَكَذٰلِكَ الْيَوْمَ تُنْسٰى$$

"But whosoever turns away from My advice (the Qur-aan and zikr), shall surely have a narrowed (difficult) life and We shall raise him up blind on the Day of Qiyaamah. He will say: 'O my Rabb, why have You raised me blind, when indeed I was one who could see.' He (Allah Ta'ala) will say, 'This (is how it shall be for you) Our Aayaat came to you, but you forgot them. In the same way you will be forgotten today.'" (Surah Taahaa – Aayah 124 - 126)

HADITH 7 - PUNISHMENT FOR THE PERSON WHO READS THE QUR-AAN FOR WORLDLY BENEFITS

عَنْ بُرَيْدَةَ رَضِىَ اللهُ عَنْهُ قَالَ قَالَ رَسُوْلُ اللهِ صَلَّى اللهُ عَلَيْهِ وَسَلَّمَ مَنْ قَرَاَ الْقُرْاٰنَ يَتَاَكَّلُ بِهِ النَّاسَ جَاءَ يَوْمَ الْقِيَامَةِ وَوَجْهُهُ عَظْمٌ لَيْسَ عَلَيْهِ لَحْمٌ

(اخرجه البيهقى فى شعب الايمان # 2384)

Hadhrat Buraydah ﷺ reports that Rasulullah ﷺ said, *"He who reads the Qur-aan so that he might get something to eat from the people, will come on the Day of Qiyaamah in such a condition that his face will only be of bones, on which there will be no flesh."*

Note: This means that those who read the Qur-aan Shareef to fulfill the needs of this world will get no share in the Aakhirah. Rasulullah ﷺ said, *"We read the Qur-aan. There are amongst us Arabs as well as non-Arabs. Go on reading the Qur-aan as you do now. Soon, some people will come who will put right the pronunciation of the letters of the Qur-aan as an arrow (i.e. they will work hard to beautify it and spend hours in improving the pronunciation of each and every letter), but all this will be for a worldly reason. They will not be concerned about the Aakhirah."* This Hadith further shows that recitation in a pleasing voice is of no use if there is no sincerity and if the purpose is only to earn worldly benefit. 'There will be no flesh' means that when a person uses the best of all things (i.e. the Qur-aan) for earning the lowly things of this world, the best of all parts of the body i.e. his face, will lose its beauty.

Once, Imraan bin Husain ﷺ happened to pass by a person giving advices after reciting the Qur-aan Shareef and then begging from the people. He was sorry to see this painful sight and recited Innaa lillaahi wa innaa ilaihi raaji'oon (verily we are from Allah Ta'ala and will return to Him). He said that he had heard from Rasulullah ﷺ that whoever recites the Qur-aan Shareef should beg for his needs only from Allah Ta'ala. Shortly, there will come a time when people will recite the Qur-aan Shareef and then beg of the people. It is reported from some Ulama that the example of a person who earns the things of this world through the knowledge of Deen is like a person who cleans his shoes with his cheeks. The shoes will no doubt be cleaned, but this act is most stupid. It is such people who are referred to in the following Aayah of the Qur-aan Shareef:

أُولَٰئِكَ الَّذِينَ اشْتَرَوُا الضَّلَالَةَ بِالْهُدَىٰ ۖ فَمَا رَبِحَت تِّجَارَتُهُمْ وَمَا كَانُوا مُهْتَدِينَ

These are the people who have purchased misguidance (error) at the price of guidance. So their trade shall neither be profitable nor will they be guided." (Surah Baqarah – Aayah 16)

Hadhrat Ubayy ibn Ka'b رَضِيَ اللَّهُ عَنْهُ says, "I taught a Surah of the Qur-aan to a man who gave me a bow as a gift. I mentioned this to Rasulullah صَلَّى اللَّهُ عَلَيْهِ وَسَلَّمَ who said that I had accepted a bow from Jahannam."

A similar story has been mentioned by 'Ubaadah ibn Saamit رَضِيَ اللَّهُ عَنْهُ in whose case Rasulullah صَلَّى اللَّهُ عَلَيْهِ وَسَلَّمَ said, "You have hung between your shoulders a spark from Jahannam." According to another Hadith Rasulullah صَلَّى اللَّهُ عَلَيْهِ وَسَلَّمَ said, "If you are prepared to put a yoke (steel buckle) of Jahannam around your neck, you may accept it."

Some words of advice for Huffaaz who are working in Madrasahs only for the sake of money. It is humbly requested that they should think about their position and responsibility. This improper conduct on their part is being made an excuse by some people for stopping the reading or memorising of the Qur-aan Shareef. Those people are not only responsible for the evil consequences, but the huffaaz are also responsible for stopping the teaching of the Qur-aan Shareef. These huffaaz think that they are engaged in the propagation of the Qur-aan, but in reality they are obstructing it through their misconduct and bad intentions. The Ulama have not permitted the acceptance of salary for teaching the Qur-aan Shareef so that it becomes the primary motive. In fact, the real motive of the teachers should only be to promote the teaching and propagation of the knowledge of the Qur-aan. No salary can be a return for the noble act of teaching the Qur-aan. The salary is only for meeting personal needs and has been permitted when forced by circumstances, in case of dire necessity.

CHAPTER 3
FINAL NOTE - SUMMARY OF THE FORTY AHAADITH MENTIONED IN PART ONE

The purpose of describing the beauties and virtues of the Qur-aan Shareef in the previous pages is to promote love for it. Love for the Qur-aan Shareef is needed for developing a love for Allah Ta'ala and vice versa. Love for one leads to the love for the other.

The purpose of creation of man in this world is that he recognises Allah Ta'ala, and all other creation are created for the service of man.

As a Persian poet says:

ابرو باد ومہ وخورشید وفلک درکارند   تا تونا نے بکف آری وبغفلت نخوری

ہمہ از بہر تو سرگشتہ وفرمانبردار   شرط انصاف نہ باشد کہ تو فرماں نبری

The clouds, the winds, the moon, the sun and the sky are constantly at work,

So that you earn your living and do not eat in forgetfulness, The whole creation is involved in working for you in obedience,

The law of justice will not be fulfilled if you fail to obey (Allah Ta'ala).

So man should learn a lesson from their punctuality and obedience in their functions of rendering service to Him.

Temporary changes are sometimes caused in their functions by Allah Ta'ala as a warning and reminder. There is no rain when it should rain; no wind blows when it should blow; similar changes are seen in the moon and the sun through their eclipses. In short, everything is subject to some change, to caution and warn those who do not fulfil their duty to their Creator. How surprising indeed that all these things are made obedient to fulfil man's needs, yet their obedience does not lead man to his own submission to the Creator. Love alone provides the best help for obedience and submission to Allah Ta'ala.

اِنَّ الْمُحِبَّ لِمَن يُحِبُّ مُطِيْعٌ

Verily, the lover submits to his beloved.

When a person falls in love with someone, submission and obedience to the beloved becomes his habit and a second nature. Disobedience to the beloved becomes difficult, just as being obedient to someone whom one does not love.

One way of developing love for someone is to look at his beauty and excellence. Looking at his beauty may be through physically seeing him or pondering over his beauty. If a look at a beautiful face can lead to natural love, then a sweet heart-captivating voice can also sometimes produce a magnetic effect.

A Persian poet says:

نه تنها عشق از دیدار خیزد بسا کیں دَوْلَت اَزْ گُفْتار خیزد

Looks alone do not inspire love, Often this wealth is attained through charming words.

Sometimes it is the sweetness of the voice which draws the heart unconsciously and sometimes it is the beauty and wisdom of speech or words which causes one to fall in love. Experienced men have suggested that in order to develop love, one should think about the fine qualities of the beloved and none other than the beloved should find a place in one's heart. It is true even in the case of earthly love that the sight of a beautiful face or a hand urges one to see the other parts of the body of the beloved, so that love may increase and the yearning of the heart may be satisfied, but that stage of satisfaction is never reached.

As an Urdu poet says:

مرض بڑھتا گیا جوں جوں دوا کی

The disease worsened as the treatment progressed.

If after sowing the seeds in a field, one does not care to water it, no crop will grow there. Similarly, after falling in love unintentionally, if one does not pay attention to the beloved, this love will disappear in time to come. But if one keeps on thinking about and imagining the charming features, the built as well as the habits, behaviour and the manner of speaking of the beloved, love will go on increasing every moment.

مکتبِ عشق کے انداز نرالے دیکھے   اس کو چھٹی نہ ملی جس نے سبق یاد کیا

Unusual are the ways in the school of love, One who learns his lesson gets no leave.

If you forget the lesson of love, you will be left out at once by the beloved. But the more you learn it, the more you are caught up in it. In the same way, if a man wants to develop love with someone worthy of love, he should find out the excellence, the charms and the valued qualities of the beloved and should not be satisfied with what he knows, but should always be eager to know more about them.

When, even in the case of a human, the lover is not satisfied with a partial view of the beloved, and is always on the lookout for more chances to see as much of the beloved as he can, then Allah Ta'ala, the Pure and Blessed, Who is the source of all beauty and elegance, (and in fact there is no beauty in this world except His) is certainly such a beloved Whose loveliness and perception knows no bounds and is limitless. One of the ways He shows His beauty and excellence is through the Qur-aan Shareef, which is the Word of Allah Ta'ala Himself. What greater pleasure can there be for a Aashiq (lover of Allah Ta'ala), than the fact that the Qur-aan is Allah Ta'ala's own Revelation. A poet says:

اے گل بتو خرسندم تو بوئے کسے داری

O, flower! How pleased am I with you, you have the smell of someone (beloved).

Even if we leave aside the consideration that the Qur-aan Shareef was revealed by Allah Ta'ala and it is His word, the relationship that the Qur-aan Shareef has with Rasulullah ﷺ is enough for a Muslim to adore it. Study of the Qur-aan itself makes one realise that there is no excellence elsewhere that cannot be found in the Glorious Qur-aan.

A poet says:

دامان نِگہ تَنگ و گلِ حُسنِ تُو بِسیار   گُل چِین بَہارِ تُو زَ دَاماں گِلَہ دارد

The limits of sight are narrow and the flowers of your beauty numerous;
He who plucks the flowers of your spring complains of not being fully capable of his hold.

There is another verse to this effect:

فدا ہو آپ کی کس کس ادا پر   ادائیں لاکھ اور بیتاب دل ایک

How many of your graces can be adored; Your charms are innumerable and my restless heart is one.

It is evident to the careful reader of the above Ahaadith, that there is hardly any important thing of this world to which our attention has not been drawn. Whatever taste for love and beauty one may possess, its excellence and perfection will be found in the Qur-aan Shareef. Whatever enjoyment and beauty one enjoys from the entire or portion of the world can all be found in the Qur-aan Shareef. In the first Hadith, the excellence of the Qur-aan Shareef has been compared against all the beauty of the worldly things. Take any example of love. If a person has love for someone for any number of reasons then we should know that the Qur-aan Shareef has unlimited number of reasons to be loved.

The Qur-aan Shareef is superior to all other lovable things, taken individually or collectively in every respect. If one loves somebody because of obtaining a great number of benefits from him, Allah Ta'ala has promised (Hadith two) that He will give to the reader of the Qur-aan Shareef more than what was begged of Him by all other persons.

If somebody is adored for his personal greatness, attainment or excellence, Allah Ta'ala has said (in the same Hadith) that the superiority of the Qur-aan Shareef over all other books is like the superiority of Allah Ta'ala Himself over His creation, of the master over his slave and of the king over his subjects.

If anybody is fond of wealth, property, servants and animals, and loves to raise and breed animals of a particular kind, he is warned (in Hadith three) that the knowledge of the Qur-aan Shareef is far more valuable than any number of good animals acquired even without labour or crime.

If a Sufi seeks piety and fear of Allah Ta'ala, and works hard to acquire them, Rasulullah ﷺ has said (Hadith four) that those who become an expert in the study of the Qur-aan Shareef will be reckoned amongst the Malaaikah. The piety of the Malaaikah cannot be excelled by anybody, because they cannot pass even a moment in disobedience to Allah Ta'ala.

Also if anybody takes pride in getting double the reward or if he likes that his words should carry a double weight, he should consider how even the reader who falters in his recitation gets double the reward.

If any jealous person finds joy in evil conduct, and jealousy has become a part and parcel of his nature and he cannot give up this vice, he can be rightly jealous of a Haafiz whose excellence is worth being jealous of, as said by Rasulullah ﷺ (Hadith five).

Let one who enjoys fruit and cannot live without it, know that the Qur-aan Shareef is like a citron. If anybody is fond of sweets, he should know that Qur-aan Shareef is sweeter than dates (Hadith six refers to this).

If anybody is desirous of honour and dignity and cannot resist being a member of some council, he should know that the Qur-aan Shareef raises the rank of its reader, both in this world as well as in the Aakhirah (This is mentioned in Hadith seven).

If anybody wants a sincere and dedicated companion, who should be ready to defend him in every dispute, he should know that the Qur-aan Shareef is ready to defend its devotee in the court of the Emperor of all emperors (as mentioned in Hadith eight).

If a person devotes his life to the in-depth study of the finer points of different subjects and appreciates these finer points, and it turns him away from the greatest pleasure of this world, then he should know that the contents of the Qur-aan Shareef is a treasure full of fine points (as described in Hadith eight).

If somebody attaches importance to discovering hidden secrets, and considers expertise in the criminal investigation department as an accomplishment and devotes his life to acquiring it, he should know that the body of the Qur-aan Shareef reveals those mysteries whose depths are boundless (which is referred to in Hadith eight).

If one likes the construction of lofty buildings and wants his special house to be on the 7th floor, then verily the Qur-aan Shareef raises its devotee to the 7000th floor in Jannah (as referred to in Hadith nine).

If anybody desires to do business which should bring maximum profit with a minimum amount of effort, he should know that the recitation of each letter of the Qur-aan Shareef will earn him ten blessings (as referred to in Hadith ten).

If anybody wants to be a king and desires the crown and a throne, and has to fight battles in this world to attain it, he should consider that the Qur-aan gets for the parents of those devoted to it, a crown whose brilliance cannot be compared to in this world (This is mentioned in Hadith eleven).

If there is any expert in acts of juggling who can catch a burning coal in his hand or can put a burning match-stick in his mouth, he should realise that the Qur-aan Shareef provides safety even against the fire of Jahannam (For this see Hadith twelve).

There are people who want to have good relations with government officers and take pride in relating how, as a result of their recommendation to an officer, an accused had not been punished but had been set free. For having contact with these officers, they spend their time and money in flattering and arranging dinners for them and so on. Those reciting the Qur-aan Shareef will intercede on behalf of ten people who had been condemned to Jahannam (This is mentioned in Hadith thirteen).

Now let us consider Hadith fourteen. If somebody is fond of flowers and gardens and loves sweet smells, he should realise that the Qur-aan Shareef has been compared to musk. If someone loves perfumes and wants to bathe in dried musk, then the example of the Qur-aan Shareef is like a musk vase. This is only as an example. In reality musk has no comparison with the fragance of the Qur-aan Shareef. The particles of this earth cannot be likened to the Heavenly ones.

A Persian Poet says:

کارِ زلفِ تُست مشک افشانی اما عاشقاں مصلحت را تهمتے برآ ہُوئے چیں بَستہ اَند

That sprinkling of musk is in fact the act of your looks; It is out of expediency that lovers accuse the Chinese deer (reported to yield musk).

A person who is often punished and only works because of the fear of receiving punishment, and encouraging him to do work is useless, will be benefited to know that one whose heart is empty of the Qur-aan, is like a ruined house (as mentioned in Hadith fifteen).

If a person is in search of the best form of all ibaadah and is careful to devote himself to that ibaadah which brings him the maximum reward, he should know that recitation of the Qur-aan Shareef is superior to all other forms of ibaadah, and it is specially mentioned in Hadith sixteen that it is superior to nafl Salaah, fasting, tasbeeh and tahleel (recitation of Kalimah Tayyibah).

Some people are deeply interested in pregnant animals, as they fetch more price than the ordinary ones. Rasulullah ﷺ has specifically said that the recitation of the Qur-aan Shareef is far more precious than such animals (see Hadith seventeen).

Many people are always worried about their health. They exercise by running or going for a walk in the morning and have a bath every day. There are others who suffer from worry and anxiety. Rasulullah ﷺ has said that Surah Fatihah provides treatment for every disease and the Qur-aan Shareef cures the sickness of the hearts.

People take pride in so many things that to list all is difficult, for example, some boast of their lineage or good habits, others of their popularity or foresight. Rasulullah ﷺ has said that the thing of real pride is the Qur-aan Shareef, which possesses all beauty and perfection.

As a Persian verse says:

آں چہ خوباں ہمہ دارند تو تنہا داری

"What all the other beloveds possess collectively, You alone possess all that." *(For this see Hadith twenty)*

Many people are fond of accumulating wealth. For this purpose, they practise miserliness in their food and dress, undergo many hardships and develop a craze that is not satisfied by any amount of wealth. Rasulullah ﷺ has advised us that the only thing that should be treasured as much as possible is the Qur-aan Shareef. No treasure of wealth is better than this (Hadith twenty-one refers to this).

Similarly, if anybody likes a bright environment and uses ten electric bulbs to light up his room, he should know that the Qur-aan Shareef provides the best of light. People have a desire to receive presents and they expect gifts from their friends every day. They try to get more friends only with this motive. If any of their friends does not send them their share of fruit from his garden, they complain about him. They should realise that the Qur-aan Shareef is the best giver of gifts. Peace descends on those who recite the Qur-aan Shareef. If you want someone to die due to him making demands on you, then the Qur-aan Shareef will take revenge on your behalf.

Some people flatter or praise the minister so that he may take their name in the court of the ruler and some flatter the workers of the minister so that they may praise him before the minister. Sometimes a person pleads with others so that they may mention his name in the presence of his beloved. Let all such people learn that through the Qur-aan Shareef, they may make themselves worthy of being mentioned by our beloved Allah Ta'ala Himself (see Hadith twenty-two).

If a person is always eager to know about the most favourite thing of the beloved and he is prepared to carry out even the most difficult task to get it, he should know that there is nothing more beloved to Allah Ta'ala than the Qur-aan Shareef. (We find this mentioned in Hadith twenty-three).

Some people want to have access to the court of the ruler, and with this object in mind, they plan and struggle all their lives. Through the Qur-aan Shareef we can become the special favourites of Allah Ta'ala, before Whom the greatest of kings is completely helpless. It is strange that in order to become a member of some council, or to join the hunting party of some man in authority, people make sacrifices of time, money and comfort. They use all sorts of tactics for approaching them and thereby spoil their Deeni as well as their worldly efforts, only for the sake of gaining some false honour. Is it then not necessary to make some effort to win the real honour by seeking it from Allah Ta'ala only? If they can spend their whole life in attaining the false honour of this world, we must spend at least a part of our lives in pleasing the Being Who gave us this life (see Hadith twenty-four).

If you are fond of *'Chistiyyat'* (one of the four branches of Sufism) and do not find comfort except in their Majlis (gatherings), you should know that gatherings for recitation of the Qur-aan are far more attracting to the heart and it also attracts the ears of the most unmindful person. If you want to attract the attention of our Great Master, you must devote yourself to the recitation of the Qur-aan Shareef (This is discussed in Ahaadith twenty-five and twenty-six).

If we declare ourselves to be Muslims and also feel proud of Islam, then we should know that it is the command of Rasulullah ﷺ that the Qur-aan Shareef should be recited in a suitable manner. If our Islam is not just lip service and it has really something to do with obedience to Allah Ta'ala and His Rasul ﷺ, then we should realise that Allah Ta'ala and Rasulullah ﷺ have commanded us to recite the Qur-aan Shareef.

If you are a staunch nationalist and love a Turkish hat because you consider it to be a part of your Islamic dress, or if you are interested in national culture and promoting it by all possible means, and if you write articles in the newspapers for this purpose and pass resolutions in public meetings, then you should know that Rasulullah ﷺ has commanded us to do our best to propagate the Qur-aan Shareef (see Hadith twenty-seven).

At this stage, it will not be out of place to express disappointment about the attitude of our national leaders in respect of the Qur-aan Shareef. They do not assist in its propagation but rather help in obstructing it. Learning the Qur-aan Shareef is looked upon by them as useless and a waste of time and effort. It is also considered an act whereby one uses his mind and physical effort in some useless work. It may be that some of them are not in favour of this attitude, but when a group of people are engaged in anti-Qur-aanic propaganda, silence on the part of our national leaders is just like helping them in the crime.

An Urdu poet says:

ہم نے مانا کہ تغافُل نہ کروگے لیکن   خاک ہو جائیں گے ہم تم کو خبر ہونے تک

We admit, you will not disregard us, but We will be reduced to dust, before you become aware.

There are many who claim that the Madrasah where the Qur-aan Shareef is taught is only promoted by the Ulama for earning their sustenance. This is a serious attack on the intentions of all such teachers and Ulama. Those who make such accusations are responsible for this slander, which they will have to prove in the Aakhirah. Such people are humbly requested to consider the results of the efforts of these so-called 'selfish teachers' and also what the results of their own unselfish ideas would be. Rasulullah ﷺ has commanded us to teach and propagate the Qur-aan Shareef. They should judge for themselves how far they have personally contributed in carrying out the command of Rasulullah ﷺ.

Their attention is drawn to another misunderstanding. Some people might think that they are not a party to this anti-Quranic propaganda and therefore remain unconcerned, but this cannot save them from the anger of Allah Ta'ala.

The Sahaabah رضى الله عنهم said to Rasulullah ﷺ;

اَنَهْلِكُ وَفِيْنَا الصَّالِحُوْنَ قَالَ نَعَمْ اِذَا كَثُرَ الْخَبَثُ (صحيح البخارى # 3346)

"Shall we be destroyed while there are righteous people amongst us."

Rasulullah ﷺ replied, "Yes (it will be so), when evil shall become widespread." There is another Hadith to the same effect where; "Allah Ta'ala ordered that a certain village should be overturned. Jibraa'eel *(alayhis salaam)* submitted that in that village there was a person who had never committed any sin. Allah Ta'ala said that it was true, however, in spite of him witnessing so much disobedience to Me (around him), there never appeared a frown on his face (in its disapproval)." In fact, it is because of these Ahaadith that the Ulama do not hesitate to point out the wrong when they see any disobedience to Allah Ta'ala being committed. It is unacceptable that some of our so-called intelligent people consider it to be narrow mindedness on the part of Ulama. This so-called broad-mindedness on the part of such people does not free them of their responsibility. They should understand that it is not the duty of the Ulama alone to check disobedience to the Commandments of Allah Ta'ala, but rather it is the duty of every Muslim who sees disobedience being committed and has the power to stop it.

Bilaal bin Sa'd رَضِيَ اللَّهُ عَنْهُ has said; "If evil deeds are committed secretly, only the evil-doers suffer for it, but if they are committed openly and nobody stops them, then all the people are punished."

There are some who are fond of history and they travel to consult old books of history wherever they may find them. Such people should rather devote themselves to the study of the Qur-aan Shareef, in which they will find information that will compare to all the books put together that are the most authentic on history. (Hadith twenty-eight refers to this).

If you want to acquire a high position that even the Ambiyaa *(alayhis salaam)* are asked to sit in your company and participate in your gathering, you can do so through the Qur-aan (Hadith twenty-nine refers to this).

If you are so lazy that you cannot do hard work, even then you can earn an honourable position without any hard work by means of the Qur-aan Shareef. You should sit down and keep listening silently to children reciting the Qur-aan Shareef in a Madrasah. Thereby you shall earn a lot of reward without any hard work on your part (This is referred to in Hadith Thirty).

If you are fond of variety, you can find it in the various ideas and different subjects of the Qur-aan Shareef, some dealing with mercy, others with punishment, some relating to different stories and others to various commandments and so on. You can also change your mode of recitation, low at times and loud at others (see Hadith thirty-one).

If your sins have exeeded all limits and you believe that you will die one day, Ahaadith thirty-two to thirty-four will encourage you to lose no time and start the recitation of the Qur-aan, because you can never find such an influential intercessor, whose intercession is certain to be accepted. On the other hand, if you are very respectful and your sense of respect and honour makes you avoid disputes with quarrelsome people, even at the cost of your valuable rights, you should try to avoid dispute with the Qur-aan on the Day of Qiyaamah, when it will be the strongest complainant, whose argument will be upheld and there will be nobody to defend you.

If you are in need of a guide who would lead you to the house of your beloved, and you would pay him any price for leading you, you should resort to the recitation of the Qur-aan Shareef. Again if you want to safeguard yourself against imprisonment, you have no way out except the recitation of the Qur-aan Shareef. (Hadith 34)

If you want to acquire the knowledge of the Ambiyaa *(alaihimus salaam)* and you are keen about its knowledge, Hadith thirty-five shows that you can specialise in it through study of the Qur-aan Shareef. Similarly, if you are keen to develop the best of character, you can do so through the recitation of the Qur-aan Shareef. (Hadith 35)

If you are very fond of mountainous areas and they alone provide you with the best recreation and satisfaction, you should know that the Qur-aan Shareef will provide recreation for you on mounds of musk on the Day of Qiyaamah, when the entire creation will be in a state of terror (Hadith thirty-six refers to this).

If you want to excel in the worship of Allah Ta'ala by remaining busy in Nafl Salaah day and night, you should know that teaching and learning the Qur-aan Shareef is a better means of doing so (See Hadith 37-39).

If you want to keep yourself away from all troubles and save yourself from all worries, you can do so simply by devoting yourself to the Qur-aan Shareef (This is pointed out in Hadith Forty).

CONCLUSION

1. If you need to consult a doctor, you should know that Surah Faatihah provides treatment for all diseases (see Hadith one of part two Concluding Section).

2. If your many daily needs remain unfulfilled, why should you not recite Surah Yaaseen (see Hadith two of part two, Concluding Section).

3. If you chase after money, you should read Surah Waaqi'ah (see Hadith three of Part two, Concluding Section).

4. If fear of punishment in the grave worries you, it can also be relieved by the Qur-aan Shareef (see Hadith four of Part two Concluding Section).

5. If you are looking for a profession that will keep you busy all the time, you can find none better than the Qur-aan Shareef (see Hadith five of Part two, Concluding Section).

6. If one has acquired the wealth of the Qur-aan Shareef, he should carefully guard it so as not to lose it. To lose such a blessing after acquiring it is a great tragedy.

7. He should also abstain from such unworthy acts as might convert this blessing into a curse (see Ahaadith six and seven of Part two, Concluding Section).

$$\text{وَمَا عَلَيْنَا اِلَّا الْبَلَاغُ}$$

I know that I am not capable enough to point out the beauties of the Glorious Qur-aan Shareef. I have explained them according to my humble understanding. However, this has opened up a field of contemplation for Ulama of deep understanding. According to those who are well versed in the art of love, the following five qualities of the beloved will arouse love. First, it is the existence of the beloved, which one loves. The passage of time does not change the Qur-aan Shareef, therefore this guarantees that it exists in all times and it is secure from any changes. Secondly, there should be a natural relationship between the lover and the beloved. The Qur-aan Shareef is the attribute of Allah Ta'ala. The relationship between the Creator and His creation, the Master and His servants, needs no explanation.

A Persian poet says:

The Creator of mankind has, with the life of Man, a connection that is incomprehensible and unimaginable.

An Urdu poet says:

He has a relationship of friendliness with all; He reaches out to the heart of each and everyone.

The third, fourth and fifth qualities are Jamaal (beauty), kamaal (perfection) and Ihsaan (kindness), respectively.

If the previous Ahaadith are studied, keeping the above three qualities in view, the Ulama will not be satisfied with what has been written by me, but they will themselves arrive at the conclusion that everything that promotes love and liking, such as the sense of respect and position, fondness and faithfulness, beauty and perfection, greatness and compassion, peace and pleasure, wealth and property, in short all such things that promote love are pointed out by Rasulullah ﷺ to be possessed in a wonderful way by the Glorious Qur-aan Shareef. It is but natural that some of these virtues may be hidden and may not be directly visible as is the case with most of the worldly valuables. We do not throw away a sweet litchi because of its rough outer cover. Nobody starts hating his beloved because she wears a purdah. He would try all possible means that she unveils herself. But if he does not succeed in unveiling her, the very sight of the purdah will excite him, provided he is sure that it is indeed his beloved behind the purdah. No doubt, the Qur-aan Shareef exceeds in all the virtues that bring about love, but if we fail to understand and realise those virtues due to some deficiency in us which then becomes a veil between us and the Qur-aan Shareef, then this veil should not make an intelligent person have a don't care attitude and become indifferent towards the Qur-aan Shareef. We should attribute this failure to our own shortcomings and feel sorry at our loss. We should think more and more about the beauties of the Qur-aan Shareef and become worthy of understanding the kitaab of Allah Ta'ala.

Usmaan ؓ and Huzaifah ؓ have reported that, if hearts become clean of all filth, then one would never be satisfied with reading the Qur-aan Shareef. Saabit Bunaani *(rahmatullahi alayh)* said, "I put in twenty years of effort to learn the Qur-aan Shareef and it has been giving me comfort for these twenty years." Thus it is obvious that whoever makes taubah over his sins and then ponders upon the Qur-aan Shareef, will find it to possess all the beauties that all the beloveds collectively possess.

I wish I were also such a person. However, I request the readers that they should not look at the humble personality of the writer, because it will prevent them from realising their objective, but they should consider the subject-matter and its source. I am only a means of drawing their attention to these important matters.

At this stage, it is just possible that some reader of this book might be blessed by Allah Ta'ala with a desire to learn the Qur-aan Shareef by heart and become a haafiz. If anyone has a desire to make his child a haafiz, then no special effort is required, because this tender age is most conducive to memorising the Qur-aan Shareef. But if some grown-up person desires to memorise the Qur-aan Shareef, I suggest that he should start with a special dua, which was recommended by Rasulullah ﷺ and has been found effective by many people. It has been reported by Tirmizi, Haakim and others *(rahmatullahi alayhim)* as follows:

Hadhrat Ibn Abbas رضي الله عنه reports that he was once in the company of Rasulullah ﷺ when Hadhrat Ali رضي الله عنه came in and said; "O, Nabi of Allah Ta'ala! You are dearer to me than my father and mother. I try to memorise the Qur-aan but cannot do so, as it disappears from my memory." Rasulullah ﷺ said; "Shall I tell you of a method that will benefit you as well as those to whom it is conveyed by you? You will then be able to remember whatever you learn." At the request of Hadhrat Ali رضي الله عنه Rasulullah ﷺ said; "When the night preceding Friday comes, rise up in its last third portion, if possible, for that would be excellent, because this is the best part of the night, as this is the time when Malaaikah come down and Duas are specially accepted at this time. It was for this time that Hadhrat Ya'qoob *(alayhis salaam)* had been waiting when he had said to his sons that he would, in the near future, pray to his Rabb for forgiveness for them. If it is difficult to get up at that time, then you should get up in the middle part of the night and if even that is not possible, offer the four rakaat in the early part of the night.

After reciting Surah Faatihah in each rakaat, Surah Yaaseen should be recited in the first rakaat, Surah Dukhaan in the second, Surah Alif Laam Meem Sajdah in the third and Surah Mulk (Tabarakal-Lazi) in the fourth. After completing *at-tahiyyaat* (glorification of Allah Ta'ala in the sitting posture in Salaat) you should praise and glorify Allah Ta'ala abundantly, send Durood on me and on all the Ambiyaa *(alayhimus* salaam) and seek forgiveness for all believers and those Muslims who have passed away before you, and then recite the following Dua."

Note: Before the dua it may be mentioned that several forms of hamd and sana (praise and glorification), etc., which are required to be recited before this dua are reported in other Ahaadith given in *'Shurooh-e-Hisn'* and *'Munaajaat Maqbul'*. Those who can consult these kitaabs should find the details themselves and thereby enrich their dua. For the convenience of those who cannot read these books, brief extracts are given hereunder:

اَلْحَمْدُ لِلّٰهِ رَبِّ الْعَالَمِيْنَ عَدَدَ خَلْقِهِ وَرِضٰى نَفْسِهِ وَزِنَةَ عَرْشِهِ وَمِدَادَ كَلِمَاتِهِ اَللّٰهُمَّ لَا اُحْصِىْ ثَنَاءً عَلَيْكَ اَنْتَ كَمَا اَثْنَيْتَ عَلٰى نَفْسِكَ اَللّٰهُمَّ صَلِّ وَسَلِّمْ وَبَارِكْ عَلٰى سَيِّدِنَا مُحَمَّدٍ النَّبِيِّ الْاُمِّيِّ الْهَاشِمِيِّ وَعَلٰى اٰلِهِ وَاَصْحَابِهِ الْبَرَرَةِ الْكِرَامِ وَعَلٰى سَائِرِ الْاَنْبِيَاءِ وَالْمُرْسَلِيْنَ وَالْمَلَائِكَةِ الْمُقَرَّبِيْنَ رَبَّنَا اغْفِرْ لَنَا وَلِاِخْوَانِنَا الَّذِيْنَ سَبَقُوْنَا بِالْاِيْمَانِ وَلَا تَجْعَلْ فِىْ قُلُوْبِنَا غِلًّا لِّلَّذِيْنَ اٰمَنُوْا رَبَّنَا اِنَّكَ رَءُوْفٌ رَّحِيْمٌ اَللّٰهُمَّ اغْفِرْ لِىْ وَلِوَالِدَىَّ وَلِجَمِيْعِ الْمُؤْمِنِيْنَ وَالْمُؤْمِنَاتِ وَالْمُسْلِمِيْنَ وَالْمُسْلِمَاتِ اِنَّكَ سَمِيْعٌ مُّجِيْبُ الدَّعْوَاتِ

All praise be to Allah Ta'ala, the Lord of the Worlds, praises up to the (countless) number of His creatures, matching His pleasure, weighty as the weight of His Throne and expansive as the ink (needed) for the writing of His Words. O, Allah Ta'ala! I cannot comprehend the praise due to You. You are as You have praised Yourself. O, Allah Ta'ala! Send Your peace, blessings and prosperity upon our leader, the Ummi (not taught by anyone), the Hashimite Nabi Muhammad and upon all the Ambiyaa and Rasuls and upon Your favourite Malaaikah. O, Allah Ta'ala! Forgive us and our brethren who preceded us in faith, and place not in our hearts any hatred towards those who believe. O our Lord! You are Most Compassionate and Most Merciful. O, Master of the Worlds! Forgive me and my parents and all believers and Muslims, whether male or female. Verily, You are the Hearer and Granter of our Duas.

After this, the following dua which was taught by Rasulullah ﷺ to Hadhrat Ali ؓ, as mentioned in the above Hadith, should be read:

اَللّٰهُمَّ ارْحَمْنِيْ بِتَرْكِ الْمَعَاصِيْ اَبَدًا مَّا اَبْقَيْتَنِيْ وَارْحَمْنِيْ اَنْ اَتَكَلَّفَ مَا لَا يَعْنِيْنِيْ وَارْزُقْنِيْ حُسْنَ النَّظَرِ فِيْمَا يُرْضِيْكَ عَنِّيْ اَللّٰهُمَّ بَدِيْعَ السَّمٰوَاتِ وَالْأَرْضِ ذَا الْجَلَالِ وَالْإِكْرَامِ وَالْعِزَّةِ الَّتِيْ لَا تُرَامُ اَسْئَلُكَ يَا اَللهُ يَا رَحْمٰنُ بِجَلَالِكَ وَنُوْرِ وَجْهِكَ اَنْ تُلْزِمَ قَلْبِيْ حِفْظَ كِتَابِكَ كَمَا عَلَّمْتَنِيْ وَارْزُقْنِيْ اَنْ اَتْلُوَهُ عَلَى النَّحْوِ الَّذِيْ يُرْضِيْكَ عَنِّيْ اَللّٰهُمَّ بَدِيْعَ السَّمٰوَاتِ وَالْأَرْضِ ذَا الْجَلَالِ وَالْإِكْرَامِ وَالْعِزَّةِ الَّتِيْ لَا تُرَامُ اَسْئَلُكَ يَا اَللهُ يَا رَحْمٰنُ بِجَلَالِكَ وَنُوْرِ وَجْهِكَ اَنْ تُنَوِّرَ بِكِتَابِكَ بَصَرِيْ وَاَنْ تُطْلِقَ بِهِ لِسَانِيْ وَاَنْ تُفَرِّجَ بِهِ عَنْ قَلْبِيْ وَاَنْ تَشْرَحَ بِهِ صَدْرِيْ وَاَنْ تَغْسِلَ بِهِ بَدَنِيْ فَاِنَّهُ لَا يُعِيْنُنِيْ عَلَى الْحَقِّ غَيْرُكَ وَلَا يُؤْتِيْهِ اِلَّا اَنْتَ وَلَا حَوْلَ وَلَا قُوَّةَ اِلَّا بِاللهِ الْعَلِيِّ الْعَظِيْمِ (سنن الترمذى # 3570)

O, Allah Ta'ala! Have mercy upon me, so that I always abstain from sinful deeds as long as I am alive, be kind to me so that I do not toil in vain pursuits, and bless me with solace in that which pleases You. O, Allah Ta'ala! The Originator of Heavens and Earth, Master of Glory and Honour, Lord of such Majesty, attainment of which cannot even be conceived. O, Allah Ta'ala! the Most Beneficent, I beg in the name of Your Majesty and the Noor of Your Countenance, to impose upon my heart the memorising of Your Book, as You have taught me the same, and grant me such a manner of recitation as pleases You. O; Allah Ta'ala! The Originator of Heavens and Earth, Master of Glory and Honour, Rabb of such Majesty, attainment of which cannot even be conceived! O, Allah Ta'ala, the Most Beneficent, I pray in the name of Your Majesty and the noor of Your Countenance, to brighten my vision with the noor of Your Book, bless my tongue with a flow in its reading, and, through its blessing, remove the heaviness of my heart, open my mind, and wash away (the sins of) my body. Certainly, there is none except You to support me in the cause of truth, and none except You can fulfil this desire of mine. There can be no safeguard (against evil) nor any power (over virtue) except with the help of Allah Ta'ala, the Most High, the Most Great.

Rasulullah ﷺ then said to Hadhrat Ali ؓ, "Repeat this act for three, five or seven Fridays. If Allah Ta'ala so wills, your Dua will certainly be granted. I swear by Him Who made me a Nabi that the acceptance of the Dua of a Muslim will never go unanswered."

Ibn Abbaas ؓ reports that hardly had five or seven Fridays passed when Hadhrat Ali ؓ came to Rasulullah ﷺ and said, "Previously I used to learn about four Aayaat but I was not able to remember them. Now I learn about forty Aayaat and I can remember them as clearly as if I have the Qur-aan Shareef open before me. Previously when I heard a Hadith and then repeated it, I could not remember it, but now when I hear Ahaadith and narrate them to others, I do not miss a single word."

May Allah Ta'ala bless both me and you with memorising of the Qur-aan Shareef and the Ahaadith by the mercy and tufail of His Nabi ﷺ.

وَصَلَّى اللهُ تَبَارَكَ وَتَعَالٰى عَلٰى خَيْرِ خَلْقِهِ سَيِّدِنَا وَمَوْلَانَا مُحَمَّدٍ وَّاٰلِهٖ وَصَحْبِهٖ وَسَلَّمَ بِرَحْمَتِكَ يَا اَرْحَمَ الرَّاحِمِيْنَ

O, Allah Ta'ala! By Your Mercy, send Your Peace and blessings on Muhammad ﷺ, the best of Your creation and our leader, and on his Family and on his Companions. You are the Most Compassionate of all the Most Merciful ones.

CHAPTER 4
40 AHAADITH OF HADHRAT SALMAAN ﷺ

The forty Ahaadith given in the previous pages relate to a special subject-matter and as such it has not been possible to keep it short. These days, we have become easy going and it is difficult to bear even slight hardships in the cause of Deen. In view of this, I give here another set of forty Ahaadith, which are very short and are reported at one place from Rasulullah ﷺ. The beauty about it is that it embraces all the vital teachings of Islam and is unique in this respect. It is given in *'Kanzul Ummaal'* and attributed to a group of the earliest Muhadditheen. Of the Ulama of later times, Moulana Qutbuddin Muhaajir Makki *(rahmatullahi alayh)* has also mentioned it. Let those having an eagerness for Deen, memorise at least this Hadith and earn a great reward for doing so little. This Hadith is given below:

عَنْ سَلْمَانَ رَضِىَ اللهُ عَنْهُ قَالَ سَأَلْتُ رَسُوْلَ اللهِ صَلَّى اللهُ عَلَيْهِ وَاٰلِهٖ وَسَلَّمَ عَنِ الْأَرْبَعِيْنَ حَدِيْثًا الَّتِىْ قَالَ مَنْ حَفِظَهَا مِنْ أُمَّتِىْ دَخَلَ الْجَنَّةَ فَقُلْتُ وَمَا هُوَ يَا رَسُوْلَ اللهِ قَالَ اَنْ تُؤْمِنَ بِاللهِ وَالْيَوْمِ الْاٰخِرِ وَالْمَلَائِكَةِ وَالْكُتُبِ وَالنَّبِيِّيْنَ وَالْبَعْثِ بَعْدَ الْمَوْتِ وَالْقَدْرِ خَيْرِهٖ وَشَرِّهٖ مِنَ اللهِ وَاَنْ تَشْهَدَ اَنْ لَّا اِلٰهَ اِلَّا اللهُ وَاَنَّ مُحَمَّدًا رَسُوْلُ اللهِ وَتُقِيْمَ الصَّلَاةَ بِوُضُوْءٍ سَابِغٍ لِّوَقْتِهَا وَتُؤْتِىَ الزَّكَاةَ وَتَصُوْمَ رَمَضَانَ وَتَحُجَّ الْبَيْتَ اِنْ كَانَ لَكَ مَالٌ وَتُصَلِّىَ اثْنَتَىْ عَشْرَةَ رَكْعَةً فِىْ كُلِّ يَوْمٍ وَّلَيْلَةٍ وَّالْوِتْرَ لَا تَتْرُكُهُ فِىْ كُلِّ لَيْلَةٍ وَّلَا تُشْرِكَ بِاللهِ شَيْئًا وَّلَا تَعُقَّ وَالِدَيْكَ وَلَا تَأْكُلَ مَالَ الْيَتِيْمِ ظُلْمًا وَّلَا تَشْرَبَ الْخَمْرَ وَلَا تَزْنِ وَلَا تَحْلِفَ بِاللهِ كَاذِبًا وَّلَا تَشْهَدَ شَهَادَةَ زُوْرٍ وَّلَا تَعْمَلَ بِالْهَوٰى وَلَا تَغْتَبَ اَخَاكَ الْمُسْلِمَ وَلَا

$$\text{تَقْذِفِ الْمُحْصَنَةَ وَلَا تَغُلَّ أَخَاكَ الْمُسْلِمَ وَلَا تَلْعَبْ وَلَا تَلْهَ مَعَ اللَّاهِينَ وَلَا تَقُلْ}$$
$$\text{لِلْقَصِيرِ يَا قَصِيرُ تُرِيدُ بِذَلِكَ عَيْبَهُ وَلَا تَسْخَرْ بِأَحَدٍ مِنَ النَّاسِ وَلَا تَمْشِ بِالنَّمِيمَةِ بَيْنَ}$$
$$\text{الْإِخْوَانِ وَاشْكُرِ اللهَ عَلَى نِعْمَتِهِ وَتَصْبِرْ عِنْدَ الْبَلَاءِ وَالْمُصِيبَةِ وَلَا تَأْمَنْ مِنْ عِقَابِ اللهِ}$$
$$\text{وَلَا تَقْطَعْ أَقْرِبَائَكَ وَصِلْهُمْ وَلَا تَلْعَنْ أَحَدًا مِنْ خَلْقِ اللهِ وَأَكْثِرْ مِنَ التَّسْبِيحِ}$$
$$\text{وَالتَّكْبِيرِ وَالتَّهْلِيلِ وَلَا تَدَعْ حُضُورَ الْجُمُعَةِ وَالْعِيدَيْنِ وَاعْلَمْ أَنَّ مَا أَصَابَكَ لَمْ يَكُنْ}$$
$$\text{لِيُخْطِيَكَ وَمَا أَخْطَاكَ لَمْ يَكُنْ لِيُصِيبَكَ وَلَا تَدَعْ قِرَاءَةَ الْقُرْآنِ عَلَى كُلِّ حَالٍ}$$

(اخرجه الرافعی فی التدوین 3/375-376)

Hadhrat Salmaan ﷺ narrates that he had asked Rasulullah ﷺ about the forty 'Ahaadith' concerning which he had said that, if anyone from amongst his Ummah memorised them, he would enter Jannah. I asked which Ahaadith are they? Rasulullah ﷺ replied: "You should believe:

(1) in Allah Ta'ala, i.e. in His Person and Attributes; and
(2) The Last Day; and
(3) The Malaaikah; and
(4) The earlier Divine Books; and
(5) All the Ambiyaa; and
(6) The life after death; and
(7) Destiny (Taqdeer), i.e. all that is good or bad is from Allah Ta'ala; and
(8) That you bear witness that there is none worthy of worship except Allah Ta'ala, and that Muhammad ﷺ is His Messenger; and
(9) That at the time of each Salaah, you perform the Salaah at its proper time after performing a perfect wudhu. And perfect wudhu is performed with keeping in mind the aadaab (etiquettes) and mustahabbaat (plural of mustahab desirable action). A fresh wudhu should preferably be performed at the time of each Salaah, although the previous wudhu would suffice, and this is mustahab. To make a good Salaah means to be mindful of the faraaidh, sunnan and mustahabaat. In another Hadith, it is said;

$$\text{إِنَّ تَسْوِيَةَ الصُّفُوفِ مِنْ إِقَامَةِ الصَّلَاةِ}$$ (صحیح البخاری # 723)

that during Salaah the saffs (rows) should be straight, i.e. the saffs should not be curved and there should be no gaps between the people. This is also included in the meaning of establishing Salaah.

(10) Pay the Zakaat (obligatory charity on wealth exceeding the nisaab); and
(11) Fast during the month of Ramadhaan; and
(12) Perform Hajj if you have wealth;
(The availability of wealth has particularly been mentioned, because the lack of wealth is generally made an excuse for not performing Hajj. Otherwise it is evident that the other requirements that make the ajj obligatory should also be fulfilled.)
(13) You should perform the twelve rakaats sunnat-e-mu'akkadah Salaah every day; (According to other Ahaadith these twelve rakaats are the two rakaats before the two fardh of Fajr Salaah, four rakaats before and two after the four fardh of Zuhr Salaah, two rakaats after the three fardh of Maghrib Salaah and two rakaats after the four fardh of Esha Salaah).
(14) You should never miss the Witr Salaah at night; Witr Salaah is waajib (compulsory, but less than fardh and more important than sunnat) and is, therefore, specially emphasised;
(15) You should not ascribe partners unto Allah Ta'ala;
(16) You should not disobey your parents;
(17) You should not use the property of orphans unjustly; (Unjustly implies that there is no harm in using the belongings of an orphan in a lawful manner, as is the case under certain circumstances.)
(18) You should not drink wine;
(19) You should not commit adultery;
(20) You should not take false oaths;
(21) You should not give false evidence;
(22) You should not give in to your base desires (nafs);
(23) You should not backbite a Muslim brother;
(24) You should not slander a pure chaste woman (or a chaste man);
(25) You should not have ill feelings towards your Muslim brethren;
(26) You should not indulge in play and futile activities
(27) You should join those who involve themselves in useless amusemnets

(28) You should not call a short person; "O, you short one!" with the intention of finding fault with him; (there is no harm in a person being called by a nickname which has become associated with him, provided that the nickname is neither used to tease nor as a term of abuse. Using it to tease is not permissible.)
(29) You should not indulge in jokes at the cost of others;
(30) You should not indulge in slander amongst Muslims;
(31) You should be ever grateful to Allah Ta'ala for His bounties;
(32) You should be steadfast in suffering and calamity;
(33) You should not be unmindful of the punishment of Allah Ta'ala;
(34) You should not cut family ties with your relatives;
(35) You should maintain good family ties with your relatives;
(36) You should not curse any creation of Allah Ta'ala;
(37) You should make the zikr and glorify Allah Ta'ala by repeating the words **Subhaanallaah, Al-hamdulillaah** (all praise is for Allah Ta'ala), **Laa ilaaha illallaah** (there is no god but Allah Ta'ala) and **Allaahu Akbar** frequently;
(38) You should not miss the Friday and Eid Salaah;
(39) You should believe that whatever difficulty or ease befalls you was predestined and could not be avoided, and whatever you have missed, would have never come to you; and
(40) You should not give up the recitation of the Qur-aan Shareef under any circumstances."

Hadhrat Salmaan رَضِىَ اللهُ عَنْهُ says that he asked Rasulullah ﷺ: "What reward would be given to one who memorises these Ahaadith?" Rasulullah ﷺ said, "Allah Ta'ala will raise him up in the company of the Ambiyaa (alayhis salaam) and the Ulama."

May Allah Ta'ala, through His Grace, forgive all our sins and include us in the company of His obedient servants by His mercy alone. This is not beyond His generous grace. The readers are humbly requested to remember this sinner in their duas.

وَمَا تَوْفِيْقِىْ إِلَّا بِاللهِ عَلَيْهِ تَوَكَّلْتُ وَإِلَيْهِ أُنِيْبُ

(Hadhrat Moulana) Muhammad Zakariyya Kandhlavi (RA),
Mazahirul-Uloom Saharanpur.
29 Zul Hijjah 1348 HIJRI.

فضائلِ صلاة

Virtues of Salaah

Contents

Author's Foreword 370
Importance of Salaah 371

PART 2

CHAPTER 1 THE REWARDS FOR PERFORMING SALAAH   373

Hadith 1 – Five fundemental aspects of Islam 373
Hadith 2 - Salaah makes ones sins fall off like leaves in autumn 374
Taubah is Necessary for Forgivenss of Major Sins 375
Hadith 3 - Salaah makes the sins fall off like leaves 375
The virues of using a miswaak 377
Hadith 4 (a) - Salaah washes off sins just as bathing in a stream washes off dirt and dust 378
Hadith 4 (b) 378
Hadith 5 - Turning to Salaah in all difficulties 380
Salaatul Haajah 382
The Story of a Porter 383
Hadith 6 - Fardh Salaah eliminates ones sins 384
Hadith 7 – One who performs Salaah entering Jannah before a Shaheed 386
Hadith 8 – Extingusihing the fire of Jahannam through Salaah 388
Hadith 9 – Guarantee of entering Jannah through Salaah 389
Hadith 10 - Two rakaats of Salaah is more valuable than thousands of Rands 390
The final bequest of Rasulullah ﷺ 391
The virtues of Ishraaq Salaah 391

40 Ahaadith explaining the importance and virtues of Salaah 392

CHAPTER 2 WARNINGS FOR NEGLECTING SALAAH   399

Hadith 1 – The barrier between a person and kufr is Salaah ... 399
Hadith 2 – 7 advices of Rasulullah ﷺ 400
Hadith 3 – Allah Ta'ala does not care for someone who neglects his Fardh Salaah 401
Tarbiyat of children and Emphasis on Salaah 402
Hadith 4 – Missing a Salaah is like losing one's family and wealth 403
Hadith 5 – Delaying Salaah is a major sin 403
Hadith 6 – Salaah is a defense in the Aakhirah 404
Hadith 7 – Five favours for a person who is mindful of his Salaah 406
Those who will go to Jannah without any hisaab 410

Ishraaq Salaah 412
Tahiyyatul Wudhu 414
Hadith 8 – Making your Salaah Qadhaa 415
Hadith 9 – Salaah is like the head in the body 417

PART 2

CHAPTER ONE REWARDS FOR PERFORMING SALAAH WITH JAMAAT   420

Hadith 1 – Salaah with Jamaat is twenty-seven times better 420
Hadith 2 – Salaah with Jamaat is twenty-five times better 422
Hadith 3 – Importance of Salaah in the Masjid 425
Hadith 4 – The first Takbeer 426
Hadith 5 – Trying to get Salaah with Jamaat 427
Hadith 6 – The bigger the congregation, the more the reward 428
Hadith 7 – Going to the Masjid in the hours of darkness 429

CHAPTER TWO WARNINGS FOR NOT PERFORMING SALAAH WITH JAMAAT   433

Hadith 1 – Performing Salaah in the Masjid after hearing the Azaan .. 433
Hadith 2 – Not going to the Masjid after hearing the Azaan 434
Hadith 3 – Setting fire to the houses of those who perform their Salaah at home 435
Hadith 4 – Making Jamaat out in the fields 436
Hadith 5 – The importance of Fardh over Nafl 437
Hadith 6 - Aayaat revealed about Fardh Salaah in the scriptures of Allah Ta'ala 437

PART 3

CHAPTER 1 AAYAAT FROM THE QUR-AAN SHAREEF   441

Aayah 1 - It is your Taqwa that reaches Allah Ta'ala 441
Aayah 2 – Curse on those who are unmindful of their Salaah 442
Aayah 3 – To perform Salaah lazily 442
Aayah 4 – People who destroy their Salaah will be thrown into Jahannam 442
Aayah 5 – The Salaah of a lazy person 443
Aayah 6 – Those who are concerned about Salaah will get Jannatul Firdaus 443
Aayah 7 – Humility in Salaah 444
Aayah 8 – Rewards for those who are not distracted by business 444
Aayah 9 – The faithful slaves of Allah Ta'ala 445
Aayah 10 – Leaving their beds to worship Allah 446

Aayah 11 – Reward for those who sleep little 447
Aayah 12 – Those who devote themselves to ibaadah at night 447
Aayah 13 – Qualities of man 447

CHAPTER TWO A FEW STORIES FROM THE LIVES OF THE PIOUS 450

Story 1 – A saint performs Esha and Fajr Salaah for forty years with the same wudhu 450
Story 2 – A saint sees women in a dream making the zikr of Allah Ta'ala 450
Story 3 – A saint goes to sleep at night without standing up for Ibaadah 451
Story 4 – A saint is reminded to get up and recite the Qur-aan in Tahajjud 451
Story 5 – Salaah of a slave girl 451
Story 6 – Another incident of a slave girl 452
Story 7 – Crying of a slave girl in Tahajjud Salaah 452
Story 8 – A porter stops work at the time of Salaah 453
Story 9 – The leg of a pious person is amputated whilst performing Salaah 454
Story 10 – A slave girl dies whilst reciting Qur'aan in Salaah 454
Story 11 – The sacrifices of a Sayyed 454
Story 12 – Salaah of Umar-bin-Abdul Aziz *(rahmatullahi alayh)* 455
Story 13 – Imaam Ahmad bin Hambal *(rahmatullahi alayh)* 456
Story 14 – The crying of Muhammad-bin-Munkadir *(rahmatullahi alayh)* in Tahajjud Salaah 456
Story 15 – Saabit Bunaani *(rahmatullahi alayh)* performs Salaah in the grave 457

Salaah of the Pious 457

CHAPTER 3 QUOTATIONS FROM AHAADITH 460

Hadith 1 – Rewards for Salaah is in proportion to one's sincerity 460
Hadith 2 – A perfect Salaah purifies one from sins 461
Hadith 3 – Nafl acts will compensate for the deficiency in the Fardh .. 462
Hadith 4 – The first thing to be questioned about on the day of Qiyaamah will be Salaah 464
Hadith 5 – Stealing in Salaah 465
Hadith 6 – Prohibition of moving about in Salaah 466
Hadith 7 – Salaah saves one from shameful acts 468
Hadith 8 – The virtues of reading long rakaats in Salaah 470

There are 12 000 virtues in Salaah 473
The Translation of Sanaa and its Significance 476

Incidents of the pious and their fear for Allah 477

1. Hadhrat Hasan's رَضِىَاللهُعَنْهُ preparation for Salaah 477
2. The Salaah of Zainul Aabideen *(rahmatullahi alayh)* 478
3. The reaction of Hadhrat Ali رَضِىَاللهُعَنْهُ at the time of Salaah 478
4. The reaction of Hadhrat Abdullah bin Abbaas رَضِىَاللهُعَنْهُ on hearing the Azaan 478
5. The Salaah of Zunnoon Misri *(rahmatullahi alayh)* 479
6. Uwais Qarni *(rahmatullahi alayh)* spending the night in ruku or sajda 479
7. I'saam *(rahmatullahi alayh)* asks Haatim Zaahid Balkhi *(rahmatullahi alayh)* how he read his Salaah 479
8. Sa'eed bin Musayyab *(rahmatullahi alayh)* in the Masjid before Azaan 480
9. Muhammad bin Waasi *(rahmatullahi alayh)* loves Salaah with jamaat 480
10. The attack of shaytaan on Hadhrat Abu Ubaidah bin Jarraah رَضِىَاللهُعَنْهُ while he was in Salaah 480
11. Maimoon bin Mahraan *(rahmatullahi alayh)* misses Jamaat 480
12. Speak to Allah Ta'ala at any time you desire 481
13. The behaviour of Rasulullah ﷺ at the time of Salaah 481
14. Sa'eed Tannookhi *(rahmatullahi alayh)* crying in Salaah 481
15. Khalaf bin Ayyub *(rahmatullahi alayh)* is not distracted in Salaah 481
16. Salaah more valuable than worldly possessions 482
17. Arrow removed from the thigh of Ali رَضِىَاللهُعَنْهُ whilst he was in Salaah 482
18. The talking of family members does not distract Muslim bin Yasaar *(rahmatullahi alayh)* in Salaah 482
19. Aamir bin Abdullah *(rahmatullahi alayh)* in the thoughts of Aakhirah in Salaah 482
20. A limb is amputated whilst performing Salaah 483
21. A pious man is not distracted by the thoughts of this world in Salaah 483
22. Shaikh busies himself in Salaah and Zikr 483
23. A saint spends the night in Salaah 484

Final appeal 484
An Important Note 485

Author's Foreword

بِسْمِ اللَّهِ الرَّحْمَنِ الرَّحِيمِ

نَحْمَدُهُ وَنَشْكُرُهُ وَنُصَلِّيْ عَلٰى رَسُوْلِهِ الْكَرِيْمِ وَعَلٰى اٰلِهِ وَصَحْبِهِ وَاَتْبَاعِهِ الْحُمَاةِ لِلدِّيْنِ الْقَوِيْمِ وَبَعْدُ: فَهٰذِهِ اَرْبَعُوْنَةٌ فِيْ فَضَائِلِ الصَّلَاةِ جَمَعْتُهَا اِمْتِثَالًا لِاَمْرِ عَمِّيْ وَصِنْوُ اَبِيْ رَقَّاهُ اللّٰهُ اِلَى الْمَرَاتِبِ الْعُلْيَا وَوَفَّقَنِيْ وَاِيَّاهُ لِمَا يُحِبُّ وَيَرْضٰى اَمَّا بَعْدُ:

"We glorify Allah Ta'ala and ask for blessings and salaams on His noble Rasul ﷺ, his Sahaabah رضي الله عنه and those who follow him in upholding the cause of the right Deen."

The indifference of Muslims towards practising Deen these days is too well known. So much so that even Salaah, which is the most important pillar of Islam (after Imaan) and the first and foremost thing to be questioned for on the Day of Qiyaamah, is being badly neglected. Although every call to Islam, nowadays, seems to be only a cry in the wilderness, yet experience shows that efforts in this direction are not altogether unsuccessful. The Ahaadith of Nabi ﷺ are sure to benefit those with an open and obedient frame of mind. With this idea in mind and to comply with the long-standing request of some of my seniors, I have taken upon myself to write this book, which is the second of the series on 'Tabligh', the first one being, *'Virtues of Tabligh'*.

وَمَا تَوْفِيْقِيْ اِلَّا بِاللّٰهِ ۚ عَلَيْهِ تَوَكَّلْتُ وَاِلَيْهِ اُنِيْبُ

"And my ability is only from Allah Ta'ala! Only on Him do I rely and only to Him do I turn." (Surah Hood - Aayah 88)

The present-day Muslims can be divided into three groups, as far as their commitment towards Salaah is concerned.

1. A large number of them are totally unmindful of their Salaah.

2. Then you get quite a few of them who observe their Salaah, but are not particular about Jamaat.

3. Then there are those who are regular with their Salaah (with Jamaat), but take no care as far its quality and demands are concerned.

Therefore I have divided this book into three parts to suit the requirements of each group. In each part, the illustrious Ahaadith of the Nabi ﷺ are quoted with their simple translation. It is not a word to word translation but rather the overall meaning is given. Explanatory notes have been added wherever necessary. The names of the books of Hadith from which the quotations are taken have also been mentioned for reference.

IMPORTANCE OF SALAAH

There are two Chapters in this part. The first one is on Importance of Salaah and the second of Warnings for those who neglect or discard Salaah.

PART 1

IMPORTANCE OF SALAAH

CHAPTER 1
THE REWARDS FOR PERFORMING SALAAH

HADITH 1 – FIVE FUNDAMENTAL ASPECTS OF ISLAM

عَنِ ابْنِ عُمَرَ رَضِيَ اللهُ عَنْهُ قَالَ قَالَ رَسُوْلُ اللهِ صَلَّى اللهُ عَلَيْهِ وَسَلَّمَ بُنِيَ الْإِسْلَامُ عَلَى خَمْسٍ شَهَادَةِ اَنْ لَّا اِلٰهَ اِلَّا اللهُ وَاَنَّ مُحَمَّدًا رَسُوْلُ اللهِ وَاِقَامِ الصَّلَاةِ وَاِيْتَاءِ الزَّكَاةِ وَصَوْمِ رَمَضَانَ وَحَجِّ الْبَيْتِ (اخرجه المنذري فى الترغيب # 521)

Hadhrat Abdullah bin Umar ﷺ narrates that he heard Rasulullah ﷺ saying: "Islam is based on five pillars; Believing that there is no god but Allah, and Muhammad ﷺ is His servant and messenger; establishment of Salaah; paying of Zakaat; fasting in Ramadhaan; and performance of Haj."

Note: Rasulullah ﷺ has compared Islam to a tent resting on five supports. The Kalimah is the central support and the other four pillars of Islam are the remaining four supports; one at each corner of the tent. Without the central support, the tent cannot possibly stand. If any one of the corner supports is missing, then that corner will collapse. Now, let us judge for ourselves how much we have kept up the tent of Islam. Is there really any pillar that is being held in its proper place?

The five pillars of Islam mentioned in this Hadith explain the most important duties of a Muslim. Although a Muslim cannot do without any one of them, Salaah in Islam holds second position after Imaan. Hadhrat Abdullah bin Mas'ood ﷺ says: "Once, I asked Rasulullah ﷺ which act (of man) was the dearest to Allah Ta'ala? Rasulullah ﷺ replied, 'Salaah'. I then asked which act came next (in order of importance) and Rasulullah ﷺ replied, 'Kindness to parents'. I again asked what was next. He answered, Jihaad."

Mulla Ali Qaari *(rahmatullahi alayh)* has used this Hadith in support of the belief that Salaah is the most important duty after Imaan. This is further supported by a Hadith, in which Nabi ﷺ says:

اَلصَّلَاةُ خَيْرُ مَوْضُوعٍ (اخرجه العسقلانی فی فتح الباری 3/479)

"Salaah is the best of all that has been commanded by Allah Ta'ala."

This topic has been discussed clearly in many other Saheeh Ahaadith that the best of all actions is that of Salaah. It is for this reason that in Jaamius Sagheer, Hadhrat Sawbaan, Ibn Amr, Salamah, Abu Umaamah and Ubaadah *(radiyallahu anhum)* have narrated this Hadith. Hadhrat Ibn Masood ﷺ and Hadhrat Anas ﷺ have narrated that the greatest action is to perform one's salaah in its correct time. It has been narrated from Hadhrat Ibn Umar ﷺ and Umm-e-Farwa ﷺ that one should read one's salaah in the awwal waqt (immediately when the time sets in). The objective of all is about the same.

HADITH 2 - SALAAH MAKES ONES SINS FALL OFF LIKE LEAVES IN AUTUMN

عَنْ أَبِي ذَرٍّ رَضِيَ اللهُ عَنْهُ أَنَّ النَّبِيَّ صَلَّى اللهُ عَلَيْهِ وَسَلَّمَ خَرَجَ فِي الشِّتَاءِ وَالْوَرَقُ يَتَهَافَتُ فَأَخَذَ بِغُصْنٍ مِّنْ شَجَرَةٍ قَالَ فَجَعَلَ ذَلِكَ الْوَرَقُ يَتَهَافَتُ فَقَالَ يَا أَبَا ذَرٍّ قُلْتُ لَبَّيْكَ يَا رَسُوْلَ اللهِ قَالَ إِنَّ الْعَبْدَ الْمُسْلِمَ لَيُصَلِّى الصَّلَاةَ يُرِيْدُ بِهَا وَجْهَ اللهِ فَتَهَافَتُ عَنْهُ ذُنُوْبُهُ كَمَا يَتَهَافَتُ هَذَا الْوَرَقُ عَنْ هَذِهِ الشَّجَرَةِ

(اخرجه المنذری فی الترغیب # 560)

"Hadhrat Abu Zar ﷺ narrates that once Rasulullah ﷺ came out of his house. It was winter and the leaves were falling off the trees. He caught hold of a branch of a tree and its leaves began to drop

in large numbers. While doing this he said, 'O, Abu Zar ﷺ! When a Muslim performs his Salaah to please Allah Ta'ala, his sins fall away from him just as these leaves are falling off this tree.'"

Note: In winter, usually, the leaves of the trees fall in large numbers, that on some trees not a single leaf is left behind. The same is the effect of Salaah performed with sincerity and devotion. All the sins of the person offering Salaah are wiped off.

TAUBAH IS NECESSARY FOR FORGIVENSS OF MAJOR SINS

However, it should be remembered that according to the Ulama, it is only the minor sins that are forgiven by the performance of Salaah and other acts of ibaadah. The major sins are not forgiven without taubah. Therefore, in addition to performing Salaah, we should be particular about making *taubah* (repentance) and *istighfaar* (seeking forgiveness). Allah Ta'ala, by His bountiful Grace, may also forgive the major sins of any person because of his Salaah.

HADITH 3 - SALAAH MAKES THE SINS FALL OFF LIKE LEAVES

عَنْ أَبِي عُثْمَانَ رَحِمَهُ اللهُ قَالَ كُنْتُ مَعَ سَلْمَانَ رَضِيَ اللهُ عَنْهُ تَحْتَ شَجَرَةٍ فَأَخَذَ غُصْنًا مِنْهَا يَابِسًا فَهَزَّهُ حَتَّى تَحَاتَّ وَرَقُهُ ثُمَّ قَالَ يَا أَبَا عُثْمَانَ أَلَا تَسْأَلُنِيْ لِمَ أَفْعَلُ هٰذَا قُلْتُ وَلِمَ تَفْعَلُهُ قَالَ هٰكَذَا فَعَلَ بِيْ رَسُوْلُ اللهِ صَلَّى اللهُ عَلَيْهِ وَسَلَّمَ وَأَنَا مَعَهُ تَحْتَ شَجَرَةٍ وَأَخَذَ مِنْهَا غُصْنًا يَابِسًا فَهَزَّهُ حَتَّى تَحَاتَّ وَرَقُهُ فَقَالَ يَا سَلْمَانُ أَلَا تَسْأَلُنِيْ لِمَ أَفْعَلُ هٰذَا قُلْتُ وَلِمَ تَفْعَلُهُ قَالَ إِنَّ الْمُسْلِمَ إِذَا تَوَضَّأَ فَأَحْسَنَ الْوُضُوْءَ ثُمَّ صَلَّى الصَّلَوَاتِ الْخَمْسَ تَحَاتَّتْ خَطَايَاهُ كَمَا تَحَاتَّ هٰذَا الْوَرَقُ وَقَالَ وَأَقِمِ الصَّلٰوةَ طَرَفَيِ النَّهَارِ وَزُلَفًا مِنَ الَّيْلِ ۚ إِنَّ الْحَسَنٰتِ يُذْهِبْنَ السَّيِّاٰتِ ۚ ذٰلِكَ ذِكْرٰى لِلذَّاكِرِيْنَ (اخرجه المنذرى فى الترغيب # ٥٣٨)

Hadhrat Abu Usmaan (rahmatullahi alayh) says: "I was once sitting under a tree with Hadhrat Salmaan ﷺ. He caught hold of a dry branch of a tree and shook it till all its leaves fell off. He then said to me, 'O, Abu Usmaan! Will you not ask me why I am doing this?' 'Do tell me,' I replied. He said, 'Rasulullah ﷺ had done exactly like this before me, while I was with him under a tree. He caught a dry branch and shook it, till all its leaves fell off.' At this he said: 'O, Salmaan! Will you not ask me why I am doing this?' I replied: 'Do tell me why you are doing this?' He remarked: 'Verily, when a Muslim makes wudhu properly and then reads his Salaah five times a day, his sins fall off just as these leaves have fallen off.' He then recited the following aayah of the Qur-aan Shareef:

وَأَقِمِ الصَّلٰوةَ طَرَفِي النَّهَارِ وَزُلَفًا مِنَ الَّيْلِ ۚ إِنَّ الْحَسَنٰتِ يُذْهِبْنَ السَّيِّاٰتِ ۚ ذٰلِكَ ذِكْرٰى لِلذّٰكِرِيْنَ

'Establish Salaah at the two ends of the day, and during portions of the night. Verily, good deeds wipe out evil acts. This is advice to those who will take heed.'" *(Surah Hud - Aayah 114)*

Note: The behaviour of Hadhrat Salmaan ﷺ in the above Hadith shows the deep love which the Sahaabah ﷺ had for Rasulullah ﷺ. They would often remember the sweet memories of the time when Rasulullah ﷺ was living amongst them. While quoting him, they would do exactly what they had seen him doing at a particular moment.

It is really very difficult to cover all the Ahaadith of Rasulullah ﷺ, which deal with the importance of Salaah and which declare forgiveness for those who guard it. As had already been said before, the Ulama restrict the asking of forgiveness to minor sins only, but, in the wording of the Hadith, there is no such restriction. My learned father gave me two reasons for this. Firstly, a devoted Muslim will not commit any major sins, and if perhaps any major sins are committed by him, then he will not be able to rest in peace (due to the fear of Allah Ta'ala in him) until he washes them with his tears of taubah in crying before Allah Ta'ala. Secondly, the person who performs his Salaah properly with sincerity, does make istighfaar a number of times daily. Look for instance at the closing Dua of Salaah:

اَللّٰهُمَّ اِنِّيْ ظَلَمْتُ نَفْسِيْ ظُلْمًا كَثِيْرًا وَّلَا يَغْفِرُ الذُّنُوْبَ اِلَّا اَنْتَ فَاغْفِرْ لِيْ مَغْفِرَةً مِّنْ عِنْدِكَ وَارْحَمْنِيْ اِنَّكَ اَنْتَ الْغَفُوْرُ الرَّحِيْمُ (سنن النسائى # 7663)

"O, My Lord! I have wronged myself a great wrong, and none forgives sins but You alone. Please forgive me and have mercy on me. Verily, You are the Most Forgiving, and Most Merciful."

THE VIRUES OF USING A MISWAAK

In the above Hadith, mention is made of wudhu to be done properly. We should, therefore, be sure of the rules of wudhu and try to make it correctly. For example, using a miswaak is a Sunnah of wudhu, but is very often left out. It is said in a Hadith that the Salaah offered after making miswaak is seventy times more rewarding than the Salaah performed without making miswaak. In another Hadith, the use of miswaak has been encouraged very strongly. These are some of the benefits of using miswaak:

1. It cleans the mouth.
2. It makes Allah Ta'ala happy
3. It displeases shaytaan.
4. Allah Ta'ala and His Malaaikah love the person who makes miswaak.
5. It strengthens the gums
6. It clears out phlegm.
7. It creates a good smell in the mouth.
8. It clears out bile.
9. It improves the eye sight.
10. It removes the stench from the mouth.

The most important benefit is that, "It is the Sunnah of our beloved Rasulullah ﷺ."

As many as seventy virtues of the miswaak have been counted by the Ulama. It is said that a person who is in the habit of making miswaak dies with the Kalimah Shahaadat on his lips.

On the other hand, there are 70 harms of taking opium (kind of drug) one of which is that at the time of death one will not remember to read the kalimah.

The rewards of making wudhu properly are many. It is mentioned in the Ahaadith that the parts of the body that are washed in wudhu shall shine on the Day of Qiyaamah and by this (sign), Rasulullah ﷺ will at once recognise his followers.

HADITH 4 (A) - SALAAH WASHES OFF SINS JUST AS BATHING IN A STREAM WASHES OFF DIRT AND DUST

عَنْ اَبِيْ هُرَيْرَةَ رَضِيَ اللهُ عَنْهُ قَالَ سَمِعْتُ رَسُوْلَ اللهِ صَلَّى اللهُ عَلَيْهِ وَسَلَّمَ يَقُوْلُ اَرَاَيْتُمْ لَوْ اَنَّ نَهْرًا بِبَابِ اَحَدِكُمْ يَغْتَسِلُ فِيْهِ كُلَّ يَوْمٍ خَمْسَ مَرَّاتٍ هَلْ يَبْقٰى مِنْ دَرَنِهٖ شَيْءٌ قَالُوْا لَا يَبْقٰى مِنْ دَرَنِهٖ شَيْءٌ قَالَ فَذٰلِكَ مَثَلُ الصَّلَوَاتِ الْخَمْسِ يَمْحُو اللهُ بِهِنَّ الْخَطَايَا (سنن النسائى # 319)

Hadhrat Abu Hurayrah رضي الله عنه narrates that once Rasulullah ﷺ asked the Sahaabah رضي الله عنهم, "Do you believe that dirt can remain on a person who has a bath five times a day in a stream flowing in front of his door?" "No", replied the Sahaabah رضي الله عنهم, "No dirt can remain on his body." Rasulullah ﷺ said: "So, exactly similar is the effect of Salaah offered five times a day. With the Grace of Allah Ta'ala, it washes away all sins."

HADITH 4 (B)

عَنْ جَابِرٍ رَضِيَ اللهُ عَنْهُ قَالَ قَالَ رَسُوْلُ اللهِ صَلَّى اللهُ عَلَيْهِ وَسَلَّمَ مَثَلُ الصَّلَوَاتِ الْخَمْسِ كَمَثَلِ نَهْرٍ جَارٍ غَمْرٍ عَلٰى بَابِ اَحَدِكُمْ يَغْتَسِلُ مِنْهُ كُلَّ يَوْمٍ خَمْسَ مَرَّاتٍ (صحيح مسلم # 668)

Hadhrat Jaabir رَضِىَ اللّٰهُ عَنْهُ narrates that he heard Rasulullah صَلَّى اللّٰهُ عَلَيْهِ وَسَلَّمَ saying: *"The example of the five daily Salaah is like a deep stream flowing in front of the door of a person who has a bath in it five times a day."*

Note: Running water is generally free from dirt and the deeper it runs the cleaner and purer it is. A bath in such water surely removes dirt from the body and makes it clean. Salaah performed properly, keeping in mind all the etiquettes of Salaah, also cleanses the soul of all sins. There are many Ahaadith with the same meaning, but with slight differences in narration, narrated by different Sahaabah of Rasulullah صَلَّى اللّٰهُ عَلَيْهِ وَسَلَّمَ. Hadhrat Abu Sa'eed Al-Khudri رَضِىَ اللّٰهُ عَنْهُ narrates that he heard Rasulullah صَلَّى اللّٰهُ عَلَيْهِ وَسَلَّمَ saying: *"Each of the five Salaah cancels the sins committed since the Salaah before it."*

To explain, let us take the case of a person working in a factory. His job is such that his body gets covered with dust. But there are five streams of running water in-between the factory and his house. When he is returning, he takes a bath in each stream. The effect of the five daily Salaah is very similar. Any sins committed between two Salaahs are forgiven because of the *istighfaar* and *taubah* in each Salaah.

Through such examples Rasulullah صَلَّى اللّٰهُ عَلَيْهِ وَسَلَّمَ is showing us that Salaah has the wonderful power of removing sins. If we fail to attain the mercy, grace and kindness of Allah Ta'ala, then surely we ourselves are the losers.

To make a mistake is human. We are likely to commit many sins and deserve the punishment of Allah Ta'ala, but look how forgiving Allah is. He has most beautifully shown us the way to earn His mercy and forgiveness. It is a great misfortune if we do not take advantage of this great favour. Allah Ta'ala is always eager to shower us with His mercy for every small wrong we do.

It is said in a Hadith, that if a person goes to bed with the intention of getting up for Tahajjud and somehow does not wake up, he receives the full reward for Tahajjud, although he has been enjoying his sleep at the time of Tahajjud. How wonderful is the grace of Allah Ta'ala? What a tremendous loss if we do not receive blessings from Him?

HADITH 5 - TURNING TO SALAAH IN ALL DIFFICULTIES

عَنْ حُذَيْفَةَ رَضِىَ اللهُ عَنْهُ قَالَ كَانَ رَسُوْلُ اللهِ صَلَّى اللهُ عَلَيْهِ وَسَلَّمَ اِذَا حَزَبَهُ اَمْرٌ فَزِعَ اِلَى الصَّلَاةِ (اخرجه السيوطى فى الدر المنثور 1/163)

Hadhrat Huzayfah ﷺ says, "Whenever Rasulullah ﷺ happened to face any difficulty, he would at once turn to Salaah."

Note: Salaah is a great blessing of Allah Ta'ala. To turn to Salaah at the time of worry is to hasten towards His mercy. When the mercy of Allah Ta'ala comes to our rescue, there can remain absolutely no worry. There are many Ahaadith concerning this practice of Rasulullah ﷺ. Similar was the practice of the Sahaabah ﷺ, who followed him in every small thing. Hadhrat Abu Darda ﷺ says: "Whenever a strong wind blew, Rasulullah ﷺ would immediately enter the Masjid and would not leave until the wind had stopped." Similarly, at the time of a solar or lunar eclipse, Rasulullah ﷺ would begin offering Salaah.

Hadhrat Suhaib ﷺ was informed by Rasulullah ﷺ that all the previous Ambiyaa of Allah Ta'ala *(alayhimus salaam)* also turned to Salaah in all difficulties.

Hadhrat Ibn Abbaas ﷺ was once on a journey. On his way he received the news of the death of his son. He got down from his camel and performed two rakaats of Salaah, sitting in *tashahhud* for a long time. He then recited '*Innaa lillaahi wa innaa ilaihi raaji-oon*' and said, "I have done what Allah Ta'ala has ordered us to do in the Qur-aan Shareef, that is;

وَاسْتَعِيْنُوْا بِالصَّبْرِ وَالصَّلٰوةِ

"Seek Allah's help with patience and Salaah" (Surah Baqarah - Aayah 45)

Another similar story is narrated about him. He was once on a journey when he received the news about the death of his brother, Qusum. He got down from his camel by the roadside and performed two rakaats of Salaah and kept sitting in Tashahhud for a long time. After finishing his

Salaah, he rode his camel, reciting the following Aayah of the Qur-aan Shareef:

$$وَاسْتَعِيْنُوْا بِالصَّبْرِ وَالصَّلٰوةِ ۚ وَاِنَّهَا لَكَبِيْرَةٌ اِلَّا عَلَى الْخٰشِعِيْنَ$$

"Seek Allah's help with patience and Salaah. Truly this is indeed difficult except for the humble ones." (Surah Baqarah - Aayah 45)

There is also another story about him. On hearing about the demise of one of the wives of Nabi ﷺ, he fell down in sajdah. When somebody asked him the reason he said, "Our dear Nabi ﷺ had ordered us to make sajdah (in Salaah) whenever we were faced with a calamity. What calamity can be greater than the death of one of the Ummul Mu'mineen?"

When Hadhrat Ubaadah رضى الله عنه was about to breathe his last, he said to the people around him, "I prohibit everyone from crying over me. When my rooh (soul) departs, I ask everyone to perform wudhu, observing all its etiquettes, to go to the masjid and make dua for my forgiveness, because our Merciful Allah Ta'ala has enjoined on us to, 'Seek help with patience and Salaah.' After that, lay me down in my grave."

Hadhrat Abdur Rahmaan رضى الله عنه, the husband of Hadhrat Umm-e-Kulsoom *(raidiyallahu anha)*, fell ill. Once, he fell into a state of unconsciousness that everyone around him thought that he had passed away. Hadhrat Umm-e-Kulsoom *(radiyallahu anha)* stood up and started to perform Salaah. After she completed her Salaah, Hadhrat Abdur Rahmaan رضى الله عنه regained consciousness. He asked the people if it seemed that he had passed away. The people replied, "Yes" He then said, "Two angels came to me and said, 'Come with us to Allah Ta'ala. Your condition will be decided over there.' They began to take me with them when suddenly a third angel appeared and said to the two of them that they should go away as he is from those people whom good fortune has been written for him from the time he was in the stomach of his mother. His children are still to take benefit from him." He remained alive for another month thereafter and then only did he pass away.

Hadhrat Nadhr *(rahmatullahi alayh)* narrates, "Once it became very dark during the day in Madinah Munawwarah. I hurriedly went to

Hadhrat Anas ﷺ to find out if he had ever experienced similar conditions during the lifetime of Rasulullah ﷺ. He said to me, 'Ma'aazallaah! During those blessed days, whenever the wind blew strong, we would hurry to the Masjid, fearing that it should be the coming of the Last Day.'"

Hadhrat Abdullah bin Salaam ﷺ narrates that whenever the members of the family of Rasulullah ﷺ experienced difficulty, Rasulullah ﷺ would instruct them to perform Salaah, and would recite the following Aayat of the Qur-aan:

وَ أْمُرْ أَهْلَكَ بِالصَّلٰوةِ وَ اصْطَبِرْ عَلَيْهَا ۖ لَا نَسْـَٔلُكَ رِزْقًا ۖ نَحْنُ نَرْزُقُكَ ۗ وَالْعَاقِبَةُ لِلتَّقْوٰى

"And instruct your family to perform Salaah and you yourself remain steadfast on it. We do not ask you to provide sustenance, but We provide it for you. And the best result (rewards in the Aakhirah) is for adopting Taqwa." *(Surah Tahaa - Aayah 132)*

SALAATUL HAAJAH

It is mentioned in a Hadith that when somebody has a need, whether it is of this life or the Aakhirah, whether it concerns Allah Ta'ala or some person, he should make a perfect wudhu and offer two rakaats of Salaah, glorify Allah Ta'ala and then send Durood on Nabi ﷺ, and then make the following dua:

لَا إِلٰهَ إِلَّا اللهُ الْحَلِيْمُ الْكَرِيْمُ سُبْحَانَ اللهِ رَبِّ الْعَرْشِ الْعَظِيْمِ الْحَمْدُ لِلهِ رَبِّ الْعَالَمِيْنَ أَسْأَلُكَ مُوْجِبَاتِ رَحْمَتِكَ وَعَزَائِمَ مَغْفِرَتِكَ وَالْغَنِيْمَةَ مِنْ كُلِّ بِرٍّ وَّالسَّلَامَةَ مِنْ كُلِّ إِثْمٍ لَا تَدَعْ لِيْ ذَنْبًا إِلَّا غَفَرْتَهُ وَلَا هَمًّا إِلَّا فَرَّجْتَهُ وَلَا حَاجَةً هِيَ لَكَ رِضًا إِلَّا قَضَيْتَهَا يَا أَرْحَمَ الرَّاحِمِيْنَ

(سنن الترمذى # 479)

"There is no god besides Allah, the Clement, the Bountiful. Glorified be Allah, the Lord of the tremendous throne. Praise be to Allah, the Lord of the worlds. I ask You all that leads to Your Mercy and deserves Your forgiveness. I ask You abundance in all that is good and refuge *from all that is evil. Leave me no sin but You pardon it, and no distress but You remove it, and no need but You fulfil it. O the most Merciful of those who show mercy!"*

THE STORY OF A PORTER

Wahb bin Munabbih *(rahmatullahi alayh)* writes: "Have your needs fulfilled by Allah Ta'ala through Salaah. In the past, if people were afflicted by a calamity or difficulty, they would hurry towards Salaah."

It is said that a porter (delivery man), who lived in Kufa, was well known for his honesty. People trusted him with their valuables and money, which he carried from one place to another. Once he was doing his job as usual when a person met him and asked him where he was going. The person said, "I am also going to the same place. If I could walk, I would have accompanied you on foot. Will you kindly give me a ride on your donkey for one Dinar?" The porter agreed and allowed him to share the donkey with him. They then arrived at a crossing.

The person asked, "Which road will you take?" "The main road, of course," replied the porter. The person said. "No brother, we should go by the other road which is a shortcut and there is plenty of grass to feed the animal." The porter said, "I have never been on this road." The person remarked, "I have travelled on this road many times." The porter believed him and proceeded. After some distance, the road ended in a terrifying forest where a large number of dead bodies were lying about. The person suddenly jumped off the donkey, drew out his knife, intending to kill the porter. "Stop", shouted the porter, "Take the animal and its load, but do not kill me." The porter begged him but the person refused to listen. He wanted to kill the porter and take the animal and the goods.

Seeing that the robber was not going to listen, the porter said to him, "All right, if you must kill me, then allow me to perform two rakaats of Salaah." The person agreed and remarked, "You can please yourself. All the dead you see made the same request. Their Salaah did not help them." The porter began his Salaah but could not remember any Surah to read after Surah Faatihah. Meanwhile the person grew impatient and angrily asked him to hurry up with his Salaah. All of a sudden, this Aayah flashed in his mind;

$$\text{اَمَّنْ يُّجِيْبُ الْمُضْطَرَّ اِذَا دَعَاهُ وَ يَكْشِفُ السُّوْٓءَ}$$

"Is it not He who responds to the distressed (helpless) person when he calls out to Him (for help), and removes the evil. . ."
(Surah Naml – Aayah 62)

Whilst the porter was reciting the Aayah, tears welled up in his eyes. Just then a horseman suddenly appeared on the scene. He was wearing a shining helmet and held a spear in his hand. He stabbed the merciless thief and killed him. A flame of fire rose from the spot where the body of the thief fell. The porter fell down in sajdah and thanked Allah Ta'ala. After finishing his Salaah, he ran towards the horseman and asked him who he was. He replied. "I am a slave of Allah Ta'ala who answers the wronged one. You are now safe and can go wherever you like." Saying this, the horseman rode away and disappeared.

Indeed, Salaah is a great gift. Besides pleasing Allah Ta'ala, it often saves us from the problems of this life and provides us with peace of mind. Ibn Seereen *(rahmatullahi alayh)* writes: "If I was allowed to choose between Jannah and a Salaah of two rakaats, I would prefer Salaah. The reason is quite clear. Jannah is for my own pleasure while Salaah is for the pleasure of my beloved Allah Ta'ala."

Nabi ﷺ has said: "Enviable is that Muslim who has little burden (i.e. of the world. He does not have much family and wealth etc.), he has lots of salaah in his life, he remains satisfied with what is provided for him, he makes the ibaadat of Allah Ta'ala with full devotion, he remains unkown to people and dies an early death, leaving very little behind and very few to mourn him."

It is mentioned in a Hadith that Rasulullah ﷺ said: "Offer your Salaah at your homes frequently, so that it may be blessed with the Grace and Mercy of Allah Ta'ala." (This refers to nafl Salaah).

HADITH 6 - FARDH SALAAH ELIMINATES ONES SINS

عَنْ اَبِىْ مُسْلِمٍ التَّغْلِبِىِّ قَالَ دَخَلْتُ عَلٰى اَبِىْ اُمَامَةَ رَضِىَ اللهُ عَنْهُ وَهُوَ فِى الْمَسْجِدِ فَقُلْتُ يَا اَبَا اُمَامَةَ اِنَّ رَجُلًا حَدَّثَنِىْ عَنْكَ اَنَّكَ سَمِعْتَ رَسُوْلَ اللهِ صَلَّى اللهُ عَلَيْهِ وَسَلَّمَ

يَقُوْلُ مَنْ تَوَضَّأَ فَأَسْبَغَ الْوُضُوْءَ فَغَسَلَ يَدَيْهِ وَوَجْهَهُ وَمَسَحَ عَلٰى رَأْسِهٖ وَأُذُنَيْهِ ثُمَّ قَامَ اِلٰى صَلَاةٍ مَفْرُوْضَةٍ غَفَرَ اللهُ لَهٗ فِىْ ذٰلِكَ الْيَوْمِ مَا مَشَتْ اِلَيْهِ رِجْلَاهُ وَقَبَضَتْ عَلَيْهِ يَدَاهُ وَسَمِعَتْ اِلَيْهِ اُذُنَاهُ وَنَظَرَتْ اِلَيْهِ عَيْنَاهُ وَحَدَّثَ بِهٖ نَفْسُهٗ مِنْ سُوْءٍ فَقَالَ وَاللهِ قَدْ سَمِعْتُهٗ مِنَ النَّبِيِّ صَلَّى اللهُ عَلَيْهِ وَسَلَّمَ مِرَارًا (اخرجه المنذرى فى الترغيب # 532)

Abu Muslim (rahmatullahi alayh) narrates: "I went to see Abu Umaamah رضى الله عنه while he was in the Masjid. I asked him if he had heard Rasulullah ﷺ saying, 'When a person performs wudhu properly and then reads his Fardh Salaah, Allah Ta'ala forgives all the sins he committed that day by his feet in going towards evil, by his hands in doing evil, by his ears in listening to evil, by his eyes in looking at evil and by his heart in thinking of evil.' He replied, 'By Allah, I have heard these words from Rasulullah ﷺ again and again.'"

Note: Many of the Sahaabah رضى الله عنهم viz. Hadhrat Usmaan رضى الله عنه, Hadhrat Abu Hurayrah رضى الله عنه, Hadhrat Anas رضى الله عنه, Hadhrat Abdullah Sanaabihi رضى الله عنه, Hadhrat Amr ibn Abasah رضى الله عنه and others have narrated this Hadith with slight differences. Those who are gifted with the power of Kashf can even witness the sins falling away.

It is said about Imaam Abu Haneefah *(rahmatullahi alayh)* that he could tell from the water falling down from the limbs of the person performing wudhu as to which sins had been washed off.

In a Hadith narrated by Hadhrat Usmaan رضى الله عنه that, Rasulullah ﷺ has warned people against committing sins in the hope of getting them forgiven through Salaah. We have absolutely no reason to behave like that. After all, what is the quality of the Salaah that we perform? If Allah Ta'ala only accepts our Salaah, it is His very special favour and grace. We would be very ungrateful if we disobey Allah Ta'ala just because He is Merciful and Forgiving.

HADITH 7 – ONE WHO PERFORMS SALAAH ENTERING JANNAH BEFORE A SHAHEED

عَنْ أَبِي هُرَيْرَةَ رَضِيَ اللهُ عَنْهُ قَالَ كَانَ رَجُلَانِ مِنْ بَلِيٍّ حَيٌّ مِنْ قُضَاعَةَ أَسْلَمَا مَعَ رَسُوْلِ اللهِ صَلَّى اللهُ عَلَيْهِ وَسَلَّمَ فَاسْتُشْهِدَ أَحَدُهُمَا وَأُخِّرَ الْآخَرُ سَنَةً قَالَ طَلْحَةُ بْنُ عُبَيْدِ اللهِ فَرَأَيْتُ الْمُؤَخَّرَ مِنْهُمَا أُدْخِلَ الْجَنَّةَ قَبْلَ الشَّهِيْدِ فَتَعَجَّبْتُ لِذٰلِكَ فَأَصْبَحْتُ فَذَكَرْتُ ذٰلِكَ لِلنَّبِيِّ صَلَّى اللهُ عَلَيْهِ وَسَلَّمَ أَوْ ذُكِرَ لِرَسُوْلِ اللهِ صَلَّى اللهُ عَلَيْهِ وَسَلَّمَ فَقَالَ أَلَيْسَ قَدْ صَامَ بَعْدَهُ رَمَضَانَ وَصَلَّى سِتَّةَ الْآفِ رَكْعَةٍ وَّكَذَا وَكَذَا رَكْعَةَ صَلَاةِ سَنَةٍ (اخرجه المنذري في الترغيب # 548)

Hadhrat Abu Hurayrah ؓ narrates, "Two people of one tribe came to Rasulullah ﷺ and accepted Islam together. One of them was made shaheed (martyred) in a battle and the other died a year later. Hadhrat Talha bin Ubaidullah ؓ says that he saw in his dream that the person who had died later entered Jannah before the shaheed (martyr). This surprised him. I do not remember whether it was he or somebody else who narrated this dream." Rasulullah ﷺ then said: "Has not the person dying later fasted for one additional month of Ramadhaan, and has he not read more than 6000 rakaats of Salaah during the year he lived after the shaheed (martyr)?"

Note: If we have to say that each month in the year has 29 days and we have to only count the rakaats of the fardh and witr salaah, it will amount to 20 rakaats. That alone will amount to 6960 rakaats. And those months that have 30 days, you will increase the rakaats for each of those days. And if you have to count the rakaats of the sunnat and nafal salaah, then how much will that amount to?

In Ibnu Majah this incident has been mentioned with more detail. Hadhrat Talha ؓ, who saw the dream, narrates that two men from one tribe once came to Rasulullah ﷺ. They both accepted Islam together. One was very brave and courageous. He was martyred in a battle. The other man passed away a year later. I saw myself at the entrance of Jannah and both of them were standing there. One person came from inside and said to the one who passed away a year later that he has permission to enter and the one who was made Shaheed was still waiting there. After some time another person came from inside and permitted the Shaheed to also enter. He then said to me, "Your time for entry has not yet come. You should go back now." In the morning I mentioned my dream to the people. Everyone was amazed as to why the Shaheed was given permission to enter later on, whereas he should have entered first. Eventually they went to Rasulullah ﷺ and mentioned the dream to him. Rasulullah ﷺ mentioned, "What is there for you to be so surprised about?" The people said, "Ya Rasulullah! The first person was Shaheed and he had more courage and bravery and here we see that the second person entered before him." Rasulullah ﷺ said, "Did he not make ibaadat for one extra year." They replied, "Yes." He further mentioned, "Did he not fast for one extra Ramadhaan?" They replied, "Yes. Most definitely." He further mentioned, "Did he not make so many more sajdahs in the one year." They replied, "Yes, indeed." Rasulullah ﷺ then said, "Between them is the difference of the skies and the earth." This incident has been narrated by many other people as well.

Abu Dawood Shareef mentions a similar incident of two Sahaabah رضي الله عنها who passed away 8 days apart. The second person passed away one week later. He still entered Jannah before the other person. In reality we do not know how valuable Salaah is. There must have been a reason why Rasulullah ﷺ was often heard saying, *"The comfort of my eyes is in Salaah."* This is an expression of his deep love for Salaah. What else can be more valuable than Salaah?

It is mentioned in one Hadith that there were two brothers. One passed away 40 days before the other. The first brother was known for his piety and people had lots of respect for him. Rasulullah ﷺ asked, "Was the second brother not a Muslim? The Sahaabah *(radiyallahu anhum)* mentioned, "Yes, he was a Muslim but an ordinary Muslim." Rasulullah ﷺ mentioned, "What do you know that these 40 days of Salaah that he had performed would have taken him to such great heights." Salaah is like the example of a sweet and deep river which flows in front of one's door. Is it ever possible for dirt to remain on the body of the person who bathes in this river five times a day?" Again Rasulullah ﷺ mentioned, that "What do you know as to what heights he must have reached through the extra Salaah he performed."

HADITH 8 – EXTINGUSIHING THE FIRE OF JAHANNAM THROUGH SALAAH

عَنْ عَبْدِ اللهِ بْنِ مَسْعُوْدٍ رَضِىَ اللهُ عَنْهُ عَنْ رَسُوْلِ اللهِ صَلَّى اللهُ عَلَيْهِ وَسَلَّمَ أَنَّهُ قَالَ يُبْعَثُ مُنَادٍ عِنْدَ حَضْرَةِ كُلِّ صَلَاةٍ فَيَقُوْلُ يَا بَنِىْ اٰدَمَ قُوْمُوْا فَاَطْفِئُوْا مَا اَوْقَدْتُّمْ عَلٰى اَنْفُسِكُمْ فَيَقُوْمُوْنَ فَيَتَطَهَّرُوْنَ وَيُصَلُّوْنَ الظُّهْرَ فَيُغْفَرُ لَهُمْ مَّا بَيْنَهُمَا فَاِذَا حَضَرَتِ الْعَصْرُ فَمِثْلُ ذٰلِكَ فَاِذَا حَضَرَتِ الْمَغْرِبُ فَمِثْلُ ذٰلِكَ فَاِذَا حَضَرَتِ الْعَتَمَةُ فَمِثْلُ ذٰلِكَ فَيَنَامُوْنَ فَمُدْلِجٌ فِىْ خَيْرٍ وَمُدْلِجٌ فِىْ شَرٍّ (اخرجه المنذرى فى الترغيب # 529)

Hadhrat Abdullah Ibn Mas'ood ؓ narrates that he heard Rasulullah ﷺ saying: "When the time of Salaah comes close, an Angel announces, 'Get up, O children of Aadam (mankind), and put out the fire that you have lit (by doing sins) to burn yourselves.' So, the (pious) people rise up, perform wudhu and offer their Zuhr Salaah. This causes forgiveness of their sins committed since sunrise. The same is repeated at Asr, Maghrib and Esha. After Esha people go to bed, but there are some who busy themselves in good, while others are busy in evil deeds."

Note: The meaning of this Hadith has been mentioned in many other Hadith kitaabs that Allah Ta'ala, through His Mercy, forgives the sins of those who perform Salaah. It has been mentioned previously that due to Istighfaar being present in Salaah, both the minor and major sins are forgiven by Allah Ta'ala. The condition for the forgiveness of major sins is to have sincere regret in the heart.

Allah Ta'ala Himself says in the Qur-aan Shareef as it has already been explained under Hadith three;

$$\text{وَأَقِمِ الصَّلٰوةَ طَرَفِيِ النَّهَارِ وَزُلَفًا مِّنَ الَّيْلِ ۚ اِنَّ الْحَسَنٰتِ يُذْهِبْنَ السَّيِّاٰتِ}$$

"Establish Salaah at the two ends of the day, and during portions of the night. Verily, good deeds wipe out evil acts." *(Surah Hood - Aayah 114)*

Hadhrat Salmaan ؓ who is a famous Sahaabi, says, "After Esha, people are divided into three groups. There are some for whom the night is a source of blessings and gain. They are those who spend it in the *ibaadah* (worship) of Allah Ta'ala, while others are asleep. For them the night brings great rewards from Allah Ta'ala. There are others who turn their night into a curse for themselves, since they commit sins in the darkness of the night. To them the night brings curses and misery. Then, there is the third group of people who go to bed immediately after Esha. They neither gain nor lose."

HADITH 9 – GUARANTEE OF ENTERING JANNAH THROUGH SALAAH

$$\text{عَنْ أَبِيْ قَتَادَةَ بْنِ رِبْعِيٍّ رَضِىَ اللهُ عَنْهُ قَالَ قَالَ رَسُوْلُ اللهِ صَلَّى اللهُ عَلَيْهِ وَسَلَّمَ قَالَ اللهُ تَبَارَكَ وَتَعَالَى اِنِّيْ افْتَرَضْتُ عَلٰى أُمَّتِكَ خَمْسَ صَلَوَاتٍ وَعَهِدْتُّ عِنْدِيْ عَهْدًا اَنَّهُ مَنْ حَافَظَ عَلَيْهِنَّ لِوَقْتِهِنَّ اَدْخَلْتُهُ الْجَنَّةَ فِيْ عَهْدِيْ وَمَنْ لَّمْ يُحَافِظْ عَلَيْهِنَّ فَلَا عَهْدَ لَهُ عِنْدِيْ}$$

(اخرجه السيوطى فى الدر المنثور 1/704)

Hadhrat Abu Qataadah bin Rab'iyy ؓ says that he heard Rasulullah ﷺ saying: "Allah Ta'ala has said, 'O Muhammad ﷺ! I have fixed five times daily Salaah for your followers. I have made a promise with myself that whoever is regular in performing his Salaah in its correct time, shall be admitted into Jannah. Those of your followers who do not guard their Salaah, are not included in this promise."

Note: In another Hadith, it is said that Allah Ta'ala has fixed five times Salaah, and whosoever is mindful of his Salaah by making wudhu properly and performing it in its correct time with sincerity and devotion is assured by Allah Ta'ala of entry into Jannah. Whoever does not guard his Salaah, there is no such guarantee for him. He may or may not be forgiven. Salaah has indeed great value. It gives us an opportunity to receive the guarantee of Allah Ta'ala for Jannah.

When an honourable person who is wealthy or someone who has some position or power gives us a guarantee for fulfilling any of our worldly requirements, we feel quite satisfied and happy and we consider it our duty to remain grateful and dedicated to him. Allah Ta'ala, who is the only king of both the worlds, is giving us the guarantee for the real success after death in return for five times daily Salaah, which does not involve much effort on our part. If even then we do not take benefit of the opportunity, we cannot blame anyone besides ourselves for the dreadful punishment that awaits us.

HADITH 10 - TWO RAKAATS OF SALAAH IS MORE VALUABLE THAN THOUSANDS OF RANDS

عَنِ ابْنِ سَلْمَانَ اَنَّ رَجُلًا مِّنْ اَصْحَابِ النَّبِيِّ صَلَّى اللهُ عَلَيْهِ وَسَلَّمَ حَدَّثَهُ قَالَ لَمَّا فَتَحْنَا خَيْبَرَ اَخْرَجُوْا غَنَائِمَهُمْ مِّنَ الْمَتَاعِ وَالسَّبْيِ فَجَعَلَ النَّاسُ يَتَبَايَعُوْنَ غَنَائِمَهُمْ فَجَاءَ رَجُلٌ فَقَالَ يَا رَسُوْلَ اللهِ لَقَدْ رَبِحْتُ رِبْحًا مَّا رَبِحَ الْيَوْمَ مِثْلَهُ اَحَدٌ مِّنْ اَهْلِ هٰذَا الْوَادِىْ قَالَ وَيْحَكَ وَمَا رَبِحْتَ قَالَ مَا زِلْتُ اَبِيْعُ وَاَبْتَاعُ حَتّٰى رَبِحْتُ ثَلَاثَ مِائَةِ اُوْقِيَّةٍ فَقَالَ رَسُوْلُ اللهِ صَلَّى اللهُ عَلَيْهِ وَسَلَّمَ اَنَا اُنَبِّئُكَ بِخَيْرِ رَجُلٍ رَبِحَ قَالَ مَا هُوَ يَا رَسُوْلَ اللهِ قَالَ رَكْعَتَيْنِ بَعْدَ الصَّلَاةِ (سنن ابی داود # 2785)

Ibn Salmaan (rahmatullahi alayh) says that he heard one of the Sahaabah of Rasulullah ﷺ narrating, "When we had won the battle of Khaibar, we began to buy and sell the booty, that we had received, amongst ourselves. One of us went to Nabi ﷺ and said, 'O, Nabi of Allah, no one has earned so much profit as I have in today's business.' 'How much did you earn?' asked Rasulullah ﷺ. He replied, 'I kept on selling and buying till I earned a total profit of 300 Awqiyyah of silver.' Rasulullah ﷺ said, *'Shall I inform you of something better than that?'* He replied, *'Do tell me, O, Nabi of Allah!'* Rasulullah ﷺ remarked *'Two rakaats nafl after the (fardh) Salaah.'"*

Note: 300 Awqiyyah of silver is equivalent to about 3000 Rupees. According to Nabi ﷺ, the money of this world cannot compare with the everlasting gain of the Aakhirah. Our life will be prosperous if we build our Imaan to the level that two rakaats of Salaah is more valuable in our sight than all the riches of this world.

THE FINAL BEQUEST OF RASULULLAH ﷺ

Salaah is really a great treasure and that is why Rasulullah ﷺ has called it 'the comfort of his eyes'. He had been commanding us to read Salaah right up to His last breath. Ummu Salamah ﷺ narrates that the last words of Rasulullah ﷺ, which he could hardly utter, were regarding guarding the Salaah and kindness towards the slaves. There is a similar Hadith narrated by Hadhrat Ali ﷺ as well.

THE VIRTUES OF ISHRAAQ SALAAH

Once, Rasulullah ﷺ sent a group of Sahaabah ﷺ in Jihaad towards Najd. They returned victorious very quickly with lots of booty. When Rasulullah ﷺ saw the people envying them and wondering at their quick bargain, he said, "Shall I inform you of a group of people who earn much more in a much shorter time? They are those who perform their Fajr with Jamaat and then remain seated till a little while after sunrise and thereafter read two rakaats of Salaah."

According to Shaqeeq Balkhi *(rahmatullahi alayh)*, a very famous Shaikh, we can acquire five things by doing five things; an increase in provisions through 'Chaasht' (Nafl Salaah before midday), a light in the grave through Tahajjud, correct answers to Munkar and Nakeer (the Malaaikah who will question us in our graves) through the recitation of the Qur-aan, an easy crossing of Siraat (the bridge over Jahannam) through fasting and charity, and a place under the shade of the Throne of Allah Ta'ala on the Day of Qiyaamah through seclusion.

40 Ahaadith Explaining the Importance and Virtues of Salaah

In the books of Hadith, there are many sayings of Rasulullah ﷺ about Salaah and its rewards and virtues. It is very difficult to cover all of them in this small book.

A few of them are mentioned below:

1. "Salaah is the first command of Allah Ta'ala upon my Ummah, and it shall be the first thing to be questioned about on the Day of Qiyaamah."

2. "Fear Allah Ta'ala in the matter of Salaah! Fear Allah Ta'ala in the matter of Salaah! Fear Allah Ta'ala in the matter of Salaah!"

3. "Salaah comes in-between a person and Shirk."

4. "Salaah is the sign of Islam. A person who reads his Salaah at the correct time with sincerity and devotion, following all its rules including the Mustahabbaat (those acts that are preferable to do), is surely a Mu'min."

5. "Of all things that have been commanded by Allah Ta'ala, Imaan and Salaah are the most valued. If there was anything better than Salaah, Allah Ta'ala would have commanded it for His Malaaikah, some of whom are always in ruku and others in sajdah."

6. "Salaah is the pillar of Islam."

7. "Salaah disgraces shaytaan."

8. "Salaah is the light of a Believer."

9. "Salaah is the best Jihaad."

10. "When a person commences his Salaah, Allah Ta'ala turns His full attention towards him and when he terminates his salaah Allah Ta'ala also turns away His attention from him."

11. "When a calamity descends from the skies, people who regularly go to the Masjid are saved."

12. "If a person lands himself in Jahannam due to some reason, the fire will not burn those limbs of his body which have touched the ground while he was in sajdah during his Salaah."

13. "Fire has been forbidden by Allah Ta'ala upon those limbs of the body which touch the ground while performing sajdah."

14. "Of all the practices, Salaah read at the correct time is most loved by Allah Ta'ala."

15. "Allah Ta'ala likes the posture of a person most when he is in sajdah, pressing his forehead on the ground in humility."

16. "A person in sajdah is nearest to Allah Ta'ala."

17. "Salaah is the key to Jannah."

18. "When a person stands in Salaah, the gates of Jannah are opened and all the veils between him and Allah Ta'ala are raised (provided he does not spoil his Salaah by coughing, etc.)."

19. "A person in Salaah knocks at the divine door of Allah Ta'ala, and the door is always opened for him who knocks on it."

20. "The position of Salaah in Islam is like the position of the head in the body."

21. "Salaah is the light of the heart. Let those who wish, brighten their hearts (through Salaah)."

22. "If a person wishes to have his sins forgiven by Allah Ta'ala, he should perform wudhu properly, perform two or four rakaats of Fardh or Nafl Salaah, with devotion, and then make dua to Allah Ta'ala. Allah Ta'ala will forgive him."

23. "Any piece of land on which Allah Ta'ala is remembered in Salaah, takes pride over the rest of the earth."

24. "Allah Ta'ala accepts the dua of a person who makes dua to Him after having performed two rakaats of Salaah. Allah Ta'ala grants him what he asks for, sometimes immediately and sometimes (for his own good) later."

25. "A person who performs two rakaats of Salaah alone, where nobody except Allah Ta'ala and His Malaaikah see him, receives a certificate of being saved from Jahannam."

26. "Allah Ta'ala accepts the dua of a person after each Fardh Salaah."

27. "Jahannam is forbidden and Jannah becomes compulsory for a person who performs his wudhu properly and performs his Salaah properly."

28. "Shaytaan remains scared of a Muslim provided he is particular about his Salaah. As soon as he neglects it, shaytaan gets hold of him and tries his best to mislead him."

29. "The most excellent practice is to perform Salaah in its awwal waqt (first time)."

30. "Salaah is an act of sacrifice for every pious person."

31. "Salaah performed in its awwal waqt (first time) is a practice most liked by Allah Ta'ala."

32. "At dawn, some people go to the Masjid and some to the market. Those going to the Masjid carry the flag of Imaan and those leaving for the market carry the flag of shaytaan."

33. "The four rakaats before Zuhr have the same reward as the four rakaats of Tahajjud."

34. "The four rakaats before Zuhr are counted equal (in reward) to the four rakaats of Tahajjud."

35. "The Mercy of Allah Ta'ala is directed towards a person standing in Salaah."

36. "Salaah at night (when everyone is asleep) is most virtuous, but there are very few who observe it."

37. "Jibraa-eel *(alayhis salaam)* came to me and said, O, Muhammad ﷺ! However long you live, you will die one day. Whoever you may love, you will leave him one day. Surely, you will receive the reward of whatever (good or evil) you do. No doubt, the honour of a believer is in Tahajjud and his respect is in contentment and staying away (from sin)."

38. "Two rakaats in the late hours of the night are more valuable than all the riches of this world. But for fear of hardship on my followers, I would have made it compulsory."

39. "Keep offering Tahajjud Salaah. It is the way of the pious and a means of coming close to Allah Ta'ala. Tahajjud safeguards one from sins, causes forgiveness of sins and improves the health of the body."

40. "Allah Ta'ala says, 'O, son of Aadam! Do not be lazy in offering four rakaats in the early part of the day. I shall fulfil your needs for the rest of the day."

Books of Hadith repeatedly mention the rewards of Salaah and also the encouragement towards performing it. The forty short Ahaadith given above can be memorised and thus the reward of knowing forty Ahaadith can be earned. In fact, Salaah is really a big favour, but this is only realised by those who have its taste. Rasulullah ﷺ called it the comfort of his eyes. He would spend most of the night standing before Allah Ta'ala. It was for the very same reason that, our dear Rasulullah ﷺ, even on his deathbed, commanded and enjoined us to be particular about Salaah. It has been reported in many Ahaadith that Rasulullah ﷺ would often say;

اِتَّقُوا اللهَ فِى الصَّلَاةِ (شعب الايمان # 10542)

"Fear Allah Ta'ala concerning Salaah."

Abdullah bin Mas'ood رضي الله عنه narrates that he heard Nabi ﷺ saying, "Of all the practices, Salaah is the dearest to me."

One of the Sahaabah رضي الله عنهم narrates, "One night I happened to go to the Masjid. I found Rasulullah ﷺ in Salaah. I really wanted to join him. I made my intention and stood behind him. He was reciting 'Surah Baqarah' at that time. I thought he would finish the qiraat and go for ruku at the end of the 100th Aayah, but he did not do so. I thought that he would perhaps go for ruku after finishing the 200th Aayaat, but he did not. I was sure that he would finish the first rakaat at the end of the Surah. When the Surah ended, he said *'Allahumma Lakal hamd'* (O Allah! All praise belongs to you) a number of times and then began

'Surah Aal-e-Imraan'. On finishing that surah, he again said 'Allahumma lakal hamdu' three times and began 'Surah Maa'idah'. He then went into ruku after finishing that Surah. In ruku and sajdah he recited tasbeeh and some other duas, which I could not hear. In the second rakaat he started 'Surah An'aam' after 'Surah Faatihah'. I could not continue with him any longer and broke away helplessly."

What Rasulullah ﷺ recited in one rakaat comes to about 5 Paras of the Qur-aan. Besides, Rasulullah ﷺ was reciting at ease with proper Tajweed. We can well imagine how long the rakaat would have been. It was because of this that his feet would often get swollen. No amount of strain and difficulty in Salaah is too much for the one whose heart has tasted the sweetness of Salaah.

Abu Ishaaq Subaihi *(rahmatullahi alayh)* is a famous Muhaddith. He died when he was over the age of 100 years. He would often exclaim in his old age, "Alas! This illness and old age have deprived me of the delight of performing long Salaah. I am now only able to recite 'Surah Baqarah' and 'Surah Aal-e-Imraan' in my Salaah of two rakaats." These two surahs comprise about one eighth of the whole Qur-aan.

Muhammad bin Sammaak *(rahmatullahi alayh)*, the famous Soofi, writes, "My neighbour at Kufa had a son. The boy fasted during the day and made ibaadah during the night. This constant strain made him so thin that his body was reduced to a skeleton. His father requested me to caution him. I was once sitting at my door when the boy passed by. He greeted me with 'Assalaamu alaikum' and sat down. I had hardly said anything when he interrupted me saying, 'Dear Uncle! Maybe you intend to advise me to reduce my efforts. Listen to my story first. I had a few friends in the locality. We decided amongst ourselves to compete with one another in ibaadah and acquiring the love of Allah Ta'ala. They all applied themselves so hard that they were soon sent for by Allah Ta'ala. They embraced death delightedly and peacefully. Now I am the only one left behind. What will they think of me when they know of my lagging behind? Dear Uncle! My friends really strived very hard and achieved their goal.' He then began to relate the pursuits and accomplishments of his late friends, which surprised all the listeners. After this he left me. Few days later, I heard that the boy too had passed away (May Allah Ta'ala bless him)."

Even nowadays there are people who remain engaged in Salaah for the major portion of the night and devote the whole day to Tableegh, Ta'leem and other services in the path of Allah Ta'ala. Hadhrat Mujaddid Alf-e-Saani *(rahmatullahi alayh)* is famously known to one and all in India. His Khalifa, Moulana Abdul Waahid Lahori *(rahmatullahi alayh),* was a famous saint who lived about two centuries ago. He sighed and wept when he learnt that there was no Salaah in Jannah, because it is the place for payment and not of effort. He sighed and remarked, "How shall we ever enjoy Jannah without Salaah!" It is because of such people that the world still functions. These are those noble people who really take the true benefit of this worldly life. May Allah Ta'ala give us also their strength of Imaan and love for His ibaadah! *Aameen.*

Before I finish this chapter, let me mention a very interesting incident which is mentioned in the following Hadith from *'Munabbihaat'* by Ibn Hajar *(rahmatullahi alayh),* "Once Rasulullah ﷺ was sitting with the Sahaabah رضي الله عنهم when he said, "Three things of this world are very dear to me; Itr (good smelling fragrance), my wives and Salaah which is the comfort of my eyes." "Quite true," said Hadhrat Abu Bakr رضي الله عنه, "The three things that I love are; to look at your face, spending my wealth on you and that my daughter be your wife, O Nabi of Allah!" "Quite true," said Hadhrat Umar رضي الله عنه, "The three things that I love most are; enforcing that which is right, forbidding the evil and wearing old clothes." "Quite true," said Hadhrat Usmaan رضي الله عنه, "The three things that I love most are; feeding the hungry, clothing the naked and reciting the Qur-aan." "Quite true," said Hadhrat Ali رضي الله عنه. "The three things that I love most are; serving a guest, fasting on a very hot day and striking the enemy with my sword." At this, Jibraa-eel *(alayhis salaam)* appeared and said to Rasulullah ﷺ, "Allah Ta'ala has sent me to tell you what I would love if I had been a human." "Yes, do tell us Jibraa-eel," said Rasulullah ﷺ. Jibraa-eel *(alayhis salaam)* replied, "If I had been a human like you, the three things I would have loved are; guiding the people who have gone away from Islam, loving those who make *ibaadah* (worship Allah Ta'ala) in poverty and helping the poor family men. As for Allah Ta'ala, the three things He loves most in His slaves are; striving in His Path (with one's life or wealth), crying at the time of making taubah and being patient in poverty and hunger."

Haafiz Ibn Qayyim *(rahmatullahi alayh)* writes: "Salaah brings our rizq (sustenance), promotes good health, drives out diseases, strengthens the heart, brings light and beauty to the face, pleases the soul, refreshes the body, cures laziness, relieves the mind, feeds the soul, brightens the heart and guarantees the favour of Allah Ta'ala. It grants protection against the punishment of Allah Ta'ala. It keeps shaytaan away and brings us closer to Allah Ta'ala. In short, Salaah is a guarantee for all that is good and a protection against all that is undesirable for both, body and soul, equally in this world and in the Aakhirah."

CHAPTER 2
WARNINGS FOR NEGLECTING SALAAH

The books of Hadith mention very severe punishments for those who neglect Salaah. A few Ahaadith are mentioned in this chapter. A single warning from Rasulullah ﷺ should be enough. Out of love and mercy for his followers, he has warned them again and again in different ways, so that they do not neglect Salaah and suffer the punishment. In spite of this, we are still unmindful of Salaah, and have the audacity to consider ourselves the followers of Rasulullah ﷺ and the champions of Islam.

HADITH 1 – THE BARRIER BETWEEN A PERSON AND KUFR IS SALAAH

عَنْ جَابِرِ بْنِ عَبْدِ اللهِ قَالَ قَالَ رَسُوْلُ اللهِ صَلَّى اللهُ عَلَيْهِ وَسَلَّمَ بَيْنَ الرَّجُلِ وَبَيْنَ الْكُفْرِ تَرْكُ الصَّلَاةِ

وَقَالَ بَيْنَ الرَّجُلِ وَبَيْنَ الشِّرْكِ وَالْكُفْرِ تَرْكُ الصَّلَاةِ

وَقَالَ بَيْنَ الْكُفْرِ وَالْإِيْمَانِ تَرْكُ الصَّلَاةِ

(اخرجه المنذري في الترغيب # 807)

Hadhrat Jaabir bin Abdillah ؓ narrates that he heard Rasulullah ﷺ saying:

1. "To leave out Salaah is to be joined with kufr."

2. *"To leave out Salaah is to be joined with kufr and shirk."*

3. *"Leaving out of Salaah is the only difference between Imaan and kufr."*

Note: There are a number of Ahaadith on this subject. On one occasion, Rasulullah ﷺ is reported to have said: "Hasten in your Salaah when it is cloudy (in case you make a mistake and miss the correct time). To leave out Salaah is to become a kaafir." What a stern warning against even missing the correct time of Salaah, as (according to this quotation) to miss the correct time of Salaah is like leaving it out. Although, according to the interpretation of the Ulama, the verdict of kufr is given against a person only when he rejects (and not simply neglects) Salaah, yet the words of Rasulullah ﷺ in these Ahaadith should be very weighty for those who have any regard for him. However, it may be noted that some of the very important Sahaabah of Rasulullah ﷺ like Hadhrat Umar ؓ, Abdullah bin Mas'ood ؓ, Abdullah bin Abbas ؓ, etc. and eminent Fuqahaa like Imaam Ahmad bin Hambal, Ishaaq bin Raahwayh, Ibn Mubaarak, *(rahmatullahi alayhim)*, etc. are definitely of the opinion that the verdict of kufr can be given against the person who intentionally leaves out his Salaah. May Allah Ta'ala save us!

HADITH 2 – SEVEN ADVICES OF RASULULLAH ﷺ

عَنْ عُبَادَةَ بْنِ الصَّامِتِ رَضِيَ اللهُ عَنْهُ قَالَ اَوْصَانِىْ خَلِيْلِىْ رَسُوْلُ اللهِ صَلَّى اللهُ عَلَيْهِ وَسَلَّمَ بِسَبْعِ خِصَالٍ فَقَالَ لَا تُشْرِكُوْا بِاللهِ شَيْئًا وَاِنْ قُطِّعْتُمْ اَوْ حُرِّقْتُمْ اَوْ صُلِّبْتُمْ وَلَا تَتْرُكُوا الصَّلَاةَ مُتَعَمِّدِيْنَ فَمَنْ تَرَكَهَا مُتَعَمِّدًا فَقَدْ خَرَجَ مِنَ الْمِلَّةِ وَلَا تَرْكَبُوا الْمَعْصِيَةَ فَاِنَّهَا سَخَطُ اللهِ وَلَا تَشْرِبُوا الْخَمْرَ فَاِنَّهَا رَأْسُ الْخَطَايَا كُلِّهَا اَلْحَدِيْثِ (اخرجه المنذرى فى الترغيب # 809)

Hadhrat Ubaadah bin Saamit ؓ narrates; "My dear friend, Rasulullah ﷺ, instructed me with seven good practices, 'Do not ascribe anything as a partner to Allah Ta'ala, though you may be cut into pieces or burnt alive or crucified. Do not leave out Salaah intentionally; otherwise you would go out of the fold of Islam. Do not disobey Allah Ta'ala, otherwise He will be angry with you. Do not drink wine, for that is the mother of all evils.'"

Note: In another Hadith, Hadhrat Abu Darda ﷺ says, "My dear Rasul ﷺ warned me saying, 'Do not ascribe anything as partner unto Allah Ta'ala even if you may be cut into pieces or burnt alive or crucified; do not discard Salaah intentionally, as Allah Ta'ala is free from any obligation to a person who knowingly neglects Salaah, and do not take wine, for that is the key to all evils.'"

HADITH 3 – ALLAH TA'ALA DOES NOT CARE FOR SOMEONE WHO NEGLECTS HIS FARDH SALAAH

عَنْ مُعَاذِ بْنِ جَبَلٍ رَضِيَ اللهُ عَنْهُ قَالَ اَوْصَانِيْ رَسُوْلُ اللهِ صَلَّى اللهِ عَلَيْهِ وَسَلَّمَ بِعَشْرِ كَلِمَاتٍ قَالَ لَا تُشْرِكْ بِاللهِ شَيْئًا وَاِنْ قُتِلْتَ وَحُرِّقْتَ وَلَا تَعُقَّنَّ وَالِدَيْكَ وَاِنْ اَمَرَاكَ اَنْ تَخْرُجَ مِنْ اَهْلِكَ وَمَالِكَ وَلَا تَتْرُكَنَّ صَلَاةً مَّكْتُوبَةً مُّتَعَمِّدًا فَاِنَّ مَنْ تَرَكَ صَلَاةً مَّكْتُوبَةً مُّتَعَمِّدًا فَقَدْ بَرِئَتْ مِنْهُ ذِمَّةُ اللهِ وَلَا تَشْرَبَنَّ خَمْرًا فَاِنَّهُ رَأْسُ كُلِّ فَاحِشَةٍ وَاِيَّاكَ وَالْمَعْصِيَةَ فَاِنَّ بِالْمَعْصِيَةِ حَلَّ سَخَطُ اللهِ وَاِيَّاكَ وَالْفِرَارَ مِنَ الزَّحْفِ وَاِنْ هَلَكَ النَّاسُ وَاِنْ اَصَابَ النَّاسَ مَوْتٌ فَاثْبُتْ وَاَنْفِقْ عَلٰى اَهْلِكَ مِنْ طَوْلِكَ وَلَا تَرْفَعْ عَنْهُمْ عَصَاكَ اَدَبًا وَاَخِفْهُمْ فِى اللهِ (اخرجه المنذرى فى الترغيب # 3785)

Hadhrat Mu'aaz bin Jabal ﷺ narrates: "Rasulullah ﷺ instructed me with ten things:

1. 'Do not believe in anything as a partner with Allah Ta'ala, though you may be killed or burnt alive.

2. Do not disobey your parents, though you may have to leave your wife or all your wealth.

3. Do not neglect the Fardh Salaah intentionally, for Allah Ta'ala does not care about a person who neglects the Fardh Salaah intentionally.

4. Do not drink wine, for it is an evil habit and the root of every evil.

5. Do not disobey Allah Ta'ala, for that brings about the anger of Allah Ta'ala.

6. Do not turn your back to the enemy in battle, though all your companions may have died.

7. Do not escape from a locality where a disease has broken out.

8. Spend on your family members according to your capacity.

9. Let your rod be hanging on them as a warning and

10. Keep on instilling the fear of Allah in them."

TARBIYAT OF CHILDREN AND EMPHASIS ON SALAAH

According to this Hadith, we should not spare the rod in checking the children from becoming reckless in doing whatever they like. Sometimes it is necessary to use the rod. It is a pity that, out of love, we do not use the rod in the beginning and when the children get spoilt, we cry and complain about them. To spare the rod and spoil the child is no kindness at all. Who would like to save a child from a surgical operation under advice from a doctor for the simple reason that it would cause pain to him? Rasulullah ﷺ has said: "Command your child with Salaah when he is seven years old and punish him if he neglects it when he reaches ten." Hadhrat Abdullah bin Mas'ood رضي الله عنه says, "Guard the Salaah of your children and inculcate good habits in them." Luqmaan عليه السلام the wise used to say, "The use of the rod on a child is as necessary as is water for the fields." Rasulullah ﷺ has said, "A person advising his children earns more reward from Allah Ta'ala than spending about (seven pounds) 3kg of grain in His path." In another Hadith Rasulullah ﷺ has said, "May Allah Ta'ala bless a person who keeps a lash hanging in his house for the warning of his house people."

He also said, "No father can give anything better to his children than teaching them good manners."

Hadith 4 – Missing a Salaah is like losing one's family and wealth

عَنْ نَوْفَلِ بْنِ مُعَاوِيَةَ رَضِيَ اللهُ عَنْهُ اَنَّ النَّبِيَّ صَلَّى اللهُ عَلَيْهِ وَسَلَّمَ قَالَ مَنْ فَاتَتْهُ الصَّلَاةُ فَكَاَنَّمَا وُتِرَ اَهْلُهُ وَمَالُهُ (صحيح ابن حبان # 1468)

Hadhrat Naufal ibn Mu'aawiyah ﷺ narrates that he heard Rasulullah ﷺ saying, "A person who has missed one Salaah is like one who has lost all his family and wealth."

Note: Salaah is missed usually when a person is in the company of his family members or whilst he is earning money. According to this Hadith, the ultimate loss suffered in missing a single Salaah is in no way less than losing one's entire family and property. In other words, if we miss a Salaah, we should be as much grieved as when we lose all our family and belongings. If we are warned by some truthful person about gangsters on a certain road, where people are robbed and killed during the night, we need to be very brave to ignore the warning and travel on that road even during the daytime. It is strange that we have been warned again and again by Rasulullah ﷺ and we definitely believe that he was the true Nabi of Allah Ta'ala, yet we do not take heed and go on missing Salaah one after the other.

Hadith 5 – Delaying Salaah is a major sin

عَنِ ابْنِ عَبَّاسٍ رَضِيَ اللهُ عَنْهُ قَالَ قَالَ رَسُوْلُ اللهِ صَلَّى اللهُ عَلَيْهِ وَسَلَّمَ مَنْ جَمَعَ بَيْنَ الصَّلَاتَيْنِ مِنْ غَيْرِ عُذْرٍ فَقَدْ اَتٰى بَابًا مِّنْ اَبْوَابِ الْكَبَائِرِ (اخرجه الحاكم فى المستدرك # 1020)

Hadhrat Ibn Abbaas ﷺ narrates that he heard Rasulullah ﷺ saying, "A person who joins two Salaahs without any strong excuse, reaches one of the doors of kabaa'ir (major sins)."

Note: Hadhrat Ali ؓ reports that Rasulullah ﷺ once said. "Do not delay in three things; Salaah when its time has set in, burial when the Janaazah is ready and the marriage of a woman when her match is found."

Many people, who consider themselves as pious and punctual on their salaah, perform many Salaah together on returning home, on the very weak excuse of travel, business or job. To delay Salaah without a strong excuse (e.g. illness, etc.) is a major sin. Although it is not as bad as not reading Salaah at all, yet it is quite serious.

HADITH 6 – SALAAH IS A DEFENSE IN THE AAKHIRAH

عَنْ عَبْدِ اللَّهِ بْنِ عَمْرٍو رَضِيَ اللَّهُ عَنْهُ عَنِ النَّبِيِّ صَلَّى اللَّهُ عَلَيْهِ وَسَلَّمَ أَنَّهُ ذَكَرَ الصَّلَاةَ يَوْمًا فَقَالَ مَنْ حَافَظَ عَلَيْهَا كَانَتْ لَهُ نُوْرًا وَّبُرْهَانًا وَّنَجَاةً يَوْمَ الْقِيَامَةِ وَمَنْ لَّمْ يُحَافِظْ عَلَيْهَا لَمْ يَكُنْ لَّهُ نُوْرٌ وَّلَا بُرْهَانٌ وَّلَا نَجَاةٌ وَكَانَ يَوْمَ الْقِيَامَةِ مَعَ قَارُوْنَ وَفِرْعَوْنَ وَهَامَانَ وَأُبَيِّ بْنِ خَلَفٍ (مسند احمد # 6576)

Hadhrat Abdullah bin Amr ؓ narrates that once Rasulullah ﷺ, while talking about Salaah, said: "For the one who used to perform Salaah, it shall be a light for him on the Day of Qiyaamah, an argument in his favour, and a means of saving him from Jahannam. There will be no light, no defence and no safety from punishment for him who does not guard his Salaah. He shall be raised up with Qaaroon, Firaun, Haamaan and Ubayy bin Khalaf."

Note: Everybody knows that Firaun the disbeliever had been so proud that he claimed himself to be 'God'. He ordered his people to worship him. Haamaan was his Chief Minister and friend. Ubayy bin Khalaf was the worst enemy of Islam among the disbelievers of Makkah. Before Hijrah, he would say to Rasulullah ﷺ most rudely, "I have trained a horse which I feed very well. I will kill you one day riding on its back." Once, Nabi ﷺ replied to him, "Insha-Allah! I will kill you."

In the battle of Uhud, he ran about the field in search of Nabi ﷺ saying, "If Muhammad ﷺ is not killed today, then I stand no chance of surviving." At last he found Rasulullah ﷺ and went forward to attack him. The Sahaabah رضي الله عنهم decided to kill him before he reached Rasulullah ﷺ, but Rasulullah ﷺ stopped them. When he approached, Nabi ﷺ took a spear from one of the Sahaabah رضي الله عنهم and struck him, causing a little scratch on his neck. He stumbled and fell from his horse and ran towards his camp crying, "By Allah! Muhammad ﷺ has killed me!" His people tried to calm him down by saying, "It was only a scratch and there was nothing to worry about." He said, "Muhammad (ﷺ) had once told me in Makkah that he would kill me. By Allah, if he only spat at me, I would have died." He cried like a bull. Abu Sufyaan, who was very active on that day, put him to shame for crying so profusely over a slight wound. He said, "Do you know who caused me this injury? It was none other than Muhammad (ﷺ). By Laat and Uzza! (Names of his idols) If my pain was to be distributed over all the people of Arabia, none of them would survive. Since the time he had said that he would kill me, I was sure that I would die at his hands. If he only spat at me, I would have fallen dead." He died on his return to Makkah.

Look! A disbeliever like Ubayy bin Khalaf is so sure about the truth of the words of Rasulullah ﷺ that he does not have the slightest doubt about his own death. Where do we stand? Although we believe in him as the greatest Nabi of Allah, consider his words to be most genuine and boast of our love for him, yet how much do we practice on his advice. How much do we fear the punishments about which he has warned us! It is for us all to think about.

Ibn Hajar *(rahmatullahi alayh)*, while quoting this Hadith, has also mentioned Qaaroon with Firaun and others. He writes: "Sharing the fate of these people on the Day of Qiyaamah will be due to the fact that these people were guilty of those causes that make us neglect our Salaah. Therefore, if a person neglects Salaah due to a craving for wealth, he will meet the fate of Qaaroon; if due to love for power, then that of Firaun; if due to a desire for attachment to a ruler, then that of Haamaan; and if due to business, then that of Ubbay Bin Khalaf." Meeting the same fate as theirs, explains fully the severest tortures in store for those who neglect

Salaah. Although the disbelievers shall have to suffer their punishment forever, the believers will be released after their period of punishment is over and will then be allowed to enter Jannah. But who knows that this period of punishment may last for thousands of years.

HADITH 7 – FIVE FAVOURS FOR A PERSON WHO IS MINDFUL OF HIS SALAAH

قَالَ بَعْضُهُمْ وَرَدَ فِي الْحَدِيْثِ أَنَّ مَنْ حَافَظَ عَلَى الصَّلَاةِ أَكْرَمَهُ اللهُ بِخَمْسِ خِصَالٍ يَرْفَعُ عَنْهُ ضِيْقَ الْعَيْشِ وَعَذَابَ الْقَبْرِ وَيُعْطِيْهِ اللهُ كِتَابَهُ بِيَمِيْنِهِ وَيَمُرُّ عَلَى الصِّرَاطِ كَالْبَرْقِ وَيَدْخُلُ الْجَنَّةَ بِغَيْرِ حِسَابٍ وَمَنْ تَهَاوَنَ عَنِ الصَّلَاةِ عَاقَبَهُ اللهُ بِخَمْسَ عَشْرَةَ عُقُوبَةً خَمْسَةٌ فِي الدُّنْيَا وَثَلَاثَةٌ عِنْدَ الْمَوْتِ وَثَلَاثٌ فِي قَبْرِهِ وَثَلَاثٌ عِنْدَ خُرُوْجِهِ مِنَ الْقَبْرِ فَأَمَّا اللَّوَاتِي فِي الدُّنْيَا فَالْأُوْلَى تُنْزَعُ الْبَرَكَةُ مِنْ عُمْرِهِ وَالثَّانِيَةُ تُمْحَى سِيْمَاءُ الصَّالِحِيْنَ مِنْ وَجْهِهِ وَالثَّالِثَةُ كُلُّ عَمَلٍ يَعْمَلُهُ لَا يَأْجُرُهُ اللهُ عَلَيْهِ وَالرَّابِعَةُ لَا يُرْفَعُ لَهُ دُعَاءٌ إِلَى السَّمَاءِ وَالْخَامِسَةُ لَيْسَ لَهُ حَقٌّ فِي دُعَاءِ الصَّالِحِيْنَ وَأَمَّا الَّتِي تُصِيْبُهُ عِنْدَ الْمَوْتِ فَإِنَّهُ يَمُوْتُ ذَلِيْلًا وَالثَّانِيَةُ يَمُوْتُ جَائِعًا وَالثَّالِثَةُ يَمُوْتُ عَطْشَانًا وَلَوْ سُقِيَ بِحَارَ الدُّنْيَا مَا رَوَى مِنْ عَطَشِهِ وَأَمَّا الَّتِي تُصِيْبُهُ فِي قَبْرِهِ فَالْأُوْلَى يَضِيْقُ عَلَيْهِ الْقَبْرُ حَتَّى تَخْتَلِفَ أَضْلَاعُهُ وَالثَّانِيَةُ يُوْقَدُ عَلَيْهِ الْقَبْرُ نَارًا فَيَتَقَلَّبُ عَلَى الْجَمْرِ لَيْلًا وَنَهَارًا وَالثَّالِثَةُ يُسَلَّطُ عَلَيْهِ فِي قَبْرِهِ ثُعْبَانٌ اسْمُهُ الشُّجَاعُ الْأَقْرَعُ عَيْنَاهُ مِنْ نَارٍ وَأَظْفَارُهُ مِنْ حَدِيْدٍ طُوْلُ كُلِّ ظُفْرٍ مَسِيْرَةُ يَوْمٍ يُكَلِّمُ الْمَيِّتَ فَيَقُوْلُ أَنَا الشُّجَاعُ الْأَقْرَعُ وَصَوْتُهُ مِثْلُ الرَّعْدِ الْقَاصِفِ يَقُوْلُ أَمَرَنِي رَبِّي أَنْ أَضْرِبَكَ عَلَى تَضْيِيْعِ صَلَاةِ الصُّبْحِ إِلَى بَعْدِ طُلُوْعِ الشَّمْسِ وَأَضْرِبَكَ عَلَى تَضْيِيْعِ صَلَاةِ الظُّهْرِ إِلَى الْعَصْرِ وَأَضْرِبَكَ عَلَى تَضْيِيْعِ صَلَاةِ الْعَصْرِ إِلَى الْمَغْرِبِ وَأَضْرِبَكَ عَلَى تَضْيِيْعِ صَلَاةِ الْمَغْرِبِ إِلَى الْعِشَاءِ وَأَضْرِبَكَ عَلَى صَلَاةِ الْعِشَاءِ إِلَى الْفَجْرِ فَكُلَّمَا ضَرَبَهُ ضَرْبَةً يَغُوْصُ فِي الْأَرْضِ سَبْعِيْنَ ذِرَاعًا فَلَا يَزَالُ فِي الْقَبْرِ مُعَذَّبًا إِلَى يَوْمِ الْقِيَامَةِ وَأَمَّا الَّتِي تُصِيْبُهُ عِنْدَ خُرُوْجِهِ مِنَ الْقَبْرِ فِي مَوْقِفِ الْقِيَامَةِ فَشِدَّةُ الْحِسَابِ

وَسَخَطُ الرَّبِّ وَدُخُوْلُ النَّارِ وَفِىْ رِوَايَةٍ فَإِنَّهُ يَأْتِىْ يَوْمَ الْقِيَامَةِ وَعَلٰى وَجْهِهِ ثَلَاثَةُ أَسْطُرٍ مَّكْتُوْبَاتٍ اَلسَّطْرُ الْأَوَّلُ يَا مُضَيِّعَ حَقَّ اللهِ اَلسَّطْرُ الثَّانِىْ يَا مَخْصُوْصًا بِغَضَبِ اللهِ اَلثَّالِثُ كَمَا ضَيَّعْتَ فِى الدُّنْيَا حَقَّ اللهِ فَأْيِسْ اَلْيَوْمَ اَنْتَ مِنْ رَحْمَةِ اللهِ

(اخرجه ابن حجر المکی فی الزواجر 1/226-227)

It is said in a Hadith that Allah Ta'ala gives five favours to a person who is mindful of his Salaah. His rizq (sustenance) is made easy for him; he is saved from the punishment in the grave; he shall receive his book of deeds in his right hand on the Day of Qiyaamah; (the details of this has been mentioned in Surah Al-Haaqqah that those who receive their book of deeds in their right hand will be extremely happy, showing their results to all), he shall cross the bridge of Siraat with the speed of lightning and he shall enter Jannah without being questioned.

As for him who neglects his Salaah, he shall meet five types of punishments in this world, three at the time of death, three in the grave and three in the Aakhirah.

Those in this world are: He is not blessed in his life. He will not have the noor (light) of piety on his face. He receives no rewards for his good practices. His duas are not answered and he has no share in the duas of the pious.

Those at the time of death are: He dies disgracefully. He dies hungry. He dies with such thirst that the water in the oceans of the world cannot quench.

Those in the grave are: He is squeezed so tightly that the ribs of one side go into the ribs of the other, fire is burnt inside the grave and he is rolled on burning coal day and night, a snake with fiery eyes and iron nails equal in length to a day's journey is let loose on him and shouts in a thundering voice, "Allah Ta'ala has instructed me to lash you till sunrise for neglecting Fajr, till Asr for neglecting Zuhr, till sunset for neglecting Asr, till Esha for neglecting Maghrib and till morning for neglecting Esha." The snake will keep on lashing him till the Last Day. Each blow pushes him to a depth of seventy arm's length. This punishment will last till the Day of Qiyaamah.

Those in the Aakhirah are: His questioning will be made difficult. Allah Ta'ala will be angry with him and he will be thrown into Jahannam. According to one report, he will have the following three lines written on his forehead:

'O you who neglected Allah's duties.'

'O you who has deserved Allah's anger.'

'Lose all hope of Allah's mercy, as you neglected your duty to Allah Ta'ala.'

Note: Famous Ulama like Ibn Hajr, Abu Lais Samarqandi *(rahmatullah alayhim)* and others, have mentioned this Hadith in their kitaabs. Although I have not been able to find the text in the original books of Hadith, yet other Ahaadith, some of which have already been mentioned and some are to follow, support its meaning. Neglect of Salaah, as has been stated above, leads one to kufr. Therefore no punishment is too severe for this offence. But we should remember that even after a person is guilty, Allah Ta'ala is free to forgive him as and when He pleases. Allah says in the Qur-aan Shareef:

$$\text{اِنَّ اللهَ لَا يَغْفِرُ اَنْ يُشْرَكَ بِهٖ وَيَغْفِرُ مَا دُوْنَ ذٰلِكَ لِمَنْ يَّشَآءُ}$$

"Verily Allah Ta'ala shall not forgive that shirk be committed but will forgive all other sins for whom He wills."

(Surah Nisaa' – Aayah 116)

If then it pleases Allah Ta'ala to forgive anybody neglecting Salaah, it will be most fortunate; but who can be sure of this fortune?

It is also stated in a Hadith that there will be three courts to be held by Allah Ta'ala on the Day of Qiyaamah. The first will judge between kufr and Islam and there will be no forgiveness. The second will be to judge our duties and conduct towards other people. All the aggrieved shall be repaid by either the people who had wronged them or by Allah

Ta'ala Himself, i.e. if He pleases to forgive anybody. The third will deal with our duties towards Allah Ta'ala. Here the doors of the mercy of Allah Ta'ala will be thrown wide open and He will forgive anybody He wills. Taking into account what has been said above, it must be clearly understood that we deserve the punishments that have been laid down because of our committing of sins, but the all-embracing mercy of Allah Ta'ala overrides everything and knows no bounds.

In Bukhaari Shareef there is a narration that it was the habit of Rasulullah ﷺ to ask the Sahaabah رضي الله عنهم after Fajr if anybody had seen a dream. He would then interpret the dream. One day, after asking, Rasulullah ﷺ himself narrated a long dream in which two men came and took him. He reported certain things which he saw in his dream. He said: "I saw the head of a person being crushed with a heavy stone. It was struck with such force that, after crushing the head, the stone rolled over a long distance. The head would return to its normal shape and the stone repeated the process. This continued non-stop. Rasulullah ﷺ asked his two companions that who is this person (being punished). He was told that this is that person who learnt the Qur-aan Shareef, but never used to recite it nor practice upon it. He would also go to sleep without reading the Fardh Salaah." There is a similar narration, in which Rasulullah ﷺ had seen (in his dream) a group of people being treated in the same manner. Jibraa-eel عليه السلام informed him that those were the people who used to neglect their Salaah.

Mujaahid *(rahmatullahi alayh)* says, "Allah Ta'ala blesses the people who guard their Salaah, just as he blessed Hadhrat Ibraheem *(alayhis salaam)* and his descendants."

Hadhrat Anas رضي الله عنه narrates that he heard Rasulullah ﷺ saying, "If a person dies with sincere Imaan, observing the commandments of Allah Ta'ala, performing Salaah and paying Zakaat, Allah Ta'ala is pleased with him when he dies."

Hadhrat Anas رضي الله عنه narrates that he heard Rasulullah ﷺ saying, "Allah Ta'ala says, 'I hold back the punishment from an area when I see people who always go to the Masjid, love one another for My sake, and make dua asking for forgiveness in the hours of darkness.'"

Hadhrat Abu Darda رضي الله عنه wrote to Hadhrat Salmaan رضي الله عنه saying: "Spend most of your time in the Masjid. I have heard Rasulullah

ﷺ saying, 'The Masjid is the place of the pious. Allah Ta'ala blesses the person who spends most of his time in the Masjid. Allah Ta'ala shall keep him in comfort and shall enable him to cross the bridge of Siraat with ease. Surely Allah Ta'ala is pleased with such a person.'"

Hadhrat Abdullah bin Mas'ood رضي الله عنه narrates that he heard Rasulullah ﷺ saying: "The Masaajid are the Houses of Allah Ta'ala and people who go there are His visitors. When everybody treats his visitors kindly, why should Allah Ta'ala not be kind to His visitors?"

Hadhrat Abu Sa'eed Khudri رضي الله عنه narrates that he heard Rasulullah ﷺ saying: "Allah Ta'ala loves the person who is attached to the Masjid."

Hadhrat Abu Hurayrah رضي الله عنه, narrates that he heard Rasulullah ﷺ saying, "After a dead person is laid in the grave, even before the people present at his burial go away, Munkar and Nakeer visit him. Then if the person is a believer, his good actions encircle him; Salaah comes close to his head, Zakaat to his right, Fast to his left, and the remaining good actions towards his feet, so that no one can approach him. Even the Malaaikah do the necessary questioning while standing at a distance."

One of the Sahaabah رضي الله عنهم reports that, when the people of Rasulullah's ﷺ house were in difficulty, he would ask them to perform Salaah and recite the following Aayah:

وَأْمُرْ أَهْلَكَ بِالصَّلٰوةِ وَاصْطَبِرْ عَلَيْهَا ۖ لَا نَسْـَٔلُكَ رِزْقًا ۖ نَحْنُ نَرْزُقُكَ ۗ وَالْعَاقِبَةُ لِلتَّقْوٰى

"And instruct your family to perform Salaah and you yourself remain steadfast on it. We do not ask you to provide sustenance, but We provide it for you. And the best result (rewards in the Aakhirah) is for adopting Taqwa." (Surah Taahaa – Aayah 132)

THOSE WHO WILL GO TO JANNAH WITHOUT ANY HISAAB

Hadhrat Asma رضي الله عنها narrates that she heard Rasulullah ﷺ saying, "All the people will be gathered together on the Day of Qiyaamah and they will all hear the voice of the announcing angel. He will say: 'Where are those who glorified Allah Ta'ala in ease and difficulty?' A group will rise up and enter Jannah without questioning. It will then be announced: 'Where are those who left their beds and spent their nights in ibaadah?' Another group will rise up and enter Jannah without questioning. The angel will again announce: 'Where are those whom trade and business did not distract them from the remembrance of Allah Ta'ala?' Yet another group will rise up and enter Jannah."

In another Hadith, the same account is given, with the addition that in the beginning the angel will say: "All those gathered here will see today who are the honoured people," and with the addition that the angel at the time of third announcement will say: "Where are those whom their engagement in trade and business did not distract from Salaah and the remembrance of Allah Ta'ala?"

Shaikh Nasar Samarqandi *(rahmatullahi alayh)* after quoting this lengthy Hadith in Tambeehul Ghaafileen, writes, "When all the three groups will have entered Jannah without questioning, a monster with a long neck, shining eyes and most well-spoken tongue will rise up from Jahannam and say; 'I have been appointed for all who are proud and ill-tempered.' It will then pick up all such persons from the crowd, as a fowl picks up grain, and then it will fling them into the Jahannam. It will rise up again saying; 'This time I have been appointed for all those who spoke bad about Allah Ta'ala and His Rasul ﷺ.' It will then pick up all such people and throw them into Jahannam. It will appear for the third time and will, in a similar manner, take away all those who made images and pictures. The questioning will then begin only after these three groups have been dealt with.

Previously, people could see shaytaan. A person came to shaytaan saying that he wanted to be like him. Shaytaan told him that no one had ever asked him such a question before and asked him why he made such a request. The person replied that he wished it from his heart. Shaytaan asked him to neglect his Salaah and to take false oaths very often, not caring about being honest in this regard. The person told Shaytaan that, By Allah Ta'ala! Never will he give up Salaah and never will he take false oaths. Shaytaan told him that he had never been tricked before by a human being. He also made a promise never to advise a human again.

Hadhrat Ubayy ﷺ narrates that he heard Rasulullah ﷺ saying, "Give good news to the Muslims that they shall be honoured and their Deen shall become powerful. There is no share in the Aakhirah for those who use Islam for the dunya (world)."

Rasulullah ﷺ is reported to have said, "I saw Allah Ta'ala in His best form. He said to me, 'O Muhammad! What are the most exalted Malaaikah (Al-Malaul'alaa) arguing about?' I said, 'I have no knowledge about that.' Allah Ta'ala placed His gracious hand on my chest. I felt its comforting coolness right through my heart and the entire universe was revealed to me. I said, 'They are arguing about the things which elevate a person's rank, those things that cause a person's sins to be forgiven, the rewards for the steps taken when going for Salaah (with Jamaat), the rewards of performing wudhu properly when it is very cold and the blessings that a person deserves when, after performing one Salaah, keeps on sitting in the masjid till the next Salaah. A person particular on these shall live a blessed life and shall have a good death."

Ishraaq Salaah

Rasulullah ﷺ is reported (in many Ahaadith) to have said, "Allah Ta'ala says, 'O, Son of Aadam! Perform four rakaats of Salaah in the early part of the day, I shall help you in completing all your work during the rest of the day."

In Tambeehul Ghaafileen there is a Hadith: "Salaah is the cause of the pleasure of Allah Ta'ala, it is loved by the Malaaikah, it is a practice of the Ambiyaa *(alayhimus salaam)*, it enables you to recognise Allah Ta'ala, it causes our duas to be accepted, it is a means of barakah in our rizq, it is the root of Imaan, it refreshes the body, it is a weapon against the enemy, it shall beg forgiveness on behalf of its reader, it is a light in the darkness of the grave, it is a source of comfort in the loneliness of the grave, it is a reply to the questioning of the Malaaikah, it is a shade against the sun on the day of Qiyaamah, it is a protection against the fire of Jahannam, it is a weight for the scales of good deeds, it is a means of crossing quickly over the bridge of Siraat and it is a key to Jannah."

Hadhrat Usmaan ﷺ is reported to have said, "Allah Ta'ala grants nine favours to a person who guards his Salaah and is particular in performing it at the correct time, viz.

1. He is loved by Allah Ta'ala,

2. He enjoys good health,
3. He is always under the protection of the Malaaikah,
4. His home is blessed,
5. There is noor (light of righteousness) on his face,
6. His heart is made soft,
7. He shall cross the bridge of Siraat with the speed of lightning,
8. He is saved from Jahannam, and
9. His neighbours in Jannah are those about whom Allah Ta'ala has said;

وَلَا خَوْفٌ عَلَيْهِمْ وَلَا هُمْ يَحْزَنُوْنَ

"And there shall neither be any fear upon them, nor shall they grieve"
(Surah Baqarah – Aayah 36)

Rasulullah ﷺ says, "Salaah is the pillar of Islam and it has ten virtues, viz;
1. It enlightens the face,
2. It is a light of the heart,
3. It is a source of comfort and refreshment for the body,
4. It is a company in the grave,
5. It is a means for the Mercy of Allah Ta'ala coming down.
6. It is a key to Jannah,
7. It is a weight for the scales (of good deeds),
8. It is a means of winning the pleasure of Allah Ta'ala,
9. It is the price of Jannah and
10. It is a protection against the fire of Jahannam.

A person who is particular on his Salaah, in fact establishes Deen, and one who neglects it, demolishes (so to say, the structure of) Deen."

It is mentioned in one Hadith that to perform Salaah in one's home is a noor (a light). So brighten up your homes with Salaah.

It is a famous Hadith that my Ummah, on the day of Qiyaamah, will have faces and limbs shining because of Wudhu and Sajdah. This will be the distinguishing factor between us and other Ummats.

It is mentioned in another Hadith that when any calamity descends from the skies, it is removed from those who frequent the Masjid.

It is mentioned in many Ahaadith that Allah Ta'ala has forbidden Jahannam to burn the places of sajdah. (If, per chance, a person has to enter Jahannam due to his evil deeds, the fire will not affect those areas where there are signs of sajdah.

In one Hadith it is mentioned that Salaah blackens the face of the devil and Sadaqah breaks his back.

According to one Hadith, Salaah is a cure. Once, when Rasulullah ﷺ saw Hadhrat Abu Hurayrah رضي الله عنه lying on his stomach, he asked him, "Are you suffering from stomach pain?" He replied, 'Yes'. Rasulullah ﷺ said, "Then get up and busy yourself in Salaah, because Salaah will cure you."

Tahiyyatul Wudhu

Once, Rasulullah ﷺ saw Jannah in his dream and heard the footsteps of Hadhrat Bilaal رضي الله عنه. The next morning he asked Hadhrat Bilaal رضي الله عنه: "What action of yours helped you to follow me even in Jannah?" He replied: "When my wudhu breaks at night, I make a fresh wudhu and perform as many rakaats of Nafl Salaah as I can."

Safeeri *(rahmatullahi alayh)* writes: "The Malaaikah address a person who misses Fajr as; 'O you wrongdoer', and one who neglects Zuhr as; 'O you loser', and one who ignores Asr as; 'O you transgressor', and one who omits Maghrib as; 'O you kaafir', and one who does not perform Esha as; 'O you violator of Allah Ta'ala's commandments."

Allama Sha'raani *(rahmatullahi alayh)* writes: "It should be clearly understood that punishment is taken away from a locality where the people are particular about Salaah, whereas a locality where the people neglect Salaah is often afflicted by punishments. Earthquakes, storms and sinking of houses are not unexpected where people are not particular about Salaah. Just guarding one's own Salaah is not enough, because when a punishment comes, it does not affect the wrongdoers only, but rather affects everybody in that locality. Once, the Sahaabah رضي الله عنهم asked Rasulullah ﷺ; "Can we be destroyed while there are pious people amongst us?" Rasulullah ﷺ replied, "Yes, if evil actions overtake good actions." It is therefore necessary that other people should also be encouraged to obey the commandments of Allah Ta'ala and stay away from wrongdoing.

Hadith 8 – Making your Salaah Qadhaa

رُوِىَ أَنَّهُ عَلَيْهِ الصَّلَاةُ وَالسَّلَامُ قَالَ مَنْ تَرَكَ الصَّلَاةَ حَتَّى مَضَى وَقْتُهَا ثُمَّ قَضَى عُذِّبَ فِى النَّارِ حُقْبًا وَالْحُقْبُ ثَمَانُونَ سَنَةً وَالسَّنَةُ ثَلَاثُ مِائَةٍ وَسِتُّونَ يَوْمًا كُلُّ يَوْمٍ كَانَ مِقْدَارُهُ أَلْفَ سَنَةٍ (كذا فى مجالس الابرار ص– 75)

Rasulullah ﷺ said, "A person neglecting his Salaah (even though he performs it later) shall remain in Jahannam for a period of one Huqb. A Huqb is equal to eighty years of 360 days each, and a day in the Aakhirah shall equal 1000 years of this world." (One huqb will be 28 800 000 years)

Note: Huqb in Arabic means a very long time. In most Ahaadith the meaning of Huqb has been explained as eighty years as mentioned above. This same amount has also been narrated in Durr-e-Mansoor from different narrations. Hadhrat Ali رضى الله عنه once asked Hilaal Hijri *(rahmatullahi alayh)* what was the amount of a Huqb. He said that a Huqb is equal to 80 years and each year is equal to 12 months and each month is equal to 30 days and one day is equal to 1000 years.

80 years has also been narrated from Abdullah Ibn Masood رضى الله عنه from authentic sources.

Hadhrat Abu Hurayrah رضى الله عنه has narrated from Rasulullah ﷺ that one Huqb is equal to 80 years and one year is equal to 360 days and one day will be equal to a 1000 years according to the days of this world. This information has also been narrated by Hadhrat Abdullah ibn Umar رضى الله عنه from Rasulullah ﷺ. Thereafter, Hadhrat Abdullah ibn Umar رضى الله عنه mentions that, "Don't just rely on this that because of your Imaan you will eventually come out of Jahannam. You may only come out after so many years. i.e. 28 800 000 years. And that is if there are no other reasons for you to remain therein." There are other durations mentioned in different Ahaadith which explain more or less days. But this amount mentioned above has come in many Ahaadith. Hence, this has been given preference. It is also possible that this duration may increase or decrease depending on the condition of the person.

Abul Lais Samarqandi *(rahmatullahi alayh)* has mentioned a Hadith in which Rasulullah ﷺ is reported to have said; "The name of a person who neglects even a single Fardh Salaah intentionally is written on the gate of Jahannam, which he must enter." Hadhrat Ibnu Abbaas رضى الله عنه narrates that once, Rasulullah ﷺ said, "Please, O Allah! Let not anyone of us be a miserable poor person." He then asked: "Do you know who is a miserable poor person?" When the Sahaabah رضى الله عنهم asked, he explained to them saying, "A miserable poor person is the one who neglects his Salaah. In Islam there is nothing for him." In another Hadith it is said, "Allah Ta'ala will not care a bit for the person who had been neglecting his Salaah intentionally and there shall be a terrible end for him."

It is said in a Hadith that ten people will be given extra punishment. One of them will be the person who neglects his Salaah. His hands will be tied while the Malaaikah shall beat him on his face and back. Jannah will say to him, "There is no place for you in me." Jahannam will say to him, "Come to me. You are for me and I am for you." It is also said that there is a valley in Jahannam named Lamlam. This valley is filled with snakes as fat as the neck of a camel and as long as one month's journey. A person neglecting Salaah will be punished in this valley. In another Hadith it is said that there is a place in Jahannam which is known as the pit of grief. It is inhabited by scorpions as huge as donkeys. This place is for punishing the people who neglect Salaah. Of course, there is no reason to worry if the most merciful Allah Ta'ala forgives our sins. But are we really prepared to ask for His forgiveness?

Ibn Hajar *(rahmatullahi alayh)* writes in his book Zawaajir that; "A woman died. Her brother was present at her burial and mistakenly his wallet fell into the grave and was buried with the dead person. The brother realised this only after he had returned home and was very sorry for the loss. He decided to dig up the grave secretly and remove the wallet. When he dug it up, he saw that the grave was in flames. He returned home full of grief and narrated the incident to his mother. He asked her if she knew why it was so. His mother informed him that his sister used to delay in Salaah and read it after its correct time. May Allah Ta'ala save us from these habits!

HADITH 9 – SALAAH IS LIKE THE HEAD IN THE BODY

عَنْ اَبِيْ هُرَيْرَةَ رَضِيَ اللهُ عَنْهُ قَالَ قَالَ رَسُوْلُ اللهِ صَلَّى اللهُ عَلَيْهِ وَسَلَّمَ لَا سَهْمَ فِي الْإِسْلَامِ لِمَنْ لَّا صَلَاةَ لَهُ وَلَا صَلَاةَ لِمَنْ لَّا وُضُوْءَ لَهُ (مسند البزار # 8539)

Hadhrat Abu Hurayrah رضى الله عنه says that he heard Rasulullah ﷺ saying: "There is no place in Islam for a person who does not perform his Salaah, and there is no Salaah without wudhu." Hadhrat Abdullah bin Umar رضى الله عنه also heard Rasulullah ﷺ saying: "There is no Islam in a person who has no Salaah by him. The position of Salaah in Islam is like the position of the head in a body."

Note: Let those who do not offer Salaah and not only call themselves Muslims, but also boast of their being champions of the Muslim cause, ponder over these words of Nabi ﷺ. They dream of reviving the past glory of Islam, but would not care to know how the people responsible for that glory stuck steadfastly to the practices of Islam.

Hadhrat Abdullah bin Abbaas رضى الله عنه suffered from cataract of the eye. People told him that the disease could be treated, but he would have to miss his Salaah for a few days. He said: "This is not possible! I have heard Rasulullah ﷺ saying, 'A person who does not perform his Salaah, will stand before Allah Ta'ala while Allah Ta'ala will be angry with him.'" The Sahaabah رضى الله عنهم of Rasulullah ﷺ would prefer to become blind rather than to leave out Salaah even for a few days. When Hadhrat Umar رضى الله عنه was stabbed by a kaafir, he often remained unconscious and eventually passed away due to heavy bleeding. On his deathbed he was made aware of the time of Salaah and he performed Salaah in that very condition and would say: "There is no place in Islam for a person who does not perform his Salaah." These days it is considered unkind and improper to make the patient perform salaah or even allow him to perform it. What a world of difference there is between the view points and approach of the Muslims of these two ages!

ببیں تفاوت راہ از کجاست تا بہ کجا

Look at the difference between the paths; what a great deviation!

Hadhrat Ali ﷺ once asked Nabi ﷺ to give him a servant. Nabi ﷺ said; "Here are three slaves. Take the one you prefer." Hadhrat Ali ﷺ said, "Can you please choose one for me." Rasulullah ﷺ pointed towards a certain man, saying, "Take this one. He is particular about his Salaah. You are not to hit him. We are not allowed to hit anyone who performs Salaah." There is another incident mentioned in this regard about Abul Haysam ﷺ who also requested a slave from Rasulullah ﷺ. We, on the other hand, mock our servants and consider him a liability if he goes for Salaah.

Sufyaan Sauri *(rahmatullahi alayh)*, the famous Sufi once fell into a state of ecstasy. He remained in his house for seven days without taking sleep, food and drink. When his Shaikh was informed of his condition, he inquired if Sufyaan *(rahmatullahi alayh)* was observing the hours of his Salaah. He was told that his Salaah was quite regular and safe. At this, the Shaikh remarked,

$$\text{اَلْحَمْدُ لِلّٰهِ الَّذِىْ لَمْ يَجْعَلْ لِلشَّيْطَانِ عَلَيْهِ سَبِيْلًا}$$

"All praise be to Allah Ta'ala, Who has not allowed Shaytaan to have an upper hand on him!"

PART 2

IMPORTANCE OF SALAAH WITH JAMAAT

It has already been mentioned in the foreword that although there are many who perform their Salaah regularly, but they are not very particular about performing the salaah with jamaat. Rasulullah ﷺ has stressed on joining the Jamaat Salaah just as he was particular about Salaah itself. This part also consists of two Chapters. The first deals with the rewards of Jamaat Salaah and the second with the consequences of neglecting Jamaat Salaah.

CHAPTER ONE
REWARDS FOR PERFORMING SALAAH WITH JAMAAT

HADITH 1 – SALAAH WITH JAMAAT IS TWENTY-SEVEN TIMES BETTER

عَنْ عَبْدِ اللهِ بْنِ عُمَرَ رَضِيَ اللهُ عَنْهُ اَنَّ رَسُوْلَ اللهِ صَلَّى اللهُ عَلَيْهِ وَسَلَّمَ قَالَ صَلَاةُ الْجَمَاعَةِ اَفْضَلُ مِنْ صَلَاةِ الْفَذِّ بِسَبْعٍ وَّعِشْرِيْنَ دَرَجَةً (موطا امام مالك # 322)

Hadhrat Abdullah bin Umar ﷺ says that he heard Rasulullah ﷺ saying: *"Salaah performed with Jamaat is twenty-seven times better than Salaah performed alone."*

Note: When we perform our Salaah with the intention of receiving reward from Allah Ta'ala, then why should it not be done in the Masjid, where the reward is twenty-seven times more. No one is so foolish to leave a profit that is twenty-seven times greater with a little extra work.

But we are so indifferent about the profits promised for our ibaadaat! This can be due to nothing but our indifference for Deen and the rewards for it. It is a pity that we work so hard to acquire the petty gains of this material world, but are unmindful of the gains in the Aakhirah, which bring us twenty-seven times more reward with a little extra effort. We often argue that by going to the masjid for Jamaat we will have to close the shop and therefore lose business. These and other excuses cannot stand in the way of those who have perfect Imaan in the Greatness of

Allah Ta'ala and in His word; and who realise the value of the blessings and reward in the Aakhirah. It is because of such people that Allah Ta'ala says:

$$رِجَالٌ لَّا تُلْهِيْهِمْ تِجَارَةٌ وَّ لَا بَيْعٌ عَنْ ذِكْرِ اللهِ وَ اِقَامِ الصَّلٰوةِ$$

"Men, whom neither their trade nor commerce distracts them from the zikr (remembrance) of Allah Ta'ala and establishment of Salaah."
(Surah Noor – Aayah 37)

In the Stories of Sahaabah (chapter 5) the details of how the Sahaabah رَضِىَ اللهُ عَنْهُمْ would react in their businesses at the time of Azaan has been mentioned briefly.

It is said of Saalim Haddaad *(rahmatullahi alayh)*, who was a businessman and a great Sufi that on hearing Azaan he would turn pale and grow restless. He would stand up immediately, leaving his shop open and recite these couplets:

$$اِذَا مَا دَعَا دَاعِيْكُمْ قُمْتُ مُسْرِعًا \qquad مُجِيْبًا لِمَوْلٰى جَلَّ لَيْسَ لَهٗ مِثْلُ$$

"When Your summoner stands up to summon, quickly I stand up." "To respond to (the summons of) The Mighty Lord Who has no peer."

$$أُجِيْبُ اِذَا نَادٰى بِسَمْعٍ وَّطَاعَةٍ \qquad وَبِىْ نَشْوَةٌ لَبَّيْكَ يَا مَنْ لَّهُ الْفَضْلُ$$

"I reply to the summons with complete submission and cheer, 'Here am I, O Bountiful One.'"

$$وَيَصْفَرُّ لَوْنِىْ خِيْفَةً وَّمَهَابَةً \qquad وَيَرْجِعُ لِىْ عَنْ كُلِّ شُغْلٍ بِهٖ شُغْلُ$$

"My face grows pale with awe and fear, and occupation in You distracts me from all other occupations."

$$وَحَقِّكُمْ مَا الَّذِىْ غَيْرُ ذِكْرِكُمْ \qquad وَذِكْرُ سِوَاكُمْ فِىْ فَمِىْ قَطُّ لَا يَحْلُوْ$$

"I swear by You, nothing is dear to me, besides Your remembrance." "Nothing is more beautiful for me than Your sweet name."

$$\text{مَتٰى يَجْمَعُ الْأَيَّامُ بَيْنِيْ وَبَيْنَكُمْ} \quad \text{وَيَفْرَحُ مُشْتَاقٌ اِذَا جَمَعَ الشَّمْلَ}$$

"O, will there be a time for us to be together?"
"A lover is happy only when he is with his Beloved."

$$\text{فَمَنْ شَاهَدَتْ عَيْنَاهُ نُوْرَ جَمَالِكُمْ} \quad \text{يَمُوْتُ اِشْتِيَاقًا نَحْوَكُمْ قَطُّ لَا يَسْلُوْ}$$

"He, whose eyes have seen the light of Your beauty, can never be comforted. He must die desiring for You."

It is said in a Hadith: "People frequenting the Masjid are its pegs. The Malaaikah are their companions, who visit them when they are sick and help them when they are at their jobs.

HADITH 2 – SALAAH WITH JAMAAT IS TWENTY-FIVE TIMES BETTER

عَنْ اَبِيْ هُرَيْرَةَ رَضِيَ اللهُ عَنْهُ قَالَ قَالَ رَسُوْلُ اللهِ صَلَّى اللهُ عَلَيْهِ وَسَلَّمَ صَلَاةُ الرَّجُلِ فِيْ جَمَاعَةٍ تُضَعَّفُ عَلٰى صَلَاتِهٖ فِيْ بَيْتِهٖ وَفِيْ سُوْقِهٖ خَمْسًا وَّعِشْرِيْنَ ضِعْفًا وَّذٰلِكَ اَنَّهٗ اِذَا تَوَضَّاَ فَاَحْسَنَ الْوُضُوْءَ ثُمَّ خَرَجَ اِلَى الْمَسْجِدِ لَا يُخْرِجُهٗ اِلَّا الصَّلَاةُ لَمْ يَخْطُ خَطْوَةً اِلَّا رُفِعَتْ لَهٗ بِهَا دَرَجَةً وَّحُطَّ عَنْهُ بِهَا خَطِيْئَةً فَاِذَا صَلّٰى لَمْ تَزَلِ الْمَلَائِكَةُ تُصَلِّيْ عَلَيْهِ مَا دَامَ فِيْ مُصَلَّاهُ مَا لَمْ يُحْدِثْ اَللّٰهُمَّ صَلِّ عَلَيْهِ اَللّٰهُمَّ ارْحَمْهُ وَلَا يَزَالُ فِيْ صَلَاةٍ مَّا انْتَظَرَ الصَّلَاةَ

(اخرجه المنذرى فى الترغيب # 585)

Hadhrat Abu Hurayrah ﷺ narrates that he heard Rasulullah ﷺ saying, "Salaah with Jamaat is twenty-five times better than Salaah which is read in a house or in a shop. When a person performs wudhu correctly and walks to the Masjid, with the intention of performing Salaah, then for each step that he takes, Allah Ta'ala gives him a reward and wipes out a sin for him. If he remains sitting in the Masjid with wudhu after the Salaah, the Malaaikah continue making dua for him, "O Allah, Have mercy on him". As long as he keeps sitting in the Masjid waiting for Salaah, he continues to earn rewards as if he is busy in Salaah."

Note: In Hadith No. 1, the superiority of Salaah performed with Jamaat compared to Salaah performed alone is described as being twenty-seven times more rewarding, while this Hadith mentions only twenty-five times. Various Ulama have discussed this difference. The following are some of the explanations:

1. This difference from twenty-five to twenty-seven is due to the level of ikhlaas (sincerity) in different individuals.

2. In Sirri (quiet) Salaah (i.e., Zuhr and Asr), it is twenty-five times, while in Jahri (loud) Salaah (i.e. Fajr, Maghrib and Ishaa), it is twenty-seven times.

3. In Fajr and Esha, when it is inconvenient to go out due to the cold and darkness, it is twenty-seven times, but in other Salaahs it is twenty-five times.

4. In the beginning it was twenty-five times, but subsequently, Allah Ta'ala (by special favour on the Ummah of Rasulullah ﷺ) raised the reward to twenty-seven times.

Some others have put forward a still finer explanation. They say that the reward for Salaah with Jamaat mentioned in this Hadith is not only twenty-five times but two raised to the power twenty-five (i.e. 2^{25}) which adds up to thirty-three million five hundred and fifty-four thousand four hundred and thirty-two (33 554 432). This is something not beyond the bountiful Mercy of Allah Ta'ala. When leaving out a single Salaah can be a cause of punishment in Jahannam for one Huqb (as we have seen in the last chapter), then the huge reward for one Salaah with Jamaat is also quite possible.

Rasulullah ﷺ has also explained to us how the reward goes on increasing in the case of a person who, after performing wudhu, leaves his house only with the intention of joining the Salaah with Jamaat in the Masjid. Each step he takes, brings one reward as well as washes away one sin.

The houses of Banu Salama, a group of people in Madinah Munawwarah, were situated far away from the Masjid. They chose to move closer to the Masjid. Rasulullah ﷺ said to them: "Stay where you are. Every step that you take to the Masjid is a means of

Sawaab (reward) for you." It is said in a Hadith: "The example of a person who performs wudhu at home and then leaves for the Masjid is like a person who, after wearing the ihraam at home, leaves for Haj."

Further, in the same Hadith, Rasulullah ﷺ points to another act of great value; i.e., as long as one remains sitting in masjid after the Salaah is over, the Malaaikah make dua for him by asking for forgiveness and mercy. The Malaaikah are the innocent and obedient creation of Allah Ta'ala, so the effect that their Duas will have is obvious.

Muhammad bin Sammaak *(rahmatullahi alayh)* is a famous Shaikh. He was the student of Imaam Abu Yusuf *(rahmatullahi alayh)* and Imaam Muhammad *(rahmatullahi alayh)*. He died at the age of 103. He would perform 200 rakaats of Nafl Salaah daily. He writes: "For forty years, I never missed the first takbeer of Salaah with Jamaat, except once when my mother had passed away." The same Shaikh writes: "Once, I missed the Jamaat Salaah. I knew that Salaah with Jamaat was twenty-five times more rewarding. I, therefore, repeated the Salaah (on my own) twenty-five times to compensate for it. I heard in my dream, 'Muhammad! You have repeated your Salaah twenty-five times (to cover up), but what about the *'Aameen'* by the Malaaikah?'" It is reported in many Ahaadith that when the Imaam says *'Ameen'* after Surah Faatihah, the Malaaikah also say *Aameen*. All the past sins of a person, who's *Aameen* coincides with that of the Malaaikah, are forgiven. This is possible by performing Salaah with Jamaat. Therefore, Moulana Abdul Hayy *(rahmatullahi alayh)*, when quoting this story about the Shaikh, writes: "If a person repeats his Salaah (by himself) a thousand times, he cannot receive the sawaab of one Salaah with Jamaat." He not only loses the *'Ameen'* with the Malaaikah, but also the sawaab of Jamaat and the duas of the Malaaikah after Salaah and many other benefits. The duas of the Malaaikah can only be earned when the Salaah is a proper one. If the Salaah of a person is not as it should be (according to Hadith), it is flung back like a dirty rag at his face. How then can the Malaaikah make dua for him?

Part 2 Ch.1 – Rewards for Performing Salaah with Jamaat

HADITH 3 – IMPORTANCE OF SALAAH IN THE MASJID

عَنِ ابْنِ مَسْعُوْدٍ رَضِيَ اللهُ عَنْهُ قَالَ مَنْ سَرَّهُ اَنْ يَلْقَى اللهَ غَدًا مُسْلِمًا فَلْيُحَافِظْ عَلَى هٰؤُلَاءِ الصَّلَوَاتِ حَيْثُ يُنَادٰى بِهِنَّ فَاِنَّ اللهَ تَعَالٰى شَرَعَ لِنَبِيِّكُمْ صَلَّى اللهُ عَلَيْهِ وَسَلَّمَ سُنَنَ الْهُدٰى وَاِنَّهُنَّ مِنْ سُنَنِ الْهُدٰى وَلَوْ اَنَّكُمْ صَلَّيْتُمْ فِيْ بُيُوْتِكُمْ كَمَا يُصَلِّيْ هٰذَا الْمُتَخَلِّفُ فِيْ بَيْتِهِ لَتَرَكْتُمْ سُنَّةَ نَبِيِّكُمْ وَلَوْ تَرَكْتُمْ سُنَّةَ نَبِيِّكُمْ لَضَلَلْتُمْ وَمَا مِنْ رَجُلٍ يَتَطَهَّرُ فَيُحْسِنُ الطُّهُوْرَ ثُمَّ يَعْمِدُ اِلٰى مَسْجِدٍ مِّنْ هٰذِهِ الْمَسَاجِدِ اِلَّا كَتَبَ اللهُ لَهُ بِكُلِّ خُطْوَةٍ يَخْطُوْهَا حَسَنَةً وَيَرْفَعُهُ بِهَا دَرَجَةً وَيَحُطُّ عَنْهُ بِهَا سَيِّئَةً وَلَقَدْ رَاَيْتُنَا وَمَا يَتَخَلَّفُ عَنْهَا اِلَّا مُنَافِقٌ مَعْلُوْمُ النِّفَاقِ وَلَقَدْ كَانَ الرَّجُلُ يُؤْتٰى بِهِ يُهَادٰى بَيْنَ الرَّجُلَيْنِ حَتّٰى يُقَامَ فِي الصَّفِّ وَفِيْ رِوَايَةٍ لَقَدْ رَاَيْتُنَا وَمَا يَتَخَلَّفُ عَنِ الصَّلَاةِ اِلَّا مُنَافِقٌ قَدْ عُلِمَ نِفَاقُهُ اَوْ مَرِيْضٌ اِنْ كَانَ الرَّجُلُ لَيَمْشِيْ بَيْنَ رَجُلَيْنِ حَتّٰى يَأْتِيَ الصَّلَاةَ وَقَالَ اِنَّ رَسُوْلَ اللهِ صَلَّى اللهُ عَلَيْهِ وَسَلَّمَ عَلَّمَنَا سُنَنَ الْهُدٰى وَاِنَّ مِنْ سُنَنِ الْهُدٰى الصَّلَاةَ فِي الْمَسْجِدِ الَّذِيْ يُؤَذَّنُ فِيْهِ

(اخرجه المنذري فى الترغيب # 587)

Hadhrat Abdullah bin Mas'ood ﷺ says: "If one wishes to meet Allah Ta'ala on the Day of Qiyaamah as a Muslim, he must perform his Salaah at a place where Azaan is called out (a Masjid). Allah Ta'ala has ordered, through His Nabi ﷺ, such practices which are nothing but complete guidance, and Salaah with Jamaat is one of them. If you start to perform your Salaah at your houses as so and so is doing, then you will be leaving out the Sunnah of Rasulullah ﷺ, and when you leave out his Sunnah, then you will go astray. When a person performs wudhu correctly and then leaves for the Masjid, for each step that he takes, he receives one sawaab (reward) and has one sin wiped out. During the lifetime of Rasulullah ﷺ, no one would miss Jamaat except an open munaafiq (a non-Muslim pretending to be a Muslim) or a really sick person. Even the munaafiq dared not miss the Jamaat. A sick person who could be taken to the Masjid with the help of two men would be helped to join the Jamaat. And he said that Rasulullah ﷺ taught us those sunnats that are acts of Ibaadat. And amongst these sunnats is to perform salaah in a Masjid where Azaan is called out."

Note: This shows the extreme care the Sahaabah رضى الله عنهم took concerning Salaah with Jamaat. Even a sick person would be brought to the Masjid somehow or the other, even if it needed two men to help him. This concern was understandable as they found Rasulullah ﷺ himself so particular about it. It is said that when Rasulullah ﷺ was on his deathbed, he would often faint. He made wudhu after trying several times. Though he could hardly stand up, he went to the Masjid with the help of Hadhrat Abbaas رضى الله عنه and another Sahaabi in a condition that his mubaarak feet were dragging on the ground. Hadhrat Abu Bakr رضى الله عنه led the Salaah, and Rasulullah ﷺ himself joined the Jamaat."

Hadhrat Abu Darda رضى الله عنه narrates that Nabi ﷺ once said to him, "Worship Allah Ta'ala as if you see Him before you. Count yourself amongst the dead. (Don't even regard yourself to be amongst the living. In this way, nothing will please you and nothing will cause you grief). Beware of the curse of the oppressed. Do not miss Esha and Fajar with Jamaat even if you could crawl to the Masjid."

It is said in another Hadith, "Esha and Fajr are very hard on the munaafiq. If they knew the reward of Salaah with Jamaat, they would go to the Masjid and join the Jamaat even if they had to crawl."

HADITH 4 – THE FIRST TAKBEER

عَنْ أَنَسِ بْنِ مَالِكٍ رَضِىَ اللهُ عَنْهُ قَالَ قَالَ رَسُوْلُ اللهِ صَلَّى اللهُ عَلَيْهِ وَسَلَّمَ مَنْ صَلَّى لِلَّهِ أَرْبَعِيْنَ يَوْمًا فِىْ جَمَاعَةٍ يُدْرِكُ التَّكْبِيْرَةَ الْأُوْلَىٰ كُتِبَ لَهُ بَرَاءَتَانِ بَرَاءَةٌ مِّنَ النَّارِ وَبَرَاءَةٌ مِّنَ النِّفَاقِ (سنن الترمذى # 241)

Hadhrat Anas bin Maalik ﷺ narrates that he heard Rasulullah ﷺ saying, "A person who is particular about his Salaah with Jamaat for forty days, without missing the first takbeer, receives two certificates: One of being saved from Jahannam and the other of freedom from nifaaq (being a hypocrite)."

Note: If a person is regular with his Salaah (with sincerity) for forty days and he joins the Jamaat from the very beginning (i.e. when the Imaam says the first takbeer), he shall neither be a munaafiq nor shall he go to Jahannam. A munaafiq is a person who pretends to be a Muslim, but there is kufr (disbelief) in his heart. Changes in a man takes place in periods of forty days (according to the Hadith). The sequence of man's creation takes place in periods of 40 days. From a drop of liquid to a piece of flesh and in this way changes take place every forty days. This seems to be the significance of forty days in this Hadith. Therefore, the Sufis attach importance to this period (called Chilla in Urdu) for purposes of spiritual discipline.

Fortunate are those who do not miss their first takbeer for years on end.

HADITH 5 – TRYING TO GET SALAAH WITH JAMAAT

عَنْ اَبِيْ هُرَيْرَةَ رَضِيَ اللهُ عَنْهُ قَالَ قَالَ رَسُوْلُ اللهِ صَلَّى اللهُ عَلَيْهِ وَسَلَّمَ مَنْ تَوَضَّأَ فَاَحْسَنَ وُضُوْءَهُ ثُمَّ رَاحَ فَوَجَدَ النَّاسَ قَدْ صَلَّوْا اَعْطَاهُ اللهُ مِثْلَ اَجْرِ مَنْ صَلَّاهَا وَحَضَرَهَا لَا يَنْقُصُ ذٰلِكَ مِنْ اَجْرِهِمْ شَيْئًا (اخرجه الحاكم فى المستدرك # 754)

Hadhrat Abu Hurayrah ﷺ narrates that he heard Nabi ﷺ saying, "A person who performs wudhu properly, and, when he arrives at the Masjid, finds that the Jamaat is over, receives the reward of Jamaat. He will not receive a reward lesser than those who have performed their Salaah with Jamaat."

Note: It is the favour and kindness of Allah Ta'ala that a slight effort is enough to earn us the reward of Jamaat, although we had missed it. Who is the loser then if we ourselves remain deprived of the gifts of the Most

Kind? This Hadith also shows that we should not leave out going to the Masjid thinking that the Jamaat is over. Even if we find, on reaching the Masjid, that the Jamaat is over, we will get the full reward. However, if we are certain that the Jamaat is already over, then there is of course no point in going to the Masjid.

HADITH 6 – THE BIGGER THE CONGREGATION, THE MORE THE REWARD

عَنْ قُبَاثِ بْنِ اَشْيَمَ اللَّيْثِيْ رَضِىَ اللهُ عَنْهُ قَالَ قَالَ رَسُوْلُ اللهِ صَلَّى اللهُ عَلَيْهِ وَسَلَّمَ صَلَاةُ الرَّجُلَيْنِ يَؤُمُّ اَحَدُهُمَا صَاحِبَهُ اَزْكىٰ عِنْدَ اللهِ مِنْ صَلَاةِ اَرْبَعَةٍ تَتْرىٰ وَصَلَاةُ اَرْبَعَةٍ اَزْكىٰ عِنْدَ اللهِ مِنْ صَلَاةِ ثَمَانِيَةٍ تَتْرىٰ وَصَلَاةُ ثَمَانِيَةٍ يَؤُمُّهُمْ اَحَدُهُمْ اَزْكىٰ عِنْدَ اللهِ مِنْ صَلَاةِ مِائَةٍ تَتْرىٰ (اخرجه المنذرى فى الترغيب # 597)

Hadhrat Qubaas bin Ashyam Allaysi رضى الله عنه narrates that he heard Rasulullah صلى الله عليه وسلم saying, "Two people performing Salaah together with one as the Imaam, are liked by Allah Ta'ala more than four people performing Salaah on their own. Similarly four people performing Salaah with Jamaat are liked by Allah Ta'ala more than eight people performing it alone. Similarly, eight people performing Salaah with Jamaat are liked by Allah more than 100 people performing it alone."

In another Hadith it is said, "A big Jamaat is liked more by Allah Ta'ala than a small Jamaat."

Note: People think that there is no harm in having a small Jamaat of their own at their houses or at their shops. This is not correct. Firstly, they lose the reward of performing Salaah in the Masjid and secondly, they lose the reward of Salaah with a big Jamaat. The bigger the Jamaat, the more pleasing it is to Allah Ta'ala. When our only aim is to please Allah Ta'ala, why should we not do that which is more pleasing to Him. Allah Ta'ala is pleased to see three things; a row of Musallis offering Salaah with Jamaat, a person busy in Salaah at the time of Tahajjud in the darkness of night and a person fighting in the path of Allah Ta'ala.

HADITH 7 – GOING TO THE MASJID IN THE HOURS OF DARKNESS

عَنْ سَهْلِ بْنِ سَعْدٍ السَّاعِدِيِّ رَضِيَ اللهُ عَنْهُ قَالَ قَالَ رَسُوْلُ اللهِ صَلَّى اللهُ عَلَيْهِ وَسَلَّمَ بَشِّرِ الْمَشَّائِيْنَ فِي الظُّلَمِ اِلَى الْمَسَاجِدِ بِالنُّوْرِ التَّامِّ يَوْمَ الْقِيَامَةِ

(اخرجه الحاكم فى المستدرك # 768)

Hadhrat Sahl bin Sa'd رَضِىَ اللهُ عَنْهُ narrates that he heard Rasulullah صَلَّى اللهُ عَلَيْهِ وَسَلَّمَ saying, "Give good news to those who go to the Masjid during the hours of darkness. They will have perfect light on the Day of Qiyaamah."

Note: The importance of going to the Masjid in the darkness of the night will be realised on the dreadful Day of Qiyaamah. A person going to the Masjid in the hours of darkness in this world will be rewarded greatly in the Aakhirah. He will carry with him a light more brilliant than that of the sun. In a Hadith it is reported that such people shall sit on thrones of noor, with no worry at all while others will be in total confusion. In another Hadith it is said, on the Day of Qiyaamah Allah Ta'ala will ask, "Where are My neighbours?" The Malaaikah will ask, "Who are Your neighbours, O Allah?" Allah Ta'ala will reply, "Those who would frequent the Masjid."

In a Hadith it is said, "Of all the places on this earth, the Masaajid (plural of Masjid) are the dearest to Allah Ta'ala, and the shopping centres are the most hated by Him." In another Hadith, the Masaajid are called, "The gardens of Jannah."

Hadhrat Abu Sa'eed رَضِىَ اللهُ عَنْهُ narrates in a Saheeh Hadith that, Rasulullah صَلَّى اللهُ عَلَيْهِ وَسَلَّمَ once said, "Bear testimony to the Imaan of the person frequenting the masjid and then he recited the following aayah of the Qur-aan;

اِنَّمَا يَعْمُرُ مَسٰجِدَ اللهِ مَنْ اٰمَنَ بِاللهِ وَالْيَوْمِ الْاٰخِرِ

"Only those should attend (and care for) Allah Ta'ala's Masaajid (places for Allah Ta'ala's worship) who believes in Allah Ta'ala and the Last Day." (Surah Taubah – Aayah 18)

The following are few more Ahaadith regarding the rewards of Salaah with Jamaat:-

1. "Making wudhu when it is difficult, walking towards the Masjid and waiting for Salaah, wipes out one's sins."

2. "The further a person lives from the Masjid, the greater the sawaab (reward) he receives." This is so because a person coming from far will have to walk more. Every step will earn him a reward. Therefore, some Sahaabah رضي الله عنهم would take small steps in going to the Masjid to earn more sawaab.

3. "There are three things in this world for which people would fight with one another if only they knew their rewards. These are: To call out the Azaan, to go to the Masjid for Zuhr in the scorching heat of the sun, and to be in the first row in Salaah with Jamaat."

4. "Seven people will be given place under the shade of the mercy of Allah Ta'ala on the Day of Qiyaamah, when everybody will be suffering under the scorching heat of the sun. One of them will be the person whose heart remains attached to the Masjid. He is anxious to return to the Masjid if per chance he had to leave for some reason." Another Hadith says that, "Allah Ta'ala loves those who love the Masjid."

Every command of the pure Shariah is a source of innumerable blessings and rewards from Allah Ta'ala and carries many benefits which are showered on those who follow it. Besides, no commandment of Allah Ta'ala is void of goodness, blessings and reward. It is often difficult to understand the full benefits of the commandments of Allah Ta'ala, as no one can understand His Knowledge and Wisdom. Some of the Ulama have tried to explain the importance of Salaah with Jamaat, but their explanations differ according to their ability to understand the commands of Allah Ta'ala.

Our respected Shaikh, Shah Waliullah Dehlawi *(rahmatullahi alayh)*, writes in his famous Book '*Hujjatullahil Balighah*': "To save the people, whether they are learned or illiterate, from the evil effects of their own customs and rituals, we have to make one of the Deeni practices so common that it may be practiced openly by everybody. The people of the city and the villages will both desire to practice it. It should become a matter of competition and pride among all of them, and it should be so commonly practised that it becomes part and parcel of their day to day life, so much so, that life without it may be worthless for them. If this is achieved, it will help to establish the ibaadah and obedience of Allah Ta'ala and it will substitute those rituals and customs which could cause serious harm. Since Salaah is the only Deeni practice that is most important and common, it becomes therefore absolutely necessary to establish it in the entire world by propagating it and reading it in Jamaat, where it can be performed collectively with unity."

"Further, in every community there are a few who have the ability to lead, while the rest of the people just follow. There are some people who can be corrected with a little advice or criticism. Then there is a third group of people with very weak Imaan. If they are not encouraged to make ibaadah in public, they are likely to leave it out altogether. It is therefore in the best interest of the Muslim community that all its members perform Salaah collectively in Jamaat, so that those who neglect their ibaadah may be identified from those that observe their ibaadah. This will also cause the people with less knowledge to follow the Ulama and make the ignorant to learn from the learned the specific requirements of ibaadah. Those who are making ibaadah will differentiate right from wrong and genuine from fake, so that the right and the genuine may prevail and the wrong and the fake may be stopped."

"That group of people who love Allah Ta'ala, who seek His Mercy, always fear Him and have their hearts and souls turned to Him alone, are a cause of His blessings and Mercy to come down from the skies."

"The Muslim community has been given the responsibility of establishing the word of Allah Ta'ala which must be held in high regard and our Deen to be dominant over all others. This object cannot be achieved unless all the Muslims, big and small, the rich and the poor, the people of the cities and the villages, all perform the highest service and the most sacred commandment of Islam (i.e., Salaah) by gathering together in one place. It is for this reason that the Shariat (Islamic Law) lays special stress on Jumuah and Salaah with jamaat, by explaining the rewards that one gets for observing it and the punishments for neglecting it. For fulfilling this important duty, two types of Jamaat Salaah are required; one for people at their local Masjid and the other for the people of the whole town. Since gathering at your local Masjid is convenient and that of gathering the entire town is a little difficult, therefore, the five times daily Salaah (with Jamaat) will be performed at their local Masjid, and the weekly Jumuah Salaah will be performed at the common town Masjid (Jaami Masjid)."

CHAPTER TWO
WARNINGS FOR NOT PERFORMING SALAAH WITH JAMAAT

Just as Allah Ta'ala has promised rewards and blessings for fulfilling His commandments, He has also warned us of the dreadful punishments for neglecting it. We are the slaves of Allah Ta'ala and, therefore, it is obligatory for us to obey Him. No payment or reward is due to us for our obedience to Him. If He gives us a reward, it is surely His extreme favour on us. Similarly, no punishments can be too much for us if we disobey Allah Ta'ala, because there can be no greater crime for a slave than disobedience to his Master. Thus, no warning was required to be given by Allah Ta'ala and His Rasul ﷺ, yet they have so kindly warned us in different ways of the punishments and explained to us again and again just to save us from disaster. If even then we don't take a lesson, who could there be to save us from the unavoidable consequences?

HADITH 1 – PERFORMING SALAAH IN THE MASJID AFTER HEARING THE AZAAN

عَنِ ابْنِ عَبَّاسٍ رَضِيَ اللهُ عَنْهُمَا قَالَ قَالَ رَسُوْلُ اللهِ صَلَّى اللهُ عَلَيْهِ وَسَلَّمَ مَنْ سَمِعَ النِّدَاءَ فَلَمْ يَمْنَعْهُ مِنَ اتِّبَاعِهِ عُذْرٌ قَالُوْا وَمَا الْعُذْرُ قَالَ خَوْفٌ أَوْ مَرَضٌ لَمْ تُقْبَلْ مِنْهُ الصَّلَاةُ الَّتِيْ صَلَّى (اخرجه المنذري في الترغيب # 616)

Hadhrat Ibn Abbaas ﷺ narrates that Rasulullah ﷺ said, "If a person, in spite of hearing the Azaan, does not go to the Masjid (and he prefers to read his Salaah at home) without a strong excuse, then his Salaah is not accepted." When the Sahaabah ﷺ inquired as to what could be a strong excuse, he replied, "Illness or fear."

Note: It may perhaps appear from this Hadith that Salaah performed at home (after hearing the Azaan) is no Salaah at all. The Hanafis do not hold this view. According to them, though the reward and blessings promised for Fardh Salaah will not be awarded, but the person performing Salaah at home frees himself of this obligation. But in the opinion of some of the Sahaabah ﷺ and their successors, Salaah with jamaat (after hearing the Azaan) is fardh, and not to join the jamaat is haraam. According to many other Ulama, such a person has not even fulfilled the obligation of that particular Salaah. However, he is surely committing the sin of leaving out jamaat. In another Hadith narrated by Hadhrat Ibn Abbaas ﷺ, it is stated that such a person is guilty of disobedience to Allah Ta'ala and His Rasul ﷺ. Hadhrat Ibn Abbaas ﷺ also says, "The person who does not join the jamaat after hearing the Azaan, did not intend to do good nor was any good intended for him." Hadhrat Abu Hurayrah ﷺ says, "It is better to pour hot lead into the ears of a person who does not join the Jamaat."

Hadith 2 – Not going to the Masjid after hearing the Azaan

عَنْ مُعَاذِ بْنِ أَنَسٍ رَضِيَ اللهُ عَنْهُ عَنْ رَسُوْلِ اللهِ صَلَّى اللهُ عَلَيْهِ وَسَلَّمَ أَنَّهُ قَالَ الْجَفَاءُ كُلُّ الْجَفَاءِ وَالْكُفْرُ وَالنِّفَاقُ مَنْ سَمِعَ مُنَادِيَ اللهِ يُنَادِيْ إِلَى الصَّلَاةِ فَلَا يُجِيْبُهُ (اخرجه المنذرى فى الترغيب # 620)

Hadhrat Mu'aaz bin Anas ﷺ narrates that he heard Nabi ﷺ saying, "A person who does not go for Salaah after hearing the Azaan is doing a great wrong. He is doing an act of kufr and nifaaq."

Note: According to this Hadith, not to join the Jamaat after hearing the Azaan is improper for a Muslim. It is the practice of a kaafir or a munaafiq. What a strong warning!

In another Hadith, it is said, "Not to join Jamaat after hearing the Azaan causes a person to be the most unfortunate and the most worthless."

Hadhrat Sulaymaan bin Abi Hasamah ﷺ is one of the famous people of the early days of Islam. He was born during the lifetime of Nabi ﷺ, but was too young at that time to have had the honour of listening to any Hadith directly from him. During the khilaafat of Hadhrat Umar ﷺ he was made in charge of the market. One day, Hadhrat Umar ﷺ found him missing in Fajr Salaah. Hadhrat Umar ﷺ went to his house and asked his mother why Sulaymaan was not present for Fajr Salaah. She replied, "He kept on reading Nafl Salaah throughout the night, and sleep overpowered him at the time of Fajr Salaah." At this, Hadhrat Umar ﷺ said, "I would prefer reading Fajr Salaah with Jamaat than reading Nafl Salaah all night long."

HADITH 3 – SETTING FIRE TO THE HOUSES OF THOSE WHO PERFORM THEIR SALAAH AT HOME

عَنْ اَبِيْ هُرَيْرَةَ رَضِىَ اللهُ عَنْهُ قَالَ قَالَ رَسُوْلُ اللهِ صَلَّى اللهُ عَلَيْهِ وَسَلَّمَ لَقَدْ هَمَمْتُ اَنْ اٰمُرَ فِتْيَتِىْ فَيَجْمَعُوْا حُزَمًا مِنْ حَطَبٍ ثُمَّ اٰتِىَ قَوْمًا يُّصَلُّوْنَ فِىْ بُيُوْتِهِمْ لَيْسَتْ بِهِمْ عِلَّةٌ فَأُحَرِّقَهَا عَلَيْهِمْ (سنن ابی داود # 549)

Hadhrat Abu Hurairah ﷺ narrates that he heard Rasulullah ﷺ saying, "I desire to ask the boys to collect a huge amount of firewood. I would then go around and set fire to the houses of those who perform their Salaah at their homes without any excuse."

Note: Rasulullah ﷺ, who was most kind and merciful towards his followers and who would be greatly pained to see them even in a little difficulty, becomes so angry that he is ready to set fire to the homes of those who read their Salaah at home.

HADITH 4 – MAKING JAMAAT OUT IN THE FIELDS

عَنْ أَبِي الدَّرْدَاءِ رَضِيَ اللهُ عَنْهُ قَالَ سَمِعْتُ رَسُوْلَ اللهِ صَلَّى اللهُ عَلَيْهِ وَسَلَّمَ يَقُوْلُ مَا مِنْ ثَلَاثَةٍ فِيْ قَرْيَةٍ وَلَا بَدْوٍ لَا تُقَامُ فِيْهِمُ الصَّلَاةُ إِلَّا قَدِ اسْتَحْوَذَ عَلَيْهِمُ الشَّيْطَانُ فَعَلَيْكُمْ بِالْجَمَاعَةِ فَإِنَّمَا يَأْكُلُ الذِّئْبُ مِنَ الْغَنَمِ الْقَاصِيَةَ

(اخرجه المنذري في الترغيب # 618)

Hadhrat Abu Darda ﷺ narrates that he heard Rasulullah ﷺ saying, "If there are (even) three people in a village or in a desert and they do not read their Salaah with Jamaat, shaytaan gets hold of them. Remember that Salaah with Jamaat is very necessary for you. Surely a wolf eats up a lonely sheep, and shaytaan is the wolf for the people."

Note: People busy in farming etc. should make arrangements to read their Salaah with Jamaat when they are three or more in number. Even if they are two, it is better to read with Jamaat. The farmers in our country are generally negligent of Salaah and consider their farming a sufficient excuse for their neglect and even those who are considered pious prefer to perform their Salaah individually. If the farmers working in the fields get together and perform Salaah with Jamaat, they will receive the blessings of Allah Ta'ala. Despite the sun, rain, heat and cold, they remain busy for the sake of small worldly gains, but lose a huge amount of reward given by Allah Ta'ala by neglecting their Salaah. They could earn a reward fifty times more by reading their Salaah with Jamaat in the fields. It is stated in a Hadith, "When a shepherd calls out the Azaan at the foot of a hill (or in the fields) and begins his Salaah, Allah Ta'ala is greatly pleased with him. He says proudly to the Malaaikah, Look at My slave! He has called out the Azaan and is performing his Salaah. He does all this out of fear for Me. I therefore grant him forgiveness and announce his entrance into Jannah."

HADITH 5 – THE IMPORTANCE OF FARDH OVER NAFL

عَنِ ابْنِ عَبَّاسٍ رَضِىَ اللهُ عَنْهُمَا أَنَّهُ سُئِلَ عَنْ رَجُلٍ يَصُوْمُ النَّهَارَ وَيَقُوْمُ اللَّيْلَ وَلَا يَشْهَدُ الْجَمَاعَةَ وَلَا الْجُمُعَةَ فَقَالَ هٰذَا فِى النَّارِ (اخرجه المنذرى فى الترغيب # 629)

Somebody asked Ibn Abbaas ﵁, "What about a person who keeps fast all day and performs Nafl Salaah all night, but does not go to the Masjid for Jamaat and Jumu'ah?" "He is doomed to Jahannam," replied Hadhrat Ibn Abbaas ﵁.

Note: Such a person, being a Muslim, may finally be freed from Jahannam, but who knows after how long? The ignorant Sufis and Shaikhs are very particular about Zikr and Nafl Salaah and consider this important in attaining piety, while they are not particular about Salaah with jamaat. It must be clearly borne in mind at all times that no person can achieve piety without holding on to the Sunnah of our beloved Nabi ﷺ.

It is stated in a Hadith that Allah Ta'ala curses three people:
1. An Imaam who insists on leading the people in Salaah, although they are unhappy with him for a valid reason;
2. A woman whose husband is angry with her; and
3. A person who hears the Azaan but does not go to the Masjid for Salaah with Jamaat.

HADITH 6 - AAYAAT REVEALED ABOUT FARDH SALAAH IN THE SCRIPTURES OF ALLAH TA'ALA

اَخْرَجَ ابْنُ مَرْدَوَيْهِ عَنْ كَعْبِ الْأَحْبَارِ رَحْمَةُ اللهِ عَلَيْهِ قَالَ وَالَّذِىْ اَنْزَلَ التَّوْرَاةَ عَلٰى مُوْسٰى وَالْإِنْجِيْلَ عَلٰى عِيْسٰى وَالزَّبُوْرَ عَلٰى دَاوُدَ وَالْفُرْقَانَ عَلٰى مُحَمَّدٍ أُنْزِلَتْ هٰذِهِ الْاٰيَاتُ فِى الصَّلَوَاتِ الْمَكْتُوْبَاتِ حَيْثُ يُنَادٰى بِهِنَّ يَوْمَ يُكْشَفُ عَنْ سَاقٍ وَّ يُدْعَوْنَ اِلَى السُّجُوْدِ فَلَا يَسْتَطِيْعُوْنَ ۞ خَاشِعَةً اَبْصَارُهُمْ تَرْهَقُهُمْ ذِلَّةٌ ۖ وَ قَدْ كَانُوْا يُدْعَوْنَ اِلَى

$$\text{السُّجُودِ وَ هُمْ سٰلِمُوْنَ ۞ اَلصَّلَوَاتُ الْخَمْسُ اِذَا نُوْدِىَ بِهَا}$$

(اخرجه السيوطى فى الدر المنثور ٢٥٦/٨)

Ka'b Ahbaar (rahimahullah) says, "By Him who revealed the Taurah to Moosa (alayhis salaam), the Injeel to Isa (alayhis salaam), the Zaboor to Dawood (alayhis salaam), and the Qur-aan to Muhammad ﷺ, the following aayaat were revealed in respect of saying the Fardh Salaah in those places (masjids) where the Azaan is called out: "On the day when the glory of Saaq is revealed (this is a special kind of tajalli) and people are ordered to make sajdah, but they will be unable to do so, their gazes will be lowered with shame and they will be covered in disgrace. This will be because they had been commanded to make sajdah when they were quite well and healthy." (Surah Qalam - Aayaat 42-43).

Note: The *'glory of Saaq'* refers to a particular type of glory to be displayed on the Day of Qiyaamah. All the Muslims will fall into sajdah on seeing this glory, but there will be some whose backs will turn stiff and they will not be able to fall into sajdah. Different interpretations have been given by different commentators as to who these unlucky people will be. According to this Hadith, which is also supported by another which is narrated by Hadhrat Ibn Abbaas ﷺ, those shall be the people who were called for Salaah with jamaat, but did not go for it. A few other interpretations of the same are given below:

1. Hadhrat Abu Sa'eed Khudri ﷺ narrates on the authority of Rasulullah ﷺ that these shall be the people who used to perform Salaah so that they could be seen by other men.
2. These shall be the disbelievers who did not perform their Salaah at all.
3. These shall be the munaafiqeen. (Allah Ta'ala knows best and His knowledge is most perfect).

What a terrible thing to be so humiliated and disgraced on the Day of Qiyaamah that, while all the Muslims will fall into sajdah on seeing the glory of Allah Ta'ala, those who neglected Salaah with jamaat will be identified because they will not be able to make sajdah.

Besides these, many other warnings have been given against the neglect of jamaat. As a matter of fact, none of these warnings is necessary for a good Muslim for whom the word of Allah Ta'ala and His Rasul ﷺ is most important. All these warnings are meaningless for the person who has no regard for the word of Allah Ta'ala and His Rasul ﷺ. A time will come when every soul will be called to account and punished for his misdeeds and then no amount of taubah shall be of any help.

PART 3

KHUSHOO AND KHUDOO
IMPORTANCE OF SINCERITY, CONCENTRATION AND DEVOTION IN SALAAH

There are many people who read their five daily Salaah. Many are particular about Jamaat as well, but they read it so incorrectly, that instead of them getting sawaab (reward), Allah Ta'ala rejects their Salaah. This is not as bad as neglecting Salaah altogether, which as we have already learnt, is very serious. Although we are deprived of the rewards by performing our Salaah incorrectly, which is not accepted, yet we are saved from the sin of neglecting and disobeying the commandments of Allah Ta'ala altogether. However, when we spend our time, leave our work and undergo inconvenience, then why should we not see that we get the best return for our time and effort by performing our Salaah as best as we can?

This third part is divided into three chapters. In the first chapter, a few Aayaat are given from the Qur-aan Shareef about the people who were reprimanded for not performing their Salaah correctly and those who were praised for performing their Salaah correctly. In the second Chapter, stories are given about the Salaah of those few people who had extreme love for Allah Ta'ala. The third chapter consists of the sayings of Rasulullah ﷺ on this subject.

CHAPTER 1
AAYAAT FROM THE QUR-AAN SHAREEF

AAYAH 1 - IT IS YOUR TAQWA THAT REACHES ALLAH TA'ALA

$$\text{لَن يَنَالَ اللّهَ لُحُومُهَا وَلَا دِمَاؤُهَا وَلَـٰكِن يَنَالُهُ التَّقْوَىٰ مِنكُمْ}$$

"Their flesh and their blood will never reach Allah Ta'ala, but it is your Taqwa that will reach Him." (Surah Hajj - Aayah 37)

Although this particular aayah refers to the sacrificing of an animal, it also applies to all other ibaadah. It is the sincerity and devotion in our ibaadah by which it is accepted and would be judged by Allah Ta'ala. Hadhrat Mu'aaz رَضِىَ اللّٰهُ عَنْهُ says, "When Rasulullah صَلَّى اللّٰهُ عَلَيْهِ وَسَلَّمَ sent me to Yemen, I requested him to give me some parting advice. He replied, "Be sincere in all your duties, as sincerity will increase the value of an action, however small it may be."

Hadhrat Saubaan رَضِىَ اللّٰهُ عَنْهُ narrates that he heard Rasulullah صَلَّى اللّٰهُ عَلَيْهِ وَسَلَّمَ saying, "Blessed are the sincere ones, for they are the lamps of guidance. They cause the worst evils to be driven off through their sincerity." It is said in another Hadith, "It is through the presence of the weak and due to their Salaah and their sincerity that the help of Allah Ta'ala comes to all the people."

Aayah 2 – Curse on those who are unmindful of their Salaah

فَوَيْلٌ لِّلْمُصَلِّيْنَ ۞ الَّذِيْنَ هُمْ عَنْ صَلَاتِهِمْ سَاهُوْنَ ۞ الَّذِيْنَ هُمْ يُرَآءُوْنَ

"Destruction be for those performers of salaah who are heedless of their Salaah, those who show off (when performing salaah)."
(Surah Maa'oon – Aayaat 4-6)

"To be heedless," has been given the following different interpretations:

1. To be so careless that you miss the correct time of Salaah.
2. To be inattentive, (i.e. your mind wandering everywhere) in Salaah.
3. To forget the number of rakaats.

Aayah 3 – To perform Salaah lazily

وَ إِذَا قَامُوْٓا اِلَى الصَّلٰوةِ قَامُوْا كُسَالٰى ۙ يُرَآءُوْنَ النَّاسَ وَلَا يَذْكُرُوْنَ اللّٰهَ اِلَّا قَلِيْلًا

"And when they (the hypocrites) stand up for Salaah, they stand up lazily (reluctantly) and want to be seen by people and they remember Allah Ta'ala only a little." *(Surah Nisaa' – Aayah 142)*

Aayah 4 – People who destroy their Salaah will be thrown into Jahannam

فَخَلَفَ مِنْۢ بَعْدِهِمْ خَلْفٌ اَضَاعُوا الصَّلٰوةَ وَاتَّبَعُوا الشَّهَوٰتِ فَسَوْفَ يَلْقَوْنَ غَيًّا

"They (these Ambiyaa عَلَيْهِمُ السَّلَام) were followed by such evil successors who destroyed salaah and pursued (followed) their passions (did as they pleased). Soon they shall meet devastation (in the Aakhirah)."
(Surah Maryam – Aayah 59)

In the dictionary, *'Ghayy'* is explained as dishonesty, which points towards the dreadful punishment and destruction in the Aakhirah.

According to many commentators, *'Ghayy'* is a pit in Jahannam full of blood and pus. The people who had destroyed their Salaah shall be thrown into this pit.

AAYAH 5 – THE SALAAH OF A LAZY PERSON

وَمَا مَنَعَهُمْ اَنْ تُقْبَلَ مِنْهُمْ نَفَقٰتُهُمْ اِلَّا اَنَّهُمْ كَفَرُوْا بِاللّٰهِ وَبِرَسُوْلِهٖ وَلَا يَأْتُوْنَ الصَّلٰوةَ اِلَّا وَهُمْ كُسَالٰى وَلَا يُنْفِقُوْنَ اِلَّا وَهُمْ كٰرِهُوْنَ

"The only thing that prevents their spending (acts of charity) from being accepted is that they disbelieve in Allah Ta'ala and His Rasul ﷺ and they perform their salaah lazily and only spend reluctantly in charity" (Surah Taubah – Aayah 54)

The Aayaat one to five above relate to those who destroy their Salaah. On the other hand, the following Aayaat speak of those whom Allah Ta'ala praises for performing a good Salaah.

AAYAH 6 – THOSE WHO ARE CONCERNED ABOUT SALAAH WILL GET JANNATUL FIRDAUS

قَدْ اَفْلَحَ الْمُؤْمِنُوْنَ ۙ الَّذِيْنَ هُمْ فِيْ صَلَاتِهِمْ خٰشِعُوْنَ ۙ وَالَّذِيْنَ هُمْ عَنِ اللَّغْوِ مُعْرِضُوْنَ ۙ وَالَّذِيْنَ هُمْ لِلزَّكٰوةِ فٰعِلُوْنَ ۙ وَالَّذِيْنَ هُمْ لِفُرُوْجِهِمْ حٰفِظُوْنَ ۙ اِلَّا عَلٰٓى اَزْوَاجِهِمْ اَوْ مَا مَلَكَتْ اَيْمَانُهُمْ فَاِنَّهُمْ غَيْرُ مَلُوْمِيْنَ ۚ فَمَنِ ابْتَغٰى وَرَآءَ ذٰلِكَ فَاُولٰٓئِكَ هُمُ الْعٰدُوْنَ ۚ وَالَّذِيْنَ هُمْ لِاَمٰنٰتِهِمْ وَعَهْدِهِمْ رٰعُوْنَ ۙ وَالَّذِيْنَ هُمْ عَلٰى صَلَوٰتِهِمْ يُحَافِظُوْنَ ۘ اُولٰٓئِكَ هُمُ الْوٰرِثُوْنَ ۙ الَّذِيْنَ يَرِثُوْنَ الْفِرْدَوْسَ ۗ هُمْ فِيْهَا خٰلِدُوْنَ

*"Successful indeed are the believers who are humble in their Salaah, who turn away from futility **(talk and actions that have no benefit),** who fulfil the act of paying Zakaat and those who safeguard*

their private orphans, except when it comes to their spouses and the slave women whom they own, then they will surely not be blamed **(about cohabiting with them)**. Whoever seeks more than this **(by fulfilling their desires in a manner the shari'ah forbids)**, then such persons are indeed transgressors (sinners). **(The successful believers are also)** Those who give due regard to (fulfil) their trust and their pledges, and are particular about their Salaah. These are the heirs who will inherit Firdaus (the highest level of Jannah) where they will live forever."

(Surah Mu'minoon – Aayaat 1-11)

Rasulullah ﷺ says, "Firdaus is the highest and the best portion of Jannah, from where all its rivers originate. The Arsh of Allah Ta'ala will be placed there. When you make dua for Jannah, always ask for Jannatul Firdaus."

AAYAH 7 – HUMILITY IN SALAAH

وَاِنَّهَا لَكَبِيرَةٌ اِلَّا عَلَى الْخٰشِعِيْنَ ۞ الَّذِيْنَ يَظُنُّوْنَ اَنَّهُمْ مُّلٰقُوْا رَبِّهِمْ وَاَنَّهُمْ اِلَيْهِ رٰجِعُوْنَ

"And truly it (Salaah) is difficult except for the humble ones; who are convinced (of the fact) that they will meet their Rabb, and that to Him they will return." (Surah Baqarah - Aayaat 45-46)

AAYAH 8 – REWARDS FOR THOSE WHO ARE NOT DISTRACTED BY BUSINESS

فِيْ بُيُوْتٍ اَذِنَ اللّٰهُ اَنْ تُرْفَعَ وَ يُذْكَرَ فِيْهَا اسْمُهٗ يُسَبِّحُ لَهٗ فِيْهَا بِالْغُدُوِّ وَ الْاٰصَالِ ۞ رِجَالٌ ۙ لَّا تُلْهِيْهِمْ تِجَارَةٌ وَّ لَا بَيْعٌ عَنْ ذِكْرِ اللّٰهِ وَاِقَامِ الصَّلٰوةِ وَاِيْتَآءِ الزَّكٰوةِ ۪ۙ يَخَافُوْنَ يَوْمًا تَتَقَلَّبُ فِيْهِ الْقُلُوْبُ وَ الْاَبْصَارُ ۞ لِيَجْزِيَهُمُ اللّٰهُ اَحْسَنَ مَا عَمِلُوْا وَ يَزِيْدَهُمْ مِّنْ فَضْلِهٖ ؕ وَاللّٰهُ يَرْزُقُ مَنْ يَّشَآءُ بِغَيْرِ حِسَابٍ

"In the houses (Masaajid) which Allah Ta'ala has commanded that they be exalted (honoured and respected), and His name be taken in them, they **(men whom Allah Ta'ala guided)** glorify Him morning and evening. **(These rightly guided men are)** Men whom neither their trade nor commerce distracts them from the zikr (remembrance) of Allah Ta'ala, establishment of Salaah and paying of Zakaat. They fear that Day when their hearts and eyes will be overturned. So that Allah Ta'ala may reward them with the best of rewards for their (good) actions and grant them an increase from His bounty. Allah provides for whoever He wills without any measure." *(Surah Noor – Aayaat 36-38)*

تُو وہ داتا ہے کہ دینے کے لے دَر تری رحمت کے ہیں ہر دم کھلے

You are that Master, Who always keeps His doors of mercy open for our sake.

Hadhrat Abdullah bin Abbaas رَضِىَ اللهُ عَنْهُ says, "Establishment of Salaah means performance of Ruku and Sajdah properly and continuous concentration in Salaah with complete humility and submission." Hadhrat Qataadah *(rahmatullahi alayh)* says: "Wherever the words 'Establishment of Salaah' occurs in Qur-aan Shareef, it means to guard its correct time, to perform wudhu correctly and to make Ruku and Sajdah properly."

AAYAH 9 – THE FAITHFUL SLAVES OF ALLAH TA'ALA

وَعِبَادُ الرَّحْمٰنِ الَّذِيْنَ يَمْشُوْنَ عَلَى الْأَرْضِ هَوْنًا وَّ اِذَا خَاطَبَهُمُ الْجٰهِلُوْنَ قَالُوْا سَلٰمًا ۝ وَالَّذِيْنَ يَبِيْتُوْنَ لِرَبِّهِمْ سُجَّدًا وَّ قِيَامًا

"The (faithful) slaves of Ar-Rahmaan (the Beneficent) are those who walk upon the earth with humility and when the ignorant talk to them, they (excuse themselves) saying "salaam" (leave us in peace) and spend the night in prostrating and standing before their Rabb."
(Surah Furqaan – Aayaat 63-64)

After describing a few more qualities of His faithful slaves, Allah Ta'ala says in the same context:

$$\text{أُولَٰئِكَ يُجْزَوْنَ الْغُرْفَةَ بِمَا صَبَرُوا وَيُلَقَّوْنَ فِيهَا تَحِيَّةً وَسَلَامًا ۝ خَالِدِينَ فِيهَا ۚ حَسُنَتْ مُسْتَقَرًّا وَمُقَامًا}$$

"These people, because of their steadfastness (Imaan and Islam), shall be rewarded with balconies (in Jannah) where they will be met (by the Malaaikah) with greetings (of welcome) and salaam. They will live there (in Jannah) forever. It is surely a beautiful residence and abode."
(Surah Furqaan – Aayaat 75-76)

$$\text{وَالْمَلَائِكَةُ يَدْخُلُونَ عَلَيْهِمْ مِنْ كُلِّ بَابٍ ۝ سَلَامٌ عَلَيْكُمْ بِمَا صَبَرْتُمْ ۚ فَنِعْمَ عُقْبَى الدَّارِ}$$

"And the Malaaikah shall come to them from every door (proclaiming) 'Salaam (peace) be on you for the sabr that you exercised. How blissful is the outcome of the Aakhirah."
(Surah Ra'd – Aayaat 23-24)

Aayah 10 – Leaving Their Beds to Worship Allah

$$\text{تَتَجَافَىٰ جُنُوبُهُمْ عَنِ الْمَضَاجِعِ يَدْعُونَ رَبَّهُمْ خَوْفًا وَطَمَعًا وَمِمَّا رَزَقْنَاهُمْ يُنْفِقُونَ ۝ فَلَا تَعْلَمُ نَفْسٌ مَا أُخْفِيَ لَهُمْ مِنْ قُرَّةِ أَعْيُنٍ جَزَاءً بِمَا كَانُوا يَعْمَلُونَ}$$

"(The ones who believe in our revelations are) Those who forsake their beds / their sides (bodies) part from their beds, making dua to their Rabb in fear (for His punishment) and hope (in His mercy) and they spend (in charity) from what We provided for them. No soul knows what pleasures are hidden for him (in Jannah) as a reward for the deed they used to carry out."
(Surah Sajdah – Aayaat 16-17)

Aayah 11 – Reward for those who sleep little

اِنَّ الْمُتَّقِيْنَ فِىْ جَنّٰتٍ وَّ عُيُوْنٍ ۙ اٰخِذِيْنَ مَآ اٰتٰىهُمْ رَبُّهُمْ ۚ اِنَّهُمْ كَانُوْا قَبْلَ ذٰلِكَ مُحْسِنِيْنَ ۗ كَانُوْا قَلِيْلًا مِّنَ الَّيْلِ مَا يَهْجَعُوْنَ ۞ وَ بِالْاَسْحَارِ هُمْ يَسْتَغْفِرُوْنَ

"Verily those with Taqwa shall be (enjoying themselves) in Jannah with springs, receiving whatever their Rabb gives them, for indeed these people use to carry out good deeds before (in this world). They used to sleep but little at night. During the closing portions of the night they would be seeking forgiveness."

(Surah Zaariyaat - Aayaat 15-18)

Aayah 12 – Those who devote themselves to Ibaadah at night

اَمَّنْ هُوَ قَانِتٌ اٰنَآءَ الَّيْلِ سَاجِدًا وَّ قَآئِمًا يَّحْذَرُ الْاٰخِرَةَ وَ يَرْجُوْا رَحْمَةَ رَبِّهٖ ۗ قُلْ هَلْ يَسْتَوِى الَّذِيْنَ يَعْلَمُوْنَ وَ الَّذِيْنَ لَا يَعْلَمُوْنَ ۗ اِنَّمَا يَتَذَكَّرُ اُولُوا الْاَلْبَابِ

"(is this kaafir better) or the person who is engrossed (engaged) in ibaadah (of Allah Ta'ala) throughout the hours of the night, prostrating and standing, fearing the Aakhirah and hoping for the mercy of his Rabb? (to be counted equal with a disbeliever)? Say (to them, O Muhammad ﷺ): 'Can those who have knowledge be equal with those who do not have knowledge? But only men of understanding will pay heed. Only those with (spiritual) intelligence (wisdom) will take heed.'"

(Surah Zumar – Aayah 9)

Aayah 13 – Qualities of Man

اِنَّ الْاِنْسَانَ خُلِقَ هَلُوْعًا ۙ اِذَا مَسَّهُ الشَّرُّ جَزُوْعًا ۙ وَّ اِذَا مَسَّهُ الْخَيْرُ مَنُوْعًا ۙ اِلَّا الْمُصَلِّيْنَ ۙ الَّذِيْنَ هُمْ عَلٰى صَلَاتِهِمْ دَآئِمُوْنَ

"Verily man was created very impatient. When difficulty afflicts him, he panics. And when he experiences any good, he becomes miserly. **(this is the condition of all people)** Except those (believers) who perform salaah, those who are constant (regular) in their Salaah."
(Surah Ma'aarij – Aayaat 19-23)

After giving some more qualities of these blessed people, Allah Ta'ala says in the same context;

وَ الَّذِيْنَ هُمْ عَلٰى صَلَاتِهِمْ يُحَافِظُوْنَ ۚ أُولٰٓئِكَ فِيْ جَنّٰتٍ مُّكْرَمُوْنَ

"And those who guard their Salaah **(the time, condition and method of performing it)**. These people shall be honoured in the gardens of Jannah." (Surah Ma'aarij – Aayaat 34-35)

Besides the quotations given above, there are many Aayaat of the Qur-aan Shareef commanding Salaah and praising those who perform their Salaah properly. Salaah is indeed a great favour. That is why Rasulullah ﷺ has called it, 'the comfort of my eyes', and Ibraaheem *(alayhis salaam)* made dua to Allah Ta'ala,

رَبِّ اجْعَلْنِيْ مُقِيْمَ الصَّلٰوةِ وَمِنْ ذُرِّيَّتِيْ ۖ رَبَّنَا وَتَقَبَّلْ دُعَآءِ

"O my Rabb! Make me one who establishes Salaah and my progeny as well. O our Rabb! Accept my dua."
(Surah Ibraaheem - Aayah 40)

Here, the famous Nabi of Allah Ta'ala, whom Allah Ta'ala has called '*Khaleel*', is asking Allah Ta'ala to allow him to perform his Salaah properly and regularly. Allah Ta'ala Himself is ordering His beloved Nabi ﷺ thus:

وَأْمُرْ أَهْلَكَ بِالصَّلٰوةِ وَاصْطَبِرْ عَلَيْهَا ۖ لَا نَسْئَلُكَ رِزْقًا ۖ نَحْنُ نَرْزُقُكَ ۗ وَالْعَاقِبَةُ لِلتَّقْوٰى

"And instruct (encourage) your family to perform Salaah and you yourself remain steadfast on it. We do not ask provision (sustenance)

from you but We provide for you. And the best result is for (adopting) taqwa." (Surah Taaha – Aayah 132)

It is said in a Hadith that whenever the people of the house of Rasulullah ﷺ experienced any difficulty, he instructed them to perform Salaah and used to recite this Aayah. All the Ambiyaa *(alayhimus salaam)* of Allah Ta'ala are reported to have turned to Salaah whenever they faced any difficulty. Unfortunately, we are so unmindful and indifferent about Salaah that in spite of all that we speak about Islam and Islamic practices, we pay no attention to it. But on the other hand, if anybody stands up to invite us and to draw our attention towards Salaah, we make jokes and mock him and oppose him, thereby harming no one but ourselves.

Even those who perform their Salaah, often perform it in such a way that it will not be wrong to call it a mockery of Salaah, because all its requirements are not observed and it also lacks concentration and devotion. The practical example of Rasulullah ﷺ and his Sahaabah ﷢ should be the guiding factor in our lives. I have collected the stories about the Salaah of the Sahaabah ﷢ in a separate book, named *"Stories of Sahaabah,"* and I need not repeat them here. However, I am giving a few stories from the lives of some pious people in the following pages. The practices and sayings of Rasulullah ﷺ about this subject would appear in Chapter three.

CHAPTER TWO
A FEW STORIES FROM THE LIVES OF THE PIOUS

STORY 1 – A SAINT PERFORMS ESHA AND FAJR SALAAH FOR FORTY YEARS WITH THE SAME WUDHU

Shaikh Abdul Waahid *(rahmatullahi alayh)* says, "One day I was so much overpowered by sleep that I went to bed before finishing my zikr for the night. I saw in my dream a most beautiful girl dressed in green silk. All parts of her body and even her shoes were engaged in zikr. She said to me, 'Desire to possess me as I desire to possess you.' She then recited a few couplets showing the eagerness of a lover. When I woke up from the dream, I vowed not to sleep any more during the night." It is reported that for full forty years he never slept at night, and performed both Esha and Fajr Salaah with the same wudhu.

STORY 2 – A SAINT SEES WOMEN IN A DREAM MAKING THE ZIKR OF ALLAH TA'ALA

Shaikh Mazhar Sa'di *(rahmatullahi alayh)*, the famous saint, kept weeping for sixty years in love and eagerness for Allah Ta'ala. One night he saw in a dream a few women by the side of pearl trees with gold branches, on the bank of a river full with fluid musk, pure and fragrant. The women were making the zikr of Allah Ta'ala. He asked them who they were. They replied by reciting two couplets, which meant, "We have been created by the Sustainer of mankind and the Rabb of Nabi

Muhammad ﷺ for those people who keep standing before Allah Ta'ala all night long, remembering Him and asking from Him."

STORY 3 – A SAINT GOES TO SLEEP AT NIGHT WITHOUT STANDING UP FOR IBAADAH

Abu Bakr Dhareer *(rahmatullahi alayh)* says, "There lived a young slave with me. He fasted the entire day and stood in Tahajjud Salaah the entire night. One day he came to me and related: 'Last night, against my usual practice, I went to sleep. I saw in my dream that the wall of the Mihraab was cracked and from the crack appeared a few damsels. One of them was very ugly. I asked one of the pretty damsels who they were. She replied that they were my previous nights and that the ugly one was this night.'"

STORY 4 – A SAINT IS REMINDED TO GET UP AND RECITE THE QUR-AAN IN TAHAJJUD

A famous Shaikh says: "One night I was in a deep sleep and could not get up for Tahajjud Salaah. I saw in my dream a girl of such beauty which I had never seen in my life. A fragrance came out from her which I had never smelt before. She handed over to me a piece of paper on which were written three couplets, which meant, "You are enjoying such a deep sleep that you have become forgetful of the high balconies of Jannah, where you have to stay forever with no fear of death. Wake up! It is better to recite the Qur-aan Shareef in Tahajjud than to sleep." Since then, whenever I feel sleepy, these couplets come to my mind and the sleep goes away.

STORY 5 – SALAAH OF A SLAVE GIRL

Hadhrat Ataa *(rahmatullahi alayh)* writes, "I once went to the market. A person was selling a slave girl who was known to be mad. I bought her for seven Dinaar (gold coins) and brought her home. After some part of the night had passed, I noticed that she got up, performed wudhu and began her Salaah. She cried so much that I thought she would die. On finishing her Salaah, she made dua to Allah Ta'ala thus, 'O my Allah!

Because of the love You have for me, show mercy on me.' I corrected her by telling her that she should rather say; 'Because of the love I have for You ...' She got annoyed and said, 'By Allah Himself! Had He not loved me, I would not be standing here before Him while you are in your bed.' She then fell into sajdah and recited a few poems saying, 'I am growing more and more restless. How can one rest whose peace of mind is taken away by love (of Allah Ta'ala)? O Allah! Show mercy and give me some good news.' She then made dua. 'O Allah! The matter between me and You had been a secret. Now, people have come to know of it. O, Allah! Call me back.' After saying this, she cried aloud and passed away on the spot."

STORY 6 – ANOTHER INCIDENT OF A SLAVE GIRL

Hadhrat Sirri *(rahmatullahi alayh)* writes: "I once bought a slave woman to work for me. She served me for some time. I didn't realise her secret. She had a corner in the house for her Salaah. After finishing her work, she would go there and offer Salaah. One night, I noticed her performing Salaah and then making dua to Allah Ta'ala. While making her dua, she said, 'Because of the love You have for me, do such and such a thing for me.' I said to her, 'O woman, say, by the love that I have for You.' She answered, 'My Master, if He had not loved me, He would not have allowed me to stand in Salaah and deprive you of it.' Next morning, I said to her, 'You are wasting your time in your present job. You are meant for the service of Allah.' I then gave her some gifts and set her free."

STORY 7 – CRYING OF A SLAVE GIRL IN TAHAJJUD SALAAH

Hadhrat Sirri Saqati *(rahmatullahi alayh)* writes about a woman: "Upon getting up for Tahajjud she would say, 'O Allah! Shaytaan is Your creation. You have full power over him. He sees me and I cannot see him. You see him and have control over all his actions, while he has no control over You. O, Allah! Stop the evil that he wishes to do to me. Forgive the wrong he may do to trick me. I seek your help from his evil plans and with Your help I chase him away.' She would cry bitterly until she became blind in one eye. People begged her to stop crying so much in case she loses her other eye. She replied, 'If it is an eye of Jannah, Allah Ta'ala will grant me better than this, but if it is an eye of Jahannam, then the sooner it is lost the better.'"

STORY 8 – A PORTER STOPS WORK AT THE TIME OF SALAAH

Shaikh Abu Abdullah Jilaa *(rahmatullahi alayh)* says: "My mother asked my father to buy some fish from the market. My father left for the market and I went with him. After buying the fish, we required someone to carry it. We paid a boy who was prepared to do the job. He put the load on his head and followed us.

On the way, we heard the Azaan. The boy exclaimed, 'The caller of Allah Ta'ala has called me. I need to make wudhu. I shall now carry the fish after Salaah. If you like, you may wait, otherwise, here it is.' Saying this, he put the load down and left for the Masjid. My father thought that if the poor boy could trust Allah Ta'ala so much, we must do so as well. He, therefore, left the fish there and took me to the Masjid. Having performed Salaah, we found the fish lying in the same place as we had left it. The boy carried it to our house. My father mentioned this strange story to my mother who insisted that the boy should be invited to eat with us.

On inviting him, he said, 'Excuse me, I am fasting.' My father then asked him to have iftaar at our house. To this he said, 'It is not possible for me to return once I am gone. Maybe I will stay in a Masjid close to your house. I shall then join you for meals.' Saying this he went to the Masjid and returned after Maghrib. When supper was over, I showed him the room where he could rest without being disturbed.

There lived a crippled woman in our neighbourhood. We were surprised to see her walking normally. Upon asking her how she got cured, she said, 'I made dua to Allah Ta'ala to cure me through the blessings of your guest. As soon as I made this dua I was cured.' When we went to look for the boy in the room where we had left him in, we found that the door was closed and he was nowhere to be seen."

STORY 9 – THE LEG OF A PIOUS PERSON IS AMPUTATED WHILST PERFORMING SALAAH

A pious man had a severe sore on his foot. According to the doctors, if his foot was not amputated, the sore might cause him to die. His mother suggested the operation be done while he was reading Salaah. The operation was done whilst he was in Salaah and he felt no pain at all.

STORY 10 – A SLAVE GIRL DIES WHILST RECITING QUR'AAN IN SALAAH

Abu 'Aamir *(rahmatullahi alayh)* says, "I saw a slave woman for sale at a very cheap price. She was very thin and her hair was dirty. I took pity on her and bought her. I said to her, 'Come woman, let us go and buy some things for Ramadhaan.' She said, '*Alhamdulillah*, all the months are same for me.' She fasted daily and stood in Salaah every night. When Eid approached, I said to her, 'O Woman! You will accompany me tomorrow to buy some things for Eid.' She replied, 'My master! You love this world too much.' She then went into her room and commenced her Salaah. She was reciting Surah Ibraheem. When she reached the 16th aayah of the Surah;

مِّن وَرَآئِهِ جَهَنَّمُ وَيُسْقَىٰ مِن مَّآءٍ صَدِيدٍ

"Before him is Jahannam where he will be given boiling, stinking water to drink." (Surah Ibraaheem – Aayah 16)

which describes the punishment of a disbeliever. She continued reciting this aayat when she suddenly gave out a cry and fell down dead."

STORY 11 – THE SACRIFICES OF A SAYYED

A story is mentioned about a Sayyed (A person from the family of Nabi ﷺ), who read Salaah for twelve days with the same wudhu and did not get the opportunity to lie down for fifteen years. There were many days wherein he did not get anything to eat.

Many similar incidents are mentioned about those people who had sacrificed for the sake of Allah Ta'ala. To emulate such people is very difficult as Allah Ta'ala had created them only for this reason (i.e. Allah

Ta'ala had bestowed them with the strength to endure such sacrifice). For the common people like us, leave alone following these people, even following those pious people who were serving Deen and also busy in their worldly responsibilities is difficult.

Story 12 – Salaah of Umar-bin-Abdul Aziz
(Rahmatullahi Alayh)

Everybody knows Umar bin Abdul Aziz *(rahmatullahi alayh)*. He is the most famous Khalifah after the four Khulafaa-e-Raashideen. His wife says, "There may be other people more particular about wudhu and Salaah, but I have never seen anybody fearing Allah Ta'ala more than my husband. After Esha, he would sit on his musalla and raise his hands in dua. He would continue crying before Allah Ta'ala till sleep overpowered him. When he awoke during the night, he would again make dua and cry before Allah Ta'ala."

It is said that since his becoming Khalifah, he never shared the bed with his wife. His wife was the daughter of the great King, Abdul Malik. Her father had given her a lot of jewellery in dowry, which included a beautiful diamond. He said to his wife, "Either part with all your jewellery for the sake of Allah Ta'ala, so that I may deposit it in the Baitul Maal or be separated from me. I would not like to live in a house where there is so much wealth." His wife replied, "I can part with a thousand times more wealth, but I cannot leave you." She then deposited everything she had in the Baitul Maal. After the death of Umar bin Abdul Aziz, when Yazeed, the son of Abdul Malik, succeeded him as Khalifah, he said to his sister, "If you like, you may have your jewellery back from the Baitul Maal. She replied, "How can the wealth I discarded during the lifetime of my husband satisfy me after his death."

Umar bin Abdul Aziz *(rahmatullahi alayh)* was on his deathbed when he asked the people around him about the cause of his disease. Someone said, "People think it is the effect of black magic." He said, "No, it is not magic." He then sent for a particular slave and asked him, "What made you poison me?" He replied, "One hundred Dinaar and a promise of freedom." Umar bin Abdul Aziz *(rahmatullahi alayh)* took away those Dinaars from the slave and put them in the Baitul Maal. He then advised the slave to run away where he could not be arrested.

Just before his death, Maslamah *(rahmatullahi alayh)* came to him and said, "Nobody has ever treated his children as you are doing. None of your thirteen sons have anything to live on." He sat up in his bed and said, "I have not held back from my sons what was due to them. I have refused them what was actually due to others. If my sons are pious, then Allah Ta'ala will surely look after them as He has said in His Book:

$$\text{وَهُوَ يَتَوَلَّى الصَّالِحِيْنَ}$$

"And He is the guardian of the righteous."

If they are wrong-doers, why should I care for them?"

STORY 13 – IMAAM AHMAD BIN HAMBAL *(RAHMATULLAHI ALAYH)*

Hadhrat Imaam Ahmad bin Hambal *(rahmatullahi alayh)* is a famous Imaam in Fiqh. Despite him being so busy the entire day in Masaail, he would perform 300 rakaats of Nafal Salaah at night. Hadhrat Sa'eed bin Jubair *(rahmatullahi alayh)* used to read the entire Qur-aan in one rakaat of Salaah.

STORY 14 – THE CRYING OF MUHAMMAD-BIN-MUNKADIR *(RAHMATULLAHI ALAYH)* IN TAHAJJUD SALAAH

Muhammad bin Munkadir *(rahmatullahi alayh)* was a Haafiz of Hadith (a person who has memorised at least 100 000 Ahaadith). One night, he cried bitterly in Tahajjud. When someone enquired, he said, "While reading, I came across the following words of the Qur-aan:

$$\text{وَبَدَا لَهُمْ مِّنَ اللّٰهِ مَا لَمْ يَكُوْنُوْا يَحْتَسِبُوْنَ}$$

"Such things will then become apparent to them from Allah Ta'ala, which they had never imagined." (Surah Zumar – Aayah 47)

In the beginning of this aayat it is mentioned that if the wrong doers possessed everything of this world and double that amount, then on the Day of Qiyaamah, in order to save themselves from the punishment, they will be prepared to give over everything they possess to save themselves.

Thereafter this aayat (above) is mentioned. At this point, all his eveil deeds will be made apparent to him.

Hadhrat Muhammad bin Munkadir *(rahmatullahi alayh)* was very worried at the time of his death saying that he feared these Aayaat of the Qur-aan.

STORY 15 – SAABIT BUNAANI *(RAHMATULLAHI ALAYH)* PERFORMS SALAAH IN THE GRAVE

Saabit Bunaani *(rahmatullahi alayh)* is a Hafiz of Hadith. He would cry a lot while making dua to Allah Ta'ala. Someone warned him that he would lose his eyesight. He replied, "Of what use are these eyes if they do not weep before Allah Ta'ala."

He used to ask in his dua, "O, Allah! Allow me to read Salaah in the grave." Abu Sanaan *(rahmatullahi alayh)* says, "By Allah! I was among those present at the burial of Saabit Bunaani *(rahmatullahi alayh)*. Just after he was placed in his grave, one of the bricks from the side fell off. I peeped into the grave, and to my amazement, Saabit *(rahmatullahi alayh)* was performing Salaah. I said to a person standing by my side, 'Look at that.' He advised me to keep quiet. After the burial, we went to his daughter and enquired, 'What was the special practice of your father?' She wanted to know what made us ask her that question. We told her the story of the grave. She said, 'He has been punctual in Tahajjud Salaah for fifty years and made dua to Allah Ta'ala to allow him to perform Salaah in the grave if that privilege could be granted to anybody.'"

Before finishing this chapter, I will write a few more stories about the Salaah of some pious people.

SALAAH OF THE PIOUS

1. Hadhrat Imaam Abu Yusuf *(rahmatullahi alayh)* was the Qaadhiul Qudhaat (supreme judge). Everyone knows very well about his ilmi pursuits. The work of qadhaa (being a judge) was a separate work. Despite all of this, he would perform 200 Rakaats of Nafl Salaah daily.
2. Muhammad bin Nasr *(rahmatullahi alayh)* is a famous Muhaddith. His devotion to Salaah cannot be compared. Once, while in Salaah, he was stung on the forehead by a wasp. Although blood oozed out, he neither moved nor did he allow it to disturb his concentration in

Salaah. It is said that in Salaah, he stood still like a stick planted in the ground.

3. It is said about Baqi bin Makhlad *(rahmatullahi alayh)* that he would recite the complete Qur-aan every night in thirteen rakaats of Tahajjud and Witr.

4. Hannaad *(rahmatullahi alayh)* is a great Muhaddith. One of his pupils says, "Hannaad used to weep a lot. After finishing the lesson in the morning, he would perform Nafl Salaah till midday. He would go home for a short break, returning for Zuhr. He would then perform Nafl Salaah till Asr. Between Asr and Maghrib, he recited the Qur-aan Shareef. I left him after Maghrib. I said to one of his neighbours, 'Our Shaikh performs so much of Salaah. It is really wonderful.' He said, 'He has been doing this for the last seventy years. You will be even more surprised if you saw his Salaah during the night.'"

5. Masrooq *(rahmatullahi alayh)* is another great Muhaddith. His wife says, "He used to read such long rakaats that his legs would get swollen. I would sit behind him, weeping out of pity for him."

6. It is said about Sa'eed bin Musayyab *(rahmatullahi alayh)* that for fifty years he read his Fajr Salaah with the wudhu made at Esha. It is also mentioned about Abul Mu'tamir that he had done the same for 40 years. Imaam Ghazaali *(rahmatullahi alayh),* on the authority of Abu Taalib Makki, reported the same practice by no less than forty Taabi'een, some of whom had been doing it for forty years continuously.

7. Imaam Abu Haneefah *(rahmatullahi alayh)* is famous for his ibaadah. It is said that for thirty, forty or fifty years (according to the information of different people) he read his Fajr Salaah with the wudhu for Esha (meaning that he did not sleep the entire night). This difference in numbers is because of the different narrators. The person who knew him for so many years narrated the number of years that he knew Imaam Saahib. He would go to sleep only for a few minutes in the afternoon saying, "It is Sunnah to sleep in the afternoon."

8. Imaam Shaafi'ee *(rahmatullahi alayh),* another famous Imaam of Fiqh, would complete reciting the Qur-aan Shareef sixty times in his Salaah during Ramadhaan. A person says, "I remained with Imaam

Shaafi'ee *(rahmatullahi alayh)* for several days and found him sleeping only for a little while at night."

9. Imaam Ahmad bin Hambal *(rahmatullahi alayh)* is one of the famous four Imaams of Fiqh. Besides being busy with his usual work, he used to read 300 rakaats of Nafl Salaah daily. After being lashed by the king, he became very weak and reduced his Nafl Salaah to 150 rakaats. We should not forget that he was eighty years old at that time.

10. Abu Itaab Sulami *(rahmatullahi alayh)* is said to have been fasting during the day and weeping during the night for forty years.

Besides the above stories, there are many other stories of the pious people in our Islamic History. It is difficult to cover all of them in this book. All that has been said here is sufficient to serve as an example. May Allah Ta'ala, through His Grace, grant me and the readers of this book the strength to follow in the footsteps of these blessed people. *Aameen.*

CHAPTER 3
QUOTATIONS FROM AHAADITH

HADITH 1 – REWARDS FOR SALAAH IS IN PROPORTION TO ONE'S SINCERITY

عَنْ عَمَّارِ بْنِ يَاسِرٍ رَضِيَ اللهُ عَنْهُ قَالَ سَمِعْتُ رَسُوْلَ اللهِ صَلَّى اللهُ عَلَيْهِ وَسَلَّمَ يَقُوْلُ اِنَّ الرَّجُلَ لَيَنْصَرِفُ وَمَا كُتِبَ لَهُ اِلَّا عُشْرُ صَلَاتِهِ تُسْعُهَا ثُمْنُهَا سَبْعُهَا سُدُسُهَا خُمْسُهَا رُبْعُهَا ثُلْثُهَا نِصْفُهَا (سنن ابی داود # 796)

Hadhrat Ammaar bin Yaasir رَضِيَ اللهُ عَنْهُ says that he heard Rasulullah صَلَّى اللهُ عَلَيْهِ وَسَلَّمَ saying: *"When a person finishes his Salaah, he gets one tenth, one ninth, one eighth, one seventh, one sixth, one fifth, one fourth, one third or half of the full reward (according to the quality of Salaah performed by him)."*

Note: Reward is granted according to the sincerity and concentration with which Salaah is performed. Therefore, some get only one tenth of the total reward. There are others who get a reward from one tenth to half of the total. Some people receive the reward in full and there are others who get no reward at all.

It is stated in a Hadith that Allah Ta'ala has a special scale for Fardh Salaah. An account is kept of the measure by which a Salaah falls short of that standard.

It is mentioned in a Hadith that concentration in Salaah will be the first thing to be taken away from the world. Not a single person in the whole Jamaat will read his Salaah with proper concentration.

HADITH 2 – A PERFECT SALAAH PURIFIES ONE FROM SINS

رُوِیَ عَنْ اَنَسِ بْنِ مَالِكٍ رَضِیَ اللهُ عَنْهُ قَالَ قَالَ رَسُوْلُ اللهِ صَلَّی اللهُ عَلَیْهِ وَسَلَّمَ مَنْ صَلَّی الصَّلَوَاتِ لِوَقْتِهَا وَاَسْبَغَ لَهَا وُضُوْءَهَا وَاَتَمَّ لَهَا قِیَامَهَا وَخُشُوْعَهَا وَرُكُوْعَهَا وَسُجُوْدَهَا خَرَجَتْ وَهِیَ بَیْضَاءُ مُسْفِرَةٌ تَقُوْلُ حَفِظَكَ اللهُ كَمَا حَفِظْتَنِیْ وَمَنْ صَلَّاهَا لِغَیْرِ وَقْتِهَا وَلَمْ یُسْبِغْ لَهَا وُضُوْءَهَا وَلَمْ یُتِمَّ لَهَا خُشُوْعَهَا وَلَا رُكُوْعَهَا وَلَا سُجُوْدَهَا خَرَجَتْ وَهِیَ سَوْدَاءُ مُظْلِمَةٌ تَقُوْلُ ضَیَّعَكَ اللهُ كَمَا ضَیَّعْتَنِیْ حَتّٰی اِذَا كَانَتْ حَیْثُ شَاءَ اللهُ لُفَّتْ كَمَا یُلَفُّ الثَّوْبُ الْخَلِقُ ثُمَّ ضُرِبَ بِهَا وَجْهُهُ

(اخرجه المنذری فی الترغیب # 584)

Hadhrat Anas ﷺ says that he heard Nabi ﷺ saying, "When a person reads his Salaah at its correct time with proper wudhu, with concentration and with qiyaam, ruku and sajdah done properly, such a Salaah rises up in a bright and beautiful form, making dua for the person saying: 'May Allah Ta'ala guard you as you have guarded me.' If a person is not punctual with his Salaah nor does he perform wudhu, qiyaam, ruku and sajdah properly, his Salaah rises up in an ugly and dark shape, cursing the person, saying, 'May Allah Ta'ala destroy you as you have destroyed me!' It is then flung like a dirty rag at the face of the person."

Note: Fortunate are those whose Salaah is so perfect that their Salaah makes dua for them. What can we say about the Salaah of most people nowadays? They go into sajdah direct from ruku. They hardly raise their heads from the first sajdah and they go for the second like a crow pecking at something. The curse for such a person is mentioned in this Hadith. When Salaah is cursing us then what else can save us? This is the reason why the condition of the Muslims is so miserable in the entire world.

This description is also given in another Hadith, with the addition that a Salaah read by a person with sincerity and concentration rises up very bright. The gates of Jannah are opened for it. It makes dua to Allah Ta'ala for its reader.

Nabi ﷺ has said, "The likeness of a person not bowing fully in ruku is that of a pregnant woman aborting just before delivery."

In a Hadith, it is stated, "There are many people who fast but get nothing out of their fast except hunger and thirst. There are many who make lots of ibaadah at night but get nothing from their ibaadah except losing their sleep."

Hadhrat Aa'ishah رضي الله عنها says that she heard Nabi ﷺ saying, "Allah Ta'ala will save (from the punishment of the Aakhirah) that person who has read his five times daily Salaah at its correct time with sincerity and concentration after having made proper wudhu. As for a person who does not do so (i.e. he did not guard his Salaah), there is no guarantee for him; he may be forgiven by Allah Ta'ala's special mercy or punished."

Once, Nabi ﷺ came to his Sahaabah رضي الله عنهم and said. "Do you know what Allah Ta'ala has said?" The Sahaabah رضي الله عنهم replied, "Allah Ta'ala and His Rasul ﷺ know best." He repeated the question and the Sahaabah رضي الله عنهم gave the same reply each time. He then said, "Allah Ta'ala says: 'By My Greatness and My Glory, I will certainly enter into Jannah that person who reads his five daily Salaah at its correct times. As for the person who does not read his Salaah, I may forgive him by My mercy or punish him."

HADITH 3 – NAFL ACTS WILL COMPENSATE FOR THE DEFICIENCY IN THE FARDH

عَنْ اَبِىْ هُرَيْرَةَ رَضِىَ اللهُ عَنْهُ سَمِعْتُ رَسُوْلَ اللهِ صَلَّى اللهُ عَلَيْهِ وَسَلَّمَ يَقُوْلُ اِنَّ اَوَّلَ مَا يُحَاسَبُ بِهِ الْعَبْدُ يَوْمَ الْقِيَامَةِ مِنْ عَمَلِهِ صَلَاتُهُ فَاِنْ صَلُحَتْ فَقَدْ اَفْلَحَ وَاَنْجَحَ وَاِنْ فَسَدَتْ فَقَدْ خَابَ وَخَسِرَ فَاِنِ انْتَقَصَ مِنْ فَرِيْضَتِهِ شَىْءٌ قَالَ الرَّبُّ اُنْظُرُوْا هَلْ لِعَبْدِىْ

مِنْ تَطَوُّعٍ فَيُكَمَّلَ بِهَا مَا انْتَقَصَ مِنَ الْفَرِيْضَةِ ثُمَّ يَكُوْنُ سَائِرُ عَمَلِهٖ عَلٰى ذٰلِكَ (سنن الترمذى # 413)

Hadhrat Abu Hurayrah رَضِىَ اللّٰهُ عَنْهُ says, "We heard Rasulullah ﷺ saying, 'The first thing that a person will be questioned about on the Day of Qiyaamah shall be his Salaah. A person will be successful if his Salaah is accepted, and he will be a miserable loser if it is rejected. If any deficiency is found in his Fardh Salaah, Allah Ta'ala will say (to the Malaaikah): 'Look at his nafl Salaah.' Whatever shortage is found in his Fardh Salaah will be covered up by his nafl Salaah. The rest of his ibaadah (Fast, Zakaat, etc.) will be treated in the same manner."

Note: This Hadith shows that we should read abundant Nafl Salaah to make up for any deficiency in our Fardh Salaah. It is a habit with many people to say, "It is enough to read the Fardh Salaah. Nafl Salaah is meant for the very pious." No doubt it is enough to offer the Fardh Salaah properly, but is it so easy to read it absolutely correctly? There will always be some shortfall, and there is no way to make up for that shortfall except through Nafl Salaah.

There is another Hadith which deals with this point in more detail. It says, "Salaah is the most important duty ordered by Allah Ta'ala. It is the first thing to be presented before Allah Ta'ala, and the first thing that will be asked about on the Day of Qiyaamah. If the Fardh Salaah is of a poor quality, its shortfall will be made up through Nafl Salaah. Then the fasts of Ramadhaan will be asked about and any shortfall will be made good through the Nafl Fasts. Then Zakaat shall be asked about. If after adding the nafl, the good deeds are found to be heavier, this person shall be sent to Jannah. Otherwise he shall go to Jahannam."

When anyone accepted Islam by Nabi ﷺ, the first thing he taught him was Salaah.

HADITH 4 – THE FIRST THING TO BE QUESTIONED ABOUT ON THE DAY OF QIYAAMAH WILL BE SALAAH

عَنْ عَبْدِ اللهِ بْنِ قُرْطٍ رَضِىَ اللهُ عَنْهُ قَالَ قَالَ رَسُوْلُ اللهِ صَلَّى اللهُ عَلَيْهِ وَسَلَّمَ أَوَّلُ مَا يُحَاسَبُ بِهِ الْعَبْدُ يَوْمَ الْقِيَامَةِ الصَّلَاةُ فَاِنْ صَلُحَتْ صَلُحَ سَائِرُ عَمَلِهِ وَاِنْ فَسَدَتْ فَسَدَ سَائِرُ عَمَلِهِ (اخرجه المنذرى فى الترغيب # 551)

Hadhrat Abdullah bin Qurt رَضِىَاللَّهُعَنْهُ says that he heard Rasulullah صَلَّىاللَّهُعَلَيْهِوَسَلَّمَ saying: "Salaah will be the first thing to be asked about on the Day of Qiyaamah. If this is found to be satisfactory, the rest of the actions will also be so. If this is not proper, the remaining actions are sure to be found deficient."

Note: During his khilaafat, Hadhrat Umar رَضِىَاللَّهُعَنْهُ had given an order to all his officials, saying, "I regard Salaah as the most important duty. A person who guards his Salaah, will follow the other laws of Islam. If he neglects his Salaah, he will most definitely destroy the rest of Islam." The above saying of Nabi صَلَّىاللَّهُعَلَيْهِوَسَلَّمَ and the order of Hadhrat Umar رَضِىَاللَّهُعَنْهُ are also explained in another Hadith, "Shaytaan is scared of a Muslim if he is mindful of his Salaah, and if he neglects his Salaah, then shaytaan becomes hopeful of misleading him. He can then easily be led to do more serious wrongs and sins." This is exactly what is meant by Allah Ta'ala when He says,

اِنَّ الصَّلٰوةَ تَنْهٰى عَنِ الْفَحْشَآءِ وَالْمُنْكَرِ

"Verily Salaah prevents one from immoral behaviour and evil things."
(Surah A'nkaboot – Aayah 45)

Hadith 5 – Stealing in Salaah

عَنْ عَبْدِ اللهِ بْنِ اَبِيْ قَتَادَةَ عَنْ اَبِيْهِ رَضِيَ اللهُ عَنْهُ قَالَ قَالَ رَسُوْلُ اللهِ صَلَّى اللهُ عَلَيْهِ وَسَلَّمَ اَسْوَاُ النَّاسِ سَرِقَةً اَلَّذِىْ يَسْرِقُ صَلَاتَهُ قَالُوْا يَا رَسُوْلَ اللهِ وَكَيْفَ يَسْرِقُ صَلَاتَهُ قَالَ لَا يُتِمُّ رُكُوْعَهَا وَلَا سُجُوْدَهَا (سنن الدارمى # 1367)

Hadhrat Abdullah bin Abi Qataadah ؓ says, Rasulullah ﷺ once said, "The worst thief is one who steals from his Salaah." The Sahaabah ؓ asked, "How can one steal from his Salaah, O' Nabi of Allah?" He replied, "When one does not do his ruku and sajdah properly."

Note: There are many other Ahaadith with the same meaning. Stealing is a very disgraceful act and a thief is hated by everybody. What do we say about a person who is called 'the worst thief' by Nabi ﷺ himself?

Hadhrat Abu Darda ؓ says, "Once Nabi ﷺ looked up towards the sky and said, 'The knowledge of Deen is soon to be taken away from this world.' Ziyaad ؓ, who was also present, asked, 'How can the knowledge of Deen be taken way, O Nabi of Allah ﷺ, when we teach the Qur-aan to our children and this process will continue?' Nabi ﷺ replied, 'Ziyaad! I always thought you to be an intelligent person. Don't you see that the Jews and the Christians also teaching their scriptures to their children. Has this prevented their decline?'"

One of Hadhrat Abu Darda's ؓ student says, "On hearing this Hadith from Hadhrat Abu Darda ؓ, I went to Hadhrat Ubaadah ؓ and narrated the Hadith to him." He said, "Abu Darda ؓ is quite right. May I tell you the first thing that will be taken away from this world? It is concentration in Salaah. You will not find a single person in the Jamaat performing his Salaah with concentration." Hadhrat Huzayfah ؓ was also heard saying, "Concentration in Salaah shall be the first thing to disappear."

It is said in a Hadith, "Allah Ta'ala does not pay attention to that Salaah in which ruku and sajdah are not performed properly."

Another Hadith says, "A person has been reading Salaah for sixty years, but not a single Salaah of his is accepted by Allah Ta'ala. This is because he has been careless in his ruku in some Salaahs and in his sajdah in others."

Great stress is laid on the proper performance of Salaah in the famous writings of Mujaddid Alf-e-Saani (Shaikh Ahmad Sirhindi) *(rahmatullah alayh)*. This subject covers a good portion of the writings. In one of them he writes, "We should keep the fingers of our hands together while in sajdah and separated while in ruku. These rules are not without a reason." He also writes, "To look at the place of sajdah while standing, on our feet while in ruku, on our nose while in sajdah, and on our hands while in Qa'dah, which helps with concentration in Salaah." When these rules, which are mustahab (preferable), increase the value of our Salaah, you can well imagine how much benefit we will derive if we are careful of the other rules, which are either Sunnah or more important.

HADITH 6 – PROHIBITION OF MOVING ABOUT IN SALAAH

عَنْ أُمِّ رُوْمَانَ وَالِدَةِ عَائِشَةَ رَضِيَ اللهُ عَنْهُمَا قَالَتْ رَاٰنِيْ أَبُوْ بَكْرٍ الصِّدِّيْقُ رَضِيَ اللهُ عَنْهُ اَتَمَيَّلُ فِيْ صَلَاتِيْ فَزَجَرَنِيْ زَجْرَةً كِدْتُّ اَنْصَرِفُ مِنْ صَلَاتِيْ قَالَ سَمِعْتُ رَسُوْلَ اللهِ صَلَّى اللهُ عَلَيْهِ وَسَلَّمَ يَقُوْلُ اِذَا قَامَ اَحَدُكُمْ فِي الصَّلَاةِ فَلْيُسْكِنْ اَطْرَافَهُ لَا يَتَمَيَّلُ تَمَيُّلَ الْيَهُوْدِ فَاِنَّ سُكُوْنَ الْاَطْرَافِ فِي الصَّلَاةِ مِنْ تَمَامِ الصَّلَاةِ

(اخرجه السيوطى فى الدر المنثور 85/6)

Hadhrat Ummu Roomaan رَضِيَ اللهُ عَنْهَا (the mother of Hadhrat Aa'ishah رَضِيَ اللهُ عَنْهَا) says, "I was reading my Salaah, when I unknowingly began leaning sometimes to one side and sometimes to the other. Hadhrat Abu Bakr رَضِيَ اللهُ عَنْهُ saw me doing this. He scolded me so harshly that I was about to break my Salaah out of fear. He told me that he had heard Rasulullah ﷺ saying, 'When a person stands for Salaah, he should keep his body still and he should not behave like the Jews. Remaining still is one of the qualities of Salaah.'"

Part 3 Ch.3 – Quotations from Ahaadith

Note: Keeping the body still during Salaah is ordered in many Ahaadith. Initially it was the habit of Rasulullah ﷺ to look towards the heavens, expecting Hadhrat Jibra-eel عليه السلام to bring some Wahi (message from Allah Ta'ala), so much so that his eyes would sometimes look up unconsciously even during Salaah. When the following Aayaat were revealed, he began looking down in Salaah.

قَدْ اَفْلَحَ الْمُؤْمِنُوْنَ ۙ الَّذِيْنَ هُمْ فِيْ صَلَاتِهِمْ خٰشِعُوْنَ

"Successful indeed are the believers who are humble in their Salaah."
(Surah Mu'minoon – Aayah 1-2)

It is said about the Sahaabah رضي الله عنهم that in the beginning they would look around during their Salaah. After these Aayaat were revealed, they gave up this habit of looking around. Explaining these Aayaat, Hadhrat Abdullah bin Umar رضي الله عنه says, "When the Sahaabah رضي الله عنهم stood for Salaah, they never looked here and there. They remained attentive in Salaah with their eyes looking at the place of sajdah, totally absorbed in Allah Ta'ala."

Someone asked Hadhrat Ali رضي الله عنه, "What is Khushoo?" He replied, "Khushoo is a state of the heart/mind." (i.e. to remain focused with ones heart and mind in Salaah.) It also includes that one should not turn his attention towards anything else whilst in Salaah.

Hadhrat Ibn-e-Abbaas رضي الله عنه says, "Khushoo (mentioned in the above Aayaat) are those who fear Allah Ta'ala and remain still in Salaah."

Hadhrat Abu Bakr رضي الله عنه says, "Once Nabi ﷺ said, 'Seek refuge in Allah Ta'ala from a hypocritical devotion.' We inquired, 'What is hypocritical devotion, O Nabi of Allah! ﷺ.' He replied, 'To pretend to have concentrate, but there is nifaaq (hypocrisy) in the heart.'"

Hadhrat Abu Darda رضي الله عنه relates a similar Hadith in which Nabi ﷺ is reported to have said, "Hypocritical devotion is that in which a person outwardly pretends concentration, while his heart is devoid of that"

Hadhrat Qataadah *(rahmatullahi alayh)* says, "For devotion in Salaah, the heart should be full of the fear of Allah Ta'ala and the gaze should be kept down."

Nabi ﷺ once saw a person playing with his beard while in Salaah. He remarked, "If his heart was blessed with khushoo', then his entire body would be at ease."

Hadhrat Aa'ishah رضي الله عنها once asked Nabi ﷺ about looking around whilst in Salaah. He said, "This is how shaytaan snatches away (the rewards) of salaah."

Nabi ﷺ said, "People who are in the habit of looking upwards while in Salaah should give up that habit, otherwise their sight may be taken away from them and it may not return to them."

It has been said by many of the Sahaabah رضي الله عنهم and their successors that Khushoo means calmness in Salaah. Rasulullah ﷺ said, "Read each Salaah with such (devotion) as if it was the last Salaah of your life."

HADITH 7 – SALAAH SAVES ONE FROM SHAMEFUL ACTS

عَنْ عِمْرَانَ بْنِ حُصَيْنٍ رَضِيَ اللهُ عَنْهُ قَالَ سُئِلَ النَّبِيُّ صَلَّى اللهُ عَلَيْهِ وَسَلَّمَ عَنْ قَوْلِ اللهِ اِنَّ الصَّلٰوةَ تَنْهٰى عَنِ الْفَحْشَآءِ وَالْمُنْكَرِ قَالَ مَنْ لَّمْ تَنْهَهُ صَلَاتُهُ عَنِ الْفَحْشَاءِ وَالْمُنْكَرِ فَلَا صَلَاةَ لَهُ

(اخرجه ابن ابى حاتم فى تفسيره # 17339)

Hadhrat Imraan bin Husain رضي الله عنه says, "Someone asked Nabi ﷺ about the meaning of the verse in the Qur-aan:

اِنَّ الصَّلٰوةَ تَنْهٰى عَنِ الْفَحْشَاءِ وَالْمُنْكَرِ

'Indeed! Salaah stops you from shameful and bad actions.'" *(Surah A'nkaboot – Aayah 45)* He replied, "Salaah is no Salaah if it does not save you from shameful and bad actions."

Note: No doubt, Salaah is a very valuable ibaadah and if it is read properly, it will save one from all bad actions. If it does not, there is something seriously wrong with our Salaah. There are many other Ahaadith with this meaning. Hadhrat Ibn Abbaas رضي الله عنه says, "Salaah has the power to stop you from sins."

Hadhrat Abul Aaliyah *(rahmatullahi alayh)* explaining the same Aayah of the Qur-aan, writes: "There are three important parts of Salaah: Sincerity, fear of Allah Ta'ala, and His zikr. Salaah is no Salaah if these three are missing. Sincerity causes you to do good actions, fear of Allah Ta'ala stops you from sin, and His zikr is the Qur-aan, which in itself is guidance towards good and a guard against evil."

Hadhrat Ibn Abbaas رَضِيَ اللّٰهُ عَنْهُ says that Rasulullah ﷺ once said, "The Salaah that does not prevent you from shameful and bad actions, instead of bringing you closer to Allah Ta'ala, drives you away from Him."

Hadhrat Hasan رَضِيَ اللّٰهُ عَنْهُ has also narrated the same thing from Rasulullah ﷺ that a Salaah which does not prevent a person from sins is in reality not a Salaah. Such a Salaah actually distances a person away from Allah Ta'ala.

Hadhrat Ibn-e-Umar رَضِيَ اللّٰهُ عَنْهُ has also narrated a similar topic from Rasulullah ﷺ.

Hadhrat Ibn Mas'ood رَضِيَ اللّٰهُ عَنْهُ narrates that he heard Rasulullah ﷺ saying, "A person who does not follow the demands of Salaah, has actually offered no Salaah. To follow up the demands of Salaah means to avoid shamelessness and sin."

Hadhrat Abu Hurayrah رَضِيَ اللّٰهُ عَنْهُ says, "A person came to Rasulullah ﷺ saying that a certain man was in the habit of offering Salaah for the whole night and then involved himself in burglary and theft before the morning." Rasulullah ﷺ said, "His Salaah will very soon prevent him from that sin." Reading Salaah with proper sincerity is a means of getting rid of evil habits. It is difficult to make taubah for each and every bad habit. It is easier and quicker to read Salaah properly and then through the blessings that follow it, bad habits are sure to disappear one by one. May Allah Ta'ala grant us the strength to perform our Salaah properly! *Aameen.*

Hadith 8 – The Virtues of Reading Long Rakaats in Salaah

عَنْ جَابِرٍ رَضِيَ اللّٰهُ عَنْهُ قَالَ قَالَ رَسُوْلُ اللّٰهِ صَلَّى اللّٰهُ عَلَيْهِ وَسَلَّمَ أَفْضَلُ الصَّلَاةِ طُوْلُ الْقُنُوْتِ (صحيح مسلم # 756)

Hadhrat Jaabir ﷺ says that he heard Rasulullah ﷺ saying, "The best Salaah is one with long rakaats."

وَقُوْمُوْا لِلّٰهِ قٰنِتِيْنَ

"And stand up humbly (obediently and silently) before Allah Ta'ala."
(Surah Baqarah – Aayah 238)

Mujahid *(rahmatullahi alayh)* while explaining the above Aayah says, Qunoot includes making proper ruku, (khushoo) devotion, long rakaats, keeping the eyes down and lowering of the shoulders in submission and fear of Allah Ta'ala. When the Sahaabah of Rasulullah ﷺ stood for Salaah, they would not look here and there or play and fiddle with anything, or think of any worldly thing intentionally due to the fear of Allah Ta'ala.

Note: Many meanings have been given to the word Qunoot, which comes in the Qur-aan in the Aayah mentioned in this Hadith. According to one of the meanings, Qunoot means silence. In the beginning of Islam, it was permissible to talk or to make salaam during Salaah, but when this Aayah was revealed, talking during Salaah was absolutely forbidden. Hadhrat Abdullah Ibn Mas'ood ﷺ says, "In the beginning, whenever I visited Nabi ﷺ, I would greet him with *'assalamu alaykum'* and he would reply with *'wa alaykumus salaam'* even if he was performing Salaah. Once I visited him while he was in Salaah and greeted him as usual, but he did not reply. I became worried, fearing that his silence might be because Allah Ta'ala was displeased with me. All sorts of worried thoughts began to enter my mind. I would think Nabi ﷺ was angry with me due to something that had happened. When Nabi ﷺ finished his Salaah, he said, "Allah Ta'ala changes His commandments as He pleases. He has now forbidden any talking during Salaah." He then recited the above Aayah, ***'And stand up with***

humility before Allah' *(Surah Baqarah - Aayah 238)* and said, "Salaah is now meant exclusively for the remembrance, zikr and praise of Allah Ta'ala."

Hadhrat Mu'aawiyah bin Hakam Sulami رَضِىَ اللّٰهُ عَنْهُ says, "When I visited Madinah Munawwarah to accept Islam, I was taught many things. One of those was that when anybody sneezed and said, '*Alhamdulillaah*' I should reply, '*Yarhamukallaah*'. As I was new in Islam, I did not know that this was not to be done during Salaah. We were all standing in Salaah when somebody sneezed. I immediately shouted, '*Yarhamukallaah*'. The Sahaabah رَضِىَ اللّٰهُ عَنْهُمْ stared at me. As I did not know then that we were not allowed to talk in Salaah, I protested saying, 'Why are you all giving me angry looks?' By showing me a sign, they asked me to keep quiet. I could not understand their behaviour, but I decided to then keep quiet. When Salaah was over, Rasulullah صَلَّى اللّٰهُ عَلَيْهِ وَسَلَّمَ called me. He did not hit or scold me. He simply said, 'It is not permitted to talk in Salaah. Salaah is the occasion for praising Allah Ta'ala and reciting the Qur-aan.' By Allah Ta'ala, never before or after have I met a teacher as kind as Rasulullah صَلَّى اللّٰهُ عَلَيْهِ وَسَلَّمَ."

Another meaning is given by Hadhrat Ibn-e-Abbaas رَضِىَ اللّٰهُ عَنْهُ in which he says that Qunoot means devotion. The words of Mujaahid *(rahmatullahi alayh)* given above are based on this interpretation. Hadhrat Abdullah ibn Abbaas رَضِىَ اللّٰهُ عَنْهُ says, "In the beginning, Rasulullah صَلَّى اللّٰهُ عَلَيْهِ وَسَلَّمَ would tie himself up with a string while in Tahajjud, so that he would not fall off to sleep. It was for this reason that the following Aayah was revealed in the Qur-aan:

$$\text{مَآ اَنْزَلْنَا عَلَيْكَ الْقُرْاٰنَ لِتَشْقٰى}$$

"We have not revealed the Qur-aan to you (Muhammad صَلَّى اللّٰهُ عَلَيْهِ وَسَلَّمَ) to cause you difficulty." (Surah Taahaa – Aayah 2)

It is said in many Ahaadith that the feet of Rasulullah صَلَّى اللّٰهُ عَلَيْهِ وَسَلَّمَ would get swollen due to standing for long hours during Tahajjud Salaah. However, due to his kindness and affection for us, he advised us to be moderate in our Ibaadah, because if any person over exerts himself then it may cause him to leave out making Ibaadat altogether. That is why we find him stopping a woman from tying herself up for avoiding sleep during Salaah.

We should remember that a Salaah with long rakaats is surely superior and more valuable, provided a person does not over exert himself. After all, there is some meaning in Nabi's ﷺ offering such lengthy Salaah that would give him swollen feet. When the Sahaabah رضى الله عنهم requested him to reduce his effort in his ibaadah because he had been guaranteed forgiveness as stated in Surah Fath:

$$\text{لِيَغْفِرَ لَكَ اللهُ مَا تَقَدَّمَ مِنْ ذَنْبِكَ وَ مَا تَأَخَّرَ}$$

"So that Allah Ta'ala may forgive you (O Muhammad ﷺ) for your past shortcomings and those that may occur in the future."
(Surah Fatah – Aayah 2)

He used to say, "Should I not be a grateful slave of Allah Ta'ala?"

It is stated in a Hadith that, when Nabi ﷺ offered his Salaah, his chest would give a constant groaning sound, which resembled that of a grinding mill. In another Hadith, this sound is compared to a boiling kettle. Hadhrat Ali رضى الله عنه narrates, "On the night of the Battle of Badr, I noticed that Rasulullah ﷺ stood under a tree, busy in Salaah and crying before Allah Ta'ala all night long till the morning." It is said in a number of Ahaadith that, "Allah Ta'ala is very pleased with certain people, one of them is he who leaves his bed shared with his dear and lovely wife and engages in Tahajjud Salaah on a cold winters night. Allah Ta'ala is very pleased with him, takes pride in him and in spite of being All-knowing, asks the Malaaikah, 'What made this slave of mine leave his bed and stand up like this?' The Malaaikah reply, 'The hope of winning Your Bounty and Grace, and the fear of your displeasure.' At this Allah Ta'ala says, 'Listen, I give him what he hopes for and grant him refuge from what he is afraid of.'"

Rasulullah ﷺ says, "No one receives a better reward from Allah Ta'ala than he who reads two rakaats of Salaah."

It has often been mentioned in the Qur-aan and Ahaadith that the Malaaikah are always busy in ibaadah. There are some who remain forever in ruku and others in sajdah. Allah Ta'ala has joined all these postures in our Salaah, so that we may get our share from each type of their ibaadah. Reading of the Qur-aan in Salaah is an extra devotion, over and above their ibaadah. While Salaah has all the postures of all the methods of ibaadah of the Malaaikah, it gives out its best when it is offered by a person who possesses the habits of the Malaaikah. That is why Rasulullah ﷺ said, "For (a good) Salaah, keep your back and stomach light." The back of a person is said to be light when he has very few of the worldly burdens, and his stomach is light when he eats moderately to avoid laziness, which is a sure outcome of greed and over eating.

THERE ARE 12 000 VIRTUES IN SALAAH

The Sufis write: There are 12 000 virtues in Salaah, which can be achieved through twelve points. If a person wants to get the full benefit from Salaah, then he must take care of these points. Sincerity is of course essential at every step. These points are as follows:

1. Knowledge: An action performed without knowledge is far inferior to the one done with full knowledge about it. We should therefore know:

   (a) What is fardh and what is sunnat in Salaah.

   (b) What is fardh and what is sunnat in wudhu and Salaah.

   (c) How shaytaan causes distraction in our Salaah.

2. Wudhu: We must try to:

   (a) Clean our heart of jealously and malice, just as we wash the other parts of our body.

   (b) Keep ourselves clean of sins.

   (c) We must neither waste nor use too little water but rather be moderate.

3. Dress: It should be:

   (a) obtained through honest living.

   (b) clean.

(c) according to the Sunnat, e.g. the ankles should not be covered.

(d) simple, and should not display vanity and pride.

4. Time: We should be:

(a) able to tell correct time at any moment.

(b) always watchful about the Azaan.

(c) particular about the time of Salaah, lest we should be too late for it.

5. Qiblah: There are three things to be ensured in facing Qiblah:

(a) We must face the Qiblah physically.

(b) Have the heart in union with Allah Ta'ala, for He is the Qiblah of the heart.

(c) Be as attentive as a slave is before his master.

6. Intention: For this we need to be particular about three things:

(a) We must be sure as to what Salaah we are performing.

(b) Remain constantly conscious of our presence before Allah Ta'ala, Who always sees us.

(c) Have perfect Imaan that Allah Ta'ala knows all that is in our hearts.

7. Takbeer Tahreemah (The First Takbeer): The essentials of Takbeer Tahreemah are:

(a) To pronounce the words correctly.

(b) To raise both hands right up to the ears. This signifies that we have cut-off our connection with all, except Allah Ta'ala.

(c) To feel the greatness of Allah Ta'ala in our heart when we say Allahu Akbar.

8. Qiyaam (Standing Posture): While in Qiyaam we should:

(a) Keep our gaze at the place of sajdah.

(b) Feel in our heart that we are standing before Allah Ta'ala.

(c) Not to think of anything else. It is said that the person who looks around in salaah is like the example of a beggar who has come in the presence of the king. Now, when the king turns his attention towards him, he starts looking around here and there. How can the king then focus his attention to him?

9. Qiraat: The essentials of Qiraat are:

   (a) To recite the Qur-aan with Tajweed.

   (b) To ponder on the meanings of what we recite.

   (c) To practice on what we recite.

10. Ruku: The essentials of Ruku are:

    (a) To keep the back straight i.e. the whole body above the legs should be in one straight line.

    (b) To hold the knees firmly with fingers spread apart.

    (c) To recite Tasbeeh with respect, humility and devotion.

11. Sajdah: The essentials of Sajdah are:

    (a) To place the hands flat and close to the ears.

    (b) To keep the elbows raised above the ground.

    (c) To recite Tasbeeh with respect and devotion.

12. Qa'dah (Sitting Posture): The essentials of Qa'dah are:

    (a) To sit up on the left foot, keeping the right one erect.

    (b) To recite Tashahhud with devotion, keeping the meaning in mind, for it contains Salaams for Rasullulah ﷺ and Dua for the Muslim Ummah.

    (c) To consider the concluding Salaam a definite greeting to the Malaaikah as well as the people on the right and on the left.

It has already been mentioned that, sincerity is the essence of all these points, which requires us:

1. To perform Salaah only to please Allah Ta'ala.

2. To understand that it is only through the grace and favour of Allah Ta'ala that we are able to perform Salaah.

3. To hope for the reward promised by Allah Ta'ala.

THE TRANSLATION OF SANAA AND ITS SIGNIFICANCE

Salaah is really a very blessed and auspicious practice. Every word said in it is filled with the greatness and blessedness of Allah Ta'ala. Sanaa, the opening Dua of Salaah, contains extremely virtuous and sacred meaning;

(1) *Subhaanakallaahumma:* O, Allah! I praise Your Sanctity. You are free from all faults and defects.

(2) *Wabihamdika:* I praise Your Glory. All virtues and beauties are admittedly for You and befit You.

(3) *Watabaarakasmuka:* Your name is blessed and in fact so blessed that it blesses everything over which it is mentioned.

(4) *Wata'aalaajadduka:* Your eminence is most exalted. Your magnificence is most sublime.

(5) *Walaailaaha ghairuk:* There is no deity but You. None has ever been and none shall ever be fit to be worshipped but You.

Similary in **ruku** we recite *"Subhaana Rabbiyal Azeem,"* which means: "My magnificent and great Allah Ta'ala is free from all faults. I express my humbleness and weakness before His Greatness by bowing my head before Him (for the bowing of head is the symbol of humbleness and submission, just as a stiff neck is the sign of haughtiness and pride). I submit before all your commandments and I take it as my responsibility to obey You and be at Your service. I am at Your command. You are really very great and I submit before Your greatness."

Similarly, in **Sajdah**, we recite *"Subhaana Rabbiyal A'alaa.* We express our submission before Allah Ta'ala the Highest, and declare Him above all defects. Our head, which is considered as the most excellent part of our body along with our eyes, ears, nose and tongue, is placed on the ground before Him in the hope that He would show mercy and grant His blessings on us.

Standing with our hands folded before Him was the first expression of our humbleness and submission. This was further supported and reinforced by the bowing of our head in ruku and it reached its peak when we placed our head on the ground before Allah. In fact the whole Salaah is an indication of humbleness and submission and therefore a means of success in the world and in the Aakhirah. May Allah Ta'ala, through His Kindness, give me and all the Muslims taufeeq to offer such a Salaah.

Mujaahid *(rahmatullahi alayh)* has mentioned that this was the kind of Salaah read by the Sahaabah. When they used to stand up for Salaah they feared Allah Ta'ala.

INCIDENTS OF THE PIOUS AND THEIR FEAR FOR ALLAH

1. HADHRAT HASAN'S ﷺ PREPARATION FOR SALAAH

It is said about Hadhrat Hasan ﷺ that, whenever he performed wudhu, he became very worried. When someone asked him why, he replied. "It is time to stand before Allah Ta'ala the Greatest and the most Powerful King." On reaching the gate of the Masjid he would say;

اِلٰهِىْ عَبْدُكَ بِبَابِكَ يَا مُحْسِنُ قَدْ اَتَاكَ الْمُسِىْءُ

وَقَدْ اَمَرْتَ الْمُحْسِنَ مِنَّا اَنْ يَّتَجَاوَزَ عَنِ الْمُسِىْءِ

فَاَنْتَ الْمُحْسِنُ وَاَنَا الْمُسِىْءُ

فَتَجَاوَزْ عَنْ قَبِيْحِ مَا عِنْدِىْ بِجَمِيْلِ مَا عِنْدَكَ يَا كَرِيْمُ

"O Allah! Your slave is at Your door, O the most Beneficent! Here is a sinner before You. You have ordered the good amongst us to forgive the faults of the bad. O Allah! You are good and I am bad, so for the sake of all that is most beautiful in You, forgive all that is evil in me, O! The Most Bountiful."

He would then enter the Masjid.

2. THE SALAAH OF ZAINUL AABIDEEN *(RAHMATULLAHI ALAYH)*

Hadhrat Zainul Aabideen *(rahmatullahi alayh)* used to read 1000 rakaats of Nafl Salaah daily. He never missed his Tahajjud, whether he was on a journey or at home. His face became pale when he performed his wudhu. He would tremble when he stood in Salaah. Somebody asked him the reason for that, he said, "Don't you know before Whom am I going to stand?" Once when he was busy in Salaah, a fire broke out in his house. He continued his Salaah most calmly. When asked about it, he said, "The fire of Jahannam caused me to forget the fire of this world." He once said, "The person who is proud surprises me. The day before, he was a drop of dirty fluid and tomorrow he will be carrion and still he is proud." He used to say, "It is strange that people do so much for the world, which is temporary, and do nothing for the Aakhirah where they are going to live for ever." He used to help the poor in the darkness of night in such a way that they did not even know who helped them. People only came to know after his death that he was supporting more than 100 families.

3. THE REACTION OF HADHRAT ALI ﷺ AT THE TIME OF SALAAH

It is said about Hadhrat Ali ﷺ that the colour of his face would change and he would tremble when the time of Salaah approached. When he was asked by someone he said, "This is the time for fulfilling the trust which the Heaven and the Earth and even the mountains were afraid to bear. I do not know if I shall be able to fulfil it."

4. THE REACTION OF HADHRAT ABDULLAH BIN ABBAAS ﷺ ON HEARING THE AZAAN

It is said about Hadhrat Abdullah bin Abbaas ﷺ that when he heard the Azaan, he wept so much that his shawl would get wet. His veins would swell and his eyes would become red. Somebody said to him, "We do not see anything in the Azaan that should cause you to be terrified." He replied, "If people understood what the Muazzin announced to them, they would give up their sleep and leave their comfort." He then explained to him the warning contained in each word of the Azaan.

5. THE SALAAH OF ZUNNOON MISRI *(RAHMATULLAHI ALAYH)*

A person says, "I read my Asr Salaah with Zunnoon Misri *(rahmatullahi alayh)*. When he said 'Allah' (in takbeer), he was so overawed with the greatness of Allah Ta'ala, that he almost passed away. When he said 'Akbar' I felt as if my heart would burst with the fear of Allah Ta'ala."

6. UWAIS QARNI *(RAHMATULLAHI ALAYH)* SPENDING THE NIGHT IN RUKU OR SAJDA

Uwais Qarni *(rahmatullahi alayh)*, a famous saint and the highest of all the Taabi'een, would spend the whole night either in ruku or in sajdah.

7. I'SAAM *(RAHMATULLAHI ALAYH)* ASKS HAATIM ZAAHID BALKHI *(RAHMATULLAHI ALAYH)* HOW HE READ HIS SALAAH

I'saam *(rahmatullahi alayh)* once asked Haatim Zaahid Balkhi *(rahmatullahi alayh)* how he read his Salaah. He replied: "When it is time for Salaah, I perform my wudhu properly and go to the place of Salaah. When I stand for Salaah, I picture the Ka'bah Shareef in front of me, the Pul-Siraat (bridge over Jahannam) under my feet, Jannah on my right, Jahannam on my left and the Angel of death over my head. I think this to be my last Salaah so that I may not have the opportunity to say another Salaah again. Allah Ta'ala alone knows what goes through my heart at that time. I then say 'Allahu Akbar' with total humility and recite the Qur-aan Shareef, pondering over its meaning. I perform my ruku and sajdah with complete humbleness, finishing my Salaah calmly, hoping that Allah Ta'ala will accept it through His mercy, and fearing that it may be rejected if it is judged on its quality."

I'saam *(rahmatullahi alayh)* asked him, "Since when have you been reading this type of Salaah?" Haatim *(rahmatullahi alayh)* replied, "I have been doing it for the last thirty years." I'saam *(rahmatullahi alayh)* wept and said, "I have not been fortunate enough to read a single Salaah like that."

It is said that Haatim *(rahmatullahi alayh)* once missed his Salaah with Jamaat and felt extremely remorseful over it. A few people came to comfort him on this loss. He started weeping and then said, "If I had lost one of my sons, half the population of Balkh would have come to sympathise with me, but on the loss of my jamaat, you are the only person sympathising with me. It is only because people regard the afflictions in the Aakhirah as lighter than the affliction of this world."

8. Sa'eed bin Musayyab *(Rahmatullahi Alayh)* in the Masjid before Azaan

Sa'eed bin Musayyab *(rahmatullahi alayh)* says, "For the last twenty years, I have never been out of the Masjid at the time of the Azaan."

9. Muhammad bin Waasi *(Rahmatullahi Alayh)* loves Salaah with Jamaat

Muhammad bin Waasi *(rahmatullahi alayh)* says, "I love only three things in this life; a friend who could warn me on my mistakes, just enough sustenance which is obtained without a fight and Salaah with Jamaat such that Allah Ta'ala may forgive its faults and give me reward for anything good in it.

10. The attack of shaytaan on Hadhrat Abu Ubaidah bin Jarraah رضي الله عنه while he was in Salaah

Hadhrat Abu Ubaidah bin Jarraah رضي الله عنه was once leading the Salaah. When the Salaah was over, he said; "Shaytaan made a dangerous attack on me while I was leading the Salaah. He caused me to think that I am the best of all of you. I shall never lead the Salaah again."

11. Maimoon bin Mahraan *(Rahmatullahi Alayh)* misses Jamaat

Maimoon bin Mahraan *(rahmatullahi alayh)* once reached the Masjid when the Jamaat was over. He recited '*Innaa lillaahi wa innaa ilaihi raaji-oon'* and said, "The reward of this Salaah with Jamaat was dearer to me than being the king of Iraq."

It is said that the Sahaabah رَضِىَ اللّٰهُ عَنْهُم would mourn for three days if they happened to miss the first takbeer and for seven days if they missed Jamaat.

12. SPEAK TO ALLAH TA'ALA AT ANY TIME YOU DESIRE

Bakr bin Abdullah *(rahmatullahi alayh)* once said, "You can speak to Allah Ta'ala, Who is our master, at any time you desire." "How?" asked somebody. He replied, "Perform your wudhu properly and stand up for Salaah."

13. THE BEHAVIOUR OF RASULULLAH ﷺ AT THE TIME OF SALAAH

Hadhrat Aa'ishah رَضِىَ اللّٰهُ عَنْهَا says, "Rasulullah ﷺ would be talking with his family members, but at the time of Salaah, he would suddenly behave as if he had never known us. He would become completely absorbed in Allah Ta'ala."

14. SA'EED TANNOOKHI *(RAHMATULLAHI ALAYH)* CRYING IN SALAAH

It is said of Sa'eed Tannookhi *(rahmatullahi alayh)* that, as long as he remained in Salaah, tears would flow from his eyes continuously.

15. KHALAF BIN AYYUB *(RAHMATULLAHI ALAYH)* IS NOT DISTRACTED IN SALAAH

Somebody asked Khalaf bin Ayyub *(rahmatullahi alayh),* "Don't the flies annoy you in Salaah?" He answered: "Even the criminals patiently bear the lashes of the police and boast of their endurance. Why should I be disturbed by flies whilst standing in front of my Creator?"

16. SALAAH MORE VALUABLE THAN WORLDLY POSSESSIONS

It is written in a kitaab titled *'Bahjatun Nufoos'* that one of the Sahaabah رَضِىَ اللّٰهُ عَنْهُم was once reading Tahajjud when a thief took away his horse. He noticed it, but did not break his Salaah. Somebody asked him, "Why did you not break your Salaah and catch the thief?" He replied, "I was busy in something far more valuable than a horse."

17. ARROW REMOVED FROM THE THIGH OF ALI رَضِىَ اللّٰهُ عَنْهُ WHILST HE WAS IN SALAAH

It is said about Hadhrat Ali رَضِىَ اللّٰهُ عَنْهُ that once an arrow got stuck in his thigh. This could not be removed because of the severe pain felt by him. When he was busy in Nafl Salaah, the people removed the arrow. On finishing his Salaah, he asked the people; "Have you gathered to remove the arrow?" When they told him that it was already removed, he informed them that he had not felt any pain.

18. THE TALKING OF FAMILY MEMBERS DOES NOT DISTRACT MUSLIM BIN YASAAR *(RAHMATULLAHI ALAYH)* IN SALAAH

Muslim bin Yasaar *(rahmatullahi alayh)* would say to his family members when standing up for Salaah, "You may keep on talking; I shall not be aware of what you talk."

Rabi *(rahmatullahi alayh)* says that, "When I stand in Salaah, I get so overcome with this concern that what will I be questioned about."

19. AAMIR BIN ABDULLAH *(RAHMATULLAHI ALAYH)* IN THE THOUGHTS OF AAKHIRAH IN SALAAH

It is said of Aamir bin Abdullah *(rahmatullahi alayh)* that, he would not even hear the beating of a drum while in Salaah, leave alone the talking of people around him. A person asked him, "Are you aware of anything while in Salaah?" He replied, "Yes, I know that I have to stand one day before Allah Ta'ala, and I shall either be sent to Jannah or Jahannam." The person said, "No, I do not mean that. Do you hear what we talk?" He replied, "It is better that spears cut through my body than I hear your conversation whilst in Salaah." He used to say, "My yaqeen in the things of the Aakhirah is so perfect that it is impossible for it to improve, even if I happen to see those things with my physical eyes."

20. A LIMB IS AMPUTATED WHILST PERFORMING SALAAH

One person had some sickness in a limb which needed to be amputated. People suggested that when he starts his Salaah, then it should be amputated. He won't even know that it is cut off. Thus, whilst he was performing Salaah, that limb was amputated.

21. A PIOUS MAN IS NOT DISTRACTED BY THE THOUGHTS OF THIS WORLD IN SALAAH

A pious man was asked, "Do you ever think of this world while you are in Salaah?" He replied, "I never think of this world, either in Salaah or out of it." Another such man was asked, "Do you think of anything whilst in Salaah?" He replied, "Is there anything more attractive than Salaah itself to think of?"

22. SHAIKH BUSIES HIMSELF IN SALAAH AND ZIKR

In *'Bahjatun Nufoos'* it is written about a person who came to meet a saint whilst he was busy offering the Zuhr Salaah. He sat down to wait for him. When he completed his Fardh Salaah, he immediately commenced with Nafal Salaah until the Asar Salaah. This person kept on waiting. Then he started off the Asar Salaah. After the Asar Salaah, he got busy engaged in dua till Maghrib. After performing the Maghrib Salaah he commenced with Nafal Salaah till Esha. This poor person kept on waiting. After performing the Esha Salaah, he once again commenced with Nafal Salaah until the morning. Then he performed the Fajar Salaah and started making Zikr and reading other Wazaaif. Whilst sitting on the musalla he was overpowered by sleep. Immediately he rubbed his eyes and woke up reciting Istighfaar and the following Dua:

اَعُوْذُ بِاللهِ مِنْ عَيْنٍ لَا تَشْبَعُ مِنَ النَّوْمِ

"I seek refuge in Allah from the eye that does not get satisfied with sleep."

23. A SAINT SPENDS THE NIGHT IN SALAAH

It is said about another Shaikh that he would go to bed. When he could not fall off to sleep, he would get up and busy himself in Salaah saying, "O Allah! You know very well that it is the fear of the Fire of Jahannam that has caused my sleep to disappear."

There are so many stories about the pious people spending their nights in the ibaadah of Allah Ta'ala which cannot be covered in this book. We have in fact lost the taste for the pleasure of ibaadah, so much so that we have begun to doubt the truth of such stories. These stories have been told so often and continuously that if we doubt them, then we can as well doubt history. If a story is told frequently and continuously, then its authenticity is guaranteed without dispute. We see people spending the entire night (sometimes even standing) in a cinema. They neither get tired nor does sleep overpower them. When such sinful actions have such an attraction, then what makes us doubt that Deeni sacrifices can be so attractive and tasteful?. People sacrificing for Deen are specially gifted with additional spiritual strength and stamina by Allah Ta'ala. The only reason we doubt these stories is because of our ignorance, which is like that of an immature child about the experiences of puberty. May Allah Ta'ala enable us to attain the heights where we may be able to taste the pleasures of His ibaadah.

FINAL APPEAL

According to the Sufis, Salaah is in fact a dua and speech with Allah Ta'ala and therefore needs thorough concentration. In the case of other practices, we do not need to be so attentive. For example, the spirit of Zakaat is to spend money for the pleasure of Allah Ta'ala. Spending in itself is so hard on a person that, even if he does it absent-mindedly, he would still feel the pinch of it. Similarly, fasting requires giving up eating, drinking and fulfilling your carnal desires. All these restrictions are really very hard, even if not observed by paying proper attention and devotion. On the other hand, Zikr and recitation of the Qur-aan are the main parts of Salaah. If these are done unmindfully and inattentively, then they cannot be regarded as speaking to or pleading with Allah Ta'ala. They are just like the speech of a person with high fever, who blurts out what is in his heart. It neither requires any careful thought nor carry any meaning for the listener. Therefore, it is necessary that we should be completely attentive when in Salaah, otherwise our Salaah will be like the talk of a person in his sleep, which neither carries meaning for the listeners, nor will we get any benefit from it. In the same way, Allah Ta'ala pays no attention to a Salaah that is offered inattentively and without concentration.

AN IMPORTANT NOTE

Even if our Salaah is not up to standard, as compared with that of the pious people in the past, we should not give up the practice. It is absolutely incorrect to think that there is no use in offering Salaah unless it is perfect. To offer an imperfect Salaah is far better than to give it up completely, as this will result in us being punished in the Aakhirah. Some Ulama have declared a person to be a kaafir who intentionally leaves out Salaah (as discussed in full in chapter one).

It is therefore important for us to make sincere and genuine efforts to do justice to our Salaah and make dua to Allah Ta'ala to grant us the taufeeq (ability) to offer Salaah similar to that of the pious people of the past, so that we may have at least one Salaah of that nature to our credit to present before Allah Ta'ala.

In conclusion, it may be pointed out that the Muhaditheen are rather liberal in accepting the authenticity of the Ahaadith relating to the rewards of different Deeni practices. As for the stories about saints and pious people, these are part of ordinary history and therefore its status is far below the level of Ahaadith.

وَمَا تَوْفِيْقِيْٓ اِلَّا بِاللّٰهِ ۗ عَلَيْهِ تَوَكَّلْتُ وَ اِلَيْهِ اُنِيْبُ، رَبَّنَا ظَلَمْنَآ اَنْفُسَنَا ۖ وَاِنْ لَّمْ تَغْفِرْلَنَا وَ تَرْحَمْنَا لَنَكُوْنَنَّ مِنَ الْخٰسِرِيْنَ، رَبَّنَا لَا تُؤَاخِذْنَآ اِنْ نَّسِيْنَآ اَوْ اَخْطَاْنَا ۚ

رَبَّنَا وَلَا تَحْمِلْ عَلَيْنَآ اِصْرًا كَمَا حَمَلْتَهٗ عَلَى الَّذِيْنَ مِنْ قَبْلِنَا ۚ رَبَّنَا وَلَا تُحَمِّلْنَا مَا لَا طَاقَةَ لَنَا بِهٖ ۚ وَاعْفُ عَنَّا ۗ وَاغْفِرْ لَنَا ۗ وَارْحَمْنَا ۗ اَنْتَ مَوْلٰىنَا فَانْصُرْنَا عَلَى الْقَوْمِ الْكٰفِرِيْنَ،

وَصَلَّى اللهُ تَعَالٰى عَلٰى خَيْرِ خَلْقِهٖ سَيِّدِ الْاَوَّلِيْنَ وَالْاٰخِرِيْنَ وَعَلٰى اٰلِهٖ وَاَصْحَابِهٖ وَاَتْبَاعِهٖ وَحَمَلَةِ الدِّيْنِ الْمَتِيْنِ بِرَحْمَتِكَ يَا اَرْحَمَ الرَّاحِمِيْنَ

My ability is only from Allah. Only on him do I rely and only to Him do I turn. O our Rabb! We have oppressed our souls and if You do not forgive us and show mercy to us, we will surely be of the losers. O our Rabb! Do not take us to task if we forget or make mistakes. Our Rabb, do not place such responsibilities on us as You had placed on those before us. Our Rabb, do not impose on us that which we do not have the strength to bear. Overlook (our sins), forgive us and have mercy on us. You are our Protector, so assist us against the nation of the disbelievers. And may Allah Ta'ala send salutations on the best of His creation, the leader of the first and the last and on his family and his companions and his followers and those who carry forward the pristine Deen by Your mercy, O! the most merciful of those who show mercy.

فضائلِ ذکر

Virtues of Zikr

Contents

Foreword 489

CHAPTER 1 VIRTUES OF ZIKR IN GENERAL 491

Section 1 Aayaat of the Qur-aan relating to Zikr 491

Section 2 Ahaadith on the virtues of 'Zikr' 505

CHAPTER 2 VIRTUES OF KALIMAH TAYYIBAH 563

Section 1 Aayaat pertaining to Kalimah Tayyibah 565

Conclusion: 576

Section 2 Aayaat pertaining to the Kalimah Tayyibah wherein the Kalimah appears in full or in part 577

Section 3 Ahaadith pertaining to the Kalimah Tayyibah 589

CHAPTER 3 VIRTUES OF THE THIRD KALIMAH 647

Section 1 Aayaat pertaining to the 3rd Kalimah 647

Section 2 Ahaadith pertaining to the 3rd Kalimah 677

Conclusion 719

Foreword

بِسْمِ اللهِ الرَّحْمٰنِ الرَّحِيْمِ

نَحْمَدُهٗ وَنُصَلِّيْ عَلٰى رَسُوْلِهِ الْكَرِيْمِ وَعَلٰى اٰلِهٖ وَاَصْحَابِهٖ وَاَتْبَاعِهٖ حَمَلَةِ الدِّيْنِ الْقَوِيْمِ

The sacred name of Allah Ta'ala carries blessings, enjoyment, sweetness, ecstasy and peace of mind. This is invariably experienced by one who has practiced and remained absorbed in His zikr for a considerable amount of time. The name of Allah Ta'ala brings joy and peace to the heart. Allah Ta'ala has said:

اَلَا بِذِكْرِ اللهِ تَطْمَئِنُّ الْقُلُوْبُ

"Behold! The Zikr of Allah provides satisfaction for the hearts."
(Surah R'ad - Aayah 152)

There is general discontentment in the world today. The letters, which I receive daily, mostly contain reports of people's worries and anxieties. The object of this book is that people, who are in difficulty and lack peace of mind, whether in an individual or collective capacity, may find a solution to their problems. Others may also benefit from this publication, **"Virtues of the zikr of Allah Ta'ala"**. It is possible that the study of this book may inspire some people to make the zikr of Allah Ta'ala with sincerity (ikhlaas). This may prove useful to me also at a time when only good deeds will prove to be helpful. Allah Ta'ala can, through His sheer grace, forgive those who have no good deeds to their credit.

What prompted me to undertake this task was that Allah Ta'ala, through His extreme Benevolence and Grace, has blessed my uncle, Hadhrat Moulana Muhammad Ilyaas Kandhlawi, who resides in Nizaamuddin with a special insight and zeal for the work of Tableegh, the activities of which are no longer confined to India, but have reached Hejaz as well. This movement is well known and needs no introduction. Its good results were seen in India and abroad, but it was particularly found in the region of Mewat. The fundamental principles of this movement are very sound and strong, which would naturally yield beneficial results. One of the very important principles is that those who are engaged in Tableegh work should be particular about making zikr, more so when they are actively busy in the work of Tabligh. After observing the wonderful results of this practice, I found the need of writing this book. I was also directed by my respected uncle that the virtues of zikr should be compiled and made available to them. Those who are regular with their zikr may improve their steadfastness on the virtues of zikr and thereby realise that zikr is indeed a great wealth.

It is neither possible for a humble person like myself to compile a detailed book on the virtues of zikr, nor is it humanly possible to do full justice to this subject. I have however briefly described some Ahaadith relating to this subject. I have divided the book into three chapters:

First Chapter: The virtues of zikr in general
Second Chapter: The virtues of Kalimah Tayyibah (The most virtuous of zikr)
Third Chapter: The virtues of the Third Kalimah (also known as Tasbeeh-Faatimah)

(Hadhrat Moulana) Muhammad Zakariyya
Kaandhalwi *(rahmatullahi alayh)*

CHAPTER 1
VIRTUES OF ZIKR IN GENERAL

Even if there were no Aayaat or Ahaadith relating to zikr, we should never be forgetful of our real Benefactor, our Rabb, whose blessings and favours on us are unlimited at all times and have no parallel. It is natural that we should remember Allah Ta'ala, make His zikr (i.e. remember Him), and always thank Him.

خداوندِعالم کے قربان میں کرم جس کے لاکھوں ہیں ہر آن میں

May I be sacrificed for the sake of the master of the worlds, whose favours rain upon me every moment

There are many virtues of zikr described in the Qur-aan Shareef, Hadith Shareef and the sayings of our elders that support the making of zikr. No doubt, the zikr of Allah Ta'ala is full of blessings and noor (spiritual light).

I wish to first explain a few Aayaat from the Qur-aan Shareef and then some Ahaadith of Rasulullah ﷺ on the subject of Zikr.

SECTION 1
AAYAAT OF THE QUR-AAN RELATING TO ZIKR

١) فَاذْكُرُوْنِيْ اَذْكُرْكُمْ وَاشْكُرُوْا لِيْ وَلَا تَكْفُرُوْنِ

1. Remember me, I will remember you. Be grateful to me and do not be ungrateful." *(Surah Baqarah - Aayah 152)*

$$ ٢) \quad فَإِذَآ أَفَضْتُم مِّنْ عَرَفَٰتٍ فَٱذْكُرُوا۟ ٱللَّهَ عِندَ ٱلْمَشْعَرِ ٱلْحَرَامِ ۖ وَٱذْكُرُوهُ كَمَا هَدَىٰكُمْ وَإِن كُنتُم مِّن قَبْلِهِۦ لَمِنَ ٱلضَّآلِّينَ $$

2. "When (during Hajj) you leave Arafaat, remember Allah by Al-Masha'arul Haraam (the spot where Rasulullah ﷺ stopped at in Muzdalifah). Remember Him as He had guided you. Verily before this you were from those who were astray." *(Surah Baqarah - Aayah 198)*

$$ ٣) \quad فَإِذَا قَضَيْتُم مَّنَٰسِكَكُمْ فَٱذْكُرُوا۟ ٱللَّهَ كَذِكْرِكُمْ ءَابَآءَكُمْ أَوْ أَشَدَّ ذِكْرًا ۗ فَمِنَ ٱلنَّاسِ مَن يَقُولُ رَبَّنَآ ءَاتِنَا فِى ٱلدُّنْيَا وَمَا لَهُۥ فِى ٱلْءَاخِرَةِ مِنْ خَلَٰقٍ ۝ وَمِنْهُم مَّن يَقُولُ رَبَّنَآ ءَاتِنَا فِى ٱلدُّنْيَا حَسَنَةً وَفِى ٱلْءَاخِرَةِ حَسَنَةً وَقِنَا عَذَابَ ٱلنَّارِ ۝ أُو۟لَٰٓئِكَ لَهُمْ نَصِيبٌ مِّمَّا كَسَبُوا۟ ۚ وَٱللَّهُ سَرِيعُ ٱلْحِسَابِ $$

3. "And when you have completed your Hajj rites, then remember Allah as you remember your fathers, or with a more lively remembrance. There are men who say, "Our Rabb! Give us, (your bounties) in this world, but they will have no portion in the hereafter. There are men (also) who say, "Our Rabb! Give us good in this world and in the hereafter, and guard us from the punishment of the fire." For them there will be allotted a share for what they have earned. Allah Ta'ala is swift at reckoning." *(Surah Baqarah - Aayah 200)*

Note: It is related in a Hadith that the 'Dua' of three people are not rejected. It is surely accepted.

(1) He who remembers Allah Ta'ala profusely.
(2) An oppressed person.
(3) A ruler who rules justly and does not oppress anyone.

$$ ٤) \quad وَٱذْكُرُوا۟ ٱللَّهَ فِىٓ أَيَّامٍ مَّعْدُودَٰتٍ $$

Chapter 1 – Virtues of Zikr

4. "(During the Hajj) Remember Allah Ta'ala during the appointed days." *(Surah Baqarah – Aayah 203)*

٥) وَاذْكُرْ رَّبَّكَ كَثِيْرًا وَّسَبِّحْ بِالْعَشِيِّ وَالْإِبْكَارِ

5. "Remember your Rabb in abundance and glorify him in the early hours of the night and the morning." *(Surah Aali I'mraan - Aayah 41)*

٦) اَلَّذِيْنَ يَذْكُرُوْنَ اللهَ قِيَامًا وَّقُعُوْدًا وَّعَلٰى جُنُوْبِهِمْ وَيَتَفَكَّرُوْنَ فِيْ خَلْقِ السَّمٰوٰتِ وَالْأَرْضِ ۚ رَبَّنَا مَا خَلَقْتَ هٰذَا بَاطِلًا ۚ سُبْحٰنَكَ فَقِنَا عَذَابَ النَّارِ

6. "(Talking of the wise men, they) remember Allah, standing, sitting, and lying down, and think deeply about the creation of the heavens and the earth, and say, (after deliberation) "Our Rabb! You have not created this in vain. Glory be to Thee! Save us from the punishment of Jahannam." *(Surah Aali I'mraan – Aayah 191)*

٧) فَإِذَا قَضَيْتُمُ الصَّلٰوةَ فَاذْكُرُوا اللهَ قِيَامًا وَّقُعُوْدًا وَّعَلٰى جُنُوْبِكُمْ

7. When you have performed Salaah, remember Allah Ta'ala, standing, sitting and lying down. (i.e. we should remember Allah Ta'ala in all circumstances.) *(Surah Nisaa - Aayah 103)*

٨) وَإِذَا قَامُوْا إِلَى الصَّلٰوةِ قَامُوْا كُسَالٰى ۙ يُرَآءُوْنَ النَّاسَ وَلَا يَذْكُرُوْنَ اللهَ إِلَّا قَلِيْلًا

8. "(The Hypocrites) When they stand up for Salaah, they perform it with laziness and to be seen by men, and they do not remember Allah Ta'ala but little." *(Surah Nisaa - Aayah 142)*

٩) إِنَّمَا يُرِيْدُ الشَّيْطٰنُ أَنْ يُّوْقِعَ بَيْنَكُمُ الْعَدَاوَةَ وَالْبَغْضَآءَ فِي الْخَمْرِ وَالْمَيْسِرِ وَيَصُدَّكُمْ عَنْ ذِكْرِ اللهِ وَعَنِ الصَّلٰوةِ ۚ فَهَلْ أَنْتُمْ مُّنْتَهُوْنَ

9. "Shaytaan wants only to incite enmity and hatred between you by means of intoxicating drinks and gambling, and turn you away from

the remembrance of Allah Ta'ala and from Salaah. Will you then not abstain? (from these bad habits) *(Surah Maaidah - Aayah 91)*

(١٠) وَلَا تَطْرُدِ الَّذِيْنَ يَدْعُوْنَ رَبَّهُمْ بِالْغَدٰوةِ وَالْعَشِيِّ يُرِيْدُوْنَ وَجْهَهٗ

10. "And do not turn away from those who call unto their Rabb morning and evening, seeking His countenance (pleasure)."
(Surah An'aam - Aayah 52)

(١١) وَّادْعُوْهُ مُخْلِصِيْنَ لَهُ الدِّيْنَ

11) "And call unto Him, making your devotions purely for Him (only)"
(Surah A'araaf – Aayah 29)

(١٢) اُدْعُوْا رَبَّكُمْ تَضَرُّعًا وَّخُفْيَةً ۚ اِنَّهٗ لَا يُحِبُّ الْمُعْتَدِيْنَ ۚ وَلَا تُفْسِدُوْا فِي الْاَرْضِ بَعْدَ اِصْلَاحِهَا وَادْعُوْهُ خَوْفًا وَّطَمَعًا ۚ اِنَّ رَحْمَتَ اللّٰهِ قَرِيْبٌ مِّنَ الْمُحْسِنِيْنَ

12. "Call unto your Rabb with humility and in secret. He does not like the transgressors. Do not do mischief in the earth after it has been set in order, and call onto Him with fear and hope. Surely the mercy of Allah Ta'ala is near unto the good doers." *(Suarh A'araaf - Aayah 55 & 56)*

(١٣) وَلِلّٰهِ الْاَسْمَآءُ الْحُسْنٰى فَادْعُوْهُ بِهَا

13. "And for Allah is the most beautiful names. Invoke Him by them."
(Surah A'araaf - Aayah 180)

(١٤) وَاذْكُرْ رَّبَّكَ فِيْ نَفْسِكَ تَضَرُّعًا وَّخِيْفَةً وَّدُوْنَ الْجَهْرِ مِنَ الْقَوْلِ بِالْغُدُوِّ وَالْاٰصَالِ وَلَا تَكُنْ مِّنَ الْغٰفِلِيْنَ

14. "And remember your Rabb within yourself humbly and with fear, not in a loud voice in the morning and evenings. Do not be from those who are neglectful." *(Surah A'araaf - Aayah 205)*

Chapter 1 – Virtues of Zikr

١٥) اِنَّمَا الْمُؤْمِنُوْنَ الَّذِيْنَ اِذَا ذُكِرَ اللهُ وَجِلَتْ قُلُوْبُهُمْ وَ اِذَا تُلِيَتْ عَلَيْهِمْ اٰيٰتُهٗ زَادَتْهُمْ اِيْمَانًا وَّعَلٰى رَبِّهِمْ يَتَوَكَّلُوْنَ

15. "Only those are the (true) believers whose hearts feel a tremor when Allah is mentioned, and when the aayaat of Allah are recited to them, their Imaan is increased and they place their trust in their Rabb." *(Surah Anfaal – Aayah 2)*
(Thereafter mentioning the observance of Salaah by them it is stated)
"They are the true believers and they shall enjoy dignified positions with their Rabb and forgiveness and a generous sustenance."
(Surah Anfaal – Aayah 4)

١٦) وَيَهْدِيْٓ اِلَيْهِ مَنْ اَنَابَ ۚ اَلَّذِيْنَ اٰمَنُوْا وَتَطْمَئِنُّ قُلُوْبُهُمْ بِذِكْرِ اللهِ ۗ اَلَا بِذِكْرِ اللهِ تَطْمَئِنُّ الْقُلُوْبُ

16. "And He guides towards Himself all those who turn to Him in repentance. Those who have believed (in the oneness of Allah) and whose hearts find contentment in the remembrance of Allah. Verily in the remembrance of Allah do hearts find contentment"
(Sura R'ad – Aayah 27-28)

١٧) قُلِ ادْعُوا اللهَ اَوِ ادْعُوا الرَّحْمٰنَ ۗ اَيًّا مَّا تَدْعُوْا فَلَهُ الْاَسْمَآءُ الْحُسْنٰى

17. "Say (unto mankind): Call upon Allah, or call upon Rahmaan (the most gracious). Whatever name you call unto Him, (it is the same). For to Him belongs the best names." *(Surah Bani Israaeel - Aayah 110)*

١٨) وَاذْكُرْ رَّبَّكَ اِذَا نَسِيْتَ

18. "And remember your Rabb when you forget" *(Surah Kahf - Aayah 24)*

$$\text{(١٩) وَاصْبِرْ نَفْسَكَ مَعَ الَّذِيْنَ يَدْعُوْنَ رَبَّهُمْ بِالْغَدٰوةِ وَالْعَشِيِّ يُرِيْدُوْنَ وَجْهَهٗ وَلَا تَعْدُ عَيْنٰكَ عَنْهُمْ ۚ تُرِيْدُ زِيْنَةَ الْحَيٰوةِ الدُّنْيَا ۚ وَلَا تُطِعْ مَنْ اَغْفَلْنَا قَلْبَهٗ عَنْ ذِكْرِنَا وَاتَّبَعَ هَوٰىهُ وَكَانَ اَمْرُهٗ فُرُطًا}$$

19. "Keep yourself patiently with those who call upon their Rabb morning and evening, seeking His pleasure; and let not your eyes overlook them, desiring the pomp of this worldly life; and do not obey those whose heart we have made heedless of our remembrance, and who follows his own lust and whose affairs (deeds) has been lost."
(Surah Kahf - Aayah 28)

$$\text{(٢٠) وَّ عَرَضْنَا جَهَنَّمَ يَوْمَئِذٍ لِّلْكٰفِرِيْنَ عَرْضَا ۙ الَّذِيْنَ كَانَتْ اَعْيُنُهُمْ فِيْ غِطَاءٍ عَنْ ذِكْرِیْ}$$

20. "On that day, we shall present Jahannam to the disbelievers, plain to view; those whose eyes had been under a veil from my remembrance." (the Qur-aan). (Surah Kahf - Aayah 100 & 101)

$$\text{(٢١) ذِكْرُ رَحْمَتِ رَبِّكَ عَبْدَهٗ زَكَرِيَّا ۖ اِذْ نَادٰى رَبَّهٗ نِدَآءً خَفِيًّا}$$

21. "(This is) a mention of the mercy of your Rabb to His servant Zakariyya; when he made dua to His Rabb secretly."
(Surah Maryam - Aayah 2 & 3)

$$\text{(٢٢) وَاَدْعُوْا رَبِّیْ ۖ عَسٰۤى اَلَّاۤ اَكُوْنَ بِدُعَآءِ رَبِّیْ شَقِيًّا}$$

22. "And I shall make dua to my Rabb. I am hopeful that I shall not be deprived in my dua to my Rabb." (Surah Maryam – Aayah 48)

$$\text{(٢٣) اِنَّنِیْۤ اَنَا اللّٰهُ لَاۤ اِلٰهَ اِلَّاۤ اَنَا فَاعْبُدْنِیْ ۙ وَاَقِمِ الصَّلٰوةَ لِذِكْرِیْ ۞ اِنَّ السَّاعَةَ اٰتِيَةٌ اَكَادُ اُخْفِيْهَا لِتُجْزٰى كُلُّ نَفْسٍ بِمَا تَسْعٰى}$$

23. "Verily! I am Allah. There is no God besides me. So worship me and establish Salaah for my remembrance. Verily! The hour is surely coming. But I will keep it hidden, that every person may be rewarded for that which he strives." *(Surah Taahaa - Aayah 14 & 15)*

(٢٤) وَلَا تَنِيَا فِىْ ذِكْرِىْ

24. "And do not slacken and become weak in my remembrance. (this is a piece of advice for Hadhrat Moosa and Haroon (alayhimas salaam)" *(Surah Taahaa - Aayah 42)*

(٢٥) وَنُوْحًا اِذْ نَادٰى مِنْ قَبْلُ

25. "And (remember) Nooh عَلَيْهِ ٱلسَّلَام when he cried (to us) before (the time of Ibraheem عَلَيْهِ ٱلسَّلَام)" *(Surah Ambiyaa - Aayah 76)*

(٢٦) وَاَيُّوْبَ اِذْ نَادٰى رَبَّهٗٓ اَنِّىْ مَسَّنِىَ الضُّرُّ وَاَنْتَ اَرْحَمُ الرّٰحِمِيْنَ

26. "And (remember) Ayoob عَلَيْهِ ٱلسَّلَام when he cried to his Rabb, 'Verily! Difficulty has afflicted me, and you are the most merciful of all those who show mercy." *(Surah Ambiyaa - Aayah 83)*

(٢٧) وَذَا النُّوْنِ اِذْ ذَّهَبَ مُغَاضِبًا فَظَنَّ اَنْ لَّنْ نَّقْدِرَ عَلَيْهِ فَنَادٰى فِى الظُّلُمٰتِ اَنْ لَّآ اِلٰهَ اِلَّآ اَنْتَ سُبْحٰنَكَ اِنِّىْ كُنْتُ مِنَ الظّٰلِمِيْنَ

27. "And (remember) Zun-Noon, Yunus عَلَيْهِ ٱلسَّلَام when he went off in anger (displeased with his community) and imagined that we had no power over him; but he cried out in the darkness (of the whale) saying "There is no Lord besides you: you be glorified! Truly I have been of the wrong-doers." *(Surah Ambiyaa - Aayah 87)*

(٢٨) وَزَكَرِيَّآ اِذْ نَادٰى رَبَّهٗ رَبِّ لَا تَذَرْنِىْ فَرْدًا وَّاَنْتَ خَيْرُ الْوٰرِثِيْنَ

28. "And (remember) Zakariyya عَلَيْهِ السَّلَام when he cried to his Rabb, "O My Rabb! Do not leave me single (childless), and You are the best of inheritors." *(Surah Ambiyaa - Aayah 89)*

(٢٩) اِنَّهُمْ كَانُوْا يُسَارِعُوْنَ فِي الْخَيْرَاتِ وَيَدْعُوْنَنَا رَغَبًا وَّرَهَبًا ۚ وَكَانُوْا لَنَا خٰشِعِيْنَ

29. "Verily! They (the Ambiyaa (alayhimus salaam) mentioned before) used to hasten in doing good deeds, and they cried to us in hope and in fear, and they used to humble themselves before us." *(Surah Ambiyaa - Aayah 90)*

(٣٠) وَبَشِّرِ الْمُخْبِتِيْنَ ۙ الَّذِيْنَ اِذَا ذُكِرَ اللّٰهُ وَجِلَتْ قُلُوْبُهُمْ

30. "And give good tidings to those who are humble, whose hearts fear when Allah is mentioned." *(Surah Hajj - Aayah 34 & 35)*

(٣١) اِنَّهٗ كَانَ فَرِيْقٌ مِّنْ عِبَادِيْ يَقُوْلُوْنَ رَبَّنَاۤ اٰمَنَّا فَاغْفِرْ لَنَا وَارْحَمْنَا وَاَنْتَ خَيْرُ الرَّاحِمِيْنَ ۚ فَاتَّخَذْتُمُوْهُمْ سِخْرِيًّا حَتّٰۤى اَنْسَوْكُمْ ذِكْرِىْ وَكُنْتُمْ مِّنْهُمْ تَضْحَكُوْنَ ۝ اِنِّىْ جَزَيْتُهُمُ الْيَوْمَ بِمَا صَبَرُوْۤا ۙ اَنَّهُمْ هُمُ الْفَآئِزُوْنَ

31. (While talking to the unbelievers on the Day of Qiyaamah, they will be asked whether they remember). Lo! There was a party of My servants who said, "Our Rabb! We believe, therefore forgive us and have mercy on us, for You are the best of all those who show mercy. But you ridiculed them, until this caused you to forget Me, while you used to laugh at them. Verily I have rewarded them this day for their patience and they are indeed the ones who are successful. *(Surah M'uminoon - Aayah 109-111)*

(٣٢) رِجَالٌ ۙ لَّا تُلْهِيْهِمْ تِجَارَةٌ وَّلَا بَيْعٌ عَنْ ذِكْرِ اللّٰهِ

32. (While praising men with perfect Imaan) "Men whom neither trade nor commerce diverts them from the remembrance of Allah." *(Surah Noor - Aayah 37)*

(٣٣) وَلَذِكْرُ اللّٰهِ اَكْبَرُ

33. *"Indeed, the remembrance of Allah is the greatest."*
(Surah Ankaboot - Aayah 45)

(٣٤) تَتَجَافٰى جُنُوْبُهُمْ عَنِ الْمَضَاجِعِ يَدْعُوْنَ رَبَّهُمْ خَوْفًا وَّطَمَعًا ۖ وَّمِمَّا رَزَقْنٰهُمْ يُنْفِقُوْنَ ۝ فَلَا تَعْلَمُ نَفْسٌ مَّآ اُخْفِيَ لَهُمْ مِّنْ قُرَّةِ اَعْيُنٍ ۚ جَزَآءًۢ بِمَا كَانُوْا يَعْمَلُوْنَ

34. *(Those) who their sides forsake their beds and they make dua to their Rabb in fear and hope, and they spend from what we have bestowed on them. No person knows what is kept hidden for them as a reward for what they used to do."* (Surah Sajdah - Ayah 16 & 17)

Note: It is mentioned in a Hadith that the one who worshipped Allah Ta'ala in the last portion of the night gains the acceptance of Allah Ta'ala. If possible, you should remember Allah Ta'ala at this hour.

(٣٥) لَقَدْ كَانَ لَكُمْ فِيْ رَسُوْلِ اللّٰهِ اُسْوَةٌ حَسَنَةٌ لِّمَنْ كَانَ يَرْجُوا اللّٰهَ وَالْيَوْمَ الْاٰخِرَ وَذَكَرَ اللّٰهَ كَثِيْرًا

35. *"Verily indeed in the messenger of Allah Ta'ala you have a good example to follow for him who long for (meeting) with Allah Ta'ala and the last day, and remembers Allah Ta'ala a lot."*
(Surah Ahzaab - Aayah 20)

(٣٦) اَلذَّاكِرِيْنَ اللّٰهَ كَثِيْرًا وَّالذَّاكِرَاتِ ۙ اَعَدَّ اللّٰهُ لَهُمْ مَّغْفِرَةً وَّاَجْرًا عَظِيْمًا

36. *"(While talking of the virtues of the believers) and men and women who remember Allah much (with their hearts and tongues) Allah has prepared for them His forgiveness and a great reward (i.e. paradise)."*
(Surah Ahzaab - Aayah 35)

(٣٧) يٰٓاَيُّهَا الَّذِيْنَ اٰمَنُوا اذْكُرُوا اللّٰهَ ذِكْرًا كَثِيْرًا ۙ ۝ وَّسَبِّحُوْهُ بُكْرَةً وَّاَصِيْلًا

37. *"O you who believe! Remember Allah with much remembrance. And glorify Him morning and evening."* (Surah A'hzaab – Aayah 41 & 42)

(۳۸) وَلَقَدْ نَادَانَا نُوْحٌ فَلَنِعْمَ الْمُجِيْبُوْنَ

38. "And Nooh عَلَيْهِ السَّلَام called out to us, and we are the best who answer (the request)." (Surah Saaffaat Aayah 75)

(۳۹) فَوَيْلٌ لِّلْقٰسِيَةِ قُلُوْبُهُمْ مِّنْ ذِكْرِ اللّٰهِ ۚ أُولٰٓئِكَ فِيْ ضَلٰلٍ مُّبِيْنٍ

39. "Then woe unto those whose hearts are hardened from the remembrance of Allah. They are in plain error."
(Surah Zumar - Aayah 22)

(٤٠) اَللّٰهُ نَزَّلَ اَحْسَنَ الْحَدِيْثِ كِتٰبًا مُّتَشَابِهًا مَّثَانِيَ ۖ تَقْشَعِرُّ مِنْهُ جُلُوْدُ الَّذِيْنَ يَخْشَوْنَ رَبَّهُمْ ۚ ثُمَّ تَلِيْنُ جُلُوْدُهُمْ وَقُلُوْبُهُمْ اِلٰى ذِكْرِ اللّٰهِ ۚ ذٰلِكَ هُدَى اللّٰهِ يَهْدِيْ بِهٖ مَنْ يَّشَآءُ

40. "Allah has revealed the most beautiful message of the Qur-aan, its parts resemble each other (in goodness and truth) (and) often repeated. The skins of those, who fear their Rabb, tremble (when they recite it or hear it), their skin and their hearts soften to the remembrance of Allah. That is the guidance of Allah. He guides with it whom He wills." (Surah Zumar – Aayah 23)

(٤۱) فَادْعُوا اللّٰهَ مُخْلِصِيْنَ لَهُ الدِّيْنَ وَلَوْ كَرِهَ الْكٰفِرُوْنَ

41. "Therefore make dua to Allah Ta'ala, making Ibaadah (worship) only for Him even though the disbelievers may dislike it."
(Surah Mu'min – Aayah 14)

(٤۲) هُوَ الْحَيُّ لَآ اِلٰهَ اِلَّا هُوَ فَادْعُوْهُ مُخْلِصِيْنَ لَهُ الدِّيْنَ ۚ اَلْحَمْدُ لِلّٰهِ رَبِّ الْعٰلَمِيْنَ

42. "He is the ever living, besides Whom there is no other god worthy of worship, so make dua to Him making Ibaadah (worship) only for Him. All praise is for Allah Ta'ala, the Rabb of the universe."
(Surah Mu'min – Aayah 65)

(٤۳) وَمَنْ يَّعْشُ عَنْ ذِكْرِ الرَّحْمٰنِ نُقَيِّضْ لَهُ شَيْطٰنًا فَهُوَ لَهُ قَرِيْنٌ

43. "And he who turns a blind eye to the remembrance (advice) of Ar-Rahmaan (The Beneficent), we shall appoint a shaytaan on him who will be his companion." *(Surah Zukhruf – Aayah 36)*

٣٣) مُحَمَّدٌ رَّسُوْلُ اللهِ ۗ وَالَّذِيْنَ مَعَهٗٓ اَشِدَّآءُ عَلَى الْكُفَّارِ رُحَمَآءُ بَيْنَهُمْ تَرَاهُمْ رُكَّعًا سُجَّدًا يَّبْتَغُوْنَ فَضْلًا مِّنَ اللهِ وَرِضْوَانًا ۗ سِيْمَاهُمْ فِيْ وُجُوْهِهِمْ مِّنْ اَثَرِ السُّجُوْدِ ۗ ذٰلِكَ مَثَلُهُمْ فِي التَّوْرٰىةِ ۛ وَمَثَلُهُمْ فِي الْاِنْجِيْلِ ۛ كَزَرْعٍ اَخْرَجَ شَطْـَٔهٗ فَاٰزَرَهٗ فَاسْتَغْلَظَ فَاسْتَوٰى عَلٰى سُوْقِهٖ يُعْجِبُ الزُّرَّاعَ لِيَغِيْظَ بِهِمُ الْكُفَّارَ ۗ وَعَدَ اللهُ الَّذِيْنَ اٰمَنُوْا وَعَمِلُوا الصّٰلِحٰتِ مِنْهُمْ مَّغْفِرَةً وَّاَجْرًا عَظِيْمًا

44. Muhammad ﷺ is the Rasool of Allah Ta'ala. And those with him (the Sahaabah رضي الله عنهم) are hard against the disbelievers and merciful among themselves. You will see them sometimes making ruku and sometimes making sajdah (worshiping Allah Ta'ala), seeking Allah Ta'ala's bounty and His pleasure. Their mark on their faces are from the traces of making sajdah. This is their description in the Torah. Their description in the Injeel is like a plant that sprouts its shoots and strengthens it, after which it becomes thick and stands on its own stem, delighting the farmers. (In the same manner, the Sahaabah رضي الله عنهم were weak in the beginning and then grew in strength and numbers day by day), so that the kuffaar may be enraged with (seeing) them. Allah Ta'ala has promised forgiveness and a grand reward for those who have Imaan and do good deeds."
(Surah Fatah – Aayah 29)

Note: Though the emphasis in these verses obviously is on the blessings occurring from 'Ruku' 'Sujud' and 'Salaah', but there is also an indication about the blessings associated with the second part of the Kalimah i.e. (Muhammadur-Rasulullah). Imaam Raazi *(rahmatullahi alayh)* has related that in the treaty of Hudaybiyya, on the refusal and insistence of the unbelievers not to write (Muhammad Rasulullah) and to substitute it with 'Muhammad bin Abdullah', Allah Ta'ala asserts that He Himself bears testimony to the Nubuwat of Nabi Muhammad ﷺ. When the sender personally confirms a particular person to be his messenger, then the rejection by any number of people does not matter. To confirm this testimony, Allah Ta'ala made the statement of 'Muahmmadur Raoulullah' (Muhammad (ﷺ) is a messenger of Allah Ta'ala).

There are other important subjects in these Aayaat as well. One of them relates to the glow on the face of a blessed person (Their marks on their foreheads from the traces of sajdah). It has been explained that a person who stays awake at night in Salaah, develops a glow on his face.

Imaam Raazi *(rahmatullahi alayh)* considers it as an established fact that if two people keep awake at night, one spending it in sensual and idle pleasures and the other uses his time in reciting the Qur-aan Shareef, learning Deeni knowledge and offering Salaah; they will wake up with different facial expressions the next morning. The latter described above will show himself to be a different person because of his spiritual glow. That person who was involved in sensual pleasures and entertainment can never be like the one who spent the night in ibaadah.

The third important thing that Imaam Maalik *(rahmatullahi alayh)* and a group of Ulama have established is 'Kufr' for those people who talk ill of the Sahaabah ﷺ and bear hatred against them.

(٤٥) اَلَمْ يَأْنِ لِلَّذِيْنَ اٰمَنُوْۤا اَنْ تَخْشَعَ قُلُوْبُهُمْ لِذِكْرِ اللّٰهِ

45. "Has not the time come for the hearts of the Mu'mineen (those who believe) to submit to Allah Ta'ala's remembrance."
(Surah Hadeed - Aayah 16)

(٤٦) اِسْتَحْوَذَ عَلَيْهِمُ الشَّيْطٰنُ فَاَنْسٰىهُمْ ذِكْرَ اللّٰهِ ؕ اُولٰٓئِكَ حِزْبُ الشَّيْطٰنِ ؕ اَلَاۤ اِنَّ حِزْبَ الشَّيْطٰنِ هُمُ الْخٰسِرُوْنَ

46. "(mentioning the hypocrites) shaytaan has overpowered them and caused them to forget the remembrance of Allah Ta'ala. They are the group of shaytaan. Verily! The group of shaytaan are the losers? *(Surah Mujaadalah - Aayah 19)*

Chapter 1 – Virtues of Zikr

٤٧) فَإِذَا قُضِيَتِ الصَّلٰوةُ فَانْتَشِرُوْا فِي الْأَرْضِ وَابْتَغُوْا مِنْ فَضْلِ اللهِ وَاذْكُرُوا اللهَ كَثِيْرًا لَّعَلَّكُمْ تُفْلِحُوْنَ

47. "And when the (Friday) Salaah has been completed, then disperse in the land and seek the bounty of Allah Ta'ala, (with the permission to engage yourself in worldly pursuits but even then) and remember Allah Ta'ala a lot, so that you may be successful."
(Surah Jumu'ah – Aayah 10)

٤٨) يٰٓأَيُّهَا الَّذِيْنَ اٰمَنُوْا لَا تُلْهِكُمْ أَمْوَالُكُمْ وَلَآ أَوْلَادُكُمْ عَنْ ذِكْرِ اللهِ ۚ وَمَنْ يَّفْعَلْ ذٰلِكَ فَأُولٰٓئِكَ هُمُ الْخٰسِرُوْنَ

48. "O you who believe! Let not your wealth nor your children distract you from the remembrance of Allah Ta'ala. Those who do so, they are the losers." (These things will not last beyond the grave and the remembrance of Allah Ta'ala will prove useful in the Aakhirah).
(Surah Munaafiqoon – Aayah 9)

٤٩) وَإِنْ يَّكَادُ الَّذِيْنَ كَفَرُوْا لَيُزْلِقُوْنَكَ بِأَبْصَارِهِمْ لَمَّا سَمِعُوا الذِّكْرَ وَيَقُوْلُوْنَ إِنَّهٗ لَمَجْنُوْنٌ

49. "It seems as if the kuffaar could almost make you (Muhammad ﷺ) slip with their gazes when they hear the reminder (Quraan) and they say, 'He is indeed insane.'" (Surah Qalam – Aayah 51)

Note: Using their eyes in this manner indicates their extreme enmity. Hadhrat Hasan Basri *(rahmatullahi alayh)* advises that if a person is affected with *nazar* (the evil eye) it will be beneficial to read this Aayah and blow on him.

٥٠) وَمَنْ يُّعْرِضْ عَنْ ذِكْرِ رَبِّهٖ يَسْلُكْهُ عَذَابًا صَعَدًا

50. "And whoever turns away from the remembrance of his Rabb, he shall enter him into a severe punishment." (Surah Jinn – Aayah 17)

(۵۱) وَاَنَّهٗ لَمَّا قَامَ عَبْدُ اللّٰهِ يَدْعُوْهُ كَادُوْا يَكُوْنُوْنَ عَلَيْهِ لِبَدًا ۞ قُلْ اِنَّمَاۤ اَدْعُوْا رَبِّیْ وَلَاۤ اُشْرِكُ بِهٖۤ اَحَدًا

51. "And when the slave of Allah Ta'ala (Muhammad ﷺ) stood up to supplicate / worship Him, they (the kuffaar) densely crowded around him. Say (to them, O Muhammad), I only worship my Rabb, and I do not ascribe anyone as His partner."
(Surah Jinn – Aayah 19 & 20)

(۵۲) وَاذْكُرِ اسْمَ رَبِّكَ وَتَبَتَّلْ اِلَيْهِ تَبْتِيْلًا

52. "So remember the name of your Rabb and cut yourself off from everything (of this world) to focus your attention solely on Him." (All other attachments should be cut off at that time and devotion to Allah Ta'ala should dominate) (Surah Muzzammil – Aayah 8)

(۵۳) وَاذْكُرِ اسْمَ رَبِّكَ بُكْرَةً وَّاَصِيْلًا ۞ وَمِنَ الَّيْلِ فَاسْجُدْ لَهٗ وَسَبِّحْهُ لَيْلًا طَوِيْلًا ۞ اِنَّ هٰۤؤُلَآءِ يُحِبُّوْنَ الْعَاجِلَةَ وَيَذَرُوْنَ وَرَآءَهُمْ يَوْمًا ثَقِيْلًا

53. "Remember the name of your Rabb in the morning and the evening; and make sajdah to Him (perform Salaah) during the night, and glorify Him during the long portions of the night. Indeed! These people (the kuffaar) love the world, and put behind them (the remembrance of) a weighty day." (Surah Dahr – Aayah 25-27)

(۵۴) قَدْ اَفْلَحَ مَنْ تَزَكّٰى ۞ وَذَكَرَ اسْمَ رَبِّهٖ فَصَلّٰى

54. "Successful indeed is he who has purified (himself of all types of evil) and remembers the name of his Rabb and performs Salaah."
(Surah A'alaa - Aayah 14 & 15)

SECTION 2
AHAADITH ON THE VIRTUES OF 'ZIKR'

When the importance of zikr has been emphasized in so many aayaat of the Qur-aan Shareef, the number of Ahaadith on this subject will naturally be much more, because there are many books of Ahaadith, while the Qur-aan Shareef is one book with 30 chapters. The books of Ahaadith are many and each book contains a large number of Ahaadith. For example, the Bukhaari Shareef alone consists of 30 voluminous parts, and similarly Abu Dawood Shareef has 32 parts. There is no book of Hadith, which does not contain several Ahaadith on the subject of 'zikr', and it is, therefore impossible to quote all such Ahaadith in this small booklet. Of course, a single Aayah of the Qur-aan Shareef or a single Hadith is sufficient to move the faithful one to do good actions. On the other hand, a library full of books will be of no use to an unwilling person to practice. He is like a donkey carrying a load of books on its back.

Hadith 1 - Allah Ta'ala Treats People according to their Expectations of Him

عَنْ اَبِيْ هُرَيْرَةَ رَضِىَ اللهُ عَنْهُ قَالَ قَالَ النَّبِىُّ صَلَّى اللهُ عَلَيْهِ وَسَلَّمَ: يَقُوْلُ اللهُ تَعَالٰى: اَنَاعِنْدَ ظَنِّ عَبْدِىْ بِىْ وَاَنَا مَعَهُ اِذَا ذَكَرَنِىْ فَاِنْ ذَكَرَنِىْ فِىْ نَفْسِهٖ ذَكَرْتُهٗ فِىْ نَفْسِىْ وَاِنْ ذَكَرَنِىْ فِىْ مَلَاٍ ذَكَرْتُهٗ فِىْ مَلَاٍ خَيْرٍ مِّنْهُمْ وَاِنْ تَقَرَّبَ اِلَىَّ بِشِبْرٍ تَقَرَّبْتُ اِلَيْهِ ذِرَاعًا وَاِنْ تَقَرَّبَ اِلَىَّ ذِرَاعًا تَقَرَّبْتُ اِلَيْهِ بَاعًا وَاِنْ اَتَانِىْ يَمْشِىْ اَتَيْتُهٗ هَرْوَلَةً (صحيح البخارى # ٧٤٠٥)

Hadhrat Abu Hurayrah ﷺ narrated that Rasulullah ﷺ has said, "Allah Ta'ala says, 'I treat my slaves according to his expectations from Me, and I am with him when he remembers Me. If he remembers Me in his heart, I remember him in My heart. If he remembers Me in a gathering, I remember him in a better and nobler gathering (i.e. the gathering of Malaaikah). If he comes closer to Me by one hand's span, I go towards him a cubit's length. If he comes toward Me by a cubit's length, I go towards him an arm's length, and if he walks towards Me, I run towards him."

Note: There are several points mentioned in this Hadith. The first point is that Allah Ta'ala deals with man according to his expectations of Him. One should therefore always be hopeful of the mercy and benevolence of Allah Ta'ala. Never becomes despondent of His blessings. Certainly, we are extremely sinful and justly deserve punishment on account of our evil deeds, yet in no case should we feel despondent of the mercy of Allah Ta'ala, as He may perhaps totally forgive us out of His sheer grace and mercy.

اِنَّ اللهَ لَا يَغْفِرُ اَنْ يُشْرَكَ بِهٖ وَ يَغْفِرُ مَا دُوْنَ ذٰلِكَ لِمَنْ يَّشَآءُ

"Verily Allah Ta'ala does not forgive the sin of shirk (i.e. that a partner be ascribed to Him) and forgives besides that whoever he wishes." (Surah An Nisaa - Aayah 48)

Allah Ta'ala may or may not forgive; that is why the 'Ulama say that true Imaan lies in between hope (forgiveness of Allah Ta'ala) and fear (of His anger). Rasulullah ﷺ once visited a young Sahaabi (companion), who was in the throes of death and asked him about his condition. He replied, "O Messenger of Allah! I am hopeful of the mercy of Allah, yet I am afraid of my sins." On this Rasulullah ﷺ said, "When the heart of a Muslim is filled with these two feelings of hope and fear, Allah Ta'ala fulfils his hopes and saves him from what he is afraid of."

It is mentioned in one Hadith that a Muslim regards his sin to be as dangerous as if he is sitting under a huge rock that is threatening to fall on him. On the other hand, a sinner regards his sin as insignificant as a fly which is easily scared off (i.e., he takes his sins very lightly). In short, one should be appropriately afraid of ones sins and remain hopeful of the mercy of Allah Ta'ala.

Hadhrat Muaaz ؓ was martyred in a plague and in the moments before his death, he fainted many times. Whenever he regained consciousness for a moment, he would say, "O Allah! You know that I love You. By Your Honour and Glory, You know this very well." When the moment of death came close, he said, "O Death! You are a welcomed guest but have come at a time when there is no food in the house." Then he said, "O Allah! You know very well that I had always feared You and today I am dying hopeful of Your forgiveness. O Allah! I enjoyed life, not for digging canals and planting gardens, but in remaining thirsty in the hot weather and in undergoing hardships for the sake of Islam, and in taking part in the gatherings engaged in zikr in the company of the Ulama."

Some Ulama have written that "the fulfilment of expectations" promised by Allah Ta'ala in this Hadith is in its most general sense. It gives assurance not only in respect of forgiveness of ones sins, but also in respect of ones duas, health, wealth and safety, etc. For instance when a person makes dua to Allah Ta'ala and sincerely believes that Allah Ta'ala shall accept his dua, then his dua is definitely accepted, but if he has doubt (that Allah Ta'ala would not accept his dua), it would not be accepted.

In another Hadith it is stated that the dua of a person is answered as long as he does not say: "My duas do not get answered." The same applies to all matters relating to health, prosperity, etc. According to one Hadith, if a person experiences hunger and he discloses it to people, he will not be relieved of his poverty, but if he shows total submission to Allah Ta'ala, who is most Gracious, and begs only from Him, his condition may soon change for the better.

However, having hope and good expectations from Allah Ta'ala is one thing, and being over-confident and bold of His help and forgiveness is another thing. Allah Ta'ala has warned us against such an attitude in several Aayaat of the Qur-aan Shareef;

$$\text{وَلَا يَغُرَّنَّكُم بِاللّٰهِ الْغَرُورُ}$$

"Let not the deceiver (shaytaan) deceive you in regard to Allah Ta'ala." (Surah Luqmaan – Aayah 33)

i.e. one should not be misled by shaytaan to commit sins just because Allah Ta'ala is the most Merciful and the Forgiver of sins. There is another Aayah,

$$\text{اَطَّلَعَ الْغَيْبَ اَمِ اتَّخَذَ عِنْدَ الرَّحْمٰنِ عَهْدًا ۞ كَلَّا}$$

"Does He have knowledge of the Unseen, or has he made a pact with the (Allah who is most) Merciful. No! Never." (Surah Maryam – Aayah 78)

The second point in this Hadith is, "Whenever a slave of Mine remembers Me, I am with him." In another Hadith, it is stated, "So long as one's lips move in My remembrance, I remain with him." i.e. Allah Ta'ala bestows His special care and mercy on him during all this time.

The third point is that Allah Ta'ala mentions him favorably to the Malaaikah, which signifies the value of zikr. Firstly, this is because Allah Ta'ala created man such that, naturally he is liable to be good as well as to go astray. (Refer to Hadith No.8). Obedience on his part therefore deserves special appreciation. Secondly, at the time of the creation of Hadhrat Aadam (alayhis salaam), the Malaaikah (who have no inclination for doing evil) objected, that why is such a creation being created who would cause blood-shed and chaos in the world, while we (the Malaaikah) are always engaged in the praise and glorification of Allah Ta'ala. Thirdly, man's worship of Allah Ta'ala and submission to His will is more admirable than that of the Malaaikah, because he worships Allah Ta'ala because of his belief in the *ghaib* (unseen) whilst the Malaaikah witness and see all aspects of the unseen. It is to this fact that Allah Ta'ala refers to in the Hadith-e-Qudsi: "If man had only seen Jannah and Jahannam one can well imagine how he would have worshipped Allah Ta'ala." It is for this reason that Allah Ta'ala praises the noble deeds of those who worship and glorify Him without seeing Him.

The fourth point contained in the above mentioned Hadith is that when man turns his attention to Allah Ta'ala, the mercy and kindness of Allah Ta'ala descend upon him even more. "Getting near" and "running" signify a great and immediate increase in His blessings and mercy upon the person. Thus, it is up to a person, if he wants to enjoy more kindness and favours from Allah Ta'ala, he should increase his devotion and Ibaadah to Him.

The fifth point in the above mentioned Hadith is that the Malaaikah have been mentioned to be superior to man, whilst it is commonly known that man is the best creation of Allah Ta'ala. One reason for this has already been explained in the translation (of the Hadith), that the Malaaikah are superior because they are sinless and do not commit sins. Secondly, they are superior because in general they are better than the majority of men, including even the majority of the Muslims. However, some special believers like the Ambiyaa *(alayhimus salaam)* are superior to the Malaaikah. Besides these, there are other explanations as well, which are not mentioned in order to prevent the discussion from getting too long.

Hadith 2 – Keeping the Tongue Busy with Zikrullah

عَنْ عَبْدِ اللهِ بْنِ بُسْرٍ رَضِيَ اللهُ عَنْهُ اَنَّ رَجُلًا قَالَ: يَا رَسُوْلَ اللهِ اِنَّ شَرَائِعَ الْاِسْلَامِ قَدْ كَثُرَتْ عَلَيَّ فَاَخْبِرْنِيْ بِشَيْءٍ اَسْتَنُّ بِهٖ قَالَ: لَا يَزَالُ لِسَانُكَ رَطْبًا مِّنْ ذِكْرِ اللهِ

(سنن الترمذى #ﷺ)

Abdullah ibnu Busr ؓ narrates that a Sahaabi said, "O, Rasulullah ﷺ, I know that the commandments of the Shariah are many, but of these tell me one that I may diligently practice on." Rasulullah ﷺ, replied, "Keep your tongue always moist (i.e. busy) with the zikr of Allah."

According to another Hadith, Hadhrat Mu'aaz ؓ said, "At the time of my departure from Rasulullah ﷺ, I asked him to advise me of such an action which is most pleasing to Allah Ta'ala, whereupon he replied, 'Death should come to you in such a condition that your tongue is busy with the zikr of Allah Ta'ala.'"

Note: By "my departure", Hadhrat Mu'aaz ؓ refers to the occasion when he was appointed by Rasulullah ﷺ as the governor of Yemen and sent there to teach and propagate Islam. It was at the time of his departure that Rasulullah ﷺ had given him some parting advices.

By saying that, "the commandments of Shariah are many", the Sahaabi ؓ had meant that although it is necessary to fulfill every commandment, it is difficult to specialize and attain perfection in every aspect. He, therefore, wanted Rasulullah ﷺ to recommend something to him which was of over-riding importance that he may hold fast onto, and practice at all times and in all conditions, whether sitting, standing or walking.

According to another Hadith, a person who possesses the following four things is truly blessed, from the worldly as well as Deeni point of view:

1. A tongue that is always busy in the zikr of Allah Ta'ala.
2. A heart that is filled with shukar (gratitude) of Allah Ta'ala.
3. A body that is capable of tolerating hardships.
4. A wife who does not betray her husband's trust in respect of her chastity and his wealth. (This means, that she does not engage in any shameless activities).

The expression, "moist tongue" according to most Ulama means making zikr abundantly. Even in our general speech if someone praises another person excessively it said (in Urdu)

فلاں کی تعریف میں رطب اللسان ہے

"His tongue is moist in the praise of that person."

But in my (i.e. the author's) humble opinion it can have another meaning as well. It is always very sweet and pleasant to talk of one's beloved as is the common feeling and experience of every lover. On this basis, the phrase "moist tongue" would therefore mean that one should take with love the name of Allah Ta'ala, so as to feel the beloved's sweetness in the mouth. I have observed many times that when some of my elders make zikr aloud, the sweetness enjoyed by them is transmitted to the listeners in such a way that their mouths also taste the sweetness and they also share in the enjoyment of the zikr. This is possible only where there is a genuine desire for zikr, and the tongue is accustomed to excessive zikr. It is stated in one Hadith that the sign of one's love for Allah Ta'ala lies in one's love for the zikr of Allah Ta'ala, and, in the same way, the proof for one's enmity for Allah Ta'ala lies in one's dislike for the zikr of Allah Ta'ala. Hadhrat Abu Darda رَضِيَ اللهُ عَنْهُ said that those who keep their tongues moist with the zikr of Allah Ta'ala will enter Jannah laughing.

Hadith 3 – Zikr, the Best of all Deeds

عَنْ اَبِي الدَّرْدَاءِ رَضِيَ اللهُ عَنْهُ قَالَ قَالَ النَّبِيُّ صَلَّى اللهُ عَلَيْهِ وَسَلَّمَ: اَلَا اُنَبِّئُكُمْ بِخَيْرِ اَعْمَالِكُمْ وَاَزْكَاهَا عِنْدَ مَلِيْكِكُمْ وَاَرْفَعِهَا فِي دَرَجَاتِكُمْ وَخَيْرٌ لَّكُمْ مِنْ اِنْفَاقِ الذَّهَبِ وَالْوَرِقِ وَخَيْرٌ لَّكُمْ مِنْ اَنْ تَلْقَوْا عَدُوَّكُمْ فَتَضْرِبُوْا اَعْنَاقَهُمْ وَيَضْرِبُوْا اَعْنَاقَكُمْ قَالُوْا: بَلٰى قَالَ: ذِكْرُ اللهِ تَعَالٰى (سنن الترمذی #۳۳۷۷)

Hadhrat Abu Darda ﷺ *narrates that Rasulullah* ﷺ *once said to the Sahaabah* ﷺ*, "Shall I tell you of something that is the best of all deeds, it is the best act of piety in the eyes of your Rabb, it will elevate your status in the hereafter, and carry more virtue than spending gold and silver in the service of Allah Ta'ala or taking part in jihaad and slaying or being slain in the path of Allah Ta'ala. The Sahaabah* ﷺ *said, "Please do inform us". Rasulullah* ﷺ *replied, "It is the zikr of Allah Ta'ala."*

Note: This Hadith is general. Otherwise, at times, due to specific needs and emergencies, sadaqah (charity) and jihaad (fighting in the path of Allah Ta'ala), etc., become more desirable as mentioned in other Ahaadith. These acts are given superiority on specific occasions; however, the zikr of Allah Ta'ala is for all times and therefore generally more important and virtuous.

According to another Hadith, Rasulullah ﷺ is reported to have said, "For everything there is a purifier or a cleanser. (For example, soap is used for cleaning the body and clothes, while a furnace is used for cleaning iron, etc.). The zikr of Allah Ta'ala cleanses and purifies the heart. There is nothing more effective in protecting a person from the punishment of Allah Ta'ala than zikrullah." This Hadith describes zikr as the purifier of the heart, and as such it also establishes the superiority of zikr over all other actions, because the value of every act of worship depends upon ikhlaas (sincerity of the intention), which in turn depends on the purity of the heart. Therefore, according to some Sufis, the zikr referred to in this Hadith refers to the zikr of the heart as against to the zikr of the tongue. By the zikr of the heart, they mean that the heart always remains conscious of Allah Ta'ala, and is always in communication with Allah Ta'ala. This condition is undoubtedly superior to all kinds of ibaadah because, when this state is achieved, then it is not possible to leave out any good act. All our limbs and faculties, external and internal, are under the command of the heart. When the heart is attached to something, all the limbs and faculties follow (in submission). The conduct of true lovers bear ample testimony to this fact. There are many more Ahaadith that describe the superiority of zikr over all other actions.

Somebody enquired from Hadhrat Salmaan رَضِيَ اللهُ عَنْهُ as to what action of man is most virtuous. He replied, "Have you not read in the Qur-aan Shareef,

$$وَلَذِكْرُ اللّٰهِ اَكْبَرُ$$

'Certainly the zikr of Allah is the greatest'"
(Surah Ankaboot - Aayah 45)

Hadhrat Salmaan رَضِيَ اللهُ عَنْهُ is referring to the first aayat of Para/Juz twenty one of the Qur-aan Shareef. The author of Majaalisul Abraar, whilst commenting on this Hadith, has written that the zikr of Allah Ta'ala is described to be superior to sadaqah, jihaad, and all other forms of ibaadah (worship) because *zikrullah* (Allah consciousness) is the ultimate objective and all other types of ibaadaat are manifestations of this.

Zikr is of two types: One is done with the tongue and one is done with the heart. Zikr with the heart is more virtuous than zikr done by the tongue. This refers to *muraqaabah* (meditation) and contemplation. This is meant in the Hadith which states that *muraqabah* (meditation) for one moment is better than ibaadah (worship) for seventy years. This Hadith is reported in *'Musnad-e-Ahmad'*. Hadhrat Sahal رَضِيَ اللهُ عَنْهُ reports that Rasulullah صَلَّى اللهُ عَلَيْهِ وَسَلَّمَ said, "The reward of the zikr of Allah Ta'ala is 700 000 times more than spending wealth in the path of Allah Ta'ala."

From the above discussion it becomes evident that jihaad and sadaqah, etc., assume more importance and become more virtuous due to the need of the hour. The Ahaadith which describe their superiority are therefore understandable in such situations. For instance, it is mentioned in one Hadith that standing up for a short while in the path of Allah Ta'ala is more valuable than offering Salaah at home for seventy years. Although Salaah is unanimously known to be the best form of ibaadah, yet taking part in jihaad at the time of being overwhelmed by the kuffaar (disbelievers) carries far greater reward.

Hadith 4 - The one who makes zikr in his soft bed will enter Jannah

عَنْ اَبِيْ سَعِيْدٍ الْخُدْرِيَ رَضِيَ اللهُ عَنْهُ اَنَّ رَسُوْلَ اللهِ صَلَّى اللهُ عَلَيْهِ وَسَلَّمَ قَالَ:
لَيَذْكُرَنَّ اللهَ اَقْوَامٌ فِي الدُّنْيَا عَلَى الْفُرُشِ الْمُمَهَّدَةِ يُدْخِلُهُمُ الدَّرَجَاتِ الْعُلٰى

(صحيح ابن حبان #)

Hadhrat Abu Saeed Khudri ﷺ *narrates that Rasulullah* ﷺ *said, "There are many a people who make the zikr of Allah Ta'ala, while lying comfortably in their soft beds, and for this, they will be rewarded with the highest positions in Jannah by Allah Ta'ala."*

Note: Generally, the greater the sufferings and hardships one undergoes in the path of Allah Ta'ala, the higher will be his status in the hereafter. But the zikr of Allah Ta'ala is such a blessed act that even if it is done in soft beds in this world, it will bring high rewards and elevated positions in the Aakhirah. Rasulullah ﷺ has said, "If you keep yourselves busy in zikr all the time, the Malaaikah will shake hands with you in your beds as well as on the road."

Once, Rasulullah ﷺ said, "The *mufarrideen* have gone far ahead." "Who are the *mufarrideen*?" enquired the Sahaabah ﷺ. Rasulullah ﷺ replied, "Those who are extremely devoted to the zikr of Allah Ta'ala." On the basis of this Hadith the Sufis have mentioned that the kings and rulers should be encouraged to make the zikr of Allah Ta'ala. They can also attain a lofty rank in the Aakhirah by making zikr.

Hadhrat Abu Darda ﷺ says, "Glorify Allah Ta'ala by making His zikr during the time of prosperity and happiness. It will help you in times of distress and trouble."

Hadhrat Salmaan Faarsi ﷺ said, "If a person remembers Allah Ta'ala in times of peace, pleasure and prosperity, then whenever he is in trouble and difficulty, the Malaaikah recognize the voice of this helpless servant and intercede before Allah Ta'ala (for his forgiveness). But if one does not remember Allah Ta'ala in his time of pleasure and happiness and then pleads for help at the time of difficulty, the Malaaikah find his voice to be quite unfamiliar and therefore do not intercede for him."

Hadhrat Ibnu Abbaas رَضِىَ اللهُ عَنْهُ said, "Jannah has eight gates, one of which is exclusively reserved for those who are engaged in zikr." It is said in one Hadith, "A person who makes the zikr of Allah Ta'ala in abundance is safe from hypocrisy (nifaaq)," and according to another Hadith, "He is loved by Allah Ta'ala."

Once, during his return journey to Madinah Munawwarah, Rasulullah صَلَّى اللهُ عَلَيْهِ وَسَلَّمَ said, "Where are those who have gone ahead?" The Sahaabah رَضِىَ اللهُ عَنْهُمْ replied, "The fast travelers have gone ahead." Rasulullah صَلَّى اللهُ عَلَيْهِ وَسَلَّمَ then said, "Those who have gone ahead are those who remain constantly absorbed in the zikr of Allah Ta'ala. Whoever desires to enjoy himself in Jannah should make the zikr of Allah Ta'ala excessively."

Hadith 5 – The one who makes the Zikr of Allah Ta'ala is like a Living Person

عَنْ أَبِىْ مُوْسَى رَضِىَ اللهُ عَنْهُ قَالَ قَالَ النَّبِىُّ صَلَّى اللهُ عَلَيْهِ وَ سَلَّمَ: مَثَلُ الَّذِىْ يَذْكُرُ رَبَّهُ وَالَّذِىْ لَا يَذْكُرُ رَبَّهُ مَثَلُ الْحَىِّ وَ الْمَيِّتِ (صحيح البخارى #٦٤٠٧)

Hadhrat Abu Musa رَضِىَ اللهُ عَنْهُ narrates that Rasulullah صَلَّى اللهُ عَلَيْهِ وَسَلَّمَ said, "The example of a person who makes the zikr of Allah Ta'ala and the one who does not make the zikr of Allah Ta'ala is like the example of the living and the dead. (The one who makes zikr is like a living person and the one who does not make zikr is like a dead person)."

Note: Every person loves life and fears death. Rasulullah صَلَّى اللهُ عَلَيْهِ وَسَلَّمَ has mentioned that the one who does not make the zikr of Allah Ta'ala, though bodily alive, is spiritually dead and his life is worthless.

زندگانی نتواں گفت حیاتیکہ مراست   زندہ آنست کہ با دوست وصالے دارد

"(The lover says) My life (of loneliness) is no life; his is the life who lives in contact with the beloved."

Some Ulama have said that the example refers to the condition of the heart. The one that remembers Allah Ta'ala, his heart is really alive, while the one that does not, his heart dies. Some Ulama say that the contrast is in respect of gain and loss. A man who harasses a zaakir is like one harassing a living being who can take revenge for this harassment. While one who ill-treats a neglectful person is like the one who ill-treats a dead body, which cannot avenge for itself. Some Sufis say that the Hadith refers to the eternal life of the zaakireen. Those who glorify Allah Ta'ala constantly with sincerity never really die, but instead remain spiritually alive even after leaving this world (and going to the *aalame barzakh*). The zaakireen also enjoy a special life after death, like the martyrs, mentioned in a Aayah of the Qur-aan Shareef:

$$\text{بَلْ اَحْيَآءٌ عِنْدَ رَبِّهِمْ يُرْزَقُوْنَ}$$

"Nay, they are alive and they are sustained by their Rabb"
(Surah Aale I'mraan – Aayah 169)

Hakeem Tirmizi *(rahmatullahi alayh)* writes, "Zikr of Allah Ta'ala moistens the heart and softens it." A heart that is devoid of zikr becomes dry and hard, due to the excessive heat of lust and base desires. All parts of the body likewise become stiff and cannot bend to the command of Allah Ta'ala. If you force them to bend, they break, like a dry piece of wood which can only be used as firewood.

Hadith 6 - Zikr of Allah Ta'ala is Greater than distributing Charity

$$\text{عَنْ اَبِىْ مُوْسَى رَضِىَ اللهُ عَنْهُ قَالَ قَالَ رَسُوْلُ اللهِ صَلَّى اللهُ عَلَيْهِ وَسَلَّمَ: لَوْ اَنَّ رَجُلًا فِىْ حِجْرِهِ دَرَاهِمْ يَقْسِمُهَا وَاٰخَرُ يَذْكُرُ اللهَ كَانَ الذَّاكِرُ لِلهِ اَفْضَلَ}$$

(اخرجه الطبرانى فى الاوسط #)

Hadhrat Abu Musa (رضى الله عنه) narrates that Rasulullah ﷺ has said, *"If a person has lots of wealth and distributes it amongst the needy, whilst another person is only busy with the zikr of Allah Ta'ala, the latter, who is engaged in zikr, is the better of the two."*

Note: Spending in the path of Allah Ta'ala is of great virtue, but the zikr of Allah Ta'ala is even more virtuous. How fortunate are those wealthy people who spend for the pleasure of Allah Ta'ala, whilst also remaining devoted to His zikr.

According to one Hadith, Allah Ta'ala also distributes sadaqah every day, i.e. He showers His favours on the people and everybody gets what he deserves. The most fortunate is that person who is favoured with the *tawfeeq* (ability given by Allah Ta'ala) to make His zikr. People who are engaged in different occupations, such as trade, farming or other employment, should spare some time for zikr every day and earn these great rewards. It is not difficult to devote an hour or two out of twenty four hours in the day, for this noble purpose. A lot of our time is wasted in useless pursuits. What difficulty would it entail to take out some time for this beneficial work?

In another Hadith, Rasulullah ﷺ is reported to have said, "The wisest of all people are those who keep track of time, with the help of the sun, the moon, the stars, and the shadows, to make their zikr regularly." Although nowadays we can determine time with the help of watches, we should still be able to work out the time with the help of these means and agents so that no time gets wasted in case the watch stops or is out of order. In another Hadith, it is stated that the piece of ground till the depths of the earth where zikr is made takes pride over other parts of the earth.

Hadith 7 - Regret over the Time spent without making Zikr

عَنْ مُعَاذِ بْنِ جَبَلٍ رَضِىَ اللهُ عَنْهُ قَالَ قَالَ رَسُوْلُ اللهِ صَلَّى اللهُ عَلَيْهِ وَسَلَّمَ: لَيْسَ يَتَحَسَّرُ اَهْلُ الْجَنَّةِ اِلَّا عَلٰى سَاعَةٍ مَرَّتْ بِهِمْ لَمْ يَذْكُرُوا اللهَ تَعَالٰى فِيْهَا

(اخرجه الطبراني في الكبير #)

Hadhrat Muaaz bin Jabal ؓ *narrates that Rasulullah* ﷺ *said, "Those who are admitted into Jannah will not regret anything of this world, except that moment spent without making zikr."*

Note: After the people of Jannah enter Jannah, they will see the great rewards (as large as mountains) for remembering Allah Ta'ala just once. This will make them feel extremely sad over their loss for the time spent without making zikr. This can be well imagined. In this world, there are such blessed people who would not enjoy this life if it were spent without the zikr of Allah Ta'ala.

Hafiz Ibn Hajar *(rahmatullahi alayh)* writes in his book *"Munabbihaat"* that Yahya bin Mu'aaz Raazi *(rahmatullahi alayh)* used to say in his dua:

اِلٰهِیْ لَا یَطِیْبُ اللَّیْلُ اِلَّا بِمُنَاجَاتِكَ وَلَا یَطِیْبُ النَّهَارُ اِلَّا بِطَاعَتِكَ وَلَا تَطِیْبُ الدُّنْیَا اِلَّا بِذِكْرِكَ وَلَا تَطِیْبُ الْاٰخِرَةُ اِلَّا بِعَفْوِكَ وَلَا تَطِیْبُ الْجَنَّةُ اِلَّا بِرُؤْیَتِكَ

O Allah! The night is no good unless spent in talking with You, the day is no good unless spent in worshipping You. This life is no good without Your zikr, the next life will be no good without forgiveness from You and Jannah will not be enjoyable without seeing You.

Hadhrat Sirri Saqati *(rahmatullahi alayh)* says, "I saw Ali Jurjani *(rahmatullahi alayh)* swallowing plain barley flour. I asked him, 'Why are you swallowing this plain barley flour?' He told me that he had compared the time taken in chewing bread and in eating plain barley flour. Eating bread took so much longer that in that time one could say *"Subhanallah"* seventy times. Therefore, he had not eaten bread for forty years, and had lived on swallowing barley flour."

It is said about Mansoor bin Mu'tamir *(rahmatullahi alayh)* that he never spoke to anybody after Isha Salaah for forty years. Similarly, it is said about Rabee' bin Haysam *(rahmatullahi alayh)* that it was his practice for twenty years that he noted down what he spoke during the day, and would check at night whether that talk was necessary or not.

Hadith 8 – Malaaikah surround those making Zikr

عَنْ اَبِيْ هُرَيْرَةَ وَاَبِيْ سَعِيْدٍ الْخُدْرِيِّ رَضِيَ اللهُ عَنْهُمَا اَنَّهُمَا شَهِدَا عَلَى النَّبِيِّ صَلَّى اللهُ عَلَيْهِ وَسَلَّمَ اَنَّهُ قَالَ: لَا يَقْعُدُ قَوْمٌ يَذْكُرُوْنَ اللهَ عَزَّ وَجَلَّ اِلَّا حَفَّتْهُمُ الْمَلَائِكَةُ وَغَشِيَتْهُمُ الرَّحْمَةُ وَنَزَلَتْ عَلَيْهِمُ السَّكِيْنَةُ وَذَكَرَهُمُ اللهُ فِيْمَنْ عِنْدَهُ (صحيح مسلم #۰)

Hadhrat Abu Hurayrah ﷺ and Hadhrat Abu Saeed Al-Khudri ﷺ both bore testimony to having heard from Rasulullah ﷺ that the gathering engaged in zikr of Allah Ta'ala is surrounded by Malaaikah on all sides. The grace of Allah Ta'ala and sakeenah (peace and tranquility) descend upon them and Allah Ta'ala speaks about them (boastfully) to His Malaaikah.

Hadhrat Abu Zar (رضي الله عنه) related that Rasulullah (صلى الله عليه وسلم) had said to him, "I advise you to fear Allah Ta'ala as this is the root (i.e. foundation) of all virtues. Remain engaged in the recitation of the Qur-aan Shareef and in the zikr of Allah Ta'ala, you will be remembered in the Heavens and it will be a light (noor) in this world. Keep silent most of the time, so that you speak nothing but good, as this will keep shaytaan away from you and make it easy for you to perform your religious duties. Abstain from too much of laughter, because excessive laughter kills the heart and removes the spiritual glow from the face. Always take part in Jihaad as this is the Rahbaaniyat (a sign of piety and isolating oneself from the world to seek Allah Ta'ala) for my Ummah. Love the poor and keep their company, compare what you have with people who are lower than you in rank and never look up to those higher than you, otherwise you will forget the bounties of Allah Ta'ala and become ungrateful to Him. Be diligent in maintaining good ties with your relatives even-though they may try to break them. Do not hesitate to speak the truth, though it may be bitter for others. In matters concerning Allah Ta'ala (i.e. laws of shariah) do not be bothered by the adverse criticism. Let your focus on your own faults prevent you from finding faults in others. Do not get angry at others for the shortcomings that you suffer from. O Abu Zar! There is no wisdom better than farsightedness. Abstinence from what is haraam (the unlawful) is the best act of piety and good manners is a sign of true nobility."

Note: The word 'sakeenah' according to various Ulama means tranquility and peace, as well as the special mercy of Allah Ta'ala, as explained briefly in my book *Fazaail-e-Qur-aan*. Imam Nawawi *(rahmatullahi alayh)* states that sakeenah is a special favour consisting of tranquility, mercy, etc. and is brought down from the Heavens by the Malaaikah.

This appreciation, in the presence of the Malaaikah, from Allah Ta'ala for those engaged in zikr is for two reasons:

Firstly, it is because the Malaaikah had objected and commented at the time of the creation of Hadhrat Aadam *(alayhis salaam)*, that man would commit mischief in the world (as mentioned under the first Hadith).

Secondly, it is because although the Malaaikah are always engaged in Salaah, submission and obedience to Allah Ta'ala, they do not think of sin at all, whereas man has the ability of obedience as well as of committing sin. He is surrounded by things that lead him to negligence and disobedience and has desires and lust within him. Therefore, Salaah, submission and abstinence from sin, despite all his obstacles, are more praiseworthy and commendable on his part.

In one Hadith, it is mentioned that, when Allah Ta'ala created Jannah, he told Hadhrat Jibra-eel *(alayhis salaam)* to go and visit it. On his return from Jannah, he reported, "O Allah! By Your Greatness, whoever comes to know of it, will do his best to enter it," i.e. its pleasures, comforts, enjoyments and blessings are so great that anybody who believes in it will strive his utmost to enter it. Allah Ta'ala then covered Jannah with hardships and difficulties. He has made it compulsory to offer Salaah, observe fasts, take part in jihaad, go for Haj, etc. for those who will enter it. Allah Ta'ala then sent Hadhrat Jibra-eel *(alayhis salaam)* to visit it again. He then said, "O Allah! I fear that hardly anybody will be able to enter it."

Similarly, after creating Jahannam, Allah Ta'ala ordered Hadhrat Jibra-eel *(alayhis salaam)* to visit it. After witnessing the punishments, horrors, afflictions and tortures of Jahannam, he submitted, "I swear by Your Greatness that one who comes to know of the conditions in Jahannam will never go near it." Then Allah Ta'ala covered Jahannam with acts of indulging in sin, such as adultery, drinking of wine, cruelty, disregard of the Divine commandments, etc. and then asked Hadhrat Jibra-eel *(alayhis salaam)* to visit it again. He saw it and submitted, "O Allah! I fear that hardly anybody will be able to escape it." It is for this reason that, when a person obeys Allah Ta'ala and abstains from sins, he becomes praiseworthy in the sight of Allah Ta'ala and therefore Allah Ta'ala expresses His pleasure regarding him.

The Malaaikah who are mentioned in this Hadith and in so many other similar Ahaadith belong to a special group who are duty-bound to visit the places and attend the gathering where people are engaged in zikr. This is supported by another Hadith wherein it is stated that there is a special group of Malaaikah who are delegated especially for this purpose that when and wherever they hear the zikr of Allah Ta'ala being recited, they flock and gather to that place and listen. It is mentioned in another Hadith that a group of Malaaikah traverse the earth and at whichever place they hear the zikr of Allah Ta'ala, they call their companions saying, "This is the place you have been searching for." Then all the Malaaikah gather, layer upon layer (group upon group) until they reach the sky as it will be mentioned in Chapter three, section two under Hadith number fourteen.

Hadith 9 – Allah Ta'ala boasts to the Malaaikah about those who make Zikr

عَنْ مُعَاوِيَةَ رَضِيَ اللهُ عَنْهُ اَنَّ رَسُوْلَ اللهِ صَلَّى اللهُ عَلَيْهِ وَسَلَّمَ خَرَجَ عَلَى حَلْقَةٍ مِّنْ اَصْحَابِهٖ فَقَالَ: مَا اَجْلَسَكُمْ قَالُوْا: جَلَسْنَا نَذْكُرُ اللهَ وَنَحْمَدُهٗ عَلٰى مَا هَدَانَا لِلْاِسْلَامِ وَمَنَّ بِهٖ عَلَيْنَا قَالَ: آللهِ مَا اَجْلَسَكُمْ اِلَّا ذَاكَ قَالُوْا: وَاللهِ مَا اَجْلَسَنَا اِلَّا ذَاكَ قَالَ: اَمَا اِنِّىْ لَمْ اَسْتَحْلِفْكُمْ تُهْمَةً لَّكُمْ وَلٰكِنَّهٗ اَتَانِىْ جِبْرِيْلُ فَاَخْبَرَنِىْ اَنَّ اللهَ عَزَّ وَجَلَّ يُبَاهِىْ بِكُمُ الْمَلَائِكَةَ (صحيح مسلم #۲۷۰۱)

"Hadhrat Muaawiyah ﷺ narrates that once Rasulullah ﷺ went to a group of Sahaabah ﷺ and said to them, "Why are you sitting here?" They replied, "We are engaged in the zikr of Allah Ta'ala, and are glorifying Him for His extreme kindness to us in that He has blessed us with the wealth of Islam. This is indeed a great favour of Allah Ta'ala upon us." Rasulullah ﷺ said, "By Allah, Are you here only for this reason?" "By Allah!" replied the Sahaabah ﷺ, "We are sitting here only for this reason." Rasulullah ﷺ then said, "I did not ask you to take an oath due to any doubt or negative thought, but because Jibra-eel (alayhis salaam) came to me and informed me just now that Allah Ta'ala was boasting about you before the Malaaikah."

Note: Rasulullah ﷺ was making an enquiry on oath simply to find out whether there was any other special reason, besides zikr, which may have been the cause of Allah Ta'ala being proud of them. It became clear that it was only because of the zikr of Allah Ta'ala that He was proud of them. How fortunate were those people whose ibaadah was accepted, and the news of the recognition of the zikr of Allah Ta'ala on their part was revealed to them in this very earthly life through

Rasulullah ﷺ. Certainly, their magnificent deeds deserved this kind of appreciation. Their feats and achievements are briefly described in my book named '*Hikaayaat-e-Sahaabah* رضى الله عنهم', (i.e. '*The Stories of Sahaabah* رضى الله عنهم').

Mulla Ali Qari *(rahmatullahi alayh)* interprets the pride on the part of Allah Ta'ala to mean that He wants the Malaaikah to realise that despite the fact that these humans are filled with temptations; shaytaan is on their backs; the world is chasing them; they have desires and worldly needs; despite all this, they are engaged in making the zikr of Allah Ta'ala. All these distractions cannot prevent them from making zikr, so therefore, the zikr and glorifications of the Malaaikah in the absence of any such temptations and distractions is comparatively insignificant.

Hadith 10 – Allah Ta'ala forgives those who assemble for His Zikr

عَنْ أَنَسِ بْنِ مَالِكٍ رَضِيَ اللهُ عَنْهُ عَنْ رَسُوْلِ اللهِ صَلَّى اللهُ عَلَيْهِ وَسَلَّمَ قَالَ: مَا مِنْ قَوْمٍ اِجْتَمَعُوْا يَذْكُرُوْنَ اللهَ عَزَّ وَجَلَّ لَا يُرِيْدُوْنَ بِذَالِكَ إِلَّا وَجْهَهُ إِلَّا نَادَاهُمْ مُنَادٍ مِنَ السَّمَاءِ: أَنْ قُوْمُوْا مَغْفُوْرًا لَكُمْ فَقَدْ بُدِّلَتْ سَيِّئَاتُكُمْ حَسَنَاتٍ

(اخرجه الهيثمى فى مجمع الزوائد # ۲۰)

Hadhrat Anas رضى الله عنه *reported that Rasulullah* ﷺ *had said, "When people assemble for the zikr of Allah Ta'ala with the sole purpose of earning His pleasure, an Angle proclaims from the sky, 'You people have been forgiven, your sins have been replaced by virtues.'"*

On the opposite end, in another Hadith (narrated by Hadhrat Abdullah ibnu Mughaffal رضى الله عنه), it is mentioned: "A gathering devoid of the zikr of Allah Ta'ala would be the cause of disappointment and sorrow on the Day of Qiyaamah."

Note: It means that the participants of such a gathering will regret that they earned no blessings and wasted their time and perhaps it led them to afflictions. In another Hadith, it is stated that the members of a gathering devoid of the zikr of Allah Ta'ala and durood on Rasulullah ﷺ are like those who get up from the dead body of an ass.

It is mentioned in another Hadith that, by reciting the following dua at the end of a gathering, then the sins committed (unintentionally) in that gathering will be forgiven:

$$\text{سُبْحَانَ اللهِ وَبِحَمْدِهٖ سُبْحَانَكَ اللّٰهُمَّ وَبِحَمْدِكَ اَشْهَدُ اَنْ لَّا اِلٰهَ اِلَّا اَنْتَ اَسْتَغْفِرُكَ وَاَتُوْبُ اِلَيْكَ}$$

"Glory be to Allah with all kinds of praises. Glory be to You, O Allah! with all Your Praise; I stand witness that there is no one to be worshipped except You. I seek Your forgiveness and turn (for mercy) to You."

It is narrated in another Hadith that any gathering devoid of the zikr of Allah Ta'ala and durood upon Rasulullah ﷺ will be a cause of regret and loss on the day of Qiyaamah. Then, out of His sheer mercy, Allah Ta'ala may grant forgiveness, or He may demand an explanation and punish. It is stated in another Hadith, "Do proper justice to a gathering by remembering Allah Ta'ala profusely, show the way to a traveler (when necessary), and keep your gazes lowered or close them (when you come across something that is forbidden to see).

Hadhrat Ali *(karamallaahu wajhahu)* said, "Whosoever desires that his reward be weighed on the Day of Qiyaamah in a large scale (i.e. his reward should be very big, as only weighty things and not the small things are weighed in big scales), should recite the following dua at the end of a meeting:

$$\text{سُبْحٰنَ رَبِّكَ رَبِّ الْعِزَّةِ عَمَّا يَصِفُوْنَ وَسَلٰمٌ عَلَى الْمُرْسَلِيْنَ وَالْحَمْدُ لِلّٰهِ رَبِّ الْعٰلَمِيْنَ}$$

(Glory) to Your Rabb, the Rabb of Honour and Power. (He is free) from what they ascribe (to Him). And peace be on the messengers, and Praise to Allah, the Rabb and Sustainer of the Worlds.
(Surah Saaffaat - Aayah 180 -182)

The above Hadith also includes glad tidings that sins will be replaced by virtues. Even in the Qur-aan Shareef, at the end of surah Furqaan, Allah Ta'ala mentions the good qualities of the Muslims and says:

Chapter 1 – Virtues of Zikr

فَأُولَٰٓئِكَ يُبَدِّلُ اللّٰهُ سَيِّاٰتِهِمْ حَسَنٰتٍ ۗ وَ كَانَ اللّٰهُ غَفُوْرًا رَّحِيْمًا

"These people are such that Allah Ta'ala will change their evil deeds to good deeds and Allah Ta'ala is ever forgiving and most merciful."
(Surah Furqaan - Aayah 70)

The following are some comments made by the commentators on this Aayah:
1. All sins will be forgiven and only the good deeds would remain (in the account). No sin being left behind (in the account) is in itself a big change.
2. Instead of committing bad deeds, Allah Ta'ala will enable them to do good deeds. As it is sometimes said, "Instead of it being hot, we are experiencing cold."
3. Their actions are converted to virtues instead of vices, so much so that their habits change from bad things to good things.

This requires some explanation. Habits once formed become second nature, which do not change. The Persian proverb "A mountain can move, but not the habit" refers to this fact. This proverb is also deduced from another Hadith, "If you hear that a mountain has moved from one place to another, you could accept this possibility, but do not believe if you are told that the habits of somebody have changed." This Hadith implies that the changing of a habit is more unlikely than a mountain moving from its place. The question then arises what is meant when it is said that the Sufis and religious teachers reform the behavior of their followers. The answer is that habits do not change, but the form and application of the habit changes. For instance, if a man's temperament is such that he is prone to anger, then for the mashaaikh to remove this quality of anger through training and discipline would be difficult. They would reform him in such a way that, previously his anger had led him to show pride and injustice. It will now be directed against the breaking of the commandments of Allah Ta'ala. At one time, Hadhrat Umar رَضِىَ اللّٰهُ عَنْهُ had left no stone unturned in causing harm to the Muslims, but after embracing Islam and remaining in the company of Rasulullah صَلَّى اللّٰهُ عَلَيْهِ وَسَلَّمَ, he became equally hard on the kuffaar and transgressors. The same is the case with other aspects of one's conduct and character. This clarification leads us to the conclusion that Allah Ta'ala shifts the direction of the conduct of such people from vices to virtues.

4. Allah Ta'ala guides him to repent for his sins. He remembers his old sins with regret and sorrow and asks for forgiveness. Thus, for every sin previously committed, he gets the reward of one repentance.

5. If Allah Ta'ala is pleased with the good deeds of someone and then through His sheer benevolence grants him virtues equal to his sins. Nobody can question His authority. He is the Rabb, He is the King, He is all powerful and His mercy is boundless. Who can close the door of His forgiveness? Who can stop His bounties? He gives everything from His treasures. He will show His power and unlimited forgiveness on the Day of Qiyaamah. Various ways of reckoning on the Day of Qiyaamah are described in the Ahaadith. It is briefly given in the book, *Bahjatun Nufoos*. It is mentioned that reckoning will be conducted in different ways. Some people will be examined in secret under the cover of the Mercy of Allah Ta'ala. Their sins will be described to them and they will be reminded of the occasion when each sin was committed. There will be no alternative for them but to confess to all their sins. Due to the abundance of his sins, he will think that he is doomed. Then Allah Ta'ala will say, "I had covered your sins during the worldly life and now I have covered them and also forgive them all." When such a person, along with others like him, will return from the place of reckoning, the people will see him and exclaim, "What a blessed person. He never committed any sin." This is because they will have no knowledge of his sins. Similarly, in another instance of reckoning, the people will have minor as well as major sins to their account. Allah Ta'ala will order that their minor sins be converted into good deeds at which they (in order to get more virtues) will exclaim that many of their other sins are not mentioned. Similarly other types of reckoning are also mentioned in the Ahaadith.

An anecdote is mentioned in one Hadith, wherein Rasulullah ﷺ is reported to have said, "I will recognise the last person who will be transferred from Jahannam into Jannah. He will be called for and the Malaaikah will be commanded that his major sins should not be mentioned and that only his minor sins should be read out to him and he should be asked to give an explanation for them. This trial will start and his sins will be described to him with the time and place where they were committed. How can he deny them? He will confess to them all. Allah Ta'ala will then order that for every sin he must be given a virtue (good deed). At this, the man will hastily say, "There are still many sins that have not been mentioned so far." While narrating this part of the story, even Rasulullah ﷺ laughed.

It is necessary to mention over here that regarding the last person to come out of Jahannam has been mentioned in many different Ahaadith but there is no contradiction in this. If a large group of people come out from Jahannam, then too each person that comes out will be regarded as the last person to emerge. And the one who comes out almost at the end is also regarded as coming out last. It could also mean those specific groups that will emerge last from Jahannam.

The main point contained in this Hadith is that of ikhlaas (i.e. doing things only for the pleasure of Allah Ta'ala). That ikhlaas which is the pre-requisite for all good deeds is found in several other Ahaadith. In fact, the acceptance by Allah Ta'ala depends only on ikhlaas. Every deed will be evaluated according to the degree of ikhlaas involved therein. According to the Sufis, ikhlaas on one's part requires that one's words and actions should always be compliant and in conformity. A Hadith will be discussed later which says that ikhlaas is that quality which prevents one from committing sins.

Two incidents of Ikhlaas

1. The cruel king who forgives a man who destroys the consignment of wine

A story of a cruel king who was notorious for his tyranny and cruelty is related in the book '*Bahjatun Nufoos*'. Once, a large consignment of wine was being brought for him in a ship. A man who happened to travel by that ship broke all the bottles or barrels of wine except one and nobody could stop him from that act. Everybody wondered how he dared to do this, for nobody had the courage to face the cruelty of the king. When the king was informed about it, he was surprised to learn how an ordinary person had the courage to do that and also wondered why he left one barrel intact. The man was summoned by the king and interrogated. He replied, "My heart had urged me to do this. You may punish me as you like." He was then asked why he had not broken one barrel? He replied, "At first I broke the barrels of wine out of my Deeni fervor, but when only one barrel was left, my heart felt happy at having stopped that act which is forbidden. I then felt that breaking this last barrel would be for the satisfaction of my nafs, I therefore, did not break it." Finding him selfless in what he did, the king ordered that he be set free.

2. Shaytaan tries to stop a pious man from chopping down a tree which was being worshipped

It is narrated in *'Ihyaa-ul Uloom'* that there was an Aabid (worshiper) among the Bani Israeel who always remained busy in the ibaadah of Allah Ta'ala. A group of people came to him and told him that a tribe who was living nearby worshipped a tree. The news upset him and with an axe on his shoulder he went to cut down that tree. On the way shaytaan met him in the form of an old man and asked him where he was going. He said that he was going to cut a particular tree. Shaytaan said, "What concerns you regarding this tree? Keep yourself busy in your ibaadah and do not give it up for the sake of something that does not concern you." "This is also ibaadah", said the man. Then shaytaan tried to prevent him from cutting the tree and there was a fight between the two of them, in which the pious man overpowered shaytaan. Shaytaan, finding himself completely helpless, begged for mercy. When the pious man released him, shaytaan said, "Allah Ta'ala has not made the cutting of this tree obligatory on you. You will not lose anything if you do not cut it. If its cutting was necessary, Allah Ta'ala could have got it done through one of his many Ambiyaa *(alayhis salaam).*" The man insisted on cutting the tree. Again there was a fight between the two and again the man overpowered shaytaan. "Well, listen" said shaytaan, "I propose a settlement that will be to your advantage." The man told him to explain. Shaytaan said, "You are a poor man. Your living is a burden on this earth. If you desist from this act, I will give you three gold coins every day. You will find them lying under your pillow daily. With this money you can fulfil your own needs, you can look after your relatives, help the needy, and do so many other virtuous actions. Cutting the tree will be only one virtue, which will eventually be of no use because the people will then grow another tree." This proposal appealed to the man and he accepted it. He found the money on the next two days, but on the third day there was nothing. He got enraged, picked up his axe, and went to cut the tree. The old man again met him on the way and asked him where he was going. "To cut the tree", shouted the man. "You will not be able to do it", replied shaytaan. An encounter ensued between the two and this time shaytaan had the upper-hand and overpowered the pious man. The man was surprised that he was defeated and asked shaytaan how he had overpowered him. Shaytaan replied, "At first, your anger was purely for earning the pleasure of Allah Ta'ala, and therefore Allah Ta'ala helped you to overpower me, but now the love of the gold coins has contaminated your intention and therefore you lost."

Truly speaking, a deed performed purely for the pleasure of Allah Ta'ala alone has a lot of strength.

Hadith 11 - Zikr can save one from the punishment of the grave

عَنْ مُعَاذِ بْنِ جَبَلٍ رَضِىَ اللهُ عَنْهُ قَالَ قَالَ رَسُوْلُ اللهِ صَلَّى اللهُ عَلَيْهِ وَسَلَّمَ: مَا عَمِلَ اٰدَمِىٌّ عَمَلًا اَنْجٰى لَهُ مِنْ عَذَابِ الْقَبْرِ مِنْ ذِكْرِ اللهِ (اخرجه الهيثمى فى مجمع الزوائد #)

Hadhrat Muaaz bin Jabal ﷜ narrates that Rasulullah ﷺ said, "No action of a person can surpass the zikr of Allah Ta'ala in saving him from the punishment in the grave."

Note: The seriousness of the punishment in the grave can only be realised by those who have the knowledge of the Hadith on this subject. Whenever Hadhrat Usmaan ﷜ visited a grave, he would weep so much that his beard would become wet with tears. Someone asked him, "How is it that mention of Jannah and Jahannam does not make you weep so much as you do when you come across a grave?" He replied, "The grave is the first of the many stages of the Aakhirah. For him who is successful during this stage, the later stages will also be easy. For a person who is not exempted in this stage, the later stages will be even more difficult." He then quoted Rasulullah ﷺ as having said, "I have not come across any sight more terrifying than that of the grave." Hadhrat Aa'ishah ﷜ said that Rasulullah ﷺ used to make dua after every Salaah for protection against the punishment of the grave. Hadhrat Zaid رَضِىَ اللهُ عَنْهُ reported that Rasulullah ﷺ said, "If it was not out of fear that you might give up burying your dead, I would have made dua to Allah Ta'ala to let you hear the punishment of the grave. With the exception of men and jinn, all other creatures hear the punishment in the grave."

According to a Hadith, once when Rasulullah ﷺ was going on a journey, his she camel began shaking out fear. Someone asked him what had happened to it. Rasulullah ﷺ replied that somebody was being punished in the grave and the cries of the punished person had frightened the she camel.

Once, Rasulullah ﷺ entered the masjid and saw that some people were laughing very loudly. He said to them, "If you had remembered death quite often, you would not have laughed like this. Not a day passes when the grave does not proclaim. 'I am the house of wilderness, the house of loneliness, and the abode of worms and insects.' When a true Muslim is buried in a grave, it welcomes him saying, 'You are welcome here, you have done well to have come here. Of all the people walking upon the earth, you were the dearest to me. Now that you have been made over to me, you will see my excellent conduct towards you.' The grave then expands to the farthest point of sight and a door of Jannah opens into it. Through this door comes the scented air of Jannah.

But when a disbeliever or a transgressor is buried, the grave says, 'Your coming here is unwelcome and detestable. Why did you even come here? Of all the people who have been walking upon me, I hated you the most. Today you have been made over to me, you will see my treatment.' Then it narrows down and presses him mercilessly till his ribs pierce into each other as the fingers of the two hands interlock each other. Then ninety or ninety-nine serpents are let loose upon him and they will continue clawing at him till the Day of Qiyaamah." Rasulullah ﷺ has said that if one of those serpents were to blow on the earth, it will be rendered incapable of growing any grass till the Day of Qiyaamah. Then Rasulullah ﷺ continued, "The grave is either a garden of Jannah or a pit of Jahannam."

According to another Hadith, Rasulullah ﷺ happened to pass by two graves. He said, "The two people buried in these graves are being punished; one for carrying tales and the other for not being careful about his urine." (i.e. he did not prevent the urine from soiling his body and clothing). It is so unfortunate that many of our so-called civilized people regard istinjaa (washing the private parts after urinating) as an undignified act and even ridicule it. Some Ulama regard such pollution of urine as a major sin. Ibn-e-Hajar Makki *(rahmatullahi alayh)* has stated that according to an authentic Hadith, the punishment in the grave is generally due to neglect of cleanliness from urine.

It is narrated in one Hadith that interrogation in the grave will first be about urine. In short, the punishment of the grave is a very serious affair. Just as some types of sins lead to this affliction, in the same way certain virtuous acts provide special safeguard against it. It is mentioned in several Ahaadith that the recitation of Surah Mulk *(Tabarakal lazi)* every night guarantees security from the punishment in the grave as well as from the punishment of Jahannam. The value of zikr in this respect is evident from the above-mentioned Hadith.

Hadith 12 – Those who assemble for the remembrance of Allah

عَنْ اَبِى الدَّرْدَاءِ رَضِىَ اللهُ عَنْهُ قَالَ قَالَ رَسُوْلُ اللهِ صَلَّى اللهُ عَلَيْهِ وَسَلَّمَ: لَيَبْعَثَنَّ اللهُ اَقْوَامًا يَوْمَ الْقِيَامَةِ فِىْ وُجُوْهِهِمْ النُّوْرُ عَلَىٰ مَنَابِرِ اللُّؤْلُوْ يَغْبِطُهُمُ النَّاسُ لَيْسُوْا بِاَنْبِيَآءَ وَلَا شُهَدَآءَ قَالَ: فَجَثَا اَعْرَابِىٌّ عَلَىٰ رُكْبَتَيْهِ فَقَالَ: يَا رَسُوْلَ اللهِ حِلِّهِمْ لَنَا نَعْرِفْهُمْ قَالَ: هُمُ الْمُتَحَابُّوْنَ فِى اللهِ مِنْ قَبَائِلَ شَتّٰى وَبِلَادٍ شَتّٰى يَجْتَمِعُوْنَ عَلَىٰ ذِكْرِ اللهِ يَذْكُرُوْنَهُ

(اخرجه الهيثمى فى مجمع الزوائد # ١٦٧٧٠)

Hadhrat Abu Darda ؓ narrates that Rasulullah ﷺ had said, "Allah Ta'ala will, on the Day of Qiyaamah, resurrect certain groups of people in such a state that their faces will be radiant with light, they will be sitting on mimbars of pearls and others will envy their lot. They will neither be from among the Ambiyaa nor from among the Shuhadaa. Somebody sat on his knees and asked Rasulullah ﷺ to explain more details about these people so that we may be able to recognise them. Rasulullah ﷺ replied,

'They will be people who belong to different families and from different places, but assemble at one place only for the love of Allah Ta'ala and are engaged in His zikr.'"

It is said in another Hadith, "In Jannah there will be pillars of emeralds, supporting balconies of houses made of rubies and with open doors on all four sides. These will shine like brilliant stars and will be occupied by those people who love each other for the sake of Allah Ta'ala and who assemble at a place and meet each other only for His pleasure."

Note: Geologists differ as to whether *zabarjad* (emeralds) and *zumurrud* (rubies) are different names for the same stone or whether it is two separate stones of the same origin. Nevertheless, it is a stone which is extremely bright and radiant.

Many modernist and western orientated people criticise and ridicule those who spend time in the khanqah. Today these (modernist) may criticise and ridicule them as much as they wish, but in the hereafter, when they will see the reality, they will realise how these humble people have been able to earn such high stages and occupy such grand pulpits and apartments, whereas those who criticised and ridiculed them had earned nothing but misery and despair:

فَسَوْفَ تَرٰى اِذَا انْكَشَفَ الْغُبَارُ   اَفَرَسٌ تَحْتَ رِجْلِكَ اَمْ حِمَارُ

"Soon the dust will settle and it will be seen whether you are riding a horse or a donkey."

How blessed are the khanqahs (places where zikr is practiced) in the eyes of Allah Ta'ala. These can be judged from this Hadith in their favour, yet they have become the targets of abuse from all quarters. It is mentioned in one Hadith that the houses where zikr is practiced shine unto the dwellers of the Heavens, as the stars shine unto the inhabitants of the Earth. According to another Hadith, *sakeenah* (a very special blessing) descends on gatherings engaged in zikr. The Malaaikah surround them and divine mercy covers them. Allah Ta'ala speaks about them on His Throne.

Hadhrat Abu Razeen رَضِىَ اللّٰهُ عَنْهُ, a Sahaabi, narrated that Rasulullah صَلَّى اللّٰهُ عَلَيْهِ وَسَلَّمَ had said, "Shall I tell you something that will strengthen your Imaan and earn you the blessings of Allah Ta'ala in both the worlds? It is the gatherings of those who make the zikr of Allah Ta'ala. You should make it a point to take part in them and when you are alone, do as much zikr as you can."

Hadhrat Abu Hurayrah رَضِىَ اللّٰهُ عَنْهُ has explained that the houses in which zikr is made, appear to be as bright and shining as the stars to the dwellers of the Earth. These houses are so bright because of the noor of zikr that they shine like stars. There are some people who are gifted by Allah Ta'ala with spiritual vision and are capable of seeing this noor in this very world. There are some pious people who can recognise the saintly buzurgs and their houses from the special noor (radiance) emitted from them. Hadhrat Fudhail bin Ayaaz, *(rahmatullahi alayh)* was a famous saint. He has mentioned that the houses in which zikr is practiced shine like a lamp unto the dwellers of the Heavens. Shaikh Abdul Aziz Dabbaagh *(rahmatullahi alayh)*, a saint of recent times, was illiterate but he could clearly distinguish between the Aayah of the Qur-aan Shareef, Hadith-e-Qudsi and Hadith-e-Nabawi. He used to say that words coming out from the mouth of the speaker carry a distinguishing light, and that the words of Allah Ta'ala carry a different kind of radiance, whereas the words of Rasulullah صَلَّى اللّٰهُ عَلَيْهِ وَسَلَّمَ carry another kind of radiance. The words of others are devoid of these two types of radiance.

It is mentioned in Tazkiratul Khaleel, the biography of Hadhrat Moulana Khaleel Ahmad Sahranpuri *(rahmatullahi alayh)*, that Moulana Zafar Ahmad Usmaani Saahib *(rahmatullahi alayh)* had related, "When Moulana Khaleel Ahmad Saahib *(rahmatullahi alayh)*, on the occasion of his fifth Hajj, entered the Masjidul Haraam for Tawaaful Qudoom, he was sitting in the company of Moulana Muhibbuddeen *(rahmatullahi alayh)*, who was one of the Khulafaa of Haji Imdaadullah Muhaajir Makki *(rahmatullahi alayh)* and was well known for his divine foresight (kashf). He was engaged in his usual recitation of Durood Shareef from a book, when all of a sudden he turned to me and asked, "Who has entered the Haram Shareef? The whole Haram has been engulfed with his noor (radiance and light)." I kept quiet. After a short while, Moulana Khaleel Ahmad Saharanpuri *(rahmatullahi alayh),* after completing his tawaaf, happened to pass by us. On seeing him, Moulana Muhibbuddeen *(rahmatullahi alayh)* stood up, smiled and said, "Now indeed I see who has entered the Haram Shareef today."

The virtues of gathering together for the sake of zikr have been described in different ways in so many other Ahaadith. In one Hadith, it is stated that Salaah and gatherings of zikr are the best Ribaat. Ribaat means; guarding the boundaries of Darul Islam (Muslim territory) against invasion by the infidels.

Hadith 13 – The gatherings of zikr

عَنْ اَنَسِ بْنِ مَالِكٍ رَضِيَ اللهُ عَنْهُ اَنَّ رَسُوْلَ اللهِ صَلَّى اللهُ عَلَيْهِ وَسَلَّمَ قَالَ: اِذَا مَرَرْتُمْ بِرِيَاضِ الْجَنَّةِ فَارْتَعُوْا قَالُوْا وَمَا رِيَاضُ الْجَنَّةِ قَالَ حِلَقُ الذِّكْرِ (رواه الترمذى # ٣٥١٠)

Hadhrat Anas رَضِيَ اللهُ عَنْهُ narrates that Rasulullah صَلَّى اللهُ عَلَيْهِ وَسَلَّمَ said, "When you pass the gardens of Jannah, graze to your heart's content." Someone asked, 'O Rasulullah صَلَّى اللهُ عَلَيْهِ وَسَلَّمَ, What is meant by the gardens of Jannah?' He replied, 'Gatherings of zikr.'"

Note: What is meant is that if somebody is lucky enough to take part in such gatherings, then he should take full advantage of this, as these are the gardens of Jannah on Earth.

The words, "Graze to your heart's content" is similar to an animal grazing in a green pasture. It does not give up grazing in spite of being driven or beaten by its owner. Similarly a zaakir (one who practices zikr) should not get distracted from the gatherings of zikr by worldly attractions. The gatherings of zikr are likened to the gardens of Jannah, because there are no worries in Jannah. Similarly gatherings of zikr are safeguarded against every kind of calamity.

It is mentioned in one Hadith that the zikr of Allah Ta'ala cures all diseases of the heart, such as arrogance, jealousy, malice, etc. The author of *'Fawaaid fis Salaah wal Awaaid'* has stated: "Constancy in zikr is a safeguard against all kinds of calamities." According to an authentic Hadith, Rasulullah صَلَّى اللهُ عَلَيْهِ وَسَلَّمَ has said, "I enjoin on you to make the zikr of Allah Ta'ala profusely. It is like taking refuge in a fort against a strong enemy. One who practices zikr is as if he were in the company of Allah Ta'ala." Can there be any benefit greater than that of being in the company of Almighty Allah Ta'ala? Besides this, it leads to the satisfaction of the heart. It enlightens the heart and removes the hardness of the heart. In addition, there are many other material and spiritual benefits, up to a hundred, which have been enumerated by some Ulama.

A man once came to see Hadhrat Abu Umaamah, رضي الله عنه and said to him, "I saw in a dream that whenever you entered your home or came out, sat or stood up, the Malaaikah made dua for you." Hadhrat Abu Umaamah رضي الله عنه replied, "If you wish, you can also earn their dua," and then recited this aayah:

يَٰٓأَيُّهَا ٱلَّذِينَ ءَامَنُوا۟ ٱذْكُرُوا۟ ٱللَّهَ ذِكْرًا كَثِيرًا ۝ وَسَبِّحُوهُ بُكْرَةً وَأَصِيلًا ۝ هُوَ ٱلَّذِى يُصَلِّى عَلَيْكُمْ وَمَلَٰٓئِكَتُهُۥ لِيُخْرِجَكُم مِّنَ ٱلظُّلُمَٰتِ إِلَى ٱلنُّورِ ۚ وَكَانَ بِٱلْمُؤْمِنِينَ رَحِيمًا ۝

"O you who believe! Celebrate the praises of Allah and do this excessively and glorify Him morning and evening. He sends blessings on you, as also His Malaaikah that He may bring you out from the depths of darkness into light, and He is full of Mercy to the believers."
(Surah Ahzaab - Aayah 41)

These Aayaat indicate that the Mercy of Allah Ta'ala and the duas of the Malaaikah can be earned through zikr. The more we remember Allah Ta'ala, the more Allah Ta'ala remembers us.

Hadith 14 – Deficiency in Nafl Ibaadah can be Compensated by Abundant Zikr

عَنِ ابْنِ عَبَّاسٍ رَضِيَ اللهُ عَنْهُمَا قَالَ قَالَ رَسُولُ اللهِ صَلَّى اللهُ عَلَيْهِ وَسَلَّمَ: مَنْ عَجَزَ مِنْكُمْ عَنِ اللَّيْلِ أَنْ يُكَابِدَهُ، وَبَخِلَ بِالْمَالِ أَنْ يُنْفِقَهُ وَجَبُنَ عَنِ الْعَدُوِّ أَنْ يُجَاهِدَهُ فَلْيُكْثِرْ ذِكْرَ اللهِ (رواه الطبراني # ١١١٢١)

Hadhrat Ibnu Abbaas رضي الله عنه narrates that Rasulullah صلى الله عليه وسلم said, "One who is unable to bear the difficulty in keeping awake at night (in the worship of Allah Ta'ala), is too miserly to spend his wealth in the path of Allah Ta'ala and is too cowardly to take part in jihaad, is advised to remain constantly engaged in the zikr of Allah Ta'ala."

Note: A shortage in respect to nafl ibaadah can be made up by making abundant zikr of Allah Ta'ala. Hadhrat Anas رَضِيَ اللَّهُ عَنْهُ reported that Rasulullah ﷺ has said, "Zikr of Allah Ta'ala is a sign of Imaan and it safeguards one from hypocrisy and protects one against shaytaan and is a protection from the fire of Jahannam." Because of all these benefits, zikr has been regarded as more virtuous than many other forms of ibaadah. It is especially effective in providing protection against shaytaan. It is mentioned in one Hadith that shaytaan sits in a kneeling position and clings to the heart of a person. When the person makes the zikr of Allah Ta'ala, shaytaan becomes helpless and frustrated and therefore pulls back. Whenever he finds the person neglecting the Zikr of Allah Ta'ala, he pollutes the heart with evil thoughts. The Sufis advise practicing zikr abundantly so that the heart remains free from evil thoughts and becomes strong enough to resist shaytaan. The Sahaabah رَضِيَ اللَّهُ عَنْهُمْ who had developed this inner strength through the blessed company of Rasulullah ﷺ were not in such a need to make abundant zikr. But with the passage of time after Rasulullah ﷺ, the power of the heart to resist sin became weaker and weaker and the need to remedy this weakness through zikr became much greater. In the present age, the hearts have become so polluted that no amount of treatment can restore their strength to compare with that of the Sahaabah رَضِيَ اللَّهُ عَنْهُمْ. Nevertheless, whatever little improvement is attained, is worthwhile, as any decrease in this widespread illness is to be appreciated.

It is related about a pious man that he made dua to Allah Ta'ala that he may be shown how shaytaan prevails over the hearts of people. He was shown that shaytaan sits like a mosquito over the left side of the heart under the shoulder and then advances his needle-like snout towards the heart. If he finds the heart busy in zikr, he withdraws at once, but if the heart is idle, he injects the poison of evil and sinful thoughts into it.

It is stated in one Hadith that shaytaan keeps on sitting with the top of his nose over the heart of a person. If the heart is busy in zikr, he withdraws in disgrace, but if it is idle, he makes a morsel of it.

After the demise of Rasulullah ﷺ, it became very difficult for the heart to remember Allah Ta'ala and it became very weak to resist sin. Thus the remedy for strengthening the heart is to make zikr abundantly.

Hadith 15 – Excessives zikr

عَنْ أَبِيْ سَعِيْدٍ الْخُدْرِيِّ رَضِيَ اللهُ عَنْهُ اَنَّ رَسُوْلَ اللهِ صَلَّى اللهُ عَلَيْهِ وَسَلَّمَ قَالَ:
اَكْثِرُوْا ذِكْرَ اللهِ حَتّٰى يَقُوْلُوْا: مَجْنُوْنٌ (رَوَاهُ اَحْمَدُ # ١١٦٥٣)

Hadhrat Abu Saeed Al-Khudri رضي الله عنه narrates that Rasulullah ﷺ said, "Make zikr so excessively that people regard you as majnoon (an insane person)." "It is mentioned in another Hadith, "Make so much of zikr that the hypocrite may regard you as an insincere person."

Note: It is clear from this Hadith that the taunts of madness and hypocrisy by the munaafiqs and foolish people, should not make one give up the spiritual wealth of zikr. In fact, it should be done so abundantly that people may think that you are mad and they leave you alone. They will consider you to be mad only if you make excessive zikr loudly and not if you make zikr silently.

Ibn Kaseer *(rahmatullahi alayh)* has narrated, on the authority of Hadhrat Abdullah bin Abbaas رضي الله عنه: "Nothing has been made obligatory by Allah Ta'ala without fixing a maximum limit for it and no excuse is accepted for any shortcomings in respect of it, except His zikr, for which no limit has been fixed and no person, as long as he is sane, is exempted from it." Allah Ta'ala has ordered in the Qur-aan Shareef:

اُذْكُرُوا اللهَ ذِكْرًا كَثِيْرًا

"Make the zikr of Allah Ta'ala excessively." (Surah Ahzaab - Aayah 41)

A person should make zikr under all conditions, whether by day or by night, in the jungle or at sea, whilst travelling or at home, in affluence or poverty, in sickness or health, loudly or silently.

In his book *'Munabbihaat'*, Hafiz Ibn Hajar *(rahmatullahi alayh)* writes that Hadhrat Usmaan رضي الله عنه, whilst explaining the Qur-aanic Aayah said:

$$\text{وَكَانَ تَحْتَهُ كَنْزٌ لَهُمَا}$$

"Beneath it there was a treasure for them" (Surah Kahf - Aayah 82)

The treasure meant a golden tablet on which were written the following seven lines:

1. I am surprised at the man who knows that he is to die and he indulges in laughter.
2. I am surprised at the man who knows that this world will come to an end one day, but runs or hankers after it.
3. I am surprised that a man who knows that everything is predestined and he complains about the loss of anything.
4. I am surprised that a man who believes in the reckoning in the Aakhirah should accumulate wealth.
5. I am surprised that a man who has the knowledge of the fire of Jahannam should commit any sin.
6. I am surprised that a man who believes in Allah Ta'ala, should remember anybody besides Him.
7. I am surprised that a man who believes in Jannah, should feel pleasure in anything of this world.

In some editions of that book, it is also added, "I am surprised that a man who knows that shaytaan is his everlasting enemy and he still obeys and follows him."

Hafiz *(rahmatullahi alayh)* has also stated on the authority of Hadhrat Jaabir ؓ that Rasulullah ﷺ once said, "Hadhrat Jibra-eel *(alayhis salaam)* laid so much stress on making zikr that I felt that without zikr nothing else is of benefit."

The above mentioned quotations show that one should continue making zikr as much as possible and should not give it up simply because others may call one mad or a hypocrite. This will cause serious loss to oneself. The Sufis have written that it is also a trap of shaytaan that he first discourages one from making zikr to avoid any comments from people. If one falls for this trap, then shaytaan will thereafter stop one completely from making zikr. It is therefore necessary to not abstain from any good action just because of what people might say. Yes, one should not do any good deed for the sake of show. One should keep on making zikr regularly.

Hadhrat Abdullah Zul Bujaadayn رضى الله عنه was a Sahaabi who became an orphan in his childhood. He lived with his uncle who looked after him very well. He embraced Islam secretly and when his uncle came to know of it, he became so angry that he chased him out of the house naked. His mother was also displeased, but a mother is a mother after all. She took pity on him and gave him a sheet of coarse cloth which he tore into two pieces, using one piece as a lower garment and the other piece as an upper covering for his body. He migrated to Madinah Munawwarah and was always found in front of the house of Rasulullah صلى الله عليه وسلم. He used to make zikr very loudly. Hadhrat Umar رضى الله عنه remarked, "Is this man a hypocrite that he makes zikr so loudly?" "No" said Rasulullah صلى الله عليه وسلم, "He is from amongst the Awwaaheen." i.e. those who always turn to Allah Ta'ala. He passed away in the battle of Tabook. One night, the Sahaabah رضى الله عنهم saw a lamp burning in the graveyard. On approaching it they found Rasulullah صلى الله عليه وسلم standing in the grave and asking Hadhrat Abu Bakr رضى الله عنه and Hadhrat Umar رضى الله عنه to make over their brother to him. The two great Sahaabah made over the dead body for burial. After the burial, Rasulullah صلى الله عليه وسلم made dua, "O Allah! I am pleased with him, You also be pleased with him." On seeing this scene, Hadhrat Abdullah Ibn Masood رضى الله عنه wished that it should have been his janaazah.

Hadhrat Fudhail *(rahmatullahi alayh)* (who was one of the great Sufis) said, "To abstain from a virtuous act for fear of being seen by people is also an aspect of riya (showing off), and a good action done with the intention of showing off amounts to Shirk."

It is stated in one Hadith that some people are the keys to zikr, i.e. looking at them inspires others to make the zikr of Allah Ta'ala. According to another Hadith, such people are the friends of Allah Ta'ala whose very sight makes others remember Allah Ta'ala. It is stated in one Hadith, 'The best amongst you are those, who, looking at them, reminds you of Allah Ta'ala.' Similarly it is stated in another Hadith; 'The best amongst you are those, who, when you look at them, you remember Allah Ta'ala. Their words increase your knowledge and their actions encourage you to work for the Aakhirah.' Of course, such a condition can be attained only by one who makes zikr excessively. One who is lazy in this respect will not be able to inspire others to remember Allah Ta'ala.

Some people regard zikr in a loud voice as bid'ah (innovation) and forbidden in Deen. This view is due to lack of insight into the knowledge of Hadith. Hadhrat Moulana Abdul Hay Saahib *(rahmatullahi alayh)* has written a booklet *'Sabaahatul Fikr'* on this subject, wherein he has quoted about fifty Ahaadith in support of zikr in a loud voice. However, it is necessary that it is done correctly within its limitations so that it does not become a means of disturbing and annoying others.

Hadith 16 – Underneath the Shade of Allah Ta'ala

عَنْ اَبِيْ هُرَيْرَةَ رَضِىَ اللهُ عَنْهُ عَنِ النَّبِيِّ صَلَّى اللهُ عَلَيْهِ وَسَلَّمَ قَالَ: سَبْعَةٌ يُظِلُّهُمُ اللهُ فِيْ ظِلِّهِ يَوْمَ لَا ظِلَّ اِلَّا ظِلُّهُ اَلْاِمَامُ الْعَادِلُ وَشَابٌّ نَشَاَ فِيْ عِبَادَةِ رَبِّهِ وَرَجُلٌ قَلْبُهُ مُعَلَّقٌ فِى الْمَسَاجِدِ وَرَجُلَانِ تَحَابَّا فِى اللهِ اِجْتَمَعَا عَلَيْهِ وَتَفَرَّقَا عَلَيْهِ وَرَجُلٌ طَلَبَتْهُ امْرَاَةٌ ذَاتُ مَنْصَبٍ وَّجَمَالٍ فَقَالَ: اِنِّىْ اَخَافُ اللهَ وَرَجُلٌ تَصَدَّقَ اَخْفٰى حَتّٰى لَا تَعْلَمَ شِمَالُهُ مَا تُنْفِقُ يَمِيْنُهُ وَرَجُلٌ ذَكَرَ اللهَ خَالِيًا فَفَاضَتْ عَيْنَاهُ (رواه البخارى # ٦٦٠)

Hadhrat Abu Hurayrah ﷺ narrates that Rasulullah ﷺ has said: "The following seven people will be accommodated by Allah Ta'ala in the shade of His Mercy on the day when there will be no other shade except His:

1. A just ruler.
2. A young man who worships Allah Ta'ala in his youth.
3. A person whose heart yearns for the masjid.
4. Those two people who love, meet and depart only for the pleasure of Allah Ta'ala.
5. A man who is tempted by a beautiful woman from a good lineage and he refuses to respond to her saying: 'I fear Allah Ta'ala.'
6. A person who gives charity so secretly that the charity of one hand is unaware of what the other hand has given.
7. A person who makes the zikr of Allah Ta'ala in solitude and tears flow from his eyes."

Note: The flowing of tears could mean deliberate weeping, due to repentance over one's past sins, but it may also mean a natural outburst of tears due to the overwhelming passion of love. Saabit Bunaani *(rahmatullahi alayh)* has quoted the words of a pious man, "I know when a dua of mine is accepted." When asked as to how he comes to know of it, he said, "I know that my dua is accepted by Allah Ta'ala when the hair on my body stands up, my heart starts beating rapidly and my eyes shed tears." Also included among the seven people mentioned in the above Hadith, is the person who weeps while making zikr in solitude. He combines two sublime qualities. First is ikhlaas, which makes him remember Allah Ta'ala in solitude, and secondly the fear or love of Allah Ta'ala, which makes him weep. Both these things are extremely virtuous. According to a poet,

ہمارا کام ہے راتوں کو رونا یادِ دلبر میں

ہماری نیند ہے محوِ خیالِ یار ہو جانا

"My work is to weep at night in remembering my beloved; and my sleep is to remain absorbed in thoughts of my beloved."

In the Arabic text of the Hadith: وَرَجُلٌ ذَكَرَ اللهَ خَالِيًا (a person who remembers Allah Ta'ala when he is unoccupied), the word 'unoccupied' according to Sufis, has two meanings. It means in solitude, as is generally understood but it also signifies the heart being free from all thoughts except Allah Ta'ala which constitutes real solitude. The best is to have both forms of solitude, physical as well as mental. But if a person, even whilst in the company of others, has his heart free from all worldly thoughts and, being absorbed in the zikr of Allah Ta'ala, happens to weep thereby, he will also be rewarded as mentioned in this Hadith. The presence or absence of others makes no difference to him. His heart is free from thoughts, not only of his companions, but also of everything other than Allah Ta'ala. The presence of others cannot distract him from his attention towards Allah Ta'ala.

To be able to weep for the fear or love of Allah Ta'ala implies possession of great spiritual wealth. Fortunate is he who is blessed with it by Allah Ta'ala. It is mentioned in one Hadith that a person who weeps for the fear of Allah Ta'ala will not be sent to Jahannam till the milk goes back into the udders of an animal (which is obviously impossible). Similarly it is impossible for such a person to go to Jahannam. According to another Hadith, a person who weeps out of the fear of Allah Ta'ala and some of his tears fall onto the ground will not be punished on the Day of Qiyaamah.

It is mentioned in one Hadith that Jahannam is forbidden for two eyes; one that sheds tears for the fear of Allah Ta'ala and the other that has remained awake in guarding the Muslims and Islam against the kuffaar. In another Hadith, it is mentioned that the fire of Jahannam is forbidden on the eyes that wept for the fear of Allah Ta'ala, the eye that has remained awake in the path of Allah Ta'ala, the eye that has refrained from looking at what is unlawful (e.g. non-mahram men and woman, etc.) and also on the eye that has been lost in the path of Allah Ta'ala.

Yet another Hadith mentions that a person who remembers Allah Ta'ala in solitude is like one who goes all alone to fight against the kuffaar.

Hadith 17 - Who are the Wise Ones?

عَنْ اَبِيْ هُرَيْرَةَ رَضِيَ اللهُ عَنْهُ قَالَ قَالَ رَسُوْلُ اللهِ صَلَّى اللهُ عَلَيْهِ وَسَلَّمَ: يُنَادِىْ مُنَادٍ يَوْمَ الْقِيَامَةِ اَيْنَ اُولُوا الْاَلْبَابِ قَالُوْا: اَىُّ اُوْلِى الْاَلْبَابِ تُرِيْدُ قَالَ: اَلَّذِيْنَ يَذْكُرُوْنَ اللهَ قِيَامًا وَّقُعُوْدًا وَّعَلٰى جُنُوْبِهِمْ وَيَتَفَكَّرُوْنَ فِىْ خَلْقِ السَّمٰوَاتِ وَالْاَرْضِ رَبَّنَا مَا خَلَقْتَ هٰذَا بَاطِلًا سُبْحَانَكَ فَقِنَا عَذَابَ النَّارِ عُقِدَ لَهُمْ لِوَاءٌ فَاتَّبَعَ الْقَوْمُ لِوَاءَهُمْ وَقَالَ لَهُمْ: اُدْخُلُوْهَا خَالِدِيْنَ (اخرجه الاصبهانى فى الترغيب # ٦٦٧)

Hadhrat Abu Hurayrah ﷺ narrates that Rasulullah ﷺ said, "An announcer will call out on the Day of Qiyaamah, 'Where are the wise ones?' People will enquire. 'Who are meant by the wise ones?' The reply will be, They are those who always remembered Allah Ta'ala, whether sitting, standing or reclining, (in other words they are busy in the zikr of Allah Ta'ala in all conditions) and they ponder over the creation of the Heavens and the Earth, and would say,

رَبَّنَا مَا خَلَقْتَ هٰذَا بَاطِلًا سُبْحَانَكَ فَقِنَا عَذَابَ النَّارِ

'O Allah! You have not created all this in vain. We glorify You. Please save us from the fire of Jahannam.' *(Surah Aale I'mraan - Aayah 191)*

Thereafter a flag will appear for them, and they will follow this flag and will be told to enter Jannah and stay forever."

Note: By "pondering over the creation of the Heaven and the Earth" is meant that they think of the power, majesty and wisdom of Allah Ta'ala as manifested in the beauty of things which are created by Allah Ta'ala and thereby strengthen their spiritual knowledge and understanding.

الہی یہ عالم ہے گلزار تیرا

"The whole universe is like a garden planned and planted by Allah Ta'ala."

As narrated by Ibn Abid Dunyaa, Rasulullah ﷺ once approached a group of Sahaabah ؓ who were sitting in silence. He asked them what they were thinking about. The Sahabah ؓ replied that they were pondering over the wonderful creations of Allah Ta'ala. Rasulullah ﷺ appreciated it and said "Do not ever ponder over the Being of Allah Ta'ala, (He is beyond our knowledge and understanding), but do ponder over His creation."

Somebody once asked Hadhrat Aa'ishah ؓ to relate something significant about Rasulullah ﷺ. She replied, "There was nothing about him that was not significant. Once he came home at night and lay down in my bed. After a short while, he said, 'Let me worship my Rabb.' Saying this, he got up, performed wudhu and stood up in Salaah, during which he wept so profusely that tears flowed onto his chest. He then continued weeping in the same manner while performing ruku and sajdah. He spent the whole night like this, till Hadhrat Bilaal ؓ came to call the azaan for the Fajar Salaah. I pleaded with him, 'O Rasool of Allah (ﷺ)! Allah Ta'ala has promised you His forgiveness, then why did you weep so much?' He replied, 'Should I not be a grateful slave of my Allah Ta'ala', and continued, 'Why should I not weep when these Aayaat have been revealed to me today:

اِنَّ فِیْ خَلْقِ السَّمٰوٰتِ وَالْاَرْضِ وَاخْتِلَافِ الَّیْلِ وَالنَّهَارِ لَاٰیٰتٍ لِّاُولِی الْاَلْبَابِ ۞ الَّذِیْنَ یَذْکُرُوْنَ اللهَ قِیَامًا وَّقُعُوْدًا وَّعَلٰی جُنُوْبِهِمْ وَیَتَفَکَّرُوْنَ فِیْ خَلْقِ السَّمٰوٰتِ وَالْاَرْضِ ۚ رَبَّنَا مَا خَلَقْتَ هٰذَا بَاطِلًا ۚ سُبْحٰنَکَ فَقِنَا عَذَابَ النَّارِ

Surely! In the creation of the heaven and earth, and in the alternating of the night and day, are signs (of His power) for those who have intelligence. (The intelligent ones are) those who remember Allah standing, sitting and reclining and they think about the creation of the heavens and the earth. (Then amazed by the creation of Allah Ta'ala they say) O! Our Rabb, you have not created all this without any purpose. All praise be to you, so save us from the punishment of the fire.' (Surah Aali Imraan – Aayah 191)

He then added, 'Destruction is for the person who, in spite of reading these Aayaat, does not ponder over His creation.'"

Aamir bin Abdul Qais *(rahmatullahi alayh)* said, "I heard from the Sahaabah رضى الله عنهم, not from one or two or three, but from many of them, that the light and radiance of Imaan lies in contemplation and meditation."

Hadhrat Abu Hurayrah رضى الله عنه narrated from Rasulullah ﷺ that a person, lying on the roof of his house, was looking at the sky and stars for some time and then said, "I swear by Allah and I believe there is somebody who has created you all. O Allah! Forgive me for my sins." Thereupon the mercy of Allah Ta'ala turned towards him and he was forgiven.

Hadhrat Ibn Abbas رضى الله عنهما (as well as Hadhrat Abu Darda رضى الله عنه and Hadhrat Anas رضى الله عنه) have reported that meditation for a short duration of time is better than Ibaadah throughout the night. Hadhrat Anas رضى الله عنه narrated that meditation over the different creations of Allah Ta'ala is better than making Ibaadah for eighty years. Somebody asked Hadhrat Umme Darda رضى الله عنها as to what had been the best kind of Ibaadah done by her husband, Hadhrat Abu Darda رضى الله عنه. She replied it was meditation and contemplation. According to Abu Hurayrah رضى الله عنه, Rasulullah ﷺ had said that, meditation and contemplation for a short duration of time is better than ibaadah for sixty years. It should not be deduced from the various quotations given above that meditation removes the necessity of Ibaadah. If anybody neglects any form of ibaadah whether fardh, waajib, Sunnah or mustahab, the relevant warning and punishment will apply for each, when it is left out.

Imam Ghazaali *(rahmatullahi alayh)* has written that meditation is regarded to be superior to zikr because, in addition to it being zikr itself, it also includes two additional things. One is the recognition of Allah Ta'ala, for which meditation is the key and secondly the love of Allah Ta'ala which is brought about by deep thinking and pondering. It is this meditation which the Sufis call '*muraaqabah*', and the virtues of which is narrated in many Ahaadith.

It is reported in '*Musnad Abu Ya'la*' that Hadhrat Aa'ishah رَضِىَ اللّٰهُ عَنْهَا reported that Rasulullah ﷺ said that: "Zikr made softly, which is not even heard by the Malaaikah, is rewarded seventy times more. On the Day of Qiyaamah, Allah Ta'ala will call for all the creation for reckoning and the Malaaikah who do the recording will bring the records of all people. Allah Ta'ala will ask them to check if there are any more good deeds to the credit of a certain individual. They will say that they had not left out anything from his records. Allah Ta'ala will then say that, "In our knowledge there is one good deed to his credit, which is not known to you and that, is his zikr which he made in silence." Baihaqi *(rahmatullahi alayh)* has quoted on the authority of Hadhrat Aa'ishah رَضِىَ اللّٰهُ عَنْهَا that the zikr which is not heard even by the Malaaikah is seventy times superior to the zikr heard by them. The following Persian couplet refers to the same thing:

میانِ عاشق و معشوق رمزے است   کرامًا کاتبین راہم خبر نیست

"Between the lover and the beloved, there is a code of communication that is not known even to the reporting Malaaikah."

How fortunate are the people who do not remain idle from zikr even for a moment. In addition to the reward that they will get for their outward ibaadah, their zikr and meditation throughout their lives will earn for them seventy times extra reward. It is for this reason that shaytaan remains worried.

Hadhrat Junaid *(rahmatullahi alayh)* said that he had seen shaytaan without any clothes in a dream. He asked him whether he did not feel ashamed of the people around him. "Are these men?" replied shaytaan, "The men are those who are sitting in the masjid of Shonezia, who have annoyed me so much that my body has become lean and thin and my heart is burnt." Hadhrat Junaid *(rahmatullahi alayh)* writes that he went to the Masjid of Shonezia and saw few men sitting there, absorbed in meditation. When they saw Hadhrat Junaid *(rahmatullahi alayh)* they told him not to be misled by the deceptive words of shaytaan. Similarly Masoohi *(rahmatullahi alayh)* has also written about a dream. On seeing shaytaan naked, he asked him whether he did not feel ashamed of being naked in the company of men. Shaytaan replied, "By Allah! If they were men, I would not have played around with them as boys do with their playball. Real men are those who made me ill," and he indicated to the group of Sufis. Abu Sa'eed Khazzaaz *(rahmatullahi alayh)* also mentions that he once saw in a dream that shaytaan attacked him and he tried to hit him back with a stick but shaytaan did not care for this beating. He then heard a heavenly voice saying that shaytaan is not scared off by the beating, he is only frightened by the spiritual light in one's heart.

Hadhrat Ubaadah ﷺ quoted Rasulullah ﷺ to have said, "The best zikr is the silent one, and the best livelihood is that which just suffices," (i.e. it should neither be insufficient to make ends meet nor should it be so abundant as to drive one to extravagance and sin). Ibne Hibbaan and Abu Ya'ala have mentioned that this Hadith is Saheeh (authentic).

In another Hadith, Rasulullah ﷺ is reported to have said, "Remember Allah Ta'ala through perfect zikr." When somebody asked; "What is a perfect zikr." He replied, "Silent zikr." All the above quoted narrations establish the excellence of zikr in silence. We have also just read the Hadith that said, "You should make zikr in such a way that people will say you are insane." These are two different methods which are applied under different sets of conditions. It is for the Shaikh (religious guide) of a person to prescribe the best form of zikr for him at a particular time.

Hadith 18 - Staying in the Company of those who are busy in the Zikr of Allah Ta'ala.

عَنْ عَبْدِ الرَّحْمٰنِ بْنِ سَهْلِ بْنِ حُنَيْفٍ رَضِيَ اللهُ عَنْهُ قَالَ نَزَلَتْ هٰذِهِ الْاٰيَةُ عَلَى النَّبِيِّ صَلَّى اللهُ عَلَيْهِ وَسَلَّمَ وَهُوَ فِيْ بَعْضِ اَبْيَاتِهٖ {وَاصْبِرْ نَفْسَكَ مَعَ الَّذِيْنَ يَدْعُوْنَ رَبَّهُمْ بِالْغَدَاةِ وَالْعَشِيِّ} خَرَجَ يَلْتَمِسُ فَوَجَدَ قَوْمًا يَذْكُرُوْنَ اللهَ مِنْهُمْ ثَائِرُ الرَّأْسِ وَحَافِي الْجِلْدِ وَذُو الثَّوْبِ الْوَاحِدِ فَلَمَّا رَاٰهُمْ جَلَسَ مَعَهُمْ فَقَالَ: اَلْحَمْدُ لِلّٰهِ الَّذِيْ جَعَلَ فِيْ اُمَّتِيْ مَنْ اَمَرَنِيْ اَنْ اَصْبِرَ نَفْسِيْ مَعَهُمْ (اخرجه السيوطى فى الدر المنثور ۳۸۱/۵)

Hadhrat Abdur Rahmaan ibnu Sahl ibnu Hunaif ؓ *narrates that Rasulullah* ﷺ *was in his house when the Aayah:*

وَاصْبِرْ نَفْسَكَ مَعَ الَّذِيْنَ يَدْعُوْنَ رَبَّهُمْ بِالْغَدٰوةِ وَالْعَشِيِّ

"Keep yourself bound to the company of those who invoke their Lord, morning and evening." *(Surah Kahf - Aayah 28)*

was revealed to him. On this revelation, he went out in search of such people; He found a group of men who were engaged in zikr. Some of them were with disheveled hair, parched skins, and clad in a single cloth (i.e. except for one cloth (the lungi), the whole body was exposed). On seeing them, Rasulullah ﷺ *sat down by them and said, "All praise is for Allah Ta'ala who has created such people in my Ummah that I have been ordered to sit in their company."*

Note: According to another Hadith, Rasulullah ﷺ went out in search of them and found them in the furthest part of the masjid, where they were busy in the zikr of Allah Ta'ala. He said, "All praise is for Allah Ta'ala Who has created such people during my lifetime that I have been ordered to sit with." Then he continued, "My life will be spent with you and my death will be with you." (i.e. You are my companions in life and death.) It is mentioned in one Hadith that a group of Sahaabah ؓ, including Hadhrat Salmaan Faarsi ؓ, were engaged in the zikr of Allah Ta'ala, when Rasulullah ﷺ came to them. They all became silent. In reply to his enquiry as to what they were doing, they said that they were engaged in the zikr of Allah Ta'ala. Rasulullah

ﷺ said, "I saw that the mercy of Allah Ta'ala was descending upon you, and so I desired that I should join your company. *Alhamdulillah* (All praise is for Allah Ta'ala)" he then continued, "Allah Ta'ala has raised such people in my Ummah that He ordered me to sit in their company."

Ibraheem Nakhaee *(rahmatullahi alayh)* says that the meaning of *"al lazeena yad'oona"* is the group of zaakireen (those engaged in the zikr of Allah Ta'ala).

It is from such commands of Allah Ta'ala that the Sufis have deduced that it is necessary for the Shaikh to also sit with his mureeds. In addition to the benefit that the mureeds will get, it will also be a great *mujaahadah* (sacrifice) for the nafs of the Shaikh. Sitting in the company of his mureeds and exercising patience over their uncultured and uncivilized ways, develops submission and humility in him. In addition to this, the unity of the hearts is important for attracting the mercy and grace of Allah Ta'ala. It was for this reason that Salaah with jamaat was prescribed, and because of this all the pilgrims (in one condition) make the ibaadah of Allah Ta'ala together on the plains of Arafaat. This point has been repeatedly and specially stressed by Shah Waliullah *(rahmatullahi alayh)* in his book, '*Hujjatullaahil Baalighah*'.

All these virtues, as mentioned in many Ahaadith, relate to those people who are engaged in zikr. On the other hand, if one somehow happens to be in a group of negligent people, and even there he keeps himself busy with the zikr of Allah Ta'ala, then a great reward is also promised for him. On such occasions, it is all the more necessary that one should remain absorbed in the remembrance of Allah Ta'ala so that he is protected from the evil effect of such company.

According to one Hadith, a person who remains engaged in zikr, while in the company of the negligent is like one who remains steadfast in his allotted position in jihaad, while his companions are fleeing. In another Hadith, the one who makes zikr when he is in the company of the negligent is like one who fights the kuffaar single-handed, whilst his companions have fled. He is also compared to a lamp in a dark house or a beautiful green tree in the midst of trees that have shed their leaves. Allah Ta'ala will show him his abode in Jannah even whilst he is alive. All his sins, even if equal to the number of all men and animals will be forgiven. All these rewards are subject to the condition that one remains engaged in zikr while in the company of the negligent; although it is forbidden even to join in such company.

According to one Hadith, one should keep away from those so-called friendly gatherings where there is nothing but idle talk and merrymaking. Azeezi *(rahmatullahi alayh)* says that these are such gathering where there is talk of everything else besides Allah Ta'ala and people indulge in futile merrymaking.

A pious man once took his maid-servant to the bazaar. He left her at a certain place and asked her to wait for his return there. He went about the market and when he returned to that place, he was upset to find her missing. He went home, and found the maid-servant there. She came to him and said, "O Master! Do not be hasty in expressing your anger. You left me in the midst of such people who were negligent of the remembrance of Allah Ta'ala. I feared that some calamity should befall them, or that they should sink into the earth and I too suffer this punishment with them."

Hadith 19 – Engaging in Zikr after Fajar and after Asar

عَنْ أَبِيْ هُرَيْرَةَ رَضِيَ اللهُ عَنْهُ قَالَ قَالَ رَسُوْلُ اللهِ صَلَّى اللهُ عَلَيْهِ وَسَلَّمَ: فِيْمَا يَذْكُرُ عَنْ رَبِّهِ عَزَّ وَجَلَّ اُذْكُرْنِيْ بَعْدَ الْفَجْرِ وَبَعْدَ الْعَصْرِ سَاعَةً اَكْفِكَ فِيْمَا بَيْنَهُمَا

(رواه احمد فى الزهد # ٢٠٣)

Hadhrat Abu Hurayrah ﷺ narrates that Rasulullah ﷺ said that Allah Ta'ala says, "Make My zikr for some time after Fajar Salaah and after Asar Salaah and I will suffice you during the interim period."

In one Hadith it is mentioned; "Make the zikr of Allah Ta'ala, He will look after your interests."

Note: Even though we don't make as much effort for the Hereafter as we do for this worldly life, what will we lose if we take out some time after Fajar and after Asar for the zikr of Allah Ta'ala (And in return Allah Ta'ala will suffice for our needs of the entire day). Many virtues have been mentioned for making zikr at these two times. When Allah Ta'ala promises to suffice for our needs, what more is needed?

According to one Hadith, Rasulullah ﷺ has said, "I prefer sitting with those who remain busy in making the zikr of Allah Ta'ala after the Fajar Salaah up to sunrise to the noble act of setting four Arab slaves free. Similarly I prefer sitting with the group who remain busy in the zikr of Allah Ta'ala after Asar Salaah up to sunset to setting four slaves free." According to another Hadith, if a person performs Fajar Salaah with jamaat and thereafter remains busy in the zikr of Allah Ta'ala until sunrise and then offers two rakaats of nafl Salaah, his reward will equal to that of a perfect Hajj and Umrah. Rasulullah ﷺ has said, "Performing Fajar Salaah with jamaat, and then remaining busy in zikr until sunrise is more precious to me than this world and all that it contains. Similarly, remaining busy in zikr with a group after Asar Salaah till sunset is preferred by me to this world and everything that it contains." It is for this reason that the time after Fajar and Asar Salaah is especially reserved by the Sufis for zikr as part of their routine. The time after Fajar Salaah is reserved for zikr even by the Fuqahaa i.e. the jurists.

It is written in the book *'Mudawwanah'* on the authority of Imaam Maalik *(rahmatullahi alayh)* that it is makrooh (undesirable) to engage in useless talk during the time between Fajr and sunrise. From amongst the Hanafees, the author of *'Durrul Mukhtaar'* also regarded it undesirable (makrooh) to engage in talking during this time. According to one Hadith, if after Fajar Salaah a person continues to sit in the same posture before talking, reciting the following kalimah ten times, ten virtues will be recorded to his account, ten sins forgiven, his position in Jannah will be raised by ten stages and he will be protected from Shayataan and other evils throughout the day.

لَا اِلٰهَ اِلَّا اللّٰهُ وَحْدَهٗ لَا شَرِيْكَ لَهٗ لَهُ الْمُلْكُ وَلَهُ الْحَمْدُ يُحْيِىْ وَيُمِيْتُ وَهُوَ عَلٰى كُلِّ شَىْءٍ قَدِيْرٌ

"There is none worthy of worship except Allah; He is one, and He has no partner. This world and the Hereafter belong to Him and He is worthy of all praise; life and death are controlled by Him, and He controls everything."

According to another Hadith, after Fajar and Asar Salaah, whoever recites three times the following Istighfaar:

$$\text{اَسْتَغْفِرُ اللّٰهَ الَّذِىْ لَا اِلٰهَ اِلَّا هُوَ الْحَىُّ الْقَيُّوْمُ وَاَتُوْبُ اِلَيْهِ}$$

"I seek the forgiveness of Allah, Whom there is nobody worthy of worship besides Him and Who is living and eternal. And I turn to Him in repentance."

All his sins will be forgiven even if it is as much as the foam on the sea.

Hadith 20 – Ilm (knowledge) & Zikr

$$\text{عَنْ اَبِىْ هُرَيْرَةَ رَضِىَ اللّٰهُ عَنْهُ قَالَ سَمِعْتُ رَسُوْلَ اللّٰهِ صَلَّى اللّٰهُ عَلَيْهِ وَسَلَّمَ يَقُوْلُ: اَلدُّنْيَا مَلْعُوْنَةٌ وَمَلْعُوْنٌ مَّا فِيْهَا اِلَّا ذِكْرَ اللّٰهِ وَمَا وَالَاهُ وَعَالِمًا وَمُتَعَلِّمًا}$$

(رواہ الترمذی # ۲۳۲۲)

Hadhrat Abu Hurayrah رَضِىَ اللّٰهُ عَنْهُ narrates that Rasulullah صَلَّى اللّٰهُ عَلَيْهِ وَسَلَّمَ has said, *"The world and all its contents are accursed (i.e. they are devoid of the mercy of Allah Ta'ala), except the following three:*
(1) zikr of Allah Ta'ala and everything that is near it,
(2) an Aalim
(3) a student of Deen."

Note: Firstly, 'The zikr of Allah Ta'ala and everything near it' could mean all the things that are helpful in making zikr. In this context, eating and drinking in reasonable quantities and all other necessities of life are included therein. 'Everything near to zikr' may also mean nearness (Qurb) to Allah Ta'ala, in which case it will mean all forms of ibaadah of Allah Ta'ala and 'zikr of Allah Ta'ala' would mean a special form of zikr i.e. zikr-e-lisaani or zikr-e-qalbi (i.e. zikr of the lips or zikr of the heart). In both cases, ilm (knowledge of Deen) is included therein because firstly it is ilm that leads one to zikr. An ignorant man cannot recognize Allah Ta'ala. Secondly ilm (i.e. Deeni knowledge) is the best form of ibaadah. In spite of this, the Aalim and the student of Deen have been specially mentioned separately for emphasis. Indeed, Ilm is a great wealth.

Virtues of Knowledge

According to one Hadith, *"Acquiring ilm for the pleasure of Allah Ta'ala is a proof of the fear of Allah Ta'ala. Travelling in search of it is an ibaadah, memorizing it is like glorifying Allah Ta'ala, making research in* it is like jihaad, studying it is like charity and spending on those involved in knowledge brings one close to Allah Ta'ala. This is because ilm enables one to distinguish between right and wrong. It is a sign indicating the way to Jannah; it provides consolation in the wilderness and a companion while travelling, (because reading a book serves this dual purpose). Further, it is like a companion to talk to when you are all alone, a guide during pain and pleasure and a weapon for friends against enemies. Because of knowledge, Allah Ta'ala raises the position of some people (i.e. the Ulama) who propagate what is right and provide guidance for others to follow their deeds and their advice. The Malaaikah love to befriend them and rub their wings over them to be blessed or to show their love. All things, whether on land or in the sea, including fish in the sea, beasts of the jungle, animals and even poisonous insects and reptiles like the snakes, make dua for their forgiveness. Ilm is a light for the heart as well as for the eyes. By virtue of knowledge, one can become the best of the Ummah and enables one to attain high positions in this life and also in the Aakhirah. Its study is as virtuous as fasting, and its memorising is like performing Tahajjud Salaah. Knowledge assists in maintaining good relations and it helps to distinguish between halaal and haraam. It is a prerequisite for good deeds and good deeds are dependent on knowledge. Fortunate people are inspired by it and the unfortunate are deprived of it."

Though some authorities have debated the overall authenticity of this Hadith, yet the virtues mentioned herein are partly supported by many other Ahaadith. In fact, many additional virtues are mentioned in the books of Ahaadith. It is for this reason that the Aalim and the student of ilm have been mentioned separately in the Hadith under discussion.

Virtues of Zikr

Hafiz Ibn Qayyim *(rahmatullahi alayh)* is a well-known Muhaddith. He has written an authentic book named '*Al-Waabilus Sayyib*', on the virtues of zikr. He has stated therein that there are more than one hundred virtues of zikr and he has listed seventy nine of these which are briefly given below in the same order. Some of these include multiple benefits and for this reason their actual number is more than one hundred:

(1) Zikr keeps away shaytaan and weakens his strength.

Chapter 1 – Virtues of Zikr

(2) It is the cause of the pleasure of Allah Ta'ala.
(3) It relieves the mind of anxieties and worries.
(4) It produces joy and happiness in the heart.
(5) It strengthens the body and the mind.
(6) It brightens the face and the heart.
(7) It attracts one's sustenance.
(8) It covers the zaakir with respect and sweetness i.e. those who see him are filled with awe and they perceive his sweetness (his companions enjoy his company).
(9) It induces love for Allah Ta'ala and this is in fact the spirit of Islam and the pivot of Deen and the basis of success and salvation in the Aakhirah. He who wants the love of Allah Ta'ala should make zikr profusely. Just as reading and repetition is the door of knowledge so too the zikr of Allah Ta'ala is the gateway to His love.
(10) Zikr leads one to *muraaqabah* (deep meditation), through which one reaches the stage of *Ihsaan*. At this stage a person worships Allah Ta'ala as if he is actually seeing Him. (To reach or attain this stage of *Ihsaan* is the ultimate objective of the Sufis).
(11) It makes him turn to Allah Ta'ala whereby he gradually begins to develop conviction that Allah Ta'ala is his only Cherisher, Guardian and Master and he turns unto Him, in all afflictions.
(12) It is the key to the nearness to Allah Ta'ala; the greater the zikr, the greater the nearness to Allah Ta'ala, and, the greater the indifference to zikr, the greater the distance from Him.
(13) It opens the door of *ma'rifat* (recognition) of Allah Ta'ala.
(14) The heart is filled with the greatness and grandeur of Allah Ta'ala and it strengthens the consciousness of his omnipresence.
(15) Zikr of Allah Ta'ala is a means of one being mentioned in the court of Allah Ta'ala, as mentioned in the Qur-aan.

$$\text{فَاذْكُرُونِيٓ أَذْكُرْكُمْ}$$

"Remember me, and I will remember you" (Surah Baqarah - Aayah 152)

and as stated in a Hadith

$$\text{مَنْ ذَكَرَنِيْ فِيْ نَفْسِهِ ذَكَرْتُهُ فِيْ نَفْسِيْ}$$

"Whosoever remembers me in his heart, I remember him in My heart."

It has been explained earlier under other Aayaat and Ahaadith that even if there were no other virtues on zikr, except that mentioned above, this alone would have established its superiority over other acts of ibaadah. Nevertheless, there are many more virtues and benefits of zikr.

(16) It gives life to the heart. Hafiz Ibn Taymiyyah *(rahmatullahi alayh)* says that zikr is as necessary for the heart as water is for the fish. Imagine the condition of a fish out of water.

(17) It is food for the heart and soul. Depriving them of zikr is like depriving the body of its food.

(18) It cleanses the heart of its rust. It has been mentioned in an earlier Hadith; everything rusts according to its nature, and the heart rusts with worldly desires and negligence. To purify it, zikr is necessary.

(19) It safeguards one against mistakes and errors.

(20) The heart of a neglectful person is beset by a feeling of bewilderment from Allah Ta'ala and nothing other than the engagement of zikr can rid the heart of this feeling.

(21) The zikr one makes, mentions one's name around the Arsh of Allah Ta'ala. As stated in a Hadith.

(22) If one remembers Allah Ta'ala in happiness, Allah Ta'ala will remember him in his afflictions.

(23) It is a means to save one from the punishment of Allah Ta'ala.

(24) It causes the peace and mercy of Allah Ta'ala to descend, while the Malaaikah surround the person engaged in zikr.

(25) It saves the tongue from indulging in backbiting, loose talk, lies and other abuses. It is a common experience that a man whose tongue remains engaged in zikr does not commit these sins. On the other hand, the tongue that is not used to zikr falls an easy prey to all kinds of useless talk.

(26) The gatherings of zikr are gathering of Malaaikah and gatherings without zikr are gatherings of shaytaan. A person is free to have a

choice which gathering he wishes to choose, and verily man, by instinct, is drawn towards that which is appeasing to his temperament.

(27) By virtue of zikr, the zaakir and also those people sitting around him are blessed. Similarly the one who is unmindful and is involved in useless activities and also those people who are sitting around him are accursed.

(28) Zikr will save one from regret on the Day of Qiyaamah. This is confirmed by an Ahaadith which says that the gathering which is devoid of the zikr of Allah Ta'ala will be a cause of sorrow and losses on that day.

(29) If zikr is joint with tears and taubah in loneliness, the zaakir will be blessed to be under the shade of the throne of Allah Ta'ala on the Day of Qiyaamah, when everyone will be in distress due to the unbearable heat of that day.

(30) Those who remain busy in zikr are rewarded more by Allah Ta'ala than those who remain busy in dua. According to one Hadith, Allah Ta'ala says that I will give better reward to the one who was unable to make dua because of his engrossment in zikr.

(31) In spite of the fact that zikr is the easiest form of ibaadah (the movement of the tongue being easier than the movement of any other part of the body), yet it is the most virtuous form of ibaadah.

(32) The zikr of Allah Ta'ala are the plants of Jannah. (Details of this will follow in Section 3 Chapter 2 under Hadith No.4)

(33) The reward and forgiveness promised for zikr is greater than for any other action. According to one Hadith, if on any day a person repeats one hundred times the kalimah:

لَا اِلٰهَ اِلَّا اللهُ وَحْدَهَ لَا شَرِيْكَ لَهُ لَهُ الْمُلْكُ وَلَهُ الْحَمْدُ وَهُوَ عَلٰى كُلِّ شَىْءٍ قَدِيْرٌ

"There is none worthy of worship except Allah, the One. There is no partner with Him; His is the kingdom, and for Him is all praise, and He is All-powerful to do everything."

He will be rewarded as freeing ten slaves. In addition one hundred virtues are written to his account and one hundred sins are forgiven. He remains protected against shaytaan throughout the day, and no one is considered as having acted better than him except one who has recited these words more than him. Similarly, there are many other Ahaadith mentioning the superiority of zikr over all other good deeds.

(34) Due to continuous zikr, one is protected from being unmindful of his nafs. When one is negligent of the remembrance of Allah Ta'ala, one will end up being negligent of one's nafs and all its interests and this will result in one's failure in both worlds. Allah Ta'ala says in the Qur-aan Shareef:

وَلَا تَكُوْنُوْا كَالَّذِيْنَ نَسُوا اللهَ فَاَنْسٰهُمْ اَنْفُسَهُمْ ۚ اُولٰٓئِكَ هُمُ الْفٰسِقُوْنَ

"And be not like those who forgot Allah Ta'ala and therefore He caused them to forget themselves. Such are the evil-doers."
(Surah Hashr – Aayah 19)

Thus, when one forgets one's self, he becomes restless and forgets his real interests, which lead to his ruin. Like a garden or field is ruined when its owner fails to look after it. Protection against this ruin can only be achieved by keeping one's tongue always busy in zikr. Zikr should become as indispensable as water is at the time of extreme thirst, or food at the time of hunger, or the house and clothes for protection against extreme heat and cold. As a matter of fact, one should be more mindful of zikr than any of these material necessities. The absence of these material necessities can result in physical death, which is a small loss as compared with spiritual death.

(35) Zikr is the source of one's spiritual upliftment whether done in one's bed or in the market, in good health or in sickness, or even when one is enjoying the (permissible) pleasures of life. No other Ibaadah can cause spiritual enhancment in all these different conditions but zikr. His heart is so illuminated with the light of zikr that, even whilst asleep, one is more wakeful than a neglectful person who stays awake all through the night.

(36) The noor (radiance) of zikr remains with a person in this life as well as in the grave. It will be in front of him on the Siraat in the Hereafter. Allah Ta'ala says in the Qur-aan:

اَوَ مَنْ كَانَ مَيْتًا فَاَحْيَيْنٰهُ وَجَعَلْنَا لَهٗ نُوْرًا يَّمْشِيْ بِهٖ فِي النَّاسِ كَمَنْ مَّثَلُهٗ فِي الظُّلُمٰتِ لَيْسَ بِخَارِجٍ مِّنْهَا

"Can he who was dead (astray) then We granted him life (gave him Imaan), and blessed him with a light with which he may walk among people, be like one who is in multitude darkness from which he cannot come out." (Surah An'aam – Aayah 122)

The person mentioned first is the Muslim who believes in Allah Ta'ala and shines with the light of His love, zikr, and recognition, while the second person is devoid of all these virtues. In reality, this radiance is a great blessing and leads to perfect success. That is why Rasulullah ﷺ used to beg for it in his lengthy duas, and made dua for noor for every part of his body. As mentioned in many Ahaadith Rasulullah ﷺ made dua that Allah Ta'ala may bless his flesh, bones, muscles, hair, skin, eyes and ears with noor, and that he may be surrounded with noor on all sides. He even made dua that he may be blessed with noor from top to bottom and that his whole body be made into noor. One's deeds will shine according to the noor in oneself so much so that the good deeds of some people (while going up to the heaven) will shine like the sun. Similar noor will be found on their faces on the Day of Qiyaamah.

(37) Zikr is the basic principle of Tasawwuf (Sufism) and is taught in all the schools of Sufism. A person who enters the gateway of zikr is sure to reach the door of Allah Ta'ala, and he will get whatever he wants, as the treasures of Allah Ta'ala are unlimited.

(38) There is a portion in the heart of man which cannot be filled except by the zikr of Allah Ta'ala. When zikr dominates the heart, not only does it fill up this portion, but it also leads the zaakir to become rich, independent of wealth and it will give him respect independent of family amongst people, which one's family or friends would fail to give. It will make him a king independent of kingdom. On the other hand, one who is unmindful of the zikr of Allah Ta'ala is disgraced, despite having wealth, riches, friends and kingdom.

(39) Zikr transforms scattered thoughts into concentration and concentration into scattered thoughts. It brings close that which is far and distances that which near. This means that one is relieved of one's troubles, worries and fears, and is blessed with peace of mind. His mistakes and sins are forgiven, and the shayaateen, who are after him, are chased away. It makes him remember that the Aakhirah is not far away, and the worldly life has little attraction for him.

(40) Zikr awakens one's heart from slumber and changes forgetfulness to alertness. While the heart of a person is asleep, it remains in a state of loss.

(41) Zikr is like a tree, the fruit of which is the recognition of Allah Ta'ala. The more zikr that is done, then the root of this tree shall grow stronger and this will result in bearing abundant fruit.

(42) Zikr of Allah Ta'ala promotes nearness to Him and thereby earns His closeness. It is mentioned in the Qur-aan Shareef:

$$اِنَّ اللّٰهَ مَعَ الَّذِيْنَ اتَّقَوْا$$

"No doubt Allah Ta'ala is with those who fear Him."
(Surah Nahl – Aayah 128)

It is stated in one Hadith:

$$اَنَا مَعَ عَبْدِيْ مَا ذَكَرَنِيْ$$

"I am with my slave as long as he remembers Me."

According to another Hadith, Allah Ta'ala says, "Those who remember Me are My men, and I do not deprive them of My mercy. When they keep making taubah, I befriend them, but if they do not make taubah, I am their physician. I put them into difficulties to forgive their sins."

Nearness to Allah Ta'ala resulting from zikr has no parallel. No words or writing can describe this nearness. Its taste is known only to those who are blessed with it (May Allah Ta'ala also bless me with the same).

(43) Zikr of Allah Ta'ala is as meritorious as freeing slaves, and spending in charity and jihaad in the path of Allah Ta'ala.

(Many virtues of this kind have already been described and more will further be narrated in this book Insha Allah).

(44) Zikr is the root of shukar (gratitude to Allah Ta'ala). One who does not make zikr cannot thank Allah Ta'ala. It is stated in one Hadith that Hadhrat Moosa *(alayhis salaam)* had asked Allah Ta'ala "O My Rabb! You have done me countless favours; teach me how I should thank you in the correct manner." Allah Ta'ala said, "The more zikr you make, the more thanks you offer." According to another Hadith, Hadhrat Moosa *(alayhis salaam)* is reported to have said, "O, My Rabb! How can I offer thanks worthy of Your greatness." Allah Ta'ala replied, "Let your tongue always remain engaged in zikr."

(45) According to Allah Ta'ala, the best of those people with Taqwa, close to Allah Ta'ala are those that always remain busy in the zikr of Allah Ta'ala, because the end result of Taqwa is Jannah, while the end result of zikrullah is the nearness of Allah Ta'ala (Himself).

(46) There is a sort of hardness in the human heart which is not softened by anything except zikr.

(47) Zikr is a remedy for all ills of the heart.

(48) Zikr of Allah Ta'ala is the root of His friendship and neglecting zikr is the root of His enmity.

(49) Nothing is more effective than zikr in attracting the blessings of Allah Ta'ala and keeping away His punishment.

(50) Allah Ta'ala grants His grace to those who make zikr and the Malaaikah make dua for them.

(51) One who wants to remain in the gardens of Jannah, even in this life, should sit in the gatherings of zikr, because these are compared to the gardens of Jannah.

(52) Gatherings of zikr are also the gatherings of Malaaikah. (This has been explained in detail).

(53) Allah Ta'ala praises those who make zikr in front of the Malaaikah.

(54) One who is always making zikr will enter Jannah smiling.

(55) All acts of worship are only prescribed for the remeberence of Allah.

(56) A good deed becomes superior compared to others of its kind because of abundant zikr. For example, the fast (saum) with more zikr is the best and the Hajj with excessive zikr is more virtuous. Similar is the case with other good deeds like jihaad etc.

(57) Zikr is a substitute of nafl Salaah and other nafl observances. It is related in one Hadith that the poor people once complained to Rasulullah ﷺ of the higher reward available to the rich because of their wealth. They said, "These rich men offer Salaah and fast, just as we do, but they surpass us by performing Umrah and Hajj, and taking part in jihaad on account of their wealth." Rasulullah ﷺ replied, "Should I tell you something, so that none except the one who practices it can surpass you." He then advised them to recite after every Salaah:

$$\text{سُبْحَانَ اللهِ الْحَمْدُ لِلّٰهِ اللهُ اَكْبَرُ}$$

Subhaanallah, Alhamdulillah and Allahu-Akbar.

(As will be mentioned in Section 3, Chapter 2, Hadith No.7). Rasulullah ﷺ had indicated the importance of zikr, to be the substitute for various kinds of Ibaadaat, like Umrah, Hajj, Jihaad, etc.

(58) Zikr assists one in performing all other forms of Ibaadah. Excessive zikr creates love for various forms of Ibaadah. One begins enjoying performing Ibaadah and never feels bored or burdened while offering them.

(59) Zikr is a solution to all difficulties and a remedy for all hardships. It lightens every burden, and relieves every affliction.

(60) Zikr removes the fear of the heart. It has a special effect in promoting peace of mind and for relieving the heart of its fear. To free the heart of its fears and the mind of its anxieties is one of the special qualities of zikr. The greater the amount of zikr, the greater the freedom from fear.

(61) By doing zikr, one is blessed with the help of Allah Ta'ala in all his work so that he accomplishers things that would normally be very difficult. Sometimes man achieves things which are beyond his ability and he gets what was seemingly beyond his reach. This is

perhaps the reason why Rasulullah ﷺ advised his daughter Hadhrat Faatimah رضي الله عنها to recite "سُبْحَانَ اللهِ" and "اَلْحَمْدُ لِلّٰهِ" thirty three times each and "اَللهُ اَكْبَرُ" thirty four times before going to bed at night, when she approached him for a helper to assist her in her difficult work of grinding the wheat and doing other house-hold chores. Rasulullah ﷺ further said, "The recitation of this zikr is better for you than a servant."

(62) Those who are striving for the life of the Aakhirah are in a race, wherein the zaakirs shall remain ahead of all on account of their zikr. Umar Maula Gafra *(rahmatullahi alayh)* says that, on the day of Qiyaamah, when people will be rewarded for their good deeds, many shall regret why they neglected zikr when it was the easiest of all good deeds and the highest in reward. In one Hadith, Rasulullah ﷺ is quoted to have said, "The *mufarrideen* have surpassed all." He was asked, "Who were the *mufarrideen*?" Rasulullah ﷺ replied, "Those who work hard making zikr (Those who are passionately devoted to making zikr) as zikr lightens their burdens."

(63) Those who make zikr are regarded as truthful by Allah Ta'ala, and those who Allah Ta'ala regards as truthful cannot be raised up among the liars on the Day of Qiyaamah. It is quoted on the authority of Rasulullah ﷺ that when a man utters,

لَا اِلٰهَ اِلَّا اللهُ وَاللهُ اَكْبَرُ

Allah Ta'ala announces, "My slave has spoken the truth, and nobody is worthy of worship except Me, and I am the Greatest of all."

(64) Zikr is a means of houses being built in Jannah. When the zikr is stopped, the Malaaikah also stop the construction of the houses. When asked why a particular construction was stopped, they reply, "The construction had to be stopped because funds for that were stopped."

This fact is confirmed by a Hadith which says that when a man recites the following seven times; a tower is raised for him in Jannah.

$$\text{سُبْحَانَ اللهِ وَبِحَمْدِهِ سُبْحَانَ اللهِ الْعَظِيْمِ}$$

"Subhaanallahi wa bi Hamdihi Subhaanallahil Azeem"

(65) Zikr becomes a barrier from Jahannam. If, due to any misdeed, a zaakir becomes liable for punishment in Jahannam, his zikr will become a barrier between him and Jahannam. The more his zikr, the stronger will be this barrier.

(66) The Malaaikah make dua for the forgiveness of those who make zikr. It is related on the authority of Hadhrat Amr ibnul Aas رضي الله عنه that when a man says either one of the following, then the Malaaikah make dua to Allah Ta'ala for his forgiveness.

$$\text{سُبْحَانَ اللهِ وَبِحَمْدِهِ}$$

or

$$\text{اَلْحَمْدُ لِلّٰهِ رَبِّ الْعَالَمِيْنَ}$$

(67) The mountain or ground on which zikr is made feels proud. According to a Hadith, one mountain asks another if any zaakir has crossed over it during the day. If the reply is yes, then it feels happy.

(68) Zikr guarantees protection from nifaaq (hypocrisy), for Allah Ta'ala has described the munaafiq (hypocrite) as;

$$\text{لَا يَذْكُرُوْنَ اللهَ اِلَّا قَلِيْلًا}$$

"They do not remember Allah except very rarely."
(Surah Nisaa – Aayah 142)

It is also related on the authority of Ka'b Ahbaar رضي الله عنه that he who makes the zikr of Allah Ta'ala frequently is free from hypocrisy.

(69) Compared to other good deeds, zikr carries a special enjoyment, which is not to be found in any other action. Even if there were no other virtues for zikr, this enjoyment alone would have been a sufficient reward to justify it. Maalik bin Dinaar *(rahmatullahi*

alayh) has said that nothing is more enjoyable than the sweetness of zikr.

(70) The faces of those who make zikr remain bright in this life, and will carry a special radiance in the Aakhirah.

(71) One who is frequently engaged in zikr, in or out of his house, or when he is stationary or travelling, will find on the Day of Qiyaamah, a large number of witnesses in his favour. Allah Ta'ala has described the Day of Qiyaamah as,

$$يَوْمَئِذٍ تُحَدِّثُ اَخْبَارَهَا$$

"The day when the Earth will tell all that it knows."
(Surah Zilzaal - Aayah 4)

Rasulullah ﷺ asked his companions if they knew what that news would be. They expressed their ignorance. Then Rasulullah ﷺ said, "Whatever deed is done, good or bad, by any man or woman, on the face of the Earth, the Earth will describe it all, with date, time and place." Therefore, one who makes zikr at many places will find many witnesses in his favour.

(72) As long as the tongue is busy in zikr, it cannot indulge in lies, backbiting or any other kind of evil. The tongue will engage in useless talk if it is not in zikr, because it cannot remain quiet. So is the case with the heart if it is devoid of the love for Allah Ta'ala, it will be filled with the love of worldly things.

(73) The shayaateen are outright enemies of man and always frighten him and surround him. The miserable condition of a person who remains surrounded by enemies can well be imagined; especially when the enemies are vengeful and every one of them wants to harm him in every possible way. Nothing except zikr can protect him against these enemies. Many forms of duas are mentioned in the Ahaadith. If any of these are recited by a person, then shaytaan will not dare come near him. If the dua is recited at the time of going to bed, one remains safe from shaytaan throughout the night. Hafiz Ibn Qayyim *(rahmatullahi alayh)* has also mentioned many such duas.

In addition to these, the author Hafiz Ibn Qayyim *(rahmatullahi alayh)* has also mentioned in detail under six headings the merits of making zikr and also some of its virtues, which are specific to zikr alone. He has also given seventy five chapters on special duas, which are suited to specific times and occasions. For the sake of keeping it short and brief, these have been excluded from this book. For those blessed with determination to practice on it, the virtues of zikr detailed above are more than enough. And for those who are disinclined to act, thousands of such virtues would be of little benefit.

وَمَا تَوْفِيْقِيْ اِلَّا بِاللّٰهِ عَلَيْهِ تَوَكَّلْتُ وَاِلَيْهِ اُنِيْبُ

"Whatever good I have done is through the grace of Allah Ta'ala. I, therefore, depend on Him and turn to Him."

CHAPTER 2
VIRTUES OF KALIMAH TAYYIBAH

لَا اِلٰهَ اِلَّا اللهُ مُحَمَّدٌ رَّسُوْلُ اللهِ

Kalimah Tayyibah, which is also called Kalimah Tauheed, has been mentioned in the Qur-aan and the Hadith more frequently than anything else. Since all Ambiyaa *(alayhimus salaam)* and their shariats have been sent specifically with the primary aim of propagating the Oneness of Allah Ta'ala, its excessive mention can well be understood. In the Qur-aan Shareef, this kalimah has been referred to by various names and in different contexts. It has been referred to as Kalimah Tayyibah (excellent utterance), قَوْلٌ ثَابِتٌ (firm statement), كَلِمَةُ التَّقْوٰى (utterance of piety), مَقَالِيْدُ السَّمٰوٰتِ وَالْأَرْضِ (keys to the heavens and earth), etc. as will be found in the Aaayaat of the Qur-aan Shareef given in the following pages. Imaam Ghazaali *(rahmatullahi alayh)* has written in his book Ihyaa that it is كَلِمَةُ التَّوْحِيْدِ (The word of the oneness of Allah Ta'ala), كَلِمَةُ الْإِخْلَاصِ (statement of sincerity), كَلِمَةُ التَّقْوٰى (The word of piety), كَلِمَةٌ طَيِّبَةٌ (excellent word), عُرْوَةُ الْوُثْقٰى (strong handhold), دَعْوَةُ الْحَقِّ (call of truth) and ثَمَنُ الْجَنَّةِ (price of Jannah).

As this kalimah has been mentioned in various contexts in the Qur-aan Shareef, this chapter is divided into three parts. The first part includes those Aayaat in which the actual words of Kalimah Tayyibah do not occur, but are implied therein. Each Aayah is followed by a brief explanation, as given by the Sahaabah ﷺ and by Rasulullah ﷺ himself.

The second part consists of those Aayaat which contain the text of Kalimah Tayyibah i.e. لَا اِلٰهَ اِلَّا اللّٰهُ *(Laailaaha illallaah)* or a slight variation, such as لَا اِلٰهَ اِلَّا هُوَ *(Laailaaha illaahu)*. As the words of the kalimah occur in these Aayaat, their translation has not been considered necessary. Only the name of the surah and Aayah number, in which the Aayah occurs, has been indicated.

The third part includes the translation and explanation of those Ahaadith that describe the virtues and importance of this kalimah.

وَ مَا تَوْفِيْقِيْ اِلَّا بِاللّٰهِ

"Whatever has been done is merely through grace of Allah Ta'ala."

Chapter 2 – Virtues of Kalimah Tayyibah

SECTION 1
AAYAAT PERTAINING TO KALIMAH TAYYIBAH

This chapter contains those Aayaat in which the words of the Kalimah Tayyibah do not occur, although it is implied therein:

١) اَلَمْ تَرَ كَيْفَ ضَرَبَ اللهُ مَثَلًا كَلِمَةً طَيِّبَةً كَشَجَرَةٍ طَيِّبَةٍ اَصْلُهَا ثَابِتٌ وَفَرْعُهَا فِى السَّمَآءِ ۙ تُؤْتِىْۤ اُكُلَهَا كُلَّ حِيْنٍۭ بِاِذْنِ رَبِّهَا ؕ وَيَضْرِبُ اللهُ الْاَمْثَالَ لِلنَّاسِ لَعَلَّهُمْ يَتَذَكَّرُوْنَ ۞ وَمَثَلُ كَلِمَةٍ خَبِيْثَةٍ كَشَجَرَةٍ خَبِيْثَةِ ِۨاجْتُثَّتْ مِنْ فَوْقِ الْاَرْضِ مَا لَهَا مِنْ قَرَارٍ

1) *"Don't you see how Allah Ta'ala explains through an example of the pure word as a pure tree that is firmly rooted and its branches reach the sky. It brings fruit at all times by the command of its Rabb. So Allah explains through examples for people so that they may reflect (ponder and understand). And the example of the evil word is like a miserable tree that is uprooted from the ground having no stability."* (Surah Ibraaheem - Aayah 24-26)

Note: Hadhrat Ibn Abbaas ؓ has explained that the words "Kalimah Tayyibah" in this aayat mean the Kalimah Shahaadat

اَشْهَدُ اَنْ لَّا اِلٰهَ اِلَّا اللهُ

which is like a tree with its roots in the hearts of the Muslims and its branches spread out up to the Heavens, by means of which the deeds of the faithful climb up to the Heavens; and كَلِمَةٌ خَبِيْثَةٌ (i.e. evil word) is the utterance of shirk, which prevents any good deed from being accepted. In another Hadith, it is stated by Ibn Abbaas ؓ that, "bearing of fruit all the time" means that Allah Ta'ala be remembered day and night.

It was narrated by Hadhrat Qataadah *(rahmatullahi alayh)* a Tabi'ee, that somebody had said to Rasulullah ﷺ, "The rich have taken all the great rewards (by virtue of spending their wealth in charity)." Rasulullah ﷺ replied, "Tell me, can anybody reach the sky by piling up his goods one over the other. I am telling you of something, which has its roots in the Earth and its branches spread out in the Heavens. It is the recitation of the kalimah ten times each after every Salaah."

لَا اِلٰهَ اِلَّا اللّٰهُ وَاللّٰهُ اَكْبَرُ وَسُبْحَانَ اللّٰهِ وَالْحَمْدُ لِلّٰهِ

٢) مَنْ كَانَ يُرِيْدُ الْعِزَّةَ فَلِلّٰهِ الْعِزَّةُ جَمِيْعًا ۚ اِلَيْهِ يَصْعَدُ الْكَلِمُ الطَّيِّبُ وَالْعَمَلُ الصَّالِحُ يَرْفَعُهُ

2. "Whosoever desires honour (should know that) all honour belongs to Allah Ta'ala alone. The pure word ascends up to Him, propelled by good deeds." (Surah Faatir – Aayah 10)

Note: According to the majority of commentators, the Kalimah Tayyibah in this Aayah means لَا اِلٰهَ اِلَّا اللّٰهُ, but some are of the opinion that it implies the kalimah of tasbeeh, as will be described in part two.

٣) وَتَمَّتْ كَلِمَتُ رَبِّكَ صِدْقًا وَعَدْلًا

3. "The word of your Rabb is perfect with regards to truth and justice." (Surah An'aam - Aayah 115)

Note: According to Hadhrat Anas رَضِىَ اللّٰهُ عَنْهُ, Rasulullah صَلَّى اللّٰهُ عَلَيْهِ وَسَلَّم had said that the kalimah of the Rabb means the kalimah of لَا اِلٰهَ اِلَّا اللّٰهُ (laailaaha illallaah). But most commentators (due to other Ahaadith) are of the opinion that it means the Qur-aan Shareef.

٤) يُثَبِّتُ اللّٰهُ الَّذِيْنَ اٰمَنُوْا بِالْقَوْلِ الثَّابِتِ فِى الْحَيٰوةِ الدُّنْيَا وَفِى الْاٰخِرَةِ ۚ وَيُضِلُّ اللّٰهُ الظّٰلِمِيْنَ ۚ وَيَفْعَلُ اللّٰهُ مَا يَشَآءُ

4. "Allah Ta'ala keeps those who have Imaan steadfast by a firm word (i.e. the Kalimah) in this world and in the Aakhirah, and Allah Ta'ala allows the oppressors (wrong doers/ kuffaar) to go astray. Allah Ta'ala does as He wills." (Surah Ibraaheem - Aayah 27)

Chapter 2 – Virtues of Kalimah Tayyibah

Note: Hadhrat Baraa ﷺ stated that Rasulullah ﷺ said, "When, at the time of questioning in the grave, a Muslim bears witness to this kalimah لَا اِلٰهَ اِلَّا اللهُ مُحَمَّدٌ رَّسُوْلُ اللهِ and this is what is meant by the words (firm statement) in this aayah. Hadhrat Aa'ishah ﷺ narrated that this refers to the questioning in the grave. Hadhrat Ibn Abbaas ﷺ said, "When a Muslim is about to die, the Malaaikah come to him, greet him, and convey glad tidings of Jannah. After his death, they accompany him and join his Janaazah Salaah. After he is buried, they make him sit up in the grave and then they question him. He replies

اَشْهَدُ اَنْ لَّا اِلٰهَ اِلَّا اللهُ وَاَشْهَدُ اَنَّ مُحَمَّدًا رَّسُوْلُ اللهِ

"I bear witness that there is nobody worthy of worship except Allah, and I bear witness that Muhammad is the messenger of Allah."

this is what is implied in this aayat."

Hadhrat Abu Qataadah ﷺ said that قَوْلُ ثَابِتٌ (firm statement) refers to the Kalimah Tayyibah in this life, and an answer to the interrogation in the grave after death. Hadhrat Taa'oos *(rahmatullahi alayh)* also gave the same interpretation.

٥) لَهُ دَعْوَةُ الْحَقِّ ۖ وَالَّذِيْنَ يَدْعُوْنَ مِنْ دُوْنِهٖ لَا يَسْتَجِيْبُوْنَ لَهُمْ بِشَىْءٍ اِلَّا كَبَاسِطِ كَفَّيْهِ اِلَى الْمَاۤءِ لِيَبْلُغَ فَاهُ وَمَا هُوَ بِبَالِغِهٖ ۚ وَمَا دُعَاۤءُ الْكٰفِرِيْنَ اِلَّا فِىْ ضَلٰلٍ

5. *The true call (the Kalimah) in only for Him. Those whom they call besides Him does not respond to them at all. They are like a person who stretches out his hand for water so that it may reach his mouth but it will never reach. The prayer of the disbelievers is wasted."*
(Surah R'ad - Aayah 14)

Note: According to Hadhrat Ali ﷺ, the words دَعْوَةُ الْحَقِّ (Da'watul Haqq, i.e. the propagation of truth) means tauheed (i.e, the Kalimah). Ibn Abbaas ﷺ as well as many others are reported to have said 'Da'watul Haqq' means the Shahaadah (i.e. this Kalimah).

٦) قُلْ يَٰٓأَهْلَ الْكِتَٰبِ تَعَالَوْا إِلَىٰ كَلِمَةٍ سَوَآءٍۭ بَيْنَنَا وَبَيْنَكُمْ أَلَّا نَعْبُدَ إِلَّا اللَّهَ وَلَا نُشْرِكَ بِهِۦ شَيْـًٔا وَلَا يَتَّخِذَ بَعْضُنَا بَعْضًا أَرْبَابًا مِّن دُونِ اللَّهِ ۚ فَإِن تَوَلَّوْا فَقُولُوا اشْهَدُوا بِأَنَّا مُسْلِمُونَ

6. "Say: O people of the book! Come to a word (matter of belief) that is common between us and you; that we worship none other but Allah Ta'ala and that we do not ascribe any partner to Him, and none of us shall take others as gods besides Allah Ta'ala. And if they turn away, then say, 'Be witness that we are Muslims.'"
(Surah Aali I'mraan - Aayah 64)

Note: This sacred aayah is self-explanatory. The word 'kalimah' in this aayah implies tauheed and the Kalimah Tayyibah. The same view-point has been categorically confirmed by Hadhrat Abu Aaliyah and Hadhrat Mujaahid *(rahmatullahi alayhima)*.

٧) كُنتُمْ خَيْرَ أُمَّةٍ أُخْرِجَتْ لِلنَّاسِ تَأْمُرُونَ بِالْمَعْرُوفِ وَتَنْهَوْنَ عَنِ الْمُنكَرِ وَتُؤْمِنُونَ بِاللَّهِ ۗ وَلَوْ ءَامَنَ أَهْلُ الْكِتَٰبِ لَكَانَ خَيْرًا لَّهُم ۚ مِّنْهُمُ الْمُؤْمِنُونَ وَأَكْثَرُهُمُ الْفَٰسِقُونَ

7. "You (the followers of Muhammad ﷺ) are the best of all nations, who have been raised for (the benefit of) mankind enjoining what is right, forbidding what is wrong and believing in Allah Ta'ala. If only the people of the book had Imaan, it would be better for them; among them are some who have Imaan while most of them are transgressors / disobedient (kuffaar)." (Surah Aali I'mraan – Aayah 110)

Note: Hadhrat Ibn Abbaas ﷺ has stated تَأْمُرُونَ بِالْمَعْرُوفِ (i.e. you enjoin good) means that you encourage people to believe in and obey Allah Ta'ala and that this kalimah is, by far, the best and foremost of all the good things.

Chapter 2 – Virtues of Kalimah Tayyibah

$$ \text{٨) وَأَقِمِ الصَّلٰوةَ طَرَفِيِ النَّهَارِ وَزُلَفًا مِنَ الَّيْلِ ۚ اِنَّ الْحَسَنٰتِ يُذْهِبْنَ السَّيِّاٰتِ ۚ ذٰلِكَ ذِكْرٰى لِلذّٰكِرِيْنَ} $$

8. "Establish Salaah at the two ends of the day and during portions of the night. Verily good deeds wipe out evil deeds. This is advice for those who will take heed (remember)." *(Surah Hood – Aayah 114)*

Note: The explanation of this sacred aayah is to be found in many Ahaadith. Rasulullah ﷺ, while referring to this aayah had said that good deeds wipe out sins from one's account. Hadhrat Abu Zar رضي الله عنه says that he had once requested Rasulullah ﷺ to give him some advice and Rasulullah ﷺ replied "Fear Allah Ta'ala. If maybe you commit any sin, hurry up at once to do some virtuous deed so that the sin committed is compensated for and it is wiped off." Then Abu Zar رضي الله عنه continued to say that he asked Rasulullah ﷺ if this kalimah (لَا إِلٰهَ إِلَّا الله) was also counted amongst the virtues. At this, Rasulullah ﷺ replied that this kalimah is the highest of all virtues. It is also quoted from Hadhrat Anas رضي الله عنه that Rasulullah ﷺ had said "Whosoever, at any time during the day or night, recites the kalimah (لَا إِلٰهَ إِلَّا الله), his sins will be washed off (his account)."

$$ \text{٩) اِنَّ اللهَ يَأْمُرُ بِالْعَدْلِ وَالْاِحْسَانِ وَاِيْتَآئِ ذِى الْقُرْبٰى وَيَنْهٰى عَنِ الْفَحْشَآءِ وَالْمُنْكَرِ وَالْبَغْىِ ۚ يَعِظُكُمْ لَعَلَّكُمْ تَذَكَّرُوْنَ} $$

9. "Verily Allah Ta'ala instructs with justice, Ihsaan and giving (charity) to relatives and He forbids shameful/ immoral deeds, evil and oppression. He advises you so that you may take heed."
(Surah Nahl – Aayah 90)

Note: There are different versions regarding the interpretation of the word عَدْل (justice). In one version, Hadhrat Abdullah bin Abbaas رضي الله عنه says that عَدْل (justice) means to say لَا إِلٰهَ إِلَّا الله and believe that nobody is worthy of worship except Allah Ta'ala, while اِحْسَان (goodness) means adherence to the commands of Allah Ta'ala.

١٠) يٰٓاَيُّهَاالَّذِيْنَ اٰمَنُوا اتَّقُوا اللهَ وَقُوْلُوْا قَوْلًا سَدِيْدًا ۙ يُّصْلِحْ لَكُمْ اَعْمَالَكُمْ وَيَغْفِرْ لَكُمْ ذُنُوْبَكُمْ ؕ وَمَنْ يُّطِعِ اللهَ وَرَسُوْلَهٗ فَقَدْ فَازَ فَوْزًا عَظِيْمًا

10. "O, you who believe! Fear Allah Ta'ala and speak what is right, (if you do this) Allah Ta'ala will correct your (good) deeds and forgive your sins. Whoever obeys Allah Ta'ala and His Rasool صَلَّى اللهُ عَلَيْهِ وَسَلَّمَ, he has succeeded tremendously."
(Surah Ahzaab - Aayah 69 & 70)

Note: Hadhrat Abdullah bin Abbaas رَضِيَ اللهُ عَنْهُمَا and Hadhrat Ikramah رَضِيَ اللهُ عَنْهُ both are said to have been of the view that the meaning of قُوْلُوْا قَوْلًا سَدِيْدًا (and speak what is right) is to recite the kalimah لَا إِلٰهَ إِلَّا اللهُ.

According to one Hadith, three things constitute the best of all actions.
1. The first is to make zikr of Allah Ta'ala under all circumstances; in happiness and in grief; in poverty and in affluence;
2. The second is to conduct oneself with justice even if one's own interest is at stake; it must not be that you are hard on others while lenient on yourself. (i.e. regarding your own matters you try to find excuses).
3. The third is to help one's brother financially.

١١) فَبَشِّرْ عِبَادِ ۙ الَّذِيْنَ يَسْتَمِعُوْنَ الْقَوْلَ فَيَتَّبِعُوْنَ اَحْسَنَهٗ ؕ اُولٰٓئِكَ الَّذِيْنَ هَدٰىهُمُ اللهُ وَاُولٰٓئِكَ هُمْ اُولُوا الْاَلْبَابِ

11. "So give glad tidings to my servants, who listen attentively to the speech (advice) and follow the best of it. These are the ones whom Allah Ta'ala has guided, and these are the men who possess intelligence (understanding)." (Surah Zumar – Aayah 17 & 18)

Chapter 2 – Virtues of Kalimah Tayyibah

Note: Hadhrat Ibn Umar رَضِىَ اللهُ عَنْهُمَا said that Hadhrat Sa'eed bin Zaid, Hadhrat Abu Zar Ghifaari and Hadhrat Salmaan Faarsi رَضِىَ اللهُ عَنْهُمْ, would recite the Kalimah لَا اِلٰهَ اِلَّا الله (laailaaha illallaah) even before they embraced Islam. What is meant by the words اَحْسَنَ الْقَوْلِ (the best utterance) in this sacred aayah is this kalimah. Hadhrat Zaid bin Aslam رَضِىَ اللهُ عَنْهُ had also said that this aayah relates to three persons who used to recite the Kalimah لَا اِلٰهَ اِلَّا الله even in their days of ignorance. They were Hadhrat Zaid bin Amr bin Nufail, Hadhrat Abu Zar Ghifaari and Hadhrat Salmaan Faarsi رَضِىَ اللهُ عَنْهُمْ.

۱۲) وَالَّذِىْ جَآءَ بِالصِّدْقِ وَ صَدَّقَ بِهٖۤ اُولٰٓئِكَ هُمُ الْمُتَّقُوْنَ ۝ لَهُمْ مَّا يَشَآءُوْنَ عِنْدَ رَبِّهِمْ ۚ ذٰلِكَ جَزَآؤُا الْمُحْسِنِيْنَ ۝ لِيُكَفِّرَ اللهُ عَنْهُمْ اَسْوَاَ الَّذِىْ عَمِلُوْا وَ يَجْزِيَهُمْ اَجْرَهُمْ بِاَحْسَنِ الَّذِىْ كَانُوْا يَعْمَلُوْنَ

12. "He who brings the truth and confirms it; these are the people who have Taqwa. They shall have whatever they desire by their Rabb. This is the reward of those who do good. So that Allah Ta'ala may cancel their evil deeds and grant them the best reward for the good deeds they carried out." *(Surah Zumar - Aayah 33-35)*

Note: Those who brought the message from Allah Ta'ala are the messengers *(alayhimus salaam)*. The people who brought the message from Rasulullah صَلَّى اللهُ عَلَيْهِ وَسَلَّمَ are the Ulama (May Allah accept their efforts). Hadhrat Ibnu Abbaas رَضِىَ اللهُ عَنْهُمَا is stated to have said that, "the true thing" means the Kalimah لَا اِلٰهَ اِلَّا الله (laailaaha illallaah). According to some commentators, the words اَلَّذِىْ جَآءَ بِالصِّدْقِ (one who brought the true message from Allah Ta'ala) refers to Rasulullah صَلَّى اللهُ عَلَيْهِ وَسَلَّمَ and the words صَدَّقَ بِهٖ (those who confirmed it) refer to the believers.

$$١٣) \text{ إِنَّ الَّذِينَ قَالُوا رَبُّنَا اللّٰهُ ثُمَّ اسْتَقَامُوا تَتَنَزَّلُ عَلَيْهِمُ الْمَلٰٓئِكَةُ اَلَّا تَخَافُوا وَلَا تَحْزَنُوا وَاَبْشِرُوا بِالْجَنَّةِ الَّتِيْ كُنْتُمْ تُوْعَدُوْنَ ۞ نَحْنُ اَوْلِيٰٓؤُكُمْ فِى الْحَيٰوةِ الدُّنْيَا وَفِى الْاٰخِرَةِ ۚ وَلَكُمْ فِيْهَا مَا تَشْتَهِيْٓ اَنْفُسُكُمْ وَلَكُمْ فِيْهَا مَا تَدَّعُوْنَ ۞ نُزُلًا مِّنْ غَفُوْرٍ رَّحِيْمٍ}$$

13. "Verily those who say, "Our Rabb is Allah Ta'ala" and are then steadfast, the Malaaikah shall surely descend upon them (saying) "Have no fear nor any grief but glad tidings of the Jannah which you were promised. We are your friends in this world and in the Aakhirah (Hereafter). There you shall have whatever your heart desires, and you shall have whatever you ask for. This is the hospitality from the most Forgiving, the most Merciful."
(Surah Haa Meem Sajdah – Aayah 30)

Note: Hadhrat Ibn Abbaas رضي الله عنه said that the words ثُمَّ اسْتَقَامُوا (then remained steadfast) means that they remained steadfast in their belief in the kalimah. Hadhrat Ibraahim and Hadhrat Mujaahid *(rahmatullahi alayhima)* both supported the interpretation "they remained steadfast to the kalimah لا إله إلا الله until their death, and never indulged in shirk of any kind."

$$١٤) \text{ وَمَنْ اَحْسَنُ قَوْلًا مِّمَّنْ دَعَآ اِلَى اللّٰهِ وَعَمِلَ صَالِحًا وَّقَالَ اِنَّنِيْ مِنَ الْمُسْلِمِيْنَ}$$

14. "Whose speech can be better than one who calls (men) to Allah Ta'ala, does righteous deeds and says, 'I am among the Muslims.'"
(Surah Haa Meem Sajdah – Aayah 33)

Note: Hadhrat Hasan رضي الله عنه said that the words دَعَا إِلَى اللهِ (invite towards Allah) refers to the calling of لا إله إلا الله by the Muazzins. Aasim bin Hubairah *(rahmatullahi alayh)* advised, "After finishing azaan, one should recite

$$\text{لَا إِلٰهَ إِلَّا اللهُ وَاللهُ اَكْبَرُ وَاَنَا مِنَ الْمُسْلِمِيْنَ}$$

"Nobody is worthy of worship except Allah; Allah is the greatest and I am from among the Muslims."

١٥) هَلْ جَزَآءُ الْاِحْسَانِ اِلَّا الْاِحْسَانُ ۚ فَبِاَيِّ اٰلَآءِ رَبِّكُمَا تُكَذِّبٰنِ

15. "Can the reward of good be anything but good? So which favours of your Rabb do the two of you deny?" *(Surah Rahmaan - Aayah 60 & 61)*

Note: Hadhrat Ibn Abbaas ﷺ narrated that Rasulullah ﷺ had said regarding this aayah, that Allah Ta'ala says, "Can there be any other reward besides Jannah in the Aakhirah for the one who is blessed in this worldly life by the recitation of the kalimah." Hadhrat Ikramah and Hadhrat Hasan ﷺ both have also said that the reward of لَا اِلٰهَ اِلَّا اللّٰه *(laailaaha illallaah)* cannot be anything but Jannah.

١٦) فَاَنْزَلَ اللّٰهُ سَكِيْنَتَهٗ عَلٰى رَسُوْلِهٖ وَعَلَى الْمُؤْمِنِيْنَ وَاَلْزَمَهُمْ كَلِمَةَ التَّقْوٰى وَكَانُوْا اَحَقَّ بِهَا وَاَهْلَهَا

16. "Then Allah sent down His tranquility upon His Rasool and upon the believers and kept them firm upon the word of taqwa as they are most deserving of it and worthy of it." *(Surah Fath - Aayah 26)*

Note: كَلِمَةُ التَّقْوٰى *(the word taqwa)* in this aayah means Kalimah Tayyibah as explained in many narrations. Hence, Hadhrat Abu Hurayrah ﷺ and Hadhrat Salama ﷺ quoted Rasulullah ﷺ as having said that it means لَا اِلٰهَ اِلَّا اللّٰه *(laailaaha illallaah)*. The same view was expressed by Hadhrat Ubayy bin Ka'b, Hadhrat Ali, Hadhrat Umar, Hadhrat Ibn Abbaas, Hadhrat Ibn Umar, and many other Sahaabah ﷺ. Ataa Khurasani *(rahmatullahi alayh)* was of the view that it meant the whole Kalimah Tayyibah i.e. لَا اِلٰهَ اِلَّا اللّٰه مُحَمَّدٌ رَّسُوْلُ اللّٰه while Hadhrat Ali ﷺ had said that it meant لَا اِلٰهَ اِلَّا اللّٰهُ اللّٰهُ اَكْبَرُ *(laailaaha illallaah Allahu-Akbar)*. Tirmizi *(rahmatullahi alayh)* is stated to have quoted on the authority of Baraa ﷺ that this implied لَا اِلٰهَ اِلَّا اللّٰه *(laailaaha illallaah)*.

١٦) قَدْ اَفْلَحَ مَنْ تَزَكَّىٰ

17. "Successful indeed is he who has purified (himself from kufr, shirk and spiritual diseases)." *(Surah A'la - Aayah 14)*

Note: Hadhrat Jaabir ﷺ has quoted Rasulullah ﷺ to have said that تَزَكَّىٰ (purified) means that he declared his Imaan in لَا إِلٰهَ إِلَّا اللهُ مُحَمَّدٌ رَّسُوْلُ اللهِ (Laailaaha illallaah Muhammadur Rasulullah) and gave up idol-worship. According to Hadhrat Ikramah ﷺ, تَزَكَّىٰ means he proclaimed *laailaaha illallaah* and this was also the viewpoint held by Ibn Abbaas ﷺ.

١٨) فَاَمَّا مَنْ اَعْطٰى وَاتَّقٰىۙ وَصَدَّقَ بِالْحُسْنٰىۙ فَسَنُيَسِّرُهٗ لِلْيُسْرٰىۗ

18. "As for him who gives (charity) and has taqwaa; and who believes in the most beautiful word. Surely we shall make the Great comfort (Jannah) easy for him." *(Surah Layl - Aayah 5-7)*

Note: لِلْيُسْرٰى (the great comfort) means Jannah, because in Jannah all kinds of comforts and facilities will be available. Further Allah Ta'ala will grace a man to make good deeds easy for him, which will hasten his entry into Jannah. Many commentators are of the view that the above-mentioned aayah was revealed in favour of Hadhrat Abu Bakr ﷺ. According to Hadhrat Ibn Abbaas ﷺ the word اَلْحُسْنٰى (good thing) mentioned in this aayah means the kalimah. Hadhrat Abu Abdur Rahmaan Sulami ﷺ also shares this view. Hadhrat Imaam-e-A'zam Abu Hanifah *(rahmatullahi alayh)*, quoting on the authority of Hadhrat Abu Zubair and Hadhrat Jaabir ﷺ says, that Rasulullah ﷺ read the words صَدَّقَ بِالْحُسْنٰى (saddaqa bil husna) and explained that it means testifying in لَا إِلٰهَ إِلَّا اللهُ (laailaaha illallaah) and then he read بِالْحُسْنٰى كَذَّبَ (kazzaba bil husna) and said that it refers to the one who has rejected لَا إِلٰهَ إِلَّا اللهُ (laailaaha illallaah).

Chapter 2 – Virtues of Kalimah Tayyibah

١٩) مَنْ جَآءَ بِالْحَسَنَةِ فَلَهُ عَشْرُ اَمْثَالِهَا ۚ وَمَنْ جَآءَ بِالسَّيِّئَةِ فَلَا يُجْزٰى اِلَّا مِثْلَهَا وَهُمْ لَا يُظْلَمُوْنَ

19. "He who does a good deed will receive (reward) ten times as much. (and on the other hand) He who does an evil deed will be punished only according to as much as his evil and they will not be oppressed."
(Surah An'aam - Aayah 160)

Note: When this aayah was revealed, someone asked Rasulullah ﷺ if the reciting of *laailaaha illallaah* was also among their virtuous deeds. Rasulullah ﷺ replied that *laailaaha illallaah* is the best of all virtues. Hadhrat Abdullah bin Abbaas رضي الله عنه and Hadhrat Abdullah bin Mas'ood رضي الله عنه say that حَسَنَة 'hasanah' (virtue) means *laailaaha illallaah*. Hadhrat Abu Hurayrah رضي الله عنه also holds the same view. Similar meanings were also narrated by Hadhrat Abu Zar Ghifaari رضي الله عنه on the authority of Rasulullah ﷺ who held the view that *laailaaha illallaah* was the best amongst all virtuous deeds.

According to Hadhrat Abu Hurayrah رضي الله عنه, one good deed is multiplied ten times over as a general principle, but, for the muhaajireen, reward for one good deed is multiplied seven hundred times.

٢٠) حٰمٓ ۚ تَنْزِيْلُ الْكِتٰبِ مِنَ اللهِ الْعَزِيْزِ الْعَلِيْمِ ۙ غَافِرِ الذَّنْۢبِ وَقَابِلِ التَّوْبِ شَدِيْدِ الْعِقَابِ ۙ ذِى الطَّوْلِ ۗ لَاۤ اِلٰهَ اِلَّا هُوَ ۗ اِلَيْهِ الْمَصِيْرُ

20. "Ha-Meem. This Book is revealed from Allah Ta'ala, the Mighty (Exalted in power), the All Knowing, Who forgives sins and accepts repentance, Severe in punishment and All Powerful. There is no god but He. All shall return to Him." (Surah Mu'min – Aayah 1-3)

Note: In an explanation of this aayah, Hadhrat Abdullah bin Umar رضي الله عنهما says that Allah Ta'ala is the forgiver of sins for those who say *laailaaha illallaah*. He is the acceptor of the taubah for one who recites *laailaaha illallaah*, and is the giver of severe punishment for one who does not proclaim the words *laailaaha illallaah*. The meaning of ذِى الطَّوْلِ *(Zit Taul)* is the One who is extremely rich, and *laailaaha illallaah* is a refutation to the Quraish, who did not believe in the Oneness of Allah Ta'ala; اِلَيْهِ الْمَصِيْرُ (ilayhil maseer) implies that one who says laailaaha illallaah will return to Allah Ta'ala for entry into Jannah, while one who rejects laailaaha illallaah will return to Him for entry into Jahannam.

$$\text{(٢١)} \quad فَمَنْ يَكْفُرْ بِالطَّاغُوْتِ وَيُؤْمِنْ بِاللهِ فَقَدِ اسْتَمْسَكَ بِالْعُرْوَةِ الْوُثْقَىٰ لَا انْفِصَامَ لَهَا$$

21. *"He who rejects false deities (shaytaan and idols) and believes in Allah Ta'ala has grasped the firm / strong handhold, which will never break."* (Surah Baqarah - Aayah 256)

Note: Hadhrat Ibn Abbaas رضي الله عنهما says that عُرْوَةُ الْوُثْقَىٰ (u'rwatul wusqaa) "a firm grasp" means proclaiming *laailaaha illallaah*. The same interpretation is also related from Sufyaan *(rahmatullahi alayh)* that عُرْوَةُ الْوُثْقَىٰ (u'rwatul wusqaa) refers to the kalimah of ikhlaas.

CONCLUSION:

قُلْتُ وَقَدْ وَرَدَ فِيْ تَفْسِيْرِ اٰيَاتٍ اُخَرَ عَدِيْدَةٍ اَيْضًا اَنَّ الْمُرَادَ بِبَعْضِ الْاَلْفَاظِ فِيْ هٰذِهِ الْاٰيَاتِ كَلِمَةُ التَّوْحِيْدِ عِنْدَ بَعْضِهِمْ فَقَدْ قَالَ الرَّاغِبُ فِيْ قَوْلِهٖ فِيْ قِصَّةِ زَكَرِيَّا عَلَيْهِ السَّلَامُ مُصَدِّقًا بِكَلِمَةٍ قِيْلَ كَلِمَةُ التَّوْحِيْدِ وَكَذَا قَالَ فِيْ قَوْلِهٖ تَعَالٰى اِنَّا عَرَضْنَا الْاَمَانَةَ الْاٰيَةَ قِيْلَ هِيَ كَلِمَةُ التَّوْحِيْدِ وَاقْتَصَرْتُ عَلٰى مَا مَرَّ لِلْاِخْتِصَارِ

Chapter 2 – Virtues of Kalimah Tayyibah

SECTION 2
AAYAAT PERTAINING TO THE KALIMAH TAYYIBAH WHEREIN THE KALIMAH APPEARS IN FULL OR IN PART

This chapter includes such Aayaat which contains the Kalimah Tayyibah in full or in part, or its equivalent in different words but having the same meaning. The Kalimah Tayyibah *(laailaaha illallaah)* means that there is no deity except Allah Ta'ala. The words مَا مِنْ اِلٰهٍ غَيْرُهُ *(maa min ilaahin ghairuh)* also has the same meaning, that there is no deity except Allah Ta'ala. This is also the meaning of لَا اِلٰهَ اِلَّا هُوَ *(laailaaha illaa hu)*, and the words لَا نَعْبُدُ اِلَّا اللهَ *(laa na'budu illallaah)*, we do not worship anyone besides Allah Ta'ala, have a similar meaning. This is also the meaning of لَا نَعْبُدُ اِلَّآ اِيَّاهُ *(laa na'budu illaa iyyaah)*, we do not worship anybody other than Allah Ta'ala and اِنَّمَا هُوَ اِلٰهٌ وَّاحِدٌ *(innamaa huwa ilaahu waahid)* (He is the only one worthy of worship). There are other similar Aayaat, which have the same meaning as Kalimah Tayyibah. The surah and aayah number in which each such aayah is found has been indicated below. In fact, the whole Qur-aan Shareef is an explanation of the Kalimah Tayyibah, because the basic objective of the Qur-aan Shareef and of the Deen of Islam is Tauheed. It was to propagate tauheed that the messengers of Allah Ta'ala were sent to people at different times. Tauheed is the common objective of all the divine religions, and it is for this reason that the subject of tauheed has all along been dealt with under different headings to establish its truth. (to confirm the concept of Tauheed, different acts of Ibaadat have been prescribed) And this is the objective of Kalimah Tayyibah.

١) وَاِلٰهُكُمْ اِلٰهٌ وَّاحِدٌ لَآ اِلٰهَ اِلَّا هُوَ الرَّحْمٰنُ الرَّحِيْمُ

1. *"Your God is one God. There is no other God besides Him; The Most Beneficent, The Most Merciful." (Surah Baqarah – Aayah 163)*

٢) اَللّٰهُ لَآ اِلٰهَ اِلَّا هُوَ اَلْحَيُّ الْقَيُّوْمُ

2. "Allah Ta'ala (is such that) there is no god besides Him. He is Ever Living, The Maintainer (of everything)." (Surah Baqarah - Aayah 255)

(٣) اَللّٰهُ لَآ اِلٰهَ اِلَّا هُوَ ۚ الْحَىُّ الْقَيُّوْمُ

3. "Allah Ta'ala (is such that) there is no god besides Him. He is Ever Living, The Maintainer (of everything)." (Surah Aali I'mraan – Aayah 2)

(٤) شَهِدَ اللّٰهُ اَنَّهٗ لَآ اِلٰهَ اِلَّا هُوَ ۙ وَالْمَلٰٓئِكَةُ وَاُولُوا الْعِلْمِ

4. "Allah Ta'ala Himself is witness that there is no god but Him. And the Malaaikah and the men of knowledge (are also witnesses to this)."
(Surah Aalil'mraan - Aayah 18)

(٥) لَآ اِلٰهَ اِلَّا هُوَ الْعَزِيْزُ الْحَكِيْمُ

5. "There is no god but Him. The Mighty, The Wise."
(Surah Aali I'mraan - Aayah 18)

(٦) وَمَا مِنْ اِلٰهٍ اِلَّا اللّٰهُ ۚ وَاِنَّ اللّٰهَ لَهُوَ الْعَزِيْزُ الْحَكِيْمُ

6. "And there is no god besides Allah Ta'ala, and verily Allah Ta'ala is The Mighty, The Wise." (Surah Aali I'mraan - Aayah 62)

(٧) تَعَالَوْا اِلٰى كَلِمَةٍ سَوَآءٍ بَيْنَنَا وَبَيْنَكُمْ اَلَّا نَعْبُدَ اِلَّا اللّٰهَ

7. "Come to a word (agreement) that is common between us and you, that we worship none other but Allah." (Surah Aali I'mraan – Aayah 64)

(٨) اَللّٰهُ لَآ اِلٰهَ اِلَّا هُوَ ۚ لَيَجْمَعَنَّكُمْ اِلٰى يَوْمِ الْقِيٰمَةِ

8. "Allah Ta'ala (is such that) there is no god besides Him; He will most definitely gather all of you on the Day of Qiyaamah."
(Surah Nisaa'- Aayah 87)

(٩) وَمَا مِنْ اِلٰهٍ اِلَّآ اِلٰهٌ وَّاحِدٌ

Chapter 2 – Virtues of Kalimah Tayyibah

9. "And there is no god besides one Allah Ta'ala."
(Surah Maa'idah - Aayah 73)

١٠) قُلْ اِنَّمَا هُوَ اِلٰهٌ وَّاحِدٌ

10. "Say: 'He (Allah Ta'ala) is One God.'" (Surah An'aam - Aayah 19)

١١) مَنْ اِلٰهٌ غَيْرُ اللّٰهِ يَأْتِيْكُمْ بِهٖ

11. "Which god besides Allah Ta'ala can restore them to you?"
(Surah An'aam - Aayah 46)

١٢) ذٰلِكُمُ اللّٰهُ رَبُّكُمْ ۖ لَآ اِلٰهَ اِلَّا هُوَ

12. That is Allah, your Rabb. There is no god besides Him.
(Surah An'aam - Aayah 102)

١٣) لَآ اِلٰهَ اِلَّا هُوَ ۚ وَاَعْرِضْ عَنِ الْمُشْرِكِيْنَ

13. "There is no god besides Allah, and turn away from those who join partners with Allah Ta'ala." (Surah An'aam - Aayah 106)

١٤) قَالَ اَغَيْرَ اللّٰهِ اَبْغِيْكُمْ اِلٰهًا

14. "He said: Shall I seek for you a god other than Allah."
(Surah A'araaf – Aayah 140)

١٥) لَآ اِلٰهَ اِلَّا هُوَ يُحْيٖ وَيُمِيْتُ

15. There is no god besides He (Allah). It is He that gives both life and death. (Surah A'araaf – Aayah 158)

١٦) وَمَآ اُمِرُوْٓا اِلَّا لِيَعْبُدُوْٓا اِلٰهًا وَّاحِدًا ۚ لَآ اِلٰهَ اِلَّا هُوَ

16. "They were commanded to worship only the One God (Allah Ta'ala). There is no god besides Him." (Surah Taubah – Aayah 31)

(١٠) حَسۡبِيَ اللّٰهُ ۖ لَاۤ اِلٰهَ اِلَّا هُوَ ۖ عَلَيۡهِ تَوَكَّلۡتُ وَهُوَ رَبُّ الۡعَرۡشِ الۡعَظِيۡمِ

17. "Allah Ta'ala is sufficient for me. There is none worthy of worship but Him (Allah Ta'ala). On Him only I have put my trust and He is the Rabb of the glorious Throne." (Surah Taubah – Aayah 129)

(١٨) ذٰلِكُمُ اللّٰهُ رَبُّكُمۡ فَاعۡبُدُوۡهُ

18. "This is Allah Ta'ala your Rabb, therefore you should worship Him." (Surah Yunus – Aayah 3)

(١٩) فَذٰلِكُمُ اللّٰهُ رَبُّكُمُ الۡحَقُّ

19. "That Allah is your true Rabb." (Surah Yunus – Aayah 32)

(٢٠) قَالَ اٰمَنۡتُ اَنَّهٗ لَاۤ اِلٰهَ اِلَّا الَّذِيۡۤ اٰمَنَتۡ بِهٖ بَنُوۡۤا اِسۡرَآءِيۡلَ وَاَنَا مِنَ الۡمُسۡلِمِيۡنَ

20. "He said, there is none worthy of worship except Him (Allah), in Whom the Banu Israaeel believe, and I am of those who surrender (to Him)." (Surah Yunus – Aayah 90)

(٢١) فَلَاۤ اَعۡبُدُ الَّذِيۡنَ تَعۡبُدُوۡنَ مِنۡ دُوۡنِ اللّٰهِ

21. "I do not worship what you worship besides Allah Ta'ala." (Surah Yunus – Aayah 104)

(٢٢) فَاعۡلَمُوۡۤا اَنَّمَاۤ اُنۡزِلَ بِعِلۡمِ اللّٰهِ وَاَنۡ لَّاۤ اِلٰهَ اِلَّا هُوَ

22. "Be assured that this (Qur-aan) has been revealed by the knowledge of Allah Ta'ala, and there is no god besides Him (Allah Ta'ala)." (Surah Hood - Aayah 14)

(٢٣) اَنۡ لَّا تَعۡبُدُوۡۤا اِلَّا اللّٰهَ

23. "That you worship none but Allah Ta'ala," (Surah Hood - Aayah 26)

(٢٤، ٢٥، ٢٦) قَالَ يٰقَوۡمِ اعۡبُدُوا اللّٰهَ مَا لَكُمۡ مِّنۡ اِلٰهٍ غَيۡرُهٗ

Chapter 2 – Virtues of Kalimah Tayyibah

24. 25. 26. "He said: O my people worship Allah; you have no other god but Him." *(Surah Hood – Aayah 50, 61 & 84)*

(٢٦) ءَاَرْبَابٌ مُّتَفَرِّقُوْنَ خَيْرٌ اَمِ اللّٰهُ الْوَاحِدُ الْقَهَّارُ

27. "Are many gods better or Allah Ta'ala who is One and The Almighty? *(Surah Yusuf - Aayah 39)*

(٢٨) اَمَرَ اَلَّا تَعْبُدُوْٓا اِلَّآ اِيَّاهُ

28. "He has commanded that you worship none but Him." *(Surah Yusuf - Aayah 40)*

(٢٩) قُلْ هُوَ رَبِّيْ لَآ اِلٰهَ اِلَّا هُوَ

29. "Say, He is my Rabb, there is none worthy of worship but Him (Allah)." *(Surah Ra'd - Aayah 30)*

(٣٠) وَلِيَعْلَمُوْٓا اَنَّمَا هُوَ اِلٰهٌ وَّاحِدٌ

30. "And that they may know that He (Allah) is only One God." *(Surah Ibraaheem - Aayah 52)*

(٣١) اَنَّهٗ لَآ اِلٰهَ اِلَّآ اَنَا فَاتَّقُوْنِ

31. "There is none worthy of worship but Myself, so fear Me." *(Surah Nahl - Aayah 2)*

(٣٢) اِلٰهُكُمْ اِلٰهٌ وَّاحِدٌ

32. "Your Allah is one Allah." *(Surah Nahl - Aayah 22)*

(٣٣) اِنَّمَا هُوَ اِلٰهٌ وَّاحِدٌ

33. "He is just one Allah." *(Surah Nahl - Aayah 51)*

(٣٤) لَا تَجْعَلْ مَعَ اللّٰهِ اِلٰهًا اٰخَرَ

34. "And do not set up with Allah any other god."
(Surah Bani Israa-eel - Aayah 22)

(٣٥) قُلْ لَّوْ كَانَ مَعَهٗۤ اٰلِهَةٌ كَمَا يَقُوْلُوْنَ

35. "Say if there had been other gods with Him (Allah), as they say / claim." (Surah Bani Israa-eel - Aayah 42)

(٣٦) فَقَالُوْا رَبُّنَا رَبُّ السَّمٰوٰتِ وَالْاَرْضِ لَنْ نَّدْعُوَا۟ مِنْ دُوْنِهٖۤ اِلٰهًا

36. "They said: Our Rabb is the Rabb of the heavens and the earth. Never shall we call upon any other god besides Him (Allah)." We will never accept another god besides Him. (Surah Kahf - Aayah 14)

(٣٧) هٰۤؤُلَآءِ قَوْمُنَا اتَّخَذُوْا مِنْ دُوْنِهٖۤ اٰلِهَةً

37. "These are our people who have taken other gods besides Him (Allah Ta'ala)." (Surah Kahf - Aayah 15)

(٣٨) يُوْحٰۤى اِلَيَّ اَنَّمَاۤ اِلٰهُكُمْ اِلٰهٌ وَّاحِدٌ

38. "Revelation has come to me that your Allah is one Allah."
(Surah Kahf - Aayah 110)

(٣٩) وَاِنَّ اللّٰهَ رَبِّيْ وَرَبُّكُمْ فَاعْبُدُوْهُ

39. "Verily, Allah Ta'ala is my Rabb and your Rabb, so worship Him."
(Surah Maryam - Aayah 36)

(٤٠) اَللّٰهُ لَاۤ اِلٰهَ اِلَّا هُوَ

40. "Allah! There is none worthy of worship but Him (Allah Ta'ala)."
(Surah Taahaa - Aayah 8)

Chapter 2 – Virtues of Kalimah Tayyibah

(٤١) اِنَّنِىْٓ اَنَا اللّٰهُ لَآ اِلٰهَ اِلَّآ اَنَا فَاعْبُدْنِىْ

41. "Verily, I am Allah. There is none worthy of worship besides Me, so worship Me." *(Surah Taahaa - Aayah 14)*

(٤٢) اِنَّمَآ اِلٰهُكُمُ اللّٰهُ الَّذِىْ لَآ اِلٰهَ اِلَّا هُوَ

42. "But your Rabb is the one Allah, besides whom there is none worthy of worship." *(Surah Taahaa - Aayah 98)*

(٤٣) لَوْ كَانَ فِيْهِمَآ اٰلِهَةٌ اِلَّا اللّٰهُ لَفَسَدَتَا

43. If there were (in the Heavens and the Earth) other gods besides Allah Ta'ala, there would have been disorder in both of them. (The two would be in chaos)." *(Surah Ambiyaa - Aayah 22)*

(٤٤) اَمِ اتَّخَذُوْا مِنْ دُوْنِهٖٓ اٰلِهَةً

44. "Have they taken others to be worthy of worship besides Him (Allah Ta'ala)." *(Surah Ambiyaa - Aayah 24)*

(٤٥) اِلَّا نُوْحِىْٓ اِلَيْهِ اَنَّهٗ لَآ اِلٰهَ اِلَّآ اَنَا فَاعْبُدُوْنِ

45. "We (Allah Ta'ala) have revealed to him (The Rasool) that there is none worthy of worship besides Me (Allah Ta'ala), so make my Ibaadah." *(Surah Ambiyaa - Aayah 25)*

(٤٦) اَمْ لَهُمْ اٰلِهَةٌ تَمْنَعُهُمْ مِّنْ دُوْنِنَا

46. "Or do they have gods who can protect them from us?" *(Surah Ambiyaa - Aayah 43)*

(٤٧) اَفَتَعْبُدُوْنَ مِنْ دُوْنِ اللّٰهِ مَا لَا يَنْفَعُكُمْ شَيْئًا وَّلَا يَضُرُّكُمْ

47. "Do you then worship such things besides Allah Ta'ala that can neither be of any good to you, nor do you harm?" *(Surah Ambiyaa - Aayah 66)*

(٤٨) لَّا اِلٰهَ اِلَّا اَنْتَ سُبْحٰنَكَ

48. "There is no god besides You: Glory be to You."
(Surah Ambiyaa - Aayah 87)

(٤٩) اِنَّمَا يُوْحٰٓى اِلَيَّ اَنَّمَآ اِلٰهُكُمْ اِلٰهٌ وَّاحِدٌ

49. "It has come to me by revelation that your God is only One God (Allah)." (Surah Ambiyaa - Aayah 108)

(٥٠) فَاِلٰهُكُمْ اِلٰهٌ وَّاحِدٌ فَلَهٗٓ اَسْلِمُوْا

50. "Your God is One God, so submit unto Him."
(Surah Hajj - Aayah 34)

(٥١، ٥٢) اُعْبُدُوا اللّٰهَ مَا لَكُمْ مِّنْ اِلٰهٍ غَيْرُهٗ

51. & 52. "Worship only Allah Ta'ala, you have no other god but Him (Allah Ta'ala)." (Surah Mu'minoon - Aayaat 23 & 32)

(٥٣) وَمَا كَانَ مَعَهٗ مِنْ اِلٰهٍ

53. "Nor is there any god along with Him." (Surah Mu'minoon - Aayah 91)

(٥٤) فَتَعٰلَى اللّٰهُ الْمَلِكُ الْحَقُّ لَآ اِلٰهَ اِلَّا هُوَ

54. "Exalted is Allah Ta'ala, the True King! There is no god besides Him (Allah Ta'ala)." (Surah Mu'minoon - Aayah 116)

(٥٥) وَمَنْ يَّدْعُ مَعَ اللّٰهِ اِلٰهًا اٰخَرَ لَا بُرْهَانَ لَهٗ بِهٖ فَاِنَّمَا حِسَابُهٗ عِنْدَ رَبِّهٖ

55. "He who calls on (worships) any other god with Allah Ta'ala, has no proof for it. His reckoning is only with his Rabb."
(Surah Mu'minoon - Aayah 117)

(٥٦) ءَاِلٰهٌ مَّعَ اللّٰهِ

56. "Can there be another god besides Allah?" (Surah Naml - Aayah 61-64)

Chapter 2 – Virtues of Kalimah Tayyibah

(٥٧) وَهُوَ اللهُ لَآ اِلٰهَ اِلَّا هُوَ لَهُ الْحَمْدُ

57. "And He is Allah. There is no god but He. To Him belongs all praise." *(Surah Qasas - Aayah 70)*

(٥٨) مَنْ اِلٰهٌ غَيْرُ اللهِ يَأْتِيْكُمْ بِلَيْلٍ

58. "Is there any god other than Allah Ta'ala, who can bring night to you?" *(Surah Qasas - Aayah 72)*

(٥٩) وَلَا تَدْعُ مَعَ اللهِ اِلٰهًا اٰخَرَ لَآ اِلٰهَ اِلَّا هُوَ

59. "And do not call on (worship) any other god besides Allah Ta'ala. There is none worthy of worship but He." *(Surah Qasas - Aayah 72)*

(٦٠) وَاِلٰهُنَا وَاِلٰهُكُمْ وَاحِدٌ

60. "And our Allah and Your Allah is One." *(Surah A'nkaboot - Aayah 46)*

(٦١) لَآ اِلٰهَ اِلَّا هُوَ فَاَنّٰى تُؤْفَكُوْنَ

61. "There is none worthy of worship but He. So to where are you wandering?" *(Surah Faatir - Aayah 3)*

(٦٢) اِنَّ اِلٰهَكُمْ لَوَاحِدٌ

62. "Verily your Rabb is surely One." *(Surah Saaffaat – Aayah 4)*

(٦٣) اِنَّهُمْ كَانُوْٓا اِذَا قِيْلَ لَهُمْ لَآ اِلٰهَ اِلَّا اللهُ يَسْتَكْبِرُوْنَ

63. "For when it was said to them: There is none worthy of worship besides Allah Ta'ala, they were too proud."
(Surah Saaffaat - Aayah 35)

(٦٤) اَجَعَلَ الْاٰلِهَةَ اِلٰهًا وَّاحِدًا

64. "Has he made all the gods (that we worship) into One God (Allah)?" *(Surah Saad - Aayah 5)*

(٦٥) وَمَا مِنْ اِلٰهٍ اِلَّا اللهُ الْوَاحِدُ الْقَهَّارُ

65. "There is no god besides Allah, The One, The Being who controls everything." *(Surah Saad – Aayah 65)*

(٦٦) هُوَ اللهُ الْوَاحِدُ الْقَهَّارُ

66. "He is Allah, The One, The Being who controls everything." *(Surah Zumar - Aayah 4)*

(٦٧) ذٰلِكُمُ اللهُ رَبُّكُمْ لَهُ الْمُلْكُ ۖ لَآ اِلٰهَ اِلَّا هُوَ

67. "That is Allah. Your Rabb (the Cherisher) to Whom all kingdoms belong. There is none worthy of worship but He." *(Surah Zumar - Aayah 6)*

(٦٨) لَآ اِلٰهَ اِلَّا هُوَ ۖ اِلَيْهِ الْمَصِيْرُ

68. "There is none worthy of worship but Him, all shall return to Him." *(Surah Mu'min – Aayah 3)*

(٦٩) لَآ اِلٰهَ اِلَّا هُوَ ۖ فَاَنّٰى تُؤْفَكُوْنَ

69. "There is no god besides Allah. So to where are you wandering?" *(Surah Mu'min – Aayah 62)*

(٧٠) هُوَ الْحَيُّ لَآ اِلٰهَ اِلَّا هُوَ فَادْعُوْهُ

70. "He is the Living besides Whom no other deserves to be worshiped, so worship Him." *(Surah Mu'min – Aayah 65)*

(٧١) يُوْحٰى اِلَيَّ اَنَّمَآ اِلٰهُكُمْ اِلٰهٌ وَّاحِدٌ

71. "It is revealed to me that your deity is One Deity."
(Surah Haameem Sajdah - Aayah 6)

(٧٢) اَلَّا تَعْبُدُوْٓا اِلَّا اللّٰهَ

72. "You should not worship (any god) but Allah."
(Surah Haameem Sajdah - Aayah 14)

(٧٣) اَللّٰهُ رَبُّنَا وَرَبُّكُمْ

73. "Allah is our Rabb and your Rabb." (Surah Shooraa – Aayah 15)

(٧٤) اَجَعَلْنَا مِنْ دُوْنِ الرَّحْمٰنِ اٰلِهَةً يُّعْبَدُوْنَ

74. "Did we appoint gods to be worshipped besides Rahmaan (the Beneficent?)." (Surah Zukhruf – Aayah 45)

(٧٥) رَبِّ السَّمٰوٰتِ وَالْاَرْضِ وَمَا بَيْنَهُمَا

75. "The Rabb of the heavens and the earth and all that is between them." (Surah Dukhaan - Aayah 7)

(٧٦) لَآ اِلٰهَ اِلَّا هُوَ يُحْيٖ وَيُمِيْتُ

76. "There is no god but He. It is He who gives life and gives death."
(Surah Dukhaan - Aayah 8)

(٧٧) اَلَّا تَعْبُدُوْٓا اِلَّا اللّٰهَ

77. "You should not worship (any god) except Allah Ta'ala."
(Surah A'hqaaf – Aayah 21)

(٧٨) فَاعْلَمْ اَنَّهٗ لَآ اِلٰهَ اِلَّا اللّٰهَ

78. "Know that there is no god but Allah Ta'ala."
(Surah Muhammad - Aayah 19)

٧٩) وَلَا تَجْعَلُوْا مَعَ اللّٰهِ اِلٰهًا اٰخَرَ

79. *"And do not ascribe any other god along with Allah."*
(Surah Zaariyaat - Aayah 51)

٨٠) هُوَ اللّٰهُ الَّذِيْ لَآ اِلٰهَ اِلَّا هُوَ

80. *"He is Allah besides Whom there is no other god.*
(Surah Hashr - Aayah 22)

٨١) اِنَّا بُرَءٰٓؤُا مِنْكُمْ وَمِمَّا تَعْبُدُوْنَ مِنْ دُوْنِ اللّٰهِ

81. *"We absolve (free) ourselves from you and from that which you worship beside Allah Ta'ala."* (Surah Mumtah'inah – Aayah 4)

٨٢) اَللّٰهُ لَآ اِلٰهَ اِلَّا هُوَ

82. *"Allah! There is none worthy of worship but He."*
(Surah Taghaabun - Aayah 13)

٨٣) رَبُّ الْمَشْرِقِ وَالْمَغْرِبِ لَآ اِلٰهَ اِلَّا هُوَ فَاتَّخِذْهُ وَكِيْلًا

83. *"He is the Rabb of the East and the West; there is no god but He (Allah Ta'ala), so adopt Him as your guardian."*
(Surah Muzzammil - Aayah 9)

٨٤) لَآ اَعْبُدُ مَا تَعْبُدُوْنَ ۞ وَلَآ اَنْتُمْ عٰبِدُوْنَ مَآ اَعْبُدُ

84. *"I (as a Muslim) do not worship what you worship, nor do you worship that which I worship (Allah Ta'ala)."*
(Surah Kaafiroon - Aayah 2-3)

٨٥) قُلْ هُوَ اللّٰهُ اَحَدٌ

85. *"Say, He, Allah Ta'ala is One."* (Surah Ikhlaas - Aayah 1)

The above are the eighty-five Aayaat, in which, text of the Kalimah Tayyibah or its equivalent in meaning are mentioned. There are still many more Aayaat, which equally convey the same meaning of the Kalimah. I have stated this in the beginning of this section. Tauheed is the fundamental basis of Deen, and therefore the more a man is grounded in Tauheed, the more steadfast he shall be on Deen. Tauheed in the Qur-aan Shareef has been described from various viewpoints and in various forms and aspects, so that it may penetrate through the very depths of the heart and it firmly settles there, leaving no room for anything besides the remembrance of Allah Ta'ala to enter.

SECTION 3
AHAADITH PERTAINING TO THE KALIMAH TAYYIBAH

This chapter includes such Ahaadith which describe the virtues and blessings of reciting Kalimah Tayyibah. When there are so many Aayaat on this subject, then what can one say about the number of Ahaadith; it is therefore difficult to record all of them here. Only a few will be given by way of example.

Hadith 1 - The Best Zikr and the Best Dua

عَنْ جَابِرِ بْنِ عَبْدِ اللهِ رَضِيَ اللهُ عَنْهُ يَقُوْلُ سَمِعْتُ رَسُوْلَ اللهِ صَلَّى اللهُ عَلَيْهِ وَسَلَّمَ يَقُوْلُ اَفْضَلُ الذِّكْرِ لَا اِلٰهَ اِلَّا اللهُ وَاَفْضَلُ الدُّعَاءِ اَلْحَمْدُ لِلّٰهِ (رواه الترمذى # ٣٣٨٣)

Hadhrat Jaabir ﷺ narrates that Rasulullah ﷺ has said, "Of all the azkaar (plural of zikr), the repetition of laailaaha illallaah is the best, and of all the du'as, Alhamdulillaah is the best."

Note: That it is the best of all azkaar is quite evident; this is mentioned in many Ahaadith. In fact when the whole of Deen depends on this Kalimah Tauheed, there can be no doubt that it is the highest of all azkaar. Alhamdulillaah has been regarded as the best dua, because praising the one who is the most benevolent being is in fact a form of begging from him. It is quite common that by writing poetry in praise of a wealthy person or authority does not mean anything else other than begging for his favours or riches.

Hadhrat Ibn Abbaas ﷺ says that one who recites *laailaaha illallaah* should follow it by reciting *alhamdulillaah*, because in the Qur-aan Shareef the Aayah:

$$\text{فَادْعُوْهُ مُخْلِصِيْنَ لَهُ الدِّيْنَ}$$

Ask Allah with sincere devotion. (Surah Mu'min - Aayah 65)

is followed by اَلْحَمْدُ لِلّٰهِ رَبِّ الْعَالَمِيْنَ (All praise is for Allah Who is the Cherisher of the universe).

Mulla Ali Qari *(rahmatullahi alayh)* has stated: "There is not the slightest doubt that Kalimah Tayyibah is by far the best and foremost of all azkaar because it is that foundation of Deen around which the whole religion of Islam rotates. Therefore, the Sufis and saints emphasize its importance and prefer it over all other azkaar and advise their followers to make extensive zikr. Experience has shown that the benefits of Kalimah Tayyibah far out-weigh those from other forms of zikr.

There is a well-known story of Sayyid Ali bin Maymoon Maghrabi *(rahmatullahi alayh)*. Once, Shaikh Ulwani Hamawi, who was a great scholar, Mufti and teacher of his age, came to learn zikr from Sayyid Ali bin Maymoon Maghrabi *(rahmatullahi alayh)*. The Sayyid *(rahmatullahi alayh)* devoted special attention to him and made him give up all his other routines, such as teaching and writing fataawa, etc. and to take up zikr all the time. Noticing this, the common people (who have no work other than criticizing and hurling abuse) started finding fault and began condemning and criticizing the Shaikh that this Aalim has now been lost to them and they were being deprived of benefiting from him etc. A few days later, when the Sayyid *(rahmatullahi alayh)* came to know that Shaikh Ulwani was occasionally reciting the Qur-aan Shareef, he stopped him from this recitation also. At this, the people lost their senses and openly accused the Sayyid of irreligiousness and deviation. After some time, when the Shaikh observed that the zikr has had its effect on his heart, the Sayyid allowed him to resume the recitation of the Qur-aan Shareef. When he opened the Qur-aan Shareef, every word and aayah emerged with new meanings and significance he had never thought of before. The Sayyid *(rahmatullahi alayh)* then explained: "Allah Forbid, My intention was not to stop him from reciting the Qur-aan Shareef, but rather it was to help him achieve these insights."

Chapter 2 – Virtues of Kalimah Tayyibah

This Kalimah constitutes the fundamental basis of Deen and the root of Imaan (faith). Therefore, the greater the devotion to this Kalimah, the more firmly will Imaan be rooted. Imaan depends on this Kalimah and the very existence of this world depends on it. According to a Hadith, the Day of Qiyaamah will not dawn as long as there exists on Earth a single person reciting the Kalimah. In other Ahaadith it is mentioned that as long as there lives a single man on Earth who remembers Allah Ta'ala, Qiyaamah will not take place.

Hadith 2 – **The special Zikr of Moosa** (alayhis salaam)

عَنْ اَبِيْ سَعِيْدٍ الْخُدْرِيِّ رَضِيَ اللهُ عَنْهُ عَنْ رَسُوْلِ اللهِ صَلَّى اللهُ عَلَيْهِ وَسَلَّمَ اَنَّهُ قَالَ قَالَ مُوْسَى عَلَيْهِ السَّلَامُ يَا رَبِّ عَلِّمْنِيْ شَيْئًا اَذْكُرُكَ بِهِ وَاَدْعُوْكَ بِهِ قَالَ قُلْ لَّا اِلٰهَ اِلَّا اللهُ قَالَ يَا رَبِّ كُلُّ عِبَادِكَ يَقُوْلُ هٰذَا قَالَ قُلْ لَّا اِلٰهَ اِلَّا اللهُ قَالَ اِنَّمَا اُرِيْدُ شَيْئًا تَخُصُّنِيْ بِهِ قَالَ يَا مُوْسٰى لَوْ اَنَّ السَّمٰوَاتِ السَّبْعَ وَالْاَرَضِيْنَ السَّبْعَ فِيْ كَفَّةٍ وَّلَا اِلٰهَ اِلَّا اللهُ فِيْ كَفَّةٍ مَالَتْ بِهِمْ لَا اِلٰهَ اِلَّا اللهُ (رواه النسائى # ١٠٦٠٢)

Hadhrat Abu Saeed Khudri ﷺ narrates that Rasulullah ﷺ is reported to have said: "Once Hadhrat Moosa (alayhis salaam) made dua to Allah Ta'ala to teach him some form of zikr for his remembrance. He was advised to recite laailaaha illallaah. He submitted: 'O my Lord! This zikr is recited by all the creation.' Again came the reply was: 'Recite laailaaha illallaah.' He submitted: 'O my Sustainer, I want something special, exclusively meant for me.' Then Allah Ta'ala said: 'If the seven heavens and the seven earths were placed in one pan of the scale, and the Kalimah laailaaha illallaah in the other, the Kalimah will outweigh the seven heavens and earths.'"

Note: It is the way of Allah Ta'ala that those things whose need is greater are provided in abundance. It will be observed that Allah Ta'ala has provided the most essential necessities of life such as air and water plentiful and in abundance. It is, however, Ikhlaas (purity of intention) that determines the value of things in the eye of Allah Ta'ala. The greater the Ikhlaas in an action, the greater will be its value. And if Ikhlaas and devotion is less, then lesser is the value. Nothing is more effective than this Kalimah for this purpose. This Kalimah is also known as the purifier of hearts (جِلَاءُ الْقُلُوْبِ). Sufis prescribe zikr of this Kalimah for purification of the heart and advise its recitation as a daily routine; not only in hundreds but in thousands.

Mulla Ali Qari *(rahmatullahi alayh)* writes that a mureed once complained to his Shaikh that, despite making zikr, his heart remained inattentive. The Shaikh replied: "Go on with your zikr firmly, and thank Allah Ta'ala for His Grace that He enabled one part of your body, i.e. the tongue, to remain busy in His zikr, and make dua to Allah Ta'ala for a devoted heart." A similar incident is related in *'Ihyaaul Uloom'* about Abu Usmaan Maghribi, who gave the same reply to a similar complaint made by one of his mureeds, and he prescribed the same remedy. As a matter of fact, zikr is the best cure.

Allah Ta'ala says in the Qur-aan, "If you show gratitude to Me, I will grant you even more than before." Likewise the Hadith says, "Zikr of Allah Ta'ala is a great blessing; be thankful to Him for having enabled you to make His zikr."

Hadith 3 – Who will Benefit most from the Intercession of Nabi ﷺ?

عَنْ اَبِيْ هُرَيْرَةَ رَضِيَ اللهُ عَنْهُ اَنَّهُ قَالَ قُلْتُ يَا رَسُوْلَ اللهِ مَنْ اَسْعَدُ النَّاسِ بِشَفَاعَتِكَ يَوْمَ الْقِيَامَةِ قَالَ رَسُوْلُ اللهِ صَلَّى اللهُ عَلَيْهِ وَسَلَّمَ لَقَدْ ظَنَنْتُ يَا اَبَا هُرَيْرَةَ اَنْ لَّا يَسْاَلَنِيْ عَنْ هٰذَا الْحَدِيْثِ اَحَدٌ اَوَّلَ مِنْكَ لِمَا رَاَيْتُ مِنْ حِرْصِكَ عَلَى الْحَدِيْثِ اَسْعَدُ النَّاسِ بِشَفَاعَتِيْ يَوْمَ الْقِيَامَةِ مَنْ قَالَ لَاۤ اِلٰهَ اِلَّا اللهُ خَالِصًا مِّنْ قَلْبِهٖ اَوْ نَفْسِهٖ (رواه البخاری # ٩٩)

Hadhrat Abu Hurayrah ؓ once enquired from Rasulullah ﷺ as to who would be most benefitted by his intercession on the Day of Qiyaamah. Rasulullah ﷺ replied, "Knowing your desire for Ilm (knowledge) of Ahaadith, I could expect that none other than you would have asked this question earlier." Thereafter Rasulullah ﷺ told Abu Hurayrah ؓ that the most blessed or the most benefitted by my intercession will be the person who proclaims laailaaha illallaah with Ikhlaas (sincerity).

Chapter 2 – Virtues of Kalimah Tayyibah

Note: The meaning of good fortune here is to get something good through the Grace of Allah Ta'ala. That the person reciting the Kalimah with Ikhlaas will be most deserving to be benefitted by the intercession of Rasulullah ﷺ, can be interpreted in two ways. Firstly, such a person could be one who has just embraced Islam with sincerity, and has done no other good deed except the recitation of the Kalimah. Evidently he can be helped only by virtue of this intercession, because he has no good deed to his credit. In this case, this Hadith is supported by other Ahaadith, in which it is stated that the intercession will be for those guilty of major sins who shall have been sent to the Jahannam because of their sins, but by virtue of their recitation of the Kalimah Tayyibah they will be released through the intercession of Rasulullah ﷺ. Secondly, the most deserving people to be benefitted will be those who continually recite this Kalimah with sincerity and they have to their credit other good deeds as well. Being most fortunate means that they will be benefitted most by the intercession of Rasulullah ﷺ in raising their status in Jannah.

Allamah Ainee *(rahmatullahi alayh)* has stated that Rasulullah ﷺ will intercede in six different ways on the Day of Qiyaamah. Firstly, it will be for relief from the intolerable distress and suspense in the maydaan-e-hashar (plain of judgement), where all the people will be afflicted in various ways and will even prefer to be sent to Jahannam so that their present worries may come to an end. They will go to all the high-ranking Ambiyaa *(alayhimus salaam)*, one by one, and beg them to intercede before Allah Ta'ala, but none of them will dare to do so. At last, Rasulullah ﷺ will intercede and this intercession will be in favour of all the people, including jinn and mankind, believers and non-believers, all of whom will be benefitted by it, as explained in detail in the Ahaadith describing Qiyaamah. Secondly, Rasulullah ﷺ will intercede for easing of punishment to some non-believers; as mentioned in the Hadith about Abu Taalib. Thirdly, his intercession will be for the release from Jahannam of some of the Believers who have already been thrown in there. Fourthly, it will be for the pardon from Jahannam of some Believers, who on account of their misdeeds had been condemned to it. Fifthly, it will be in favour of some Believers for their admittance into Jannah, without requiring them to render an account of their deeds. Sixthly, it will be for raising the status of the Believers in general.

Hadith 4 – Reading the Kalimah with Ikhlaas

عَنْ زَيْدِ بْنِ اَرْقَمَ رَضِىَ اللهُ عَنْهُ قَالَ قَالَ رَسُوْلُ اللهِ صَلَّى اللهُ عَلَيْهِ وَسَلَّمَ مَنْ قَالَ لَا اِلٰهَ اِلَّا اللهُ مُخْلِصًا دَخَلَ الْجَنَّةَ قِيْلَ وَمَا اِخْلَاصُهَا قَالَ اَنْ تَحْجِزَهُ عَنْ مَحَارِمِ اللهِ

(رواه الطبرانى # ۱۲۳۵)

Hadhrat Zaid bin Arqam ﷺ narrates that Rasulullah ﷺ had said, "One who recites laailaaha illallaah with Ikhlaas will enter Jannah." Somebody asked, "What is the sign of Ikhlaas?" He explained "That it (i.e. laailaaha illallaah) prevents one from indulging in forbidden things.

Note: It is apparent that one who abstains from forbidden things and professes Imaan in *laailaaha illallaah*, will directly be admitted into Jannah. But if one has indulged in some forbidden things and has been sent to Jahannam, even then, through the blessings of this Kalimah, he will, sometime, after undergoing punishment for his sins, certainly be transferred to Jannah. But if his sins have been such that it took him out of the fold of Islam and Imaan, he will remain condemned in Jahannam forever.

Faqih Abul Laith of Samarkand has written in his book *'Tambeeh-ul-Ghaafileen'*, "It is important for everyone to hymn *laailaaha illallaah* often, and also make dua to Allah Ta'ala for steadfastness in Imaan, and abstain from sins because there are many people whose sinful deeds destroy their Imaan and they die as non-believers. There can be no greater sorrow than that a man should be a Muslim throughout his life, but on the Day of Qiyaamah his name should appear in the list of non-believers. This is indeed the greatest misfortune. One does not feel sorry for a person who has, throughout his life, worshipped in a church or a temple and in the Aakhirah be listed among the non-believers, but it is a matter of great grief that he who had remained in the masjid should be counted as one of the non-believers. This happens as a result of excessive sinning and secretly being involved in forbidden things. Many people get unlawful possession of something knowingly, but they delay in returning it or having it forgiven and they happen to die before returning it or getting forgiven, then they are in deep trouble. There are some who divorce their wives and knowingly continue living together (and continue sharing the bed), till death overtakes them. In such cases, one does not get a chance of making Taubah (repentance) and, as a result, is completely deprived of his Imaan.

اَللّٰهُمَّ احْفَظْنَا مِنْهُ

May Allah Ta'ala save us!

In the books of Ahaadith, the story of a young man who was unable to recite the Kalimah at the time of his death, is related. This was brought to the notice of Rasulullah ﷺ who went to the young man and asked him what the matter was. He replied that it felt as if a lock was placed on his heart. On enquiry, it transpired that his mother was angry with him because of his misbehavior. She was called by Rasulullah ﷺ and when she came, he asked her: "If somebody lights a big fire and wants to throw your son into it, will you have mercy on him?" "I will certainly do so," she replied. "If it is so, then forgive his faults," said Rasulullah ﷺ. At this she forgave her son, and thereafter when the young man was asked to recite the kalimah he readily did so. Rasulullah ﷺ thanked Allah Ta'ala that, through his effort, the man was saved from the fire of Jahannam. There are hundreds of cases like the one mentioned above, where the evil effect of the sins, in which we get involved, results in our worldly as well as spiritual loss.

The great author of *Ihyaaul-Uloom* has related that once Rasulullah ﷺ delivered a khutba in which he said: "One who recites *laailaaha illallaah* in the manner that he does not mix it up, he becomes entitled to Jannah." Hadhrat Ali ؓ asked for the clarification of the meaning of mixing it up. Rasulullah ﷺ said: "It is to love the worldly life and hanker after it. There are many who talk like the Prophets, but act like the arrogant people and tyrants. If one recites this Kalimah while not indulging in anything of this sort, he becomes entitled to Jannah."

Hadith 5 – The Doors of the Heavens Open up for the Kalimah

عَنْ اَبِىْ هُرَيْرَةَ رَضِىَ اللهُ عَنْهُ قَالَ قَالَ رَسُوْلُ اللهِ صَلَّى اللهُ عَلَيْهِ وَسَلَّمَ مَا قَالَ عَبْدٌ لَا اِلٰهَ اِلَّا اللهُ اِلَّا فُتِحَتْ لَهُ اَبْوَابُ السَّمَاءِ حَتّٰى تُفْضِيَ اِلَى الْعَرْشِ مَا اجْتَنَبَ الْكَبَائِرَ

(رواه الترمذى # ٣٥٩٠)

Hadhrat Abu Hurayrah رَضِىَ اللهُ عَنْهُ narrates that Rasulullah ﷺ said, "There is nobody who recites laailaaha illallaah and the doors of the Heavens do not get opened to allow this Kalimah to reach the Arsh-e-Ilaahi (throne of Allah Ta'ala), provided he abstains from major sins."

Note: The excellence and acceptability of this Kalimah is proved by its going straight to the Arsh-e-Ilaahi (throne of Allah Ta'ala). It has already been stated that its recitation, even by a person who commits major sins, is not without benefit. Mulla Ali Qari *(rahmatullahi alayh)* says that the condition of being free from major sins is the key to quick acceptance and for the opening of all the doors of the Heavens. Otherwise the recitation of the Kalimah is not without reward and acceptance, in spite of major sins. Some Ulama have explained this Hadith to mean that after the death of such a person, all the doors of the Heavens are opened to welcome and honour his soul. According to another Hadith, there are two special Kalimahs, one does not stop before reaching the Throne of Allah, and the other fills the Heaven and Earth with its light or reward. One is *laailaaha illallaah* and the other is *Allahu Akbar*.

Hadith 6 – Allah Ta'ala has Promised Jannah for those who proclaim the Kalimah

عَنْ يَعْلٰى بْنِ شَدَّادٍ قَالَ حَدَّثَنِىْ اَبِىْ شَدَّادُ بْنُ اَوْسٍ وَعُبَادَةُ بْنُ الصَّامِتِ رَضِىَ اللهُ عَنْهُمَا حَاضِرٌ يُصَدِّقُ قَالَ كُنَّا عِنْدَ النَّبِىِّ صَلَّى اللهُ عَلَيْهِ وَسَلَّمَ فَقَالَ هَلْ فِيْكُمْ غَرِيْبٌ يَعْنِىْ اَهْلَ الْكِتَابِ قُلْنَا لَا يَا رَسُوْلَ اللهِ فَاَمَرَ بِغَلْقِ الْبَابِ وَقَالَ ارْفَعُوْا اَيْدِيَكُمْ وَقُوْلُوْا لَا اِلٰهَ اِلَّا اللهُ فَرَفَعْنَا اَيْدِيَنَا سَاعَةً ثُمَّ قَالَ الْحَمْدُ لِلّٰهِ اَللّٰهُمَّ اِنَّكَ بَعَثْتَنِىْ بِهٰذِهِ الْكَلِمَةِ وَوَعَدْتَنِىْ

عَلَيْهَا الْجَنَّةَ وَاَنْتَ لَا تُخْلِفُ الْمِيْعَادَ ثُمَّ قَالَ اَبْشِرُوْا فَاِنَّ اللهَ قَدْ غَفَرَ لَكُمْ (رواه احمد # ۱۷۱۲۱)

Hadhrat Shaddaad ibnu Aws رَضِىَ اللهُ عَنْهُ relates and Hadhrat Ubaadah رَضِىَ اللهُ عَنْهُ confirms that, "Once we were sitting with Rasulullah صَلَّى اللهُ عَلَيْهِ وَسَلَّمَ and he asked if there was any stranger (i.e. non-Muslim) sitting in the gathering. We replied that there was none. He then had the door closed and asked us to raise our hands and recite laailaaha illallaah. We raised our hands for some time and recited the Kalimah (Tayyibah). He then exclaimed: O Allah! You have sent me with this Kalimah. You have promised Jannah for those who profess it, and Your promise never remains unfulfilled. Then he turned to us and said: 'Be happy, Allah has blessed you with His forgiveness'."

Note: Rasulullah صَلَّى اللهُ عَلَيْهِ وَسَلَّمَ had made sure that no stranger was present, and he had got the door closed because most probably he had every hope that those particular people would be forgiven by virtue of reciting the Kalimah. And he had no such hope in respect of non-believers.

The Sufis quote this Hadith as an argument for making their mureeds engage in zikr collectively. It is stated in *'Jaamiul-Usool'* that there were instances when Rasulullah صَلَّى اللهُ عَلَيْهِ وَسَلَّمَ made his companions make zikr collectively and also individually. This Hadith is quoted as authority for making zikr collectively. The closing of the door would be to help those present to concentrate better. The enquiry about the presence of any stranger might also be for the same reason; it may not have distracted Rasulullah صَلَّى اللهُ عَلَيْهِ وَسَلَّمَ, but there was likelihood of others getting distracted.

چہ خوش است با تو بزمے بنہفتہ ساز کردن

در خانہ بند کردن سرِ شیشہ باز کردن

How exciting is it to be in solitude with you, to close the door behind me and open the lid of the bottle

Hadith 7 – Renewing our Imaan

عَنْ اَبِیْ هُرَيْرَةَ رَضِیَ اللهُ عَنْهُ قَالَ قَالَ رَسُوْلُ اللهِ صَلَّى اللهُ عَلَيْهِ وَسَلَّمَ جَدِّدُوْا اِيْمَانَكُمْ قِيْلَ يَا رَسُوْلَ اللهِ وَكَيْفَ نُجَدِّدُ اِيْمَانَنَا قَالَ اَكْثِرُوْا مِنْ قَوْلِ لَا اِلٰهَ اِلَّا اللهُ

(رواه احمد #)

Hadhrat Abu Hurayrah ﷺ narrates that Rasulullah ﷺ said: "Keep on renewing your Imaan." "O Rasulullah! how should we renew our Imaan?" enquired the Sahaabah. "Recite laailaaha illallaah in abundance," was the reply.

Note: In one Hadith, Rasulullah ﷺ is reported to have said, "Like old clothes, Imaan also gets worn out. Therefore, keep on making dua to Allah Ta'ala to renew it." Imaan getting weak means that it loses strength and radiance on account of sins. Thus it is stated in one Hadith that, when a man commits a sin, a dark spot appears on his heart. If he makes sincere Taubah (repentance), this spot gets washed away, otherwise it remains there. When he commits another sin, another black dot appears on the heart. Thus, on account of further sins, the black dots continue to increase, until ultimately the heart is all blackened and rusted, as described in the Qur-aan Shareef in Surah Mutaffifeen.

كَلَّا بَلْ ۫ رَانَ عَلٰى قُلُوْبِهِمْ مَّا كَانُوْا يَكْسِبُوْنَ

Nay, but that which they have earned is rust upon their hearts.
(Surah Mutaffifeen - Aayah 14)

When such a stage is reached, the heart is no longer influenced by the truth. It is said in one Hadith, "Four things cause ruin to the heart; debating with foolish people, excessive sinning, excessive mixing with women and remaining in the company of dead people." Somebody enquired, "What is meant by 'dead people'?" Rasulullah ﷺ explained that it meant such wealthy persons who have pride because of their wealth.

Chapter 2 – Virtues of Kalimah Tayyibah

Hadith 8 - Recite *"laailaaha illallaah"* very often before your death

وَعَنْ اَبِىْ هُرَيْرَةَ رَضِىَ اللهُ عَنْهُ قَالَ قَالَ رَسُوْلُ اللهِ صَلَّى اللهُ عَلَيْهِ وَسَلَّمَ اَكْثِرُوْا مِنْ شَهَادَةِ اَنْ لَّا اِلٰهَ اِلَّا اللهُ قَبْلَ اَنْ يُّحَالَ بَيْنَكُمْ وَبَيْنَهَا (اخرجه المنذرى فى الترغيب # ٢٣٥٥)

Hadhrat Abu Hurayrah ﵁ narrates that Rasulullah ﷺ said, "Recite laailaaha illallaah very often, before the time (of death) comes when you will not be able to say it."

Note: No deed is possible after death. This life is very short, and it is time for action and for sowing seeds. This life after death is infinitely long, and it is over there that we will reap whatever we have sown here.

Hadith 9 – Jahannam becomes forbidden on the one who recites the Kalimah

عَنْ عُمَرَ بْنِ الْخَطَّابِ رَضِىَ اللهُ عَنْهُ قَالَ سَمِعْتُ رَسُوْلَ اللهِ صَلَّى اللهُ عَلَيْهِ وَسَلَّمَ يَقُوْلُ اِنِّىْ لَاَعْلَمُ كَلِمَةً لَّا يَقُوْلُهَا عَبْدٌ حَقًّا مِّنْ قَلْبِهِ فَيَمُوْتُ عَلٰى ذٰلِكَ اِلَّا حُرِّمَ عَلَى النَّارِ لَا اِلٰهَ اِلَّا اللهُ (رواه الحاكم # ٢٤٢)

Hadhrat Umar ﵁ narrates that Rasulullah ﷺ said, "I know of a Kalimah, that if anybody recites it regarding it to be true from his heart and then dies upon that belief, Jahannam becomes forbidden for him. This Kalimah is laailaaha illallaah."

Note: This subject matter has been related in many Ahaadith. If the person referred to in the above Hadith has been a new convert to Islam, then there can be no doubt about the meaning, because it is unanimously agreed that on embracing Islam all one's sins committed as a non-Muslim are forgiven. But if it refers to a born Muslim, who recites the Kalimah with sincerity just before his death, even then it is hoped that Allah Ta'ala, through His sheer Grace, may forgive all his sins. Allah Ta'ala has Himself said that He may forgive any sin He wishes, except Shirk.

Mulla Ali Qari *(rahmatullahi alayh)* has stated that some Ulama are of the view that these Ahaadith apply to the very early period of Islam when detailed commandments had not yet been revealed. Some scholars have stated that the Hadith implies declaration of the Kalimah with proper discharge of one's obligations enjoined by it as given under Hadith number four above. Hasan Basri *(rahmatullahi alayh)* and many others also hold this view. According to the considered view of Imaam Bukhaari *(rahmatullahi alayh)*, this promise holds true if the declaration of the Kalimah before death is accompanied by sincerity and regret, which is the essence of taubah. According to Mulla Ali Qari *(rahmatullahi alayh)*, the reciter will not be doomed to Jahannam forever. It is a matter of common observation that sometimes the inherent quality of a thing becomes ineffective due to some obstacle. For instance, a laxative may become ineffective if it is followed by medication that causes constipation. This does not mean that the laxative doesn't work; its effect did not manifest itself because of an opposing medication.

Hadith 10 – The keys to Jannah

عَنْ مُعَاذِ بْنِ جَبَلٍ رَضِيَ اللّٰهُ عَنْهُ قَالَ قَالَ رَسُوْلُ اللّٰهِ صَلَّى اللّٰهُ عَلَيْهِ وَسَلَّمَ مَفَاتِيْحُ الْجَنَّةِ شَهَادَةُ اَنْ لَّا اِلٰهَ اِلَّا اللّٰهُ (رواه احمد # ٢٢١٠٢)

Hadhrat Muaaz bin Jabal ﷺ narrates that Rasulullah ﷺ said, "Professing faith in laailaaha illallaah is the keys to Jannah."

Note: The Kalimah has been described as the keys of Jannah, because it serves as the key for opening every door and every part of Jannah. Therefore, the Kalimah has all the keys. Alternatively, it is called the keys, because the Kalimah itself is made up of two parts; one is *laailaaha illallaah* and the other is *Muhammadur Rasulullah*. Thus, Jannah may be said to open with these two keys. In these Ahaadith, wherever the Kalimah is stated to cause entry into Jannah or protection against Jahannam, it means the complete Kalimah comprising both the parts. In one Hadith, it is said that the price of Jannah is *laailaaha illallaah*.

Hadith 11 – Sins are replaced by Virtues

عَنْ اَنَسٍ رَضِىَ اللهُ عَنْهُ قَالَ قَالَ رَسُوْلُ اللهِ صَلَّى اللهُ عَلَيْهِ وَسَلَّمَ مَا مِنْ عَبْدٍ قَالَ لَا اِلٰهَ اِلَّا اللهُ فِىْ سَاعَةٍ مِّنْ لَيْلٍ اَوْ نَهَارٍ اِلَّا طُمِسَتْ مَا فِى الصَّحِيْفَةِ مِنَ السَّيِّاٰتِ حَتّٰى تَسْكُنَ اِلٰى مِثْلِهَا مِنَ الْحَسَنَاتِ (اخرجه المنذرى فى الترغيب # ٢٣٥٧)

Hadhrat Anas ؓ narrates that Rasulullah ﷺ said, "Whosoever recites laailaaha illallaah any time during the day or the night, his sins are deleted from his record of deeds and virtues are written in its place."

Note: The replacement of sins by virtues has been fully described under Hadith number ten of Chapter one Part two, where various meanings of all the aayaat and Ahaadith of this kind are given. According to every version, this Hadith definitely states that sins are washed away from the account of a person's deeds, provided there is Ikhlaas, i.e. sincerity of intention. In any case, making zikr of the blessed name of Allah Ta'ala and excessive recitation of Kalimah Tayyibah also develops Ikhlaas. Therefore, this blessed Kalimah is also called the "Kalimah of Ikhlaas."

Hadith 12 – The pillar of noor shakes when one recites the Kalimah

عَنْ اَبِىْ هُرَيْرَةَ رَضِىَ اللهُ عَنْهُ عَنِ النَّبِىِّ صَلَّى اللهُ عَلَيْهِ وَسَلَّمَ قَالَ اِنَّ لِلّٰهِ تَبَارَكَ وَتَعَالٰى عَمُوْدًا مِّنْ نُوْرٍ بَيْنَ يَدَىِ الْعَرْشِ فَاِذَا قَالَ الْعَبْدُ لَا اِلٰهَ اِلَّا اللهُ اِهْتَزَّ ذٰلِكَ الْعَمُوْدُ فَيَقُوْلُ اللهُ تَبَارَكَ وَتَعَالٰى اُسْكُنْ فَيَقُوْلُ كَيْفَ اَسْكُنُ وَلَمْ يُغْفَرْ لِقَائِلِهَا فَيَقُوْلُ اِنِّىْ قَدْ غَفَرْتُ لَهٗ فَيَسْكُنُ عِنْدَ ذٰلِكَ (رواه البزار # ٨٠٦٥)

Hadhrat Abu Hurayrah ؓ narrates that Rasulullah ﷺ said, "There is a pillar of Noor (Divine Light) in front of the Arsh (the Throne of Allah Ta'ala). When somebody recites laailaaha illallaah, this pillar starts shaking. When Allah Ta'ala tells it to stop shaking, it says, 'How can I stop, when the reciter of the Kalimah has not yet been granted forgiveness?' Thereupon Allah Ta'ala says: 'Well, I have forgiven him,' and then that pillar stops shaking."

Note: Some scholars of Hadith have debated the authenticity of this Hadith, but Allama Suyuti *(rahmatullahi alayh)* has written that this Hadith has been narrated with some differences in wordings through many sources. According to some narrations, Allah Ta'ala also says, "I have made him utter the Kalimah in order that I may grant him forgiveness." How kind and benevolent is Allah Ta'ala that He himself graces a person with the power to do this virtuous act, and then grants forgiveness on this basis to complete His extreme favour.

In this connection, the well-known story about Hadhrat Ataa *(rahmatullahi alayh)* is told and this story is quite popular. He once happened to go to the market where a mad slave woman was on sale. He purchased her. At midnight she got up, performed wudhu, and began offering Salaah. During her Salaah she wept so profusely that her breath was getting choked. Then she said: "O my Rabb! In the name of the love that You have for me, bestow Your Mercy on me." Hearing this, Ataa said "O slave woman, say: 'O Allah, in the name of the love that I have for You.'" Upon hearing this she got upset and said, "By Allah! If He had not loved me, He would not have let you sleep and made me stand in Salaah as you see!" Then she recited the following couplets:

$$\text{اَلْكَرْبُ مُجْتَمِعٌ وَالْقَلْبُ مُحْتَرِقٌ وَالصَّبْرُ مُفْتَرِقٌ وَالدَّمْعُ مُسْتَبِقٌ}$$

My restlessness is increasing, and my heart is burning. Patience has forsaken me and my tears are flowing.

$$\text{كَيْفَ الْقَرَارُ عَلٰى مَنْ لَّا قَرَارَ لَهُ مِمَّا جَنَاهُ الْهَوٰى وَالشَّوْقُ وَالْقَلَقُ}$$

How can one have peace of mind, when one is all affected by the pangs of love and restlessness?

$$\text{يَا رَبِّ اِنْ كَانَ شَىْءٌ فِيْهِ لِىْ فَرَجٌ فَامْنُنْ عَلَىَّ بِهٖ مَا دَامَ بِىْ رَمَقٌ}$$

O Allah! If there is anything which can help me to get rid of my grief, please bestow it upon me as a favour!

Then she said, O Allah! Until now no one knew about the deal between You and me, since it is no more a secret now, take me away from here. Saying this, she uttered a shriek and breathed her last. There have been many other incidents similar to this. It is a fact that Allah Ta'ala alone grants the power to do good.

وَمَا تَشَآءُوْنَ اِلَّآ اَنْ يَّشَآءَ اللهُ رَبُّ الْعٰلَمِيْنَ

"And if Allah, the Sustainer of the Universe does not will it, you cannot even wish for anything." (Surah Takweer - Aayah 29)

Hadith 13 – Those who believe in the Kalimah will have no fear

عَنِ ابْنِ عُمَرَ رَضِيَ اللهُ عَنْهُ قَالَ قَالَ رَسُوْلُ اللهِ صَلَّى اللهُ عَلَيْهِ وَسَلَّمَ لَيْسَ عَلٰى اَهْلِ لَا اِلٰهَ اِلَّا اللهُ وَحْشَةٌ فِيْ قُبُوْرِهِمْ وَلَا مَنْشَرِهِمْ وَكَاَنِّيْ اَنْظُرُ اِلٰى اَهْلِ لَا اِلٰهَ اِلَّا اللهُ وَهُمْ يَنْفُضُوْنَ التُّرَابَ عَنْ رُءُوْسِهِمْ وَيَقُوْلُوْنَ اَلْحَمْدُ لِلهِ الَّذِيْ اَذْهَبَ عَنَّا الْحَزَنَ

(رواه الطبراني # ٩٤٧٨)

Hadhrat Ibnu Umar ؓ narrates that Rasulullah ﷺ said, "The people of laailaaha illallaah will neither have fear in the grave nor on the Day of Qiyaamah. It is as if I see the scene when they will rise from their graves, wiping dust from their heads and saying: 'All praise is for Allah, who has cast off (forever) all worry and fear from us.'"

It is stated in another Hadith that those who profess *laailaaha illallaah* will neither experience affliction at the time of death nor in the grave.

Note: Hadhrat Ibn Abbaas ؓ says: "Once Hadhrat Jibra-eel *(alayhis salaam)* came to Rasulullah ﷺ when he was very worried and Jibra-eel *(alayhis salaam)* said: 'Allah Ta'ala has sent His salaams to you and has enquired: "Why do you look so sad and worried!" (Although Allah Ta'ala knows whatever is hidden in the hearts, yet by such questions Allah Ta'ala shows honour, respect and favours). Rasulullah ﷺ replied, "O Jibra-eel! I am very worried about my Ummat, as to how they will fare on the Day of Qiyaamah!" "Is it about the non-believers or about the Muslims?" asked Jibra-eel *(alayhis salaam)*. "About the Muslims" replied Rasulullah ﷺ. Jibra-eel *(alayhis salaam)* then took Rasulullah ﷺ along to a graveyard where the people of the tribe of Banu Salama were buried. There he struck a grave with his wing and said قُمْ بِإِذْنِ اللهِ (stand up by the order of Allah). Out of that grave, an extremely handsome man stood up, and he was reciting لَا إِلٰهَ إِلَّا اللهُ مُحَمَّدٌ رَسُوْلُ اللهِ الْحَمْدُ لِلهِ رَبِّ الْعَالَمِيْنَ.

Hadhrat Jibra-eel *(alayhis salaam)* told him to go back to his place, which he did. Then he struck another grave with his wing. Out of it stood up an extremely ugly person with black face and worried eyes, who was saying, "Alas, there is nothing but sorrow, shame and horror!" Hadhrat Jibra-eel *(alayhis salaam)* told him to go back to his place, and then explained to Rasulullah ﷺ, "The people will rise up on the Day of Qiyaamah in the same state that they were at the time of their death."

In the Hadith under discussion, the people of *laailaaha illallaah* apparently imply those who have a special and close attachment to the Kalimah and remain busy with its recitation, just as in common usage descriptions such as milkman, shoe-man, pearl-man and ice-man etc. are used for people who have a special interest and involvement in those things. Thus, there is no doubt whatsoever that the people of this Kalimah, will receive this extraordinary treatment. In Surah Faatir of the Qur-aan Shareef, three categories of this Ummat have been described; one category is named سَابِقٌ بِالْخَيْرَاتِ (leaders in virtues), about whom it is stated in a Hadith that they will enter Jannah without any reckoning. According to one Hadith, a person who recites *laailaaha illallaah* one hundred times daily will be raised up on the Day of Qiyaamah with his face shining like the full moon. Hadhrat Abu Darda ؓ narrated that those whose tongues remain busy in the zikr of Allah Ta'ala will enter Jannah smiling (happily).

Hadith 14 – Ninety-nine registers of sins weighed against the Kalimah on the scale

عَنْ عَبْدِ اللهِ بْنِ عَمْرِو بْنِ الْعَاصِ رَضِيَ اللهُ عَنْهُ أَنَّ رَسُوْلَ اللهِ صَلَّى اللهُ عَلَيْهِ وَسَلَّمَ قَالَ إِنَّ اللهَ يَسْتَخْلِصُ رَجُلًا مِّنْ أُمَّتِيْ عَلَى رُءُوْسِ الْخَلَائِقِ يَوْمَ الْقِيَامَةِ فَيَنْشُرُ عَلَيْهِ تِسْعَةً وَّتِسْعِيْنَ سِجِلًّا كُلُّ سِجِلٍّ مِثْلُ مَدِّ الْبَصَرِ ثُمَّ يَقُوْلُ أَتُنْكِرُ مِنْ هٰذَا شَيْئًا أَظَلَمَكَ كَتَبَتِيَ الْحَافِظُوْنَ فَيَقُوْلُ لَا يَا رَبِّ فَيَقُوْلُ أَفَلَكَ عُذْرٌ فَيَقُوْلُ لَا يَا رَبِّ فَيَقُوْلُ اللهُ تَعَالٰى

Chapter 2 – Virtues of Kalimah Tayyibah

بَلْ اِنَّ لَكَ عِنْدَنَا حَسَنَةً فَاِنَّهُ لَا ظُلْمَ عَلَيْكَ الْيَوْمَ فَتُخْرَجُ بِطَاقَةٌ فِيْهَا اَشْهَدُ اَنْ لَّا اِلٰهَ اِلَّا اللهُ وَاَشْهَدُ اَنَّ مُحَمَّدًا عَبْدُهُ وَرَسُوْلُهُ فَيَقُوْلُ اُحْضُرْ وَزْنَكَ فَيَقُوْلُ يَا رَبِّ مَا هٰذِهِ الْبِطَاقَةُ مَعَ هٰذِهِ السِّجِلَّاتِ فَقَالَ فَاِنَّكَ لَا تُظْلَمُ الْيَوْمَ فَتُوْضَعُ السِّجِلَّاتُ فِيْ كَفَّةٍ وَّالْبِطَاقَةُ فِيْ كَفَّةٍ فَطَاشَتِ السِّجِلَّاتُ وَثَقُلَتِ الْبِطَاقَةُ فَلَا يَثْقُلُ مَعَ اللهِ شَيْءٌ

(رواه الترمذى # ٢٦٣٩)

Hadhrat Abdullah ibnu Amr ibnul Aas ﷺ narrates that Rasulullah ﷺ said, "On the Day of Qiyaamat, Allah Ta'ala will select a man from my Ummat and will call him in the presence of all mankind, and then 99 registers of his sins will be opened before him, each register as long as one can see. He will then be asked if he denies anything recorded in his account of deeds, or whether the Malaaikah who were appointed to record his deeds had been unjust to him in any respect. He will reply in the negative (i.e. he will neither deny anything nor blame the Malaaikah for any injustice to him). Then Allah Ta'ala will ask him if he can justify his misdeeds, but he will reply that he has no excuse to offer. Then Allah Ta'ala will say, "Well, there is indeed one virtue to your credit. Today no injustice will be done to you." Then a small piece of paper with the Kalimah written on it will be handed over to him, and he will be asked to go and get it weighed. He will submit that this small piece of paper will be of little avail against so many lengthy registers. Allah will say, "This day, no injustice will be done to you." Then all the registers will be placed in one pan and the piece of paper in the other pan. The pan with the registers will fly up in the air on account of the excessive weight of that piece of paper. The truth of the matter is that nothing is weightier than the name of Allah Ta'ala."

Note: This is purely the blessed result of Ikhlaas that, a single recitation of the Kalimah Tayyibah with sincerity can outweigh all the misdeeds recorded in so many registers. Therefore, it is necessary that one should not look down upon any Muslim and think himself to be superior to him. Who knows that Allah Ta'ala may accept from him some deeds which may suffice for his salvation. And, on the other hand nobody can be sure about himself whether any of his deeds will be found worthy of acceptance.

The story of two people belonging to the Bani Israa-eel is related in one Hadith; one of whom was a worshipper and the other was a sinner. The worshipper always criticised the latter, who used to reply: "Leave me to my Creator." One day, the worshipper, in a fit of anger, said: "By Allah! you will never be forgiven." Allah Ta'ala assembled them in His presence and pardoned the sinner because he had always expected mercy from Allah Ta'ala, but ordered punishment for the worshipper due to the oath he took. No doubt the oath was terrible and it was directly conflicting with declaration of forgiveness by Allah Ta'ala in the Aayah;

اِنَّ اللّٰهَ لَا يَغْفِرُ اَنْ يُّشْرَكَ بِهٖ وَيَغْفِرُ مَا دُوْنَ ذٰلِكَ لِمَنْ يَّشَآءُ

(Allah Ta'ala will not forgive Kufr and Shirk but apart from that, He may forgive any sin as He may like).

So how can anybody take such an oath that a particular person will not be forgiven? This does not mean that we should not warn others against sins and undesirable things, and remind others to abstain from these. At hundreds of places in the Qur-aan Shareef and in the books of Hadith, there are warnings for not forbidding people from evil. It is stated in many Ahaadith that the people who see a sin being committed and do not stop it, in spite of their having power to do so, will also share in the punishment for that sin. This point has been discussed by me in detail in my book, Fazaail-e-Tabligh, which can be consulted if desired.

At this point an important word of caution should be heeded to. Just as it is extremely wrong to condemn sinful Muslims as absolute dwellers of Jahannam, it is equally dangerous on the part of ignorant people to accept any person as their spiritual guide, in spite of him being devoid of good practices and his making senseless and un-Islamic statements. Rasulullah ﷺ has said: "Whosoever respects a bidati (innovator) in Islam is counted from amongst those who helped in demolishing Islam." It is stated in several Ahaadith that in times to come, there will appear many imposters, cheats and liars, who will relate Ahaadith that you will have never heard before. Beware of such people, lest they should mislead you and put you into trouble (fitnah).

Hadith 15 – The weight of the Kalimah will outweigh the weight of the Skies and the Earth

عَنِ ابْنِ عَبَّاسٍ رَضِيَ اللهُ عَنْهُ قَالَ قَالَ رَسُوْلُ اللهِ صَلَّى اللهُ عَلَيْهِ وَسَلَّمَ وَالَّذِيْ نَفْسِيْ بِيَدِهِ لَوْ جِئْءَ بِالسَّمَاوَاتِ وَالْأَرْضِ وَمَنْ فِيْهِنَّ وَمَا بَيْنَهُنَّ وَمَا تَحْتَهُنَّ فَوُضِعْنَ فِيْ كَفَّةِ الْمِيْزَانِ وَوُضِعَتْ شَهَادَةُ اَنْ لَّا اِلٰهَ اِلَّا اللهُ فِى الْكَفَّةِ الْأُخْرَى لَرَجَحَتْ بِهِنَّ

(اخرجه الهيثمى فى مجمع الزوائد # ٣٩١٦)

Hadhrat Ibn Abbaas ﷺ narrates that Rasulullah ﷺ said: "I swear by Allah Who controls my life that if all the skies and the earth, with all the people and all the things between them and all that may be within them, are placed together in one pan of the scale, and Imaan in laailaaha illallaah is put in the other pan, the latter will outweigh the former."

Note: This subject matter has been discussed in many Ahaadith. It declares that undoubtedly nothing can be equal to the blessed name of Allah Ta'ala. It is really a great misfortune and deprivation for those who take it lightly. However, the weight of this Kalimah is proportionate to the Ikhlaas with which it is uttered. The greater the Ikhlaas, the weightier becomes the Kalimah. To achieve this Ikhlaas, one has to remain in the service of the Mashaaikh. According to one Hadith, the above-mentioned saying of Rasulullah ﷺ was in connection with another subject matter. He has said: "Encourage a dying person to recite *laailaaha illallaah* because he who recites this Kalimah at the time of his death gets entry into Jannah." The Sahaabah ﷺ enquired: "O Rasulullah! (ﷺ) what about reciting it during good health?" He replied, "Then it is even more effective in making the individual worthy of Jannah," and then stated, on oath, the Hadith related above.

Hadith 16 - What is most weighty in Testimony

عَنِ ابْنِ عَبَّاسٍ رَضِيَ اللهُ عَنْهُ قَالَ جَاءَ النَّحَّامُ بْنُ زَيْدٍ وَقُرْدُ بْنُ كَعْبٍ وَبَحْرِىُّ بْنُ عَمْرٍو فَقَالُوْا يَا مُحَمَّدُ مَا تَعْلَمُ مَعَ اللهِ اِلٰهًا غَيْرَهُ فَقَالَ رَسُوْلُ اللهِ صَلَّى اللهُ عَلَيْهِ وَسَلَّمَ

$$\text{لَا اِلٰهَ اِلَّا اللّٰهُ بِذٰلِكَ بُعِثْتُ وَاِلٰى ذٰلِكَ اَدْعُوْ فَاَنْزَلَ اللّٰهُ تَعَالٰى فِىْ قَوْلِهِمْ ۚ قُلْ اَىُّ شَىْءٍ اَكْبَرُ شَهَادَةً الْاٰيَةَ ....(اخرجه السيوطى فى الدر المنثور ۲۵٦/۱)}$$

Hadhrat Ibn Abbaas رضى الله عنه narrates that once there came to Rasulullah ﷺ three non-Muslims who said to him: "O Muhammad! (ﷺ) don't you recognise anybody, except Allah as worthy of worship?" In reply, Rasulullah ﷺ recited (laailaaha illallaah) (Nobody is worthy of worship except Allah), and added: "I have been deputed specifically for the propagation of this Kalimah, and I invite all mankind towards it."

It was in this connection that the following aayah was revealed.

$$\text{قُلْ اَىُّ شَىْءٍ اَكْبَرُ شَهَادَةً}$$

"What is most weighty in testimony?" (Surah An'aam - Aayah 19)

Note: The words of Rasulullah ﷺ, "I have been appointed (as a Nabi) specifically for the propagation of this Kalimah and I invite all mankind to it," did not mean that only he had been sent on this special mission. In fact, all the Ambiyaa *(alayhimus salaam)* had been sent for the propagation of this Kalimah, and all of them had invited mankind to it. From Hadhrat Aadam *(alayhis salaam)* to Rasulullah ﷺ the last and the best of all the Ambiyaa *(alayhimus salaam)*, there was not a single Nabi who had not propagated this sublime Kalimah. So blessed and sublime is this Kalimah that, all the Ambiyaa *(alayhimus salaam)* and all true religions propagated it and served its cause. In fact, every true religion is based on this Kalimah. It is in support of this Kalimah that the Qur-aanic Aayah;

$$\text{قُلْ اَىُّ شَىْءٍ اَكْبَرُ شَهَادَةً}$$

had been revealed, in which Allah Ta'ala is a witness in favour of Rasulullah ﷺ. According to one Hadith, when somebody recites *laailaaha illallaah* then Allah Ta'ala testifies to it and says: "My slave has spoken the truth; there is none worthy of worship except I."

Hadith 17 – The Deeds of this Ummah would be the weightiest because of the Kalimah

عَنْ لَيْثٍ قَالَ قَالَ عِيْسَى ابْنُ مَرْيَمَ عَلَيْهِمَا السَّلَامُ أُمَّةُ مُحَمَّدٍ صَلَّى اللهُ عَلَيْهِ وَسَلَّمَ اَثْقَلُ النَّاسِ فِى الْمِيْزَانِ ذَلَّتْ اَلْسِنَتُهُمْ بِكَلِمَةٍ ثَقُلَتْ عَلٰى مَنْ كَانَ قَبْلَهُمْ لَا اِلٰهَ اِلَّا اللهُ

(اخرجه السيوطى فى الدر المنثور ٤٢٣/٦)

Hadhrat Laith رضى الله عنه narrates that Hadhrat Isa (alayhis salaam) had said: "The deeds of the Ummat of Hadhrat Muhammad ﷺ would be the weightiest on the Day of Qiyaamah because their tongues are used to the recitation of the Kalimah, which was found too hard by the Ummats of other Ambiyaa, and this Kalimah is laailaaha illallaah."

Note: It is a fact that the Ummat of Rasulullah ﷺ is devoted to this Kalimah, much more than any other Ummat. There have not only been thousands, but indeed millions of Sufis (pious persons) who had hundreds of mureeds, all of whom recited the Kalimah thousands of times daily as a matter of routine. It is stated in *'Jaamiul-Usool'* that the word "Allah" should be repeated a minimum number of five thousand times daily and there is no maximum limit for it. The Sufis are required to repeat "Allah" daily at least 25 000 times. With regards to the amount of *laailaaha illallaah*, one should read this zikr at least 5000 times daily. This number varies according to the advice of the Mashaaikh. I have related all this in support of the above saying of Hadhrat Isa *(alayhis salaam)* that the Mashaaikh have prescribed these amounts daily for each individual. Hadhrat Shah Waliullah *(rahmatullahi alayh)* has stated in his book '*Al-Qowlul Jameel*' that his father, in his early stages in Sufism, used to recite *laailaaha illallaah* 200 times in one breath.

Virtue of Reading the Kalimah 70 000 times

Shaikh Abu Yazeed Qurtubi *(rahmatullahi alayh)* writes: "When I learnt that one who recites *laailaaha illallaah* 70 000 times is safe from the fire of Jahannam, I completed this number once for my wife and then several times for myself as a provision for the Aakhirah. A young man who lived near us was known to be blessed with the power of Kashf (blessed with the ability by Allah Ta'ala to see the unseen things), even in respect of

Jannah and Jahannam, but I hesitated to believe it. Once when this young man was eating with us, he uttered a cry of agony, his breathing became difficult and he exclaimed, "I see my mother burning in the fire of Jahannam." When I saw him so worried, I thought of giving one of my complete 70 000 recitations of the Kalimah to his mother, so that the truth of what the young man said could be tested. I quietly did so in my heart, without telling anybody else about it. But as soon as I did this, the young man felt relieved and said, 'Uncle! My mother has been relieved of the punishment of Jahannam!' This incident proved useful to me in two ways: firstly, the blessing of reciting the Kalimah 70 000 times was proven by actual experience, and secondly it was established that the young man was truly blessed with the power of kashf.

This is but one of many such incidents in the lives of various individuals of this Ummat. The Sufis make their followers practice zikr so that there is no breath that goes in or comes out without the zikr of Allah Ta'ala. There are millions of people from the Ummat of Nabi Muhammad ﷺ who have adopted this practice. There is, therefore no denying the fact stated by Hadhrat Isa *(alayhis salaam)* that their tongues are especially accustomed to the recitation of the Kalimah.

Hadith 18 – Inscribed on the Door of Jannah

عَنِ ابْنِ عَبَّاسٍ رَضِيَ اللهُ عَنْهُمَا اَنَّ رَسُوْلَ اللهِ صَلَّى اللهُ عَلَيْهِ وَسَلَّمَ قَالَ مَكْتُوْبٌ عَلٰى بَابِ الْجَنَّةِ اِنَّنِيْ اَنَا اللهُ لَا اِلٰهَ اِلَّا اَنَا لَا اُعَذِّبُ مَنْ قَالَهَا (اخرجه السيوطى فى الدر المنثور ٥٦٠/٥)

Hadhrat Ibn Abbaas رضى الله عنه narrates that Rasulullah ﷺ has said: "There is inscribed on the gate of Jannah

اِنَّنِيْ اَنَا اللهُ لَا اِلٰهَ اِلَّا اَنَا لَا اُعَذِّبُ مَنْ قَالَهَا

(Indeed, I am Allah, none except Me is worthy of worship. Whosoever keeps reciting this Kalimah will not be punished by Me.)

Note: It is mentioned in many other Ahaadith that one will be punished for his sins. If the word punishment mentioned in the above Hadith means eternal punishment, then there is no doubt with regards to finally being forgiven by Allah Ta'ala. But if any fortunate person recites this

Kalimah with such sincerity of heart that he is altogether saved from punishment in spite of his sins, then no one can question the mercy of Allah Ta'ala, as already stated under Hadith 9 and 14 of this chapter.

Hadith 19 – Entering into the Fort of Allah Ta'ala

عَنْ عَلِيٍّ رَضِيَ اللهُ عَنْهُ قَالَ حَدَّثَنَا رَسُوْلُ اللهِ صَلَّى اللهُ عَلَيْهِ وَسَلَّمَ عَنْ جَبْرَئِيْلَ عَلَيْهِ السَّلَامُ قَالَ قَالَ اللهُ عَزَّ وَجَلَّ اِنِّىْ اَنَا اللهُ لَا اِلٰهَ اِلَّا اَنَا فَاعْبُدْنِىْ مَنْ جَاءَنِىْ مِنْكُمْ بِشَهَادَةِ اَنْ لَا اِلٰهَ اِلَّا اللهُ بِالْاِخْلَاصِ دَخَلَ فِىْ حِصْنِىْ وَمَنْ دَخَلَ فِىْ حِصْنِىْ اَمِنَ مِنْ عَذَابِىْ (اخرجه ابو نعيم فى الحلية ۲؍۱۹۲)

Hadhrat Ali رَضِىَ اللهُ عَنْهُ narrates that Rasulullah ﷺ related that he was told by Jibra-eel (alayhis salaam) that Allah Ta'ala says: "Only I am Allah, there is none worthy of worship except I, therefore worship Me only. Whosoever will come to Me with firm Imaan in laailaaha illallaah will enter My fort and whosoever enters My fort will be safe from My punishment."

Note: If the abovementioned blessing is on condition that one does not commit major sins, as mentioned under Hadith No 5, then there can be no objection about it, but if recitation of the Kalimah, together with committing major sins, is meant, then the word 'punishment' implies eternal punishment.

However, the Mercy of Allah Ta'ala is not bound by any law. It is mentioned in the Qur-aan Shareef that Allah Ta'ala will not forgive the sin of Shirk, but will forgive any other sin as He may please. According to one Hadith, Allah Ta'ala punishes only such people who revolt against Him and refuse to recite *laailaaha illallaah*. According to another Hadith, the recitation of *laailaaha illallaah* removes the anger of Allah Ta'ala, as long as one does not attach more importance to the worldly things over the matters of Deen. But if one starts preferring dunya over Deen, then recitation of *laailaaha illallaah* will prove to be of little use, because then Allah Ta'ala says: "You are not true in what you profess."

Hadith 20 – The Best Zikr and the Best Dua

عَنْ عَبْدِ اللّٰهِ بْنِ عَمْرٍو رَضِيَ اللّٰهُ عَنْهُ عَنِ النَّبِيِّ صَلَّى اللّٰهُ عَلَيْهِ وَسَلَّمَ قَالَ اَفْضَلُ الذِّكْرِ لَآ اِلٰهَ اِلَّا اللّٰهُ وَاَفْضَلُ الدُّعَاءِ اَلْاِسْتِغْفَارُ ثُمَّ قَرَاَ "فَاعْلَمْ اَنَّهٗ لَآ اِلٰهَ اِلَّا اللّٰهُ وَاسْتَغْفِرْ لِذَنْۢبِكَ اَلْاٰيَةِ (رواه الطبرانى # ١٢٩)

Hadhrat Abdullah ibn Amr ﷺ narrates that Rasulullah ﷺ said: "The best form of zikr is laailaahaillallaah and the best form of dua is Istighfaar (seeking the forgiveness of Allah Ta'ala)"

Then, in support thereof, he recited from Surah Muhammad, the following Aayah:

فَاعْلَمْ اَنَّهٗ لَآ اِلٰهَ اِلَّا اللّٰهُ وَاسْتَغْفِرْ لِذَنْۢبِكَ

"So know that none is worthy of worship but Allah and seek forgiveness for your sins." (Surah Muhammad - Aayah 19)

Note: It is already mentioned in Hadith No. 1 of this chapter that *laailaaha illallaah* is superior to all other forms of zikr. The reason for this superiority, according to the Sufis, is that zikr has a special cleansing effect on the heart. By virtue of this zikr, the heart gets purified of all its filth and if it is supplemented by Istighfaar, this becomes most effective. It is stated in one Hadith that when the fish had swallowed Hadhrat Yunus *(alayhis salaam)* he recited this dua,

لَآ اِلٰهَ اِلَّآ اَنْتَ سُبْحٰنَكَ اِنِّىْ كُنْتُ مِنَ الظّٰلِمِيْنَ

There is none worthy of worship but You, glory be to You. Indeed I am from the wrong doers.

Whosoever makes dua in these words, his dua will definitely be accepted.

It has also been mentioned in Hadith No. 1 of this chapter, namely that the best form of zikr is *laailaaha illallaah*, and that *alhamdulillaah* is mentioned to be the best of duas whereas over here it is stated to be Istighfaar. This apparent difference is according to different situations. For a pious man, *alhamdulillaah* is the best form of zikr, whereas a sinner is more in need of Taubah and Istighfaar, and Istighfaar is naturally the most suitable zikr for such persons. Also, for getting benefits, praising and glorifying Allah Ta'ala is more effective, whilst Istighfaar proves to be more effective in relieving difficulties and hardships. There are also other reasons given for this difference.

Hadith 21 – Efforts of shaytaan in misleading mankind

عَنْ اَبِيْ بَكْرٍ رَضِىَ اللهُ عَنْهُ عَنْ رَسُوْلِ اللهِ صَلَّى اللهُ عَلَيْهِ وَسَلَّمَ عَلَيْكُمْ بِلَا اِلٰهَ اِلَّا اللهُ وَالْاِسْتِغْفَارِ فَاَكْثِرُوْا مِنْهُمَا فَاِنَّ اِبْلِيْسَ قَالَ اَهْلَكْتُ النَّاسَ بِالذُّنُوْبِ وَاَهْلَكُوْنِيْ بِلَا اِلٰهَ اِلَّا اللهُ وَالْاِسْتِغْفَارِ فَلَمَّا رَاَيْتُ ذٰلِكَ اَهْلَكْتُهُمْ بِالْاَهْوَاءِ وَهُمْ يَحْسَبُوْنَ اَنَّهُمْ مُهْتَدُوْنَ (اخرجه السيوطى فى الجامع الصغير # ٨٢٣٢)

Hadhrat Abu Bakr رَضِىَ اللهُ عَنْهُ narrates that Rasulullah ﷺ said: "Recite laailaaha illallaah and Istighfaar as frequently as you can, because shaytaan says: 'I ruin the people by inclining them to commit sins but they frustrate me through their recitation of laailaaha illallaah and Istighfaar. When I find this so, I mislead them to indulge in bid'at and thereby make them follow their base desires in the belief that, they are still on the right path.'"

Note: The main object of shaytaan is to inject poison into one's mind, as stated under Hadith No. 14 in part 2 of Chapter 1. He is successful in doing so only when the heart is not engaged in zikr, otherwise he has to go away in disgrace. In fact, zikr of Allah Ta'ala purifies the heart. It is narrated in *'Mishkaat Shareef'* that Rasulullah ﷺ had said: "For everything there is a cleanser, and the heart is cleansed by means of the zikr of Allah Ta'ala." The effect of Istighfaar is similar, as mentioned in many Ahaadith that it removes the dirt and rust from the heart. Abu Ali Daqqaaq *(rahmatullahi alayh)* writes that when a person recites *laailaaha* with sincerity, his heart is cleansed of all dirt (just as a mirror is cleaned with a wet cloth), and when he says *illallaah* his heart shines with its light. It is clear that under these situations, the whole effort of shaytaan is wasted.

Ruining through base desires means that one may begin to consider wrong as right, and clothe one's desires in the garb of Deen. This practice has been condemned in the Qur-aan Shareef at several places. At one place it is said:

$$\text{اَفَرَءَيْتَ مَنِ اتَّخَذَ اِلٰهَهٗ هَوٰىهُ وَاَضَلَّهُ اللّٰهُ عَلٰى عِلْمٍ وَّ خَتَمَ عَلٰى سَمْعِهٖ وَقَلْبِهٖ وَجَعَلَ عَلٰى بَصَرِهٖ غِشْوَةً ۭ فَمَنْ يَّهْدِيْهِ مِنْۢ بَعْدِ اللّٰهِ ۭ اَفَلَا تَذَكَّرُوْنَ}$$

"Have you seen him who made his desire his god and Allah made him astray knowingly and sealed up his hearing and his heart, and set on his sight a covering? Then who can guide him, after Allah (condemned him)? Will you not then heed?" (Surah Jaasiyah - Aayah 23)

It is said at another place in the Qur-aan Shareef:

$$\text{وَمَنْ اَضَلُّ مِمَّنِ اتَّبَعَ هَوٰىهُ بِغَيْرِ هُدًى مِّنَ اللّٰهِ ۭ اِنَّ اللّٰهَ لَا يَهْدِى الْقَوْمَ الظّٰلِمِيْنَ}$$

"Who is further astray than one who follows his lust without any guidance from Allah Ta'ala? Verily Allah Ta'ala does not guide the wrong-doing nation." (Surah Qasas - Aayah 50)

There are many other Aayaat on the same subject. It is the most severe attack of shaytaan that he presents an irreligious deed as a religious one, so that one practices on it believing it to be good and hopes to get reward for it. Because the person performs it as a religious act, there is no likelihood of him making Taubah. If somebody is in the habit of committing sins like adultery and theft, there is a possibility that he may make Taubah and give them up, but if somebody is doing a wrong thing under the impression that it is an act of Ibaadat, the question of him making Taubah does not arise. Rather, he will get more involved in it day by day. This explains the words of shaytaan: "I involved them in sins, but they frustrated my efforts through zikr, taubah, and istighfaar. Then I entrapped them in such a manner that their escape becomes impossible."

Thus, it is essential that in all matters of Deen, guidance be sought from the ways of Rasulullah ﷺ and his Sahaabah ؓ. Taking an opposite path will lead to sin and destruction.

Imam Ghazaali *(rahmatullahi alayh)* has reported from Hasan Basri, *(rahmatullahi alayh)* that shaytaan says: "I presented sinful deeds in an attractive form to the Muslims, but they destroyed my efforts through istighfaar. Then I presented before them vices in the garb of virtues, thus leaving them with no initiative for istighfaar." Instances of such vices are self-made innovations in Deeni practices.

Wahb bin Munabbih *(rahmatullahi alayh)* says: "Fear Allah Ta'ala, who knows everything. You curse shaytaan in the presence of others, but you quietly obey and befriend him." Some Sufis have narrated: "It is most unfortunate that, in spite of knowing Allah Ta'ala as our real benefactor and acknowledging His favours, we still show disobedience to Him and obey shaytaan, whom we know and believe to be most treacherous and our greatest enemy."

Hadith 22 – Benefit of Professing Sincere Belief in the Kalimah

عَنْ مُعَاذِ بْنِ جَبَلٍ رَضِيَ اللهُ عَنْهُ قَالَ قَالَ رَسُوْلُ اللهِ صَلَّى اللهُ عَلَيْهِ وَسَلَّمَ لَا يَمُوْتُ عَبْدٌ يَشْهَدُ اَنْ لَّا اِلٰهَ اِلَّا اللهُ وَاَنَّ رَسُوْلُ اللهِ يَرْجِعُ ذٰلِكَ اِلٰى قَلْبٍ مُوْقِنٍ اِلَّا دَخَلَ الْجَنَّةَ وَفِيْ رِوَايَةٍ اِلَّا غُفِرَ لَهٗ (اخرجه السيوطى فى الدر المنثور ٧/٤٩٣)

Hadhrat Muaaz bin Jabal راضى الله عنه narrates that Rasulullah صلى الله عليه وسلم says: "Whosoever professes sincere belief in laailaaha illallaah Muhammadur Rasulullah at the time of his death, shall certainly enter Jannah." According to another Hadith, "He shall certainly be pardoned by Allah Ta'ala."

Note: Rasulullah صلى الله عليه وسلم is reported to have said: "Listen to glad tidings, and convey them to others as well, that whosoever believes in *laailaaha illallaah* with sincerity, shall enter Jannah." It is Ikhlaas that is valued by Allah Ta'ala. A small deed done with Ikhlaas (sincerity) earns a great reward, but anything done for the sake of show or to please people, will earn no rewards, but instead punishment from Allah Ta'ala. That is why a person who recites the Kalimah with sincerity will certainly be forgiven and admitted into Jannah. It may or may not be that he suffers some punishment for his sins before going to Jannah but, if Allah Ta'ala is really pleased with a particular deed of a sinful Muslim, He may forgive all his sins in the very first instance. When Allah Ta'ala is so Merciful and Gracious, it is our greatest misfortune if we do not serve and obey Him in full. In short, great rewards are promised in these Ahaadith for one who believes in the Kalimah Tayyibah. However, two possibilities are there: he may have to suffer some punishment for his sins according to the general rule before being forgiven, or he may be forgiven without any punishment by Allah Ta'ala, out of his sheer Mercy and Grace.

Yahya bin Aksam *(rahmatullahi alayh)* is a Muhaddith. After his death, somebody saw him in a dream and asked him how he had fared. He replied: "I appeared before Allah Ta'ala, and He said to me: 'You sinful old man. You did this and you did that, till all my sins were recounted one by one. I was asked if I had any explanation in my defense. I replied that no Hadith to that effect had been conveyed to me. Then Allah Ta'ala asked: 'What Hadith had been conveyed to you?' I said: "I was told by Abdur Razzaaq who was told by Muammar who was told by Zuhri who was told by Urwah who was told by Hadhrat 'Aa-ishah رضى الله عنها, who was told by Rasulullah ﷺ, who was told by Jibra-eel *(alayhis salaam)*, who was told by You: 'A person who grows to old age in Islam may have deserved punishment on account of his sins, yet as a token of respect for his old age, I forgive him,' and You know that I am very old." Allah Ta'ala then said, "Abdur Razzaaq spoke the truth, Muammar spoke the truth, Zuhri spoke the truth, Urwah spoke the truth, 'Aa-ishah رضى الله عنها spoke the truth, Rasulullah ﷺ spoke the truth, Jibra-eel *(alayhis salaam)* spoke the truth, and what I had said is true. After that, it was ordered that I should be admitted into Jannah."

Hadith 23 – Two acts for which there is no obstacle before it reaches Allah Ta'ala

عَنْ أَنَسٍ رَضِىَ اللهُ عَنْهُ قَالَ قَالَ رَسُوْلُ اللهِ صَلَّى اللهُ عَلَيْهِ وَسَلَّمَ لَيْسَ شَىْءٌ إِلَّا بَيْنَهُ وَبَيْنَ اللهِ حِجَابٌ إِلَّا قَوْلَ لَا اِلٰهَ اِلَّا اللهُ وَدُعَاءَ الْوَالِدِ (اخرجه السيوطى فى الدر المنثور ٤٩٣/٦)

Hadhrat Anas رضى الله عنه *narrates that Rasulullah* ﷺ *said: "There are obstacles in the way of every action before it reaches Allah Ta'ala, but the recitation of laailaaha illallaah and the dua of a father in favour of his children goes up to Allah Ta'ala unchecked."*

Note: Going unchecked up to Allah Ta'ala means that these two actions are accepted without any delay. Whereas there are stages in between for other deeds before they reach Allah Ta'ala, these two things go to Him directly.

Story of a cruel kaafir king

There is a story of a Kaafir king, who was extremely cruel against the Muslims. It so happened that he was captured alive in a battle against the Muslims. As he had caused a lot of sufferings to the Muslims, they were naturally very vengeful. They put him in a cauldron which was placed on a fire. At first, he begged his idols for help, but finding no response from them, he then accepted Islam and started continuous recitation of *laailaaha illallaah*. How sincerely and devotedly he must have been reciting can well be imagined. Immediately help came from Allah Ta'ala in the form of heavy rain, which extinguished the fire and cooled the cauldron. It was then followed by a powerful cyclone which carried the cauldron away and dropped it in a city inhabited by non-believers. He was still engaged in the recitation of the Kalimah. The people there were wonderstruck by this scene, and after listening to his whole story, all of them embraced Islam.

Hadith 24 – Reciting the Kalimah for the pleasure of Allah Ta'ala

عَنْ عِتْبَانَ بْنِ مَالِكٍ الْأَنْصَارِيِّ رَضِيَ اللهُ عَنْهُ قَالَ قَالَ رَسُوْلُ اللهِ صَلَّى اللهُ عَلَيْهِ وَسَلَّمَ لَنْ يُوَافِيَ عَبْدٌ يَوْمَ الْقِيَامَةِ يَقُوْلُ لَا اِلٰهَ اِلَّا اللهُ اِلَّا اللهُ يَبْتَغِيْ بِذٰلِكَ وَجْهَ اللهِ اِلَّا حُرِّمَ عَلَى النَّارِ (اخرجه السيوطى فى الدر المنثور ٧/٤٩٤)

Hadhrat Itbaan bin Maalik ﷺ narrates that Rasulullah ﷺ says: "On the Day of Qiyaamah, Jahannam would be forbidden for all those who had recited laailaaha illallaah with the sole aim of earning the pleasure of Allah Ta'ala."

Note: A person who recites Kalimah Tayyibah with sincerity, on condition that he is free from major sins, will be safe from the fire of Jahannam. Being saved from Jahannam for such a person may off course mean that his everlasting stay therein is forbidden, but who is there to question Allah Ta'ala if he altogether saves the sincere reciter of the Kalimah from Jahannam, in spite of his sins. Mention is made in the Ahaadith of such people whose sins will be enumerated by Allah Ta'ala on the Day of Qiyaamah such that they will feel sure of being doomed to severe punishment, but after their confession, Allah Ta'ala will say to them: "I covered your sins in your worldly life, and I will now cover them and forgive you." Many similar cases have been related in the Ahaadith. Thus, it is not far-fetched that the zaakireen (those who make zikr) may be treated in this way. There are many blessings and benefits in reciting the exalted name of Allah Ta'ala. One should do it as often as possible. How fortunate are those blessed souls who understood the virtues of this Kalimah, and devoted their lives fully to its recitation.

Hadith 25 – Reciting the Kalimah at the time of death

عَنْ يَحْيَى بْنِ طَلْحَةَ بْنِ عَبْدِ اللهِ رَضِيَ اللهُ عَنْهُ قَالَ رُؤِيَ طَلْحَةُ حَزِيْنًا فَقِيْلَ لَهُ مَا لَكَ قَالَ اِنِّيْ سَمِعْتُ رَسُوْلَ اللهِ صَلَّى اللهُ عَلَيْهِ وَسَلَّمَ يَقُوْلُ اِنِّيْ لَاَعْلَمُ كَلِمَةً لَا يَقُوْلُهَا عَبْدٌ عِنْدَ مَوْتِهِ اِلَّا نَفَّسَ اللهُ عَنْهُ كُرْبَتَهُ وَاَشْرَقَ لَوْنُهُ وَرَاٰى مَا يَسُرُّهُ وَمَا مَنَعَنِيْ اَنْ اَسْاَلَهُ عَنْهَا اِلَّا الْقُدْرَةُ عَلَيْهِ حَتّٰى مَاتَ فَقَالَ عُمَرُ اِنِّيْ لَاَعْلَمُهَا فَقَالَ فَمَا هِيَ قَالَ لَا نَعْلَمُ كَلِمَةً هِيَ اَعْظَمُ مِنْ كَلِمَةٍ اَمَرَهَا عَمَّهُ لَا اِلٰهَ اِلَّا اللهُ قَالَ فَهِيَ وَاللهِ هِيَ

(اخرجه السيوطى فى الدر المنثور ٦/٤٩٤)

Hadhrat Yahya bin Talha bin Abdullah ﷺ narrates that once Hadhrat Talhah ﷺ was seen sitting in a very sad mood. Somebody asked him why he was so sad. He said: "I had heard from Rasulullah ﷺ that he knew the words, which, if recited by a dying person at the time of his death, brings him relief from the pangs of death, so that his face brightens and he dies in happiness. Unfortunately I could not enquire about those words from Rasulullah ﷺ, and therefore I am feeling so sad." Hadhrat Umar ﷺ said that he knew those words. Hadhrat Talhah ﷺ joyously asked what those were and Hadhrat Umar ﷺ said: "We know that no words are better than the Kalimah which was offered by Rasulullah ﷺ to his uncle Abu Taalib and it is laailaaha illallaahu." Hadhrat Talhah ﷺ said "By Allah! it is this, By Allah! it is this."

Note: It is learnt from many Ahaadith that the Kalimah Tayyibah generates light and happiness through and through. Haafiz Ibn Hajar *(rahmatullahi alayh)* has stated in his book '*Munabbihaat*': "There are five kinds of darknesses for which there are five specific lights.
1) The love of the world is a darkness, the light for it is piety;
2) sin is a darkness, the light for which is Taubah;
3) the grave is a darkness, the light for which is the Kalimah *laailaaha illallaah Muhammadur Rasulullah,*
4) the next life is a darkness, the light for which is good deeds; and
5) the Pulsiraat is a darkness, the light for which is Yaqeen (Faith and conviction)."

Raabiah Adawiyyah *(rahmatullahi alayha),* a well-known female saint, used to remain busy in Salaah throughout the night. She would sleep a little after early dawn and would wake up abruptly just before the Fajr Salaah, blaming herself and saying: "How long will you lie asleep; soon you will be in the grave, where you will sleep till Qiyaamah." At the time of her death, she told her servant that she should be buried in the patched woolen cloak, which she used to wear at the time of Tahajjud Salaah and that nobody should be informed of her death. After her burial according to her wishes, the servant saw her in a dream wearing a very beautiful dress. When asked what happened to her old woolen dress, she replied that it had been deposited with her deeds. The servant requested her for some advice and she replied: "Make zikr of Allah Ta'ala as much as you can, by virtue of this, you will be worthy of envy in the grave."

Hadith 26 – **The Requirement for Salvation**

عَنْ عُثْمَانَ بْنِ عَفَّانَ رَضِيَ اللهُ عَنْهُ قَالَ اِنَّ رِجَالًا مِنْ اَصْحَابِ النَّبِيِّ صَلَّى اللهُ عَلَيْهِ وَسَلَّمَ حِيْنَ تُوُفِّيَ النَّبِيُّ صَلَّى اللهُ عَلَيْهِ وَسَلَّمَ حَزِنُوْا عَلَيْهِ حَتَّى كَادَ بَعْضُهُمْ يُوَسْوِسُ قَالَ عُثْمَانُ رَضِيَ اللهُ عَنْهُ وَكُنْتُ مِنْهُمْ فَبَيْنَا اَنَا جَالِسٌ مَرَّ عَلَيَّ عُمَرُ رَضِيَ اللهُ عَنْهُ وَ سَلَّمَ فَلَمْ اَشْعُرْ بِهٖ فَاشْتَكٰى عُمَرُ رَضِيَ اللهُ عَنْهُ اِلٰى اَبِيْ بَكْرٍ رَضِيَ اللهُ عَنْهُ ثُمَّ اَقْبَلَا حَتّٰى سَلَّمَا عَلَيَّ جَمِيْعًا فَقَالَ اَبُوْ بَكْرٍ رَضِيَ اللهُ عَنْهُ مَا حَمَلَكَ عَلٰى اَنْ لَّا تَرُدَّ عَلٰى اَخِيْكَ عُمَرَ رَضِيَ اللهُ عَنْهُ سَلَامَهٗ قُلْتُ مَا فَعَلْتُ فَقَالَ عُمَرُ رَضِيَ اللهُ عَنْهُ بَلٰى وَاللهِ لَقَدْ فَعَلْتَ

قَالَ قُلْتُ وَاللّٰهِ مَا شَعُرْتُ اَنَّكَ مَرَرْتَ وَلَا سَلَّمْتَ قَالَ اَبُوْ بَكْرٍ رَضِيَ اللّٰهُ عَنْهُ صَدَقَ عُثْمَانُ رَضِيَ اللّٰهُ عَنْهُ قَدْ شَغَلَكَ عَنْ ذٰلِكَ اَمْرٌ فَقُلْتُ اَجَلْ قَالَ مَا هُوَ قُلْتُ تَوَفّٰى اللّٰهُ تَعَالٰى نَبِيَّهُ صَلَّى اللّٰهُ عَلَيْهِ وَسَلَّمَ قَبْلَ اَنْ نَسْئَلَهُ عَنْ نَجَاةِ هٰذَا الْاَمْرِ قَالَ اَبُوْ بَكْرٍ رَضِيَ اللّٰهُ عَنْهُ قَدْ سَئَلْتُهُ عَنْ ذٰلِكَ فَقُمْتُ اِلَيْهِ وَقُلْتُ لَهُ بِاَبِيْ اَنْتَ وَاُمِّيْ اَنْتَ اَحَقُّ بِهَا قَالَ اَبُوْ بَكْرٍ رَضِيَ اللّٰهُ عَنْهُ قُلْتُ يَا رَسُوْلَ اللّٰهِ مَا نَجَاةُ هٰذَا الْاَمْرِ فَقَالَ رَسُوْلُ اللّٰهِ صَلَّى اللّٰهُ عَلَيْهِ وَسَلَّمَ مَنْ قَبِلَ مِنِّيْ الْكَلِمَةَ الَّتِيْ عَرَضْتُ عَلٰى عَمِّيْ فَرَدَّهَا فَهِيَ لَهُ نَجَاةٌ (رواه احمد #)

(٢٠)

Hadhrat Usmaan ؓ narrates that at the time of the demise of Rasulullah ﷺ, his companions were so shocked and grieved that many of them became overwhelmed with frustration and doubts of various sorts. Hadhrat Usmaan ؓ said: "I was also amongst those who were gripped with these doubts. Hadhrat Umar ؓ came to me and made salaam to me, but I was too absorbed to be aware of his coming. He complained to Hadhrat Abu Bakr ؓ that I was displeased with him, so much so that I did not respond even to his salaam. Then both of them came to me and made salaam to me and Hadhrat Abu Bakr ؓ asked me the reason why I had not responded to Hadhrat Umar's salaam. Hadhrat Umar ؓ said: "Yes, I swear by Allah, Most certainly you did." Hadhrat Usmaan ؓ denied having behaved like this, and told them, "I did not even know of his coming and making salaam to me." Hadhrat Abu Bakr ؓ accepted my explanation and said that it must have happened so, and that probably I must have been absorbed in some deep thought. I confessed that I was indeed absorbed in some deep thought. Hadhrat Abu Bakr ؓ enquired what it was and I submitted that I was worried because Rasulullah ﷺ passed away and we failed to enquire from him the basic thing required for salvation. Hadhrat Abu Bakr ؓ said that he had asked Rasulullah ﷺ about that. I got up, and praised him saying, "May my parents be sacrificed for you. Only you are worthy of having asked such a question, (because you always excelled in matters of Deen)." Hadhrat Abu Bakr

رَضِىَ اللّٰهُ عَنْهُ then said, I had asked Rasulullah ﷺ what basic thing was necessary for one's salvation, and he had replied that whoever accepts the Kalimah that he had offered to his uncle Abu Taalib at the time of his death (but which he rejected), that is the Kalimah of salvation."

Note: All the Sahaabah رَضِىَ اللّٰهُ عَنْهُمْ were very upset and overcome with grief and sorrow so much so that even Hadhrat Umar رَضِىَ اللّٰهُ عَنْهُ, in spite of him being so brave, held his sword in his hand and proclaimed: "I will chop off the head of whosoever says that Rasulullah ﷺ is dead. He has only gone to meet his Allah, as Hadhrat Moosa *(alayhis salaam)* had gone to Mount Toor." Some of the Sahaabah رَضِىَ اللّٰهُ عَنْهُمْ feared that the death of Rasulullah ﷺ meant the end of Islam. Some thought that there was no longer any chance for the progress of Islam, whereas some were dumbfounded and could not even speak. It was only Hadhrat Abu Bakr رَضِىَ اللّٰهُ عَنْهُ, who, in spite of his extreme love and attachment with Rasulullah ﷺ, remained firm, calm, and collected. He got up and delivered his forceful address, beginning with the Aayah,

وَمَا مُحَمَّدٌ اِلَّا رَسُوْلٌ ...

"Muhammad ﷺ is but a messenger (he is not god who will not die). Many messengers have passed away before him. Will it be that when he dies or is slain, you will turn away from Deen? He who turns away from his Deen does not harm Allah Ta'ala in the least. (He will cause harm to himself)." *(Surah Aali I'mraan - Aayah 144)*

This story has been briefly related in my book 'Stories of Sahaabah'.

Another point made in the abovementioned Hadith is on what essential basic things does salvation depend. It can be interpreted in two ways. Firstly, it may mean: The matters of Deen are many, but on which things does Deen depend on, and which is indispensable? According to this interpretation, the reply given above is clearly understood. The whole of Deen depends on the Kalimah, which is the fundamental belief of Islam. Secondly it can mean that there are hardships in the path of Deen viz. doubts and the whispers of shaytaan crop up. They are a constant source of trouble. Also, worldly needs demand one's attention, etc.; How can these be overcome? In this case, the saying of Rasulullah ﷺ would mean that frequent recitation of Kalimah Tayyibah will help overcome all these difficulties, for it develops sincerity of intention, it cleanses the heart, it causes defeat of shaytaan and has many other benefits, as mentioned in all these Ahaadith. It is said in one Hadith that the Kalimah *laailaaha illallaah* keeps away ninety-nine kinds of calamities, the least of which is grief, which is a constant worry for man.

Hadith 27 – The Kalimah that will Forbid the Fire of Jahannam

عَنْ عُثْمَانَ بْنِ عَفَّانَ رَضِيَ اللهُ عَنْهُ قَالَ سَمِعْتُ رَسُوْلَ اللهِ صَلَّى اللهُ عَلَيْهِ وَسَلَّمَ يَقُوْلُ اِنِّيْ لَاَعْلَمُ كَلِمَةً لَّا يَقُوْلُهَا عَبْدٌ حَقًّا مِّنْ قَلْبِهِ اِلَّا حُرِّمَ عَلَى النَّارِ فَقَالَهُ عُمَرُ بْنُ الْخَطَّابِ رَضِيَ اللهُ عَنْهُ اَنَا اُحَدِّثُكَ مَا هِيَ هِيَ كَلِمَةُ الْاِخْلَاصِ الَّتِيْ اَعَزَّ اللهُ تَبَارَكَ وَتَعَالَى بِهَا مُحَمَّدًا صَلَّى اللهُ عَلَيْهِ وَسَلَّمَ وَاَصْحَابَهُ وَهِيَ كَلِمَةُ التَّقْوَى الَّتِيْ اَلَاصَ عَلَيْهَا نَبِيُّ اللهِ صَلَّى اللهُ عَلَيْهِ وَسَلَّمَ عَمَّهُ اَبَا طَالِبٍ عِنْدَ الْمَوْتِ شَهَادَةَ اَنْ لَّا اِلٰهَ اِلَّا اللهُ

(رواه احمد # ٤٤٧)

Hadhrat Usmaan ؓ narrated that he heard Rasulullah ﷺ saying: "I know of a Kalimah which, if recited by a person with sincerity, makes the fire of Jahannam haraam on him." Hadhrat Umar ؓ said: "Shall I tell you which Kalimah is that? It is the same Kalimah by virtue of which Allah Ta'ala honoured Rasulullah ﷺ and his companions, it is the same Kalimah of piety that was offered by Rasulullah ﷺ to his uncle Abu Taalib at the time of his death. It is laailaaha illallaah."

Note: This well-known incident of Abu Taalib, the uncle of Rasulullah ﷺ, is given in the books of Hadith, Tafseer, and History. He had been helping Rasulullah ﷺ and the Muslims. Rasulullah ﷺ went to him when he was about to die and said: "O my uncle, recite *laailaaha illallaah* even now, so that I may be able to intercede on your behalf on the Day of Qiyaamah and I may bear witness before Allah Ta'ala that you embraced Islam." Abu Taalib replied: "People will taunt me for having accepted the Deen of my nephew for fear of death, otherwise I would have pleased you by reciting this Kalimah *laailaaha illallaah*." Rasulullah ﷺ returned from there deeply grieved. It was in this connection that the following Aayah of the Qur-aan was revealed;

$$\text{اِنَّكَ لَا تَهْدِيْ مَنْ اَحْبَبْتَ}$$

"Verily you cannot guide who you love, but Allah guides whom He wills." (Surah Qasas - Aayah 56)

It is evident from this incident that those who are involved in sins and bad deeds, and disobey Allah Ta'ala and His Rasul ﷺ, but think that they will get forgiven because of the dua of some pious person in their favour, are sadly mistaken. All power rests with Allah Ta'ala, to whom we should always turn to and with whom we should establish our real contact. However, the company of pious men, their duas and their blessings can help us in achieving this end.

Hadith 28 – The Dua of Hadhrat Aadam *(alayhis salaam)*

عَنْ عُمَرَ بْنِ الْخَطَّابِ رَضِيَ اللهُ عَنْهُ قَالَ قَالَ رَسُوْلُ اللهِ صَلَّى اللهُ عَلَيْهِ وَسَلَّمَ لَمَّا اَذْنَبَ اٰدَمُ الذَّنْبَ الَّذِىْ اَذْنَبَهُ رَفَعَ رَأْسَهُ اِلَى السَّمَاءِ فَقَالَ اَسْئَلُكَ بِحَقِّ مُحَمَّدٍ اِلَّا غَفَرْتَ لِىْ فَاَوْحَى اللهُ اِلَيْهِ مَنْ مُحَمَّدٌ فَقَالَ تَبَارَكَ اسْمُكَ لَمَّا خَلَقْتَنِىْ رَفَعْتُ رَأْسِىْ اِلٰى عَرْشِكَ فَاِذَا فِيْهِ مَكْتُوْبٌ لَا اِلٰهَ اِلَّا اللهُ مُحَمَّدٌ رَسُوْلُ اللهِ فَعَلِمْتُ اَنَّهُ لَيْسَ اَحَدٌ اَعْظَمَ عِنْدَكَ قَدْرًا عَمَّنْ جَعَلْتَ اسْمَهُ مَعَ اسْمِكَ فَاَوْحَى اللهُ اِلَيْهِ يَا اٰدَمُ اِنَّهُ اٰخِرُ النَّبِيِّيْنَ مِنْ ذُرِّيَّتِكَ وَلَوْ لَا هُوَ مَا خَلَقْتُكَ (اخرجه الطبرانى فى الصغير # ٩٩٢)

Hadhrat Umar ؓ narrates that Rasulullah ﷺ said: "After Hadhrat Aadam (alayhis salaam) happened to commit the mistake (as a result of which he was transferred from Jannah to this Earth, he wept all the time, making dua and taubah), and once he looked up towards the Heavens and made dua: "O Allah! I beg Your forgiveness in the name of Muhammad ﷺ." "Who is Muhammad?" came the enquiry through Divine revelation. He replied: "When you had created me I saw the words 'laailaaha illallaah Muhammadur Rasulullah' written on Your Arsh, and since then I believed that no human being is superior to Muhammad ﷺ, whose name appeared along with Yours." In reply, it was revealed, "He is to be the last of all the Ambiyaa, and will be your descendant. If he were not to be created, you would not have been created."

Note: The manner in which Aadam *(alayhis salaam)* must have made dua, wept and asked for forgiveness has been described in many Ahaadith. Only those who have experienced the agony of the displeasure of a master can have some idea about the plight of Hadhrat Aadam *(alayhis salaam)*. On account of the displeasure of earthly masters, a servant gets very worried, but in the case of Hadhrat Aadam *(alayhis salaam)*, it was the displeasure of our Rabb, Allah Ta'ala, the Sustainer of the whole universe. In spite of Aadam *(alayhis salaam)* being the favorite of Allah Ta'ala and the Malaaikah were made to bow to him, Allah Ta'ala still directed his anger towards him. The higher the position of a favourite, the more he feels the anger of the Master, provided he is not a mean person, and in this case a Nabi was involved.

Hadhrat Ibn Abbaas ﷜ narrated that Hadhrat Aadam *(alayhis salaam)* wept so much that his weeping exceeded the total weeping by all the people of this world and he remained in sajdah for forty years without lifting up his head even once. Hadhrat Buraydah ﷜ also narrated that Rasulullah ﷺ had said: "The weeping of Hadhrat Aadam *(alayhis salaam)*, if compared, will exceed the weeping by all the people of the world." It is stated in another Hadith that his tears would outweigh the tears shed by all his descendants. Under these circumstances, in how many ways he must have grieved and repented can well be imagined.

یاں لب پے لاکھ لاکھ سخن اضطراب میں
واں ایک خامشی تری سب کے جواب میں

One million words on my lips due to uneasiness
Your silence is a reply to all

In addition to this, he even begged to be pardoned through the means of Rasulullah ﷺ.

The other aspect mentioned here that the Kalimah *laailaaha illallaah Muhammadur Rasulullah* is written on the Arsh is supported by many other Ahaadith. Rasulullah ﷺ had said: "When I entered Jannah, I saw three lines written in gold on both sides. In the first line it was written

$$ \text{لَا اِلٰهَ اِلَّا اللهُ مُحَمَّدٌ رَسُوْلُ اللهِ} $$

In the second line it was written

$$ \text{مَاقَدَّمْنَا وَجَدْنَا وَمَااَكَلْنَا رَبِحْنَا وَمَاخَلَفْنَا خَسِرْنَا} $$

What we sent in advance (i.e. charity, etc.), we found, what we consumed, we enjoyed, and what we left behind we lost,

and in the third line was written

$$ \text{أُمَّةٌ مُذْنِبَةٌ وَرَبٌّ غَفُوْرٌ} $$

People are sinful, but a Rabb that is forgiving.

A pious person relates: "I happened to visit a town in India, and there I came across a tree, the fruit of which resembles the almond and has a double shell. When it is broken, a rolled green leaf comes out with *laailaaha illallaah* inscribed on it in red. When I spoke about it to Abu Yaqoob, the hunter, he was not surprised at all and told me that in Aylah he had caught a fish, which had *laailaaha illallaah* inscribed on one ear and *Muhammadur Rasulullah* on the other.

Hadith 29 – Ismul A'zam

عَنْ أَسْمَاءَ بِنْتِ يَزِيْدَ بْنِ السَّكَنِ رَضِيَ اللهُ عَنْهَا عَنْ رَسُوْلِ اللهِ صَلَّى اللهُ عَلَيْهِ وَسَلَّمَ أَنَّهُ قَالَ اِسْمُ اللهِ الْأَعْظَمُ فِىْ هَاتَيْنِ الْآيَتَيْنِ {وَاِلٰهُكُمْ اِلٰهٌ وَاحِدٌ لَّا اِلٰهَ اِلَّا هُوَ الرَّحْمٰنُ الرَّحِيْمُ} وَ{الٓمٓ ۚ اللهُ لَا اِلٰهَ اِلَّا هُوَ الْحَيُّ الْقَيُّوْمُ} (رواه الترمذى # ٣٤٧٨)

Hadhrat Asma ﷺ relates that Rasulullah ﷺ said: "The greatest name of Allah, which is generally known as Ismul A'zam, is *contained in the following two Aayaat (as long as these are recited with Ikhlaas)."*

$$\text{وَاِلٰـهُكُمْ اِلٰـهٌ وَّاحِدٌ ۚ لَّآ اِلٰهَ اِلَّا هُوَ الرَّحْمٰنُ الرَّحِيْمُ}$$

$$\text{الٓمٓ ۚ اللّٰهُ لَآ اِلٰهَ اِلَّا هُوَ الْحَيُّ الْقَيُّوْمُ}$$

Note: It is stated in several Ahaadith that whatever dua is made after the recitation of Ismul A'zam is granted by Allah Ta'ala. However, the Ulama differ in specifying the Ismul A'zam as is the case with some of the most precious things that Allah Ta'ala keeps them partly secret. This results in difference of opinion about their exact specification. Thus, there is difference of opinion about Laylatul Qadr (The Night of Power) and in respect of the special time of acceptance of duas on Friday. This difference of opinion in such matters is a blessing in disguise, as explained in detail in my book on Fazaail-e-Ramadhaan. Thus, there have been different narrations in respect to the Ismul-A'zam and the above is one of these. There have been other Ahaadith too in regard to these two aayaat as follows:

Hadhrat Anas ﷺ reported that Rasulullah ﷺ said that no Aayah falls so heavy on the mischievous and wicked shayaateen as the two aayaat beginning with

$$\text{وَاِلٰـهُكُمْ اِلٰـهٌ وَّاحِدٌ}$$

According to Ibrahim bin Wasma *(rahmatullahi alayh)*, the recitation of the following aayah is very effective, in cases of mental illnesses, and cases of the evil eye, etc. Whosoever is particular in their recitation will be safeguarded against such maladies.

$$\text{وَاِلٰـهُكُمْ اِلٰـهٌ وَّاحِدٌ ..... الآية}$$

(Surah Baqarah - Aayah 163)

$$\text{اللّٰهُ لَآ اِلٰهَ اِلَّا هُوَ الْحَيُّ الْقَيُّوْمُ ..... الآية}$$

(Surah Baqarah - Aayah 255)

Chapter 2 – Virtues of Kalimah Tayyibah

$$ اِنَّ رَبَّكُمُ اللهُ الَّذِىْ ..... الْمُحْسِنِيْنَ $$

(Surah A'araaf - Aayah 54-56)

$$ هُوَ اللهُ الَّذِىْ لَآ اِلٰهَ اِلَّا هُوَ ..... الْحَكِيْمُ $$

(Surah Hashr - Aayah 24)

It has reached us that all these aayaat are written on the corner of the Arsh and Ibrahim *(rahmatullahi alayh)* used to also say that these aayaat must be written down for children who have fear or there is fear of them being affected with the evil eye.

Allamah Shami *(rahmatullahi alayh)* has quoted Imaam Abu Hanifa *(rahmatullahi alayh)* as saying that Ismul-A'zam is the word "Allah". He has also stated that Allamah Tahaawi *(rahmatullahi alayh)* as well as other Ulama supported this view. The great Buzurgs and Sufis also have reached the same conclusion, and that is why the zikr of this holy name is practiced more than anything else by their followers. The leader of the Auliyaa, Hadhrat Shaikh Abdul Qadr Jilaani *(rahmatullahi alayh)*, is also of the same view that "Allah" is the Ismul-A'zam, provided at the time of its recitation, there is nothing but Allah Ta'ala in one's heart. He further advised that during its recitation, ordinary people should think of His grandeur and fear Him, while the specialists in zikr should also concentrate on His attributes and the selected few should have in their mind thoughts of nothing else except Allah Ta'ala. He also stated that it was for this reason that this blessed name is mentioned so many times, in fact 2360 times in the Qur-aan Shareef.

Shaikh Ismail Farghaani *(rahmatullahi alayh)* relates: "For a long time I had a keen desire to learn this Ismul-A'zam and for this purpose I had undergone great hardships. I would fast for days on end, so much so that sometimes I would fall unconscious on account of severe hunger. One day, I was sitting in a masjid in Damascus, when two men entered there and stood beside me. I sensed that they were Malaaikah. One of them said to the other: "Do you want to learn the Ismul-A'zam?" "Yes", replied the other, "please tell me." On hearing this conversation, I became more attentive. The former said, "It is the word "Allah", provided it is recited with Sidqul-laja, which according to Shaikh Ismail *(rahmatullahi alayh)* is the state of mind comparable to that of a person drowning in the ocean when there is nobody to save him, and he calls Allah Ta'ala for help with extreme sincerity.

In order to learn the Ismul A'zam, one should possess very sublime qualities as well as endurance and self-restraint. There is a story of a pious person who knew the Ismul-A'zam. Once a man came to him and begged that he should be taught the Ismul-A'zam: "You lack the required capability," said the pious person. "No, I am capable of learning it," said the man. The pious person then asked him to go and sit at a particular place and then come back and relate to him his observations. This man went there and saw an old man who was bringing firewood on his donkey from the jungle. A policeman came from the other direction and started beating the old man and snatched away his firewood. The man was extremely enraged at the policeman and came back to report the whole incident before the pious person and said that, if he had known the Ismul-A'zam, he would have made dua against that policeman. The pious man said: "I learnt the Ismul-A'zam from that very old man who was bringing the firewood."

Hadith 30 – Imaan Equivalent to an iota

عَنْ اَنَسٍ رَضِيَ اللهُ عَنْهُ قَالَ قَالَ رَسُوْلُ اللهِ صَلَّى اللهُ عَلَيْهِ وَسَلَّمَ يَقُوْلُ اللهُ تَبَارَكَ وَتَعَالٰى اَخْرِجُوْا مِنَ النَّارِ مَنْ قَالَ لَا اِلٰهَ اِلَّا اللهُ وَفِيْ قَلْبِهٖ مِثْقَالُ ذَرَّةٍ مِّنَ الْاِيْمَانِ اَخْرِجُوْا مِنَ النَّارِ مَنْ قَالَ لَا اِلٰهَ اِلَّا اللهُ اَوْ ذَكَرَنِيْ اَوْ خَافَنِيْ فِيْ مَقَامٍ (رواه الحاكم)

Hadhrat Anas ﷺ narrates that Rasulullah ﷺ said that Allah Ta'ala will order on the Day of Qiyaamah: "Take out of Jahannam all those who professed laailaaha illallaah and who had an iota of Imaan in their hearts; take out from Jahannam all those who recited laailaaha illallaah or remembered Me in any way or feared me on any occasion."

Note: The great blessings that Allah Ta'ala grants on account of this Kalimah can be imagined from the fact that if a hundred year old man, who practiced Kufr and Shirk all his life, happens to recite this Kalimah once with Imaan and sincerity, becomes a Muslim and all the sins committed by him are washed away. Even if he happens to commit any sins after he had become a Muslim, then too, by virtue of this Kalimah, he will sooner or later be freed from Jahannam.

Hadhrat Huzayfah ﷺ, who was a confidant of Rasulullah ﷺ, narrated that Rasulullah ﷺ had once said: "A time will come when Islam will become weak like the worn-out prints on hazy old clothing. Nobody will even know about fasting, Hajj or Zakaat, till one night even the Qur-aan Shareef will be lifted from this world, so that no one will remember any aayah. At this time, the old men and women will say that they had heard their elders reciting the Kalimah *laailaaha illallaah* and that they would recite it too." A pupil of Hadhrat Huzayfah ﷺ enquired: "When there is no Hajj, Zakaat, Fasting or any other fundamental of Islam, will the mere Kalimah then be of any use to us?" Hadhrat Huzayfah ﷺ did not answer, but when his pupil repeated his enquiry a second and a third time, he replied: "Sooner or later it will free one from Jahannam, free one from Jahannam, free one from Jahannam." He meant that the Kalimah will free one from Jahannam after one has undergone the punishment for not observing the basics of Islam. This is what is meant by the above mentioned Hadith that a person with even an iota of Imaan will be freed from Jahannam one day. It is also narrated in one Hadith: "Whosoever recites the Kalimah *laailaaha illallaah*, it will come to his rescue on some day, which may be after he has undergone some punishment."

Hadith 31 – Advice of Nooh (alayhis salaam) to his sons

عَنْ عَبْدِ اللهِ بْنِ عَمْرٍو رَضِيَ اللهُ عَنْهُ قَالَ أَتَى النَّبِيَّ صَلَّى اللهُ عَلَيْهِ وَسَلَّمَ أَعْرَابِيٌّ عَلَيْهِ جُبَّةٌ مِنْ طَيَالِسَةٍ مَكْفُوفَةٍ بِالدِّيبَاجِ فَقَالَ إِنَّ صَاحِبَكُمْ هٰذَا يُرِيدُ يَرْفَعُ كُلَّ رَاعٍ وَابْنَ رَاعٍ وَيَضَعُ كُلَّ فَارِسٍ وَابْنَ فَارِسٍ فَقَامَ النَّبِيُّ صَلَّى اللهُ عَلَيْهِ وَسَلَّمَ مُغْضَبًا فَأَخَذَ بِمَجَامِعِ ثَوْبِهِ فَاجْتَذَبَهُ وَقَالَ أَلَا أَرَى عَلَيْكَ ثِيَابَ مَنْ لَا يَعْقِلُ ثُمَّ رَجَعَ رَسُولُ اللهِ صَلَّى اللهُ عَلَيْهِ وَسَلَّمَ فَجَلَسَ فَقَالَ إِنَّ نُوحًا لَمَّا حَضَرَتْهُ الْوَفَاةُ دَعَا ابْنَيْهِ فَقَالَ إِنِّي قَاصٌّ عَلَيْكُمَا الْوَصِيَّةَ آمُرُكُمَا بِاثْنَتَيْنِ وَأَنْهَاكُمَا عَنِ اثْنَتَيْنِ أَنْهَاكُمَا عَنِ الشِّرْكِ وَالْكِبْرِ وَآمُرُكُمَا بِلَا إِلٰهَ إِلَّا اللهُ فَإِنَّ السَّمَاوَاتِ وَالْأَرْضَ وَمَا فِيهِنَّ لَوْ وُضِعَتْ فِي كَفَّةِ الْمِيزَانِ

$$\text{وَوُضِعَتْ لَا اِلٰهَ اِلَّا اللّٰهُ فِى الْكِفَّةِ الْاُخْرٰى كَانَتْ اَرْجَحَ مِنْهُمَا وَلَوْ اَنَّ السَّمَاوَاتِ وَالْاَرْضَ وَمَا فِيْهِمَا كَانَتْ حَلْقَةً فَوُضِعَتْ لَا اِلٰهَ اِلَّا اللّٰهُ عَلَيْهَا لَقَصَعَتْهُمَا وَاْمُرْكُمَا بِسُبْحَانَ اللّٰهِ وَبِحَمْدِهٖ فَاِنَّهُمَا صَلَاةُ كُلِّ شَىْءٍ وَبِهِمَا يُرْزَقُ كُلُّ شَىْءٍ (رواه الحاكم # ١٥٤)}$$

Hadhrat Abdullah ibn Amr ؓ narrates that once a villager, who was wearing a long silken robe bordered with silken lace, came to Rasulullah ﷺ, and said to the Sahaabah ؓ: *"This friend of yours wants to exalt every ordinary shepherd and his children, and to degrade every (noble) horseman and his children."* Rasulullah ﷺ got up in anger and pulling his robe by the collar said to him: *"Are you dressed like the people who have no understanding?"* Then after going back to his seat, he added: *"At the time of death, Hadhrat Nooh (alayhis salaam) called his two sons and said to them: 'I recommend to you two things and warn you against two things. The two things against which I warn you are shirk and arrogance. And of the two things which I recommend, one is the Kalimah (laailaaha illallaah), which weighs heavier than the Universe together with all its contents. In fact if this kalimah is placed on it, it will get crushed and crumble on account of its weight; and the second is Subhanallahi wabihamdihi, which two words constitute the dua of all the creation, and by virtue of its blessings, everything gets its sustenance.'"*

Note: The comments of Rasulullah ﷺ on the clothes indicates that the outward appearance provides an indication of one's inner self. When a person's outward behavior is incorrect, his mind is bound to be defective as well. Hence, every effort has to be made to improve the exterior because the interior is dependent on it. The Sufis lay stress on outward cleanliness through wudhu, etc., as a first step for attaining inner purity. Those who talk of internal improvement and ignore the external betterment are incorrect. The external rectification is an independent objective and the internal improvement is a separate objective. One of the duas of Rasulullah ﷺ was:

$$\text{اَللّٰهُمَّ اجْعَلْ سَرِيْرَتِىْ خَيْرًا مِّنْ عَلَانِيَتِىْ وَاجْعَلْ عَلَانِيَتِىْ صَالِحَةً}$$

"O Allah! Make my interior better than my exterior, and make my exterior noble and good."

Hadhrat Umar ﷺ narrates that this dua was taught to me by Rasulullah ﷺ.

Hadith 32 - Benefit of the Kalimah when it is recited by the living and by the one about to pass away

عَنْ أَنَسٍ رَضِيَ اللّٰهُ عَنْهُ أَنَّ أَبَا بَكْرٍ رَضِيَ اللّٰهُ عَنْهُ دَخَلَ عَلَى النَّبِيِّ صَلَّى اللّٰهُ عَلَيْهِ وَسَلَّمَ وَهُوَ كَئِيْبٌ فَقَالَ لَهُ النَّبِيُّ صَلَّى اللّٰهُ عَلَيْهِ وَسَلَّمَ مَالِيْ أَرَاكَ كَئِيْبًا قَالَ يَا رَسُوْلَ اللّٰهِ كُنْتُ عِنْدَ ابْنِ عَمٍّ لِيْ فُلَانٍ اَلْبَارِحَةَ وَهُوَ يَكِيْدُ بِنَفْسِهِ قَالَ فَهَلْ لَقَّنْتَهُ لَا اِلٰهَ اِلَّا اللّٰهُ قَالَ قَدْ فَعَلْتُ يَا رَسُوْلَ اللّٰهِ قَالَ فَقَالَهَا قَالَ نَعَمْ قَالَ وَجَبَتْ لَهُ الْجَنَّةُ قَالَ أَبُوْ بَكْرٍ يَا رَسُوْلَ اللّٰهِ كَيْفَ هِيَ لِلْاَحْيَاءِ قَالَ هِيَ أَهْدَمُ لِذُنُوْبِهِمْ هِيَ أَهْدَمُ لِذُنُوْبِهِمْ

(رواه البزار # ٦٤٩٩)

Hadhrat Anas ﷺ narrates that once Hadhrat Abu Bakr ﷺ came to Rasulullah ﷺ in a very sad mood. Rasulullah ﷺ asked him: "You look very sad. What is the matter with you?" He replied: "My cousin died last night, and I was sitting near him when he breathed his last." "Did you encourage him to recite laailaaha illallaah?" asked Rasulullah ﷺ; "Yes", said he. "Did he recite it?" asked Rasulullah ﷺ. "Yes, he had recited it," said he. "Then certainly he will go to Jannah." said Rasulullah ﷺ. "What do the living people get if they recite this Kalimah?" enquired Abu Bakr ﷺ. Rasulullah ﷺ said twice: "This Kalimah will demolish and eliminate their sins."

Note: Stress is laid in many Ahaadith on reciting the Kalimah near the dead and in the graveyard. It is said in one Hadith that, the Kalimah *(laailaaha illallaah)* should be recited abundantly during a funeral. In another Hadith it is said that *laailaaha illa anta* (none is worthy of worship except You) will be the distinguishing mark of this Ummah when they pass over the Siraat (the Bridge). In yet another Hadith, it is related that when they will rise from their graves on the Day of Qiyaamah, they will be reciting;

لَا اِلٰهَ اِلَّا اللّٰهُ وَعَلَى اللّٰهِ فَلْيَتَوَكَّلِ الْمُؤْمِنُوْنَ

"Nobody is worthy of worship except Allah, and on Him the faithful will rely."

In a third Hadith, it is said that their mark of distinction in the darkness of Qiyaamah will be *laailaaha illa anta*.

The blessings of frequent recitation of the Kalimah becomes apparent just before one's death, and in the case of some pious people, these blessings appear even earlier in their life. Abul Abbaas *(rahmatullahi alayh)* related: "I was lying sick in the town of Ashbila. I saw a large flock of huge birds of different colours, white, red, green, etc., which were spreading their wings all together and there were many men who were carrying something in big covered trays. I understood them to be gifts for a dying person and started reciting the Kalimah Tayyibah hurriedly. Then one of those men said to me that the time of my death had not yet come, and that this was a gift for another believer for whom the time of death had approached."

Just before his death, Hadhrat Umar bin Abdul Aziz *(rahmatullahi alayh)* asked those around him to make him sit up. After they did so, he said: "O Allah! You ordered me to do many things, which I could not do, and You prohibited me from certain things, but I disobeyed you in them." He repeated these words thrice, and then after reciting *laailaaha illallaah* began to stare in one direction. Somebody asked him what was he looking at. He said: "There are some green figures who are neither men nor jinn," and then breathed his last. Somebody saw Zubaidah *(rahmatullahi alayha)* in a dream and asked her how she fared. She replied that she had been forgiven because of reciting these four Kalimahs.

لَا اِلٰهَ اِلَّا اللّٰهُ اُفْنِيْ بِهَا عُمْرِيْ   لَا اِلٰهَ اِلَّا اللّٰهُ اَدْخُلُ بِهَا قَبْرِيْ

لَا اِلٰهَ اِلَّا اللّٰهُ اَخْلُوْ بِهَا وَحْدِيْ   لَا اِلٰهَ اِلَّا اللّٰهُ اَلْقٰى بِهَا رَبِّيْ

1. I will hold fast unto *laailaaha illallaah* until I die.

2. I will take laailaaha illallaah with me into my grave.
3. I will pass my time of solitude with laailaaha illallaah.
4. I will take laailaaha illallaah with me when I meet my Rabb.

Hadith 33 – The Kalimah is the Best of Good Actions

عَنْ اَبِىْ ذَرٍّ رَضِىَ اللهُ عَنْهُ قَالَ قُلْتُ يَا رَسُوْلَ اللهِ اَوْصِنِىْ قَالَ اِذَا عَمِلْتَ سَيِّئَةً فَاَتْبِعْهَا حَسَنَةً تَمْحُهَا قُلْتُ يَا رَسُوْلَ اللهِ اَمِنَ الْحَسَنَاتِ لَا اِلٰهَ اِلَّا اللهُ قَالَ هِىَ اَفْضَلُ الْحَسَنَاتِ (رواه احمد # ٢١٤٨٧)

Hadhrat Abu Zar Ghifaari ﷺ submitted: "O, Rasulullah ﷺ, favour me with some advice." Rasulullah ﷺ said: "When you happen to commit a sin, hasten to do a virtue in atonement, so that the effect of the sin may be washed away." Abu Zar ﷺ then further enquired: "O Rasulullah! ﷺ is the recitation of laailaaha illallaah also a virtue?" "It is the best of all virtues," was the reply of Rasulullah ﷺ.

Note: No doubt, a minor sin is washed away by a virtuous deed, but a major one is wiped off, as a rule, through taubah or of course through the Mercy of Allah Ta'ala, as explained earlier in this book. In either case, the wiped out sin is neither written in the account of deeds nor mentioned anywhere else. It is said in one Hadith that, when a man makes taubah, Allah Ta'ala makes the recording angels forget about that sin. It is forgotten even by the hands and feet of the sinner and even by the piece of land where it was committed, so that there is nobody to give evidence for that sin on the Day of Qiyaamah; when the hands, feet, and other parts of the body of the person himself will stand witness for his good or bad deeds, as will be explained in Hadith No. 18 of Chapter 2 part 3.

The subject matter of the above mentioned Hadith is supported by many other Ahaadith. There are many Ahaadith to the effect that taubah from a sin washes it away, as if one had never committed it. Taubah means to repent and feel ashamed of the sin that has been committed, and make a firm resolution not to repeat it.

According to one Hadith, Rasulullah ﷺ has said: "Worship Allah Ta'ala only, and do not ascribe any partner to Him. Be sincere in all your actions as if you are standing before Allah Ta'ala. Consider yourself among the dead. Remember Allah Ta'ala near every stone and every tree, so that there are many witnesses in your favour on the Day of Qiyaamah. If you happen to commit a sin, do some good deed immediately in place thereof. If the sin is committed in secret, the good deed should also be done in secret, and if the sin is committed openly, the good deed should also be done openly."

Hadith 34 - Forty Thousand Virtues

عَنْ تَمِيْمِ الدَّارِيِّ رَضِيَ اللهُ عَنْهُ قَالَ قَالَ رَسُوْلُ اللهِ صَلَّى اللهُ عَلَيْهِ وَسَلَّمَ مَنْ قَالَ لَا إِلٰهَ إِلَّا اللهُ وَاحِدًا أَحَدًا صَمَدًا لَّمْ يَتَّخِذْ صَاحِبَةً وَّلَا وَلَدًا وَّلَمْ يَكُنْ لَّهُ كُفُوًا أَحَدٌ عَشْرَ مَرَّاتٍ كُتِبَ لَهُ أَرْبَعُوْنَ أَلْفَ حَسَنَةٍ (رواه احمد # ١٦٩٥٢)

Hadhrat Tameem Daari ﷺ narrates that Rasulullah ﷺ has said: "Whosoever recites the following ten times will be rewarded with forty thousand virtues,"

لَا إِلٰهَ إِلَّا اللهُ وَاحِدًا أَحَدًا صَمَدًا لَّمْ يَتَّخِذْ صَاحِبَةً وَّلَا وَلَدًا وَّلَمْ يَكُنْ لَّهُ كُفُوًا أَحَدٌ

Note: Great rewards are mentioned in the books of Hadith for reciting Kalimah Tayyibah a certain number of times. It is said in one Hadith: "When you offer a Fardh Salaah, thereafter recite ten times,

لَا إِلٰهَ إِلَّا اللهُ وَحْدَهُ لَا شَرِيْكَ لَهُ لَهُ الْمُلْكُ وَلَهُ الْحَمْدُ وَهُوَ عَلٰى كُلِّ شَيْءٍ قَدِيْرٌ

its reward is equivalent to that of freeing a slave."

Hadith 35 – Two Million Virtues

عَنْ عَبْدِ اللهِ بْنِ اَبِيْ اَوْفٰى رَضِيَ اللهُ عَنْهُ قَالَ قَالَ رَسُوْلُ اللهِ صَلَّى اللهُ عَلَيْهِ وَسَلَّمَ مَنْ قَالَ لَا إِلٰهَ إِلَّا اللهُ وَحْدَهُ لَا شَرِيْكَ لَهُ أَحَدًا صَمَدًا لَّمْ يَلِدْ وَلَمْ يُوْلَدْ وَلَمْ يَكُنْ لَّهُ كُفُوًا أَحَدٌ كَتَبَ اللهُ لَهُ أَلْفَيْ أَلْفِ حَسَنَةٍ (اخرجه المنذري فى الترغيب # ٢٣٧١)

Hadhrat Abdullah ibn Abi Aufa ﷺ has narrated that Rasulullah ﷺ said: "Whoever recites:

Chapter 2 – Virtues of Kalimah Tayyibah

لَا اِلٰهَ اِلَّا اللّٰهُ وَحْدَهٗ لَا شَرِيْكَ لَهٗ اَحَدًا صَمَدًا لَمْ يَلِدْ وَلَمْ يُوْلَدْ وَلَمْ يَكُنْ لَّهٗ كُفُوًا اَحَدٌ

two million virtues will be written to his credit."

Note: How great is the kindness and benevolence of Allah Ta'ala, that He bestows thousands and millions of virtues just for reciting this Kalimah, which does not involve hard labour or much time; but unfortunately, we are negligent and remain so much absorbed in our worldly pursuits that we never care to take advantage of these bounties.

Allah Ta'ala grants at least ten times reward for every virtue, provided it is done with Ikhlaas. This reward multiplies further according to the degree of sincerity. Rasulullah ﷺ has said: "When a person embraces Islam, all his previous sins are forgiven. Thereafter a record is kept, for every virtue he is rewarded ten to seven hundred times or even more than that as Allah Ta'ala may please. A sin is indicated as a single action, and if it is forgiven by Allah Ta'ala then it is not even mentioned in the account of deeds. According to another Hadith, a virtue is noted in the account of a person as soon as he intends to do it, but when it is actually done its reward is increased from ten to seven hundred times, and even more, as Allah Ta'ala may please. There are many Ahaadith to this effect, that the bounty of Allah Ta'ala knows no limits, provided a person tries to make an effort for it. The pious people keep this in view, so they are not deceived by any amount of worldly wealth.

اللّٰهُمَّ اجْعَلْنِيْ مِنْهُمْ

"O Allah! Make me one of them."

Rasulullah ﷺ had said: "There are six kinds of deeds and four categories of people. Of the deeds, the first two kinds lead to definite results, two carry equivalent rewards while the reward is ten times for the fifth and seven hundred times for the remaining one. Of the first two kinds of deed, one is certain to lead a person to Jannah; who is free from Shirk at the time of his death, and the other is certain to lead a person to Jahannam; who died in a state of Shirk. Of the two kinds of deeds which bring equal rewards, one is to make firm intention for a virtuous deed (before its actual performance), and the other is to commit a sin which is also recorded as only one. The fifth is to do a noble deed, the reward for which is ten times, while the sixth is to spend wealth in the path of Allah Ta'ala, in which case the reward is increased seven hundred times.

Of the four categories of people, the first is of those who enjoy prosperity in this world but will face hardship in the Aakhirah. The second is of those who face difficulty in this world but will enjoy prosperity in the Aakhirah. The people in the third category face difficulty in both the worlds, i.e. they are poor in this life and will be punished in the Aakhirah, and the fourth category includes those who are well off in both the worlds.

A person came to Hadhrat Abu Hurayrah رَضِيَ اللهُ عَنْهُ and asked him if he had narrated that Allah Ta'ala multiplies the reward of some virtues one million times. He replied: "What is surprising about this and swore in confirmation that he had heard it exactly like that." According to another version, he had heard it from Rasulullah ﷺ that the reward of some virtues is up to two million times. Allah Ta'ala says in the Qur-aan Shareef;

$$يُضْعِفْهَا وَيُؤْتِ مِنْ لَدُنْهُ اَجْرًا عَظِيْمًا$$

"that He multiplies the virtues and grants from His treasure great rewards." (Surah Nisaa - Aayah 40)

Can we imagine the great extent of the reward which Allah Ta'ala has described?

According to Imaam Ghazaali *(rahmatullahi alayh)*, the great reward will be possible only if we recite these words with full concentration on their meanings and with the awareness of the great attributes of Allah Ta'ala.

Hadith 36 – Reciting the shahaadatain after wudhu

عَنْ عُمَرَ بْنِ الْخَطَّابِ رَضِيَ اللهُ عَنْهُ قَالَ قَالَ رَسُوْلُ اللهِ صَلَّى اللهُ عَلَيْهِ وَسَلَّمَ مَا مِنْكُمْ مِنْ اَحَدٍ يَتَوَضَّأُ فَيُبْلِغُ اَوْ فَيُسْبِغُ الْوُضُوْءَ ثُمَّ يَقُوْلُ اَشْهَدُ اَنْ لَّا اِلٰهَ اِلَّا اللهُ وَاَشْهَدُ اَنَّ مُحَمَّدًا عَبْدُهُ وَرَسُوْلُهُ اِلَّا فُتِحَتْ لَهُ اَبْوَابُ الْجَنَّةِ الثَّمَانِيَةُ يَدْخُلُ مِنْ اَيِّهَا شَاءَ (رواه مسلم # ٢٣٤)

Hadhrat Umar Ibnul Khattaab ؓ narrates that Rasulullah ﷺ said, "When a person performs wudhu and performs the wudhu properly (i.e. observing all its essentials as well as details) and then recites:

اَشْهَدُ اَنْ لَّا اِلٰهَ اِلَّا اللهُ وَاَشْهَدُ اَنَّ مُحَمَّدًا عَبْدُهُ وَرَسُوْلُهُ

(I bear witness that there is none worthy of worship except Allah, the One who has no partner, and also that Muhammad ﷺ is His slave and Rasool) all the eight gates of Jannah are thrown open for him, so that he may enter as he likes, through anyone of them."

Note: One gate is enough for entering Jannah, but to open up all the eight gates is a mark of special welcome and an extreme favour. According to another Hadith, a person who did not indulge in Shirk before his death, and never committed any unlawful murder, is allowed to enter Jannah as he may like through any one of its gates.

Hadith 37 – Reciting the Kalimah 100 times a day

عَنْ أَبِي الدَّرْدَاءِ رَضِيَ اللهُ عَنْهُ عَنِ النَّبِيِّ صَلَّى اللهُ عَلَيْهِ وَسَلَّمَ قَالَ لَيْسَ مِنْ عَبْدٍ يَقُوْلُ لَا اِلٰهَ اِلَّا اللهُ مِائَةَ مَرَّةٍ اِلَّا بَعَثَهُ اللهُ يَوْمَ الْقِيَامَةِ وَوَجْهُهُ كَالْقَمَرِ لَيْلَةَ الْبَدْرِ وَلَمْ يُرْفَعْ لِاَحَدٍ يَوْمَئِذٍ عَمَلٌ اَفْضَلُ مِنْ عَمَلِهِ اِلَّا مَنْ قَالَ مِثْلَ قَوْلِهِ اَوْ زَادَ

(اخرجه السيوطى فى مجمع الزوائد # ١٦٨٣٠)

Hadhrat Abu Darda ؓ narrates that Rasulullah ﷺ mentioned that, "One who recites laailaaha illallaah one hundred times a day, will be raised with his face shining like the full moon on the Day of Qiyaamah, and no one can surpass him in excellence on that day except one who recites this Kalimah more than him."

Note: Many Ahaadith and Aayaat confirm that *laailaaha illallaah* is a light for the heart as well as for the face. It has been observed that the pious people who are used to reciting this Kalimah excessively have a sort of brightness over their faces, even during their worldly life.

Hadith 38 – Reciting the kalimah at the time of death

عَنِ ابْنِ عَبَّاسٍ رَضِيَ اللهُ عَنْهُ عَنِ النَّبِيِّ صَلَّى اللهُ عَلَيْهِ وَسَلَّمَ قَالَ افْتَحُوْا عَلَى صِبْيَانِكُمْ أَوَّلَ كَلِمَةٍ بِلَا اِلٰهَ اِلَّا اللهُ وَلَقِّنُوْهُمْ عِنْدَ الْمَوْتِ لَا اِلٰهَ اِلَّا اللهُ فَاِنَّهُ مَنْ كَانَ أَوَّلُ كَلَامِهِ لَا اِلٰهَ اِلَّا اللهُ وَاٰخِرُ كَلَامِهِ لَا اِلٰهَ اِلَّا اللهُ ثُمَّ عَاشَ اَلْفَ سَنَةٍ لَمْ يُسْئَلْ عَنْ ذَنْبٍ وَّاحِدٍ (رواه البيهقى فى شعب الايمان # ٨٢٨٢)

Hadhrat Ibn Abbaas رَضِيَ اللهُ عَنْهُ narrates that Rasulullah ﷺ says, "Teach the Kalimah laailaaha illallaah to a child when he starts speaking and encourage a dying person to recite laailaaha illallaah. He who has had his beginning with laailaaha illallaah and has his end with laailaaha illallaah, will not be required to account for any of his sins, even though he lives for a thousand years, (i.e. either he would commit no sin, or if he happened to commit any sin, it would be written off because of taubah or through the sheer mercy of Allah Ta'ala)."

Note: Talqeen means to encourage a dying man to recite the Kalimah. Those sitting near him should recite it audibly, so that on hearing it he may also do the same. He should not be forced to do so, because he may be in a state of agony. 'A dying person should be persuaded to recite the Kalimah' has been stressed in many Ahaadith. In several Ahaadith, Rasulullah ﷺ is reported to have said, "The sins of a person who is blessed to recite the Kalimah at the time of death are washed off just as a building is washed away by flood water." According to other Ahaadith, one who recites this blessed Kalimah before his death gets all his past sins forgiven. It is said in one Hadith that a munaafiq (hypocrite) is never able to recite it (at the time of his death). It is said in another Hadith that we should give *laailaaha illallaah* as a provision to our deceased ones. According to a Hadith, one who brings up a child till he is able to recite *laailaaha illallaah*, will not be required to give any account for him. In one Hadith it is said, "When a person, who has been steadfast in offering Salaah, is about to die, an angel comes to him, drives away shaytaan and encourages him to recite the Kalimah *laailaaha illallaah*."

However, it is often observed that this sort of encouragement is only useful in the case of those who are used to the recitation of the Kalimah during their lifetime. A story is related about a person who used to trade in straw. When he was about to die, people tried to encourage him to recite the Kalimah, but he only cried out, "The price of this bundle is so much and of that is so much." Many such incidents, which had been actually observed, have been described in the book, *'Nuzhatul Basaateen'*.

The harms of opium and the benefits of miswaak

Many a time, sins prevent a dying person from reciting the Kalimah. The Ulama say that opium has seventy disadvantages, one of which is that the person who takes opium cannot remember the Kalimah at the time of his death. On the other hand, brushing one's teeth (with miswaak) carries seventy benefits, one of which is to recite the Kalimah at the time of his death. It is related about one man that, when he was persuaded to recite the Kalimah before his death, he expressed his inability to recite, because he said he used to cheat through under weighing. There is a story of another person who, when persuaded to recite the Kalimah, said, "I cannot say it, because I was tempted to cast sinful glances on a woman who had come to purchase towels from my shop." Many such stories are related in the book, *'Tazkirah Qurtubiyyah'*. Taking the abovementioned into account, it is necessary for a person to ask and seek the help of Allah Ta'ala, forgiveness of his sins, and to recite the Kalimah at the time of his death.

Hadith 39 – The Kalimah washes away one's sins

عَنْ أُمِّ هَانِئٍ رَضِيَ اللهُ عَنْهَا قَالَتْ قَالَ رَسُوْلُ اللهِ صَلَّى اللهُ عَلَيْهِ وَسَلَّمَ لَا اِلٰهَ اِلَّا اللهُ لَا يَسْبِقُهَا عَمَلٌ وَّلَا تَتْرُكُ ذَنْبًا (رواه ابن ماجه # ٣٧٩٧)

Hadhrat Umm-e-Haani ﷺ narrates that Rasulullah ﷺ said, "No deed can excel the recitation of laailaaha illallaah and this Kalimah does not let any sin remain unwashed."

Note: No deed can excel this Kalimah is quite obvious, because without belief in this Kalimah no action carries any reward. It is a requirement for the acceptance of Salaah, Fasting, Haj and Zakaat, because without Imaan, no action is acceptable. Recitation of Kalimah Tayyibah, which is a declaration of our faith, is not dependent on anything else. If a person has only Imaan and no other virtue in his account, sooner or later he is bound (through the grace of Allah Ta'ala) to get admission into Jannah. On the other hand, if a person does not possess Imaan, then no amount of good deeds will be sufficient for his salvation.

The second part of the above-mentioned Hadith is that the Kalimah does not let any sin remain unwashed. It is unanimously agreed that if a person embraces Islam in his old age and immediately after recitation of the Kalimah he happens to meet his death, then all his sins which he had committed as a disbeliever before his declaration of Imaan are forgiven. However, if recitation of the Kalimah in an earlier stage is implied, then the Hadith means that the Kalimah purifies and polishes the heart and its excessive recitation will cleanse the heart, to such an extent that he must make Taubah, which will result in the forgiveness of his sins. According to one Hadith, if a person is particular on reciting *laailaaha illallaah* before going to sleep and after getting up, even his worldly affairs will lead to the betterment of his life in the Aakhirah, and he will be guarded against misfortune and trouble.

Hadith 40 – Seventy branches of Imaan

عَنْ أَبِيْ هُرَيْرَةَ رَضِيَ اللهُ عَنْهُ قَالَ قَالَ رَسُوْلُ اللهِ صَلَّى اللهُ عَلَيْهِ وَسَلَّمَ اَلْإِيْمَانُ بِضْعٌ وَسَبْعُوْنَ شُعْبَةً فَأَفْضَلُهَا قَوْلُ لَا اِلٰهَ اِلَّا اللهُ وَاَدْنَاهَا اِمَاطَةُ الْأَذٰى عَنِ الطَّرِيْقِ وَالْحَيَاءُ شُعْبَةٌ مِّنَ الْاِيْمَانِ (رواه مسلم # ٣٥)

Hadhrat Abu Hurayrah ﷺ narrates that Rasulullah ﷺ has said, "Imaan has more than seventy branches (according to some, seventy seven), of which the greatest is the recitation of *laailaaha illallaah* and the lowest is to remove some obstacle (stone, wood, thorns, etc.) from the path and modesty also is a special branch of Imaan."

Note: Modesty has been specially mentioned because it serves as a safeguard against many sins like adultery, theft, dirty talk, nakedness, abusive language, etc. Similarly, the fear of bad reputation often becomes the reason for doing some virtuous acts. In fact, the fear of getting a bad name in this world as well as in the next life influences a man towards good deeds, including Salaah, Hajj, Zakaat, etc, and also obedience in all respects to Allah Ta'ala. Thus, there is the well-known proverb, "Become shameless and then do whatever you like." There is also one Hadith to this effect

اِذَا لَمْ تَسْتَحْيِ فَاصْنَعْ مَا شِئْتَ (رواه البخارى # ٣٤٨٤)

"If you do not have shame, then do as you please."

The fact is that we abstain from misdeeds for fear of disgrace and shame. A sense of modesty and shame makes one think, "If I do not offer Salaah, I will face disgrace in the Aakhirah." But if one has lost all sense of shame, he will say "What does it matter if others speak low about me?"

Seventy Branches of Imaan

Important Note: According to the above-mentioned Hadith, there are more than seventy branches of Imaan. In many Ahaadith, this number is given as seventy-seven. The Ulama have written detailed commentaries on these seventy-seven branches. Imaam Abu Haatim ibn Hibbaan *(rahmatullahi alayh)* wrote; "I pondered on the meaning of this Hadith for a long time. When I counted the different forms of ibaadat (worship), the number far exceeded seventy-seven. If I counted the things which are specially mentioned in the Ahaadith as branches of Imaan, their number was less. The things counted as part of Imaan in the Qur-aan Shareef would also total less than this. However, I found that the total of such things mentioned in both the Qur-aan Shareef as well as the Hadith, conformed with this number. I therefore concluded that the above-mentioned Hadith implied all these things."

Qaadhi Iyaadh *(rahmatullahi alayh)* writes, "Some people have made special efforts to give details of these branches of Imaan by means of Ijtihaad, but failure to know all these details does not cause any defect in one's Imaan, as its basic principles (with their details) are so well known". Khattaabi *(rahmatullahi alayh)* says that full details of the exact number is known only to Allah Ta'ala and His Rasul ﷺ, but they are there in the Islamic Code (Shariat), and therefore does not matter if their details are not known.

Imaam Nawawi *(rahmatullahi alayh)* has written that Rasulullah ﷺ has said that the Kalimah Tauheed i.e. *(laailaaha illallaah)* is the most important branch of Imaan. This proves that it is the highest aspect of Imaan, and that no other branch of Imaan is superior to it.

Thus, belief in Tauheed is the most important requirement of Imaan and is compulsory on every believer. The least thing (in the order of merit) is the removal of anything that is likely to cause obstruction or inconvenience to any Muslim. The degree of importance of all the remaining essentials of Imaan lies in between the two; it is enough to believe in them in a general way just as it is necessary to believe in the Malaaikah without knowing all the details. Some Muhadditheen have however written books about their details. Abu Abdullah Haleemi *(rahmatullahi alayh)* wrote a book, *'Fawaaidul Minhaaj'* on this topic. Imaam Bayhaqi *(rahmatullahi alayh)* and Shaikh Abdul Jaleel *(rahmatullahi alayh)* wrote books both of which are called *'Shu-abul Imaan'*. Ishaaq Qurtubi *(rahmatullahi alayh)* wrote *'Kitabun Nasaa-ih'* and Imam Abu Haatim wrote *'Wasful Imaan wa Shu-abihi'*.

The commentators of *'Bukhari'*, the most famous collection of Ahaadith, have summarised the contents of these books at one place. The gist of this summary is that complete Imaan in reality consists of three components:

1. Firstly, confirmation by the heart of all the essentials of Imaan,
2. Secondly, confirmation by the mouth; and
3. Thirdly, confirmation by our actions.

Thus, the branches of Imaan are divided into three categories, the first of which concerns the intention, belief and action of the heart, the second concerns the use of the tongue, and the third concerns all the remaining parts of the body. All the things of Imaan are included in these three categories. The first category includes thirty articles of Imaan which are as follows:

1. To believe in Allah Ta'ala, in His Being and His Attributes, and that He is One, has no partner, and that there is no one like Him.
2. To believe that everything besides Allah Ta'ala was created afterwards by Allah Ta'ala and that only Allah Ta'ala has been forever.
3. To believe in the Malaaikah.
4. To believe in the revealed Books.
5. To believe in the messengers of Allah Ta'ala.
6. To believe in Taqdeer (fate or destiny), i.e. whether it is good or bad, it is ordained by Allah Ta'ala.

7. To believe in the life after death, including questioning in the grave, punishment in the grave, resurrection on the Day of Qiyaamah, giving an account of one's deeds, and passing over the bridge of Siraat.
8. To believe in the existence of Jannah, and that (by the grace of Allah Ta'ala) the Muslims will live in it forever.
9. To believe in the existence of Jahannam, with its severest punishments, and that it will last forever.
10. To love Allah Ta'ala.
11. To love or hate people for the pleasure of Allah Ta'ala (i.e. to love the pious and hate the disobedient). It includes, loving the Sahaabah رَضِىَ اللهُ عَنْهُم, especially the Muhaajireen, Ansaar, and the descendants of Rasulullah صَلَّى اللهُ عَلَيْهِ وَسَلَّم.
12. To love Rasulullah صَلَّى اللهُ عَلَيْهِ وَسَلَّم, which includes having the highest respect and regard for him, offering Durood on him, and following the Sunnah i.e. his way of life.
13. To practice Ikhlaas, which includes avoiding show and hypocrisy.
14. To make Taubah i.e. to repent over one's sins from the bottom of the heart, and to be determined not to repeat them ever again.
15. To fear Allah Ta'ala.
16. To hope and pray for the mercy of Allah Ta'ala.
17. Not to lose hope of the mercy of Allah Ta'ala.
18. To remain thankful to Allah Ta'ala.
19. To be faithful in one's promise.
20. To have patience.
21. To have humility, which includes respect for the elders.
22. To show kindness and pity, which includes kindness to children.
23. To be pleased with whatever Allah Ta'ala has destined for us.
24. To have tawakkul i.e. to have complete trust in Allah Ta'ala.
25. To refrain from self-praise and self-admiration which is part of self-reformation.
26. Not to have hatred and jealousy for others.
27. To cultivate modesty. (This point was left out in Allamah Aini's kitaab because of the error of the scribe. Hadhrat Shaikh (rahmatullahi alayh) has added it on.)
28. Not to get angry.
29. Not to deceive, cheat or have suspicions for others.

30. To expel the love of worldly things from one's heart, including that for wealth and status.

According to Allamah Ainee *(rahmatullahi alayh)*, this list covers all the functions of the heart. If anything is found apparently missing, then pondering a little will show that it is covered by one item or the other in this list.

The second category includes the functions of the tongue, and there are seven essentials in this respect, as follows:
1. Recitation of Kalimah Tayyibah.
2. Recitation of the Qur-aan Shareef.
3. Acquisition of the Ilm of Deen (religious knowledge).
4. Propagation of Deeni knowledge to others.
5. Dua, i.e. supplication.
6. Zikr of Allah Ta'ala, including Istighfaar (asking for forgiveness).
7. To abstain from useless talk.

The third category includes physical actions. In this respect, there are forty essentials which are divided into three parts. The first part which includes actions that relate to the person himself. These are sixteen, as follows:
1. Observing cleanliness of the body, clothes and place. The cleanliness of the body include wudhu and obligatory bath, purification from haiz and nifaas (menstruation and post-birth blood).
2. Establishing Salaah, including Fardh, Nafl and Qadhaa Salaah. This would mean offering Salaah in such a manner that all its requirements and etiquettes are fulfilled.
3. Giving sadaqah (charity), which includes Zakaat, Sadaqatul-Fitr, voluntary charity, feeding people, entertaining guests and freeing slaves.
4. Fasting, obligatory as well non-obligatory.
5. Performing Hajj, obligatory or non-obligatory. It includes making Umrah and Tawaaf.
6. I'tikaaf (remaining in a masjid in full devotion), which includes searching for Lailatul Qadr.
7. Leaving one's home for the defense of the Deen. This includes Hijrat (migration for the sake of Allah Ta'ala).
8. Fulfilling one's vows.

9. Steadfastness in one's oaths.
10. Payment of kaffarah (money in lieu of unfulfilled obligations), if it is due.
11. Covering the essential parts of the body, as required by Islam, during Salaah and outside Salaah.
12. Offering of Qurbaani and taking care of the animals to be sacrificed.
13. Making arrangements for the funeral.
14. Payment of debts.
15. To correct our dealings and abstaining from usury and interest.
16. Giving correct evidence and not concealing the truth.

The second part, which concerns the relationship with one's relatives and others, has six essentials:

1. Getting married to protect one's chastity.
2. To discharge obligations towards one's family members, servants and subordinates.
3. Good treatment towards one's parents and being kind and obedient to them.
4. Bringing up one's children in a proper way.
5. Remaining on good terms with one's relatives.
6. Obeying one's elders, and following their advice.

The third part includes eighteen essentials, which relates to our social obligations to society in general:

1. To rule one's domain with justice.
2. To support the party that is on the truth.
3. To obey the rulers, provided their orders are not against Deen.
4. To work for the betterment of mutual relations, including punishing the wrong-doers and making Jihaad against the rebels.
5. To help others in their noble deeds.
6. To enjoin the good and forbid the evil. It includes work and speech for propagation of Deen.
7. To carry out the punishments enjoined by the Shariat (for specific offences).
8. To take part in Jihaad i.e. to fight in the path of Allah Ta'ala. It includes guarding the defense lines.
9. To pay off your dues and return amaanats; this includes payment of Khums (payment of tax equal to one fifth of the booty).

10. To lend (to the needy) and to pay back debts.
11. To discharge our obligations to our neighbours and to be kind and helpful to them.
12. To be fair in one's business dealings. This includes earning and saving in a lawful manner.
13. To be careful in one's expenditure. One should guard against extravagance as well as miserliness.
14. To make salaam and respond to the salaam.
15. To say *Yarhamukallah* (May Allah Ta'ala have mercy on you) to the person who sneezes.
16. Not to be the cause of any trouble and loss to others.
17. To avoid idle and useless pursuits.
18. To clear any obstructions from the way.

The seventy-seven branches of Imaan have been counted above. Some of these can be merged together; for example earning and spending can be put together, under fair dealings. Careful consideration can enable one to cut down the total to seventy or sixty-seven, which are the totals given in some Ahaadith.

The above list has been prepared mainly from the commentary of Allamah Ainee *(rahmatullahi alayh)* on *'Bukhaari Shareef*, wherein these things are mentioned in their order of merit. Selection has also been made from other books, i.e. *Fathul-Baari* of Ibnu Hajar *(rahmatullahi alayh)* and *Mirqaat* of Mulla Ali Qaari *(rahmatullahi alayh).*

Ulama have written that the essentials of Imaan are given above. One should ponder over these and be thankful to Allah Ta'ala for the good qualities acquired already, because all goodness is possible only through His grace and mercy. In case there is a shortfall with respect to any quality, one should strive for it and keep on making dua that Allah Ta'ala grace him with His blessings.

وَمَا تَوْفِيْقِيْ اِلَّا بِاللهِ

CHAPTER 3
VIRTUES OF THE THIRD KALIMAH

سُبْحَانَ اللهِ وَالْحَمْدُ لِلّٰهِ وَلَا اِلٰهَ اِلَّا اللهُ وَاللهُ اَكْبَرُ

The virtues of the third Kalimah, i.e.

سُبْحَانَ اللهِ وَالْحَمْدُ لِلّٰهِ وَلَا اِلٰهَ اِلَّا اللهُ وَاللهُ اَكْبَرُ

According to some narrations it is also followed by *laahowla walaaquwwata illaa billah*, as will be described in this chapter. These words are also known as Tasbihaat-e-Faatimah, because Rasulullah ﷺ had advised his most beloved daughter, Hadhrat Faatimah رضي الله عنها, to recite these tasbeehs regularly, as will be described later on. There are many Aayaat of the Qur-aan Shareef and several Ahaadith in respect of this Kalimah. This chapter is divided into two parts. The first part contains Aayaat from the Qur-aan Shareef and the second part the sayings of Rasulullah ﷺ.

SECTION 1
AAYAAT PERTAINING TO THE 3ʳᴰ KALIMAH

This part includes Aayaat of the Qur-aan Shareef that relate to the Kalimah;

$$\text{سُبْحَانَ اللهِ وَالْحَمْدُ لِلهِ وَلَا اِلٰهَ اِلَّا اللهُ وَاللهُ اَكْبَرُ}$$

It is an accepted rule that the greater the importance of the subject matter, more stress will be laid on the method of explaining it, so that it is properly understood. Therefore, the meanings and significance of these words have been explained in various ways in the Qur-aan Shareef.

The first of these phrases is *Subhaanallah*. It means that Allah Ta'ala is free from all defects and shortcomings and it is a declaration of firm belief in His being absolutely pure. Allah Ta'ala has ordered its recitation and has also informed us that the Malaaikah and all other creation remain busy in reciting it. It is also the case with the other words of this Kalimah in that their significance and importance is stressed in so many ways in the Qur-aan Shareef.

Aayaat of Tasbeeh *(Subhaanallah)*

$$١. \quad \text{وَنَحْنُ نُسَبِّحُ بِحَمْدِكَ وَنُقَدِّسُ لَكَ}$$

1. (At the time of creation of man, the Malaaikah had said) "We (always) glorify You with Your praises and proclaim Your purity."
(Surah Baqarah - Aayah 30)

$$٢. \quad \text{قَالُوْا سُبْحَانَكَ لَا عِلْمَ لَنَآ اِلَّا مَا عَلَّمْتَنَا ۖ اِنَّكَ اَنْتَ الْعَلِيْمُ الْحَكِيْمُ}$$

2. (When the Malaaikah were put to a test) "They (the Malaaikah) submitted, "We proclaim Your purity! We have no knowledge except that which You have taught us; You are the All Knowing, the Wise."
(Surah Baqarah - Aayah 32)

$$٣. \quad \text{وَاذْكُرْ رَّبَّكَ كَثِيْرًا وَّسَبِّحْ بِالْعَشِيِّ وَالْاِبْكَارِ}$$

3. "Remember your Rabb exceedingly, and praise / glorify (Him) by night and day." (Surah Aali I'mraan - Aayah 41)

$$٤. \quad \text{رَبَّنَا مَا خَلَقْتَ هٰذَا بَاطِلًا ۚ سُبْحَانَكَ فَقِنَا عَذَابَ النَّارِ}$$

4. (Wise men are those who remain busy in the zikr of Allah, and ponder over the wonders of Nature and say,) "O our Rabb! You have

not created all this without any purpose, Glory be to You, so save us from the punishment of Jahannam." *(Surah Aali I'mraan - Aayah 191)*

$$سُبْحٰنَهٗٓ اَنْ يَّكُوْنَ لَهٗ وَلَدٌ$$

5. "He is Pure from having any children." *(Surah Nisaa' - Aayah 171)*

$$قَالَ سُبْحٰنَكَ مَا يَكُوْنُ لِيْٓ اَنْ اَقُوْلَ مَا لَيْسَ لِيْ ۛ بِحَقٍّ$$

6. (On the day of Qiyaamah when Allah Ta'ala would enquire from Hadhrat Isa (alayhis salaam) whether he had preached the belief of Trinity to his people), he would say "I express Your purity! It does not befit me to say what I have no right to say." *(Surah Maaidah - Aayah 116)*

$$سُبْحٰنَهٗ وَتَعٰلٰى عَمَّا يَصِفُوْنَ$$

7. "He is Pure from and Exalted above all those things that they (the disbelievers) ascribe (to Him)." *(Surah An'aam - Aayah 100)*

$$فَلَمَّآ اَفَاقَ قَالَ سُبْحٰنَكَ تُبْتُ اِلَيْكَ وَاَنَا اَوَّلُ الْمُؤْمِنِيْنَ$$

8. (When, on the mountain of Toor, Hadhrat Moosa (alayhis salaam) could not withstand even a glimpse of the glory of Allah Ta'ala and became unconscious), "and when he recovered he said, 'I declare Your purity. I repent to You and I am the first of the true believers (Mu'mineen)." *(Surah A'araaf - Aayah 143)*

$$اِنَّ الَّذِيْنَ عِنْدَ رَبِّكَ لَا يَسْتَكْبِرُوْنَ عَنْ عِبَادَتِهٖ وَيُسَبِّحُوْنَهٗ وَلَهٗ يَسْجُدُوْنَ$$

9. "Verily those who are near to your Rabb (i.e. the Malaaikah) are not too proud to worship Him. They praise Him (His purity) and make sajdah to Him alone." *(Surah A'araaf - Aayah 206)*

The Sufis have written that not to be proud (i.e. getting rid of pride) is being mentioned before anything else. This indicates that to be free from pride is a requirement for constancy in ibaadah and that pride makes one neglectful in one's ibaadah.

$$\text{١٠. } \text{سُبْحٰنَهٗ عَمَّا يُشْرِكُوْنَ}$$

10. "He (Allah Ta'ala) is pure from all that they (the disbelievers) ascribe as partners (to Him)." *(Surah Taubah - Aayah 31)*

$$\text{١١. } \text{دَعْوٰىهُمْ فِيْهَا سُبْحٰنَكَ اللّٰهُمَّ وَتَحِيَّتُهُمْ فِيْهَا سَلٰمٌ ۚ وَاٰخِرُ دَعْوٰىهُمْ اَنِ الْحَمْدُ لِلّٰهِ رَبِّ الْعٰلَمِيْنَ}$$

11. "Their (i.e. of dwellers of Jannah) dua there (in Jannah) shall be 'O Allah! You are Pure', and their greetings will be 'Salaam (peace)' and the conclusion of their dua will be 'All praise belongs to Allah Ta'ala, the Rabb of the universe.'" *(Surah Yunus - Aayah 10)*

$$\text{١٢. } \text{سُبْحٰنَهٗ وَتَعٰلٰى عَمَّا يُشْرِكُوْنَ}$$

12. "He (Allah Ta'ala) is Pure and exalted above all that they (non-believers) ascribe to Him." *(Surah Yunus - Aayah 18)*

$$\text{١٣. } \text{قَالُوا اتَّخَذَ اللّٰهُ وَلَدًا سُبْحٰنَهٗ ۖ هُوَ الْغَنِيُّ}$$

13. "They (the kuffaar) say, 'Allah has taken a son.' He is Pure (from this). He is independent." *(Surah Yunus - Aayah 68)*

$$\text{١٤. } \text{وَسُبْحٰنَ اللّٰهِ وَمَآ اَنَا مِنَ الْمُشْرِكِيْنَ}$$

14. "Glory be to Allah, and I am not from the idolaters."
(Surah Yusuf - Aayah 108)

$$\text{١٥. } \text{وَيُسَبِّحُ الرَّعْدُ بِحَمْدِهٖ وَالْمَلٰٓئِكَةُ مِنْ خِيْفَتِهٖ}$$

15. "And the thunder (Malaaikah in charge of the thunder) praises Him (Allah Ta'ala) together with glorifying Him, and the (other) Malaaikah also do so out of fear for Him." *(Surah R'ad - Aayah 13)*

It is mentioned by the Ulama that if anybody, on hearing thunder, recites the following, will be protected from the harm of the lightening.

Chapter 3 – Virtues of the Third Kalimah

سُبْحَانَ الَّذِىْ يُسَبِّحُ الرَّعْدُ بِحَمْدِهٖ وَالْمَلَائِكَةُ مِنْ خِيْفَتِهٖ

Subhannallazi yusabbihur R'adu bi hamdihi wal Malaaikatu min kheefatihi

It is narrated in one Hadith, "Make zikr of Allah Ta'ala when you hear the thunder of lightening, because it cannot harm one who is making zikr." It is narrated in another Hadith, "At the time of thunder say *Subhaanallah* and not *Allahu-Akbar.*

16. وَلَقَدْ نَعْلَمُ اَنَّكَ يَضِيْقُ صَدْرُكَ بِمَا يَقُوْلُوْنَ ۞ فَسَبِّحْ بِحَمْدِ رَبِّكَ وَ كُنْ مِّنَ السّٰجِدِيْنَ ۞ وَاعْبُدْ رَبَّكَ حَتّٰى يَأْتِيَكَ الْيَقِيْنُ

16. "We know very well that your bosom (heart) is tightened (distressed / hurt) by what they say. So glorify the praises of your Rabb and be of those who make sajdah (perform Salaah). And worship your Rabb until the certainty (i.e. death) comes to you."
(Surah Hijr - Aayah 97-99)

17. سُبْحٰنَهٗ وَتَعٰلٰى عَمَّا يُشْرِكُوْنَ

17. "He is Pure and Exalted above all that they associate (as partners with Him)." (Surah Nahl - Aayah 1)

18. وَيَجْعَلُوْنَ لِلّٰهِ الْبَنٰتِ سُبْحٰنَهٗ وَلَهُمْ مَّا يَشْتَهُوْنَ

18. "And they (the Mushrikeen) assign daughters to Allah Ta'ala. He is Pure (from needing a family)! Yet they have for themselves what they desire." (Surah Nahl - Aayah 57)

19. سُبْحٰنَ الَّذِىْ اَسْرٰى بِعَبْدِهٖ لَيْلًا مِّنَ الْمَسْجِدِ الْحَرَامِ اِلَى الْمَسْجِدِ الْاَقْصَا

19. "Pure is that Being Who transported His slave (Rasulullah ﷺ) by night from Masjidul Haraam to Masjidul Aqsa."
(Surah Bani Israaeel - Aayah 1)

$$ \text{٢٠. سُبْحَٰنَهُۥ وَتَعَٰلَىٰ عَمَّا يَقُولُونَ عُلُوًّا كَبِيرًا} $$

20. "Glorified is He; He (Allah Ta'ala) is Pure, exalted and extremely high above what they say." (Surah Bani Israaeel - Aayah 43)

$$ \text{٢١. تُسَبِّحُ لَهُ السَّمَٰوَٰتُ السَّبْعُ وَالْأَرْضُ وَمَن فِيهِنَّ} $$

21. "The seven heavens and earth together with what is within them glorify / praise Him (Allah Ta'ala)."
(Surah Bani Israaeel - Aayah 44)

$$ \text{٢٢. وَإِن مِّن شَيْءٍ إِلَّا يُسَبِّحُ بِحَمْدِهِۦ وَلَٰكِن لَّا تَفْقَهُونَ تَسْبِيحَهُمْ} $$

22. "And there is not a thing that does not glorify His praises, but you do not understand their praises." (Surah Bani Israaeel - Aayah 44)

$$ \text{٢٣. قُلْ سُبْحَانَ رَبِّي هَلْ كُنتُ إِلَّا بَشَرًا رَّسُولًا} $$

23. (In reply to the absurd demands of the Kuffar Rasulullah ﷺ was commanded) "Say, 'My Rabb is Pure! I am but a human and a Rasool.'" (Surah Bani Israaeel - Aayah 93)

$$ \text{٢٤. وَيَقُولُونَ سُبْحَٰنَ رَبِّنَا إِن كَانَ وَعْدُ رَبِّنَا لَمَفْعُولًا} $$

24. (When the Qur-aan is recited before those who are blessed with the knowledge of Deen, they go down in sajdah) "And they say, 'Glory be to our Rabb. Without doubt, the promise of our Rabb has surely come to pass.'" (Surah Bani Israaeel - Aayah 108)

$$ \text{٢٥. فَخَرَجَ عَلَىٰ قَوْمِهِۦ مِنَ الْمِحْرَابِ فَأَوْحَىٰ إِلَيْهِمْ أَن سَبِّحُوا بُكْرَةً وَعَشِيًّا} $$

25. "So when he (Hadhrat Zakariyya alayhis salaam) came to his people from the mihraab (his place where he engaged in Ibaadah), he indicated to them, 'Glorify your Rabb morning and evening.'"
(Surah Maryam - Aayah 11)

Chapter 3 – Virtues of the Third Kalimah

٢٦. مَا كَانَ لِلّٰهِ اَنْ يَّتَّخِذَ مِنْ وَّلَدٍ سُبْحٰنَهٗ

26. "It does not befit Allah Ta'ala that He should take a son, He is pure." (Surah Maryam - Aayah 35)

٢٧. وَسَبِّحْ بِحَمْدِ رَبِّكَ قَبْلَ طُلُوْعِ الشَّمْسِ وَقَبْلَ غُرُوْبِهَا وَمِنْ اٰنَآئِ الَّيْلِ فَسَبِّحْ وَاَطْرَافَ النَّهَارِ لَعَلَّكَ تَرْضٰى

27. "So (O Muhammad ﷺ), patiently bear with what they (the kuffaar) say and glorify the praises of your Rabb before the rising of the sun and before it sets. And glorify Him during the hours of the night and at the ends of the day, so that you will become pleased. (because of the rewards you could expect)." (Surah Taahaa - Aayah 130)

٢٨. يُسَبِّحُوْنَ الَّيْلَ وَالنَّهَارَ لَا يَفْتُرُوْنَ

28. "They (The pious people) glorify Him (Allah Ta'ala) night and day without being tired." (Surah Ambiyaa - Aayah 20)

٢٩. فَسُبْحٰنَ اللّٰهِ رَبِّ الْعَرْشِ عَمَّا يَصِفُوْنَ

29. "Allah Ta'ala, the Rabb of the Arsh (throne), is Pure from all that they attribute (to Him as equals)." (Surah Ambiyaa - Aayah 22)

٣٠. وَقَالُوا اتَّخَذَ الرَّحْمٰنُ وَلَدًا سُبْحٰنَهٗ

30. "And they (the mushrikeen) say, Ar Rahmaan (the Beneficent) has taken children (for Himself). He is Pure (from needing children)." (Surah Ambiyaa - Aayah 26)

٣١. وَسَخَّرْنَا مَعَ دَاوٗدَ الْجِبَالَ يُسَبِّحْنَ وَالطَّيْرَ

31. "And We subjugated the mountains and the birds to Dawood (alayhis salaam) and they all engage in the glorification of Allah Ta'ala." (Surah Ambiyaa - Aayah 79)

٣٢. لَّآ اِلٰهَ اِلَّآ اَنْتَ سُبْحٰنَكَ ۖ اِنِّىْ كُنْتُ مِنَ الظّٰلِمِيْنَ

32. (Yunus Alayhis Salaam cried out in the darkness of the belly of the fish saying) "There is no god but You (O Allah Ta'ala), You are Pure. I have certainly been from among the wrongdoers."
(Surah Ambiyaa - Aayah 87)

٣٣. سُبْحٰنَ اللهِ عَمَّا يَصِفُوْنَ

33. "Allah Ta'ala is Pure of all (the partners) that they attribute to Him." (Surah Mu'minoon - Aayah 91)

٣٤. سُبْحٰنَكَ هٰذَا بُهْتَانٌ عَظِيْمٌ

34. "Glory be to You. All of this (that they falsely allege against Hadhrat Aaishah رَضِىَ اللهُ عَنْهَا) is a great slander." (Surah Noor - Aayah 16)

٣٥. يُسَبِّحُ لَهٗ فِيْهَا بِالْغُدُوِّ وَالْاٰصَالِ ۙ رِجَالٌ ۙ لَّا تُلْهِيْهِمْ تِجَارَةٌ وَّلَا بَيْعٌ عَنْ ذِكْرِ اللهِ وَاِقَامِ الصَّلٰوةِ وَاِيْتَآءِ الزَّكٰوةِ ۙ يَخَافُوْنَ يَوْمًا تَتَقَلَّبُ فِيْهِ الْقُلُوْبُ وَالْاَبْصَارُ

35. "Therein (in the Masaajid) they glorify Him (Allah Ta'ala) morning and evening, (these rightly guided men are) Men whom neither their trade nor commerce distracts them from the zikr (remembrance) of Allah Ta'ala, the establishment of Salaah and the paying of zakaat. They fear a day (the day of Qiyaamah) when the hearts and eyes will be overturned." (Surah Noor - Aayah 36-37)

٣٦. اَلَمْ تَرَ اَنَّ اللهَ يُسَبِّحُ لَهٗ مَنْ فِى السَّمٰوٰتِ وَالْاَرْضِ وَالطَّيْرُ صٰٓفّٰتٍ ۖ كُلٌّ قَدْ عَلِمَ صَلَاتَهٗ وَتَسْبِيْحَهٗ ۗ وَاللهُ عَلِيْمٌۢ بِمَا يَفْعَلُوْنَ

36. "Do you not see that everyone in the heavens and earth glorifies Allah Ta'ala, including the birds with their wings spread out? Each one knows its Salaah (mode of ibaadah) and method of glorification.

Chapter 3 – Virtues of the Third Kalimah

And Allah Ta'ala has knowledge of what you do."
(Surah Noor - Aayah 41)

٣٧. قَالُوْا سُبْحٰنَكَ مَا كَانَ يَنْۢبَغِىْ لَنَآ اَنْ نَّتَّخِذَ مِنْ دُوْنِكَ مِنْ اَوْلِيَآءَ وَلٰكِنْ مَّتَّعْتَهُمْ وَاٰبَآءَهُمْ حَتّٰى نَسُوا الذِّكْرَ ۚ وَكَانُوْا قَوْمًۢا بُوْرًا

37. (On the Day of Qiyaamah when Allah Ta'ala will haul up the non-believers and those whom they worshipped, and enquire from the latter whether they had misled the former). They (the gods) will say, "You are pure (from having partners). It was not right for us to take (as gods) any friends besides You; but what happened was that You granted enjoyment (wealth, comfort and luxuries) to them and their fathers until they forgot to remember (You) and they were a destroyed nation." *(Surah Furqaan - Aayah 18)*

٣٨. وَتَوَكَّلْ عَلَى الْحَىِّ الَّذِىْ لَا يَمُوْتُ وَسَبِّحْ بِحَمْدِهٖ ؕ وَكَفٰى بِهٖ بِذُنُوْبِ عِبَادِهٖ خَبِيْرَا

38. "And place your trust on the Living One (i.e. Allah Ta'ala) Who cannot die, and glorify His praises. He (Allah Ta'ala) is sufficient as the Knower of His bondsman's sins." *(Surah Furqaan - Aayah 58)*

٣٩. وَسُبْحٰنَ اللّٰهِ رَبِّ الْعٰلَمِيْنَ

39. "Glorified is Allah, the Rabb of the worlds." *(Surah Naml - Aayah 8)*

٤٠. سُبْحٰنَ اللّٰهِ وَتَعٰلٰى عَمَّا يُشْرِكُوْنَ

40. "Allah Ta'ala is Pure and Exalted above all that they ascribe as His partners." *(Surah Qasas - Aayah 68)*

٤١. فَسُبْحٰنَ اللّٰهِ حِيْنَ تُمْسُوْنَ وَحِيْنَ تُصْبِحُوْنَ ۞ وَلَهُ الْحَمْدُ فِى السَّمٰوٰتِ وَالْاَرْضِ وَعَشِيًّا وَّحِيْنَ تُظْهِرُوْنَ

41. "So glorify Allah Ta'ala as you spend the evenings and the mornings. All praise in the heavens and the earth belongs to Him and (glorify him) during the latter parts of the day and during the afternoons." (Surah Room – Aayah 17 & 18)

٤٢. سُبْحٰنَهٗ وَتَعٰلٰى عَمَّا يُشْرِكُوْنَ

42. "He (Allah Ta'ala) is Pure and Exalted from what they ascribe to Him." (Surah Room - Aayah 40)

---

٤٣. اِنَّمَا يُؤْمِنُ بِاٰيٰتِنَا الَّذِيْنَ اِذَا ذُكِّرُوْا بِهَا خَرُّوْا سُجَّدًا وَّسَبَّحُوْا بِحَمْدِ رَبِّهِمْ وَهُمْ لَا يَسْتَكْبِرُوْنَ

43. "Only those people (truly) believe in Our Aayaat who, when they are reminded of them (the aayaat), they fall into Sajdah, glorify the praises of their Rabb and they do not behave arrogantly." (Surah Sajdah - Aayah 15)

٤٤. يٰٓاَيُّهَا الَّذِيْنَ اٰمَنُوا اذْكُرُوا اللّٰهَ ذِكْرًا كَثِيْرًا ۙ وَّسَبِّحُوْهُ بُكْرَةً وَّاَصِيْلًا

44. "O you who believe! Remember Allah Ta'ala in abundance, and glorify Him during the morning and evening." (Surah Ahzaab – Aayah 41 & 42)

٤٥. قَالُوْا سُبْحٰنَكَ اَنْتَ وَلِيُّنَا مِنْ دُوْنِهِمْ

45. (On the Day of Qiyaamah, when the entire creation would be assembled, Allah Ta'ala will ask the Malaaikah whether they were being worshipped). "They (Malaaikah) will say, 'You (O Allah Ta'ala) are pure, and You are our protecting friend, not them.'" (Surah Saba - Aayah 41)

٤٦. سُبْحٰنَ الَّذِيْ خَلَقَ الْاَزْوَاجَ كُلَّهَا

46. "Glory be to Him Who created every pair (male and female)..." (Surah Yaaseen - Aayah 36)

Chapter 3 – Virtues of the Third Kalimah

٤٧۔ فَسُبْحٰنَ الَّذِیْ بِیَدِهٖ مَلَکُوْتُ کُلِّ شَیْءٍ وَّ اِلَیْهِ تُرْجَعُوْنَ

47. "Therefore, glory be to that Being in Whose hand is the control of everything, and to Whom you will all be returned."
(Surah Yaaseen - Aayah 83)

٤٨۔ فَلَوْلَاۤ اَنَّهٗ کَانَ مِنَ الْمُسَبِّحِیْنَ ۙ لَلَبِثَ فِیْ بَطْنِهٖۤ اِلٰی یَوْمِ یُبْعَثُوْنَ

48. "And if he (Yunus alayhis salaam) had not been one of those who glorify Him (Allah Ta'ala), he would have remained inside its (the fish's) belly till the day people will be resurrected."
(Surah Saaffaat – Aayah 143 & 144)

٤٩۔ سُبْحٰنَ اللهِ عَمَّا یَصِفُوْنَ

49. "Glorified is Allah Ta'ala who is pure from all (the partners) that they ascribe to Him." (Surah Saaffaat - Aayah 159)

٥٠۔ وَاِنَّا لَنَحْنُ الْمُسَبِّحُوْنَ

50. "Indeed we (the Malaaikah) are hymning His praises."
(Surah Saaffaat - Aayah 166)

٥١۔ سُبْحٰنَ رَبِّکَ رَبِّ الْعِزَّةِ عَمَّا یَصِفُوْنَ ۚ وَسَلٰمٌ عَلَی الْمُرْسَلِیْنَ ۚ وَالْحَمْدُ لِلّٰهِ رَبِّ الْعٰلَمِیْنَ

51. "Your Rabb, the Rabb of all honour is pure (free) from what they attribute (to Him). And peace be upon the Ambiyaa, and praise be to Allah Ta'ala, the Rabb of the worlds." (Surah Saaffaat - Aayah 182)

٥٢۔ اِنَّا سَخَّرْنَا الْجِبَالَ مَعَهٗ یُسَبِّحْنَ بِالْعَشِیِّ وَالْاِشْرَاقِ ۙ وَالطَّیْرَ مَحْشُوْرَةً ؕ کُلٌّ لَّهٗۤ اَوَّابٌ

52. "Verily We subjugated the mountains that would glorify Allah Ta'ala with him (Hadhrat Dawood alayhis salaam) at nightfall and at

daybreak. And We subjugated the birds to him, who all assembled together. They all turned towards Him (Allah Ta'ala)."
(Surah Saad – Aayah 18)

$$\text{۵۳. سُبْحٰنَهٗ هُوَ اللّٰهُ الْوَاحِدُ الْقَهَّارُ}$$

53. "Glory be to Him. He is Allah, the One, the Being Who controls everything." (Surah Zumar - Aayah 4)

$$\text{۵۴. سُبْحٰنَهٗ وَ تَعٰلٰى عَمَّا يُشْرِكُوْنَ}$$

54. "He (Allah Ta'ala) is Pure and exalted from all that they ascribe as partners to Him." (Surah Zumar - Aayah 67)

$$\text{۵۵. وَ تَرَى الْمَلٰٓئِكَةَ حَآفِّيْنَ مِنْ حَوْلِ الْعَرْشِ يُسَبِّحُوْنَ بِحَمْدِ رَبِّهِمْ وَقُضِيَ بَيْنَهُمْ بِالْحَقِّ وَ قِيْلَ الْحَمْدُ لِلّٰهِ رَبِّ الْعٰلَمِيْنَ}$$

55. "And (on the day of Qiyaamah) you (O! Muhammad ﷺ) will see the Malaaikah thronging around the Arsh, glorifying the praises of their Rabb. Then with justice, judgement will be made between the people and it will be said, 'All praise belongs to Allah Ta'ala, the Rabb of the universe.'" (Surah Zumar - Aayah 75)

$$\text{۵۶. اَلَّذِيْنَ يَحْمِلُوْنَ الْعَرْشَ وَ مَنْ حَوْلَهٗ يُسَبِّحُوْنَ بِحَمْدِ رَبِّهِمْ وَ يُؤْمِنُوْنَ بِهٖ وَ يَسْتَغْفِرُوْنَ لِلَّذِيْنَ اٰمَنُوْا رَبَّنَا وَسِعْتَ كُلَّ شَيْءٍ رَحْمَةً وَّ عِلْمًا فَاغْفِرْ لِلَّذِيْنَ تَابُوْا وَ اتَّبَعُوْا سَبِيْلَكَ وَقِهِمْ عَذَابَ الْجَحِيْمِ}$$

56. "Those (Malaaikah) who carry the Throne, and all those who are around them, hymn the praise of their Rabb, believe in Him and ask forgiveness for all those who have Imaan. (They make dua) saying: 'O our Rabb, Your mercy and knowledge encompass everything, so forgive those who repent and follow Your path, and save them from the punishment of Jahannam.'" (Surah Mu'min - Aayah 7)

$$\text{۵۷. وَ سَبِّحْ بِحَمْدِ رَبِّكَ بِالْعَشِيِّ وَ الْإِبْكَارِ}$$

Chapter 3 – Virtues of the Third Kalimah

57. "And hymn the praise of your Rabb morning and evening."
(Surah Mu'min - Aayah 55)

٥٨. فَالَّذِيْنَ عِنْدَ رَبِّكَ يُسَبِّحُوْنَ لَهٗ بِالَّيْلِ وَ النَّهَارِ وَهُمْ لَا يَسْئَمُوْنَ

58. "Then those (Malaaikah) who are near your Rabb glorify Him day and night, and they never feel tired."
(Surah Haameem Sajdah - Aayah 38)

٥٩. وَالْمَلٰٓئِكَةُ يُسَبِّحُوْنَ بِحَمْدِ رَبِّهِمْ وَيَسْتَغْفِرُوْنَ لِمَنْ فِي الْاَرْضِ

59. "And the Malaaikah hymn the praises of their Rabb and seek forgiveness for those on the earth." (Surah Shooraa - Aayah 5)

٦٠. وَتَقُوْلُوْا سُبْحٰنَ الَّذِيْ سَخَّرَ لَنَا هٰذَا وَمَا كُنَّا لَهٗ مُقْرِنِيْنَ ۞ وَاِنَّآ اِلٰى رَبِّنَا لَمُنْقَلِبُوْنَ

60. "Glorified is He (your Rabb) Who has placed this (conveyance) at your service, whereas we would never have been able to control it. And our return shall certainly be to our Rabb."
(Surah Zukhruf - Aayah - ۱۳ & 14)

٦١. سُبْحٰنَ رَبِّ السَّمٰوٰتِ وَالْاَرْضِ رَبِّ الْعَرْشِ عَمَّا يَصِفُوْنَ

61. "The Rabb of the heavens and the earth, the Rabb of the Throne is Pure from whatever they ascribe (to Him)." (Surah Zukhruf - Aayah 82)

٦٢. وَتُسَبِّحُوْهُ بُكْرَةً وَّ اَصِيْلًا

62. "And glorify Him at morning and evening." (Surah Fath - Aayah 9)

٦٣. فَاصْبِرْ عَلٰى مَا يَقُوْلُوْنَ وَسَبِّحْ بِحَمْدِ رَبِّكَ قَبْلَ طُلُوْعِ الشَّمْسِ وَقَبْلَ الْغُرُوْبِ ۞ وَمِنَ الَّيْلِ فَسَبِّحْهُ وَاَدْبَارَ السُّجُوْدِ

63. "Therefore (O Muhammad ﷺ) patiently bear whatever they (the kuffaar) say, and hymn the praises of your Rabb before sunrise and before sunset, and glorify Him during a portion of the night as well and after making sajdah (performing Salaah)."
(Surah Qaaf - Aayah 39-40)

٦٤. سُبْحٰنَ اللّٰهِ عَمَّا يُشْرِكُوْنَ

64. "Allah Ta'ala is Pure from all that they ascribe as partners (to Him)." (Surah Toor - Aayah 43)

٦٥. وَسَبِّحْ بِحَمْدِ رَبِّكَ حِيْنَ تَقُوْمُ ۞ وَمِنَ الَّيْلِ فَسَبِّحْهُ وَاِدْبَارَ النُّجُوْمِ

65. "And hymn the praises of your Rabb when you rise (from sleep and stand in Salaah). And glorify Him during a portion of the night and even after the stars have vanished." (Surah Toor - Aayah 48-49)

٦٦-٦٧. فَسَبِّحْ بِاسْمِ رَبِّكَ الْعَظِيْمِ

66 & 67. "Therefore (O Muhammad ﷺ), glorify the name of your Majestic Rabb." (Surah Waaqi'ah - Aayah 74 & 96)

٦٨. سَبَّحَ لِلّٰهِ مَا فِي السَّمٰوٰتِ وَالْاَرْضِ ۚ وَهُوَ الْعَزِيْزُ الْحَكِيْمُ

68. "Everything that is in the heavens and the earth glorifies Allah Ta'ala, and He is the Mighty, the Wise." (Surah Hadeed - Aayah 1)

٦٩. سَبَّحَ لِلّٰهِ مَا فِي السَّمٰوٰتِ وَمَا فِي الْاَرْضِ ۚ وَهُوَ الْعَزِيْزُ الْحَكِيْمُ

69. "Everything that is in the heavens and Everything in the earth glorifies Allah Ta'ala, and He is the Mighty, the Wise."
(Surah Hashr - Aayah 1)

٧٠. سُبْحٰنَ اللّٰهِ عَمَّا يُشْرِكُوْنَ

70. "Allah Ta'ala is Pure from all that they ascribe as partners (to Him)." (Surah Hashr - Aayah 23)

Chapter 3 – Virtues of the Third Kalimah

۷۱. يُسَبِّحُ لَهُ مَا فِى السَّمٰوٰتِ وَالْأَرْضِ ۚ وَهُوَ الْعَزِيْزُ الْحَكِيْمُ

71. "Everything that is in the heavens and the earth glorifies Allah Ta'ala, and He is the Mighty, the Wise." *(Surah Hashr - Aayah 24)*

۷۲. سَبَّحَ لِلّٰهِ مَا فِى السَّمٰوٰتِ وَمَا فِى الْأَرْضِ ۚ وَهُوَ الْعَزِيْزُ الْحَكِيْمُ

72. *"Everything that is in the heavens and everything that is in the Earth glorifies Allah, and He is the Mighty, the Wise."*
(Surah Saff - Aayah 1)

۷۳. يُسَبِّحُ لِلّٰهِ مَا فِى السَّمٰوٰتِ وَمَا فِى الْأَرْضِ الْمَلِكِ الْقُدُّوْسِ الْعَزِيْزِ الْحَكِيْمِ

73. *"Everything that is in the heavens and everything that is in the earth glorifies Allah, the Sovereign, the Most Holy, the Mighty, the Wise."* *(Surah Jumu'ah - Aayah 1)*

۷٤. يُسَبِّحُ لِلّٰهِ مَا فِى السَّمٰوٰتِ وَمَا فِى الْأَرْضِ ۚ لَهُ الْمُلْكُ وَلَهُ الْحَمْدُ ۖ وَهُوَ عَلٰى كُلِّ شَىْءٍ قَدِيْرٌ

74. *"Everything that is in the heavens and everything that is in the earth glorifies Allah Ta'ala. All kingdom and all praise belongs to Him and He has power over everything."* *(Surah Tagaabun - Aayah 1)*

۷۵ & ۷٦. قَالَ أَوْسَطُهُمْ أَلَمْ أَقُلْ لَكُمْ لَوْلَا تُسَبِّحُوْنَ ۞ قَالُوْا سُبْحٰنَ رَبِّنَآ إِنَّا كُنَّا ظٰلِمِيْنَ

75 & 76. *"The good one among them said. 'Did I not tell you, why don't you now glorify Allah Ta'ala?' They said, 'Glorified is our Rabb, indeed we were wrong doers.'"* *(Surah Qalam - Aayah 28-29)*

۷۷. فَسَبِّحْ بِاسْمِ رَبِّكَ الْعَظِيْمِ

77. *"So glorify the name of your Majestic Rabb."*
(Surah Al-Haaqqah - Aayah 52)

$$\text{وَ اذْكُرِ اسْمَ رَبِّكَ بُكْرَةً وَّاَصِيْلًا ۚ وَ مِنَ الَّيْلِ فَاسْجُدْ لَهٗ وَ سَبِّحْهُ لَيْلًا طَوِيْلًا}$$

78. *"Remember the name of your Rabb morning and evening, and worship Him during a portion of the night, and glorify Him through the long night."* (Surah Dahr - Aayah 25-26)

$$\text{سَبِّحِ اسْمَ رَبِّكَ الْاَعْلَى}$$

79. *"Glorify the name of your your Rabb, the most High."*
(Surah A'alaa - Aayah 1)

$$\text{فَسَبِّحْ بِحَمْدِ رَبِّكَ وَاسْتَغْفِرْهُ}$$

80. *"Then hymn the praise of your Rabb and seek forgiveness from Him."* (Surah Nasr - Aayah 3)

In the eighty Aayaat quoted above, there is either a clear commandment of Allah Ta'ala for hymning His glory or else its importance is stressed. What has been repeatedly mentioned and especially stressed in Qur-aan Shareef is undoubtedly most virtuous.

Aayaat of Tahmeed *(Alhamdulillah)*

Along with the commandment for glorification of Allah Ta'ala, it has been stressed in many of the above mentioned Aayaat to hymn His praise and recite *Alhamdulillah*. In addition to these Aayaat, there are other Aayaat as well, given below, which describe specifically the importance of hymning His praise and reciting *Alhamdulillah*. It is most significant that the Qur-aan Shareef starts with the Aayah **Alhamdulillahi Rabbil Aalameen** which indicates the excellence of this sacred phrase.

$$\text{اَلْحَمْدُ لِلّٰهِ رَبِّ الْعٰلَمِيْنَ}$$

1. *"All praise belongs to Allah Ta'ala, the Rabb of the worlds."*
(Surah Faatihah - Aayah 1)

Chapter 3 – Virtues of the Third Kalimah

٢. اَلْحَمْدُ لِلّٰهِ الَّذِيْ خَلَقَ السَّمٰوٰتِ وَالْاَرْضَ وَجَعَلَ الظُّلُمٰتِ وَالنُّوْرَ ۖ ثُمَّ الَّذِيْنَ كَفَرُوْا بِرَبِّهِمْ يَعْدِلُوْنَ

2. "All praise belongs to Allah Ta'ala, Who created the heavens and the earth, and Who made multitudes of darkness (evil) and light (guidance). Then too the kuffaar (disbelievers) ascribe equals with their Rabb." *(Surah An'aam - Aayah 1)*

٣. فَقُطِعَ دَابِرُ الْقَوْمِ الَّذِيْنَ ظَلَمُوْا ۗ وَالْحَمْدُ لِلّٰهِ رَبِّ الْعٰلَمِيْنَ

3. "Thus the roots of the oppressive people were cut (none survived). All praise is for Allah Ta'ala, the Rabb of the worlds." *(Surah An'aam - Aayah 45)*

٤. وَقَالُوا الْحَمْدُ لِلّٰهِ الَّذِيْ هَدٰىنَا لِهٰذَا ۖ وَمَا كُنَّا لِنَهْتَدِيَ لَوْلَاۤ اَنْ هَدٰىنَا اللّٰهُ

4. "And they (the people of Jannah) will say, 'All praise is for Allah Ta'ala, Who has guided us to this, we would have never been rightly guided had Allah Ta'ala not guided us.'" *(Surah A'araaf - Aayah 43)*

٥. اَلَّذِيْنَ يَتَّبِعُوْنَ الرَّسُوْلَ النَّبِيَّ الْاُمِّيَّ الَّذِيْ يَجِدُوْنَهٗ مَكْتُوْبًا عِنْدَهُمْ فِى التَّوْرٰىةِ وَالْاِنْجِيْلِ

5. "Those who follow the Rasool, The Nabi who could neither read nor write (Nabi Muhammad ﷺ), whom they find (his name and description) in the Torah and Injeel (both of which they have) with them." *(Surah A'araaf - Aayah 157)*

٦. اَلتَّآئِبُوْنَ الْعٰبِدُوْنَ الْحٰمِدُوْنَ السَّآئِحُوْنَ الرّٰكِعُوْنَ السّٰجِدُوْنَ الْاٰمِرُوْنَ بِالْمَعْرُوْفِ وَالنَّاهُوْنَ عَنِ الْمُنْكَرِ وَالْحٰفِظُوْنَ لِحُدُوْدِ اللّٰهِ ۗ وَبَشِّرِ الْمُؤْمِنِيْنَ

6. (While talking about the qualities of those who have sold their lives and wealth to Allah Ta'ala, Allah Ta'ala says) "Those who repent, those who worship (Allah Ta'ala alone), those who praise (Him), those

who fast, those who bow down (make Ruku), those who fall prostrate (make sajdah), those who command (others to do) good and forbid (others from) evil, and those who maintain the limits set by Allah Ta'ala. Convey the good news (of an everlasting Jannah) to the Mu'mineen (believers)." (Surah Taubah - Aayah 112)

٦. وَاٰخِرُ دَعْوٰىهُمْ اَنِ الْحَمْدُ لِلّٰهِ رَبِّ الْعٰلَمِيْنَ

7. "And the conclusion of their dua will be, 'All praise is for Allah Ta'ala, the Rabb of the worlds (universe).'" (Surah Yunus - Aayah 10)

٨. اَلْحَمْدُ لِلّٰهِ الَّذِىْ وَهَبَ لِىْ عَلَى الْكِبَرِ اِسْمٰعِيْلَ وَاِسْحٰقَ

8. "All praise is for Allah Ta'ala, Who has gifted me with (my sons) Ismaa'eel (alayhis salaam) and Ishaaq (alayhis salaam) despite (my) old age." (Surah I'braaheem - Aayah 39)

٩. اَلْحَمْدُ لِلّٰهِ بَلْ اَكْثَرُهُمْ لَا يَعْلَمُوْنَ

9. "All praise is for Allah, but most of them do not know."
(Surah Nahl - Aayah 75)

١٠. يَوْمَ يَدْعُوْكُمْ فَتَسْتَجِيْبُوْنَ بِحَمْدِهٖ وَتَظُنُّوْنَ اِنْ لَّبِثْتُمْ اِلَّا قَلِيْلًا

10 "The day (i.e. the Resurrection day) when He will call you (from your graves), you shall respond by praising Him, and you will think that you have stayed only for a little while."
(Surah Bani Israaeel - Aayah 52)

١١. وَقُلِ الْحَمْدُ لِلّٰهِ الَّذِىْ لَمْ يَتَّخِذْ وَلَدًا وَّلَمْ يَكُنْ لَّهٗ شَرِيْكٌ فِى الْمُلْكِ وَلَمْ يَكُنْ وَلِىٌّ مِّنَ الذُّلِّ وَكَبِّرْهُ تَكْبِيْرًا

11. "And say, 'All praise is for Allah Ta'ala, Who has not taken a child, has no partner in kingdom and is not so weak that He requires an assistant. (so) Declare His greatness in abundance.'"
(Surah Bani Israaeel - Aayah 111)

Chapter 3 – Virtues of the Third Kalimah

١٢. اَلْحَمْدُ لِلّٰهِ الَّذِيْ اَنْزَلَ عَلٰى عَبْدِهِ الْكِتٰبَ وَلَمْ يَجْعَلْ لَّهُ عِوَجًا

12. "All praise belongs to Allah Ta'ala, Who has revealed the Book (the Qur-aan) to His slave (Muhammad ﷺ), and has not placed therein any crookedness (misguidance)." *(Surah Kahf - Aayah 1)*

١٣. فَقُلِ الْحَمْدُ لِلّٰهِ الَّذِيْ نَجّٰنَا مِنَ الْقَوْمِ الظّٰلِمِيْنَ

13. (Addressing Hadhrat Nooh (alayhis salaam), Allah Ta'ala commanded him) "Then say, 'All praise is for Allah Ta'ala, Who has saved us from the oppressive nation.'" *(Surah Mu'minoon - Aayah 28)*

١٤. وَقَالَا الْحَمْدُ لِلّٰهِ الَّذِيْ فَضَّلَنَا عَلٰى كَثِيْرٍ مِّنْ عِبَادِهِ الْمُؤْمِنِيْنَ

14. "They two (Nabi Sulaimaan alayhis salaam and Nabi Dawood alayhis salaam) said, 'All praise is for Allah Ta'ala, Who has favoured us more than many of his bondsmen who have Imaan.'"
(Surah Naml - Aayah 15)

١٥. قُلِ الْحَمْدُ لِلّٰهِ وَسَلٰمٌ عَلٰى عِبَادِهِ الَّذِيْنَ اصْطَفٰى

15. "Say (O Muhammad ﷺ!) 'All praise be to Allah Ta'ala, and peace be on those bondsmen of His whom He has chosen."
(Surah Naml - Aayah 59)

١٦. وَقُلِ الْحَمْدُ لِلّٰهِ سَيُرِيْكُمْ اٰيٰتِهٖ فَتَعْرِفُوْنَهَا

16. "And say, 'All praise is for Allah Ta'ala, Who will soon show you His aayaat (signs of Qiyaamah), which you will recognize."
(Surah Naml - Aayah 93)

١٧. لَهُ الْحَمْدُ فِى الْاُوْلٰى وَالْاٰخِرَةِ ۖ وَلَهُ الْحُكْمُ وَاِلَيْهِ تُرْجَعُوْنَ

17. "All praise belongs to Him in the first (this world) and in the next (the Aakhirah). All command (control over everything) is His and to Him shall you all be returned." *(Surah Qasas - Aayah 70)*

١٨. قُلِ الْحَمْدُ لِلّٰهِ ۚ بَلْ اَكْثَرُهُمْ لَا يَعْقِلُوْنَ

18. "Say, 'All praise belongs to Allah Ta'ala, but most of them do not understand.'" *(Surah A'nkaboot - Aayah 63)*

١٩. وَمَنْ كَفَرَ فَاِنَّ اللّٰهَ غَنِيٌّ حَمِيْدٌ

19. "As for him who is ungrateful, Allah Ta'ala is certainly Independent, Most Worthy of praise." *(Surah Luqmaan - Aayah 12)*

٢٠. قُلِ الْحَمْدُ لِلّٰهِ ۚ بَلْ اَكْثَرُهُمْ لَا يَعْلَمُوْنَ

20. "Say, 'All praise belongs to Allah Ta'ala. However, most of them do not know.'" *(Surah Luqmaan - Aayah 25)*

٢١. اِنَّ اللّٰهَ هُوَ الْغَنِيُّ الْحَمِيْدُ

21. "Verily Allah Ta'ala, He is most Independent, most Worthy of all praise." *(Surah Luqmaan - Aayah 26)*

٢٢. اَلْحَمْدُ لِلّٰهِ الَّذِيْ لَهٗ مَا فِي السَّمٰوٰتِ وَمَا فِي الْاَرْضِ وَلَهُ الْحَمْدُ فِي الْاٰخِرَةِ

22. "All praise belongs to Allah Ta'ala, to Whom belongs whatever is in the heavens and whatever is in the earth. All praise belongs to Him in the Aakhirah (hereafter) as well." *(Surah Saba' - Aayah 1)*

٢٣. اَلْحَمْدُ لِلّٰهِ فَاطِرِ السَّمٰوٰتِ وَالْاَرْضِ

23. "All praise be to Allah, the Creator of Heavens and the Earth." *(Surah Faatir - Aayah 1)*

٢٤. يٰاَيُّهَا النَّاسُ اَنْتُمُ الْفُقَرَآءُ اِلَى اللّٰهِ ۚ وَاللّٰهُ هُوَ الْغَنِيُّ الْحَمِيْدُ

24. "O Mankind! You are all beggars (in need) before Allah Ta'ala, and Allah Ta'ala is Independent, most Worthy of praise." *(Surah Faatir - Aayah 15)*

Chapter 3 – Virtues of the Third Kalimah

٢٥. وَقَالُوا الْحَمْدُ لِلّٰهِ الَّذِىٓ اَذْهَبَ عَنَّا الْحَزَنَ ؕ اِنَّ رَبَّنَا لَغَفُوْرٌ شَكُوْرُ ۙ الَّذِىٓ اَحَلَّنَا دَارَ الْمُقَامَةِ مِنْ فَضْلِهٖ ۚ لَا يَمَسُّنَا فِيْهَا نَصَبٌ وَّلَا يَمَسُّنَا فِيْهَا لُغُوْبٌ

25. "And (in Jannah) they will say, 'All praise is for Allah Ta'ala, Who has removed grief from us. Undoubtedly our Rabb is Most Forgiving, Most Appreciative. He (our Rabb) has settled us in an eternal home by His grace. Here (in Jannah) no difficulty will ever afflict us nor shall any tiredness touch us." (Surah Faatir - Aayah 34-35)

٢٦. وَسَلٰمٌ عَلَى الْمُرْسَلِيْنَ ۚ وَالْحَمْدُ لِلّٰهِ رَبِّ الْعٰلَمِيْنَ

26. "And peace be upon the Ambiyaa, and all praise belongs to Allah Ta'ala, the Rabb of the worlds." (Surah Saaffaat - Aayah 181-182)

٢٧. اَلْحَمْدُ لِلّٰهِ ؕ بَلْ اَكْثَرُهُمْ لَا يَعْلَمُوْنَ

27. "All praise belongs to Allah Ta'ala; but most of them do not know." (Surah Zumar - Aayah 29)

٢٨. وَقَالُوا الْحَمْدُ لِلّٰهِ الَّذِىْ صَدَقَنَا وَعْدَهٗ وَاَوْرَثَنَا الْاَرْضَ نَتَبَوَّاُ مِنَ الْجَنَّةِ حَيْثُ نَشَآءُ ۚ فَنِعْمَ اَجْرُ الْعٰمِلِيْنَ

28. "(After entry into Jannah) they would say, 'All praise be to Allah Ta'ala, Who has fulfilled His promise to us, made us inheritors of this land (Jannah) so that we may settle wherever we wish in Jannah. Excellent indeed is the reward of those who do good deeds." (Surah Zumar - Aayah 74)

٢٩. فَلِلّٰهِ الْحَمْدُ رَبِّ السَّمٰوٰتِ وَرَبِّ الْاَرْضِ رَبِّ الْعٰلَمِيْنَ

29. "All praise belongs to Allah Ta'ala, the Rabb of heavens and the Rabb of the earth, the Rabb of the worlds. (Surah Jaasiyah - Aayah 36)

٣٠. وَمَا نَقَمُوْا مِنْهُمْ اِلَّا اَنْ يُّؤْمِنُوْا بِاللهِ الْعَزِيْزِ الْحَمِيْدِ ۞ الَّذِىْ لَهٗ مُلْكُ السَّمٰوٰتِ وَالْاَرْضِ

30. (Talking of a kuffar ruler, who was oppressing the believers) "And they (the kuffar) found no fault in them (no excuse to kill the Mu'mineen) except that they believed in Allah Ta'ala, the Mighty, the Most Worthy of praise, to Whom belongs the kingdom of the heavens and the earth." *(Surah Burooj - Aayah 8-9)*

Note: The aayaat above describe the attributes of Allah Ta'ala and the virtues of reciting His praises. They also contain encouragement and commandments for doing so. Those who hymn His praises have been specially praised in many Ahaadith. According to one Hadith, the first to be called for admittance into Jannah will be those who used to hymn His praise under all conditions, whether good or bad. It is stated in another Hadith that Allah Ta'ala likes the hymning of His praises and it should be so, because He alone is worthy of real praise. Nobody else (in reality) deserves any praise, because nobody has real control over anything, not even over his own person.

It is narrated in one Hadith that the most virtuous of people on the Day of Qiyaamah will be those who hymn the praise of Allah Ta'ala excessively. According to one Hadith, recitation of the praise of Allah Ta'ala is the essence of expressing gratitude to Him, and one who does not recite His praise has not expressed his thanks to Him. It is stated in a Hadith that, when one receives any bounty, then reciting the praise of Allah Ta'ala acts as a safeguard against its loss.

Rasulullah ﷺ is stated to have said, "Saying *alhamdulillah* by anyone from my Ummat is more beneficial to him than his getting possession of the whole world."

It is narrated in one Hadith that when Allah Ta'ala bestows a favour upon someone and that person recites His Praise, this act of his is more in value than that of the bounty, however big it might be.

A Sahaabi رَضِىَ اللهُ عَنْهُ, while sitting near Rasulullah ﷺ, happened to recite in a low voice;

اَلْحَمْدُ لِلّٰهِ حَمْدًا كَثِيْرًا طَيِّبًا مُّبَارَكًا فِيْهِ

alhamdulillah hamdan kaseeran tayyiban mubaarakan feeh
All praise is due to Allah Ta'ala, many pure blessed praises.

Rasulullah ﷺ enquired as to who had recited that dua. Thinking that he had done something which he should not have done at that time, the Sahaabi رضي الله عنه kept quiet. Rasulullah ﷺ assured that there was no harm in saying it, because it was not anything undesirable, after which the Sahaabi رضي الله عنه admitted that the dua had been uttered by him. Then Rasulullah ﷺ said, "I saw thirteen Malaaikah, all of whom were trying to surpass each other in taking this dua to Allah Ta'ala."

There is the well-known Hadith, wherein it is stated that any great work that commences without the praises of Allah Ta'ala will be void of barkat (blessings). Therefore, it is for this reason that every book is commenced with the praises of Allah Ta'ala.

It is narrated in one Hadith that when somebody's child dies, Allah Ta'ala asks the Malaaikah if they have taken out the soul of His servant's child. On receiving the reply in the affirmative, He adds that they have taken out (so to say) a part of his heart. The Malaaikah reply in the affirmative. Allah Ta'ala then enquires "What did my servant say on that?" They say, "He praised You and recited

اِنَّا لِلّٰهِ وَاِنَّا اِلَيْهِ رَاجِعُوْنَ

We belong to Allah, and to Him we shall return."

On this, Allah Ta'ala orders that a house should be built in Jannah for him, and that it should be named Baitul-Hamd (House of Praise).

According to another Hadith, Allah Ta'ala is greatly pleased with a person who says اَلْحَمْدُ لِلّٰهِ *(alhamdulillah)* when he eats a morsel of food or on getting a sip of water.

The third part of this Kalimah is لَا اِلٰهَ اِلَّا اللهُ *(laailaaha illallaah)* which has been described in detail in the last chapter.

Aayaat of Takbeer (Allahu Akbar)

The fourth part is known as Kalimah Takbeer - اللهُ اَكْبَرُ *(Allahu Akbar)* which means acknowledging His greatness and affirmation of His grandeur and His splendour. The importance of this fourth part of the Kalimah has also been described in many of the Aayaat given already. There are other aayaat which specifically describe the greatness and grandeur of Allah Ta'ala. A few of these will be mentioned:

١. وَلِتُكَبِّرُوا اللهَ عَلَىٰ مَا هَدٰىكُمْ وَلَعَلَّكُمْ تَشْكُرُوْنَ

1. "So that you glorify Allah Ta'ala for Him guiding you, and so that you may show gratitude." *(Surah Baqarah Aayah 185)*

٢. عٰلِمُ الْغَيْبِ وَالشَّهَادَةِ الْكَبِيْرُ الْمُتَعَالِ

2. "(He is) the knower of the unseen and that which can be seen, The Great, The Most High." *(Surah Ra'd - Aayah 9)*

٣. كَذٰلِكَ سَخَّرَهَا لَكُمْ لِتُكَبِّرُوا اللهَ عَلَىٰ مَا هَدٰىكُمْ ۚ وَبَشِّرِ الْمُحْسِنِيْنَ

3. "Thus Allah Ta'ala has subjugated it (the Qurbaani animal) to you so that you may proclaim the greatness of Allah Ta'ala for the guidance that He has granted you. And (O Muhammad ﷺ) convey good news (of Jannah) to those who do good."
(Surah Hajj - Aayah 37)

٤-٥. وَأَنَّ اللهَ هُوَ الْعَلِيُّ الْكَبِيْرُ

4 & 5. "And indeed Allah Ta'ala, He is The Highest, The Greatest."
(Surah Hajj - Aayah 62 & Surah Luqmaan - Aayah 30)

٦. حَتَّىٰ إِذَا فُزِّعَ عَنْ قُلُوْبِهِمْ قَالُوْا مَاذَا ۙ قَالَ رَبُّكُمْ ۖ قَالُوا الْحَقَّ ۚ وَهُوَ الْعَلِيُّ الْكَبِيْرُ

6. (When the Malaaikah receive any command from Allah Ta'ala, they become overwhelmed with fear. They remain in this condition of fear) "until when the fear leaves their heart and they say, 'What has your Rabb said?' They say, '(He speaks) the truth and He is the Exalted, the Great.'" *(Surah Saba' - Aayah 23)*

Chapter 3 – Virtues of the Third Kalimah

٦. فَالْحُكْمُ لِلّٰهِ الْعَلِيِّ الْكَبِيْرِ

7. "So, the command belongs only to Allah Ta'ala, The Highest, The Greatest." *(Surah Mu'min - Aayah 12)*

٨. وَلَهُ الْكِبْرِيَآءُ فِي السَّمٰوٰتِ وَالْاَرْضِ وَهُوَ الْعَزِيْزُ الْحَكِيْمُ

8. "And all Majesty (supreme power) belongs to Him (Allah Ta'ala) in the heavens and the earth, and He is the Mighty, the Wise." *(Surah Jaasiyah - Aayah 37)*

٩. هُوَ اللّٰهُ الَّذِيْ لَآ اِلٰهَ اِلَّا هُوَ الْمَلِكُ الْقُدُّوْسُ السَّلٰمُ الْمُؤْمِنُ الْمُهَيْمِنُ الْعَزِيْزُ الْجَبَّارُ الْمُتَكَبِّرُ

9. "He is Allah, there is no other god besides Him, the King, The Most Pure, the Giver of peace, the Giver of security (shelter), The Vigilant, The Mighty, The Overpowering, the Glorious." *(Surah Hashar - Aayah 23)*

Note: We have been encouraged and commanded in the above Aayaat to Glorify and proclaim the greatness of Allah Ta'ala. In many other Ahaadith we have been encouraged to glorify and proclaim the Greatness of Allah Ta'ala.

It is stated in one Hadith, "When you see that fire has broken out somewhere, say اَللهُ اَكْبَرُ *(Allahu Akbar - Takbeer)* excessively, which will put out the fire." Another Hadith also states that the recitation of اَللهُ اَكْبَرُ *(Allahu Akbar)* puts out the fire. It is said in one Hadith that when a person says اَللهُ اَكْبَرُ *(Allahu Akbar)*, its Noor (Light) covers everything between the earth and the sky. According to one Hadith, Rasulullah ﷺ has said, "Hadhrat Jibreel *(alayhis salaam)* ordered me to recite *Allahu Akbar*."

In addition to the Aayaat and Ahaadith given above, the greatness of Allah Ta'ala and His splendour has been described and recitation of it has been stressed under different headings and in different words at many places in the Qur-aan Shareef.

There are many other aayaat, which do not contain the specific words of these Kalimahs, but they imply these Kalimahs. Some of these Aayaat are as follows:

١. فَتَلَقّٰى اٰدَمُ مِنْ رَّبِّهٖ كَلِمٰتٍ فَتَابَ عَلَيْهِ ۚ اِنَّهٗ هُوَ التَّوَّابُ الرَّحِيْمُ

1. *"Aadam (alayhis salaam) learnt a few words from his Rabb, and He (Allah Ta'ala) pardoned him. Without doubt He (Allah Ta'ala) is the Most Forgiving, the Most Merciful."* (Surah Baqarah - Aayah 37)

Note: There are different versions and explanations from the Hadith about the words referred to in this aayah. According to some of these versions, these words were as follows:

لَا اِلٰهَ اِلَّا اَنْتَ سُبْحَانَكَ وَبِحَمْدِكَ رَبِّ عَمِلْتُ سُوْءًا وَّظَلَمْتُ نَفْسِيْ فَاغْفِرْ لِيْ اِنَّكَ اَنْتَ خَيْرُ الْغَافِرِيْنَ لَا اِلٰهَ اِلَّا اَنْتَ سُبْحَانَكَ وَبِحَمْدِكَ رَبِّ عَمِلْتُ سُوْءًا وَّظَلَمْتُ نَفْسِيْ فَارْحَمْنِيْ اِنَّكَ اَنْتَ اَرْحَمُ الرَّاحِمِيْنَ لَا اِلٰهَ اِلَّا اَنْتَ سُبْحَانَكَ وَبِحَمْدِكَ رَبِّ عَمِلْتُ سُوْءًا وَّظَلَمْتُ نَفْسِيْ فَتُبْ عَلَىَّ اِنَّكَ اَنْتَ التَّوَّابُ الرَّحِيْمُ

(a) There is no god except You. You are above all shortcomings and are worthy of all kinds of praise. O my Rabb! I have acted incorrectly and wronged myself, therefore forgive me, surely you are the best of forgivers.

(b) There is no god except You. You are above all defects, you are worthy of all praise. O my Rabb! I have acted incorrectly and wronged myself. Kindly show mercy upon me, surely You are most Compassionate, most Merciful.

(c) There is no god except You. You are above all defects and shortcomings, and are worthy of all praise. O my Rabb! I have acted incorrectly and wronged myself. Forgive me, as You are Most Forgiving and Merciful.

There are other Ahaadith of a similar nature, as narrated by Allamah Suyuti *(rahmatullahi alayh)* in *Durrul Mansoor* wherein words meaning glorification and hymning praise of Allah Ta'ala occur.

Chapter 3 – Virtues of the Third Kalimah

٢. مَنْ جَآءَ بِالْحَسَنَةِ فَلَهٗ عَشْرُ اَمْثَالِهَا ۚ وَمَنْ جَآءَ بِالسَّيِّئَةِ فَلَا يُجْزٰٓى اِلَّا مِثْلَهَا وَهُمْ لَا يُظْلَمُوْنَ

2. "Whoever brings a good deed will receive ten times the like thereof, while whosoever carries out a sin will be punished only equal to the sin and they will not be wronged." *(Surah An'aam - Aayah 160)*

Note: Rasulullah ﷺ said, "There are two routines, which, if followed by a Muslim, will enable him to enter into Jannah. Both these routines are very easy to follow, but very few people act on them. One is to recite *(subhaanallah, alhamdulillah and Allahu Akbar)* ten times after every fardh Salaah i.e. five times a day. In this way, one is able to glorify Allah Ta'ala 150 times and thereby earn 1500 rewards every day, because every good act is multiplied by ten. The second routine is to recite; اَللهُ اَكْبَرُ *(Allahu Akbar)* thirty four times, اَلْحَمْدُ لِلّٰهِ *(Alhamdulillah)* thirty three times, and سُبْحَانَ اللهِ *(Subhanallah)* thirty three times at the time of going to bed every night. One glorifies Allah Ta'ala 100 times in this way, and thereby earns 1000 rewards. Thus, the virtues earned during the day total 2500. On the Day of Qiyaamah, when deeds will be weighed, will there be anybody who will have committed 2500 evil deeds every day, which can counter-act so many rewards?"

Although there were none among the Sahaabah رضي الله عنهم, who could have committed 2500 evil deeds during a day, yet in this age, our daily misdeeds far exceed this number. Therefore, it was extremely kind of Rasulullah ﷺ to have told us the prescription for increasing our good deeds over our evil deeds. The prescription has been given and it is now for the sick to act on it.

According to one Hadith, the companions of Rasulullah ﷺ asked him the reason why only a few people are able to act upon the above mentioned two things in spite of their being so easy. He replied that at night shaytaan makes one sleep before he has recited it and at the time of Salaah he reminds him of something which makes him get up and go away at once without having recited it.

According to one Hadith Rasulullah ﷺ said, "Is it not possible for you to earn 1000 virtues daily? Someone enquired, "How can we earn 1000 virtues daily O Rasulullah ﷺ?" He replied, "Recite سُبْحَانَ اللهِ (Subhaanallah) one hundred times, and you will have earned 1000 virtues."

٣. اَلْمَالُ وَالْبَنُوْنَ زِيْنَةُ الْحَيٰوةِ الدُّنْيَا ۚ وَالْبٰقِيٰتُ الصّٰلِحٰتُ خَيْرٌ عِنْدَ رَبِّكَ ثَوَابًا وَّ خَيْرٌ اَمَلًا

3. "Wealth and children are merely adornments of this worldly life. The lasting good deeds are best in the sight of your Rabb in terms of reward and best in terms of expectations." (i.e. we should base our hope and expectations on good deeds instead of on our wealth and children). (Surah Kahf - Aayah 46)

٤. يَزِيْدُ اللهُ الَّذِيْنَ اهْتَدَوْا هُدًى ۚ وَالْبٰقِيٰتُ الصّٰلِحٰتُ خَيْرٌ عِنْدَ رَبِّكَ ثَوَابًا وَّ خَيْرٌ مَّرَدًّا

4. "Allah Ta'ala will increase the guidance (insight) of those who are rightly guided. And the lasting good deeds are best in the sight of your Rabb in terms of reward, and best in terms of consequences." (Surah Maryam - Aayah 76)

Note: Although اَلْبٰقِيٰتُ الصّٰلِحٰتُ (Baaqiyaatus Saalihaat - good deeds which last forever) include all those good deeds whose reward continue for ever, yet according to some Ahaadith it implies these very Kalimahs. Rasulullah ﷺ has said, Hymn these اَلْبٰقِيٰتُ الصّٰلِحٰتُ (baaqiyaatus Saalihaat) excessively." Somebody enquired what it was. Rasulullah ﷺ replied, "It is to recite Takbeer اللهُ اَكْبَرُ (Allahu Akbar), Tahleel لَا إِلٰهَ إِلَّا اللهُ (laailaaha illallaah), Tasbeeh سُبْحَانَ اللهِ (Subhaanallah), Tahmeed اَلْحَمْدُ لِلّٰهِ (Alhamdulillah) and لَا حَوْلَ وَلَا قُوَّةَ إِلَّا بِاللهِ (lahaw la walaquwwata illa billah)." According to another Hadith, Rasulullah ﷺ said, "Pay

Chapter 3 – Virtues of the Third Kalimah

attention, سُبْحَانَ اللهِ اَلْحَمْدُ لِلّٰهِ لَا اِلٰهَ اِلَّا اللهُ اَللهُ اَكْبَرُ (Subhanallah, Alhamdulillah, laailaha illallah, Allahu Akbar) constitute اَلْبٰقِيٰتُ الصّٰلِحٰتُ (Baaqiyaatus Saalihaat - good deeds which last forever)."

It is stated in one Hadith that Rasulullah ﷺ had said, "Beware, be on your guard." Somebody enquired "O, Rasulullah ﷺ, is it against some future invasion by some enemy?" Rasulullah ﷺ replied, "No, arrange to guard yourself against the fire of Jahannam, through the recitation of سُبْحَانَ اللهِ اَلْحَمْدُ لِلّٰهِ لَا اِلٰهَ اِلَّا اللهُ اَللهُ اَكْبَرُ because these Kalimahs will go forward to intercede for you on the Day of Qiyaamah (or they will move you forward towards Jannah), these will guard you from behind, these will favour and benefit you and these are the اَلْبٰقِيٰتُ الصّٰلِحٰتُ (Baaqiyaatus Saalihaat - good deeds which last forever)."

Similarly, there are many other Ahaadith on this topic, as given in '*Durul Mansoor*', by Allamah Suyuti.

ه. لَهٗ مَقَالِيْدُ السَّمٰوٰتِ وَ الْاَرْضِ

5. *"To Him belong the keys of the heavens and the earth."*
(Surah Zumar - Aayah 63)

Note: It is narrated by Hadhrat Uthmaan ﷺ that in reply to his enquiry about *maqaaleedus samaawaati wal ardh* (keys of the heavens and the earth), Rasulullah ﷺ had said that it was;

لَا اِلٰهَ اِلَّا اللهُ وَاللهُ اَكْبَرُ سُبْحَانَ اللهِ اَلْحَمْدُ لِلّٰهِ اَسْتَغْفِرُ اللهَ الَّذِيْ لَا اِلٰهَ اِلَّا هُوَ الْاَوَّلُ وَالْاٰخِرُ وَالظَّاهِرُ وَالْبَاطِنُ يُحْيٖ وَيُمِيْتُ وَهُوَ حَىٌّ لَا يَمُوْتُ بِيَدِهِ الْخَيْرُ وَهُوَ عَلٰى كُلِّ شَىْءٍ قَدِيْرٌ

According to another Hadith, the keys of the heavens and the earth means سُبْحَانَ اللهِ اَلْحَمْدُ لِلّٰهِ لَا اِلٰهَ اِلَّا اللهُ وَاللهُ اَكْبَرُ (*subhaanallah, alhamdulillah, laailaaha illallaah and Allahu Akbar*) which had been sent down from the treasure of the Arsh i.e. the Throne of Allah Ta'ala. This subject has been discussed in many other Ahaadith.

٦. اِلَيْهِ يَصْعَدُ الْكَلِمُ الطَّيِّبُ وَالْعَمَلُ الصَّالِحُ يَرْفَعُهُ

6. "The Pure Word (the Kalimah and other forms of zikr) climbs up to Him (Allah Ta'ala), and good deeds propel it." (coupled with good deeds, a Muslim's zikr is readily accepted by Allah Ta'ala).
(Surah Faatir - Aayah 10)

Note: This aayah has already been mentioned under the section of Kalimah Tayyibah. Hadhrat Abdullah bin Masood رضى الله عنه said, "Whenever I recite some Hadith, I also quote from the Qur-aan Shareef in support thereof. When a Muslim reads,

سُبْحَانَ اللهِ وَبِحَمْدِهِ اَلْحَمْدُ لِلّٰهِ لَا اِلٰهَ اِلَّا اللّٰهُ اَللّٰهُ اَكْبَرُ تَبَارَكَ اللّٰهُ

an angel carefully takes these words towards heaven in his wings and whichever sky he crosses, the Malaaikah there make dua for the forgiveness of the reciter." This is supported by the above aayah.

Hadhrat Ka'ab Ahbaar رضى الله عنه had said that hymning of

سُبْحَانَ اللهِ اَلْحَمْدُ لِلّٰهِ لَا اِلٰهَ اِلَّا اللّٰهُ وَاللّٰهُ اَكْبَرُ

goes buzzing round the Arsh, mentioning the name of the reciter. Another Sahaabi by the name of Hadhrat Numaan رضى الله عنه has also narrated a similar Hadith from Rasulullah صلى الله عليه وسلم.

SECTION 2
AHAADITH PERTAINING TO THE 3ʳᴰ KALIMAH

This part deals with the Ahaadith in which Rasulullah ﷺ mentioned the rewards of these kalimahs and recommended their recitation.

Hadith 1 – The virtue of reading سُبْحَانَ اللهِ وَبِحَمْدِهِ سُبْحَانَ اللهِ الْعَظِيْمِ

عَنْ اَبِيْ هُرَيْرَةَ رَضِيَ اللهُ عَنْهُ قَالَ قَالَ رَسُوْلُ اللهِ صَلَّى اللهُ عَلَيْهِ وَ سَلَّمَ كَلِمَتَانِ خَفِيْفَتَانِ عَلَى اللِّسَانِ ثَقِيْلَتَانِ فِي الْمِيْزَانِ حَبِيْبَتَانِ اِلَى الرَّحْمٰنِ سُبْحَانَ اللهِ وَبِحَمْدِهِ سُبْحَانَ اللهِ الْعَظِيْمِ (رواه البخارى # ٦٦٨٢)

Hadhrat Abu Hurayrah ؓ narrates that Rasulullah ﷺ said, "There are two kalimahs which are very light on the tongue (i.e. easy to utter) but very weighty in reward and very pleasing to Allah Ta'ala. These are سُبْحَانَ اللهِ وَبِحَمْدِهِ سُبْحَانَ اللهِ الْعَظِيْمِ (Glory be to Allah Ta'ala with all praises, Glory be to Allah Ta'ala, the Majestic)."

Note: Light on the tongue means that these kalimahs are so brief that little time is spent in their recitation and no difficulty is experienced in memorizing them. In spite of their being so easy, they will be found very weighty when good deeds will be weighed. The fact that they are so dear to Allah Ta'ala more than anything else, surpasses all other advantages. Imam Bukhaari *(rahmatullahi alayh)* concluded his book *'Saheeh Bukhaari'* with these two kalimahs and the above mentioned Hadith was given at the end of the kitaab.

According to one Hadith, Rasulullah ﷺ had said, "None of you should miss earning 1000 virtues daily. Recite سُبْحَانَ اللهِ وَبِحَمْدِهِ *(subhanaalahi wa bihamdihi)* 100 times and you will get 1000 virtues. Hopefully through the grace of Allah Ta'ala, your daily sins will be less than this number. Then the reward of your good deeds, other than reciting this kalimah, will be in addition."

According to another Hadith a person who recites سُبْحَانَ اللهِ وَبِحَمْدِهِ *(subhanallahi wabihamdihi)* 100 times in the morning and in the evening has all his sins forgiven, even if they are more than the foam on the sea. It is stated in one Hadith that recitation of سُبْحَانَ اللهِ الْحَمْدُ لِلَّهِ لَا إِلَهَ إِلَّا اللهُ وَاللهُ اَكْبَرُ causes the sins to fall off like the leaves of trees (during the winter season).

Hadith 2 – **The virtue of reciting** سُبْحَانَ اللهِ وَبِحَمْدِهِ

عَنْ اَبِيْ ذَرٍّ رَضِيَ اللهُ عَنْهُ قَالَ قَالَ رَسُوْلُ اللهِ صَلَّى اللهُ عَلَيْهِ وَسَلَّمَ اَلَا اُخْبِرُكَ بِاَحَبِّ الْكَلَامِ اِلَى اللهِ قُلْتُ يَارَسُوْلَ اللهِ اَخْبِرْنِيْ بِاَحَبِّ الْكَلَامِ اِلَى اللهِ فَقَالَ اِنَّ اَحَبَّ الْكَلَامِ اِلَى اللهِ سُبْحَانَ اللهِ وَبِحَمْدِهِ (رواه مسلم # ٢٧٣١)

Hadhrat Abu Zar ؓ narrated that once Rasulullah ﷺ had said, "Should I tell you what speech is most liked by Allah?" "Do tell me", said I. He said, "It is سُبْحَانَ اللهِ وَبِحَمْدِهِ (Subhanallahi wabihamdihi)." In another Hadith, it is سُبْحَانَ رَبِّيْ وَبِحَمْدِهِ (Subhana Rabbi wa bihamdihi). Another Hadith relates, "The thing that Allah Ta'ala ordered His Malaaikah to hymn is undoubtedly the best one, and it is سُبْحَانَ اللهِ وَبِحَمْدِهِ (Subhanallahi wa bihamdihi)."

Note: It is mentioned in several aayaat in Part 1 that those Malaaikah who are near the Arsh and all others, remain ever hymning the glory and praise of Allah Ta'ala, which is their sole duty. This is why, when Allah Ta'ala created Hadhrat Aadam *(alayhis salaam)* the Malaaikah submitted,

نَحْنُ نُسَبِّحُ بِحَمْدِكَ وَنُقَدِّسُ لَكَ

"We hymn Your praises and glorify You."

as given in the first aayah in Part 1.

According to one Hadith, Rasulullah ﷺ had said, "The heaven crackles due to the awe of the greatness of Allah Ta'ala, as does a bed under a heavy weight, and the Heaven is justified in doing so (due to the awe of Allah Ta'ala). I swear by Allah Ta'ala, Who controls my life, that in the heaven there is not an inch of space where some angel is not in sajdah and glorifying the praises of Allah Ta'ala."

Hadith 3 – Entry into Jannah is Guaranteed

عَنْ اِسْحَاقَ بْنِ عَبْدِ اللهِ بْنِ اَبِيْ طَلْحَةَ عَنْ اَبِيْهِ عَنْ جَدِّهِ رَضِىَ اللهُ عَنْهُ قَالَ قَالَ رَسُوْلُ اللهِ صَلَّى اللهُ عَلَيْهِ وَسَلَّمَ مَنْ قَالَ لَا اِلٰهَ اِلَّا اللهُ دَخَلَ الْجَنَّةَ وَ وَجَبَتْ لَهُ الْجَنَّةُ وَمَنْ قَالَ سُبْحَانَ اللهِ وَبِحَمْدِهٖ مِائَةَ مَرَّةٍ كَتَبَ اللهُ لَهٗ اَلْفَ حَسَنَةٍ وَاَرْبَعًا وَّعِشْرِيْنَ اَلْفَ حَسَنَةٍ قَالُوْا يَا رَسُوْلَ اللهِ اِذًا لَّا يَهْلِكُ مِنَّا اَحَدٌ قَالَ بَلٰى اِنَّ اَحَدَكُمْ لَيَجِيْءُ بِالْحَسَنَاتِ لَوْ وُضِعَتْ عَلٰى جَبَلٍ اَثْقَلَتْهُ ثُمَّ تَجِیْءُ النِّعَمُ فَتَذْهَبُ بِتِلْكَ ثُمَّ يَتَطَاوَلُ الرَّبُّ بَعْدَ ذٰلِكَ بِرَحْمَتِهٖ (رواه الحاكم # ٧٦٣٨)

Hadhrat Ishaaq ibn Abdullah bin Abu Talha narrates from his father who narrates from his grandfather that Rasulullah ﷺ said, "Whosoever says laailaaha illallaah, his admittance into Jannah is guaranteed, and whosoever hymns one hundred times, subhanallahi wa bihamdihi, is credited with 124 000 rewards." The Sahaabah ﵃ said, "O, Rasulullah! ﷺ if such is the case, then none of us will be destroyed on the Day of Qiyaamah because the virtues are sure to outweigh the sins." Rasulullah ﷺ said, "Some people will have so many virtues that a mountain may crumble under its weight, but these will be nothing in comparison with the favours of Allah Ta'ala. However, Allah Ta'ala, out of His extreme mercy and grace, will then rescue them."

Note: The large number of rewards will look like nothing as compared with the bounties of Allah Ta'ala, shows that whereas rewards and sins will be weighed on the Day of Qiyaamah, a person will also be called to account for whether he had made proper use of the bounties of Allah Ta'ala and had shown gratitude to Him. As a matter of fact, everything we have is granted by Allah Ta'ala, and for everything we owe a duty, and it will be checked whether we have discharged this duty properly. Rasulullah ﷺ has said,

$$\text{يُصْبِحُ عَلٰى كُلِّ سُلَامٰى مِنْ اَحَدِكُمْ صَدَقَةٌ} \text{ (رواه مسلم # 720)}$$

It is obligatory on a person to give sadaqah every morning in exchange of every joint and bone.

According to another Hadith, there are 360 joints in the human body, and it is obligatory on a person to give sadaqah for each joint. This is a token of gratitude to Allah Ta'ala that, after the night's sleep (which is similar to death), Allah Ta'ala gave him life again, with each part of the body in good order. The Sahaabah رَضِيَ اللّٰهُ عَنْهُمْ asked, "Who can afford to do so many sadaqahs every day?" Rasulullah ﷺ replied, "Saying subhanallah is a sadaqah, saying alhamdulillah is sadaqah, saying Allahu Akbar is sadaqah, saying *laailaaha illallaah* is sadaqah, removing some obstacle from the way is sadaqah (and so on)." In short, he enumerated several such items of sadaqah. There are other similar Ahaadith, wherein the bounties of Allah Ta'ala in one's own body are enumerated, and then there are, in addition, the bounties in respect of food, drink, comfort and so many other blessings of Allah Ta'ala also.

Appreciating the bounties of Allah Ta'ala

This subject is mentioned in the Qur-aan Shareef in Surah at-Takaathur, that on the Day of Qiyaamah, one will be questioned about the bounties of Allah Ta'ala. Hadhrat Ibn Abbaas رَضِيَ اللّٰهُ عَنْهُ stated that one will be reminded about the health of his body, of his ears, of his eyes, that Allah Ta'ala had bestowed on him. All such bounties are purely because of His mercy. And a person will be questioned as to how he had used these for the service of Allah Ta'ala. Did he use them like the animals for his own desires or otherwise? Thus, in the Qur-aan Shareef in Surah Bani Israa-eel, Allah Ta'ala says,

$$\text{اِنَّ السَّمْعَ وَالْبَصَرَ وَالْفُؤَادَ كُلُّ اُولٰٓئِكَ كَانَ عَنْهُ مَسْئُوْلًا}$$

"the hearing and the sight, and the heart of each person will be questioned" (Surah Bani I'sraaeel - Aayah 36),

i.e. everybody will be required to give an account for the proper use of his ears, eyes, and heart. Rasulullah ﷺ remarked that the favours for which one will be questioned about include peace of mind, which is a great blessing and also physical health. Mujaahid *(rahmatullahi alayh)* has stated that every worldly pleasure is a bounty, for which one will have to give an account. Hadhrat Ali ؓ said that security is also one of the bounties of Allah Ta'ala. A person asked Hadhrat Ali ؓ the meaning of the aayah,

$$ ثُمَّ لَتُسْـَٔلُنَّ يَوْمَئِذٍ عَنِ النَّعِيْمِ $$

"then on the Day, you will be questioned about the bounties."
(Surah Takaathur - Aayah 8)

He replied that one will be questioned about the wheat bread eaten and of cold water, as well as about the house in which he lived. It is stated in one Hadith that when this aayah was revealed, some Sahaabah ؓ said, "O Rasulullah ﷺ, what are the bounties about which we shall be questioned? We get only half a meal and that too of barley bread." Then came the revelation, "Do you not wear shoes? Do you not drink cold water? These are also bounties of Allah Ta'ala." According to one Hadith, when this aayah was revealed, some Sahaabah ؓ asked, "O Rasulullah ﷺ! About what bounties shall we be questioned? We get only dates to eat and water to drink, and we have to remain always with our swords on our shoulders, ready to fight some enemy (on account of which even these two things cannot be enjoyed by us in peace)." Rasulullah ﷺ replied, "The bounties are about to become available in the near future."

It is stated in one Hadith that Rasulullah ﷺ had said, "The first of the bounties to be accounted for on the Day of Qiyaamah, will be physical health, (i.e. whether we discharged our obligation in respect of it, and did any service for the pleasure of Allah Ta'ala) and the other is the cold drinking-water." Cold water is, in fact, a great gift of Allah Ta'ala and is realised as such where it is not (readily) available. It is indeed a great blessing of Allah Ta'ala, but we never acknowledge it to be as such; let alone speaking of thanking Allah Ta'ala for it and discharging our duty in respect of it.

It is said in one Hadith, "The bounties to be accounted for include the piece of bread eaten to satisfy the hunger, the water drunk to quench the thirst, and the cloth used to cover the body."

Once, at midday, when it was very hot, Hadhrat Abu Bakr رضى الله عنه felt extremely hungry and left his house and went to the Masjid. Soon after his arrival in the Masjid, Hadhrat Umar رضى الله عنه also reached there in a similar condition and asked him why he was there at that unusual time. "My hunger has become unbearable", was the reply. Hadhrat Umar رضى الله عنه said, "By Allah, the same thing has compelled me to also come out." The two were talking thus, when Rasulullah صلى الله عليه وسلم also came there and asked them how was it that they were there. They replied, "Hunger made us restless and compelled us to come out here." Rasulullah صلى الله عليه وسلم said, "I have come here for the same reason." All three of them went to the house of Hadhrat Abu Ayoob Ansari رضى الله عنه. He was not at home so his wife welcomed them. She was overjoyed to have them in her house. Rasulullah صلى الله عليه وسلم enquired about Abu Ayoob رضى الله عنه. She replied that he had gone out for some need and would soon be back. After a little while, Hadhrat Abu Ayoob رضى الله عنه also came back. On seeing them, he was overwhelmed with joy, and cut a big bunch of dates to entertain them. Rasulullah صلى الله عليه وسلم remarked, "Why did you cut the whole bunch? The raw and the half-ripe dates have also been cut thereby. You could have selected and plucked the ripe ones only." He replied, "I plucked the whole bunch so that all kind of dates may be before you, and you may eat the kind you may like." (Sometimes, one likes the half ripe dates in preference to the ripe ones). Leaving the dates before them, he slaughtered a small goat, roasted some of its meat, and cooked the rest. Rasulullah صلى الله عليه وسلم took some bread and a piece of roasted meat and giving it to Abu Ayoob رضى الله عنه said, "Take this to Faatimah رضى الله عنها. She also did not get anything to eat for several days." Hadhrat Abu Ayoob رضى الله عنه hastened to comply with the orders and then returned. All of them ate to their hearts content. Then Rasulullah صلى الله عليه وسلم said, "See, these are the bounties of Allah Ta'ala. The bread, the meat, the raw dates and the ripe ones." While uttering these words, tears began to flow from his eyes and he said, "By Allah! Who controls my life, these are the bounties about which one will be questioned on the Day of Qiyaamah." Considering the circumstances under which these things had become available, the Sahaabah رضى الله عنهم felt perplexed and worried that an account was required to be given for these things, which became available under such difficult conditions of helplessness. Rasulullah ﷺ said, "It is necessary to express our gratitude to Allah Ta'ala. When you put your hand on such things, say *bismillah* before starting to eat, and after eating recite,

اَلْحَمْدُ لِلّٰهِ الَّذِىْ هُوَ اَشْبَعَنَا وَاَنْعَمَ عَلَيْنَا وَاَفْضَلَ

All praise is for Allah who satiated us, and favoured us, and bestowed upon us plentifully

Its recitation will suffice as your expression of shukr (gratitude). Many incidents of this nature are narrated under different headings in the books of Hadith. Rasulullah ﷺ said the same things when he happened to visit the house of Abul Haysam Maalik bin Tayhaan رضي الله عنه and once when he visited a Sahaabi whose name was Waqifi رضي الله عنه.

Once Hadhrat Umar رضي الله عنه came across a leper who was blind, deaf and dumb. He said to his companions, "Do you see any bounties of Allah Ta'ala on this person?" "Apparently none," they replied. "Can he not urinate easily?" asked Umar رضي الله عنه.

Hadhrat Abdullah bin Mas'ood رضي الله عنه said, "There will be three courts on the Day of Qiyaamah. In one of these, the accounts of virtues will be examined, in the second, the bounties of Allah Ta'ala will be counted, and in the third, the sins will have to be accounted for. The virtues will be counter-balanced by the bounties of Allah Ta'ala, so that the sins will remain outstanding and their disposal will depend on the mercy of Allah Ta'ala."

All this means that a man is duty bound to show his gratitude to Allah Ta'ala for His unlimited favours at all times and under all conditions. Therefore, he should strive his utmost to earn as many virtues as possible and should not be content at any stage, because it will be on the Day of Qiyaamah that he will realize how many sins had been committed through his eyes, nose, ears, and other parts of the body, much of which he was not even aware off.

Rasulullah ﷺ had said, "Every one of you will have to appear before Allah Ta'ala, and will have to face Him, with no barrier in between. There will be no lawyer or interpreter to fight your case. There will be heaps of your deeds, good and bad, on either side of you. The fire of Jahannam will be in front of you. Therefore you should try your best to ward off this fire through sadaqah (voluntary charity), even if it be with a single date (or even a piece of a date)." It is stated in one Hadith, "On the Day of Qiyaamah, you will first be reminded about how you were blessed with good health and were given cold water to drink" (which implies, whether you showed gratitude for these favours). According to another Hadith, "You will not be allowed to move away from the court of Allah Ta'ala until you have answered five questions:

a. How did you spend your life?
b. How did you utilize your youth?
c. How did you earn your wealth?
d. How did you spend it? (i.e. whether earning and spending was in a lawful manner).
e. How did you act upon the knowledge which you acquired?"

Hadith 4 – Planting trees in Jannah

عَنِ ابْنِ مَسْعُوْدٍ رَضِيَ اللهُ عَنْهُ قَالَ قَالَ رَسُوْلُ اللهِ صَلَّى اللهُ عَلَيْهِ وَسَلَّمَ لَقِيْتُ اِبْرَاهِيْمَ لَيْلَةَ اُسْرِيَ بِيْ فَقَالَ يَا مُحَمَّدُ اَقْرِأْ اُمَّتَكَ مِنِّي السَّلَامَ وَاَخْبِرْهُمْ اَنَّ الْجَنَّةَ طَيِّبَةُ التُّرْبَةِ عَذْبَةُ الْمَاءِ وَاَنَّهَا قِيْعَانٌ وَاَنَّ غِرَاسَهَا سُبْحَانَ اللهِ وَالْحَمْدُ لِلهِ وَلَا اِلٰهَ اِلَّا اللهُ وَاللهُ اَكْبَرُ (رواه الترمذي # ٣٤٦٢)

Hadhrat Abdullah ibn Masood رَضِيَ اللهُ عَنْهُ narrates that Rasulullah صَلَّى اللهُ عَلَيْهِ وَسَلَّمَ says, "On the night of Me'raaj, when I met Hadhrat Ibrahim (alayhis salaam) he asked me to convey his salaams to my Ummat and tell them that the soil of Jannah is very fine and fertile and there is lots of water to irrigate it, but the land is all plain and its plants are

سُبْحَانَ اللهِ وَالْحَمْدُ لِلهِ وَلَا اِلٰهَ اِلَّا اللهُ وَاللهُ اَكْبَرُ

subhanallah, alhamdulillah, laailaaha illallaah and Allahu Akbar (so that one can plant there as much as he likes)."

According to one Hadith, the above Kalimah is also followed by لَا حَوْلَ وَلَا قُوَّةَ اِلَّا بِاللهِ laahawla wa laaquwwata illa billaah. According to

Chapter 3 – Virtues of the Third Kalimah

another Hadith it was said, "A tree for every part of this Kalimah is planted in Jannah." It is stated in one Hadith, "Whosoever recites سُبْحَانَ اللهِ الْعَظِيْمِ وَبِحَمْدِهِ *subhaanallaahil azeem wa bihamdihi*, a tree is planted for him in Jannah." It is stated in one Hadith, "Rasulullah ﷺ was going somewhere when he saw that Hadhrat Abu Hurayrah ؓ was planting something. He asked him what he was doing, 'I am planting a tree,' was the reply. Thereupon Rasulullah, ﷺ said, 'Should I tell you about the best plantation? It is

سُبْحَانَ اللهِ وَالْحَمْدُ لِلَّهِ وَلَا اِلٰهَ اِلَّا اللهُ اللهُ اَكْبَرُ

subhanallah walhamdulillah wa laailaaha illallaah wallaahu akbar, the recitation of each of these Kalimahs causes a tree to grow for you in Jannah.'"

Note: Hadhrat Ibraahim *(alayhis salaam)* sent his salaams through Rasulullah ﷺ to this Ummat. The Ulama have written that whosoever hears this Hadith, should say in return,

وَعَلَيْهِ السَّلَامُ وَرَحْمَةُ اللهِ وَبَرَكَاتُهُ

wa alyhis salaam warahmtullaahi wa barakaatuhu

(May peace be upon him as well as Allah's mercy and His blessings). The second thing mentioned in the Hadith is that the soil of Jannah is very fertile and its water very sweet. This can be interpreted in two ways. Firstly, it is the description of that place which is extremely fine, its soil (according to some Ahaadith) is of saffron and musk, and its water is very sweet, so that everybody loves to have a house there and as it has all facilities for recreation and for planting gardens, etc., nobody will like to leave it. The second interpretation is that wherever there is fertile soil and excellent water, there is always lush growth. In that case, it means that saying *subhaanallah* once will cause a tree to be planted and then by virtue of the fertile soil and excellent water, this tree will continue to grow by itself. Only the seed is required to be planted once, the growth afterwards is all automatic.

In this Hadith, Jannah is stated to have a totally plain land. In other Ahaadith where Jannah has been described it is stated that there are all kinds of fruit trees in it, so much so that the literal meaning of the word Jannah is "garden". There is thus a sort of outward contradiction here.

The Ulama explain that originally Jannah is a plain land without any trees, but when it will be handed over to the various people, they will find gardens and trees there in accordance with their deeds. The second explanation by some Ulama is that the gardens in Jannah will be awarded according to the deeds of good people and, as such, it is the deeds that are said to have caused these trees to grow for them.

The third explanation is that the smallest Jannah that anybody will get will be bigger than the whole world. Some parts of it are covered with original gardens and other parts of it are without any growth, so that trees will get automatically planted there according to the Zikr and glorification done by its recipient.

Hadhrat Moulana Gangohi *(rahmatullahi alayh)*, a great Shaikh and Aalim, has stated in his book *'Al-Kaukabud Durree'* that all the trees are available there in the form of seedlings and are planted according to the good deeds, after which they continue to grow.

Hadith 5 – More valuable than a mountain of gold

عَنْ أَبِي أُمَامَةَ رَضِيَ اللهُ عَنْهُ أَنَّ رَسُوْلَ اللهِ صَلَّى اللهُ عَلَيْهِ وَسَلَّمَ قَالَ مَنْ هَالَهُ اللَّيْلُ اَنْ يُّكَابِدَهُ اَوْ بَخِلَ بِالْمَالِ اَنْ يُنْفِقَهُ اَوْ جَبُنَ عَنِ الْعَدُوِّ اَنْ يُقَاتِلَهُ فَلْيُكْثِرْ مِنْ سُبْحَانَ اللهِ وَبِحَمْدِهٖ فَإِنَّهَا أَحَبُّ إِلَى اللهِ مِنْ جَبَلِ ذَهَبٍ يُنْفِقُهُ فِيْ سَبِيْلِ اللهِ (رواه الطبراني # ٧٨٠٠)

Hadhrat Abu Umaamah رَضِيَ اللهُ عَنْهُ narrates that Rasulullah ﷺ said, "One who is unable to toil at night i.e., he cannot keep awake and worship at night, or is too miserly to spend money, or is too cowardly to take part in Jihaad (fighting in the path of Allah Ta'ala) should say subhaanallaahi wa bi hamdihi excessively, because this action is more valuable to Allah Ta'ala than spending a mountain load of gold in His path."

Note: How great is the grace of Allah Ta'ala that even those who cannot bear hardship in the path of Allah Ta'ala are not deprived from earning virtues and huge rewards. One who cannot keep awake at night, cannot spend in the path of Allah Ta'ala, because of miserliness, and cannot take part in Jihaad, because of cowardice, but still has value for Deen in his heart and is anxious to improve his life in the Aakhirah, is still eligible to earn the favours of Allah Ta'ala. It is one's extreme misfortune if he cannot earn something even then.

Hadith 6 – Zikr is most liked by Allah Ta'ala

عَنْ سَمُرَةَ بْنِ جُنْدُبٍ رَضِيَ اللهُ عَنْهُ قَالَ قَالَ رَسُوْلُ اللهِ صَلَّى اللهُ عَلَيْهِ وَسَلَّمَ اَحَبُّ الْكَلَامِ اِلَى اللهِ اَرْبَعٌ سُبْحَانَ اللهِ وَالْحَمْدُ لِلهِ وَلَا اِلٰهَ اِلَّا اللهُ وَاللهُ اَكْبَرُ لَا يَضُرُّكَ بِاَيِّهِنَّ بَدَأْتَ (رواه مسلم # ٢١٣٧)

Hadhrat Samurah bin Jundub ﷺ *narrates that Rasulullah* ﷺ *said, "The words most liked by Allah Ta'ala consist of four Kalimahs, viz; Subhaanallah, Alhamdulillaah, laailaaha illallaah and Allahu Akbar which may be recited in any sequence."*

Note: According to one Hadith, these Kalimahs are also mentioned in the Qur-aan Shareef. These Kalimahs occur very frequently in the Qur-aan Shareef, wherein there is the command and persuasion for their recitation as described in detail in Part one. It is stated in one Hadith, "Adorn the festivals of Eid with these words by their frequent recitation."

Hadith 7 – The poor surpassing the wealthy

عَنْ اَبِيْ هُرَيْرَةَ رَضِيَ اللهُ عَنْهُ اَنَّ فُقَرَاءَ الْمُهَاجِرِيْنَ اَتَوْا رَسُوْلَ اللهِ صَلَّى اللهُ عَلَيْهِ وَسَلَّمَ فَقَالُوْا ذَهَبَ اَهْلُ الدُّثُوْرِ بِالدَّرَجَاتِ الْعُلٰى وَالنَّعِيْمِ الْمُقِيْمِ فَقَالَ مَا ذَاكَ قَالُوْا يُصَلُّوْنَ كَمَا نُصَلِّيْ وَيَصُوْمُوْنَ كَمَا نَصُوْمُ وَيَتَصَدَّقُوْنَ وَلَا نَتَصَدَّقُ وَيُعْتِقُوْنَ وَلَا نُعْتِقُ فَقَالَ رَسُوْلُ اللهِ صَلَّى اللهُ عَلَيْهِ وَسَلَّمَ اَفَلَا اُعَلِّمُكُمْ شَيْئًا تُدْرِكُوْنَ بِهٖ مَنْ سَبَقَكُمْ وَتَسْبِقُوْنَ بِهٖ مَنْ بَعْدَكُمْ وَلَا يَكُوْنُ اَحَدٌ اَفْضَلَ مِنْكُمْ اِلَّا مَنْ صَنَعَ مِثْلَ مَا صَنَعْتُمْ قَالُوْا بَلٰى يَا رَسُوْلَ اللهِ قَالَ تُسَبِّحُوْنَ وَتُكَبِّرُوْنَ وَتَحْمَدُوْنَ دُبُرَ كُلِّ صَلَاةٍ ثَلَاثًا وَّثَلَاثِيْنَ مَرَّةً قَالَ اَبُوْ صَالِحٍ فَرَجَعَ فُقَرَاءُ الْمُهَاجِرِيْنَ اِلٰى رَسُوْلِ اللهِ صَلَّى اللهُ عَلَيْهِ وَسَلَّمَ فَقَالُوْا سَمِعَ اِخْوَانُنَا

اَهْلُ الْاَمْوَالِ بِمَا فَعَلْنَا فَفَعَلُوْا مِثْلَهُ فَقَالَ رَسُوْلُ اللهِ صَلَّى اللهُ عَلَيْهِ وَسَلَّمَ ذٰلِكَ فَضْلُ اللهِ يُؤْتِيْهِ مَنْ يَّشَاءُ (رواه مسلم) وَفِىْ رِوَايَةٍ اَوَلَيْسَ قَدْ جَعَلَ اللهُ لَكُمْ مَّا تَصَّدَّقُوْنَ اِنَّ بِكُلِّ تَسْبِيْحَةٍ صَدَقَةً وَبِكُلِّ تَحْمِيْدَةٍ صَدَقَةً وَّفِىْ بُضْعِ اَحَدِكُمْ صَدَقَةً قَالُوْا يَا رَسُوْلَ اللهِ اَيَأْتِىْ اَحَدُنَا شَهْوَتَهُ يَكُوْنُ لَهُ فِيْهَا اَجْرٌ قَالَ اَرَاَيْتُمْ لَوْ وَضَعَهَا فِى الْحَرَامِ اَكَانَ عَلَيْهِ فِيْهَا وِزْرٌ وَّكَذٰلِكَ اِذَا وَضَعَهَا فِى الْحَلَالِ كَانَ لَهُ فِيْهَا اَجْرٌ (مسند احمد #٢٣)

Hadhrat Abu Hurayrah ﷺ narrates that once a group of poor Muhaajirs came to Rasulullah ﷺ and said, "O Rasulullah ﷺ! Only the rich attain the higher spiritual grades, and the eternal bounties of Allah fall only to their lot." "How?" enquired Rasulullah ﷺ. They replied, "They offer Salaah and observe fasting in the same manner as we do, but, being rich, they are able to perform other good deeds, like giving sadaqah and freeing slaves, which we being poor are unable to do." Rasulullah ﷺ said, "Should I tell you something, by acting upon which, you may overtake your predecessors and surpass your successors and nobody may be better than you unless he also acts upon the same thing." "Do tell us," said the Sahaabah ﷺ. "Recite Subhaanallah, Alhamdulillah and Allahu Akbar thirty-three times each after every Salaah," said Rasulullah ﷺ. They acted upon his advice, but the rich of those days came to know of it and started doing the same. The poor again came to Rasulullah ﷺ and complained, "Our rich brothers have come to learn what you told us and are also acting upon it." Rasulullah ﷺ then remarked, "It is the favour of Allah Ta'ala which He bestows on whomsoever He likes. Nobody can stop Him." According to another Hadith, Rasulullah ﷺ is also reported to have said to them, "Allah Ta'ala has also favoured you with a substitute of sadaqah. Reciting Subhaanallah once is sadaqah, saying Alhamdulillah once is sadaqah, intercourse with one's wife is sadaqah." The Sahaabah ﷺ were astonished to hear this, and asked, "O Rasulullah! ﷺ indulgence with one's wife is an act of satisfying one's lust, and you say this is also sadaqah?" Rasulullah

ﷺ said, "Would it not be a sin to indulge in the unlawful?" "Yes", said the Sahaabah رضي الله عنهم. "In the same manner, engaging in halaal will amount to sadaqah and reward," explained Rasulullah ﷺ.

Note: From this it is clear that to share the bed with one's wife in order to save oneself from adultery brings reward from Allah Ta'ala.

In another Hadith, the reply of Rasulullah ﷺ to the query by the Sahaabah رضي الله عنهم that sharing the bed with the wife is for the satisfaction of one's lust was, "Just tell me, if a child is born as a result thereof, and when he grows up to youth and becomes the center of your expectations, and then he happens to die, will you then not hope for a reward from Allah Ta'ala in lieu of this loss?" Their reply was in the affirmative, and then Rasulullah ﷺ continued, "Why this expectation of reward? Did you create him? Did you guide him or did you sustain him? On the other hand, it was Allah Ta'ala who created him, guided him and sustained him. Similarly, you put your semen in the lawful place, then it is up to Allah Ta'ala to make it into a child or prevent it from becoming a child." In short, this Hadith implies that the reward from Allah Ta'ala is for one's having become the cause of the birth of the child.

Hadith 8 – Tasbeehaat after the Fardh Salaah

عَنْ أَبِي هُرَيْرَةَ رَضِيَ اللهُ عَنْهُ قَالَ قَالَ رَسُولُ اللهِ صَلَّى اللهُ عَلَيْهِ وَسَلَّمَ مَنْ سَبَّحَ اللهَ فِي دُبُرِ كُلِّ صَلَاةٍ ثَلَاثًا وَّثَلَاثِيْنَ وَحَمِدَ اللهَ ثَلَاثًا وَّثَلَاثِيْنَ وَكَبَّرَ اللهَ ثَلَاثًا وَّثَلَاثِيْنَ فَتِلْكَ تِسْعَةٌ وَّتِسْعُوْنَ وَقَالَ تَمَامَ الْمِائَةِ لَا إِلٰهَ إِلَّا اللهُ وَحْدَهُ لَا شَرِيْكَ لَهُ لَهُ الْمُلْكُ وَلَهُ الْحَمْدُ وَهُوَ عَلٰى كُلِّ شَيْءٍ قَدِيْرٌ غُفِرَتْ خَطَايَاهُ وَإِنْ كَانَتْ مِثْلَ زَبَدِ الْبَحْرِ

(رواه مسلم # ٥٩٧)

Hadhrat Abu Hurayrah رضي الله عنه narrates that Rasulullah ﷺ said, "Whosoever reads 33 times Subhaanallah, 33 times Alhamdulillah, 33 times Allahu Akbar after every Salaah and then reads once the following

$$\text{لَا إِلٰهَ إِلَّا اللهُ وَحْدَهُ لَا شَرِيْكَ لَهُ لَهُ الْمُلْكُ وَلَهُ الْحَمْدُ وَهُوَ عَلٰى كُلِّ شَىْءٍ قَدِيْرٌ}$$

all his sins are forgiven, even though they may be (countless) like the foam in the sea."

Note: "sins are forgiven" (by virtue of zikr) has already been discussed under several Ahaadith. According to the Ulama, it is only the minor sins that are forgiven. In this Hadith, it is stated that three Kalimahs should be recited 33 times each, and then *Laailaaha illallaahu wahdahu la shareekalahu lahul mulku walahul hamdu wahuwa 'alaa kulli shayin qadeer* once. According to the next Hadith, two of the three Kalimahs should be recited 33 times each and the third one i.e. Allahu Akbar 34 times.

Hadhrat Zaid رَضِيَ اللهُ عَنْهُ has narrated, "Rasulullah ﷺ had ordered us to recite *Subhaanallah, Alhamdulillah* and *Allahu-Akbar* thirty-three times each after every Salaah. An Ansaari Sahaabi رَضِيَ اللهُ عَنْهُ saw in a dream that a person advised reciting the three Kalimahs 25 times each and then *laailaaha illallaah* also 25 times. When Rasulullah ﷺ was told about this dream, he permitted him to recite it in that way". According to one Hadith, *Subhaanallah, Alhamdulillah* and *Allahu-Akbar* should be read 11 times each after every Salaah, and according to another Hadith it is ten times each. In one Hadith, the recitation of *Laailaaha illallaah* is ten times and that of the other three Kalimahs is 33 times each. According to one Hadith, each of the four kalimahs should be read hundred times each. All these Ahaadith are narrated in the book *'Hisnul Haseen'*. The apparent difference in these versions is due to the different circumstances of the persons who were advised by Rasulullah ﷺ. Those who were busy with other (important) work were advised the lesser number and those who were free were advised a greater number. The Muhaqqiqeen, religious authorities, however, advise that one should conform to the numbers narrated in the Ahaadith just as the quantity of a thing that is used as a medicine is also specified.

Chapter 3 – Virtues of the Third Kalimah

Hadith 9 – Tasbeehaat after every Fardh Salaah

عَنْ كَعْبِ بْنِ عُجْرَةَ رَضِىَ اللهُ عَنْهُ قَالَ قَالَ رَسُوْلُ اللهِ صَلَّى اللهُ عَلَيْهِ وَسَلَّمَ مُعَقِّبَاتٌ لَا يَخِيْبُ قَائِلُهُنَّ اَوْ فَاعِلُهُنَّ دُبُرَ كُلِّ صَلَاةٍ مَكْتُوْبَةٍ ثَلَاثٌ وَّثَلَاثُوْنَ تَسْبِيْحَةً وَّثَلَاثٌ وَّثَلَاثُوْنَ تَحْمِيْدَةً وَّاَرْبَعٌ وَّثَلَاثُوْنَ تَكْبِيْرَةً (رواه مسلم # ٥٩٦)

Hadhrat Ka'b bin Ujrah ﷺ narrates that Rasulullah ﷺ said, "The following words are such that one who recites them is never disappointed. These are which should be recited, 33 times Subhaanallah, 33 times Alhamdulillah and 34 times Allahu-Akbar respectively after every fardh Salaah."

Note: These Kalimahs have been termed as Mu'aqqibaat (things that will follow), either because these are recited after the Salaah or because the recitation of these after committing sins results in washing them off, or because these are recited one after the other. Hadhrat Abu Darda ﷺ narrated, "We have been directed to recite *Subhaanallah* 33 times, *Alhamdulillah* 33 times and *Allahu-Akbar* 34 times after every Salaah."

Hadith 10 – Reward greater than mount Uhud

عَنْ عِمْرَانَ بْنِ حُصَيْنٍ رَضِىَ اللهُ عَنْهُ رَفَعَهُ اَمَا يَسْتَطِيْعُ اَحَدُكُمْ اَنْ يَّعْمَلَ كُلَّ يَوْمٍ مِثْلَ اُحُدٍ عَمَلًا قَالُوْا يَا رَسُوْلَ اللهِ وَمَنْ يَّسْتَطِيْعُهُ قَالَ كُلُّكُمْ يَسْتَطِيْعُهُ قَالُوْا يَا رَسُوْلَ اللهِ مَاذَا قَالَ سُبْحَانَ اللهِ اَعْظَمُ مِنْ اُحُدٍ وَّلَا اِلٰهَ اِلَّا اللهُ اَعْظَمُ مِنْ اُحُدٍ وَّالْحَمْدُ لِلّٰهِ اَعْظَمُ مِنْ اُحُدٍ وَّاللهُ اَكْبَرُ اَعْظَمُ مِنْ اُحُدٍ (اخرجه ابن طاهر السوسى فى جمع الفوائد # ٩٥٢٠)

Hadhrat Imraan bin Husain ﷺ narrates that Rasulullah ﷺ once said, "Is there anybody amongst you who may be able to do good deeds every day which are equal to Uhud (a mountain near Madinah Shareef)." The Sahaabah ﷺ said, "O Rasulullah! Who has the strength to do that?" "Everybody has the strength to do it," replied Rasulullah ﷺ, "How is it?" enquired the Sahaabah ﷺ. He explained, "The reward of Subhaanallah is greater than the mountain Uhud, that of laailaaha illallaah is greater than Uhud, that of *Alhamdulillah* is greater than Uhud and that of *Allahu Akbar* is greater than Uhud."

Note: Therefore, the reward of each of these Kalimahs is greater than the mountain of Uhud, or rather it is even greater than many such mountains. It is said in one Hadith that the reward of *Subhaanallah* and *Alhamdulillah* fills all the Heavens and the Earths. It is said in another Hadith that the reward of *Subhaanallah* occupies half the pan of the scale (in which deeds will be weighed), the reward of *Alhamdulillah* occupies the remaining half, and the reward of *Allahu-Akbar* fills the space between the Earth and the sky. It is stated in one Hadith that Rasulullah ﷺ had said,

سُبْحَانَ اللهِ اَلْحَمْدُ لِلهِ لَا اِلٰهَ اِلَّا اللهُ اَللهُ اَكْبَرُ

is more dear to me than all the things under the Sun."

Mulla Ali Qari *(rahmatullahi alayh)* explained it to mean that it is more dear than spending in the path of Allah Ta'ala all that which this world contains.

It is said that once Hadhrat Sulaymaan *(alayhis salaam)* was flying somewhere on his throne, when the birds spread their wings to protect him from the sun, and the armies of men and jinn were accompanying him. On seeing this, a pious person praised Allah Ta'ala for the grandeur of this vast kingdom. Hadhrat Sulaymaan *(alayhis salaam)* remarked, "The credit in the account of deeds of a believer for reciting *Subhaanallah* once is more than the whole kingdom of Sulaymaan Bin Dawood, because this kingdom is temporary but the reward of reciting *Subhaanallah* is everlasting."

Hadith 11 – Five things are very weighty on the scales

عَنْ أَبِيْ سَلَامٍ رَضِيَ اللهُ عَنْهُ عَنْ مَوْلٰى رَسُوْلِ اللهِ صَلَّى اللهُ عَلَيْهِ وَسَلَّمَ أَنَّ رَسُوْلَ اللهِ صَلَّى اللهُ عَلَيْهِ وَسَلَّمَ قَالَ بَخٍّ بَخٍّ خَمْسٌ مَا أَثْقَلَهُنَّ فِي الْمِيْزَانِ لَا اِلٰهَ اِلَّا اللهُ وَاللهُ اَكْبَرُ وَسُبْحَانَ اللهِ وَالْحَمْدُ لِلهِ وَالْوَلَدُ الصَّالِحُ يُتَوَفّٰى لِلْمَرْءِ الْمُسْلِمِ فَيَحْتَسِبُهُ

(رواه احمد # ١٥٦٦٢)

Chapter 3 – Virtues of the Third Kalimah

Hadhrat Abu Salaam ﷺ narrates that Rasulullah ﷺ said, "Bakh! Bakh! How weighty in the scales are five things, viz. لَا إِلٰهَ إِلَّا اللهُ وَاللهُ أَكْبَرُ وَسُبْحَانَ اللهِ وَالْحَمْدُ لِلهِ (laailaaha illallaah, Allahu Akbar, Subhaanallah, Alhamdulillah) and the exercising of patience by the father (or the mother) over the death of his (or her) obedient child."

Note: The subject-matter of this Hadith is narrated by many Sahaabah ﷺ in so many other Ahaadith. The words *(Bakh! Bakh)* are exclaimed at the time of extreme joy and pleasure. These things are of great joy and pleasure to Rasulullah ﷺ and are therefore, stressed so much by him. Is it not therefore, incumbent upon us, who claim to love him, that we should show extreme devotion to these Kalimahs, because doing so also amounts to showing respect, obedience and gratitude to Him.

Hadith 12 – The advice of Hadhrat Nooh (alayhis salaam) to his son

عَنْ سُلَيْمَانَ بْنِ يَسَارٍ رَضِيَ اللهُ عَنْهُ عَنْ رَجُلٍ مِنَ الْأَنْصَارِ اَنَّ النَّبِيَّ صَلَّى اللهُ عَلَيْهِ وَسَلَّمَ قَالَ قَالَ نُوْحٌ لِابْنِهِ: اِنِّي مُوْصِيْكَ بِوَصِيَّةٍ وَقَاصِرُهَا لِكَيْ لَا تَنْسَاهَا أُوْصِيْكَ بِاثْنَيْنِ وَاَنْهَاكَ عَنِ اثْنَيْنِ اَمَّا اللَّتَانِ أُوْصِيْكَ بِهِمَا فَيَسْتَبْشِرُ اللهُ بِهِمَا وَصَالِحُ خَلْقِهِ وَهُمَا يُكْثِرَانِ الْوُلُوْجَ عَلَى اللهِ تَعَالٰى أُوْصِيْكَ بِلَا اِلٰهَ اِلَّا اللهُ فَاِنَّ السَّمٰوَاتِ وَالْأَرْضَ لَوْ كَانَتَا حَلْقَةً قَصَمَتْهُمَا وَلَوْ كَانَتَا فِيْ كَفَّةٍ وَزَنَتْهُمَا وَأُوْصِيْكَ بِسُبْحَانَ اللهِ وَبِحَمْدِهٖ فَاِنَّهُمَا صَلَاةُ الْخَلْقِ وَبِهَا يُرْزَقُ الْخَلْقُ وَاِنْ مِنْ شَيْءٍ اِلَّا يُسَبِّحُ بِحَمْدِهٖ وَلٰكِنْ لَا تَفْقَهُوْنَ تَسْبِيْحَهُمْ اِنَّهٗ كَانَ حَلِيْمًا غَفُوْرًا وَاَمَّا اللَّتَانِ اَنْهَاكَ عَنْهُمَا فَيَحْتَجِبُ اللهُ مِنْهُمَا وَصَالِحُ خَلْقِهِ اَنْهَاكَ عَنِ الشِّرْكِ وَالْكِبْرِ (رواه النسائي # ١٠٦٠٠)

Hadhrat Sulaymaan bin Yasaar (rahmatullahi alayh) narrates from an Ansaari Sahaabi ﷺ that Rasulullah ﷺ said, "Hadhrat Nooh (alayhis salaam) said to his son, "I will give you a piece of advice, and in order that you may not forget it, I will say it very briefly. I advise you to do two things and forbid you from doing two things. The two things which I recommend are such that Allah Ta'ala and His noble creation are greatly pleased with them, and both of these have easy access to Allah Ta'ala. One of the two things is laailaaha illallaah, which, if it were enclosed in the mighty sky, will break through it and reach Allah Ta'ala and if all the heavens and the earth were placed in one pan of the scale and this kalimah were put in the other pan, the latter would out weight the former. The second thing that I recommend to you is the recitation of subhaanallahi wabihamdihi which is the Ibaadah (form of worship) of all the creation and by virtue of which all the creation get their sustenance. There is none among the creation that do not make the tasbeeh of Allah Ta'ala but you do not understand their speech. And the two things from which I forbid you, are shirk (polytheism) and arrogance, because these two keep you away from Allah Ta'ala and His noble creation."

Note: The subject matter of this Hadith has also been discussed before when describing the virtues of laailaaha illallaah. It is mentioned in the Qur-aan Shareef, that the entire creation hymns the glory of Allah Ta'ala. One of these aayaat is:

$$وَاِنْ مِّنْ شَىْءٍ اِلَّا يُسَبِّحُ بِحَمْدِهٖ$$

"There is none among the creation who does not hymn His glory."
(Surah Israa - Aayah 44)

It is narrated in many Ahaadith that on the night of Mi'raaj, Rasulullah ﷺ had heard all the heavens hymning the glory of Allah Ta'ala.

Once Rasulullah ﷺ happened to pass by a group of men who, though halted, were still sitting on the backs of their horses and camels. He said to them, "Do not use the backs of your animals as chairs and pulpits. Many a times they are better than their riders and make zikr of Allah Ta'ala more than their riders."

Hadhrat Ibn Abbas ؓ said that even the crops hymn the glory of Allah Ta'ala, and the owner gets the reward for it.

Once, a bowl was presented to Rasulullah ﷺ, in which there was sareed (a special dish made with gravy, bread and meat). He remarked that the food was making the tasbeeh of Allah Ta'ala.

Somebody asked if he understood its tasbeeh. He replied in the affirmative, and then he asked that it be taken to a certain person. When the cup was brought to him, he heard it hymning the glory of Allah Ta'ala. In the same way, it was presented to another person who also heard it. Somebody requested that all those present should be allowed to hear it. Rasulullah ﷺ said, "If someone fails to hear it, others will think that he is a sinner." This is known as kashf which the Ambiyaa *(alayhimus salaam)* possessed to a highest degree. The Sahaabah ؓ, at times, also experienced it as a result of their nearness and company with Rasulullah ﷺ.

Kashf

Hundreds of incidents can be cited as a proof thereof. Even the Sufis often develop this quality through their *mujaahadah* (spiritual exertion), as a result of which they are able to understand what the rocks and animals recite and speak. But according to the authentic Ulama, expertise in this line is not necessarily proof of one's high spiritual attainment or nearness to Allah Ta'ala. Whoever makes mujaahadah (exerts himself) for this can develop it, irrespective of whether he attains nearness to Allah Ta'ala or not. Therefore, the Ulama do not attach any importance to it. On the other hand, they regard it as harmful for a beginner who may get so much absorbed and involved in it that it becomes a hindrance to his spiritual progress.

Some mureeds of Moulana Khalil Ahmad Sahaaranpuri *(rahmatullahi alayh)* happened to develop a sort of kashf. In order to prevent its further progress, Moulana *(rahmatullahi alayh)* stopped them from making all forms of zikr. Furthermore, the Ulama avoid development of kashf, because this leads to the sins of others being exposed, which according to them is a means of polluting the heart.

Allamah Sha'raani *(rahmatullahi alayh)* has related in his book Meezaanul Kubra about Hadhrat Imam Abu Hanifa *(rahmatullahi alayh)* that when he happened to see somebody performing wudhu, he could also see the sins being washed away in the water, so much so that he could even distinguish whether the sins were major, minor or merely undesirable deeds, just as one is able to see the material things. Once he happened to go into the wudhu khana in the main masjid of Koofa, where a young man was making wudhu. After looking at the water used by him, he quietly advised him, "My brother! Make taubah from disobeying your parents," which he did. Then he saw another person and said to him, "My brother! Refrain from adultery, it is a major sin," and the man made taubah from adultery. He saw that the water used by yet another man indicated the sins of drinking and sinful amusement. He advised the man accordingly who also made taubah immediately. Afterwards, Hadhrat Imam Abu Hanifa *(rahmatullahi alayh)* made dua, "O Allah! Take away this thing from me. I do not want to see the shortcomings of other people." His dua was accepted by Allah Ta'ala, and he was relieved of this ability. It is related that it was during that period that he had declared the water once used for wudhu to have become impure. When he saw the dirt and bad smell of sins in it, he could not regard it as clean. After he was relieved of this power, he also retracted his view of declaring this water as impure.

It is related of a mureed of our Shaikh Moulana Abdur Rahim Raipuri *(rahmatullahi alayh)*, may Allah Ta'ala enlighten his grave, that for many days on end, he could not go out to answer the call of nature, because he found spiritual light prevailing all over. Similarly, there are hundreds and thousands of incidents proving beyond any doubt that those who experience kashf can see hidden things, according to the degree of their attainment.

Hadith 13 – An easy zikr for old and weak people

عَنْ أُمِّ هَانِئٍ رَضِيَ اللهُ عَنْهَا قَالَتْ: مَرَّ بِىْ رَسُوْلُ اللهِ صَلَّى اللهُ عَلَيْهِ وَسَلَّمَ فَقُلْتُ: يَا رَسُوْلَ اللهِ إِنِّىْ قَدْ كَبِرْتُ وَضَعُفْتُ أَوْ كَمَا قَالَتْ فَمُرْنِىْ بِعَمَلٍ أَعْمَلُهُ وَأَنَا جَالِسَةٌ قَالَ: سَبِّحِىْ اللهَ مِائَةَ تَسْبِيْحَةٍ فَإِنَّهَا تَعْدِلُ لَكِ مِائَةَ رَقَبَةٍ تُعْتِقِيْنَهَا مِنْ وُلْدِ إِسْمَاعِيْلَ وَاحْمَدِىْ اللهَ مِائَةَ تَحْمِيْدَةٍ فَإِنَّهَا تَعْدِلُ لَكِ مِائَةَ فَرَسٍ مُسْرَجَةٍ مُلْجَمَةٍ تَحْمِلِيْنَ عَلَيْهَا فِىْ سَبِيْلِ اللهِ وَكَبِّرِىْ اللهَ مِائَةَ تَكْبِيْرَةٍ فَإِنَّهَا تَعْدِلُ لَكِ مِائَةَ بَدَنَةٍ مُقَلَّدَةٍ مُتَقَبَّلَةٍ وَهَلِّلِى اللهَ مِائَةَ تَهْلِيْلَةٍ قَالَ أَبُوْ خَلَفٍ: أَحْسِبُهُ قَالَ تَمْلَأُ مَا بَيْنَ السَّمَاءِ وَالْأَرْضِ وَلَا يُرْفَعُ لِأَحَدٍ عَمَلٌ أَفْضَلُ مِمَّا يُرْفَعُ لَكِ إِلَّا أَنْ يَأْتِىَ بِمِثْلِ مَا أَتَيْتِ (رواه احمد # ٢٦٩١١)

Chapter 3 – Virtues of the Third Kalimah

Hadhrat Umme Haani ﷺ related that once when Rasulullah ﷺ visited her, she said to him, "O Rasulullah ﷺ! I have grown very old and weak. Tell me something that I may be able to do while sitting." Rasulullah ﷺ said to her, Recite Subhaanallah 100 times and you will get a reward as if you set free 100 Arab slaves, recite alhamdulillah 100 times, which will fetch you a reward as if you present 100 horses, fully equipped, for the Jihaad, say Allahu Akbar 100 times, which is as if you sacrificed 100 camels for the sake of Allah Ta'ala; and say laailaaha illallaah 100 times, the reward of which will fill all the space between the earth and the sky. There is no other commendable action that can surpass it."

Hadhrat Salma ﷺ, the wife of Abu Raafe' ﷺ, had also requested Rasulullah ﷺ to prescribe for her some zikr which may not be very lengthy. Rasulullah ﷺ advised her, "Recite Allahu Akbar ten times, because Allah Ta'ala says in reply, 'This is for Me,' recite Subhaanallah ten times, because Allah Ta'ala says in reply, 'This is for Me', and then recite Allahummaghfirli (O Allah! forgive me) ten times, because then Allah Ta'ala says, 'Yes, I have forgiven you.' If you recite Allahummaghfirli ten times, Allah Ta'ala will also say to each time, 'I have forgiven you.'"

Note: What a brief and easy zikr has been taught by Rasulullah ﷺ for old and weak people, especially women. It is very brief and involves no effort or going about, and yet what a tremendous reward is promised for it. It is really a pity if we fail to earn this great reward.

Hadhrat Umm-e-Sulaim ﷺ has narrated that she also requested Rasulullah ﷺ to prescribe for her something that she should recite before her dua to Allah Ta'ala at the time of Salaah, and that she was told, "Recite Subhaanallah, Alhamdulillah and Allahu-Akbar ten times each, and then make dua for whatever you like." In another Hadith, Allah Ta'ala will say; "Yes, Yes, I accept it." How simple and common are these words, that no effort is required to memorise them. We engage in such useless talk throughout the day but if, whilst doing our business or sitting in the shop or working on the field, we make this zikr as well, then along with our work for the worldly life we can also earn lots of wealth and reward for the next life of the Aakirah.

Hadith 14 – The Malaaikah go out in search of people making zikr

عَنْ اَبِيْ هُرَيْرَةَ رَضِيَ اللهُ عَنْهُ قَالَ قَالَ رَسُوْلُ اللهِ صَلَّى اللهُ عَلَيْهِ وَسَلَّمَ اِنَّ لِلهِ مَلَائِكَةً يَطُوْفُوْنَ فِى الطُّرُقِ يَلْتَمِسُوْنَ اَهْلَ الذِّكْرِ فَاِذَا وَجَدُوْا قَوْمًا يَذْكُرُوْنَ اللهَ تَنَادَوْا هَلُمُّوْا اِلٰى حَاجَتِكُمْ فَيَحُفُّوْنَهَا بِاَجْنِحَتِهِمْ اِلَى السَّمَاءِ فَاِذَا تَفَرَّقُوْا عَرَجُوْا وَصَعِدُوْا اِلَى السَّمَاءِ فَيَسْاَلُهُمْ رَبُّهُمْ وَهُوَ يَعْلَمُ مِنْ اَيْنَ جِئْتُمْ فَيَقُوْلُوْنَ: جِئْنَا مِنْ عِنْدِ عِبَادٍ لَكَ يُسَبِّحُوْنَكَ وَيُكَبِّرُوْنَكَ وَيَحْمَدُوْنَكَ فَيَقُوْلُ: هَلْ رَاَوْنِيْ فَيَقُوْلُوْنَ: لَا فَيَقُوْلُ: وَكَيْفَ لَوْ رَاَوْنِيْ فَيَقُوْلُوْنَ: لَوْ رَاَوْكَ كَانُوْا اَشَدَّ لَكَ عِبَادَةً وَّاَشَدَّ لَكَ تَمْجِيْدًا وَّاَكْثَرَ لَكَ تَسْبِيْحًا فَيَقُوْلُ: فَمَا يَسْاَلُوْنَ فَيَقُوْلُوْنَ: يَسْاَلُوْنَكَ الْجَنَّةَ فَيَقُوْلُ: وَهَلْ رَاَوْهَا فَيَقُوْلُوْنَ: لَا فَيَقُوْلُ: فَكَيْفَ لَوْ رَاَوْهَا فَيَقُوْلُوْنَ: لَوْ اَنَّهُمْ رَاَوْهَا كَانُوْا اَشَدَّ عَلَيْهَا حِرْصًا وَّاَشَدَّ لَهَا طَلَبًا وَّاَعْظَمَ فِيْهَا رَغْبَةً قَالَ: فَمِمَّ يَتَعَوَّذُوْنَ فَيَقُوْلُوْنَ: مِنَ النَّارِ فَيَقُوْلُ: وَهَلْ رَاَوْهَا فَيَقُوْلُوْنَ: لَا فَيَقُوْلُ: فَكَيْفَ لَوْ رَاَوْهَا فَيَقُوْلُوْنَ: لَوْ اَنَّهُمْ رَاَوْهَا كَانُوْا اَشَدَّ مِنْهَا فِرَارًا وَّاَشَدَّ لَهَا مَخَافَةً فَيَقُوْلُ: اُشْهِدُكُمْ اَنِّيْ قَدْ غَفَرْتُ لَهُمْ فَيَقُوْلُ مَلَكٌ مِّنَ الْمَلَائِكَةِ: فُلَانٌ لَيْسَ مِنْهُمْ اِنَّمَا جَاءَ لِحَاجَةٍ قَالَ: هُمُ الْقَوْمُ لَا يَشْقٰى بِهِمْ جَلِيْسُهُمْ (رواه البخاری # ٦٤٠٨)

Hadhrat Abu Hurayrah ﷺ narrates that Rasulullah ﷺ said: "There is a class of Malaaikah who keep moving about on the pathways and wherever they find some people engaged in the zikr of Allah Ta'ala, they call each other and gather around them and pile up over each other right up to the sky. When that assembly for zikr is over, the Malaaikah ascend to the Heavens and then Allah Ta'ala, dispite knowing everything, asks them where they had come from? They say that they have come from such and such group of His servants who were busy in making zikr of tasbeeh (Subhaanallah), takbeer (Allahu Akbar) and tahmeed (alhamdulillah). Allah Ta'ala askes, "Have those people seen Me?" "No, our Rabb", confirm the Malaaikah? "How would they have acted if they had actually seen me?" says Allah Ta'ala. "They would have busied themselves with even greater zeal in worshiping You and in hymning Your praise and Glory," reply the Malaaikah. "What do they desire for?" "They want Jannah", reply the Malaaikah. "Have they ever seen Jannah?" asks Allah Ta'ala. "No our Rabb" say the Malaaikah. "If they had seen it, how would they have acted?" says Allah Ta'ala. "Their zeal, yearning, and their duas for it would have been even greater," reply the Malaaikah. "What were they seeking refuge from?" says Allah Ta'ala. "They were seeking refuge from Jahannam", say the Malaaikah. "Have they seen Jahannam?" "They have not seen it." "How would they have acted if they had seen it?" says Allah. "They would have been more scared of it, and would have tried more for protection against it," say the Malaaikah. Then Allah Ta'ala says, "Alright then, all of you bear witness that I grant forgiveness to all those present in that assembly." One angel says, "O Allah! A person happened to be there only by chance; he had come for some other purpose and had not taken part in what they did." Allah Ta'ala says, "That group was so blessed that whosoever sat with them, even by the way, is not deprived of the blessings (and thus he is also forgiven)."

Note: It is described in several Ahaadith that there is a group of Malaaikah who go about in search of gatherings and individuals engaged in zikr, and wherever they find them, they sit near them and listen to their zikr. This subject matter is already included in Hadith No. 8 in Chapter 1, wherein it is also explained why Allah Ta'ala praises these people in the presence of the Malaaikah.

The enquiry by an angel that there was a person in that assembly who had come there for his personal work was only a statement of facts, because on that occasion those Malaaikah were acting as the witnesses that those people were engaged in Ibaadah and zikr of Allah Ta'ala. That is why they had to clarify the position, in case there should be any objection. But it is the extreme benevolence of Allah Ta'ala that, because of the blessed people engaged in zikr, a man who is just sitting with them coincidently, is not deprived of blessings. Allah Ta'ala says in the Qur-aan Shareef:

$$\text{يَٰٓأَيُّهَا ٱلَّذِينَ ءَامَنُوا۟ ٱتَّقُوا۟ ٱللَّهَ وَكُونُوا۟ مَعَ ٱلصَّٰدِقِينَ}$$

"O you who believe! Fear Allah Ta'ala and be with the truthful."
(Surah Taubah - Aayah 119)

The Sufis say, "Remain with Allah Ta'ala, and if this is not possible, then be in the company of those people who remain with Allah Ta'ala." Remaining with Allah Ta'ala is a reference to the Hadith in *'Bukhaari Shareef'* where in it is mentioned that Allah Ta'ala says, "By means of nafl Salaah, My servants keep on getting nearer and nearer to Me, till I make him My beloved. And at that stage, I become his ears with which he listens, his eyes with which he sees, his hands with which he holds, his feet with which he walks and whatever he begs of Me I grant it to him." Allah Ta'ala becomes his hands and feet, etc., means that he performs his actions for earning the pleasure and love of Allah Ta'ala and that he does not do anything against the will of Allah Ta'ala. The books of history relate the lives of many sufis of this level. A booklet, known as *'Nuzhatul Basaateen'* is specially devoted to the account of such Sufis.

Shaikh Abu Bakr Kattaani *(rahmatullahi alayh)* related, "Once, at the time of Hajj, there was a gathering in Makkah Mukarramah of some Sufis, the youngest among whom was Junaid Baghdadi *(rahmatullahi alayh)*. In that gathering, there was a discussion on the subject of the Love of Allah Ta'ala and as to who is the lover of Allah! Many of them expressed their views on the subject, but Junaid Baghdadi *(rahmatullahi alayh)* remained silent. He was pressed to say something. With his head bowed down and tears in his eyes, he said, 'A lover (of Allah Ta'ala) is he who forgets his own self, remains engaged in the zikr of Allah Ta'ala with due regard to all its requirements; sees Allah Ta'ala with the eyes of his heart, which is burnt by the heat of the fear of Allah Ta'ala, the zikr of Allah Ta'ala intoxicates him like a cup of wine, he speaks the word of Allah Ta'ala as if Allah Ta'ala speaks through his mouth. If he moves he does so under the command of Allah Ta'ala. He derives peace of mind only through obedience to Allah Ta'ala and when such a stage is reached, his eating, drinking, sleeping, awaking and, in short, all his actions are for the pleasure of Allah Ta'ala. He neither pays any heed to the worldly customs, nor does he attach any importance to negative criticism by the people."

Incident of the son-in-law of Sa'eed bin Musayyib (rahmatullahi alayh)

Hadhrat Sa'eed bin Musayyib *(rahmatullahi alayh)* was a well-known Tabi'ee, and is counted amongst the great Muhaditheen. A person by

Chapter 3 – Virtues of the Third Kalimah

the name of Abdullah bin Abi Widaa-ah, who used to go to him very often, related as follows: "I could not go to him for a few days, and when I went to him, Hadhrat Sa'eed *(rahmatullahi alayh)* asked me where I had been. I told him that my wife had passed away and that I remained busy getting work done. He said, "Had you informed me, I could have also joined the funeral." When, after a little while, I got up to leave he said, "Have you married again?" I replied, "Who would marry a penniless person such as I?" He said that he would arrange it, and immediately he read out the marriage sermon and made my nikaah (marriage declaration) with his own daughter, fixing the mehr at a minimal sum of eight or ten aanas." (This small amount as mehr may be permissible according to them, as it is according to some Imaams, but according to Imam Abu Hanifa *(rahmatullahi alayh)* a sum less than two rupees and eight annas is not permissible). After the nikaah, I left the place. Only Allah Ta'ala knows how overjoyed I was. In my happiness, I was thinking where to borrow the money from for expenses to bring the wife to my house. I remained absorbed in these thoughts till it was evening. I was fasting, and I broke my fast at sunset. After the Maghrib Salaah I reached home and lighting the lamp, I started eating my bread with olive oil, when somebody knocked at the door. "Who is there?" I asked, "Sa'eed", came the reply. I started thinking which Sa'eed it was. It did not occur to me that it could be Hadhrat Sa'eed *(rahmatullahi alayh)*, because for forty years, he had never been to any place except the masjid and his own house. I was surprised to see him standing outside, and said to him that he should have rather called for me. He replied, "It was proper for me to come. I thought that since you have been married, you should not spend the night alone in your house. I have, therefore, brought your wife to live with you." Saying this, he sent his daughter in, closed the door and went away. The girl, being overwhelmed with modesty, fell down on the ground. I bolted the door from inside, removed the bread and olive oil from near the lamp lest she should see it, climbed up on the roof of my house and called out to my neighbours. When people gathered, I told them that Hadhrat Sa'eed *(rahmatullahi alayh)* had given his daughter to me in marriage and that he had himself brought her and left her in my house. They were all greatly surprised, and exclaimed, "Is it true that she is already in your house?" "Yes", I confirmed. The news spread and also reached my mother, who at once came there and said, "If you touch her within three days, I will not see your face. In three days we will make all the preparations." After three days, when I met the girl, I found her extremely beautiful. She was a Haafizah of the Qur-aan Shareef, very conversant with the Sunnah of Rasulullah ﷺ and well acquainted with her obligations to her husband. For one month, neither Hadhrat Sa'eed *(rahmatullahi alayh)* came to me, nor did I go to him. After one month, when I went to him, there was a big gathering. After making salaam to him, I sat down. When all the others left, he asked me how I found my wife. I replied, "She is most excellent, so much so that friends become happy for me and foes become envious." He further said, "If you find anything undesirable, you may rectify her." After I returned from there, he sent me through a special messenger a gift of 24 000 Dirhams (which comes to about five thousand rupees). This girl had been demanded by King Abdul Malik bin Marwaan for marriage with his son, Waleed, who was the crown prince, but Hadhrat Sa'eed *(rahmatullahi alayh)* had declined the offer. In this way, he had earned the wrath of King Abdul Malik, who, on some other excuse, got him punished with a hundred lashes in the bitter cold weather and then had a utensil of cold water poured on him."

Hadith 15 – Ten virtues for each letter of this kalimah

عَنِ ابْنِ عُمَرَ رَضِيَ اللهُ عَنْهُ قَالَ: سَمِعْتُ رَسُوْلَ اللهِ صَلَّى اللهُ عَلَيْهِ وَسَلَّمَ يَقُوْلُ: مَنْ قَالَ: سُبْحَانَ اللهِ وَالْحَمْدُ لِلهِ وَلَا اِلٰهَ اِلَّا اللهُ وَاللهُ اَكْبَرُ كُتِبَتْ لَهُ بِكُلِّ حَرْفٍ عَشْرُ حَسَنَاتٍ وَمَنْ اَعَانَ عَلٰى خُصُوْمَةٍ بَاطِلٍ لَمْ يَزَلْ فِيْ سَخَطِ اللهِ حَتّٰى يَنْزِعَ وَمَنْ حَالَتْ شَفَاعَتُهُ دُوْنَ حَدٍّ مِّنْ حُدُوْدِ اللهِ فَقَدْ ضَادَّ اللهَ فِيْ اَمْرِهٖ وَمَنْ بَهَتَ مُؤْمِنًا اَوْ مُؤْمِنَةً حَبَسَهُ اللهُ فِيْ رَدْغَةِ الْخَبَالِ يَوْمَ الْقِيَامَةِ حَتّٰى يَخْرُجَ مِمَّا قَالَ وَلَيْسَ بِخَارِجٍ

(رواه الطبراني # ١٣٤٣٥)

Hadhrat Ibn Umar ﷺ *narrates that Rasulullah* ﷺ *said, "Whosoever recites* سُبْحَانَ اللهِ وَالْحَمْدُ لِلهِ وَلَا اِلٰهَ اِلَّا اللهُ وَاللهُ اَكْبَرُ *(Subhanallahi walhamdulillaahi walaailaaha illallaahu wallaahu Akbar) will be rewarded with ten virtues for each letter thereof. Whosoever supports an unjust party in a dispute incurs the wrath of Allah Ta'ala until he repents and makes taubah. Whosoever intercedes to prevent infliction of punishment according to Islamic law is considered to oppose Allah Ta'ala and whosoever slanders a Muslim man or woman will be imprisoned in the Aakhirah in Radghatul Khabaal (a deep part of Jahannam), until he gets forgiven from this sin, which will hardly be possible there."*

Note: Backing an unjust cause has nowadays become our second nature. In spite of knowing that we are at fault, we become unjust and bias for the sake of our relatives and our party. We are not afraid of the anger, displeasure, and punishment of Allah Ta'ala when our relatives and friends are involved. Let alone telling them that they should abstain from committing wrong, we cannot even keep quiet and remain neutral, but we go to the extreme in supporting them. If anybody puts up a claim against them, we try to oppose him. If a friend of ours commits theft, oppresses somebody, or indulges in adultery, we encourage and help him in all possible ways. Is this according to the dictates of our Imaan and our Deen? Is this according to the Islam that we feel proud of? Do we not thus degrade our Islam in the eyes of others, and degrade ourselves before Allah Ta'ala? It is stated in one Hadith that the one who deals or fights with somebody on the basis of race (sectionalism) is not one of us. According to another Hadith, sectionalism means to help one's own people in their wrong cause.

"Radghatul Khabaal" is the mud formed by the blood and pus of those in Jahannam. How dirty and horrible would be that place where such people, who slander the Muslims, will be imprisoned. In this life, we take it very lightly to make accusations against whosoever we like, but we will realise the seriousness of our offence in the Aakhirah when we will be required to justify and prove whatever we have said here, and the proof to be given there will have to be what was acceptable from the Shariah point of view. Flowery talk based on lies will be of no help there. What we said here and what the consequences were, will all be known there. Rasulullah ﷺ had said, "Sometimes one talks merely to amuse others, but, because of it, he is thrown into Jahnnam to a depth which exceeds the distance between the earth and the sky. A slip of the tongue is worse than the slip of the foot." It is said in one Hadith, "Whosoever mocks somebody else for his sin will find himself involved in it before his death." Imam Ahmad *(rahmatullahi alayh)* explained that this Hadith refers to such sins from which the sinner has made taubah. Hadhrat Abu Bakr Siddeeq ﷺ used to hold his tongue and say, "Because of you, we fall into trouble." Ibnul Munkadir *(rahmatullahi alayh)*, a famous Muhaddith and a Taabi'ee, was seen weeping when he was about to die. Someone asked why he wept. He replied, "I do not remember to have committed any sin, but I might have said something which, though insignificant in my sight, may turn out to be something very serious before Allah Ta'ala."

Hadith 16 – Dua to recite at the end of a meeting

عَنْ اَبِىْ بَرْزَةَ الْاَسْلَمِىِّ رَضِىَ اللهُ عَنْهُ قَالَ: كَانَ رَسُوْلُ اللهِ صَلَّى اللهُ عَلَيْهِ وَسَلَّمَ يَقُوْلُ بِاٰخِرِهٖ اِذَا اَرَادَ اَنْ يَّقُوْمَ مِنَ الْمَجْلِسِ سُبْحَانَكَ اللّٰهُمَّ وَبِحَمْدِكَ اَشْهَدُ اَنْ لَّا اِلٰهَ اِلَّا اَنْتَ اَسْتَغْفِرُكَ وَاَتُوْبُ اِلَيْكَ فَقَالَ رَجُلٌ يَا رَسُوْلَ اللهِ اِنَّكَ لَتَقُوْلُ قَوْلًا مَّا كُنْتَ تَقُوْلُهٗ فِيْمَا مَضٰى قَالَ: كَفَّارَةٌ لِّمَا يَكُوْنُ فِىْ الْمَجْلِسِ (رواه النسائى # ١٠١٨٧)

"Hadhrat Abu Barzah Aslami ﷺ narrates that during the last period of his life, whenever Rasulullah ﷺ got up from a meeting, he used to recite,

سُبْحَانَكَ اللّٰهُمَّ وَبِحَمْدِكَ اَشْهَدُ اَنْ لَّا اِلٰهَ اِلَّا اَنْتَ اَسْتَغْفِرُكَ وَاَتُوْبُ اِلَيْكَ

(Glory be to You O Allah, with the highest of Praises; I bear witness that there is none worthy of worship except You, I seek Your forgiveness and turn to You.)"

Someone said, "You have begun reciting this recently and you had not been reciting in the past." Rasulullah ﷺ said, "It is the kaffaarah (atonement) of the sitting." According to another version Rasulullah ﷺ has said, "These words constitute the kaffaarah of the sitting and were taught to me by Hadhrat Jibra-eel (alayhis salaam)."

Note: Hadhrat Aa-ishah ﷺ also related, "Whenever Rasulullah ﷺ got up from a meeting, he would recite:

سُبْحَانَكَ اللّٰهُمَّ رَبِّيْ وَبِحَمْدِكَ لَا اِلٰهَ اِلَّا اَنْتَ اَسْتَغْفِرُكَ وَاَتُوْبُ اِلَيْكَ

When I asked him the reason for reciting this dua so often, he said, 'If a person recites it at the end of a meeting, then all his mistakes and shortcomings during the meeting are forgiven.'" We are all likely to do some irrelevant and useless talk during a meeting. This dua is very brief, but whosoever recites either of the two versions of this dua will get saved from the adverse results of that meeting. Allah Ta'ala has provided so many facilities for our benefit.

Hadith 17 – Your name mentioned in the presence of Allah Ta'ala

عَنِ النُّعْمَانِ بْنِ بَشِيْرٍ رَضِىَ اللهُ عَنْهُ قَالَ قَالَ رَسُوْلُ اللهِ صَلَّى اللهُ عَلَيْهِ وَسَلَّمَ: اَلَّذِيْنَ يَذْكُرُوْنَ مِنْ جَلَالِ اللهِ مِنْ تَسْبِيْحِهِ وَتَحْمِيْدِهِ وَتَكْبِيْرِهِ وَتَهْلِيْلِهِ يَتَعَاطَفْنَ حَوْلَ الْعَرْشِ لَهُنَّ دَوِيٌّ كَدَوِيِّ النَّحْلِ يَذْكُرْنَ بِصَاحِبِهِنَّ اَلَا يُحِبُّ اَحَدُكُمْ اَنْ لَّا يَزَالَ لَهُ عِنْدَ اللهِ شَىْءٌ يَّذْكُرُ بِهٖ (رواه احمد # ١٨٣٦٢)

Hadhrat Numaan bin Basheer ؓ narrates that Rasulullah ﷺ said, "When a person hymns the greatness of Allah, i.e. recites

سُبْحَانَ اللهِ اَلْحَمْدُ لِلّٰهِ اَللّٰهُ اَكْبَرُ لَا اِلٰهَ اِلَّا اللهُ

these kalimahs revolve round the Arsh (throne of Allah Ta'ala) with a low humming tone, and mention the name of the reciter. Do you not wish that there should be somebody near Allah Ta'ala to mention and recommend you before Him?"

Note: People who try to get close to the rulers or hanker after positions, get overwhelmed with joy and feel so proud if they are praised before a governor, not to speak of even the viceroy or the minister or the king, even though such a recommendation does not benefit them in Deen or dunya. It is quite clear that this brings no Deeni benefit to them. In dunya also they have no benefit because if there is some benefit in these recommendations, the harms are far more greater than the benefits. In order to approach high officials, some people squander their property, get involved in debt, earn the enmity of others and thus disgrace themselves in so many ways. All this is experienced during the election period.

On the other hand, just imagine the blessings and honour of one's name being mentioned before the Arsh of Allah Ta'ala, the Rabb of all Rabbs, who controls this world as well as the Hereafter and in fact everything in the universe, Who controls the hearts of the kings, Who grants success or failure, gain or loss; so that, all the people of the world, including the rulers and the ruled, the kings and their subjects, cannot harm or help anybody against His will. They cannot give even a drop of water to anybody if He does not will it. No worldly wealth or honour can be compared to this blessing that one's name should be mentioned with favour before such a Supreme Rabb. If a person attaches more importance to any worldly honour, he does a great wrong to himself.

Hadith 18 – Counting on ones fingers

عَنْ يُسَيْرَةَ رَضِيَ اللهُ عَنْهَا وَكَانَتْ مِنَ الْمُهَاجِرَاتِ قَالَتْ قَالَ لَنَا رَسُوْلُ اللهِ صَلَّى اللهُ عَلَيْهِ وَسَلَّمَ: عَلَيْكُنَّ بِالتَّسْبِيْحِ وَالتَّهْلِيْلِ وَالتَّقْدِيْسِ وَاعْقِدْنَ بِالْاَنَامِلِ فَاِنَّهُنَّ مَسْئُوْلَاتٌ مُسْتَنْطَقَاتٌ وَلَا تَغْفُلْنَ فَتَنْسَيْنَ الرَّحْمَةَ (رواه الترمذي # ٣٥٨٣)

Hadhrat Yusayrah رضى الله عنها, one of the Muhaajir women, related that Rasulullah ﷺ had said, "Make it a point of reading Subhaanallah, Laailaaha illallaah, Taqdees (Subhaanal Malikil Quddoos; Subbuhun Quddusun Rabbul Malaaikati war rooh) and counting on your fingers, because the fingers will also be questioned on the Day of Qiyaamah about the deeds performed by them and will speak out what they did. You should not neglect doing zikr of Allah Ta'ala, otherwise you would get deprived of His Mercy."

Note: On the Day of Qiyaamah, not only the body of a person, but even his hands, feet, and every limb will be questioned about the good and bad actions performed by them, as stated in the Qur-aan Shareef at so many places. At one place, it is stated,

يَوْمَ تَشْهَدُ عَلَيْهِمْ اَلْسِنَتُهُمْ وَاَيْدِيْهِمْ

"The day when their tongues, hands and feet will stand witness against them about the sins they committed." *(Surah Noor - Aayah 24)*

At another place, it is said:

وَ يَوْمَ يُحْشَرُ اَعْدَآءُ اللهِ اِلَى النَّارِ

At this place, the subject matter is described in several aayaat, which are translated as follows:

"On that Day (Day of Qiyaamah), the enemies of Allah Ta'ala will be driven towards Jahannam. Then they will be checked at one place, till they have all reached near Jahannam. At that time, their ears, eyes, skin, etc., will bear witness against them, (and will speak out about the sins committed through these by each person). At this, those people will (in utter surprise) say to them, "Why do you give witness against us?" (it was for you that, in the worldly life, we indulged in sins?) These organs will reply, "Allah Ta'ala has given us the ability of speech, as He gave the ability of speech to all things. It is He Who created you the first time, and unto Him you have returned."
(Surah Haa meem Sajdah - Aayah 19)

There are many Ahaadith that describe this sort of testimony. In one Hadith, it is stated, "On the Day of Qiyaamah, the non-believer, in spite of knowing his own sins, will deny that he had ever committed them. He will be told that his neighbours stand witness against him. He will reply that the neighbours speak lies out of enmity against him. He will be told that his own family testify against him, but he will say that they are also false. Then his own limbs will be made to give evidence against him. According to one Hadith, the thigh will be the first to testify the evil deeds committed by it.

It is stated in one Hadith, "The last one to cross the Siraat Bridge will pass stumbling to this side and that side, just as a child does when his father gives him a beating. The Malaaikah will ask him whether he would confess to his sins if he were helped to cross it with ease. He will promise that he will confess the truth, and he will swear by Allah that he will not hide any fact. The Malaaikah will make him stand erect and pass the Siraat Bridge. When he has crossed over, he will be asked by the Malaaikah to give his statement. Thinking that, if he confesses, he may be sent back to Jahannam, he will flatly deny having committed any sin.

The Malaaikah will tell him that they can produce witnesses against him. He will look around and as there will be nobody, he will think that since everybody has now reached their destination, no witness can be available against him, and therefore, he will agree to face the witnesses. His own limbs will be asked to speak the truth, and when they start speaking he will be left with no option but to accept. Then he will say, "There are many serious sins that are still to be told." Allah Ta'ala will then say that he has been granted forgiveness.

Therefore, it is necessary for us that we should make our limbs do as many good acts as possible, so that they may give witness in our favour. It is for this reason that Rasulullah ﷺ had ordered (his followers) to make zikr on the fingers. For the same reason, it is mentioned in another Hadith that we should attend the masjid very frequently, so that the foot-steps will bear witness in our favour, and reward will be granted for these.

How fortunate are those people against whom there is nobody to stand witness, either because no sins were committed or because they were washed off through taubah etc., and who (on the other hand) have hundreds and thousands of witnesses to testify to their good deeds and virtues. The easy way to become one such person is: Firstly, if a sin is committed, it should be wiped out at once by means of taubah (because in this way the sin is wiped away, as stated in Hadith No 33 of Section 2, Chapter II) and secondly, the virtues should be accumulated in the account of deeds and there should be witnesses to testify to them. The limbs used for good deeds will all stand witness in one's favour.

Counting (of zikr) on the fingers by Rasulullah ﷺ himself is mentioned in various words in several Ahaadith. Hadhrat Abdullah bin Amr رضي الله عنه related that Rasulullah ﷺ used to make zikr by counting on his fingers.

In the Hadith under discussion, there is warning against neglecting the zikr of Allah Ta'ala, which deprives one of His Mercy. It is learnt from this that people who neglect zikr are ignored in respect of the Mercy of Allah Ta'ala. It is said in the Qur-aan Shareef, "You remember Me, then I will remember you (with My Mercy)." Allah Ta'ala has thus made making His zikr a condition for granting His favours. The Qur-aan Shareef says:

Chapter 3 – Virtues of the Third Kalimah

وَمَنْ يَعْشُ عَنْ ذِكْرِ الرَّحْمٰنِ نُقَيِّضْ لَهُ شَيْطٰنًا فَهُوَ لَهُ قَرِيْنٌ ۝ وَاِنَّهُمْ لَيَصُدُّوْنَهُمْ عَنِ السَّبِيْلِ وَيَحْسَبُوْنَ اَنَّهُمْ مُّهْتَدُوْنَ

"And a person who intentionally blinds himself to the of zikr Allah Ta'ala (which may be recitation of the Qur-aan or any other zikr), We appoint a shaytaan on him, who remains with him all the time and who (with other such shaytaans) keeps on misleading all such people (who have become blind to the zikr of Allah Ta'ala), and yet they feel they are rightly guided." (Surah Zukhruf - Aayah 37)

It is stated in one Hadith that a shaytaan is appointed to remain with every person. In the case of a non-believer, he takes part in everything he does; he is with him even when he eats, drinks and sleeps. In the case of a believer, he remains at some distance, but is always on the lookout for a chance to attack him unawares when he is not making the zikr of Allah Ta'ala. Allah Ta'ala says at another place in the Qur-aan Shareef:

يٰۤاَيُّهَا الَّذِيْنَ اٰمَنُوْا لَا تُلْهِكُمْ اَمْوَالُكُمْ وَلَاۤ اَوْلَادُكُمْ عَنْ ذِكْرِ اللّٰهِ (اِلٰى اٰخِرِ السُّوْرَةِ)

"O, you who believe! Let not your wealth or your children (and other similar things) distract you from the remembrance of Allah Ta'ala. Those who do so are the losers. And spend of that wherewith We have provided you, before death overtakes one of you and then he says, 'My Rabb: if only You would give me respite for a little while, then I would give charity and be amongst Your pious ones,' But Allah Ta'ala will never give respite to any soul when its time has come and Allah Ta'ala is aware of all that you do."
(Surah Munaafiqoon - Aayah 9-11)

There are some people who are mindful of the remembrance of Allah Ta'ala at any given time. Hadhrat Shibli *(rahmatullahi alayh)* writes, "I happened to see a lunatic on whom some boys were throwing stones at. I scolded the boys, who said, "This man claims that he sees Allah." I went near him and found that he was murmuring something. On listening to him attentively, I heard him saying, "You have done so well to have set these boys after me." I said to him, "These boys accuse you of something." "What do they say?" he enquired. I said, "They say that you claim to see Allah Ta'ala." He yelled a shriek and said, "O Shibli, I swear by Him, who has afflicted me with His Love and Who keeps me wandering restlessly sometimes near Him and at times away from Him. If I were to lose sight of Him even for a while, my heart would burst into pieces on account of the pangs of separation." Saying this, he turned and ran away from me reciting the following couplet:

$$\text{خِيَالُكَ فِيْ عَيْنِيْ وَذِكْرُكَ فِيْ فَمِيْ وَمَثْوَاكَ فِيْ قَلْبِيْ فَأَيْنَ تَغِيْبُ}$$

Your appearance is constantly before my eyes, your remembrance is always on my tongue, your abode is in my heart, then where can you hide from me.

When Junaid Baghdadi *(rahmatullahi alayh)* was about to die, someone advised him to recite the kalimah. He said, "I have never forgotten it at any time." (you should remind it to someone who may have neglected it). When Hadhrat Mumshaad Dinwari *(rahmatullahi alayh)* was about to die someone made dua to Allah Ta'ala for granting of such and such blessings to him in Jannah. He smiled, and said, "For the last thirty years, Jannah with all its blessings has been appearing before me, but I have not even once diverted my attention from Allah Ta'ala towards it."

When somebody reminded Hadhrat Ruwaym *(rahmatullahi alayh)* at the time of his death, to recite the kalimah, he said, "I have no acquaintance with anyone except Allah Ta'ala."

When Hadhrat Ahmad bin Khadhrawayh *(rahmatullahi alayh)* was about to die, somebody asked him something. With tears in his eyes he said, "For the last ninety-five years, I have been knocking at a door which is now about to open. I am not aware whether it will be a good or a bad fortune for me. I am too absorbed to talk to anybody at this time."

Hadith 19 – A special zikr taught to Hadhrat Juwayriyyah رَضِيَ اللهُ عَنْهَا

عَنْ جُوَيْرِيَةَ رَضِيَ اللهُ عَنْهَا اَنَّ النَّبِيَّ صَلَّى اللهُ عَلَيْهِ وَسَلَّمَ خَرَجَ مِنْ عِنْدِهَا بُكْرَةً حِيْنَ صَلَّى الصُّبْحَ وَهِيَ فِيْ مَسْجِدِهَا ثُمَّ رَجَعَ بَعْدَ اَنْ اَضْحٰى وَهِيَ جَالِسَةٌ قَالَ: مَا زِلْتِ عَلَى الْحَالِ الَّتِيْ فَارَقْتُكِ عَلَيْهَا قَالَتْ: نَعَمْ قَالَ النَّبِيُّ صَلَّى اللهُ عَلَيْهِ وَسَلَّمَ: لَقَدْ قُلْتُ

Chapter 3 – Virtues of the Third Kalimah

بَعْدَكِ أَرْبَعَ كَلِمَاتٍ ثَلَاثَ مَرَّاتٍ لَوْ وُزِنَتْ بِمَا قُلْتِ مُنْذُ الْيَوْمِ لَوَزَنَتْهُنَّ سُبْحَانَ اللهِ وَبِحَمْدِهِ عَدَدَ خَلْقِهِ وَرِضَا نَفْسِهِ وَزِنَةَ عَرْشِهِ وَمِدَادَ كَلِمَاتِهِ (رواه مسلم # ٢٧٢٦)

Hadhrat Juwayriyyah رَضِىَ اللهُ عَنْهَا related, "When Rasulullah ﷺ left my house for the Fajar Salaah, I was sitting on the musalla (busy in the zikr of Allah Ta'ala). When he came back after Chaasht Salaah (just before midday), I was still sitting in the same position. He asked me whether I had continued in that position right from the time he left in the morning. I replied in the affirmative. He then said, "After I left you, I recited four kalimahs three times which, if compared to all that you have recited since the morning, will be found to outweigh it. These kalimahs are:

سُبْحَانَ اللهِ وَبِحَمْدِهِ عَدَدَ خَلْقِهِ وَرِضَا نَفْسِهِ وَزِنَةَ عَرْشِهِ وَمِدَادَ كَلِمَاتِهِ

(Glory and praise be to Allah Ta'ala equal in number to His creation, according to His will and pleasure, equal in weight to His Arsh and equal to the ink of his words)."

عَنْ سَعْدِ بْنِ اَبِىْ وَقَّاصٍ رَضِىَ اللهُ عَنْهُ اَنَّهُ دَخَلَ مَعَ النَّبِىِّ صَلَّى اللهُ عَلَيْهِ وَسَلَّمَ عَلَى امْرَاَةٍ وَّبَيْنَ يَدَيْهَا نَوًى اَوْ حَصًى تُسَبِّحُ بِهِ فَقَالَ اَلَا اُخْبِرُكِ بِمَا هُوَ اَيْسَرُ عَلَيْكِ مِنْ هٰذَا اَوْ اَفْضَلُ فَقَالَ سُبْحَانَ اللهِ عَدَدَ مَا خَلَقَ فِى السَّمَاءِ وَسُبْحَانَ اللهِ عَدَدَ مَا خَلَقَ فِى الْاَرْضِ وَسُبْحَانَ اللهِ عَدَدَ مَا بَيْنَ ذٰلِكَ وَسُبْحَانَ اللهِ عَدَدَ مَا هُوَ خَالِقٌ وَّاللهُ اَكْبَرُ مِثْلَ ذٰلِكَ وَالْحَمْدُ لِلهِ مِثْلَ ذٰلِكَ وَلَا اِلٰهَ اِلَّا اللهُ مِثْلَ ذٰلِكَ وَلَا حَوْلَ وَلَا قُوَّةَ اِلَّا بِاللهِ مِثْلَ ذٰلِكَ (سنن الترمذى # ٣٥٦٨)

It is mentioned in another Hadith that Hadhrat Sa'ad رَضِىَ اللهُ عَنْهُ accompanied Rasulullah ﷺ to the house of a Sahaabi woman رَضِىَ اللهُ عَنْهَا, who had before her some date seeds and pebbles, on which she was counting her zikr. Rasulullah ﷺ said to her, "May I tell you something which may be easier (or better) than this?" (i.e. easier than counting zikr on the stones)

$$\text{سُبْحَانَ اللهِ عَدَدَ مَا خَلَقَ فِى السَّمَاءِ وَسُبْحَانَ اللهِ عَدَدَ مَا خَلَقَ فِى الْأَرْضِ وَسُبْحَانَ اللهِ عَدَدَ مَا بَيْنَ ذٰلِكَ وَسُبْحَانَ اللهِ عَدَدَ مَا هُوَ خَالِقٌ وَّاللهُ اَكْبَرُ مِثْلَ ذٰلِكَ وَالْحَمْدُ لِلّٰهِ مِثْلَ ذٰلِكَ وَلَا اِلٰهَ اِلَّا اللهُ مِثْلَ ذٰلِكَ وَلَا حَوْلَ وَلَا قُوَّةَ اِلَّا بِاللهِ مِثْلَ ذٰلِكَ}$$

I glorify Allah equal to the number of His creation in the Heaven, I glorify Allah equal to the number of His creation on the earth, and I glorify Allah equal to the number of His creation in between the two (i.e. between the Heaven and the Earth), and I glorify Allah equal to the number of things He is to create. And likewise Allahu Akbar, Alhamdulillaah, Laailaaha illallaah and laahawla walaa quwwata illaa billaah.

Note: Mulla Ali Qari *(rahmatullahi alayh)* has written that the zikr in the words mentioned above is more rewarding because one concentrates on the attributes of Allah Ta'ala mentioned therein, and then meditates over them. It is evident that the more one meditates and contemplates over the zikr one does, the better it is. It is for this reason that the recitation of even a few aayaat of the Qur-aan Shareef, with proper contemplation on what is read, is far better than considerably more recitation done without proper understanding.

Some Ulama consider that this zikr is superior because there is in it an expression of one's utter helplessness in respect of counting the praises and favours of Allah Ta'ala, which is the best form of submission to Him. It is for this reason that some Sufis say that we commit countless sins, but we recite the name of Allah Ta'ala a limited number of times by counting. This does not mean that we should not count zikr. If it were so, then counting in particular cases would not have been stressed in the Ahaadith. In many of the Ahaadith, special rewards are promised for doing a particular zikr a specific number of times. It really means that one should not feel satisfied after completing the specified number, and that after completing the zikr specified for particular timings of the day, one should still remain engaged in other various forms of zikr in one's free moments, because zikr is such a precious wealth that it should not be confined to any number or any other limitation.

Chapter 3 – Virtues of the Third Kalimah

The Tasbeeh

These Ahaadith also indicate the permissibility of using a tasbeeh (i.e. a string of beads) for keeping a count of the zikr. Some people think this to be a bidat (innovation), but this is not correct, because its source is found in the time of Nabi ﷺ. Rasulullah ﷺ saw others counting on pebbles and date-seeds whilst making zikr, but did not object to it, which proves its justification. Stringing or not stringing these beads together does not make any difference in its ruling. Therefore, all Ulama and Fuqahaa have been using it. Moulana Abdul Hay Saahib *(rahmatullahi alayh)* wrote a book named *Nuzhatul Fikr* on this subject. Mulla Ali Qari *(rahmatullahi alayh)* says: "This Hadith provides a valid proof for the commonly used string of beads, because Rasulullah ﷺ saw his companions counting on date-seeds and pebbles, and did not disapprove of it, which proves its justification, and stringing or not stringing the beads does not make any difference. Therefore, the statement of the people who call this practice a bidat (innovation) is not reliable. In the terminology of the Sufis, the string of beads is called a whip for Shaytaan". Someone once saw a tasbeeh in the hands of Hadhrat Junaid Baghdadi *(rahmatullahi alayh)* at a time when he was at the height of his spiritual glory, and questioned him about it. He replied that he could not give up a thing by means of which he had attained nearness to Allah Ta'ala.

It is narrated about many Sahaabah ﺭﺿﻲﺍﻟﻠﻪﻋﻨﻬﻢ that they kept date-seeds and pebbles for counting zikr. It is related about a Sahaabi named Abu Safiyyah ﺭﺿﻲﺍﻟﻠﻪﻋﻨﻪ that he used to do zikr whilst counting on small pebbles or stones. It is related about Hadhrat Sa'ad bin Abi Waqqaas ﺭﺿﻲﺍﻟﻠﻪﻋﻨﻪ that he used both date stones as well as pebbles. Hadhrat Abu Sa'eed ﺭﺿﻲﺍﻟﻠﻪﻋﻨﻪ is also reported to have used pebbles for counting zikr. It is mentioned in Mirqaat that Hadhrat Abu Hurayrah ﺭﺿﻲﺍﻟﻠﻪﻋﻨﻪ used to count on a string with knots on it. It is mentioned in '*Sunan Abi Dawood*', a book of Ahaadith, that Hadhrat Abu Hurayrah ﺭﺿﻲﺍﻟﻠﻪﻋﻨﻪ used to keep a bag full of date-seeds and pebbles for counting zikr and that when the bag would get empty, his servant would put the date-seeds and pebbles back into the bag and place it near him again. The bag would get empty because the stones were placed outside the bag whilst counting the zikr, till all the stones would be placed outside the bag. The servant would then put the same stones back into the bag and place it near him. It is also narrated about Hadhrat Abu Darda رضى الله عنه that he had a bag containing ajwah date-seeds, on which he would commence zikr after the Fajar Salaah and would continue till all the seeds were emptied from the bag.

Hadhrat Abu Safiyyah رضى الله عنه, a slave of Rasulullah ﷺ, used to spread a piece of skin with pebbles on it before him and he would count his zikr with these pebbles from morning to midday. When this skin with pebbles used to be removed from there, he would then attend to his other needs. After the Zuhr Salaah, the skin was again spread before him and he would continue with his zikr on the pebbles till the evening.

The grandson of Hadhrat Abu Hurayrah رضى الله عنه narrated that, his grandfather used to have a string with two thousand knots in it, and he would not go to bed until he had completed making zikr on these. Hadhrat Faatimah رضى الله عنها, the daughter of Hadhrat Husain رضى الله عنه, also had a string with knots on which she used to count her zikr.

In the language of the Sufis, the tasbeeh is also known as muzakkirah (that which reminds), because when it is held in one's hand, there is a sort of urge for doing zikr, and therefore, it is termed as such. In this connection a Hadith is also narrated through Hadhrat Ali رضى الله عنه that Rasulullah ﷺ had said, "What a good muzakkirah (reminder) is the tasbeeh."

In this regard, a Hadith is narrated by Moulana Abdul Hay *(rahmatullahi alayh);* "Every Shaikh (teacher) in my line right up to a pupil of Hadhrat Junaid Baghdadi *(rahmatullahi alayh)* had bestowed a tasbeeh on his pupil and recommended him to make zikr on it." The pupil of Hadhrat Junaid *(rahmatullahi alayh)* had stated, "On seeing a tasbeeh in the hand of my Shaikh, I enquired if he still needed the tasbeeh after having reached such a spiritual height." He replied that he had seen this tasbeeh in the hand of his Shaikh, Sirri Saqati *(rahmatullahi alayh)* and had put the same question to him, and Hadhrat Sirri Saqati *(rahmatullahi alayh)* had also replied that on seeing a tasbeeh in the hand of his Shaikh, Hadhrat Ma'roof Karkhi *(rahmatullahi alayh), he* had put the same question to his Shaikh Hadhrat Bishr Haafi *(rahmatullahi alayh),* who said that he had also put the question to his Shaikh Umar Makki *(rahmatullahi alayh),* who had also stated that he had asked the same question from his Shaikh Hadhrat Hasan Basri *(rahmatullahi alayh)*, as to why he kept a tasbeeh in his hand in spite of his having attained such spiritual heights, to which the Shaikh replied, "It had proved very useful in my initial stages of tasawwuf and I had made progress because of it. I do not want to leave it in the last stage when I want to use my heart, tongue, hands and everything in making the zikr of Allah Ta'ala." There is some discussions in the field of Hadith in this regard.

Hadith 20 – **Tasbeeh-e-Faatimah**

عَنِ ابْنِ اَعْبُدَ قَالَ قَالَ عَلِيٌّ رَضِيَ اللهُ عَنْهُ اَلَا اُحَدِّثُكَ عَنِّيْ وَعَنْ فَاطِمَةَ بِنْتِ رَسُوْلِ اللهِ صَلَّى اللهُ عَلَيْهِ وَسَلَّمَ وَكَانَتْ مِنْ اَحَبِّ اَهْلِهِ اِلَيْهِ قُلْتُ: بَلٰى قَالَ: اِنَّهَا جَرَّتْ بِالرَّحٰى حَتّٰى اَثَّرَ فِيْ يَدِهَا وَاسْتَقَتْ بِالْقِرْبَةِ حَتّٰى اَثَّرَ فِيْ نَحْرِهَا وَكَنَسَتِ الْبَيْتَ حَتَّى اغْبَرَّتْ ثِيَابُهَا فَاَتَى النَّبِيَّ صَلَّى اللهُ عَلَيْهِ وَسَلَّمَ خَدَمٌ فَقُلْتُ: لَوْ اَتَيْتِ اَبَاكِ فَسَاَلْتِهِ خَادِمًا فَاَتَتْهُ فَوَجَدَتْ عِنْدَهُ حِدَّاثًا فَرَجَعَتْ فَاَتَاهَا مِنَ الْغَدِ فَقَالَ: مَا كَانَ حَاجَتُكِ فَسَكَتَتْ فَقُلْتُ: اَنَا اُحَدِّثُكَ يَا رَسُوْلَ اللهِ جَرَّتْ بِالرَّحٰى حَتّٰى اَثَّرَتْ فِيْ يَدِهَا وَحَمَلَتْ بِالْقِرْبَةِ حَتّٰى اَثَّرَتْ فِيْ نَحْرِهَا فَلَمَّا اَنْ جَاءَكَ الْخَدَمُ اَمَرْتُهَا اَنْ تَأْتِيَكَ فَتَسْتَخْدِمَكَ خَادِمًا يَقِيْهَا حَرَّ مَا هِيَ فِيْهِ قَالَ: اِتَّقِي اللهَ يَا فَاطِمَةُ وَاَدِّيْ فَرِيْضَةَ رَبِّكِ وَاعْمَلِيْ عَمَلَ اَهْلِكِ فَاِذَا اَخَذْتِ مَضْجَعَكِ فَسَبِّحِيْ ثَلَاثًا وَّثَلَاثِيْنَ وَاحْمَدِيْ ثَلَاثًا وَّثَلَاثِيْنَ وَكَبِّرِيْ اَرْبَعًا وَّثَلَاثِيْنَ فَتِلْكَ مِائَةٌ فَهِيَ خَيْرٌ لَكِ مِنْ خَادِمٍ قَالَتْ: رَضِيْتُ عَنِ اللهِ وَعَنْ رَسُوْلِهِ

(رواه ابو داود # ٢٩٨٨)

Hadhrat Ali رَضِىَ اللهُ عَنْهُ said to one of his students, "May I tell you a story relating to me and my wife, Faatimah رَضِىَ اللهُ عَنْهَا, the daughter of Rasulullah صَلَّى اللهُ عَلَيْهِ وَسَلَّمَ and the most beloved one in his family?" "Do tell us," replied the student. Hadhrat Ali رَضِىَ اللهُ عَنْهُ said, "Most definitely I will tell you. She used to grind the corn herself, as a result of which there were marks of calluses on her hands. She used to fetch the water in a skin bag, the strings of which left marks on her chest. She swept the house herself as a result her clothes remained dirty. Once

Rasulullah ﷺ received a few slaves, both men and women and I persuaded Faatimah رضي الله عنها to go to her father and ask for a servant who could help her in her work. She went, but on seeing a big crowd with Rasulullah ﷺ, she came back. The next day, Rasulullah ﷺ came to our house and asked her why she had come to him the previous day. She kept silent (out of modesty), so I said, 'O Rasulullah! ﷺ, her hands have become rough on account of working the grindstone, the skin bag used by her for fetching water has left marks on her chest, and her clothes remain dirty because of sweeping the house. Therefore, I had sent her to ask for a slave so that she would get some relief in her work.' Rasulullah ﷺ said, 'O Faatimah! Keep fearing Allah Ta'ala, discharge your obligatory duties to Him, do all the work in the house yourself and at the time of going to bed recite Subhaanallah 33 times, Alhamdulillaah 33 times and Allahu Akbar 34 times, which totals 100, because this is better for you than a servant.' She said, 'I submit to the Will of Allah Ta'ala and the advice of His Rasool ﷺ.'

According to another Hadith, a similar story is related of two cousins of Rasulullah ﷺ who, along with his daughter, Faatimah رضي الله عنها, went to him and told him of their hardships and asked for a servant. Rasulullah ﷺ replied to them, "As for giving you a servant, the orphans of the Battle of Badr deserve preference over you but I can tell you something that is better than a servant. After every Salaah, recite these three Kalimahs (i.e. *Subhaanallah, Alhamdulillah and Allahu Akbar*) thirty-three times each and then recite once,

لَا اِلٰهَ اِلَّا اللهُ وَحْدَهُ لَا شَرِيْكَ لَهُ لَهُ الْمُلْكُ وَلَهُ الْحَمْدُ وَهُوَ عَلٰى كُلِّ شَيْءٍ قَدِيْرٌ

This will be more useful than a servant."

Note: Rasulullah ﷺ recommended this zikr especially to members of his family and his relatives. According to one Hadith, he would advise his wives to recite *Subhaanallah, Alhamdulillaah* and *Allahu Akbar* thirty-three times each at the time of going to bed.

In the Hadith under discussion, he recommended this zikr to be beneficial for worldly labour and hardship. The reason is obvious that worldly labour and hardship is not a matter of serious consequence for a

Muslim. He is always anxious to provide for the comforts and joys in the life after death. It was therefore that Rasulullah ﷺ diverted the attention of his dear ones from the hardships and worries of this life to making provision for the comforts in the Aakhirah.

That this particular zikr is most rewarding in the Aakhirah has been described in the Hadith given in this chapter.

The other reason why Rasulullah ﷺ recommended these tasbeehaat for zikr is that, in addition to spiritual and religious gains, these tasbeehaat bring many worldly benefits as well. There are many things in the Book of Allah Ta'ala and in the sayings of Rasulullah ﷺ which result not only in spiritual benefits but also in worldly benefits. Thus, it is said in one Hadith that during the time of Dajjaal the food of the believers will be the same as that of the Malaaikah, i.e. reciting *Subhaanallah*, etc.. Allah Ta'ala will satisfy their hunger. This Hadith proves that in this life one can also live upon the zikr of Allah Ta'ala without eating and drinking anything. When a common believer can acquire this at the time of Dajjaal, it is no wonder that the pious servants of Allah Ta'ala can attain this blessing even in present times. Therefore, one should not deny or refute that on certain occasions there were some Buzroogs who had lived without (or on insufficient) food for days on end.

It is stated in one Hadith that when a fire breaks out anywhere, Takbeer (Allahu Akbar) should be recited excessively, because it will help in extinguishing the fire. It is written in the book *'Al-Hisnul Haseen'* that if somebody feels difficult or tired in doing some job and requires additional strength to overcome his shortcoming, he should recite *Subhaanallah* 33 times, *Alhamdulillaah* 33 times and *Allahu Akbar* 34 times, before going to bed, or each of the three tasbeehaat should be recited 33 times or any one of the three may be said 34 times.

Hafiz Ibn Taymiyah *(rahmatullahi alayh)* has deduced from the Ahaadith in which Rasulullah ﷺ, instead of giving a servant to Hadhrat Faatimah ؓ, advised her to recite these tasbeehaat, that one who does this zikr with constancy will not get tired while doing difficult jobs. Hafiz Ibn Hajar *(rahmatullahi alayh)* has stated that even if he feels a little tired, it will not harm him in any way by reading these tasbeehaat. Mulla Ali Qaari *(rahmatullahi alayh)* has mentioned that it had been experienced that the recitation of this zikr before going to bed removes tiredness and increases one's strength.

Allamah Suyuti *(rahmatullahi alayh)* has written in his book *'Mirqaatus-Sa'ood'* that the recitation of these tasbeehaat is better than a servant is true in respect of the life in the Aakhirah. Because the benefits that will add up in the Aakhirah as a result of this zikr cannot be compared to the small benefit and usefulness of a servant in this world. Even from the worldly perspective it is also better, because the strength that will be acquired through doing this zikr enables one to accomplish more than is possible even with the help of a servant.

According to one Hadith, Rasulullah ﷺ has said, "There are two routines which, if followed by a Muslim, will enable him to enter Jannah. Both these routines are very easy to follow, but very few people will act on them. One is to recite these three tasbeehaat ten times each after every Salaah. In this way, one glorifies Allah Ta'ala 150 times and thereby earns 1500 rewards every day. The second routine is to recite *Subhaanallah* 33 times, *Alhamdulillaah* 33 times and *Allahu Akbar* 34 times before going to bed every day. In this way, one does 100 good deeds but actually earns 1000 rewards. Someone asked the reason why only a few people will be able to act upon this? Rasulullah ﷺ said, "At the time of Salaah, shaytaan comes and reminds him of something, which makes him get up and go away, and at night shaytaan reminds him of other work, which makes him neglect the recitation of this zikr."

In these Ahaadith there is one thing especially noteworthy that Hadhrat Faatimah ؓ, who will be the leader of women in Jannah, and the daughter of the leader of mankind in both the worlds, used to grind the corn flour herself, as a result of which her hands developed calluses on them, would herself fetch the water in the skin water bag, which left impressions on her chest and would sweep the house herself, so that her clothes remained dirty and did all other household duties like cooking meals and preparing bread, etc. Do our womenfolk do this much work or even half of that with their own hands? If it is not so and our lives have little resemblance with the lives of those whom we profess to be our leaders, then it is a matter of great shame. It ought to have been that we, who claim to be their servants, should put in more labour than our masters, but it is a matter of great disappointment that the actual position is quite the opposite.

فَإِلَى اللهِ الْمُشْتَكَى وَاللهُ الْمُسْتَعَانُ

CONCLUSION

Salaatut Tasbeeh

Now I will describe something that is really very important and thereby conclude this section of this book. The tasbeehaat mentioned above are very important and very useful from a worldly as well as a spiritual point of view as mentioned in the Ahaadith given above. As these tasbeehaat are very important and rewarding, Rasulullah ﷺ prescribed a special Salaah, which is known as Salaatut Tasbeeh (i.e. Salaah of these tasbeehaat). It is called Salaatut Tasbeeh, because these kalimahs are recited 300 times during this Salaah. Rasulullah ﷺ greatly stressed this and encouraged us to offer this Salaah as is evident from the following Ahaadith;

عَنِ ابْنِ عَبَّاسٍ رَضِيَ اللهُ عَنْهُ أَنَّ النَّبِيَّ صَلَّى اللهُ عَلَيْهِ وَسَلَّمَ قَالَ لِلْعَبَّاسِ بْنِ عَبْدِ الْمُطَّلِبِ يَا عَبَّاسُ يَا عَمَّاهُ أَلَا أُعْطِيكَ أَلَا أَمْنَحُكَ أَلَا أَحْبُوكَ أَلَا أَفْعَلُ بِكَ عَشْرَ خِصَالٍ إِذَا أَنْتَ فَعَلْتَ ذَلِكَ غَفَرَ اللهُ لَكَ ذَنْبَكَ أَوَّلَهُ وَآخِرَهُ قَدِيمَهُ وَحَدِيثَهُ خَطَأَهُ وَعَمْدَهُ صَغِيرَهُ وَكَبِيرَهُ سِرَّهُ وَعَلَانِيَتَهُ عَشْرَ خِصَالٍ أَنْ تُصَلِّيَ أَرْبَعَ رَكَعَاتٍ تَقْرَأُ فِي كُلِّ رَكْعَةٍ فَاتِحَةَ الْكِتَابِ وَسُورَةً فَإِذَا فَرَغْتَ مِنَ الْقِرَاءَةِ فِي أَوَّلِ رَكْعَةٍ وَأَنْتَ قَائِمٌ قُلْتَ سُبْحَانَ اللهِ وَالْحَمْدُ لِلهِ وَلَا إِلَهَ إِلَّا اللهُ وَاللهُ أَكْبَرُ خَمْسَ عَشْرَةَ مَرَّةً ثُمَّ تَرْكَعُ فَتَقُولُهَا وَأَنْتَ رَاكِعٌ عَشْرًا ثُمَّ تَرْفَعُ رَأْسَكَ مِنَ الرُّكُوعِ فَتَقُولُهَا عَشْرًا ثُمَّ تَهْوِي سَاجِدًا فَتَقُولُهَا وَأَنْتَ سَاجِدٌ عَشْرًا ثُمَّ تَرْفَعُ رَأْسَكَ مِنَ السُّجُودِ فَتَقُولُهَا عَشْرًا ثُمَّ تَسْجُدُ فَتَقُولُهَا عَشْرًا ثُمَّ تَرْفَعُ رَأْسَكَ فَتَقُولُهَا عَشْرًا فَذَلِكَ خَمْسٌ وَسَبْعُونَ فِي كُلِّ رَكْعَةٍ تَفْعَلُ

ذٰلِكَ فِیْ اَرْبَعِ رَكَعَاتٍ اِنِ اسْتَطَعْتَ اَنْ تُصَلِّيَهَا فِیْ كُلِّ يَوْمٍ مَّرَّةً فَافْعَلْ فَاِنْ لَّمْ تَفْعَلْ فَفِیْ كُلِّ جُمْعَةٍ مَّرَّةً فَاِنْ لَّمْ تَفْعَلْ فَفِیْ كُلِّ شَهْرٍ مَّرَّةً فَاِنْ لَّمْ تَفْعَلْ فَفِیْ كُلِّ سَنَةٍ مَّرَّةً فَاِنْ لَّمْ تَفْعَلْ فَفِیْ عُمُرِكَ مَرَّةً (رواه ابو داود # ۱۲۹۷)

(1) Once Rasulullah ﷺ said to his uncle, Hadhrat Abbaas رضى الله عنه, "O, Abbaas, my uncle! I want to make a special gift to you i.e. to tell you something special, so that if you act upon it, Allah Ta'ala will forgive all your sins, whether past or present, intentional or unintentional, minor or major, open or secret. That action is to offer four rakaats of nafl Salaah and during each rakaat, after you have recited Surah Faatihah and one more Surah, then you should say:

سُبْحَانَ اللهِ وَالْحَمْدُ لِلّٰهِ وَلَا اِلٰهَ اِلَّا اللهُ وَاللهُ اَكْبَرُ

15 times, while standing, then repeat it 10 times when you are in ruku, 10 times when you stand up from the ruku, 10 times in the first sajdah, 10 times when you rise from the first sajdah, 10 times in the second sajdah, and 10 times when you sit up after the second sajdah. The total in each rakaat comes to 75. If possible, you should offer this Salaah once every day and if you cannot do it daily, then offer it every Friday, or once a month, or once a year or at least once in your lifetime."

عَنْ اَبِی الْجَوْزَاءِ رَحِمَهُ اللهُ عَنْ رَجُلٍ كَانَتْ لَهُ صُحْبَةٌ يَّرَوْنَ اَنَّهُ عَبْدُ اللهِ بْنُ عَمْرٍو رَضِىَ اللهُ عَنْهُ قَالَ قَالَ لِیْ النَّبِیُّ صَلَّى اللهُ عَلَيْهِ وَسَلَّمَ اِئْتِنِیْ غَدًا اَحْبُوْكَ وَاُثِيْبُكَ وَاُعْطِيْكَ حَتّٰى ظَنَنْتُ اَنَّهُ يُعْطِيْنِیْ عَطِيَّةً قَالَ اِذَا زَالَ النَّهَارُ فَقُمْ فَصَلِّ اَرْبَعَ رَكَعَاتٍ فَذَكَرَ نَحْوَهُ وَفِيْهِ قَالَ فَاِنَّكَ لَوْ كُنْتَ اَعْظَمَ اَهْلِ الْاَرْضِ ذَنْبًا غُفِرَ لَكَ بِذٰلِكَ قَالَ قُلْتُ فَاِنْ لَمْ اَسْتَطِعْ اَنْ اُصَلِّيَهَا تِلْكَ السَّاعَةَ قَالَ صَلِّهَا مِنَ اللَّيْلِ وَالنَّهَارِ (رواه ابو داود # ۱۲۹۸)

(2) A Sahaabi narrates, "Once Rasulullah ﷺ said to me, 'Come to me tomorrow morning, I will grant you something. I will give you a special gift.' I thought that I would be given something of material value. When I went to him he said to me, 'Offer four rakaats

Chapter 3 – Virtues of the Third Kalimah

of Salaah after midday.' Then Rasulullah ﷺ explained the method of offering this Salaah (as given in the above Hadith). Rasulullah ﷺ also told me that even if I were more sinful than all the people of the world, my sins would be forgiven. I asked him what I should do if for some reason, I am not able to offer this Salaah at the given time. He told me to offer it whenever I could during the day or night."

عَنْ نَافِعٍ رَحِمَهُ اللهُ عَنِ ابْنِ عُمَرَ رَضِيَ اللهُ عَنْهُ قَالَ: وَجَّهَ رَسُوْلُ اللهِ صَلَّى اللهُ عَلَيْهِ وَسَلَّمَ جَعْفَرَ بْنَ أَبِيْ طَالِبٍ رَضِيَ اللهُ عَنْهُ اِلٰى بِلَادِ الْحَبَشَةِ فَلَمَّا قَدِمَ اعْتَنَقَهُ وَقَبَّلَ بَيْنَ عَيْنَيْهِ ثُمَّ قَالَ اَلَا اَهَبُ لَكَ اَلَا اُبَشِّرُكَ اَلَا اَمْنَحُكَ اَلَا اُتْحِفُكَ قَالَ نَعَمْ يَا رَسُوْلَ اللهِ قَالَ تُصَلِّيْ اَرْبَعَ رَكَعَاتٍ فَذَكَرَ نَحْوَهُ (رواه الحاكم # ١١٩٦)

(3) Rasulullah ﷺ had sent his cousin, Hadhrat Ja'far, رضي الله عنه to Ethiopia. When he returned from there and reached Madinah Shareef, Rasulullah ﷺ embraced him, kissed him on his forehead, and said to him, "Shall I give you something, give you good tidings, give you a gift, grant you a present?" He replied in the affirmative and then Rasulullah ﷺ asked him to offer four rakaats of Salaah in the manner explained already. In this Hadith the four tasbeehaat are also followed by,

لَا حَوْلَ وَلَا قُوَّةَ اِلَّا بِاللهِ الْعَلِيِّ الْعَظِيْمِ

laahawla walaa quwwata illaa billaahil a'liyyil a'zeem.

عَنِ الْعَبَّاسِ بْنِ عَبْدِ الْمُطَّلِبِ قَالَ قَالَ لِيْ رَسُوْلُ اللهِ صَلَّى اللهُ عَلَيْهِ وَسَلَّمَ اَلَا اَهَبُ لَكَ اَلَا اُعْطِيْكَ اَلَا اَمْنَحُكَ فَظَنَنْتُ اَنَّهُ يُعْطِيْنِيْ شَيْئًا مِّنَ الدُّنْيَا شَيْئًا لَّمْ يُعْطِهِ اَحَدًا مِّنْ قَبْلِيْ قَالَ اَرْبَعَ رَكَعَاتٍ اَلْحَدِيْثِ (اتحاف السادة المتقين ٥/٥٥)

(4) Hadhrat Abbaas رضي الله عنه narrated, "Rasulullah ﷺ said to me 'Should I grant you a present, give you a gift, bestow something on

you?' I thought that he wanted to give me some material thing which had not been given to anybody else. Then he taught me the method of offering four rakaats, as explained above. He also told me that when I sit for at-tahiyyaat, I should repeat this tasbeehaat before reciting at-tahiyyaatu ..."

قَالَ التِّرْمِذِيُّ وَقَدْ رَوَى ابْنُ الْمُبَارَكِ وَغَيْرُ وَاحِدٍ مِّنْ اَهْلِ الْعِلْمِ صَلَاةَ التَّسْبِيْحِ وَذَكَرُوا الْفَضْلَ فِيْهِ حَدَّثَنَا اَحْمَدُ بْنُ عَبْدَةَ قَالَ: حَدَّثَنَا اَبُوْ وَهْبٍ قَالَ: سَاَلْتُ عَبْدَ اللهِ بْنَ الْمُبَارَكِ عَنِ الصَّلَاةِ الَّتِيْ يُسَبَّحُ فِيْهَا فَقَالَ: يُكَبِّرُ ثُمَّ يَقُوْلُ: سُبْحَانَكَ اللّٰهُمَّ وَبِحَمْدِكَ وَتَبَارَكَ اسْمُكَ وَتَعَالٰى جَدُّكَ وَلَا اِلٰهَ غَيْرُكَ ثُمَّ يَقُوْلُ خَمْسَ عَشْرَةَ مَرَّةً: سُبْحَانَ اللهِ وَالْحَمْدُ لِلّٰهِ وَلَا اِلٰهَ اِلَّا اللهُ وَاللهُ اَكْبَرُ ثُمَّ يَتَعَوَّذُ ثُمَّ يَقْرَأُ: بِسْمِ اللهِ الرَّحْمٰنِ الرَّحِيْمِ وَفَاتِحَةَ الْكِتَابِ وَسُوْرَةً ثُمَّ يَقُوْلُ عَشْرَ مَرَّاتٍ: سُبْحَانَ اللهِ وَالْحَمْدُ لِلّٰهِ وَلَا اِلٰهَ اِلَّا اللهُ وَاللهُ اَكْبَرُ ثُمَّ يَرْكَعُ فَيَقُوْلُهَا عَشْرًا ثُمَّ يَرْفَعُ رَأْسَهُ فَيَقُوْلُهَا عَشْرًا ثُمَّ يَسْجُدُ فَيَقُوْلُهَا عَشْرًا ثُمَّ يَرْفَعُ رَأْسَهُ فَيَقُوْلُهَا عَشْرًا ثُمَّ يَسْجُدُ الثَّانِيَةَ فَيَقُوْلُهَا عَشْرًا يُصَلِّيْ اَرْبَعَ رَكَعَاتٍ عَلٰى هٰذَا فَذٰلِكَ خَمْسٌ وَسَبْعُوْنَ تَسْبِيْحَةً فِيْ كُلِّ رَكْعَةٍ

(سنن الترمذي #)

(5) Hadhrat Abdullah bin Mubaarak *(rahmatullahi alayh)* and many other Ulama, while narrating the virtues of Salaatut Tasbeeh, also narrate the following method of offering this Salaah. "After reciting sanaa and before starting Surah Faatihah repeat these kalimahs 15 times. Then start with ta'awwuz and tasmiyyah and, after completing Surah Faatihah and some surah, these tasbeehaat should be repeated ten times before the ruku, ten times during the ruku, ten times after rising from the ruku, ten times in each sajdah and ten times while sitting between the two sajdahs. This completes seventy-five times in one rakaat (so that these tasbeehaat do not have to be read in the sitting position after the two sajdahs). In the ruku *subhaana rabbiyal azeem* and in sajdah *subhaana rabbiyal a'ala* should be recited before reciting the tasbeehaat." (This method is also narrated to have been advised by Rasulullah ﷺ).

Note: (1) Salaatut Tasbeeh is a very important Salaah as is evident from the Ahaadith given above. Rasulullah ﷺ enjoined it as a matter of great kindness and favour and stressed its importance. As such, the Ulama, Muhaddiseen, Fuqaha and Sufis, throughout the past centuries, have been particular in offering this Salaah.

Haakim *(rahmatullahi alayh),* who is an authority on Hadith, has written that the authenticity of this Hadith is supported by the fact that, from the Tab-e-Taabi'een (The second generation after the Sahaabah رضى الله عنهم) to our times with continuity, all the great Ulama of Deen have been offering this Salaah constantly and have been advising people to do so. Amongst such great people was Abdullah bin Mubaarak *(rahmatullahi alayh).* He was the teacher of the teachers of Imaam Bukhaari *(rahmatullahi alayh).* Imaam Bayhaqi *(rahmatullahi alayh)* stated that even before Ibnul Mubaarak, Abul Jauzaa *(rahmatullahi alayh)*, a great Taabi'ee (one who had seen the Sahaabah رضى الله عنهم) and whose narrations are considered to be reliable, used to be very particular in offering this Salaah. As soon as he heard the azaan for the Zuhr Salaah, he would go to the Masjid and would complete this Salaah before the Zuhr Salaah daily.

Abdul Aziz bin Abi Rawwaad *(rahmatullahi alayh),* who was the teacher of Ibnul Mubaarak *(rahmatullahi alayh),* and who was a great devotee, buzroog and pious man, stated that one who desires to go to Jannah should be very constant in offering Salaatut Tasbeeh.

Abu Usmaan Hayree *(rahmatullahi alayh)* who was a great buzroog stated that nothing is as effective as Salaatut Tasbeeh in providing relief from misfortunes and sorrows.

Allama Taqi Subki *(rahmatullahi alayh)* stated, "This Salaah is very important and one should not get misled if some people happen to deny its importance. One who ignores it even after learning about its reward, is negligent in Deeni matters, fails to act like virtuous people, and should not be considered as a reliable person."

It is stated in Mirqaat that Hadhrat Abdullah bin Abbaas رضى الله عنه used to offer this Salaah every Friday.

(2) Some Ulama do not accept this Hadith to be authentic, because they cannot reconcile that there could be so much reward, especially forgiveness of major sins, for offering only four rakaats of Salaah. But since it has been narrated by many Sahaabah رضى الله عنهم, its authenticity

cannot be denied. However, according to many Aayaat and other Ahaadith, taubah remains an essential condition for the forgiveness of major sins.

(3) In the Ahaadith given above, two slightly different methods of offering this Salaah have been described. The first method is that;

$$\text{سُبْحَانَ اللهِ ٱلْحَمْدُ لِلّٰهِ لَا اِلٰهَ اِلَّا اللهُ ٱللّٰهُ اَكْبَرُ}$$

should be recited fifteen times while standing, after reciting Surah Faatihah and one surah, ten times after reciting *subhaana rabbiyal azeem* in the ruku, ten times after rising from ruku, ten times, after reciting *subhaana rabbiyal a'ala* in each sajdah, ten times while sitting between the two sajdahs; and ten times after the second sajdah, when after saying *subhaana rabbiyal a'ala* one should repeat it ten times before standing after the first and third rakaats and before reciting At-Tahiyyaat in the second and fourth rakaats.

According to the second method of offering this Salaah, the tasbeehaat should be recited fifteen times after reciting sanaa and before reciting Surah Faatihah, ten times after reciting Surah Faatihah and a surah, and the rest is like the first method, except that it is not necessary to recite this tasbeehaat after the second sajdah in any rakaat. The Ulama have stated, "It is better if this Salaah is offered sometimes according to the first method and sometimes the second method."

Masaail of Salaatut Tasbeeh

As this Salaah is not a general practice, a few rules are mentioned below for the ease of those who offer it:

(1) In this Salaah, no surah is particularly specified. Any surah may be recited. But some Ulama have stated that four out of the five surahs, namely Hadeed, Hashr, Saf, Jumu'ah and Taghaabun should be recited. According to some Ahaadith, at least twenty aayaat should be recited. According to some, it should be any of the following surahs, Zilzaal, Aadiyaat, Takaasur, Asr, Kaafiroon, Nasr, and Ikhlaas.

2) Counting should not be done verbally as this act will break or nullify the Salaah. Counting on the fingers or by means of a string of beads is permissible but Makrooh (not desirable). The best way is that the fingers should be kept in their position, but should be pressed on the hand or body one by one for counting.

Chapter 3 – Virtues of the Third Kalimah

(3) If one forgets to recite the tasbeeh at any stage, he should make up the number in the next act of Salaah, except that no such deficiency should be made up after rising from ruku, between the two sajdahs or after the second sajdah. In these three positions, one should recite the tasbeehaat as specified and then make up the deficiency in the next position. For instance, if one forgets recitation of the kalimah in the ruku one should make up this deficiency in the first sajdah. Similarly, the deficiency of the first sajdah should be made up in the second sajdah and that of second sajdah in the second rakaat while standing or, if one forgets to do so, then in the last rakaat while sitting and before reciting at tahiyyaat.

(4) If, for some reason, sajdatus sahw becomes necessary, the tasbeehaat should not to be recited then, because the number of 300 has already been completed. However, if the total has been less than 300, the deficiency can then be made up in sajdatus sahwu as well.

(5) According to some Ahaadith the following dua should be recited after at-tahiyyaat and before the salaam:

اَللّٰهُمَّ اِنِّيْ اَسْئَلُكَ تَوْفِيْقَ اَهْلِ الْهُدٰى وَاَعْمَالَ اَهْلِ الْيَقِيْنِ وَمُنَاصَحَةَ اَهْلِ التَّوْبَةِ وَعَزْمَ اَهْلِ الصَّبْرِ وَجِدَّ اَهْلِ الْخَشْيَةِ وَطَلَبَ اَهْلِ الرَّغْبَةِ وَتَعَبُّدَ اَهْلِ الْوَرَعِ وَعِرْفَانَ اَهْلِ الْعِلْمِ حَتّٰى اَخَافَكَ اَللّٰهُمَّ اِنِّيْ اَسْئَلُكَ مَخَافَةً تَحْجُزُنِيْ بِهَا عَنْ مَعَاصِيْكَ حَتّٰى اَعْمَلَ بِطَاعَتِكَ عَمَلًا اَسْتَحِقُّ بِهٖ رِضَاكَ وَحَتّٰى اُنَاصِحَكَ بِالتَّوْبَةِ خَوْفًا مِنْكَ وَحَتّٰى اُخْلِصَ لَكَ النَّصِيْحَةَ حُبًّا لَّكَ وَحَتّٰى اَتَوَكَّلَ عَلَيْكَ فِى الْاُمُوْرِ حُسْنَ ظَنٍّ بِكَ سُبْحَانَ خَالِقِ النُّوْرِ رَبَّنَا اَتْمِمْ لَنَا نُوْرَنَا وَاغْفِرْ لَنَا اِنَّكَ عَلٰى كُلِّ شَيْءٍ قَدِيْرٌ بِرَحْمَتِكَ يَا اَرْحَمَ الرَّاحِمِيْنَ (رواه الطبرانى # ٢٣١٨)

O Allah! I ask of you to grant me taufeeq (ability) like that of the people of guidance, actions like that of the people of yaqeen (conviction), sincerity like those who make taubah for their sins, courage like those who make sabr (patience), sacrifice like those who have fear, aspirations as possessed by those who are endowed with Your love, ibaadah (worship) like that of the pious and recognition like that of the Ulama. And allow all of these (blessings) to remain with me till I meet with You. O Allah! I beg of You to bless me with such fear which would prevent me from committing sins so that I may do acts of obedience for You in a way that I will receive Your pleasure, and I may make taubah sincerely before You out of fear for You, that I may be encouraged to do acts of ibaadah (worship) out of special regards for You, and I may rely purely on You in all matters and hope for the best from You, O The Unblemished Creator of light. You are above all defects. O our Sustainer! Grant us complete light (noor) and forgive us; no doubt You have complete control over everything. O! You, the Most Merciful, grant my dua out of Your Mercy.

(6) Except the three forbidden times, this Salaah can be offered at any time of the day or night. However, the preferred time is after Zawwaal (midday), then any time during the day and thereafter any time during the night.

(7) According to some Ahaadith, the third kalimah should also be followed by *lahawla wal quwwata illa billah* as also stated in Hadith No. three given above. It is, therefore, better to recite it sometimes in addition to the third kalimah.

وَاٰخِرُ دَعْوَانَا اَنِ الْحَمْدُ لِلّٰهِ رَبِّ الْعَالَمِيْنَ

(Hadhrat Shaikh) ZAKARIYYA KANDHALVI
Friday Night 26th Shawwal 1358 (A.H.)

فضائلِ تبلیغ

Virtues of Tableegh

Contents

Foreword 729

Chapter 1 Verses of the Qur-aan concerning Tableegh 731

Chapter 2 Ahaadith, Sayings of Nabi ﷺ concerning
          Tableegh 737
    Hadith 1 – When one sees sin being committed then he must prevent
          it 737
    Hadith 2 – The pious should advise the sinners 738
    Hadith 3 – The downfall of Bani Israa-eel 739
    Hadith 4 – Punishment before death for not stopping sins 741
    Hadith 5 – The rights of the Kalimah 743
    Hadith 6 – The Khutbah of Nabi ﷺ regarding enjoining
          good and preventing evil 743
    Hadith 7 – When people begin to give importance to the worldly
          things 745

Chapter 3 Practice what you preach 753

Chapter 4 The Importance of Ikraam (honouring/respecting
          other Muslims) 756

Chapter 5 Importance of Ikhlaas (Sincerity) 759

Chapter 6 Respect for learning Deen and the Ulama 763

Chapter 7 Keeping company of the pious (Ahlullah) 767

FOREWORD

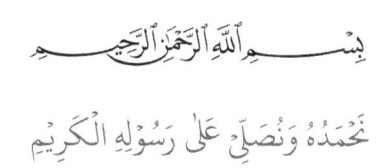

$$\bismillah$$

نَحْمَدُهُ وَنُصَلِّيْ عَلٰى رَسُوْلِهِ الْكَرِيْم

We praise Allah Ta'ala, and we ask His blessings and send Salutations on His noble Nabi Muhammad ﷺ.

Firstly, I give thanks to Allah Ta'ala, Who has given me the ability to write this booklet on Tableegh. One of the best Aalim of this age has advised me to select a few Aayaat of the Qur-aan Shareef and some Ahaadith of Rasulullah ﷺ on Tableegh and explain the same. Since my humble services to such sincere believers can be a means of my everlasting success, I present this kitaab to every Islamic School, Islamic organization, Islamic Government, rather to every Muslim and request them to serve the sacred cause of Tableegh in their own way.

During this age there is a day-to-day decline in our devotion to Deen and, against our true Deen, objections are raised not only by the kuffaar, but also by the so called 'Muslims'. The fardh and waajib actions are being neglected, not only by the common Muslims, but also by those who hold important positions. Millions of Muslims have become involved in shirk and kufr, not to speak of neglecting Salaah and fasting; and they are not even conscious of their actions being shirk and kufr. Breaking the commands of Allah Ta'ala has become very common and making a mockery of Deen has become a fashion of the day. That is why the Ulama have even begun to ignore the common people and a result of this is that jahaalat (ignorance) about the teachings of Islam is increasing day by day.

People offer the excuse that no one is interested in teaching them the Deen of Islam and the Ulama have an excuse that no one listens to them. But none of these excuses is valid before Allah Ta'ala. As a matter of fact, Allah Ta'ala will never accept the excuse of the common people that they were ignorant about Deen; because to learn Deen and to make an effort to acquire ilm (knowledge) is the personal responsibility of every Muslim. Since ignorance of the law is no excuse under any government, then why should it be accepted by the Lord of all rulers, Allah Ta'ala? They say, making excuses for a crime is worse than the crime itself. Similarly, the excuse of the Ulama that no one listens to them is not valid. They boast of representing the great Mashaaikh of the past, but never consider how much sacrifices and hardships those Mashaaikh had to tolerate to call towards the true Deen! Were they not pelted with stones? Were they not abused and oppressed to the extreme degree? But in spite of all these obstacles and hardships, they fulfilled their responsibilities of Tableegh and gave the Dawat of Islam regardless of the opposition.

Generally, the Muslims have limited Tableegh to the Ulama only, whereas every Muslim has been commanded by Allah Ta'ala to stop the people from doing forbidden things. If we admit for a moment that Tableegh is the responsibility of the Ulama only and they do not fulfil it properly, then it becomes the responsibility of every Muslim to do so. The importance that has been laid on Tableegh by the Qur-aan Shareef and Hadith, will be proved by the Qur-aanic Aayaat and sayings of Nabi ﷺ that are going to be quoted in the following pages. Therefore, you can neither leave the duty of Tableegh to the Ulama only, nor can it be an excuse for you to neglect it. I would request every Muslim to devote his time and energy to Tableegh as much as he can:

هر وقت خوش کہ دست دہد مغتنم شمار کسرا و قوف نیست کہ انجام کار چیست

"Consider, the time at your disposal, as a blessing; for no one knows what his end will be."

You do not necessarily have to be an Aalim to do the work of Tableegh, i.e. encouraging the good and preventing the evil. Whatever little knowledge of Islam you have, you must teach it to others. Whenever a morally wrong or a sin is committed in your presence, then, as a Muslim, it is your duty to stop the sinner, as far as it lies in your power. I have described all the important things about Tableegh briefly in seven chapters and hope that every Muslim will benefit from them.

Shaikhul-Hadith, Hafiz Mohammad Zakariyya
Madrasah Mazaahirul-Uloom, Saharanpur

CHAPTER 1
VERSES OF THE QUR-AAN CONCERNING TABLEEGH

I wish to mention a few Aayaat of the Qur-aan Shareef concerning Tableegh and Amr bil ma'roof (calling people towards Allah Ta'ala). The readers can easily see how important Allah Ta'ala regards calling people to Islam. I have come across as many as sixty Aayaat on this particular subject, and Allah Ta'ala alone knows how many more Aayaat could be found by another keen observer. I quote a few of them here for the benefit of every true Muslim.

وَ مَنْ اَحْسَنُ قَوْلًا مِّمَّنْ دَعَآ اِلَى اللّٰهِ وَ عَمِلَ صَالِحًا وَّ قَالَ اِنَّنِيْ مِنَ الْمُسْلِمِيْنَ

"And whose words can be better than his, who calls (people) towards Allah, performs good deeds, and says: 'I am one of those who obey Allah!'" (Surah Haameem Sajdah - Aayah 33)

Some commentators have written that whoever invites people to Allah Ta'ala in any way deserves the honour mentioned in the above Aayah. The Ambiyaa *(alayhimus salaam)* called people to Allah Ta'ala with miracles. The Ulama invite them by lectures, the Mujaahideen call them by means of the sword and the muazzins call them by means of the azaan. In short, whoever invites people to good deeds deserves this reward, whether he calls them to the external ibaadaat (e.g. Salaat, reciting the Qur-aan, etc.) or to reform the inner self, like the Sufis who stress on the purification of the heart and the recognition of Allah Ta'ala's attributes.

In the concluding verse quoted above, some commentators say that such a person should also be proud of the honour bestowed on him by Allah Ta'ala, of being categorised as a Muslim and he should proclaim this honour in words.

Some other commentators interpret that he should not be proud of being a preacher but should consider himself as an ordinary Muslim.

وَذَكِّرْ فَاِنَّ الذِّكْرٰى تَنْفَعُ الْمُؤْمِنِيْنَ

"(O Nabi ﷺ), Continue advising (reminding) because advice is beneficial for the Believers. (Surah Zaariyaat - Aayah 55)

The Mufassireen have written that 'calling people to the truth' means educating the Muslims through the Aayaat of the Qur-aan Shareef, as this would guide them to the right path. This method can also be useful for non-Muslims, because they may also accept Islam.

The intention for people doing Tableegh should not be to show off their ability to deliver beautiful speeches. Rasulullah ﷺ has said: "Whoever learns the art of giving speeches in order to attract people towards himself, his ibaadat, whether fardh or nafl, will not be accepted on the Day of Qiyaamah."

وَأْمُرْ اَهْلَكَ بِالصَّلٰوةِ وَاصْطَبِرْ عَلَيْهَا ۖ لَا نَسْـَٔلُكَ رِزْقًا ۖ نَحْنُ نَرْزُقُكَ ۗ وَالْعَاقِبَةُ لِلتَّقْوٰى

"And command your family to perform Salaah, and also perform these yourself regularly. We do not ask you for sustenance (rizq). We will give you sustenance, and the final reward is for those who fear Allah Ta'ala." (Surah Taaha - Aayah 132)

Many Ahaadith mention that whenever anyone complained of poverty to Rasulullah ﷺ, he recited this Aayah and advised him to perform Salaah regularly. A person who is regular with his Salaah will receive abundant *rizq* (provision).

It has been stressed in this Aayah to first do actions yourself before commanding others. This is a more effective and successful method of Tableegh. All the Ambiyaa *(alayhimus salaam)* first practiced upon what they preached. They became examples for their followers who would then not think that the teachings of their Deen would be difficult to carry out.

Allah Ta'ala has promised abundant rizq (sustenance) for those who perform Salaah regularly. They should never feel that Salaah interferes with the earning of their wealth through business, jobs, etc. Thereafter it is stated that ultimate success and salvation will be achieved only by those fearing Allah Ta'ala.

يٰبُنَىَّ اَقِمِ الصَّلٰوةَ وَأْمُرْ بِالْمَعْرُوْفِ وَانْهَ عَنِ الْمُنْكَرِ وَاصْبِرْ عَلٰى مَآ اَصَابَكَ ۖ اِنَّ ذٰلِكَ مِنْ عَزْمِ الْاُمُوْرِ

"O my beloved son! Establish Salaah, instruct others to do good deeds and prevent them from wrong, and patiently bear whatever (difficulty) comes to you (while preaching the truth). Surely this is from those matters which demand determination!"
(Surah Luqmaan - Aayah 17)

In this Aayah, several important commands for a Muslim have been mentioned, which can be a means of our eternal success, but has been neglected by us. Leave alone calling towards the truth, we have even neglected our Salaah, which is a pillar of Islam, in fact the most important after Imaan. There are so many people who do not perform their Salaah at all and even those who do perform it neglect its requirements, such as Salaah with jamaat. It is only the poor who perform their Salaah with jamaat in the Masjid, while the rich feel it below their dignity to go to the Masjid.

فَاِلَى اللهِ الْمُشْتَكٰى

Ah! My complaint is to Allah Ta'ala only!

آنچہ عارِتُست اوفخرِ من است

"O careless person! What is an insult for you, is a matter of pride for me."

وَلْتَكُنْ مِنْكُمْ اُمَّةٌ يَّدْعُوْنَ اِلَى الْخَيْرِ وَيَأْمُرُوْنَ بِالْمَعْرُوْفِ وَيَنْهَوْنَ عَنِ الْمُنْكَرِ وَأُولٰٓئِكَ هُمُ الْمُفْلِحُوْنَ

"O Muslims, there must be a group among you who would invite people to good and command them to do good deeds and prevent them from wrong things and these are the people who will be successful."
(Surah Aali Imraan - Aayah 104)

Allah Ta'ala clearly commands the Muslims to prepare a group who would call people to Islam throughout the world. However, the Muslims have totally forgotten this command. On the other hand, non-Muslims are preaching their religion day and night. For instance, some Christians have been specially chosen to spread their religion in the whole world. Similarly, other religions are also doing their best to preach their religions. The question is, is there such a group among the Muslims?

If any individual or group among the Muslims tries to preach Islam, then instead of assisting them, we find faults with them. It is the duty of every Muslim to assist those who call people to Islam and also correct their mistakes. Most people neither do anything themselves to preach Islam nor do they help those who have given their lives in calling towards Allah Ta'ala. Thus, even those who are sincere, are disappointed and give up preaching.

كُنْتُمْ خَيْرَ اُمَّةٍ اُخْرِجَتْ لِلنَّاسِ تَأْمُرُوْنَ بِالْمَعْرُوْفِ وَتَنْهَوْنَ عَنِ الْمُنْكَرِ وَتُؤْمِنُوْنَ بِاللهِ

"(O Muslims!) You are the best of nations who have been chosen for the guidance of mankind, you command them to do good deeds and prevent them from doing wrong and you have firm faith in Allah."
(Surah Aali I'mraan - Aayah 110)

It has also been mentioned in the Ahaadith of Rasulullah ﷺ that, 'Muslims are the best of all people' and there are some Aayaat of the

Qur-aan Shareef that support this. The above Aayah gives us the title of 'Best Nation' provided that we call people to Islam, command people to do good and prevent them from evil.

In this Aayah, commanding people to do good and preventing them from evil has been mentioned even before Imaan, whereas Imaan is the root of all Islamic beliefs and actions. The reason is that Imaan has been a common factor among all the nations of the world, but the special thing that has mainly distinguished the Ummah of Rasulullah ﷺ, is enjoining people to do good and preventing them from evil. The real basis for the superiority of the Muslims of this Ummah was because they fulfilled this command, and since in Islam good actions are of little value without Imaan, it is therefore specifically mentioned at the end of the Aayah.

In fact, the real object in this Aayah is to stress the importance of enjoining people to do good deeds, and this is the distinguishing feature of the Muslim Ummah. It is not enough to enjoin good and to prevent from evil only now and then, but rather this practice should continue at all times and on all occasions regularly. The responsibility of enjoining the good is also found in earlier religions, but what makes the Muslim Ummah unique is that it is taken up as a regular responsibility. This is not a temporary work, but a permanent one.

$$\text{لَا خَيْرَ فِيْ كَثِيْرٍ مِّنْ نَّجْوٰىهُمْ اِلَّا مَنْ اَمَرَ بِصَدَقَةٍ اَوْ مَعْرُوْفٍ اَوْ اِصْلَاحٍ بَيْنَ النَّاسِ ۚ وَمَنْ يَّفْعَلْ ذٰلِكَ ابْتِغَآءَ مَرْضَاتِ اللّٰهِ فَسَوْفَ نُؤْتِيْهِ اَجْرًا عَظِيْمًا}$$

"There is no good in most of their secret consultations (discussions) except in him who instructs (people to give) charity, to do good deeds or (to take part in) making peace between people. Whoever does this, seeking Allah Ta'ala's pleasure, We shall soon grant him a great reward." (Surah Nisaa - Aayah 114)

Allah Ta'ala promises great reward for those who call towards the truth. How great will be the reward that has been called 'great' by Allah Ta'ala Himself?

Rasulullah ﷺ has said, "A man's words may become a burden (sin) for him, except those words that he has spoken calling people to do good deeds and preventing others from forbidden acts, or in remembering Allah Ta'ala."

In another Hadith, Rasulullah ﷺ has said, "Shall I tell you a reward which is better than Nafl Salaah, fasting and charity?" The Sahaabah رضي الله عنهم asked, "Please do tell us, O Messenger of Allah ﷺ!" Rasulullah ﷺ replied: "Making peace between people, for hatred and disputes wipe out good deeds just as a razor removes hair."

There are many more aayaat of the Qur-aan Shareef and sayings of Nabi ﷺ that teaches us to make peace between people. To make peace between people is another form of instructing them to do good and stopping them from evil. It is very important to bring about peace between people.

CHAPTER 2
AHAADITH, SAYINGS OF NABI ﷺ CONCERNING TABLEEGH

In this chapter, I will quote certain Ahaadith of Rasulullah ﷺ that explain the meaning of the above-mentioned Aayaat of the Qur-aan Shareef. Our intention is not to cover all the relevant Ahaadith. If I quote all the Aayaat and the Ahaadith on this subject, I fear no one will read them, for now-a-days people hardly take out the time for such things. I give below a few sayings of Nabi ﷺ to show the importance of Tableegh and what serious consequences follow if we neglect it.

HADITH 1 – WHEN ONE SEES SIN BEING COMMITTED THEN HE MUST PREVENT IT

عَنْ أَبِيْ سَعِيْدٍ الْخُدْرِيِّ رَضِيَ اللهُ عَنْهُ عَنْ رَسُوْلِ اللهِ صَلَّى اللهُ عَلَيْهِ وَسَلَّمَ قَالَ مَنْ رَأَى مِنْكُمْ مُنْكَرًا فَلْيُغَيِّرْهُ بِيَدِهِ فَإِنْ لَمْ يَسْتَطِعْ فَبِلِسَانِهِ فَإِنْ لَمْ يَسْتَطِعْ فَبِقَلْبِهِ وَذٰلِكَ أَضْعَفُ الْإِيْمَانِ (صحيح مسلم # 49)

It is reported by Hadhrat Abu Sa'eed Al-Khudri ؓ that Rasulullah ﷺ said: "Whoever sees a haraam action being done, should prevent it with his hand; and if he cannot do this, then he should prevent it with his tongue and if he cannot do this even, then he should at least think of it as a sin in his heart, and this is the lowest level of Imaan."

In another Hadith, it has been said that if a person can prevent evil with his tongue then he should prevent it. He should otherwise at least think it to be evil in his heart. Another Hadith says that the person who hates sin within his heart, is a true believer, but this is the weakest form of Imaan. This subject is discussed in many sayings of Nabi ﷺ. How many Muslims are there who practice on this Hadith? How many of us stop evil by force? How many with the tongue, and how many of us seriously hate it within our hearts? We have to take stock of ourselves regarding this.

HADITH 2 – THE PIOUS SHOULD ADVISE THE SINNERS

عَنِ النُّعْمَانِ بْنِ بَشِيْرٍ رَضِيَ اللهُ عَنْهُمَا عَنِ النَّبِيِّ صَلَّى اللهُ عَلَيْهِ وَسَلَّمَ قَالَ مَثَلُ الْقَائِمِ عَلىٰ حُدُوْدِ اللهِ وَالْوَاقِعِ فِيْهَا كَمَثَلِ قَوْمٍ اسْتَهَمُوْا عَلىٰ سَفِيْنَةٍ فَصَارَ بَعْضُهُمْ أَعْلَاهَا وَبَعْضُهُمْ أَسْفَلَهَا فَكَانَ الَّذِيْنَ فِيْ أَسْفَلِهَا إِذَا اسْتَقَوْا مِنَ الْمَاءِ مَرُّوْا عَلىٰ مَنْ فَوْقَهُمْ فَقَالُوْا لَوْ أَنَّا خَرَقْنَا فِيْ نَصِيْبِنَا خَرْقًا وَّلَمْ نُؤْذِ مَنْ فَوْقَنَا فَإِنْ يَّتْرُكُوْهُمْ وَمَا أَرَادُوْا هَلَكُوْا جَمِيْعًا وَإِنْ أَخَذُوْا عَلىٰ أَيْدِيْهِمْ نَجَوْا وَنَجَوْا جَمِيْعًا (صحيح البخاري # 2493)

It has been reported by Nu'maan bin Basheer ؓ that Rasulullah ﷺ said: "There are people who do not break the limits (laws) of Allah Ta'ala, and there are others who do so. They are like two groups of people on a ship, one of them on the upper deck (storey) and the other, on the lower deck of the ship. So, when the people of the lower deck needed water, they said: 'Why should we cause discomfort to the people of the upper deck when we can easily have plenty of water by making a hole in our deck.' Now if the people of the upper deck do not stop this group from such foolishness, all of them will drown, but if they stop them, then they will all be saved."

The Sahaabah ؓ asked Rasulullah ﷺ: "O Messenger of Allah (ﷺ), can we people be destroyed even when there are pious

Allah-fearing people amongst us?" He answered: "Yes, when evil deeds are plentiful in a community (more than their good deeds)."

The Muslims are generally worried about the downfall of this Ummah and they give some ideas about how to stop this downfall. Did they ever think as to what is the main cause of our downfall? They fail to see that the true reason of our spiritual and moral downfall, especially when the proper solution has been given to us by Allah Ta'ala and His Rasool ﷺ. It is a pity that the wrong diagnosis and incorrect remedies, including the continued neglect of the responsibility of Tableegh, is causing the Ummah to fall even further. In fact, the main cause of our downfall is that we neither do the effort of Tableegh nor do we help those who are doing Tableegh.

میر کیا سادہ ہیں بیمار ہوئے جس کے سبب

اسی عطار کے لڑکے سے دوا لیتے ہیں

How simple minded are you, O Meer! The cause of your sickness is the very same person who you buy medication from

HADITH 3 – THE DOWNFALL OF BANI ISRAA-EEL

عَنْ عَبْدِ اللهِ بْنِ مَسْعُودٍ رَضِيَ اللهُ عَنْهُ قَالَ قَالَ رَسُوْلُ اللهِ صَلَّى اللهُ عَلَيْهِ وَسَلَّمَ أَوَّلُ مَا دَخَلَ النَّقْصُ عَلَى بَنِىْ إِسْرَائِيْلَ أَنَّهٗ كَانَ الرَّجُلُ يَلْقَى الرَّجُلَ فَيَقُوْلُ يَا هٰذَا اتَّقِ اللهَ وَدَعْ مَا تَصْنَعُ بِهٖ فَإِنَّهٗ لَا يَحِلُّ لَكَ ثُمَّ يَلْقَاهُ مِنَ الْغَدِ وَهُوَ عَلٰى حَالِهٖ فَلَا يَمْنَعُهٗ ذٰلِكَ اَنْ يَّكُوْنَ اَكِيْلَهٗ وَشَرِيْبَهٗ وَقَعِيْدَهٗ فَلَمَّا فَعَلُوْا ذٰلِكَ ضَرَبَ اللهُ قُلُوْبَ بَعْضِهِمْ بِبَعْضٍ ثُمَّ قَالَ لُعِنَ الَّذِيْنَ كَفَرُوْا مِنْ بَنِىْ إِسْرَائِيْلَ عَلٰى لِسَانِ دَاوٗدَ وَعِيْسَى ابْنِ مَرْيَمَ إِلٰى قَوْلِهٖ فَاسِقُوْنَ ثُمَّ قَالَ كَلَّا وَاللهِ لَتَأْمُرُنَّ بِالْمَعْرُوْفِ وَلَتَنْهَوُنَّ عَنِ الْمُنْكَرِ وَلَتَأْخُذُنَّ عَلٰى يَدِ الظَّالِمِ وَلَتَأْطُرُنَّهٗ عَلَى الْحَقِّ أَطْرًا (سنن ابی داود # 4336)

It has been reported by Ibn Mas'ood ﷺ that Rasulullah ﷺ said: "The destruction of the Bani Israa-eel began like this. When the pious among them saw sins being committed by the sinners, they stopped them. When these sinners did not make taubah, the pious, because of their relationship and friendship, continued to mix with them. Allah Ta'ala thus caused their hearts to be cursed in the same manner." (i.e. their hearts were also affected with the sins of the sinners). In support of the above, Rasulullah ﷺ read a verse of the Qur-aan which says: "The disobedient and the sinners among the Bani Israa-eel were cursed by Allah." Rasulullah ﷺ then advised the Sahaabah رضى الله عنهم: "You must encourage others to do good deeds and stop them from doing evil. You should stop every tyrant from tyranny (oppressing others) and invite him towards truth and justice."

Another Hadith says that Rasulullah ﷺ was resting comfortably when, suddenly overcome with emotion, he sat up and said: "I swear by Allah that you people cannot attain najaat (salvation) unless you prevent the tyrants from tyranny."

Another Hadith says that Rasulullah ﷺ said: "You people must call to the truth, and stop the sinners from doing haraam things and stop the tyrants. Bring them towards the right path, otherwise you will be cursed and your hearts will be corrupted, just as Allah Ta'ala did with the Bani Israa-eel." Rasulullah ﷺ read certain Aayaat of the Qur-aan Shareef to show the importance of this subject. The Bani Israa-eel were cursed because among other sins, they also did not stop others from haraam.

Nowadays it is considered as good manners to be at peace with all and please everyone including the sinners. This is definitely a wrong practice, because in extreme cases you may be excused for keeping quiet, but never for falling in line with the tyrants and sinners. At the very least, one must command those people to do good whom they can easily influence, for instance: those who are under him, his servants, his wife, his children, and his relatives. In such situations, to remain silent about Tableegh, cannot be forgiven before Allah Ta'ala.

Hadhrat Sufyaan Sauri *(rahmatullahi alayh)* says: "Whoever is very popular and loved by his relatives and neighbours, we suspect him to be compromising in preaching the true teachings of Deen."

Many Ahaadith mention that when a sin is committed secretly, it affects the sinner only, but when it is committed openly and it is not prevented by those who are able to prevent it, then it affects everybody.

How many sins are committed openly in front us every day? Although we have the ability to stop it, we fail to do so. It is a pity that if anyone makes an effort to stop the wrong, these ignorant and shameless people find faults with him instead of helping him.

وَسَيَعْلَمُ الَّذِيْنَ ظَلَمُوْٓا اَىَّ مُنْقَلَبٍ يَّنْقَلِبُوْنَ

"Shortly (after death) the oppressors (wrongdoers) will come to know to which place they will return (Jahannam)." *(Surah Shu'araa - Aayah 227)*

HADITH 4 – PUNISHMENT BEFORE DEATH FOR NOT STOPPING SINS

عَنْ جَرِيْرِ بْنِ عَبْدِ اللهِ رَضِىَ اللهُ عَنْهُ قَالَ سَمِعْتُ رَسُوْلَ اللهِ صَلَّى اللهُ عَلَيْهِ وَ سَلَّمَ يَقُوْلُ مَا مِنْ رَجُلٍ يَكُوْنُ فِيْ قَوْمٍ يُعْمَلُ فِيْهِمْ بِالْمَعَاصِيْ يَقْدِرُوْنَ عَلٰى اَنْ يُّغَيِّرُوْا عَلَيْهِ وَلَا يُغَيِّرُوْنَ اِلَّا اَصَابَهُمُ اللهُ بِعِقَابٍ قَبْلَ اَنْ يَّمُوْتُوْا (سنن ابی داود # 4339)

Hadhrat Jareer bin Abdullah ﷺ says, "I heard Rasulullah ﷺ saying: 'When a sin is done in front of people and they do not stop it in spite of being able to, Allah Ta'ala will punish them a severe punishment before their death.'"

My dear friends! You wish to see the rise of Islam and the Muslims. You have clearly seen the cause of our downfall. Leave alone the general people, we do not even stop from sin our own family members and others who are under us. We do not even think about stopping evil, let alone doing something about it. We do not even check our own son when he breaks the commandments of Allah Ta'ala, but if he takes some interest in politics, or joins a certain political party, we then worry not only about him but also about our own safety and honour. We then warn him and also think about some plans to be safe and secure from any harm. On the other hand, when he breaks the commandments of Allah Ta'ala, we are not concerned about the life in the Hereafter and about the questioning of the Day of Qiyaamah.

Sometimes you are aware that your son is addicted to some useless things like playing chess and is careless about his Salaah, but you have no courage to prevent him from such habits, or to discipline him, although Allah Ta'ala has clearly commanded you to be firm in uprooting such evils and even cut off relations with the sinner which has been discussed earlier.

ببیں تفاوت راہ از کجاست تا کجا

Look at the difference between the paths; what a great deviation!

Many times a father will be angry with his son, because he is lazy and does not pay attention to his studies or job or business properly, but is there anyone who is angry with his son, because he does not have concern for Salaah with jamaat or he makes his Salaah qadha?

My dear friends! As a matter of fact, the ill effects of breaking the commandments of Allah Ta'ala is not only a great loss in the Hereafter but also to our worldly affairs and interests which are so dear to us. This blindness of ours has no limits, for Allah Ta'ala says:

مَنْ كَانَ فِيْ هٰذِهٖ اَعْمٰى فَهُوَ فِي الْاٰخِرَةِ اَعْمٰى وَاَضَلُّ سَبِيْلًا

"Whoever is blind (to the way of guidance and salvation) in this world, will surely be blind in the Hereafter/ Aakhirah (unable to see the way to Jannah) and will be even more astray."
(Surah Bani Israaeel - Aayah 72)

And the reality is that:

خَتَمَ اللهُ عَلٰى قُلُوْبِهِمْ وَعَلٰى سَمْعِهِمْ ۗ وَعَلٰٓى اَبْصَارِهِمْ غِشَاوَةٌ

"Allah has placed a seal on their hearts (so that no good enters it) and on their hearing/ ears, while there is a veil over their eyes (so that they neither hear nor see the truth)." (Surah Baqarah - Aayah 7)

HADITH 5 – THE RIGHTS OF THE KALIMAH

رُوِىَ عَنْ اَنَسِ بْنِ مَالِكٍ رَضِىَ اللهُ عَنْهُ اَنَّ رَسُوْلَ اللهِ صَلَّى اللهُ عَلَيْهِ وَسَلَّمَ قَالَ لَا تَزَالُ لَا اِلٰهَ اِلَّا اللهُ تَنْفَعُ مَنْ قَالَهَا وَتَرُدُّ عَنْهُمُ الْعَذَابَ وَالنِّقْمَةَ مَا لَمْ يَسْتَخِفُّوْا بِحَقِّهَا قَالُوْا يَا رَسُوْلَ اللهِ وَمَا الْاِسْتِخْفَافُ بِحَقِّهَا قَالَ يَظْهَرُ الْعَمَلُ بِمَعَاصِى اللهِ فَلَا يُنْكَرُ وَلَا يُغَيَّرُ (اخرجه الاصبهانى فى الترغيب # 307)

It has been reported by Hadhrat Anas ﷺ that Rasulullah ﷺ said: "As long as a person says 'Laailaaha illallaah' (no one is worthy of worship but Allah Ta'ala), he receives reward, and he is saved from miseries and problems, unless he ignores its rights." The Sahaabah ﷺ asked: "O Messenger of Allah ﷺ, how are its rights ignored?" He answered, "When sins are committed openly, and the person who recites the kalimah does not stop the sinners from sin."

How many sins are committed without any serious effort to stop it? With so many sins being committed around us, the very existence of the Muslims is a great favour of Allah Ta'ala. We are rather inviting the anger of Allah Ta'ala in different ways.

Hadhrat Aa'ishah ﷺ asked Rasulullah ﷺ, "When the punishment of Allah Ta'ala comes to the people of any area, does it affect the pious, just as it affects the sinners?" Rasulullah ﷺ answered: "Yes, it does affect all of them in this world but on the day of Qiyaamah the pious will be separated from the sinners." Therefore, those who are satisfied with their own piety and do not stop others from evil, should not feel that they are safe from the punishment of Allah Ta'ala. If a punishment comes from Allah Ta'ala, they too will be punished.

HADITH 6 – THE KHUTBAH OF NABI ﷺ REGARDING ENJOINING GOOD AND PREVENTING EVIL

عَنْ عَائِشَةَ رَضِىَ اللهُ عَنْهَا قَالَتْ دَخَلَ عَلَىَّ النَّبِىُّ صَلَّى اللهُ عَلَيْهِ وَسَلَّمَ فَعَرَفْتُ فِىْ وَجْهِهِ اَنْ قَدْ حَضَرَهُ شَىْءٌ فَتَوَضَّاَ وَمَا كَلَّمَ اَحَدًا فَلَصِقْتُ بِالْحُجْرَةِ اَسْتَمِعُ مَا يَقُوْلُ فَقَعَدَ

$$\text{عَلَى الْمِنْبَرِ فَحَمِدَ اللهَ وَاَثْنٰى عَلَيْهِ وَقَالَ يَا اَيُّهَا النَّاسُ اِنَّ اللهَ تَعَالٰى يَقُوْلُ لَكُمْ مُرُوْا}$$
$$\text{بِالْمَعْرُوْفِ وَانْهَوْا عَنِ الْمُنْكَرِ قَبْلَ اَنْ تَدْعُوْا فَلَا اُجِيْبَ لَكُمْ وَتَسْئَلُوْنِىْ فَلَا}$$
$$\text{اُعْطِيَكُمْ وَتَسْتَنْصِرُوْنِىْ فَلَا اَنْصُرَكُمْ فَمَا زَادَ عَلَيْهِنَّ حَتّٰى نَزَلَ}$$

(صحيح ابن حبان # 209)

Hadhrat Aa'ishah ﵂ says: "Once Rasulullah ﷺ entered the house and I saw from his face that something very important had happened. He did not talk to anyone, and after making wudhu he entered the Masjid. I stood behind the wall to hear what he said. He sat on the mimbar and after praising Allah Ta'ala, he said, 'O Muslims! Allah has commanded you to encourage people to good deeds, and stop them from sins. Otherwise a time will come when you will make dua to Him, but He will not listen to you. You will ask for your needs of Him, but He will not grant them. You will ask for His help against your enemies, but He will not help you.' After saying this, he stepped down from the mimbar."

Those people who want to fight the enemies of Islam but neglect to fulfil the basics of Islam, should ponder over this Hadith. They forget that the strength and stability of the Ummah depends upon the propagation of Deen.

Hadhrat Abu Darda ﵁, who is a great Sahaabi of Rasulullah ﷺ, says: "You must command people to do good and stop them from evil, otherwise Allah Ta'ala will cause such a tyrant to rule over you, who will not respect your elders, and will not have mercy on your youngsters. You will make dua to Allah Ta'ala, but He will not accept your dua. You will ask Him for help, but He will not help you. You will ask for His forgiveness but He will not forgive you." Allah Ta'ala Himself says:

$$\text{يٰۤاَيُّهَا الَّذِيْنَ اٰمَنُوْۤا اِنْ تَنْصُرُوا اللهَ يَنْصُرْكُمْ وَيُثَبِّتْ اَقْدَامَكُمْ}$$

"O Believers, if you help (in the propagation of the Deen of) Allah Ta'ala, He will help you, and will keep your feet firm (give you strength against your enemies)." (Surah Muhammad - Aayah 7)

Allah Ta'ala says in another verse:

$$اِنْ يَنْصُرْكُمُ اللّٰهُ فَلَا غَالِبَ لَكُمْ ۚ وَاِنْ يَخْذُلْكُمْ فَمَنْ ذَا الَّذِيْ يَنْصُرُكُمْ مِنْ بَعْدِهٖ ۚ وَعَلَى اللّٰهِ فَلْيَتَوَكَّلِ الْمُؤْمِنُوْنَ$$

"O Believers! If Allah Ta'ala helps you, then no one can overpower you and if He does not help you, then who can come to your help. And only in Allah Ta'ala should the Believers trust."
(Surah Aali I'mraan - Aayah 160)

It has been reported in Durr-e-Mansoor from Imaam Tirmizi and others that Hadhrat Huzayfah رَضِىَ اللّٰهُ عَنْهُ said that Rasulullah صَلَّى اللّٰهُ عَلَيْهِ وَسَلَّمَ took on oath: "You must command people to do good and stop them from doing haraam, otherwise Allah Ta'ala will send a severe punishment upon you. Then, even your duas will not be accepted by Him."

Here my respected readers should think and ponder about how many times we break the commandments of Allah Ta'ala. Therefore, this is why our attempts to reform the people fail and our duas are of no use. Instead of sowing the seeds of progress, we cause its downfall.

HADITH 7 – WHEN PEOPLE BEGIN TO GIVE IMPORTANCE TO THE WORLDLY THINGS

$$عَنْ اَبِىْ هُرَيْرَةَ رَضِىَ اللّٰهُ عَنْهُ قَالَ قَالَ رَسُوْلُ اللّٰهِ صَلَّى اللّٰهُ عَلَيْهِ وَسَلَّمَ اِذَا عَظَّمَتْ اُمَّتِىْ الدُّنْيَا نُزِعَتْ مِنْهَا هَيْبَةُ الْاِسْلَامِ وَاِذَا تَرَكَتِ الْاَمْرَ بِالْمَعْرُوْفِ وَالنَّهْىَ عَنِ الْمُنْكَرِ حُرِمَتْ بَرَكَةَ الْوَحْىِ وَاِذَا تَسَابَّتْ اُمَّتِىْ سَقَطَتْ مِنْ عَيْنِ اللّٰهِ$$

(اخرجه الحكيم الترمذى فى نوادر الاصول 2/270)

It has been reported by Hadhrat Abu Hurayrah رَضِىَ اللّٰهُ عَنْهُ that Rasulullah صَلَّى اللّٰهُ عَلَيْهِ وَسَلَّمَ said, "When my followers will begin to give importance to their worldly possessions, their hearts will lose the love of Islam. When they stop calling to the truth, and stop preventing evil, they will lose the blessings of Wahi (revelation) and when they will swear each other, they will lose their respect in the eyes of Allah Ta'ala."

Those who are concerned about the plight of the Ummah should ponder why their efforts result in failure instead of success. If you people do believe your Rasool ﷺ and his teachings to be true and beneficial, then why do you take those things as useful that he has declared harmful? He says such and such thing will worsen your disease, but you think that they will bring health to you.

Rasulullah ﷺ said: *"None of you can be a true Muslim unless his wishes are according to the Deen that I have brought."*

But you think that Deen is an obstacle with regards to your individual and national progress like that of other nations. Allah Ta'ala says in the Qur-aan Shareef:

$$مَنْ كَانَ يُرِيدُ حَرْثَ الْآخِرَةِ نَزِدْ لَهُ فِىْ حَرْثِهٖ ۚ وَمَنْ كَانَ يُرِيدُ حَرْثَ الدُّنْيَا نُؤْتِهٖ مِنْهَا وَمَالَهٗ فِى الْآخِرَةِ مِنْ نَصِيْبٍ$$

"Whoever desires the harvest of the hereafter, We shall increase his harvest for him. And whoever desires the harvest of this world, We shall give him a part thereof but there is no share for him in the Hereafter." (Surah Shura - Aayah 20)

A hadith says:
"The heart of a Muslim whose object is the life of the Hereafter does not care for the worldly pleasures, yet the world is brought to his feet, on the other hand, whoever hankers after the world, he is overpowered by miseries and calamities, yet he cannot receive more than his allotted portion."

Rasulullah ﷺ read the above Aayah and said: *"Allah Ta'ala says: 'O son of man, give yourself to My worship, and I will free your heart from worldly worries and will remove your poverty. Otherwise, I will fill your heart with a thousand worries and will not remove your poverty.'"*

These are the words of Allah Ta'ala and His Rasool ﷺ, but you think that Deen and the teachings of Ulama interferes with your worldly progress. Don't you think that your worldly progress can be very helpful to the Ulama, for then you would be in a better position to serve them? Then why should they oppose you as this will be a loss to them? The Ulama are sacrificing their own worldly interests by speaking out the truth, by preaching Islam, in order to bring you to the right path. Whatever your Ulama tell you is based on the teachings of the Qur-aan Shareef, and is it sensible for you to turn away from them? If you deny them, then you cannot be a true believer. Those doing Tableegh might have some personal faults, but as long as they are conveying to you the commandments of Allah Ta'ala from the Qur-aan Shareef and the Ahaadith of Rasulullah ﷺ, you are obliged to listen to them and to obey their instructions. If you disobey them, then you have to answer for your disobedience to Allah Ta'ala. Not even a fool would say that the government's orders should not be obeyed, just because an ordinary servant told you about those orders.

Never accuse those who have devoted themselves to the work of Tableegh that, they do it for worldly gains and interest. The true preachers of Islam are never selfish and never ask anything for themselves. The more they make the ibaadah of Allah Ta'ala and devote themselves to the work of Deen, the less attention they pay to worldly efforts. However, if they do ask help of you, then it will be entirely for the sake of Deen (i.e. to propagate Deen and the teachings of the Qur-aan Shareef), wherein they find more satisfaction than in any personal interest. Why should you then hesitate to help them?

Generally, the people say that Islam does not ask us to give up our worldly interests and with regards to this the Aayaat of the Qur-aan Shareef are often misunderstood. For instance, there is an Aayah that says:

رَبَّنَآ اٰتِنَا فِی الدُّنْیَا حَسَنَۃً وَّ فِی الْاٰخِرَۃِ حَسَنَۃً وَّ قِنَا عَذَابَ النَّارِ

"O our Rabb, grant us good in this world, and good in the Hereafter; and save us from the punishment of the Fire (of Jahannam)."
(Surah Baqarah - Aayah 201)

Some ignorant people stress that in this Aayah the worldly good is favoured and appreciated by Islam, as much as the good in the Hereafter. In other words, there is no giving up or rejecting of the world in Islam. Such people claim to be 'learned Ulama' after having seen only some translations of the Qur-aan Shareef. The true meanings of the Qur-aan Shareef can only be properly understood by those who have looked deep into its Aayaat and are learned on this subject.

Different interpretations of the above Aayah have been explained by the Sahaabah ﷺ, who were the companions of Nabi ﷺ, and the Mufassireen (commentators) are as follows:

Hadhrat Qatadah ﷺ says: "By *good in this world* is meant peaceful existence and necessary livelihood."

Hadhrat Ali ﷺ says that by *good in this world* is meant a pious wife.

Hadhrat Hasan Basri *(rahmatullahi alayh)* says that by *good in this world* is meant knowledge of Islam and ibaadah.

Hadhrat Suddi *(rahmatullahi alayh)* says that by *good in this world* is meant lawful earnings.

Hadhrat Ibn 'Umar ﷺ says that by *good in this world* is meant pious children and other people speaking good about you.

Hadhrat Ja'far ﷺ says that by *good in this world* is meant good health, honest living, understanding of the Qur-aan Shareef, victory over the enemies of Islam, and the company of the pious.

I would add that if *good in this world* meant our material progress, even then the emphasis in the Aayah is on making dua to Allah Ta'ala for such a *good* but not entirely busying ourselves in chasing after the material world. To ask from Allah Ta'ala, even if it is the fixing of a shoe lace, is in itself a part of Deen. Even if it means honest living, or to be prosperous and self-sufficient, then that too is not forbidden in Islam. However, making effort for Deen should be equal to or even more than making effort for your living in this world. The point is that our efforts for the sake of Deen should at least be as much as for our efforts for the worldly things, if not more, because Islam teaches us to value both this life and the Hereafter.

The following verses of the Qur-aan Shareef show more stress and importance on the life Hereafter:

$$مَنْ كَانَ يُرِيْدُ حَرْثَ الْاٰخِرَةِ نَزِدْ لَهٗ فِيْ حَرْثِهٖ$$

"Whoever desires the harvest of the Hereafter, We shall increase its harvest for him." *(Surah Shuraa - Aayah 20)*

مَنْ كَانَ يُرِيدُ الْعَاجِلَةَ عَجَّلْنَا لَهُ فِيهَا مَا نَشَآءُ لِمَنْ نُّرِيدُ ثُمَّ جَعَلْنَا لَهُ جَهَنَّمَ يَصْلٰىهَا مَذْمُومًا مَّدْحُورًا ۞ وَمَنْ أَرَادَ الْأٰخِرَةَ وَسَعٰى لَهَا سَعْيَهَا وَهُوَ مُؤْمِنٌ فَأُولٰٓئِكَ كَانَ سَعْيُهُمْ مَّشْكُورًا

"Whoever desires this present world (and its benefits), We shall soon grant him/ her whatever We desire (not necessarily what he/ she desires) for whoever We will (not for everyone who desires it); then We will appoint Jahannam for him. He will be thrown headlong, with disgrace. And whoever desires the Aakhirah, and exerts himself for it as he ought to, and he is a Mu'min (true believer), then those are such people whose efforts will be appreciated (rewarded)."
(Surah Bani Israaeel - Aayah 18-19)

ذٰلِكَ مَتَاعُ الْحَيٰوةِ الدُّنْيَا ۖ وَاللّٰهُ عِنْدَهُ حُسْنُ الْمَاٰبِ

"These are the luxuries of the worldly life, but with Allah Ta'ala is a very good abode (Jannah)." *(Surah Aali I'mraan - Aayah 14)*

مِنْكُمْ مَنْ يُرِيدُ الدُّنْيَا وَمِنْكُمْ مَنْ يُرِيدُ الْأٰخِرَةَ

"And amongst you are those who desire the world only; and amongst you are those who desire the Aakhirah (life of the hereafter)."
(Surah Aali I'mraan -Aayah 152)

قُلْ مَتَاعُ الدُّنْيَا قَلِيلٌ ۗ وَالْأٰخِرَةُ خَيْرٌ لِمَنِ اتَّقٰى

"(O, Rasulullah ﷺ) Tell them, "The comforts (enjoyments) of this world is very short. The Aakhirah (life of the hereafter) is much better for those who have Taqwa (fear Allah)." *(Surah Nisaa - Aayah 77)*

وَمَا الْحَيٰوةُ الدُّنْيَا إِلَّا لَعِبٌ وَّلَهْوٌ ۗ وَلَلدَّارُ الْأٰخِرَةِ خَيْرٌ لِّلَّذِينَ يَتَّقُوْنَ

"The life of this world is nothing but a play (pastime) and sport, and the home of the Aakhirah (hereafter) is best for those with Taqwa (The pious)." *(Surah An'aam - Aayah 32)*

وَذَرِ الَّذِيْنَ اتَّخَذُوْا دِيْنَهُمْ لَعِبًا وَّ لَهْوًا وَّ غَرَّتْهُمُ الْحَيٰوةُ الدُّنْيَا

"And leave aside those who regard their religion (Islam) as a play and sport (make a mockery of it), and whom the worldly life has deceived."
(Surah An'aam - Aayah 70)

تُرِيْدُوْنَ عَرَضَ الدُّنْيَا ۖ وَاللّٰهُ يُرِيْدُ الْاٰخِرَةَ

"You people desire the things (wealth) of this world only, while Allah Ta'ala desires the Aakhirah/ Hereafter (for you)."
(Surah Anfaal - Aayah 67)

أَرَضِيْتُمْ بِالْحَيٰوةِ الدُّنْيَا مِنَ الْاٰخِرَةِ ۚ فَمَا مَتَاعُ الْحَيٰوةِ الدُّنْيَا فِى الْاٰخِرَةِ اِلَّا قَلِيْلٌ

"Do you prefer the life of this world instead of the (the great rewards in store in the) Hereafter? The benefits of this worldly life is but little (insignificant) compared to the (comforts and pleasures of the) Hereafter." *(Surah Taubah - Aayah 38)*

مَنْ كَانَ يُرِيْدُ الْحَيٰوةَ الدُّنْيَا وَ زِيْنَتَهَا نُوَفِّ اِلَيْهِمْ اَعْمَالَهُمْ فِيْهَا وَهُمْ فِيْهَا لَا يُبْخَسُوْنَ ۞ أُولٰٓئِكَ الَّذِيْنَ لَيْسَ لَهُمْ فِى الْاٰخِرَةِ اِلَّا النَّارُ ۖ وَ حَبِطَ مَا صَنَعُوْا فِيْهَا وَ بٰطِلٌ مَّا كَانُوْا يَعْمَلُوْنَ

"Whoever desires the life of this world and all its adornments, We shall grant them the full rewards for their (good) deeds in this very world and they will not be wronged. They are the ones who shall have nothing but the fire for themselves in the Aakhirah. Whatever (good actions) they did in this world will be lost to them (in the Aakhirah) and all their (good) deeds will be in vain." *(Surah Hood - Aayah 15-16)*

$$\text{وَفَرِحُوا بِالْحَيَوةِ الدُّنْيَا ۚ وَمَا الْحَيَوةُ الدُّنْيَا فِي الْاٰخِرَةِ اِلَّا مَتَاعٌ}$$

"And they (the Kuffaar) rejoice (boast) about the life of this world; but the worldly life, when compared to the Hereafter, is but something worthless." (Surah Ra'd - Aayah 26)

$$\text{فَعَلَيْهِمْ غَضَبٌ مِنَ اللّٰهِ ۖ وَلَهُمْ عَذَابٌ عَظِيْمٌ ۞ ذٰلِكَ بِاَنَّهُمُ اسْتَحَبُّوا الْحَيَوةَ الدُّنْيَا عَلَى الْاٰخِرَةِ}$$

"They shall have Allah Ta'ala's wrath on them and they shall suffer a terrible punishment. This (punishment) is because they preferred the life of this world to the Hereafter." (Surah Nahl - Aayah 106-107)

There are many other Aayaat in which the life of this world and the Hereafter has been compared. I cannot mention all of them here, but I have quoted a few of them as examples. Basically, the moral of all the Aayaat is that those who prefer this world to the hereafter will be losers in the long run. If you cannot properly deal with both the worlds, then the life of the hereafter is preferable, and you should fulfil its requirements. We cannot avoid the needs and necessities of this worldly life. For example, we will not sit in the toilet the whole day, but rather only spend that amount of time which is necessary to relieve ourselves.

If we carefully study the Shariah, we will have to admit that Islam has shown us the proper place for our worldly jobs and our Islamic duties. We have been commanded to use at least half of our time for our Ibaadaat and spend the other half in our necessities such as resting or earning a living. According to this plan, we can carry out our Islamic duties as well as fulfil our worldly needs. If we totally busy ourselves only with our worldly needs, then we will be unjust and unfair. Justice requires that we should do both, that is, see to our needs of this life as well as the hereafter, so that both are taken care of, because Islam does not ask us to withdraw from this world. This is what is meant by the Aayah:

$$\text{رَبَّنَآ اٰتِنَا فِي الدُّنْيَا حَسَنَةً وَّ فِي الْاٰخِرَةِ حَسَنَةً وَّ قِنَا عَذَابَ النَّارِ}$$

"O our Rabb! Give us good in this world and in the Hereafter, and save us from the punishment of the Fire (of Jahannam)."
(Surah Baqarah - Aayah 201)

In this chapter, my real object was to quote the sayings of Rasulullah ﷺ about the work of Tableegh. The seven that I have quoted above are sufficient for true believers. As for the disbelievers, Allah Ta'ala says:

$$وَسَيَعْلَمُ الَّذِيْنَ ظَلَمُوْٓا اَىَّ مُنْقَلَبٍ يَّنْقَلِبُوْنَ$$

"Shortly the oppressors (wrongdoers) will come to know to which place they will return (Jahannam)." (Surah Shu'araa - Aayah 227)

Some sayings of Rasulullah ﷺ indicate that there will come a time when everyone will follow his own desires and temptations and no one will pay any attention to the teachings of Deen or the commandments of Allah Ta'ala. In those times, Rasulullah ﷺ has advised us not to worry about the reformation of others and to engage ourselves in the ibaadah of Allah Ta'ala in seclusion, rather than delivering lectures to the people. But the pious ones say that such a period has not yet come; therefore, try your best to reform yourself and to encourage others, before such a time comes. We must avoid those shortcomings pointed out above by Rasulullah ﷺ, as these are the doors through which corruption will occur in our personal life as well as in the Ummah. Rasulullah ﷺ has counted these shortcomings among the causes of our destruction.

$$اَللّٰهُمَّ احْفَظْنَا مِنَ الْفِتَنِ مَا ظَهَرَ مِنْهَا وَمَا بَطَنَ$$

"O Allah! Save us from the tests of sins, whether they are visible or hidden." Aameen.

CHAPTER 3
PRACTICE WHAT YOU PREACH

In this chapter it is intended to draw our attention to a specific shortcoming. Just as most educated Muslims and Ulama of the day have neglected the duty of Tableegh work, similarly there are those who preach Islam to others through speech and by writings, but they neglect practising what they say. In fact they, as preachers, should worry more about reforming themselves than to reform others. Rasulullah ﷺ has strictly forbidden such people to preach who are themselves guilty of sin.

On the night of Mi'raaj, Rasulullah ﷺ saw a group of people whose lips were being clipped with burning scissors. When he asked who they were, Jibreel عليه السلام said that these people preached to others but did not act on what they preached. A Hadith says:

"Some of the people of Jannah will ask those in Jahannam: 'How is it that you people are here, whereas we followed your preaching, and got into Jannah?' They will answer: 'We did not practice ourselves what we preached to others.'"

Another Hadith says: "The punishment of Allah Ta'ala will come down more quickly upon the evil Ulama than on the common sinners. They will be surprised to see this, and will say: "Why is the punishment of Allah Ta'ala coming upon us before even the idol worshipers?" The answer they will receive is that: "Those who committed sins in spite of having the knowledge of Deen are more guilty than those who did not have this knowledge." The pious elders have written that the dawat of those who do not practise Deen themselves, cannot leave an impression on others. That is why Deeni talks, writings and articles today have no effect on the listeners and the readers.

Allah Ta'ala says in the Qur-aan Shareef:

$$\text{اَتَأْمُرُوْنَ النَّاسَ بِالْبِرِّ وَتَنْسَوْنَ اَنْفُسَكُمْ وَاَنْتُمْ تَتْلُوْنَ الْكِتٰبَ ۚ اَفَلَا تَعْقِلُوْنَ}$$

"Do you command people to do good but forget your own selves, even though you read the Book? Don't you understand?"
(Surah Baqarah – Aayah 44)

Rasulullah ﷺ said:

$$\text{مَا تَزَالُ قَدَمَا عَبْدٍ يَوْمَ الْقِيَامَةِ حَتّٰى يُسْئَلَ عَنْ اَرْبَعٍ عَنْ عُمرِهِ فِيْمَ اَفْنَاهُ وَعَنْ شَبَابِهِ فِيْمَ اَبْلَاهُ وَعَنْ مَّالِهِ مِنْ اَيْنَ اكْتَسَبَهُ وَفِيْمَ اَنْفَقَهُ وَعَنْ عِلْمِهِ مَاذَا عَمِلَ فِيْهِ}$$

(اخرجه المنذرى فى الترغيب # 2676)

"On the Day of Qiyaamah, no one will be permitted to move one step until he is asked four questions: (1) How did he spend his life? (2) What use did he make of his youth? (3) How did he earn his wealth and (4) where did he spend it? (5) How much did he act upon his knowledge?"

Hadhrat Abu Darda رضى الله عنه says: "The thing I fear most on the Day of Qiyaamah is the question that I will be asked in front of all the people: 'Did you act upon the knowledge that you had?'" One of the Sahaabah of Rasulullah ﷺ asked him: "Who is the worst of all creation?" He answered: "Don't ask me questions about bad things, but ask me good things. The worst of all creation are the evil Ulama, (i.e. those who do not practise what they say)."

Rasulullah ﷺ says in another Hadith: "Knowledge is of two types: One which remains on the tongue and does not affect the heart and the other which goes into the heart and benefits the rooh (soul) and that is the useful type."

A Muslim should not only learn the knowledge of the external ibaadat (e.g. Salaat, reciting the Qur-aan Shareef, etc.) but also the knowledge of the inner self which would purify his heart and enlighten his mind. We will be questioned on the Day of Qiyaamah as to how much we acted upon our knowledge. Similar warnings are found in several other Ahaadith.

Therefore, I would request all the people doing the work of Tableegh to reform their outer and inner-selves and to practise themselves what they preach to others, otherwise only preaching without *amal* (practicing) cannot be accepted by Allah Ta'ala, as has been shown by various Aayaat of the Qur-aan Shareef, as well as the Ahaadith of Rasulullah ﷺ. I make dua to Allah Ta'ala that He should enable me to also improve myself externally and internally and practise what I preach, for I totally depend upon His favours to hide my shortcomings.

اِلَّا اَن يَّتَغَمَّدَنِيَ اللّٰهُ بِرَحْمَتِهِ الْوَاسِعَةِ

Except that Allah Ta'ala will envelope me in His encompassing mercy

CHAPTER 4
THE IMPORTANCE OF IKRAAM
(HONOURING/RESPECTING OTHER MUSLIMS)

This chapter is about another very important part of Tableegh, which, through a little carelessness of those doing Tableegh, can cause much harm instead of good. For instance, when trying to stop someone from sins, or save him from a bad habit, you should advise him secretly and not openly disgrace him. The respect and honour of a Muslim is very valuable as explained in the following Ahaadith of Rasulullah ﷺ:

عَنْ أَبِيْ هُرَيْرَةَ رَضِيَ اللهُ عَنْهُ مَرْفُوْعًا مَنْ سَتَرَ عَلَىٰ مُسْلِمٍ سَتَرَهُ اللهُ فِي الدُّنْيَا وَالْآخِرَةِ وَاللهُ فِيْ عَوْنِ الْعَبْدِ مَا كَانَ الْعَبْدُ فِيْ عَوْنِ أَخِيْهِ (صحيح مسلم # 2699)

It has been reported by Hadhrat Abu Hurayrah ﷺ that Rasulullah ﷺ said: "Whoever hides the sins of a Muslim, Allah Ta'ala will hide his sins in this world and in the hereafter, and Allah helps His servant so long as he helps his Muslim brother."

عَنِ ابْنِ عَبَّاسٍ رَضِيَ اللهُ عَنْهُ مَرْفُوْعًا مَنْ سَتَرَ عَوْرَةَ أَخِيْهِ الْمُسْلِمِ سَتَرَ اللهُ عَوْرَتَهُ يَوْمَ الْقِيَامَةِ وَمَنْ كَشَفَ عَوْرَةَ أَخِيْهِ الْمُسْلِمِ كَشَفَ اللهُ عَوْرَتَهُ حَتّىٰ يُفْضِحَهُ بِهَا فِيْ بَيْتِهِ

(سنن ابن ماجه # 2546)

It has been reported by Ibn Abbaas رَضِىَ اللّٰهُ عَنْهُ that Rasulullah صَلَّى اللّٰهُ عَلَيْهِ وَسَلَّمَ said: "Whoever hides the faults of a Muslim brother. Allah will hide his faults on the Day of Qiyaamah, and whoever will tell others about the faults of his Muslim brother, Allah will inform others about his faults, so much so that he will be disgraced sitting in his own house."

There are many other Ahaadith on this subject. Therefore, people who call towards Allah Ta'ala should always hide the faults and protect the respect of our brothers in Islam. Another Hadith says: "Whoever does not help his Muslim brother when he is being disgraced, Allah Ta'ala will not worry about him when he is in need of help." Yet another Hadith says: "The worst form of interest is disgracing a Muslim."

In many Ahaadith, the disrespecting of a Muslim has been made haraam. Those doing Tableegh should be very cautious in this regard. The correct method is to advise people secretly on the sins that we come to know secretly and openly advise those on the sins that they commit openly. However, advice should be given in such a way that the sinner is not disgraced, otherwise the advice will have the opposite effect. In short, the sinners must be corrected according to the command of Allah Ta'ala, but let us not forget the instruction of respecting every Muslim.

The person doing Tableegh must be polite and kind when speaking to people. Bad manners and bad words have the opposite effect. Adopting a soft approach is also from the etiquettes of Tableegh.

A person once spoke harshly to the Khalifah Ma'moon Ar-Rasheed while advising him. The Khalifah said: "Please be polite and kind to me because Fir'aun was a worse person than me, and Hadhrat Musa عَلَيْهِ السَّلَام was a much better person than you. When Hadhrat Musa عَلَيْهِ السَّلَام and Hadhrat Haroon عَلَيْهِ السَّلَام were sent to advise Fir'aun, Allah Ta'ala commanded them:

$$\text{فَقُوْلَا لَهُ قَوْلًا لَّيِّنًا لَّعَلَّهُ يَتَذَكَّرُ أَوْ يَخْشٰى}$$

"Speak to him in soft words so that he may turn to the Right Path, or maybe he will fear Me!" (Surah Tahaa - Aayah: 44)

A youth from an outlying area came to Rasulullah صَلَّى اللّٰهُ عَلَيْهِ وَسَلَّمَ and said: "Please allow me to commit adultery." The Sahaabah of Rasulullah صَلَّى اللّٰهُ عَلَيْهِ وَسَلَّمَ took this very badly and were angry at his words; but

Rasulullah ﷺ asked him: "Come nearer to me. Would you like anyone to commit adultery with your mother?" He replied: "Not at all." Rasulullah ﷺ then said: "Other people will also never tolerate such a shameful act with their mothers." Then Rasulullah ﷺ asked him the same question about his daughter, sister, aunt, etc., and each time he answered in the negative. Then Rasulullah ﷺ put his hand on the youth's chest and made dua: "O Allah! Purify his heart, forgive his sins, and guard him against adultery." The reporters say that, after this, nothing was more hateful to him than adultery.

In short, one should employ the means of dua, advice, softness, etc. when advising or correcting someone. One should think to himself that, "If I was in such a position, how would I like someone to advise or correct me."

CHAPTER 5
IMPORTANCE OF IKHLAAS (SINCERITY)

The people doing Tableegh should be very sincere as far as their talks, writings and actions are concerned. Even a small good deed with sincerity will be greatly rewarded by Allah Ta'ala. Without sincerity, they will have no reward in this world or in the Hereafter.

عَنْ اَبِىْ هُرَيْرَةَ رَضِىَ اللهُ عَنْهُ قَالَ قَالَ رَسُوْلُ اللهِ صَلَّى اللهُ عَلَيْهِ وَسَلَّمَ اِنَّ اللهَ لَا يَنْظُرُ اِلٰى صُوَرِكُمْ وَاَمْوَالِكُمْ وَلٰكِنْ يَنْظُرُ اِلٰى قُلُوْبِكُمْ وَاَعْمَالِكُمْ (صحيح مسلم # 2564)

Hadhrat Abu Hurayrah ؓ narrates that Rasulullah ﷺ says about sincerity: "Allah does not look at your faces or towards your riches; but He sees (the sincerity of) your hearts and your deeds."

On another occasion, Rasulullah ﷺ was asked as to what is the meaning of 'Imaan'. He answered, "It means Ikhlaas (sincerity)."

Hadhrat Mu'aaz ؓ was made the governor of Yemen. When he was about to leave for Yemen, he asked for advice from Rasulullah ﷺ who said: "Be sincere in all your beliefs and actions, for it will increase the reward of your good deeds." Another Hadith says: "Allah Ta'ala accepts only those deeds of His servants, which are done with complete sincerity for Him."

Another Hadith says:

$$\text{قَالَ اللهُ تَعَالٰى اَنَا اَغْنَى الشُّرَكَاءِ عَنِ الشِّرْكِ مَنْ عَمِلَ عَمَلًا اَشْرَكَ فِيْهِ مَعِىْ غَيْرِىْ تَرَكْتُهُ وَشِرْكَهُ وَفِىْ رِوَايَةٍ: فَاَنَا مِنْهُ بَرِىْءٌ فَهُوَ لِلَّذِىْ عَمِلَهُ}$$ (صحیح مسلم # 2985)

> "Allah Ta'ala has said: 'I am the most independent of all partners. Whoever brings a partner to Me in any action (i.e. whoever does some action to show off to someone), I give him over to that partner, (and will not help him at all). Then I have no value for his actions, which are all given to the partner.'"

It has been stated in another Hadith that it will be announced on the Day of Qiyaamah:

> "Whoever has made a partner to Allah Ta'ala in any action, he should ask for his reward from that partner because Allah Ta'ala does not need any partner."

Another Hadith says:

$$\text{مَنْ صَلّٰى يُرَائِىْ فَقَدْ اَشْرَكَ وَمَنْ صَامَ يُرَائِىْ فَقَدْ اَشْرَكَ وَمَنْ تَصَدَّقَ يُرَائِىْ فَقَدْ اَشْرَكَ}$$ (مسند احمد # 17140)

> "Whoever does ibaadat for show, he becomes guilty of false worship and whoever fasts for show, he also becomes guilty of false worship and whoever gives charity for show, he also becomes guilty of false worship."

To be guilty of false worship means that he does not perform good deeds sincerely for the sake of Allah Ta'ala only. By making a show of it, he wants to look good in front of people, which indirectly makes them look like partners to Allah Ta'ala.

Another Hadith says:

$$\text{اِنَّ اَوَّلَ النَّاسِ يُقْضٰى عَلَيْهِ يَوْمَ الْقِيَامَةِ رَجُلٌ اُسْتُشْهِدَ فَاُتِىَ بِهٖ فَعَرَّفَهٗ نِعَمَهٗ فَعَرَفَهَا قَالَ فَمَا عَمِلْتَ فِيْهَا قَالَ قَاتَلْتُ فِيْكَ حَتّٰى اسْتُشْهِدْتُ قَالَ كَذَبْتَ وَلٰكِنَّكَ قَاتَلْتَ لِاَنْ يُّقَالَ جَرِىْءٌ فَقَدْ قِيْلَ ثُمَّ اُمِرَ بِهٖ فَسُحِبَ عَلٰى وَجْهِهٖ حَتّٰى اُلْقِىَ فِى النَّارِ وَرَجُلٌ تَعَلَّمَ}$$

Ch.5 – The Importance of Ikhlaas

الْعِلْمَ وَعَلَّمَهُ وَقَرَاَ الْقُرْآنَ فَأتِيَ بِهِ فَعَرَّفَهُ نِعَمَهُ فَعَرَفَهَا قَالَ فَمَا عَمِلْتَ فِيْهَا قَالَ تَعَلَّمْتُ الْعِلْمَ وَعَلَّمْتُهُ وَقَرَأْتُ فِيْكَ الْقُرْآنَ قَالَ كَذَبْتَ وَلٰكِنَّكَ تَعَلَّمْتَ الْعِلْمَ لِيُقَالَ اِنَّكَ عَالِمٌ وَقَرَأْتَ الْقُرْآنَ لِيُقَالَ هُوَ قَارِئٌ فَقَدْ قِيْلَ ثُمَّ أُمِرَ بِهِ فَسُحِبَ عَلٰى وَجْهِهِ حَتّٰى اُلْقِيَ فِي النَّارِ وَرَجُلٌ وَسَّعَ اللّٰهُ عَلَيْهِ وَاَعْطَاهُ مِنْ اَصْنَافِ الْمَالِ كُلِّهِ فَأتِيَ بِهِ فَعَرَّفَهُ نِعَمَهُ فَعَرَفَهَا قَالَ فَمَا عَمِلْتَ فِيْهَا قَالَ مَا تَرَكْتُ مِنْ سَبِيْلٍ تُحِبُّ اَنْ يُنْفَقَ فِيْهَا اِلَّا اَنْفَقْتُ فِيْهَا لَكَ قَالَ كَذَبْتَ وَلٰكِنَّكَ فَعَلْتَ لِيُقَالَ هُوَ جَوَادٌ فَقَدْ قِيْلَ ثُمَّ أُمِرَ بِهِ فَسُحِبَ عَلٰى وَجْهِهِ ثُمَّ اُلْقِيَ فِي النَّارِ (صحيح مسلم # 1905)

"Some people will be called before everybody for questioning on the Day of Qiyaamah. A shaheed will be asked by Allah Ta'ala, 'Did I not give you such and such favour?' He will admit those favours. Allah Ta'ala will then ask him: 'How did you make use of My favours?' He will answer: 'I went in Jihaad to please You, and was killed for Your sake.' Allah Ta'ala will say: 'You lie! You went in Jihaad to be called a hero by people, and this has been done.' He will be thrown head first into the fire of Jahannam. Next, an Aalim will be called and the same questions will be put to him. In reply he will admit the favours of Allah Ta'ala. He will be asked: 'How did you make use of My favours?' He will answer, 'I learnt the knowledge of Islam and taught it to others only to please You.' Allah Ta'ala will say: 'You lie! You learnt knowledge in order to be called an Aalim and you read the Qur-aan to be called a Qaari.' He too will be thrown head first into the fire of Jahannam. Thereafter a rich man will be called, and the same questions will be put to him. He will say: 'I always spent money to please You.' Allah Ta'ala will say: 'You lie! You spent money in order to be called a generous man, and this has been said.' He also will be thrown headfirst into the fire of Jahannam."

Therefore, we should avoid showing off. We should invite people to Islam and serve Deen only to please Allah Ta'ala. We should follow the Sunnah of Rasulullah ﷺ and should neither desire to become famous nor to receive favours from people. If our intention is incorrect, we should ask Allah Ta'ala to protect us and should ask His forgiveness.

May Allah Ta'ala, through His kindness and through the sadaqah of His beloved (Rasul ﷺ) and through the barkat of his pure work, grant us sinners the taufeeq of ikhlaas (sincerity) and may Allah also bless the readers as well. Aameen.

CHAPTER 6
RESPECT FOR LEARNING DEEN AND THE ULAMA

In this chapter, I would write down a few points for the Muslims so that they may know how to respect the Ulama and those doing Tableegh. Today it is normal to find faults with the Ulama as well as those doing Tableegh. This is very harmful from an Islamic point of view. Everywhere in the world, there are good as well as bad people. If there are a few bad Ulama also, it is understandable. Take note of two important points! Firstly, you should not think bad about anyone, unless you have solid proof.

Allah Ta'ala says in the Qur-aan Shareef:

وَلَا تَقْفُ مَا لَيْسَ لَكَ بِهِ عِلْمٌ ۚ إِنَّ السَّمْعَ وَالْبَصَرَ وَالْفُؤَادَ كُلُّ أُولَٰئِكَ كَانَ عَنْهُ مَسْئُولًا

"And do not pursue something which you have no knowledge of, because everyone will be questioned as to how he used his ears and eyes and the heart." (Surah Bani Israaeel - Aayah: 36)

Obviously, it is wrong to reject the good advice of a person doing Tableegh just because you have some doubts about him.

The Jews translated their holy books into Arabic, and would read them to the Muslims. Rasulullah ﷺ was so careful that he advised: "O Muslims, you should neither accept nor reject what they say. You should rather say: 'We believe in everything which Allah Ta'ala has revealed.'" In other words, he stopped us from rejecting even a kaafir's word without first verifying it. We are such that we do not pay attention to those doing Tableegh and attack them even though we know that they are pious and sincere.

The second thing that you must remember is that the pious Ulama and those doing Tableegh are human beings. They too may have some weaknesses. They will answer for their good or bad deeds and the final decision belongs to Allah Ta'ala. I hope that by His mercy and kindness He forgives them. They have been sacrificing and serving His Deen throughout their lives. In short, to doubt and find faults with those doing Tableegh, or to speak bad about them, will drive people away from Deen. This will be a cause of great worry for those who are doing the work of Deen.

Rasulullah ﷺ has said:

إِنَّ مِنْ إِجْلَالِ اللهِ تَعَالَى إِكْرَامَ ذِى الشَّيْبَةِ الْمُسْلِمِ وَحَامِلِ الْقُرْآنِ غَيْرِ الْغَالِىْ فِيْهِ وَلَا الْجَافِىْ عَنْهُ وَإِكْرَامَ ذِى السُّلْطَانِ الْمُقْسِطِ (سنن ابى داود # 4843)

"Whoever respects the following three, he really shows respect to Allah Ta'ala: (1) An old Muslim, (2) One who takes care of the Qur-aan without going against its orders himself (i.e. transgress its limits), (3) A ruler who is just to the people."

The following saying of Rasulullah ﷺ tells us:

لَيْسَ مِنْ أُمَّتِىْ مَنْ لَمْ يُجِلَّ كَبِيْرَنَا وَيَرْحَمْ صَغِيْرَنَا وَيَعْرِفْ عَالِمَنَا (مسند احمد # 22755)

"That person who does not respect our elders, nor is he merciful to our youngsters, and he does not respect our Ulama is not one of us."

عَنْ أَبِىْ أُمَامَةَ رَضِىَ اللهُ عَنْهُ عَنْ رَسُوْلِ اللهِ صَلَّى اللهُ عَلَيْهِ وَسَلَّمَ قَالَ ثَلَاثٌ لَا يَسْتَخِفُّ بِهِمْ إِلَّا مُنَافِقٌ ذُو الشَّيْبَةِ فِى الْإِسْلَامِ وَذُو الْعِلْمِ وَإِمَامٌ مُقْسِطٌ (اخرجه المنذرى فى الترغيب # 174)

"Whoever disgraces the following three people is not a Muslim, but rather a hypocrite: first, an old Muslim, second, an Aalim (of Deen) and third, a just ruler."

Rasulullah ﷺ has also said:

"I fear especially three problems in my followers. First, with an increase in worldly possessions, they will become jealous of one another; second, discussing the Qur-aan will become so common that even the ignorant (those who don't know) will say that they know the meanings of the Qur-aan, although many meanings are such that cannot be understood by anyone except the learned Ulama of the Qur-aan, who say: 'We have strong belief in it, and that it is from Allah Ta'ala', so how much more careful should the common people be; third, the Ulama will be neglected and people will not benefit from them." (Targheeb)

Many similar Ahaadith are found in the books of Hadith. It has been mentioned in *'Fataawa Aalamgiri'* that the sort of insulting words used today by the ignorant people about the Ulama may seriously damage their Imaan. Therefore, people must be careful to avoid such words. Suppose for a moment there are no true and sincere Ulama in the world, even then, nothing is gained by calling them evil Ulama. Rather, it is the Islamic and moral duty of every Muslim to form such an Islamic organization (Jamaat) that will produce sincere servants of Islam. Only when such a Jamaat exist, should we be content.

One common objection is that the differences amongst the Ulama have brought about destruction to the general masses. It is possible that this objection is correct to a certain extent. But, in reality, difference of opinion amongst the Ulama is not something new. It is not something that only came into existence in the last century or so but rather it is in existence from the golden era of Rasulullah ﷺ.

There is a Hadith that says: "Rasulullah ﷺ gave his shoes to Hadhrat Abu Hurayrah رضي الله عنه, and said: 'Take my shoes as a sign and announce among the Muslims that whoever will say *'Laa ilaaha illallaah Muhammadur Rasulullah,'* from the bottom of his heart, will certainly enter Jannah.'" Hadhrat Umar رضي الله عنه met Hadhrat Abu Hurayrah رضي الله عنه on the way and asked him where he was going. He told him the message of Rasulullah ﷺ, Hadhrat Umar رضي الله عنه was annoyed, because he did not agree with such a plan. Therefore, he hit the messenger on the chest which caused him to fall on his back. Yet no one raised any objections against Hadhrat Umar ﷺ, nor was any demonstration arranged against him because of this difference of opinion.

Many differences of opinion existed among the Sahaabah ﷺ and later on the four Imaams of Fiqh differed amongst themselves on many issues. There have been many minor differences of opinion about Salaah between the four Imaams. I myself know of about 200. There may be many more. Besides "The raising of the hands (*rafa hadain*)" and "Saying Aameen loudly (aameen bil jahr)" people probably never heard of anything else. This does not mean that their followers should doubt the Imaan of one another, calling each other 'kaafir'. The fact is that the common people do not know the finer points on which various Ulama and Imaams differ in their views. These differences are a blessing in disguise. As a matter of fact, good preachers and sincere servants of Islam do not attach any importance to such minor issues, but continue their attempt to bring people to the right path. We know that doctors and lawyers also have differences, but people still take their advice. But those who are ignorant, selfish and lazy, raise objections against the Ulama simply because of the differences of opinions that the Ulama have. Every Muslim has been commanded to follow those Ulama whom he respects and knows to be the followers of the Sunnah. He should not find fault with those whom he does not like. Anyone who has no proper knowledge of Islam and the Qur-aan has no right to find faults with the Ulama. The Ulama should always keep this saying of Rasulullah ﷺ in mind and act accordingly: "It is a waste of knowledge to pass it on to those who are not fit for it."

In this corrupt age, when even the commandments of Allah Ta'ala and the sayings of Rasulullah ﷺ are being criticised, I have no reason to be surprised if the people do not hear the advices of Ulama and do not follow the Qur-aan Shareef.

Allah Ta'ala says in the Qur-aan Shareef:

$$\text{وَمَن يَتَعَدَّ حُدُودَ اللّٰهِ فَأُولَٰٓئِكَ هُمُ الظَّٰلِمُونَ}$$

"And whoever transgresses the limits of Allah Ta'ala, surely these are the unjust." *(Surah Baqarah - Aayah 229)*

CHAPTER 7
KEEPING COMPANY OF THE PIOUS (AHLULLAH)

In this last chapter, I would like to remind the Muslims to follow the Sunnah of Rasulullah ﷺ and to make friends with those who practice Islam fully and remember Allah Ta'ala day and night. This will make them stronger in Islam. Even Rasulullah ﷺ was commanded to remain with the pious people.

Rasulullah ﷺ says:

اَلَا اَدُلُّكَ عَلَى مِلَاكِ هٰذَا الْأَمْرِ الَّذِىْ تُصِيْبُ بِهِ خَيْرَ الدُّنْيَا وَالْاٰخِرَةِ عَلَيْكَ بِمَجَالِسِ اَهْلِ الذِّكْرِ وَاِذَا خَلَوْتَ فَحَرِّكْ لِسَانَكَ مَا اسْتَطَعْتَ بِذِكْرِ اللّٰهِ

(اخرجه البيهقى فى شعب الايمان # 8608)

"Shall I tell you something through which you will acquire the good of this world and the Aakhirah? Frequent the gatherings of the people of zikr and when you are alone, then keep your tongue busy with the zikr of Allah Ta'ala as much as you can."

It is important for a person to first investigate and find out who are the true lovers of Allah Ta'ala. They are the true followers of the Sunnah. Allah Ta'ala has sent his beloved Nabi ﷺ as an example for the guidance of the Muslims.

Allah Ta'ala says in the Qur-aan Shareef:

$$\text{قُلْ إِنْ كُنْتُمْ تُحِبُّونَ اللَّهَ فَاتَّبِعُونِيْ يُحْبِبْكُمُ اللَّهُ وَيَغْفِرْ لَكُمْ ذُنُوْبَكُمْ ۗ وَاللَّهُ غَفُوْرٌ رَّحِيْمٌ}$$

"O Nabi ﷺ, say: If you people (really) love Allah, then follow me so that Allah will love you, and will forgive your sins, and Allah is Forgiving, Merciful." *(Surah Aali I'mraan - Aayah 31)*

Whoever follows Rasulullah ﷺ sincerely, is nearer to Allah Ta'ala. Whoever does not follow him, is far away from Allah Ta'ala and cannot acquire his favours. The Ulama have written that whoever claims to be a lover of Allah Ta'ala, but does not follow the Sunnah of Rasulullah ﷺ is a liar. A true lover loves everything of the beloved. It is a law of love that if you love someone then you will also love his house, the walls of his house, the courtyard of his house, his garden and even his dog and donkey.

$$\text{أَمُرُّ عَلَى الدِّيَارِ دِيَارِ لَيْلٰى ۞ أُقَبِّلُ ذَا الْجِدَارَ وَذَا الْجِدَارَ}$$

$$\text{وَمَا حُبُّ الدِّيَارِ شَغَفْنَ قَلْبِيْ ۞ وَلٰكِنْ حُبُّ مَنْ سَكَنَ الدِّيَارَا}$$

Majnoon said, "Whenever I pass by the house of Laila, I kiss every brick and every wall. Really, it is not the love of the house that I am infatuated with, but rather it is the love of the one who resides in the house."

Another poet says:

$$\text{تَعْصِى الْإِلٰهَ وَأَنْتَ تُظْهِرُ حُبَّهُ ۞ وَهٰذَا لَعَمْرِيْ فِى الْفِعَالِ بَدِيْعُ}$$

$$\text{لَوْ كَانَ حُبُّكَ صَادِقًا لَأَطَعْتَهُ ۞ إِنَّ الْمُحِبَّ لِمَنْ يُحِبُّ مُطِيْعُ}$$

"You pretend to be a lover of Allah Ta'ala, and yet you do not obey His commandments! I take an oath that this is indeed really strange. If

Ch.6 – Respect for Learning Deen & the Ulama

it was really that your love was true, you would definitely obey Him, for a lover is always obedient to his beloved."

Rasulullah ﷺ said: "All my followers will enter Jannah except those who have denied (not accepted) me." The Sahaabah رضى الله عنهم asked: "Who would deny you?" Rasulullah ﷺ replied: "Those who follow me will enter Jannah, but those who disobey me have in fact denied me." In another Hadith, Nabi ﷺ has said. "None of you can be a true Muslim unless his desires are according to that which I have brought, that is the Qur-aan Shareef."

Those who claim to love Islam and the Muslims would never disobey Allah Ta'ala and His Nabi ﷺ. When told that some action is against the Sunnah, they get upset. How can they be true followers of Rasulullah ﷺ?

Sa'di (rahmatullahi alayh) has said:

خلافِ پیمبر کسے رہ گزید   کہ ہرگز بمنزل نہ خواہدرَسید

"Whoever follows a way opposite to the Sunnah of Rasulullah ﷺ, will never reach his destination."

After understanding the above explanation, if any person is a lover of Allah Ta'ala, then increasing ones link and connection with him, trying to spend as much time in his khidmat and service and taking benefit from his knowledge is the means of progress in one's Deen. This is also the command of Rasulullah ﷺ.

Rasulullah ﷺ said:

"Whenever you pass through the gardens of Jannah, then eat of its fruits." The Sahaabah رضى الله عنهم asked: "What are the gardens of Jannah?" Rasulullah ﷺ answered: "The gatherings where the knowledge of Deen is taught."

Rasulullah ﷺ also said: "Luqmaan (alayhis salaam) instructed his son in these words: 'Remain with the Ulama, and pay attention to the words of the wise, as Allah Ta'ala revives the dead hearts, just as He revives the dead earth with heavy rains, and only the wise understand Deen.'"

A Sahaabi ﷺ asked Rasulullah ﷺ, "Who can be a best friend to us?" He answered: "Such a person that, when you see him, you remember Allah Ta'ala, when you listen to him, your knowledge of Islam is increases and when you see his actions, you are reminded of the Aakhirah." (Targheeb)

Again, "The most devoted servants of Allah Ta'ala are such that, when you see them you remember Allah Ta'ala."

Allah Ta'ala says in the Qur-aan Shareef:

$$\text{يَاأَيُّهَا الَّذِينَ آمَنُوا اتَّقُوا اللهَ وَ كُونُوا مَعَ الصَّادِقِينَ}$$

"O those who believe! Fear Allah, and remain with the truthful (faithful) people!" (Surah Taubah - Aayah 119)

The commentators have written that by truthful it is meant the Sufis and the true lovers of Allah Ta'ala, for whoever attaches himself to them and listens to their advices, he attains very high levels of spirituality.

Shaikh Akbar *(rahmatullahi alayh)* has written: "You cannot get rid of your evil desires, though you may try for your whole life, unless your wishes are according to the orders of Allah Ta'ala and the Sunnah of Rasulullah ﷺ. When you do find a true lover of Allah Ta'ala, submit yourself fully before him, serve him well and follow him as though you have no desire of your own. Obey him in all your matters, including those concerning your spiritual, religious and personal problems, even those concerning your employment. He may then lead you to the right path and take you closer to Allah Ta'ala."

Rasulullah ﷺ says, "When a group of people remember Allah Ta'ala in a meeting, the Malaaikah surround that gathering, Allah Ta'ala's mercy comes down on them and Allah Ta'ala remembers them in the group of Malaaikah."

What honour can be greater for the Muslims than that of Allah Ta'ala remembering and acknowledging them.

Rasulullah ﷺ says: "An angel is sent to those who remember Allah Ta'ala sincerely. He says 'Allah Ta'ala has forgiven your past sins, and has changed your bad deeds into good ones.'"

In another Hadith, Rasulullah ﷺ says: "That group of Muslims who did not remember Allah Ta'ala, (did not) send salaams to His Nabi ﷺ, will be disappointed on the Day of Qiyaamah."

The following is a dua of Hadhrat Dawood عَلَيْهِ السَّلاَم: "O Allah! if you see me staying away from the gatherings of Zikr and attending the gatherings of sinners, then break my feet (so that I may not be able to walk towards them)."

A poet has said.

جب اس کی صوت وصورت سے ہے محرومی تو بہتر ہے

مرے کانوں کا کر ہونا اور آنکھیں کور ہو جانی

"When I do not listen to Him and see His face, it is better for me to be deaf and blind."

Hadhrat Abu Hurayrah رَضِىَ اللهُ عَنْهُ says; "A gathering where Allah Ta'ala is remembered and glorified, shines to the people of the skies, just as the stars shine for the people of the earth."

Hadhrat Abu Hurayrah رَضِىَ اللهُ عَنْهُ once went to a bazaar and called out to the people: "O brothers! You are sitting here whilst the 'wealth' of Rasulullah صَلَّى اللهُ عَلَيْهِ وَسَلَّم is being distributed in the Masjid." The people hurried to the Masjid. Since no 'wealth' was being distributed, they returned disappointed. Hadhrat Abu Hurayrah رَضِىَ اللهُ عَنْهُ asked them, "What was being done there?" They answered: "A few people were reading the Qur-aan Shareef, and a few were busy in the zikr of Allah Ta'ala." He said: "This is what we call the 'wealth' of Rasulullah صَلَّى اللهُ عَلَيْهِ وَسَلَّم."

Imaam Ghazaali *(rahmatullahi alayh)* has mentioned many similar Ahaadith. Even Rasulullah صَلَّى اللهُ عَلَيْهِ وَسَلَّم has been ordered by Allah Ta'ala:

وَاصْبِرْ نَفْسَكَ مَعَ الَّذِيْنَ يَدْعُوْنَ رَبَّهُمْ بِالْغَدٰوةِ وَالْعَشِيِّ يُرِيْدُوْنَ وَجْهَهٗ وَلَا تَعْدُ عَيْنٰكَ عَنْهُمْ ۚ تُرِيْدُ زِيْنَةَ الْحَيٰوةِ الدُّنْيَا ۚ وَلَا تُطِعْ مَنْ اَغْفَلْنَا قَلْبَهٗ عَنْ ذِكْرِنَا وَاتَّبَعَ هَوٰىهُ وَكَانَ اَمْرُهٗ فُرُطًا

"(O Rasulullah صَلَّى اللهُ عَلَيْهِ وَسَلَّم) Restrain (keep) yourself (in the company of) those who call upon their Rabb morning and evening, seeking His pleasure only and do not shift your attention from them with the intention of acquiring the attractions of the worldly life and do not

obey them (the wealthy Kuffaar) whose hearts We have turned away from our zikr (remembrance), and who follow their desires, and whose (every) affairs entail transgressing (by not living within the laws of Allah Ta'ala)." (Surah Kahf - Aayah 28)

Rasulullah ﷺ would thank Allah Ta'ala for making such pious people from his followers that he was ordered to remain with them. In the same Aayah, Rasulullah ﷺ has been ordered to stay away from those who follow their desires and disobey Allah Ta'ala. He has been instructed time and again not to follow them.

Those who blindly follow the ways of the sinners and non-Muslims should look deep into their hearts and see how far they have drifted from being true Muslims. Imitating the non-Muslims has taken them far away from the Right Path:

ترسم نه رسی بکعبه اے اعرابی

کیں رہ کہ تو میروی بترکستان است

"O innocent villager! I fear that you won't be able to reach the Ka'bah; because the road that you are travelling on goes to Turkey."

مرادِ ما نصیحت بود و کردیم

حوالت باخدا کردیم ورفتیم

I intended to advise you about Deeni matters, and I have done my duty. Now I leave you to Allah Ta'ala. The Ambiyaa عَلَيْهِمُ السَّلَام were also ordered only to say the truth.

وَمَا عَلَى الرُّسُلِ اِلَّا الْبَلَاغُ

Please do remember me in your duas
Muhammad Zakariyya Kandhlawi,
Mazahirul-Uloom, Saharanpur
29th ZulHijjah 1348 A.H.

فضائلِ رمضان

VIRTUES OF RAMADHAAN

Contents

Foreword	777
Introduction	778
Chapter 1 The Virtues of Ramadhaan	**780**
Hadith 1 - The khutbah of Rasulullah ﷺ on the last day of Sha'baan	780
Nafal Ibaadaat	783
Our Faults	783
The practice of Moulana Khalil Ahmad Saharanpuri (RA) during Ramadhaan	784
The practice of Shaikhul Hind (RA) during Ramadhaan	785
Advice	785
All Divine Books were revelaed in Ramadhaan	786
Some specialities of this month	787
Kindness for the Poor & Unfortunate	787
The three parts of this month	789
Kindness to ones workers	790
Hadith 2 - Five special things given to the Ummah of Rasulullah ﷺ	791
The fragrance of the mouth	792
Using the miswaak whilst fasting	793
Fish seeking forgiveness on our behalf	793
Jannah is Decorated	794
Shaytaans are chained up	794
Those who fast are forgiven	796
Hadith 3 – The curse of Jibra-eel (alayhis salaam) and the Aameen of Rasulullah ﷺ	796
Hadith 4 – Show Allah Ta'ala Your Good deeds in Ramadhaan	799
Hadith 5 – Freedom from Jahannam and acceptance of Dua	800
Hadith 6 - Three People whose Dua is surely accepted	802
Hadith 7 – The Importance of Sehri (the meal before Dawn)	805

HADITH 8 - MANY PEOPLE FAST AND WORSHIP AT NIGHT BUT EARN NOTHING BESIDES HUNGER AND LOST SLEEP 808

HADITH 9 - FASTING IS A PROTECTIVE SHIELD 808

HADITH 10 - FASTING PERSON EATING WITHOUT A VALID REASON 816

CHAPTER 2 LAYLATUL QADR 819

THE ORIGIN 819

HADITH 1 - STANDING UP IN IBAADAH ON LAYLATUL QADR 824

HADITH 2 - ONE WHO MISSES LAYLATUL QADR 825

HADITH 3 – DUAS ACCEPTED AND SINS FORGIVEN ON THE OCCASION OF EID 829

HADITH 4 - LOOKING FOR LAYLATUL QADR 830

Advice 831

HADITH 5 - ACTUAL DATE OF LAYLATUL QADR TAKEN AWAY BECAUSE OF TWO PEOPLE ARGUING 832

HADITH 6 - A SAHAABI ﺭﺿﻲﺍﻟﻠﻪﻋﻨﻪ ENQUIRING ABOUT LAYLATUL QADR 839

HADITH 7 - WHAT DUA TO MAKE ON LAYLATUL QADR 840

CHAPTER 3 I'TIKAAF (STAYING IN THE MASJID) 842

a) Waajib Itikaaf: 842
b) Sunnah Itikaaf: 842
c) Nafl (optional) Itikaaf: 842

OBJECTS AND ADVANTAGES OF ITIKAAF 843

WHERE TO PERFORM ITIKAAF 845

HADITH 1 - RASULULLAH ﺻﻠﻰﺍﻟﻠﻪﻋﻠﻴﻪﻭﺳﻠﻢ IN ITIKAAF 846

HADITH 2 - REWARDS FOR ITIKAAF 847

HADITH 3 - TO HELP SOMEONE TO FULFIL A NEED IS BETTER THAN PERFORMING ITIKAAF FOR TEN YEARS 849

HADITH 4 - GREAT REWARDS GIVEN TO THIS UMMAH IN RAMADHAAN AND ON THE DAY OF EIDUL FITR 851

Point of note 860

مناجات 862

FOREWORD

بِسْمِ اللَّهِ الرَّحْمَنِ الرَّحِيمِ

This book is a simple English translation of a famous book in Urdu by Shaikhul-Hadith Moulana Zakariyya of Saharanpur, India.

Moulana Zakariyya *(rahmatullahi alaih)* was one of the world's greatest scholars on Hadith and was undoubtedly one of the greatest spiritual teachers of his age, having thousands of mureeds all over India, Pakistan, Malaysia, South Africa, etc. He needs no introduction as an Aalim and Sheikh (spiritual guide) since he is following in the footsteps of the illustrious sons of Islam such as Shaikhul-Hind Moulana Mahmoodul-Hasan, Moulana Raipuri, Moulana Thanwi, Moulana Madani, Moulana Khalil Ahmad, Moulana 'Usmaani and Moulana Ilyaas *(rahmatullahi alaihim)* etc. His numerous works in Urdu and Arabic have benefitted millions and have spread far and wide as a result of the activities of the Tablighi Jamaats all over the world.

Because of the beneficial nature of this book, we felt that it should be translated into English. This humble effort is being placed before the English speaking public. May Allah Ta'ala accept this work and may it benefit us all. Our fervent dua is that Allah Ta'ala grants us the ability to serve Islam and the Muslims at all times, Ameen.

A humble appeal is made to all Jamaats going out in Tabligh and to the Imaams of Masjids to read this book or to arrange for it to be read to the congregation for about ten minutes daily, after the Maghrib or Esha Salaah, in the weeks preceding Ramadhaan, and also during the blessed month at a suitable time so that, Inshaa Allah, as many Muslims as possible may be inspired to observe Ramadhaan in the most fulfilling manner, Aameen.

Yusuf Karaan

INTRODUCTION

$$\text{بِسْمِ اللهِ الرَّحْمٰنِ الرَّحِيْمِ}$$

$$\text{نَحْمَدُهُ وَنُصَلِّيْ عَلٰى رَسُوْلِهِ الْكَرِيْمِ حَامِدًا وَمُصَلِّيًا وَمُسَلِّمًا}$$

All praise is due to Allah Ta'ala only and blessings be upon His chosen Rasul ﷺ.

In the following pages I have quoted a few Ahaadith with reference to the blessed month of Ramadhaan. Rasulullah ﷺ has advised us in these Ahaadith to change our lives by acquiring the great virtues and blessings of this month. True appreciation would be that we fully carry out these teachings. These days, our negligence has become so obvious that, we neither act upon his advice nor pay any heed to it, so much so that very few of us even know about the great good we can obtain from it.

My object in collecting these Ahaadith in this book is to assist the Imaams of the Masaajid, the Huffaaz and other learned Muslims who have the interest of our Deen at heart, to read out and explain this book in the Masjid before and also during the first few days of Ramadhaan, so that through the mercy and the blessings of Allah Ta'ala and His beloved Rasul ﷺ, we may pay due attention to it and receive the blessings Allah Ta'ala during this mubaarak month. This can lead us towards acting on His commandments and keeping us away from sins.

Rasulullah ﷺ has said, "Should Allah Ta'ala guide one person on the right path through you, it shall be better for you than a red camel (something that is pricey, and also considered a most precious possession)."

Ramadhaan is a very great favour for the Muslims. This favour can only be considered as such if we appreciate it, otherwise Ramadhaan will come and go without us gaining anything.

It is stated in the Hadith, "If my Ummah realize what Ramadhaan really is, they would wish that the whole year be Ramadhaan." Every person knows that fasting for a full year is a very difficult task, and only because of the great rewards for Ramadhaan mentioned by Rasulullah ﷺ, will they desire the full year to be Ramadhaan.

In another Hadith we are told, "The fasting of Ramadhaan and fasting three days of every month keeps evil away from the heart."

The Sahaabah (companions) of Rasulullah ﷺ used to fast even during jihaad and on tiresome journeys, in spite of getting permission from Rasulullah ﷺ not to fast. Finally, Rasulullah ﷺ had to instruct them not to fast. Imaam Muslim *(rahmatullahi alaih)* reports that once the Sahaabah رضي الله عنهم were on a journey for Jihaad. It was extremely hot and due to poverty, they did not even have a cloth for shade to protect themselves against the heat. In this condition, when they stopped at one place, many of them used their hands for shade from the sun. In this condition too, many of them were fasting. They were so overcome with weakness that they could not bear the excessive heat and fell down. Some Sahaabah رضي الله عنهم fasted throughout the year.

There are many Ahaadith in which the blessings of Ramadhaan are explained. It is not possible for me to collect them all here, and if I am to narrate and explain them all in detail, then the readers may find it too lengthy and difficult. However, now is the time to refresh our mind with them. After all, we do not have to explain how disinterested we have become in our Deen. It is self-evident. I have mentioned only twenty-one Ahaadith in this book and have divided them into three chapters.

a) **Chapter one**, on the **Virtues of Ramadhaan** (Ten Ahaadith)
b) **Chapter two**, on **Laylatul Qadr** (Seven Ahaadith)
c) **Chapter three**, on **Itikaaf** (Three Ahaadith)

In conclusion, at the end of this book, I have included one long Hadith. May Allah Ta'ala accept this work through His Grace and the blessings of His beloved Nabi Muhammad ﷺ and grant me and all the Muslims hidaayah to derive benefit from it. Most surely He encompasses all Good, is Generous and Most Kind. Aameen.

Chapter 1
The Virtues of Ramadhaan

Hadith 1 - The khutbah of Rasulullah ﷺ on the last day of Sha'baan

عَنْ سَلْمَانَ رَضِىَ اللهُ عَنْهُ قَالَ خَطَبَنَا رَسُوْلُ اللهِ صَلَّى اللهُ عَلَيْهِ وَسَلَّمَ فِىْ اٰخِرِ يَوْمٍ مِنْ شَعْبَانَ فَقَالَ يَا اَيُّهَا النَّاسُ قَدْ اَظَلَّكُمْ شَهْرٌ عَظِيْمٌ مُبَارَكٌ فِيْهِ لَيْلَةٌ خَيْرٌ مِّنْ اَلْفِ شَهْرٍ جَعَلَ اللهُ صِيَامَهٗ فَرِيْضَةً وَّقِيَامَ لَيْلِهٖ تَطَوُّعًا مَنْ تَقَرَّبَ فِيْهِ بِخَصْلَةٍ كَانَ كَمَنْ اَدّٰى فَرِيْضَةً فِيْمَا سِوَاهُ وَمَنْ اَدّٰى فَرِيْضَةً فِيْهِ كَانَ كَمَنْ اَدّٰى سَبْعِيْنَ فَرِيْضَةً فِيْمَا سِوَاهُ وَهُوَ شَهْرُ الصَّبْرِ وَالصَّبْرُ ثَوَابُهُ الْجَنَّةُ وَشَهْرُ الْمُوَاسَاةِ وَشَهْرٌ يُّزَادُ فِىْ رِزْقِ الْمُؤْمِنِ فِيْهِ مَنْ فَطَّرَ فِيْهِ صَائِمًا كَانَ مَغْفِرَةً لِّذُنُوْبِهٖ وَعِتْقَ رَقَبَتِهٖ مِنَ النَّارِ وَكَانَ لَهٗ مِثْلُ اَجْرِهٖ مِنْ غَيْرِ اَنْ يَّنْقُصَ مِنْ اَجْرِهٖ شَئٌ قَالُوْا يَا رَسُوْلَ اللهِ لَيْسَ كُلُّنَا نَجِدُ مَا يُفَطِّرُ الصَّائِمَ فَقَالَ رَسُوْلُ اللهِ صَلَّى اللهُ عَلَيْهِ وَسَلَّمَ يُعْطِىْ اللهُ هٰذَا الثَّوَابَ مَنْ فَطَّرَ صَائِمًا عَلٰى تَمْرَةٍ اَوْ شَرْبَةِ مَاءٍ اَوْ مَذْقَةِ لَبَنٍ وَهُوَ شَهْرٌ اَوَّلُهٗ رَحْمَةٌ وَّاَوْسَطُهٗ مَغْفِرَةٌ وَّاٰخِرُهٗ عِتْقٌ مِّنَ النَّارِ مَنْ خَفَّفَ عَنْ مَّمْلُوْكِهٖ فِيْهِ غَفَرَ اللهُ لَهٗ وَاَعْتَقَهٗ مِنَ النَّارِ وَاسْتَكْثِرُوْا فِيْهِ مِنْ اَرْبَعِ خِصَالٍ خَصْلَتَيْنِ تُرْضُوْنَ بِهِمَا رَبَّكُمْ وَخَصْلَتَيْنِ لَا غِنَاءَ بِكُمْ عَنْهُمَا فَاَمَّا الْخَصْلَتَانِ اللَّتَانِ

Ch. 1 - The Virtues of Ramadhaan

تُرْضُوْنَ بِهِمَا رَبَّكُمْ فَشَهَادَةُ اَنْ لَّا اِلٰهَ اِلَّا اللهُ وَتَسْتَغْفِرُوْنَهٗ وَاَمَّا الْخَصْلَتَانِ اللَّتَانِ لَا غِنَاءَ بِكُمْ عَنْهُمَا فَتَسْأَلُوْنَ اللهَ الْجَنَّةَ وَتَعَوَّذُوْنَ بِهٖ مِنَ النَّارِ وَمَنْ سَقٰى فِيْهِ صَائِمًا سَقَاهُ اللهُ مِنْ حَوْضِيْ شَرْبَةً لَا يَظْمَأُ حَتّٰى يَدْخُلَ الْجَنَّةَ (صحيح ابن خزيمة # 1887)

Hadhrat Salmaan ؓ says that on the last day of Sha'baan, Rasulullah ﷺ spoke to us and said: "O People, there comes to you now a great month, a most blessed month, in which there is a night greater in value and goodness than a thousand months. It is a month in which Allah Ta'ala has made fasting fardh during the day and has made Sunnah the Taraaweeh Salaah at night. Whosoever wants to be close to Allah Ta'ala by doing any good deed, for such a person there shall be the reward like the one who had performed a fardh in any other time and whoever performs a fardh, shall be given the reward of seventy faraaidh in any other time. This is indeed the month of patience and the reward for true patience is Jannah. It is the month of showing kindness to everyone. It is the month in which a true believer's rizq (food, money, etc.) are increased. Whosoever feeds a fasting person in order to break the fast at the time of iftaar, for him there shall be forgiveness of sins and freedom from the fire of Jahannam and he shall receive the same reward as the fasting person (whom he fed) without the fasting person losing any reward. Thereupon we said, 'O Messenger of Allah Ta'ala, not all of us can afford to give a fasting person something to break his fast with.' Rasulullah ﷺ replied, 'Allah Ta'ala gives the same reward to the one who gives a fasting person to break the fast, just one date or a drink of water or a sip of milk.'
This is a month, the first of which brings the mercy of Allah Ta'ala, the middle of which brings His forgiveness and the last of which brings freedom from the fire of Jahannam.
Whosoever lessons the work of his workers (who are also fasting in this month), Allah Ta'ala will forgive him and free him from the fire of Jahannam.
In this month four things you should perform in great number, two of which shall be to please Allah Ta'ala, while the other two shall be those which you cannot do without. Those which shall be to please

Allah Ta'ala, are that you should recite the Kalimah Tayyibah - Laailaaha illallah (i.e. To bear witness that there is no god except Allah Ta'ala) abundantly and to recite istighfaar (beg for the forgiveness of Allah Ta'ala by saying Astaghfirullah). And as for those which you cannot do without; you should beg of Allah Ta'ala for entrance into Jannah and ask protection in Him from Jahannam. And whoever gives a fasting person water to drink, Allah Ta'ala shall grant him to drink from my fountain, such a drink, after which that person shall never feel thirsty again until he enters Jannah."

Note: Muhaditheen have some reservations regarding some of the narrators of this Hadith. However, in aspects of Fazaail (Virtues), such reservations can be tolerated. Secondly, all the points in this Hadith have been explained in many other Ahaadith on the great rewards of Ramadhaan. Quite a number of important points are brought to our notice.

Rasulullah ﷺ gave this lecture at the end of Sha'baan, because he wanted to show us the great importance of Ramadhaan so that we do not allow one second of this month to go to waste. Thereafter our attention is drawn to Laylatul Qadr (this is discussed in detail in the section on Laylatul Qadr). Then attention is drawn to the fact that Fasting has been made fardh by Allah Ta'ala who has also made sunnah the Taraaweeh Salaah at night.

From this Hadith we learn that the command for Taraaweeh Salaah too comes from Allah Ta'ala Himself. Besides this, in all the Ahaadith where Rasulullah ﷺ says, "I have made it Sunnah," is to stress its importance. All the Ulama are agreed upon the fact that Taraaweeh is Sunnah. It is written in Burhaan that no one rejects this besides the Shias.

Moulana Shah Abdul Haq Muhaddith Dehlawi *(rahmatullahi alayh)* in his book, *'Maa Sabata bis Sunnah',* states that if the people of any town do not perform Taraaweeh Salaah, the Muslim ruler should make them do so by force.

Many people say that you may listen to the full Qur-aan being read in a certain Masjid in eight or ten nights and then stop performing Taraaweeh with jamaat as the Sunnah will have been fulfilled. This is wrong, because by doing this, only one Sunnah will be fulfilled and the other will be neglected. We should remember that there are two separate Sunnats. Firstly, it is Sunnah to hear the full Qur-aan being read in the

Taraaweeh in Ramadhaan. Secondly, it is Sunnah to perform Taraaweeh Salaah with jamaat for men in the Masjid for the entire Ramadhaan. Both the Sunnats should be fulfilled.

For those who are musaafir (travelling) and are unable to fulfil both the Sunnats, because of not knowing as to the different places they will be at during their travels, then for them it is advisable that they should complete the full Quraan Shareef in Taraaweeh in the first few days of Ramadhaan. Thereafter they should perform Taraaweeh wherever they find the opportunity. In this way the Qur-aan will be completed and their work will also not be hampered.

Nafal Ibaadaat

Another point we learn in the Hadith is that Rasulullah ﷺ told us that any nafl done in Ramadhaan is rewarded as much as a fardh in normal times and a fardh done in Ramadhaan has the reward of seventy faraaidh in other times.

Our Faults

Here we should ponder over our ibaadah. Is our ibaadah or worship in Ramadhaan important to us? How many nawaafil do we perform? As far as our fardh is concerned, how many people do we see who after having eaten sehri, go back to bed without performing the Fajr Salaah. Many people do perform fajr, but not with jamaat. How do we show our thanks to Allah Ta'ala for the food we had eaten for sehri by not performing the most important fardh or by not performing it with jamaat. Such a Salaah is (not complete and) considered as defective.

Rasulullah ﷺ said: "There is no Salaah for those near the Masjid except in the Masjid." In the kitaab *'Mazhaahir-e-Haq'* it is mention that there is no reward for a person who does not perform his Salaah with jamaat without any good reason or excuse.

Similarly, in many cases at the time of iftaar, Maghrib Salaah is missed and many do not come to the Masjid. From those people who come to the masjid, some miss the first takbeer or the first rakaat. Many people hurry to get over with the Taraaweeh Salaah and perform the Esha Salaah even before the time of Esha sets in. (Some people do not perform their Salaah at all, even in Ramadhaan).

This is the condition of our fardh Salaah in Ramadhaan. Whilst performing one fardh of fasting, three others are destroyed. How often do we see that the time of Zuhr Salaah passes by because we are asleep, while the time of Asr goes by because we are too busy buying, selling or cooking to prepare for iftaar.

If such is the case with the faraaidh, then we can imagine how much less importance is given to the nafl actions. One finds that because of sleep, the times of Salaatul Ishraaq (after sunrise) and Salaatud Dhuhaa (before noon) goes by. Then what about Salaatul Awwabeen (just after Maghrib)? Here we find ourselves busy with iftaar and when taking into account the Taraaweeh Salaah after Esha, this Salaah is also neglected. Further, we find that the time for Salaatut Tahajjud is the same as that for sehri, as a result, this too is neglected. One may make a thousand excuses for not finding time for these nawaafil. These are all excuses only for not performing these Salaah.

تو ہی اگر نہ چاہے تو باتیں ہزار ہیں

If you do not wish to do something then you will make up a thousand excuses for it

THE PRACTICE OF MOULANA KHALIL AHMAD SAHARANPURI (RA) DURING RAMADHAAN

We see that there are many who do find the time to engage themselves in ibaadah during these precious moments. I had personally observed my ustaad, Moulana Khalil Ahmad *(rahmatullahi alayh)*, during many a Ramadhaan. He was a weak sickly person and of advanced age but in spite of these difficulties he used to read one and a quarter juz of the Qur-aan in nafl Salaah after Maghrib. Thereafter he used to have meals for about half an hour. After performing all other necessities in preparation for Taraaweeh Salaah, he used to stand in Taraaweeh for about two and a half hours when he was in India, and when he was in Madinah Munawwarah the duration was three hours. Thereafter he used to sleep for about two or three hours (depending on the season). Then he used to again recite the Qur-aan in Tahajjud Saalah until about half an hour before Fajr. He then ate sehri. From sehri until Fajr he remained busy with reciting the Qur-aan or wazifas. With the greyness of dawn he performed Fajr Salaah and thereafter remained in meditation (muraaqabah) until Ishraaq. After having performed Ishraaq he used to write his famous kitaab, *'Bazlul Majhood'*, which is a commentary on Abu Dawood. He would then normally attend to letters and dictating replies up to midday. Then he would rest until Zuhr Salaah. Between Zuhr and Asr he used to recite the Qur-aan. From Asr Salaah until Maghrib he used to be busy with tasbeeh and answering the queries of those who visited him. When he completed *'Bazlul Majhood'*, then part of the morning used to be spent in tilaawah and studying some great Deeni kitaabs, especially *'Bazlul Majhood'* and *'Wafa al Wafa'*. This was his daily programme for nafl ibaadat throughout the year. However, in Ramadhaan he used to spend a bit more time in his ibaadah, making the rakaats in Salaah longer. For an ordinary person to carry out the daily routine that our pious elders had for Ramadhaan would be difficult.

The practice of Shaikhul Hind (RA) during Ramadhaan

Shaikhul Hind Moulana Mahmoodul Hasan *(rahmatullahi alayh)* used to remain in nafl Salaah from after Taraaweeh until Fajr, while also listening to the Qur-aan recited by various huffaaz one after the other.

Moulana Shah Abdurraheem Raipuri remained busy with tilaawah (recitation) of the Qur-aan day and night in Ramadhaan. There was no time for attending to correspondence or meeting visitors. Only his special persons were allowed to wait on him after Taraaweeh for a short period while he drank a cup of tea.

Advice

The reason for mentioning the manner in which these pious people spent their Ramadhaan is not that we may just read about it without deriving any benefit or pass a casual remark. Rather it is written with the object that we, in our own way, may build up courage and to the best of our ability try to copy and follow their noble examples. Every pious elder's program was unique. How wonderful would it be if those who are not occupied and are free (of duties), try their utmost to commit themselves more to ibaadah in this one month after having allowed eleven months of the year go by wasted.

As for those who have to report to their offices at eight, nine or ten in the morning; there should be no difficulty for them if they at least spend the time from Fajr until their office hours in reciting the Qur-aan in Ramadhaan. After all, for fulfilling all our necessities we do find time in spite of our office hours.

For those who are engaged in farming and are self-employed, nothing prevents them from reciting the Qur-aan on their farms or adjusting their daily routine. As far as the businessmen, shopkeepers and wholesalers are concerned, nothing prevents them from reciting the Qur-aan in Ramadhaan during their business hours or cutting short the trading time in order to make time for Tilaawah.

ALL DIVINE BOOKS WERE REVELAED IN RAMADHAAN

There is a very strong link between Ramadhaan and the Tilaawah of the Qur-aan. Many great divine books of Allah Ta'ala were revealed in this month. Similarly, in this month the Qur-aan Shareef was brought down from the *'Lowhul Mahfoozh'* (preserved tablet) to the *'samaaud dunyaa'* (Earthly sky), from where it was revealed in small passages and verses to Rasulullah ﷺ in a period of twenty-three years. Nabi Ibrahim *(alayhis salaam)* received his scriptures on the first and third of this sacred month. Nabi Dawood *(alayhis salaam)* received the Zaboor on the twelfth or eighteenth. Nabi Moosa *(alayhis salaam)* received the Towrah on the sixth. Nabi Essa *(alayhis salaam)* received the Injeel on the twelfth or thirteenth. From this we note the great connection between the divine books of Allah Ta'ala and the month of Ramadhaan. Therefore, as much tilaawah of the Qur-aan Shareef as possible should be made during this month. This was the habit of our Mashaaikh.

Jibra-eel *(alayhis salaam)* would recite the whole Qur-aan to our Nabi ﷺ in the month of Ramadhaan. In some reports it is stated that Rasulullah ﷺ would recite and Jibra-eel *(alayhis salaam)* used to listen. By combining these reports, the Ulama have deduced that it is Mustahab to read Qur-aan in such a manner that while one recites, the other listens. Thereafter, another recites while the other listens. So recite the Qur-aan as much as possible. Whatever time remains thereafter should be spent in Ibaadah.

Rasulullah ﷺ drew our attention to four things and advised us that we should practice on them as much as possible. They are: the recitation of Kalimah Tayyibah, Istighfaar, begging for Jannah and asking safety from Jahannam. Therefore, it will be ones good fortune to spend as much time as possible reciting these. This will be the true appreciation of the teachings of Rasulullah ﷺ. It is easy in keeping the tongue busy with the recitation of Durood Shareef or *'Laa Ilaaha illallaah'* while being engaged in our daily works?

میں گو رہا رہین ستمہائے روزگار   لیکن تمہاری یاد سے غافل نہیں رہا

"I never forget you, even though I face so many difficulties of life."

SOME SPECIALITIES OF THIS MONTH

In the same Hadith, Rasulullah ﷺ has mentioned a few specialties and etiquettes of this month. Firstly, Ramadhaan is the month of patience. So if great difficulty is experienced in fasting, one should bear it with patience. One should not complain as people are fond of doing during hot days. If by chance sehri is missed out, then too one should not complain. Similarly, should any difficulty or trial be experienced in Taraaweeh Salaah, one should bear it with happiness and not as a burden, otherwise these deeds may possibly be empty of barakah (blessings). When we have avoided the worldly pleasures and given up our eating and drinking, then, for the sake of the pleasure of Allah Ta'ala, then what are these difficulties?

KINDNESS FOR THE POOR & UNFORTUNATE

The Hadith also says that it is the month of sympathy and kindness, especially for the poor and needy. Sympathy should be of a practical nature. When ten things are placed before us for iftaar, at least two or four of them should be set aside for the poor and needy. Actually they should be treated more favourably, if not, then at least equally, and should certainly be given some food at least. The Sahaabah ﷺ were living examples in showing sympathy for the poor and therefore it is our duty to follow or at least try to follow them. As far as sacrifice and sympathy is concerned, only the brave people can follow the examples of the Sahaabah ﷺ. There are many examples which will leave one astonished.

By way of example one incident is narrated, Abu Jahm ﷺ relates that, during the battle of Yarmook, he went in search of his cousin, taking with him water in a water bag to give him to drink and also wash his wounds if he was found alive or wounded. He found him lying among the wounded. When I asked him whether he wanted some water, he replied 'Yes'. At that moment someone near him moaned. My cousin pointed to that person indicating that I should first give him the water. I went to him and found that he too needed water, but just as I was about to give him the water, a third person groaned near him. The second one pointed to this third person, indicating that I should give the third person to drink first. I went to the third person but before he could drink, I found out that he had passed away, I then returned to the second one only to find that he too had passed away. When I came back to my cousin, he too had become a shaheed.

This is the type of caring character the Sahaabah رضي الله عنهم had. They preferred to die thirsty rather than to drink before another Muslim brother. May Allah Ta'ala be pleased with them all and grant us the ability to follow in their footsteps. *Aameen*.

Roohul Bayaan quotes from Imaam Suyuti's *(rahmatullahi alayh) Jaami'us Sagheer* and Imam Sakhaawi's *Maqaasid* the narration of Hadhrat Ibn Umar رضي الله عنه that Nabi صلى الله عليه وسلم said, "At all times in my Ummah there will be 500 chosen servants and forty abdaal (pious ones, totally devoted to Allah Ta'ala). When anyone of them passes away then immediately he is succeeded by another." The Sahaabah رضي الله عنهم inquired, "What are their exclusive deeds?" Rasulullah صلى الله عليه وسلم replied, "They overlook the injustices of the sinners and show kindness to those who ill treat them, and from the rizq provided for them by Allah Ta'ala, they promote sympathy and graciousness (by spending on the creation of Allah Ta'ala)."

Another Hadith says that whoever feeds the hungry, clothes the unclothed and gives shelter to the traveler, Allah Ta'ala shall save him from the terrors of Qiyaamah.

Yahya Barmaki *(rahmatullahi alayh)* would give Imaam Sufyaan Sauri *(rahmatullahi alayh)* 1000 Dirhams every month, whereupon Imaam Sufyaan *(rahmatullahi alayh)* used to make sajdah before Allah Ta'ala making dua, "O Allah! Yahya has seen sufficiently to my worldly needs. You see, through Your Great Mercy, to his necessities in the Hereafter." After the death of Yahya some people saw him in their dreams and on inquiring what had happened to him in the hereafter, he replied: "Through the duas of Sufyaan I have been forgiven by Allah Ta'ala."

Further, Rasulullah ﷺ mentioned the virtue of feeding a fasting person at the time of breaking the fast. In one Hadith it is reported that one who feeds a person out of his Halaal earnings to break the fast, the Malaaikah grant mercy upon him during the nights of Ramadhaan and Jibra-eel *(alayhis salaam)* shakes his hands on Laylatul Qadr. The sign of this is that his heart becomes soft and tears flow from his eyes.

During Ramadhaan, Hammaad bin Salamah, a very famous Muhaddith, would feed fifty people every day at the time of iftaar.

THE THREE PARTS OF THIS MONTH

Thereafter, the Hadith of Rasulullah ﷺ called the first section (i.e. first ten days) of Ramadhaan the coming of mercy, which means that Allah's Ta'ala showers His mercy on all the believers. For those who are thankful to Allah Ta'ala for His bounties, they will receive even more. The Qur-aan Shareef says:

$$لَئِنْ شَكَرْتُمْ لَأَزِيْدَنَّكُمْ$$

"If you are grateful, I will surely grant you more."
(Surah Ibraaheem - Aayah 7)

During the second section (i.e. the second ten days) of Ramadhaan, forgiveness begins to come down as a reward for fasting during the first section. The last section (i.e. the last ten days) of Ramadhaan brings protection from entrance into Jahannam. This is supported by many similar Ahaadith.

In my personal opinion, Ramadhaan has been divided into three sections because people are normally of three different types. Firstly, there are those who have no sins. They receive Allah Ta'ala's Mercy and Bounties from the very beginning of Ramadhaan. Secondly, there are those whose sins are not too much. They receive forgiveness after one third of Ramadhaan has passed. Thirdly, there are the real sinners. They receive forgiveness after having fasted most of Ramadhaan. Those who received Allah Ta'ala's mercy right at the beginning are the most fortunate ones because of the great amount of mercy they have received. (And Allah Ta'ala knows best).

KINDNESS TO ONES WORKERS

Another point mentioned in the Ahaadith is that employers should be merciful to their workers (employees) in Ramadhaan because, after all, they are also fasting. Unnecessary hard work or too much of it will be difficult for them. An extra worker should be hired when the work is too much. That of course, only applies when the employee himself is fasting; otherwise there is no difference for them between Ramadhaan and any other month.

Words cannot describe the position of the shameless and oppressive employer who himself does not fast and unnecessarily burdens his employees with extra work, and if there is any delay caused by the employee due to Salaah or fasting, then he is outraged. Regarding such persons the Qur-aan states;

وَسَيَعْلَمُ الَّذِيْنَ ظَلَمُوْٓا اَىَّ مُنْقَلَبٍ يَنْقَلِبُوْنَ

"And soon the oppressor will come to know where his abode is. (In Jahannam)" (Surah Shua'raa - Aayah 227)

Lastly, Rasulullah ﷺ encouraged four things in the Hadith that should be repeated constantly. Firstly, the recitation of Kalimah Tayyibah, which in the Ahaadith is called the highest form of zikr. In *'Mishkaat'*, Abu Saeed Khudri ؓ reports: "Once Nabi Moosa *(alayhis salaam)* begged Allah Ta'ala to grant him a special zikr by which he can remember Allah Ta'ala and also (by which he could) ask from Him in dua. Allah Ta'ala told him to recite the Kalimah Tayyibah. Sayyidina Moosa *(alayhis salaam)* said, 'O Allah! This is a zikr recited by all your servants, I wish for a special zikr.' Allah Ta'ala replied, 'O Moosa, if the seven heavens, the earth and all its occupants including the Malaaikah but excluding Myself (i.e. excluding Allah Ta'ala Himself) are placed on one side of a scale and this Kalimah on the other side, then this Kalimah will weigh heavier than everything else."

In another Hadith it is stated, "Should anyone sincerely recite this Kalimah, the doors of Jannah open up immediately for him and nothing can stop him from reaching Allah Ta'ala's arsh (throne)." The only condition is that the reciter should stay away from major sins.

Allah Ta'ala's system is that He grants our basic needs in abundance. We see all over the world that whatever is generally required is found in abundance. For example, water, which is a basic necessity, has been made common by Allah Ta'ala in His infinite mercy, and how uncommon He has made the useless art of alchemy. The Kalimah Tayyibah is the most excellent form of zikr. Allah Ta'ala has made it common for everybody, so that no one is deprived of it. Therefore, if any person is deprived of it, it is his own fault. There are many Ahaadith showing its rewards which I have left out for the sake of brevity.

The second thing which should be recited plentifully is istighfaar. The Ahaadith report many rewards of istighfaar. In one Hadith we read, "Whoever makes abundant Istighfaar, Allah Ta'ala opens a way out for him from all problems and removes all sadness from him. He also receives rizq (food, money, etc.) from unexpected places." In another Hadith, Rasulullah ﷺ said, "Every man is a sinner, but the best among the sinners are those who make taubah and ask for forgiveness." In one Hadith it is mentioned, "When a man commits a sin, a black spot forms on his heart, but when he asks for forgiveness, it is washed away, if not, then the black spot remains."

Thereafter, Rasulullah ﷺ commanded us to beg two things which we cannot do without. Firstly to beg Allah Ta'ala for entrance into Jannah and secondly to ask for protection in Him from Jahannam. May Allah Ta'ala grant us this good fortune. (Aameen)

HADITH 2 - FIVE SPECIAL THINGS GIVEN TO THE UMMAH OF RASULULLAH ﷺ

عَنْ اَبِيْ هُرَيْرَةَ رَضِيَ اللهُ عَنْهُ قَالَ قَالَ رَسُوْلُ اللهِ صَلَّى اللهُ عَلَيْهِ وَسَلَّمَ اُعْطِيَتْ اُمَّتِيْ خَمْسَ خِصَالٍ فِيْ رَمَضَانَ لَمْ تُعْطَهُنَّ اُمَّةٌ قَبْلَهُمْ خُلُوْفُ فَمِ الصَّائِمِ اَطْيَبُ عِنْدَ اللهِ مِنْ رِيْحِ الْمِسْكِ وَتَسْتَغْفِرُ لَهُمُ الْحِيْتَانُ حَتَّى يُفْطِرُوْا وَيُزَيِّنُ اللهُ عَزَّ وَجَلَّ كُلَّ يَوْمٍ جَنَّتَهُ ثُمَّ يَقُوْلُ يُوْشِكُ عِبَادِيَ الصَّالِحُوْنَ اَنْ يُلْقُوْا عَنْهُمُ الْمَؤُنَةَ وَيَصِيْرُوْا اِلَيْكَ وَتُصَفَّدُ فِيْهِ مَرَدَةُ الشَّيَاطِيْنِ فَلَا يَخْلُصُوْا فِيْهِ اِلٰى مَا كَانُوْا يَخْلُصُوْنَ اِلَيْهِ فِيْ غَيْرِهِ وَيُغْفَرُ لَهُمْ فِيْ آخِرِ لَيْلَةٍ قِيْلَ يَا رَسُوْلَ اللهِ صَلَّى اللهُ عَلَيْهِ وَسَلَّمَ اَهِيَ لَيْلَةُ الْقَدْرِ قَالَ لَا وَلٰكِنِ الْعَامِلُ اِنَّمَا يُوَفّٰى اَجْرُهُ اِذَا قَضٰى عَمَلَهُ (اخرجه المنذري فى الترغيب # 1476)

Hadhrat Abu Hurairah ﷺ says that Rasulullah ﷺ said, "My Ummah has been given five special things in Ramadhaan that were not given to anyone before them. The smell from the mouth of a fasting person is sweeter to Allah Ta'ala than the sweet smell of musk. The fish in the sea continue asking for forgiveness for them until they break their fast. Allah Ta'ala prepares and decorates Jannah every day for them and then says: 'The time is near when My pious servants shall throw away the trials (of the world) and come to you.' The evil shayaateen are chained up in the month of Ramadhaan so as not to take people towards evils which they normally do during other months. On the last night of Ramadhaan, the fasting Muslims are forgiven."

The Sahaabah ﷺ then asked, "O Rasulullah ﷺ, is that the night of Laylatul Qadr?" Rasulullah ﷺ replied, "No, but it is only right that a servant should be given his reward on having completed his duty."

Note: Rasulullah ﷺ has mentioned in this Hadith five gifts from Allah Ta'ala which were not granted to the (fasting) people before Islam. If only we could truly appreciate how great this gift from Allah Ta'ala really is, we will sincerely try to get these special favours.

THE FRAGRANCE OF THE MOUTH

First, we are told that the smell from the mouth of the fasting person is more pleasing to Allah Ta'ala than the smell of musk. The commentators of Hadith have mentioned eight opinions in this regard which I have explained in detail in the commentary of 'Muatta' but according to this humble soul there are three most acceptable explanations in this regard:

Some say that, in the Aakhirah (Hereafter), Allah Ta'ala shall reward that smell from the mouth with a pleasant smell which is sweeter and more refreshing than musk. This opinion is quite clear and is supported by another narration in Durre Mansoor.

The second opinion is that on the day of Qiyaamah when we shall rise from our graves, a sweet smell shall come from the mouths of those who fasted and that shall be better than musk.

The third opinion which is most acceptable to me, is the opinion that in this very world the smell is more pleasing to Allah Ta'ala than musk. This shows the love between Allah Ta'ala and His fasting slaves.

We all know that even a bad smell from a person whom one loves truly and sincerely, is in itself attractive to the lover, who in this case is Allah Ta'ala Himself. What is being shown here is how close to Allah Ta'ala a fasting person is.

اے حافظ مسکین چہ کنی مشکِ ختن را   از گیسوئے احمد بستان عطر عدن را

O Poor Hafiz, what will you do with the musk of khutan
Enjoy the fragrance of Jannah from the tresses of Ahmad ﷺ

Fasting is one of the most pleasing forms of ibaadah in the sight of Allah Ta'ala and for this reason a Hadith states that for every deed the reward is brought by the Malaaikah, but Allah Ta'ala says, "The reward for fasting, I Myself will give, because it is for Me alone." Another report of the same Hadith (when read in a different way) says; "I Myself become his reward." What greater reward can there be for the lover than to meet the Beloved?

In another Hadith we read, "Fasting is the door to all other forms of ibaadah of Allah Ta'ala." This means that the heart becomes illuminated and a person is able to perform other forms of ibaadah through fasting. This is only the case if the fast is kept properly (as shall be explained later), and is not merely remaining hungry and thirsty.

USING THE MISWAAK WHILST FASTING

At this juncture I wish to draw attention to one point. Because of this Hadith some Imaams (especially Imaam Shafi'ee) prohibited cleansing of the teeth with miswaak in the afternoon, whereas the Hanafis consider it to be mustahab at all times. The Imaam's reason is that, through miswaak, the smell from the teeth is removed. The odour referred to here is the smell resulting from the stomach being empty, having nothing to do with miswaak.

FISH SEEKING FORGIVENESS ON OUR BEHALF

The second special favour is that the fish in the sea ask for forgiveness for the person who fasts. The purpose here is to explain that many living things make dua for him. This has been already explained in many other

Ahaadith. In some narrations it is mentioned that the Malaaikah make dua for his forgiveness. My uncle, Moulana Muhammad Ilyaas Saahib *(rahmatullahi alayh),* used to say that this is so because Allah Ta'ala says in the Qur-aan Shareef,

$$إِنَّ الَّذِيْنَ اٰمَنُوْا وَعَمِلُوا الصّٰلِحٰتِ سَيَجْعَلُ لَهُمُ الرَّحْمٰنُ وُدًّا$$

"Certainly those who believe and do righteous deeds, Allah Ta'ala shall make them beloved (in this world)" (Surah Maryam – Aayah 96)

One Hadith explains this further, "When Allah Ta'ala loves a person, He says to the angel Jibra-eel *(alayhis salaam),* 'I love that person, so you also love him.' Jibra-eel *(alayhis salaam)* then also loves that person and announces in the first heaven that, 'That person is loved by Allah Ta'ala, you all should also love him.' Then all the creations of the heavens begin to love him. Then, love for that person spreads all over the earth." Normally only those who are near to a person seem to love him, but here that love spreads all over, even the animals in the jungle and the fish in the sea do the same. They all then make dua on his behalf.

JANNAH IS DECORATED

The third favour given to the fasting persons is that Jannah is decorated for them. The Hadith states that at the beginning of every year, Jannah begins to be decorated for Ramadhaan. We know that when an important person is expected to arrive, great care is taken in the preparations for his welcome. For example, in a marriage, preparations start months in advance, likewise it should be the same with Ramadhaan.

SHAYTAANS ARE CHAINED UP

The fourth favour is that evil shayaateen are chained, as a result of which evil becomes much less. One would have expected that, because of the great desire for Ibaadah of Allah Ta'ala in the blessed month of Ramadhaan, the shayaateen would try just as hard to mislead the faithful away from the right path, so that much more evil would be committed. That is not the case. Instead we see so much less evil. How many drunkards we see that just because of the blessed month of Ramadhaan, do not drink alcohol. How many other sinners we see giving up evil acts during the mubaarak month of Ramadhaan.

Committing sins during the month of Ramadhaan does not contradict the meaning of the Hadith, because the Hadith mentions only the rebellious shayaateen. Therefore, sin could be committed due to the influence of the non-rebellious shayaateen. In some Ahaadith the chaining of the shayaateen is general, but this could be explained by those Ahaadith in which the rebellious shayaateen is mentioned.

You may wonder that, when the shayaateen are chained, how is it possible that we still see sins being committed, even though in lesser amounts? The reply to this is that all evil may not necessarily be caused by the evil shayaateen. A person who had lived for eleven months in obedience to the wishes of the shayaateen and, as a result, the doing of evil actions became a habit; therefore, evil is committed by him both in Ramadhaan and also out of Ramadhaan. For this reason, we find that those who normally commit sins, continue to do some of it in Ramadhaan. Thus, even though the shayaateen have been chained, their effect on us has become so strong that we follow their ways from our own side even in Ramadhaan.

Another important point is that Nabi ﷺ has said, "When a person commits a sin, a black spot forms on his heart, but when he sincerely makes *taubah* (repents), it is removed, otherwise it remains. When he again commits a sin another spot forms (and so on), until his heart becomes completely black. Then nothing good can enter his heart." Referring to this, Allah Ta'ala says in the Qur-aan Shareef,

كَلَّا بَلْ ۜ رَانَ عَلَىٰ قُلُوبِهِم مَّا كَانُوا يَكْسِبُونَ

"Never! But on their heart is the stain (of evil)."
(Surah Muthaffifeen – Aayah 14)

When their hearts become totally stained, then these hearts are obviously attracted towards sins. This is the reason why many people commit one type of sin without any fear, but when thinking of another similar sin, then their hearts stop them from committing it.

For example, if those people who drink wine are told to eat pork, they would hate it, whereas these two evils are equally sinful. Similarly, the heart is stained by committing these sins out of Ramadhaan, thus resulting in these sins being done even without any action of the shayaateen in Ramadhaan. If we take the meaning of the Hadith to mean that all the shayaateen are locked up in Ramadhaan, then too we are aware as to why a person commits sins in Ramadhaan. If it means that it is only the evil shayaateen that are locked up, then it is obvious as to why sins are committed.

My personal opinion is that not all the shayaateen are chained, but only the most evil ones. All of us can see that in Ramadhaan, it does not require a great amount of effort and energy to perform a good act. It also does not need a great amount of self-control and effort to avoid sin, as in other times. Shah Muhammad Ishaaq *(rahmatullahi alayh)* was of the opinion that for the evil people, only the most evil shayaateen are chained, whereas for the pious people, all the shayaateen are chained.

THOSE WHO FAST ARE FORGIVEN

The fifth favour is that forgiveness is granted on the last night of Ramadhaan (See previous Hadith). Because of this great favour, the Sahaabah ﷺ thought that this night was Laylatul Qadr. They knew the great blessings of that night and therefore asked whether it was Laylatul Qadr. The reply was that it was not. This is just a favour granted for having fasted till the end of Ramadhaan.

HADITH 3 – THE CURSE OF JIBRA-EEL (ALAYHIS SALAAM) AND THE AAMEEN OF RASULULLAH ﷺ

عَنْ كَعْبِ بْنِ عُجْرَةَ رَضِيَ اللهُ عَنْهُ قَالَ قَالَ رَسُوْلُ اللهِ صَلَّى اللهُ عَلَيْهِ وَسَلَّمَ أُحْضُرُوا الْمِنْبَرَ فَحَضَرْنَا فَلَمَّا ارْتَقَى دَرَجَةً قَالَ آمِيْنَ فَلَمَّا ارْتَقَى الدَّرَجَةَ الثَّانِيَةَ قَالَ آمِيْنَ فَلَمَّا ارْتَقَى الدَّرَجَةَ الثَّالِثَةَ قَالَ آمِيْنَ فَلَمَّا نَزَلَ قُلْنَا يَا رَسُوْلَ اللهِ لَقَدْ سَمِعْنَا مِنْكَ الْيَوْمَ شَيْئًا مَا كُنَّا نَسْمَعُهُ قَالَ إِنَّ جِبْرَيِيْلَ عَلَيْهِ الصَّلَاةُ وَالسَّلَامُ عَرَضَ لِيْ فَقَالَ بَعُدَ مَنْ أَدْرَكَ رَمَضَانَ فَلَمْ يُغْفَرْ لَهُ قُلْتُ آمِيْنَ فَلَمَّا رَقِيْتُ الثَّانِيَةَ قَالَ بَعُدَ مَنْ ذُكِرْتَ عِنْدَهُ فَلَمْ يُصَلِّ عَلَيْكَ قُلْتُ آمِيْنَ فَلَمَّا رَقِيْتُ الثَّالِثَةَ قَالَ بَعُدَ مَنْ أَدْرَكَ أَبَوَيْهِ الْكِبَرَ عِنْدَهُ أَوْ أَحَدَهُمَا فَلَمْ يُدْخِلَاهُ الْجَنَّةَ قُلْتُ آمِيْنَ (المستدرك للحاكم # 7256)

Hadhrat Ka'b Ibn Ujrah ﷺ says that Rasulullah ﷺ said, "Come close to the mimbar." We came close to the mimbar. When He climbed the first step of the mimbar, He said "Aameen". When He climbed the second step, He said "Aameen". When He climbed the third step, He said "Aameen". When He came down, we said "O Rasul of Allah ﷺ, today we have heard from you something which we had never heard before." Rasulullah ﷺ said, "When I climbed the first step, Jibra-eel *(alayhis salaam)* appeared before me and said, "Destruction to the person who found the blessed month of Ramadhaan and let it pass by without gaining his forgiveness," I said "Aameen." When I climbed the second step, he said, "Destruction to the person before whom your (i.e. Nabi's ﷺ) name is taken and he does not send Durood and Salaam on you (for example by saying, Sallallahu alayhi wasallam)." I replied "Aameen." When I climbed the third step, he said, "Destruction on that person in whose lifetime both his parents or either one of them reaches old age, and (because of not serving them) he is not allowed to enter Jannah." I said "Aameen."

Note: In this Hadith, Jibra-eel *(alayhis salaam)* made three curses, upon which Rasulullah ﷺ said "Aameen" each time. In '*al Durrul Mansoor*', it is said that Jibra-eel *(alayhis salaam)* asked Rasulullah ﷺ to say 'Aameen'. The curses of Jibra-eel *(alayhis salaam)*, an angel of such high position, are sure to be accepted. May Allah Ta'ala, in His mercy, grant us His help and save us from these three curses.

The first person described above is he who, even in the blessed month of Ramadhaan, spends his days in sin and does not worry about his duties, as a result of which he does not receive forgiveness. Ramadhaan is the month of Allah Ta'ala's mercy and if even this month is spent carelessly, how can he expect to be forgiven for his sins? If he cannot gain Allah Ta'ala's forgiveness in Ramadhaan, then when will he do so? The way to seek Allah Ta'ala's forgiveness for his sins is to complete his duties in Ramadhaan as ordered by Allah Ta'ala, such as fasting, reading Taraaweeh Salaah and making abundant taubah and istighfaar.

The second unfortunate person is he who hears the name of Rasulullah ﷺ and does not send Durood and Salaam on him. For this reason, some Ulama consider it compulsory to recite Durood whenever the name of Muhammad ﷺ is mentioned. In some Ahaadith, the person who fails to do so is called unfortunate and stingy.

Such people are described as those who are disloyal and of those who would lose the way to Jannah, or even among those who will enter Jahannam or those who will not be allowed to look at the blessed face of Rasulullah ﷺ. The Ulama give us many meanings to these Ahaadith. But who can deny that not sending Durood and Salaam on Nabi ﷺ is indeed very severe.

Why should it not be? After all, the favours on us by Rasulullah ﷺ cannot be described neither our writings nor our lectures. His favours on us are very very great. Therefore, any warning for the neglect of sending Durood and Salaam on Nabi ﷺ is acceptable.

On the other hand, the reward for reciting Durood is very great. The Hadith teaches us that whosoever recites Durood once, Allah Ta'ala sends ten blessings on him and the Malaaikah make dua for him. All his sins are forgiven, his position is raised and his reward will be as big as mount Uhud, and on the day of Qiyaamah, the Shafaa'at of Rasulullah ﷺ (asking Allah Ta'ala to forgive him) will become waajib.

More promises of reward are: Obtaining Allah Ta'ala's happiness, mercy and safety against His anger, safety from the fears of Qiyaamah, seeing your abode in Jannah while still alive on this earth. There are many virtues promised for reading Durood shareef in specific numbers. Besides these, there is the promise of never being worried about poverty and of enjoying nearness to Rasulullah ﷺ, the promise of help against our enemies, cleansing the heart from rust and hypocrisy, and the promise of being loved by others. There are many other Ahaadith that explain the virtues of reciting Durood Shareef abundantly.

The Fuqaha have explained that it is compulsory to recite Durood at least once in a lifetime and all the Ulama are agreed upon this fact. However, some Ulama say that Durood Shareef must be recited whenever the name of Rasulullah ﷺ is mentioned while others say it is preferable.

The third person described in the Hadith above is he in whose lifetime either one or both of his parents reach old age, and he is deprived of Jannah by not serving them. The Ulama have stated that in every permissible act, it is compulsory to obey your parent's commands. You should not be disrespectful to them, but rather be humble towards them, even though they may be non-muslims. You must neither raise your voice above theirs, nor call them by their names. They should be given the preference to do anything before you, (viz. eating, walking, sitting, etc.). When they have to be called towards good and stopped from evil, it should be done gently and you should continue to make dua for them even if they refuse to accept. In short, at all times they should be honored and respected and dua for their guidance should be made.

In a Hadith it is also related that the best of doors for entering Jannah is the father. If you wish, look after it and if you wish, destroy it. A Sahaabi رَضِىَ اللهُ عَنْهُ asked Rasulullah صَلَّى اللهُ عَلَيْهِ وَسَلَّمَ, "What are the rights due to parents?" He replied, "They are your Jannah or your Jahannam!" i.e. if they are happy, it leads you to Jannah while their unhappiness leads you to Jahannam. It is stated in a Hadith that when an obedient son looks with love and affection at his parents, the reward for that look shall be an accepted Hajj. In another Hadith, it is stated that Allah Ta'ala forgives all sins as He pleases except the sin of shirk (i.e. joining partners with Allah Ta'ala). However, He punishes a person for being disobedient to his parents, right in this world before death.

A Sahaabi رَضِىَ اللهُ عَنْهُ said, "O Rasul of Allah صَلَّى اللهُ عَلَيْهِ وَسَلَّمَ, I want to go for Jihaad." Rasulullah صَلَّى اللهُ عَلَيْهِ وَسَلَّمَ asked, "Is your mother alive?" "Yes," he replied. Rasulullah صَلَّى اللهُ عَلَيْهِ وَسَلَّمَ then said, "Serve her, Jannah lies under her feet." Again, another Hadith says, "The pleasure of Allah Ta'ala is in pleasing your father, and Allah Ta'ala's displeasure is in displeasing your father." Many other Ahaadith explain their great rights and virtues

However, if one's parents were not respected and treated properly during their lifetime and have now passed away, according to the shariat, there is still something that their children can do. The Hadith teaches us that, in such cases, one should always make abundant dua for their forgiveness. By doing so, you will be counted among those who are obedient. Another Hadith says that the best action a person can do after the death of his father is to treat his friends in a friendly manner (just as the father would have done).

HADITH 4 – SHOW ALLAH TA'ALA YOUR GOOD DEEDS IN RAMADHAAN

وَعَنْ عُبَادَةَ بْنِ الصَّامِتِ رَضِيَ اللهُ عَنْهُ أَنَّ رَسُولَ اللهِ صَلَّى اللهُ عَلَيْهِ وَسَلَّمَ قَالَ يَوْمًا وَحَضَرَنَا رَمَضَانُ أَتَاكُمْ رَمَضَانُ شَهْرُ بَرَكَةٍ يَغْشَاكُمُ اللهُ فِيهِ فَيُنْزِلُ الرَّحْمَةَ وَيَحُطُّ

$$\text{الْخَطَايَا وَيَسْتَجِيْبُ فِيْهِ الدُّعَاءَ يَنْظُرُ اللهُ تَعَالٰى اِلٰى تَنَافُسِكُمْ فِيْهِ وَيُبَاهِيْ بِكُمْ}$$

$$\text{مَلَائِكَتَهُ فَأَرُوا اللهَ مِنْ اَنْفُسِكُمْ خَيْرًا فَاِنَّ الشَّقِيَّ مَنْ حُرِمَ فِيْهِ رَحْمَةَ اللهِ عَزَّ وَجَلَّ}$$

(اخرجه المنذري في الترغيب # 1490)

Hadhrat Ubaadah bin Saamit ﷺ reports that, one day when Ramadhaan had come near, Rasulullah ﷺ said: "Ramadhaan, the month of blessings has come upon you, wherein Allah Ta'ala turns towards you and sends to you His special blessings, forgives your faults, accepts your duas, appreciates your competing for the greatest good and boasts to the Malaaikah about you. So, show to Allah Ta'ala your good deeds; for truly, the most pitiful and unfortunate one is he who is deprived of Allah Ta'ala's mercy in this month."

Note: In this Hadith, we read about the spirit of competition among the believers, each one trying to do more good deeds than the other. In our home, I am greatly pleased to see how the women compete with each other, each one trying to recite more Qur-aan than the other, so that together with housework, each one reads half to two thirds of the Qur-aan daily. I mention this only out of a sense of gratitude to Allah Ta'ala, indicating His favour and not to boast of it. May Allah Ta'ala accept their and our actions, and increase our ability to do good actions.

HADITH 5 – FREEDOM FROM JAHANNAM AND ACCEPTANCE OF DUA

$$\text{عَنْ اَبِيْ سَعِيْدٍ الْخُدْرِيِّ رَضِيَ اللهُ عَنْهُ قَالَ قَالَ رَسُوْلُ اللهِ صَلَّى اللهُ عَلَيْهِ وَسَلَّمَ اِنَّ لِلّٰهِ}$$

$$\text{تَبَارَكَ وَتَعَالٰى عُتَقَاءَ فِيْ كُلِّ يَوْمٍ وَلَيْلَةٍ يَعْنِيْ فِيْ رَمَضَانَ وَاِنَّ لِكُلِّ مُسْلِمٍ فِيْ كُلِّ يَوْمٍ}$$

$$\text{وَلَيْلَةٍ دَعْوَةٌ مُسْتَجَابَةٌ}$$ (اخرجه المنذري في الترغيب # 1002)

Hadhrat Abu Saeed Al-Khudree ﷺ relates that Rasulullah ﷺ said: "During each day and night of Ramadhaan, Allah Ta'ala sets free many people from Jahannam, and during each day and night, at least one dua for every Muslim is certainly accepted."

Note: Besides this Hadith, there are many others Ahaadith that the dua of a fasting person is accepted (mustajaab). In one Hadith, we read that the dua is accepted at the time of breaking the fast, but we are generally so busy with our iftaar, that we miss this opportunity of making dua. Sometimes even the dua for breaking the fast is also often forgotten. The famous dua at the time of iftaar is:

$$\text{اَللّٰهُمَّ لَكَ صُمْتُ وَبِكَ اٰمَنْتُ وَعَلَيْكَ تَوَكَّلْتُ وَعَلٰى رِزْقِكَ اَفْطَرْتُ}$$

"Allaahumma laka sumto wa bika aamantu wa alayka tawakkaltu wa alaa rizqika aftar tu"

"O Allah for You have I fasted, in You do I believe, and on You do I rely, and now I break this fast with food coming from You."

Hadhrat Abdullah Ibn Amr ؓ used to make the following dua when breaking the fast:

$$\text{اَللّٰهُمَّ اِنِّیْ اَسْئَلُكَ بِرَحْمَتِكَ الَّتِیْ وَسِعَتْ كُلَّ شَیْءٍ اَنْ تَغْفِرَ لِیْ}$$

"Allaa-humma innee as'aluka bi-rahmatikallatee wasi at kulla shay in an taghfira lee"

"O Allah, I beg You, through Your infinite mercy, which surrounds all things, to forgive me."

In some books we read that Rasulullah ﷺ used to say:

$$\text{یَا وَاسِعَ الْفَضْلِ اِغْفِرْ لِیْ}$$

"Yaa waasi al-fadli-igh-fir lee"
"O most bountiful, forgive me."

There are many other duas for breaking the fast, but no special dua is fixed. The time when breaking the fast is a time when duas are accepted. So ask Allah Ta'ala and put all your needs before Him, and if you remember, then make dua for me also.

چشمہ فیض سے گر ایک اشارہ ہو جائے

لطف ہو آپ کا اور کام ہمارا ہو جائے

If I enjoy even one glance of your mercy, it will be your grace and my work will be done.

HADITH 6 - THREE PEOPLE WHOSE DUA IS SURELY ACCEPTED

عَنْ أَبِيْ هُرَيْرَةَ رَضِيَ اللهُ عَنْهُ قَالَ قَالَ رَسُوْلُ اللهِ صَلَّى اللهُ عَلَيْهِ وَسَلَّمَ ثَلَاثَةٌ لَا تُرَدُّ دَعَوَاتُهُمْ اَلصَّائِمُ حَتَّى يُفْطِرَ وَالْإِمَامُ الْعَادِلُ وَدَعْوَةُ الْمَظْلُوْمِ يَرْفَعُهَا اللهُ فَوْقَ الْغَمَامِ وَيُفْتَحُ لَهَا أَبْوَابُ السَّمَاءِ وَيَقُوْلُ الرَّبُّ وَعِزَّتِيْ لَأَنْصُرَنَّكَ وَلَوْ بَعْدَ حِيْنٍ

(سنن الترمذى # 3598)

Hadhrat Abu Hurairah رَضِيَ اللهُ عَنْهُ reports that Rasulullah ﷺ said: "There are three people whose dua is not rejected: the fasting person until he breaks his fast, the just ruler and the oppressed person, whose dua Allah Ta'ala lifts above the clouds and opens to it the doors of the skies and Allah Ta'ala says, 'I swear by my honor, verily, I shall assist you, even though it may be after some time.'"

Note: In Durre Manssor it is reported from Hadhrat Aa'ishah رَضِيَ اللهُ عَنْهَا that, when Ramadhaan came, the colour of Rasulullah's ﷺ face used to change. He then used to increase his Salaah, become even more humble in his dua and be more fearful of Allah Ta'ala.

According to another report, he hardly ever lay down in bed until Ramadhaan came to an end. It is stated in a Hadith that the Malaaikah carrying Allah Ta'ala's throne are commanded in Ramadhaan to leave everything else and say 'Aameen' to the duas of those who fast. There are many Ahaadith stating that duas in Ramadhaan in particular are answered. When Allah Ta'ala has given us His promise and His truthful Nabi ﷺ has informed us about it, then there should be no doubt whatsoever about the truth of these promises. Yet it is strange that, in spite of these promises, we still find people who do not get what they ask for when making dua. This does not mean that their dua has been rejected. We should understand what is meant by a dua being answered.

Rasulullah ﷺ has told us that when a Muslim makes dua for anything from Allah Ta'ala, as long as he does not make dua for breaking off relationship from his near relatives or for anything sinful, then he definitely receives one of the following three things:

1. He gets the exact thing which he asked for. If he does not receive this, then;

2. Allah Ta'ala either removes from him some great difficulty or problem in exchange for what he had asked for,
3. Or the reward for that thing which he made dua for is stored for him in the Aakhirah (Hereafter).

Another Hadith it is mentioned that on the day of Qiyaamah, Allah Ta'ala will call his slave and say to him: "O My slave, I used to command you to ask of Me and promised to answer. Did you beg of Me?" The slave will answer: "Yes I did." Then Allah Ta'ala shall reply: "You did not make any dua which has not been accepted. You made dua that a certain problem should be removed, which I did for you in the worldly life. You made dua that a certain sorrow and grief should be removed from you, but the result of that dua was not known to you in the world. For that dua I have fixed for you such and such reward (in the Aakhirah)." Rasulullah ﷺ says that the man shall again be reminded of each and every dua and he shall be shown how it had been answered in the world or else what reward had been stored for him in the Aakhirah (Hereafter). On seeing that reward in the Aakhirah (Hereafter), he shall wish that not a single dua of his should have been answered in the world, so that he could receive the full rewards only in the Aakhirah (Hereafter).

Yes, dua is indeed very important and to leave it out at any time is indeed a great loss. Hope should not be lost, even when it seems that our dua is not accepted. From the long Hadith at the end of this book, it is clear that, in accepting duas, Allah Ta'ala first considers our own good and welfare. Should Allah Ta'ala find that giving us what we ask from Him is for our own good, then He gives it to us, otherwise holds it back. Actually, it is Allah Ta'ala's favour on us that we do not always get what we ask for, because, very often, due to our lack of understanding, we beg for things that are not good for us at a certain time.

Here, another important point needs to be made; many men and especially women have a bad habit of cursing their children in their anger. We should be aware of this, because there are certain times when Allah Ta'ala immediately accepts whatever dua is made. Therefore, due to our own stupidity, the child is cursed and when the effect of that same curse comes upon the child and lands him into difficulties, the parents then go about crying and complaining, not even realizing that this is the result of their own curse. Rasulullah ﷺ commanded us not to curse ourselves, our children, things that we own, or our servants. It is just possible that we curse someone at a time when duas are answered, especially in Ramadhaan, which is full of such special moments of acceptance. Hence, in this month great care should be taken.

Hadhrat Umar رضي الله عنه says that Rasulullah ﷺ said, "Whosoever remembers Allah Ta'ala in Ramadhaan, is definitely forgiven, and one who asks for a favour from Allah Ta'ala, is not refused." Hadhrat Abdullah ibn Masood رضي الله عنه says that on every night of Ramadhaan, an angel from the heavens calls out: "O You seeker of good, come near, O You seeker of evil, turn away (from evil) and open your eyes." Thereafter, that angel calls out: "Is there any seeker of forgiveness, that he may be forgiven? Is there anyone making taubah so that Allah Ta'ala accepts his taubah? Is there anyone making dua, so that his dua may be heard? Is there anyone wanting anything, so that his wish may be granted?"

Lastly, it should be remembered that there are certain conditions under which duas are accepted. Without these, duas may often be rejected. Among these is not consuming haraam food; when haraam food is eaten, then our duas are not accepted.

Rasulullah ﷺ said: "Many a time a person who is in problems and difficulties lifts up his hands to the heavens, making dua and crying out: 'O Allah! O Allah!' but the food he eats is forbidden by Allah Ta'ala, what he drinks is forbidden and his clothes had been earned by haraam means, then in such a case how can his dua ever be accepted?"

A story is related about a group of people in Kufa, whose dua would always be accepted. Whenever a cruel ruler was put over them, they used to make dua for a curse upon him, which quickly came to destroy him. When the oppressive Hajjaaj became the ruler there, he invited these people to a meal. After they had all eaten, he said to them: "I am no longer afraid of the curse upon me from these people, because haraam (forbidden) food has now entered their stomachs."

Let us think over how many things, forbidden (made haraam) by Allah Ta'ala, are being consumed in these times. People are even trying to make the taking of interest permissible. We find people going so far as to think that bribery and what is obtained through it is permissible, whilst our businessmen very often think it okay to cheat and deceive people when doing business.

Hadith 7 – The Importance of Sehri (The Meal before Dawn)

عَنِ ابْنِ عُمَرَ رَضِىَ اللهُ عَنْهُ قَالَ قَالَ رَسُوْلُ اللهِ صَلَّى اللهُ عَلَيْهِ وَسَلَّمَ اِنَّ اللهَ وَمَلَائِكَتَهُ يُصَلُّوْنَ عَلَى الْمُتَسَحِّرِيْنَ (سنن ابن حبان # 3467)

Hadhrat Ibn Umar ﷺ says that, Rasulullah ﷺ said: "Verily Allah Ta'ala and His Malaaikah send blessings upon those who eat Sehri."

Note: How great is Allah Ta'ala's favour upon us that even eating sehri before dawn for fasting is so greatly rewarded. There are many Ahaadith in which the rewards of sehri are explained. Allamah Ainee *(rahmatullahi alayh)*, a famous Aalim, has quoted the rewards of sehri from seventeen different Sahaabah ﷺ and there is ijmaa' on its being mustahab.

Many people lose this great reward because of their own laziness. Some people, after finishing the Taraaweeh Salaah, eat some food in place of sehri and go to bed. What great blessing do they lose! Sehri actually means food eaten shortly before dawn. Some Ulama say that the time for sehri starts after midnight. The author of '*Al-Kashshaaf (Az-Zamakhsharee)*' has divided the night into six parts, saying that the last one of these is the time of sehri. Therefore, when the night (from sunset till dawn) lasts twelve hours, then the last two hours would be the correct time for sehri. It must also be remembered that to eat at the last permissible time is better and greater in reward than eating earlier, on condition that sehri is completed before the time of dawn.

The virtues of sehri are mentioned in many Ahaadith Rasulullah ﷺ said, "The difference between our fasting and that of the Ahl-e-Kitaab (Jews and Christians) is that we eat sehri and they do not." Nabi ﷺ has said, "Eat sehri, because in it lies great blessings."

In another Hadith it is said, "In three things there are great blessings, in Jamaat (in a group), in eating sareed (a special dish) and in sehri." In this Hadith the use of the word Jamaat is general (for all actions). It also includes Salaah with Jamaat and all those good actions which are done in a group, as Allah Ta'ala's help comes to them. Sareed is a type of tasty food, in which baked bread is cooked with gravy and meat.

The third thing this Hadith speaks of is about sehri. When Rasulullah ﷺ would invite any of the Sahaabah رضي الله عنه to eat sehri with him, he used to say: "Come and eat this blessed food with me."

One Hadith says: "Eat sehri and strengthen yourself for the fast, Sleep in the afternoon (siesta) so that it makes it easy to wake up in the later portion of the night (for the worship of Allah Ta'ala)." Abdullah Ibn Haaris رضي الله عنه reports that one of the Sahaabah رضي الله عنه said, "I once visited Rasulullah ﷺ at a time when he was busy eating sehri." Rasulullah ﷺ then said: "This is a thing that is full of barakah, which Allah Ta'ala has granted you. Do not leave it out."

Rasulullah ﷺ often mentioned the importance of sehri to such an extent, that he said: "If there is nothing else, at least eat a date or drink some water." Therefore, when there are definitely great advantages and reward in sehri, Muslims should never miss the partaking of meals at the time of sehri. However, in all things, moderation (not too less or not too much) is important, and eating more than the required amount is harmful. Neither should so little be eaten that one feels weak while fasting nor should so much be eaten that it causes discomfort (that we burp the whole day). We have been advised not to overeat in many Ahaadith.

Ibn Hajar has listed different reasons regarding the barakah (blessings) of sehri:

- The Sunnah is followed.
- Through sehri, we separate ourselves from the ways of Ahl-e-Kitaab (Jews and Christians), which we are at all times supposed to do.
- It provides strength for the ibaadah of Allah Ta'ala.
- It causes greater concentration in the ibaadah of Allah Ta'ala.
- It aids in preventing a bad temper, which normally comes about as a result of hunger.
- Sehri is the time when duas are accepted.
- At the time of sehri, one gets the opportunity to remember Allah Ta'ala, make zikr and dua.
- Sharing ones food with the poor and needy, especially those who live close by.

The above are a few major reasons although there are other reasons as well.

Ibn Daqeequl Eid *(rahmatullahi alayh)* says that some Sufis are doubtful whether the eating of sehri is against the object of fasting. They say that the object of fasting is to stay away from food, drink and sexual desires and therefore sehri is against the object of fasting. In my humble opinion, the ideal is to reduce the amount of food eaten at iftaar and sehri. However, the amount to be eaten is different according to different persons and their activities. For example, for those students who are busy studying the knowledge of Deen, too little food at sehri as well as at breaking the fast will be harmful for them. For them it is better not to eat too little, because they are studying Deeni knowledge, which is very important (for the protection and spread of Islam). Similar is the case of those who are busy with zikr and other Deeni activities. Other people who have no hard work to do should eat little at sehri.

Once, Rasulullah ﷺ announced to those who were going for jihad; "There is no reward in fasting while travelling." That was in the month of Ramadhaan, in this situation, Jihaad had to be given preference. Of course, when one is doing some work of Deen and eating less does not cause laziness or weakness, then it is best to eat less. Allaama Sharaani *(rahmatullahi alayh)* mentions in '*Sharh Iqna*', "A promise was made with us that we shall not fill our stomachs completely when eating especially in the nights of Ramadhaan." It is better that one should eat less in the nights of Ramadhaan than on other nights. After all, there is little benefit in fasting after having filled oneself at sehri and at iftaar. The pious people have said, "Whoever remains hungry in Ramadhaan shall remain safe from the evil of Shaytaan throughout the year until the next Ramadhaan." Many other soofiya have also advocated eating less.

In the commentary of '*Ihyaa*', Awaarif *(rahmatullahi alayh)* quotes that Sahl bin Adullah Tastari *(rahmatullahi alayh)* would eat only once every fifteen days. While in Ramadhaan he ate only one morsel. In order to follow the Sunnah he used to have a drink of water for sehri and iftaar. Shaikh Junaid *(rahmatullahi alayh)* used to always fast throughout the year. However, when noble friends used to visit him occasionally, he used to break his nafl fast and eat with them saying, "The reward of breaking fast and eating with such noble friends is not less than nafl fasting."

Similarly, we can mention the experiences of numerous pious people, who, through eating little food, used to train their inner-selves. But once again we must bear in mind that it should not be carried out to such an extent that our Deeni activities and responsibilities are neglected. (as a result of weakness caused in the body.)

HADITH 8 - MANY PEOPLE FAST AND WORSHIP AT NIGHT BUT EARN NOTHING BESIDES HUNGER AND LOST SLEEP

عَنْ اَبِيْ هُرَيْرَةَ رَضِيَ اللهُ عَنْهُ قَالَ قَالَ رَسُوْلُ اللهِ صَلَّى اللهُ عَلَيْهِ وَسَلَّمَ رُبَّ صَائِمٍ لَيْسَ لَهُ مِنْ صِيَامِهِ اِلَّا الْجُوْعُ وَرُبَّ قَائِمٍ لَيْسَ لَهُ مِنْ قِيَامِهِ اِلَّا السَّهَرُ

(سنن ابن ماجه # 1690)

Hadhrat Abu Hurairah ﷺ relates that Rasulullah ﷺ said, "Many people who fast, get nothing for their fasting except hunger, and many perform Salaah by night but get nothing by it except the discomfort of staying awake."

Note: The Ulama have three different interpretations about this Hadith. Firstly, this Hadith may mean that those who fast during the day and then for breaking the fast at iftaar, eat food that is haraam. All the reward for fasting is lost because of the greater sin of eating haraam food and nothing is gained except remaining hungry.

Secondly, it may mean those who fast, but during fasting busy themselves in backbiting and falsely accusing others.

Thirdly, the person referred to may be the one, who did not stay away from evil and sin while fasting.

In this Hadith, all such possibilities are included. Similar is the case of the person performing Salaah the entire night but because of backbiting or any other sinful act (e.g. missing Fajr Salaah or keeping awake for show), loses the reward for his night of ibaadah.

HADITH 9 - FASTING IS A PROTECTIVE SHIELD

عَنْ اَبِيْ عُبَيْدَةَ رَضِيَ اللهُ عَنْهُ قَالَ سَمِعْتُ رَسُوْلَ اللهِ صَلَّى اللهُ عَلَيْهِ وَسَلَّمَ يَقُوْلُ الصَّوْمُ جُنَّةٌ مَا لَمْ يَخْرِقْهُ (السنن الكبرى للنسائ # 2555)

Hadhrat Abu Ubaydah رَضِىَ اللهُ عَنْهُ *reports, I heard Rasulullah* صَلَّى اللهُ عَلَيْهِ وَسَلَّمَ *saying, "Fasting is a protective shield (for a man), as long as he does not tear up that protection."*

Note: "Fasting is a Protective Shield," (in this Hadith) It means that just as a man protects himself with a shield, similarly fasting protects him from his enemy, Shaytaan. In other Ahaadith, we are told that fasting saves one from Allah Ta'ala's punishment and the fire of Jahannam in the Aakhirah (Hereafter).

Once, somebody asked Rasulullah صَلَّى اللهُ عَلَيْهِ وَسَلَّمَ, "What causes the fast to break?" He replied, "Speaking lies and backbiting." This Hadith, when read in combination with many other Ahaadith, actually tells us not to do those things which causes the fast to be destroyed.

These days, we like wasting time with unnecessary conversations just to pass time whilst fasting. Some Ulama say that lies, backbiting, slander (wrongly accusing somebody), etc. actually breaks the fast just like eating and drinking. But the majority of the Ulama believe that the fast is not totally broken, but loses its blessings (barakah). The Ulama tell us of six things of which care should be taken whilst fasting:

Firstly: One should keep the eyes away from any place where one should not look at. Some go so far as to forbid looking at one's own wife with desire, let alone another woman. Similarly, we should avoid looking at anything forbidden and any futile amusement or where evil is committed (e.g. T.V., DVD's, etc.).

Rasulullah صَلَّى اللهُ عَلَيْهِ وَسَلَّمَ said: "The sight is an arrow from the arrows of Shaytaan. Whosoever, out of fear of Allah Ta'ala, protects his gaze, Allah Ta'ala will give him such noor (light) of Imaan, the taste and sweetness of which he will feel in the heart."

The pious people say that this means that we should not look at all at those places and things that take the mind away from the remembrance of Allah Ta'ala.

Secondly: One should guard the tongue from lies, unnecessary talks, backbiting, arguments, etc. In '*Saheeh Bukhari*' we read that fasting is a shield for the fasting person. Those who fast should stay away from all foolish and obscene talk e.g. joking, arguments, etc. Should an understanding person start an argument, then say to him, "I am fasting." In other words, one should not start an argument and even if someone else starts it, then too, one should avoid it. And if a foolish person starts an argument, then at least one should remind oneself that; "I am fasting" and must not respond to such meaningless arguments. One should be even more careful in avoiding lies and backbiting since according to some Ulama it actually breaks the fast.

During the time of our Nabi ﷺ, two women who were fasting felt so hungry that they could not manage the fast and both were close to death. When the Sahaabah رضي الله عنهم told our Nabi ﷺ about this, he sent a bowl to the women asking both of them to vomit into it. When they both vomited into the bowl, pieces of meat and fresh blood were found in it. The Sahaabah رضي الله عنهم were greatly surprised, upon which our Nabi ﷺ said: "They fasted by not eating pure food from Allah Ta'ala, but ate food which was not permitted by Allah Ta'ala by backbiting of other people."

By backbiting during fasting, the fast becomes more difficult. Both these women were close to death. Similar is the effect of other sinful acts. This is also borne out by experience, fasting is not difficult for the pious Allah-fearing persons, whereas the sinful people find it very difficult. If one wishes the fast to be easy, he should stay away from sins, especially the major sins like backbiting and slander, which are often done to pass time. Allah Ta'ala says in the Qur-aan that backbiting is the (actual) eating of the flesh of one's dead brother. We find this description in the Hadith also. Once, when Rasulullah ﷺ saw a group of people, he said to them, "Pick your teeth." They replied; "We did not partake of meat today." Rasulullah ﷺ then said, "A certain person's meat is sticking to your teeth." This meant that they were involved in backbiting. May Allah Ta'ala keep us safe from this evil sin because we are very neglectful of this. All of us are guilty of this. Leave aside those people who are not generally regarded as religious, backbiting is common even amongst the gatherings of Ulama and those who are considered to be pious. What is most heart breaking is that we do not even consider it to be backbiting. If a person suspects that he is guilty of backbiting, then he covers it up by calling it a "narration of facts."

One of the Sahaabah رضي الله عنه asked Rasulullah ﷺ, "What is backbiting?" Rasulullah ﷺ replied: "To say something about your brother, behind his back, which he does not like." The Sahaabah رضي الله عنهم

then said: "And is it still backbiting if what is said about him is really true?" Our Nabi ﷺ said: "In that case (if that which was said is really true) it is definitely backbiting; but if what is said is false, then you have slandered (falsely accused) him."

Once when Nabi ﷺ passed by two graves, he said: "Punishment is being given to both the people of these graves. One is being punished because of backbiting and the other because of not having taken precautions (to stay clean) when passing urine." Rasulullah ﷺ also said, "There are more than seventy kinds of evil in (using) interest. The mildest form of which is like commiting adultery with your mother, and taking one Dirham of interest is a worse evil than having fornicated thirty-five times. The worst and most evil form of taking interest is disgracing a Muslim. In the Hadith we are strictly warned against backbiting and disgracing others. I very much wanted to write down here a number of Ahaadith on this subject because all our gatherings and conversations are generally filled with backbiting and slander. However, I shall suffice with what was mentioned because the subject under discussion here, is something else and not actually backbiting. So, having just noted down these few Ahaadith, I once again make dua that Allah Ta'ala keep us safe from this evil. I also beg my friends and brothers to make dua for me too, as we are all full of inner faults.

کبر و نخوت، جہل و غفلت، حقد و کینہ بد ظنی

کذب و بد عہدی، ریا و بغض و غیبت دشمنی

کون بیماری ہے یا رب جو نہیں مجھ میں ہوئی

عَافِنِيْ مِنْ كُلِّ دَاءٍ وَاقْضِ عَنِّيْ حَاجَتِيْ   اِنَّ لِيْ قَلْبًا سَقِيْمًا اَنْتَ شَافٍ لِّلْعَلِيْلِ

"Arrogance and pride, ignorance and negligence,
dislike and malice, evil thoughts, lies and the breaking of promises,
ostentation (showing off) and hatred, backbiting and animosity
(hatred).

What sickness is there O Allah, that is not in me,
Heal me from every illness and grant me my necessity,

Verily I have a heart that is ailing,
Verily you are Healer of the sick."

Thirdly: The person who fasts must be careful about what he hears. Whatever is wrong to say, is also wrong to listen too. Rasulullah ﷺ has said, "In backbiting, both the backbiter and the one who listens to it are equally sinful."

Fourthly: The rest of the body should be kept away from sin and wrong things. The hands must not touch it and the feet must not walk towards it. Special care should be taken especially at the time of breaking the fast that no doubtful or haram food enters the stomach. When a person fasts and at the time of breaking the fast, eats haraam food, he is like a sick person who takes medicine as a cure but also adds a little poison, which then kills him.

Fifthly: It is not good to completely fill the stomach while breaking the fast at iftaar even with halaal food because the purpose of fasting is then lost.

The objective of fasting is to weaken the carnal and animalistic powers of the nafs, and to strengthen the angelic and spiritual powers of the nafs. For eleven months, we eat and drink freely. In Ramadhaan this should be cut down to a minimum. We have a bad habit of filling our stomachs when breaking the fast to cover up for what was lost during the day and again at sehri in preparation for the fast, thereby actually increasing our daily food intake. For such people their appetite increases in Ramadhaan. Many such items of food are eaten that we normally do not eat at other times. This type of habit is completely against the spirit of Ramadhaan and the true spirit of fasting.

Imam Ghazaali *(rahmatullahi alayh)* asks the same question: "When the object of fasting is to decrease our bodily needs and to go against Shaytaan, then how can this possibly be done by overeating when breaking the fast thereby defeating the object of fasting?" Actually in that case we have only changed the times of eating and not really fasted. In fact, by having many types of delicious foods, we eat even more than in normal times. Instead of lessening the bodily desires, these are increased. The real benefit of fasting comes with real hunger. Our Nabi ﷺ said, "Shaytaan flows in the body of man like blood, so close up his path by remaining hungry," i.e. when the body is hungry, the rooh (spirit) receives strength, and when the body is stuffed with food, then all the limbs of the body are spiritually starved.

Apart from hunger, fasting gives us a chance to appreciate the condition of the poor and thereby feel sorry for them. This can only be felt by remaining hungry. But by filling the stomach with delicious foods at sehri, we will be losing the purpose of fasting because we will not feel hungry throughout the fast. We will only be able to identify with the poor if we ourselves experience hunger (pangs of hunger). Once a person went to Bishr Haafi *(rahmatullahi alaih)* and found him shivering from cold in spite of having warm clothes at his side. The person inquired, "Is this the time for taking off your clothes?" Bishr *(rahmatullahi alayh)* replied; "There are many poor and needy people and I am unable to sympathize with them. The most I could do is to be like them." The pious people and Fuqaha (Jurists) advise us to have the same attitude when fasting. In Maraaqil Falaah it is written: "Do not over eat at sehri like the rich people, as this is a way to lose the object of fasting." Allamah Tahthaawi *(rahmatullahi alayh)* explains this, "The reward for fasting increases when hunger is really felt and awareness is also felt for the poor and hungry ones."

Our Nabi ﷺ himself said: "Allah Ta'ala hates the filling of anything to the top more than the filling of the stomach." Rasulullah ﷺ said, "A few morsels of food, enough to keep the back upright is sufficient for a person." If anyone wants to eat more than this, he should eat so that one third should be filled with food, one third with drink, while the other third remains empty. There had to be some reason why Rasulullah ﷺ himself used to fast for many days on end without eating anything in between.

I had seen my ustaad, Moulana Khalil Ahmed *(rahmatullahi alayh),* eating only slightly more than one thin handmade roti (bread) at iftaar and sehri during the whole month of Ramadhaan. When any of his family used to ask him to eat more, he used to reply, "I am not hungry. Actually, I only sat down to eat so that I can be with my friends."

I have heard that Moulana Shah Abdurraheem Raipuri *(rahmatullahi alayh)* used to fast for days on end in Ramadhaan, having nothing else besides a few cups of tea without milk for sehri and iftaar. Once his most trusted mureed and Khalifah, Moulana Shah Abdul Qadir *(rahmatullahi alayh,)* remarked with anxiety; "Hadhrat you will become quite weak if you do not eat anything." To this Moulana Shah Raipuri *(rahmatullahi alayh)* replied; "Praise be to Allah Ta'ala, I am experiencing something of the ecstasy of Jannah." (May Allah Ta'ala grant us all the ability to follow such pious people (Aameen).

ندارند تن پروراں آگہی   کہ پُر معدہ باشد ز حکمت تہی

The one living in luxury cannot attain recognition, since a full stomach is empty of wisdom.

The sixth point: After fasting one should always have fear and anxiety as to whether one's fast has been accepted or rejected by Allah Ta'ala. This should be the case with all our other ibaadah. One never knows for which deficiency and fault, which we may take lightly (as something insignificant), our deeds may be thrown back in our faces. Rasulullah ﷺ said; "Many who are the reciters of the Qur-aan are being cursed by the Qur-aan." He also said, "On the day of Qiyaamah, one of those whom Allah Ta'ala will question first will be a shaheed (martyr). Allah Ta'ala will call him and remind him of all the favours that Allah Ta'ala bestowed upon him, to which the shaheed will admit. He will then be asked; "What have you done in return to show gratitude for those favours?" The shaheed will reply; "I fought in your path till I became a Shaheed." Allah Ta'ala will reply, "Not true. You fought so that people would call you a brave man and so it was said." Thereafter Allah Ta'ala will command that he be pulled with his face down on the ground, and thrown into Jahannam. Thereafter an Aalim will be called. He will also be reminded of the favours of Allah Ta'ala and asked the same question. He will reply, "O Allah, I strove to acquire knowledge, taught others and I recited the Qur-aan for Your sake." Allah Ta'ala will say, "Not true. You did all that just to show the people so that they will say that you are a very learned man and so it was said." Thereafter Allah Ta'ala will command that he also be pulled with his face down on the ground and thrown into Jahannam. Thereafter a rich man will be called. He will also be reminded of the favours of Allah Ta'ala to which he will admit. He will then be asked as to what he did to show his gratitude, he will reply, "There was no worthy cause in which I did not spend in charity just for Your sake." Allah Ta'ala will reply, "Not true. You did all that so that the people may say that you are very generous and so it was said." Thereafter Allah Ta'ala will command that he also be pulled with his face down on the ground and thrown into Jahannam. May Allah Ta'ala save us.

This is the result of our incorrect niyyahs (intentions). Many such examples are mentioned in the Hadith. Therefore, the fasting person must at all times safeguard his niyyat and have the fear that his actions must not be rejected. He should also constantly make dua that Allah Ta'ala makes this a cause for His pleasure. It should also be borne in mind that regarding your act as not being worthy of acceptance is one aspect and your hopes for the infinite grace and mercy of Allah Ta'ala is another aspect. This latter aspect of Allah Ta'ala's kindness is unique. Sometimes Allah Ta'ala converts our sins to good deeds (due to other good deeds that follow the sins committed by us). Then why should we not hope for rewards for our defective deeds?

خوبی ہمیں کرشمہ و ناز و خرام نیست　　　بسیار شیوہاست بتاں را کہ نام نیست

"Don't count this charisma and phenomena to be His only execellence. The beloved has so many other virtues which words cannot express."

These above six advices are compulsory for all the righteous ones. As for the extremely pious servants of Allah Ta'ala, a **seventh point** is also added to the above six. Whilst fasting, the heart should not be turned towards anyone else except Allah Ta'ala, so much so that it is one's shortcoming to worry about whether there shall be something to eat for iftaar or not. Some pious servants of Allah Ta'ala even consider it wrong to worry about how one is going to get his food for iftaar, because this shows his lack of confidence in promise of Allah Ta'ala regarding his rizq (sustenance). In the commentary of *'Ihyaa Ulumud Deen'*, it is mentioned regarding some Mashaaikh, that should any food arrive for iftaar before the time of iftaar, then it was given away, fearing that the heart will now be set on the food for the rest of the day, which in turn would reduce their reliance on Allah Ta'ala. This of course can only be practiced by the exceptionally pious people, as our Imaan is not on such a level. Should we try to follow that, then we may harm ourselves.

The Qur-aan commands, **"Fasting has been prescribed for you."** The commentators of the Qur-aan say that from this aayat it is deduced that fasting is made compulsory for every portion of the body. Therefore, fasting of the tongue means abstaining from speaking lies, etc. Fasting of the ears means not listening to evil. Fasting of the eyes means not looking at any form of evil and sin, and in the same manner all the other limbs, to this extent that fasting of the nafs means to protect oneself from greed and carnal desires. Fasting of the heart is to keep it empty of the love of the world. Fasting of the rooh (soul) means to abstain from dwelling in the pleasures of the Aakhirah. Fasting of the mind means avoiding thoughts about the presence of any other being besides Allah Ta'ala.

HADITH 10 - FASTING PERSON EATING WITHOUT A VALID REASON

عَنْ اَبِیْ هُرَیْرَةَ رَضِیَ اللهُ عَنْهُ اَنَّ رَسُوْلَ اللهِ صَلَّی اللهُ عَلَیْهِ وَسَلَّمَ قَالَ مَنْ اَفْطَرَ یَوْمًا مِّنْ رَمَضَانَ مِنْ غَیْرِ رُخْصَةٍ وَّلَا مَرَضٍ لَمْ یَقْضِهِ عَنْهُ صَوْمُ الدَّهْرِ کُلِّهِ وَاِنْ صَامَهُ

(سنن الترمذی # 723)

Hadhrat Abu Hurayrah رَضِیَ اللهُ عَنْهُ reports that Rasulullah صَلَّی اللهُ عَلَیْهِ وَسَلَّمَ said, "Whosoever eats on one day of Ramadhaan without a valid reason or excuse or genuine illness (which is acceptable in Shariah), shall never be able to compensate for that day even by fasting for the rest of his life."

Note: The view of some Ulama is that if anybody has failed to fast on any day of Ramadhaan without any valid excuse and dishonored it by eating etc., can never compensate (duly fulfil the Qadhaa) for this major sin. Even if a person fasts for the rest of his life, he cannot make up for this one day. Hadhrat Ali رَضِیَ اللهُ عَنْهُ is amongst those who hold this view. However, the vast majority of Ulama say that where a person did not fast on a particular day of Ramadhaan, then only one fast will suffice for that day as compensation. On the other hand, when a person had started to fast in Ramadhaan and then breaks it during the day without any valid excuse, then according to the Shariah, this person will have to fast consecutively for two months without a break in between. No matter what happens, the true virtue and blessings of Ramadhaan will never be attained. This is the meaning of the above Hadith that, where a fast of Ramadhaan has been missed without an excuse, then any number of fasts to compensate for it will not bring back the true blessings of that one day of Ramadhaan. This applies to those who keep the qadhaa fast.

However, those who deny the fast and do not keep it at all, are most unfortunate and misguided. Fasting is one of the fundamental pillars of

Islam. Rasulullah ﷺ has mentioned the five pillars of Islam. First and foremost is belief in the oneness of Allah Ta'ala and Muhammad ﷺ being a Rasul (Messenger of Allah Ta'ala) and thereafter the other four famous pillars: Salaah, Fasting, Zakaat and Haj.

How many people do we find who are known to be Muslims, yet do not uphold even one of these five pillars of Islam. In the records of the government, they are recorded as Muslims, whereas in Allah Ta'ala's sight they cannot be counted as Muslims.

Ibn Abbaas ؓ relates in a Hadith that, "Islam is based on three principles: 1. The Shahaadah, 2. Salaah, 3. Fasting. Whoever fails to uphold any of these principles is a disbeliever and it will be permissible to give him capital punishment (i.e. he must be killed)." The Ulama have explained that they will only be regarded as disbelievers when they deny it as an obligation, or deny its being a principle. No matter what interpretation is given, the fact remains that Rasulullah ﷺ spoke against such people most forcefully. Therefore, those who fail to keep up the faraaidh of Deen should indeed fear Allah Ta'ala's anger. No one can escape death. The pleasure and comforts of this life are temporary. Only obedience to Allah Ta'ala's commands can save us.

Much worse is the position of those who do not only refuse to fast, but speak such words whereby they mock and jeer at the month of fasting (Ramadhaan). This is something very serious and can bring one to the brink of kufr. You may have heard them mockingly say, "Fasting is for those who have no food in their homes, not for me." Or "What does Allah Ta'ala gain by making us suffer with hunger?" Such words should never be uttered. A very important point should be noted that to mock and jeer at, or poke fun at even the smallest part of our Deen becomes the cause of kufr (apostasy). If a person does not perform a single Salaah in his life, nor does he fast a single day, or fail to perform any of the fardh obligations in Islam, then that person does not become a kaafir, as long as he does not deny any part of Deen. However, he will certainly be punished for any fardh that he had neglected. But to mock and jeer at even the smallest aspect of the Deen is kufr (apostasy) and can result in all our good actions being nullified. From this it can be seen how serious this matter is. Therefore, we should never make irresponsible statements about fasting or any other part of our Deen.

However, a person who did not fast without a valid reason will be sinful, even though he did not mock and jeer at this command of Allah Ta'ala. The Ulama have clearly mentioned that the person who eats openly in Ramadhaan without a valid reason, should be killed. And if this is not possible due to being in non-Muslim country and you do not have a Muslim leader (i.e. an Ameerul Mumineen), then it is the duty of every person to express his disapproval of such behaviour, or the lowest level of Imaan is to regard such behaviour as evil.

May Allah Ta'ala, through the blessings of His obedient servants, give me the ability to do good actions, since I am the one who is most guilty of not doing good actions. *Aameen.*

I think ten Ahaadith in chapter one should be sufficient, since one Hadeeth is enough for those who are prepared to accept and similarly keeping in mind the aayat in which Allah Ta'aala has mentioned:

$$تِلْكَ عَشَرَةٌ كَامِلَةٌ$$

"This completes ten." (Surah Baqarah - Aayah 196)

As for those who are not prepared to accept, any number of Ahaadith will be insufficient for them. May Allah Ta'ala grant the Muslims the ability to practice on what has been mentioned. *Aameen.*

CHAPTER 2
LAYLATUL QADR

There is one amongst the nights of Ramadhaan, 'Laylatul Qadr. this night is of great blessings. The Qur-aan-e-Kareem describes it as being greater in blessedness and rewards than a thousand months. It is greater than eighty-three years and four months (in blessings).

Fortunate is that person who gets the full blessings of this night by spending it in the ibaadah of Allah Ta'ala, because he has then earned reward for ibaadah of eighty-three years and four months and even more. Indeed, the granting of this night to the Muslims is a great favour.

THE ORIGIN

In Durre Mansoor reported by Hadhrat Anas رَضِىَ اللّٰهُ عَنْهُ that Rasulullah صَلَّى اللّٰهُ عَلَيْهِ وَسَلَّمَ is reported to have said, "Laylatul Qadr was given to my Ummah and not to any other Ummah before this." Many reasons for the granting of Laylatul Qadr have been mentioned. One reason given according to some Ahaadith is that, Rasulullah صَلَّى اللّٰهُ عَلَيْهِ وَسَلَّمَ used to look at the longer lives of the earlier people and was saddened over the shorter lives of his Ummah. If His Ummah had wished to compete with the people before them in the doing of good deeds, because of their shorter lives, it would be impossible for them to either copy or do more good deeds than them. To cover up for this difference in their shorter lives, Allah Ta'ala, in His countless mercy, gave them this night of great blessings. If any fortunate person of this ummah spends ten such nights during his lifetime in the worship of Allah Ta'ala, he will earn the reward of eight hundred and thirty years and even more.

Rasulullah ﷺ once related to the Sahaabah رضى الله عنهم the story of a very pious man from the Bani Israa'eel, who spent 1000 months in jihaad. On hearing this, the Sahaabah رضى الله عنهم envied that person because they could not get the same reward, whereupon Allah Ta'ala granted them Laylatul Qadr (the Night of Power).

Our Nabi ﷺ once mentioned the names of the four most pious people from amongst the Bani Israa'eel who each spent eighty years in Allah Ta'ala's sincere ibaadah, worshipping Him, and not sinning at all. They were Nabi Ayyub *(alayhis salaam)*, Zakariyya *(alayhis salaam)*, Hizqeel *(alayhis salaam)* and Yushaa *(alayhis salaam)*. The Sahaabah رضى الله عنهم heard this with astonishment. Then Jibra-eel *(alayhis salaam)* appeared and recited Surah Qadr, where the blessings of this night were revealed.

Besides these Ahaadith, there are others also explaining how the Night of Power came about. The differences in narration arise because after several incidents occurred, some wahi was revealed. Those aayaat could be relevant to anyone of the incidents that took place. But no matter which of them we accept, the important fact remains is that Allah Ta'ala has granted the ummah of Muhammad ﷺ this night. This is a great favour and gift of Allah Ta'ala. To make lots of ibaadah on this night is also a blessing from Allah Ta'ala. Fortunate are those pious saints who did not miss the ibaadah of even one Laylatul Qadr from the time they became baaligh (age of maturity).

تہی دَستانِ قِسمَت راچہ سُود اَز رَہبَرِ کامِل
کہ خِضَر اَز آبِ حَیوان تَشنَہ می آرَد سِکَندَر را

Some unfortunate people do not benefit from a Shaik-e-Kaamil

Just as Alexander returned deprived from the Aab-e-Hayaat despite the guidance of Khizar عليه السلام

There are many different narrations of the Ulama regarding the specification of this night. About fifty different views of the Ulama are mentioned regarding which night is Laylatul Qadr. The numerous benefits of this night are mentioned in many books of Ahaadith. The Qur-aan Majeed itself mentions the night in Surah Qadr, of which we shall begin with a short commentary.

$$\bismillah$$

In the name of Allah, the beneficent, the Merciful.

$$\text{إِنَّا أَنزَلْنَٰهُ فِى لَيْلَةِ ٱلْقَدْرِ}$$

We have indeed revealed this (message) on Lalatul Qadr (the night of significants). (Surah Qadr - Aayah 1)

Note: On this special night, the Qur-aan was sent down from the lowhul mahfuz (The preserved tablet in a special place above the heavens) to the heavens above the earth. A great divine book like the Qur-aan-e-Kareem being revealed on this night is sufficient to explain its great significance, not to mention all its other blessings and virtues. In the very next aayaat, a question is asked:

$$\text{وَمَآ أَدْرَىٰكَ مَا لَيْلَةُ ٱلْقَدْرِ}$$

And what will explain to you what the Night of significants is?
(Surah Qadr - Aayah 2)

The question asked here is: Have you any knowledge as to the greatness and the great importance of this night? Have you any knowledge as to the great favours and gifts that this night contains? The next verse explains to us some of that greatness:

$$\text{لَيْلَةُ ٱلْقَدْرِ خَيْرٌ مِّنْ أَلْفِ شَهْرٍ}$$

The Night of Power is better than a thousand months.
(Surah Qadr - Aayah 3)

The true meaning here is that the reward for spending this night in ibaadah is better than having spent one thousand months in ibaadah. It is in fact much more, but as to how much more rewarding it is, we are not told here.

$$\text{تَنَزَّلُ الْمَلَائِكَةُ وَالرُّوحُ فِيهَا بِإِذْنِ رَبِّهِمْ مِنْ كُلِّ أَمْرٍ}$$

The Malaaikah come down therein and the Spirit (Jibra-eel) by Allah Ta'ala's permission on every task. (Surah Qadr - Aayah 4)

A good explanation is given on this aayat by Imaam Raazi *(rahmatullahi alayh)*. He explains that when man first appeared on earth, created by Allah Ta'ala as His deputy, the Malaaikah looked at him with doubt. When Allah Ta'ala informed them of His intention of placing man on earth, they even went further to ask, "Will you place someone on this earth who shall commit evil and cause bloodshed?"

Similarly, when his parents saw the drop of sperm (mani) which was his original form, they looked upon it as something dirty, so much so, that they considered it as something which made your clothing unclean and had to be washed of. But later, when Allah Ta'ala made that same dirty sperm into a fine human being, they began to love and cherish him. When this same man grew up, then on this Night of significance and virtue we see him through Allah Ta'alas taufeeq worshipping Him and displaying their obedience and submission to Him. Those very same Malaaikah who had looked down on him before with doubt now, come down towards him and are regretful for the thoughts that they had against him.

In this aayat mention is made **"and the spirit"**. This refers clearly to Jibra-eel *(alayhis salaam)*. Mufassireen (commentators of the Qur-aan Shareef) have given many meanings of this word. Let us look at some of the meanings:

(a) Majority of the mufassireen are agreed that it refers to Jibra-eel *(alayhis salaam)* and according to Imaam Raazi *(rahmatullahi alaih)*, this is the most correct meaning. Allah Ta'ala first speaks of the Malaaikah and then special mention is made of Jibra-eel *(alayhis salaam)* because of his status.

(b) Some mufassireen hold the view that "Spirit" here means one Malaaikah of such an extremely huge size, that before him, the heavens and earth appear just as a morsel (of food i.e. as almost nothing).

(c) Another group of mufassireen are of the opinion that "Spirit" here means a group of Malaaikah who never appear and only on this night are seen by the other Malaaikah.

(d) Some mufasireen believe that the "Spirit" here refers to one such creation of Allah Ta'ala which partakes of food and drink, but is neither man nor angel.

(e) There is also a view that "Spirit" here refers to Isa *(alayhis salaam)* who, on this night, comes down with the Malaaikah to view the good deeds of this ummah.

(f) The last view we wish to mention here is that "Spirit" means, Allah Ta'ala's special mercy which comes when the Malaaikah come down. Besides these there are many other views, but the first opinion is the most acceptable one.

Imaam Bayhaqi *(rahmatullahi alaih)* reports a Hadith by Hadhrat Anas رضى الله عنه wherein Rasulullah صلى الله عليه وسلم is reported to have said, "On Laylatul Qadr, Jibra-eel *(alayhis salaam)* comes down with a group of Malaaikah and makes dua of mercy for every one whom they find busy in ibaadah." This same verse which is being discussed above says,

$$بِاِذْنِ رَبِّهِمْ مِنْ كُلِّ اَمْرٍ$$

"By Allah Ta'ala's permission on every task...."

The Author of *'Mazaahirrul Haq'* writes that on this night, many ages ago, the Malaaikah were created. On this night, the substance from which Adam *(alayhis salaam)* was created, had been gathered and his creation had begun. Trees were planted in Jannah and a large number of Ahaadith state clearly that on this night dua's are accepted. Similarly, we read in the kitaab, *'Durre Manthoor'* that according to a Hadith, it was on this night that Isa *(alayhis salaam)* was lifted up bodily into the heavens and also it was on this night that the taubah (repentance) of the Bani Israa'eel was accepted.

$$سَلٰمٌ هِيَ حَتّٰى مَطْلَعِ الْفَجْرِ$$

Peace prevails until the break of dawn (Surah Qadr Aayah 5)

Yes, this is the very picture of peace. Throughout the night the Malaaikah recite salaam on the believers. As one group comes down, another goes up as is explained in the Ahaadith. Another meaning is that it is a night of complete safety from evil and mischief.

These blessings remain throughout the night until the break of dawn and are not limited to any particular hour.

Having noted the different virtues of this night as explained in the words of Allah Ta'ala it does not require any further endorsement, nevertheless we shall mention some Ahaadith on the virtues of this night.

HADITH 1 - STANDING UP IN IBAADAH ON LAYLATUL QADR

عَنْ اَبِيْ هُرَيْرَةَ رَضِيَ اللهُ عَنْهُ قَالَ قَالَ رَسُوْلُ اللهِ صَلَّى اللهُ عَلَيْهِ وَسَلَّمَ مَنْ قَامَ لَيْلَةَ الْقَدْرِ اِيْمَانًا وَّاحْتِسَابًا غُفِرَ لَهُ مَا تَقَدَّمَ مِنْ ذَنْبِهٖ (صحيح البخارى # 1901)

Hadhrat Abu Hurayrah رضي الله عنه reports that Rasulullah ﷺ said, "Whoever stands in Salaah and ibaadah on the night of qadar with firm Imaan and with sincere hope of gaining reward, his previous sins are forgiven."

Note: In the above Hadith **'standing'** refers to salaah as well as any other form of ibaadah, for example zikr, tilaawat, etc. The expression **'with sincere hope of gaining reward'**, means that one should be sincerely occupied with ibaadah only for the pleasure of Allah Ta'ala and to receive rewards from Him. This should not be done to show others or to deceive them. Khattaabi *(rahmatullahi alayh)* says that it means that one should have complete trust in the promise that any deed done will be rewarded and therefore one must stand before Allah Ta'ala with sincerity and devotion. Neither should a person think of ibaadah as a burden, nor should he doubt the reward which he will get for it. After all, when one aims at a high goal and desires to get a great reward for it, and he is certain that he will get it, then the effort of striving hard to attain that goal becomes easy. Therefore, standing for long hours in ibaadah becomes easy. This is the reason why those who reach a high spiritual rank in Allah Ta'ala's sight, find it easy to remain in ibaadah most of the time.

The Hadith speaks about **'previous sins being forgiven.'** The Ulama have said that the forgiveness which is mentioned in the Hadith above and other Ahaadith only refer to minor sins. Major sins can only be forgiven, according to the Qur-aan, after sincere taubah, with the promise never to return to such sins again. This is the reason why all the

Ulama are of the same opinion that major sins are not forgiven except by sincere taubah. Therefore, when forgiveness of sins is mentioned in the Ahaadith, the Ulama specify it to be minor sins.

My late father (May Allah Ta'ala bless him and grant him light in his qabr) used to say that, the word minor has been omitted here for two reasons. Firstly, he says, "If a true Muslim does commit a major sin, he will never rest or find peace until he has sincerely made taubah to Allah Ta'ala, begging for forgiveness and promising not to do so in future."

Secondly, my late father used to say, when we are given such great and blessed days and nights, then a true Muslim stands before Allah Ta'ala in Salaah, hoping to gain reward, he naturally feels ashamed and greatly grieved by his previous sins. This grief over sins and the determination not to return to such acts are the most important requirements of taubah. This means that on such days and nights one naturally makes taubah for major sins, (thereby leaving only minor sins to be forgiven). It is best, however, that on an occasion like Laylatul Qadr, one who has committed major sins should first of all make taubah with sincerity and ask for forgiveness so that Allah Ta'ala, in His infinite mercy, may forgive all the major and minor sins. And when you do so, also remember me in your duas. (The publishers also request your duas).

Hadith 2 - One Who Misses Laylatul Qadr

عَنْ أَنَسِ بْنِ مَالِكٍ رَضِىَ اللهُ عَنْهُ قَالَ دَخَلَ رَمَضَانُ فَقَالَ رَسُوْلُ اللهِ صَلَّى اللهُ عَلَيْهِ وَسَلَّمَ اِنَّ هٰذَا الشَّهْرَ قَدْ حَضَرَكُمْ وَفِيْهِ لَيْلَةٌ خَيْرٌ مِّنْ أَلْفِ شَهْرٍ مَنْ حُرِمَهَا فَقَدْ حُرِمَ الْخَيْرَ كُلَّهُ وَلَا يُحْرَمُ خَيْرَهَا اِلَّا مَحْرُوْمٌ (سنن ابن ماجه # 1644)

Hadhrat Anas رَضِىَ اللهُ عَنْهُ reports, "Once when Ramadhaan had commenced, the Messenger of Allah صَلَّى اللهُ عَلَيْهِ وَسَلَّمَ said, 'A month has verily dawned over you wherein lies a night better than a thousand months. Whoever is deprived of its blessings has been indeed deprived of all good. None is deprived of its good except he who is completely unfortunate.'"

Note: Who can doubt how unlucky a person is if he is deprived of the great good of Laylatul Qadr? (Who can doubt how unlucky a person will be if he misses all the favours bestowed upon him? Despite this, there are many of us who are still deprived). There are those who, because of their jobs, have to stay awake at night throughout the year. What difficulty is there for these people to stay awake at night in this month, only for the sake of gaining reward of over eighty years of ibaadah, in the service of Allah Ta'ala?

To stay awake at night in this month should not be too difficult for them, but because of lack of interest, there is no desire in the heart. If there was a desire, then not only one night, but a thousand nights in the ibaadah of Allah Ta'ala would become extremely easy.

الفت میں برابر ہے وفا ہو کہ جفا ہو

ہر چیز میں لذت ہے اگر دل میں مزا ہو

"When one is really attached, he welcomes any treatment from his beloved be it kindness, be it harshness. If the heart is satisfied, everything is enjoyable"

It is that desire that we must create. After all, there must have been some reason why Rasulullah ﷺ had performed such lengthy rakaats in Salaah that caused his feet to swell. He did this in spite of knowing of the promises and glad tidings which Allah Ta'ala had given him. We also claim to be the followers of Rasulullah ﷺ. Those who really valued these special moments for ibaadah, themselves took advantage of these moments and, as such, set an example for the Ummah to follow. They left no room for the critics to question that, "Who could fulfill the desire of Rasulullah ﷺ and who else can do it?" It is only a matter of convincing the heart, that if you have the desire to do something, then the most difficult task becomes easy. This could only be achieved by staying in the company of a recognized Shaikh for spiritual guidance.

تمنّا دردِ دل کی ہے تو کر خدمت فقیروں کی

نہیں ملتا یہ گو ہر بادشاہوں کے خزینہ میں

"If you wish to attain the love of Allah Ta'ala then humble yourself before the saintly ones. This treasure will not be found anywhere else, not even in the volts of the kings."

Ch. 2 – Laylatul Qadr

Let us look at the example of the following illustrious sons of Islam. One of them was Hadhrat 'Umar رَضِيَٱللَّهُعَنْهُ who, after performing his Isha Salaah, used to return home and then remain in Salaah throughout the night until the azaan for Fajr was heard. Then there is the example of Hadhrat Usmaan رَضِيَٱللَّهُعَنْهُ who used to fast the entire day almost throughout the year, and have a little sleep during the first third of the night and thereafter spend the rest of the night in Salaah. It is well known about him that he used to recite the whole Qur-aan during one rakaat. In *'Ihya Ulumud Deen'* by Imaam Ghazaali *(rahmatullahi alayh)*, Abu Taalib Makki *(rahmatullahi alayh)* says that about forty men from among the Taabi'een used to perform Fajr Salaah with the same wudhu with which they had performed Isha Salaah with. This has been reported by many authentic narrators.

Hadhrat Shaddaad رَضِيَٱللَّهُعَنْهُ was one of the Sahaabah who used to stay awake throughout the night, turning from side to side, until Fajr. Then he used to say, "O Allah, the fear for the fire of Jahannam has driven away sleep from my eyes." Apart from sleeping a little between Maghrib and Esha, Aswad bin Yazeed *(rahmatullahi alayh)* used to remain in Ibaadah throughout the night during Ramadhaan. Now let us look at a man like Saeed ibnul Musayyib *(rahmatullahi alayh)* of whom it is said that he used to perform Esha and Fajr with the same wudhu for fifty years. Then there is the example of Sila bin Ashyam *(rahmatullahi alayh)*, who after spending a whole night in the ibaadah Allah Ta'ala, used to say at the break of day, "O Allah, I am not fit to beg of You Jannah but all I ask is that You save me from Jahannam."

Qataadah *(rahmatullahi alayh)* was a man who used to finish the recitation of the Qur-aan every three nights of Ramadhaan but during the last ten nights he used to complete the whole Qur-aan every night. It is well known about Imaam Abu Haneefah *(rahmatullahi alayh)* that, for forty years, he performed Isha and the following morning's Fajr Salaah with the same wudhu. To doubt these incidents is to deny true historical facts. When his companions asked him as to where he had got the strength for that, he replied, "It is in answer to a special dua which I made to Allah Ta'ala in the name of the blessedness of His special names." He only slept a little in the afternoons about which he said, "In the Hadith we are advised to do that." In other words, he slept in the afternoon so that he could practice on the sunnah. Imaam Abu Haneefah (rahmatullahi alayh) used to cry so much whilst reciting the Qur-aan that his neighbours used to feel pity for him. Once he wept the whole night while repeating the following aayah again and again:

$$بَلِ السَّاعَةُ مَوْعِدُهُمْ وَ السَّاعَةُ اَدْهٰى وَ اَمَرُّ$$

"Nay the hour (of Judgement) is the time promised for them (for their recompense) and that hour will be most grievous and bitter."
(Surah Qamar - Aayah 46)

In Ramadhaan, Ibrahim Ibn Adham (rahmatullahi alaih) neither slept by night nor by day. Imaam Shaafi (rahmatullahi alaih) used to recite the Qur-aan about sixty times in his Salaah, in the days and nights of Ramadhaan. Apart from these few pious people, there are countless others who used to act on the command of the following aayat:

$$وَمَا خَلَقْتُ الْجِنَّ وَ الْاِنْسَ اِلَّا لِيَعْبُدُوْنِ$$

"I have only created jinn and human so that they may worship me."
(Surah Zaariyaat - Aayah 56)

Nothing is difficult for those who have a will to practice. These are examples of the people of the past. But even today there are also many pious servants who serve Allah Ta'ala with the same devotion. Even though their exertion does not equal those pious people of the past, their efforts are reminiscent of these great souls. In these times of evil and immorality they strictly follow the example of Rasulullah ﷺ. Leisure, comfort and our daily responsibilities should not become obstacles and prevent us from devoting ourselves to Deen.

The Messenger of Allah ﷺ said, "Allah Ta'ala says, 'O son of Aadam, spend your time in my service and I will bless you with contentment of the heart and I will remove your poverty. Otherwise I shall fill you with responsibilities and your poverty and needs will still remain.'" We see the reality and truth of this daily.

(There are people who only serve Allah Ta'ala. They need nothing, in spite of having no apparent means of earning a livelihood. On the other hand, we see people striving hard to earn the worldly things and necessities. They become so engrossed in this task that no time is left for ibaadah. In spite of spending all their time seeking material needs, they still remain full of worldly desires, necessities and obligations - Translator).

HADITH 3 – DUAS ACCEPTED AND SINS FORGIVEN ON THE OCCASION OF EID

عَنْ أَنَسِ بْنِ مَالِكٍ رَضِىَ اللهُ عَنْهُ قَالَ قَالَ رَسُوْلُ اللهِ صَلَّى اللهُ عَلَيْهِ وَسَلَّمَ اِذَا كَانَ لَيْلَةُ الْقَدْرِ نَزَلَ جِبْرِيْلُ عَلَيْهِ السَّلَامُ فِى كَبْكَبَةٍ مِنَ الْمَلَائِكَةِ يُصَلُّوْنَ عَلَى كُلِّ عَبْدٍ قَائِمٍ اَوْ قَاعِدٍ يَذْكُرُ اللهَ عَزَّ وَجَلَّ فَاِذَا كَانَ يَوْمُ عِيْدِهِمْ يَعْنِىْ يَوْمَ فِطْرِهِمْ بَاهٰى بِهِمْ مَلَائِكَتَهُ فَقَالَ يَا مَلَائِكَتِىْ مَا جَزَاءُ اَجِيْرٍ وَفٰى عَمَلَهُ قَالُوْا رَبَّنَا جَزَاؤُهُ اَنْ يُّوَفّٰى اَجْرُهُ قَالَ مَلَائِكَتِىْ عَبِيْدِىْ وَاِمَائِىْ قَضَوْا فَرِيْضَتِىْ عَلَيْهِمْ ثُمَّ خَرَجُوْا يَعِجُّوْنَ اِلَى الدُّعَاءِ وَعِزَّتِىْ وَجَلَالِىْ وَكَرَمِىْ وَعُلُوِّىْ وَارْتِفَاعِ مَكَانِىْ لَاُجِيْبَنَّهُمْ فَيَقُوْلُ ارْجِعُوْا فَقَدْ غَفَرْتُ لَكُمْ وَبَدَّلْتُ سَيِّئَاتِكُمْ حَسَنَاتٍ قَالَ فَيَرْجِعُوْنَ مَغْفُوْرًا لَهُمْ

(اخرجه البيهقى فى شعب الايمان # 3444)

Hadhrat Anas ؓ reports that Rasulullah ﷺ said, "On the Night of Power, Jibra-eel (alayhis salaam) comes down to the earth with a group of Malaaikah, making dua for blessings for every servant of Allah Ta'ala they see standing in ibaadah or sitting and engaged in the praises (zikr) of Allah Ta'ala. Then on the day of Eid, Allah Ta'ala boasts about them to the Malaaikah (this is because the Malaaikah had objected when Allah Ta'ala created man), 'O Malaaikah, what is the reward of that employee who had fully completed his work?' They reply, 'O, our Sustainer, his reward should be given to him in full.' To this Allah Ta'ala replies, 'O, My Malaaikah, verily My servants, the males among them as well as the females, have fulfilled the compulsory duty placed upon them, thereafter they went to the Eidgaah raising their voices in My praises. I swear by My honour, by My Grace and by My High position of greatness, that I shall surely answer the duas of those people. Thereafter Allah Ta'ala says (addressing the people) 'Return, I have definitely forgiven your sins and have exchanged them with good deeds.' Rasulullah ﷺ said, 'Those people then return (from the Eidgaah) in a forgiven state.'"

Note: In this Hadith it is clearly mentioned that Jibra-eel *(alayhis salaam)* comes down with the Malaaikah, as mentioned in the Qur-aan which has been explained earlier and this is also explained clearly in many Ahaadith. The last Hadith of this book explains in detail that Hadhrat Jibra-eel *(alayhis salaam)* commands all the Malaaikah to go to the homes of every person engaged in zikr and ibaadat and make musaafahah (shake hands) with them.

The author of *'Ghaaliyatul Mawaaiz'* quotes from the *'Ghunyah'* of Shaikh Abdul Qaadir Jilaani *(rahmatullahi alayh)* that in a Hadith reported by Ibn Abbas ؓ it is mentioned that Hadhrat Jibra-eel *(alayhis salaam)*, after his coming down, commands the Malaaikah to go to the houses of those busy in ibaadah and make musaafaha (shake their hand). Thereupon the Malaaikah visit every house, whether big or small, whether in the jungle or on a ship, wherein a believer engaged in ibaadah resides, and shakes his hand. However, they do not enter certain houses; the house in which there is a dog or a pig, the house in which there is a person in the state of janaabah, which has resulted from adultery or fornication and a house wherein pictures of men and animals are displayed. How unfortunate it is that many Muslim houses do not have Malaaikah entering simply because there are pictures of men and animals being displayed, only for the sake of adding a bit of decoration. Only one picture may have been hung by one careless member of the household and all the occupants are completely deprived of blessings.

HADITH 4 - LOOKING FOR LAYLATUL QADR

عَنْ عَائِشَةَ رَضِيَ اللهُ عَنْهَا قَالَتْ قَالَ رَسُوْلُ اللهِ صَلَّى اللهُ عَلَيْهِ وَسَلَّمَ تَحَرَّوْا لَيْلَةَ الْقَدْرِ فِي الْوِتْرِ مِنَ الْعَشْرِ الْأَوَاخِرِ مِنْ رَمَضَانَ (صحيح البخارى # 2017)

Hadhrat Aa'ishah ؓ reports that Rasulullah ﷺ said, "Seek Laylatul Qadr among the odd numbered nights of the last ten days of the month of Ramadhaan."

Note: We now come to the question; When is Laylatul Qadr? The above Hadith commands us to look for it in the last ten nights of Ramadhaan.

According to the majority of Ulama, the last ten nights starts on the 21st night. Whether the month of Ramadhaan consists of twenty-nine or thirty days, one should **seek Laylatul Qadr on the 21st, 23rd, 25th, 27th or the 29th night.** If the month is twenty-nine days, then too these will be regarded as the last ten (Akheer Asharah).

A great learned Aalim, Ibn Hazm *(rahmatullahi alayh)*, has a different opinion, saying that the word Asharah as used in the Hadith means ten. As such, the above calculation will only be correct when the month of Ramadhaan consists of thirty days. However, when there are only twenty-nine days in the month (as often happens), the last ten days in the month will commence with the 20th night. According to this calculation it will mean that the unevenly numbered nights will be the 20th, 22nd, 24th, 26th and 28th night.

With due respect to a greatly learned Aalim like ibn Hazm *(rahmatullahi alayh)*, However the majority of Ulama do not agree with this view, the reason being that Itikaaf is sunnah during the last ten days of Ramadhaan. All the Ulama are of the same opinion that Rasulullah ﷺ used to commence Itikaaf on the 21st night of Ramadhaan in search of Laylatul Qadr.

ADVICE

Though there is the great possibility of Laylatul Qadr being on the odd nights from the 21st onwards, there is also the likelihood that it could fall during the last ten nights. The best advice one can give here is that one should spend each night from the 20th onwards in ibaadah, so that one may be sure of having acquired the blessings of Laylatul Qadr. Ten or eleven nights is definitely not so difficult if one looks at the great reward that is granted.

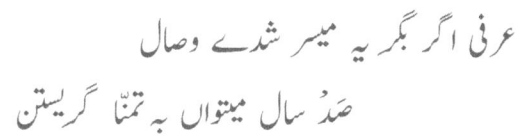

عرفی اگر بگر یہ میسر شدے وصال

صَدْ سال میتواں بہ تمنّا گریستن

"O Urfi! If it is wailing that will bring me to the beloved, then in the hope of reaching I will cry for a hundred years"

HADITH 5 - ACTUAL DATE OF LAYLATUL QADR TAKEN AWAY BECAUSE OF TWO PEOPLE ARGUING

عَنْ عُبَادَةَ بْنِ الصَّامِتِ رَضِيَ اللهُ عَنْهُ قَالَ خَرَجَ النَّبِيُّ صَلَّى اللهُ عَلَيْهِ وَسَلَّمَ لِيُخْبِرَنَا بِلَيْلَةِ القَدْرِ فَتَلَاحٰى رَجُلَانِ مِنَ الْمُسْلِمِيْنَ فَقَالَ خَرَجْتُ لِأُخْبِرَكُمْ بِلَيْلَةِ الْقَدْرِ فَتَلَاحٰى فُلَانٌ وَفُلَانٌ فَرُفِعَتْ وَعَسٰى اَنْ يَّكُوْنَ خَيْرًا لَّكُمْ فَالْتَمِسُوْهَا فِي التَّاسِعَةِ وَالسَّابِعَةِ وَالْخَامِسَةِ (صحيح البخاري # 2023)

Hadhrat Ubaadah bin Saamit رَضِيَ اللهُ عَنْهُ said, "Once Rasulullah صَلَّى اللهُ عَلَيْهِ وَسَلَّمَ came out to inform us about the true date of Laylatul Qadr, unfortunately at that time an argument took place between two men, whereupon he said, 'I came out in order to inform you as to when Laylatul Qadr was, but because two people were arguing, (the fixing of the correct date) was taken away. May be that is better for you. So, look for it among the ninth, seventh and fifth nights."

Note: Three important points are referred to in this Hadith. Firstly, there is mention of an argument which resulted in the knowledge of Laylatul Qadr being withheld from us. Arguments are always the cause of loss of barakah and blessings. Once Rasulullah صَلَّى اللهُ عَلَيْهِ وَسَلَّمَ asked the Sahaabah رَضِيَ اللهُ عَنْهُمْ, "Shall I inform you of some action that is better than Salaah, fasting and charity?" The Sahaabah رَضِيَ اللهُ عَنْهُمْ replied, "Certainly." Rasulullah صَلَّى اللهُ عَلَيْهِ وَسَلَّمَ then said, "Maintaining peaceful and good relations amongst yourselves is most virtuous, for verily arguments amongst yourselves causes one to destroy his Deen." Just as the razor removes hair from the head, similarly, arguments amongst yourselves destroys one's Deen (good deeds).

This is indeed an illness amongst us. Even those among us who appear to be extremely pious and busy with zikr, are victims of these arguments and fighting. We should carefully study the saying of Rasulullah صَلَّى اللهُ عَلَيْهِ وَسَلَّمَ and then check our conduct where pride prevents us from restoring our relationship with others. In the first chapter of this book (where the rewards and etiquette of fasting is discussed) we read that Rasulullah صَلَّى اللهُ عَلَيْهِ وَسَلَّمَ said, "To insult or disgrace a Muslim is considered as being involved in the worst type of interest (usury). We neither care for a Muslim's honour and respect when we say some bad words during an argument, nor do we take the sayings of Allah Ta'ala and His Rasul ﷺ into consideration. Allah Ta'ala says in the Qur-aan Shareef,

وَلَا تَنَازَعُوْا فَتَفْشَلُوْا وَتَذْهَبَ رِيْحُكُمْ وَاصْبِرُوْا ۚ اِنَّ اللّٰهَ مَعَ الصّٰبِرِيْنَ

"Argue not among yourselves, otherwise your courage will go and your strength will depart, and be patient and persevering, for Allah Ta'ala is with those who patiently persevere."
(Surah Anfaal - Aayah 46)

It the duty of those who want to injure and destroy the honour and dignity of others to ponder how much harm they have done to themselves. Through these despicable deeds, they should realise that they themselves have become despicable in the sight Allah Ta'ala and in the sight of the people. The person who cuts relationship with his brothers for more than three days and dies in this state, will go straight to Jahannam. Rasulullah ﷺ said that on every Monday and Thursday the actions of all the people are brought before Allah Ta'ala. Except for the idolaters, forgiveness is then granted to all through His Mercy (as a result of some of their pious deeds). However, regarding any two people between whom an argument had taken place and friendship is cut off, it shall be said, "Leave their affair aside until such time that they restore their relationship with each other."

Another Hadith states that on every Monday and Thursday, when our aamal (actions) are presented before Allah Ta'ala, He accepts the taubah of those who make taubah, and forgives those who seek forgiveness. But those who had arguments are not forgiven.

Another Hadith says that on Shabe Bara'at (the 15th night of Shabaan) Allah Ta'ala showers His mercy on His creation and forgiveness is freely granted to all, except for two types of persons. Firstly, a kaafir (disbeliever) and secondly, for the one who harbors hatred against others. In another Hadith it is stated: There are three kinds of people whose Salaah does not rise one hand span above their heads for acceptance, and one among these three are those who argue among themselves.

In the above paragraphs I have gone off the topic which is under discussion. It was not my intention to mention all these Ahaadith on arguments. I only did it to bring to our notice this great evil which we regard as insignificant, so much so that even those whom we consider to be pious are guilty of it.

فَإِلَى اللهِ الْمُشْتَكٰى وَ اللهُ الْمُسْتَعَانُ

From Allah Ta'ala do I ask, as He is the only One we seek assistance from.

We should be aware that this fighting, use of harsh words and cutting ourselves off from others, will only be regarded as a sin and evil in Islam when it is done out of enmity and hatred over worldly matters. It is permissible to break off relations with somebody because of his sins or because of some religious matters where he is in the wrong and guilty.

Once, when Hadhrat Ibn Umar رضي الله عنه quoted a saying of Rasulullah صلى الله عليه وسلم, his son said something which outwardly appears as if he objected to it. The result was that Ibn Umar رضي الله عنه never again spoke to that son for as long as he lived. There are numerous similar instances reported of the Sahaabah رضي الله عنهم.

Many a time we too cut off relations with people and claim that it is for the sake of the Deen. Allah Ta'ala is All-knowing, All-seeing and He alone knows the realty. He knows which relationships are cut off because of Deen and which are cut off because of the hurt caused to our honour, pride and dignity.

The second point to which the Hadith draws our attention to is that man should be satisfied and accept Allah Ta'ala's decision in all matters. For example, even though it seems that the loss of the knowledge as to when Laylatul Qadr actually falls is a great loss of goodness, it has to be accepted because it is from Allah Ta'ala. For this reason, Rasulullah صلى الله عليه وسلم says, "It is better for us that way." One should ponder over this as Allah Ta'ala is at all times merciful to His servants.

Even when someone is overtaken by a great calamity because of his own sins, he only needs to appeal to His Creator by admitting his own weakness and that same calamity becomes a cause of great good for him. Nothing is impossible for Allah Ta'ala.

Our Ulama have mentioned several advantages in not knowing the actual date for Laylatul Qadr.

Firstly, had we known the actual date for this blessed night, there would have been so many of us who would not have worshipped Allah Ta'ala at all during the year or on other nights. We would wait for the prescribed night only, in which to perform Ibaadah. Because of not knowing the actual date, one has to stay awake and be in ibaadah for quite a number of nights in the hope that each night is perhaps Laylatul Qadr. (This means more nights spent in Allah Ta'ala's ibaadah for which one will be rewarded).

Secondly, there are those amongst us who just do not seem to be able to avoid sin. How extremely dangerous and unfortunate for them would it be that in spite of knowing that a certain night is Laylatul Qadr, they still spend it in sin and evil? Once Rasulullah ﷺ entered the masjid and saw one of the Sahaabah رضي الله عنه sleeping on one side. He said to Hadhrat Ali رضي الله عنه; "Wake him up so that he can make wudhu." Ali رضي الله عنه did this and then addressed Rasulullah ﷺ thus, "O Messenger of Allah Ta'ala, why did you not wake him up yourself as You are always first to hurry towards any good deed?" To this Rasulullah ﷺ replied, "I fear on his behalf that this man may refuse, and refusal to my command is kufr. If he refused your command, it would not be kufr (disbelief)." Similarly, Allah Ta'ala, in His mercy, does not like that a person, in spite of knowing that it is the night of Qadr, should still spend it in sin and evil.

Thirdly, there are some who find it possible to spend one, two or three nights in ibaadah, while we do not know exactly which night is the night of Qadr. Now say for arguments sake, if we knew which night is Laylatul Qadr and in spite of that, for one reason or another, within or outside our control, we allowed that night to go by without spending it in ibaadah, then almost certainly on no other night for the rest of Ramadhaan we would have spent in ibaadah. But since we do not know the exact night of Qadr, every person gets the opportunity to wake up for either one or two nights.

Fourthly, every night spent in ibaadah in search of Laylatul Qadr is a night for which a separate reward is granted.

Fifthly, we have read that Allah Ta'ala boasts to His Malaaikah about those believers who exert themselves in ibaadah during

Ramadhaan. Therefore, when they spend more nights in ibaadah, Allah Ta'ala has more opportunities of boasting about those believers. In spite of not knowing when Laylatul Qadr is and only having a vague idea about its fixed time, they still exert themselves to the utmost in Allah Ta'ala's ibaadah night after night. They exert themselves to such an extent in spite of not knowing the actual night, how much more would they had exerted themselves if it was known to them?

Besides the above points, there are also other benefits due to which Allah Ta'ala often keeps certain things secret to Himself. For example, if we call upon Allah Ta'ala using the "Ismul Aazam" (the great name of Allah Ta'ala), He will certainly answer. Similarly, there is a special moment on the day of Jumuah when Duas are answered. The exact time of this also is not known to us. There are many other occasions which are included in this category. It is possible that because of the argument that took place, the fixing of Laylatul Qadr during that Ramadhaan was caused to be forgotten. However, because of the other benefits, the knowledge of the fixed date was not revealed.

The third point to which attention is drawn to in the above Hadith is that one should search for Laylatul Qadr on the 9th, 7th and 5th nights. By reading this together with other Ahaadith quoted earlier, we come to know that this refers to the last ten nights of Ramadhaan. So which nights are these? If we start from the 20th, counting upwards, then these three nights are the 25th, 27th and 29th. But if we start counting from the 29th downwards, where Ramadhaan has 29 days, these nights will be the 21st, 23rd, and 25th, and in the case where the month has 30 days then it will be the 22nd, 24th and 26th.

From all the above one can see how much uncertainty there is about the correct date. Among the learned Ulama there are approximately fifty different opinions. Because of this reason, some Ulama have said that Laylatul Qadr does not occur on one and the same night every year. If in one year it occurred on one night then the following year it will occur on another night. At various times Rasulullah ﷺ commanded the Sahaabah رضي الله عنهم to search among a certain number of nights, whereas at other times he used to fix a particular night.

Hadhrat Abu Hurayrah رضي الله عنه reports that, once whilst talking with the Sahaabah رضي الله عنهم, Rasulullah ﷺ spoke about Laylatul Qadr and then asked, "What is the date today?" They replied, "The 22nd of

Ramadhaan." Rasulullah ﷺ said, "Search for Laylatul Qadr in the night following this day."

Abu Zar ؓ reports that he inquired of Rasulullah ﷺ whether Laylatul Qadr was only granted for the time of the duration of Rasulullah's ﷺ life, or whether it will continue to come after him. Rasulullah ﷺ replied, "It continues until Qiyaamah." I then inquired "In which section of Ramadhaan does it come?" Rasulullah ﷺ replied, "Search for it in the first ten and in the last ten days." Thereafter Rasulullah ﷺ became busy with other work, I waited, and, finding another chance, inquired, "Please indicate in which section of those ten does Laylatul Qadr come?" Upon this Rasulullah ﷺ became so angry with me as he had never been before or after, and he said, "If it had been Allah Ta'ala's object to make it known, would He not have informed us? Search for it among the last seven nights, and ask no more." In another Hadith again Rasulullah ﷺ is reported to have told one Sahaabi that Laylatul Qadr was on the 23rd night.

Ibn Abbaas ؓ related, "Once, while sleeping, somebody said to me in my dream, 'Rise up. This is Laylatul Qadr.' I woke up and went quickly to Rasulullah ﷺ and found him in salaah. That was the 23rd night." According to other reports again, the 24th is Laylatul Qadr. Hadhrat Abdullah ibn Mas'ood ؓ said, "Whoever remains awake every night of the year in ibaadah can find Laylatul Qadr." (In other words, the blessed night moves throughout the year and does not necessarily have to come in Ramadhaan only). Ibn Mas'ood ؓ reports this view from Nabi ﷺ.

When this was mentioned to Hadhrat Ubay bin Kaab ؓ he said; "Abdullah ibn Mas'ood ؓ meant people will stay awake only on this night and become contented." Thereafter he swore by Allah Ta'ala that Laylatul Qadr comes on 27th night. This is also the view held by numerous Sahaabah ؓ as well as the Taabieen.

Among the Imaams, the well-known opinion of Imaam Abu Hanifa *(rahmatullahi alayh)* is that Laylatul Qadr moves throughout the year, while another view of his is that it moves about throughout the month of Ramadhaan. However, His famous students, Imaam Muhammad *(rahmatullahi alayh)* and Imaam Abu Yusuf *(rahmatullahi alayh)*, were of the opinion that this night is unknown and fixed on one special night during the holy month. The Shaafiee's believe that it occurs probably on the 21st and Imaam Ahmad *(rahmatullahi alayh)* and Imaam Maalik *(rahmatullahi alayh)* hold the view that it is not fixed and occurs among the odd nights of the last ten nights of Ramadhaan, changing every year. But as for the vast majority of Ulama, their hope lies in that Laylatul Qadr is on 27th night every year.

Ibn-e-Arabi *(rahmatullahi alayh)* says, "In my opinion the view of those who believe that Laylatul Qadr comes on various nights throughout the year, is most correct, because twice have I seen it in Sha'baan, once on the 15th and once on the 19th, and twice have I seen it in the middle ten nights of Ramadhaan, the 13th and the 18th. I have also seen it on every odd night of the last ten. For this reason, I am sure that it could occur on any night of the year but occurs mostly in Ramadhaan."

Shah Waliyullah *(rahmatullahi alayh)* of Delhi believed that Laylatul Qadr comes twice every year:

a) **One Laylatul Qadr** is that one on which Allah Ta'ala's commands are revealed (to the Malaaikah). This is also the night on which the Qur-aan Shareef was sent down from the Lowhul Mahfooz to the heavens. This night does not come in Ramadhaan only but moves and can come on any night of the year. However, the night on which the Qur-aan Shareef was revealed fell in Ramadhaan and mostly falls during Ramadhaan.

b) **The second Laylatul Qadr** is the one of great spiritual value, when the Malaaikah come down in large numbers while the shayaateen are held back and a time when duas and ibaadah are accepted. This comes only in Ramadhaan during the odd nights of the last ten days. (This view of Shaah Waliyullah *(rahmatullahi alayh)* used to be the most acceptable to my late father).

Anyway, whether there are only one or two Laylatul Qadr, the fact still remains that one has to search for it according to his courage and ability. If not throughout the year, then in Ramadhaan. If that also proves difficult, then during the last ten days. When that also seems a bit too much, then only in the odd numbered nights of the last ten days. If by chance one has wasted all the above mentioned opportunities too, then by no means should the 27th night be allowed to go by. If by Allah Ta'ala's blessings and your good fortune that is Laylatul Qadr, then in comparison, all the wealth and pleasures of the world would be meaningless. Thus, even though that may not be the much searched for night, then at least the reward for ibaadah is received.

The Maghrib and Isha salaah should be performed with Jamaat throughout the year because if it is Laylatul Qadr, then the reward for both is so much more. It is a great blessing of Allah Ta'ala that when one makes effort for Deen and is not successful in his efforts, he is at least still rewarded for the effort made. In spite of this, there are those who go all out to render their services for Deen. On the other hand, regarding worldly affairs, if a person doesn't achieve his desired result, then his efforts are also written off as a waste. In spite of this, many people still spend their time, effort and wealth in worldly things that are fruitless and without purpose and also do not hold any reward or peace of mind.

ببیں تفاوتِ رہ از کجا است تابک کجا

"Look at the disparity of our paths from where to where."

HADITH 6 - A SAHAABI ﷺ ENQUIRING ABOUT LAYLATUL QADR

عَنْ عُبَادَةَ بْنِ الصَّامِتِ رَضِيَ اللهُ عَنْهُ أَنَّهُ سَئِلَ رَسُولَ اللهِ صَلَّى اللهُ عَلَيْهِ وَسَلَّمَ عَنْ لَيْلَةِ الْقَدْرِ فَقَالَ فِي رَمَضَانَ فِي الْعَشْرِ الْأَوَاخِرِ فَإِنَّهَا فِي لَيْلَةٍ وِتْرٍ فِي إِحْدَى وَعِشْرِينَ أَوْ ثَلَاثٍ وَعِشْرِينَ أَوْ خَمْسٍ وَعِشْرِينَ أَوْ سَبْعٍ وَعِشْرِينَ أَوْ تِسْعٍ وَعِشْرِينَ أَوْ آخِرِ لَيْلَةٍ مِنْ رَمَضَانَ مَنْ قَامَهَا إِيْمَانًا وَاحْتِسَابًا غُفِرَ لَهُ مَا تَقَدَّمَ مِنْ ذَنْبِهِ وَمِنْ أَمَارَاتِهَا أَنَّهَا لَيْلَةٌ بَلْجَةٌ صَافِيَةٌ سَاكِنَةٌ سَاجِيَةٌ لَا حَارَّةٌ وَلَا بَارِدَةٌ كَأَنَّ فِيهَا قَمَرًا سَاطِعًا وَلَا يَحِلُّ لِنَجْمٍ أَنْ يُرْمَى بِهِ تِلْكَ اللَّيْلَةَ حَتَّى الصَّبَاحِ وَمِنْ أَمَارَاتِهَا أَنَّ الشَّمْسَ تَطْلُعُ صَبِيحَتَهَا لَا شُعَاعَ لَهَا مُسْتَوِيَةً كَأَنَّهَا الْقَمَرُ لَيْلَةَ الْبَدْرِ وَحَرَّمَ اللهُ عَلَى الشَّيْطَانِ أَنْ يَخْرُجَ مَعَهَا يَوْمَئِذٍ

(اخرجه السيوطى فى الدر المنثور 8 / 571)

Hadhrat Ubaadah bin Saamit ﷺ reports that he asked Rasulullah ﷺ about Laylatul Qadr. He replied, "It is in Ramadhaan during the last ten days, on the unevenly numbered nights, either the 21st, 23rd, 25th, 27th and 29th or the last night of the month of

Ramadhaan, Whosoever stands in ibaadah on this night with sincere Imaan and with genuine hopes of gaining reward, his previous sins will be forgiven. Among the signs of this night is that it is a peaceful, quiet, shining night, neither too hot, nor too cold and the moon remains clear without any rays (due to the presence of abundant spiritual light). No stars are flung at the shayaateen on that night until the break of dawn. Another sign is that the sun rises without any radiant beams of light, appearing rather like the moon in its fullness. On that day Allah Ta'ala prohibits the shayaateen from rising up with the sun." (contrary to other days when the shayaateen appear at the time of the rising of the sun)

Note: Some of the things mentioned in this Hadith has already been explained earlier. However, this Hadith mentions some signs about the actual night. These signs are clear and need no further explanation. Apart from these signs, there are also other signs as found in the Hadith and also in the personal accounts of those who had the good fortune to experience Laylatul Qadr. However, the sign that is most common in the Hadith and generally witnessed, is the rising of the sun without any radiant beams of light. The other signs besides this are not necessarily always found.

Hadhrat Ab'da bin Abi Lubaabah رَضِىَ اللهُ عَنْهُ says, "On the evening of the 27th, I tasted the water of the sea and it was sweet." Hadhrat Ayoob bin Khaalid *(rahmatullahi alayh)* said, "When I once had to perform ghusl (bath) with sea water, then on tasting it, I found it to be sweet. This was on the 23rd night." Some of the Mashaaikh write that on the evening of Laylatul Qadr everything makes sajdah on the ground and then return to their positions. However, these are things that are only shown to some people and are not seen by an ordinary person.

HADITH 7 - WHAT DUA TO MAKE ON LAYLATUL QADR

عَنْ عَائِشَةَ رَضِىَ اللهُ عَنْهُ قَالَتْ قُلْتُ يَا رَسُوْلَ اللهِ اَرَئَيْتَ اِنْ عَلِمْتُ اَىُّ لَيْلَةٍ لَيْلَةُ الْقَدْرِ مَا اَقُوْلُ فِيْهَا قَالَ قُوْلِىْ اَللّٰهُمَّ اِنَّكَ عُفُوٌّ تُحِبُّ الْعَفْوَ فَاعْفُ عَنِّىْ

(سنن الترمذى # 3513)

Hadhrat Aa'ishah رضى الله عنها reports that she asked Rasulullah ﷺ, "If I find myself in Laylatul Qadr, what shall I say?" Rasulullah ﷺ replied,

اَللّٰهُمَّ اِنَّكَ عُفُوٌّ تُحِبُّ الْعَفْوَ فَاعْفُ عَنِّىْ

"O Allah! Indeed, You are the One who forgives, You love to forgive, so please forgive me."

Note: This is indeed an all-inclusive dua, wherein a person begs Allah Ta'ala that through His infinite grace He should forgive our sins. What else would one require?

من نگویم که طاعتم بپذیر   قلم عفو بر گنا هم کش

"I am not asking that you accept my obedience (since I don't have anything to present) All I ask is a stroke of pardon from your pen of forgiveness"

Imaan Sufyaan Sauri *(rahmatullahi alayh)* used to say that to keep yourself busy on this night with dua is better than any other form of ibaadah. Ibn Rajab *(rahmatullahi alayh)* says that one should not only remain busy with dua but should also take part in all other forms of ibaadah as well, such as the recitation of the Qur-aan Shareef, Salaah, dua, Zikr, etc. This latter opinion is considered correct and close to what Rasulullah ﷺ has said, as already been mentioned in previous Ahaadith.

CHAPTER 3
I'TIKAAF (STAYING IN THE MASJID)

The meaning of itikaaf is to seclude oneself in the masjid with the niyyah (intention) of itikaaf. According to the Hanafi school of thought, there are three different types of itikaaf.

A) WAAJIB ITIKAAF:

This itikaaf becomes compulsory when a person makes it obligatory upon himself. An example of this is when a person makes a vow to Allah Ta'ala that if Allah Ta'ala fulfills a certain wish of his, he will undertake to perform a certain number of days in itikaaf. In this case, the moment his wish is fulfilled, itikaaf becomes compulsory. From the moment a person makes an unconditional vow whereby he makes itikaaf waajib upon himself for certain number of days, then it becomes a Waajib duty on him.

B) SUNNAH ITIKAAF:

This was the general practice of Rasulullah ﷺ and it means to seclude oneself inside the masjid for the last ten days of Ramadhaan.

C) NAFL (OPTIONAL) ITIKAAF:

There is no special time or specific number of days for Nafl itikaaf. A person may make niyyah for any number of days at any time, even for his whole life. However, Imaam Abu Haneefah *(rahmatullahi alayh)* states that it must be for at least one full day. Imaam Muhammad *(rahmatullahi alayh)* states that there is no limit on the minimum period of time. The fatwa is on this latter view. Therefore, it is desirable for anyone entering a Masjid to make the niyyah (intention) of itikaaf for the period that he will remain in the Masjid. So, while he is in ibaadah, he also gains the reward of itikaaf.

In view of the above, it is advisable that anyone going the Masjid to join the Salaah with Jamaah should make the niyyah for itikaaf when entering the masjid. As long as he remains busy with Salaah, zikr, listening to lectures or sermons, etc., he will also receive the reward for itikaaf. I always observed that my late father used to make niyyah for itikaaf while stepping into the masjid with his right foot. Occasionally, by way of teaching and reminding his followers, he used to raise his voice when reciting the niyyah.

OBJECTS AND ADVANTAGES OF ITIKAAF

The reward for itikaaf is great. Rasulullah ﷺ constantly performed itikaaf. The example of the person who stays in the Masjid in itikaaf is like that person who had gone to a certain place for something and he remained there until it was granted.

نکل جائے دم تیرے قدموں کے نیچے یہی دل کا حسرت یہی آرزو

May my soul be extracted at Your feet. This is my heart's desire, This is my heart's desire

When someone comes begging to our door and then refuses to leave until he has been granted his request, I am sure that even the one with the hardest heart amongst us will eventually give in to his request. How much more merciful is Allah Ta'ala Who grants without any reason.

تُو وہ داتا ہے کہ دینے کے لیے

در تری رحمت کے ہیں ہر دم کھلے

خدا کی دین کا موسٰی سے پوچھیے احوال

کہ آگ لینے کو جائیں پیمبری مل جائے

"You are that master whose doors of grace and mercy and perpetually open. Ask Hadhrat Moosa (alayhis salaam) about the amazing system of Allah Ta'ala's Deen, that he left in search of a flame and returned? (the lamp of nubuwat)."

Hence, when one isolates himself from all worldly things and goes to Allah Ta'ala's door, then what doubt can there be for his request and duas to be accepted. When Allah Ta'ala has favoured someone, others cannot describe the enjoyment of such limitless treasures. How could a person ever describe what he has not yet obtained? Can an under aged person describe the joys of adulthood?

جس گل کو دل دیا ہے جس پھول پر فدا ہوں
یا وہ بغل میں آئے یا جاں قفس سے چھوٹے

"That rose I gave my heart to, that flower to whom I handed over my self, either I am connected to him otherwise there is no point in being alive."

Allaamah ibn Qayyim *(rahmatullahi alayh)*, on explaining the significance of itikaaf, writes that, "The actual aim of itikaaf is to divert the heart from everything except Allah Ta'ala, and to join it to Allah Ta'ala alone, thereby forming a complete spiritual connection with our Creator. All worldly connections are thus cut off for the sake of gaining Allah Ta'ala's attention. All thoughts, desires, love and devotion become centered around Him. As a result, His love is attained, a love and friendship that will be the only friend in the loneliness of the grave. When a person has that, then we can imagine the great happiness and enjoyment with which he will spend his time in the grave?"

جی ڈھونڈتا ہے پھر وہی فُرصت کے رات دن
بیٹھا رہوں تصوّرِ جاناں کیے ہوئے

"Day and night the heart anticipates for that chance where I sit and go on thinking of my beloved."

In *'Maraaqil Falaah'*, the author writes that itikaaf is a most rewarding deed when performed properly and sincerely. One cannot possibly list all the great advantages and benefits in it. In actual fact, what takes place in itikaaf, is that the heart is drawn away from everything else except the Creator, while our entire life is laid down at His doorstep.

پھر جی میں ہے کہ ڈر پہ کسی کے پڑا رہوں

سر زیرِ بارِ منّتِ درباں کیے ہوئے

"Again my heart desires to go and remain at the threshold of someone and be indebted to the one who kindly let me in."

One remains in ibaadah all the time. Even whilst one is asleep, one is still in His service, striving for nearness to Him. Allah Ta'ala says (according to a Hadith): "Whoever draws near to Me (the length of) one hand, then I draw nearer to him (the length of) two hands, and whoever draws near to Me by walking, I draw near to him by running." In itikaaf one goes to Allah Ta'ala's house and the most Kind Host always honours a guest who visits Him. The one in itikaaf also attains safety in Allah Ta'ala's fortress where no enemy can reach him. Besides this there are numerous other virtues and distinctive features of this important ibaadah.

WHERE TO PERFORM ITIKAAF

For males, the best of all places for itikaaf is the Masjidul Haraam in Makkah Mukarramah. The next best is the Masjidun Nabawi in Madinah Munawwarah, and the next best is Baitul Muqaddas. Thereafter, comes the Jaam'i Masjid in one's own town, and last but not least, the Masjid nearest to one's home. Imaam Abu Hanifah *(rahmatullahi alayh)* specifies that the Masjid should be one wherein the five daily Salaah are performed, while Imaam Abu Yusuf *(rahmatullahi alayh)* and Imaam Muhammad *(rahmatullahi alayh)* are agreed that any Masjid according to the Shariah can be entered for itikaaf, even if there is no regular Salaah with Jamaah.

As for the females, they should perform itikaaf in the Masjid inside their homes. However, where no Masjid exists and there is a desire for itikaaf, then one room of the house should be set aside for this purpose.

In fact, itikaaf is an easier task for women. A special section of the house, most commonly the Salaah room, is set aside wherein they seclude themselves, remaining in ibaadah. The woman who is in itikaaf, in a section of her home, will also be rewarded for the domestic duties that are carried out by her daughters or servants. It is so very unfortunate that in spite of such ease, our womenfolk still remain deprived of the blessings of itikaaf.

HADITH 1 - RASULULLAH ﷺ IN ITIKAAF

عَنْ اَبِيْ سَعِيْدٍ الْخُدْرِيِّ رَضِىَ اللهُ عَنْهُ اَنَّ رَسُوْلَ اللهِ صَلَّى اللهُ عَلَيْهِ وَسَلَّمَ اِعْتَكَفَ الْعَشْرَ الْأَوَّلَ مِنْ رَمَضَانَ ثُمَّ اعْتَكَفَ الْعَشْرَ الْأَوْسَطَ فِىْ قُبَّةٍ تُرْكِيَّةٍ ثُمَّ اَطْلَعَ رَأْسَهُ فَقَالَ اِنِّىْ اِعْتَكَفْتُ الْعَشْرَ الْأَوَّلَ اَلْتَمِسُ هٰذِهِ اللَّيْلَةَ ثُمَّ اعْتَكَفْتُ الْعَشْرَ الْأَوْسَطَ ثُمَّ اُتِيْتُ فَقِيْلَ لِىْ اِنَّهَا فِى الْعَشْرِ الْأَوَاخِرِ فَمَنْ كَانَ اعْتَكَفَ مَعِىْ فَلْيَعْتَكِفِ الْعَشْرَ الْأَوَاخِرَ فَقَدْ اُرِيْتُ هٰذِهِ اللَّيْلَةَ ثُمَّ اُنْسِيْتُهَا وَقَدْ رَاَيْتُنِىْ اَسْجُدُ فِىْ مَاءٍ وَطِيْنٍ مِنْ صَبِيْحَتِهَا فَالْتَمِسُوْهَا فِى الْعَشْرِ الْأَوَاخِرِ وَالْتَمِسُوْهَا فِىْ كُلِّ وِتْرٍ قَالَ فَمَطَرَتِ السَّمَاءُ تِلْكَ اللَّيْلَةَ وَكَانَ الْمَسْجِدُ عَلٰى عَرِيْشٍ فَوَكَفَ الْمَسْجِدُ فَبَصُرَتْ عَيْنَاىَ رَسُوْلَ اللهِ صَلَّى اللهُ عَلَيْهِ وَسَلَّمَ وَعَلٰى جَبْهَتِهٖ اَثَرُ الْمَاءِ وَالطِّيْنِ مِنْ صَبِيْحَةِ اِحْدٰى وَّعِشْرِيْنَ (صحيح مسلم # 1167)

Hadhrat Abu Saeed Khudri ﷺ reports that Rasulullah ﷺ once performed itikaaf for the first ten days of Ramadhaan. Thereafter, he made itikaaf in a Turkish tent (inside the Masjid) for the middle ten days. Thereafter, he raised his head out of the tent and said, "Verily, in search of Laylatul Qadr did I perform itikaaf for the first ten days, then for the middle ten days. Then someone (a Malaaikah) came and told me, 'It is in the last ten days. Whosoever has made itikaaf with me should continue for the last ten days.' I had been shown that night and then made to forget it. (However, a sign for it is), 'I saw myself making sajdah to Allah Ta'ala with my forehead on mud the next morning. Look for Laylatul Qadr in the last ten nights of Ramadhaan. Look for it among the odd nights." Abu Saeed

Ch. 3 – I'tikaaf

رَضِىَاللَّهُعَنْهُ says; "That same night it rained. The roof of the Masjid leaked. I looked at Rasulullah's صَلَّىاللَّهُعَلَيْهِوَسَلَّمَ eyes and forehead and there were remains of water and mud. This was on the morning of the 21st after performing sujood on muddy clay."

Note: It used to be the general practice of Rasulullah صَلَّىاللَّهُعَلَيْهِوَسَلَّمَ to perform itikaaf in Ramadhaan. At times he used to remain in the Masjid for the whole month, and during the last year of his life, he was in itikaaf for twenty days. Because he always secluded himself in the Masjid for the last ten days, therefore the Ulama consider it sunnah mu'akkadah to perform itikaaf for that period.

From the above Hadith it could be understood that the major object behind itikaaf was to search for Laylatul Qadr. What better method can there be than to be in itikaaf, because one is considered to be in ibaadah all the time, whether one is awake or asleep. Furthermore, one in itikaaf is free from all daily tasks and thus has all the time to devote to zikrullah and muraaqabah (meditation). There is no better way to spend ones time for those searching for Laylatul Qadr Rasulullah صَلَّىاللَّهُعَلَيْهِوَسَلَّمَ exerted himself throughout Ramadhaan but increased his ibaadah when the last ten days came along and he had no limit in exerting himself. He himself remained awake throughout the night and awakened his family members for the same purpose. Aa'ishah رَضِىَاللَّهُعَنْهَا reports: "During Ramadhaan, Rasulullah صَلَّىاللَّهُعَلَيْهِوَسَلَّمَ tied his lungi tightly around him, staying awake all night and waking his family (for the purpose of ibaadah)." Tied his lungi tightly means that he either knew no limits in exerting himself in ibaadah or that he gave due importance and preference to ibaadah and avoided all forms of contact with his respected wives.

HADITH 2 - REWARDS FOR ITIKAAF

عَنِ ابْنِ عَبَّاسٍ رَضِىَ اللَّهُ عَنْهُ أَنَّ رَسُوْلَ اللَّهِ صَلَّى اللَّهُ عَلَيْهِ وَسَلَّمَ قَالَ فِى الْمُعْتَكِفِ هُوَ يَعْتَكِفُ الذُّنُوْبَ وَيُجْرَى لَهُ مِنَ الْحَسَنَاتِ كَعَامِلِ الْحَسَنَاتِ كُلِّهَا

(سنن ابن ماجة # 1781)

Hadhrat Ibn Abbas رَضِىَاللَّهُعَنْهُ relates that Rasulullah صَلَّىاللَّهُعَلَيْهِوَسَلَّمَ said, "The person performing itikaaf remains free from sins, and he is given *the same reward as those who do good deeds in spite of not having done those deeds because of staying in the Masjid."*

(Note that the one remaining secluded in the Masjid is not allowed to depart from there for worldly needs. He may only go outside for the call of nature, to perform wudhu or ghusl or for attending Jumu-ah Salaah when that is not performed in the same Masjid, after which he must return immediately - translator).

Note: Now this Hadith points to two great benefits of itikaaf. Firstly, one is saved from sin as it is true that it very often happens that one falls into sin without ever intending to do so. (The world all around us is full of temptations). To commit sin in the blessed month of Ramadhaan is indeed a great injustice to ourselves. By remaining secluded in the Masjid, one completely avoids the temptation to commit sin.

Secondly, it would appear outwardly that when one is secluded in the Masjid, one is automatically at a disadvantage by not being allowed to perform certain good deeds like joining the janaza Salaah, attending burials, visiting the sick, etc. That is not so, because according to this Hadith one is rewarded for these deeds even though not performing them. What a great favour from Allah Ta'ala! How great is Allah Ta'ala's bounty! By performing one ibaadah, one receives the reward of many other ibaadahs. In fact, Allah Ta'ala looks for the smallest excuse to reward His servants. These rewards could be received in abundance with a little effort and begging.

بَہَانہ می دِہد بَہَانَا نَمی دہد

"Allah Ta'ala mercy creates excuses (to usher you in)"

If only we can understand and properly appreciate these favours. The proper appreciation and understanding can only enter our minds when we have the true love and interest for our Deen.

اس کے الطاف تو ہیں عام شہیدی سب پر

تجھ سے کیا ضد تھی اگر تُو کسی قابل ہوتا

"Shaheedi! His grace covers everything. When you had some ability then why were you so adamant."

Hadith 3 - To help someone to fulfil a need is better than performing Itikaaf for ten years

وَعَنِ ابْنِ عَبَّاسٍ رَضِيَ اللهِ عَنْهُمَا اَنَّهُ كَانَ مُعْتَكِفًا فِي مَسْجِدِ رَسُوْلِ اللهِ صَلَّى اللهِ عَلَيْهِ وَسَلَّمَ فَاَتَاهُ رَجُلٌ فَسَلَّمَ عَلَيْهِ ثُمَّ جَلَسَ فَقَالَ لَهُ ابْنُ عَبَّاسٍ يَا فُلَانُ اَرَاكَ مُكْتَئِبًا حَزِيْنًا قَالَ نَعَمْ يَا ابْنَ عَمِّ رَسُوْلِ اللهِ لِفُلَانٍ عَلَى حَقٌّ وَلَا حُرْمَةُ صَاحِبِ هٰذَا الْقَبْرِ مَا اَقْدِرُ عَلَيْهِ قَالَ ابْنُ عَبَّاسٍ اَفَلَا اُكَلِّمُهُ فِيْكَ قَالَ اِنْ اَحْبَبْتَ قَالَ فَانْتَعَلَ ابْنُ عَبَّاسٍ ثُمَّ خَرَجَ مِنَ الْمَسْجِدِ فَقَالَ لَهُ الرَّجُلُ اَنَسِيْتَ مَا كُنْتَ فِيْهِ قَالَ لَا وَلٰكِنِّيْ سَمِعْتُ صَاحِبَ هٰذَا الْقَبْرِ صَلَّى اللهُ عَلَيْهِ وَسَلَّمَ وَالْعَهْدُ بِهِ قَرِيْبٌ فَدَمَعَتْ عَيْنَاهُ وَهُوَ يَقُوْلُ مَنْ مَشٰى فِيْ حَاجَةِ اَخِيْهِ وَبَلَغَ فِيْهَا كَانَ خَيْرًا لَهُ مِنِ اعْتِكَافِ عَشْرِ سِنِيْنَ وَمَنِ اعْتَكَفَ يَوْمًا اِبْتِغَاءَ وَجْهِ اللهِ جَعَلَ اللهُ بَيْنَهُ وَبَيْنَ النَّارِ ثَلَاثَ خَنَادِقَ اَبْعَدَ مِمَّا بَيْنَ الْخَافِقَيْنِ

(اخرجه المنذرى فى الترغيب # 1650)

Hadhrat Ibn Abbaas ﷺ reports that while he was once performing Itikaaf in Masjidun Nabawi (Rasulullah's ﷺ Masjid), a man came to him, greeted him and sat down. Ibn Abbaas ﷺ said to him: "I see that you seem sad and troubled." The man replied: "Yes, O son of the uncle of Rasulullah ﷺ, I am indeed troubled in that I have an obligation to fulfil to someone. I swear by the honour of the inmate of this honoured resting place (Rasulullah's ﷺ grave) that I am not able to fulfil this obligation." Ibn Abbaas ﷺ inquired: "Shall I intercede with that person on your behalf?" The man replied: "By all means if you wish so." Ibn Abbaas ﷺ put on his shoes and proceeded from the Masjid. The man, seeing this, said: "Have you forgotten that you are in Itikaaf?" With tears filling his eyes, Ibn Abbaas ﷺ replied: "No, the time is still fresh in my mind, I heard the esteemed master of this grave say, 'Whoever goes out trying to fulfil a need of his brother, that service shall be better for him than to perform Itikaaf for ten years, and whomsoever performs Itikaaf for a day, thereby seeking the pleasure of Allah Ta'ala, then

Allah Ta'ala will open three trenches between him and the fire of Jahannam, the width of each being greater than the distance between heaven and earth.'"

(If this is the virtue of one day of itikaaf then what will be the reward of ten years of itikaaf?)

Note: Two things are clear from this Hadith. Firstly, we are told that the reward of one day in itikaaf is that Allah Ta'ala opens three trenches between him and the fire of Jahannam, the width of each trench is the distance between the heavens and the earth. Therefore, for every additional day that he performs itikaaf, he is rewarded accordingly. In '*Kashful Ghummah*', Allamah Sharaani *(rahmatullahi alayh)* relates a Hadith wherein Rasulullah ﷺ said, "Whoever performs itikaaf for the final ten days of Ramadhaan, he will be rewarded with two Haj and two Umrahs, and whoever performs itikaaf from Maghrib until Ishaa, doing nothing except performing Salaah and reciting the Qur-aan, Allah Ta'ala will prepare a palace in Jannah for him."

Secondly, and even more important we are told that fulfilling the need of a brother brings a reward that is greater than ten years of itikaaf. It was for this reason that Ibn Abbaas ﺭﺿﻲﺍﻟﻠﻪﻋﻨﻪ broke off his itikaaf. It was of course possible for him to continue it afterwards. (What he actually did was to leave the Masjid to relieve some suffering of his brother, who was greatly troubled in the heart and mind). The Sufis say that the amount of sympathy which Allah Ta'ala shows towards other things cannot be compared to the sympathy He shows towards a broken heart. It is for this reason that we have been strongly warned of the plea to Allah Ta'ala of that person, whose heart we hurt through unjust treatment and persecution. Whenever Rasulullah ﷺ appointed someone as a governor, amongst the many advices he gave, he also would say,

وَ اتَّقِ دَعْوَةَ الْمَظْلُوْمِ

"Be mindful of the dua of the oppressed."

بترس از آہِ مظلوماں کہ ہنگامِ دُعا کردن

اجابت از درِ حق بہر استقبال می آید

"Fear the pain of the opresser, since the moment he engages in dua, his petition is most welcomed in the court of Allah."

Note: Itikaaf breaks when one leaves the Masjid even for fulfilling a duty on behalf of a fellow Muslim. If it was a waajib itikaaf, then it has to be performed all over again. Rasulullah ﷺ never left the Masjid except for the calls of nature and wudhu. As for Ibn Abbaas ؓ leaving the Masjid to fulfil a need of a friend, it was in the same spirit of that soldier lying on the battlefield of Yarmouk close to death, refusing to drink water until the soldier next to him had been given to drink first. On the other hand, however, it is possible that Ibn Abbaas ؓ was performing nafl itikaaf, in which case it was permissible for him to leave the Masjid.

In conclusion I now wish to quote a lengthy Hadith hereunder, in which many virtues are mentioned and with this I conclude this book.

HADITH 4 - GREAT REWARDS GIVEN TO THIS UMMAH IN RAMADHAAN AND ON THE DAY OF EIDUL FITR

عَنِ ابْنِ عَبَّاسٍ رَضِيَ اللهُ عَنْهُمَا أَنَّهُ سَمِعَ رَسُوْلَ اللهِ صَلَّى اللهُ عَلَيْهِ وَسَلَّمَ يَقُوْلُ إِنَّ الْجَنَّةَ لَتُبَخَّرُ وَتُزَيَّنُ مِنَ الْحَوْلِ إِلَى الْحَوْلِ لِدُخُوْلِ شَهْرِ رَمَضَانَ فَإِذَا كَانَتْ أَوَّلُ لَيْلَةٍ مِنْ شَهْرِ رَمَضَانَ هَبَّتْ رِيْحٌ مِنْ تَحْتِ الْعَرْشِ يُقَالُ لَهَا الْمُثِيْرَةُ فَتَصْفِقُ وَرَقَاتُ أَشْجَارِ الْجِنَانِ وَحِلَقُ الْمَصَارِيْعِ فَيُسْمَعُ لِذَلِكَ طَنِيْنٌ لَمْ يَسْمَعِ السَّامِعُوْنَ أَحْسَنَ مِنْهُ فَتَبْرُزُ الْحُوْرُ الْعِيْنُ حَتَّى يَقِفْنَ بَيْنَ شُرَفِ الْجَنَّةِ فَيُنَادِيْنَ هَلْ مِنْ خَاطِبٍ إِلَى اللهِ فَيُزَوِّجُهُ ثُمَّ يَقُلْنَ الْحُوْرُ الْعِيْنُ يَا رِضْوَانُ الْجَنَّةِ مَا هَذِهِ اللَّيْلَةُ فَيُجِيْبُهُنَّ بِالتَّلْبِيَةِ ثُمَّ يَقُوْلُ هَذِهِ أَوَّلُ لَيْلَةٍ مِنْ شَهْرِ رَمَضَانَ فُتِحَتْ أَبْوَابُ الْجَنَّةِ لِلصَّائِمِيْنَ مِنْ أُمَّةِ مُحَمَّدٍ صَلَّى اللهُ عَلَيْهِ وَسَلَّمَ قَالَ وَيَقُوْلُ اللهُ عَزَّ وَجَلَّ يَا رِضْوَانُ افْتَحْ أَبْوَابَ الْجِنَانِ وَيَا مَالِكُ أَغْلِقْ أَبْوَابَ الْجَحِيْمِ عَلَى الصَّائِمِيْنَ مِنْ أُمَّةِ أَحْمَدَ صَلَّى اللهُ عَلَيْهِ وَسَلَّمَ وَيَا جِبْرَئِيْلُ اهْبِطْ إِلَى الْأَرْضِ فَاصْفَدْ مَرَدَةَ الشَّيَاطِيْنِ وَغُلَّهُمْ بِالْأَغْلَالِ ثُمَّ اقْذِفْهُمْ فِي الْبِحَارِ حَتَّى لَا يُفْسِدُوْا

عَلٰى اُمَّةِ مُحَمَّدٍ حَبِيْبِىْ صَلَّى اللهُ عَلَيْهِ وَسَلَّمَ صِيَامَهُمْ قَالَ وَيَقُوْلُ اللهُ عَزَّ وَجَلَّ فِىْ كُلِّ لَيْلَةٍ مِّنْ شَهْرِ رَمَضَانَ لِمُنَادٍ يُّنَادِىْ ثَلَاثَ مَرَّاتٍ هَلْ مِنْ سَائِلٍ فَاُعْطِيَهٗ سُؤْلَهٗ هَلْ مِنْ تَائِبٍ فَاَتُوْبَ عَلَيْهِ هَلْ مِنْ مُّسْتَغْفِرٍ فَاَغْفِرَ لَهٗ مَنْ يَّقْرِضُ الْمَلِىَّ غَيْرَ الْعَدُوْمِ وَالْوَفِىَّ غَيْرَ الظَّلُوْمِ قَالَ وَلِلّٰهِ عَزَّ وَجَلَّ فِىْ كُلِّ يَوْمٍ مِّنْ شَهْرِ رَمَضَانَ عِنْدَ الْاِفْطَارِ اَلْفُ اَلْفِ عَتِيْقٍ مِّنَ النَّارِ كُلُّهُمْ قَدِ اسْتَوْجَبُوا النَّارَ فَاِذَا كَانَ اٰخِرُ يَوْمٍ مِّنْ شَهْرِ رَمَضَانَ اَعْتَقَ اللهُ فِىْ ذٰلِكَ الْيَوْمِ بِقَدْرِ مَا اَعْتَقَ مِنْ اَوَّلِ الشَّهْرِ اِلٰى اٰخِرِهٖ وَاِذَا كَانَتْ لَيْلَةُ الْقَدْرِ يَاْمُرُ اللهُ عَزَّ وَجَلَّ جِبْرَئِيْلَ عَلَيْهِ السَّلَامُ فَيَهْبِطُ فِىْ كَبْكَبَةٍ مِّنَ الْمَلَائِكَةِ وَمَعَهُمْ لِوَاءٌ اَخْضَرُ فَيَرْكُزُوا اللِّوَاءَ عَلٰى ظَهْرِ الْكَعْبَةِ وَلَهٗ مِائَةُ جَنَاحٍ مِّنْهَا جَنَاحَانِ لَا يُنْشِرُهُمَا اِلَّا فِىْ تِلْكَ اللَّيْلَةِ فَيُنْشِرُهُمَا فِىْ تِلْكَ اللَّيْلَةِ فَيُجَاوِزَانِ الْمَشْرِقَ اِلَى الْمَغْرِبِ فَيَحُثُّ جِبْرَئِيْلُ عَلَيْهِ السَّلَامُ الْمَلَائِكَةَ فِىْ هٰذِهِ اللَّيْلَةِ فَيُسَلِّمُوْنَ عَلٰى كُلِّ قَائِمٍ وَّقَاعِدٍ وَّمُصَلٍّ وَّذَاكِرٍ وَّيُصَافِحُوْنَهُمْ وَيُؤَمِّنُوْنَ عَلٰى دُعَائِهِمْ حَتّٰى يَطْلُعَ الْفَجْرُ فَاِذَا طَلَعَ الْفَجْرُ يُنَادِىْ جِبْرَئِيْلُ عَلَيْهِ السَّلَامُ مَعَاشِرَ الْمَلَائِكَةِ الرَّحِيْلَ الرَّحِيْلَ فَيَقُوْلُوْنَ يَا جِبْرَئِيْلُ فَمَا صَنَعَ اللهُ فِىْ حَوَائِجِ الْمُؤْمِنِيْنَ مِنْ اُمَّةِ اَحْمَدَ صَلَّى اللهُ عَلَيْهِ وَسَلَّمَ فَيَقُوْلُ نَظَرَ اللهُ اِلَيْهِمْ فِىْ هٰذِهِ اللَّيْلَةِ فَعَفَا عَنْهُمْ اِلَّا اَرْبَعَةً فَقُلْنَا يَا رَسُوْلَ اللهِ مَنْ هُمْ قَالَ رَجُلٌ مُّدْمِنُ خَمْرٍ وَّعَاقٌّ لِّوَالِدَيْهِ وَقَاطِعُ رَحِمٍ وَّمُشَاحِنٌ قُلْنَا يَا رَسُوْلَ اللهِ مَا الْمُشَاحِنُ قَالَ هُوَ الْمُصَارِمُ فَاِذَا كَانَتْ لَيْلَةُ الْفِطْرِ سُمِّيَتْ تِلْكَ اللَّيْلَةُ لَيْلَةَ الْجَائِزَةِ فَاِذَا كَانَتْ غَدَاةُ الْفِطْرِ بَعَثَ اللهُ عَزَّ وَجَلَّ الْمَلَائِكَةَ فِىْ كُلِّ بِلَادٍ فَيَهْبِطُوْنَ اِلَى الْاَرْضِ فَيَقُوْمُوْنَ عَلٰى اَفْوَاهِ السِّكَكِ فَيُنَادُوْنَ بِصَوْتٍ يَّسْمَعُ مِنْ خَلْقِ اللهِ عَزَّ وَجَلَّ اِلَّا الْجِنَّ وَالْاِنْسَ فَيَقُوْلُوْنَ يَا اُمَّةَ مُحَمَّدٍ اُخْرُجُوْا اِلٰى رَبٍّ كَرِيْمٍ يُّعْطِى الْجَزِيْلَ وَيَعْفُوْ عَنِ الْعَظِيْمِ فَاِذَا بَرَزُوْا اِلٰى مُصَلَّاهُمْ يَقُوْلُ اللهُ عَزَّ وَجَلَّ لِلْمَلَائِكَةِ مَا جَزَاءُ الْاَجِيْرِ اِذَا عَمِلَ عَمَلَهٗ قَالَ فَتَقُوْلُ الْمَلَائِكَةُ اِلٰهَنَا وَسَيِّدَنَا جَزَاؤُهٗ اَنْ تُوَفِّيَهٗ اَجْرَهٗ قَالَ فَيَقُوْلُ فَاِنِّىْ اُشْهِدُكُمْ يَا مَلَائِكَتِىْ اَنِّىْ قَدْ جَعَلْتُ ثَوَابَهُمْ مِنْ صِيَامِهِمْ شَهْرَ رَمَضَانَ

Ch. 3 – I'tikaaf

وَقِيَامِهِمْ رِضَايْ وَمَغْفِرَتِيْ وَيَقُوْلُ يَا عِبَادِيْ سَلُوْنِيْ فَوَعِزَّتِيْ وَجَلَالِيْ لَا تَسْئَلُوْنِيَ الْيَوْمَ شَيْئًا فِيْ جَمْعِكُمْ لِآخِرَتِكُمْ اِلَّا اَعْطَيْتُكُمْ وَلَا لِدُنْيَاكُمْ اِلَّا نَظَرْتُ لَكُمْ فَوَعِزَّتِيْ لَأَسْتُرَنَّ عَلَيْكُمْ عَثَرَاتِكُمْ مَا رَاقَبْتُمُوْنِيْ وَعِزَّتِيْ وَجَلَالِيْ لَا اُخْزِيْكُمْ وَلَا اُفْضِحُكُمْ بَيْنَ اَصْحَابِ الْحُدُوْدِ وَانْصَرِفُوْا مَغْفُوْرًا لَكُمْ قَدْ اَرْضَيْتُمُوْنِيْ وَرَضِيْتُ عَنْكُمْ فَتَفْرَحُ الْمَلَائِكَةُ وَتَسْتَبْشِرُ بِمَا يُعْطِيْ اللهُ عَزَّ وَجَلَّ هٰذِهِ الْأُمَّةَ اِذَا اَفْطَرُوْا مِنْ شَهْرِ رَمَضَانَ

(اخرجه المنذري فى الترغيب # 1493)

Hadhrat Ibn Abbaas ﷺ says that he heard Nabi ﷺ saying, "Jannah is perfumed with the sweetest fragrance in Ramadhaan. From the beginning of the year till the end, it is being brightly decorated for this blessed month. When the first night of Ramadhaan appears, a wind blows from beneath the Arsh (Throne). It is called 'Museerah', which causes the leaves of the trees of Jannah to rustle and the door handles to sound, causing such a beautiful sound as had never been heard before. The beautiful eyed women of Jannah then step forward till they appear in the center of the balconies of Jannah, saying: 'Is there anyone making dua to Allah Ta'ala for us that Allah Ta'ala may marry us to him?' Then these women call out: 'O Ridwaan, keeper of Jannah, what night is this?' He replies: 'Labbaik, this is the first night of Ramadhaan, when the doors of Jannah are opened to those who fast from among the Ummah of Nabi Muhammad ﷺ.'"

Rasulullah ﷺ further said, that Allah Ta'ala says, "O Ridwaan, open the doors of Jannah, and O Maalik, (keeper of Jahannam) close the doors of Jahannam for those who fast from the Ummah of Ahmad ﷺ (another name for Nabi ﷺ), O Jibra-eel! Go down to the earth and tie the evil Shayaateen, put them in chains and throw them in the oceans so that they do not make mischief, thereby spoiling the fast of the Ummah of My beloved Muhammad ﷺ."

Allah Ta'ala commands a caller from the heavens to call out three times on every night of Ramadhaan: "Is there anyone begging of Me that I may grant him his desire? Is there anyone making taubah so that I may turn in mercy to him? Is there anyone begging for forgiveness so that I may forgive him? Who is there who shall give a loan to the One whose wealth does not become less and the One who fulfils in full without giving less?"

Rasulullah ﷺ then said, "Every day at the time of iftaar, Allah Ta'ala sets free one million people from the fire of Jahannam, all of whom had already earned entrance into Jahannam. On the last night He sets free as many as had been set free throughout the month. On Laylatul Qadr, Allah Ta'ala commands Hadhrat Jibra-eel (alayhis salaam) to go down to the earth with a large army of Malaaikah (Angels). They go down carrying a green flag which is then planted on top of the Kabah Shareef. Jibra-eel (alayhis salaam) himself has 100 wings, only two of which are spread out on this night. He spreads out these wings which cover from the east to the west. Jibra-eel (alayhis salaam) then sends out the Malaaikah on this night in all directions to make salaam upon each and every one they find in ibaadah standing or sitting, or performing Salaah and making the zikr of Allah Ta'ala. They shake hands with them and say 'Aameen' to all their duas until the morning. When dawn comes, Jibra-eel (alayhis salaam) calls out; 'Depart O Malaaikah of Allah, depart.'"

The Malaaikah then inquire: "O Jibra-eel! What did Allah Ta'ala do regarding the needs of the faithful people from among the ummah of Ahmad ﷺ which they asked from Him?" Jibra-eel (alayhis salaam) replies: "Allah Ta'ala looked at them with mercy and forgave them all except four kinds of people." Then we (the Sahaabah رضی اللہ عنہم) asked: "Who are they, O Rasulullah ﷺ?" Rasulullah ﷺ replied, "They are the people who are addicted to wine, those who are disobedient to their parents, those who do not speak to their near relatives and the mushaahin." We asked, "O Rasulullah ﷺ, who are the mushaahin?" He replied: "Those who have bad feelings in their hearts for their brothers and break off relations with them."

The night of Eidul Fitr, the night that is called Laylatul Jaa'izah (The night of prize giving), comes along. On the morning of Eid, Allah Ta'ala sends down the Malaaikah to all the lands of the earth, where they stand at the entrance of roads, calling out with a voice that is heard by all except man and jinn: "O Ummah of Muhammad ﷺ, come out of your houses towards your Rabb who is noble and gracious, who grants much and forgives major sins." When they go towards the places for their Eid Salaah, Allah Ta'ala ask the Malaaikah: "What is the reward of that worker who has completed his work?" The Malaaikah reply: "O Rabb and Master, it is only right that he should receive his reward in full." Allah Ta'ala then says: "I make you a witness, O My Malaaikah, as a reward, I have granted them My pleasure and forgiveness for having fasted during the month of Ramadhaan and for having stood before Me in salaah at night. O My servants, ask now of Me, for I swear by My honour and My greatness, that whatever you will beg of Me on this day, in this gathering of yours for the needs of the Hereafter, I will grant it to you, and whatever you will ask for your worldly needs, I will grant it what is good for you. I swear by My honour that as long as you shall obey My commands, I shall cover up your faults. By My Honour and My Greatness do I swear that I shall never disgrace you together with the sinful ones and the disbelievers. Go now from here, you are forgiven. You have pleased Me and I am pleased with you."

The Malaaikah, on seeing this great reward given by Allah Ta'ala to the Ummah of Nabi Muhammad ﷺ on the day of Eidul Fitr, become greatly pleased and happy.

"O Allah Ta'ala, make us also of those lucky ones, Aameen."

Note: The previous pages of this book already dealt with almost all that is contained in this last long Hadith. However, a few points need attention. The first point and most important point is that there are a few people who are deprived of forgiveness in Ramadhaan and are unfortunate indeed in not being able to share the great gifts of Allah Ta'ala on the morning of Eid. Among them are those who fight and argue among themselves and those disobedient to their parents.

Somebody should ask them: "You have displeased Allah Ta'ala, and having done so, what other protection do you have besides Allah Ta'ala? We indeed feel sad that for some reason or the other, you have made yourselves the target for the curse of Allah Ta'ala, His Rasool ﷺ and Jibra-eel *(alayhis salaam)* while at the same time being left out from Allah Ta'ala's freely granted forgiveness. Today you have disgraced your opponent and you are standing tall; for how long is this "victory" going to last? Who else can grant you protection? Who and what can stand by your side when you carry the curse of Rasulullah ﷺ? Who can help you when Allah Ta'ala's close Malaaikah, Jibra-eel *(alayhis salaam)* has made dua against you? While Allah Ta'ala is excluding you from His forgiveness and mercy, I plead with you, my dear brother and sister, to think about your position at this moment. Think and stay away from all that draws you away from Allah Ta'ala. There is time to make amends and repent, and now is that time. Tomorrow you shall have to stand before a Judge before whom no rank, honour, position and wealth will be of any help. A Judge before whom only amaal (good deeds) will count and Who is indeed aware of everything we do. Remember that Allah Ta'ala may forgive our sins as far as our relationship with Him is concerned, but as far as our dealing with people is concerned, He will not forgive us without us repaying them for not fulfilling their rights.

Rasulullah ﷺ said, "The bankrupt one from among my Ummah is that person who shall appear on the day of Qiyaamah, bringing with him good deeds like Salaah, saum (fast) and charity. However, he had also sworn at someone, falsely accused someone and assaulted someone, with the result that all these people shall come forward complaining and bearing witness against him. As a repayment, his good deeds shall be taken away and granted to the aggrieved persons. When his good deeds are finished, the aggrieved persons sins shall be put upon him because of him not being able to repay the full penalty through lack of good deeds. Hence, in this manner he shall enter Jahannam. We cannot describe his regret and sorrow in spite of him having had many good deeds to his account. (O Allah Ta'ala, save us from that, Ameen)

وہ مایوس تمنّا کیوں نہ سُوئے آسمان دیکھے

کہ جو منزل بمنزل اپنی محنت رائیگاں دیکھے

"It is not surprising for him who's lost all hope to look towards the sky, when every leg of the journey he sees his efforts going in vain."

Another point that needs explanation is this: we have come across many occasions and actions that cause one's sins to be forgiven – the question arises that when the sins have been forgiven on the first occasion, which sin are then forgiven later? In other words, once a person had been forgiven there are no sins left on him. So why is forgiveness granted again? The answer is this: when Allah Ta'ala's mercy and forgiveness descends upon mankind, those who have (a burden of) sins, their sins are wiped out and those (fortunate) people without (a burden of) sin are blessed and favored with Allah Ta'ala's mercy (Rahmat and in'aamaat) and bounties.

A further interesting point to note is that Allah Ta'ala time and again calls the Malaaikah to witness. The question may arise why is that so? Here one should remember that the questioning of the day of Qiyaamah has been set and witnesses will be brought forward to testify. Hence, Ambiya *(alayhis salaam)* will be required to bring witnesses as to whether they had delivered the message. Very often our Nabi ﷺ used to say, "Verily you shall be asked about me (and my mission). So, bear witness that I did deliver the message."

In Bukhaari Shareef we read a Hadith: "On the day of Qiyaamah, Hadhrat Nooh *(alayhis salaam)* will be called and asked, "Did you deliver the message in the proper manner?" He shall reply, "Yes I did." Then his Ummah shall be asked, "Did he deliver the message?" They shall reply,

$$\text{مَا جَآءَنَا مِنْ بَشِيْرٍ وَّلَا نَذِيْرٍ}$$

"No, neither did a bringer of glad tiding come to us nor did the Warner." (Surah Maa'idah - Aayah 19)

"Thereupon Nooh *(alayhis salaam)* will be called to bring witnesses. He shall call upon Hadhrat Muhammad ﷺ and his Ummah. This Ummah shall be called forward and they shall testify to the truth of Nooh *(alayhis salaam's)* evidence."

In some versions of this Hadith, this Ummah shall be cross questioned, "How do you know that Nooh *(alayhis salaam)* delivered the message of Allah Ta'ala, (When you were not present at that time?)" They shall reply, "Our Nabi ﷺ informed us of that." In this same manner all the Ambiyaa *(alayhis salaam)* will be questioned. For this the Qur-aan-e-Kareem says,

$$\text{وَكَذٰلِكَ جَعَلْنٰكُمْ أُمَّةً وَّسَطًا لِّتَكُوْنُوْا شُهَدَآءَ عَلَى النَّاسِ}$$

"Thus, we made you an Ummah, justly balanced, that you might be witnesses over the nations." *(Surah Baqarah - Aayah 143)*

Imaam Fakhrud Deen Raazi *(rahmatullahi alaih)* writes that on the day of Qiyaamah there shall be four types of witnesses:

1. The Malaaikah. The Qur-aan says:

$$\text{وَجَاءَتْ كُلُّ نَفْسٍ مَّعَهَا سَائِقٌ وَشَهِيدٌ}$$

1.1. "Every soul shall come with an angel **(who will take him to the place where he will be questioned)** and a witness **(the angel who has recorded all his actions)**." *(Surah Qaaf - Aayah 21)*

$$\text{مَا يَلْفِظُ مِنْ قَوْلٍ إِلَّا لَدَيْهِ رَقِيبٌ عَتِيدٌ}$$

1.2. "Whenever a word escapes (from a persons mouth), there is a guard ready by him (an angel immediately records it, be it good or bad) *(Surah Qaaf - Aayah 18)*

$$\text{وَإِنَّ عَلَيْكُمْ لَحَافِظِينَ ۞ كِرَامًا كَاتِبِينَ ۞ يَعْلَمُونَ مَا تَفْعَلُونَ}$$

1.3. "Verily there are guardians (angels) upon you (with every person) who are noble and (continuously) recording (everything you say). They know what you do." *(Surah Infitaar - Aayah 10-12)*

2. The Ambiyaa *(alayhis salaam)*. The Qur-aan says:

$$\text{وَكُنْتُ عَلَيْهِمْ شَهِيدًا مَا دُمْتُ فِيهِمْ}$$

2.1. "And I was a witness to them as long as I was with them." *(Surah Maa'idah - Aayah 117)*

$$\text{فَكَيْفَ إِذَا جِئْنَا مِنْ كُلِّ أُمَّةٍ بِشَهِيدٍ وَجِئْنَا بِكَ عَلَىٰ هَٰؤُلَاءِ شَهِيدًا}$$

2.2. "How will it be (the condition of the kuffaar on the day of Qiyaamah) when We shall bring forth a witness from every nation and call you (O Muhammad ﷺ) to be a witness over all of them?" *(Surah Nisaa - Aayah 41)*

Ch. 3 – I'tikaaf

3. **The Ummah of Muhammad** ﷺ, the following Aayaat refer to this:

$$وَجِاْىٓءَ بِالنَّبِيِّنَ وَالشُّهَدَآءِ$$

3.1. "and the Ambiya and the witnesses will be brought."
(Surah Zumar - Aayah 69)

4. **The different parts of a man's body.** Thus, the Qur-aan Shareef states:

$$يَوْمَ تَشْهَدُ عَلَيْهِمْ اَلْسِنَتُهُمْ وَ اَيْدِيْهِمْ وَ اَرْجُلُهُمْ بِمَا كَانُوْا يَعْمَلُوْنَ$$

"On the day (of Qiyaamah) when their tongues, hands and legs will testify against them for what they did." (Surah Noor - Aayah 24)

$$اَلْيَوْمَ نَخْتِمُ عَلٰى اَفْوَاهِهِمْ وَ تُكَلِّمُنَآ اَيْدِيْهِمْ وَ تَشْهَدُ اَرْجُلُهُمْ بِمَا كَانُوْا يَكْسِبُوْنَ$$

4.1. "On this day (day of Qiyaamah) We shall seal their mouths, but their hands will speak to Us and their legs will testify to what they earned/ did." (Surah Yaaseen - Aayah 65)

The last Hadith also mentions one glad tiding for the fortunate ones. Allah Ta'ala says that those who were obedient to him will not be disgraced and humiliated in front of the disbelievers and sinners. This is the great extent of Allah Ta'ala's grace and kindness and also the regard Allah Ta'ala shows for the status of the Muslims. Another of Allah Ta'ala's blessing and favour for those who sought his pleasure is that their faults and sins will be covered up on this occasion.

Hadhrat Abdullah ibn 'Umar رضي الله عنه reports that Rasulullah ﷺ said, "On the day of Qiyaamah Allah Ta'ala will call a believer to come near to Him and a curtain will be drawn so that no one else can see. Allah Ta'ala will then remind him of each and every sin of his which he will admit to. On seeing his numerous sins, that person will feel that he had indeed failed and shall be doomed. But then Allah Ta'ala will say: 'In the world I covered your faults and today also I will hide them and forgive you.'" Thereafter his book of good deeds will be given to him.

The contents of this Hadith is also contained in many other Ahaadith as well. One should therefore be careful of not humiliating and attacking the righteous ones for their sins, because it is possible that their sins will be forgiven. In the end we may be the real losers due to backbiting, mocking and insulting those who, in their own manner, seek to please Allah Ta'ala. It is possible that Allah Ta'ala may cover their faults and forgive them through the blessings of their other good deeds, while we, who continue to backbite, mock and insult them, may be the cause of our own destruction. (May Allah Ta'ala, in His Mercy, forgive us all).

This Hadith also states that the night before the day of Eid is called the night of prize giving, the night when Allah Ta'ala gives the true reward to his servants. This night should also be properly appreciated. Once an announcement has been made that tomorrow is Eid, many of us, including the pious, go to sleep, whereas this is also a night that should be spent in Ibaadah. Rasulullah ﷺ said, "Whoever remains awake (for ibaadah) on the nights preceding both the Eids with the aim of gaining reward, his heart will not die on that day when hearts will die." The meaning here is that at the time when evil will overcome all hearts, his heart shall stay alive (guarded against evil). It may also refer to the time when the soor (trumpet) shall be blown to announce the day of Qiyaamah, then on that day his soul shall not become unconscious.

Rasulullah ﷺ is also reported to have said, "Whoever stays awake for Ibaadah on the following five nights, entrance into Jannah becomes waajib for him, Laylatut Tarwiyah (the night before the 8th Zul Hijjah), Laylatul Arafah (the night before the 9th Zul Hijjah), Laylatun Nahr (the night before the 10th Zul Hijjah), the night before Eidul Fitr and the night of 15th Sha'baan.

The fuqahaa have written that it is mustahab to remain in ibaadah on the nights before Eid. It is reported in *'Maa sabata bis Sunnah'* from Imaam Shaafiee *(rahmatullahi alayh)* that there are five nights in which duas are accepted; the night before Friday, the night before both Eids, the first night of Rajab, and Laylatul Bara'ah (15th Shabaan).

Point of Note

Among the pious, it is said that because of the exceptional greatness of Friday night, one should spend this night in ibaadah during the month of Ramadhaan. But there are some Ahaadith that prohibit us from fixing only that particular night for ibaadah. Therefore, it is advisable that one or two other nights should also be joined with it.

In conclusion, as I have now come to the end of this book, I hope that this will be of benefit to those who seek Allah Ta'ala's pleasure. I beg and plead for all the readers to make dua for me (the humble writer of these pages), during those special hours of Ramadhaan. It is possible that because of your dua, Allah Ta'ala will bestow His happiness and love upon me too, Aameen.

Readers are humbly requested to also include in their dua's the founder, past and present staff, pupils and associates of this Institute.

مناجات

گرچہ میں بدکار و نالائق ہوں اے شاہِ جہاں

پر ترے دَر کو بتا اب چھوڑ کر جاؤں کہاں

کون ہے تیرے سوا مجھ بے نوا کے واسطے

O king of the universe! Eventhough I am in the wrong and most unworthy, but then, O my beloved! Besides you where else can I go. Besides you who else can there be for a destitute like me.

دیکھ مت میرے عمل، کر لُطف پر اپنے نگاہ

کشمکش سے نا اُمیدی کی ہوا ہوں میں تباہ

یا رب اپنے رحم و احسان و عطا کے واسطے

Please do not look at my deeds (and pass judgement), instead look at me with your eye of grace. In the distress of despair I am destroyed. O my Rabb, bless me with your mercy, kindness and grace.

چرخِ عِصیاں سر پہ ہے زیرِ قدم بحرِ اَلم

چار سُو ہے فوجِ غم، کر جلد اب بَہر کَرم

کچھ رَہائی کا سبب اس مبتلا کے واسطے

Above me is my load of sin, below me is the ocean of trial. The army of distress has surrounded me from all sides. Please come quickly to my rescue. Create some exit for this distressed one.

ہے عبادت کا سہارا عابدوں کے واسطے

اور تکیہ زہد کا ہے زاہدوں کے واسطے

Munaajaat

ہے عصائے آہ مجھ بے دست و پا کے واسطے

The ones in your servitude have their worship to rely on.
Those who renounce this world have the virtue of abstinence to their account and then myself with absolutely nothing to present, I only have my cry (of regret and hope)

نے فقیری چاہتا ہوں نے امیری کی طلب

نے عبادت نے وَرَع نے خواہشِ علم و ادب

دردِ دل، پر چاہیے مجھ کو خدا کے واسطے

It is not poverty which I desire, nor is it prosperity, worship, austerity or the desire for knowledge and respect do I wish. Yes, for the sake of Allah Ta'ala, Darde Dil (your love) is what I desire

عقل و ہوش و فکر اور نُعمائے دُنیا بے شمار

کی عطا تو نے مجھے، پر اب تو اے پروردگار

بخش وہ نعمت جو کام آئے سَدا کے واسطے

I fully acknowledge your unlimited blessings upon me in this world, my understanding, my sanity, my rational etc.
Now O My Cherisher! I beg of you that bounty which will see me through forever.

حد سے اَبتَر ہو گیا ہے حال مجھ ناشاد کا

کر مری اِمداد اللہ! وقت ہے امداد کا

اپنے لُطف و رحمتِ بے انتہا کے واسطے

This unfortunate one has now reached the point of desperation. O Allah! Now is the time I need your help. Out of your shoreless grace and mercy....please assist me.

گو میں ہوں اک بندۂ عاصی غلامِ پُر قصور

جُرم میرا حوصلہ ہے نام ہے تیرا غفور

تیرا کہلاتا ہوں میں جیسا ہوں اے ربّ شکور

On the one hand I admit being a sinful slave full of faults and error. Yet it is you, O Allah, whose attributes is the most forgiving that gives me the courage (to still come to you) whatever I may be, at the end, I am still referred to you as yours.

اَنْتَ شَافٍ اَنْتَ كَافٍ فِیْ مُهِمَّاتِ الْاُمُوْرِ

اَنْتَ حَسْبِیْ اَنْتَ رَبِّیْ اَنْتَ لِیْ نِعْمَ الْوَكِیْلُ

You are the curer, you are the one sufficient for me in all my concerns. You are enough for me, you are my Rabb, you are the most execellent manager of my affairs.

(Hadhrat Moulana) Muhammad Zakariyya Kandhlawi (RA)
Resident at Madrasah Mazahirul Uloom
Saharanpur U.P. India
27th Ramadhaan, 1349 Hijri

The Current Downfall of the Muslims and it's only Remedy

Contents

Author's Preface	867
Past History	868
The Disease	868
Earlier attempts of Improvement	869
The Approach	870
Finding the cause of our problems	870
The main cause	877
First Cause	879
Second Cause	881
Third Cause	882
Fourth Cause	885
Fifth Cause	885
Sixth Cause	886
The Solution	887
Course of Action	890
Method for Tabligh	894
Etiquettes of Tableegh	895
Summary	897
Conclusion	900
Final Request	900

Author's Preface

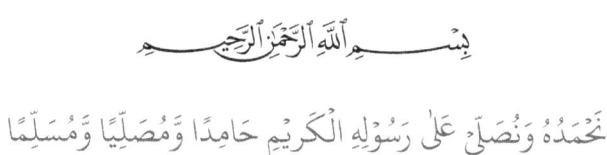

$$\text{بِسْمِ اللَّهِ الرَّحْمَنِ الرَّحِيمِ}$$

$$\text{نَحْمَدُهُ وَنُصَلِّي عَلَى رَسُولِهِ الْكَرِيْمِ حَامِدًا وَمُصَلِّيًا وَمُسَلِّمًا}$$

Through the dedication and commitment of Hadhrat Moulana Muhammad Ilyaas *(rahmatullahi alayh)* and many other learned and pious elders, the Tabligh Jamaat is attempting to establish an Islamic way of life. This is something that is known to most of the Muslims. Although unworthy for this work, I have been commanded by my pious elders to write a booklet about this work, to explain clearly what is Tabligh and the real need for this effort of Deen so that in this critical period in history, the Muslims are able to understand and benefit from this effort.

In obedience to their command, I have attempted to gather in this booklet a few thoughts and ideas, which are mere drops from the oceans of knowledge possessed by our pious elders. The collection really amounts to a handful of petals from the vast garden of the teachings of Islam, which I have hurriedly picked up to present to the readers. There may be mistakes in this book for which I beg the readers forgiveness. I also request them to please correct these mistakes.

It is my dua that Allah Ta'ala, by His special favour and kindness, may hide my faults and forgive my sins. May He make us all pious, give us His true love and enable us to follow the Deen of Islam. May He also give us the ability to follow the Deen of Islam and the strength to spread Islam in the way of His dearest Nabi Muhammad ﷺ.

Madrasah Kaashiful Uloom (Nizaamuddeen)
Muhammad Ihtishaamul Hasan (Delhi)
18 Rabi'us Saani 1358 A.H.

Fazaail-e-A'maal

بِسْمِ اللهِ الرَّحْمٰنِ الرَّحِيْمِ

اَلْحَمْدُ لِلهِ رَبِّ الْعَالَمِيْنَ وَالصَّلَاةُ وَالسَّلَامُ عَلٰى سَيِّدِ الْاَوَّلِيْنَ وَالْاٰخِرِيْنَ خَاتِمِ الْاَنْبِيَاءِ وَالْمُرْسَلِيْنَ مُحَمَّدٍ وَّاٰلِهِ وَاَصْحَابِهِ الطَّيِّبِيْنَ الطَّاهِرِيْنَ

PAST HISTORY

About 1350 years ago *(This kitaab was written in 1358 Hijri equivalent to the Gregorian year 1939)* the world was filled with darkness, ignorance and sin. The noor of true knowledge and guidance arose from the hills of Bat-haa (name of hills near Makkah). Its light spread to the East, West, North and South. Within a short period of twenty-three years, mankind reached such heights of glory as had never been reached before. The Muslims were educated and a desire was created in them to seek the right advice which would make them successful in the Aakirah. By following the right path, the Muslims moved from success to success and reached the heights of glory.

For centuries they ruled on earth with such strength that no power could challenge them, and if someone dared to do so, he did it at the risk of being destroyed. This is a historical truth which cannot be erased. But, alas! This fact of history has only become like a fairy tale which may sound strange and ridiculous, because of the present day life of Muslims, which is obviously an ugly stain on the excellent efforts and achievements of our pious elders who were the early followers of Islam.

THE DISEASE

Up to the end of the 13th century Hijri, history proves that the Muslims were people of honour, dignity, power and greatness. But when we look at the Muslims of today, we see them in disgrace. It is an Ummah, who has no real strength or power, no honour or dignity, no brotherhood or love and no real virtue or akhlaaq (moral character). We do not find any sign of those noble deeds which was found in every Muslim. Nowadays, there is hardly a person who has devotion or sincerity. Muslims are drowning in evil and sin. They have moved far away from the path of goodness. The enemies of Islam discuss the affairs of Muslims with laughter, disrespect and ridicule.

Unfortunately, the matter does not end here. The Muslim youth have been affected and influenced by modern ways or by the Western way of life. They take pleasure in ridiculing and openly criticizing the teachings of Islam which they say is not practical and out dated. The Muslims who once gave strength, happiness, honour and peace to the entire mankind are now completely demoralised, indifferent and helpless. Those who had once taught the world the golden lessons of manners and culture are today found lacking in these qualities.

EARLIER ATTEMPTS OF IMPROVEMENT

The concerned elders and Ulama have been seriously pondering over this unfortunate condition of the people. They have been working hard to correct the Muslim Ummah, but alas!

مرض بڑھتا گیا جوں جوں دوا کی

"The treatment only increased the disease."

The situation is getting worse and the future does not look promising. Doing absolutely nothing about it and being content on our part in this situation is a sin that cannot be forgiven. Before deciding what to do, it is necessary to study what the cause of this sad state of affairs is.

People have suggested many causes of this downfall and have tried to correct this problem, but unfortunately all their efforts so far have only brought more failures. Instead of improvement, hopelessness and confusion have resulted, especially among the learned preachers and the Ulama. The basic reason for this is that the actual cause of the disease has not been found. Until this is done, no proper treatment can be given. Any effort without proper examination and correct treatment would make the situation even worse. It would increase the confusion and hopelessness even more.

THE APPROACH

The Shariah is a complete way of life given by Allah Ta'ala. It guarantees everlasting success and shows us the way of life that leads to true success and piety. It very clearly gives us guidelines on the proper course of action we should take and shows us what to do when we lose direction or go astray. In other words, "Shariah-e-Muhammadiah" promises its followers their Deeni and worldly progress in all situations right up to the last day of their lives. Therefore, it would be obviously useless to look for the cause and the cure for our downfall outside the guidelines of "Shariah". Therefore, we should look closely into the Qur-aan, which is the original source of Shariah. It is the only source of wisdom for man. We should seek its help to find out what our problems are and how they could be corrected. If we really wish to recover, we must implement the solution seriously. The wisdom and guidance from the Qur-aan will never fail us, especially in the difficult times through which we are passing through. Let us search for the solution only in the Qur-aan and the Sunnah.

FINDING THE CAUSE OF OUR PROBLEMS

Allah Ta'ala, The Creator of the universe, clearly wants that leadership and khilaafat on earth to be only for the Muslims of perfect Imaan. This is clear from the following Aayah:

وَعَدَ اللهُ الَّذِيْنَ اٰمَنُوْا مِنْكُمْ وَعَمِلُوا الصَّلِحٰتِ لَيَسْتَخْلِفَنَّهُمْ فِى الْاَرْضِ

"Allah has promised those of you who have Imaan and do good actions that He would surely make them His successors (rulers) on earth." (Surah Noor - Aayah 55)

He has also promised that true believers will always rule over non-believers and that the non-believers will be left without any friend or helper. This is clear from the following Aayah:

وَلَوْ قَاتَلَكُمُ الَّذِيْنَ كَفَرُوْا لَوَلَّوُا الْاَدْبَارَ ثُمَّ لَا يَجِدُوْنَ وَلِيًّا وَّلَا نَصِيْرًا

"And if the Kuffaar were to fight you (in battle instead of signing the treaty), they would turn their backs (and flee from the battlefield), and then they would not find any protector nor any helper"
(Surah Fath - Aayah 22).

It is the promise of Allah Ta'ala to help the true Muslims. It is also His promise that such people will remain superior and honoured. This is explained by the following Aayah:

$$وَكَانَ حَقًّا عَلَيْنَا نَصْرُ الْمُؤْمِنِيْنَ$$

"And it is our duty to help the true believers." *(Surah Room - Aayah 47)*

$$وَلَا تَهِنُوْا وَلَا تَحْزَنُوْا وَأَنْتُمُ الْأَعْلَوْنَ اِنْ كُنْتُمْ مُّؤْمِنِيْنَ$$

"And do not be weak (lose courage against your enemies), and do not grieve (over your losses) for you shall be elevated, if you are true believers." *(Surah Aale I'mraan - Aayah 139)*

$$وَلِلَّهِ الْعِزَّةُ وَلِرَسُوْلِهٖ وَلِلْمُؤْمِنِيْنَ$$

"And honour is only for Allah, His *Rasul* (ﷺ) and those who believe." *(Surah Munaafiqoon - Aayah 8)*

The above Aayaat indicate that honour, greatness, superiority, fame and virtue can only be acquired by Muslims by adopting perfect Imaan. If our relationship with Allah Ta'ala and with Rasulullah ﷺ is strong, we will certainly be masters of the earth. On the other hand, if it is weak, then disaster will follow. This is clear from the following Aayah:

$$وَالْعَصْرِ ۞ اِنَّ الْاِنْسَانَ لَفِيْ خُسْرٍ ۞ اِلَّا الَّذِيْنَ اٰمَنُوْا وَعَمِلُوا الصّٰلِحٰتِ وَتَوَاصَوْا بِالْحَقِّ وَتَوَاصَوْا بِالصَّبْرِ$$

"By the oath of time! Certainly, man is at a great loss except those who believe, do good deeds, who encourage each other towards the truth and encourage each other to exercise patience."
(Surah Asr - Aayah 1-3)

History proves that the early Muslims had reached the highest level of honour and glory, whereas the Muslims of today have moved in the opposite direction. These Aayaat of the Qur-aan indicate that the early Muslims reached the highest position because of the strength of their Imaan and the beauty of their akhlaaq (character). On the other hand, the miserable condition of the present day Muslims is because of a weakness in their Imaan and akhlaaq. It would be correct to say that today we are Muslims in name only. The true Messenger of Allah Ta'ala, Nabi Muhammad ﷺ, had said:

سَيَأْتِيْ عَلَى النَّاسِ زَمَانٌ لَّا يَبْقٰى مِنَ الْإِسْلَامِ اِلَّا اسْمُهُ وَلَا مِنَ الْقُرْاٰنِ اِلَّا رَسْمُهُ

(اخرجه السيوطى فى جامع الاحاديث # 33576)

"A time will come very soon when Islam will exist only in name and the Qur-aan will exist only in writing."

This applies to the Muslims of today. We need to be concerned about the following points:

a) The type of Imaan that will be accepted by Allah Ta'ala and His Rasul ﷺ which will bring us Deeni and worldly success. What are the means to earn true Imaan?

b) What has caused the destruction of that Imaan and the true spirit of Islaam.

A study of the Qur-aan Shareef clearly shows that having true Imaan, and rising to honour and fame through it, depends on doing that effort which has been granted by Allah Ta'ala to the Muslims alone. They have been honoured in the Qur-aan with the noble position of *'Khairul-Umam'* (the best of all nations).

The purpose for the creation of this world was to declare the Oneness and the existence of Allah Ta'ala and to show His unlimited powers and qualities through man, who was to be guided by the noor of true ilm (knowledge). It is impossible for man to understand and use that knowledge without being aware of Allah Ta'ala and being cleansed of evil and sin. Only after cleansing oneself can he acquire excellence of conduct and the ability to do good. For the purpose of granting this purity and power to mankind, Allah Ta'ala sent thousands of Ambiyaa (alayhimus salaam). The last of them was Sayyidul Ambiyaa wal

Mursaleen (the greatest of all the Ambiyaa), Hadhrat Muhammad ﷺ. Through his guidance, man reached the highest stage of purity. It was then that mankind received the glad tidings of:

$$\text{اَلْيَوْمَ اَكْمَلْتُ لَكُمْ دِيْنَكُمْ وَاَتْمَمْتُ عَلَيْكُمْ نِعْمَتِیْ}$$

"And today I have perfected your Deen (religion) for you and completed My bounty upon you." (Surah Maai'dah - Aayah 3)

The purpose of man's creation had been completed, good and evil had been clearly explained, a complete practical way of life had been revealed, Nubuwwah (Prophethood) had been completed and lastly the duties that used to be given to the Ambiyaa *(alayhimus salaam)* has been given to the Ummah of Hadhrat Muhammad ﷺ. This fact has been explained in the following Aayah of the Qur-aan:

$$\text{كُنْتُمْ خَيْرَ اُمَّةٍ اُخْرِجَتْ لِلنَّاسِ تَأْمُرُوْنَ بِالْمَعْرُوْفِ وَتَنْهَوْنَ عَنِ الْمُنْكَرِ وَتُؤْمِنُوْنَ بِاللهِ}$$

"You (O followers of Muhammad ﷺ) are the best of all nations, who have been raised for (the benefit of) mankind. You command what is right, forbid the evil and believe in Allah Ta'ala."
(Surah Aali I'mraan Aayah 110)

$$\text{وَلْتَكُنْ مِنْكُمْ اُمَّةٌ يَّدْعُوْنَ اِلَى الْخَيْرِ وَيَأْمُرُوْنَ بِالْمَعْرُوْفِ وَيَنْهَوْنَ عَنِ الْمُنْكَرِ وَاُولٰٓئِكَ هُمُ الْمُفْلِحُوْنَ}$$

"And there should be a group from you who invite towards good, command what is right and forbid the evil. These are indeed the successful ones." (Surah Aali I'mraan - Aayah 104)

In the first Aayah, Allah Ta'ala has given the reason why the Muslims are called *Khairul Umam* (best of all Ummahs). It is because of commanding good and preventing evil. In the second Aayah, He has further explained that only those people shall be successful who obey that order. The command does not end here, rather it is stated in another place that not obeying will bring disaster and punishment to the Ummah. This is understood from the following Aayah:

لُعِنَ الَّذِيْنَ كَفَرُوْا مِنْ بَنِيْ اِسْرَآءِيْلَ عَلٰى لِسَانِ دَاوٗدَ وَعِيْسَى ابْنِ مَرْيَمَ ۚ ذٰلِكَ بِمَا عَصَوْا وَّكَانُوْا يَعْتَدُوْنَ ۞ كَانُوْا لَا يَتَنَاهَوْنَ عَنْ مُّنْكَرٍ فَعَلُوْهُ ۚ لَبِئْسَ مَا كَانُوْا يَفْعَلُوْنَ

"Those of the Bani Israa'eel who committed kufr (disbelieved in Allah Ta'ala) were cursed on the tongues of Dawood (alayhis salaam) and Isa (alayhis salaam) the son of Maryam (alayhas salaam). That was because they were disobedient and they overstepped the limits. They never prevented each other from the evil they used to commit. Evil indeed was that which they did." (Surah Maai'dah - Aayah 78-79)

A detailed explanation of the above Aayah of the Qur-aan Shareef can be seen from the following Hadith of Nabi Muhammad ﷺ.

عَنِ ابْنِ مَسْعُوْدٍ رَضِيَ اللهُ عَنْهُ قَالَ قَالَ رَسُوْلُ اللهِ صَلَّى اللهُ عَلَيْهِ وَسَلَّمَ اِنَّ مَنْ كَانَ قَبْلَكُمْ كَانَ اِذَا عَمِلَ الْعَامِلُ فِيْهِمْ بِالْخَطِيْئَةِ جَاءَهُ النَّاهِىْ تَعْذِيْرًا حَتَّى اِذَا كَانَ مِنَ الْغَدِ جَالَسَهُ وَوَاكَلَهُ وَشَارَبَهُ كَأَنَّهُ لَمْ يَرَهُ عَلٰى خَطِيْئَةٍ بِالْأَمْسِ فَلَمَّا رَأَى اللهُ عَزَّ وَجَلَّ ذٰلِكَ مِنْهُمْ ضَرَبَ بِقُلُوْبِ بَعْضِهِمْ عَلٰى بَعْضٍ ثُمَّ لَعَنَهُمْ عَلٰى لِسَانِ نَبِيِّهِمْ دَاوٗدَ وَعِيْسَى ابْنِ مَرْيَمَ ذٰلِكَ بِمَا عَصَوْا وَّكَانُوْا يَعْتَدُوْنَ وَالَّذِىْ نَفْسُ مُحَمَّدٍ بِيَدِهِ لَتَأْمُرُنَّ بِالْمَعْرُوْفِ وَلَتَنْهَوُنَّ عَنِ الْمُنْكَرِ وَلَتَأْخُذُنَّ عَلٰى يَدِ السَّفِيْهِ وَلَتَأْطُرُنَّهُ عَلَى الْحَقِّ أَطْرًا أَوْ لَيَضْرِبَنَّ اللهُ بِقُلُوْبِ بَعْضِكُمْ عَلٰى بَعْضٍ ثُمَّ يَلْعَنُكُمْ كَمَا لَعَنَهُمْ (المعجم الكبير # 10268)

It has been narrated by Hadhrat Abdullah bin Masood رضي الله عنه that Rasulullah ﷺ said: "In a previous Ummah, when somebody committed a sin, the other would try to stop him and would say, 'Fear

Allah, but on the following day he would befriend him and mix with him as if he had never seen him doing the sin. And when Allah Ta'ala saw them behaving like this, He sealed the hearts of some because of the (ill effect) hearts of others and cursed them through the tongues of Dawood (alayhis salaam) and Isa (alayhis salaam), son of Maryam and this was because they disobeyed Allah Ta'ala and broke His commands. I, Muhammad (ﷺ), swear by Him, Who has control over my soul, you must command the good and forbid the evil and force the ignorant wrongdoer onto the path of piety, otherwise Allah Ta'ala will seal your hearts and you will be cursed, as were those people of the past."

عَنْ جَرِيرٍ رَضِىَ اللهُ عَنْهُ قَالَ سَمِعْتُ رَسُوْلَ اللهِ صَلَّى اللهُ عَلَيْهِ وَسَلَّمَ يَقُوْلُ مَا مِنْ رَجُلٍ يَكُوْنُ فِى قَوْمٍ يُعْمَلُ فِيهِمْ بِالْمَعَاصِىْ يَقْدِرُوْنَ عَلَى اَنْ يُغَيِّرُوْا عَلَيْهِ فَلَا يُغَيِّرُوْا اِلَّا اَصَابَهُمُ اللهُ بِعَذَابٍ مِّنْ قَبْلِ اَنْ يَّمُوْتُوْا (سنن ابى داود # 4339)

Hadhrat Jareer (رضي الله عنه) has narrated that Rasulullah (ﷺ) said: "When a person in a community sins, and the community, in spite of being able to, does not prevent him from sinning, Allah Ta'ala's punishment comes to them even before death i.e. He sends to them many punishments in this very world."

عَنْ اَنَسِ بْنِ مَالِكٍ رَضِىَ اللهُ عَنْهُ اَنَّ رَسُوْلَ اللهِ صَلَّى اللهُ عَلَيْهِ وَسَلَّمَ قَالَ لَا تَزَالُ لَا اِلٰهَ اِلَّا اللهُ تَنْفَعُ مَنْ قَالَهَا وَتَرُدُّ عَنْهُمُ الْعَذَابَ وَالنِّقْمَةَ مَا لَمْ يَسْتَخِفُّوْا بِحَقِّهَا قَالُوْا يَا رَسُوْلَ اللهِ وَمَا الْاِسْتِخْفَافُ بِحَقِّهَا قَالَ يَظْهَرُ الْعَمَلُ بِمَعَاصِى اللهِ فَلَا يُنْكَرُ وَلَا يُغَيَّرُ (اخرجه الاصبهانى فى الترغيب # 307)

Hadhrat Anas (رضي الله عنه) has narrated that Rasulullah (ﷺ) said: "Laa ilaaha illal laahu always benefits those who say it, and keeps away from them problems and troubles, unless its rights are ignored.

The Sahaabah رَضِىَ اللهُ عَنْهُم asked, 'What does the ignoring of its rights mean?' Rasulullah ﷺ replied: 'It means that when sins are being committed openly, they do not prevent or stop them.'"

عَنْ عَائِشَةَ رَضِىَ اللهُ عَنْهَا قَالَتْ دَخَلَ عَلَىَّ النَّبِىُّ صَلَّى اللهُ عَلَيْهِ وَسَلَّمَ فَعَرَفْتُ فِىْ وَجْهِهٖ اَنْ قَدْ حَضَرَهُ شَىْءٌ فَتَوَضَّأَ وَمَا كَلَّمَ اَحَدًا ثُمَّ خَرَجَ فَلَصِقْتُ بِالْحُجْرَةِ اَسْتَمِعُ مَا يَقُوْلُ فَقَعَدَ عَلَى الْمِنْبَرِ فَحَمِدَ اللهَ وَاَثْنٰى عَلَيْهِ وَقَالَ يَا اَيُّهَا النَّاسُ اِنَّ اللهَ تَعَالٰى يَقُوْلُ لَكُمْ مُرُوْا بِالْمَعْرُوْفِ وَانْهَوْا عَنِ الْمُنْكَرِ قَبْلَ اَنْ تَدْعُوْنِىْ فَلَا اُجِيْبَكُمْ وَتَسْئَلُوْنِىْ فَلَا اُعْطِيَكُمْ وَتَسْتَنْصِرُوْنِىْ فَلَا اَنْصُرَكُمْ فَمَا زَادَ عَلَيْهِنَّ حَتّٰى نَزَلَ (صحيح ابن حبان # 290)

Hadhrat Aa'ishah رَضِىَ اللهُ عَنْهَا has reported: "Nabi ﷺ came to me and I could see from his noble countenance that something important had taken place. He did not speak a single word. After making wudhu, he went straight to the Masjid. I too stood by the wall of the Masjid to hear what he had to say. Rasulullah (ﷺ) climbed the mimbar and after the usual khutbah said, 'O people! Allah has ordered you to command the good and forbid the evil, otherwise a time will come when you will make dua and He may not answer it, you may ask for a favour and He may not give it and you will ask for help and He may refuse you.' He then came down from the mimbar."

عَنْ اَبِىْ هُرَيْرَةَ رَضِىَ اللهُ عَنْهُ قَالَ قَالَ رَسُوْلُ اللهِ صَلَّى اللهُ عَلَيْهِ وَسَلَّمَ اِذَا عَظَّمَتْ اُمَّتِىَ الدُّنْيَا نُزِعَتْ مِنْهَا هَيْبَةُ الْاِسْلَامِ وَاِذَا تَرَكَتِ الْاَمْرَ بِالْمَعْرُوْفِ وَالنَّهْىَ عَنِ الْمُنْكَرِ حُرِمَتْ بَرَكَةَ الْوَحْىِ وَاِذَا تَسَابَّتْ اُمَّتِىْ سَقَطَتْ مِنْ عَيْنِ اللهِ

(اخرجه الحكيم الترمذى فى نوادر الاصول 2/ 270)

Hadhrat Abu Hurayrah رَضِىَ اللهُ عَنْهُ has narrated that Rasulullah ﷺ said, "When my Ummah begins to attach more importance to the world and begins to regard it as a source of glory, the awe and importance of Islam will vanish from their hearts, and when they give up the practice of commanding the good and forbidding the evil, they will lose the blessings of Wahi and when they begin to speak ill of one another, they will fall in the eyes of Allah."

THE MAIN CAUSE

From the above Hadith it is clear that not commanding others to do good and not stopping them from evil is generally the main cause of the anger and punishment of Allah Ta'ala. If this Ummah becomes guilty of this, the punishment will be more severe than the punishments of the earlier nations, as they would have failed to recognise and fulfil their responsibility. For this reason, Nabi ﷺ has said that commanding others to do good and stopping them from evil is, "The essence and special sign of the Deen of Islam." He also said that leaving it out is the cause of the Imaan becoming weak.

عَنْ أَبِيْ سَعِيْدٍ الْخُدْرِيِّ رَضِيَ اللهُ عَنْهُ قَالَ سَمِعْتُ رَسُوْلَ اللهِ صَلَّى اللهُ عَلَيْهِ وَسَلَّمَ يَقُوْلُ مَنْ رَأَى مِنْكُمْ مُنْكَرًا فَلْيُغَيِّرْهُ بِيَدِهٖ فَاِنْ لَّمْ يَسْتَطِعْ فَبِلِسَانِهٖ فَاِنْ لَّمْ يَسْتَطِعْ فَبِقَلْبِهٖ وَذٰلِكَ أَضْعَفُ الْاِيْمَانِ (صحيح مسلم # 49)

Hadhrat Abu Sa'eed Khudree رضى الله عنه says, "I heard Rasulullah ﷺ saying, 'When anyone of you sees evil being done, he should use his hands to stop it; if he does not have the power to do this, he should use his tongue and if he does not have the power to do this, he should use his heart (by disliking the action), and this is the weakest level of Imaan.'")

Just as disliking the sin from the heart is the weakest level of Imaan, to physically stop a sin is the most complete form of Dawah and the most complete form of Imaan.

The above Hadith is more clearly explained in the Hadith of Hadhrat Ibn Masood رضي الله عنه:

اَنَّ رَسُوْلَ اللهِ صَلَّى اللهُ عَلَيْهِ وَسَلَّمَ قَالَ مَا مِنْ نَبِيٍّ بَعَثَهُ اللهُ قَبْلِىْ اِلَّا كَانَ لَهُ فِىْ اُمَّتِهٖ حَوَارِيُّوْنَ وَاَصْحَابٌ يَّأْخُذُوْنَ بِسُنَّتِهٖ وَيَقْتَدُوْنَ بِاَمْرِهٖ ثُمَّ اِنَّهَا تَخْلُفُ مِنْ بَعْدِهِمْ خُلُوْفٌ يَّقُوْلُوْنَ مَا لَا يَفْعَلُوْنَ وَيَفْعَلُوْنَ مَا لَا يُؤْمَرُوْنَ فَمَنْ جَاهَدَهُمْ بِيَدِهٖ فَهُوَ مُؤْمِنٌ وَّمَنْ جَاهَدَهُمْ بِلِسَانِهٖ فَهُوَ مُؤْمِنٌ وَّمَنْ جَاهَدَهُمْ بِقَلْبِهٖ فَهُوَ مُؤْمِنٌ وَلَيْسَ وَرَاءَ ذٰلِكَ مِنَ الْاِيْمَانِ حَبَّةُ خَرْدَلٍ (صحيح مسلم # 50)

"It is usual for Allah Ta'ala to make it such that every Nabi leaves behind a group of his companions who will carry on with His message, who follow it strictly and look after the message exactly how the Rasul left it. Then comes a time of evil and mistakes; a time that sees people move away from the path shown by their Nabi. Their actions are opposite to what they say and their doings are against Shariah. So whosoever defends the Truth and Shariah and stops the sinners with his hands is a true believer; he who cannot do this but uses his tongue, he is a believer too; and he who cannot do even this but uses his heart (by disliking the action), is also a believer; but below this there is no Imaan."

The importance of Tabligh has been explained by Imaam Ghazaali *(rahmatullahi alayh)* as follows:

"There can be no doubt that commanding others to do good and stopping them from evil is an important part of Deen. It is for this very reason that Allah Ta'ala sent all the Ambiyaa *(alayhimus salaam)*. Unfortunately, if it is ignored or forgotten and its methods are given up, then the very purpose of Nubuwwah is defeated and made meaningless. As a result people will lose their conscience and their minds will become dull. Sins, oppression and immorality will spread in the whole world. All actions of man will become harmful. Human relationships will break down and civilization will be destroyed. Mankind will become corrupt and soaked in sins. The true understanding of all this will only become clear on the day of Qiyaamah, when all the people will stand before Allah Ta'ala and answer for each and every action."

Alas! Alas! This fear has come true. That which we feared is now before our eyes.

كَانَ اَمْرُ اللهِ قَدَرًا مَّقْدُوْرًا فَاِنَّا لِلهِ وَاِنَّا اِلَيْهِ رَاجِعُوْنَ

Knowledge and guidance have been destroyed and we only see disgrace and disrespect amongst the people. There is no longer any fear of Allah Ta'ala in the hearts of people. Nothing of the beautiful relationship between man and his creator is left in human hearts and man has become like an animal, following his desires. There are very few true Muslims left in this world and it is almost impossible to meet anyone who is prepared to sacrifice for the sake of spreading Islam.

Any Muslim, who tries to take up this responsibility to change this terrible situation and revive the Sunnah of Tabligh, will surely be the noblest and the best of all people.

Imaam Ghazaali Saahib *(rahmatullahi alayh)* said this nearly 800 years ago. His words apply perfectly to us today. We must ponder about what is to be done. There are some well-known causes for the problems we face today. These are discussed below.

FIRST CAUSE

We generally believe that Tabligh is the work and responsibility of the Ulama only, even when the Aayaat of the Qur-aan clearly apply to each and every Muslim. The efforts and sacrifices of the Sahaabah of Nabi ﷺ and all those noble Muslims who immediately followed them prove that each and every Muslim is responsible for Tabligh.

To shift the responsibility of Tabligh (commanding people to do good and stopping them from evil) to the Ulama alone is a sign of great ignorance. The duty of the Ulama is to state the truth and to point out the right path. To encourage piety among the people and to keep them moving on the right path is the responsibility of all Muslims. The following Hadith is a clear warning for this.

$$\text{عَنْ عَبْدِ اللهِ رَضِيَ اللهُ عَنْهُ اَنَّ رَسُوْلَ اللهِ صَلَّى اللهُ عَلَيْهِ وَسَلَّمَ قَالَ كُلُّكُمْ رَاعٍ وَكُلُّكُمْ مَسْئُوْلٌ عَنْ رَعِيَّتِهِ فَالْأَمِيْرُ الَّذِيْ عَلَى النَّاسِ رَاعٍ عَلَيْهِمْ وَهُوَ مَسْئُوْلٌ عَنْهُمْ وَالرَّجُلُ رَاعٍ عَلٰى اَهْلِ بَيْتِهِ وَهُوَ مَسْئُوْلٌ عَنْهُمْ وَالْمَرْأَةُ رَاعِيَةٌ عَلٰى بَيْتِ بَعْلِهَا وَوَلَدِهِ وَهِيَ مَسْئُوْلَةٌ عَنْهُمْ وَالْعَبْدُ رَاعٍ عَلٰى مَالِ سَيِّدِهِ وَهُوَ مَسْئُوْلٌ عَنْهُ فَكُلُّكُمْ رَاعٍ وَكُلُّكُمْ مَسْئُوْلٌ عَنْ رَعِيَّتِهِ}$$ (صحيح مسلم # 2554)

"Indeed! All of you are trustees and shall be questioned on the day of Qiyaamah about your trust. The king is the leader of his people and shall be questioned about them. The husband is in charge of his wife and children and shall be questioned about them. The wife is responsible for her husband's house and the children and shall be questioned about them all. The slave is a guard of his owner's belongings and shall be questioned about those. So you are all trustees and you shall be questioned about those that you are in charge of."

In another Hadith, it is more clearly explained;

$$\text{عَنْ تَمِيْمٍ الدَّارِيِّ رَضِيَ اللهُ عَنْهُ اَنَّ النَّبِيَّ صَلَّى اللهُ عَلَيْهِ وَسَلَّمَ قَالَ اَلدِّيْنُ النَّصِيْحَةُ قُلْنَا لِمَنْ قَالَ لِلهِ وَلِكِتَابِهِ وَلِرَسُوْلِهِ وَلِأَئِمَّةِ الْمُسْلِمِيْنَ وَعَامَّتِهِمْ}$$ (صحيح مسلم # 55)

Rasulullah ﷺ said, "Deen is to wish well (i.e. to fulfil the obligations of everyone)." The Sahaabah رضي الله عنه asked, "Wishing well towards whom?" He said, "Towards Allah, His Rasul, the leaders of the Muslims and the Muslims at large."

Even if we suppose that this effort has to be carried out by the Ulama only, the present emergency demands that every one of us should put his shoulder to the wheel and work hard to establish Deen on the earth and to protect the Islamic way of life.

SECOND CAUSE

It is usually believed that if a person is firm and steadfast in his own Imaan, the wrong beliefs of others cannot harm him as it is pointed out in the following Aayah:

$$\text{يَاأَيُّهَا الَّذِينَ آمَنُوا عَلَيْكُمْ أَنْفُسَكُمْ لَا يَضُرُّكُمْ مَنْ ضَلَّ إِذَا اهْتَدَيْتُمْ}$$

"O you who believe! Take care of your own selves (i.e. while advising others, guard your own Imaan also). He who has strayed (from the truth) cannot harm you when (as long as) you are rightly guided."

(Surah Maai'dah - Aayah 105)

In fact, the real meaning of the above Aayah is not what is usually understood. In that case, the meaning would appear to be against the Divine wisdom and against the teachings of the Shariah. It actually means that the progress and everlasting success of the entire Muslim Ummah is the basis of Islam. Muslim people are like one body having many limbs. When any limb becomes injured, the whole body suffers from the pain.

Mankind may progress to any limit and it may reach the highest glory in all departments of life, yet there will be some who will go astray and become involved in sins. In that case, the above Aayah comforts the pious people that as long as they remain firm and keep moving on the right path, no harm can come to them by those who decide to give up the right way of life.

The reality of *Hidaayah* (guidance) is that all the rules of the law of Shariah are accepted and practiced, including all of Allah Ta'ala's commands, which also include commanding good and stopping evil.

$$\text{عَنْ أَبِي بَكْرٍ الصِّدِّيقِ رَضِيَ اللهُ عَنْهُ قَالَ يَا أَيُّهَا النَّاسُ إِنَّكُمْ تَقْرَءُونَ هَذِهِ الْآيَةَ يَا أَيُّهَا الَّذِينَ آمَنُوا عَلَيْكُمْ أَنْفُسَكُمْ لَا يَضُرُّكُمْ مَنْ ضَلَّ إِذَا اهْتَدَيْتُمْ فَإِنِّي سَمِعْتُ رَسُولَ اللهِ صَلَّى اللهُ عَلَيْهِ وَسَلَّمَ يَقُولُ إِنَّ النَّاسَ إِذَا رَأَوُا الْمُنْكَرَ فَلَمْ يُغَيِّرُوهُ أَوْشَكَ أَنْ يَعُمَّهُمُ اللهُ بِعِقَابِهِ}$$ (سنن ابن ماجه # 4005)

Hadhrat Abu Bakr ﷺ said, "O people! You quote this Aayah (quoted above), 'O you who believe! Watch out for your own selves (i.e. your deeds). When you are on the right path, those who go astray cannot harm you'. But I have heard Rasulullah ﷺ say that when people see something evil and do not try to stop it, Allah will send down a punishment to all of them."

Imaam Nawawi *(rahmatullahi alaih)* explains in his *'Sharah Muslim'* that the agreed opinion of the Mufassireen about the meaning of this Aayah is that, "When you have performed the duty given to you, the carelessness of those who refuse to listen to your advice will not harm you, as Allah Ta'ala says,

$$وَلَا تَزِرُ وَازِرَةٌ وِزْرَ اُخْرٰى$$

"And no one will bear the burden (sins) of another." *(Surah A'naam - Aayah 164, Israa - Aayah 15, Faatir - Aayah 18 & Zumar - Aayah 7)*

Of the many commandments addressed to all, one is of enjoining good and preventing evil. Therefore, when anyone has fulfilled this duty and the people do not obey, the *Muballigh* (the person doing Tabligh) shall not be questioned about it. He has fulfilled his duty of commanding the good and stopping the evil and whether people accept or reject is not his responsibility. Allah Ta'ala knows best.

THIRD CAUSE

Most people, including the common man, the educated and the uneducated have all lost hope for the Ummah. They seem to have accepted the fact, that it is difficult, rather impossible for Muslims to make progress by regaining power and once again become rulers. Whenever any plan for improvement and correction is put forward to anyone, the usual response is that how can the Muslims progress when they neither have power nor a country of their own to rule over. They also complain that they do not have any wealth, army, military equipment and influence? They do not have physical strength, disagree amongst themselves and no unity in carrying out their mission. Even the pious people seem to have decided that the downfall of Islam and the Muslims is certain, because it being the 14th century Hijri and the people have moved so far away from the teachings of Nabi ﷺ. They believe that, in these times, it will be useless to make any effort towards correcting the Muslims.

It is true that the light of Nubuwwah becomes less and less as we move further away from it, but this does not mean that no effort should be made to spread Islam and encourage the way of life taught by Nabi Muhammad ﷺ.

If the Muslims before us thought like this, there would have been no trace of Islam left. There would have been no way for the teachings of the Shariah to reach us. Therefore, we should stop having this feeling of hopelessness. We should become positive for our own sake and also for the sake of those coming after us. Time is moving fast and Islam is quickly becoming weaker and weaker. What is needed is a strong, quick and determined effort by all of us in facing the problems and stopping the Muslim Ummah from becoming weak.

Islam depends upon the determination and collective effort of its followers. Unfortunately, we seem to be falling short in these requirements. We must understand that the Qur-aan and Hadith instruct the Muslims to be active and to stand firm in the path of Allah Ta'ala. In a Hadith it is stated that a pious person who may be busy in Salaah night and day, cannot reach the level of one who struggles and sacrifices his pleasure and comfort for the sake of guiding and helping people to move towards the right path.

It is clearly mentioned in the Quraan that the one who sacrifices in the path of Allah Ta'ala, remains far better and more noble compared to others.

لَا يَسْتَوِى الْقٰعِدُوْنَ مِنَ الْمُؤْمِنِيْنَ غَيْرُ أُولِى الضَّرَرِ وَالْمُجٰهِدُوْنَ فِىْ سَبِيْلِ اللهِ بِأَمْوَالِهِمْ وَأَنْفُسِهِمْ ۚ فَضَّلَ اللهُ الْمُجٰهِدِيْنَ بِأَمْوَالِهِمْ وَأَنْفُسِهِمْ عَلَى الْقٰعِدِيْنَ دَرَجَةً ۚ وَكُلًّا وَّعَدَ اللهُ الْحُسْنٰى ۚ وَفَضَّلَ اللهُ الْمُجٰهِدِيْنَ عَلَى الْقٰعِدِيْنَ أَجْرًا عَظِيْمًا ۙ دَرَجٰتٍ مِّنْهُ وَمَغْفِرَةً وَّرَحْمَةً ۚ وَكَانَ اللهُ غَفُوْرًا رَّحِيْمًا

"The Muslims who sit back without any excuse cannot be equal to those who strive in the path of Allah Ta'ala with their wealth and lives. Allah Ta'ala has raised the positions of those who strive in His way with their wealth and lives over those who sit back. Allah Ta'ala has promised the most beautiful (Jannah) for each of them (those who strive as well as those who do not). (However) Allah Ta'ala has preferred (increased the rewards for) those who strive over those who sit back (without any excuse) by granting them a tremendous reward (in the form of) many ranks (above the rest), forgiveness and mercy from Him. Allah Ta'ala is Most Forgiving Most Merciful." *(Surah Nisaa - Aayah 95-96)*

Although the above Aayah refers directly to Jihaad against the kuffaar in order to establish the teachings of Islam and eradicate kufr and shirk and although we are unfortunate in not having the opportunity of fulfilling that great task, we should not throw away any chance of doing something, however small, in trying to spread the truth. Only if we persevere, then can we expect that one day our efforts may gather strength and increase.

وَالَّذِيْنَ جَاهَدُوْا فِيْنَا لَنَهْدِيَنَّهُمْ سُبُلَنَا

"We shall most certainly show Our avenues (of guidance and insight leading to Jannah) to those who exert themselves (strive) in Our cause." *(Surah A'nkaboot - Aayah 69)*

Certainly, Allah Ta'ala has promised protection for the way of life shown to us by Nabi Muhammad ﷺ. But, human effort and perseverance is the only means to promote it. The Sahaabah of Nabi ﷺ made untiring sacrifices and succeeded and they were greatly rewarded. They had the honour of receiving the help of Allah Ta'ala. We, being their admirers and believers, should try and follow their example by giving dawat towards the *'Kalimah'* thereby establishing the rule of Allah Ta'ala on the earth and for spreading His message. Thus, we will also be favoured with the help of Allah Ta'ala,

اِنْ تَنْصُرُوا اللهَ يَنْصُرْكُمْ وَيُثَبِّتْ أَقْدَامَكُمْ

"If you (come forward to) help the religion of Allah Ta'ala, He shall help you and make your feet firm." *(Surah Muhammad - Aayah 7)*

FOURTH CAUSE

Most of us feel that, as we ourselves do not have the proper qualities of Islam, we are not capable of inviting others. This is a total misunderstanding. We have been commanded by Allah Ta'ala to fulfil this responsibility of inviting others and we will have to obey His command. Our efforts shall, *Insha-Allah*, gather strength and make us more determined. Our continued efforts will bring us the great honour of being beloved to Allah Ta'ala. It is against the law of Allah Ta'ala that, if anyone is steadfast and strives for the sake of His Deen, He would not grant his favours and kindness on that person even if the person was not fit for carrying out this task. This point is fully explained in the following Hadith.

عَنْ اَنَسٍ رَضِيَ اللهُ عَنْهُ قَالَ قُلْنَا يَا رَسُوْلَ اللهِ لَا نَأْمُرُ بِالْمَعْرُوْفِ حَتّٰى نَعْمَلَ بِهِ كُلِّهِ وَلَا نَنْهٰى عَنِ الْمُنْكَرِ حَتّٰى نَجْتَنِبَهُ كُلَّهُ فَقَالَ رَسُوْلُ اللهِ صَلَّى اللهُ عَلَيْهِ وَسَلَّمَ بَلْ مُرُوْا بِالْمَعْرُوْفِ وَاِنْ لَمْ تَعْمَلُوْا بِهِ كُلِّهِ وَانْهَوْا عَنِ الْمُنْكَرِ وَاِنْ لَمْ تَجْتَنِبُوْهُ كُلَّهُ

(اخرجه الطبرانى فى الاوسط # 6628)

Hadhrat Anas رَضِيَ اللهُ عَنْهُ says, "We said, O Rasulullah ﷺ, should we not command with good until we practice it all and should we not stop evil until we avoid it all? He (ﷺ) said, 'No! Command with good even if you do not practice it yourself and stop evil even if you yourself are not able to avoid it.'"

FIFTH CAUSE

Many of us feel that the Madrasahs, the Ulama, the Khanqahs, Islamic books and pamphlets are sufficient for the responsibility of *"amr bil ma'ruf nahi a'nil munkar"* (i.e. to carry out tabligh). Certainly, the presence of all these is important and we must respect them and help them, as the little Islam that exists today is because of these very methods and institutions. But this is not enough to fulfil this responsibility even partially. The task we are faced with is difficult, considering our present weaknesses and the size of the problem. To be satisfied with these few methods will be foolish on our part.

To benefit fully from these methods and institutions, we have to create a true and a deep respect for the Deen of Islam and a burning desire within ourselves to bring it into our daily life. Up to fifty years ago, people had real love, urge and passion for Islam and there were clear signs and examples of the Islamic way of life. Perhaps in those days these institutions could have been enough. Today, our feelings for Islam are almost dead, because of the continuous attack on our Imaan by various outside forces. Alas! They have succeeded because, instead of loving Deen, we seem to be secretly ashamed of Islam and our Imaan.

Obviously, we must act quickly and make a strong effort through which we are able to oppose the forces of kufr, thereby revive the dead spirit of every Muslim and reawaken in him the love for Islam. Then only can we benefit from our Islamic organisations which would then serve the Ummah in a suitable manner. Unless we take this seriously, the problems will only increase and our organisations which are doing good in their limited way, may have to close up.

SIXTH CAUSE

Whenever anyone does the work of *"amr bil ma'ruf nahi a'nil munkar"* (commanding good and stopping evil), he is not received well by the people. People always treat him badly, using harsh and insulting language. People also become rude and insulting towards those who do the effort of Deen. This is true, but we must remember that we need to simply follow in the footsteps of the Ambiyaa *(alayhimus salaam)* of Allah Ta'ala, who were always the victims of the worst type of abuse. This is expected for those who do this work. Indeed, all Ambiyaa *(alayhimus salaam)* had to suffer difficulties as is clear from the following Aayah:

وَلَقَدْ اَرْسَلْنَا مِنْ قَبْلِكَ فِىْ شِيَعِ الْاَوَّلِيْنَ ۞ وَمَا يَأْتِيْهِمْ مِنْ رَّسُوْلٍ اِلَّا كَانُوْا بِهٖ يَسْتَهْزِءُوْنَ

"And undoubtedly We have sent down Ambiyaa before you to the previous groups (past nations). However they ridiculed (and denied) every one of the Rasul that came to them." *(Surah Hijr - Aayah 10-11)*

Then Nabi ﷺ once said, "No Rasul or Nabi has suffered more than me in the preaching of the truth."

It is clear, that there can be no excuse for abandoning the work of Dawah and Tableegh. We should follow the noble example of Nabi Muhammed ﷺ who himself suffered while carrying out the duty of Tabligh but cheerfully tolerated everything. We must also follow his beautiful example exercising patience and calmness while carrying out the duty of Tabligh.

THE SOLUTION

It has been clearly explained that the disease in the Ummah is due to the weakening of the true spirit of Islam in our hearts. As a result, true feelings and love for Islam are almost dead in us and our Imaan has become weak. When the very source becomes dry, the streams of justice, good deeds and fine character, which flow from it, will not be seen. This is exactly what we see today. The only way for reviving this source and receiving benefits from it is by doing the work of Tabligh which really and truly is the life blood of Islam. Unless we are able to renew it, we cannot achieve anything, because no nation or people can rise to success without high human qualities and character which only the Deen of Islam can give.

We should be aware of the disease we suffer from and take the correct treatment. It is now up to us to involve ourselves in the work of Tabligh which will result in restoring the true Deen of Islam in the people. Through Tabligh, we can recognise and truly understand both Allah Ta'ala and His Rasul ﷺ and we will be able to clearly understand and follow their commands and wishes. To achieve this, we will have to follow the ways that were shown by Rasulullah ﷺ himself when he made an effort on the idol worshipping Arabs. Allah Ta'ala says in the Qur-aan Shareef:

$$\text{لَقَدْ كَانَ لَكُمْ فِىْ رَسُوْلِ اللهِ اُسْوَةٌ حَسَنَةٌ}$$

"Indeed there is an excellent example in Rasulullah ﷺ."
(Surah A'hzaab Aayah 21)

Imaam Maalik *(rahmatullahi alayh)* said;

$$\text{لَن يُّصْلِحَ اٰخِرَ هٰذِهِ الْاُمَّةَ اِلَّا مَا اَصْلَحَ اَوَّلَهَا}$$ (الشفا 2/88)

Reformation of the last part of the Ummah of Muhammad ﷺ will never be possible until that way is adopted which was used in the beginning (by Nabi Muhammad ﷺ).

In the beginning, when Nabi ﷺ had called the people to Islam, he did not have a single supporter or any power or wealth. The idol worshipping Arabs were proud and stubborn. None of them were prepared to listen to the truth or obey another person. They hated the message of truth which Nabi ﷺ had brought. We wonder, that under these trying conditions, what gave strength to this one, single, poor man without any means, who was able to attract the whole of the Arab nation towards him.

After all, what was it that Rasulullah ﷺ called the people towards, which they initially refused, but accepted when they saw the light and stood and remained loyal to him forever? There was one message that Rasulullah ﷺ propagated:

$$\text{اَلَّا نَعْبُدَ اِلَّا اللهَ وَلَا نُشْرِكَ بِهٖ شَيْئًا وَّلَا يَتَّخِذَ بَعْضُنَا بَعْضًا اَرْبَابًا مِّنْ دُوْنِ اللهِ}$$

"That we worship nothing but Allah Ta'ala and that we don't ascribe anyone as partners with Him and that we do not take each other as gods besides Allah Ta'ala." (Surah Aali I'mraan - Aayah 64)

Inviting towards that very truth can bring the same results again. Nabi ﷺ stopped his followers from worshipping any being except Allah Ta'ala. Not only did he succeed, but he was also able to unite his people upon one system of life which they held onto steadfastly. They really became the true picture of:

$$ اِتَّبِعُوْا مَآ اُنْزِلَ اِلَيْكُمْ مِنْ رَّبِّكُمْ وَلَا تَتَّبِعُوْا مِنْ دُوْنِهٖٓ اَوْلِيَآءَ ۭ $$

"Follow that which has been revealed to you from Your Rabb, and do not leave him aside to follow other friends." *(Suarh A'araaf - Aayah 3)*

This was the message which Nabi ﷺ had been commanded by Allah Ta'ala to spread. It is also clear from the following Aayah:

$$ اُدْعُ اِلٰى سَبِيْلِ رَبِّكَ بِالْحِكْمَةِ وَالْمَوْعِظَةِ الْحَسَنَةِ وَجَادِلْهُمْ بِالَّتِيْ هِيَ اَحْسَنُ ۭ اِنَّ رَبَّكَ هُوَ اَعْلَمُ بِمَنْ ضَلَّ عَنْ سَبِيْلِهٖ وَهُوَ اَعْلَمُ بِالْمُهْتَدِيْنَ $$

"(O Muhammad ﷺ), call (the people) to the path of your Rabb (Islam) with wisdom and good advice, and debate with them (kuffaar) in a manner that is best. Indeed your Rabb knows best who strays from His path and He knows best who the rightly guided ones are."
(Surah Nahl - Aayah 125)

The method for the progress of Nabi ﷺ and his followers is described in the following Aayah:

$$ قُلْ هٰذِهٖ سَبِيْلِيْٓ اَدْعُوْٓا اِلَى اللّٰهِ ڀ عَلٰى بَصِيْرَةٍ اَنَا وَمَنِ اتَّبَعَنِيْ ۭ وَسُبْحٰنَ اللّٰهِ وَمَآ اَنَا مِنَ الْمُشْرِكِيْنَ $$

"(O Muhammad ﷺ) Say, this is my way, I call towards Allah Ta'ala with insight, I as well as those who follow me, and Allah Ta'ala is Pure, and I am not one of those who join partners with Him." *(Surah Yusuf - Aayah 108)*

$$ وَمَنْ اَحْسَنُ قَوْلًا مِّمَّنْ دَعَآ اِلَى اللّٰهِ وَعَمِلَ صَالِحًا وَّقَالَ اِنَّنِيْ مِنَ الْمُسْلِمِيْنَ $$

"And whose words can be better than the one who calls (others) towards Allah Ta'ala, does good deeds and says, 'Certainly, I am from the Muslims.'" *(Surah Haa Meem Sajdah - Aayah 33)*

To call people to Allah Ta'ala and to show the right path to all those who had gone astray was the only purpose of the life of Nabi ﷺ. For this very purpose, thousands of Ambiyaa *(alayhimus salaam)* had been sent before him. Allah Ta'ala says:

$$\text{وَمَآ اَرْسَلْنَا مِنْ قَبْلِكَ مِنْ رَسُوْلٍ اِلَّا نُوْحِیْۤ اِلَیْهِ اَنَّهٗ لَاۤ اِلٰهَ اِلَّاۤ اَنَا فَاعْبُدُوْنِ}$$

"And we did not send any Rasool before you (O Muhammad ﷺ), except that We sent revelation to Him that certainly there is no deity but Me, so worship Me" *(Surah Ambiyaa - Aayah 25)*

The noble stories about Nabi Muhammad ﷺ and other Ambiyaa *(alayhimus salaam)* show one single mission of their lives, i.e., to believe in One True Allah Ta'ala with all His qualities. This belief is the foundation of Islam. It was to practice and call towards this Imaan that man has been sent on this earth. In other words:

$$\text{وَمَا خَلَقْتُ الْجِنَّ وَالْاِنْسَ اِلَّا لِیَعْبُدُوْنِ}$$

"I have created the Jinn and Human beings only to worship (serve) Me." *(Surah Zaariyaat - Aayah 56)*

We should, by now, be able to understand the real purpose behind the creation of man and the way we, particularly Muslims, should live. We also know the true disease from which we suffer, and its treatment should, therefore, not be difficult to apply. If we act sincerely, then *Insha-Allah* (by the will of Allah Ta'ala) it will be beneficial and successful. However, a proven successful method is described below.

COURSE OF ACTION

With my very little knowledge and understanding, I have suggested a plan of action for the improvement of Muslims and their progress in Islam. Actually, what I have to say is the practical way of life which had been followed by our forefathers and early Muslims.

The first thing to do is to change the aim of our life from dunya and wealth towards giving da'wat (propagation) and spreading the *'kalimah'*, enforcing the commands of Allah Ta'ala, sincerely making a determination to obey Allah Ta'ala in a practical way, and not to disobey

Allah Ta'ala under any conditions. The fulfilment of this decision must be made the main aim of life. We can start off by doing the following:

1. To memorise and correctly recite the kalimah;

$$\text{لَا اِلٰهَ اِلَّا اللّٰهُ مُحَمَّدٌ رَسُوْلُ اللّٰهِ}$$

   To understand its exact meaning as well as what it actually requires from us. We have to bring this Imaan that, Allah Ta'ala is the only Power, the only Authority and the only Controller of all things, and He alone must be worshipped and obeyed, and He alone grants success or failure in life. Success will depend on us adopting the way of life shown and taught to us by Nabi Muhammad ﷺ and our accepting him as true and last Nabi of Allah Ta'ala. Having this as the perfect life before us, we now begin to change our own life on the requirements of the 'kalimah'.

2. To become punctual and regular in offering Salaah five times a day. The fulfilling of this fardh duty should be strictly in accordance as shown to us by Hadhrat Muhammad ﷺ. Salaah should be offered with utmost concentration and devotion. The greatness and superiority of Allah Ta'ala must be uppermost in our mind throughout Salaah, whilst maintaining our own humbleness and helplessness. In other words, Salaah should be performed as if one is actually present in front of Allah Ta'ala and in a manner befitting His Greatness and Glory. If the method of Salaah is not known, it should be properly learnt with memorising each detail.

3. To learn the knowledge of Deen and to do the sincere zikr of Allah Ta'ala. To develop attachment of body and soul to the Qur-aan Shareef in the following manner:

   a. To daily recite even a small portion of the Qur-aan, with the highest degree of devotion and respect for the Qur-aan Shareef, and if possible, by understanding its meaning also. If one is unable to understand the meaning, he may still recite the text with the hope that his everlasting success and progress depends on it. Simple recitation of the original words and lines is also a great blessing. If a person is unable to recite, he should make an effort and spend a little time daily to learn to recite.

    b. To ensure that one's own children as well as those of his neighbours and friends are taught the Qur-aan Shareef and other essential Deeni books as a first step in their learning.

4. Sometime should be set aside daily for zikr, which means concentrating on the greatness and attributes of Allah Ta'ala, and to send durood and salaam on Nabi Muhammad ﷺ. A person should seek guidance from a "Shaikh-e-Tariqat" (a spiritual guide). This Shaikh should be a pious person who follows the Shariah and Sunnah in all aspects. He may prescribe certain zikr to be recited. In a case where no such pious person can be found, it is suggested that the following zikr be recited a hundred times (one tasbih of 100 beads) each, both in the morning and in the evening:

    a) Third Kalimah,

$$\text{سُبْحَانَ اللهِ وَالْحَمْدُ لِلّٰهِ وَلَا اِلٰهَ اِلَّا اللهُ وَاللهُ اَكْبَرُ وَلَا حَوْلَ وَلَا قُوَّةَ اِلَّا بِاللهِ الْعَلِيِّ الْعَظِيْمِ}$$

    b) Durood (Sending durood and salaam on Nabi ﷺ).

    c) Istighfaar (Asking Allah Ta'ala for forgiveness).

5. Every Muslim must be considered as our real brother and must always be shown affection, sympathy and sincere attention at all times, particularly when he is in need. All Muslims should respect and honour his Muslim brother and not cause him any type of harm due to the fact that he has Imaan.

The above should be brought into our own lives, and at the same time, effort should be made so that other people may follow as well. The best way to do this is to spend some time especially for learning and practicing these fine Islamic qualities and also encouraging others to make an effort as well. Thus, a joint and collective effort will automatically bring the Deen of Islam alive in its true form, which is the real and urgent need of the day.

It was exactly this type of work which every Nabi of Allah Ta'ala had to do as his sole occupation. For the sake of this work, almost all Ambiyaa *(alayhimus salaam)* had to go through sufferings and hardships. The noble Sahaabah of Nabi Muhammad ﷺ as well as many other Muslims of the early period of Islaam, spent their whole lives sacrificing and struggling for the Deen of Islam in this very manner. Most of them sacrificed their lives in the path of Allah Ta'ala. It will be our huge loss if we do not spend a small part of our lifetime towards spreading Islam. We must agree that it is because of our carelessness that the Muslim Ummah has reached its present poor state. Therefore, we must rise and increase our efforts.

To give one's life, honour and wealth for Islam should be the object of a Muslim. Previously, if anyone did not do that, he was regarded to be an ignorant and useless person. But alas! Today, although we feel proud to be called Muslims, every part of Islam is being destroyed before our very eyes and not a finger is lifted to stop this terrible loss. If we realise this, then we can understand that the spreading of Islam is our real purpose in life and in dawah lies our everlasting success. The opposite is also true, that by neglecting this important responsibility, the Ummah will suffer greatly. The only solution for this is that all of us must sincerely make taubah for our carelessness of the past and take immediate action to restart Tabligh as our main work and effort. It is only then that we can expect the mercy and kindness of Allah Ta'ala to bring us success and happiness both in this life and the Aakhirah.

This does not mean that we should give up everything else, i.e. our jobs and businesses and do only this work. It means that, just as we give our whole hearted attention and time to our jobs, we should similarly also look after this effort. When some people get ready to start Tabligh, they should try to contact their friends or other people in their areas who may be already involved in this work and spend a few hours a week in their company. The next step will be to spend three days every month in a different locality or a village. Thereafter, as early as possible, spend a full month or, better, still forty days every year somewhere far away in a similar manner. Lastly, the real requirement in Tabligh is to spend four months once in a lifetime. All these periods are to be spent only for learning and teaching Islam and practicing the actual way of life according to the Shariah. Thus, our efforts will encourage every person, rich and poor, boss and worker, landlord and tenant, educated and uneducated to join hands in this work and become true Muslims as commanded by Allah Ta'ala and His Rasul ﷺ.

METHOD FOR TABLIGH

The most important point in Tabligh is the method and manner to be used in propagating Islam. We have to closely follow the method used by the noble Sahaabah of Nabi ﷺ according to his teachings and practices. The method used by Nabi ﷺ was as follows:

A group of at least ten people should go out for the work of Tabligh. First they should choose an Ameer from amongst themselves. They should then gather in the Masjid and after making wudhu, read two Rakaat Nafl Salaah (as long as this is done at a time of the day when Nafl Salaah is allowed). After Salaah, everyone should sit together and beg Allah Ta'ala by making dua for help, success, and the ability to remain steadfast in doing this effort. After making dua they should leave for the place, where they have decided to do the effort of Tabligh, with dignity and calmness, quietly making the zikr of Allah Ta'ala and avoiding useless talk. When they get to the place, they should once again gather together, making dua to Allah Ta'ala, asking Him for assistance in fulfilling their mission.

The area where they will do the effort of Tabligh will be in the vicinity of a Masjid of a locality. A few brothers of the jamaat will go out and meet all the people of the neighbourhood or the village, inviting them to join the ta'leem (reading and teaching from the fazaail kitaabs) being conducted in the Masjid. They should then encourage these people to join the next Salaah on the prescribed time. After Salaah, one of the brothers of the jamaat should address the people, encouraging and advising them about the importance of reviving Islam in each and every Muslim as commanded by Allah Ta'ala and His Rasul ﷺ. Then basic points of Tabligh, including how to fulfil this effort should be explained. Finally, the people should be motivated to make firm intentions to do the same effort in the same manner. They should themselves be encouraged to go out in the path of Allah Ta'ala and do the work of Tabligh.

Some members of the jamaat may accompany the people to their homes, where the womenfolk should also be addressed from behind a curtain and encourage them to do a similar effort amongst the women. They should be told to be punctual in their Salaah. All this should be done without entering the private portion of any house. The women should also be told to strictly follow the basic points of Tabligh in their daily lives and observe pardah in accordance with the Shariah.

When some people are prepared to join the work, they should be grouped into a separate jamaat and an ameer should be appointed from amongst them. They should first be made to work under the guidance of the members of the original jamaat. It is important that every person engaged in Tabligh must fully obey his ameer and the ameer, in turn, should ensure that his personal services and attention are available to each and every member of his Jamaat. He must see to every person's welfare, comfort and morale. Before taking any decision, he must make mashwarah (consult) with the entire jamaat. The following general principles of the work of Tabligh should be carefully noted at all times.

ETIQUETTES OF TABLEEGH

Tabligh is an important type of ibaadah of Allah Ta'ala and it is a great blessing. It actually means to follow in the footsteps of the Ambiyaa *(alayhimus salaam)*. Truly, since the work is so great, it must be based on certain rules, which must be always strictly followed. Each person who takes part in this effort must feel that it is he who needs to improve himself, rather than thinking of changing others. Whilst out for Tabligh or even at home, he must try to behave as a perfect Muslim, as a loyal slave of Allah Ta'ala, obeying and following the commands of Shariah and always seeking the mercy and pleasure of Allah Ta'ala. This is the main requirement and the foundation of the work of Tabligh. Once this is deeply and firmly established in the hearts of Tabligh workers, the other rules and practices, some of which are described below, will become easy to follow:

1. As far as possible, all expenses such as travelling, food, etc. must be paid for by each person himself, and the one who can afford it, may quietly help those who may be in need.

2. All the brothers in this work must be given full respect, shown tolerance, be cared for and encouraged at all times by one another. This will prove a great blessing for the whole area where the Jamaat may be working.

3. Conversation, talks and discussions must be soft and encouraging, using simple and polite language. All types of anger with each other must be avoided. The Ulama must be held in such high respect as we usually show for the Qur-aan and Hadith, because, it is through these learned Ulama that Allah Ta'ala has blessed us with the true knowledge and understanding of Islam. Any disrespect towards them, however small, may be disrespect for Islam itself, which can cause the displeasure of Allah Ta'ala for the whole community.

4. Holidays and free time must be spent either in reading good Islamic books or in the company of the pious and learned people. By doing this, one will be able to learn many important things about our Deen, about Allah Ta'ala and His Rasul ﷺ. A lot of care must be taken that the time given to the Tabligh work must be utilised correctly and no time should be wasted. Nothing unimportant, useless or senseless should be spoken, discussed or done.

5. Try to earn an honest and pure living. Be very careful in spending. Always carry out every single obligation, however big or small, towards one's family, relatives and friends.

6. No controversial topics should be discussed at any time. Maximum time must be spent in discussing, listening and pondering about the Oneness of Allah Ta'ala. Restrict all talk to the main points of Tabligh, which are in reality, the basic rules to be followed by each and every Muslim at all times.

7. Every action, work and speech must be filled with sincerity. Anything, however small, but done with sincerity, will certainly bring high rewards and plenty of goodness. On the other hand, anything done without sincerity, no matter how big, will not benefit in any way, in this life or in the Aakhirah. When Hadhrat Mu'aaz رضي الله عنه was appointed as the governor of Yemen, he begged

Nabi ﷺ to give him some special advice. Nabi ﷺ mentioned, *"Be very honest and sincere in matters of Islam, a little done with sincerity is enough."*

There is another Hadith which says that, *"Allah Ta'ala accepts only those actions and deeds which are done purely for His pleasure."* In another place it is stated that, *"Allah Ta'ala does not look at your face nor at your wealth, but only at your hearts and deeds."*

Thus the work of Tabligh must be performed with full sincerity and honesty. No acting or outward show is to be portrayed. The amount of success and progress will depend entirely on our sincerity.

Summary

We have discussed the work of Tabligh, its importance and urgent need. How will this guide us and bring us benefits in these times which are filled with confusion and difficulties? For this, once again, we have to look into the Qur-aan Shareef which says that hard work and patience for Deen is a very rewarding business:

يَاأَيُّهَا الَّذِيْنَ اٰمَنُوْا هَلْ اَدُلُّكُمْ عَلٰى تِجَارَةٍ تُنْجِيْكُمْ مِّنْ عَذَابٍ اَلِيْمٍ ۚ تُؤْمِنُوْنَ بِاللهِ وَرَسُوْلِهٖ وَتُجَاهِدُوْنَ فِيْ سَبِيْلِ اللهِ بِاَمْوَالِكُمْ وَاَنْفُسِكُمْ ۚ ذٰلِكُمْ خَيْرٌ لَّكُمْ اِنْ كُنْتُمْ تَعْلَمُوْنَ ۙ يَغْفِرْ لَكُمْ ذُنُوْبَكُمْ وَيُدْخِلْكُمْ جَنّٰتٍ تَجْرِىْ مِنْ تَحْتِهَا الْاَنْهٰرُ وَمَسٰكِنَ طَيِّبَةً فِيْ جَنّٰتِ عَدْنٍ ۚ ذٰلِكَ الْفَوْزُ الْعَظِيْمُ ۙ وَاُخْرٰى تُحِبُّوْنَهَا ۚ نَصْرٌ مِّنَ اللهِ وَفَتْحٌ قَرِيْبٌ ۚ وَبَشِّرِ الْمُؤْمِنِيْنَ

"O you who believe! Shall I not show you a business that will save you from a painful punishment? Believe in Allah Ta'ala and His Rasool ﷺ and strive in the path of Allah Ta'ala (to propagate Islaam) with your wealth and lives. This is best for you, if you know. Allah Ta'ala will forgive your sins and enter you into gardens, beneath which rivers flow and into wonderful mansions in the everlasting

Jannah. That is the supreme success. Another (bounty) which you really love is help from Allah Ta'ala and victory which is near (imminent), and give good news to those who believe (Mu'mineen)."
(Surah Saff - Aayah 10-13)

This Aayah describes a business, wherein promises of saving us from all types of sufferings and punishments are contained. The business meant here is to have firm Imaan in Allah Ta'ala and His Rasul ﷺ and to sacrifice in the path of Allah Ta'ala using one's own life and wealth. Tabligh will bring us everlasting goodness and happiness. It is this simple work that will bring us great benefits, such as the forgiveness for all our sins and mistakes and high rewards in the Aakhirah. Leave alone success in the next life, which really is the greatest joy for a Muslim, there is also success in this life also. We shall get what we like most, such as prosperity, the help of Allah Ta'ala and success against our enemies.

In other words, Allah Ta'ala asks two things from us, first to have Imaan in Him and His Rasul ﷺ, and secondly to sacrifice in His path, giving our lives and all that we own. In return for this, He has also promised us two things, firstly a beautiful and peaceful home in Jannah with everlasting happiness and secondly, honour and success in this life. The first demand on us is that of Imaan. This is exactly what Tabligh is all about, that we should all be gifted with the wealth of true Imaan. The second demand is that of sacrificing in the path of Allah Ta'ala which actually means Jihaad. Jihaad may normally mean sometimes fighting a war against the oppressors and non-believers. However, it actually means to spread the belief in Tawheed (The Oneness of Allah Ta'ala) and to establish the commandments of Allah Ta'ala, which is also the main aim of Tabligh.

It should be clear to us now that happiness and success in the Aakhirah (life of the hereafter) totally depends on having firm Imaan in Allah Ta'ala and His Rasul ﷺ and in sacrificing in His path. Similarly, success and goodness in this life also depends completely on that very Imaan and on spending all our efforts in the path of Allah Ta'ala.

When we fulfil these basic requirements, firstly of Imaan in Allah Ta'ala and His Rasul ﷺ and secondly of sacrificing in their path, then through these two qualities alone we can beautify ourselves with high noble qualities and excellence of character. Only then can we deserve to become the rulers (Khulafaa of Allah Ta'ala) on earth, which will certainly come as is promised in the Qur-aan:

وَعَدَ اللّٰهُ الَّذِيْنَ اٰمَنُوْا مِنْكُمْ وَعَمِلُوا الصّٰلِحٰتِ لَيَسْتَخْلِفَنَّهُمْ فِى الْاَرْضِ كَمَا اسْتَخْلَفَ الَّذِيْنَ مِنْ قَبْلِهِمْ ۪ وَلَيُمَكِّنَنَّ لَهُمْ دِيْنَهُمُ الَّذِى ارْتَضٰى لَهُمْ وَلَيُبَدِّلَنَّهُمْ مِّنْ بَعْدِ خَوْفِهِمْ اَمْنًا ۭ يَعْبُدُوْنَنِيْ لَا يُشْرِكُوْنَ بِيْ شَيْئًا ۭ

"Allah Ta'ala has promised those of you who have Imaan and do good actions that He will certainly make them successors (of the rulers) on earth just as He had made those before them successors. And He will certainly grant strength to the Deen that He has chosen for them and will certainly replace their fear with peace (on condition that) they worship Me and do not ascribe any partner to Me."
(Surah Noor - Aayah 55)

This Aayat describes a direct promise of governing on earth, but through Imaan and goods deeds. This was actually fulfilled in the days of Nabi ﷺ and remained right through the period of the Khulafaa-e-Raashideen (first four Khulafaa of Islam who were guided by Allah Ta'ala, viz. Hadhrat Abu Bakr رضي الله عنه, Hadhrat Umar رضي الله عنه, Hadhrat Usmaan رضي الله عنه and Hadhrat Ali رضي الله عنه). The whole of Arabia had become an Islamic country in the days of Nabi ﷺ himself, and the rest of the countries (Muslim countries of today) mostly joined Islam during the period of the first four Khulafaa or immediately after their time. Later on, the promise also continued to be fulfilled for many Muslim kings and Khulafaa and it would still happen today if someone fulfils the conditions, as is clear from the following Aayah;

اِنَّ حِزْبَ اللّٰهِ هُمُ الْغٰلِبُوْنَ

"Surely only the party of Allah Ta'ala (those with Him) shall be victorious." (Surah Maa'idah - Aayah 56).

In these few pages, a breakdown of the present situation and a practical solution for improving it has been given. In fact, the solution will be found nowhere besides the pure Islamic way of life, which was practically demonstrated by our forefathers and early Muslims.

CONCLUSION

In conclusion, it can be said that there is no way to gain honour, happiness, peace and rest in this life other than hold on to the work and system of Tabligh, for which everyone of us must use all our energies and wealth.

$$\text{وَاعْتَصِمُوْا بِحَبْلِ اللهِ جَمِيْعًا وَّلَا تَفَرَّقُوْا}$$

"Hold fast on to the rope of Allah Ta'ala all of you together, and do not separate." (Surah Aale I'mraan - Aayah 103)

FINAL REQUEST

This method has actually been recently started off in Mewaat and a few other areas around Delhi (India). Although the work in that region has not yet reached the final stage, the progress of the local Muslims has been excellent. The benefits of the system of Tabligh are clearly visible for all to see. If all Muslims collectively try to follow the noble example described above and practice the correct system of life, as described in this book, there is every hope that through that effort, Allah Ta'ala may remove all our hardships and troubles. We may also be able to increase our Imaan and the ability to do good deeds. One may then be able to attain honour, greatness and glory in this life and everlasting success in the next. The Muslims can then set an example for the rest of the world to live in peace and happiness, which is the natural desire of every man on earth.

$$\text{وَلِلهِ الْعِزَّةُ وَلِرَسُوْلِهِ وَلِلْمُؤْمِنِيْنَ}$$

"And all honour belongs to Allah Ta'ala, His Rasool ﷺ and to the believers." (Surah Munaafiqoon - Aayah 8)

The real purpose of publishing this book is to present to the readers a practical way of life, which had been started and followed by Hadhrat

Moulana Muhammad Ilyaas Saahib *(rahmatullahi alaih)* about sixty years ago (This was written in the year 1358 Hijri). He had in fact spent all his life for this noble purpose. It is up to us, the Muslims of today, to understand our duties towards Islam and fulfil them so that we, as well as the rest of mankind, can benefit. The way is clear and well set out for us. So let us begin with all seriousness and earn the pleasure and happiness of Allah Ta'ala.

میری قسمت سے الٰہی پائیں یہ رنگِ قبول   پھول کچھ میں نے چنے ہیں ان کے دامن کے لیے

O Allah, May it be my good fortune that they blossom with acceptance

These flowers which I have chosen for his remembrance

وَاٰخِرُ دَعْوَانَا اَنِ الْحَمْدُ لِلّٰهِ رَبِّ الْعَالَمِيْنَ وَالصَّلَاةُ وَالسَّلَامُ عَلٰى رَسُوْلِهٖ مُحَمَّدٍ وَّاٰلِهٖ وَاَصْحَابِهٖ اَجْمَعِيْنَ بِرَحْمَتِكَ يَا اَرْحَمَ الرَّاحِمِيْنَ

محمد ﷺ

چھ باتیں

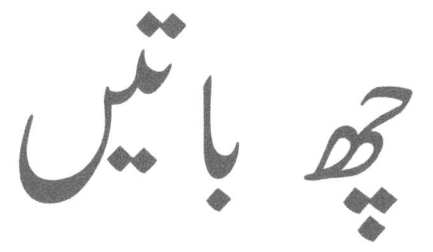

Six Fundamentals
By: Moulana Aashiq Ilaahi (RA)

Contents

SIX FUNDAMENTALS	903
FIRST LESSON KALIMAH TAYYIBAH	906
The Words and Translation of the Kalimah	906
The Meaning of the Kalimah	907
The Requirements of the Kalimah Tayyibah	907
The Benefits of the Kalimah Tayyibah	908
SECOND LESSON SALAAH	909
Salaah with Jamaat	910
The correct way to perform rukoo and sajdah	911
Performing Salaah out of its appointed time	911
THIRD LESSON ILM (KNOWLEDGE) AND ZIKR	912
Knowledge	912
The virtue of an Aalim over a common person	913
To leave home for the sake of acquiring knowledge	913
To offer service and help to a student of Deen	913
The benefits of the Halaqa (gathering) of Taleem	913
Zikr	914
The preference of zikr	915
FOURTH LESSON HONOUR FOR A MUSLIM	916
FIFTH LESSON SINCERITY OF INTENTION	918
SIXTH LESSON SPENDING TIME IN THE PATH OF ALLAH TA'ALA	920
SEVENTH LESSON TO STAY AWAY FROM VAIN (USELESS) THINGS	923
THE REQUISITES OF A JOURNEY FOR TABLIGH	925
The duties of an Ameer (leader)	927
Ilm (Knowledge) and zikr	929
The Nafl (optional) Salaah	931

Gasht (To go visit the common and the influential people for the sake of Allah Ta'ala) 932

Giving Dawat (Inviting Towards Allah Ta'ala and His Deen) 933

Obedience to the Ameer (leader) 934

The Aadaab (etiquettes) of eating 934

The Aadaab (etiquette) of going to sleep 936

Wudhu and Salaah 937

Miscellaneous 939

Directives for the workers of Tabligh 942

First Lesson
Kalimah Tayyibah

لَا اِلٰهَ اِلَّا اللهُ مُحَمَّدٌ رَّسُوْلُ اللهِ

Laa ilaaha illallaahu, Muhammadur-Rasulullaah

This Kalimah is a promise which man makes with Allah Ta'ala. That is, when a believer sincerely reads this Kalimah, he admits that he is a sincere and faithful servant of Allah Ta'ala, he will obey all His commandments and will avoid all the forbidden things. Therefore, one must keep in mind four important points about this Kalimah:
1. First, he should remember its words in the correct form.
2. Second, he should remember its correct translation.
3. Third, he should remember its exact meaning.
4. Fourth, he should see what its requirements are, and practically implement them in his life.

The Words and Translation of the Kalimah

This Kalimah has two parts; first: **"Laa ilaaha illallaah"**, and second, **"Muhammadur-Rasulullah"**, the translation of which is;
"*No one is worthy of worship but Allah, and Muhammad is His true Messenger.*"

THE MEANING OF THE KALIMAH

When a believer admits that no one is worthy of worship but Allah Ta'ala, it necessarily means that he should worship no one in the whole universe besides the Almighty Allah Ta'ala and should join no partner to Him in worship, concerning all the principles of Islam. He should believe Him to be his only Guardian and Helper in all problems and difficulties, and that Allah Ta'ala is present everywhere, seeing and hearing everything in the world. He should trust in His guidance, and should faithfully obey His commandments; moreover, he should not follow any customs and traditions that are contrary to His commandments. In all the affairs of his life, he should follow the teachings of the Qur-aan-e-Kareem, hope for His mercy and fear His anger and he should completely rely upon Allah Ta'ala for His guidance!

The second part of the Kalimah is, *"Muhammadur Rasulullah"*, which means, that after believing in the oneness of Allah Ta'ala, if one were to follow the commandments of Allah Ta'ala, then he cannot do so unless he keeps Muhammad ﷺ as his instructor and guide to the Right Path. That is, I will worship Allah Ta'ala just as Muhammad ﷺ has told me, because he was a faithful and true messenger of Allah Ta'ala, who taught us nothing of his own will or desire. The obedience of Rasulullah ﷺ, is really the obedience of Allah Ta'ala and love for him, is love for Allah Ta'ala. One must believe that to be obedient to him is a compulsory thing and we must submit to his orders, without any reservations. Whatever he has told us of the unseen like the Malaaikah (angels), Jannah, Jahannam, the incidents in the grave and the Resurrection, we must believe in them, even though we cannot understand them. We must believe that the Sunnah way of life which he has informed us about and has practically demonstrated, is the only way of life which is accepted by Allah Ta'ala and anyone who acts contrary to it, is not following the Right Path and is not loved by Allah Ta'ala.

THE REQUIREMENTS OF THE KALIMAH TAYYIBAH

When a Muslim has firm faith (Imaan) in the kalimah, he indeed becomes a true believer. He has to, therefore, abandon all the forbidden things and follow the commandments of Allah Ta'ala. That is why

Rasulullah ﷺ has said, "The first effect of *'Laa ilaaha illallaah'* is that it should prevent its reader from all the forbidden things."

Therefore, the reader of such a sacred Kalimah should give up all the forbidden things and follow all the commandments of Allah Ta'ala on all occasions. He should keep them in mind on the occasion of marriage, death, when taking meals, when going to sleep, on waking up, when conducting business and on all other occasions.

THE BENEFITS OF THE KALIMAH TAYYIBAH

This Kalimah has many spiritual benefits. Rasulullah ﷺ said, "The most famous Zikr is *'Laa ilaaha ilallaah'*". He also said, "Read the Kalimah a hundred times daily, for it is the best compensation for one's sins and no good deed is better than it," In another Hadith he says, "Whoever reads *'Laa ilaaha ilallaah'* a hundred times in the morning, and a hundred times in the evening shall be given the reward of releasing ten slaves from the progeny of Ismaa-eel *(alayhis salaam)*." In another Hadith Rasulullah ﷺ says, "Keep your Imaan fresh by reading and observing *'Laa ilaaha ilallaah.'"*

SECOND LESSON
SALAAH

When a Muslim has firmly believed in the Kalimah Tayyibah, he has made a promise to obey all the commandments of Allah Ta'ala; the first and foremost of which is Salaah which must be observed by every adult, male or female, five times a day. In other words, those who perform Salaah regularly, after believing in the Kalimah, they practically fulfil their promise with Allah Ta'ala, made through the Kalimah; and those who are not regular with Salaah, they practically go against their promise with Allah Ta'ala, i.e. to be His faithful servants. Rasulullah ﷺ mentions about those who go against their promise that, "Whoever neglects Salaah intentionally, becomes a kaafir." In another Hadith he says, "Whoever gives up Salaah, will be raised among Qaaroon, Fir'own, his minister Haamaan and the famous disbeliever, Ubayy bin Khalaf on the Day of Qiyaamah."

Next to the Kalimah, Salaah is the most important of all good deeds. It has been mentioned in the Hadith that the first thing to be brought to account on the Day of Qiyaamah, will be Salaah. If one's Salaah is perfect in every respect, he will certainly be forgiven; otherwise he will be deprived of all the blessings and favours of Allah Ta'ala and will suffer a great loss. Therefore, one should perform Salaah at the correct times, with perfect wudhu and complete devotion, so that one will not be raised up with the kuffaar and sent to Jahannam.

Whatever is read in Salaah (for example Thana (*Subhaanak-Allahumma*) and Tashahhud (*Attahiyyaat*) etc.), should be learnt well so that no mistakes occur whilst performing Salaah. One must know the Faraaidh, the Sunnan, all the conditions of Salaah, and also have concentration in Salaah, so that it is performed correctly.

One should increase the quality of his Salaah by ensuring that all his limbs viz. the hands, feet, head, waist, nose, forehead, tongue etc., are all completely devoted to Allah Ta'ala, that is every part of his body is engaged in obedience to the commandments of Allah Ta'ala. If a Muslim performs Salaah with all its conditions, it is unlikely that any of his limbs will commit sins out of Salaah. It has been mentioned in the Qur-aan-e-Kareem that Salaah prevents a Muslim from shameful and forbidden things. The believers have been commanded hundreds of times in the Qur-aan-e-Kareem to perform Salaah properly.

Salaah has been enjoined and emphasized many a time in the Ahaadith. For instance, Rasulullah ﷺ said, "One's sins between one Salaah to the next Salaah are forgiven by Allah Ta'ala."

In another Hadith he says, "If one has a stream at his door and has a bath in it five times a day; he will have no dirt left on his body. Similarly, if one performs Salaah five times a day, his sins will be forgiven by Allah Ta'ala, and he will be cleansed of them." In another Hadith Rasulullah ﷺ says, "When your children are seven years old, instruct them to perform Salaah, but when they are ten years old, beat them to perform Salaah."

Salaah with Jamaat

Rasulullah ﷺ says in a Hadith, "Salaah with Jamaat is rewarded twenty seven times more than Salaah performed alone." It has also been mentioned in a Hadith that Rasulullah ﷺ intended to burn the houses of those who did not visit the masjid to perform their Salaah with Jamaat, but he refrained from doing so, because of the children and women. Ibn Mas'ood رضى الله عنه says, "During the time of Rasulullah ﷺ only that person who was an open Munaafiq (hypocrite) dared to neglect his Salaah." It has also been mentioned in a Hadith that performing Esha Salaah with jamaat causes one to get the reward of being in Salaah till half the night; and thereafter performing Fajr Salaah with Jamaat causes one to get the reward of being in Salaah the entire night.

THE CORRECT WAY TO PERFORM RUKOO AND SAJDAH

Rasulullah ﷺ says in a Hadith, "Allah does not look at the Salaah of one who does not keep his waist straight in Salaah (i.e. he performs Salaah lazily)." In another Hadith he says, "The worst kind of thief is one who steals in Salaah." The Sahaabah رضي الله عنهم asked, "What is meant by stealing in Salaah?" Rasulullah ﷺ answered, "Stealing in Salaah is not to perform the rukoo (bowing posture) and sajdah (prostrating posture) properly, with spending sufficient time and devotion."

PERFORMING SALAAH OUT OF ITS APPOINTED TIME

Rasulullah ﷺ said, "It is the Salaah of a munaafiq to cause delay in the Salaah and to wait for sunset; so when it becomes dull, he gets up to perform it just as a custom and he remembers Allah Ta'ala but little."

THIRD LESSON
ILM (KNOWLEDGE) AND ZIKR

There are two important subjects in this lesson; firstly knowledge and secondly zikr (i.e. remembrance of Allah Ta'ala). There are so many sayings of Rasulullah ﷺ which stress on the value and distinction of these two things. For instance, a Hadith says, "Beware! This world and whatever is in it, is cursed by Allah Ta'ala, with the exception of Salaah and Zikr, the Aalim, and the student of Deen."

Therefore, every Muslim should try his best to achieve the high standard of Deeni knowledge and zikr.

KNOWLEDGE

Only that knowledge, which takes a man nearer to Allah Ta'ala, is appreciated by Him and enables him to follow His commandments. That amount of knowledge of the Deen of Islam that would purify and strengthen one's Imaan, is Fardh (obligatory) on every Muslim man and woman. When a servant of Allah Ta'ala has entirely submitted himself to Allah Ta'ala and has promised to follow His commandments, then it is necessary for him to know all His commandments, and the method of Ibaadah. Yes, he should have perfect knowledge of Salaah, fasting, Zakaat, Hajj, mutual dealings in everyday life, true Islamic Aadaab and other important aspects of an Islamic way of life. Every Muslim should particularly know these basic aspects about Islam and if he is ignorant of these, then he is likely to commit sins. When a person has the knowledge of these things, he must then observe them in a practical way, for it has been mentioned in a Hadith, "Verily, the worst punishment of Allah Ta'ala on the Day of Qiyaamah will be meted out to those who have been scholars of Deen, but did not practice it themselves."

THE VIRTUE OF AN AALIM OVER A COMMON PERSON

Rasulullah ﷺ has said in a Hadith, "Anyone who shows the Right Path to a Muslim is like one who has already followed the commandments of Allah Ta'ala." Another Hadith says, "A thousand worshippers are not so annoying and deadly to Shaytaan compared to one person who has achieved perfect knowledge about Islam." Another Hadith says, "Anyone who died whilst attaining the knowledge of Islam, his position in Jannah will be only one stage below the Ambiyaa *(alayhimus salaam)*." Another Hadith says, "The best person amongst you is he who has learned the Qur-aan Shareef and then teaches it to other Muslims." Rasulullah ﷺ says in another Hadith, "May Allah Ta'ala keep that person fresh and healthy who listens to my instructions, and then delivers them to others, exactly as I have spoken."

TO LEAVE HOME FOR THE SAKE OF ACQUIRING KNOWLEDGE

Rasulullah ﷺ has said, "Whoever left his home for the sake of acquiring knowledge (about the Qur-aan-e-Kareem and Islam), will be honoured as one who has entirely devoted himself to Allah Ta'ala."

TO OFFER SERVICE AND HELP TO A STUDENT OF DEEN

It has been mentioned in a Hadith, that Rasulullah ﷺ, whilst addressing his followers, said, "Indeed, the coming generation will follow you, for you have followed me. After me people will come to you from remote places to learn the knowledge of Islam. So when they come to you, it is my request that you should entertain them well." That is, when the students of Deen visit you, serve them properly, sit in their company and be polite to them.

THE BENEFITS OF THE HALQAH (GATHERING) OF TA'LEEM

Rasulullah ﷺ says in a Hadith, "When certain people gather in the House of Allah Ta'ala (that is a Masjid) and they recite the Book of

Allah Ta'ala (i.e. the Qur-aan-e-Kareem) to one another, they are blessed with sakinah (spiritual comfort) and the mercy of Allah Ta'ala, the Malaaikah assemble around them, and Allah Ta'ala remembers them among His Malaaikah."

ZIKR

The second part of the third lesson is zikr. The highest degree of zikr is that a believer should be entirely devoted to Allah Ta'ala and should never forget Him. This standard of zikr is achieved by constant spiritual exercise and by continuous remembrance of Allah Ta'ala. Those who have realized the spiritual benefits of Zikr, do not neglect it for a single moment of their life. Rasulullah ﷺ instructed a Sahaabi of his with the following words, "Keep your tongue always busy with the remembrance of Allah Ta'ala." In another Hadith he says, "When some people gather in an assembly and then get up without remembering Allah Ta'ala, be sure that they sat around the dead body of an ass and thereafter left. Therefore, such an assembly will be a source of sorrow to them on the Day of Qiyaamah."

The true believers should remember Allah Ta'ala most often and by pondering about the wonders of His creation, they should glorify Him, and thereby strengthen their love for Him. The more they remember Allah Ta'ala, the better will be their good deeds, the stronger their Imaan and knowledge. Then they will have more and more love for Allah Ta'ala and their service to Him will be more sincere and realistic. Particularly, during the Tabligh journey they should not forget Allah Ta'ala for a single moment. If all the daily Sunnah Duas, which are mentioned in the Hadith, viz, Dua for going to sleep and waking up, Dua at the end of a gathering, Dua for the beginning and the end of the meals, Dua for entering and leaving home, Dua at the beginning of a journey and returning from it, Dua for riding an animal (or any other mode of transport), Dua for entering a new town or a city etc., are remembered well, and are read on the relevant occasions, naturally the exercise of the remembrance of Allah Ta'ala can be improved to a great extent. No amount of time is sufficient for a sacred thing like zikr. Therefore, most of the spare time should be devoted to zikr. The least that every Muslim can do is to read the Kalimah Tayyibah, Durood Shareef and Istighfaar (100 times each) every morning and evening and a time should be fixed for the recitation of the Qur-aan-e-Kareem. Even some worldly loss can easily be tolerated for the countless favours of Allah Ta'ala that are going to be granted to a believer in the next life.

THE PREFERENCE OF ZIKR

It has been mentioned in the Hadith that zikr purifies and enlightens the heart. Another Hadith says that nothing saves a Muslim from the punishment of Allah Ta'ala more than zikr. Another Hadith says that amongst a group of negligent people, the one who remembers Allah Ta'ala most often is like a glowing lamp in a dark house. A Hadith of Bukhaari says, "One who remembers Allah Ta'ala, is remembered by Him amongst His Malaaikah (Angels)." In another Hadith Rasulullah ﷺ says, "Anyone who remembers Allah Ta'ala most often, is more preferable to a person who distributes a huge amount of money in the path of Allah Ta'ala." (Targheeb)

FOURTH LESSON
HONOURING A MUSLIM

The essence of this lesson is that every Muslim should recognize the rights of other Muslims and should fulfill them practically, according to the status of each person in Islam. Particularly, he should have great regard for the honour of a Muslim who deserves all the respect because he has the light of Imaan in his heart. Rasulullah ﷺ says in a Hadith, "He is not one of us who does not respect our elders, does not show mercy to our youngsters and is not respectful to the student of Deen." Another Hadith says. "Only a Munaafiq (hypocrite) could insult these three persons; firstly an aged Muslim, secondly an Aalim and thirdly a just Muslim king."

According to the teachings of the Qur-aan-e-Kareem and the Ahaadith, the following are the most important qualities of a true believer. He should realize the rights of the creation of Allah Ta'ala and should be polite and humble to them. He should like for others, what he likes for himself. He should neither be jealous of others nor should he show hatred towards them. He must not be proud. He should be polite and loving to all. He should be the first to greet a Muslim. He should be generous enough to forgive those who have offended him. He should visit the sick. He should respect everyone just as he respects himself. He should avoid backbiting. He should overlook the weaknesses of others. If anyone consults him, he should give him the correct and honest counsel. He should give financial help to the poor and needy. He should not rejoice in the misery of others. And the most important and valuable service to a Muslim is that he should be instructed with firm Imaan in Allah Ta'ala, in the Day of Qiyaamah and to be prepared for Day of Qiyaamah by doing a lot of good deeds, so that he may be saved from the punishment in the Aakhirah. Undoubtedly, this is the best service to a brother Muslim.

Islam has instructed all the Muslims with a collective life and has enjoined them to be united so that they should provide peace and prosperity for one another. For instance, they have been instructed to put on their best clothes and apply itr (perfume) for the Jumu'ah and the Eid Salaah; they have been prevented from jumping over the necks of those sitting in a gathering, or to sit between two persons without their permission, or to move a person from the place where he is sitting. Rasulullah ﷺ says, "A true Muslim is he, who does not offend any other Muslim with his tongue or hand and a true believer is he, who does not cause any loss to another believer." In another Hadith Rasulullah ﷺ says, "That person will not enter Jannah, whose neighbor is not safe from his mischief and evil."

These sayings of Rasulullah ﷺ clearly indicate that a believer should behave so politely towards others, that they should never fear any trouble or a loss from him.

In another Hadith Rasulullah ﷺ says, "Whoever helps a poor and miserable person, Allah Ta'ala will grant him seventy three rewards, one of which will be sufficient to fulfil his needs in this world and the remaining seventy two rewards will elevate his rank in the Aakhirah." Another Hadith says "When a Muslim leaves home to see another Muslim, seventy thousand Malaaikah see him off and all of them bless him with the mercy of Allah Ta'ala." Rasulullah ﷺ says about a person who is your companion on a journey, "Only that person, who serves his companions on a journey, is your leader or ameer and no one can surpass such a person except a Shaheed."

FIFTH LESSON
IKHLAAS (SINCERITY)

This is also called "the correction of intention" i.e. whenever a person intends to do something good, he must not be tempted by some worldly motive but rather do it purely for the pleasure of Allah Ta'ala and to expect its reward in the Aakhirah. This purity of intention can be achieved only when we have firm Imaan in the reward which Allah Ta'ala and His Rasul ﷺ have promised for our good deeds and therefore, the hope of attaining this reward should be our motive when doing good deeds. That is why Rasulullah ﷺ has said, "The reward for your deeds depends entirely on your intention and everyone is paid in accordance with the nature of his intention." It means that it is not merely the action which ensures us a reward from Allah Ta'ala, but rather it is the sincerity of our intention. If an action is void of good intention and is undertaken for the sake of passion, or to please men, or to attain some worldly interest, then it is hollow, lifeless and deserves no reward from Allah Ta'ala. A Hadith to this effect says, "All the deeds of men will be gathered before Allah Ta'ala on the Day of Qiyaamah and only those deeds which were done purely for Allah Ta'ala will be separated and the rest will be thrown into Jahannum." *(Targheeb)*

When certain good deeds are done purely for Allah Ta'ala, it is called "Ikhlaas" and whenever a believer intends to do something based on sincerity, the nafs or Shaytaan will put obstacles in his way. Therefore, it is essential for sincerity that one should forsake the worldly temptations and should believe in the everlasting blessings and favours of the

Aakhirah. Those who have realized the value of sincerity apply it to their worldly affairs also. They observe sincerity (ikhlaas) in eating, drinking, sleeping, awakening, walking, earning their livelihood, etc. This standard of sincerity cannot be achieved without the company of buzroogs (pious Allah fearing people). For example, the Ulama have told us that if someone desires reward by fasting and also good health at the same time; or if by going for Haj, one wishes reward, recreation and safety from the enemy; or if by giving Sadaqah to a beggar, one has an intention to attain reward from Allah Ta'ala, appreciation from the onlookers and to silence the beggar, then all the above-mentioned deeds will be void of sincerity. A Sahaabi of Rasulullah ﷺ asked him, "What is Imaan?" He replied, "Another name for Imaan is sincerity!" (Targheeb) In another Hadith Rasulullah ﷺ says, "Observe sincerity in your deeds, then even a few good deeds will be greatly rewarding for you!" (Targheeb) Another Sahaabi of Rasulullah ﷺ asked him, "One man participates in Jihaad for the sake of acquiring wealth and another man participates for the sake of his reputation, that he may be called a hero. O! Messenger of Allah, who is it that is really fighting in the path of Allah Ta'ala?" He answered, "Only that person who wants to propagate and establish the truth told to him (in the Qur-aan-e-Kareem) really fights in the path of Allah Ta'ala." *(Bukhaari, Muslim)*

Those who do not desire the pleasure of Allah Ta'ala for their deeds, but rather wish only for the worldly achievements are certainly hypocrites and this (hypocrisy) is a disease of the heart, which our Mashaaikh say is the root of all evils. Once Rasulullah ﷺ said to his Sahaabah ؓ, "The thing I fear most in your actions is smaller shirk." The Sahaabah ؓ asked, "What is smaller shirk?" He answered, "Showing off (of one's good deeds!)" Another Hadith says, "Whoever makes a show of his Salaah, fasting or Sadaqah, has committed shirk." Another Hadith says, "There is a pit of sorrow in Jahannam, of which even Jahannam seeks the refuge of Allah Ta'ala. Those worshippers, who make a show of their Ibaadah will be thrown into it."

SIXTH LESSON
SPENDING TIME IN THE PATH OF ALLAH TA'ALA

A believer should spare as much time as possible for inviting and encouraging others towards the commandments of Allah Ta'ala, even if he has to leave his home and family for this noble cause. Whilst spending time in the path of Allah Ta'ala one should try to bring these six qualities or lessons practically into his life because experience shows that by staying in the home environment with one's family and attending to one's business or job, one can neither easily learn or teach the different aspects of Deen, nor can one adopt the Sunnah way of life particularly in this age of materialism.

Therefore, one should temporarily set aside his worldly commitments to serve Allah Ta'ala and His true Deen. He should join a Jamaat of brothers going out in the path of Allah Ta'ala so that they could call and encourage those who are totally engrossed in their worldly commitments and have forgotten the life of the Aakhirah, to the right path.

The duty of the Ambiyaa *(alayhimus salaam)* was to invite the sinners and negligent people towards Allah Ta'ala and to encourage them to obey His commandments. This duty has now been entrusted to the Muslims. To truly follow Rasulullah ﷺ requires that every Muslim should devote himself to the mission of Rasulullah ﷺ and should sacrifice everything for inviting towards the true Deen of Islam. Just as Rasulullah ﷺ himself patiently bore so many troubles for the sake of Islam, similarly every follower of his should also follow in his footsteps.

The companions of Rasulullah ﷺ had fully understood what the mission of Tabligh required from them, and therefore tolerated the troubles of this world for the sake of attaining the blessings and favours of Allah Ta'ala in the Aakhirah. They happily devoted themselves to the service of Allah Ta'ala and preferred the needs of Deen over the needs of this worldly life. They sometimes ate leaves or a single date and walked barefoot on long journeys in the path of Allah Ta'ala. During the time of the Sahabah, it was necessary to propagate Islam so that it spread far and wide, but today we only have to revive it. We should try to follow the example of the Sahaabah who fulfilled this mission by sacrificing their lives.

Rasulullah ﷺ has clearly informed us that to leave one's home and family for the cause of Allah Ta'ala carries great rewards in the Aakirah.

Rasulullah ﷺ has said, "Whoever spends his morning or evening in the path of Allah Ta'ala, his reward will be much more than the whole world and whatever is in it." (Bukhaari and Muslim) In another Hadith he says, "The fire of Jahannam will not touch anyone whose feet becomes dusty whilst he is in the path of Allah Ta'ala."

When we invite people towards the commandments of Allah Ta'ala, then it means that we have fulfilled the responsibility of Tabligh and have revived it, regarding which Rasulullah ﷺ has said, "When people see others committing sins and do not prevent them from doing so, Allah Ta'ala will soon inflict a punishment on them, which will affect the common people as well as the pious."

A Hadith of '*Tirmizi Shareef*' says, "I swear by Allah Ta'ala, you must command people with good deeds and prevent them from forbidden things or Allah Ta'ala will soon inflict a severe punishment on you and then even your Duas will not be heard by Him!"

An Aayah of the Qur-aan Shareef says,

وَلْتَكُنْ مِنْكُمْ أُمَّةٌ يَدْعُوْنَ اِلَى الْخَيْرِ وَيَأْمُرُوْنَ بِالْمَعْرُوْفِ وَيَنْهَوْنَ عَنِ الْمُنْكَرِ وَاُولٰٓئِكَ هُمُ الْمُفْلِحُوْنَ

"There must be a group among you, who should invite people to good, and should command them with good things, and should prevent them from evil things; and certainly those will the successful."
(Surah Aale I'mraan – Aayah 104)

Another Aayah of the Qur-aan Shareef says,

$$كُنْتُمْ خَيْرَ أُمَّةٍ أُخْرِجَتْ لِلنَّاسِ تَأْمُرُونَ بِالْمَعْرُوفِ وَتَنْهَوْنَ عَنِ الْمُنْكَرِ وَتُؤْمِنُونَ بِاللهِ$$

"O Muslims! You are the best nation, who has been chosen for the guidance of mankind; you command people with good, and prevent them from evil, and have a firm faith in Allah!" (Surah Aale I'mraan – Aayah 110)

It has been reported by Abu Darda رضي الله عنه that Rasulullah ﷺ said, "You must encourage people to good deeds and prevent them from evil deeds, otherwise Allah Ta'ala will cause a tyrant to rule over you, who will neither respect your elders nor show mercy to your youngsters; then even the Duas of your pious people will not be granted by Allah Ta'ala; if you seek forgiveness from Him, He will not forgive you!"

SEVENTH LESSON
TO STAY AWAY FROM VAIN (USELESS) THINGS

This lesson will explain the most important conditions of piety. A Muslim should spend every moment of his life trying to achieve the everlasting benefits of the Aakhirah. He should not only avoid sins, but also useless and destructive customs which negatively affects our Deen and beliefs. Although many deeds and hobbies may not be sinful, yet they are an absolute waste of time and energy which could be rather used for constructive things. This is the characteristic of a true believer that he spends his time only in virtuous deeds, remembers Allah Ta'ala as much as possible, avoids all forbidden things, does not indulge in useless things, and is polite and humble towards other Muslims. If one does not avoid vain talk and vain deeds, one is likely to indulge in shameful sins. It has been mentioned in a Hadith that when a Sahaabi of Rasulullah ﷺ passed away, a Muslim said to him, "I give to you the happy news of Jannah!" When Rasulullah ﷺ heard these words, he said, "You are giving him the happy news of Jannah, while you do not know that he might have indulged in vain talk, or might have been a miser in spending his wealth for the good of others, which really does not decrease by spending in good causes." This evidently means that one should be very cautious in his speech and should avoid vain talk, for one's tongue is likely to talk nonsense.

Another Hadith says, "A man does not slip so much by his feet as by his tongue."

Another Hadith says, "Sometimes a man speaks an offensive and sinful thing subconsciously, by which he is thrown into Jahannum deeper than the distance between east and west!" *(Bukhaari & Muslim)*

Therefore, every believer should be cautious in his speech and should spend every moment of his life in good deeds. He must avoid useless things particularly during the period when he has left home to learn Deen or to invite towards Deen.

Someone asked Luqmaan Hakeem (the wise), "How did you attain so much wisdom?" He answered, "Because I speak the truth, return the trusts to their rightful owners, and avoid useless (vain) things!" *(Muatta Imaam Maalik)*

Hadhrat Sahl Tastari *(rahmatullahi alayh)* says, "Anyone who desires that the qualities and signs of the truthful be visible upon him, must not eat anything besides that which is pure and halaal and should strictly follow the Sunnah." *(Ihyaaul-Uloom)*

In another Hadith Rasulullah ﷺ said, "The perfection of one's Imaan requires that one should totally give up vain and useless things."

The Qur-aan-e-Kareem mentions a great quality of true believers,

$$وَالَّذِيْنَ هُمْ عَنِ اللَّغْوِ مُعْرِضُوْنَ$$

"Those who do not indulge in useless things!" (Surah Mu'minoon Aayah 3)

NB. All the Ahaadith, which have no references have been quoted from '*Mishkaat Shareef*'.

THE REQUISITES OF A JOURNEY FOR TABLIGH

1. When a believer has decided to undertake such a journey, he should make the following Dua,

$$\text{اَللّٰهُمَّ بِكَ اَصُوْلُ وَبِكَ اَحُوْلُ وَبِكَ اَسِيْرُ}$$

   "O Allah! I attack the enemy with your help, I plan my work with Your help, and I walk on the earth with Your help."

2. When he has left home, he should read.

$$\text{بِسْمِ اللهِ تَوَكَّلْتُ عَلَى اللهِ لَا حَوْلَ وَلَا قُوَّةَ اِلَّا بِاللهِ}$$

   "I start my journey with the name of Allah, I entirely depend on Allah; the power to do good and to avoid evil is from Allah."

3. The Jamaat going in the path of Allah Ta'ala should have an Ameer for safr (travelling), who could be another person other than the Ameer of the Jamaat.

4. When he rides and puts his feet in the stirrup, he should say بِسْمِ اللهِ *(Bismillaah)* and when he sits on the back of the animal he should say اَلْحَمْدُ لِلّٰهِ *(Alhamdu lillaah)* and then he should read this Aayah,

سُبْحَانَ الَّذِىْ سَخَّرَ لَنَا هٰذَا وَمَا كُنَّا لَهٗ مُقْرِنِيْنَ وَاِنَّا اِلٰى رَبِّنَا لَمُنْقَلِبُوْنَ

"Glory be to Allah, who has subjected this animal to us, and we could not overpower it without His help; and at last we have to return to our Sustainer"

He should then say اَلْحَمْدُ لِلّٰهِ *(Alhamdu lillaah)* thrice and then اَللّٰهُ اَكْبَرُ *(Allaahu Akbar)* thrice and he should then say,

سُبْحَانَكَ اِنِّىْ ظَلَمْتُ نَفْسِىْ فَاغْفِرْ لِىْ فَاِنَّهٗ لَا يَغْفِرُ الذُّنُوْبَ اِلَّا اَنْتَ

"O Allah! You are clear of evil; I have been unjust to my soul; therefore, forgive me, for no one forgives sins, but You!"

5. When he has ridden and the animal walks, or when he himself begins to walk, he should say,

اَللّٰهُمَّ اِنِّىْ اَعُوْذُ بِكَ مِنْ وَّعْثَآءِ السَّفَرِ وَكَآبَةِ الْمُنْقَلَبِ وَالْحَوْرِ بَعْدَ الْكَوْرِ وَدَعْوَةِ الْمَظْلُوْمِ وَسُوْءِ الْمَنْظَرِ فِى الْاَهْلِ وَالْمَالِ

"O Allah! I seek Your refuge from the hardships of this journey, and from difficulties on my return, and from failure after success, and from the curses of the oppressed, and from loss of wealth and my family."

6. When he climbs to some high place, he should say; اَللّٰهُ اَكْبَرُ *(Allaahu Akbar)* thrice and when he descends, he should say; سُبْحَانَ اللّٰهِ *(Subhaanallaah)* thrice and when he passes through a field or a stream, he should say; لَا اِلٰهَ اِلَّا اللّٰهُ *(Laa ilaaha illallaah)* and اَللّٰهُ اَكْبَرُ *(Allaahu Akbar)*. (Hisn Haseen) [1]

---

[1] The same Duas apply for the person travelling by car, bus, plane etc.

7. He should not only be pleased to walk in the path of Allah Ta'ala, but he should rather prefer to go on foot, because this is a Sunnah of Rasulullah ﷺ and his Sahaabah ﷺ. He should therefore, get himself used to the sacrifices of this journey, which is a source of blessings and favours of Allah Ta'ala in the Aakhirah.

8. If his foot slips somewhere or hits some obstacle, he should say بِسْمِ اللهِ *(Bismillah)*. (Hisn Haseen)

9. When he sets foot at some station or destination, he should say;

$$\text{اَعُوْذُ بِكَلِمَاتِ اللهِ التَّامَّاتِ مِنْ شَرِّ مَا خَلَقَ}$$

"With the complete words of Allah, I seek refuge from the evil of whatever He has created".

10. When he enters some village or a city, he should say thrice,

$$\text{اَللّٰهُمَّ بَارِكْ لَنَا فِيْهَا}$$

"O Allah! Let it be auspicious for us."

He should then recite this Dua,

$$\text{اَللّٰهُمَّ ارْزُقْنَا جَنَاهَا وَحَبِّبْنَا اِلٰى اَهْلِهَا وَحَبِّبْ صَالِحِيْ اَهْلِهَا اِلَيْنَا}$$

"O Allah! Let us enjoy the fruits of this city, and fill our love into the hearts of the people of this city, and cause the love of the pious of this city to enter our hearts." *(Hisn Haseen)*

11. He should serve his companions as much as he can and should take pride in it. It has been mentioned in a Hadith, "That person who serves his companions the most is most worthy of being an Ameer in a journey. None can attain his rank except a Shaheed." *(Mishkaat)*

THE DUTIES OF AN AMEER (LEADER)

Here are the duties of an Ameer on a journey in the path of Allah Ta'ala:
1. He should provide comfort for his companions. He should make mashwara (consult) with his companions and if he disagrees with

anyone on a certain topic, then he should not discourage him, but should rather politely inform him of someone else's opinion which maybe more useful.
2. He should not be hard upon any companion and should not speak to him in a commanding tone.
3. He should treat each of his companions according to their status.
4. If any of his companions has the ability of giving a bayaan (speech), he should give him an opportunity to deliver a speech, and if somebody's talk is not according to the aims and objects of the Jamaat, he should not allow him to give a talk. He should be told in such a way that it would not displease or dishearten him.
5. He should prevent his companions from useless things in a polite and encouraging manner.
6. He should encourage them to complete their zikr in the morning and evening, more particularly when they are out for Tabligh work.
7. He himself should appoint a person to give Dawat (Mutakallim), a person to give the talk (bayaan), and if he does not find any suitable person for this purpose then he should do it himself.
8. Even whilst travelling, he should encourage his companions to learn the Tabligh lessons (qualities) well and he should advise them to memorise and remember the Masnoon Duas for all occasions.
9. He should pair the new brothers with one of the learned ones so that they may learn the Masnoon Duas, etc. from him.
10. He should distribute various duties among his companions. For instance, some of them should awake others for Tahajjud Salaah, some of them should encourage them for Chaasht and Ish-raaq Salaah and some of them should encourage others to complete the morning and evening zikr.
11. If there is some dispute or disunity among his companions, he should reconcile them.
12. He should talk to his companions again and again about the fear of Allah Ta'ala and preparation for the next life and sincerely advise them in the following words: "We have left our homes to reform ourselves before we reform others. Our real aim and object during this journey is to be in the company of the pious and the Muttaqee (God-fearing), thereby strengthening our relationship with them and performing our Ibaadah in the best possible manner. Thus we

should remember Allah Ta'ala as much as possible, serve one another sincerely, devote ourselves to all good deeds and prevent ourselves from forbidden things. The time that we have devoted to Tabligh work is not ours at all, but rather for the promotion and establishment of the true Deen of Allah Ta'ala. We should, therefore, value this time and learn and teach our Deen. We had spent our lives in useless things, but we should now be determined to spend the rest of our lives as true Muslims. We should fulfil the object of this journey to the best of our ability."

ILM (KNOWLEDGE) AND ZIKR

1. As far as knowledge is concerned, the Tablighi Jamaat is to have a complete and reliable knowledge of Islam and to teach it to other Muslims so that they also develop a keen interest in Islam. Moreover, this Jamaat must know the promises and the commandments of Allah Ta'ala and should practically implement them in their lives.
2. Whilst out in the path of Allah Ta'ala, the learning of Salaah and the Qur-aan-e-Kareem must be given great importance. The time required to learn these cannot be acquired on this brief Tabligh journey. Therefore, the companions are expected to realize the importance of learning about Salaah and the Qur-aan-e-Kareem whilst on this journey and they should devote more time for this in the future.
3. The members of the Jamaat should also think of their past life and show remorse and regret for not devoting themselves to Tabligh work in the past for which they should seek the forgiveness of Allah Ta'ala. If they are still ignorant of their Deen, they should be sorry for this negligence, make taubah and make amends for the future.
4. In their spare time they should remember Allah Ta'ala, i.e. engage in zikr not only verbally, but also in their hearts by contemplating.
5. Those who are learned in Deen should teach it to others as a responsibility and those who are still ignorant should make an attempt to learn.
6. One cannot learn all the teachings of the Deen by studying from the books or by listening to talks only, but rather also practicing on it.

Acquiring the knowledge of Islam and thereafter practicing upon it is essential and, perfection in Imaan cannot be acquired without action. Therefore, one must practice what he knows and also encourage others with the same.

7. The correction of mistakes, that one commits whilst reciting the Qur-aan-e-Kareem or performing Salaah, should not be limited whilst out in the path of Allah Ta'ala or conducting taleem, but also during ones free time at home.

8. All the members of the Jamaat should sit silently and respectfully whilst taleem is being conducted and should not pay attention to anything else. The person conducting the taleem should point out and correct their mistakes whilst the others should keep silent. Having regard for the words of Allah Ta'ala and His Rasul ﷺ, they should sit motionless, as if birds were sitting on their heads.

9. In the halaqa of taleem, special attention should be given to the following;

   (a) The teachings of the Qur-aan-e-Kareem, particularly in relation with tajweed; all the possible mistakes concerning ذ zaal, ز Zaa, س Seen, ص Saud, ح Haa, ه Haa, ع Ayn, ءHamzah, ت Taa, ط Tau, ‗Fatha/Zabar etc., should be avoided with great care.

   (b) The words of Kalimah Tayyibah should be learnt properly and the meaning should be understood thoroughly, so much so that everyone should believe that Islam is incomplete without putting the Kalimah into practice.

   (c) The basic conditions, fundamentals and whatever is read in Salaah should be learnt and remembered well. The rewards and virtues of Salaah should be stressed and the punishment for neglecting it should be repeated again and again. Moreover, the methods to attain concentration in Salaah should be practiced.

   (d) All the punishments that are mentioned in the Qur-aan-e-Kareem and Hadith for neglecting the basics of the Kalimah, Salaah, Deeni knowledge, zikr, respect for a Muslim, Tabligh work etc., should be read out and also the virtues and rewards for observing them should be explained from reliable kitaabs.

(e) The Sunnah way of life of Rasulullah ﷺ should also be discussed in the halaqa of taleem. For instance, how he observed Salaah and led his daily life. Thus, by studying the Seerah of Rasulullah ﷺ and his Sahaabah رَضِىَ اللّٰهُ عَنْهُم, a Muslim will learn that in spite of all the difficulties and obstacles how they spread Islam far and wide, and at the same time how they fulfilled their responsibility towards their families and business. They fulfilled their Deeni and worldly responsibility by being true and just to both.

(f) All the members of Jamaat should assist one another in learning their Tabligh lessons, viz., the Kalimah, Salaah, Islamic knowledge, Zikr, honour for a Muslim, sincerity, setting aside time to do good deeds, and abstaining from useless things. They should then encourage each other to lead their life practically according to these lessons.

10. They should read one Tasbeeh of Durood Shareef, one of the Kalimah Tayyibah and one of Istighfaar, every morning and evening. If they have any authentic Dua kitaabs e.g. '*Dalaail-ul-Khairaat*', '*Hizb-ul-A'azam*', '*Munaajaate Maqbool*', they should also read them regularly.

11. They should spend all their free time in the remembrance of Allah Ta'ala and should keep their tongues busy with zikr.

THE NAFL (OPTIONAL) SALAAH

One should try to perform the "Nawaafil" (the optional Salaah) during the Tabligh journey. The Ishraaq, Chaasht, Tahajjud, Awwaabeen, the Nawaafil after fardh and the Sunnah Salaah, should be performed properly. These Salaah are generally neglected at home, but they can be performed during the journey during the free time. All the persons in the Jamaat must give preference to the Ijtimaaee Aamaal (collective Aamaal) over the optional Salaah. The Ijtimaaee Aamaal (collective Aamaal) has priority over the Nawaafil and you can easily give up the latter for the former. Complete all objects of Tabligh first and thereafter perform the Nawaafil afterwards.

GASHT
(To go visit the common and the influential people for the sake of Allah Ta'ala)

1. The real object of going around for an informal visit (Umumi Gasht) or a special visit (Khususi Gasht) whilst out in Tabligh is that the worldly and business places like bazaars, streets and the market places should also be blessed and benefitted with the remembrance of Allah Ta'ala, and the Imaan of the Jamaat would help to strengthen the Imaan of others, and vice versa. Remember, this Tabligh work is exactly following the work which was carried out by Rasulullah ﷺ, who went from house to house.
2. When you go out for Gasht, lower your gaze and keep your tongue and heart busy with the zikr of Allah Ta'ala. This attitude of yours will affect the hearts of others to a great extent.
3. Going out for Gasht must be done before the Salaah time. During your Gasht, encourage others with the basics of the Kalimah and the principles of Islam and then politely invite them to Salaah in the masjid and ask them to join your Tabligh group.
4. Neither ask anyone to recite the Kalimah nor compel them to perform Salaah, for such an attitude would sometimes discourage them. It is for this reason that we are advised to take those who are educated and also the influential people of that locality with us, so that they will talk to the people according to their status.
5. Before going out for Gasht, make Dua to Allah Ta'ala and ask Him in all humility, saying; "O Allah! We are weak and helpless and nothing can be achieved without Your assistance. Therefore, assist us in this sacred cause and direct the hearts of Your servants to Your true Deen, and to the life of the Aakhirah and let us be a means for this service. O Allah! Accept this humble service of ours, and establish Your Deen with it. O Allah! Save us from the evil of those whom we have come into contact with in this work, and also save them from the evil of ourselves. Let them benefit from the good in our souls, and let us benefit from the good in their souls!" (One could also make any other suitable Dua according to the occasion).
6. You should neither engage in controversial discussions with anyone, nor arrange any debates.

7. When going out for Gasht, take the local pious people with you, so that they can see the impiety and transgression of the people of their town with their own eyes and then they may join you in Tabligh effort.
8. When you reach a certain city or village, meet the influential people and explain to them the method, aims and objects of the effort of Tabligh, and stress the importance of this deeni responsibility, and then invite them to join your Jamaat. By the influential people we mean the pious or the wealthy who are one way or another, influential in their city, mohalla or village. One should be very cautious, reasonable and to the point, while talking to them.

GIVING DAWAT (INVITING TOWARDS ALLAH TA'ALA AND HIS DEEN)

1. Talking to people eloquently is not the real aim and object, but rather it is only a medium of instruction. One should try to make the people understand the real meaning and the purpose of the work of Tabligh. Explain yourself clearly to the listeners in simple and easy language. Do not adopt the style of a bayaan and do not talk about things which the listener would not understand. Rasulullah ﷺ repeated every sentence of his thrice, so that his audience would understand it easily. His words were spoken slowly and clearly, so that the listeners could follow.
2. In your speech you should explain the uselessness of this material world and the great and eternal blessings and enjoyments of the Aakhirah. Encourage the people to do good deeds and prepare for the life in the grave so that they would attain peace and salvation on the Day of Qiyaamah. Encourage them to live a life of piety because this will save them from the punishment of Jahannam. Explain to them about the impiety and negligence of the present day Muslims, particularly the condition of local people whom you will come to know during your Gasht visits.
3. Tell them the spiritual and Deeni benefits of joining the Tabligh Jamaat and invite them to join.

4. Explain to them the punishment for not encouraging people towards good and preventing them from evil. Explain to them the reward of being faithful to Islam during this era of sin and disobedience.
5. Do not adopt a commanding tone and an attitude of superiority while speaking to people.
6. In every speech, one should advise the people to put into practice whatever they know about Islam.

OBEDIENCE TO THE AMEER (LEADER)

Every order of the Ameer should be obeyed, provided he does not ask you to commit a sin. Obey him even though he may not be as educated as you are. Rasulullah ﷺ has said in a Hadith, "If a leader has been appointed over you, whose nose and ears are cut, you should obey him, as long as he instructs you with the Qur-aan-e-Kareem."

Sometimes the leader will honour a person or give him the right of speech, though he is inferior to you in status. In such a case, you should neither object to it nor raise any objections against him. Hadhrat Ubaadah bin Saamit رضى الله عنه says, "We took a pledge at the hands of Rasulullah ﷺ that we will obey him in affluence and in difficulty, in pleasure and sorrow and will not obey the suggestions of our nafs against his wish. We will not prefer ourselves to others against his choice and we will not try to snatch away leadership from another person. We will speak the truth wherever we are and will not mind the criticism of anyone, while obeying the commandments of Allah Ta'ala." (Mishkaat Shareef)

THE AADAAB (ETIQUETTES) OF EATING

1. Wash your hands before and after meals and rinse your mouth also.
2. Before eating say;

$$\text{بِسْمِ اللهِ وَعَلٰى بَرَكَةِ اللهِ}$$

"Bismillaah wa'alaa barkatillaah"

3. Eat with your right hand.
4. Eat the food that is in front of you. If there are different types of food in the utensil from which you are eating, then you may eat from wherever you please.

5. Place the food on a cloth (dastarkhaan) and then partake from the food.
6. Do not eat from the center of the utensil because the blessings of Allah Ta'ala descend at that point.
7. Finish all the food in the utensil. Do not leave anything for Shaytaan. When all the food is eaten, the utensil make Dua to Allah Ta'ala to save you from Jahannam.
8. Lick your fingers before washing your hands. It is mentioned in a Hadith, "One does not know in which particle of the food the blessing of Allah Ta'ala is."
9. Eat with three fingers of the right hand.
10. If a morsel falls on the cloth (dastarkhaan), pick it up and eat it and do not leave it for Shaytaan.
11. One should not lean on a cushion or arrogantly recline whilst eating.
12. Do not object to the quality of food; if you like it, eat it otherwise keep silent.
13. All of you should eat your meals together as a Jamaat and not separately.
14. Hadhrat Anas رضى الله عنه says, "I saw Rasulullah ﷺ taking his meals in a squatting position."
15. If few companions are eating sweetmeats or dates together, do not take two pieces at a time without their permission.
16. If you forget to read بِسْمِ اللهِ *(Bismillaah)* before you begin eating, then say,

$$\text{بِسْمِ اللهِ أَوَّلَهُ وَاٰخِرَهُ}$$

"Bismillaahi awwalahu wa aakhirahu"
"With the name of Allah in the beginning and at the end of it"

17. Do not eat onions while you are in the masjid and if you have eaten them out of the masjid, then do not enter until such time that there is no smell left in the mouth.
18. After eating your meals, say;

$$\text{اَلْحَمْدُ لِلّٰهِ الَّذِيْ اَطْعَمَنَا وَسَقَانَا وَجَعَلَنَا مِنَ الْمُسْلِمِيْنَ}$$

Alhamdu lillaahil lazee at'amanaa wasaqaanaa waja-alanaa minal muslimeen

"All praise is due to Allah who has nourished us and has quenched our thirst and has assisted us to be Muslims."

19. First pick up the cloth and then get up.
20. Do not eat food which is too hot.
21. If you have finished eating, do not get up before your companions, rather keep eating slowly. If you do have to get up for some reason, then excuse yourself and ask them to continue.
22. If you drink water, milk or any other liquid say, بِسْمِ اللهِ **(Bismillaah)** at the beginning and اَلْحَمْدُ لِلهِ **(Alhamdulillaah)** at the end.
23. Do not drink continuously in one gulp like a camel.
24. Do not breathe in a utensil nor blow into it.
25. If the utensil is broken or chipped at a certain point then do not eat or drink from that point of the utensil.
26. Wash your mouth after drinking milk and read this Dua;

اَللّٰهُمَّ بَارِكْ لَنَا فِيْهِ وَزِدْنَا مِنْهُ

Allaahumma baarik lanaa feehi wa zidnaa minhu.
"O Allah! Let it be a blessing for us and increase it for us."

All these Aadaab (etiquettes) of eating and drinking have been quoted from
'Mishkaat Shareef'.

THE AADAAB (ETIQUETTES) OF GOING TO SLEEP

1. Sleep with wudhu.
2. Dust the bed thrice before going to sleep.
3. Lie on the bed on your right side, place your right hand under your right cheek, and read;

اَللّٰهُمَّ بِاسْمِكَ اَمُوْتُ وَاَحْيٰى

Allahumma bismika amootu wa ahyaa
"O Allah! In Your name do I die and live."

4. Read *"Aayatul Kursi"* and *"Aamanar Rasoolu"* (up to the end of Surah) before going to sleep.
5. Read ***"Subhaanallah"***, ***"Alhamdulillaah"*** and ***"Allaahu-Akbar"***, thirty three times each, before going to sleep.
6. Read all the four Surahs beginning with "Qul", then blow on your hands and pass them over your whole body; do this thrice.
7. Read Surah *"Alif laam meem sajdah"* and *"Tabarakal-lazee beyadihil mulk"* before going to sleep.
8. When awakening from your sleep read;

اَلْحَمْدُ لِلّٰهِ الَّذِىْ اَحْيَانَا بَعْدَ مَا اَمَاتَنَا وَاِلَيْهِ النُّشُوْرُ

Alhamdu lillaahil lazee ahyaanaa ba'da maa amaata-naa wa ilayhin nushoor

"All praise to Allah who gave us life after giving us death and to Him we shall have to return."

9. Apply Surmah (collyrium) to your eyes thrice before going to sleep.
10. If you want to get up for Tahajjud Salaah, read the last few Aayaat of Surah Kahf, from *"In-nallazina aamanu"* till the end of the Surah (Ayah 107 till Ayah 110). All these Aadaab (etiquettes) of sleeping have been quoted from the Ahaadith.

WUDHU AND SALAAH

1. If you are leaving on a journey and the time of Salaah is near, then perform wudhu before leaving. Also take a Lota (utensil for the purpose of wudhu) and a six yard rope to draw water from a well if the need arises.
2. The water from the railway station taps and that from the toilet in the train is clean. If this water is not available then only will Tayammum be permissible.
3. The time for Maghrib Salaah begins after sunset and ends when the redness in the sky disappears. The general belief that Maghrib Salaah cannot be performed a short while after sunset is incorrect.

4. If the distance of your journey is more than forty eight miles (77,248 Kilometers) then instead of performing four rakaats fardh, you should perform only two.
5. Do not postpone any Salaah during the journey because postponing even a single Salaah will render your journey useless. If you have forgotten a certain Salaah, or its time has passed whilst you were asleep, then perform it as soon as possible. If the Salaah of a journey (i.e. qasr) are performed after reaching home (i.e. Qadha), then read two rakaats for Zuhr, Asr and Esha. If on the other hand, Salaah that was made Qadha at home and is performed during the journey then read four rakaats for Zuhr, Asr and Esha.
6. There are many Muslims on whom Qadha Salaah for many years is due. They are advised to perform these Salaah as soon as possible, whilst on a Tabligh journey. The opportunities are numerous, so perform as many Qadha Salaah as possible. Rather perform the Fardh Qadha instead of the Nawaafil. Remember that Qadha Salaah is only performed for the Fardh and Witr Salaah.
7. The Jamaat Salaah (congregational Salaah) is necessary even during the Tabligh journey. When the time for Salaah sets in, give the Adhaan (the call to prayer) and then say the Iqaamah and perform the Salaah with Jamaat. If for some reason all the members cannot perform the Salaah together then let them perform it in pairs.
8. If you are in a hurry, then you may leave the Sunnats before and after the fardh Salaah, but not those of the Fajr Salaah. And if you are not in a hurry then perform all the Sunnats.
9. If you have put your luggage in a railway compartment or in a bus and it is about to depart, then terminate the Salaah. Perform the Salaah in the train or vehicle if it is possible.
10. To face the qiblah is necessary even in a railway compartment, therefore perform your Salaah in the correct direction and if you do not know the direction of the qiblah, nor is there anyone to show you, then establish the qiblah by careful estimation. If the train or vehicle takes a turn, while you are performing the Salaah, then turn yourself accordingly.
11. Even if the train is moving, it is fardh for you to stand and complete your Salaah. If you are healthy and strong enough to stand, then do not sit and read Salaah. One can easily perform the Salaah in the

passage or in between the seats. You can perform the Salaah in pairs with jamaat in the space between the two rows of seats.

MISCELLANEOUS

1. Every member of the Tabligh Jamaat is responsible for his own expenditure during the journey.
2. Be courteous and polite to every Muslim whom you meet during your journey. Be courteous to the non-Muslims also and show them good akhlaaq (Islamic manners). If you sometimes talk to them, tell them that humanity is generally negligent of Allah Ta'ala; therefore, they must submit to Him for their salvation.
3. When you reach a certain destination, consult the people of the locality before you start your work of Tabligh.
4. When you reach a city, town or village, do not stay anywhere except in the masjid, even though someone may insist on doing otherwise.
5. In the masjid where you are staying, extinguish the lamp or the light at the normally fixed times, for it is not correct to use it only for personal use. Put out the lights after Esha Salaah when the musallies (worshippers) have departed; then light a candle or torch of your own if it is needed.
6. Do not ask for any bedding or any utensils from the people of the locality. Do help one another in the Jamaat if there is a shortage of bedding.
7. Fix a fee before engaging any labourer. If you employ any labourer without fixing a fee, then pay him his full remuneration. If you pay him less than the local rate and he is unhappy and kept asking for more, until he went away disappointed, then you will have to pay him on the Day of Qiyaamah. Remember, oppression or forced agreement concerning fixing a fee before engaging any labourer is not recognized. Therefore, if anyone gives up his right by oppression, then the oppressor cannot be forgiven by that person.
8. Avoid all useless talk during your Tabligh journey and be cautious of everything you do. In short, spend your time carefully during this journey and pay special attention to the Tabligh work. Neither talk too much nor laugh unnecessarily, for it is mentioned in a Hadith that, "Too much talk hardens the heart, too much laughing kills the heart and the noor of the face is lessened."

9. Every action of yours must be based on sincerity and you should not despair of the reward from Allah Ta'ala. In whatever you do, you must make a good niyyat (intention).
10. Make your return journey home also a Tabligh journey and observe the same as you had observed while going out in the path of Allah Ta'ala.
11. All the basics of Islamic Aadaab (etiquettes) that you learnt and all the Salaah that you performed during the journey, should also be maintained when you return home. Humility in Salaah, constant zikr, service to humanity, sincerity and all the good actions that you practiced during the journey, should be observed at home also because the main object of this journey was to bring all these good deeds practically in one's life.
12. If you happen to undertake a journey not purely for Tabligh work but rather for worldly reasons, even then observe Islamic Aadaab and Duas, perform your Salaah regularly with Jamaat and if there are three people travelling together, one of them should be made the ameer.
13. During the Tabligh journey keep all the books of Tabligh with you, namely *Hikaayaat-e-Sahaabah, Fadhaa'il-e-Namaaz, Fadhaa'il-e-Tabligh,* etc. and you should also keep a miswaak, lota (utensil for holding water for the purpose of wudhu), musallah (prayer mat), soap, thread and needle, cloth (dastarkhaan), mud lumps or tissue for the purpose of Istinja, matches, candle, comb, surmah daani (surmah dispenser), torch and staff (which could be used as a Sutrah – A barrier in front of the person reading Salaah).
14. If the Ameer asks you to prepare food for the Jamaat, or to do some other service, obey his orders happily. Don't think that you will be deprived of the reward of doing Tabligh work when your companions leave you with your task, because you will deserve double reward, one for making Khidmah for your companions and the other for relieving your companions of carrying out those tasks so they are able to do the Tabligh work freely.
15. The Tabligh journey is a good period in which to practice the Islamic routine. Therefore, be helpful to one another, and promote unity. Don't insist on your own proposal, but only suggest it and explain the benefits. If your companions do not accept your

proposal, then don't be disappointed. If the proposal of somebody else is accepted by the group and the outcome is not positive, then don't say, "What did I suggest to you? Had you only accepted my advice, you would have not gone wrong!"

16. During Gasht, or during the halaqa of Taleem, or at the time of giving da'wat, don't discuss any controversial subject, but rather invite people to the fundamentals of Islam and Tawheed (Oneness) of Allah Ta'ala, because when one understands the meaning of the Kalimah, he will then want to know more about Imaan and Islam.

17. Remain in any city or village that you visit as long as its inhabitants can easily understand the main object of the work of Tabligh and are prepared to observe all the rules of Tabligh work. It is not correct to be at one place in the morning, at another in the evening, at one place at Zuhr and at another at Asr. One cannot do justice to Tabligh work if you visit only a few persons, or only deliver a speech in the masjid. Your attempt in this task can be successful and beneficial only when you stay in a town for a required period of time.

18. When you are nearing your city or village when returning from a journey, read the following Dua;

$$\text{اٰئِبُوْنَ تَائِبُوْنَ عَابِدُوْنَ لِرَبِّنَا حَامِدُوْنَ}$$

Aa-iboona, taa-iboona, 'aabidoona lirabbinaa haamidoon

"We are returning (to piety); we are repenting; we are worshipping Allah; and we are giving praises to Allah."

19. When you return from the journey and enter your home say;

$$\text{اَوْبًا اَوْبًا لِرَبِّنَا تَوْبًا لَا يُغَادِرُ عَلَيْنَا حَوْبًا}$$

Owban, owban, lirabbinaa towban, laa yughaadiru alaynaa howban

"I have returned, I have returned to my Sustainer with repentance, which would cleanse us of every sin."

20. It is preferable to reach your town after sunrise. First perform two rakaats nafl Salaah in your local musjid, then talk to your Muslim

brothers for a while and then enter your home. This was the practice of Rasulullah ﷺ when he returned from a journey. *(Mishkaat)*

21. Whenever Rasulullah ﷺ returned from a journey during the night, he did not enter his home, but rather on the next morning or evening. *(Mishkaat)*
22. It has been reported by Jaabir رضي الله عنه that Rasulullah ﷺ said, "Whenever you return from a journey after sunset and wish to go home to your wife, then give her sufficient time to remove unwanted hair and to comb the hair on her head (in order that she groom herself in preparation for your return). *(Bukhaari, Muslim)*
23. After returning from a journey, one should hastily rejoin the Tabligh workers in his locality. Successful and fortunate is he who observes the requisites of this journey sincerely and returns home with a great spiritual improvement.

DIRECTIVES FOR THE WORKERS OF TABLIGH
(Selected from the sayings of Hadhrat Moulana Muhammad Ilyaas *(rahmatullahi alayh)*

1. The first and the main object of knowledge is that one should examine his actions, realize his duties and shortcomings and seek the means to overcome them. If you only judge the actions of others according to your ilm (knowledge), then this pride will destroy those who have ilm.
2. The real remembrance of Allah Ta'ala is that a Muslim should always obey the commandments of Allah Ta'ala and keep them in mind at all times.
3. The main object of our Jamaat is to teach the Muslims the original and complete Deen which was taught by Rasulullah ﷺ. This is our real object. As for our Tabligh journeys in groups, this is a preliminary means to carry out our work. The instruction of Kalimah Tayyibah and Salaah is the initiation of our course.
4. Our workers should remember that if their da'wat is not accepted anywhere, they should not be disappointed. They should remember that they are following the Sunnah of the Ambiyaa *(alayhimus salaam)* and particularly the Sunnah of Rasulullah ﷺ. How

many people there are who go out in the path of Allah Ta'ala, bear hardships and yet they are disgraced? On the other hand, if they are welcomed and honoured somewhere, they should think it to be a favour of Allah Ta'ala and should have great regard for it. When you teach Deen to those who pay attention to it, though they are common people, you should thank Allah Ta'ala for this favour.
5. Our workers should not desire for difficult and trying conditions from Allah Ta'ala. Should any misfortune befall them, they should accept it to be the mercy of Allah Ta'ala, a compensation for their sins and a means to raise their ranks.
6. When you are explaining something, you should have the intention to please Allah Ta'ala only and not your audience. In the Tabligh journey we should bear in mind that we have left our homes in obedience to the command of Allah Ta'ala and not by our own wish, therefore, it is He who will assist us. When you have such an intention, you will neither be angered by the ill treatment of the people whom you talk to nor will you be discouraged by them.
7. We become disappointed if the people we are giving Dawat to, do not follow our advice and we regard ourselves to be losers. Actually it is in fact a loss to the listeners because they refuse to obey the teachings of Deen. Our success lies in discharging our duty to deliver the truth. We should therefore, not regard ourselves to be unsuccessful due to the negligence of others, as our duty is to present Islam in the best possible manner. Even the Ambiyaa *(Alayhimus salaam)* were not held responsible when the people did not follow them. When people reject your Dawat, then it is an opportunity to learn a lesson because maybe your approach to this work may not be perfect and faultless. Therefore, you will improve your future attempts and ask Allah Ta'ala for complete guidance.
8. If the Ulama and pious people of a town show no keenness and are not sympathetic towards the work of Tabligh, then do not doubt their sincerity and don't have any ill feeling for them in your heart. You should realize that maybe the object of the Tabligh work is not clear to them as yet.
9. Wherever you go, you should visit the Ulama and pious people of that place, so that you can benefit from their knowledge and piety. You should not invite them to the work of Tabligh, for they know

their duties best and the benefits thereof. The Ulama may not understand the real object of the work of Tabligh just by giving them an explanation. Therefore, they will neither readily accept nor even acknowledge it, but rather question it, hence, meet them only for your benefit, as long as you are in their town. You should yourself make an effort to follow the lessons and principles of Tabligh very strictly. When the Ulama and pious ones come to know of your work, they will be interested in it, thereafter, in a very honourable and respectful manner explain to them what your aims and objects are.

10. One of the principles of Tabligh is that a speaker should be very polite, courteous and to the point in his speech when addressing a particular person. He should instruct a person in a general way, not picking on his personal faults. Whenever Rasulullah ﷺ came to know of the wrong actions of a particular person, he disapproved of it in general terms and said, "What will the result of such a nation be, who commits wrong actions."

11. We are used to be pleased with talks only. We merely talk about good deeds and think that our words alone are sufficient which will replace practicing on it. Therefore, try to refrain from this habit.

12. Whatever good deeds you do, attribute them to Allah Ta'ala and seek His forgiveness for verily you should keep in mind that whatever action you did was not the best and that there was fault in it. Rasulullah ﷺ used to seek the forgiveness of Allah Ta'ala at the end of his Salaah. The responsibility of the work of Allah Ta'ala cannot be completed in anyway by His servants. When we are busy with a certain work, this should not stop us from doing other work, and we should seek the forgiveness and assistance of Allah Ta'ala at the completion of all good work.

13. All your Tabligh journeys will be worthless if you do not continue to study deeni ilm (knowledge of deen) and practice regular zikrullah. There is fear that negligence of these two essential things could be a cause of confusion and you may be led astray. Without deeni ilm, Islam and Imaan is only for namesake and a customary ritual, because no good deed is possible without sound Deeni knowledge and knowledge without zikrullah is but darkness and no

noor can be derived from it and this is what our workers have neglected.

14. When Dawat is being given during the Gasht, the jamaat members are advised to remain in Zikr and Fikr. The reason for this is that whilst Dawat is being given towards the truth, all the hearts in the Jamaat must have the same fikr, because this will have an effect on the hearts of others.
15. When unfavourable and adverse conditions are encountered by the Jamaat, they must increase their zikrullah to attract the help of Allah Ta'ala. This will protect them from the evil effects of human and jinn shayaateen.
16. Sincerity and good intention is the basis of Tabligh work and steadfastness in sincerity is very important. Therefore, Tabligh workers should at all times only seek the pleasure of Allah Ta'ala and obey His commandments. The greater the extent there is sincerity and steadfastness, the greater will be your reward from Allah Ta'ala.
17. At the end of your good actions you should always admit your weakness and negligence and should have the fear that this deed may not be accepted by Allah Ta'ala.
18. In our Tabligh work, in addition to sincerity and truthfulness, unity and mashwara (mutual consultation) is essential. Without these there is a great danger of making mistakes.
19. Those high positions which Rasulullah ﷺ showed us and which was also attained by the Sahaabah رضي الله عنهم by undergoing sacrifices and hardships, could also be attained by us by showing love and dedication to Deen. Do you wish to attain that status by merely reading books? Those lofty favours and rewards were obtained through sacrifice and therefore, we should also sacrifice and work for it.
20. What benefit is there in only remembering what work we have completed. One should plan for the future to complete the remainder of the mission and take stock of the shortcomings of the work done in the past.
21. Don't be satisfied with only a single person accepting or understanding your message, but always be mindful of the millions of people who are left to whom the message of Allah Ta'ala did not

reach. How many more are there who accepted your message and were aware of it but due to your negligence did not carry out the commandments of Allah Ta'ala?

22. Many are of the view that to only convey the message is Tabligh, this is a serious misunderstanding. The meaning of Tabligh is that a person, according to his ability and experience, should convey the message of deen in such a manner that there is hope for the people to accept what is being said. This was the method practiced by the Ambiyaa *(Alayhimus salaam).*
23. Those who go out for Deeni work or for Gasht, their hearts will be affected and influenced by meeting unmindful and negligent people or visiting irreligious places. They should wipe out this influence by making zikrullah and fikr of Deen in seclusion.
24. Basically every good deed is for the pleasure of Allah Ta'ala and to gain reward in the Aakhirah. These good deeds will also benefit us as far as the worldly gains are concerned and this should also be mentioned for encouragement towards piety. In the beginning, some people do Deeni work just for worldly gain, but due to the blessing of the work, they are later favoured by Allah Ta'ala with sincerity.
25. Plan, suggest and propose ways and means to call people towards Deen and doing the work of Deen. Approach them in a manner that will draw their attention and attract them towards Deen.
26. The object of going out for the Tabligh journey is not merely to advise and guide others, but rather it is to reform ourselves and develop good habits. Hence, during the journey we should be engaged at all times with zikrullah and acquiring deeni ilm (knowledge of deen). These should be practiced with the advice and guidance of our learned elders and Ameer (leader). Be mindful of these because going out for Tabligh will be useless if these are neglected.
27. In this work of Tabligh, to establish deen firmly is more important than its expansion. The method of this is that with establishing Deen, its expansion must be simultaneous. How could this work of Tabligh be established without travelling to different villages, towns and countries?

28. One of the principles of Tabligh work is that one stays away from making independent decisions and freedom of movement. At all times one should abide by the guidance of the recognized learned elders.
29. The general practice of Tabligh workers is that they give full attention to prominent personalities and are less attentive towards other pious and humble not well to do persons who offer their services. It must be understood that this is an approach which is totally for worldly gain. Keep in mind that the pious and humble who are very poor and needy, and who offer their services out of dedication for guidance, are a blessing from Allah Ta'ala. Therefore honour and be grateful to them.
30. Womenfolk should assist the men and give them the opportunity to do Deeni work. We should make their household chores lighter for them so that they may also do deeni work without any difficulty. If the women do not cooperate with us in our deeni work, then they will be the victims of becoming a trap of Shaytaan.
31. It is very important that when one goes out for Tabligh work, one remains occupied in the activities of the jamaat and does not get involved in other things. The work of the jamaat is as follows;

   a. To go around meeting Muslims for the upliftment of Deen.
   b. The acquiring of Deeni ilm (knowledge of deen) and the development of a habit of constant zikrullah.
   c. To be helpful, particularly to your close associates.
   d. The correction of intention and working towards the development of Ikhlaas (sincerity) and exercising Ihtisaab, i.e. making a concerted effort of taking stock of oneself under the guidance of a senior to attain purity and clarity of niyyah. One must also regularly entrench the thought in his heart that his going out is solely for the pleasure of Allah Ta'ala alone. Therefore, one will definitely be blessed with the promise in the Qur-aan-e-Kareem and Hadith for his full dedication with this refined quality. It is this Ikhlaas that is kept in check by Ihtisaab (taking stock of oneself) which is termed true Imaan, and is also the essence of all our deeds.

32. Shaytaan's desire is to wipe out and destroy the progress and higher positions which would be attained by being punctual with

the Faraa'idh, therefore all ones free moments must be spent in nafl zikr (optional zikr), so that Shaytaan is unable to influence you into useless things which would result in harm.

33. One of the principles of Tabligh work is that you honour every Muslim and respect the Ulama.
34. Understand that when some of your companions intend returning home, don't desire to follow them, but rather suppress your desire and continue with the Tabligh work, because great virtues have been promised for it. The example of those who suppress their desire and remain steadfast on this work is like that of a fighter who remains fighting on the battlefield whilst his companions disappear in retreat.
35. The condition of attaining the assistance of Allah Ta'ala is that you should first assist His true Deen. If you offer assistance to His deen, then difficulties and obstacles in this world will turn into a means of pleasure, and the earth, skies and whatever it contains will be of assistance to you. Those who, after carrying out the work of Allah Ta'ala despair in the mercy and pleasure of Allah Ta'ala, would be most unfortunate and knowingly transgressing His laws.
36. What is termed to be divine assistance (i.e. help of Allah Ta'ala) and unforeseen power is not bestowed in the beginning, but is granted at the appropriate occasion and time.

Milton Keynes UK
Ingram Content Group UK Ltd.
UKHW020312101124
450803UK00006BA/113

9 784887 237827